Langenscheidt's
Pocket Italian
Dictionary

Italian-English
English-Italian

Edited by the
Langenscheidt Editorial Staff

In cooperation with Paravia

P9-CFF-260

LANGENSCHEIDT
NEW YORK · BERLIN · MUNICH

Compiled by Lexus Ltd., Glasgow,
with contributions by
Jane Goldie
Loredana Riu
Debora Mazza
Pat Bulhosen
Carla Zipoli
Peter Terrell
Francesca Logi

© *Langenscheidt KG, Berlin and Munich*
Printed in Germany

3 4 5 6 7   07 06 05 04 03

Preface

Here is a new dictionary of English and Italian, a tool with some 45,000 references for those who work with the English and Italian languages at beginner's or intermediate level.

Focusing on modern usage, the dictionary offers coverage of everyday language – and this means including vocabulary from areas such as computer use and business.

Having made the selection of vocabulary items to include, the editors of this book have set out to provide the means to enable you, the user of the dictionary, to get straight to the translation that fits a particular context of use. Is the *mouse* you need for your computer, for example, the same in Italian as the *mouse* you don't want in the house? Is *flimsy* referring to furniture the same in Italian as *flimsy* referring to an excuse? This dictionary is rich in sense distinctions like this – and in translation options tied to specific, identified senses.

Vocabulary needs grammar to back it up. So in this dictionary you'll find irregular verb forms, in both English and Italian, irregular English plural forms as well as detailed guidance on Italian plural and feminine endings.

And vocabulary items are often only clearly understood in a context. So a large number of idiomatic phrases are given to show how the two languages correspond in context.

All in all, this is a book full of information, which will, we hope, become a valuable part of your language toolkit.

Contents

How to use the dictionary

To get the most out of your dictionary you should understand how and where to find the information you need. Whether you are yourself writing text in a foreign language or wanting to understand text that has been written in a foreign language, the following pages should help.

1. How and where do I find a word?

1.1 The word list for each language is arranged in alphabetical order and also gives irregular forms of verbs and nouns in their correct alphabetical order.

Sometimes you might want to look up terms made up of two separate words, for example **falling star**, or hyphenated words, for example **absent-minded**. These words are treated as though they were a single word and their alphabetical ordering reflects this.

The only exception to this strict alphabetical ordering is made for English *phrasal verbs* – words like **go off, go out, go up**. These are positioned in an alphabetical block directly after their main verb (in this case **go**).

1.2 Italian feminine headwords of the form **-trice** are shown as follows:

> **albergatore** *m*, **-trice** *f* hotel keeper

Here **-trice** means **albergatrice**.

1.3 Pronunciation for English headwords is given in square brackets. You can look up the spelling of a word in your dictionary in the same way as you would in a spelling dictionary. American spelling variants are marked *Am*. If just a single letter is omitted in the American spelling, this is put between round brackets:

> colo(u)r — hono(u)r — travel(l)er

2. How do I split a word?

Italians find English hyphenation very difficult. All you have to do with this dictionary is look for the bold dots between syllables. These dots show you where you can split a word at the end of a line but you should avoid having just one letter before or after the hyphen as in a•mend or thirst•y. In such cases it is better to take the entire word over to the next line.

3. Swung dashes and long dashes

3.1 A swung dash (~) replaces the entire headword when the headword is repeated within an entry:

> **face** [feɪs] **1** *n* viso *m*, faccia *f*; ~ **to** ~ faccia a faccia

Here ~ **to** ~ means **face to face**.

> **incanto**[1] *m* (*incantesimo*) spell; **come per** ~ as if by magic

Here **come per** ~ means **come per incanto**.

3.2 When a headword changes form in an entry, for example if it is put in the past tense or in the plural, then the past tense or plural ending is added to the swung dash – but only if the rest of the word doesn't change:

>**flame** [fleɪm] *n* fiamma *f*; **go up in ~s** incendiarsi
>**top** [tɒp] ... **3** *v/t* (*pret & pp* **-ped**): **~ped with cream** ricoperto di crema

But:

>◆**make up 1** *v/i* ... **be made up of** essere composto da
>**sup•ply** [sə'plaɪ] ... **2** *v/t* ... **be supplied with** *fitted with etc* essere dotato di

3.3 Double headwords are replaced by a single swung dash:

>**'one-track mind** *hum*: **have a ~** essere fissato col sesso
>**sliced 'bread** [slaɪst] pane *m* a cassetta; **the greatest thing since ~** F il non plus ultra

3.4 In the Italian-English part of the dictionary, when a headword is repeated in a phrase or compound with an altered form, a long dash is used:

>**impronta** *f* impression, mark; **-e** *pl* **digitali** fingerprints

Here **-e digitali** means **impronte digitali**.

4. What do the different typefaces mean?

4.1 All Italian and English headwords and the Arabic numerals differentiating between parts of speech appear in **bold**:

>**incisivo 1** *agg* incisive **2** *m* dente incisor
>**itch** [ɪtʃ] **1** *n* prurito *m* **2** *v/i* prudere

4.2 *Italics* are used for :

a) abbreviated grammatical labels: *adj, adv, v/i, v/t* etc

b) gender labels: *m, f, mpl* etc

c) all the indicating words which are the signposts pointing to the correct translation for your needs, eg:

>**mix•ture** ['mɪkstʃə(r)] miscuglio *m*; *medicine* sciroppo *m*
>**pro•fuse•ly** [prə'fjuːslɪ] *adv thank* con grande effusione; *bleed* copiosamente
>**rugoso** rough; *pelle* wrinkled; *albero* gnarled
>**terra** *f* earth; (*regione, proprietà, terreno agricolo*) land; (*superficie del suolo*) ground; (*pavimento*) floor

4.3 All phrases (examples and idioms) are given in ***secondary bold italics***:

>**sym•pa•thet•ic** [sɪmpə'θetɪk] *adj* ... **be ~ towards an idea** simpatizzare per un'idea
>**premio** *m* (*pl* -mi) ... **~ Nobel per la pace** Nobel peace prize

4.4 The normal typeface is used for the translations. It is also used for Italian plural forms.

4.5 If a translation is given in italics, and not in the normal typeface, this means that the translation is more of an *explanation* in the other language and that an explanation has to be given because there just is no real equivalent:

> 'Mid•lands *npl regione f nell'Inghilterra centrale*
>
> ragioneria *f* book-keeping; EDU *high school specializing in business studies*

5. Stress

To indicate where to put the **stress** in English words, the stress marker ' appears before the syllable on which the main stress falls:

> on•ion ['ʌnjən] cipolla *f*
>
> rec•ord¹ ['rekɔːd] *n* MUS disco *m* ...
>
> record² [rɪ'kɔːd] *v/t* electronically registrare ...

Stress is shown either in the pronunciation or, if there is no pronunciation given, in the actual headword or compound itself.

> 'rec•ord hold•er primatista *m/f*

6. What do the various symbols and abbreviations tell you?

6.1 A solid blue diamond is used to indicate a phrasal verb:

> ♦auction off *v/t* vendere all'asta

6.2 A white diamond is used to divide up longer entries into more easily digested chunks of related bits of text:

> a *prp* ◊ *stato in luogo*: *a Roma* in Rome; *a casa* at home
>
> ◊ *moto a luogo*: *andare a Roma* go to Rome; *andare a casa* go home ◊ *tempo* ...

6.3 The abbreviation F tells you that the word or phrase is used colloquially rather than in formal contexts. The abbreviation V warns you that a word or phrase is vulgar or taboo. Be careful how you use these words. Words or phrases labelled P are slang.

These abbreviations, F, V and P are used both for headwords/phrases and for the translations of headwords/phrases. They come after the headword and before any phrase or indicated sense to be translated. They are given after the translation, but only if the translation has the same register as the headword/example. If there is no such label given, then the word or phrase is neutral.

6.4 A colon before an English or Italian phrase means that usage is restricted to this specific example (at least as far as this dictionary's translation is concerned):

> tru•ant ['truːənt]: *play* ~ marinare la scuola
>
> tuck [tʌk] ... 2 *v/t*: ~ *sth into sth* infilare qc in qc
>
> 'shoe•string *n*: *do sth on a* ~ fare qc con pochi soldi

7. Does the dictionary deal with grammar too?

7.1 All English headwords are given a part of speech label:

> tooth•less ['tuːθlɪs] *adj* sdentato
> top•ple ['tɒpl] **1** *v/i* crollare **2** *v/t government* far cadere

But if a headword can only be used as a noun (in ordinary English) then no part of speech is given:

> tooth•paste dentifricio *m*

7.2 Italian headwords are not given parts of speech in cases where the grammar of the translation matches the grammar of the Italian:

> esclusivo exclusive
> piuttosto rather

But:

> planetario (*pl* -ri) **1** *agg* planetary **2** *m* planetarium

And Italian gender markers are given, as well as Italian plural forms:

> pinacoteca *f* (*pl* -che) art gallery
> farmacista *m/f* (*mpl* -i) chemist, *Am* pharmacist

7.3 If an English translation of an Italian adjective can only be used in front of a noun, and not after it, this is marked with *attr*:

> fiabesco (*pl* -chi) fairytale *attr*

7.4 If the Italian, unlike the English, doesn't change form if used in the plural, this is marked with *inv*:

> fine settimana *m inv* weekend

7.5 If the English, in spite of appearances, is not a plural form, this is marked with *nsg*:

> mea•sles ['miːzlz] *nsg* morbillo *m*

7.6 Irregular English plurals are identified:

> the•sis ['θiːsɪs] (*pl* **theses** ['θiːsiːz]) tesi *f inv*
> thief [θiːf] (*pl* **thieves** [θiːvz]) ladro *m*, -a *f*
> trout [traʊt] (*pl* **trout**) trota *f*

7.7 Words like physics or media studies have not been given a label to say if they are singular or plural for the simple reason that they can be either, depending on how they are used.

7.8 Irregular and semi-irregular verb forms are identified:

> sim•pli•fy ['sɪmplɪfaɪ] *v/t* (*pret & pp* **-ied**) semplificare
> sing [sɪŋ] *v/t & v/i* (*pret* **sang**, *pp* **sung**) cantare

7.9 Cross-references are given to tables of Italian conjugations:

> finire <4d>   fischiare <1k>

7.10 Grammatical information is provided on the prepositions you'll need in order to create complete sentences:

> ear•mark ['ɪəmɑːk] *v/t* riservare; ~ **sth for sth** riservare qc a qc
> tremare <1b> tremble, shake (*di, per* with)

Abbreviations

see	→	vedi	feminine plural	*fpl*	femminile plurale
registered trademark	®	marchio registrato	railway	FERR	ferrovia
abbreviation	*abbr*	abbreviazione	figurative	*fig*	figurato
adjective	*adj*	aggettivo	philosophy	FIL	filosofia
adverb	*adv*	avverbio	financial	FIN	finanze
adjective	*agg*	aggettivo	physics	FIS	fisica
agriculture	AGR	agricoltura	physiology	FISIOL	fisiologia
mountaineering	ALP	alpinismo	formal usage	*fml*	uso formale
American	*Am*	inglese	photography	FOT	fotografia
English		americano	future	*fut*	futuro
anatomy	ANAT	anatomia	cooking	GASTR	gastronomia
architecture	ARCHI	architettura	generally	*gen*	generalmente
article	*art*	articolo	geography	GEOG	geografia
astronomy	AST	astronomia	geology	GEOL	geology
astrology	ASTR	astrologia	gerund	*ger*	gerundio
attributive usage	*attr*	uso attributivo	grammatical	GRAM	grammatica
motoring	AUTO	automobilismo	humorous	*hum*	uso spiritoso
civil aviation	AVIA	aviazione	imperative	*imper*	imperativo
adverb	*avv*	avverbio	imperfect	*imperf*	imperfetto
biology	BIO	biologia	indicative	*ind*	indicativo
botany	BOT	botanica	IT term	INFOR	informatica
British English	*Br*	inglese britannico	interjection	*int*	interiezione
chemistry	CHEM	chimica	invariable	*inv*	invariabile
chemistry	CHIM	chimica	ironic	*iron*	ironico
commerce,	COM	commercio	law	LAW	diritto
business			masculine	*m*	maschile
computers,	COMPUT	informatica	masculine noun	*m/agg*	sostantivo mas-
IT term			and adjective		chile e aggettivo
conditional	*cond*	condizionale	masculine and	*m/f*	maschile e
conjunction	*cong*	congiunzione	feminine		femminile
subjunctive	*congiunt*	congiuntivo	masculine plural	*mpl*	maschile plurale
conjunction	*conj*	congiunzione	nautical	MAR	marineria,
law	DIR	diritto			navigazione
et cetera	*ecc*	eccetera	mathematics	MAT	matematica
education	EDU	educazione	mathematics	MATH	matematica
for example	*eg*	per esempio	medicine	MED	medicina
electricity,	EL	elettricità,	metallurgy	METAL	metallurgia
electronics		elettronica	meteorology	METEO	meteorologia
electricity,	ELEC	elettricità,	military	MIL	militare
electronics		elettronica	mineralogy	MIN	mineralogia
especially	*esp*	specialmente	motoring	MOT	automobilismo
et cetera	*etc*	eccetera	music	MUS	musica
euphemistic	*euph*	eufemismo	noun	*n*	sostantivo
familiar, colloquial	F	familiare	nautical	NAUT	marineria,
feminine	*f*	femminile			navigazione
feminine noun	*f/agg*	sostantivo fem-	negative	*neg*	in senso negativo
and adjective		minile e aggettivo	plural noun	*npl*	sostantivo plurale

singular noun	*nsg*	sostantivo singolare	something	qc	qualcosa
optics	OPT	ottica	someone	qu	qualcuno
oneself	o.s.	sé, se stesso	radio	RAD	radio
optics	OTT	ottica	railway	RAIL	ferrovia
popular, slang	P	popolare	religion	REL	religione
painting	PAINT	pittura	skiing	SCI	sci
pejorative	*pej*	spregiativo	singular	sg	singolare
photography	PHOT	fotografia	someone	s.o.	qualcuno
physics	PHYS	fisica	sports	SP	sport
painting	PITT	pittura	humorous	*spir*	uso spiritoso
plural	*pl*	plurale	pejorative	*spreg*	spregiativo
politics	POL	politica	something	sth	qualcosa
past participle	*pp*	participio passato	theatre	TEA	teatro
			technology	TEC	tecnica
present participle	*p pr*	participio presente	technology	TECH	tecnica
			telecommuni- cations	TELEC	telecomuni- cazione
present	*pr*	presente	theatre	THEA	teatro
past historic	*p.r.*	passato remoto	typography, typesetting	TIP	tipografia
present subjunctive	*pr congiunt*	presente congiuntivo	television	TV	televisione
preposition	*prep*	preposizione	vulgar	V	volgare
preterite	*pret*	preterito	auxiliary verb	*v/aus*	verbo ausiliario
present indicative	*pr ind*	presente indicativo	auxiliary verb	*v/aux*	verbo ausiliario
			intransitive verb	*v/i*	verbo intransitivo
pronoun	*pron*	pronome	reflexive verb	*v/r*	verbo riflessivo
preposition	*prp*	preposizione	transitive verb	*v/t*	verbo transitivo
psychology	PSI	psicologia	zoology	ZO	zoologia
psychology	PSYCH	psicologia			

Italian Spelling and Pronunciation

1. The Italian Alphabet

The twenty-one letters of the Italian alphabet are listed below with their names and with their sounds given as approximate English equivalents.

LETTER	NAME	APPROXIMATE SOUND
a	a	Like *a* in English *father*, eg **facile**, **padre**.
b	bi	Like *b* in English *boat*, eg **bello**, **abate**.
c	ci	When followed by **e** or **i**, like *ch* in English *cherry*, eg **cento**, **cinque**; if the **i** is unstressed and followed by another vowel, its sound is not heard, eg **ciaria**, **cieco**. When followed by **a**, **o**, **u**, or a consonant like *c* in English *cook*, eg **casa**, **come**, **cura**, **credere**. **Ch**, which is used before **e** and **i**, has likewise the sound of *c* in English *cook*, eg **chiesa**, **perché**.
d	di	Like *d* in English *dance*, eg **dare**, **madre**.
e	e	Has two sounds. One like *a* in English *make*, eg **ferro**; and one like *e* in English *met*, eg **festa**.
f	effe	Like *f* in English *fool*, eg **farina**, **efelide**.
g	gi	When followed by **e** or **i**, like *g* in English *general*, eg **gelato**, **ginnasta**; if the **i** is unstressed and followed by another vowel, its sound is not heard, eg **giallo**, **giorno**. When followed by **a**, **o**, **u**, or a consonant, like *g* in English *go*, eg **gamba**, **goccia**, **gusto**, **grado**. **Gh**, which is used before **e** and **i**, has likewise the sound of *g* in English *go*, eg **ghisa**. When the combination **gli** (a) is a form of the definite article or the personal pronoun, (b) is final in a word, or (c) comes between two vowels, it has the sound of Castilian *ll*, which is somewhat like *lli* in English *million*, eg (a) **gli uomini**, **gli ho parlato ieri**, (b) **battagli**, (c) **figlio**, **migliore**. When it is (a) initial (except in the word **gli**, above), (b) preceded by a consonant, or (c) followed by a consonant, it is pronounced like *gli* in English *negligence*, eg (a) **glioma**, (b) **ganglio**, (c) **negligenza**. The combination **gl** followed by **a**, **e**, **o**, or **u** is pronounced like *gl* in English *globe*, eg **glabro**, **gleba**, **globo**, **gluteo**, **inglese**. **Gn** has the sound of Castilian *ñ*, which is somewhat like *ni* in English *onion*, eg **signore**, **gnocco**.
h	acca	Always silent, eg **ah**, **hanno**. See **ch** under **c** above and **gh** under **g** above.
i	i	Like *i* in English *machine*, eg **piccolo**, **sigla**.

		When unstressed and followed by another vowel, like *y* in English *yes*, eg **piatto**, **piede**, **fiore**, **fiume**.
		For **i** in *ci*, see **c** above, in *gi*, see **g** above, and in *sci*, see **s** below.
l	elle	Like *l* in English *lamb*, eg **labbro**, **lacrima**.
m	emme	Like *m* in English *money*, eg **mano**, **come**.
n	enne	Like *n* in English *net*, eg **nome**, **cane**.
o	o	Has two sounds. One like *o* in English *note*, eg **sole**; and one like *o* in English *hot*, eg **donna**.
p	pi	Like *p* in English *pot*, eg **passo**, **carpa**.
q	cu	This letter is always followed by the letter **u** and the combination has the sound of *qu* in English *quart*, eg **quanto**, **questo**.
r	erre	Like *r* in English *rubber*, with a slight trill, eg **roba**, **carta**.
s	esse	Has two sounds.
		When initial and followed by a vowel, when preceded by a consonant and followed by a vowel, and when followed by **c** [k] **f**, **p**, **q**, or **t**, like *s* in English *see*, eg **sale**, **falso**, **scappare**, **spazio**, **stoffa**.
		When standing between two vowels and when followed by **b**, **d**, **g** [g], **l**, **m**, **n**, **r** or **v**, like *z* in English *zero*, eg **paese**, **sbaglio**, **svenire**.
		However, **s** standing between two vowels in some words and initial *s* followed by **b**, **d**, **g** [g], **l**, **m**, **n**, **r**, or **v** in some foreign borrowings are pronounced like *s* in *see*, eg **casa**, **tesa**, **smoking**, **slam**.
		When initial s stands between two vowels in a compound, its pronunciation remains that of initial s, eg **autoservizio**.
		Sc, when followed by **e** or **i** has the sound of *sh* in English *shall*, eg **scelta**, **scimmia**; if the **i** is unstressed and followed by another vowel, its sound is not heard, eg **sciame**, **sciopero**.
		Sch has the sound of *sc* in English *scope*, eg **scherzo**, **schiavo**.
		An **s** coming between two vowels is generally pronounced like *z* in English *zero* in the north of Italy.
t	ti	Like *t* in English *table*, eg **terra**, **pasto**.
u	u	Like *u* in English *rule*, eg **luna**, **mulo**. When followed by a vowel, like *w* in English *was*, eg **quanto**, **guerra**, **nuovo**.
v	vu	Like *v* in English *vain*, eg **vita**, **uva**.
z	zeta	Has two sounds. One like *ts* in English *nuts*, eg **grazia**, **zuccero**; and one like *dz* in English *adze*, eg **zero**, **mezzo**.

The following five letters are found in borrowings from other languages.

LETTER	NAME	EXAMPLES
j	i lunga	**jazz**
k	cappa	**ko**
w	vu doppia	**whisky**
x	ics	**xenofobo**, *xilofono*
y	ìpsilon	**yacht, yoghurt**

Consonants written double are longer than consonants written single, that is, it takes a longer time to pronounce them, eg **camino** *chimney*, and **cammino** *road*, **capello** *hair* and **cappello** *hat*. Special attention is called to the following double consonants: **cc** followed by **e** or **i** has the sound of *ch ch* in English *beach chair*, that is a lengthened *ch*, eg **accento**; **cch** has the sound of *kk* in English *book-keeper*, eg **becchino**; **cq** has the sound of *kk* in English *book-keeper*, eg **acqua**; **gg** followed by **e** or **i** has the sound of *ge j* in English *carriage joiner*, eg **peggio**; **ggh** has the sound of *g g* in English *tag game*, eg **agghindare**.

2. Stress and Accent Marks

Whenever stress is shown as part of regular spelling, it is shown on **a, i**, and **u** by the grave accent mark, eg **libertà, giovedì, gioventù**, on close **e** and **o** by the acute accent mark, eg **perché**, and on open **e** and **o** by the grave accent mark, eg **caffè, parlò**.

Guidelines on Stress

(a)   In words of two syllables, the stress falls on the syllable next to the last, eg **casa, muro, terra**. If the syllable next to the last contains a diphthong, that is, a combination of a strong vowel (**a, e**, or **o**) and a weak vowel (**i** or **u**), the strong vowel is stressed, regardless of which vowel comes first, eg **daino, eroico, neutro, fiato, duale, siepe, fiore, buono**.

(b)   In words of more than two syllables, the stress may fall on the syllable next to the last, eg **andata, canzone, pastore** or on a preceding syllable, eg **missile, gondola, mandorla**. In these positions also the stressed syllable may contain a diphthong, eg **incauto, idraulico, fiocina**.

(c)   If a weak vowel in juxtaposition with a strong vowel is stressed, the two vowels constitute two separate syllables, eg **abba•ino**, **ero•ina, pa•ura, miriade, via**.

(d)   Two strong vowels in juxtaposition constitute two separate syllables, eg **pa•ese, aureola, idea, oceano**.

(e)   Two weak vowels in juxtaposition generally consitute a diphthong in which the first vowel is stressed in some words, eg **fluido** and the second vowel in others, eg **piuma**.

(f)   If a word ends in a diphthong, the diphthong is stressed, eg **marinai, parlai, eroi**.

English Pronunciation

Vowels

[ɑː]	*father*	[ˈfɑːðə(r)]
[æ]	*man*	[mæn]
[e]	*get*	[get]
[ə]	*about*	[əˈbaʊt]
[ɜː]	*absurd*	[əbˈsɜːd]
[ɪ]	*stick*	[stɪk]
[iː]	*need*	[niːd]
[ɒ]	*hot*	[hɒt]
[ɔː]	*law*	[lɔː]
[ʌ]	*mother*	[ˈmʌðə(r)]
[ʊ]	*book*	[bʊk]
[uː]	*fruit*	[fruːt]

Diphthongs

[aɪ]	*time*	[taɪm]
[aʊ]	*cloud*	[klaʊd]
[eɪ]	*name*	[neɪm]
[eə]	*hair*	[heə(r)]
[ɪə]	*here*	[hɪə(r)]
[ɔɪ]	*point*	[pɔɪnt]
[əʊ]	*oath*	[əʊθ]
[ʊə]	*tour*	[tʊə(r)]

Consonants

[b]	*bag*	[bæg]
[d]	*dear*	[dɪə(r)]
[f]	*fall*	[fɔːl]
[g]	*give*	[gɪv]
[h]	*hole*	[həʊl]
[j]	*yes*	[jes]
[k]	*come*	[kʌm]
[l]	*land*	[lænd]
[m]	*mean*	[miːn]
[n]	*night*	[naɪt]
[p]	*pot*	[pɒt]
[r]	*right*	[raɪt]
[(r)]	pronounced only at the end of a word followed by a word starting with a vowel: *where* [weə(r)]
[s]	*sun*	[sʌn]
[t]	*take*	[teɪk]
[v]	*vain*	[veɪn]
[w]	*wait*	[weɪt]
[z]	*rose*	[rəʊz]
[ŋ]	*bring*	[brɪŋ]
[ʃ]	*she*	[ʃiː]
[ʧ]	*chair*	[ʧeə(r)]
[dʒ]	*join*	[dʒɔɪn]
[ʒ]	*leisure*	[ˈleʒə(r)]
[θ]	*think*	[θɪŋk]
[ð]	*the*	[ðə]
[']	means that the following syllable is stressed: *ability* [əˈbɪlətɪ]

A

A *abbr* (= *autostrada*) M (= motorway)

a *prp* ◊ *stato in luogo*: **a Roma** in Rome; **a casa** at home ◊ *moto a luogo*: **andare a Roma** go to Rome; **andare a casa** go home ◊ *tempo*: **alle quattro** at four o'clock; **a Natale** at Christmas; **a maggio** in May; **a vent'anni** at the age of twenty; **a giorni** any day now; **a domani!** see you tomorrow! ◊ *modo*: **a piedi** on foot; **alla moda** in fashion; **al burro** GASTR in butter ◊ *mezzo*: **ricamato a mano** embroidered by hand, hand-embroidered; **fatto a macchina** machine-made ◊ *con valore distributivo*: **a due a due** two at a time; **a poco a poco** little by little ◊ *prezzo, misura*: **a che prezzo** at what price; **al metro** by the metre; **100 km all'ora** 100 km an hour

AAS *abbr* (= *Azienda Autonoma di Soggiorno*) tourist board

ab. *abbr* (= *abitanti*) inhabitants

abate *m* abbot

abbacchiato downhearted

abbacchio *m* (*pl* -cchi) GASTR young lamb

abbagliante 1 *agg* dazzling **2** *m gen pl* -**i** AUTO full beam

abbagliare <1g> dazzle

abbaglio *m* (*pl* -gli): **prendere un ~** make a blunder

abbaiare <1i> bark

abbandonare <1a> abandon

abbandono *m* abandon; (*rinuncia*) abandonment; **stato di ~** state of disrepair

abbassamento *m* lowering

abbassare <1a> *prezzo* lower; *radio* turn down; **~ la voce** lower one's voice

abbassarsi (*chinarsi*) bend down; *prezzo* come down; *fig* **~ a** stoop to

abbasso *int*: **~ la scuola!** down with school!

abbastanza enough; (*alquanto*) quite; **ho mangiato ~** I've had enough to eat; **sono ~ soddisfatto** I'm quite satisfied

abbattere <3a> knock down; *casa* demolish; *albero* cut down; *aereo* shoot down; *fig* dishearten

abbattersi fall; *fig* become disheartened

abbattimento *m* knocking down; *casa* demolition; *albero* cutting down; *aereo* shooting down; *fig* despondency

abbattuto disheartened

abbazia *f* abbey

abbellire <4d> embellish

abbeverare <1m> water

abbi, abbia → **avere**

abbicci *m inv* abc; *fig* basics *pl*

abbigliamento *m* clothing; **~ sportivo** sportswear; **industria** *f* **dell'~** clothing industry

abbinare <1a> match; (*combinare*) combine

abboccare <1d> *di pesce* bite; TEC join; *fig* swallow the bait

abboccato *vino* medium sweet

abbonamento *m a giornale*, TEA subscription; *a treno, bus* season-ticket; **~ annuale** yearly subscription; yearly ticket; **~ mensile** monthly subscription; monthly ticket

abbonare <1c & o> take out a subscription for; (*condonare*) deduct

abbonarsi subscribe

abbonato *m* subscriber; TELEC **elenco** *m* **degli -i** telephone directory

abbondante abundant; *porzione* generous; *vestito* loose; *nevicata* heavy

abbondanza *f* abundance

abbordabile *persona* approachable;

prezzo reasonable

abbordare <1a> **1** v/t *persona* approach; F *persona dell'altro sesso* chat up F; *argomento* tackle **2** v/t MAR board

abbottonare <1a> button up

abbozzare <1c> sketch; ~ *un sorriso* smile faintly

abbozzo m sketch

abbracciare <1f> embrace, hug; *fig* take up

abbracciarsi embrace, hug

abbraccio m (pl -cci) embrace, hug; *un ~ a fine lettera* love

abbreviare <1k & b> abbreviate

abbreviazione f abbreviation

abbronzante m sun-tan lotion; *lettino m ~* sunbed

abbronzarsi <1a> *pelle* tan

abbronzarsi get a tan

abbronzato tanned

abbronzatura f tan

abbrustolire <4d> roast

abbuffarsi <1a> stuff o.s. (*di* with)

abbuono m FIN discount

abdicare <1l & d> abdicate

abdicazione f abdication

abete m fir

abile good (*in* at); fit (*a* for)

abilità f inv ability

abilitazione f qualification

abisso m abyss

abitabile habitable; *cucina f ~* dining kitchen

abitacolo m AUTO passenger compartment

abitante m/f inhabitant

abitare <1l> **1** v/t live in **2** v/i live

abitato 1 agg inhabited **2** m built-up area

abitazione f house

abiti mpl clothes

abito m dress; *da uomo* suit; *~ da sera* evening dress

abituale usual

abituare <1l> accustom (*a* to)

abituarsi: *~ a* get used to

abitudinario (pl -ri) **1** agg of fixed habits **2** m creature of habit

abitudine f habit

abolire <4d> abolish

abolizione f abolition

abominevole abominable

aborigeno 1 agg aboriginal **2** m aboriginal

abortire <4d> MED miscarry; *volontariamente* have an abortion; *fig* fail

abortista m/f pro-choice campaigner

aborto m MED miscarriage; *provocato* abortion

abrogare <1e & c or 1l> repeal

abrogazione f repeal

abusare <1a>: *~ di* abuse; (*approfittare*) take advantage of; *~ nel bere* drink to excess

abusivo illegal

abuso m abuse; *~ sessuale* sexual abuse

a.C. abbr (= *avanti Cristo*) BC (= before Christ)

acacia f (pl -cie) acacia

acca f: *non capire un'~* not understand a thing

accademia f academy; *~ di belle arti* art college

accademico (pl -ci) academic

accadere <2c> happen

accaduto m: *raccontami l'~* tell me what happened

accaldarsi <1a> get overheated

accaldato overheated

accalorarsi <1a> *fig* get excited

accampamento m camp

accampare <1a> **1** v/t: *~ scuse* come up with excuses **2** v/i e **accamparsi** camp

accanimento m (*tenacia*) tenacity; (*furia*) rage

accanirsi <4d> (*ostinarsi*) persist; *~ contro qu* rage against s.o.

accanito *odio* fierce; *tifoso* dedicated; *fumatore* inveterate; *lavoratore m ~* hard worker

accanto 1 prp *~ a* next to **2** avv near, nearby; *abitare* next door

accantonare <1a> put aside

accappatoio m (pl -oi) bathrobe; *da mare* beachrobe

accarezzare <1a> caress; *speranza* cherish; *animale* stroke accasciarsi <1f> flop down

accatastare <1a> pile up

accattonaggio *m* begging

accattone *m* beggar

accavallare <1a> cross

accavallarsi *fig* overlap

accecare <1b & d> **1** *v/t* blind **2** *v/i* be blinding

accedere <3a>: ~ **a** enter

accelerare <1b & m> speed up; AUTO accelerate

accelerato **1** *agg* fast; *treno* slow **2** *m* slow train

acceleratore *m* AUTO accelerator

accelerazione *f* acceleration

accendere <3c> light; RAD, TV turn on

accendersi light up; *apparecchio* come on

accendino *m*, **accendisigari** *m inv* lighter

accennare <1a> indicate; *con parole* mention; ~ **a fare qc** show signs of doing sth

accenno *m* (*cenno*) gesture; (*indizio*) sign; (*allusione*) hint

accensione *f* ignition; AUTO ~ **elettronica** electronic ignition

accento *m* accent

accentuare <1b & m> accentuate

accertare <1b> check

accertarsi: ~ **di qc** check sth

acceso *colore* bright; *motore* running; *TV, luce* on

accessibile accessible; *prezzo* reasonable

accesso *m* access; *fig e* MED fit; **divieto d'** ~ no entry

accessori *mpl* accessories

accessoriato AUTO complete with accessories

accessorio secondary

accetta *f* ax(e)

accettabile acceptable

accettare <1b> accept

accettazione *f* acceptance; (*di albergo*) reception; ~ **bagagli** check-in

accetto: **bene**/**male** ~ welcome / not welcome

acchiappare <1a> catch

acciaio *m* (*pl* -ai) steel; ~ **inossi-**

dabile stainless steel

accidentale accidental

accidentato *terreno* rough

accidenti *int* F damn! F; *di sorpresa* wow!

accigliato frowning

accingersi <3d>: ~ **a fare qc** be about to do sth

acciottolato *m* cobbles *pl*

acciuffare <1a> grab

acciuga *f* (*pl* -ghe) anchovy

acclamare <1a>applaud

acclimatarsi <1m> get acclimatized

accludere <3q> enclose

accluso enclosed; **qui** ~ enclosed

accogliente welcoming

accogliere <3ss> welcome; *richiesta* grant

accollare <1c> shoulder

accollarsi take on

accollato *abito* high-necked

accoltellare <1b> knife

accolto *pp* → **accogliere**

accomodamento *m* arrangement; (*accordo*) agreement

accomodante accommodating

accomodare <1c & m> (*riparare*) mend; *lite* resolve; (*sistemare*) arrange

accomodarsi make o.s. at home; **si accomodi!** come in!; (*sedersi*) have a seat!

accompagnamento *m* accompaniment; **lettera** *f* **di** ~ covering letter

accompagnare <1a> accompany

accompagnatore *m*, **-trice** *f* escort; MUS accompanist

acconciatura *f* hairdo

acconsentire <4b> consent (**a** to)

accontentare <1b> satisfy

accontentarsi be happy (**di** with)

acconto *m* deposit

accoppiare <1k & c> couple; *animali* mate

accoppiarsi pair off

accorciare <1f> shorten

accorciarsi get shorter

accordare <1c> grant; MUS tune; (*armonizzare*) harmonize

accordarsi agree; *di colori* match

accordo *m* agreement; (*armonia*)

harmony; MUS chord; *essere d'~* agree; *mettersi d'~* reach an agreement; *d'~!* OK!

accorgersi <3d>: ~ *di* notice

accorrere <3o> hurry; ~ *in aiuto di qu* rush to help s.o.

accortezza f forethought

accorto 1 pp → *accorgersi* 2 agg shrewd

accostare <1c> approach; *porta* leave ajar

accostarsi get close

accreditare <1b & m> confirm; FIN credit

accredito m credit

accrescere <3n> increase

accrescersi grow bigger

accudire <4d> 1 v/t look after 2 v/i: ~ *a qc* attend to sth

accumulare <1m> accumulate

accumulatore m battery

accumulazione f accumulation

accuratezza f care

accurato careful

accusa f accusation; DIR charge; *Pubblica Accusa* public prosecutor

accusare <1a> accuse; DIR charge; ~ *ricevuta* acknowledge receipt

accusato m, -a f accused

accusatore m prosecutor

acerbo unripe

acero m maple

aceto m vinegar; ~ *balsamico* balsamic vinegar; *mettere sott'~* pickle

acetone m nail varnish remover

ACI abbr (= *Automobile Club d'Italia*) Automobile Club of Italy

acidità f acidity; ~ *di stomaco* heartburn

acido 1 agg acid; fig sour; *piogge fpl acide* acid rain sg 2 m acid

ACLI abbr (= *Associazione Cristiana dei Lavoratori Italiani*) Italian trade union association

acne f acne

acqua f water; ~ *corrente* running water; ~ *minerale* mineral water; ~ *potabile* drinking water; ~ *di rubinetto* tap water; ~ *ossigenata* hy-

drogen peroxide; *una teoria che fa ~* a theory that doesn't hold water; ~ *in bocca!* keep it under your hat!; *ha l'~ alla gola* (*non ha tempo*) he's pushed for time; *-e pl* waters; *-e pl territoriali* territorial waters; *in cattive -e* in deep water

acquaforte f etching

acquaio m (pl -ai) sink

acquaragia f turpentine

acquario m (pl -ri) aquarium; ASTR *Acquario* Aquarius

acquatico (pl -ci) aquatic; *sci m* ~ water skiing; *oggetto* waterski; *uccello m* ~ waterfowl

acquavite f brandy

acquazzone m downpour

acquedotto m aqueduct

acqueo: *vapore m* ~ water vapo(u)r

acquerello m water-colo(u)r

acquirente m/f purchaser

acquisizione f acquisition

acquistare <1a> 1 v/t buy; fig gain 2 v/i improve (*in* in)

acquisto m purchase; *potere m d'~* purchasing power; ~ *a rate* hire purchase, Am installment plan

acquolina f: *mi viene l'~ in bocca* my mouth's watering

acre sour; *voce* harsh

acrilico (pl -ci) acrylic

acrobata m/f acrobat

acustica f acoustics

acustico (pl -ci) acoustic

acuto 1 agg intense; *nota, dolore* sharp; *suono, voce* shrill; MED acute 2 m MUS high note

ad prp → *a* (before vowels)

adagiare <1f> *persona* lay down

adagiarsi lie down

adagio 1 avv slowly; *con cautela* cautiously 2 m (pl -gi) MUS adagio

adattamento m adaptation; (*rielaborazione*) reworking

adattare <1a> adapt

adattarsi (*adeguarsi*) adapt (*a* to); (*addirsi*) be suitable (*a* for); *questo colore non ti si adatta* this colour doesn't suit you

adattatore m adaptor

adatto right (*a* for)

addebitare <1m>: FIN ~ *qc a qu* debit s.o. with sth; *fig* ascribe sth to s.o.

addebito *m* FIN debit; *nota f di ~* debit note

addensarsi <1b> thicken

addestramento *m* training

addestrare <1b> train

addetto 1 *agg* assigned (*a* to) **2** *m*, -*a* *f* person responsible; ~ *alle pubbliche relazioni* public relations officer; *fig* ~ *ai lavori* expert; ~ *culturale* cultural attaché; *vietato l'ingresso ai non -i* authorized personnel only

addio 1 *int* goodbye **2** *m* goodbye, farewell

addirittura (*assolutamente*) absolutely; (*perfino*) even

additivo *m* additive

addizionare <1a> add

addizione *f* addition

addobbare <1c> decorate

addobbo *m* decoration

addolcire <4d> sweeten; *fig* soften

addolorare <1a> grieve

addome *m* abdomen

addomesticare <1b, d & n> tame

addominale abdominal

addormentare <1b> get (off) to sleep

addormentarsi fall asleep

addormentato asleep; (*assonnato*) sleepy

addossare <1c> (*appoggiare*) lean (*a* on); *fig colpa* put, lay (*a* on)

addossarsi lean (*a* on); *fig* shoulder

addosso 1 *prp* on; *vicino* next to **2** *avv*: *avere ~ vestiti* have on; *avere ~ qu* have s.o. breathing down one's neck

addurre <3e> produce

adeguare <1a> adjust

adeguarsi conform; ~ *alle circostanze* adjust to circumstances

adeguato adequate

adempiere <4d & g>: ~ *a dovere* carry out, do

aderente 1 *agg vestito* tight **2** *m/f* follower

aderire <4d>: ~ *a* adhere to; *partito*

support; *richiesta* agree to

adesione *f* adhesion; (*consenso*) agreement

adesivo 1 *agg* adhesive **2** *m* sticker

adesso now; *da ~ in poi* from now on; *fino ~* up to now; *per ~* for the moment

adiacente adjacent; ~ *a* next to, adjacent to

adibire <4d> use

adirarsi <1a> get angry

adirato angry

adolescente *m/f* adolescent, teenager

adolescenza *f* adolescence, teens *pl* F

adoperare <1m & c> use

adorare <1a> adore

adorazione *f* adoration

adornare <1a> adorn

adottare <1c> adopt

adottivo *genitori* adoptive; *figlio* adopted

adozione *f* adoption

adrenalina *f* adrenalin

adriatico (*pl* -ci) **1** *agg* Adriatic; *mare m Adriatico* Adriatic Sea **2** *m*: *Adriatico* Adriatic

adulare <1a> flatter

adulazione *f* flattery

adulterare <1m> adulterate

adulterio *m* (*pl* -ri) adultery

adulto 1 *agg* adult **2** *m*, -*a* *f* adult

adunare <1a> assemble

aerare <1l> air

aerazione *f* airing

aereo 1 *agg air attr; fotografia, radici* aerial; *base f -a* air base; *compagnia f -a* airline; *ponte m* ~ airlift; *posta f -a* airmail **2** *m* plane; ~ *di linea* airliner

aerobica *f* aerobics *sg*

aerobus *m inv* plane that makes short-haul flights

aerodinamico aerodynamic

aeronautica *f* aeronautics; ~ *militare* Air Force

aeroplano *m* plane, aeroplane, *Am* airplane

aeroporto *m* airport

aerosol *m inv contenitore* aerosol

aerospaziale aerospace *attr*
aerostato *m* aerostat, lighter-than-air aircraft
aerostazione *f* air terminal
afa *f* closeness, mugginess
affabile affable
affaccendarsi <1b> busy o.s. (*in* with)
affaccendato busy
affacciarsi <1f> appear
affamato starving
affannato breathless
affanno *m* breathlessness; *fig* anxiety
affare *m* matter, business; FIN transaction; *-i pl* business *sg*; **non sono -i tuoi** it's none of your business; **uomo** *m* **d'-i** businessman; **ministro** *m* **degli Affari Esteri** Foreign Secretary; **giro** *m* **d'-i** turnover
affarista *m/f* (*mpl* -i) wheeler-dealer
affascinante fascinating
affascinare <1m> fascinate
affaticare <1d> tire
affaticarsi tire o.s. out
affatto completely; **non è ~ vero!** there's not the slightest bit of truth in it!
affermare <1a> state
affermarsi become established
affermazione *f* assertion; (*successo*) achievement
afferrare <1b> seize, grab F; (*comprendere*) grasp
afferrarsi cling (*a* to), hold on (*a* to)
affettare[1] <1a> (*tagliare*) slice
affettare[2] <1b> *ammirazione ecc* affect
affettato[1] *m* sliced meat
affettato[2] *agg* affected
affettatrice *f* slicer
affetto *m* affection
affettuoso affectionate
affezionarsi <1a>: **~ a qu** become fond of s.o.
affezionato: **~ a qu** fond of s.o.
affiancare <1d> place side by side; *fig* support
affibbiare <1k>: **~ qc a qu** saddle s.o. with sth
affidabilità *f* dependability

affidamento *m* trust; **fare ~ su** rely on
affidare <1a> entrust
affidarsi: **~ a** rely on
affiggere <3mm> *avviso* put up
affilare <1a> sharpen; *fig* make thinner
affilato sharp; *naso* thin
affiliare <1g> *a una società* affiliate
affiliato 1 *m*, **-a** *f* member **2** *agg*: **società** *f* **-a** affiliate
affiliazione *f* affiliation
affinché so that
affine similar
affinità *f inv* affinity
affiorare <1a> *dall'acqua* emerge; *fig* (*mostrarsi*) appear
affissione *f* bill-posting
affisso 1 *pp* → **affiggere 2** *m* bill
affittacamere *m/f* landlord; *donna* landlady
affittare <1a> *locali, terre* let; (*prendere in affitto*) rent; **affittasi** to let
affitto *m* rent; **dare in ~** let; **prendere in ~** rent
affliggere <3cc> distress; *di malattia* trouble, plague
afflitto distressed
affluente *m* tributary
affluenza *f fig* influx
affluire <4d> flow; *di persone* pour in
afflusso *m* influx
affogare <1c & e> *v/t* & *v/i* drown
affollamento *m* crowd
affollare <1c>, **affollarsi** crowd
affollato crowded
affondare <1a> *v/t* & *v/i* sink
affrancare <1d> free; *posta* frank
affrancatura *f* franking; *tassa di spedizione* postage
affresco *m* (*pl* -chi) fresco
affrettare <1a> speed up
affrettarsi hurry
affrontare <1a> face, confront; *spese* meet
affronto *m* insult
affumicare <1d & m> *stanza* fill with smoke; *alimenti* smoke
affumicato smoked
affusolato tapering

afoso sultry

Africa f Africa

africano 1 agg African **2** m, **-a** f African

afrodisiaco m/agg aphrodisiac

agave f agave

agenda f diary

agente m/f agent; **~ di cambio** stockbroker; **~ immobiliare** estate agent, Am realtor; **~ inquinante** pollutant; **~ di pubblica sicurezza** police officer; **~ di vendita** sales representative; **~ di viaggio** travel agent

agenzia f agency; **~ di cambio** bureau de change; **~ immobiliare** estate agency, Am real estate office; **~ pubblicitaria** advertising agency; **~ di viaggi** travel agency

agevolare <1m> make easier

agevolato FIN on easy terms

agevolazione f FIN special term

agevole easy

agganciare <1f> hook; cintura, collana fasten

aggeggio m (pl -ggi) gadget

aggettivo m adjective

agghiacciante spine-chilling

aggiornamento m updating; (rinvio) postponement; **corso m d'~** refresher course

aggiornare <1a> (mettere al corrente) update; (rinviare) postpone

aggiornarsi keep up to date

aggirare <1a> surround; fig ostacolo get round

aggirarsi hang about; FIN be in the region of

aggiudicare <1d & m> award; all'asta knock down

aggiungere <3d> add

aggiunta f addition

aggiustare <1a> (riparare) repair; (sistemare) settle

agglomerato m: **~ urbano** built-up area

aggrapparsi <1a> cling, hold on (a to)

aggravante 1 agg aggravating **2** f aggravation

aggravare <1a> punizione increase; (peggiorare) make worse

aggravarsi worsen, deteriorate

aggravio m (pl -vi): **~ fiscale** tax increase

aggraziato graceful

aggredire <4d> attack

aggressione f aggression; (attacco) attack; POL **patto m di non ~** non-aggression pact

aggressività f aggressiveness

aggressivo aggressive

aggressore m attacker; POL aggressor

agguato m ambush; **tendere un ~ a qu** ambush s.o., set an ambush for s.o.

agguerrito hardened

agiatezza f comfort

agiato comfortable, well-off; (comodo) comfortable

agibile fit for human habitation

agile agile

agilità f agility; fig liveliness

agio m (pl -gi) ease; **vivere negli agi** live in comfort; **sentirsi a proprio ~** feel at ease

agire <4d> act; comportarsi behave, act; di medicina take effect; DIR take action (**contro** against)

agitare <1l> shake; fazzoletto wave; fig (turbare) upset, agitate; **~ prima dell'uso** shake before use

agitato agitated; mare rough

agitazione f agitation

agli prp **a** and art **gli**

aglio m (pl -gli) garlic

agnello m lamb

agnolotti mpl type of ravioli

ago m (pl -ghi) needle

agonia f agony

agonismo m competitiveness

agonistico (pl -ci) competitive

agopuntura f acupuncture

agorafobia f agoraphobia

agosto m August; **in ~** in August

agraria f agriculture

agrario (pl -ri) agricultural

agricolo agricultural

agricoltore m farmer

agricoltura f agriculture

agrifoglio m holly

agriturismo m farm holidays pl

agro sour

agrodolce bittersweet; GASTR sweet and sour

agronomo *m*, **-a** *f* agricultural economist

agrumi *mpl* citrus fruit *sg*

aguzzare <1a> sharpen; **~ la vista** keep one's eyes peeled

aguzzo pointed

ah! oh!

ahi! ouch!

ai *prp* **a** and *art* **i**

Aids *m o f* Aids

airbag *m inv* airbag

A.I.R.E. *abbr* (= **Anagrafe degli Italiani Residenti all'Estero**) register of Italian citizens resident overseas

airone *m* heron

aiuola *f* flower bed

aiutante *m/f* assistant

aiutare <1a> help

aiuto *m* help, assistance; **persona** assistant; **~ allo sviluppo** development aid *or* assistance; **chiedere ~ a qu** ask s.o. for help

aizzare <1a> incite

al *prp* **a** and *art* **il**

ala *f* (*pl* -i) wing

alabastro *m* alabaster

alano *m* Great Dane

alba *f* dawn; **all'~** at dawn

albanese *agg*, *m/f* Albanian

Albania *f* Albania

albeggiare <1f> dawn

alberato tree-lined

albergare <1b & e> put up

albergatore *m*, **-trice** *f* hotel keeper

alberghiero hotel *attr*

albergo *m* (*pl* -ghi) hotel; **guida** *f* **degli -ghi** hotel guide

albero *m* tree; MAR mast; AVIA, AUTO shaft; **~ genealogico** family tree; **~ motore** drive shaft; **~ di Natale** Christmas tree

albicocca *f* (*pl* -cche) apricot

albicocco *m* (*pl* -cchi) apricot (tree)

albo *m* notice board; (*registro*) register; **radiare dall'~** strike off

album *m inv* album

albume *m* albumen

alcalino alkaline

alcol *m* alcohol

alcolico (*pl* -ci) **1** *agg* alcoholic; **gradazione** *f* **-a** alcohol content **2** *m* alcoholic drink

alcolismo *m* alcoholism

alcolizzato *m*, **-a** *f* alcoholic

alcoltest *m inv* Breathalyzer®

alcuno 1 *agg* any; **non ~** no, not any **2** *pron* any; **-i** *pl* some, a few

aldilà *m*: **l'~** the next world

aletta *f* fin

alfabetico (*pl* -ci) alphabetical

alfabeto *m* alphabet

alfanumerico (*pl* -ci) INFOR alphanumeric

alfiere *m scacchi* bishop

alfine eventually

alga *f* (*pl* -ghe) seaweed

algebra *f* algebra

Algeria *f* Algeria

algerino 1 *agg* Algerian **2** *m*, **-a** *f* Algerian

aliante *m* glider

alice *f* anchovy

alienare <1b> DIR transfer; *persone* alienate

alienarsi become lienated

alienato 1 *agg* alienated **2** *m*, **-a** *f* madman; *donna* madwoman

alienazione *f* alienation; **~ mentale** madness

alimentare <1a> **1** *v/t* feed **2** *agg* food *attr*; **generi** *mpl* **-i** foodstuffs

alimentazione *f* feeding

alimento *m* food; **~ base** basic food(stuff); **-i** *pl* DIR alimony *sg*

aliquota *f* share; **~ d'imposta** rate of taxation

aliscafo *m* hydrofoil

alito *m* breath

all. *abbr* (= **allegato**) enc(l). (= enclosed)

all', **alla** *prp* **a** and *art* **l'**, **la**

allacciamento *m* TEC connection

allacciare <1f> fasten; TEC connect

allagamento *m* flooding

allagare <1e> flood

allargare <1e> widen; *vestito* let out; *braccia* open

allargarsi widen

allarmare <1a> alarm

allarmarsi become alarmed

allarme *m* alarm; **dare l'~** raise the alarm; **~ smog** smog alert

allattare <1a> *bambino* feed

alle *prp* **a** and *art* **le**

alleanza *f* alliance

allearsi <1b> ally o.s.

alleato **1** *agg* allied **2** *m*, **-a** *f* ally

allegare <1e> *documento* enclose

allegato *m* enclosure; INFOR attachment; **qui ~** enclosed

alleggerire <4d> lighten; *fig dolore* ease

allegria *f* cheerfulness

allegro **1** *agg* cheerful; *colore* bright **2** *m* MUS allegro

allenamento *m* training

allenare <1b>, **allenarsi** train (*per* for; *a* in)

allenatore *m*, **-trice** *f* trainer

allentare <1b> **1** *v/t* loosen; *fig disciplina* relax **2** *v/i e* **allentarsi** loosen

allergia *f* allergy

allergico (*pl* -ci) allergic (*a* to)

allestimento *m* preparation; MAR fitting out; TEA **~ scenico** sets *pl*, scenery

allestire <4d> prepare; MAR fit out; TEA stage

allevamento *m* BOT, ZO breeding

allevare <1b> BOT, ZO breed; *bambini* bring up, raise

allevatore *m*, **-trice** *f* breeder

alleviare <1b & k> alleviate

allievo *m*, **-a** *f* pupil, student

alligatore *m* alligator

allineamento *m* alignment

allineare <1m> line up; FIN adjust; TIP align

allinearsi line up; *fig* **~ con qu** align o.s. with s.o.

allo *prp* **a** and *art* **lo**

allodola *f* skylark

alloggiare <1f & c> **1** *v/t* put up; MIL billet **2** *v/i* stay, put up

alloggio *m* (*pl* -ggi) accommodation; **dare ~ a qu** put s.o. up; **vitto e ~** bed and board

allontanare <1a> take away; *fig pericolo, sospetto* avert

allontanarsi go away; *fig* grow apart

allora **1** *avv* then **2** *cong* then; **d'~ in poi** from then on; **fin d'~** since then

alloro *m* laurel; GASTR bay

alluce *m* big toe

allucinante F incredible, mind-blowing F

allucinazione *f* hallucination

alludere <3q> allude (*a* to)

alluminio *m* aluminium, *Am* aluminum

allungamento *m* lengthening

allungare <1e> lengthen; (*diluire*) dilute; *mano* stretch out, put out

allungarsi *di giorni* get longer; *di persona* stretch out, lie down

allusione *f* allusion

alluvione *f* flood

almeno at least

alogena *f* halogen

Alpi *fpl* Alps

alpinismo *m* mountaineering

alpinista *m/f* mountain climber

alpino Alpine

alquanto **1** *agg* some **2** *avv* a little, somewhat

alt *int* stop

altalena *f* swing

altare *m* altar

alterare <1l> alter

alterarsi (*guastare*) go bad *or* off; (*irritarsi*) get angry

alterazione *f* alteration

alterco *m* (*pl* -chi) altercation

alternare <1b>, **alternarsi** alternate

alternativa *f* alternative

alternativo *m* alternative

alternato: **corrente** *f* **-a** alternating current

alterno: **a giorni** *pl* **-i** on alternate days

altezza *f* height; *titolo* Highness

alticcio (*pl* -cci) tipsy

altitudine *f* GEOG altitude

alto **1** *agg* high; *persona* tall; **a voce -a** in a loud voice; *leggere* aloud; **in ~** at the top; *moto* up; **a notte -a** in the middle of the night **2** *m* top

altoatesino **1** *agg* South Tyrolean **2** *m*, **-a** *f* person from South Tyrol

altoforno *m* blast furnace

altoparlante *m* loudspeaker

altopiano *m* (*pl* altipiani) plateau

altrettanto *agg, pron* as much; **-i** *pl* as many

altrimenti (*in modo diverso*) differently; (*in caso contrario*) otherwise

altro **1** *agg* other; *un* ~ another; *l'altr'anno* last year; *l'~ giorno* the other day; *l'~ ieri* the day before yesterday **2** *pron* other; *l'un l'~* one another; *gli altri* other people; *tra l'~* what's more, moreover; *desidera ~?* anything else?; *tutt'~ che* anything but

altronde: *d'~* on the other hand

altrove elsewhere

altruismo *m* altruism

altura *f* hill

alunno *m*, **-a** *f* pupil, student

alzacristallo *m inv* AUTO window winder

alzare <1a> raise, lift; *prezzi* increase, raise; (*costruire*) build, erect; *~ le spalle* shrug (one's shoulders)

alzarsi stand up, rise; *da letto* get up; *di sole* come up, rise

amabile lovable; (*gentile*) pleasant, kind; *vino* sweet

amabilità *f* pleasantness

amaca *f* (*pl* -che) hammock

amalgamare <1m> amalgamate

amante *m/f* lover

amare <1a> love; *amico* be fond of

amareggiare <1f> embitter

amareggiato embittered

amarena *f* sour black cherry

amarezza *f* bitterness

amaro **1** *agg* bitter **2** *m liquore* bitters *pl*

ambasciata *f* embassy

ambasciatore *m*, **-trice** *f* ambassador

ambedue both

ambientale environmental

ambientalista **1** *agg* environmental **2** *m/f* environmentalist

ambientarsi <1b> become acclimatized

ambiente *m* BIO environment; *~ di lavoro* work environment; *protezione f dell'~* environmental protection

ambiguità *f inv* ambiguity

ambiguo ambiguous

ambito *m* sphere

ambizione *f* ambition

ambizioso ambitious

ambo **1** *agg* both; *in -i casi* in both cases **2** *m* (*lotteria*) double

ambulante **1** *agg* travel(l)ing **2** *m/f* pedlar

ambulanza *f* ambulance

ambulatorio *m* MED (*pl* -ri) outpatients

America *f* America

americano **1** *agg* American **2** *m*, **-a** *f* American **3** *m* American English

ametista *f* amethyst

amianto *m* asbestos

amichevole friendly

amicizia *f* friendship

amico (*pl* -ci) **1** *agg* friendly **2** *m*, **-a** *f* (*pl* -che) friend; *~ intimo* close friend

amido *m* starch

ammaccare <1d> dent; *frutta* bruise

ammaccatura *f* dent; *su frutta* bruise

ammaestrare <1b> teach; *animali* train

ammalarsi <1a> fall ill

ammalato **1** *agg* ill **2** *m*, **-a** *f* ill person

ammanco *m* (*pl* -chi) deficit

ammanettare <1a> handcuff, put handcuffs on

ammarare <1a> *di aereo* put down in the water; *di navetta spaziale* splash down

ammassare <1a>, **ammassarsi** mass

ammasso *m* pile; GEOL mass

ammazzare <1a> kill; *animali* slaughter

ammazzarsi (*suicidarsi*) kill o.s.

ammenda *f* (*multa*) fine; *fare ~ di* make amends for

ammesso *pp* → **ammettere**

ammettere <3ee> admit; (*supporre*) suppose; (*riconoscere*) acknowledge; *ammesso che ...* supposing (that) ...

amministrare <1a> administer; *azienda* manage, run

amministrativo administrative

amministratore *m*, **-trice** *f* administrator; *di azienda* manager; ~ **delegato** managing director

amministrazione *f* administration; ~ **comunale** local council; **pubblica** ~ public administration; **spese** *fpl* **d'~** administrative costs

ammiraglia *f* flagship

ammiraglio *m* (*pl* -gli) admiral

ammirare <1a> admire

ammiratore *m*, **-trice** *f* admirer

ammirazione *f* admiration

ammirevole admirable

ammissibile admissible

ammobiliare <1g> furnish

ammobiliato furnished

ammodo **1** *agg inv* respectable **2** *avv* properly

ammollo: **in** ~ soaking

ammonimento *m* reprimand, admonishment; (*consiglio*) warning

ammonire <4d> reprimand, admonish; (*avvertire*) warn; DIR caution

ammonizione *f* reprimand, admonishment; SP warning; DIR caution

ammontare **1** *v/i* <1a>: ~ **a** amount to **2** *m* amount; **per un** ~ **di ...** in the amount of ...

ammorbidire <4d> soften

ammortamento *m* FIN amortization

ammortizzare <1a> FIN amortize

ammortizzatore *m* AUTO shock absorber

ammucchiare <1g> pile up

ammucchiarsi pile up, accumulate

ammuffire <4d> go mo(u)ldy; *fig* mo(u)lder away

ammutolire <4d> be struck dumb

amnesia *f* amnesia

amnistia *f* amnesty

amo *m* hook; *fig* bait

amore *m* love; **per l'~ di qu** for love of s.o.; **per l'amor di Dio** for goodness' sake, for the love of God; **fare l'~ con qu** make love to s.o.

amoreggiare <1f> flirt

amorevole loving

amoroso loving, affectionate; *sguardo* amorous; *lettera*, *poesia* love *attr*

amperaggio *m* (*pl* -gi) amperage

ampiezza *f di stanza* spaciousness; *di*

gonna fullness; *fig di cultura* breadth; *fig* ~ **di vedute** broadmindedness

ampio (*pl* -pi) *stanza* spacious, large; *abito* roomy; *gonna* full

ampliamento *m* broadening, widening; *di edificio* extension

ampliare <1l> broaden, widen; *edificio* extend

amplificare <1m & d> TEC *suono* amplify

amplificatore *m* amplifier

ampolla *f* cruet

amputare <1l> amputate

amputazione *f* amputation

amuleto *m* amulet

anabbagliante dipped

anabolizzante *m* anabolic steroid

anacronistico (*pl* -ci) anachronistic

anagrafe *f ufficio* registry office

analcolico (*pl* -ci) **1** *agg* non-alcoholic **2** *m* non-alcoholic drink

anale anal

analfabeta *m/f* (*mpl* -i) illiterate person, person who cannot read or write

analfabetismo *m* illiteracy

analgesico (*pl* -ci) *m/agg* analgesic

analisi *f inv* analysis; ~ **del sangue** blood test

analista *m/f* (*mpl* -i) analyst; ~ **programmatore** systems analyst

analizzare <1a> analyse, *Am* analyze

analogia *f* analogy

analogo (*pl* -ghi) analogous

ananas *m inv* pineapple

anarchia *f* anarchy

anarchico (*pl* -ci) **1** *agg* anarchic **2** *m*, **-a** *f* anarchist

ANAS *abbr* (= **Azienda Nazionale Autonoma della Strada**) Italian Roads Department

anatomia *f* anatomy

anatomico (*pl* -ci) anatomical

anatra *f* duck

anca *f* (*pl* -che) hip

anche too, also, as well; (*perfino*) even; ~ **se** even if

ancora[1] *avv* still; *di nuovo* again; *di più* (some) more; **non** ~ not yet; ~

una volta once more, one more time; **dammene ~ un po'** give me a bit more

ancora² *f* anchor; **gettare l'~** drop anchor

ancoraggio *m* (*pl* -ggi) anchoring; *luogo* anchorage

ancorare <1l> anchor

ancorarsi anchor; *fig* **~ a** cling to

andamento *m di vendite* performance

andare <1p> **1** *v/i* go; (*funzionare*) work; **~ via** (*partire*) leave; *di macchia* come out; **~ bene** suit; *taglia* fit; **~ a cavallo** ride; **~ a passeggio** walk; **~ a male** go off; **~ a finire** turn out; **~ in bicicletta** cycle; **come va?** how are you?, how are things?; **non mi va** *di vestito* it doesn't fit me; **non mi va di venire** I don't feel like coming **2** *m*: **coll'~ del tempo** with the passage of time; **a lungo ~** in the long run

andarsene go away

andata *f* outward journey; **c'era più traffico all'~** there was more traffic on the way there; **biglietto** *m di* **~** single (ticket), *Am* oneway ticket; **biglietto** *m di* **~ e ritorno** return (ticket), *Am* roundtrip ticket

andatura *f* walk; SP pace

andirivieni *m inv* toing and froing

androne *m* hallway

aneddoto *m* anecdote

anello *m* ring; **~ di fidanzamento** engagement ring

anemia *f* an(a)emia

anemico (*pl* -ci) an(a)emic

anemone *m* anemone

anestesia *f* an(a)esthesia; *sostanza* an(a)esthetic

anestesista *m/f* (*mpl* -i) an(a)esthetist

anestetico *m* (*pl* -ci) an(a)esthetic

anfetamina *f* amphetamine

anfibio (*pl* -bi) **1** *agg* amphibious **2** *m* ZO amphibian; MIL amphibious vehicle

anfiteatro *m* amphitheatre, *Am* -theater

anfora *f* amphora

angelo *m* angel; **~ custode** guardian angel

anglicano 1 *agg* Anglican **2** *m*, **-a** *f* Anglican

anglista *m/f* student of English

anglosassone Anglo-Saxon

angolare angular

angolo *m* corner; MAT angle; **~ cottura** kitchenette; MAT **~ retto** right angle; SP **calcio d'~** corner kick;

angoloso angular

angoscia *f* (*pl* -sce) anguish

angoscioso *pieno d'angoscia* anguished; *che da angoscia* distressing, heart-rending

anguilla *f* eel

anguria *f* water melon

angusto narrow

anice *m* GASTR aniseed

anidride *f*: **~ carbonica** carbon dioxide

anima *f* soul; **non c'è ~ viva** there isn't a soul to be seen; F **rompere l'~ a qu** get on s.o.'s nerves F

animale 1 *agg* animal *attr* **2** *m* animal; **~ domestico** pet

animare <1l> give life to; *conversazione* liven up; (*promuovere*) promote

animato *strada* busy; *conversazione, persona* animated

animatore *m*, **-trice** *f di gruppo* leader

animazione *f* animation; INFOR **~ al computer** computer animation

animo *m* nature; (*coraggio*) heart; **farsi ~** be brave; **perdersi d'~** lose heart

anisetta *f* aniseed-flavoured liqueur

anitra *f* duck

annacquare <1a> water down

annaffiare <1k> water

annaffiatoio *m* (*pl* -oi) watering can

annali *mpl* annals

annata *f* vintage; (*anno*) year; *importo* annual amount

annegare <1e> **1** *v/t* drown **2** *v/i e* **annegarsi** drown

annerire <4d> **1** *v/t* blacken **2** *v/i e* **annerirsi** turn black, blacken

annessione f POL annexation
annesso 1 pp → **annettere 2** agg annexed; (allegato) enclosed, attached **3** m edificio annex(e)
annettere <3m> POL annex; ARCHI add; (allegare) enclose, attach
annidarsi <1a> nest
anniversario m (pl -ri) anniversary
anno m year; **buon ~!** Happy New Year!; **~ finanziario** financial year; **~ scolastico** school year; **quanti -i hai?** how old are you?; **ho 33 -i** I'm 33 (years old)
annodare <1c> tie (together); cravatta tie, knot
annoiare <1i> bore; (dare fastidio a) annoy
annoiarsi get bored
annoiato bored
annotare <1c> make a note of; testo annotate
annotazione f note; in testo annotation
annuale annual, yearly; di un anno year-long
annuario m (pl -ri) yearbook
annuire <4d> (assentire) assent (a to)
annullamento m cancellation; di matrimonio annulment
annullare <1a> cancel; matrimonio annul; gol disallow; (vanificare) cancel out
annunciare <1f> announce
annunciatore m, **-trice** f RAD, TV announcer
Annunciazione f REL Annunciation
annuncio m (pl -ci) announcement; in giornale advertisement; **-i** pl **economici** classified ads, classifieds; **~ pubblicitario** ad(vert), advertisement
annunziare <1a> → **annunciare**
annuo annual, yearly
annusare <1a> sniff; fig smell
annuvolarsi <1a> cloud over
anomalo anomalous
anonimo anonymous; **società** f **-a** limited company
anoressia f anorexia
anoressico anorexic

anormale abnormal
ANSA abbr (= **Agenzia Nazionale Stampa Associata**) Italian Press Agency
ansa f handle; di un fiume bend
ansia f anxiety; **con ~** anxiously
ansimare <1l> wheeze
ansioso anxious
antagonismo m antagonism
antagonista m/f (mpl -i) antagonist
antartico (pl -ci) Antarctic attr
antecedente 1 agg preceding **2** m precedent
antefatto m prior event
anteguerra m pre-war years pl
antenato m, **-a** f ancestor
antenna f RAD, TV aerial; ZO antenna; **~ parabolica** satellite dish
anteporre <3ll> put before
anteposto pp → **anteporre**
anteprima f preview
anteriore front; precedente previous
anti … anti …
antiatomico (pl -ci) anti-nuclear; **rifugio** m **~** fallout shelter
antibiotico (pl -ci) m/agg antibiotic
anticamente in ancient times
anticamera f ante-room; **fare ~** be kept waiting
antichità f inv antiquity; **negozio** m **d'~** antique shop
anticiclone m anticyclone
anticipare <1m> anticipate; denaro pay in advance; partenza, riunione ecc bring forward
anticipo m advance; (caparra) deposit; **in ~** ahead of time, early
antico (pl -chi) **1** agg ancient; mobile antique **2 gli -chi** pl the ancients
anticoncezionale m/agg contraceptive
anticonformista m/f (mpl -i) nonconformist
anticongelante m anti-freeze
anticorpo m antibody
anticostituzionale unconstitutional
antidoto m antidote
antifurto 1 adj antitheft **2** m antitheft device
antigas inv gas attr
antincendio inv fire attr

antinebbia *m inv* foglamp

antiorario: **in senso** ~ anticlockwise, *Am* counterclockwise

antipasto *m* starter

antipatia *f* antipathy

antipatico (*pl* -ci) disagreeable

antiquariato *m* antique business, antiques; **negozio** *m* **di** ~ antique shop

antiquario *m* (*pl* -ri), **-a** *f* antique dealer

antiquato antiquated

antiriflesso *inv* anti-glare

antiruggine *m* rust inhibitor

antirumore: **protezione** *f* ~ soundproofing

antisemitismo *m* anti-Semitism

antisettico (*pl* -ci) *m*/*agg* antiseptic

antisismico (*pl* -ci) earthquakeproof

antitesi *f* FIL antithesis

antiurto shockproof

antologia *f* anthology

antracite *f* anthracite

antropologia *f* anthropology

anulare *m* ring finger

anzi in fact; (*o meglio*) (or) better still

anzianità *f* old age; ~ **di servizio** seniority

anziano **1** *agg* elderly; *per servizio* (most) senior **2** *m*, **-a** *f* old man; *donna* old woman; **gli -i** the elderly

anziché rather than

anzitutto first of all

aorta *f* aorta

apatia *f* apathy

apatico (*pl* -ci) apathetic

ape *f* bee

aperitivo *m* aperitif

aperto **1** *pp* → **aprire 2** *agg* open; *di mentalità* **aperta** broad-minded; **all'** ~ *piscina* open-air; **mangiare all'**~ eat outside *or* in the open air

apertura *f* opening; PHOT aperture; ~ **di credito** loan agreement; ~ **alare** wingspan

apice *m* apex; *fig* height

apicoltore *m*, **-trice** *f* bee-keeper

apicoltura *f* bee-keeping

apnea *f* SP free diving

apolide **1** *agg* stateless **2** *m* stateless person

apolitico (*pl* -ci) apolitical

apoplessia *f* apoplexy

apostolico (*pl* -ci) apostolic

apostolo *m* apostle

apostrofare <1m & c> reprimand; GRAM add an apostrophe to

apostrofo *m* apostrophe

appagare <1e> satisfy

appaiare <1i> match

appallottolare <1c & n> roll up into a ball

appalto *m* (*contratto*) contract; **dare in** ~ contract out; **prendere in** ~ win the contract for; **gara** *f* **di** ~ call for tenders

appannare <1a> mist up

appannarsi *di vetro* mist up; *di vista* grow dim

apparato *m* TEC, *fig* apparatus; ~ **digerente** digestive system

apparecchiare <1g> *tavola* set, lay; (*preparare*) prepare

apparecchiatura *f* equipment

apparecchio *m* (*pl* -cchi) TEC device; AVIA F plane; *per denti* brace; ~ **fotografico** camera; F **portare l'**~ wear a hearing aid

apparente apparent

apparenza *f* appearance; **salvare le -e** save face

apparire <4e> appear

appariscente striking, eyecatching

apparizione *f* apparition

appartamento *m* flat, *Am* apartment

appartarsi <1a> withdraw

appartenere <2q> belong

appassionare <1a> excite; (*commuovere*) move

appassionarsi become excited (*a* by)

appassionato passionate

appassire <4d> wither

appellarsi <1b> appeal (*a* to; **contro** against)

appello *m* appeal; **fare** ~ **a qu** appeal to s.o.; DIR **ricorrere in** ~ lodge an appeal

appena **1** *avv* just **2** *cong* as soon as

appendere <3c> hang

appendiabiti *m* hatstand

appendice f appendix
appendicite f appendicitis
Appennini mpl Apennines
appesantire <4d> make heavier
appesi, **appeso** pp → **appendere**
appetito m appetite; **buon ~!** enjoy
your meal!
appetitoso appetizing
appianare <1a> level; lite smooth
over
appiattire <4d> flatten
appiccicare <1m & d> stick
appiccicarsi stick
appiccicoso sticky; fig clingy
appigliarsi <1g> grab hold (**a** of)
appiglio m (pl -gli) per mani finger-
hold; per piedi toehold; fig excuse
applaudire <4a or d> v/t & v/i applaud
applauso m applause
applicare <1l & d> etichetta attach;
regolamento apply
applicarsi: ~ **a qc** apply o.s. to sth
applicazione f application
appoggiare <1f & c> lean (**a**
against); (posare) put; fig support,
back
appoggiarsi: ~ **a** lean on; fig rely on,
lean on
appoggiatesta m inv headrest
appoggio m (pl -ggi) support
apporre <3ll> put; ~ **la firma su qc**
put one's signature to sth
apportare <1c> bring; fig (causare)
cause
apposito appropriate
apposta deliberately, on purpose;
specialmente specifically
apprendere <3c> learn; notizia hear
apprendista m/f (mpl -i) apprentice
apprendistato m apprenticeship
apprensione f apprehension
apprensivo apprehensive
appreso pp → **apprendere**
appresso 1 prp close, near; (dietro)
behind; ~ **a qu** near s.o., close to s.o.
2 avv near, close by; **portarsi qc** ~
bring sth (with one)
apprezzare <1b> appreciate
approccio m (pl -cci) approach
approdare <1c> land; di barca moor,

tie up; fig **non ~ a nulla** come to
nothing
approdo m landing; luogo landing
stage
approfittare <1a>: ~ **di qc** take advantage of sth
approfondire <4d> deepen; fig
study in depth
appropriarsi <1m & c>: ~ **di qc** appropriate sth
appropriato appropriate
approvare <1c> approve of; legge
approve
approvazione f approval
approvvigionamento m supply
appuntamento m appointment
appuntare <1a> pin; avviso pin up
appuntito pointed; matita sharp
appunto 1 m note; **prendere -i** take
notes 2 avv: (**per l'**)~ exactly
apribottiglie m inv bottle opener
aprile m April
aprire <4f> open; rubinetto turn on
aprirsi open; ~ **con qu** confide in s.o.,
open up to s.o.
apriscatole m inv can-opener, Br
tin-opener
aquila f eagle
aquilone m kite
arabesco m (pl -chi) arabesque; spir
scrawl, scribble
Arabia Saudita f Saudi (Arabia)
arabo 1 agg Arab 2 m, **-a** f Arab 3 m
Arabic
arachide f peanut
aragosta f lobster
arancia f (pl -ce) orange
aranciata f orangeade
arancio 1 agg inv orange 2 m (pl -ci)
albero orange tree; colore orange
arancione m/agg orange
arare <1a> plough, Am plow
aratro m plough, Am plow
arazzo m tapestry
arbitraggio m (pl -ggi) arbitration;
SP refereeing
arbitrare <1l> arbitrate in; SP referee
arbitrario (pl -ri) arbitrary
arbitro m arbiter; SP referee
arbusto m shrub
arca f (pl -che) (cassa) chest; REL **l'~**

di Noè Noah's Ark

arcaico (*pl* -ci) archaic

arcangelo *m* archangel

arcata *f* ANAT, ARCHI arch

archeologia *f* arch(a)eology

archeologo *m* (*pl* -gi), **-a** *f* arch(a)eologist

archetto *m* MUS bow

architetto *m* architect

architettonico (*pl* -ci) architectural

archiviare <1k> file

archivio *m* (*pl* -vi) archives, records

arcipelago *m* (*pl* -ghi) archipelago

arcivescovo *m* archbishop

arco *m* (pl -chi) bow; ARCHI arch; **~ di tempo** space of time; **orchestra *f* d'~chi** string orchestra

arcobaleno *m* rainbow

ardente *fig* ardent

ardere <3uu> *v/t & v/i* burn

area *f* surface; *zona* area; **~ fabbricabile** site that may be built on; SP **~ di rigore** penalty area; **~ di servizio** service area

arena *f* arena

arenarsi <1a> run aground; *fig* come to a halt

areo … → **aereo …**

argano *m* winch

argentato silver-plated

argenteria *f* silver(ware)

Argentina *f* Argentina

argentino **1** *agg* Argentinian **2** *m*, **-a** *f* Argentinian

argento *m* silver; **~ vivo** quicksilver; FERR **carta *f* d'~** travel pass for people over a certain age; **nozze fpl d'~** silver wedding *sg*

argilla *f* clay

argilloso clayey

arginare <1l> embank

argine *m* embankment

argomento *m* argument; (*contenuto*) subject; **cambiare ~** change the subject

arguto witty; (*perspicace*) shrewd

arguzia *f* wit; *espressione* witticism, witty remark; (*perspicacia*) shrewdness

aria *f* **1** air; **~ condizionata** air conditioning; **all'~ aperta** in the fresh air; **mandare all'~ qc** ruin sth **2** (*aspetto*) appearance; (*espressione*) air; **aver l'~ stanca** look tired; **ha l'~ di non capire** he looks as if he doesn't understand; **darsi delle -e** give o.s. airs **3** MUS tune; *di opera* aria

aridità *f* dryness

arido dry, arid

arieggiare <1f> *stanza* air

ariete *m* ZO ram; ASTR **Ariete** Aries

aringa *f* (*pl* -ghe) herring

arista *f* GASTR chine of pork

aristocratico (*pl* -ci) **1** *agg* aristocratic **2** *m*, **-a** *f* aristocrat

aristocrazia *f* aristocracy

aritmetica *f* arithmetic

arma *f* (*pl* -i) weapon; **~ da fuoco** firearm; **-i** *pl* **convenzionali** conventional weapons; **-i** *pl* **nucleari** nuclear weapons; **-i** *pl* **atomiche, biologiche e chimiche** atomic, biological and chemical weapons; **chiamare alle -i** call up; *fig* **essere alle prime -i** be a beginner, be just starting out

armadio *m* (*pl* -di) cupboard; **~ a muro** fitted cupboard

armamentario *m* (*pl* -ri) *gen spir* paraphernalia

armamento *m* armament; **industria *f* degli -i** armaments industry

armare <1a> arm; ARCHI reinforce

armarsi arm o.s. (**di** with)

armata *f* army; MAR fleet

armato armed

armatore *m* shipowner

armatura *f* armo(u)r; (*struttura*) framework

armistizio *m* (*pl* -zi) armistice

armonia *f* harmony

armonica *f* (*pl* -che) harmonica; **~ a bocca** mouth organ

armonico (*pl* -ci) harmonic

armonioso harmonious

armonizzare <1a> *v/t & v/i* harmonize

arnese *m* tool

arnia *f* beehive

aroma *m* (*pl* -i) aroma

aromatico (*pl* -ci) aromatic

aromatizzare <1a> flavo(u)r

aromaterapia f aromatherapy

arpa f harp

arpione m pesca harpoon

arrabattarsi <1a> do everything one can

arrabbiarsi <1k> get angry

arrabbiato angry; (idrofobo) rabid

arrampicarsi <1m & d> climb

arrampicata f climb

arrampicatore m, -trice f climber; ~ **sociale** social climber

arrangiamento m arrangement

arrangiare <1f> arrange

arrangiarsi (accordarsi) agree (**su** on); (destreggiarsi) manage

arrecare <1b & d> bring; fig cause

arredamento m décor; mobili furniture; arte interior design

arredare <1b> furnish

arredatore m, -trice f interior designer

arrendersi <3c> surrender; fig give up

arrendevole soft, yielding

arrestare <1b> stop, halt; DIR arrest

arrestarsi stop

arresto m coming to a stop; DIR arrest

arretrato **1** agg in arrears; paese underdeveloped; **numero** m ~ **di giornale** back number **2** -i mpl arrears

arricchire <4d> fig enrich

arricchirsi get rich

arricciare <1f> capelli curl; ~ **il naso** turn up one's nose

arringa f (pl -ghe) DIR closing speech for the defence

arrivare <1a> arrive; ~ **a** reach; ~ **primo** arrive first; ~ **puntuale** arrive on time; ~ **a fare qc** manage to do sth; F **non ci arriva** he doesn't get it F, he doesn't understand

arrivederci, **arrivederla** goodbye

arrivista m/f (mpl -i) social climber

arrivo m arrival; SP finishing line; -i **internazionali** international arrivals

arrogante arrogant

arroganza f arrogance

arrossire <4d> blush

arrostire <4d> carne roast; ai ferri grill

arrosto m roast; ~ **d'agnello** roast lamb

arrotolare <1m & c> roll up

arrotondare <1a> round off; stipendio supplement

arroventato red-hot

arruffare <1a> capelli ruffle

arruffato ruffled

arrugginire <4d> **1** v/t rust **2** v/i e arrugginirsi rust; fig become rusty

arruolamento m enlistment

arruolare <1o> enlist

arruolarsi enlist, join up

arsenale m arsenal; MAR dockyard

arso **1** pp → ardere **2** agg burnt; (secco) dried-up

arsura f blazing heat

arte f art; (abilità) gift; **le -i pl figurative** the figurative arts; **-i pl grafiche** graphic arts; **storia** f **dell'~** history of art; **un discorso fatto ad ~** a masterly speech

artefatto voce disguised

artefice m/f fig author, architect

arteria f artery; ~ **stradale** arterial road

arterioso arterial

artico (pl -ci) Arctic attr

articolare **1** agg articular **2** v/t <1m> articulate; (suddividere) divide

articolazione f ANAT articulation

articolo m item, article; GRAM ~ **determinativo** definite article; GRAM ~ **indeterminativo** indefinite article; -i **pl di consumo** consumer goods; ~ **di fondo** leading article; ~ **di prima necessità** basic

artificiale artificial

artificio m (pl -ci) artifice; **fuochi** mpl d'~ fireworks

artificioso maniere artificial

artigianale handmade, handcrafted

artigianato m craftsmanship

artigiano m, -a f craftsman; donna craftswoman

artiglieria f artillery

artiglio m (pl -gli) claw

artista m/f (mpl -i) artist

artistico (pl -ci) artistic

arto *m* limb

artrite *f* arthritis

artrosi *f* rheumatism

ascella *f* armpit

ascendente **1** *agg* ascending; *strada* sloping upwards; *movimento* upwards **2** *m* ASTR ascendant; *fig* influence

ascensione *f di montagna* ascent; REL Ascension

ascensore *m* lift, *Am* elevator

ascesa *f* ascent

ascesso *m* abscess

asceta *m* (*pl* -i) ascetic

ascia *f* (*pl* -sce) ax(e)

asciugacapelli *m* hairdryer

asciugamano *m* towel; ~ *da bagno* bath towel

asciugare <1e> dry

asciugarsi dry o.s.; ~ *i capelli* dry one's hair

asciugatrice *f* tumble dryer

asciutto **1** *agg* dry **2** *m*: *fig* *trovarsi all'*~ be stony broke

ascoltare <1a> listen to

ascoltatore *m*, **-trice** *f* listener

ascolto *m* listening; *dare / prestare* ~ listen (*a* to); *indice m di* ~ ratings *pl*

asettico (*pl* -ci) aseptic

asfaltare <1a> asphalt

asfalto *m* asphalt

asfissia *f* asphyxia

asfissiare <1k> asphyxiate

Asia *f* Asia

asiatico (*pl* -ci) **1** *agg* Asian **2** *m*, **-a** *f* Asian

asilo *m* shelter; *richiesta f di* ~ *politico* request for political asylum; ~ *infantile* nursery school; ~ *nido* day nursery

asimmetrico (*pl* -ci) asymmetrical

asino *m* ass (*anche fig*)

asma *f* asthma

asmatico (*pl* -ci) asthmatic

asociale antisocial

asola *f* buttonhole

asparago *m* (*pl* -gi) spear of asparagus; **-gi** asparagus *sg*

aspettare <1b> wait for; ~ *un bambino* be expecting a baby; *farsi*

~ keep people waiting

aspettarsi expect; *dovevo aspettarmelo* I should have expected it

aspettativa *f* expectation; *da lavoro* unpaid leave

aspetto[1] *m* look, appearance; *di problema* aspect; *sotto quest'* ~ from that point of view

aspetto[2] *m*: *sala f d'* ~ waiting room

aspirante **1** *agg* TEC suction *attr* **2** *m/f* applicant

aspirapolvere *m* vacuum cleaner

aspirare <1a> **1** *v/t* inhale; TEC suck up **2** *v/i*: ~ *a qc* aspire to sth

aspirina *f* aspirin

asportare <1c> take away

aspro sour; (*duro*) harsh; *litigio* bitter

assaggiare <1f> taste, sample

assaggio *m* (*pl* -ggi) taste, sample

assai **1** *agg* a lot of **2** *avv con verbo* a lot; *con aggettivo* very; (*abbastanza*) enough

assalire <4m> attack

assaltare <1a> → *assalire*

assalto *m* attack; *fig* *prendere d'*~ storm

assassinare <1a> murder; POL assassinate

assassinio *m* murder; POL assassination

assassino **1** *agg* murderous **2** *m*, **-a** *f* murderer; POL assassin

asse[1] *f* board; ~ *da stiro* ironing board

asse[2] *m* TEC axle; MAT axis

assecondare <1a> support; (*esaudire*) satisfy

assediare <1k> besiege

assedio *m* (*pl* -di) siege

assegnare <1a> *premio* award; (*destinare*) assign

assegno *m* cheque, *Am* check; ~ *in bianco* blank cheque (*Am* check); ~ *sbarrato* crossed cheque (*Am* check); ~ *turistico* traveller's cheque, *Am* traveler's check; *contro* ~ cash on delivery; *-i familiari* child benefit; *emettere un* ~ issue *or* write a cheque (*Am* check)

assemblea *f* meeting; ~ *generale* annual general meeting

assennato sensible

assentarsi <1b> go away, leave

assente absent, away; *fig* absent-minded

assenza *f* absence; **~ di qc** lack of sth

assessore *m* council(l)or; **~ comunale** local councillor

assetato thirsty

assetto *m* order; *MAR* trim

assicurare <1a> insure; (*legare*) secure; *lettera, pacco* register

assicurarsi make sure, ensure

assicurata *f* registered letter

assicurato 1 *agg* insured; *lettera, pacco* registered **2** *m*, **-a** *f* person with insurance

assicurazione *f* insurance; **~ dei bagagli** luggage insurance; **~ di responsabilità civile** liability insurance; **~ sulla vita** life insurance; **~ casco** comprehensive insurance

assideramento *m* exposure

assiduo (*diligente*) assiduous; (*regolare*) regular

assieme together

assillante nagging

assillare <1a> pester

assillo *m* *fig persona* pest, nuisance; (*preoccupazione*) nagging thought

assimilare <1m> assimilate

assimilazione *f* assimilation

assise *fpl*: **Corte** *f* **d'~** Crown Court

assistente *m/f* assistant; **~ sociale** social worker; **~ di volo** flight attendant

assistenza *f* assistance; **~ medica** medical care; **~ sociale** social work; **~ tecnica** after-sales service

assistere <3f> **1** *v/t* assist, help; (*curare*) nurse **2** *v/i* (*essere presente*) be present (**a** at), attend (**a** sth)

asso *m* ace; *fig* **piantare in ~** leave in the lurch

associare <1f> take into partnership; *fig* **~ qu a qc** associate s.o. with sth

associarsi enter into partnership (**a** with); (*unirsi*) join forces; (*iscriversi*) subscribe (**a** to); (*prendere parte*) join (**a** sth)

associazione *f* association; **~ per la difesa dei consumatori** consumer association

assoggettare <1b> subject

assolato sunny

assolo *m inv* MUS solo

assolto *pp* → **assolvere**

assolutamente absolutely

assoluto absolute

assoluzione *f* DIR acquittal; REL absolution

assolvere <3g> DIR acquit; *da un obbligo* release; *compito* carry out, perform; REL absolve, give absolution to

assomigliare <1g>: **~ a qu** be like s.o., resemble s.o.

assomigliarsi be like *or* resemble each other

assonnato sleepy

assorbente 1 *agg* absorbent **2** *m*: **~ igienico** sanitary towel

assorbire <4c or 4d> absorb

assordante deafening

assordare <1a> **1** *v/t* deafen **2** *v/i* go deaf

assortimento *m* assortment

assortito assorted; **essere ben ~ con** go well with

assorto engrossed

assuefare <3aa> accustom (**a** to)

assuefarsi become accustomed (**a** to)

assuefatto *pp* → **assuefare**

assuefazione *f* resistance, tolerance; *agli alcolici, alla droga* addiction

assumere <3h> *impiegato* take on, hire; *incarico* take on

assunzione *f di impiegato* employment, hiring; REL **Assunzione** Assumption

assurdità *f* absurdity

assurdo absurd

asta *f* pole; FIN auction; **mettere all'~** sell at auction, put up for auction

astemio (*pl* -mi) **1** *agg* abstemious **2** *m*, **-a** *f* abstemious person

astenersi <2q>: **~ da** abstain from

astensione *f* abstention; **~ dal voto** abstention

asterisco *m* (*pl* -chi) asterisk

astigmatismo *m* astigmatism

astinenza *f* abstinence

astio *m* (*pl* -ti) ranco(u)r

astratto abstract

astringente *m/agg* MED astringent

astro *m* star

astrologia *f* astrology

astrologo *m* (*pl* -gi), -a *f* astrologer

astronauta *m/f* (*mpl* -i) astronaut

astronave *f* spaceship

astronomia *f* astronomy

astronomico (*pl* -ci) astronomical

astronomo *m*, -a *f* astronomer

astuccio *m* (*pl* -cci) case

astuto astute

ateismo *m* atheism

ateneo *m* university

ateo *m*, -a *f* atheist

atlante *m* atlas

atlantico (*pl* -ci) Atlantic; **Oceano m Atlantico** Atlantic Ocean

atleta *m/f* (*mpl* -i) athlete

atletica *f* athletics; ~ **leggera** track and field (events)

atletico (*pl* -ci) athletic

atmosfera *f* atmosphere

atmosferico (*pl* -ci) atmospheric

atomico (*pl* -ci) atomic

atomo *m* atom

atrio *m* (*pl* -ri) foyer; ~ **della stazione** station concourse

atroce appalling

atrocità *f* atrocity

attaccabrighe *m o f inv* F troublemaker

attaccamento *m* attachment

attaccante *m* SP forward

attaccapanni *m inv* clothes hook; *a stelo* clothes hanger

attaccare <1d> 1 *v/t* attach; (*incollare*) stick; (*appendere*) hang; (*assalire*) attack; (*iniziare*) begin, start 2 *v/i* stick; F ~ **a fare qc** start doing sth

attaccarsi stick; (*aggrapparsi*) hold on (**a** to)

attacco *m* (*pl* -cchi) attack; (*punto di unione*) junction; EL socket; SCI binding; MED fit; (*inizio*) beginning

attardarsi <1a> linger

atteggiamento *m* attitude

atteggiarsi <1f>: ~ **a** pose as

attendere <3c> 1 *v/t* wait for 2 *v/i*: ~ **a** attend to

attendibile reliable

attenersi <2q> stick (**a** to)

attentare <1b>: ~ **a** attack; ~ **alla vita di qu** make an attempt on s.o.'s life

attentato *m* attempted assassination

attento 1 *agg* attentive; **stare ~ a** be careful of 2 *int* ~**!** look out!, (be) careful!

attenuante *f* extenuating circumstance

attenuare <1m & b> reduce; *colpo* cushion

attenuarsi lessen, decrease

attenzione *f* attention; ~**!** look out!, (be) careful!; **far ~ a qc** mind *or* watch sth

atterraggio *m* (*pl* -ggi) landing; ~ **di fortuna** emergency landing

atterrare <1b> 1 *v/t avversario* knock down; *edificio* demolish, knock down 2 *v/i* land

attesa *f* waiting; (*tempo d'attesa*) wait; (*aspettativa*) expectation

atteso *pp* → **attendere**

attestare <1b> certify

attestato *m* certificate; ~ **di frequenza** good attendance certificate

attico *m* (*pl* -ci) attic

attiguo adjacent (**a** to)

attimo *m* moment

attinente relevant (**a** to)

attirare <1a> attract

attitudine *f* attitude; **avere ~ per qc** have an aptitude for sth

attivare <1a> activate

attività *f* activity; *pl* FIN assets; **che ~ svolgi?** what do you do (for a living)?; **avere un'~ in proprio** have one's own business

attivo 1 *agg* active; FIN **bilancio m** ~ credit balance 2 *m* FIN assets *pl*; GRAM active voice

atto *m* act; (*gesto*) gesture; *documento* deed; ~ **di fede** act of faith; **all'~ pratico** when it comes to the crunch; **mettere in ~** carry out; **prendere ~ di** note; DIR **mettere**

agli -i enter in the court records

attorcigliare <1g>, **attorcigliarsi** twist

attore m, **-trice** f actor; *donna* actress

attorno: **~ a qc** round sth; **qui ~** around here

attraccare <1d> MAR berth, dock

attracco m (pl -cchi) MAR berth

attraente attractive

attrarre <3xx> attract

attrattiva f attraction

attratto pp → **attrarre**

attraversare <1b> *strada, confine* cross; **~ un momento difficile** be going through a bad time

attraverso across

attrazione f attraction

attrezzare <1a> equip

attrezzarsi get o.s. kitted out

attrezzato equipped

attrezzatura f equipment, gear F

attrezzo m piece of equipment; **-i** pl **da ginnastica** apparatus

attribuire <4d> attribute

attributo m attribute

attrice f → **attore**

attrito m friction

attuale current

attualità f news; **d'~** topical

attualizzare <1a> update

attuare <1l> put into effect

attuazione f putting into effect

audace bold

audacia f boldness

audioleso 1 agg hearing-impaired 2 m, **-a** f person with hearing difficulties, person who is hearing-impaired

audiovisivo audiovisual

audizione f audition

augurare <1l> wish; **~ a qu buon viaggio** wish s.o. a good trip

augurio m (pl -ri) wish; **fare gli -ri di Buon Natale a qu** wish s.o. a Merry Christmas; **tanti -ri!** all the best!

aula f **di scuola** class room; *di università* lecture theatre *or* room

aumentare <1a> 1 v/t increase; *prezzi* increase, raise, put up 2 v/i increase; *di prezzi* increase, rise, go up

aumento m increase, rise; **~ salariale** pay rise; **~ dei prezzi** increase *or* rise in prices

aureo golden

aureola f halo

auricolare m earphone

aurora f dawn; **~ boreale** northern lights pl

ausiliare 1 agg auxiliary 2 m GRAM auxiliary

ausiliario (pl -ri) auxiliary

austerità f austerity

australe southern

Australia f Australia

australiano 1 agg Australian 2 m, **-a** f Australian

Austria f Austria

austriaco (mpl -ci) 1 agg Austrian 2 m, **-a** f Austrian

autenticare <1m, d & b> authenticate

autenticità f authenticity

autentico (pl -ci) authentic

autista m/f (mpl -i) driver

auto f inv → **automobile**

autoadesivo 1 agg self-adhesive 2 m sticker

autoambulanza f ambulance

autobiografia f autobiography

autobomba f car bomb

autobus m bus; **~ di linea** city bus

autocaravan f camper van

autocarro m truck, Br lorry

autocisterna f tanker

autocontrollo m self-control

autocritica f self-criticism

autodidatta m/f (mpl -i) self-taught person

autodifesa f self-defence, Am -defense

autodromo m motor racing circuit

autofinanziamento m self-financing

autogol m inv own goal

autografo m autograph

autogrill m inv motorway café

autolavaggio m (pl -ggi) car-wash

automa m (pl -i) robot

automatico (pl -ci) 1 agg automatic 2 m *bottone* press stud fastener

automezzo m motor vehicle

automobile f car; **~ da corsa** racing

car; **~ da noleggio** hire car

automobilismo *m* driving; SP motor racing

automobilista *m/f* (*mpl* -i) driver

autonoleggio *m* (*pl* -ggi) car rental; (*azienda*) car-rental firm

autonomia *f* autonomy; TEC battery life

autonomo autonomous

autoradio *f inv* car radio

autore *m*, **-trice** *f* author; DIR perpetrator

autorevole authoritative

autorimessa *f* garage

autorità *f inv* authority; **~ portuale** port authorities *pl*

autoritario (*pl* -ri) authoritarian

autorizzare <1a> authorize

autorizzazione *f* authorization

autoscatto *m* automatic shutter release

autoscuola *f* driving school

autosilo *m inv* multistorey car park, *Am* parking garage

autosoccorso *m* self-help

autostop *m*: **fare l'~** hitchhike

autostoppista *m/f* (*mpl* -i) hitchhiker

autostrada *f* motorway, *Am* highway; **~ informatica** information highway

autotreno *m* articulated lorry, *Am* semi

autovettura *f* motor vehicle

autrice *f* → **autore**

autunno *m* autumn, *Am* fall

avambraccio *m* (*pl* -cci) forearm

avanguardia *f* avant-garde; **all'~** avant-garde *attr*; *azienda* leading-edge; **essere all'~ in** lead the way in

avanti 1 *avv* in front, ahead; **d'ora in ~** from now on; **andare ~** *di orologio* be fast; **mandare ~** be the head of; **essere ~ nel programma** be ahead of schedule **2** *int* **~!** come in! **3** *m* SP forward

avanzare <1a> **1** *v/i* advance; *fig* make progress; (*rimanere*) be left over **2** *v/t* put forward

avanzo *m* remainder; FIN surplus; **gli -i** *pl* the leftovers

avaria *f* failure

avariato damaged; *cibi* spoiled

avarizia *f* avarice

avaro 1 *agg* miserly **2** *m*, **-a** *f* miser

avena *f* oats *pl*

avere <2b> **1** *v/t* have; **~ 20 anni** be 20 (years old); **~ fame / sonno** be hungry / sleepy; **~ caldo / freddo** be hot / cold; **~ qualcosa da fare** have something to do; **avercela con qu** have it in for s.o.; **che hai?** what's up with you? **2** *v/aus* have; **hai visto Tony?** have you seen Tony?; **hai visto Tony ieri?** did you see Tony yesterday? **3** *m* FIN credit; **dare e ~** debits and credits; **-i** *mpl* wealth *sg*

avi *mpl* ancestors

aviatore *m* flyer

aviazione *f* aviation; MIL Air Force

avidità *f* avidness

avido avid

aviogetto *m* jet

AVIS *abbr* (= **Associazione Volontari Italiani del Sangue**) Italian blood donors' association

avocado *m* avocado

avorio *m* ivory

avvalersi <2r>: **~ di qc** avail o.s. of sth

avvallamento *m* depression

avvantaggiare <1f> favo(u)r

avvantaggiarsi: **~ di qc** take advantage of sth

avvedersi <2s>: **~ di qc** notice sth

avveduto astute

avvelenamento *m* poisoning

avvelenare <1a> poison

avvelenarsi poison o.s.

avvenimento *m* event

avvenire <4p> **1** *v/i* (*accadere*) happen **2** *m* future

Avvento *m* Advent

avventore *m* regular customer

avventura *f* adventure

avventurarsi <1a> venture

avventuriero *m*, **-a** *f* adventurer; *donna* adventuress

avventuroso adventurous

avvenuto *pp* → **avvenire**

avverarsi <1a> come true

avverbio *m* (*pl* -bi) adverb

avversario (*pl* -ri) **1** *agg* opposing **2** *m*, **-a** *f* opponent

avversione *f* aversion (**per** to)

avvertenza *f* (*ammonimento*) warning; (*premessa*) foreword; **avere l'~ di** be careful to; **-e** *pl* (*istruzioni per l'uso*) instructions

avvertimento *m* warning

avvertire <4b> warn; (*percepire*) catch

avviamento *m* introduction; TEC, AUTO start-up

avviare <1h> start

avviarsi set out, head off

avviato established

avvicendare <1b> alternate

avvicendarsi alternate

avvicinamento *m* approach

avvicinare <1a> approach; **~ qc a qc** move sth closer to sth

avvicinarsi approach, near (**a** sth)

avvilire <4d> depress; *mortificare* humiliate

avvilirsi demean o.s.; *scoraggiarsi* become depressed

avvilito *scoraggiato* depressed

avvio *m*: **dare l'~ a qc** get sth under way

avvisare <1a> (*informare*) inform, advise; (*mettere in guardia*) warn

avviso *m* notice; **a mio ~** in my opinion; **mettere qu sull'~** warn s.o.

avvitare <1a> screw in; *fissare* screw

avvocato *m* lawyer

avvolgere <3d> wrap

avvolgibile *m* roller blind

avvolto *pp* → **avvolgere**

avvoltoio *m* (*pl* -oi) vulture

azienda *f* business; **~ a conduzione familiare** family business; **~ autonoma di soggiorno** tourist information office

aziendale company *attr*

azionare <1a> activate; *allarme* set off

azionario share; **capitale** *m* **~** share capital

azione *f* action; (*effetto*) influence; FIN share; FIN **~ ordinaria** ordinary share; **emettere -i** issue shares

azionista *m/f* (*mpl* -i) shareholder; **maggiore ~** majority shareholder

azoto *m* nitrogen

azzannare <1a> bite into

azzardarsi <1a> dare

azzardato foolhardy

azzardo *m* hazard; **gioco** *m* **d'~** game of chance

azzerare <1b> TEC reset

azzuffarsi <1a> come to blows

azzurro 1 *agg* blue **2** *m colore* blue; SP **gli -i** *pl* the Italians, the Italian national team

B

babbo *m* F dad F, *Am* pop F; **Babbo Natale** Father Christmas, Santa (Claus)

babbuino *m* baboon

babordo *m* MAR port (side)

baby-sitter *m/f inv* baby-sitter

bacato wormeaten

bacca *f* (*pl* -cche) berry

baccalà *m inv* dried salt cod

baccano *m* din

bacchetta *f* rod; MUS **del direttore d'orchestra** baton; *per suonare il tamburo* (drum) stick; **~ magica** magic wand

bacheca *f* (*pl* -che) notice board; *di museo* showcase

baciare <1f> kiss

baciarsi kiss (each other)

bacillo *m* bacillus

bacinella *f* basin; FOT tray

B

bacino *m* basin; ANAT pelvis; MAR port

bacio *m* (*pl* -ci) kiss

baco *m* (*pl* -chi) worm; **~ da seta** silkworm

bada *f*: **tenere a ~ qu** keep s.o. at bay

badare <1a>: **~ a** look after; (*fare attenzione a*) look out for, mind; **~ ai fatti propri** mind one's own business; **non ~ a spese** spare no expense

baffo *m*: **-i** *pl* m(o)ustache; *di animali* whiskers

bagagliaio *m* (*pl* -ai) FERR luggage van, *Am* baggage car; AUTO boot, *Am* trunk

bagaglio *m* (*pl* -gli) luggage, *Am* baggage; **deposito m -i** left luggage (office), *Am* baggage checkroom; **fare i -i** pack; **spedire come ~ appresso** send as accompanied luggage

bagliore *m* glare; *di speranza* glimmer

bagnante *m/f* bather

bagnare <1a> wet; (*immergere*) dip; (*inzuppare*) soak; (*annaffiare*) water; *di fiume* flow through

bagnarsi get wet; *in mare ecc* swim, bathe

bagnato wet; **~ di sudore** dripping with sweat; **~ fradicio** soaked, wet through

bagnino *m*, **-a** *f* lifeguard

bagno *m* bath; *stanza* bathroom; *gabinetto* toilet; **~ di fango** mud bath; **fare il ~** have a bath; **mettere a ~** soak; *nel mare ecc* (have a) swim; **~ degli uomini** gents, *Am* men's room; **~ per donne** ladies' (room)

bagnomaria *m inv* double boiler, bain marie

baia *f* bay

baio *m* (*pl* bai): **cavallo m ~** bay

baita *f* mountain chalet

balaustra *f* balustrade

balbettare <1a> stammer; *bambino* babble, prattle

balbettio *m* stammering; *di bambino* babble, prattle

balbuzie *f* stutter

balbuziente *m/f* stutterer

balcanico (*pl* -ci) Balkan; **paesi mpl -ci** Balkans

balconata *f* TEA dress circle, *Am* balcony

balcone *m* balcony

baldoria *f* revelry; **fare ~** have a riotous time

balena *f* whale

balenare <1a>: *fig* **gli è balenata un'idea** an idea flashed through his mind

baleno *m* lightning; **in un ~** in a flash

balestra *f* AUTO leaf spring

balia[1] *f*: **in ~ di** at the mercy of

balia[2] *f*: **~ asciutta** nanny

balla *f* bale; *fig* F (*frottola*) fib F

ballare <1a> *v/t* & *v/i* dance

ballata *f* MUS ballad

ballerina *f* dancer; *di balletto* ballet dancer; *di rivista* chorus girl; (*scarpa*) ballet shoe; ZO wagtail

ballerino *m* dancer; *di balletto* ballet dancer

balletto *m* ballet

ballo *m* dance; (*il ballare*) dancing; (*festa*) ball; **corpo m di ~** corps de ballet; **essere in ~** *persona* be involved; **essere in gioco** be at stake; **abbiamo in ~ un lavoro importante** we've got a big job on at the moment; **tirare in ~ qc** bring sth up

balneare *località*, *centro* seaside *attr*; **stagione f ~** swimming season; **stabilimento m ~** lido; **stazione f ~** seaside resort

balocco *m* (*pl* -cchi) toy

balordo **1** *agg ragionamento* shaky; *idea* stupid; *tempo*, *consiglio* unreliable **2** *m* (*teppista*) lout

balsamico (*pl* -ci) *aceto* balsamic; *aria* balmy

balsamo *m per i capelli* hair conditioner; *fig* balm, solace

baltico (*pl* -ci) Baltic

balzare <1a> jump, leap; **~ in piedi** jump *or* leap to one's feet; *fig* **un errore che balza subito agli occhi** a mistake that suddenly jumps out at you

balzo *m* jump, leap; *fig* **cogliere la**

palla al ~ jump at the chance
bambagia *f* cotton wool, *Am* absorbent cotton
bambinaia *f* nanny
bambino *m*, **-a** *f* child; *in fasce* baby; ~ **in provetta** test-tube baby
bambola *f* doll
bambolotto *m* baby boy do!l
bambù *m* bamboo; **canna** *f* **di** ~ bamboo cane
banale banal
banalità *f inv* banality
banana *f* banana
banano *m* banana tree
banca *f* (*pl* -che) bank; INFOR ~ **dati** data bank; ~ **degli organi** organ bank
bancarella *f* stall
bancario (*pl* -ri) **1** *agg istituto, segreto* banking *attr; deposito, estratto conto* bank *attr* **2** *m*, **-a** *f* bank employee
bancarotta *f* bankruptcy
banchetto *m* banquet
banchiere *m* banker
banchina *f* FERR platform; MAR quay; *di strada* verge; *di autostrada* hard shoulder; ~ **spartitraffico** central reservation, *Am* median strip
banchisa *f* ice floe
banco *m* (*pl* -chi) FIN bank; *di magistrati, di lavoro* bench; *di scuola* desk; *di bar* bar; *di chiesa* pew; *di negozio* counter; ~ **corallino** coral reef; ~ **di sabbia** sandbank; ~ **del lotto** place *that sells State lottery tickets;* **vendere** *qc* **sotto** ~ sell sth under the counter
bancogiro *m* giro
bancone *m* (work)bench
bancomat® *m inv* (*distributore*) cash-point, *Am* ATM; (*carta*) cash card
banconota *f* banknote, *Am* bill
banda *f* band; *di delinquenti* gang; INFOR ~ **perforata** punched tape
banderuola *f* weathercock (*anche fig*)
bandiera *f* flag
bandire <4d> proclaim; *concorso* announce; (*esiliare*) banish; *fig* (*abolire*) dispense with

bandito *m* bandit
banditore *m all'asta* auctioneer
bando *m* proclamation; (*esilio*) banishment
bar *m inv* bar
bara *f* coffin
baracca *f* (*pl* -cche) hut; *spreg* hovel; F **mandare avanti la** ~ keep one's head above water
baraccopoli *f inv* shanty town
barare <1a> cheat
baratro *m* abyss
barattare <1a> barter
baratto *m* barter
barattolo *m* tin, *Am* can; *di vetro* jar
barba *f* beard; **farsi la** ~ shave; *fig* **che** ~! what a nuisance!, what a pain! F
barbabietola *f* beetroot, *Am* red beet; ~ **da zucchero** sugar beet
barbarico (*pl* -ci) barbaric
barbarie *f* barbarity
barbaro 1 *agg* barbarous **2** *m* barbarian
barbecue *m inv* barbecue
barbiere *m* barber
barboncino *m* (miniature) poodle
barbone[1] *m* (*cane*) poodle
barbone[2] *m*, **-a** *f* (*vagabondo*) tramp
barca *f* (*pl* -che) boat; ~ **a remi** rowing boat, *Am* rowboat; ~ **a vela** sailing boat, *Am* sailboat
barcaiolo *m* boatman
barcollare <1c> stagger
barcone *m* barge
barella *f* stretcher
baricentro *m* centre of gravity
barile *m* barrel
barista *m/f* (*mpl* -i) barman, *Am* bartender; *donna* barmaid; *proprietario* bar owner
baritono *m* baritone
baro *m* cardsharp
barocco (*pl* -cchi) *m/agg* Baroque
barometro *m* barometer
barone *m*, **-essa** *f* baron; *donna* baroness; *fig* ~ **dell'industria** tycoon
barra *f* bar; MAR tiller; ~ **spaziatrice** space bar
barricare <1l & d> barricade
barricata *f* barricade

B

barriera f barrier (anche fig); **~ doganale** tariff barrier

baruffa f (litigio) squabble; (zuffa) brawl; **far ~** squabble; (venirse alle mani) brawl

barzelletta f joke

basare <1a> base

basarsi be based (**su** on)

basco (pl -chi) **1** agg Basque **2** m, **-a** f Basque **3** m (berretto) beret

base f base; fig basis; **in ~ a** on the basis of

basette fpl sideburns

basilare basic

basilica f (pl -che) basilica

basilico m basil

bassezza f lowness; fig (viltà, azione meschina) vileness

basso 1 agg low; di statura short; MUS bass; fig despicable; **a capo ~** with bowed head; **a occhi -i** looking downwards, with lowered eyes; **fare man -a di qc** steal sth **2** avv: **in ~** stato down below; **più in ~** further down; **da ~ in una casa** downstairs **3** m MUS bass

bassopiano m (pl bassipiani) GEOG lowland

bassorilievo m (pl bassorilievi) bas-relief

bassotto m dachshund

basta → **bastare**

bastardo m, **-a** f cane mongrel; fig bastard

bastare <1a> be enough; (durare) last; **basta!** that's enough!; **adesso basta!** enough is enough!; **basta che** (purché) as long as

bastimento m ship

bastonare <1a> beat

bastone m stick; di pane baguette, French stick; fig **il ~ e la carota** the carrot and stick (approach); **~ da passeggio** walking stick

battaglia f battle (anche fig)

battagliero combative

battello m boat

battente m di porta wing; di finestra shutter

battere <3a> **1** v/i (bussare, dare colpi) knock **2** v/t beat; record break;

senza ~ ciglio without batting an eyelid; **~ le mani** clap (one's hands); **~ i piedi** stamp one's feet; **batteva i denti dal freddo** his teeth were chattering with cold; **~ a macchina** type; **~ bandiera** fly a flag

battersela run off

battersi fight

batteria f battery; MUS drums pl

batteri mpl bacteria

batterista m/f (pl -i) drummer

battesimo m christening, baptism

battezzare <1a> christen, baptize

battibaleno m: **in un ~** in a flash

battibecco m (pl -cchi) argument

batticuore m palpitations pl; fig **con un gran ~** with great anxiety

battimano m applause

battipanni m inv carpet beater

battistero m baptistry

battistrada m inv AUTO tread

battito m del polso pulse; delle ali flap (of its wings); della pioggia beating; **~ cardiaco** heartbeat

battuta f beat; in dattilografia keystroke; MUS bar; TEA cue; nel tennis service; **fare ~ di caccia** go hunting; **~ di spirito** wisecrack; **non perdere una ~** not miss a word

baule m trunk; AUTO boot, Am trunk

bavaglino m bib

bavaglio m (pl -gli) gag

bavero m collar

bazar m inv bazaar

bazzecola f trifle

bazzicare <1l & d> **1** v/t un posto haunt; persone associate with **2** v/i hang about

Bce abbr (= **Banca centrale europea**) Central European Bank

beatificare <1n & d> beatify

beatitudine f bliss

beato happy; REL blessed; **~ te!** lucky you!

beauty-case m inv toilet bag

bebè m inv baby

beccaccia f (pl -cce) woodcock

beccare <1d> peck; F fig (cogliere sul fatto) nab F; F fig malattia catch, pick up F

beccarsi fig bisticciare squabble; F

malattia catch, pick up F
beccheggiare <1f> MAR pitch
becchino *m* grave digger
becco *m* (*pl* -cchi) beak; *di teiera ecc* spout; CHIM ~ **Bunsen** Bunsen burner; F *chiudi il ~!* shut up! F, shut it! F; *non avere il ~ di un quattrino* be broke
befana *f kind old witch who brings presents to children on Twelfth Night*; REL Twelfth Night; *fig* old witch
beffa *f* hoax; *farsi -e di qu* make a fool of s.o.
beffardo scornful
beffare <1b> mock
beffarsi: ~ *di* mock
bega *f* (*pl* -ghe) (*litigio*) fight, argument; (*problema*) can of worms
begli → *bello*
begonia *f* begonia
Bei *abbr* (= **Banca europea per gli investimenti**) EIB (= European Investment Bank)
bei → *bello*
belare <1b> bleat
belga (*mpl* -gi) *agg*, *m/f* Belgian
Belgio *m* Belgium
belladonna *f* BOT deadly nightshade
bellezza *f* beauty; *istituto m di* ~ beauty salon; *prodotti mpl di* ~ cosmetics
bellico (*pl* -ci) (*di guerra*) war *attr*; (*del tempo di guerra*) wartime *attr*
bellicoso bellicose
bello **1** *agg* beautiful; *uomo* handsome; *tempo* fine, nice, beautiful; *questa è -a!* that's a good one!; *a -a posta* on purpose; *hai un bel dire* in spite of what you say; *nel bel mezzo* right in the middle; *farsi* ~ get dressed up; *scamparla* ~ have a narrow escape **2** *m* beauty; *sul più* ~ at the worst possible moment
belva *f* wild beast
belvedere *m inv* viewpoint
bemolle *m inv* MUS flat
benché though, although
benda *f* bandage; *per occhi* blindfold
bendare <1b> MED bandage
bene **1** *avv* well; ~*!* good!; *per* ~ properly; *stare* ~ *di salute* be well; *di*

vestito suit; *ben ti sta!* serves you right!; *va* ~*!* OK!; *andare* ~ *a qu di abito* fit s.o.; *di orario, appuntamento* suit s.o.; *di* ~ *in meglio* better and better; *sentirsi* ~ feel well **2** *m* good; *fare* ~ *alla salute* be good for you; *per il tuo* ~ for your own good; *voler* ~ *a qu* love s.o.; (*amare*) love s.o.; *-i pl* assets, property *sg*; *-i pl di consumo* consumer goods; *-i pl culturali* cultural heritage *sg*; *-i pl immobili* real estate *sg*; *-i pl pubblici* public property *sg*
benedetto **1** *pp* → *benedire* **2** *agg* blessed; REL *acqua f -a* holy water
benedire <3t> bless
benedizione *f* blessing
beneducato well-mannered
benefattore *m*, *-trice* *f* benefactor
beneficenza *f* charity; *spettacolo m di* ~ benefit (*performance*)
beneficio *m* (*pl* -ci) benefit; *a* ~ *di* for the benefit of
benefico (*pl* -ci) beneficial; *organizzazione, istituto* charitable; *spettacolo* charity *attr*
benemerito worthy
benessere *m* well-being; (*agiatezza*) affluence
benestante **1** *agg* well-off **2** *m/f* person with money
benestare *m* consent
benevolenza *f* benevolence
benevolo benevolent
benigno MED benign
beninteso of course; ~ *che* provided that
benone splendid
benpensante *m/f* moderate; *spreg* conformist
benservito *m*: *dare il* ~ *a qu* thank s.o. for their services
bensì but rather
bentornato welcome back
benvenuto **1** *agg* welcome **2** *m* welcome; *dare il* ~ *a qu* welcome s.o.
benvisto well thought of
benvolere: *farsi* ~ *da qu* win s.o. over
benvoluto well-liked
benzina *f* petrol, *Am* gas; *serbatoio*

B

m della ~ petrol (*Am* gas) tank; *~ normale* 4-star, *Am* premium; *~ senza piombo* unleaded petrol (*Am* gas); *fare ~* get petrol (*Am* gas)

benzinaio *m* (*mpl* -ai), **-a** *f* petrol *or Am* gas station attendant

bere 1 *v/t* <3i> drink; *fig* swallow; *fig darla a ~ a qu* take s.o. in **2** *m bevanda* drink; *atto* drinking

berlina *f* AUTO saloon

berlinese 1 *agg* Berlin **2** *m/f* Berliner

Berlino *m* Berlin

bermuda *mpl* Bermuda shorts

bernoccolo *m* bump; *fig* flair; *aver il ~ di qc* have a flair for sth

berretto *m* cap

berrò → **bere**

bersaglio *m* (*pl* -gli) target; *fig di scherzi* butt

besciamella *f* béchamel

bestemmia *f* swear-word

bestemmiare <1k> **1** *v/i* swear (*contro* at) **2** *v/t* curse

bestia *f* animal; *persona brutale* beast; *persona sciocca* blockhead; *fig andare in ~* fly into a rage

bestiale bestial; F (*molto intenso*) terrible

bestiame *m* livestock

bettola *f spreg* dive

betulla *f* birch

bevanda *f* drink

beve → **bere**

bevibile drinkable

bevitore *m*, **-trice** *f* drinker

bevuta *f* drink; *azione* drinking

biada *f* fodder

biancheria *f* linen; *~ intima* underwear

bianco (*pl* -chi) **1** *agg* white; *foglio* blank; *dare carta -a a qu* give s.o. a free hand, give s.o. carte blanche; *notte f -a* sleepless night **2** *m* white; *~ d'uovo* egg white; *lasciare in ~* leave blank; *di punto in ~* point-blank; GASTR *riso in ~* rice with butter and cheese; *mangiare in ~* avoid rich food; *in ~ e nero* film black and white; *in ~* *assegno* blank

biancospino *m* hawthorn

biasimare <1l> blame

biasimevole blameworthy

biasimo *m* blame

bibbia *f* bible

biberon *m inv* baby's bottle

bibita *f* soft drink

bibliografia *f* bibliography

bibliografico (*pl* -ci) bibliographical

biblioteca *f* (*pl* -che) library; *mobile* book-case

bibliotecario *m* (*pl* -ri), **-a** *f* librarian

bicamerale POL two-chamber

bicameralismo *m* two-chamber system

bicamere *m inv* two-room flat (*Am* apartment)

bicarbonato *m*: *~* (*di sodio*) bicarbonate of soda

bicchiere *m* glass; *un ~ di birra* a glass of beer; *~ da birra* beer-glass; *~ di carta* paper cup

bicentenario *m* bicentenary

bici *f inv* F bike F

bicicletta *f* bike, bicycle; *andare in ~* cycle, ride a bicycle; *~ pieghevole* folding bike; *~ da corsa* racing bike; *gita f in ~* bike ride

bidè *m inv* bidet

bidone *m* drum; *della spazzatura* (dust)bin, *Am* garbage can; F (*imbroglio*) swindle F

biella *f* TEC connecting rod

biennale 1 *agg che si fa ogni due anni* biennial; *che dura due anni* two-year **2 Biennale** *f* (*di Venezia*) Venice Arts Festival

biennio *m* (*pl* -nni) period of two years

bietola *f* beet

bifase two-phase

bifora *f* ARCHI mullioned window

biforcarsi <1d> fork

biforcazione *f* fork

bigamia *f* bigamy

bigamo *m*, **-a** *f* bigamist

bigiotteria *f* costume jewellery, *Am* costume jewelry; (*negozio*) jewel-(l)er's

bigliettaio *m* (*pl* -ai), **-a** *f* booking office clerk; *sul treno, tram* conductor

B

biglietteria f ticket office, booking office; di cinema, teatro box office

biglietto m ticket; ~ **aereo** airline or plane ticket; ~ **d'andata e ritorno** return ticket, Am roundtrip ticket; ~ **d'auguri** (greetings) card; ~ **da visita** business card; ~ **di banca** banknote, Am bill; ~ **della lotteria** lottery ticket; **un ~ da 10 dollari** a ten-dollar bill; **fare il ~** buy the ticket

bigodino m roller

bigotto 1 agg bigoted **2** m, **-a** f bigot

bikini m inv bikini

bilancia f (pl -ce) scales; FIN balance; ASTR **Bilancia** Libra; ~ **commerciale** balance of trade; ~ **dei pagamenti** balance of payments

bilanciare <1f> balance; (pareggiare) equal, be equal to; fig weigh up; FIN ~ **un conto** balance an account

bilanciarsi balance

bilancio m (pl -ci) balance; (rendiconto) balance sheet; ~ **annuale** annual accounts; ~ **consuntivo** closing balance; ~ **dello Stato** national budget; ~ **preventivo** budget; **fare il ~** draw up a balance sheet; fig take stock; **relazione** f **annuale di** ~ annual report

bilaterale bilateral

bile f bile; fig rage

biliardo m billiards sg

bilico m: **essere in** ~ be precariously balanced; fig be undecided

bilingue bilingual

bilione m (mille miliardi) million million, Am trillion; (miliardo) billion

bilocale m two-room flat (Am apartment)

bimbo m, **-a** f child

bimensile every two weeks, Br fortnightly

bimestrale ogni due mesi bimonthly; che dura due mesi two-month (long)

bimotore 1 agg twin-engine **2** m twin-engine plane

binario 1 agg binary **2** m (pl -ri) track; (marciapiede) platform

binocolo m binoculars pl

biochimica f biochemistry

biodegradabile biodegradable

biodinamica f biodynamics

biografia f biography

biografico (pl -ci) biographical

biografo m, **-a** f biographer

biologia f biology

biologico (pl -ci) biological; (verde) organic; **da culture -che** organic

biologo m (pl -gi), **-a** f biologist

biondo blonde

bioritmo m biorhythm

biossido m dioxide

biotopo m biotope

biplano m biplane

bipolare bipolar

biposto m/agg two-seater

birbante m rascal

birichino 1 agg naughty **2** m, **-a** f little devil

birillo m skittle

biro® f inv biro, ballpoint (pen)

birra f beer; ~ **chiara** lager; ~ **scura** brown ale; ~ **in lattina** canned beer; ~ **alla spina** draught (beer); **lievito** m **di** ~ brewer's yeast; **a tutta** ~ flat out

birreria f pub that sells only beer; fabbrica brewery

bis m inv, int encore

bisbetico (pl -ci) bad-tempered

bisbigliare <1g> whisper

bisbiglio m whisper

bisca f (pl -che) gambling den

biscia f (pl -sce) grass snake

biscotto m biscuit, Am cookie

bisessuale bisexual

bisestile: anno m ~ leap year

bisettimanale every two weeks, Br fortnightly

bisnonno m, **-a** f great-grandfather; **donna** great-grandmother

bisognare <1a>: **bisogna farlo** it must be done, it needs to be done; **non bisogna farlo** it doesn't have to be done, there's no need to do it

bisogno m need; (mancanza) lack; (fabbisogno) requirements; **in caso di** ~ if necessary, if need be; **avere** ~ **di qc** need sth; **non ce n'è bisogno** there is no need

bisognoso needy

B

bisonte m ZO bison

bistecca f (pl -cche) steak; ~ **ai ferri** grilled or Am broiled steak; ~ **alla fiorentina** charcoal grilled steak

bisticciare <1f> quarrel

bisticcio m (pl -cci) quarrel

bisturi m inv MED scalpel

bit m inv INFOR bit

bitter m inv aperitif

bivaccare <1d> bivouac

bivacco m (pl -cchi) bivouac

bivio m (pl -vi) junction; fig crossroads

bizantino Byzantine

bizzarro bizarre

bizzeffe: a ~ galore

blando mild, gentle

blatta f cockroach

blindare <1a> armo(u)r-plate

blindato armo(u)red

blitz m inv blitz

bloccare <1c & d> block; MIL blockade; (isolare) cut off; prezzi, conto freeze

bloccarsi di ascensore, persona get stuck; di freni, porta jam

bloccaruota m AUTO wheel clamp, Am Denver boot; **mettere il ~ a** clamp

bloccasterzo m AUTO steering lock

blocchetto m per appunti notebook

blocco m (pl -cchi) block; di carta pad; MIL blockade; di strada road block; ~ **dei fitti** rent control; **comprare in ~** buy in bulk; ~ **dei prezzi** price-freeze; ~ **delle esportazioni** export ban, embargo

bloc-notes m inv writing pad

blu blue

blusa f blouse

boa[1] m inv ZO boa constrictor

boa[2] f MAR buoy

boato m rumble

bob m inv SP bobsleigh, bobsled

bobbista m/f (pl -i) bobsledder

bobina f spool; di film reel; AUTO ~ **d'accensione** ignition coil

bocca f (pl -cche) mouth; (apertura) opening; **igiene** f **della ~** oral hygiene; **in ~ al lupo!** good luck!; **vuoi essere sulla ~ di tutti?** do you want

to be the talk of the town?; **lasciare la ~ amara** leave a bad taste; **rimanere a ~ aperta** be dumbfounded; fig **rimanere a ~ asciutta** come away empty-handed

boccaccia f (pl -cce) (smorfia) grimace

boccaglio m (pl -gli) di maschera per il nuoto mouthpiece

boccale m jug; da birra tankard

boccetta f small bottle

boccheggiare <1f> gasp

bocchino m per sigarette cigarette holder; MUS, di pipa mouthpiece

boccia f (pl -cce) (palla) bowl; **gioco** m **delle -cce** bowls

bocciare <1c & f> (respingere) reject, vote down; EDU fail; **boccia** hit, strike

bocciatura f failure

bocciolo m bud

bocconcino m morsel

boccone m mouthful; ~ **amaro** bitter pill

bocconi face down

body m inv body

boia m inv executioner; F **fa un freddo ~** it's bloody freezing F

boicottaggio m boycott

boicottare <1c> boycott

bolgia f fig bedlam

bolide m AST meteor; **come un ~** like greased lightning

bolla[1] f bubble; MED blister

bolla[2] f documento note, docket; ~ **di consegna** delivery note

bollare <1a> stamp; fig brand

bollente boiling hot

bolletta f bill; ~ **della luce** electricity bill; ~ **di consegna** delivery note; F **essere in ~** be hard up F

bollettino m: ~ **meteorologico** weather forecast

bollire <4c> v/t & v/i boil

bollito 1 agg boiled 2 m boiled meat

bollitore m kettle

bollo m stamp; ~ **(di circolazione)** road tax (disk); **marca** f **da ~** revenue stamp

bomba f bomb; **a prova di ~** bombproof; ~ **a mano** hand grenade; ~ **a**

orologeria time bomb; **~ atomica** atomic bomb

bombardamento *m* shelling, bombardment; (*attacco aereo*) air raid; *fig* bombardment

bombardare <1a> bomb; *fig* bombard

bombardiere *m* bomber

bombola *f* cylinder; **~** (**di gas**) gas bottle, gas cylinder

bomboniera *f* wedding keep-sake

bonaccia *f* MAR calm

bonaccione *m*, **-a** *f* kind-hearted person

bonario (*pl* -ri) kind-hearted

bonifica *f* (*pl* -che) reclamation

bonificare <1m & d> FIN (*scontare*) allow, discount; (*accreditare*) credit; AGR reclaim; (*prosciugare*) drain

bonifico *m* FIN (*sconto*) allowance, rebate; (*trasferimento*) (money) transfer

bontà *f inv* goodness; (*gentilezza*) kindness

bonus-malus *m inv* assicurazione no-claims bonus system

bora *f* bora (*a cold north wind*)

borbottare <1a> mumble

bordello *m* brothel; *fig* F bedlam F; (*disordine*) mess

bordo *m* (*orlo*) edge; MAR, AVIA, AUTO **a ~** on board; **salire a ~** board, go on board

boreale northern; **aurora** *f* **~** northern lights *pl*

borgata *f* village; (*rione popolare*) suburb

borghese **1** *agg* middle-class; **in ~** in civilian clothes; **poliziotto** *m* **in ~** plainclothes policeman **2** *m/f* middle-class person; **piccolo ~** petty bourgeois, lower middle-class person

borghesia *f* middle classes *pl*

borgo *m* (*pl* -ghi) village

boria *f* conceit

borico *m* (*pl* -ci): **acido** *m* **~** boric acid

borotalco *m* talcum powder, talc

borraccia *f* (*pl* -cce) flask

borsa *f* bag; (*borsetta*) handbag, *Am* purse; *per documenti* briefcase; FIN Stock Exchange; **~ della spesa** shopping bag; **~ termica** cool bag; **~ di studio** scholarship; **~ merci** Commodities Exchange; **~ nera** black market; **~ valori** Stock Exchange; **bollettino** *m* (o **listino** *m*) **di ~** share index; **metter mano alla ~** put one's hand in one's pocket

borsaiolo *m*, **-a** *f* pickpocket

borseggio *m* (*pl* -ggi) pickpocketing

borsellino *m* purse, *Am* coin purse

borsetta *f* handbag, *Am* purse

borsista *m/f* (*mpl* -i) *speculatore* speculator; *studente* scholarship holder

boscaglia *f* brush, scrub

boscaiolo *m* woodcutter

bosco *m* (*pl* -schi) wood

boscoso wooded

bossolo *m* di proiettili (shell) case

BOT, bot *abbr* (= **Buono Ordinario del Tesoro**) treasury bond

botanica *f* botany

botanico (*pl* -ci) **1** *agg* botanical **2** *m*, **-a** *f* botanist

botola *f* trapdoor

botta *f* blow; (*rumore*) bang; **fare a -e** come to blows

botte *f* barrel; ARCHI **volta** *f* **a ~** barrel vault

bottega *f* (*pl* -ghe) shop; (*laboratorio*) workshop

bottegaio *m* (*pl* -ai), **-a** *f* shopkeeper

botteghino *m* box office; (*del lotto*) *sales outlet for lottery tickets*

bottiglia *f* bottle

bottiglieria *f* wine merchant's

bottino *m* loot

botto *m* (*rumore*) bang; **di ~** all of a sudden

bottone *m* button; **~ automatico** press-stud, *Am* snap fastener; **attaccare un ~ a qu** sew a button on for s.o.; *fig* buttonhole s.o.

bovino **1** *agg* bovine **2** *m*: **-i** *pl* cattle

box *m inv* per auto lock-up garage; per bambini playpen; per cavalli loose box

boxe *f* boxing

bozza *f* draft; TIP proof

bozzetto *m* sketch

B

bozzolo m cocoon

braccetto m: **a ~** arm in arm

bracciale m bracelet; (*fascia*) armband; *di orologio* watch strap

braccialetto m bracelet

bracciante m/f day labo(u)rer

bracciata f *nel nuoto* stroke

braccio m (pl le braccia e i bracci) arm; **~ di mare** sound; **a -a aperte** with open arms; **portare in ~ qu** carry s.o.; *fig* **essere il ~ destro di qu** be s.o.'s right-hand man; **incrociare le -a** fold one's arms; *fig* go on strike

bracciolo m arm(rest)

bracco m (pl -cchi) hound

bracconiere m poacher

brace f embers pl; **alla ~** char-grilled, *Am* -broiled

braciola f GASTR chop

branca f (pl -che) branch (*anche fig*)

branchia f gill

branco m (pl -chi) ZO *di cani, lupi* pack; *di pecore, uccelli* flock; *fig spreg* gang

brancolare <1l> grope

branda f camp-bed

brandello m shred, scrap; **a -i** in shreds *or* tatters

brano m *di testo, musica* passage

brasato m GASTR *di manzo* braised beef

Brasile m Brazil

brasiliano 1 *agg* Brazilian **2** m, **-a** f Brazilian

bravata f boasting; *azione* bravado

bravo good; (*abile*) clever, good; **~!** well done!

bravura f skill

break m inv break

breccia f (pl -cce) breach

bretella f (*raccordo*) slip road, *Am* ramp; **-e** pl braces, *Am* suspenders

breve short; **in ~** briefly, in short

brevettare <1a> patent

brevetto m patent; *di pilota* licence, *Am* license; **ufficio** m **dei -i** patent office

brevità f shortness

brezza f breeze

bricco m (pl -cchi) jug, *Am* pitcher

briciola f crumb

briciolo m fig grain, scrap

bricolage m do-it-yourself

briga f (pl -ghe): **darsi la ~ di fare qc** take the trouble to do sth; **attaccar ~ con qu** pick a quarrel with s.o.

brigadiere m MIL sergeant

brigante m bandit

brigata f party, group; MIL brigade

briglia f rein; *fig* **a ~ sciolta** at breakneck speed

brillante 1 *agg* sparkling; *colore* bright; *fig* brilliant **2** m diamond

brillare <1a> **1** v/i shine **2** v/t *mina* blow up

brillo tipsy

brina f hoar-frost

brindare <1a> drink a toast (**a** to), toast (**a** sth); **~ alla salute di qu** drink to *or* toast s.o.

brindisi m inv toast

brio m liveliness; MUS brio

brioche f inv brioche

brioso lively

britannico (pl -ci) **1** *agg* British **2** m, **-a** f Briton

brivido m *di freddo, spavento* shiver; *di emozione* thrill

brizzolato *capelli* greying, *Am* graying

brocca f (pl -cche) jug, *Am* pitcher

broccato m brocade

broccoli mpl broccoli sg

brodo m (clear) soup; *di pollo, di manzo, di verdura* stock; **minestra** f **in ~** soup; **~ ristretto** consommé

brodoso watery, thin

bronchiale bronchial

bronchite f bronchitis

broncio m: **avere** (*o* **tenere**) **il ~** sulk; **mi ha tenuto il ~ per tre giorni** he sulked for three days

broncopolmonite f bronchopneumonia

brontolare <1l> grumble; *di stomaco* rumble

brontolio m grumble; *di stomaco* rumble

brontolone 1 *agg* grumbling **2** m, **-a** f grumbler

bronzo m bronze

bruciapelo: *a ~* point-blank

bruciare <1f> **1** *v/t* burn; *(incendiare)* set fire to; *~ le tappe* forge ahead **2** *v/i* burn; *fig di occhi* sting

bruciarsi burn o.s.

bruciato burnt; *dal sole* scorched, parched

bruciatura *f* burn

bruciore *m* burning sensation; *~ di stomaco* heartburn

bruco *m* (*pl* -chi) grub; *(verme)* worm

brufolo *m* spot

brughiera *f* heath, moor

brulicare <1l & d> swarm

brulichio *m* swarming

brullo bare

bruno brown; *capelli* dark

brusco (*pl* -schi) sharp; *persona, modi* brusque, abrupt; *(improvviso)* sudden

brutale brutal

brutalità *f inv* brutality

bruto **1** *agg:* **forza** *f* **-a** brute force **2** *m* brute

brutta *f*: (**copia** *f*) ~ rough copy

bruttezza *f* ugliness

brutto ugly; *(cattivo)* bad; *tempo, tipo, situazione, affare* nasty

Bruxelles *f* Brussels

buca *f* (*pl* -che) hole; *(avvallamento)* hollow; *del biliardo* pocket; *~ delle lettere* letter-box, *Am* mailbox

bucaneve *m inv* snowdrop

bucare <1d> make a hole in; *(pungere)* prick; *biglietto* punch; *~ una gomma* have a puncture, *Am* have a flat (tire); *fig* *avere le mani bucate* be a spendthrift

bucarsi prick o.s.; *con droga* shoot up

bucato *m* washing, laundry; *fare il ~* do the washing

buccia *f* (*pl* -cce) peel

bucherellare <1b> make holes in; *bucherellato dai tarli* riddled with woodworm

buco *m* (*pl* -chi) hole; *~ dell' ozono* hole in the ozone layer; *~ nero* black hole

budello *m* (*pl* le budella) gut; *(vicolo)* alley

budget *m inv* budget

budino *m* pudding

bue *m* (*pl* buoi) ox, *pl* oxen; *carne* beef

bufalo *m* buffalo

bufera *f* storm; *~ di neve* snowstorm

buffet *m inv* buffet; *mobile* sideboard

buffo funny

buffone *m*, *-a f* buffoon, fool; *di corte* fool, jester

bugia¹ *f* candle holder

bugia² *f* (*menzogna*) lie; *dire -e* tell lies, lie

bugiardo **1** *agg* lying **2** *m*, *-a f* liar

bugigattolo *m* cubby-hole

buio **1** *agg* dark **2** *m* darkness; *al ~* in the dark; *~ pesto* pitch dark

bulbo *m* BOT bulb

Bulgaria *f* Bulgaria

bulgaro **1** *agg* Bulgarian **2** *m*, *-a f* Bulgarian

bulletta *f* tack

bullone *m* bolt

buoi → *bue*

buon → *buono*

buonafede *f*: *in ~* in good faith

buonanotte *int, f* good night; *dare la ~* say good night

buonasera *int, f* good evening; *dare la ~* say good evening

buongiorno *int, m* good morning, hello; *dare il ~* say good morning *or* hello

buongustaio *m* (*pl* -ai), *-a f* gourmet

buongusto *m* good taste; *di ~* in good taste

buono **1** *agg* good; *(valido)* good, valid; *momento, occasione* right; *alla -a* informal, casual; *di buon'ora* early; *di buon grado* willingly; *avere buon naso* have a good sense of smell; *~ a nulla* good-for-nothing **2** *m* good; FIN bond; *(tagliando)* coupon, voucher; *~ del tesoro* Treasury bond; *~ pasto o mensa* luncheon voucher; *~ regalo* gift voucher; *~ sconto* money-off coupon

buonsenso *m* common sense

B

buonuscita f (*liquidazione*) golden handshake
burattino m puppet
burbero gruff, surly
burla f practical joke, trick
burlarsi <1a>: ~ *di qu* make fun of s.o.
burlone m, **-a** f joker
burocrate m bureaucrat
burocratico (*pl* -ci) bureaucratic
burocrazia f bureaucracy
burrasca f (*pl* -sche) storm
burrascoso stormy
burro m butter; GASTR **al** ~ in butter; **tenero come il** ~ soft as butter
burrone m ravine
bussare <1a> knock; ~ *alla porta* knock at the door
bussola f compass; ~ *magnetica* magnetic compass; *perdere la* ~

lose one's bearings
busta f *per lettera* envelope; *per documenti* folder; (*astuccio*) case; ~ **paga** pay packet
bustarella f bribe
bustina f: ~ *di tè* tea bag
busto m ANAT torso; *scultura* bust; (*corsetto*) girdle
buttafuori m inv TEA call-boy; *di locale notturno* bouncer
buttare <1a> **1** v/i BOT shoot, sprout **2** v/t throw; ~ *via* throw away; *fig* waste; ~ *giù* knock down; *lettera* scribble down; *boccone* gulp down; F ~ *la pasta* put the pasta on
buttarsi throw o.s.; *fig* have a go (*a* at); ~ *giù* (*saltare*) jump; *fig* lose heart, get discouraged
by-pass m inv by-pass
byte m inv INFOR byte

C

ca. abbr (= *circa*) ca (= circa)
c.a. abbr (= *corrente alternata*) AC (= alternating current)
cabaret m inv cabaret
cabina f *di nave, aereo* cabin; *di ascensore, funivia* cage; ~ *balneare* beach hut; ~ *di guida* driver's cab; ~ *elettorale* polling booth; ~ *telefonica* phone box, Am pay phone
cabinato m cabin cruiser
cabriolè, cabriolet m inv convertible
cacao m cocoa
caccia (*pl* -cce) **1** f hunting; *andare a* ~ go hunting (*di* sth); *dare la* ~ *a qu* chase after s.o. **2** m MIL *aereo* fighter; *nave* destroyer
cacciagione f GASTR game
cacciare <1f> hunt; (*scacciare*) drive out; (*ficcare*) shove; ~ (*via*) chase away
cacciarsi: *dove ti eri cacciato?*

where did you get to?
cacciatora f: GASTR **alla** ~ stewed
cacciatore m, **-trice** f hunter; ~ *di frodo* poacher
cacciavite m inv screwdriver
cachemire m inv cashmere
cachet m inv MED capsule
cacio m cheese
cactus m inv cactus
cadavere m corpse
cadente: *stella f* ~ shooting star
cadere <2c> fall; *di edificio* fall down; *di capelli, denti* fall out; *di aereo* crash; ~ *dalle nuvole* be thunderstruck; *lasciar* ~ drop; *lasciarsi* ~ *su una poltrona* collapse into an armchair
caduta f fall; ~ *massi* falling rocks; ~ *di tensione* drop in voltage
caffè m inv coffee; *locale* café; ~ *corretto* espresso with a shot of alcohol; ~ *macchiato* espresso with a

splash of milk

caffeina *f* caffeine; **senza ~** caffeine free

caffellatte *m inv* hot milk with a small amount of coffee

caffettiera *f* (*bricco*) coffee pot; (*macchinetta*) coffee maker

cafone *m* boor

cagionevole delicate, sickly

cagliare <1g> curdle

cagna *f* bitch

calabrese *agg, m/f* Calabrian

calabrone *m* hornet

calamari *mpl* squid

calamita *f* magnet

calamità *f inv* calamity; **~ naturale** natural disaster

calante: **luna** *f* **~** waning moon

calare <1a> **1** *v/t* lower; *prezzi* reduce, lower **2** *v/i di vento* drop; *di prezzi* fall, come down; *di sipario* fall; *di sole* set, go down; **~ di peso** lose weight; **è calato del 20%** it's down 20%

calca *f* throng

calcagno *m* (*pl* i calcagni *o* le calcagna) heel

calcare[1] <1d> (*pigiare*) press down; *con i piedi* tread; *parole* emphasize; **~ la mano** exaggerate; **~ le scene** become an actor, take up acting

calcare[2] *m* limestone

calcareo chalky

calce[1] *f* lime

calce[2] *m fig*: **in ~** below

calcestruzzo *m* concrete

calciare <1f> kick

calciatore *m* footballer, soccer player

calcina *f* (*malta*) mortar

calcinaccio *m* (*pl* -cci) (*intonaco*) bit of plaster; *di muro* bit of rubble

calcio *m* (*pl* -ci) kick; *attività* football, soccer; MIL butt; CHIM calcium; **giocare al ~** play football *or* soccer; **campionato** *m* **di ~** football *or* soccer championship; **~ di rigore** penalty kick

calco *m* (*pl* -chi) mo(u)ld

calcolare <1l> calculate; (*valutare*) weigh up

calcolatore *m* calculator; *fig* calculating person; *elettronico* computer

calcolatrice *f* calculator; **~ tascabile** pocket calculator; **~ da tavolo** desktop calculator

calcolo *m* calculation; MED stone; **~ preventivo** estimate

caldaia *f* boiler

caldarrosta *f* roast chestnut

caldo 1 *agg* warm; (*molto caldo*) hot; **non mi fa né ~ né freddo** it's all the same to me **2** *m* warmth; *molto caldo* heat; **ho ~** I'm warm; I'm hot

calendario *m* (*pl* -ri) calendar; **~ delle manifestazioni** calendar of events

calibrare <1l> calibrate

calibro *m* calibre, *Am* caliber; TEC callipers

calice *m* goblet; REL chalice

calle *f a Venezia* lane

calligrafia *f* calligraphy

callo *m* corn; **fare il ~ a qc** become hardened to sth

calma *f* calm; **prendersela con ~** take it easy

calmante *m* sedative

calmare <1a> calm; *dolore* soothe

calmarsi *di dolore* ease (off)

calmo calm

calo *m di peso* loss; *dei prezzi* drop, fall

calore *m* warmth; *intenso* heat

caloria *f* calorie

caloroso *fig* warm

calpestare <1a> walk on; *fig* trample over

calunnia *f* slander

calunniare <1k> slander

calura *f* heat

calvario *m* REL Calvary; *fig* ordeal

calvizie *f* baldness

calvo bald

calza *f da donna* stocking; *da uomo* sock; **~ elastica** support stocking; **fare la ~** knit

calzamaglia *f* tights *pl*, *Am* pantyhose; *da ginnastica* leotard

calzare 1 *v/t scarpe* put on; (*indossare*) wear **2** *v/i fig* fit

calzascarpe *m* shoehorn

calzatoio *m* (*pl* -oi) shoehorn

calzature *fpl* footwear *sg*

calzaturificio *m* (*pl* -ci) shoe factory

calzettone *m* knee sock

calzino *m* sock

calzolaio *m* (*pl* -ai) shoemaker

calzoleria *f* shoe shop

calzoncini *mpl* shorts; **~ da bagno** (swimming) trunks

calzone *m* GASTR folded-over pizza

calzoni *mpl* trousers, *Am* pants

camaleonte *m* chameleon

cambiale *f* bill (of exchange); **~ in bianco** blank bill; **girare una ~** endorse a bill; **pagare una ~** hono(u)r a bill; **~ a vista** sight bill; **~ a scadenza fissa** fixed-term bill

cambiamento *m* change; **~ climatico** climate change

cambiare <1k> **1** *v/t* change; (*scambiare*) exchange; AUTO **~ la marcia** change gear; **~ casa** move (house); **~ idea** change one's mind **2** *v/i e* **cambiarsi** change

cambiavalute *m o f inv* currency dealer, money-broker

cambio *m* (*pl* -bi) change; FIN, (*scambio*) exchange; AUTO, TEC gear; **~ automatico** automatic gearshift; **~ dell'olio** oil change; **~ d'indirizzo** change of address; **in ~** in exchange (**di** for); **dare il ~ a qu** relieve s.o.; **fare ~ con qu** swap *or* exchange with s.o.

camelia *f* camellia

camera *f* room; **~ da letto** bedroom; **~ singola** single room; **~ matrimoniale** double room; **~ a due letti** twin room; **~ d'albergo** hotel room; **~ blindata** strong room; **Camera dei Deputati** House of Commons; FOT **~ oscura** darkroom; **~ d'aria** inner tube; **~ dell'industria e del commercio** chamber of commerce

cameraman *m inv* cameraman

camerata *f stanza* dormitory; *in ospedale* ward

cameriera *f* waitress; (*domestica*) maid

cameriere *m* waiter; (*domestico*) manservant

camerino *m* dressing room

camice *m di medico* white coat; *di chirurgo* gown

camicetta *f* blouse

camicia *f* (*pl* -cie) shirt; **~ sportiva** sports shirt; **~ da notte** nightdress

caminetto *m* fireplace

camino *m* chimney; (*focolare*) fireplace

camion *m inv* truck, *Br* lorry

camioncino *m* van

camionista *m* (*pl* -i) truck driver, *Br* lorry driver

cammello *m* camel; *stoffa* camel hair

camminare <1a> walk; (*funzionare*) work, go

camminata *f* walk

cammino *m*: **un'ora di ~** an hour's walk; **mettersi in ~** set out

camomilla *f* camomile; (*infuso*) camomile tea

camoscio *m* (*pl* -sci) chamois; **scarpe** *fpl* **di ~** suede shoes

campagna *f* country; *fig*, POL campaign; **vivere in ~** live in the country; **~ pubblicitaria** advertising campaign; **~ elettorale** election campaign

campana *f* bell

campanello *m* bell; *della porta* doorbell; **~ d'allarme** alarm bell

campanile *m* bell tower

campanula *f* campanula

campare <1a> live; **~ alla giornata** live for the moment

campeggiare <1f> camp

campeggiatore *m* camper

campeggio *m* camping; *posto* camp site

camper *m inv* camper van

campestre rural

camping *m* camp site

campionario *m* (*pl* -ri) samples

campionato *m* championship; **~ mondiale** world championship

campione *m* sample; (*esemplare*) specimen; *di stoffa* swatch; SP champion

campo *m* field; **~ giochi** playground; **~ di golf** golf course; **~ di calcio** football *or* soccer pitch; **~ di con-**

centramento concentration camp; **~ da tennis** tennis court; **~ di ricerche** area of research; **~ sportivo** sports ground; **~ profughi** refugee camp

camposanto m (pl camposanti) cemetery

camuffare <1a> disguise

Canada m Canada

canadese 1 agg Canadian 2 m/f Canadian 3 f half-litre (Am -liter) bottle of beer

canale m channel; artificiale canal

canalizzazione f channelling; (conduttura) pipe

canapa f hemp

canarino m canary

cancellare <1b> cross out; con gomma rub out, erase; INFOR delete; debito write off, cancel; appuntamento cancel

cancellata f railings pl

cancelleria f: **articoli** mpl **di ~** stationery

cancelliere m chancellor; DIR clerk of the court

cancello m gate

cancerogeno carcinogenic

cancrena f gangrene

cancro m MED cancer; ASTR, GEOG **Cancro** Cancer

candeggiante m stain remover

candeggina f bleach

candela f candle; **~ d'accensione** spark plug

candelabro m candelabra

candeliere m candlestick

candidarsi <1l> stand (for election)

candidato m, **-a** f candidate

candidatura f candidacy, candidature

candido pure white; (sincero) frank; (innocente) innocent, pure; (ingenuo) naive

canditi mpl candied fruit

cane m dog; di arma da fuoco hammer, cock; **~ da guardia** guard dog; **freddo ~** freezing cold; **non c'era un ~** there wasn't a soul about; F **fatto da -i** botched F

canestro m basket

canguro m kangaroo

canile m (casotto) kennel; luogo kennels

canino 1 agg dog attr 2 m (dente) canine (tooth)

canna f reed; (bastone) stick; P joint P; **~ fumaria** flue; **~ da pesca** fishing rod; **~ da zucchero** sugar cane

cannella f GASTR cinnamon

cannelloni mpl cannelloni sg

cannibale m cannibal

cannocchiale m telescope

cannonata f fig: **è una ~** it's terrific

cannone m MIL gun, cannon; (asso) ace

cannuccia f (pl -cce) straw

canoa f canoe

canone m FIN rental (fee); RAD, TV licence (fee); (norma) standard

canottaggio m a pagaie canoeing; a remi rowing; **circolo** m **di ~** rowing club

canottiera f vest

canotto m rowing boat, Am rowboat; **~ pneumatico** rubber dinghy; **~ di salvataggio** lifeboat

cantante m/f singer

cantare <1a> sing

cantautore m, **-trice** f singer-songwriter

cantiere m building or construction site; MAR shipyard

cantina f cellar; locale wineshop

canto¹ m (canzone) song; (il cantare) singing; **~ popolare** folk song; **~ del cigno** swan song

canto² m: **dal ~ mio** for my part; **d'altro ~** on the other hand

cantonata f (grosso sbaglio) blunder

cantone m POL canton; **Lago** m **dei Quattro Cantoni** Lake Lucerne

canzonare <1a> tease

canzone f song; **la solita ~** the same old story

canzoniere m songbook

caos m chaos

caotico (pl -ci) chaotic

C.A.P. abbr (= **Codice di Avviamento Postale**) postcode, Am zip code

capace (abile) capable; (ampio) large, capacious; **~ di fare qc**

capable of doing sth

capacità *f inv* ability; (*capienza*) capacity; FIN **~ di acquisto** purchasing power; INFOR **~ di memoria** memory

capanna *f* hut

capannone *m* shed; AVIA hangar

caparra *f* FIN deposit

capello *m* hair; **-i** *pl* hair *sg*; GASTR **-i d'angelo** very thin noodles; **ne ho fin sopra i -i!** I've had it up to here!; **per un ~** by the skin of one's teeth

capezzolo *m* nipple

capiente large, capacious

capienza *f* capacity

capigliatura *f* hair

capillare MED capillary

capire <4d> understand; **capisco** I see; **si capisce!** naturally!, of course!; **far ~ qc a qu** make s.o. understand sth, get s.o. to see sth; **farsi ~** make o.s. understood

capitale 1 *agg* capital; *fig* major **2** *f città* capital **3** *m* FIN capital; **~ d'esercizio** working capital; **~ disponibile** available capital; **~ fisso** fixed capital; **~ iniziale** start-up capital; **fuga *f di* -i** flight of capital; **~ proprio** equity capital; **~ sociale** share capital

capitalismo *m* capitalism

capitalista *agg, m/f* (*mpl* -i) capitalist

capitaneria *f*: **~ di porto** port authorities *pl*

capitano *m* captain

capitare <1l> *di avvenimento* happen; *di persona* find o.s.; **se mi capita l'occasione di venire** if I get a chance to come; **~ in cattive mani** fall into the wrong hands; **mangio dove capita** I don't always eat in the same place; **~ a proposito** come along at the right time; **sono cose che capitano** these things happen

capitello *m* ARCHI capital

capitolo *m* chapter; **avere voce in ~** have a say in the matter

capitombolo *m* tumble, fall

capo *m* ANAT head; *persona* head, chief, boss F; GEOG cape; **~ del governo** head of government; **~ dello**

Stato head of state; **~ di vestiario** item of clothing; **da ~** from the beginning; **ti seguirò in ~ al mondo** I'll follow you to the ends of the earth; **per sommi -i** briefly; **andare a ~** start a new paragraph; **non venire a ~ di nulla** be unable to come to any kind of conclusion; **questa storia non ha né ~ né coda** this story just doesn't make sense

capobanda *m/f di delinquenti* ringleader

capodanno *m* New Year's Day

capofamiglia *m/f* head of the family

capofitto: **a ~** headlong

capogiro *m* dizzy spell

capogruppo *m/f* group leader; POL leader

capolavoro *m* masterpiece

capolinea *m* terminus

capolista *f* SP leaders *pl*

capoluogo *m* (*pl* capoluoghi) principal town

capomastro *m* (*pl* capomastri) master builder

caporeparto *m/f* (*mpl* capireparto, *fpl* caporeparto) *di fabbrica* foreman; *donna* forewoman; *di ufficio* superintendent

caposala *m/f* (*mpl* capisala, *fpl* caposala) *in ospedale* ward sister; *uomo* charge nurse

caposaldo *m* (*pl* capisaldi) stronghold

caposezione *m/f* (*mpl* capisezione, *fpl* caposezione) section chief

capostazione *m/f* (*mpl* capistazione, *fpl* capostazione) station master

capostipite *m/f* founder

capotavola: **a ~** at the head of the table

capote *f inv* AUTO hood, (soft) top

capotreno *m/f* (*mpl* capitreno, *fpl* capotreno) guard

capoufficio *m/f* (*mpl* capiufficio, *fpl* capoufficio) supervisor

capoverso *m* (*pl* capoversi) paragraph; TIP indent(ation)

capovolgere <3d> turn upside down; *piani* upset; *situazione* reverse

capovolgersi turn upside down; *di barca* capsize

capovolgimento *m* complete change

capovolto *pp* → **capovolgere**

cappa *f* (*mantello*) cloak; *di cucina* hood; ~ **del camino** cowl

cappella *f* chapel

cappellano *m* chaplain

cappelletti *mpl* pasta, shaped like little hats, with meat, cheese and egg filling

cappello *m* hat; ~ **di paglia** straw hat; **senza** ~ hatless; **mettersi il** ~ put one's hat on

cappero *m* caper

cappio *m* noose

cappone *m* capon; **far venire la pelle di** ~ **a qu** give s.o. the creeps

cappotto *m* coat

cappuccino *m bevanda* cappuccino

cappuccio *m* (*pl* -cci) hood; *di penna* top, cap

capra *f* (nanny)goat; (*cavalletto*) trestle

capretto *m* kid

capriccio *m* (*pl* -cci) whim; *di bambini* tantrum; **fare i -i** have tantrums

capriccioso capricious; *bambino* naughty; *tempo* changeable

Capricorno ASTR, GEOG Capricorn

capriola *f* somersault

capriolo *m* roe deer; GASTR venison

capro *m* billy goat; ~ **espiatorio** scapegoat

capsula *f* capsule; *di dente* crown; ~ **spaziale** space capsule

captare <1a> RAD pick up

carabina *f* carbine

carabiniere *m* police officer

caraffa *f* carafe

caramella *f* sweet

caramello *m* caramel

carato *m* carat

carattere *m* character; (*caratteristica*) characteristic; (*lettera*) character, letter; **-i** *pl* TIP typeface; INFOR font

caratteristica *f* characteristic

caratteristico (*pl* -ci) characteristic

caratterizzare <1a> characterize

caravan *m inv* caravan

caravanning *m inv* caravanning

carboidrato *m* carbohydrate

carbone *m* coal

carbonella *f* charcoal

carburante *m* fuel

carburatore *m* carburet(t)or

carcassa *f di animale* carcass; TEC (*intelaiatura*) frame; MAR, F wreck

carcerato *m*, **-a** *f* prisoner

carcerazione *f* imprisonment; ~ **preventiva** preventive detention

carcere *m* (*pl* le -ri) jail, prison

carceriere *m*, **-a** *f* jailer, gaoler

carciofo *m* artichoke

cardellino *m* goldfinch

cardiaco (*pl* -ci) cardiac, heart

cardinale 1 *agg* cardinal; **punto** *m* ~ cardinal point **2** *m* REL cardinal

cardine *m* hinge

cardiologia *f* cardiology

cardiologo *m* (*pl* -gi), **-a** *f* (*pl* -ghe) heart specialist, cardiologist

cardo *m* thistle

carena *f* MAR keel

carenza *f* lack (**di** of)

carestia *f* shortage

carezza *f* caress

carezzare <1a> caress

cargo *m aereo* air freighter; *nave* cargo ship

cariato: **dente** *m* ~ decayed tooth

carica *f* (*pl* -che) (*incarico*) office; *fig* (*slancio, energia*) drive; TEC load; MIL (*attacco*) charge; **in** ~ in office; **durata** *f* **della** ~ term of office; **tornare alla** ~ insist

caricare <1d & l> load; MIL charge; *orologio* wind up

caricarsi overload o.s. (**di** with); PSI psych o.s. up; ~ **di debiti** get heavily into debt

caricatura *f* caricature

caricaturista *m/f* (*mpl* -i) caricaturist

carico (*pl* -chi) **1** *agg* loaded; EL charged; *caffè* strong; *colore* deep; *orologio* wound up **2** *m* load; FIN charge, expense; MAR cargo; DIR **a** ~ **di** (*contro*) against; **essere a ~ di qu**

be dependent on s.o.; ~ **utile** payload; **lettera f** (o **polizza f**) **di** ~ bill of lading; ~ **di lavoro** workload

carie f inv tooth decay

carino (*grazioso*) pretty; (*gentile*) nice

carisma m charisma

carità f charity; **per** ~! for goodness sake!, for pity's sake

carnagione f complexion

carnale carnal; **fratello** m ~ blood brother

carne f flesh; GASTR meat; ~ **di maiale/manzo** pork/beef; ~ **tritata** mince

carneficina f slaughter

carnevale m carnival

carnivoro m carnivore

carnoso fleshy

caro 1 agg dear; (*costoso*) dear, expensive; **mi è molto** ~ I am very fond of him/it; **a** ~ **prezzo** dearly **2** avv a lot; **costare** ~ be very expensive; *fig* have a high price **3** m dear; **-i** pl loved ones, family

carogna f carrion; F swine

carosello m merry-go-round

carota f carrot

carotide f carotid artery

carovana f caravan

carovita m high cost of living; **indennità f di** ~ cost of living allowance

carpa f carp

carpentiere m carpenter

carpire <4d>: ~ **qc a qu** get sth out of s.o.

carponi on all fours

carrabile → **carraio**

carraio: **passo** m ~ driveway

carreggiata f roadway; **rimettersi in** ~ *fig* catch up

carrello m trolley; AVIA undercarriage; ~ **elevatore** fork-lift truck; ~ **portabagagli** baggage trolley, *Am* baggage cart

carretto m cart

carriera f career; **fare** ~ come a long way; **di gran** ~ at top speed

carriola f wheelbarrow

carro m cart; AST Bear; FERR ~ **bestiame** cattle truck; FERR ~ **merci**

goods wagon, *Am* freight car; ~ **armato** tank; ~ **attrezzi** breakdown van, tow truck, *Am* wrecker; ~ **funebre** hearse

carrozza f FERR carriage; ~ **con cuccette** sleeper; ~ **ristorante** restaurant car

carrozzella f per bambini pram; per invalidi wheelchair

carrozzeria f bodywork, coachwork

carrozziere m AUTO (*progettista*) (car) esigner; (*costruttore*) coachbuilder; *chi fa riparazioni* panel beater

carrozzina f pram

carta f paper; GASTR (*menù*) menu; GEOG ~ **geografica** map; ~ **assegni** cheque (guarantee) card; ~ **da bollo** official stamped paper; ~ **da gioco** (playing) card; ~ **da lettere** note paper; ~ **da macero** waste paper (for pulping); ~ **da parati** wallpaper; ~ **d'argento** card that entitles people over a certain age to reduced fares; ~ **di credito** credit card; ~ **d'identità** identity card; AVIA ~ **d'imbarco** boarding pass; ~ **igienica** toilet paper; ~ **stagnola** silver paper; GASTR tinfoil; ~ **stradale** road map; ~ **telefonica** phone card; ~ **velina** tissue paper; AUTO ~ **verde** green card; ~ **vetrata** sandpaper

cartacarbone f carbon paper

cartamoneta f inv paper money

cartamodello m (pl cartamodelli) pattern

cartapecora f parchment, vellum

cartapesta f papier-mâché

cartastraccia f waste paper

carteggio m (pl -ggi) correspondence

cartella f (*borsa*) briefcase; di alunno schoolbag, satchel; *copertina per documenti* folder, file; *foglio dattiloscritto* page; ~ **clinica** medical record

cartellino m (*etichetta*) label; **con prezzo** price tag; (*scheda*) card; SP ~ **giallo/rosso** yellow/red card; ~ **orario** clocking-in card

cartello m sign; *nelle dimostrazioni*

placard; FIN cartel; **~ stradale** road sign

cartellone m pubblicitario hoarding, Am billboard; TEA bill

cartiera f paper mill

cartilagine f cartilage

cartina f GEOG map; (bustina) packet; per sigarette cigarette paper

cartoccio m (pl -cci) paper bag; a cono paper cone; GASTR **al ~** baked in tinfoil, en papillote

cartografia f cartography

cartoleria f stationer's

cartolina f postcard; **~ illustrata** picture postcard; **~ postale** postcard

cartoncino m (thin) cardboard; (biglietto) card

cartone m cardboard; **-i** pl animati cartoons

cartuccia f (pl -cce) cartridge

casa f edificio house; (abitazione) home; FIN company; **~ di cura** nursing home; **~ editrice** publishing house; **~ dello studente** hall of residence; **~ a schiera** terraced house; **~ unifamiliare** single-family dwelling; **~ per le vacanze** holiday home; **case popolari** council houses; **seconda ~** second home; **essere di ~** be like one of the family; **dove stai di ~?** where do you live?; **cambiar ~** move (house); **fatto in ~** home-made; **andare a ~** go home; **essere a ~** be at home; SP **giocare in/fuori ~** play at home/away

casalinga f (pl -ghe) housewife

casalingo (pl -ghi) domestic; (fatto in casa) home-made; persona home-loving; **cucina f -a** home cooking; **-ghi** mpl household goods

cascare <1d> fall (down); fig **cascarci** fall for it

cascata f waterfall

cascina f (casa colonica) farmhouse; (caseificio) dairy farm

casco m (pl -chi) helmet; dal parrucchiere hair dryer; **-chi** pl **blu** UN forces, blue berets F

caseggiato m (edificio) block of flats, Am apartment block

caseificio m (pl -ci) dairy

casella f di schedario pigeon hole; (quadratino) square; **~ postale** post office box

casellario m (pl -ri) pigeon holes; **~ giudiziario** criminal records (office)

casello m autostradale toll booth

casereccio (pl -cci) homemade

caserma f barracks

casino P m brothel; (rumore) din, racket; (disordine) mess; **~ di caccia** hunting lodge

casinò m inv casino

caso m case; (destino) chance; (occasione) opportunity; **~ d'emergenza** emergency; **per ~** by chance; **a ~** at random; **(in) ~ che** in case; **in ~ contrario** should that not be the case; **in ogni ~** in any case, anyway; **in nessun ~** under no circumstances; **nel peggiore dei -i** if the worst comes to the worst

casolare m farmhouse

caspita! goodness (gracious)!, good heavens!

cassa f case; di legno crate; di negozio till; sportello cash desk, cashpoint; (banca) bank; **~ acustica** speaker; **~ comune** kitty; **~ continua** night safe; **~ da morto** coffin; **~ di risparmio** savings bank; **~ integrazione** form of income support; **~ malattia** department administering health insurance scheme; **~ toracica** ribcage; **orario m di ~** opening hours

cassaforte f (pl casseforti) safe

cassapanca f (pl cassapanche) chest

casseruola f (sauce)pan

cassetta f box; per frutta, verdura crate; (musicassetta) cassette; **~ delle lettere** (buca) post box, Am mailbox; (casella) letterbox, Am mailbox; **~ del pronto soccorso** first-aid kit; **~ di sicurezza** strong box; **successo m di ~** box office hit; **pane m a ~** sliced loaf

cassetto m drawer; AUTO **~ portaoggetti** glove compartment

cassettone m chest of drawers; **soffitto m a -i** panelled ceiling cassiere *m*, **-a** *f* cashier; *di banca* teller; *di supermercato* checkout assistant

cassonetto *m* dustbin

casta *f* caste

castagna *f* chestnut

castagno *m* chestnut (tree)

castano *capelli* chestnut; *occhi* brown

castello *m* castle; TEC (*impalcatura*) scaffolding; **letti** *mpl* **a ~** bunk beds

castigare <1e> punish

castigo *m* (*pl* -ghi) punishment

castità *f* chastity

castoro *m* beaver

castrare <1a> castrate; *gatto* neuter; *femmina di animale* spay

casual **1** *agg* casual **2** *m* casual clothes, casual wear

casuale chance, casual

casualità *f* chance nature

cataclisma *m* (*pl* -i) disaster

catacomba *f* catacomb

catalizzatore *m* catalyst; AUTO catalytic converter; **~ a tre vie** three-way catalytic converter

catalogare <1m & e> catalog(ue)

catalogo *m* (*pl* -ghi) catalog(ue); **~ di vendita per corrispondenza** mail order catalog(ue)

catapecchia *f* shack

catapultare <1a> catapult

catarifrangente *m* reflector; *lungo la strada* reflector, *Br* cat's eye

catarro *m* catarrh

catasta *f* pile, heap

catasto *m* land register

catastrofe *f* catastrophe

catastrofico (*pl* -ci) catastrophic

categoria *f* category; *di albergo* class; **~ a rischio** at risk category

categorico (*pl* -ci) categoric(al)

catena *f* chain; **-e** *pl* **da neve** snow chains; **reazione** *f* **a ~** chain reaction; **~ di montaggio** assembly line; **~ montuosa** mountain range, chain of mountains

catenaccio *m* (*pl* -cci) bolt; SP defensive tactics

cateratta *f* (*chiusa*) sluice(gate); (*cascata*) falls; MED cataract

catino *m* basin

catrame *m* tar

cattedra *f scrivania* desk; *incarico d'insegnamento* teaching post; **~ universitaria** university chair

cattedrale *f* cathedral

cattiveria *f* wickedness; *di bambini* naughtiness; *azione* nasty thing to do; *parole crudeli* nasty thing to say

cattività *f* captivity

cattivo bad; *bambino* naughty, bad; **con le buone o con le -e** by hook or by crook

cattolicesimo *m* (Roman) Catholicism

cattolico (*pl* -ci) **1** *agg* (Roman) Catholic **2** *m*, **-a** *f* (Roman) Catholic

cattura *f* capture; (*arresto*) arrest

catturare <1a> capture; (*arrestare*) arrest

caucciù *m* rubber

causa *f* cause; (*motivo*) reason; DIR lawsuit; **fare ~** sue (**a qu** s.o.); **a ~ di** because of; **per ~ tua** because of you

causale *f* cause, reason

causare <1a> cause

cautela *f* caution; (*precauzione*) precaution

cauto cautious

cauzione *f* (*deposito*) security; *per la libertà provvisoria* bail

Cav. *abbr* (= **Cavaliere**) *Italian title awarded for services to the country*

cava *f* quarry

cavalcare <1d> ride

cavalcata *f* ride

cavalcavia *m inv* flyover

cavalcioni: **a ~** astride

cavaliere *m* rider; *accompagnatore* escort; *al ballo* partner

cavalla *f* mare

cavallerizzo *m*, **-a** *f* horseman; *donna* horsewoman

cavalletta *f* grasshopper

cavalletto *m* trestle; FOT tripod; *da pittore* easel

cavallo *m* horse; *scacchi* knight; *dei pantaloni* crotch; **~ da corsa** race horse; AUTO **~ vapore** horsepower

andare a ~ go riding; **vivere a ~ di due secoli** straddle two centuries

cavallone *m* breaker

cavalluccio *m* (*pl* -cci): **~ marino** sea horse

cavare <1a> take out; *dente* take out, extract; **cavarsela** manage, get by

cavarsi: **~ da un impiccio** get out of trouble

cavatappi *m inv* corkscrew

caverna *f* cave

cavernoso: **una voce -a** a deep voice

cavia *f* guinea pig (*anche fig*)

caviale *m* caviar

caviglia *f* (*pl* -glie) ANAT ankle

cavillo *m* quibble

cavità *f inv* cavity

cavo 1 *agg* hollow **2** *m* cable; **~ d'accensione** plug lead; **~ di avviamento** jump leads; **~ di ormeggio** mooring rope; **~ da rimorchio** tow rope; **~ in fibra ottica** optic fibre cable; **televisione** *f* **via ~** cable TV

cavolfiore *m* cauliflower

cavolo *m* cabbage; **~ di Bruxelles** Brussels sprout; **~ rapa** kohlrabi; **~ verzotto** Savoy cabbage

cazzo *m* V prick V; **~!** fuck! V

CC *abbr* (= **Carabinieri**) Italian police force

cc *abbr* (= **centimetri cubici**) cc (= cubic centimetres)

c.c. *abbr* (= **corrente continua**) DC (= direct current)

c/c *abbr* (= **conto corrente**) current account, *Am* checking account

CD *m inv* CD; **lettore** *m* **~** CD player; **CD-Rom** *m inv* CD-Rom; **drive** *m* **per ~** CD-Rom drive

ce → ci (*before lo, la, li, le, ne*)

c'è there is

cecchino *m* sniper

cece *m* chickpea

cecità *f* blindness

ceco 1 *agg* Czech **2** *m*, **-a** *f* Czech

cecoslovacco (*pl* -cchi) **1** *agg* Czechoslovakian **2** *m*, **-a** *f* Czechoslovakian

cedere <3a> **1** *v/t* (*dare*) hand over, give up; (*vendere*) sell, dispose of; **~**

il posto give up one's seat **2** *v/i* give in, surrender (**a** to); *muro, terreno* collapse, give way; **non ~!** don't give in!

cedevole soft

cedibile transferable, assignable

cedola *f* coupon; **~ di consegna** delivery note

cedro *m del Libano* cedar

CEE, **Cee** *abbr* (= **Comunità Economica Europea**) EEC (= European Economic Community)

cefalo *m* ZO mullet

ceffone *m* slap

celebrare <1l & b> celebrate

celebrazione *f* celebration

celebre famous

celebrità *f inv* fame; (*persona*) celebrity

celere fast, speedy, swift; **posta** *f* **~** swiftair®, *Am* Fedex®

celeste sky blue; (*divino*) heavenly (*anche fig*)

celibato *m* celibacy

celibe 1 *agg* single, unmarried **2** *m* bachelor

cella *f* cell

cellula *f* cell; **~ fotoelettrica** photoelectric cell; **~ solare** solar cell

cellulare 1 *agg* cell *attr*; **telefono** *m* **~** mobile phone, *Am* cell(ular) phone **2** *m* prison van; (*telefono*) mobile

cellulite *f* cellulite

cellulosa *f* cellulose

celtico (*pl* -ci) Celtic

cemento *m* cement; **~ armato** reinforced concrete

cena *f* supper, evening meal; *importante, con ospiti* dinner; **~ in piedi** buffet

cenacolo *m* PITT Last Supper

cenare <1a> have supper; *formalmente* dine

cencio *m* (*pl* -ci) rag, piece of cloth; (*per spolverare*) duster; **bianco come un ~** white as a sheet

cenere *f* ash; **le Ceneri** *fpl* Ash Wednesday

cenno *m* sign; *della mano* wave; *del capo* nod; *con gli occhi* wink; (*breve notizia*) mention; (*allusione*) hint;

far ~ **a qu** con la mano wave to s.o.; con il capo nod to s.o.; con gli occhi wink at s.o.; **far ~ di voler andare** signal that one wants to leave; **far ~ di sì** nod (one's head); **far ~ di no** shake one's head

cenone *m* feast, banquet; ~ **di San Silvestro** special celebratory meal on New Year's Eve

censimento *m* census

censura *f* censorship

censurare <1a> censor

centenario (*pl* -ri) **1** *agg* hundred-year-old **2** *m* (*persona*) centenarian; (*anniversario*) centenary

centesimo **1** *agg* hundredth **2** *m*: ~ **di dollaro** cent; **badare al ~** count every penny

centigrado *m* centigrade

centimetro *m* centimetre, *Am* -meter; ~ **cubo** cubic centimetre (*Am* -meter); ~ **quadrato** square centimetre (*Am* -meter)

centinaio *m* (*pl* le centinaia) hundred; **un ~ di** about a hundred, a hundred or so

cento hundred; **per ~** per cent; ~ **per ~** one hundred per cent; ~ **di questi giorni** many happy returns

centrale **1** *agg* central **2** *f* station, plant; ~ **atomica o nucleare** nuclear power station

centralinista *m/f* switchboard operator

centralino *m* switchboard

centralizzare <1a> centralize

centrare <1b> TEC centre, *Am* center; ~ **il bersaglio** hit a bull's eye

centrifuga **1** *agg* centrifugal **2** *f* spin-dryer; TEC centrifuge

centrifugare <1e & m> spin-dry; TEC centrifuge

centro *m* centre, *Am* center; **di bersaglio** bull's eye; ~ **commerciale** shopping centre, *Am* center; ~ **della città** town or city centre, *Am* downtown; ~ **residenziale** residential area; ~ **storico** old (part of) town; **fare ~** hit the bull's eye; *fig* hit the nail on the head

ceppo *m*: ~ **bloccarruota** wheel

clamp; **mettere il ~** a clamp

cera[1] *f* wax; **per lucidare** polish; ~ **da scarpe** shoe polish

cera[2] *f* look; **avere una brutta ~** look awful

ceralacca *f* sealing wax

ceramica *f* (*pl* -che) *arte* ceramics *sg*; *oggetto* piece of pottery

cerata *f* oilskins *pl*

cerca *f*: **in ~ di ...** in search of ...

cercare <1d> **1** *v/t* look for **2** *v/i*: ~ **di fare** try to do

cerchia *f* circle

cerchio *m* (*pl* -chi) circle

cerchione *m* TEC rim

cereale **1** *agg* grain *attr* **2** -**i** *mpl* grain, cereals

cerealicoltura *f* grain farming

cerebrale: **commozione** *f* ~ concussion

cerimonia *f* ceremony; REL service; -**e** *pl* (*convenevoli*) pleasantries; **fare ~** stand on ceremony; **senza tante ~** (*bruscamente*) unceremoniously

cerimoniale *m/agg* ceremonial

cerimonioso *agg* ceremonious

cerino *m* (wax) match

cernia *f* grouper

cerniera *f* hinge; ~ **lampo** zip (fastener), *Am* zipper

cernita *f* selection, choice

cero *m* (large) candle

cerotto *m* (sticking) plaster

certezza *f* certainty

certificare <1m & d> certify

certificato *m* certificate; ~ **medico** medical certificate; ~ **di garanzia** guarantee; ~ **di nascita** birth certificate; ~ **di sana e robusta costituzione** certificate of good health

certo **1** *agg* (*sicuro*) certain, sure (**di** of; **che** that); **un ~ signor Federici** a (certain) Mr Federici; **ci vuole un ~ coraggio** it takes (some) courage; **di una -a età** of a certain age; -**i** some; -**e cose non si dicono** there are some things you just don't say; **un ~ non so che** a certain something, a certain je ne sais quoi **2** *avv* (*certamente*) certainly; (*naturalmente*) of course; **~ che ...** surely ... **3** *pron*: **-i, -e** some, some people

certosa *f* Carthusian monastery

cervello *m* (*pl* i cervelli, le cervella) brain; GASTR brains; **farsi saltare le -a** blow one's brains out; **lambiccarsi il ~** rack one's brains

cervo *m* deer; *carne* venison; **~ volante** stag beetle

cesareo: **taglio** *m* **~** C(a)esarean (section), C section

cesellare <1b> chisel

cesello *m* chisel

cesoie *fpl* shears

cespuglio *m* (*pl* -gli) bush, shrub

cessare <1b> stop, cease

cessate il fuoco *m* ceasefire

cessazione *f* *di contratto* termination; **~ di esercizio** closure, going out of business

cessione *f* transfer, handover

cesso *m* P bog P

cesta *f* basket

cestinare <1a> throw away, bin F

cestino *m* little basket; *per la carta* wastepaper basket

cesto *m* basket

cetaceo *m* cetacean

ceto *m* (social) class; **~ medio** middle class

cetra *f* zither

cetriolino *m* gherkin

cetriolo *m* cucumber

cf., cfr. *abbr* (= **confronta**) cf (= compare)

cg *abbr* (= **centigrammo**) cg (= centigram)

CGIL *abbr* (= **Confederazione Generale Italiana del Lavoro**) Italian trade union organization

chalet *m inv* chalet

charter *m inv* charter

che 1 *agg* what; **a ~ cosa serve?** what is that for?; **~ brutta giornata!** what a filthy day! **2** *pron persona*: soggetto who; *persona*: oggetto who, that, *fml* whom; *cosa* that, which; **~?** what?; **ciò ~** what; **non c'e di ~** don't mention it, you're welcome **3** *cong dopo il comparativo* than;

sono tre anni ~ non la vedo I haven't seen her for three years

check-in *m inv* AVIA check-in; **fare il ~** check in

chemioterapia *f* chemotherapy, chemo F

chetichella: **alla ~** stealthily

chi who; **di ~ è il libro?** whose book is this? **a ~ ha venduto la casa?** who did he sell the house to?; **c'è ~ dice che** some people say that; **~ ... ~** some ... others

chiacchiera *f* chat; (*maldicenza*) gossip; (*notizia infondata*) rumo(u)r; **far due -e con qu** have a chat with s.o.

chiacchierare <1l> chat, chatter; *spreg* gossip

chiacchierata *f* chat

chiacchierone 1 *agg* talkative, chatty; (*pettegolo*) gossipy **2** *m, -a f* chatterbox; (*pettegolo*) gossip

chiamare <1a> call; TELEC (tele)phone, ring; **andare a ~ qu** go and get s.o., fetch s.o.; **mandare a ~ qu** send for s.o.; (*convocare*) call in; TELEC **~ in teleselezione** call direct, dial direct

chiamarsi be called; **come ti chiami?** what's your name?; **mi chiamo ...** my name is ...

chiamata *f* call; TELEC (tele)phone call; **~ a carico del destinatario** reverse charge call, *Am* collect call; **~ interurbana** long-distance call

chiara *f* egg white

chiarezza *f* clarity

chiarimento *m* clarification

chiarire <4d> clarify

chiarirsi become clear

chiaro 1 *agg* clear; *colore* light, pale; (*luminoso*) bright; **~ e tondo** definite **2** *m* light; **~ di luna** moonlight; **mettere in ~** (*appurare*) throw light on; (*spiegare*) clarify **3** *avv* plainly; (*con franchezza*) frankly

chiaroscuro *m* PITT chiaroscuro

chiaroveggente *m/f* clairvoyant

chiasso *m* din, racket; **fare ~** make a din *or* racket; *fig* cause a sensation

chiassoso noisy

chiatta f barge; **ponte** m **di ~e** pontoon bridge

chiave 1 agg inv key **2** f key; MUS clef; **~ d'accensione** ignition key; **~ della macchina** car key; **~ inglese** spanner, Am monkey wrench; **sotto ~** under lock and key

chiavistello m bolt

chiazza f (macchia) stain; sulla pelle, di colore patch

chic inv chic, stylish, elegant

chicco m (pl -chi) grain; (di caffè) bean; **~ d'uva** grape

chiedere <3k> per sapere ask (**di** about); per avere ask for; (esigere) demand, require; **~ qc a qu** ask s.o. sth; **~ di qu** (chiedere notizie di) ask about s.o.; per parlargli ask for s.o.; **~ un piacere a qu** ask s.o. a favo(u)r, ask a favo(u)r of s.o.; **~ scusa a qu** apologize to s.o.

chiedersi wonder (**se** whether)

chiesa f church

chiesto pp → **chiedere**

chiglia f MAR keel

chilo m kilo; **mezzo ~** half a kilo

chilogrammo m kilogram

chilometraggio m AUTO mileage

chilometrico indennità per kilometre

chilometro m kilometre, Am -meter; **-i** pl **all'ora** kilometres (Am -meters) per hour

chilowatt m inv kilowatt

chimica f chemistry

chimico (pl -ci) **1** agg chemical; **sostanze** fpl **-che** chemicals **2** m, **-a** f chemist

chinare <1a> testa bend; occhi lower

chinarsi stoop, bend down

chincaglierie fpl knick-knacks, ornaments

chinino m quinine

chioccia f fig mother hen

chiocciola f snail; **scala f a ~** spiral staircase

chiodato: SP **scarpe** fpl **-e** spikes

chiodo m nail; **~ di garofano** clove; fig **~ fisso** obsession, idée fixe; **roba da -i!** it's unbelievable!

chioma f mane; di cometa tail

chiosco m (pl -chi) kiosk

chiostro m cloister

chip m inv chip

chiromante m/f palmist

chiropratico m, **-a** f chiropractor

chirurgia f surgery

chirurgico (pl -ci) surgical

chirurgo m (pl -ghi) surgeon

chissà who knows; (forse) maybe

chitarra f guitar

chitarrista m/f (mpl -i) guitarist

chiudere <3b> close, shut; a chiave lock; strada close off; gas, luce turn off; fabbrica, negozio per sempre close down, shut down; **~ un occhio** turn a blind eye; FIN **~ in pareggio** break even; **~ in perdita / in attivo** show a loss / a profit

chiudersi di porta, ombrello close, shut; di ferita heal up; **~ in se stesso** withdraw into o.s.

chiunque anyone; relativo whoever

chiusa f di fiume lock; di discorso conclusion

chiuso 1 pp → **chiudere 2** agg closed, shut; a chiave locked; (nuvoloso) cloudy, overcast; persona reserved

chiusura f closing, shutting; AUTO **~ centralizzata** central locking; **~ lampo** zip (fastener), Am zipper; **ora f di ~** closing time

choc m inv shock

ci 1 pron us; **non ~ ha parlato** he didn't speak to us; **~ siamo divertiti molto** we had a great time; **~ vogliamo bene** we love each other; **~ penso** I'm thinking about it **2** avv here; (lì) there; **~ sei?** are you there?; **c'è ...** there is ...; **~ sono ...** there are ...; **~ vuole tempo** it takes time

C.ia abbr (= **compagnia**) Co. (= company)

ciabatta f slipper

cialda f wafer

ciambella f GASTR type of cake, baked in a ring-shaped mo(u)ld; (salvagente) lifebelt

cianfrusaglia f knick-knack

ciao! *nell'incontrarsi* hi!; *nel congedarsi* 'bye!, cheerio!

ciarlatano *m* charlatan

ciarpame *m* junk

ciascuno 1 *agg* each; (*ogni*) every **2** *pron* everyone

cibarsi <1a> feed on, eat (*di* sth)

cibernetica *f* cybernetics

cibo *m* food; *-i pl* foodstuffs, foods; **~ pronto** fast food

cicala *f* (*insetto*) cicada

cicalino *m* buzzer, bleeper

cicatrice *f* scar

cicatrizzare <1a>, **cicatrizzarsi** heal

cicca *f* (*pl* -che) (*mozzicone*) stub, butt; (*gomma da masticare*) (chewing) gum

ciccia *f* (*grasso*) flab

ciccione *m*, **-a** *f* fatty

cicciottello chubby

cicerone *m* guide

ciclamino *m* cyclamen

ciclico cyclical

ciclismo *m* cycling, bike riding

ciclista *m/f* (*mpl* -i) cyclist

ciclistico bike *attr*, cycle *attr*

ciclo *m* cycle

ciclomotore *m* moped

ciclone *m* cyclone

cicloturismo *m* cycling holidays

cicogna *f* stork

cicoria *f* chicory

cieco (*pl* -chi) **1** *agg* blind; *vicolo m ~* dead end, blind alley **2** *m*, **-a** *f* blind man; *donna* blind woman

cielo *m* sky; REL heaven; *grazie al ~* thank heaven(s)

cifra *f* figure; (*monogramma*) monogram; (*somma*) amount, sum; (*codice*) cipher, code; *~ d'affari* turnover; *numero m di sei -e* six digit number

cifrato (*messaggio*) in cipher, in code

ciglio *m* (*pl* le ciglia) ANAT eyelash; (*pl* i cigli) (*bordo*) edge

cigno *m* swan

cigolare <1l> squeak

cigolio *m* squeak

Cile *m* Chile

cilecca: *far ~ di arma da fuoco* misfire

cileno 1 *agg* Chilean **2** *m*, **-a** *f* Chilean

ciliegia *f* (*pl* -ge) cherry

ciliegio *m* (*pl* -gi) cherry (tree)

cilindrata *f* TEC cubic capacity; *automobile f di media ~* middle of the range car

cilindrico (*pl* -ci) cylindrical

cilindro *m* cylinder; *cappello* top hat

cima *f* top; *in ~ all'armadio* on top of the wardrobe; *da ~ a fondo* from top to bottom; *fig* from beginning to end; *non è una ~* he's no Einstein

cimentarsi <1b>: *~ in* embark on

cimice *f* bug; *dei letti* bed bug; (*puntina da disegno*) drawing-pin

ciminiera *f* smokestack

cimitero *m* cemetery

Cina *f* China

cinciallegra *f* great tit

cincilla, **cincillà** *f* chinchilla

cin cin! F cheers!

cineamatore *m* video enthusiast

cineforum *m inv* film followed by a discussion; *club* film club

cinema *m inv* cinema, Am *luogo* movie theater; *~ d'essai* experimental cinema; *luogo* art cinema, art house

cinematografia *f* cinematography; *industria* film *or* movie industry

cinematografico (*pl* -ci) film *attr*, movie *attr*

cinepresa *f* cine camera

cinese *agg*, *m/f* Chinese

cineteca *f* film library

cinetico (*pl* -ci) kinetic

cingere <3d> (*circondare*) surround

cinghia *f* strap; (*cintura*) belt; *tirare la ~* tighten one's belt

cinghiale *m* wild boar; *pelle f di ~* pigskin

cinguettare <1a> twitter

cinguettio *m* twittering

cinico (*pl* -ci) **1** *agg* cynical **2** *m* -**a** *f* cynic

cinismo *m* cynicism

cinquanta fifty

cinquantenario *m* fiftieth anniversary

cinquantenne *m/f* 50-year-old
cinquantesimo *m/agg* fiftieth
cinquantina *f*: **una ~ di** about 50
cinque five
cinquecento **1** *agg* five hundred **2** *m*: **il Cinquecento** the sixteenth century
cinquemila five thousand
cintare <1a> enclose
cinto *pp* → **cingere**
cintura *f* belt; (*vita*) waist; **~ di salvataggio** lifebelt; **~ di sicurezza** seat-belt
cinturino *m* strap
ciò (*questo*) this; (*quello*) that; **~ che** what; **con tutto ~** even so, in spite of all that; **~ nonostante** nevertheless
ciocca *f* (*pl* -cche) *di capelli* lock
cioccolata *f* chocolate
cioccolatino *m* chocolate
cioccolato *m* chocolate
cioè that is, i.e.
ciondolare <1l> dangle; *fig* hang about
ciondolo *m* pendant
ciotola *f* bowl
ciottolo *m* pebble
cipolla *f* onion; *di pianta* bulb
cipollina *f* small onion; **erba** *f* **~** chives *pl*
cipresso *m* cypress (tree)
cipria *f* (face) powder
circa **1** *avv* (round) about **2** *prp* about
circo *m* (*pl* -chi) circus
circolare **1** *v/i* <1l> circulate; *di persone* move along; **le auto non possono ~** it's impossible to drive **2** *agg* circular **3** *f lettera* circular
circolazione *f* traffic; MED circulation; DIR **libera ~** freedom of movement; **~ del sangue** circulation of the blood; **mettere in ~** voci spread; **ritirare dalla ~** withdraw from circulation
circolo *m* circle; (*club*) club; **~ vizioso** vicious circle
circondare <1a> surround
circonferenza *f* circumference
circonvallazione *f* ring road
circoscrivere <3tt> circumscribe

circoscrizione *f* area, district; **~ elettorale** constituency
circostante surrounding
circostanza *f* circumstance; (*occasione*) occasion
circuito *m* SP (*percorso*) track; EL circuit; EL **corto ~** short circuit
CISL *abbr* (= **Confederazione Italiana Sindacati Lavoratori**) Italian trade union organization
cisterna *f* cistern; (*serbatoio*) tank; **nave** *f* **~** tanker
cisti *f* ANAT cyst
cistifellea *f* gall bladder
cistite *f* cystitis
CIT *abbr* (= **Compagnia Italiana del Turismo**) Italian Tourist Board
citare <1a> quote; *come esempio* cite, quote; DIR *testimone* summons; *in giudizio* sue
citazione *f* quotation, quote; DIR summons
citofono *m* entry phone; *in uffici* intercom
città *f* town; *grande* city; **~ dormitorio** dormitory town; **~ giardino** garden city; **~ universitaria** university town (*in the provinces*); **la ~ vecchia** the old (part of) town; **Città del Vaticano** Vatican City; **la ~ eterna** the Eternal City
cittadina *f* (small) town
cittadinanza *f* citizenship; (*popolazione*) citizens; **~ onoraria** freedom of the city
cittadino **1** *agg* town *attr*, city *attr* **2** *m*, **-a** *f* citizen; (*abitante di città*) city dweller
ciuccio *m* F (*succhiotto*) dummy, *Am* pacifier
ciuffo *m* tuft
civetta *f* ZO (little) owl; *fig* **far la ~** flirt
civico (*pl* -ci) (*della città*) municipal, town *attr*; *delle persone* civic; **numero ~** (street) number
civile **1** *agg* civil; *civilizzato* civilized; (*non militare*) civilian; **guerra** *f* **~** civil war; **matrimonio** *m* **~** civil marriage; **stato** *m* **~** marital status **2** *m* civilian

civiltà f inv civilization; (cortesia) civility

clacson m inv horn

clamoroso fig sensational

clandestino 1 agg clandestine; (illegale) illegal 2 m, -a f stowaway

clarinetto m clarinet

classe f class; (aula) classroom; ~ operaia working class; ~ turistica tourist class; di ~ classy

classicismo m classicism

classico (pl -ci) 1 agg classical; (tipico) classic 2 m classic

classifica f classification; (elenco) list; sportiva league standings, league table; musicale charts

classificare <1m & d> classify

classificatore m (cartella) folder; mobile filing cabinet, Am file cabinet

classismo m class consciousness

clausola f clause; (riserva) proviso

claustrofobia f claustrophobia

clavicola f collar-bone, clavicle

clemente merciful; tempo mild

clemenza f clemency; di tempo mildness

cleptomane m/f kleptomaniac

clericale clerical

clero m clergy

clessidra f hourglass

clic m inv click; mediante ~ by clicking

cliccare <1d> INFOR click (su on)

cliché m inv fig cliché

cliente m/f customer; di professionista client; di albergo guest; MED patient; ~ abituale regular

clientela f customers pl, clientele; di professionista clients pl; di medico patients pl; ~ abituale patrons pl, regular customers pl

clima m (pl -i) climate

climatico (pl -ci) climate attr, climatic; stazione f climatica health resort

clinica f (pl -che) (ospedale) clinic; (casa di cura) nursing home; ~ medica clinical medicine

clinico (pl -ci) 1 agg clinical 2 m clinician

clip m inv clip

clonare <1a> BIO clone

cloro m chlorine

clorofilla f chlorophyl(l)

cloroformio m chloroform

club m inv club

cm abbr (= centimetro) cm (= centimetre)

c.m. abbr (= corrente mese) of this month, inst.

CNR abbr (= Consiglio Nazionale delle Ricerche) Italian National Research Council

coabitare <1m> share a flat (Am an apartment), be flatmates (Am roommates)

coagularsi <1m> di sangue coagulate, clot; di latte curdle

coalizione f coalition; governo m di ~ coalition government

coalizzarsi <1a> join forces; POL form a coalition

cobra m inv cobra

cocaina f cocaine

cocainomane 1 agg addicted to cocaine 2 m/f cocaine addict

coccinella f ladybird, Am ladybug

coccio m (pl -cci) earthenware; frammento fragment (of pottery), shard

cocciuto stubborn, obstinate

cocco m (pl -cchi) coco-nut palm or tree; noce f di ~ coconut 2 m, -a f (persona prediletta) darling

coccodrillo m crocodile

coccolare <1l & c> F cuddle; (viziare) spoil

cocente scorching; fig scathing

cocktail m inv bevanda cocktail; festa cocktail party

cocomero m water melon

coda f tail; (fila) queue, Am line; di veicolo, treno rear; MUS coda; ~ di paglia guilty conscience; ~ dell'occhio corner of the eye; piano m a ~ grand piano; fare la ~ queue (up), Am stand in line

codardo 1 agg cowardly 2 m, -a f coward

codazzo m swarm

codesto 1 *agg* that **2** *pron* that one

codice *m* code; **~ a barre** bar code; **~ civile** civil code; **~ di avviamento postale** post code, *Am* zip code; **~ fiscale** tax code; **~ stradale** Highway Code

codificare <1m & d> *dati* encode; DIR codify

codino *m* pigtail, plait

coefficiente *m* coefficient

coerente coherent; *fig* consistent

coerenza *f* coherence; *fig* consistency

coesione *f* cohesion

coesistenza *f* coexistence

coetaneo 1 *agg* the same age (**di** as) **2** *m*, **-a** *f* contemporary, person of the same age

cofanetto *m* casket

cofano *m* AUTO bonnet, *Am* hood

cogestione *f* joint management; **~ aziendale** worker participation

cogliere <3ss> pick; (*raccogliere*) gather; (*afferrare*) seize; *occasione* take, seize, jump at; (*capire*) grasp; **~ di sorpresa** catch unawares, take by surprise; **~ sul fatto** catch in the act, catch red-handed

cognac *m inv* cognac

cognato *m*, **-a** *f* brother-in-law; *donna* sister-in-law

cognizione *f* knowledge; FIL cognition; **parla con ~ di causa** he knows what he's talking about

cognome *m* surname; **nome** *m* **e ~** full name

coi *prp* **con** and *art* **i**

coincidenza *f* coincidence; FERR connection; **perdere la ~** miss one's connection

coincidere <3q> coincide

coinquilino *m*, **-a** *f* in condominio fellow tenant; *in appartamento* flatmate, *Am* roommate

coinvolgere <3d> involve (**in** in)

coinvolto *pp* → **coinvolgere**

col *prp* **con** and *art* **il**

colabrodo *m inv* strainer

colapasta *m inv* colander

colare <1a> **1** *v/t* strain; *pasta* drain **2** *v/i* drip; (*perdere*) leak; *di naso* run; *di cera* melt; **~ a fondo** *o* **a picco** sink, go down

colata *f di metallo* casting; *di lava* flow

colazione *f prima* breakfast; *di mezzogiorno* lunch; **~ al sacco** picnic; **far ~** have breakfast, breakfast

colei *pron f* the one; **~ che** the one that

colera *m* cholera

colesterolo *m* cholesterol

colica *f* (*pl* -che) colic

colino *m* strainer

colla *f* glue; *di farina* paste

collaborare <1m> co-operate, collaborate; *con giornale* contribute

collaboratore *m*, **-trice** *f* collaborator; *di giornale* contributor; **~atore** *m* **esterno** freelance(r); **-trice** *f* **domestica** home help

collaborazione *f* co-operation, collaboration

collana *f* necklace; *di libri* series

collant *m inv* tights *pl*, *Am* pantyhose

collare *m* collar

collasso *m* collapse; **~ cardiaco** heart failure

collaudare <1a> test; *fig* put to the test

collaudo *m* test

colle *m* hill; (*valico*) pass

collega *m/f* (*mpl* -ghi) colleague, co-worker

collegamento *m* connection; MIL liaison; RAD, TV link; **~ aereo / ferroviario** connecting flight / train

collegare <1a> connect, link

collegarsi RAD, TV link up

collegiale 1 *agg* collective **2** *m/f* boarder

collegio *m* (*pl* -gi) boarding school; **~ elettorale** constituency

collera *f* anger; **andare in ~** get angry; **essere in ~ con qu** be angry with s.o.

collerico (*pl* -ci) irascible

colletta *f* collection

collettività *f* community

collettivo *m/agg* collective

colletto *m* collar

collezionare <1a> collect

collezione *f* collection; **fare ~ di qc** collect sth, make a collection of sth

collezionista *m/f* collector; **~ di francobolli** stamp collector

collina *f* hill

collinoso hilly

collirio *m* eyewash

collisione *f* collision; **entrare in ~** collide

collo *m* neck; (*bagaglio*) piece *or* item of luggage; (*pacco*) package; **~ del piede** instep

collocamento *m* placing; (*impiego*) employment; **agenzia *f* di ~** employment agency; **ufficio *m* di ~** Jobcentre

collocare <1l & d> place, put; **~ a riposo** retire

collocazione *f* place, job

colloquiale colloquial

colloquio *m* (*pl* -qui) talk, conversation; *ufficiale* interview; (*esame*) oral (exam)

colluttazione *f* scuffle

colmare <1a> fill (**di** with); *fig di gentilezze* overwhelm (**di** with); **~ un vuoto** bridge a gap

colmo 1 *agg* full (**di** of) **2** *m* summit, top; *fig* (*culmine*) height; **è il ~!** that's the last straw!

colomba *f* ZO, *fig* dove

colombo *m* pigeon

colon *m* colon

Colonia *f*: **acqua *f* di ~** eau de Cologne

colonia *f* colony; *per bambini* holiday camp; **~ marina** seaside holiday camp

coloniale colonial

colonico (*pl* -ci): **casa *f* -a** farmhouse

colonizzare <1a> colonize

colonna *f* column; *di veicoli* line; *fig* mainstay; **~ sonora** sound track; **~ vertebrale** spinal column

colonnato *m* colonnade

colonnello *m* colonel

colonnina *f* **della benzina** petrol (*Am* gas) pump

colorante *m* dye; **senza -i** with no artificial colo(u)rings

colorare <1a> colo(u)r; *disegno* colo(u)r in

colorato colo(u)red

colorazione *f* colo(u)ring

colore *m* colo(u)r; *carte* suit; *poker* flush; **gente *f* di ~** colo(u)red people; **scatola *f* dei -i** paint box; **~ a olio** oil (paint); **a -i** film, televisione colo(u)r *attr*; **farne di tutti i -i** get up to all sorts of mischief

colorito 1 *agg volto* rosy-cheeked; *fig* (*vivace*) colo(u)rful **2** *m* complexion

coloro *pron pl* the ones; **~ che** those who

colossale colossal

colosso *m* colossus

colpa *f* fault; REL sin; **dare a qu la ~ di qc** blame s.o. for sth; **non è ~ sua** it's not her fault; **per ~ tua** because of you; **senso *m* di ~** sense of guilt; **sentirsi in ~** feel guilty

colpevole 1 *agg* guilty **2** *m/f* culprit, guilty party

colpire <4d> hit, strike; *fig* impress, leave an impression on; **~ nel segno** hit the nail on the head

colpo *m* blow; (*fig*) blow, shock; *di pistola* shot; MED stroke; **~ apoplettico** apoplectic fit; **~ di calore** heat stroke; **~ di sole** sunstroke; **~ di stato** coup d'état; **~ di telefono** phone call; **~ di testa** whim; **fare ~** make an impact; **sul ~, di ~** suddenly

coltellata *f* **ferita** stab wound

coltello *m* knife

coltivare <1a> AGR, *fig* cultivate

coltivatore *m* farmer

coltivazione *f* cultivation; *di prodotti agricoli e piante* growing; *campi coltivati* crops

colto¹ *agg* cultured, learned

colto² *pp* → **cogliere**

coltura *f* growing; *piante* crop

colui *pron m* the one; **~ che** the one that

coma *m* coma

comandamento *m* commandment

comandante *m* commander; AVIA, MAR captain

comandare <1a> 1 v/t (*ordinare*) order, command; *esercito* command; *nave* captain, be captain of; FIN *merci* order; TEC control; ~ *a distanza* operate by remote control 2 v/i be in charge

comando *m* order, command; TEC control; ~ *a distanza* remote control

combaciare <1f> fit together; *fig* correspond

combattente *m* soldier, serviceman

combattere <3a> v/t & v/i fight

combattimento *m* fight; SP match, fight

combinare <1a> combine; (*organizzare*) arrange; ~ *un guaio* make a mess; *oggi ho combinato poco* I got very little done today

combinarsi go well together

combinazione *f* combination; (*coincidenza*) coincidence; *per ~* by chance

combustibile 1 *agg* combustible 2 *m* fuel

combustione *f* combustion

come 1 *avv* as; (*in modo simile o uguale*) like; *interrogativo, esclamativo* how; (*prego?*) pardon?; *fa' ~ ti ho detto* do as I told you; *lavora ~ insegnante* he works as a teacher; ~ *me* like me; *un cappello ~ il mio* a hat like mine; ~ *sta?* how are you?, how are things?; *com'è bello!* how nice it is!; ~ *mai?* how come?, why?; *oggi ~ oggi* nowadays; ~ *se* as if 2 *cong* (*come se*) as if, as though; (*appena, quando*) as (soon as); ~ *se niente fosse* as if nothing had happened

cometa *f* comet

comfort *m inv* comfort; *dotato di tutti i ~ moderni* with all mod cons

comicità *f* funniness

comico (*pl* -ci) 1 *agg* funny, comical; *genere* comic 2 *m*, -*a f* comedian; *donna comedienne*

comignolo *m* chimney pot

cominciare <1f> start, begin (*a* to); *a ~ da oggi* (starting) from today; *tanto per ~* to begin *or* start with

comitato *m* committee; ~ *direttivo* steering committee

comitiva *f* group, party

comizio *m* meeting

Comm. *abbr* (= *Commendatore*) *Italian title awarded for services to the country*

commando *m* commando

commedia *f* comedy; *fig* play-acting

commediografo *m*, -*a f* playwright

commemorare <1m & b> commemorate

commemorazione *f* commemoration

commentare <1a> comment on

commentatore *m*, -*trice f* commentator

commento *m* comment

commerciale commercial; *relazioni, trattative* trade *attr*; *lettera* business *attr*

commercialista *m/f* accountant

commercializzare <1a> market

commerciante *m/f* merchant; (*negoziante*) shopkeeper

commerciare <1b & f> deal (*in* in)

commercio *m* (*pl* -ci) trade, business; *internazionale* trade; *di droga* traffic; ~ *all'ingrosso* wholesale trade; ~ *al minuto* retail trade; *camera f di ~* chamber of commerce; *essere in ~* be available; *mettere in ~ qc* put sth on the market

commessa *f* (*ordinazione*) order

commesso *m*, -*a f* shop assistant, *Am* sales clerk; (*impiegato*) clerk; ~ *viaggiatore* travel(l)ing salesman

commestibile 1 *agg* edible 2 -*i mpl* foodstuffs

commettere <3ee> commit; *errore* make

commiserare <1m> feel sorry for

commissariato *m*: ~ (*di pubblica sicurezza*) police station

commissario *m* (*pl* -ri) *di polizia* (police) superintendent; *membro di commissione* commissioner

commissionare <1a> FIN commission

commissione *f* commission; (*incarico*) errand; *Commissione europea* European Commission; *-i pl* shopping *sg*; *fatto su ~* made to order

commosso **1** *pp* → *commuovere* **2** *agg fig* moved, touched

commovente moving, touching

commozione *f* emotion; *~ cerebrale* concussion

commuovere <3ff> move, touch

commuoversi be moved *or* touched

comò *m inv* chest of drawers

comodino *m* bedside table

comodità *f inv* comfort; (*vantaggio*) convenience

comodo **1** *agg* comfortable; *vestito* loose, comfortable; (*facilmente raggiungibile*) easy to get to; (*utile*) useful, handy; F *persona* laid back F; *stia ~!* don't get up! **2** *m* comfort; *con ~* at one's convenience; *far ~ di denaro* come in useful, be handy; *le fa ~ così* she finds it easier that way; *fare il propio ~* do as one pleases

compagnia *f* company; (*gruppo*) group; REL order; *~ aerea* airline; *~ di assicurazioni* insurance company; *far ~ a qu* keep s.o. company

compagno *m*, *-a f* companion; (*convivente*), FIN partner; POL comrade; *~ di scuola* schoolfriend, schoolmate; *~ di squadra* team mate; *~ di viaggio* travelling companion

comparativo *m/agg* comparative

comparire <4e> appear; (*essere pubblicato*) come out, appear; (*far figura*) stand out

comparizione *f*: DIR *mandato m di ~* summons

comparsa *f* appearance; TEA person with a walk-on part; *in film* extra

comparso *pp* → *comparire*

compartimento *m* compartment

compassione *f* compassion, pity; *provare ~ per qu* feel sorry for s.o.

compasso *m* (pair of) compasses

compatibile compatible

compatire <4d>: *~ qu* feel sorry for s.o.

compatriota *m/f* (*mpl -i*) compatriot

compatto compact; *folla* dense; *fig* united

compensare <1b> (*controbilanciare*) compensate for, make up for; (*ricompensare*) reward; (*risarcire*) pay compensation to

compenso *m* (*ricompensa, risarcimento*) compensation; (*retribuzione*) fee; *in ~* (*d'altra parte*) on the other hand; *dietro ~* for a fee

compera *f* purchase; *fare le -e* go shopping

competente competent; (*responsabile*) appropriate

competenza *f* (*esperienza*) competence; *essere di ~ di qu* be s.o.'s responsibility

competere <3a> (*gareggiare*) compete

competitività *f* competitiveness

competitivo competitive

competizione *f* competition

compiacere too eager to please

compiacenza *f* overeagerness to please

compiacere <2k> please

compiacersi (*provare piacere*) be pleased (*di* with); *mi compiaccio con te* congratulations

compiaciuto *pp* → *compiacere*

compiangere <3d> pity; *per lutto* mourn

compianto *pp* → *compiangere*

compiere <4g> (*finire*) complete, finish; (*eseguire*) carry out; *~ gli anni* have one's birthday

compiersi (*avverarsi*) happen

compilare <1a> compile; *modulo* complete, fill in

compilatore *m* INFOR compiler

compilazione *f* compilation

compimento *m* completion

compito[1] *agg* polite

compito[2] *m* task; EDU *i -i pl* homework *sg*

compiuto *lavoro, opera* completed, finished; *ha 10 anni -i* he's 10

compleanno *m* birthday; *buon ~!* happy birthday!

complementare complementary

complemento *m* complement;

GRAM object

complessato full of complexes

complessivo all-in

complesso 1 *agg* complex, complicated **2** *m* complex; MUS group; *di circostanze* set, combination; **in** o **nel ~** on the whole

completamento *m* completion

completare <1b> complete

completo 1 *agg* complete; (*pieno*) full; TEA sold out **2** *m* set; (*vestito*) suit; **al ~** (*pieno*) full (up); TEA sold out

complicare <1l & d> complicate

complicarsi get complicated

complicato complicated, complex

complicazione *f* complication

complice *m/f* DIR accomplice

complimentarsi: **~ con qu** congratulate s.o. (**per** on)

complimento *m* compliment; **fare un ~ a qu** pay s.o. a compliment; **-i!** congratulations!; **non fare -i!** help yourself!

componente 1 *m* component **2** *m/f* (*persona*) member

componibile modular; *cucina* fitted

componimento *m* composition; DIR settlement

comporre <3ll> (*mettere in ordine*) arrange; MUS compose; TELEC **~ un numero** dial a number

comporsi: **~ di** consist of, be made up of

comportamento *m* behavio(u)r

comportare <1c> involve

comportarsi behave

compositore *m*, **-trice** *f* composer

composizione *f* composition; *di fiori* arrangement

composta *f* stewed fruit; (*terricciato*) compost

composto 1 *pp* → **comporre 2** *agg* compound; *abiti*, *capelli* tidy, neat; **~ da** made up of; **stai ~** keep still; *seduto* sit properly **3** *m* compound

comprare <1a> buy, purchase; (*corrompere*) bribe, buy off

compratore *m*, **-trice** *f* buyer, purchaser

compravendita *f* buying and selling

comprendere <3c> (*includere*) comprise, include; (*capire*) understand

comprensibile understandable

comprensione *f* understanding

comprensivo (*tollerante*) understanding; **~ di** inclusive of

compreso 1 *pp* → **comprendere 2** *agg* inclusive; (*capito*) understood; **tutto ~** all in; **~ te** including you

compressa *f* (*pastiglia*) tablet; *di garza* compress

compresso *pp* → **comprimere**

comprimere <3r> press; (*reprimere*) repress; FIS compress

compromesso 1 *pp* → **compromettere 2** *m* compromise; DIR **~ di vendita** agreement to sell

compromettere <3ee> compromise

compromettersi compromise o.s.

computer *m inv* computer; **assistito dal ~** computer-assisted; **~ portatile** portable (computer), laptop

computerizzare <1a> computerize

computisteria *f* book-keeping, accountancy

comunale *del comune* municipal, town *attr*; **consiglio** *m* **~** town council; **palazzo** *m* **~** town hall

comune 1 *agg* common; *amico* mutual; (*ordinario*) ordinary, common; **in ~** in common; **non ~** unusual, uncommon; **fuori del ~** out of the ordinary **2** *m* municipality; **palazzo** *m* **del ~** town hall

comunemente commonly

comunicare <1m & d> **1** *v/t notizia* pass on, communicate; *contagio* pass on; REL give Communion to **2** *v/i* (*esprimersi*) communicate; *di persone* keep in touch, communicate

comunicato *m* announcement, communiqué; **~ stampa** press release

comunicazione *f* communication; (*annuncio*) announcement; TELEC (*collegamento*) connection; **dare ~ di qc a qu** tell s.o. about sth; TELEC **la ~ si è interrotta** I've been cut off; TELEC **~ internazionale** international call

comunione f REL communion; *di idee* sharing

comunismo m Communism

comunista m/f (mpl -i) Communist

comunità f community; *Comunità europea* European Community

comunitario community *attr*; *dell'UE* Community *attr*

comunque 1 cong however, no matter how; *~ vadano le cose* whatever happens **2** avv (in ogni modo) in any case, anyhow; (in qualche modo) somehow; (tuttavia) however

con with; (mezzo) by; *~ questo tempo* in this weather; *~ tutto ciò* for all that; *avere ~ sé* have with or on one

conato m: *~ di vomito* retching

concedere <3l> grant; *premio* award; *ti concedo che* I admit that

concedersi: *~ qc* treat o.s. to sth

concentramento m concentration

concentrare <1b>, **concentrarsi** concentrate

concentrazione f concentration

concentrico (pl -ci) concentric

concepibile conceivable

concepimento m conception

concepire <4d> conceive; (ideare) devise, conceive

concernere <3a> concern; *per quanto mi concerne* as far as I'm concerned

concerto m concert; *composizione* concerto

concessionario m (pl -ri) agent; *~ esclusivo* sole agent

concessione f concession

concesso pp → *concedere*

concetto m concept; (giudizio) opinion

concezione f conception; *fig* idea (*di* for)

conchiglia f shell

conciare <1f> *pelle* tan; (sistemare) arrange; *come ti sei conciato!* what a state or mess you're in!; *~ qu per le feste* tan s.o.'s hide, give s.o. a good hiding

conciliare <1k> reconcile; *multa* pay, settle; *~ il sonno* be conducive to sleep

conciliazione f reconciliation; DIR settlement

concimare <1a> *pianta* feed

concime m manure; *~ chimico* chemical fertilizer

conciso concise

concitato excited

concittadino m, **-a** f fellow citizen

concludere <3q> conclude; (portare a termine) achieve, carry off; *~ un affare* clinch a deal; *non ho concluso nulla* I got nowhere

concludersi end, close

conclusione f conclusion; *in ~* in short

conclusivo conclusive

concluso pp → *concludere*

concordanza f agreement

concordare <1c> **1** v/t agree (on); GRAM make agree **2** v/i (essere d'accordo) agree; (coincidere) tally

concordato 1 agg agreed on **2** m agreement; REL concordat; DIR settlement

concorde agg in agreement; (unanime) unanimous; (simultaneo) simultaneous

concordia f harmony

concorrente 1 agg (rivale) competing, rival **2** m/f in una gara, gioco competitor, contestant; FIN competitor

concorrenza f competition

concorrenziale competitive

concorrere <3o> (contribuire) concur; (competere) compete (*a* for); *di strade* converge; *~ per un posto* compete for a position

concorso 1 pp → *concorrere* **2** m (competizione) competition, contest; *bandire un ~* announce a competition

concreto concrete; (pratico) practical

condanna f DIR sentence

condannare <1a> condemn (*a* to); DIR sentence (*a* to)

condensare <1b>, **condensarsi** condense

condensazione f condensation

condimento m seasoning; *di*

insalata dressing

condire <4d> season; *insalata* dress; *fig* spice up

condito seasoned

condividere <3q> share

condiviso *pp* → **condividere**

condizionale **1** *m/agg* conditional **2** *f* suspended sentence

condizionamento *m* PSI conditioning; **~ dell'aria** air conditioning

condizionare <1a> PSI condition

condizionato: **con aria -a** with air conditioning, air-conditioned

condizionatore *m* air conditioner

condizione *f* condition; **-i** *pl* **di lavoro** working conditions; **a ~ che** on condition that

condoglianze *fpl* condolences; **fare le ~ a qu** express one's condolences to s.o.

condominio *m* (*comproprietà*) joint ownership; *edificio* block of flats, *Am* condo

condomino *m* owner-occupier, *Am* condo owner

condonare <1a> remit

condono *m* remission; **~ fiscale** conditional amnesty for tax evaders

condotta *f* (*comportamento*) behavio(u)r, conduct; (*canale*) piping

condotto **1** *pp* → **condurre 2** *m* pipe; ANAT duct

conducente *m/f* driver; **~ di autobus** bus driver

condurre <3e> lead; (*accompagnare*) take; *veicolo* drive; *azienda* run; *acque, gas* carry, take

conduttore *m*, **-trice** *f* RAD, TV presenter; FERR (*controllore*) conductor

conduttura *f* (*condotto*) pipe

confederazione *f* confederation

conferenza *f* conference; **~ al vertice** summit (conference); **~ stampa** press conference

conferimento *m* conferring

conferire <4d> **1** *v/t* (*dare*) confer; *premio* award **2** *v/i:* **~ con qu** confer with s.o.

conferma *f* confirmation

confermare <1a> confirm

confessare <1b>, **confessarsi** confess

confessione *f* confession

confessore *m* confessor

confetto *m* GASTR sugared almond; MED pill

confettura *f* jam

confezionare <1a> *merce* wrap, package; *abiti* make

confezione *f* wrapping, packaging; *di abiti* making; **~ regalo** gift wrap; **-i** *pl* (*abiti*) garments

conficcare <1d> hammer, drive

confidare <1a> **1** *v/t* confide **2** *v/i:* **~ in** trust in, rely on

confidarsi **~ con** confide in

confidenza *f* (*familiarità*) familiarity; (*fiducia*) confidence, trust; **avere ~ con qu** be familiar with s.o.; **prendere ~ con qc** familiarize o.s. with sth

confidenziale (*riservato*) confidential; **strettamente ~** strictly confidential

configurare <1a> configure

configurazione *f* configuration

confinante neighbo(u)ring

confinare <1a> border (**con** sth); *fig* confine

confine *m* border; *fra terreni, fig* boundary

confisca *f* (*pl* -che) seizure

confiscare <1d> confiscate

conflitto *m* conflict

confluire <4d> merge

confondere <3bb> confuse, mix up; (*imbarazzare*) embarrass

confondersi get mixed up

conformare <1a> (*rendere adatto*) adapt

conformarsi **~ a** conform to; (*adattarsi*) adapt to

conforme (*simile*) similar; **~ a** in accordance with; **copia** *f* **~** (certified) true copy

conformismo *m* conformity

conformista *m/f* (*mpl* -i) conformist

conformità *f* conformity; **in ~ a** in accordance with

confortare <1c> comfort

confortevole comfortable

conforto *m* comfort

confrontare <1a> compare

confronto *m* confrontation; (*comparazione*) comparison; **a ~ di, in ~ a** compared with; **maleducato nei -i di qu** rude to s.o.

confusione *f* confusion; (*disordine*) muddle, mess; (*baccano*) noise, racket; (*imbarazzo*) embarrassment

confuso 1 *pp* → **confondere 2** *agg* (*non chiaro*) confused, muddled; (*imbarazzato*) embarrassed

congedare <1b> dismiss; MIL discharge

congedarsi take leave (*da* of)

congedo *m* (*permesso*) leave; MIL *assoluto* discharge

congelare <1b> **1** *v/t* freeze **2** *v/i e* **congelarsi** freeze

congelato frozen

congelatore *m* freezer

congenito congenital

congestionare <1a> congest

congestionato congested; *volto* flushed

congestione *f* congestion

congettura *f* conjecture

congiungere <3d> join

congiungersi join (up)

congiuntivite *f* conjunctivitis

congiuntivo *m* GRAM subjunctive

congiunto 1 *pp* → **congiungere 2** *m*, **-a** *f* relative, relation

congiuntura *f* ANAT joint; **~ economica** economic situation

congiunzione *f* GRAM conjunction

congiura *f* conspiracy, plot

congratularsi <1m>: **~ con qu** congratulate s.o. (*per* on)

congratulazioni *fpl*: **fare le propie ~ a qu** congratulate s.o.; **-i!** congratulations!

congressista *m/f* (*mpl* -i) convention participant

congresso *m* convention

conguaglio *m* (*pl* -gli) balance

CONI *abbr* (= **Comitato Olimpico Nazionale Italiano**) Italian Olympic Committee

coniare <1k & c> mint; *fig* coin

conifere *fpl* conifers

coniglio *m* (*pl* -gli) rabbit

coniugare <1l, c & e> conjugate

coniugato married

coniugazione *f* conjugation

coniuge *m/f* spouse; **-i** *pl* husband and wife; **i -i Rossi** Mr and Mrs Rossi

connazionale *m/f* compatriot

connessione *f* connection

connotati *mpl* features

cono *m* cone; **~ gelato** ice-cream cone

conoscente *m/f* acquaintance

conoscenza *f* knowledge; *persona* acquaintance; (*sensi*) consciousness; *per* ~ cc; **fare la ~ di qu** make s.o.'s acquaintance, meet s.o.; **perdere** ~ lose consciousness, faint

conoscere <3n> know; (*fare la conoscenza di*) meet; **~ qu di vista** know s.o. by sight

conoscitore *m*, **-trice** *f* connoisseur

conosciuto well-known, famous

conquista *f* conquest

conquistare <1a> conquer; *fig* win

consacrare <1a> consecrate; *sacerdote* ordain; (*dedicare*) dedicate

consacrarsi devote o.s. (*a* to)

consacrazione *f* consecration; *di sacerdote* ordination

consanguineo *m*, **-a** *f* blood relative

consapevole: **~ di** conscious of, aware of

consapevolezza *f* consciousness, awareness

conscio conscious, aware

consecutivo (*di seguito*) consecutive; **tre giorni -i** three consecutive days, three days in a row

consegna *f di lavoro, documento* handing in; *di prigioniero, ostaggio* handover; **~ a domicilio** home delivery; **~ bagagli** left luggage, *Am* baggage checkroom

consegnare <1a> *lavoro, documento* hand in; *prigioniero, ostaggio* hand over; *merci, posta* deliver

conseguente consequent

conseguenza *f* consequence; **di ~** consequently; **in ~ di qc** as a result of sth

conseguire <4a> **1** v/t achieve; *laurea* obtain **2** v/i follow

consenso m (*permesso*) consent, permission

consentire <4b> **1** v/i (*accondiscendere*) consent **2** v/t allow

conserva f preserve; ~ *di pomodoro* tomato purée; ~ *di frutta* jam

conservante m preservative

conservare <1b> keep; GASTR preserve

conservarsi keep; *in salute* keep well

conservatore m, **-trice** f conservative

conservatorio m (pl -ri) music school, conservatoire

conservazione f preservation

considerare <1m> consider

considerazione f consideration; (*osservazione*) remark, comment; **prendere in** ~ take into consideration

considerevole considerable

consigliare <1g> advise; (*raccomandare*) recommend

consigliarsi ask for advice

consigliere m adviser; ~ **municipale** town council(l)or

consiglio m (pl -gli) piece of advice; (*organo amministrativo*) council; ~ **d'amministrazione** board (of directors); **Consiglio d'Europa** Council of Europe; ~ **dei ministri** Cabinet

consistente substantial; (*denso*) thick

consistenza f (*densità*) consistency, thickness; *di materiale* texture; *di argomento* basis

consistere <3f> consist (**in, di** of)

consocio m (pl -ci), **-a** f associate

consolare[1] <1c> console, comfort

consolare[2] agg consular

consolarsi console o.s.

consolato m consulate; ~ **generale** consulate general

consolazione f consolation

console[1] m diplomatico consul; ~ **generale** consul general

console[2] f mobile console

consolidare <1m & c> consolidate

consolidarsi stabilize

consonante f consonant

consorte m/f spouse; **principe** m ~ prince consort

consorzio m (pl -zi) *di imprese* consortium

constatare <1l> ascertain, determine; (*notare*) note

constatazione f statement

consueto usual

consuetudine f habit, custom; (*usanza*) custom, tradition

consulente m/f consultant; ~ **legale** legal adviser; ~ **tributario** tax consultant

consulenza f consultancy; ~ **aziendale** management consultancy

consultare <1a> consult

consultarsi: ~ **con qu** consult s.o.

consultazione f consultation; **opera** f **di** ~ reference book

consultorio m family planning clinic

consumare <1a> *acqua, gas* use, consume; (*logorare*) wear out; (*mangiare*) eat, consume; (*bere*) drink

consumarsi wear out

consumatore m, **-trice** f consumer

consumazione f food; (*bevanda*) drink

consumismo m consumerism

consumo m consumption; (*usura*) wear; **beni** mpl **di** ~ consumer goods

consuntivo m FIN closing balance

contabile m/f book keeper

contabilità f FIN *disciplina* accounting; *ufficio* accounts department; **tenere la** ~ keep the books

contachilometri m inv mileometer, clock F

contadino 1 agg rural, country attr **2** m, **-a** f peasant

contagiare <1f> infect

contagio m (pl -gi) infection; *per contatto diretto* contagion; (*epidemia*) outbreak

contagioso infectious

contagiri m inv rev(olution) counter

contagocce m inv dropper

container m inv container

contaminare <1m> contaminate, pollute

contaminazione *f* contamination, pollution

contante *m* cash; **in -i** cash

contare <1a> **1** *v/t* count **2** *v/i* count; **~ di fare qc** plan on doing sth

contascatti *m inv* time meter on *phone*

contatore *m* meter

contatto *m* contact

conte *m* count

contegno *m* behavio(u)r; *(atteggiamento)* restraint

contemplare <1b> contemplate; DIR provide for

contemplazione *f* contemplation

contemporaneamente at the same time

contemporaneo **1** *agg* contemporary *(di* with); *movimenti* simultaneous **2** *m*, **-a** *f* contemporary

contendere <3c> **1** *v/t*: **~ qc a qu** compete with s.o. for sth **2** *v/i (competere)* contend

contendersi contend for, compete for

contenere <2q> contain, hold; *(reprimere)* repress; *(limitare)* limit

contenersi contain o.s.

contenitore *m* container

contentare <1b> please

contentarsi be content *(di* with);

contentezza *f* happiness

contento pleased *(di* with); *(lieto)* glad, happy

contenuto *m* contents *pl*

contesa *f* dispute

conteso *pp* → **contendere**

contessa *f* countess

contestare <1b> protest; DIR serve

contestatore *m*, **-trice** *f* protester

contestazione *f* protest

contesto *m* context

contiene → **contenere**

contiguo adjacent *(a* to)

continentale continental

continente *m* continent

continuare <1m> **1** *v/t* continue **2** *v/i* continue, carry on *(a fare* doing)

continuazione *f* continuation; *di film* sequel; **in ~** over and over again; *(ininterrottamente)* non stop

continuità *f* continuity

continuo *(ininterrotto)* continuous; *(molto frequente)* continual; **di ~** *(ininterrottamente)* continuously; *(molto spesso)* continually; EL **corrente** *f* **-a** direct current

conto *m (calcolo)* calculation; FIN account; *in ristorante* bill, *Am* check; **~ corrente** current account, *Am* checking account; **~ corrente postale** Post Office account; **~ profitti e perdite** profit and loss account; **~ vincolato** term deposit; **rendere ~ di qc** account for sth; **rendersi ~ di qc** realize sth; **fare ~ su qu** count on s.o.; **tenere ~ di qc** take sth into account; **~ alla rovescia** countdown; **per ~ mio** *(secondo me)* in my opinion; *(da solo)* on my own; **sapere qc sul ~ di qu** know sth about s.o.; **in fin dei -i** when all's said and done, after all

contorcere <3d> twist

contorcersi: **~ dal dolore/dalle risate** roll about in pain/laughing

contorno *m* outline, contour; GASTR accompaniment

contorto twisted

contrabbandare <1a> smuggle

contrabbandiere *m* smuggler

contrabbando *m* contraband

contrabbasso *m* MUS double bass

contraccambiare <1k> return

contraccambio *m (pl* -bi) return

contraccettivo *m* contraceptive

contraccezione *f* contraception

contraccolpo *m* rebound; *di arma da fuoco* recoil

contraddire <3t> contradict

contraddizione *f* contradiction

contraffare <3aa> *(falsificare)* forge; *(imitare)* imitate

contraffatto forged; *voce* imitated

contraffazione *f (imitazione)* imitation; *(falsificazione)* forgery

contralto *m* MUS (contr)alto

contrappeso *m* counterbalance

contrapporre <3ll> set against

contrapporsi *(contrastare)* clash; **~ a** oppose

contrapposizione *f* opposition;

mettere in ~ contrast
contrapposto *pp* → **contrapporre**
contrariamente: ~ **a** contrary to
contrariare <1k> *piani* thwart, oppose; *persona* irritate, annoy
contrariato irritated, annoyed
contrarietà *fpl inv* difficulties, problems
contrario (*pl* -ri) **1** *agg* contrary; *direzione* opposite; *vento* adverse; *essere* ~ be against (*a* sth) **2** *m* contrary, opposite; *al* ~ on the contrary
contrarre <3xx> contract
contrarsi contract
contrassegnare <1a> mark
contrassegno *m* mark; FIN (*in*) ~ cash on delivery
contrastante contrasting
contrastare <1a> **1** *v/t* contrast; (*ostacolare*) hinder **2** *v/i* contrast (*con* with)
contrasto *m* contrast; (*litigio, discordia*) disagreement, dispute
contrattacco *m* (*pl* -cchi) counterattack
contrattare <1a> negotiate; *persona* hire
contrattempo *m* hitch
contratto[1] *pp* → **contrarre**
contratto[2] *m* contract; ~ **d'affitto** lease
contrattuale contractual
contravvenire <4p> contravene
contravvenzione *f* contravention; (*multa*) fine
contrazione *f* contraction; (*riduzione*) reduction
contribuente *m/f* taxpayer
contribuire <4d> contribute
contributo *m* contribution; *-i pl* **sociali** social security (*Am* welfare) contributions
contro against
controbattere <3a> (*replicare*) answer back; (*confutare*) rebut
controcorrente 1 *agg* non-conformist **2** *avv* against the current; *in fiume* upstream
controffensiva counter-offensive
controfigura *f in film* stand in
controfirmare <1a> countersign

controindicazione *f* MED contraindication
controllare <1c> control; (*verificare*) check
controllo *m* control; (*verifica*) check; MED check-up; ~ **alla frontiera** customs inspection; ~ **dei biglietti** ticket inspection; ~ (**dei**) **passaporti** passport control; ~ **della qualità** quality control
controllore *m* controller; *di bus, treno* ticket inspector; ~ **di volo** air-traffic controller
controluce *f*: *in* ~ against the light
contromano: *andare a* ~ be going the wrong way
contromarca *f* (*pl* -che) token
contromisura *f* countermeasure
controproducente counterproductive
controproposta *f* counter-proposal
contrordine *m* counterorder
controsenso *m* contradiction in terms; (*assurdità*) nonsense
controversia *f* controversy, dispute; DIR litigation
controverso controversial
controvoglia unwillingly
contusione *f* bruise
contuso bruised
convalescente 1 *agg* convalescent **2** *m/f* person who is convalescent
convalescenza *f* convalescence; *essere in* ~ be convalescing
convalidare <1m> validate
convegno *m* convention; *luogo* meeting place
convenevoli *mpl* pleasantries
conveniente (*vantaggioso*) good; (*opportuno*) appropriate
convenienza *f di prezzo, offerta* good value; *di gesto* appropriateness; *fare qc per* ~ do sth out of self-interest
convenire <4p> **1** *v/i* gather, meet; (*concordare*) agree; (*essere opportuno*) be advisable, be better **2** *v/t* (*stabilire*) stipulate
convento *m di monache* convent; *di monaci* monastery
convenuto *pp* → **convenire**

convenzionale conventional

convenzione f convention; *(accordo)* agreement, convention

convergere <3uu> converge

conversare <1b> talk, make conversation

conversazione f conversation

conversione f conversion; AUTO U-turn

convertibile convertible

convertibilità f convertibility

convertire <4b or d> convert

convertirsi be converted

convincere <3d> convince

convinto pp → **convincere**

convinzione f conviction

convivente m/f common-law husband; *donna* common-law wife

convivenza f living together, cohabitation

convivere <3zz> live together

convocare <1l, c & d> call, convene

convocazione f calling, convening

convoglio m (pl -gli) MIL, MAR convoy; FERR train

cooperare <1m & c> co-operate (*a* in); *(contribuire)* contribute (*a* to)

cooperativa f: *(società f)* ~ co-operative; ~ *di consumo* cooperative (store)

cooperativo cooperative

cooperazione f cooperation

coordinamento m co-ordination

coordinare <1m> co-ordinate

coordinata f MAT co-ordinate

coordinatore m, **-trice** f co-ordinator

coordinazione f co-ordination

coperchio m (pl -chi) lid, top

coperta f blanket; MAR deck; ~ *imbottita* quilt

copertina f cover

coperto 1 pp → **coprire 2** agg covered (*di* with); *cielo* overcast, cloudy **3** m cover, shelter; *piatti e posate* place; *prezzo* cover charge; *essere al* ~ be under cover, be sheltered

copertone m AUTO tyre, Am tire

copertura f cover; ~ *delle spese* covering one's costs

copia f copy; FOT print, copy; *in*

duplice ~ in duplicate

copiare <1k & c> copy

copione m per attore script

copioso copious, abundant

copisteria f copy centre (*Am* center)

coppa f cup; *(calice)* glass; ~ *(di) gelato* dish of ice-cream; AUTO ~ *dell'olio* oil sump

coppetta f di gelato tub

coppia f couple, pair; *gara f a -e* doubles

copricapo m inv head covering

copricostume m inv beachrobe

coprifuoco m curfew

copriletto m inv bedspread, coverlet

coprire <4f & c> cover; *errore, suono* cover up

coprirsi *(vestirsi)* put something on; *(rannuvolarsi)* become overcast

coproduzione f co-production, joint production

coraggio m courage; *(sfacciataggine)* nerve; *farsi* ~ be brave

coraggioso brave, courageous

corallo m coral

Corano m Koran

corazza f MIL armo(u)r; ZO shell

corazzata f battleship

corazzato MIL armo(u)red; fig hardened (*contro* to)

corda f cord; *(fune)* rope; *(cordicella)* string; MUS string; ~ *vocale* vocal cord; *essere giù di* ~ feel down or depressed; *tenere qu sulla* ~ keep s.o. in suspense or on tenterhooks; *tagliare la* ~ cut and run

cordame m MAR rigging

cordata f ALP rope, roped party

cordiale 1 agg cordial; *-i saluti* mpl kind regards **2** m cordial

cordialità f cordiality

cordoglio m *(dolore)* grief, sorrow; *(condoglianze)* condolences pl

cordone m cord; *di marciapiedi* kerb, Am curb; *(sbarramento)* cordon; ~ *ombelicale* umbilical cord

coreografia f choreography

coreografo m, **-a** f choreographer

coriandolo m BOT coriander; *-i* mpl confetti

coricare <1l, c & d> *(adagiare)* lay

down; (*mettere a letto*) put to bed
coricarsi lie down
cornacchia f crow
cornamusa f bagpipes pl
cornea f cornea
cornetta f MUS cornet
cornetto m (*brioche*) croissant; (*gelato*) cone, cornet
cornice f frame
cornicione m ARCHI cornice
corno m (*pl gen le corna*) horn; *ramificate* antlers; ~ **da scarpe** shoehorn; *fig* F **fare le -a a qu** cheat on s.o. F; **facciamo le -a!** touch wood!; F **non m'importa un ~** I don't give a damn F
cornuto F cheated, betrayed
coro m chorus; *cantori* choir; **in ~** (*insieme*) all together
corona f crown; (*rosario*) rosary; **~ di fiori** wreath
coronaria f ANAT coronary artery
coronario: **vasi** mpl **-i** coronary arteries
corpetto m *da donna* bodice
corpo m body; MIL corps; ~ **celeste** heavenly body; ~ **diplomatico** diplomatic corps; ~ **di ballo** dancers pl; (*a*) ~ **a** ~ hand-to-hand
corporatura f build
corporazione f corporation
corpulento stout, corpulent
Corpus Domini m Corpus Christi
corredo m equipment; *da sposa* trousseau; *da neonato* layette
correggere <3cc> correct
correggersi correct o.s.
correlazione f correlation
corrente 1 *agg* current; *acqua* running; *lingua* fluent; **di uso** ~ in common use 2 m: **essere al** ~ know (*di* sth); **tenersi qu al** ~ keep s.o. up to date, keep s.o. informed 3 f *current*; *fig di opinione* trend; *fazione* faction; ~ **continua** direct current; ~ **d'aria** draught
correre <3o> 1 v/t run; ~ **il pericolo** run the risk 2 v/i run; (*affrettarsi*) hurry; *di veicolo* speed; *di tempo* fly; ~ **in aiuto di qu** rush to help s.o.; ~ **dietro a qu** run after s.o.; **lascia** ~!

let it go!, leave it!; **corre voce** it is rumo(u)red
correttezza f correctness; (*onestà*) honesty
corretto 1 pp → **correggere** 2 *agg* correct
correzione f TIP correction
corrida f bullfight
corridoio m (*pl* -oi) corridor; *in aereo, teatro* aisle
corridore m *in auto* racing driver; *a piedi* runner
corriera f coach, bus
corriere m courier; ~ **della droga** drugs courier, mule P
corrispondente 1 *agg* corresponding 2 m/f correspondent; ~ **estero** foreign correspondent
corrispondenza f correspondence; (*posta*) post; **vendita f per** ~ mail order (shopping)
corrispondere <3hh> 1 v/t (*pagare*) pay; (*ricambiare*) reciprocate 2 v/i correspond; (*coincidere*) coincide; (*equivalere*) be equivalent
corrisposto 1 pp → **corrispondere** 2 *agg* reciprocated
corrodere <3b>, **corrodersi** corrode, rust
corrompere <3rr> corrupt; *con denaro* bribe
corrosione f corrosion
corrosivo corrosive
corroso pp → **corrodere**
corrotto 1 pp → **corrompere** 2 *agg* corrupt
corrugare <1e> wrinkle; ~ **la fronte** frown
corruzione f corruption; *con denaro* bribery
corsa f run; *attività* running; *di autobus* trip, journey; (*gara*) race; ~ **agli armamenti** arms race; ~ **a ostacoli** *ippica* steeplechase; *atletica* hurdles; **di** ~ at a run; *in fretta* in a rush; **vettura** f **da** ~ racing car; **fare una** ~ rush, dash; **-e** pl races
corsia f aisle; *di ospedale* ward; AUTO lane; ~ **di emergenza** emergency lane; ~ **di sorpasso** overtaking lane; **a tre -e** three-lane

Corsica f Corsica

corsivo m italics pl

corso[1] **1** agg Corsican **2** m, **-a** f Corsican

corso[2] **1** pp → **correre 2** m course; (strada) main street; FIN di moneta circulation; di titoli rate; **~ d'acqua** watercourse; **~ di lingue** language course; **~ dei cambi** exchange rate, rate of exchange; **~ di chiusura** closing rate; FIN **fuori ~** out of circulation; TIP **in ~ di stampa** being printed; **lavori** mpl **in ~** work in progress; **si sposeranno nel ~ dell'anno** they'll get married this year

corte f court; **Corte di giustizia europea** European Court of Justice

corteccia f (pl -cce) bark

corteggiare <1f> court

corteo m procession

cortese polite, courteous

cortesia f politeness, courtesy; **per ~!** please!

cortile m courtyard

cortina f curtain

corto short; **tagliar ~** cut it short; **essere a ~ di quattrini** be short of money

cortocircuito m short (circuit)

cortometraggio m short

corvo m rook; **~ imperiale** raven

cosa f thing; (che) **~** what; **qualche ~** something; **dimmi una ~** tell me something; **una ~ da nulla** a trifle; **un'altra** another thing; **-e** pl **da vedere** sights; **fra le altre -e** among other things; **tante belle -e!** all the best!

coscia f (pl -sce) thigh; GASTR leg

cosciente conscious

coscienza f conscience; (consapevolezza) consciousness; **agire secondo ~** listen to one's conscience; **senza coscienza** unscrupulous

coscienzioso conscientious

così so; (in questo modo) like this; **~ ~** so-so; **e ~ via** and so on; **per ~ dire** so to speak; **proprio ~!** exactly!; **basta ~!** that's enough!

cosicché and so

cosiddetto so called

cosiffatto such

cosmesi f cosmetics pl

cosmetico (pl -ci) **1** agg cosmetic **2** m cosmetic

cosmico (pl -ci) cosmic

cosmo m cosmos

cosmonauta m/f (pl -ti) cosmonaut

cosmopolita cosmopolitan

coso m F what-d'you-call-it F

cospargere <3uu> sprinkle; (coprire) cover (di with)

cosparso pp → **cospargere**

cospirare <1a> conspire

cospiratore m, **-trice** f conspirator

cospirazione f conspiracy

costa f coast, coastline; (pendio) hillside; ANAT rib; di libro spine

costante 1 agg constant, steady; MAT constant **2** f MAT constant

costanza f perseverance

costare <1c> cost; **~ caro** be expensive, cost a lot; fig cost dearly; **quanto costa?** how much is it?

costata f rib steak; **~ di agnello** lamb chop

costeggiare <1f> skirt, hug

costellazione f constellation

costiero coastal

costituire <4d> constitute; società form, create

costituirsi give o.s. up

costituzionale constitutional

costituzione f constitution

costo m cost; **~ della vita** cost of living; **prezzo** m **di ~** cost price; **-i** pl **di produzione** production costs; **a ~ di perdere** even if it means losing; **ad ogni ~** at all costs

costola f rib; di libro spine

costoletta f GASTR cutlet

costoro pron pl they; complemento them

costoso expensive, costly

costretto pp → **costringere**

costringere <3d> force, compel

costrizione f constraint

costruire <4d> build, construct

costruttivo fig constructive

costruttore m, **-trice** f builder; (fab-

bricante) manufacturer

costruzione *f* building, construction; GRAM construction

costui *pron m* he; *complemento* him

costume *m* (*usanza*) custom; (*condotta*) morals *pl*; (*indumento*) costume; **~ da bagno** swimming costume, swimsuit; *da uomo* (swimming) trunks; **~ nazionale** national costume

cotechino *m* kind of pork sausage

cotenna *f* pigskin; *della pancetta* rind

cotoletta *f* cutlet; **~ alla milanese** breaded cutlet fried in butter

cotone *m* cotton; MED **~ idrofilo** cotton wool, *Am* absorbent cotton

cotta *f* F crush

cottimo *m*: **lavorare a ~** do piecework

cotto 1 *pp* → **cuocere 2** *agg* done, cooked; F *fig* head over heels in love (**di** with)

cottura *f* cooking

coupon *m inv* coupon

covare <1a> **1** *v/t* sit on, hatch; *fig malattia* sicken for, come down with; *rancore* harbo(u)r **2** *v/i* sit on eggs

covo *m* den; (*nido*) nest; *fig* hideout

covone *m* sheaf

cozza *f* mussel

cozzare <1c>: **~ contro** crash into; *fig* clash with

C.P. *abbr* (= **Casella Postale**) PO Box (= Post Office Box)

crac *m inv fig* crash

crampo *m* cramp

cranio *m* (*pl* -ni) skull

crash *m* INFOR: **andare in ~** crash

cratere *m* crater

cravatta *f* tie; **~ a farfalla** bow-tie

crawl *m* SP crawl, freestyle

creare <1b> create; *fig* (*causare*) cause

creatività *f* creativity

creativo 1 *agg* creative **2** *m* copywriter

creato 1 *pp* → **creare 2** *m* creation

creatore 1 *agg* creative **2** *m* Creator **3** *m*, **-trice** *f* creator

creatura *f* creature

creazione *f* creation

credente *m/f* believer

credenza[1] *f* belief

credenza[2] *f* mobile dresser

credenziali *fpl* credentials

credere <3a> **1** *v/t* believe; (*pensare*) believe, think; **lo credo bene!** I should think so too!; **credersi** believe *or* think o.s. to be **2** *v/i* believe; **~ a qu** believe s.o.; **~ in qu** believe in s.o.; **credo in Dio** I believe in God; **non ci credo** I don't believe it; **non credevo ai miei occhi** I couldn't believe my eyes

credibile credible

credibilità *f* credibility

credito *m* credit; *fig* trust; (*attendibilità*) reliability; **comprare a ~** buy on credit; **dare ~ a qc** believe sth; **fare ~ a qu** give s.o. credit

creditore *m*, **-trice** *f* creditor

credo *m inv* credo

crema *f* cream; *di latte e uova* custard; **~ da barba** shaving foam; **~ idratante** moisturizer, moisturizing cream; **~ solare** suntan lotion

cremare <1b> cremate

cremazione *f* cremation

cren *m* horseradish

crepa *f* crack

crepaccio *m* (*pl* -cci) cleft; *di ghiacciaio* crevasse

crepare <1b> (*spaccarsi*) crack; F (*morire*) kick the bucket; F: **~ dalle risa** split one's sides laughing

crêpe *f inv* pancake

crepitare <1l & b> crackle

crepuscolo *m* twilight

crescendo *m* MUS crescendo

crescente growing; *luna* waxing

crescere <3n> **1** *v/t* bring up, raise **2** *v/i* grow; (*aumentare*) grow, increase

crescione *m* watercress

crescita *f* growth; (*aumento*) growth, increase; **~ economica** economic growth

cresima *f* confirmation

cresimare <1l & b> confirm

crespo *capelli* frizzy

cresta *f* crest; *di montagna* peak

creta *f* clay

cretino F **1** *agg* stupid, idiotic **2** *m*, **-a** *f* idiot

CRI *abbr* (= **Croce Rossa Italiana**) Italian Red Cross

cric *m inv* AUTO jack

criminale **1** *agg* criminal **2** *m/f* criminal; **~ di guerra** war criminal

criminalità *f* crime

criminalizzare <1a> criminalize

crimine *m* crime

criniera *f* mane

cripta *f* crypt

crisantemo *m* chrysanthemum

crisi *f* crisis; MED fit; **~ energetica** energy crisis; **~ degli alloggi** housing shortage

cristallizzare, **cristallizzarsi** <1a> crystallize

cristallo *m* crystal; **bicchiere** *m* **di ~** crystal glass

cristianesimo *m* Christianity

cristianità *f* (*i cristiani*) Christendom

cristiano **1** *agg* Christian **2** *m*, **-a** *f* Christian

Cristo *m* Christ

criterio *m* (*pl* -ri) criterion; (*buon senso*) common sense

critica *f* (*pl* -che) criticism

criticare <1l & d> criticize

critico (*pl* -ci) **1** *agg* critical **2** *m*, **-a** *f* critic

croato **1** *agg* Croatian **2** *m*, **-a** *f* Croat, Croatian

Croazia *f* Croatia

croccante **1** *agg* crisp, crunchy **2** *m* GASTR nut brittle

crocchetta *f* GASTR potato croquette

croce *f* cross; **Croce Rossa** Red Cross; **farsi il segno della ~** cross o.s.; **a occhio e ~** at a rough guess

crocevia *m* crossroads *inv*

crociata *f* crusade

crociera *f* cruise; ARCHI crossing; **velocità** *f* **di ~** cruising speed

crocifiggere <3mm> crucify

crocifissione *f* crucifixion

crocifisso **1** *pp* → **crocifiggere 2** *m* crucifix

croco *m* BOT crocus

crollare <1c> collapse

crollo *m* collapse

cromare <1c> chromium-plate

cromatico (*pl* -ci) MUS chromatic

cromo *m* chrome

cronaca *f* (*pl* -che) chronicle; *di partita* commentary; **fatto di ~** news item; **~ nera** crime news; **essere al centro della ~** be front-page news

cronico (*pl* -ci) chronic

cronista *m/f* (*mpl* -i) reporter; *di partita* commentator

cronologia *f* chronology

cronologico (*pl* -ci) chronological

cronometrare <1a> time

cronometro *m* chronometer; SP stopwatch

crosta *f* crust; MED scab; *di formaggio* rind

crostacei *mpl* shellfish

crostata *f* GASTR tart

crostino *m* GASTR crouton

cruciale crucial

cruciverba *m inv* crossword (puzzle)

crudele cruel

crudeltà *f* cruelty

crudo raw

crumiro *m*, **-a** *f* scab

crusca *f* bran

cruscotto *m* dashboard; *scomparto* glove compartment

c.s. *abbr* (= **come sopra**) as above

CSI *abbr* (= **Comunità di Stati Indipendenti**) CIS (= Commonwealth of Independent States)

c.to *abbr* (= **conto**) acct (= account)

Cuba *f* Cuba

cubano **1** *agg* Cuban **2** *m*, **-a** *f* Cuban

cubetto *m* (small) cube; **~ di ghiaccio** ice cube

cubico (*pl* -ci) cubic

cubo **1** *agg* cubic **2** *m* cube

cuccagna *f*: (**paese** *m* **della**) **~** land of plenty

cuccetta *f* FERR couchette; MAR berth

cucchiaiata *f* spoonful

cucchiaino *m* teaspoon

cucchiaio *m* (*pl* -ai) spoon; **~ da**

tavola tablespoon

cuccia f (pl -cce) dog's basket; *esterna* kennel

cucciolo m cub; *di cane* puppy

cucina f kitchen; *cibi* food; ~ **casalinga** home cooking; ~ **a gas** gas cooker or stove; *libro di* ~ cook book

cucinare <1a> cook

cucinino m kitchenette

cucire <4a> sew; **macchina** f **da** ~ sewing-machine

cucito 1 agg sewn **2** m sewing

cucitura f seam

cuculo m cuckoo

cuffia f *da piscina* swimming cap; RAD, TV headphones pl; ~ **da bagno** shower cap

cugino m, **-a** f cousin

cui *persona* who, whom *fml*; *cose* which; *la casa in* ~ **abitano** the house they live in, the house in which they live, the house where they live; *il* ~ **nome** whose name; **per** ~ so

culinario cookery *attr*, culinary; *arte* f **-a** culinary art, cookery

culla f cradle

cullare <1a> rock

culminante: *punto* m ~ climax

culminare <1l> culminate

culmine m peak

culo V m arse V, Am ass V

culto m cult; *religione* religion

cultura f culture; ~ **di massa** mass culture; ~ **generale** general knowledge

culturale cultural

culturismo m body-building

cumulativo cumulative; **biglietto** m ~ group ticket

cumulo m heap, pile

cuneo m wedge

cunetta f *fondo stradale* bump

cuocere <3p> cook; *pane* bake

cuoco m (pl -chi), **-a** f cook

cuoio m leather; ~ **capelluto** scalp; F

tirare le -a kick the bucket F

cuore m heart; *carte* **-i** pl hearts; **di** ~ wholeheartedly; **senza** ~ heartless; *fig* **nel** ~ **di** in the heart of; **nel** ~ **della notte** in the middle of the night; **stare a** ~ **a** qu be very important to s.o.

cupo gloomy; *suono* deep

cupola f dome

cura f care; MED treatment; ~ **dimagrante** diet; **avere** ~ **di** qc take care of sth; **casa** f **di** ~ nursing home

curabile curable

curare <1a> take care of; MED treat

curarsi look after o.s.; **non curarti di loro** don't care about them

curato m parish priest

curatore m, **-trice** f *fiduciario* trustee; *di testo* editor; ~ **fallimentare** official receiver

curia f curia

curiosare <1a> have a look around; *spreg* pry (**in** into)

curiosità f inv curiosity

curioso curious

cursore m INFOR cursor

curva f curve

curvare <1a> curve; *schiena* bend

curvarsi bend

curvatura f curve

curvo curved; *persona* bent

cuscinetto m TEC bearing; ~ **a sfere** ball bearing; POL **stato** m ~ buffer state

cuscino m cushion; (*guanciale*) pillow

custode m/f caretaker; **angelo** m ~ guardian angel

custodia f care; DIR custody; (*astuccio*) case

custodire <4d> (*conservare*) keep

cute f skin

CV abbr (= **Cavallo Vapore**) HP (= horsepower); (= **curriculum vitae**) CV (= curriculum vitae)

cyclette f exercise bike

D

da *prp stato in luogo* at; *moto da luogo* from; *moto a luogo* to; *tempo* since; *con verbo passivo* by; *viene ~ Roma* he comes from Rome; *sono ~ mio fratello* I'm at my brother's (place); *ero ~ loro* I was at their place; *passo ~ Firenze* I'm going via Florence; *vado dal medico* I'm going to the doctor's; *~ ieri* since yesterday; *~ oggi in poi* from now on, starting from today; *~ bambino* as a child; *l'ho fatto ~ me* I did it myself; *qualcosa ~ mangiare* something to eat; *francobollo ~ 1000 lire* 1000 lire stamp; *la donna ~i capelli grigi* the woman with grey hair

dà → dare

daccapo → capo

dado *m* dice; GASTR stock cube; TEC nut

dagli *prp da and art gli*

dai[^1] *prp da and art i*

dai[^2] → dare

daino *m* deer; (*pelle*) buckskin

dal *prp da and art il*

dalia *f* dahlia

dall', dalla, dalle, dallo *prp da and art l', la, le, lo*

daltonico *agg* (*pl* -ci) colo(u)r-blind

dama *f* lady; *gioco* draughts, *Am* checkers

damasco *m* (*pl* -chi) damask

damigiana *f* demijohn

danaro *m* → denaro

danese 1 *m/agg* Danish 2 *m/f* Dane

Danimarca *f* Denmark

danneggiare <1f> (*rovinare*) damage; (*nuocere*) harm

danno *m* damage; (*a persona*) harm; *risarcire i -i a qu* compensate s.o. for the damage; *-i pl all'ambiente* environmental damage, damage to the environment

dannoso harmful

danza *f* dance; *~ classica* ballet

danzare <1a> *v/t & v/i* dance

dappertutto everywhere

dappoco *agg inv* (*inetto*) worthless; (*irrilevante*) minor, unimportant

dapprima at first

dare <1r> 1 *v/t* give; *~ qc a qu* give s.o. sth, give sth to s.o.; *~ uno sguardo a qc* have a look at sth; *dammi del tu* call me 'tu'; *mi dia del lei* address me as 'lei'; SP *~ il via* give the off; *fig ~ il via a qc* get sth under way 2 *v/i di finestra* overlook (*su* sth); *di porta* lead into (*su* sth); *fig ~ nell'occhio* attract attention, be noticed 3 *m* FIN debit; *~ e avere* debit and credit

darsi *v/r* give each other; (*dedicarsi*) devote o.s. (*a* to); *~ al commercio* go into business; *darsela a gambe* take to one's heels; *può ~* perhaps

darsena *f* dock

data *f* date; *~ di nascita* date of birth; *~ di scadenza* expiry date; *senza indicazione di ~* undated

datare <1a> 1 *v/t* date; *lettera* date, put the date on 2 *v/i*: *a ~ da oggi* from today

dato 1 *pp* → dare 2 *agg* (*certo*) given, particular; (*dedito*) addicted (*a* to); *in -i casi* in certain cases; *~ che* given that 3 *m* piece of data; *-i pl* data; INFOR *elaborazione f dei data* data processing; *supporto m ~* data medium

datore *m*, *-trice f*: *~ di lavoro* employer

dattero *m* date; (*albero*) date palm

dattilografare <1n> type

dattilografia *f* typing

dattilografo *m*, *-a f* typist

davanti 1 *prp*: *~ a* in front of 2 *avv* in front; (*dirimpetto*) opposite; *se mi stai ~* if you stand in front of me

[^1]: dai

3 *agg inv* front **4** *m* front

davanzale *m* window sill

davanzo more than enough

davvero really

dazio *m* (*pl* -zi) duty; (*posto*) customs; ~ **d'importazione** import duty; ~ **d'esportazione** export duty; **esente da** ~ duty-free

d.C. *abbr* (= **dopo Cristo**) AD (= **anno domini**)

dea *f* goddess

debito 1 *agg* due, proper **2** *m* debt; (*dovere*) duty; FIN ~ **pubblico** national debt; **avere un** ~ **con qu** be in debt to s.o.; *fig* **sentirsi in** ~ **verso qu** feel indebted to s.o.

debitore *m*, **-trice** *f* debtor; **essere** ~ **di qc a qu** owe s.o. sth, owe sth to s.o.

debole 1 *agg* weak; (*voce*) weak, faint; (*luce*) dim **2** *m* weakness; **avere un** ~ **per qu** have a soft spot for s.o.

debolezza *f* weakness

debuttante *m/f* beginner; *artista* performer at the start of his / her career

debuttare <1a> make one's début

debutto *m* début

decadente decadent

decadenza *f* decadence

decaffeinato decaffeinated, decaff F

decalcomania *f* transfer, *Am* decal

decano *m* dean

decappottabile *f/agg* AUTO convertible

decathlon *m* decathlon

decedere <3ll> **è deceduto ieri** he died yesterday

decelerare <1b & m> *v/t & v/i* slow down

decennio *m* (*pl* -ni) decade

decente *agg* decent

decentramento *m* decentralization

decentrare <1b> decentralize

decesso *m* death

decidere <3q> **1** *v/t questione* settle; *data* decide on, settle on; ~ **di fare qc** decide to do sth **2** *v/i* decide

decidersi decide (**a** to), make up one's mind (**a** to)

decifrare <1a> decipher

decimale *m/agg* decimal

decimetro *m* decimetre, *Am* -meter

decimo *m/agg* tenth

decina *f* MATH ten; **una** ~ about ten

decisione *f* decision; (*risolutezza*) decisiveness; **prendere una** ~ make a decision; ~ **della maggioranza** majority decision

decisivo decisive

deciso 1 *pp* → **decidere 2** *agg* (*definito*) definite; (*risoluto*) determined; (*netto*) clear; (*spiccato*) marked

declassare <1a> *oggetto* downgrade; *persona* demote

declinare <1a> **1** *v/t* decline; ~ **ogni responsabilità** disclaim all responsibility **2** *v/i* (*tramontare*) set; (*diminuire*) decline

declinazione *f* GRAM declension

declino *m fig* decline

decodificatore *m* decoder

decollare <1c> take off

decollo *m* take-off

decomporre <3ll> **1** *v/i* (*putrefarsi*) decompose **2** *v/t* CHIM break down

decomposizione *f* decomposition; CHIM breaking down

decompressione *f* decompression

decongestionare <1a> *strada*, MED relieve congestion in; ~ **il traffico** relieve traffic congestion

decorare <1b> decorate

decoratore *m*, **-trice** *f* decorator

decorazione *f* decoration

decoro *m* decorum

decoroso decorous

decorrenza *f*: **con immediata** ~ with immediate effect

decorrere <3o> *v/i* pass; **a** ~ **da oggi** with effect from today

decorso 1 *pp* → **decorrere 2** *m di malattia* course

decrepito decrepit

decrescere <3n> decrease, fall

decreto *m* decree; **~-legge** *m* decree passed in exceptional circumstances that has the force of law

dedica *f* (*pl* -che) dedication

dedicare <1b & d> dedicate

dedicarsi dedicate o.s.

dedito dedicated (**a** to); *a un vizio* addicted (**a** to)

dedizione f dedication

dedurre <3e> deduce; FIN deduct; (*derivare*) derive

deduttivo deductive

deduzione f deduction

defalcare <1d> deduct

defalco m (*pl* -chi) deduction

defezione f defection

deficiente 1 agg (*mancante*) deficient, lacking (*di* in) **2** m/f backward person; *insulto* idiot, moron

deficienza f (*scarsezza*) deficiency, lack (*di* of)

deficit m inv deficit; ~ *del bilancio pubblico* budget deficit, public spending deficit

definire <4d> define; (*risolvere*) settle

definitivo definitive

definizione f definition; DIR settlement

deflettore m AUTO quarterlight

deflusso m ebb

deformare <1a> deform; *legno* warp; *metallo* buckle; *fig* distort

deformarsi *di legno* warp; *di metallo* buckle; *di scarpe* lose their shape

deformazione f deformation; *di legno* warping; *di metallo* buckling; *fisica* deformity; *fig*, OTT distortion

deforme deformed

defunto 1 agg dead; *fig* defunct **2** m, -a f DIR: *il ~* the deceased

degenerare <1m & b> degenerate (*in* into)

degente m/f patient

degenza f stay (in bed / hospital)

degli prp *di* and art *gli*

degnare <1a> **1** v/t: ~ *qu di una parola* deign to speak to s.o. **2** v/i e **degnarsi**: ~ *di* deign to, condescend to

degno worthy; ~ *di nota* noteworthy; ~ *di un re* fit for a king

degradante degrading, demeaning

degradare <1a> degrade; *da un rango* demote

degradarsi demean o.s., lower o.s.; CHIM degrade; *di ambiente, edifici* deteriorate

degradazione f degradation

degrado m deterioration; ~ *ambientale* damage to the environment

degustazione f tasting; ~ *del vino* wine tasting

dei[1] prp *di* and art *i*

dei[2] (*pl di* **dio**): *gli ~* mpl the Gods

del prp *di* and art *il*

delatore m, **-trice** f informer

delega f (*pl* -ghe) delegation; (*procura*) proxy

delegare <1b & e> delegate

delegato 1 agg: *amministratore* m ~ managing director **2** m, **-a** f delegate; ~ *sindacale* (trade) union delegate

delegazione f delegation

delfino m dolphin

deliberare <1m> **1** v/t decide **2** v/i DIR deliberate (*su* on)

delicatezza f delicacy; (*discrezione*) tact, delicacy; (*debolezza*) frailty, delicacy

delicato delicate; (*persona*) frail, delicate; (*colore*) soft

delimitare <1m> define

delineare <1m> outline

delinquente m/f criminal; *fig* scoundrel; ~ *minorile* juvenile delinquent

delinquenza f crime; ~ *minorile* juvenile delinquency; ~ *organizzata* organized crime

delirare <1a> be in raptures, rave; MED be delirious

delirio m (*pl* -ri) delirium; *fig* frenzy

delitto m crime; *corpo* m *del* ~ corpus delicti

delizia f delight

delizioso delightful; *cibo* delicious

dell', della, delle, dello prp *di* and art *l', la, le, lo*

delta m delta

deltaplanista m/f (*mpl* -ti) hang-glider

deltaplano m hang-glider; *attività* hang-gliding

deludere <3q> disappoint

delusione f disappointment

deluso disappointed

demagogo m (*pl* -ghi) demagog(ue)

demanio *m* State property

demente *m/f* MED person with dementia; F lunatic F

demenza *f* MED dementia; F lunacy F, madness F

democratico (*pl* -ci) **1** *agg* democratic **2** *m*, **-a** *f* democrat

democrazia *f* democracy

democristiano *m/agg* Christian Democrat

demografia *f* demography

demografico demographic

demolire <4d> demolish (*anche fig*); *macchine* crush

demolizione *f* demolition; *di macchine* crushing

demone *m* spirit

demonio *m* (*pl* -ni) devil

demoralizzarsi <1a> become demoralized, lose heart

demotivato demotivated

denaro *m* money; **~ contante** cash

denatalità *f* decline in the birth rate

denaturato CHIM: **alcol** *m* ~ methylated spirits *pl*

denominare <1m & c> name, call

denominazione *f* name; **~ di origine controllata** term signifying that a wine is of a certain origin and quality

denotare <1l & b or c> denote, be indicative of

densità *f* density; *della nebbia* thickness, density; **~ della popolazione** population density

denso dense; *fumo, nebbia* thick, dense

dentario (*pl* -ri) dental

dentata *f* bite; *segno* toothmark

dente *m* tooth; **~ del giudizio** wisdom tooth; **~ di leone** dandelion; **mal** *m* **di -i** toothache; *fig* **stringere i -i** grit one's teeth; *parlare fra i -i* mumble; GASTR **al ~** al dente, still slightly firm

dentice *m* fish native to the Mediterranean

dentiera *f* dentures

dentifricio *m* (*pl* -ci) toothpaste

dentista *m/f* (*mpl* -ti) dentist

dentro 1 *prp* in, inside; (*entro*) within;

~ di sé inwardly **2** *avv* in, inside; (*nell' intimo*) inwardly; **qui / lì ~** in here / there; F **metter ~** put inside or away F

denuclearizzato nuclear-free, denuclearized

denuncia *f* (*pl* -ce) denunciation; *alla polizia, alla società di assicurazione* complaint, report; *di nascita, morte* registration; **~ dei redditi** income tax return

denunciare <1f> denounce; *alla polizia, alla società di assicurazione* report; *nascita* register

denunzia → **denuncia**

denutrito undernourished

deodorante *m* deodorant

depilare <1a> *con pinzette* pluck; *con rasoio* shave; *con ceretta* wax

depilatorio (*pl* -ri) **1** *agg* depilatory **2** *m* hair-remover, depilatory

dépliant *m inv* leaflet; (*opuscolo*) brochure

deplorare <1c> deplore

deplorevole deplorable

deporre <3ll> **1** *v/t* put down; *uova* lay; *re, presidente* depose; **~ il falso** commit perjury **2** *v/i* DIR testify, give evidence (**a favore di** for, **a carico di** against)

deportare <1c> deport

depositare <1m & c> deposit; (*posare*) put down, deposit; (*registrare*) register

depositato: marchio *m* ~ registered trademark

deposito *m* deposit; (*magazzino*) warehouse; MIL, *rimessa* depot; FERR **~ bagagli** left-luggage office, *Am* baggage checkroom; **~ di munizioni** ammunition dump; FIN **~ vincolato** term deposit

deposizione *f* deposition; *da un'alta carica* removal; *di regnante*; overthrow

deposto *pp* → **deporre**

depravato *m*, **-a** *f* depraved person

depressione *f* depression; **~ atmosferica** atmospheric depression; **zona** *f* **di ~ atmosferica** area of low pressure, low

depresso 1 *pp* → **deprimere 2** *agg* depressed

deprezzamento *m* depreciation

deprezzare <1b> lower the value of

deprezzarsi depreciate

deprimente depressing

deprimere <3r> depress

deprimersi get depressed

depurare <1a> purify

depuratore *m* purifier

depurazione *f* purification; *impianto m di ~* purification plant

deputato *m*, **-a** *f* Member of Parliament, *Am* Representative

deragliare <1g> FERR go off *or* leave the rails; *far ~* derail

deridere <3g> deride

derisione *f* derision

deriso *pp* → **deridere**

deriva *f* MAR drift; *andare alla ~* drift

derivare <1a> **1** *v/t* derive **2** *v/i*: *~ da* come from, derive from

derivazione *f* derivation; *(discendenza)* origin; EL shunt; TELEC extension

dermatologia *f* dermatology

dermatologo *m* (*pl* -gi), **-a** *f* dermatologist

derrate *fpl* food

derubare <1a> rob

descritto *pp* → **descrivere**

descrivere <3tt> describe

descrizione *f* description

deserto 1 *agg* deserted; *isola f -a* desert island **2** *m* desert

desiderare <1m> *(volere)* want, wish; *intensamente* long for, crave; *sessualmente* desire; *desidera?* can I help you?; *farsi ~* play hard to get; *(tardare)* keep people waiting; *lascia a ~* it leaves a lot to be desired

desiderio *m* (*pl* -ri) wish (*di* for); *intenso* longing (*di* for); *sessuale* desire (*di* for)

design *m inv* design

designare <1a> *(nominare)* appoint, name; *(fissare)* fix, set

designer *m/f inv* designer

desistere <3f>: *~ da* desist from

desolante distressing

desolato desolate; *sono ~!* I am so sorry

desolazione *f* desolation; *(dolore)* distress

dessert *m inv* dessert

destare <1a> *fig* (a)rouse, awaken

destarsi *fig* be aroused, be awakened

destinare <1a> destine; *(assegnare)* assign; *con il pensiero* mean, intend; *data* fix, set; *(indirizzare)* address (*a* to)

destinatario *m* (*pl* -ri), **-a** *f di lettera* addressee

destinazione *f*: *(luogo m di)* ~ destination

destino *m* destiny

destra *f* right; *(mano)* right hand; *a ~ stato* on the right, to the right; *moto* to the right

destreggiarsi <1f> manœuvre, *Am* maneuver

destrezza *f* skill, dexterity

destro right; *(abile)* skil(l)ful, dexterous

destrorso 1 *agg persona* right-handed; TEC clockwise **2** *m*, **-a** *f* right-hander, right-handed person

detenere <2q> hold; *in prigione* detain, hold

detenuto *m*, **-a** *f* prisoner

detenzione *f imprigionamento* detention; *~ abusiva di armi* possession of illegal weapons

detergente *m* detergent; *per cosmesi* cleanser

deteriorabile perishable

deteriorarsi <1a> deteriorate

determinare <1m & b> determine, establish; *(causare)* cause, lead to

determinato certain; *(specifico)* particular, specific; *(risoluto)* determined

determinazione *f* determination

detersivo *m* detergent; *per piatti* washing-up liquid, *Am* dishwashing liquid; *per biancheria* detergent, *Br* washing powder

detestare <1b> hate, detest

detonare <1c> detonate

detrarre <3xx> deduct (*da* from)

detratto *pp* → **detrarre**

detrazione *f* deduction

detrito *m* debris; GEOL detritus

detta *f*: *a ~ di* according to

dettaglio *m* (*pl* -gli) detail; FIN *commercio m al ~* retail trade

dettare <1a> dictate; *~ legge* lay down the law

dettato *m* dictation

dettatura *f* dictation; *scrivere sotto ~* take dictation

detto 1 *pp* → **dire**; *~ fatto* no sooner said than done; *come non ~* let's forget it **2** *agg* said; (*soprannominato*) known as **3** *m* saying

devastare <1a> devastate

devastazione *f* devastation

deve, devi → **dovere**

deviare <1h> **1** *v/t traffico, sospetti* divert **2** *v/i* deviate

deviazione *f* deviation; *di traffico* diversion

devo → **dovere**

devolvere <3g> POL devolve

devoluto *pp* → **devolvere**

devoluzione *f* POL devolution

devoto 1 *agg* devoted; REL devout **2** *m*, *-a f* devotee; REL *i -i* the devout

devozione *f* devotion; REL devoutness

di 1 *prp* of; *con il comparativo* than; *~ ferro* (made of) iron; *io sono ~ Roma* I'm from Rome; *l'auto ~ mio padre* my father's car; *una tazza ~ caffè* a cup of coffee; *~ giorno* by day; *parlare ~ politica* talk about politics; *d'estate* in the summer; *~ questo passo* at this rate; *~ chi è questo libro?* whose is this book?, who does this book belong to?; *più bello ~* prettier than **2** *art* some; *interrogativo* any, some; *neg* any; *del vino* some wine

di' → **dire**

dia → **dare**

diabete *m* diabetes

diabetico (*pl* -ci) **1** *agg* diabetic **2** *m*, *-a f* diabetic

diadema *m* diadem

diaframma *m* (*pl* -i) diaphragm

diagnosi *f inv* diagnosis

diagnosticare <1n, c & d> diagnose

diagonale 1 *agg* diagonal **2** *f* diagonal (line)

diagramma *m* (*pl* -i) diagram

dialetto *m* dialect

dialisi *f inv* dialysis

dialogo *m* (*pl* -ghi) dialog(ue)

diamante *m* diamond

diametro *m* diameter

diapason *m inv* tuning fork

diapositiva *f* FOT slide

diario *m* (*pl* -ri) diary

diarrea *f* diarrh(o)ea

diavolo *m* devil; *un buon ~* a good fellow; *mandare qu al ~* tell s.o. to get lost

dibattere <3a> debate, discuss

dibattersi struggle; *fig* struggle (*in* with)

dibattito *m* debate

dicembre *m* December

diceria *f* rumo(u)r

dichiarare <1a> state; *ufficialmente* declare; *nei giochi di carte* bid; *ha qualcosa da ~?* anything to declare?

dichiararsi declare o.s.

dichiarazione *f* declaration; *~ dei redditi* income tax statement; *~ doganale* customs declaration

diciannove nineteen

diciannovesimo *m/agg* nineteenth

diciassette seventeen

diciassettesimo *m/agg* seventeenth

diciottenne *m/f* eighteen-year-old

diciotto eighteen

diciottesimo *m/agg* eighteenth

didattica *f* didactics

dieci ten; *alle/verso le ~* at/about ten (o'clock)

diesel *m* diesel

dieta *f* diet; *essere a ~* be on a diet

dietetica *f* dietetics

dietetico (*pl* -ci) diet *attr*

dietista *m/f* dietitian, dietician

dietro 1 *prp* behind; *~ l'angolo* round the corner; *~ di me* behind me; *uno ~ l'altro nello spazio* one behind the other; *nel tempo* one after the other; *~ ricevuta* on receipt

2 *avv* behind; *in auto* in the back; *di ~ stanza, porta* back; *zampe* hind; AUTO rear **3** *m inv* back

difatti *cong* in fact

difendere <3c> defend; (*proteggere*) protect

difensiva *f* defensive; *stare sulla ~* be on the defensive

difensivo defensive

difensore *m* defender; *~ d'ufficio* legal aid lawyer, *Am* public defender

difesa *f* defence, *Am* defense; *~ dei consumatori* consumer protection; *legittima ~* self-defence (*Am* -defense)

difeso *pp* → **difendere**

difetto *m* (*imperfezione*) defect; *morale* fault, flaw; (*mancanza*) lack; *far ~* be lacking

difettoso defective

diffamare <1a> slander; *scrivendo* libel

diffamazione *f* defamation of character

differente different (*da* from, *Am* than)

differenza *f* difference; *~ di prezzo* difference in price; *a ~ di* unlike

differenziare <1f> differentiate

differenziarsi differ (*da* from)

differire <4d> postpone

difficile difficult; (*improbabile*) unlikely

difficoltà *f inv* difficulty; *senza ~* easily, without any difficulty

diffida *f* DIR injunction

diffidare <1a> **1** *v/t* DIR issue an injunction against; *~ qu dal fare qc* warn s.o. not to do sth **2** *v/i:* *~ di qu* distrust s.o., mistrust s.o.

diffidente distrustful, mistrustful

diffidenza *f* distrust, mistrust

diffondere <3bb> diffuse; *fig* spread

diffondersi *fig* spread; (*dilungarsi*) enlarge

diffusione *f di luce, calore* diffusion; *di giornale* circulation

diffuso 1 *pp* → **diffondere 2** *agg* widespread; (*luce*) diffuse

difterite *f* diphtheria

diga *f* (*pl* -ghe) *fluviale* dam; *litoranea*

dyke; *portuale* breakwater

digerire <4d> digest; F (*tollerare*) stomach F

digestione *f* digestion

digestivo 1 *agg* digestive **2** *m* after-dinner drink, digestif

digitale digital; *impronta ~* fingerprint

digitare <1l> INFOR key

digiunare <1a> fast

digiuno 1 *agg* fasting; *fig privo* lacking (*di* in); *essere ~ di notizie* have no news, not have any news **2** *m* fast; *a ~* on an empty stomach

dignità *f* dignity

dignitoso dignified

digrignare <1a> gnash

dilagare <1e> flood; *fig* spread rapidly

dilaniare <1k> tear apart

dilapidare <1m> squander

dilatare <1a> FIS expand; *occhi* open wide

dilatarsi *di materiali, metalli* expand; *di pupilla* dilate

dilatazione *f* expansion; *di pupilla* dilation

dilazionare <1a> defer, delay

dilazione *f* extension

dileguarsi <1a> vanish, disappear

dilemma *m* (*pl* -i) dilemma

dilettante *m/f* amateur; *spreg* dilettante

dilettare <1b> delight

dilettarsi: *~ di qc* dabble in sth, do sth as a hobby; *~ a fare qc* take delight in doing sth

diletto[1] **1** *agg* beloved **2** *m*, **-a** *f* beloved

diletto[2] *m* (*piacere*) delight; *fare qc per ~* do sth for pleasure

diligente diligent; (*accurato*) accurate

diligenza *f* diligence

diluire <4d> dilute

dilungarsi <1e> *fig* dwell (*su* on)

diluviare <1k> pour down

diluvio *m* downpour; *fig* deluge; *~ universale* Flood

dimagrante: *cura f ~* diet

dimagrire <4d> lose weight

dimenare <1a> wave; *coda* wag

dimenarsi throw o.s. about

dimensione *f* dimension; (*grandezza*) size; (*misure*) dimensions

dimenticanza *f* forgetfulness, absent-mindedness; (*svista*) oversight

dimenticare <1m & d> forget

dimenticarsi forget (*di* sth; *di fare qc* to do sth)

dimestichezza *f* familiarity

dimettere <3ee> dismiss (*da* from); *da ospedali* discharge, release (*da* from); *da carceri* release (*da* from)

dimettersi resign (*da* from)

dimezzare <1b> halve; (*dividere*) halve, divide in two

diminuire <4d> **1** *v/t* reduce, diminish; *prezzi* reduce, lower **2** *v/i* decrease, diminish; *di prezzi, valore* fall, go down; *di vento, rumore* die down

diminuzione *f* decrease; *di prezzi, valore* fall, drop (*di* in)

dimissioni *fpl* resignation *sg*; **dare le ~** resign, hand in one's resignation

dimora *f* residence; **senza fissa ~** of no fixed abode

dimostrare <1a> demonstrate; (*interesse*) show; (*provare*) prove, show

dimostrarsi prove to be

dimostrazione *f* demonstration; (*prova*) proof

dinamica *f* dynamics

dinamico (*pl* -ci) dynamic

dinamismo *m* dynamism

dinamite *f* dynamite

dinamo *f inv* dynamo

dinanzi *prp*: **~ a** al cospetto di before

dinastia *f* dynasty

dingo *m inv* dingo

dinosauro *m* dinosaur

dintorno **1** *avv* around **2** *m*: **-i** *pl* neighbo(u)rhood

dio *m* (*pl* gli dei) *idolo* god; **Dio** God; **grazie a Dio!** thank God!, thank goodness!; **per l'amor di Dio** for God's *or* goodness sake

diocesi *f inv* diocese

diossina *f* dioxin

dipartimento *m* department

dipendente **1** *agg* dependent **2** *m/f* employee

dipendenza *f* dependence; (*edificio*) annex(e); **essere alle ~ di** work for

dipendere <3c>: **~ da** (*essere subordinato a*) depend on; (*essere mantenuto da*) be dependent on; (*essere causato da*) derive from, be due to; **dipende** it depends; **questo dipende da te** it's up to you

dipeso *pp* → **dipendere**

dipingere <3d> paint; *fig* describe, depict

dipinto 1 *pp* → **dipingere 2** *m* painting, picture

diploma *m* (*pl* -i) diploma, certificate; **~ di laurea** degree (certificate)

diplomarsi <1c> obtain a diploma

diplomatico (*pl* -ci) **1** *agg* diplomatic **2** *m* diplomat

diplomato 1 *agg* qualified **2** *m*, **-a** *f* holder of a diploma

diplomazia *f* diplomacy

diporto *m*: **imbarcazione** *f* **da ~** pleasure boat

diradare <1a> thin out

diradarsi thin out; *di nebbia* clear, lift

dire <3t> **1** *v/t* say; (*raccontare*) tell; **~ qc a qu** tell s.o. sth; **vale a ~** that is, in other words; **a ~ il vero** to tell the truth; **come si dice … in inglese?** what's the English for … ?; **voler ~** mean **2** *v/i* **~ bene di qu** speak highly of s.o.; **dico sul serio** I'm serious **3** *m*: **per sentito ~** by hearsay; **hai un bel ~** say what you like

direttissima *f* ALP shortest *or* most direct route; DIR **processo** *m* **per ~** summary proceedings *pl*

direttiva *f* directive

direttivo 1 *agg di direzione di società* managerial; *comitato, consiglio,* POL executive *attr* **2** *m di società* board (of directors); POL leadership

diretto 1 *pp* → **dirigere 2** *agg* (*immediato*) direct; **~ a** aimed at; *lettera* addressed to; **essere ~ a casa** be heading for home; RAD, TV **in (ripresa) -a** live **3** *m* direct train; SP straight

direttore *m*, **-trice** *f* manager; *più in alto nella gerarchia* director; MUS conductor; EDU headmaster, headmistress *f*, *Am* principal; *di giornale, rivista* editor (in chief); **~ generale** chief executive officer; **~ delle vendite** sales manager; **~ d'orchestra** conductor; **~ tecnico** technical manager; SP coach and team manager

direzione *f* direction; *di società* management; *di partito* leadership; *ufficio* office; *sede generale* head office; **in ~ di Roma** in the direction of Rome

dirigente 1 *agg* classe, partito ruling; *personale* managerial **2** *m/f* executive; POL leader

dirigere ‹3u› direct; *azienda* run, manage; *orchestra* conduct

dirigersi head (**a**, **verso** for, towards)

dirigibile *m* airship, dirigible

dirimpetto opposite, across the way; **~ a** facing, in front of

diritto 1 *agg* straight **2** *avv* straight **3** *m* right; DIR law; **-i** *pl* (*il compenso*) fees; **-i d'autore** copyright; **~ commerciale** commercial law; **~ costituzionale** constitutional law; **~ internazionale** international law; **~ di precedenza** right of way; **~ di voto** right to vote; **-i** *pl* **umani** human rights; **parità** *f* **di -i** equal rights; **aver ~ a** be entitled to; **di ~** by rights

dirittura *f* straight line; SP straight; *fig* rectitude; **in ~ d'arrivo** in the home straight

diroccato ramshackle

dirottamento *m* hijack(ing)

dirottare ‹1c› *traffico* divert; *aereo* reroute; *con intenzioni criminali* hijack

dirottatore *m*, **-trice** *f* hijacker

dirotto: *piove a* **~** it's pouring

dirupo *m* precipice

disabile 1 *agg* disabled **2** *m/f* disabled person

disabitato uninhabited

disabituare ‹1n›: **~ qu a qc** get s.o. out of the habit of sth

disaccordo *m* disagreement

disadattato 1 *agg* maladjusted **2** *m/f* (social) misfit

disadatto unsuitable (**a** for); *persona* unsuited (**a un lavoro** to a job)

disadorno bare, unadorned

disagiato uncomfortable; *vita* hard

disagio *m* (*pl* -gi) (*difficoltà*) hardship; (*scomodità*) discomfort; (*imbarazzo*) embarrassment; **essere a ~** be ill at ease

disambientato out of place

disapprovare ‹1c› disapprove of

disapprovazione *f* disapproval

disappunto *m* disappointment

disarmare ‹1a› disarm

disarmato unarmed; *fig* defenceless

disarmo *m* POL disarmament

disastro *m* disaster

disastroso disastrous

disattento inattentive

disattenzione *f* inattention, lack of attention; *errore* careless mistake

disavanzo *m* deficit; **~ della bilancia commerciale** trade deficit; **~ commerciale con l'estero** foreign trade deficit

disavventura *f* misadventure

disboscamento *m* deforestation

disboscare ‹1d› deforest

disbrigo *m* (*pl* -ghi) dispatch

discapito *m*: **a ~ di qu** to the detriment *or* disadvantage of s.o.

discarica *f* (*pl* -che) dumping; (*luogo*) dump

discendente 1 *agg inv* descending **2** *m/f* descendant

discendenza *f* descent; (*discendenti*) descendants

discendere ‹3c› descend; (*trarre origine*) be a descendant (**da** of), be descended (**da** from); *da veicoli, da cavallo* alight (**da** from)

discepolo *m* disciple

discesa *f* descent; (*pendio*) slope; *di bus* exit; SCI **~ libera** downhill (race); **strada** *f* **in ~** street that slopes downwards

dischetto *m* INFOR diskette, floppy F

disciogliere ‹3ss› dissolve; *neve* melt

disciolto pp → **disciogliere**

disciplina f discipline

disciplinare **1** agg disciplinary **2** v/t <1a> discipline

disciplinato disciplined

disco m (pl -chi) disc, Am disk; SP discus; MUS record; INFOR disk; INFOR ~ **rigido** hard disk; AUTO ~ **orario** parking disc; ~ **volante** flying saucer

discobolo m discus thrower

discografia f elenco recordings, discography; attività record industry

discolo **1** agg wild, unruly **2** m troublemaker

discolpare <1a> clear

discontinuo intermittent; (disuguale) erratic

discorde not in agreement, clashing

discordia f discord; (differenza di opinioni) disagreement; (litigio) argument

discorrere <3o> talk (**di** about)

discorso **1** pp → **discorrere 2** m pubblico, ufficiale speech; (conversazione) conversation, talk; **che –i!** what rubbish!

discoteca f (pl -che) locale disco; raccolta record library

discrepanza f discrepancy

discreto (riservato) discreet; (abbastanza buono) fairly good; (moderato) moderate, fair

discrezione f discretion; **a ~ di** at the discretion of

discriminare <1m> **1** v/i discriminate **2** v/t stranieri, donne discriminate against

discriminazione f discrimination

discussione f discussion; (litigio) argument

discusso pp → **discutere**

discutere <3v> **1** v/t proposta, caso discuss, talk about; questione debate; (mettere in dubbio) question; (contestare) dispute **2** v/i talk; (litigare) argue; (negoziare) negotiate

discutibile debatable

disdegnare <1a> disdain

disdetta f DIR notice; fig bad luck

disdetto pp → **disdire**

disdire <3t> impegno cancel; contratto terminate

disegnare <1a> draw; (progettare) design

disegnatore m, -trice f draughtsman, Am draftsman; donna draughtswoman, Am draftswoman; (progettista) designer

disegno m drawing; (progetto) design; ~ **di legge** bill

diserbante m weed-killer, herbicide

diserbare <1a> weed

diseredare <1b> disinherit

diseredato underprivileged, disadvantaged

disertare <1b> **1** v/t desert; ~ **una riunione** not attend a meeting **2** v/i desert

disertore m deserter

diserzione f desertion

disfare <3aa> undo; letto strip; (distruggere) destroy; ~ **la valigia** unpack

disfarsi di neve, ghiaccio melt; ~ **di** get rid of

disfatta f defeat

disfatto pp → **disfare**

disfunzione f MED disorder

disgelo m thaw

disgrazia f misfortune; (incidente) accident; (sfavore) disgrace; **per ~** unfortunately

disgraziato **1** agg (sfortunato) unlucky, unfortunate **2** m, -a f poor soul; F (farabutto) bastard F

disgregare <1b> break up

disgregarsi break up, disintegrate

disguido m hiccup, hitch

disgustare <1a> disgust

disgustarsi be disgusted (**di** by)

disgusto m disgust

disgustoso disgusting

disidratato dehydrated

disilludere <3b> disillusion

disillusione f disillusionment

disilluso disillusioned

disimparare <1a> forget

disinfettante m disinfectant

disinfettare <1b> disinfect

disinfezione f disinfection

disingannare <1a> disillusion

disinibito uninhibited

disinnescare <1d> *bomba* defuse

disinnestare <1a> AUTO *marcia* disengage

disinquinare <1a> clean up

disinserire <4d> disconnect

disinteressarsi take no interest (**di** in)

disinteressato disinterested

disinteresse *m* lack of interest; (*generosità*) unselfishness

disintossicare <1m, c & d> detoxify

disintossicazione *f* treatment for drug / alcohol addiction, *Am* detox F

disinvolto confident

disinvoltura *f* confidence

dislessia *f* dyslexia

dislessico dyslexic

dislivello *m* difference in height; *fig* difference

disobbedire → **disubbidire**

disoccupato **1** *agg* unemployed, jobless **2** *m*, **-a** *f* person who is unemployed, person without a job; *i -i* the unemployed, the jobless

disoccupazione *f* unemployment; **~ giovanile** unemployment among the young, youth unemployment

disonestà *f* dishonesty

disonesto dishonest

disonorare <1a> bring dishono(u)r on

disonore *m* dishono(u)r

disopra **1** *avv* above; *al ~ di* above **2** *agg* upper **3** *m* top

disordinato untidy, messy

disordine *m* untidiness, mess; *in ~* untidy, in a mess; *-i pl* riots, public disorder *sg*

disorganizzazione *f* disorganization, lack of organization

disorientare <1b> disorient(ate)

disorientamento *m* disorientation

disorientato disorient(at)ed

disotto **1** *avv* below; *al ~ di* beneath **2** *agg* lower **3** *m* underside

dispari odd

disparità *f* disparity

disparte: *in ~* aside, to one side

dispendio *m* waste

dispendioso expensive

dispensa *f stanza* larder; *mobile* cupboard; *pubblicazione* instal(l)ment; DIR exemption; *~* **universitaria** duplicated lecture notes

dispensare <1b> dispense; (*esonerare*) exonerate

disperare <1b> despair (**di** of); *far ~ qu* drive s.o. to despair

disperarsi despair

disperato desperate

disperazione *f* despair, desperation

disperdere <3uu> disperse; *energie, sostanze* squander; **non ~ nell'ambiente** please dispose of carefully

disperdersi disperse

dispersione *f* dispersal; CHIM, FIS dispersion; *fig di energie* waste

disperso **1** *pp* → **disperdere 2** *agg* scattered; (*sperduto*) lost, missing

dispetto *m* spite; *per ~* out of spite; *a ~ di qc* in spite of sth; *fare -i a qu* annoy or tease s.o.

dispettoso mischievous

dispiacere **1** *v/i* <2k> (*causare dolore*) upset (**a** s.o.); (*non piacere*) displease (**a** s.o.); *mi dispiace* I'm sorry; *le dispiace se apro la finestra?* do you mind if I open the window? **2** *m* (*rammarico*) regret, sorrow; (*dolore*) grief, sadness; (*delusione*) disappointment; *-i* (*preoccupazioni*) worries, troubles

display *m* display

disponibile available; (*cortese*) helpful, obliging

disponibilità *f* availability; (*cortesia*) helpfulness

disporre <3ll> **1** *v/t* arrange; (*stabilire*) order **2** *v/i* (*decidere*) make arrangements; *abbiamo già disposto diversamente* we've made other arrangements; *~ di qc* have sth (at one's disposal)

dispositivo *m* TEC device

disposizione *f* arrangement; (*norma*) provision; (*attitudine*) aptitude (**a** for); *stare / mettere a ~ di qu* be / put at s.o.'s disposal

disposto **1** *pp* → **disporre 2** *agg*: *~ a* ready to, willing to; *essere ben ~*

verso qu be well disposed to s.o.

dispotico (*pl* -ci) despotic

disprezzare <1b> despise

disprezzo *m* contempt

disputa *f* dispute, argument

disputare <1l> **1** *v/i* argue **2** *v/t* SP take part in; **disputarsi qc** compete for sth

dissanguare <1a> *fig* bleed dry, bleed white

disseminare <1m> scatter, disseminate; *fig* spread

dissenso *m* dissent; (*dissapore*) argument, disagreement

dissenteria *f* dysentery

dissentire <4b> disagree (**da** with)

disseppellire <4d> exhume

dissertazione *f* dissertation

disservizio *m* (*pl* -zi) poor service; (*inefficienza*) inefficiency; (*cattiva gestione*) mismanagement

dissestare <1b> FIN destabilize

dissestato *strada* uneven; *finanze* precarious

dissesto *m* ruin, failure; **~ ecologico** environmental meltdown

dissetante thirst-quenching

dissetare <1a> **~ qu** quench s.o.'s thirst

dissetarsi quench one's thirst

dissidente *m/f* dissident

dissimulare <1m> conceal, hide

dissimulazione *f* concealment

dissipare <1l> dissolve; (*sperperare*) squander

dissociare <1f> dissociate

dissociarsi dissociate o.s. (**da** from)

dissodare <1c> till

dissoluto dissolute

dissolvere <3g> dissolve; *dubbi*, *nebbia* dispel

dissolversi dissolve; (*svanire*) vanish

dissonante dissonant; *fig* discordant

dissonanza *f* MUS dissonance; *fig* clash

dissuadere <2i> **~ qu da fare qc** dissuade s.o. from doing sth

dissuaso *pp* → **dissuadere**

distaccare <1d> detach; SP leave behind

distaccarsi *da persone* detach o.s.

(**da** from)

distacco *m* (*pl* -cchi) detachment (*anche fig*); (*separazione*) separation; SP lead

distante distant, remote, far-off; **~ da** far from

distanza *f* distance (*anche fig*); **comando m a ~** remote control

distanziare <1g> **1** *v/t* space out; SP leave behind; (*superare*) overtake

distare <1a>: **l'albergo dista 100 metri dalla stazione** the hotel is 100 metres from the station; **quanto dista da qui?** how far is it from here?

distendere <3c> (*adagiare*) lay; *gambe*, *braccia* stretch out; *muscoli* relax; *bucato* hang out; *nervi* calm

distendersi lie down; (*rilassarsi*) relax

distensione *f* relaxation; POL détente

distensivo relaxing

distesa *f* expanse

disteso **1** *pp* → **distendere** **2** *agg* stretched out; (*rilassato*) relaxed

distillare <1a> distil, *Am* distill

distilleria *f* distillery

distinguere <3d> distinguish

distintivo **1** *agg* distinctive **2** *m* badge

distinto **1** *pp* → **distinguere** **2** *agg* (*diverso*) different, distinct; (*chiaro*) distinct; *fig* distinguished; **-i saluti** yours faithfully

distinzione *f* distinction

distorsione *f* distortion; MED sprain

distrarre <3xx> distract; (*divertire*) entertain

distrarsi (*non essere attento*) get distracted; (*svagarsi*) take one's mind off things

distratto **1** *pp* → **distrarre** **2** *agg* absent-minded

distrazione *f* absent-mindedness; (*errore*) inattention; (*svago*) amusement; **che distrae da un'attività** distraction

distretto *m* district

distribuire <4d> distribute; *premi* award, present

distributore *m* distributor; ~ (*di benzina*) (petrol, *Am* gas) pump; ~ **automatico** vending machine; ~ **automatico di biglietti** ticket machine

distribuzione *f* distribution; *posta* delivery

distruggere <3cc> destroy

distruttivo destructive

distrutto *pp* → **distruggere**

distruzione *f* destruction

disturbare <1a> disturb; (*dare fastidio a*) bother; (*sconvolgere*) upset

disturbarsi: **non si disturbi** please don't bother

disturbi *mpl* RAD interference *sg*

disturbo *m* trouble, bother; MED -*i pl* **di circolazione** circulation problems

disubbidiente disobedient

disubbidienza *f* disobedience

disubbidire <4d>: ~ **a** disobey

disuguaglianza *f* disparity, difference

disuguale different; *terreno* uneven; *fig* inconsistent, erratic

disumano inhuman

disuso *m*: **in** ~ in disuse, disused

ditale *m* thimble

dito *m* (*pl* le dita) finger; *del piede* toe; **un ~ di vino** a drop of wine

ditta *f* company, firm; ~ **fornitrice** supplier; ~ **di vendite per corrispondenza** mail-order company

dittafono® *m* dictaphone®

dittatore *m* dictator

dittatura *f* dictatorship

diurno daytime *attr*; **albergo** *m* ~ place where travellers can have a shower/shave

diva *f* diva

divagare <1e> digress

divampare <1a> *di rivolta, incendio* break out; *di passione* blaze

divano *m* sofa; ~ **letto** sofa bed

divaricare <1m & d> open (wide)

divario *m* (*pl* -ri) difference

divenire <4p> become

diventare <1b> become; *rosso, bianco* turn, go; ~ **grande** grow up

diverbio *m* (*pl* -bi) argument

divergente diverging, divergent

divergenza *f* divergence; *di opinioni* difference

divergere <3uu & 3a> diverge

diversamente differently; (*altrimenti*) otherwise

diversificare <1n & d> **1** *v/t* diversify **2** *v/i e* **diversificarsi** differ

diversità *f* difference; (*varietà*) diversity

diversivo *m* diversion, distraction

diverso 1 *agg* (*differente*) different (*da* from, *Am* than); -*i pl* several; *da* -*i giorni* for the past few days **2** *mpl* -*i* several people

divertente amusing

divertimento *m* amusement; **buon ~!** have a good time!, enjoy yourself/yourselves!

divertire <4b> amuse

divertirsi enjoy o.s., have a good time

dividendo *m* dividend

dividere <3q> divide; (*condividere*) share

dividersi *di coppia* separate; (*scindersi*) be split, be divided (*in* into)

divieto *m* ban; ~ **d'importazione** import ban; AUTO ~ **di segnalazioni acustiche** please do not use your horn; ~ **di sosta** no parking

divincolarsi <1m> twist, wriggle

divinità *f inv* divinity

divino divine

divisa *f* uniform; FIN currency

divisione *f* division; ~ **del lavoro** division of labo(u)r

divisorio (*pl* -ri) **1** *agg* dividing; **parete** *f* -*a* partition wall, stud wall **2** *m* partition

divo *m* star

divorare <1c> devour

divorziare <1c & g> get a divorce

divorziato divorced

divorzio *m* (*pl* -zi) divorce

divulgare <1e> divulge, reveal; (*rendere accessibile*) popularize

divulgazione *f* divulging; *scientifica ecc* popularization

dizionario *m* (*pl* -ri) dictionary

DNA *abbr* (= *acido deossiribonu-cleico*) DNA (= deoxyribonucleic acid)

do[1] → *dare*

do[2] *m inv* MUS C; *nel solfeggio della scala* doh

dobbiamo → *dovere*

D.O.C., doc *abbr* (= *Denominazione d'Origine Controllata*) term signifying that a wine is of a certain origin and quality

doccia *f* (*pl* -cce) shower; *fare la ~* take a shower

docente 1 *agg* teaching; *personale m* ~ teaching staff **2** *m/f* teacher

docile docile

documentare <1a> document

documentarsi collect information

documentario *m* documentary

documentazione *f* documentation

documento *m* document; *-i pl* papers; *-i dell'autoveicolo* car documents

dodici twelve

dogana *f* customs; (*dazio*) (customs) duty

doganale customs *attr*; **controllo** *m* ~ customs check; **dichiarazione** *f* ~ customs declaration; **formalità** *fpl* -i customs formalities

doganiere *m* customs officer

doglie *fpl*: *avere le -e* be in labo(u)r

dogma *m* (*pl* -i) dogma

dolce 1 *agg* sweet; *carattere, voce, pendio* gentle; *acqua* fresh; *clima* mild; *ricordo* pleasant; *suono* soft **2** *m* (*portata*) dessert, sweet; *di sapore* sweetness; (*torta*) cake; *-i pl* sweet things

dolcezza *f* sweetness; *di carattere, voce* gentleness; *di clima* mildness; *di ricordo* pleasantness; *di suono* softness

dolciastro sweetish; *fig* syrupy, sugary

dolcificante *m* sweetener

dolciumi *mpl* sweets, *Am* candy *sg*

dolente painful, sore

dolere <2e> hurt, be painful; *mi duole la schiena* my back hurts, I have a sore back

dolersi be sorry (*di* for); (*lagnarsi*) complain (*di* about)

dollaro *m* dollar

dolo *m* malice

Dolomiti *fpl* Dolomites

dolorante sore, painful

dolore *m* pain

doloroso painful

doloso malicious

domanda *f* question; (*richiesta*) request; FIN demand; *fare una ~ a qu* ask s.o. a question; *~ e offerta* supply and demand

domandare <1a> **1** *v/t* *per sapere*: *nome, ora, opinione ecc* ask; *per ottenere*: *informazioni, aiuto ecc* ask for; *~ un favore a qu* ask s.o. a favour; *~ scusa* apologize **2** *v/i*: *~ a qu* ask s.o.; *~ di qu* per sapere come sta ask after s.o.; *per parlargli* ask for s.o.

domandarsi wonder, ask o.s.

domani 1 *avv* tomorrow; *~ mattina* tomorrow morning; *~ sera* tomorrow evening; *a ~!* see you tomorrow! **2** *m* tomorrow

domare <1a> tame; *fig* control

domattina tomorrow morning

domenica *f* (*pl* -che) Sunday; *la ~, di ~* on Sundays

domestico (*pl* -ci) **1** *agg* domestic; *animale m* ~ pet **2** *m*, *-a f* servant; *donna* maid

domiciliato: *~ a* domiciled at

domicilio *m* domicile; (*casa*) home

dominante dominant; *idee* prevailing; *classe* ruling

dominare <1l & c> **1** *v/t* dominate; *materia* master; *passioni* master, overcome **2** *v/i* rule (*su* over), be master (*su* of); *fig di confusione* reign

dominazione *f* domination

dominio *m* (*pl* -ni) (*controllo*) control, power; *fig* (*campo*) domain, field

domino *m* mask, domino

donare <1a> donate, give; *sangue* give

donatore *m*, *-trice f* donor; *~ di sangue* blood donor

donazione *f* donation

dondolare <1l> **1** *v/t culla* rock; *testa* nod **2** *v/i* sway; (*oscillare*) swing

dondolarsi *su altalena* swing; *su sedia* rock; *fig* hang around

dondolio *m* (gentle) rocking

dondolo *m*: **cavallo** *m* **a ~** rocking horse; **sedia** *f* **a ~** rocking chair

donna *f* woman; *carte da gioco* queen; **~ di servizio** home help; **scarpe** *fpl* **da ~** women's *or* ladies' shoes

donnola *f* weasel

dono *m* gift

dopo 1 *prp* after; **~ di te** after you; **~ mangiato** after eating, after meals; **subito ~ il bar** just past the bar **2** *avv* (*in seguito*) afterward(s), after; (*poi*) then; (*più tardi*) later; **il giorno ~** the day after, the next day **3** *conj*: **~ che** after

dopobarba *m inv* aftershave

dopodomani the day after tomorrow

dopoguerra *m inv* post-war period

dopopranzo *m* afternoon

doposci *m inv* après-ski; **~ pl stivali** après-ski boots

dopotutto after all

doppiaggio *m* di film dubbing

doppiare <1k> *film* dub; SP lap; MAR round

doppiatore *m*, **-trice** *f* dubber

doppio (*pl* -pi) **1** *agg* double **2** *m* double; SP doubles

doppine *m inv* duplicate

doppipetto *m* double-breasted jacket

dorare <1c> gild; GASTR brown

dorato 1 *pp* → **dorare 2** *agg* gilded; *sabbia*, *riflessi* golden; GASTR browned

dorico (*pl* -ci) ARCHI Doric

dormicchiare <1k> doze

dormiglione *m*, **-a** *f* late riser

dormire <4c> sleep

dormita *f* (good) night's sleep

dormitorio *m* (*pl* -ri) dormitory

dormiveglia *m*: **essere nel ~** be only half awake

dorso *m* back; (*di libro*) spine; SP backstroke

dosaggio *m* (*pl* -gi) proportion; *di medicina* dosage

dosare <1c> measure out; *fig* be sparing with; *parole* weigh

dose *f* quantity, amount; MED dose; **una buona ~ di coraggio** a lot of courage

dosso *m* di strada hump; **togliersi gli abiti di ~** get undressed, take one's clothes off

dotare <1c> provide, supply (**di** with); *fig* provide, endow (**di** with)

dotato gifted; **~ di** equipped with

dotazione *f* equipment; *finanziaria* endowment; **dato in ~ a qu** issued with

dote *f* dowry; *fig* gift

dott. *abbr* (= **dottore**) Dr (= doctor)

dotto 1 *agg* learned **2** *m* scholar

dottorato *m* doctorate; **~ di ricerca** doctorate in scientific research

dottore *m* doctor (**in** of)

dottoressa *f* (woman) doctor

dottrina *f* doctrine

dott.ssa *abbr* (= **dottoressa**) Dr (= doctor)

dove where; **~ sei?** where are you?; **di ~ sei?** where are you from?; **fin ~?** how far?; **per ~ si passa?** which way do you go?; **mettilo ~ vuoi** put it wherever you like

dovere <2f> **1** *v/i* have to, must; **devo averlo** I must have it, I have to have it; **non devo dimenticare** I mustn't forget; **deve arrivare oggi** she is supposed to arrive today; **come si deve** (*bene*) properly; *persona* very decent; **doveva succedere** it was bound to happen; **dovresti avvertirlo** you ought to *or* should let him know **2** *v/t* owe **3** *m* duty; **per ~** out of duty

dovunque 1 *avv* (*dappertutto*) everywhere; (*in qualsiasi luogo*) anywhere **2** *conj* wherever

dovuto 1 *pp* → **dovere 2** *agg* due; **~ a** because of, due to

dozzina *f* dozen; **una ~ di uova** a dozen eggs; **se ne vendono a ~** they are sold by the dozen

dragare <1e> dredge

drago *m* (*pl* -ghi) dragon

dragoncello *m* tarragon

dramma *m* (*pl* -i) drama

drammatico (*pl* -ci) dramatic

drammatizzare <1a> dramatize

drammaturgia *f* theatre, *Am* theater

drammaturgo *m* (*pl* -ghi) playwright

drastico (*pl* -ci) drastic

drenaggio *m* drainage

drenare <1a> drain

dribblare <1a> SP dribble

dritto **1** *agg* straight **2** *avv* straight (ahead) **3** *m di indumento, tessuto* right side **4** *m*, **-a** *f* F crafty devil F

drive *m inv* INFOR drive

drizzare <1a> (*raddrizzare*) straighten; (*erigere*) put up, erect; **le orecchie** prick up one's ears

drizzarsi: **~ in piedi** rise to one's feet

droga *f* (*pl* -ghe) drug; **-ghe** *pl* **pesanti/leggere** hard/soft drugs

drogare <1c & e> drug

drogarsi SP take drugs

drogato *m*, **-a** *f* drug addict

drogheria *f* grocer's

dubbio (*pl* -bbi) **1** *agg* doubtful; (*equivoco*) dubious **2** *m* doubt; **essere in ~ fra** hesitate between; **mettere qc in ~** doubt sth; **senza ~** undoubtedly, without a doubt

dubbioso doubtful

dubitare <1l> doubt (*di* sth); **dubito che venga** I doubt whether he'll come

duca *m* (*pl* -chi) duke

ducato *m* (*territorio*) duchy

duchessa *f* duchess

due two; *a ~ a ~* in twos, two by two

tutt'e ~ both of them; **vorrei dire parole** I'd like to say a word or two

duecento **1** *agg* two hundred **2** *m*: **Duecento** the thirteenth century

duello *m* duel

duemila two thousand

duepezzi *m inv* bikini; (*vestito*) two piece (suit)

duetto *m* duet; (*persone*) duo, couple

duna *f* (sand) dune

dunque **1** *conj* so; (*allora*) well (then) **2** *m*: **venire al ~** come to the crunch

duomo *m* cathedral

duplex *m inv* party line

duplicato *m* duplicate

duplice double; **in ~ copia** in duplicate

durante *prp* during; **vita natural ~** for ever and ever

durare <1a> last; (*conservarsi*) keep, last

durata *f* duration, length; *di prodotto* life; **per tutta la ~ di** throughout; **~ di volo** flight time

duraturo lasting

durevole lasting

durezza *f* hardness; *di carne* toughness; (*asprezza*) harshness

duro **1** *agg* hard; *carne, persona* tough; *inverno, voce* harsh; *congegno, meccanismo* stiff; *pane* stale; (*ostinato*) stubborn; F (*stupido*) thick F; **~ d'orecchi** hard of hearing; **tieni ~!** don't give up!, hang in there! **2** *m* tough guy

durone *m* callous

duttile ductile; *fig* malleable

E *abbr* (= *est*) E (= east)

e and

è → *essere*

ebanista *m/f* (*mpl* -i) cabinet maker

ebano *m* ebony

ebbe, ebbi → *avere*

ebbene well

ebbrezza *f* drunkenness; *fig* thrill

ebbro (*pl* -ci) **1** *agg* Hebrew; *religione* Jewish **2** *m* Hebrew

ebreo 1 *m*, **-a** *f* Jew; **gli -i** the Jews **2** *agg* Jewish

ecc. *abbr* (= *eccetera*) etc (= et cetera)

eccedente excess

eccedenza *f* excess; (*il di più*) surplus; *peso m in ~* excess weight

eccedere <3a> **1** *v/t* exceed, go beyond **2** *v/i* go too far; *~ nel bere* drink too much

eccellente excellent

eccentrico (*pl* -ci) eccentric

eccessivo excessive

eccesso *m* excess; *~ di personale* overmanning; *~ di velocità* speeding

eccetera et cetera

eccetto except

eccettuare <1m & b> except

eccezionale exceptional; *in via ~* as an exception

eccezionalmente exceptionally

eccezione *f* exception

ecchimosi *f inv* bruise

eccitante 1 *agg* exciting **2** *m* stimulant

eccitare <1l & b> excite

eccitarsi get excited

eccitazione *f* excitement

ecclesiastico (*pl* -ci) **1** *agg* ecclesiastical **2** *m* priest

ecco (*qui*) here; (*là*) there; *~ come* this is how; *~ fatto* that's that; *~ tutto* that's all; *~mi* here I am; *~li*

here they are; *~ti il libro* here is your book

eclissare <1a> eclipse

eclissarsi *fig* slip away

eclisse *f*, **eclissi** *f inv* eclipse; *~ solare* solar eclipse; *~ lunare* lunar eclipse

eco *m/f* (*pl* gli echi) echo

ecografia *f* scan

ecologia *f* ecology

ecologico (*pl* -ci) ecological

ecologista 1 *m/f* ecologist **2** *agg* ecological

ecologo *m* (*pl* -gi), **-a** *f* ecologist

economia *f* economy; *scienza* economics *sg*; *fare ~* economize (*di* on); *~ di mercato* market economy; *università Economia e Commercio* business school; *-e pl* savings

economico (*pl* -ci) economic; (*poco costoso*) economical; *classe f ~* economy class

economista *m/f* (*mpl* -i) economist

economizzare <1a> **1** *v/t* save **2** *v/i* economize (*su* on)

economo 1 *agg* thrifty **2** *m*, **-a** *f* bursar

ecosistema *m* ecosystem

eczema *m* (*pl* -i) eczema

ed and

edera *f* ivy

edicola *f* newspaper kiosk

edificare <1m & d> build; *fig* edify

edificio *m* (*pl* -ci) building; *fig* structure

edile construction *attr*, building *attr*

edilizia *f* construction, building; (*urbanistica*) town planning

editare <1a> INFOR edit

editore 1 *agg* publishing **2** *m* publisher; (*curatore*) editor

editoria *f* publishing

editoriale 1 *agg* publishing **2** *m* editorial

edizione f edition; ~ **straordinaria** *di telegiornale* special news bulletin; *di giornale* extra (edition); **la quarta** ~ **del congresso XY** the fourth XY conference

educare <1l, b & d> educate; (*allevare*) bring up; *gusto, orecchio, mente* train

educativo education *attr*; (*istruttivo*) educational

educato: (**ben**) ~ well brought-up, polite

educazione f education; *dei figli* upbringing; (*buone maniere*) (good) manners; ~ **fisica** physical education

effervescente *bibita* fizzy, effervescent; *aspirina* soluble; *personalità* bubbly, effervescent

effettivamente (*in effetti*) in fact; *per rafforzare un'affermazione* really, actually

effettivo 1 *agg* (*reale*) real, actual; (*efficace*) effective; *personale* permanent; MIL regular **2** *m* FIN sum total

effetto *m* (*conseguenza*) effect; (*impressione*) impression; FIN (*cambiale*) bill (of exchange); ~ **serra** greenhouse effect; **fare** ~ (*funzionare*) work; (*impressionare*) make an impression; **fare l'**~ **di essere …** give the impression of being …; **-i** *pl* **collaterali** side effects; **-i** *pl* **personali** personal effects *or* belongings; **a tutti gli -i** to all intents and purposes; **in -i** in fact

effettuare <1m & b> carry out; *pagamento* make

effettuarsi take place; **il servizio non si effettua la domenica** there is no Sunday service

efficace effective

efficacia f effectiveness

efficiente efficient; (*funzionante*) in working order

efficienza f efficiency

Egitto *m* Egypt

egiziano 1 *agg* Egyptian **2** *m*, **-a** f Egyptian

egizio ancient Egyptian

egli *pron m* he

egocentrico egocentric

egoismo *m* selfishness, egoism

egoista 1 *agg* selfish **2** *m/f* (*mpl* -i) selfish person, egoist

egr. *abbr* (= **egregio**) *form of address used in correspondence*

egregio (*pl* -gi) distinguished; *nelle lettere* ~ **signore** Dear Sir

eguale → **uguale**

eh? eh?, what?

ehi! oi!

E.I. *abbr* (= **Esercito Italiano**) Italian army

elaborare <1m> elaborate; *dati* process; *piano* draw up, work out

elaborato elaborate

elaboratore *m*: ~ **elettronico** computer

elaborazione f elaboration; ~ **elettronica dei dati** electronic data processing; ~ **dei testi** word processing

elasticità f elasticity; (*agilità*) agility, suppleness; *fig* flexibility; *della mente* quickness

elastico (*pl* -ci) **1** *agg* elastic; *norme, orari* flexible **2** *m* rubber band

elefante *m* elephant

elegante elegant

eleganza f elegance

eleggere <3cc> elect

elementare elementary; *scuola* f ~ primary school, *Am* elementary school

elemento *m* element; (*componente*) component; **-i** *pl* (*rudimenti*) rudiments; (*fatti*) data

elemosina f charity; **chiedere l'**~ beg

elemosinare <1n & c> *v/t & v/i* beg

elencare <1b & d> list

elenco *m* (*pl* -chi) list; ~ **telefonico** phone book F, telephone directory

eletto 1 *pp* → **eleggere 2** *agg* chosen

elettorale electoral

elettorato *m* electorate

elettore *m*, **-trice** f voter

elettrauto *m inv auto* electrics garage; *persona* car electrician

elettricista *m/f* (*pl* -i) electrician

elettricità f electricity

elettrico (pl -ci) electric; **centrale** f **-a** power station

elettrocardiogramma m (pl -i) electrocardiogram

elettrodo m electrode

elettrodomestico m (pl -ci) household appliance

elettrolisi f electrolysis

elettromagnetico electromagnetic

elettromotore m electric motor

elettromotrice f FERR electric locomotive

elettrone m electron

elettronica f electronics

elettronico electronic

elettroshock electroshock

elettrotecnica f electrical engineering

elettrotecnico (pl -ci) **1** agg electrical **2** m electrical engineer

elevare <1b> raise; costruzioni erect; (promuovere) promote; fig migliorare better

elevato high; fig elevated, lofty

elevazione f elevation

elezione f election

eliambulanza f air ambulance

elica f (pl -che) MAR propeller, screw; AVIA propeller

elicottero m helicopter

eliminare <1m> eliminate

eliminatoria f SP heat

eliminazione f elimination

elio m helium

eliporto m heliport

élite f elite, élite

ella pron f she

ellenico (pl -ci) Hellenic

ellenismo m Hellenism

ellepì m inv LP

elmetto m helmet

elmo m helmet

elogiare <1f & c> praise

elogio m (pl -gi) praise

eloquente eloquent

eloquenza f eloquence

eludere <3q> elude; sorveglianza, domanda evade

elusivo elusive

elvetico (pl -ci) Swiss

emanare <1a> **1** v/t give off; legge pass **2** v/i emanate, come (**da** from)

emanazione f di calore, raggi emanation; di legge passing

emancipare <1m> emancipate

emanciparsi become emancipated

emancipazione f emancipation

emarginare <1m> marginalize

emarginato m, **-a** f person on the fringes of society

ematoma m (pl -i) h(a)ematoma

embargo m (pl -ghi) embargo

emblema m (pl -i) emblem

embolia f embolism

embrione m embryo

emergenza f emergency; **freno** m **d'~** emergency brake; **in caso di ~** in an emergency

emergere <3uu> emerge; (distinguersi) stand out

emersione f emersion

emerso pp → **emergere**

emesso pp → **emettere**

emettere <3ee> luce give out, emit; grido, verdetto give; calore give off; FIN issue; TEC emit

emicrania f migraine

emigrante m/f emigrant

emigrare <1a> emigrate

emigrato m, **-a** f person who has emigrated

emigrazione f emigration

emisfero m hemisphere

emissario m (pl -ri) GEOG outlet; (agente segreto) emissary

emissione f emission; di denaro, francobolli issue; RAD broadcast; **banca** f **di ~** bank of issue, issuing bank; **data** f **di ~** date of issue; **-i** pl **inquinanti** toxic emissions

emittente 1 agg issuing; (trasmittente) broadcasting **2** f RAD transmitter; TV channel; **~ privata** commercial channel

emoglobina f h(a)emoglobin

emorragia f h(a)emorrhage

emorroidi fpl h(a)emorrhoids

emostatico m h(a)emostat

emotivo emotional; (sensibile) sensitive

emozionante exciting, thrilling

emozionato excited; (*agitato*) nervous; (*commosso*) moved; (*turbato*) upset

emozionare <1a> (*appassionare*) excite; (*commuovere*) move; (*turbare*) upset

emozionarsi get excited; (*commuoversi*) be moved

emozione *f* emotion; (*agitazione*) excitement

empirico (*pl* -ci) empirical

emporio *m* (*pl* -ri) *negozio* department store

emulsione *f* emulsion

enciclopedia *f* encyclop(a)edia

enciclopedico (*pl* -ci) encyclop(a)edic

endovenoso intravenous

ENEL *abbr* (= **Ente Nazionale per l'Energia Elettrica**) Italian electricity board

energetico *fabbisogno, consumo ecc* energy *attr*; *alimento* energy-giving

energia *f* energy; **~ eolica** wind power; **~ nucleare** nuclear energy; **~ solare** solar power

energico (*pl* -ci) strong, energetic

enfasi *f* emphasis

enfatizzare <1a> emphasize

ENI *abbr* (= **Ente Nazionale Idrocarburi**) state-owned oil company

enigma *m* (*pl* -i) enigma

enigmatico (*pl* -ci) enigmatic

ENIT *abbr* (= **Ente Nazionale Italiano per il Turismo**) Italian tourist board

ennesimo MAT nth; F **per l'-a volta** for the hundredth time F

enorme enormous

enoteca *f* (*pl* -che) (*negozio*) wine merchant's (*specializing in fine wines*)

ente *m* organization; FIL being; **~ per il turismo** tourist board; **gli enti locali** the local authorities

entrambi both

entrare <1a> (*andare dentro*) go in, enter; (*venire dentro*) come in, enter; **la chiave non entra** the key won't go in, the key doesn't fit; *fig* **questo non c'entra** that has noth-

ing to do with it; **~ in una stanza** enter a room, go into/come into a room; **~ in carica** take up one's duties; **non entro più nei pantaloni** I can't get into my trousers any more

entrata *f* entrance; *in parcheggio* entrance, way in; *in un paese* entry; INFOR input; FIN **-e** *pl* (*reddito*) income; (*guadagno*) earnings; **~ libera** admission free

entro within

entroterra *m inv* hinterland

entusiasmare <1a> arouse enthusiasm in

entusiasmo *m* enthusiasm

entusiasta enthusiastic

entusiastico (*pl* -ci) enthusiastic

enumerare <1m> enumerate

enumerazione *f* enumeration

enzima *m* (*pl* -i) enzyme

epatite *f* hepatitis; **~ virale** viral hepatitis

epica *f* epic

epicentro *m* epicentre, *Am* -center; *fig* centre

epidemia *f* epidemic; **~ di influenza** flu epidemic

epidermide *f* skin; MED epidermis

Epifania *f* Epiphany

epilessia *f* epilepsy

epilettico (*pl* -ci) **1** *agg* epileptic **2** *m*, **-a** *f* epileptic

episodio *m* (*pl* -di) episode

epistolare: *stile* *m* **~** style of letter-writing

epoca *f* (*pl* -che) age; (*periodo*) period, time; *auto f d'~* vintage car; *mobili mpl d'~* period furniture

epurare <1a> *fig* purge

eppure (and) yet

E.P.T. *abbr* (= **Ente Provinciale per il Turismo**) provincial tourist board

equatore *m* equator

equatoriale equatorial

equazione *f* equation

equilatero equilateral

equilibrare <1a> balance

equilibrato balanced; *fig* well-balanced

equilibrio *m* (*pl* -ri) balance; *fig* common sense

equino horse *attr*; **carne** *f* **-a** horse-meat

equinozio *m* (*pl* -zi) equinox

equipaggiamento *m* equipment

equipaggiare <1f> equip; MAR, AVIA *con personale* man, crew

equipaggio *m* (*pl* -ggi) crew

equiparare <1m> make equal

equiparazione *f* equalization; **~ di diritti** equal rights

équipe *f inv* team; **lavoro** *m* **di ~** team work

equitazione *f* horse riding

equivalente *m/agg* equivalent

equivalenza *f* equivalence

equivoco (*pl* -ci) **1** *agg* ambiguous; (*sospetto*) suspicious; F (*losco*) shady F **2** *m* misunderstanding

era *f* (*epoca*) age, era; GEOL era; **~ atomica** atomic age; **~ glaciale** Ice Age

era, erano → **essere**

erba *f* grass; GASTR **-e** *pl* herbs; **-e aromatiche** herbs; **alle -e** with herbs; *fig* **in ~** budding

erbaccia *f* (*pl* -cce) weed

erborista *m/f* (*pl* -i) herbalist

erboristeria *f* herbalist's

erboso grassy

erede *m/f* heir; *donna* heiress

eredità *f* inheritance; BIO heredity

ereditare <1m & b> inherit

ereditarietà *f* heredity

ereditario (*pl* -ri) hereditary

ereditiera *f* heiress

eremita *m* (*pl* -i) hermit

eresia *f* heresy

eretico 1 *agg* heretical **2** *m* (*pl* -ci), **-a** *f* heretic

eretto 1 *pp* → **erigere 2** *agg* erect

erezione *f* building; FISIOL erection

ergastolano *m*, **-a** *f* person serving a life sentence, lifer F

ergastolo *m* life sentence

ergonomico (*pl* -ci) ergonomic

erica *f* heather

erigere <3u> erect; *fig* (*fondare*) establish, found

erigersi *fig* set o.s. up (**a** as)

eritema *m* (*pl* -i) *cutaneo* rash; **~ solare** sunburn

ermafrodito *m* hermaphrodite

ermellino *m* ermine

ermetico (*pl* -ci) (*a tenuta d'aria*) airtight; *fig* obscure

ernia *f* MED hernia; **~ del disco** slipped disc

ero → **essere**

eroe *m* hero

erogare <1l, b & e> *denaro* allocate; *gas, acqua* supply

erogazione *f di denaro* allocation; *di gas ecc* supply

eroico (*pl* -ci) heroic

eroina *f droga* heroin; *donna* eroica heroine

eroinomane *m/f* heroin addict

erosione *f* GEOL erosion

erotico (*pl* -ci) erotic

erotismo *m* eroticism

errare <1b> wander, roam; (*sbagliare*) be mistaken

errata corrige *m inv* correction

erroneamente mistakenly

errore *m* mistake, error; **~ di battitura** typographical error, typo F; **~ di calcolo** mistake in the addition; **~ di ortografia** spelling mistake; **~ di stampa** misprint; **~ giudiziario** miscarriage of justice; **per ~** by mistake

erta *f*: **stare all'~** be on the alert

erudito 1 *agg* erudite, learned **2** *m*, **-a** *f* erudite person

erudizione *f* erudition, learning

eruttare <1a> *di vulcano* erupt

eruzione *f* eruption; MED rash

es. *abbr* (= **esempio**) eg (= for example)

esagerare <1m> **1** *v/t* exaggerate **2** *v/i* exaggerate; (*eccedere*) go too far (**in** in)

esagerato 1 *agg* exaggerated; *zelo* excessive; *prezzo* exorbitant **2** *m*, **-a** *f*: **sei il solito ~!** you're exaggerating as usual!

esagerazione *f* exaggeration

esagonale hexagonal, six-sided

esagono *m* hexagon

esalare <1a> **1** *v/t odori* give off; **~ il respiro** exhale **2** *v/i* come, emanate (**da** from)

esaltare <1a> exalt; (*entusiasmare*) elate

esaltarsi become elated

esaltato 1 *agg* elated; (*fanatico*) fanatical **2** *m* fanatic

esaltazione *f* exaltation; (*eccitazione*) elation

esame *m* exam(ination); MED (*test*) test; (*visita*) examination; ~ *d'idoneità* aptitude test; ~ *di guida* driving test; **prendere in** ~ examine

esaminare <1m> examine (*anche* MED)

esaminatore *m*, **-trice** *f* examiner

esasperante exasperating

esasperare <1m> (*inasprire*) exacerbate; (*irritare*) exasperate

esasperarsi become exasperated

esasperato exasperated

esasperazione *f* exasperation

esattezza *f* accuracy; **con** ~ exactly; **per l'**~ to be precise

esatto 1 *pp* → **esigere 2** *agg* exact; *risposta* correct, right; *in punto* exactly; ~*!* that's right!

esattoria *f* tax office

esaudire <4d> grant; *speranze* fulfil

esauriente exhaustive

esaurimento *m* exhaustion; FIN **svendita** *f* **fino a** ~ **della merce** clearance sale; MED ~ **nervoso** nervous breakdown

esaurire <4d> exhaust; *merci* run out of

esaurito (*esausto*) exhausted; FIN sold out; *pubblicazioni* out of print; TEA **fa il tutto** ~ it is playing to a full house

esausto exhausted

esca *f* (*pl* -che) bait (*anche fig*)

esce → **uscire**

eschimese *agg*, *m/f* Inuit, Eskimo

esclamare <1a> exclaim

esclamazione *f* exclamation

escludere <3q> exclude; *possibilità, ipotesi* rule out

esclusione *f* exclusion

esclusiva *f* exclusive right, sole right; FIN ~ **di vendita** sole agency

esclusivo exclusive

escluso 1 *pp* → **escludere 2** *agg* excluded; (*impossibile*) out of the question, impossible **3** *m*, **-a** *f* person on the fringes of society

esco → **uscire**

escogitare <1m & c> contrive

escoriazione *f* graze

escrementi *mpl* excrement *sg*

escursione *f* trip, excursion; *a piedi* hike; ~ *di un giorno* day trip

escursionismo *m* touring; *a piedi* hiking, walking

escursionista *m/f* tourist; *a piedi* hiker, walker

esecutivo *m/agg* executive

esecutore *m*, **-trice** *f* DIR executor; MUS performer; ~ **testamentario** executor

esecuzione *f* (*realizzazione*) carrying out; MUS performance; DIR execution; ~ **capitale** execution

eseguire <4b or 4d> carry out; MUS perform

esempio *m* (*pl* -pi) example; **per** ~, **ad** ~ for example; **prendere** ~ **da qu** follow s.o.'s example

esemplare 1 *agg* exemplary **2** *m* specimen; (*copia*) copy

esentare <1b> exempt (**da** from)

esente exempt; ~ **da tasse** tax free

esequie *fpl* funeral (service) *sg*

esercente *m/f* shopkeeper

esercitare <1m & b> exercise; (*addestrare*) train; *professione* practise

esercitarsi practise

esercitazione *f* exercise

esercito *m* army

esercizio *m* (*pl* -zi) exercise; (*pratica*) practice; *di impianti* operation, use; (*anno finanziario*) financial year, *Am* fiscal year; FIN *azienda* business; *negozio* shop; ~ **pubblico** commercial premises

esibire <4d> *documenti* produce; *mettere in mostra* display

esibirsi *in uno spettacolo* perform; *fig* show off

esibizione *f* exhibition; (*ostentazione*) showing off; (*spettacolo*) performance

esibizionista *m/f* show-off; PSI exhibitionist

esigente exacting, demanding

esigenza f demand; (*bisogno*) need

esigere <3w> demand; (*riscuotere*) exact

esile slender; (*voce*) faint

esiliare <1k> exile

esilio m (pl -li) exile

esistente existing

esistenza f existence

esistere <3f> exist

esitare <1l & b> hesitate

esitazione f hesitation

esito m result, outcome; FIN sales, turnover

eskimo m inv giacca parka

esodo m exodus; *di capitali* flight

esofago m (pl -ghi) œsophagus, Am esophagus

esonerare <1m & c> exempt (*da* from)

esonero m exemption

esorbitante exorbitant

esordiente m/f beginner

esordio m (pl -di) introduction, preamble; (*inizio*) beginning; TEA début

esordire <4d> begin; TEA make one's début

esortare <1c> (*incitare*) urge; (*pregare*) beg

esortazione f urging

esoterico (pl -ci) esoteric

esoterismo m esotericism

esotico (pl -ci) exotic

espandere <3uu> expand

espandersi expand; (*diffondersi*) spread

espansione f expansion

espansività f fig warmth, friendliness

espansivo FIS, TEC expansive; fig warm, friendly

espatriare <1m & k> leave one's country

espatrio m (pl -i) expatriation

espediente m expedient; *vivere di -i* live by one's wits

espellere <3y> expel

esperienza f experience; *per ~* from experience

esperimento m experiment

esperto m/agg expert

espiare <1h> atone for

espirare <1a> breathe out, exhale

espirazione f exhalation

esplicito explicit

esplodere <3q> **1** v/t *colpo* fire **2** v/i explode

esplorare <1c> explore

esploratore m, **-trice** f explorer; *giovane* m ~ boy scout

esplorazione f exploration

esplosione f explosion; fig ~ **demografica** population explosion

esplosivo m/agg explosive

esploso pp → **esplodere**

esponente m/f exponent

esporre <3ll> expose (*anche* PHOT); *avviso* put up; *in una mostra* exhibit, show; (*riferire*) present; *ragioni, caso* state; *teoria* explain

esporsi expose o.s. (*a* to); (*compromettersi*) compromise o.s.

esportare <1c> export

esportatore 1 agg exporting; *paese* m ~ exporting country, exporter **2** m, **-trice** f exporter

esportazione f export

esposimetro m FOT exposure meter

espositore m, **-trice** f exhibitor

esposizione f (*mostra*) exhibition; (*narrazione*) presentation; FOT exposure

esposto 1 pp → **esporre 2** agg in *mostra* on show; ~ *a* exposed to; *critiche* open to; ~ *a sud* south facing **3** m statement; (*petizione*) petition

espressione f expression

espressivo expressive

espresso 1 pp → **esprimere 2** agg express **3** m posta express letter; FERR express; (*caffè* m) ~ espresso; *macchina* f ~ espresso machine; *per* ~ express

esprimere <3r> express

esprimersi express o.s.

espropriare <1m & c> expropriate

espropriazione f expropriation

esproprio m expropriation

espulsione f expulsion

espulso *pp* → **espellere**

essa *pron f persona* she; *cosa, animale* it

essenza *f* essence

essenziale **1** *agg* essential **2** *m*: l'~ è the main thing is

essere <3z> **1** *v/i* be; ~ *di* (*provenire di*) be or come from; ~ *di qu* (*appartenere a*) belong to s.o.; **lei è di Roma** she is or comes from Rome; **è di mio padre** it is my father's, it belongs to my father; **c'è** there is; **ci sono** there are; **sono io** it's me; **cosa c'è?** what's the matter?, what's wrong?; **non c'è di che!** don't mention it!; **chi è?** who is it?; **ci siamo!** here we are!; **sono le tre** it's three o'clock; **siamo in quattro** there are four of us; **se fossi in te** if I were you; **sarà!** if you say so! **2** *v/aus*: **siamo arrivati alle due** we arrived at two o'clock; **non siamo ancora arrivati** we haven't arrived yet; **è stato investito** he has been run over **3** *m* being; ~ **umano** human being

esso *pron m persona* he; *cosa, animale* it

est *m* east; **a ~ di** east of

estasi *f* ecstasy

estate *f* summer; ~ **di San Martino** Indian summer; **in ~, d'~** in (the) summer

estendere <3c> extend

estendersi *di territorio* extend; (*allungarsi*) stretch; *fig* (*diffondersi*) spread

estensione *f* extension; (*vastità*) expanse; MUS range

estenuante exhausting

esteriore *m/agg* exterior, outside

esteriorità *f* appearance

esterno **1** *agg* external; **per uso ~** for external use only **2** *m* outside; *in film* location shot; **all'~** on the outside

estero **1** *agg* foreign; **ministro m degli Affari -i** Foreign Secretary, *Am* Secretary of State **2** *m* foreign countries; **all'~** abroad

esteso **1** *pp* → **estendere 2** *agg*

extensive; (*diffuso*) widespread; **per ~** in full

estetica *f* (a)esthetics

estetista *f* beautician

estinguere <3d> extinguish, put out; *debito* pay off; *sete* quench

estinguersi die out

estinto **1** *pp* → **estinguere 2** *agg* extinct; *debito* paid off **3** *m*, **-a** *f* deceased

estintore *m* fire extinguisher

estinzione *f* extinction; FIN redemption, paying off

estirpare <1a> uproot; *dente* extract; *fig* eradicate

estivo summer *attr*

estorcere <3d> *denaro* extort

estorsione *f* extortion

estorto *pp* → **estorcere**

estradare <1a> extradite

estradizione *f* extradition

estraneo **1** *adj* outside (**a** sth); **corpo m ~** foreign body **2** *m*, **-a** *f* stranger; *persona non autorizzata* unauthorized person

estrarre <3xx> extract; *pistola* draw out; ~ **a sorte** draw

estratto **1** *pp* → **estrarre 2** *m* extract; *documento* abstract; FIN ~ **conto** statement (of account)

estrazione *f* extraction

estremista *m/f* (*pl* -i) extremist

estremità *f inv* extremity; *di corda* end; (*punta*) tip; (*punto superiore*) top

estremo **1** *agg* extreme; (*più lontano*) farthest; (*ultimo nel tempo*) last, final; **l'-a sinistra** the far or extreme left; **l'Estremo Oriente** the Far East **2** *m* (*estremità*) extreme; **gli -i** *di un documento* the main points

estro *m* (*ispirazione artistica*) inspiration

estromettere <3ee> expel, *Am* expell

estroverso extrovert(ed)

estuario *m* (*pl* -ri) estuary

esuberante (*vivace*) exuberant

esuberanza *f* exuberance

esule *m/f* exile

esultare <1a> rejoice

età *f inv* age; **all'~ di** at the age of; **~ della pietra** Stone Age; **raggiungere la maggiore ~** come of age; **limiti** *mpl* **d'~** age limit; **avere la stessa ~** be the same age; **di mezz' ~** middle-aged

etere *m* ether

eternità *f* eternity

eterno eternal; *(interminabile)* endless, never-ending; *questione, problema* age-old; **in ~** for ever and ever

eterogeneo heterogen(e)ous

eterosessuale heterosexual

etica *f* ethics

etichetta *f* label; *cerimoniale* etiquette

etico ethical

etimologia *f* etymology

etiope *agg*, *m/f* Ethiopian

Etiopia *f* Ethiopia

etiopico *m/agg* Ethiopian

etnico *(pl -ci)* ethnic

etrusco *(pl -chi)* **1** *agg* Etruscan **2** *m*, **-a** *f* Etruscan

ettaro *m* hectare

etto *m* hundred grams

ettogrammo *m* *(pl -i)* hundred grams *pl*, hectogram

ettolitro *m* hectolitre, *Am* -liter

eucalipto *m* eucalyptus

eucaristia *f* REL Eucharist

euforia *f* euphoria

euforico *(pl -ci)* euphoric

euro *m inv* euro

eurocheque *m inv* Eurocheque

eurodeputato *m*, **-a** *f* Euro MP

eurodollaro *m* Eurodollar

euromercato *m* euromarket

Europa *f* Europe

europeo **1** *agg* European **2** *m*, **-a** *f* European

eurovisione *f* Eurovision

evacuare <1m> evacuate

evacuazione *f* evacuation

evadere <3q> **1** *v/t* evade; *(sbrigare)* deal with; **~ le tasse** evade taxes **2** *v/i* escape *(da* from)

evaporare <1m> evaporate

evaporazione *f* evaporation

evasione *f* escape; *fig* escapism; **~ fiscale** *f* tax evasion

evasivo evasive

evaso 1 *pp* → **evadere 2** *m*, **-a** *f* fugitive

evasore *m*: **~ fiscale** tax evader

evenienza *f* eventuality

evento *m* event

eventuale possible

eventualità *f inv* eventuality; **nell'~ che** in the event that; **per ogni ~** for every eventuality

eventualmente if necessary

evidente evident

evidenza *f* evidence; **mettere in ~** emphasize, highlight

evidenziatore *m* highlighter

evitare <1l & b> avoid; **~ il fastidio a qu** spare s.o. the trouble

evoluto 1 *pp* → **evolvere 2** *agg* developed; *(progredito)* progressive, advanced; *senza pregiudizi* open minded, broad-minded

evoluzione *f* evolution

evolvere <3s> **1** *v/t* develop **2** *v/i e* **evolversi** evolve, develop

evviva hurray

ex ... *(nelle parole composte)* ex-, former

expertise *f inv* expertise

extra 1 *agg inv* extra; **di qualità ~** top quality **2** *m inv* extra

extracomunitario 1 *agg* non-EC, non-EU **2** *m*, **-a** *f* non-EC or non-EU citizen

extraconiugale extramarital

extraeuropeo non-European

extraterrestre *agg*, *m/f* extraterrestrial

E

F

fa **1** → *fare* **2** *avv:* **5 anni ~** 5 years ago **3** *m* MUS F; *nel solfeggio della scala* fa(h)

fabbisogno *m* needs *pl*, requirements *pl*

fabbrica *f* (*pl* -che) factory, *Am* plant

fabbricante *m/f* manufacturer

fabbricare <1l & d> manufacture; ARCHI build; *fig* fabricate

fabbricato *m* building

fabbricazione *f* manufacturing; ARCHI building

fabbro *m:* ~ (*ferraio*) blacksmith

faccenda *f* matter

faccende *fpl* housework *sg*

facchino *m* porter

faccia *f* (*pl* -cce) face; (*risvolto, aspetto*) facet; (*lato*) side; ~ **tosta** cheek; ~ **a ~** face to face; *di ~ a* opposite, in front of; *in ~* in the face; *gliel'ha detto in* ~ he told him to his face

facciata *f* ARCHI front, façade; *di foglio* side; *fig* (*esteriorità*) appearance

faccio → *fare*

facile easy; *di carattere* easy-going; (*incline*) prone (*a* to); *è ~ a dirsi!* easier said than done!; *è ~ che venga* he is likely to come; *non è mica una cosa* ~ it isn't that easy

facilità *f* ease; (*attitudine*) aptitude, facility; *con* ~ easily; INFOR ~ **d'uso** user-friendliness

facilitare <1m> facilitate

facilitazione *f* facility; *-i pl di prezzo* easy terms

facilmente easily

facoltà *f inv* faculty; (*potere*) power; *avere la ~ di scelta* have a choice, be able to choose

facoltativo optional

facoltoso wealthy

facsimile *m* facsimile

faggio *m* (*pl* -ggi) beech (tree)

fagiano *m* pheasant

fagiolini *mpl* green beans

fagiolo *m* bean

fagotto *m* bundle; MUS bassoon; *fig far ~* pack up and leave

fai → *fare*

fai da te *m inv* do-it-yourself, DIY

falce *f* scythe

falciare <1f> cut (with a scythe); *fig* mow down

falciatrice *f* lawn-mower

falco *m* (*pl* -chi) hawk

falda *f* layer; GEOL stratum; *di cappello* brim; (*pendio*) slope; (*piede di monte*) foot; ~ **acquifera** water table

falegname *m* carpenter

falegnameria *f* carpentry

falena *f* moth

falla *f* MAR leak; *tappare una ~* stop *or* plug a leak (*anche fig*)

fallimento *m* failure; FIN bankruptcy

fallire <4d> **1** *v/t* miss **2** *v/i* fail; FIN go bankrupt

fallito **1** *agg* unsuccessful, failed; FIN bankrupt **2** *m* failure; FIN bankruptcy

fallo *m* fault; (*errore*) error, mistake; SP foul; *mettere il piede in* ~ lose one's footing; *cogliere in* ~ *qu* catch s.o. out; (*in flagrante*) catch s.o redhanded

falò *m inv* bonfire

falsare <1a> *verità, fatti* distort

falsario *m* (*pl* -ri) forger

falsificare <1m & d> forge

falsificazione *f* forgery

falsità *f* falsity, falseness; (*menzogna*) lie; (*ipocrisia*) insincerity

falso **1** *agg* false; (*sbagliato*) incorrect, wrong; *oro, gioielli* imitation, fake F; (*falsificato*) forged, fake F **2** *m* (*falsità*) falsehood; *oggetto falsificato* forgery, fake F; DIR forgery

fama *f* fame; (*reputazione*) reputation; *di ~ mondiale* world-famous

fame *f* hunger; *aver ~* be hungry

famiglia *f* family; *~ numerosa* large family

familiare 1 *agg* family *attr*; (*conosciuto*) familiar; (*semplice*) informal **2** *m/f* relative, relation

familiarità *f* familiarity

familiarizzare <1a> familiarize

familiarizzarsi familiarize o.s.

famoso famous

fanale *m* AUTO, MAR, AVIA, FERR light; (*lampione*) street lamp

fanalino *m* AUTO: *~ di coda* tail-light; *fig essere il ~ di coda* bring up the rear

fanatico (*pl* -ci) **1** *agg* fanatical **2** *m*, *-a* *f* fanatic

fanciullo *m*, *-a* *f* *lit* (young) boy; *ragazza* (young) girl

fandonia *f* lie

fango *m* (*pl* -ghi) mud; MED *-ghi pl* mud-baths

fangoso muddy

fannullone *m*, *-a* *f* lazy good-for-nothing

fantascienza *f* science fiction

fantasia *f* fantasy; (*immaginazione*) imagination; (*capriccio*) fancy; MUS fantasia

fantasma *m* (*pl* -i) ghost

fantasticare <1m & d> day-dream (*di* about)

fantastico (*pl* -ci) fantastic

fante *m* *carte da gioco* jack

fanteria *f* MIL infantry

fantoccio *m* (*pl* -cci) puppet (*anche fig*)

farabutto *m* nasty piece of work

faraona *f*: (*gallina f*) *~* guinea fowl

farcire <4d> GASTR stuff; *torta* fill

farcito stuffed; *dolce* filled

fard *m inv* blusher

fardello *m* bundle; *fig* burden

fare <3aa> **1** *v/t* do; *vestito, dolce, errore* make; *biglietto, benzina* buy, get; *~ (dello) sport* play sport; *~ il pieno* fill up; *~ un bagno* have a bath; *~ il conto* al ristorante prepare the bill; *~ il medico / l'insegnante* be a doctor / teacher; *non fa niente* it

doesn't matter; *~ vedere qc a qu* show sth to s.o.; *farcela* manage; *non c'e la faccio più* I can't take any more; *2 più 2 fa 4* 2 and 2 make(s) 4; *quanto fa?* how much is it?; *far ~ qc a qu* get s.o. to do sth **2** *v/i*: *questo non fa per me* this isn't for me; *faccia pure!* go ahead!, carry on!; *qui fa bello / brutto* the weather here is nice / awful; *fa freddo / caldo* it's cold / warm

farsi (*diventare*) grow; F (*drogarsi*) shoot up F; *~ grande* grow tall; *si sta facendo tardi* it's getting late; *~ avanti* step forward; *~ la barba* shave; *~ male* hurt o.s.

farfalla *f* butterfly

farina *f* flour

farinaceo 1 *agg* starchy **2** *-cei mpl* starchy foodstuffs

faringe *f* pharynx

faringite *f* inflammation of the pharynx

farmaceutico (*pl* -ci) pharmaceutical

farmacia *f* pharmacy; *negozio* chemist's, *Am* drugstore

farmacista *m/f* (*mpl* -i) chemist, *Am* pharmacist

farmaco *m* (*pl* -ci) drug

faro *m* MAR lighthouse; AVIA beacon; AUTO headlight; *-i pl fendinebbia* fog lamps *or* lights

farsa *f* farce

fascia *f* (*pl* -sce) band; MED bandage; *~ elastica* crepe bandage; *~ oraria* (time) slot

fasciare <1f> MED bandage

fasciatura *f* (*fascia*) bandage; *azione* bandaging

fascicolo *m* (*opuscolo*) booklet, brochure; (*incartamento*) file, dossier

fascino *m* fascination, charm

fascio *m* (*pl* -sci) bundle; *di fiori* bunch; *di luce* beam

fascismo *m* Fascism

fascista *agg, m/f* (*mpl* -i) Fascist

fase *f* phase; AUTO stroke; *fig essere fuori ~* be out of sorts; *~ di lavorazione* production stage

fastidio *m* (*pl* -di) bother, trouble;

dare ~ a qu bother s.o.; **le dà ~ se … ?** do you mind if … ?; **un sacco di -i** a lot of bother

fastidioso (*irritante*) irritating, annoying; (*irritabile*) irritable

fasto *m* pomp

fastoso sumptuous

fata *f* fairy

fatale fatal; **era ~ che non si sarebbero mai più rivisti** they were fated never to meet again

fatalità *f inv* (*il fato*) fate; (*disavventura*) misfortune

fatato magic, enchanted

fatica *f* (*pl* -che) (*sforzo*) effort; (*stanchezza*) fatigue; **a ~** with a great deal of effort; **faccio ~ a crederci** I find it hard to believe

faticare <1d> toil; **~ a** find it difficult to

faticoso tiring; (*difficile*) laborious

fatt. *abbr* (= **fattura**) *inv* (= invoice)

fattibile feasible

fatto 1 *pp* → **fare 2** *agg* done; AGR ripe; **~ a mano** hand-made; **~ di legno** made of wood; **~ in casa** home-made; **~ per qu/qc** (tailor-)made for s.o./sth **3** *m* fact; (*avvenimento*) event; (*faccenda*) affair, business; **il ~ è che …** the fact is that …; **cogliere sul ~** catch red-handed; **di ~** *agg* real; *avv* in fact, actually; **passare a vie di ~** come to blows; **in ~ di** as regards

fattore *m* (*elemento*) factor; AGR farm manager; **~ di protezione antisolare** sun protection factor

fattoria *f* farm; (*casa*) farmhouse

fattorino *m* messenger; *per consegne* delivery man; *posta* postman, *Am* mailman

fattura *f* (*lavorazione*) workmanship; *di abiti* cut; FIN invoice; **rilasciare una ~ a qu** invoice s.o.

fatturare <1a> FIN invoice

fatturato *m* FIN (*giro d'affari*) turnover

fauna *f* fauna

fava *f* broad bean

favola *f* (*fiaba*) fairy tale; (*storia*) story; *morale* fable; (*meraviglia*)

dream; **una vacanza da ~** a dream holiday

favoloso fabulous

favore *m* favo(u)r; **prezzo** *m* **di ~** special deal; **a ~ di qu** in favo(u)r of s.o.; **per ~!** please!; **fare un ~ a qu** do s.o. a favo(u)r

favorevole favo(u)rable

favorire <4d> **1** *v/t* favo(u)r; (*promuovere*) promote **2** *v/i*: **vuol ~?** would you care to join me/us?; **favorisca i documenti!** your papers, please!; **favorisca nello studio** would you go into the study please

favorito *m/agg* favo(u)rite

fax *m inv* fax; **mandare un ~ a qc** send s.o. a fax, fax s.o.

faxare <1a> fax

fazione *f* faction

fazolettino *m*: **~ di carta** tissue

fazzoletto *m* handkerchief; *per la testa* headscarf

f.co *abbr* (= **franco**) free

febbraio *m* February

febbre *f* fever; **ha la ~** he has *or* is running a temperature; **~ da fieno** hay fever

febbrifugo *m* (*pl* -ghi) MED *drug that reduces the temperature*

febbrile feverish

fecondare <1a> fertilize

fecondazione *f* fertilization; **~ artificiale** artificial insemination

fecondità *f* fertility

fecondo fertile

fede *f* faith; (*fedeltà*) loyalty; *anello* wedding ring; **aver ~ in** have faith in s.o.; **tener ~ a una promessa** keep a promise

fedele 1 *agg* faithful; (*esatto, conforme all'originale*) true **2** *m* REL believer; **i -i** *pl* the faithful

fedeltà *f* faithfulness; MUS **alta ~** hi-fi, high fidelity

federa *f* pillowcase

federale federal

federazione *f* federation

fegato *m* liver; *fig* courage, guts *pl* F

felce *f* fern

felice happy; (*fortunato*) lucky

felicità *f* happiness

felicitarsi <1m>: ~ *con qu per qc* congratulate s.o. on sth

felicitazioni *fpl* congratulations

felino feline

felpa *f* sweatshirt

feltro *m* felt

femmina *f* (*figlia*) girl, daughter; ZO, TEC female

femminile 1 *agg* feminine; (*da donna*) women's **2** *m* GRAM feminine

femminilità *f* feminity

femminismo *m* feminism

femminista *m/f* (*mpl* -i) feminist

femore *m* femur

fendinebbia *m inv* fog lamp *or* light

fenicottero *m* flamingo

fenomeno *m* phenomenon

feriale: *giorno m ~* weekday

ferie *fpl* holiday *sg, Am* vacation *sg*; *andare in ~* go on holiday (*Am* vacation)

ferimento *m* wounding

ferire <4d> wound; *in incidente* injure; *fig* hurt

ferirsi injure o.s.

ferita *f* wound; *in incidente* injury

ferito 1 *agg* wounded; *in incidente* injured; *fig sentimenti* hurt; *orgoglio* injured **2** *m* casualty

fermacarte *m inv* paperweight

fermacravatta *m* tiepin

fermaglio *m* (*pl* -gli) clasp; *per capelli* hair slide; (*gioiello*) brooch

fermare <1a> stop; DIR detain

fermarsi stop; (*restare*) stay, remain

fermata *f* stop; ~ *dell' autobus* bus stop; ~ *facoltativa o ~ a richiesta* request stop

fermentare <1a> ferment

fermentazione *f* fermentation

fermento *m* yeast; *fig* ferment

fermezza *f* firmness

fermo 1 *agg* still, motionless; *veicolo* stationary; (*saldo*) firm; *mano* steady; *star ~* (*non muoversi*) keep still; *l'orologio è ~* the watch has stopped **2** *int ~!* (*alt!*) stop!; (*immobile!*) keep still! **3** *m* DIR detention

fermoposta *m* poste restante

feroce fierce, ferocious; *animale* wild; (*insopportabile*) dreadful

ferocia *f* ferocity

ferragosto *m* August 15 public holiday; *periodo* August holidays

ferramenta *f* hardware; *negozio* hardware store, ironmonger's *Br*

ferrato FERR: *strada f -a* railway line, *Am* railroad; *fig essere ~ in qc* be well up in sth

ferro *m* iron; (*arnese*) tool; *fig di ~ memoria, salute* excellent; *stomaco* cast-iron; ~ *da calza* knitting needle; ~ *da stiro a vapore* steam iron; ~ *di cavallo* horseshoe; ~ *battuto* wrought iron; GASTR *ai -i* grilled, *Am* broiled

ferrovia *f* railway, *Am* railroad; ~ *metropolitana o sotterranea* underground, *Am* subway

ferrovecchio *m* (*pl* -cchi) scrap merchant

ferroviario (*pl* -ri) rail(way) *attr, Am* railroad *attr*

ferroviere *m* rail (*Am* railroad) worker

fertile fertile

fertilità *f* fertility

fertilizzante *m* fertilizer

fesso *m* F idiot F; *far ~ qu* con s.o F

fessura *f* (*spaccatura*) crack; (*fenditura*) slit, slot

festa *f* feast; *di santo* feast day; (*ricevimento*) party; (*compleanno*) birthday; (*onomastico*) name day; ~ *della mamma / del papà* Mother's / Father's Day; ~ *nazionale* national holiday; *buone -e! a Natale* Merry Christmas and a happy New Year!

festeggiamenti *mpl* celebrations

festeggiare <1f> celebrate; *persona* have a celebration for

festival *m inv* festival

festività *f inv* festival; ~ *pl* celebrations, festivities

festivo festive; *giorno m ~* holiday

festoso happy, cheerful

feto *m* f(o)etus

fetta *f* slice; *a -e* sliced

feudale feudal

fiaba *f* fairy tale

fiabesco (*pl* -chi) fairytale *attr*

fiacca *f* weariness; (*svogliatezza*)

laziness; **battere la ~** slack, be a shirker

fiacco (pl -cchi) (debole) weak; (svogliato) lazy; FIN mercato sluggish

fiaccola f torch

fiala f phial

fiamma f flame; MAR pennant; GASTR **alla ~** flambé

fiammante: **rosso ~** m fiery red; **nuovo ~** brand new

fiammifero m match

fiancheggiare <1f> border; fig support

fianco m (pl -chi) side; ANAT hip; **~ a ~** side by side; **di ~ a qu** beside s.o.; **al tuo ~** by your side

fiasco m (pl -chi) flask; fig fiasco

fiato m breath; **senza ~** breathless; MUS **strumento a ~** wind instrument; **tutto d'un ~** in one go; **riprendere ~** catch one's breath

fibbia f buckle

fibra f fibre, Am fiber; **di forte ~** robust, sturdy; **~ morale** moral fibre (Am fiber); **~ sintetica** synthetic; **~ di vetro** fibreglass, Am fiberglass

fibroso fibrous

ficcanaso m/f F nosy parker F

ficcare <1d> thrust; F (mettere) shove F

ficcarsi get; **~ nei guai** get into hot water; **~ qc in testa** get sth into one's head; **dove s'è ficcato?** where can it / he have got to?

fico m (pl -chi) frutto fig; albero fig (tree); **~ d'India** prickly pear

fidanzamento m engagement

fidanzarsi <1a> get engaged

fidanzata f fiancée

fidanzato m fiancé; **i -i** pl the engaged couple

fidarsi: **~ di qu/qc** trust s.o. / sth, rely on s.o. / sth; **non mi fido di chiederlo a mio padre** I don't dare ask my father

fidato trustworthy

fideiussione f DIR guarantee

fido 1 agg trusted, trusty **2** m FIN credit

fiducia f confidence; **avere ~ in qu** have faith in s.o.; **di ~ persona** reli-

able, trustworthy; incarico responsible

fiduciaria f ~ FIN trust company

fiduciario (pl -ri) **1** agg DIR atto, società trust attr **2** m trustee

fiducioso trusting

fienile m barn

fieno m hay

fiera¹ f animale wild beast

fiera² f mostra fair

fierezza f pride

fiero proud

fifa F f nerves, jitters F; **aver ~** have the jitters, be jittery

figlia f daughter

figliastra f stepdaughter

figliastro m stepson

figlio m (pl -gli) son; **avere -gli** have children; **essere ~ unico** be an only child

figlioccia f (pl -cce) goddaughter

figlioccio m (pl -cci) godson

figura f figure; (illustrazione) illustration; (apparenza) appearance; **far brutta ~** make a bad impression

figurare <1a> **1** v/t fig imagine; **figurati!** just imagine!, just think!; **si figuri!** not at all!, of course not! **2** v/i (apparire) appear; (far figura) make a good impression

figurato (illustrato) illustrated; linguaggio, espressione figurative

figurina f da raccolta collector card, trading card

figurino m fashion sketch

fila f line, row; (coda) queue, Am line. **di ~** in succession; **tre giorni di ~** three days running, three days in succession; **in ~ indiana** in single file; **fare la ~** queue, Am wait in line

filamento m filament

filare <1a> **1** v/t spin **2** v/i di ragno spin; di ragionamento make sense; di formaggio go stringy; di veicolo travel; F (andarsene) take off F; **fila!** go away!, shoo!; **~ diritto** (comportarsi bene) behave (o.s.) **3** m di alberi row

filarmonico (pl -ci) philharmonic

filastrocca f (pl -cche) m nursery rhyme

filatelia f philately

filato 1 agg (logico) logical; **andare di ~ a casa** go straight home; **per 10 ore filate** for ten hours straight **2** m yarn; per cucire thread

file m inv INFOR file

filetto m GASTR fillet; TEC thread

filiale f branch; (società affiliata) affiliate

filigrana f su carta watermark; in oreficeria filigree

film m inv film, movie; **~ giallo** thriller; **~ in bianco e nero** black and white film

filmare <1a> film

filmato m short (film)

filo m (pl anche le -a) thread; metallico wire; di lama edge; d'erba blade; fig **un ~ di vergogna / rispetto** an ounce of shame / respect; fig **~ conduttore** lead; **~ interdentale** (dental) floss; **~ spinato** barbed wire; **~ di voce** whisper; **per ~ e per segno** in detail; **dare del ~ da torcere a qu** make things difficult for s.o.

filobus m inv trolley(bus)

filodrammatica f amateur dramatic society

filologia f philology

filologo m (pl -gi) philologist

filone m MIN vein; pane French stick; fig tradition

filosofia f philosophy

filosofico (pl -ci) philosophic(al)

filosofo m philosopher

filovia f trolley(bus)

filtrare <1a> **1** v/t strain, filter **2** v/i fig filter out

filtro m filter; **~ dell'olio** oil filter; **~ di carta** filter paper

fin → **fine, fino**

finale 1 agg final **2** m end **3** f SP final

finalista m/f finalist

finalmente (alla fine) at last; (per ultimo) finally

finanza f finance; **-e** pl finances; **ministro m delle -e** Minister of Finance

finanziamento m funding

finanziare <1g> fund, finance

finanziario (pl -ri) financial

finanziere m financier; (guardia di finanza) Customs and Excise officer; lungo le coste coastguard

finché until; (per tutto il tempo che) as long as

fine 1 agg fine; (sottile) thin; udito, vista sharp, keen; (raffinato) refined **2** m aim; **al ~ di ...** in order to ...; **secondo ~** ulterior motive **3** f end; **alla ~** in the end; **alla fin ~, in fin dei conti** after all, when all's said and done; **senza ~** endless

fine settimana m inv weekend

finestra f window

finestrino m window; AUTO **~ posteriore** rear window

finezza f fineness; (sottigliezza) thinness; (raffinatezza) refinement

fingere <3d> **1** v/t: **~ sorpresa / dolore** pretend to be surprised / to be in pain **2** v/i: **~ di** pretend to

fingersi pretend to be

finire <4d> **1** v/t finish, end; **finiscila!** stop it! **2** v/i end, finish (in in); **andrà a ~ male** cosa this will all end in tears; **persona** he / she will come to no good

finito finished; (venduto) sold out; **è finita** it's over; **farla finita con qc** put an end to sth

finlandese 1 m/agg Finnish **2** m/f Finn

Finlandia f Finland

fino¹ agg fine; (acuto) sharp; oro pure

fino² prp tempo till, until; luogo as far as; **~ a domani** until tomorrow; **~ a che** (per tutto il tempo che) as long as; (fino al momento in cui) until; **fin da ieri** since yesterday

fino³ avv even; **fin troppo** more than enough

finocchio m (pl -cchi) fennel

finora so far

finta f pretence, Am pretense, sham; SP feint; **far ~ di** pretend to be

fintantoché until

finto 1 pp → **fingere 2** agg false; (artificiale) artificial; (simulato) feigned

finzione f pretence, Am pretense, sham

fiocco m (pl -cchi) bow; ~ **di neve** snowflake; **-cchi** pl **d'avena** oat flakes, rolled oats; fig **coi -cchi** first-rate

fioco (pl -chi) weak; luce dim

fionda f catapult

fioraio m (pl -ai), **-a** f florist

fiordaliso m cornflower

fiordo m fiord

fiore m flower; fig **il** (**fior**) ~ the cream; nelle carte **-i** pl clubs; **disegno** m a **-i** floral design; **a fior d'acqua** on the surface of the water; **essere in** ~ be in flower

fiorente flourishing

fiorentino 1 agg Florentine 2 m, **-a** f Florentine; GASTR **alla -a** with spinach; bistecca charcoal grilled 3 f GASTR T-bone steak

fioretto m SP foil

fiorire <4d> flower; fig flourish

fioritura f flowering (anche fig)

Firenze f Florence

firma f signature; (il firmare) signing; FIN **avere la** ~ be an authorized signatory

firmamento m firmament

firmare <1a> sign

firmatario m (pl -ri) signatory

firmato abito, borsa designer attr

fisarmonica f (pl -che) accordion

fiscale tax, fiscal; fig spreg rigid, unbending

fiscalità f taxation; (pignoleria) rigidity, lack of flexibility

fischiare <1k> 1 v/t whistle; ~ **qu** boo s.o. 2 v/i di vento whistle

fischio m (pl -chi) whistle; SP ~ **finale** final whistle

fisco m tax authorities pl, Inland Revenue, Am Internal Revenue; **il** ~ the taxman

fisica f physics; ~ **nucleare** nuclear physics

fisico (pl -ci) 1 agg physical 2 m physicist; ANAT physique

fisiologia f physiology

fisionomia f face; fig di popolo, città appearance; (carattere) character

fisioterapia f physiotherapy

fisioterapista m/f (mpl -i) physiotherapist

fissare <1a> (fermare) fix; (guardare intensamente) stare at; (stabilire) arrange; (prenotare) book

fissarsi (stabilirsi) settle; (ostinarsi) set one's mind (**di** on); (avere un'idea fissa) become obsessed (**di** with); ~ **in mente** memorize

fissatore m (per capelli) hair-spray; FOT fixer

fissazione f (mania) fixation (**di** about)

fisso 1 agg fixed; stipendio, cliente regular; lavoro permanent 2 avv fixedly

fitta f sharp pain

fitto[1] 1 agg (denso) thick; ~ **di** full of 2 avv nevicare, piovere hard

fitto[2] m rent

fiume m river; fig flood, torrent; **letto** m **del** ~ river bed

fiutare <1a> smell; cocaina snort; ~ **un imbroglio** smell a rat

fiuto m sense of smell; fig nose

flacone m bottle

flagrante flagrant; **cogliere qu in** ~ catch s.o. red-handed

flanella f flannel

flash m inv FOT flash; stampa newsflash

flatulenza f flatulence

flauto m flute

flemma f calm

flemmatico (pl -ci) phlegmatic

flessibile flexible

flessione f bending; GRAM inflection; (diminuzione) dip, (slight) drop

flipper m inv pinball machine; **giocare a** ~ play pinball

flirt m inv flirtation

flirtare <1a> flirt

F.lli abbr (= **fratelli**) Bros (= brothers)

floppy disk m inv floppy (disk)

flora f flora

floreale floral

floricultura f flower-growing industry

florido flourishing

floscio (*pl* -sci) limp; *muscoli* flabby

flotta *f* fleet

fluido *m/agg* fluid

fluorescente fluorescent

fluoro *m* fluorine

flusso *m* flow; **~ e riflusso** ebb and flow

fluttuare <1l> FIN, *fig* fluctuate

fluttuazione *f* fluctuation; **~ dei prezzi** price fluctuation

fluviale river *attr*

f.m. *abbr* (= **fine mese**) end of the month

FMI *abbr* (= **Fondo Monetario Internazionale**) IMF (= International Monetary Fund)

f.to *abbr* (= **firmato**) sgd (= signed)

foca *f* (*pl* -che) seal

focaccia *f* (*pl* -cce) focaccia; *dolce sweet type of bread*; **rendere pan per ~** give tit for tat

focalizzare <1a> focus on

foce *f* mouth

focolaio *m* (*pl* -ai) *fig* hotbed

focolare *m* hearth; TEC furnace

focoso *m* fiery

fodera *f interna* lining; *esterna* cover

foderare <1l & c> *all'interno* line; *all'esterno* cover

fodero *m* sheath

foggia *f* (*pl* -gge) *f di abito, acconciatura* style

foglia *f* leaf

fogliame *m* foliage

foglio *m* (*pl* -gli) sheet; INFOR **~ elettronico** spreadsheet; **~ rosa** *provisional driving licence*; **~ di via obbligatorio** expulsion order

fogna *f* sewer

fognatura *f* sewers *pl*, sewage pipes *pl*

folata *f* gust

folclore *m* folklore

folcloristico (*pl* -ci) folk *attr*

folgorare <1l> *di fulmine, idea* strike; *di corrente elettrica* electrocute; **~ qu con lo sguardo** glare at s.o.

folgorato struck

folklore *m* → **folclore**

folla *f* crowd; *fig* host

folle[1] *agg* mad

folle[2] AUTO: **in ~** in neutral

follia *f* madness

folto thick

fondale *m* MAR sea bed; TEA backcloth, backdrop

fondamentale fundamental

fondamento *m* foundation; **le -a** *fpl* the foundations; **senza ~** unfounded

fondare <1a> found

fondarsi be based (**su** on)

fondato founded

fondatore *m*, **-trice** *f* founder

fondazione *f* foundation

fondere <3bb> **1** *v/t* (*liquefare*) melt; METAL smelt; *colori* blend **2** *v/i* melt

fondersi melt; FIN merge

fonderia *f* foundry

fondiario (*pl* -ri) land *attr*

fondo **1** *agg* deep **2** *m* bottom; (*sfondo*) background; *terreno* property; FIN fund; SP long-distance; SCI cross-country, langlauf; **-i** *pl denaro* funds; **a ~** (*profondamente*) in depth; *fig* **in ~** basically; **in ~ alla strada / al corridoio** at the end *or* bottom of the road / of the corridor; **essere in ~ al treno** be at the rear of the train; FIN **~ d'ammortamento** depreciation fund; **andare a ~** (*affondare*) sink; (*approfondire*) get to the bottom (**di** of); **-i** *pl di magazzino* old *or* unsold stock *sg*

fondotinta *m inv* foundation

fonduta *f cheese* fondue

fonetica *f* phonetics

fontana *f* fountain

fonte *m/f* spring; *fig* source; **~ energetica** source of energy; **da ~ attendibile** from a reliable source

footing *m* jogging

foraggio *m* (*pl* -ggi) forage

forare <1a> *di proiettile* pierce; *con il trapano* drill; *biglietto* punch; *pneumatico* puncture

foratura *f di pneumatico* puncture

forbici *fpl* scissors; **un paio di ~** a pair of scissors

forca *f* (*forcone*) pitchfork

forcella *f* TEC fork

forchetta *f* fork; **essere una buona**

~ have a big appetite

forcina f hairpin

forcipe m forceps pl

forcone m pitchfork

foresta f forest

forestale forest attr

foresteria f guest accommodation

forestiero 1 agg foreign **2** m, **-a** f foreigner

forfait m inv lump sum; SP withdrawal; **a ~** on a lump-sum basis

forfettario flat-rate, all in; **prezzo** m ~ lump sum

forfora f dandruff

forma f form; (sagoma) shape; TEC (stampo) mo(u)ld; **essere in ~** be in good form

formaggiera f dish for grated cheese

formaggino m processed cheese

formaggio m (pl -ggi) cheese

formale formal

formalità f inv formality

formare <1a> shape; TELEC ~ **il numero** dial the number

formarsi form; (svilupparsi) develop; di un'idea take shape

formato m size; di libro format

formattare <1a> INFOR format

formazione f formation; fig addestramento training; SP line-up; ~ **professionale** vocational training

formica[1] f (pl -che) ZO ant

formica[2]® Formica®

formicaio m (pl -ai) anthill

formicolare <1m> di mano, gamba tingle; fig ~ **di** teem with

formicolio m sensazione pins and needles pl

formidabile (straordinario) incredible; (poderoso) powerful

formula f formula

formulare <1l> teoria, ipotesi formulate; (esprimere) express

fornaio m (pl -ai) baker; negozio bakery

fornello m stove

fornire <4d> supply (**qc a qu** s.o. with sth)

fornirsi get (**di** sth), get hold (**di** of)

fornitore m supplier

fornitura f supply

forno m oven; (panetteria) bakery; ~ **a microonde** microwave (oven); GASTR **al** ~ carne, patate roast; mele, pasta baked

foro[1] m (buco) hole

foro[2] m romano forum; DIR (tribunale) (law) court

forse perhaps, maybe; **mettere in ~** cast doubt on

forte 1 agg strong; suono loud; pioggia heavy; taglia large; somma considerable, substantial; dolore severe **2** avv (con forza) hard; (ad alta voce) loudly; (velocemente) fast **3** m (fortezza) fort; **questo è il suo ~** it's his strong point

fortezza f MIL fortress; ~ **d'animo** strength of character

fortificare <1m & d> rendere più forte strengthen; MIL fortify

fortino m MIL blockhouse

fortuito chance

fortuna f fortune; **avere ~** be successful; (essere fortunato) be lucky; **buona ~!** good luck!; **fare ~** make a fortune; **per ~** luckily; **di ~** makeshift; **atterraggio** m **di ~** emergency landing

fortunatamente fortunately

fortunato lucky, fortunate

foruncolo m pimple

forza f strength; (potenza) power; muscolare force; ~ **di gravità** force of gravity; **per cause di ~ maggiore** because of circumstances beyond my/our control; **a viva ~** by force; **a ~ di ...** by dint of ...; **per ~** against my/our will; **per ~!** (naturalmente) of course!; **~!** come on!; **-e** pl (armate) MIL armed forces

forzare <1c> force

foschia f haze

fosco (pl -schi) dark

fosfato m phosphate

fosforescente phosphorescent

fosforo m phosphorus

fossa f pit, hole; (tomba) grave; ~ **comune** mass grave

fossato m ditch; di fortezza moat

fossetta f dimple

fossile 1 agg fossil attr **2** m fossil

fosso *m* ditch

foto *f inv* photo, snap

fotocellula *f* photocell

fotocopia *f* photocopy

fotocopiare <1k & c> photocopy

fotocopiatrice *f* photocopier

fotogenico (*pl* -ci) photogenic

fotografare <1m & c> photograph

fotografia *f arte* photography; (*foto*) photograph; *~ formato tessera* passport-size photograph; *~ aerea* aerial photograph; *~ a colori* colo(u)r photograph

fotografico (*pl* -ci) photographic; *macchina f -a* camera; *articoli mpl -ci* photographic equipment

fotografo *m* photographer

fotomontaggio *m* (*pl* -gi) photo-montage

fotoreporter *m/f inv* photo journalist

fotoromanzo *m* story told in pictures

fra *prp* ◊ between; *~ Roma e Londra* between Rome and London ◊ among; *~ questi ragazzi* out of all these boys; *~ di noi* between you and me; *~ l'altro* what's more ◊ in; *~ breve* in a very short time, soon; *~ tre giorni* in three days ◊ *~ sé e sé* to himself / herself

frac *m inv* tails

fracassare <1a> smash

fracasso *m di persone* din; *di oggetti che cadono* crash

fradicio (*pl* -ci) rotten; (*bagnato*) soaked, soaking wet; *ubriaco ~* blind drunk F, blotto F

fragile fragile; *persona* frail, delicate

fragola *f* strawberry

fragore *m* roar; *di tuono* rumble

fraintendere <3c> misunderstand

frammentario (*pl* -ri) fragmentary

frammento *m* fragment

frana *f* landslide

franare <1a> collapse

francamente frankly

francese **1** *m/agg* French **2** *m/f* Frenchman; *donna* Frenchwoman; *i -i pl* the French

franchezza *f* frankness

franchigia *f* FIN exemption; *posta* freepost; *~ doganale* exemption from customs duties

Francia *f* France

franco (*pl* -chi) **1** *agg* frank; FIN free; *farla -a* get away with it; *~ domicilio* free delivery, carriage paid **2** *m* FIN franc

francobollo *m* stamp; *due -i da ... lire* two ... lire stamps

frangente *m* (*onda*) breaker; (*situazione*) (difficult) situation

frangia *f* (*pl* -ge) fringe

frantumare <1a> shatter

frantumi *mpl* splinters; *in ~* in smithereens; *mandare in ~* smash to smithereens

frappé *m inv* milkshake

frase *f* phrase; *~ fatta* cliché

frassino *m* ash (tree)

frastagliato: *costa f -a* jagged coastline

frastuono *m* racket

frate *m* REL friar, monk

fratellastro *m* step-brother; *con legami di consanguineità* half-brother

fratello *m* brother; *-i pl fratello e sorella* brother and sister

fraterno brotherly, fraternal

frattaglie *fpl* GASTR offal *sg*; *di pollo* giblets

frattanto meanwhile, in the meantime

frattempo *m*: *nel ~* meanwhile, in the meantime

frattura *f* fracture

fratturare <1a> fracture

fratturarsi: *~ una gamba* break one's leg

frazionare <1a> (*dividere in parti*) break up, split up

frazionarsi split (*in* into)

frazione *f* fraction; POL small group; (*borgata*) hamlet; *~ decimale* decimal fraction; *una ~ di secondo* a split second

freccia *f* (*pl* -cce) arrow; AUTO ~ (*di direzione*) indicator

freddezza *f* coldness

freddo **1** *agg* cold; *fig a sangue ~* in cold blood **2** *m* cold; *ho ~* I'm cold;

fa ~ it's cold

freddoloso: essere ~ feel the cold

freddura f pun, play on words

freezer m inv freezer

fregare <1e> rub; F (imbrogliare) swindle F; F (battere) beat, wipe the floor with F; F a un esame fail; F (rubare) pinch F, lift F; P me ne frego di quello che pensano I don't give a damn what they think F

fregata f MAR frigate

fregatura f F (imbroglio) rip-off F; (ostacolo, contrarietà) pain F

fregio m ARCHI frieze

fremere <3a> (tremare) tremble, quiver

frenare <1a> AUTO brake; folla, lacrime, risate hold back; entusiasmo, impulso restrain

frenarsi (dominarsi) restrain o.s.

frenata f braking; fare una ~ brake; segni mpl di ~ tyre marks

freno m AUTO brake; del cavallo bit; ~ d'allarme emergency brake; ~ a mano handbrake, Am parking brake; ~ a pedale foot-brake; porre ~ a qc curb sth; fig senza ~ without restraint; tenere a ~ la lingua curb one's tongue

frequentare <1b> luoghi frequent; scuola, corso attend; persona associate with

frequentato popular; strada busy

frequente frequent; di ~ frequently

frequenza f frequency; scolastica attendance; un'alta ~ di spettatori a large audience; con ~ frequently

freschezza f freshness; di temperatura coolness

fresco (pl -chi) **1** agg fresh; temperatura cool; fig F stai ~! you're for it! F, you've had it! F **2** m coolness; prendere il ~ take the air; fa ~ it's cool; mettere in ~ put in a cool place; fig F al ~ inside F

frescura f cool(ness)

fretta f hurry; aver ~ be in a hurry; non c'è ~ there's no hurry, there's no rush; in tutta ~, in ~ e furia in great haste

frettoloso saluto, sorriso hurried;

lavoro rushed; persona in a hurry

fricassea f GASTR fricassee

friggere <3cc> **1** v/t fry **2** v/i sizzle

friggitoria f shop that sells deep fried fish etc

friggitrice f deep fryer

frigido MED frigid

frigo m fridge

frigorifero 1 agg cold attr; camion, nave, vagone refrigerated **2** m refrigerator

fringuello m chaffinch

frittata f GASTR omelette, Am omelet; fig ormai la ~ è fatta the damage is done

frittella f fritter; fig (macchia) grease stain

fritto 1 pp → friggere **2** agg fried **3** m fried food; ~ misto assortment of deep-fried food

frittura f metodo frying; ~ di pesce fried fish

frivolo frivolous

frizionare <1a> rub

frizione f friction; AUTO clutch

frizzante bevanda fizzy, sparkling; aria crisp; fig parola, motto biting, sharp

frodare <1c> defraud (di of); ~ il fisco evade or dodge F tax

frode f fraud

frontale frontal; scontro m ~ head-on collision

fronte 1 f forehead; di ~ a (dirimpetto) opposite, facing; in presenza di before; a confronto di compared to or with; la casa, vista dal di ~ the house, seen from the front **2** m front; ~ caldo warm front; far ~ agli impegni face up to one's responsibilities; far ~ alle spese make ends meet

fronteggiare <1f> (stare di fronte a) face; (far fronte a) face, confront

frontespizio m (pl -zi) title page; ARCHI frontispiece

frontiera f border, frontier; guardia f di ~ border guard; valico m di ~ border crossing

frontone m ARCHI pediment

fronzolo m frill

frottola f F fib F

frugale frugal

frugare <1e> **1** v/i (*rovistare*) rummage **2** v/t (*cercare con cura*) search, rummage through

fruire <4d>: **~ di qc** benefit from sth

frullare <1a> GASTR blend, liquidize; *uova* whisk

frullato m milk-shake

frullatore m liquidizer, blender

frullino m whisk

frumento m wheat

frusciare <1f> rustle

fruscio m rustle

frusta f whip; GASTR whisk

frustare <1a> whip

frustino m riding crop

frustrare <1a> frustrate

frustrazione f frustration

frutta f fruit; ~ **candita** candied fruit; ~ **fresca** fresh fruit; ~ **secca** nuts

fruttare <1a> **1** v/t yield **2** v/i fruit

frutteto m orchard

fruttifero fruitful; FIN interest-bearing

fruttivendolo m, **-a** f greengrocer

frutto m fruit; **-i pl di mare** seafood sg

fruttuoso profitable

FS abbr (= **Ferrovie dello Stato**) Italian State railways

fu → **essere**

fucilare <1a> shoot

fucilata f shot

fucile m rifle

fucina f forge

fuga f (pl -ghe) escape; MUS fugue; ~ **di gas** gas leak; FIN ~ **di capitali** flight of capital

fuggevole fleeting

fuggiasco m (pl -schi) fugitive

fuggifuggi m inv stampede

fuggire <4a> flee

fuggitivo m fugitive

fulcro m fulcrum

fuliggine f soot

fulizginoso sooty

fulminante *sguardo* withering; *malattia* which strikes suddenly

fulminare <1l> *di sguardo* look daggers at, glare at; **rimanere fulminato** da fulmine be struck by light-

ning; *da elettricità* be electrocuted; *fig* be thunderstruck

fulminarsi *di lampadina* blow

fulmine m lightning

fulmineo fast, rapid

fumaiolo m MAR funnel; FERR chimney; *di casa* chimney pot

fumare <1a> smoke

fumatore m, **-trice** f smoker; ~ **scompartimento** m **per -i/non -i** smoking/non-smoking compartment

fumetto m comic strip; **-i pl per ragazzi** comics

fumo m smoke; (*vapore*) steam; *fig* **andare in** ~ (*fallire*) go up in smoke; (*svanire*) come to nothing; **mandare in** ~ shatter

fumoso smoky; *fig* (*oscuro*) muddled

fune f rope; (*cavo*) cable; **tiro** m **alla** ~ tug-of-war

funebre funeral attr; *fig* gloomy, funereal; **carro** m ~ hearse

funerale m funeral

fungere <3d> act (**da** as)

fungo m (pl -ghi) mushroom; MED fungus; ~ **velenoso** poisonous mushroom; ~ **prataiolo** field mushroom

funicolare f funicular railway

funivia f cableway

funzionamento m operation, functioning

funzionare <1a> operate, function; **non** ~ be out of order; *di orologio* have stopped

funzionario m (pl -ri) official, civil servant

funzione f function; (*carica*) office; REL service, ceremony; **mettere in** ~ put into operation; **in** ~ **di ...** depending on; **variare in** ~ **di ...** vary with ...

fuoco m (pl -chi) fire; FIS, FOT focus; **dar** ~ **a qc** set fire to sth; **-chi d'artificio** fireworks; MIL **far** ~ (open) fire; FOT **mettere a** ~ focus

fuorché except

fuori 1 prp *stato* outside, out of; *moto* out of, away from; ~ **di casa** outside the house; ~ **città** out of town; ~

luogo out of place; **~ mano** out of the way; **~ di sé** beside o.s.; **~ uso** out of use **2** *avv* outside; *all'aperto* out of doors; SP out; *di* ~ outside; ~*!* out!

fuoribordo *m inv* motorboat; *motore* outboard motor

fuoriclasse *agg*, *m/f inv* champion

fuorigioco *m inv* offside; **essere nel ~** be offside

fuoriserie 1 *agg* made to order, custom made **2** *f inv* AUTO custom-built model

fuoristrada *m inv* off-road vehicle

fuoriuscita *f di gas* leakage, escape

fuoriuscito *m* exile

fuorviare <1h> **1** *v/i* go astray **2** *v/t* lead astray

furbizia *f* cunning

furbo cunning, crafty

furfante *m* rascal, rogue

furgoncino *m* (small) van

furgone *m* van

furia *f* fury, rage; **a ~ di ...** by dint of ...

furibondo furious, livid

furioso furious; *vento*, *lotta* violent

furore *m* fury, rage; **far ~** be all the rage

furtivo furtive

furto *m* theft; **~ con scasso** burglary

fusa *fpl*: **fare le ~** purr

fuscello *m* twig

fuseaux *mpl* leggings

fusibile *m* EL fuse

fusione *f* fusion; FIN merger; **~ nucleare** nuclear fusion

fuso[1] *pp* → **fondere**; METAL molten; *burro* melted

fuso[2] *m* spindle; **~ orario** time zone

fusto *m* (*tronco*) trunk; (*stelo*) stem, stalk; *di metallo* drum; *di legno* barrel

futile futile

futilità *f* futility

futuristico futuristic

futuro *m/agg* future; **in ~** in future; **in un lontano / prossimo ~** in the distant / near future

G

g *abbr* (= **grammo**) g (= gram)

gabbia *f* cage; **~ di mattia** *fig* madhouse; **~ toracica** rib cage

gabbiano *m* (sea)gull

gabinetto *m* toilet; POL cabinet; **~ medico / dentistico** doctor's / dentist's surgery; POL **~ ombra** shadow cabinet

gaffe *f* blunder, gaffe

gaelico *m* Gaelic

gala *f* (*ricevimento*) gala; **serata *f* di ~** gala evening

galante gallant

galanteria *f* gallantry

galantuomo (*pl* -uomini) *m* gentleman

galassia *f* galaxy

galateo *m libro* book of etiquette; *comportamento* etiquette, (good) manners

galera *f* (*prigione*) jail, prison

galla *f* BOT gall; **a ~** afloat; **venire a ~** (come to the) surface; *fig* come to light; **tenersi a ~** stay *or* keep afloat

galleggiante 1 *agg* floating **2** *m* (*boa*) buoy

galleggiare <1f> float

galleria *f* gallery; *passaggio con negozi* (shopping) arcade; FERR, MIN tunnel; TEA circle

Galles *m* Wales

gallese 1 *m/agg* Welsh **2** *m/f* Welshman; *donna* Welshwoman

gallina *f* hen

gallo *m* cock; SP **peso** *m* **~** bantamweight

gallone *m* MIL stripe; *unità di misura* gallon

galoppare <1c> gallop

galoppo *m* gallop; *al ~* at a gallop

gamba *f* leg; *fig* **in ~** (*capace*) smart, bright; (*in buona salute*) healthy, (*fighting*) fit; *persona anziana* spry, sprightly; *darsela a -e* take to one's heels

gamberetto *m* shrimp

gambero *m* prawn

gambo *m* *di fiore, bicchiere* stem; *di pianta, fungo* stalk

gamma *f* range; MUS scale

gancio *m* (*pl* -ci) hook; *~ di traino* tow-hook

gara *f* competition; *di velocità* race; *~ automobilistica* car race; *~ eliminatoria* heat; *fare a ~* compete

garage *m inv* garage; *~ sotterraneo* underground car park (*Am* parking garage)

garagista *m* (*pl* -i) (*custode*) garage attendant; (*meccanico*) mechanic

garante *m* guarantor.

garantire <4d> 1 *v/t* guarantee; (*assicurare*) ensure 2 *v/i* (*farsi garante*) stand guarantor (*per* for)

garantito guaranteed

garanzia *f* guarantee; *essere in ~* be under guarantee

garbato courteous, polite

garbo *m* courtesy, politeness; (*modi gentili*) good manners *pl*; (*tatto*) tact

gardenia *f* gardenia

gareggiare <1f> compete

gargarismo *m* gargle; (*collutorio*) mouthwash; *fare i -i* gargle

garofano *m* carnation; GASTR *chiodi mpl di ~* cloves

garza *f* gauze

garzone *m* boy

gas *m inv* gas; *a ~* gas *attr*; AUTO *dare ~* accelerate; *~ asfissiante* poison gas; *~ lacrimogeno* tear gas; *~ naturale* natural gas; *~ di scarico* exhaust (*fumes*)

gasato 1 *agg* *bibita* fizzy; (*eccitato*) excited 2 *m*, *-a f* bighead

gasolio *m per riscaldamento* oil; AUTO diesel fuel

gastrico (*pl* -ci) gastric; *succhi mpl -ci* digestive juices

gastrite *f* gastritis

gastronomia *f* gastronomy

gastronomico (*pl* -ci) gastronomic

gatta *f* (*female*) cat

gattino *m* kitten

gatto *m* cat; *maschio* (tom) cat; *c'erano quattro -i* there was hardly anybody there

gavetta *f* MIL mess tin; *fare la ~* come up through the ranks

gay *m*/*agg* gay

gazza *f* magpie

gazzella *f* gazelle

gazzetta *f* gazette; *~ ufficiale* official journal, gazette

gazzosa *f* fizzy drink

GB *abbr* (= *Gran Bretagna*) GB (= Great Britain)

G.d.F. *abbr* (= *Guardia di Finanza*) Customs and Excise

gel *m inv* gel

gelare <1b> 1 *v/t* freeze 2 *v/i e* *gelarsi* freeze; *mi si è gelato il sangue* my blood ran cold

gelata *f* frost

gelateria *f* ice-cream parlo(u)r

gelatina *f* gelatine; *~ di frutta* fruit jelly

gelato 1 *agg* frozen 2 *m* ice cream; *~ alla vaniglia* vanilla ice cream; *~ di fragola* strawberry ice cream

gelido freezing

gelo *m* (*brina*) frost; *fig* chill

gelosia *f* jealousy

geloso jealous (*di* of)

gelso *m* mulberry (tree)

gelsomino *m* jasmine

gemellaggio *m* twinning

gemello 1 *agg* twin 2 *m di camicia* cuff link 3 *m*, *-a f* twin; ASTR *Gemelli pl* Gemini

gemere <3a> groan

gemito *m* groan

gemma *f* (*pietra preziosa*) gem, jewel; BOT bud; *fig* gem

gene *m* BIO gene

genealogia *f* genealogy

genealogico (*pl* -ci) genealogical; *albero m ~* family tree

generale 1 *agg* general; **in ~** in general **2** *m* MIL general

generalità *f inv* general nature; **le ~** *pl* personal details

generalizzare <1a> generalize

generalmente generally

generare <1l & b> (*dar vita a*) give birth to; (*causare*) generate, create; *sospetti* arouse; *elettricità, calore* generate

generatore *m* EL generator

generazione *f* generation

genere *m* (*tipo, specie*) kind; BIO genus; GRAM gender; **in ~** generally; **unico nel suo ~** unique; **-i** *pl* **alimentari** foodstuffs; **-i** *pl* **di consumo** consumer goods; **~ umano** mankind, humanity

generico (*pl* -ci) generic

genero *m* son-in-law

generosità *f* generosity

generoso generous (**con** to)

genesi *f* genesis

genetico (*pl* -ci) genetic; **ingegneria** *f* **-a** genetic engineering

gengiva *f* gum

geniale ingenious; *idea* brilliant

genialità *f* genius; (*ingegnosità*) ingeniousness

genio *m* (*pl* -ni) genius; (*inclinazione*) talent; **andare a ~** be to one's liking; **lampo** *m* **di ~** brainwave

genitali *mpl* genitals

genitori *mpl* parents

gennaio *m* January

genocidio *m* genocide

Genova Genoa

genovese *m/agg* Genoese

gentaglia *f* scum

gente *f* people *pl*; **quanta ~ !** what a crowd!; *iron* **~ bene** upper-crust

gentile kind; *nelle lettere* **~ signora** Dear Madam

gentilezza *f* kindness

gentiluomo (*pl* -uomini) *m* gentleman

genuino genuine; *prodotto alimentare* traditionally made; *risata* spontaneous

genziana *f* gentian

geografia *f* geography; **~ economica** economic geography

geografico (*pl* -ci) geographic

geologia *f* geology

geologico (*pl* -ci) geological

geologo *m* (*pl* -gi), **-a** *f* geologist

geometra *m/f* surveyor

geometria *f* geometry

geometrico (*pl* -ci) geometric(al)

geranio *m* (*pl* -ni) geranium

gerarchia *f* hierarchy

gerarchico (*pl* -ci) hierarchical; **per via -a** through the proper channels

gerente *m/f* manager

gergo *m* (*pl* -ghi) slang; *di una professione* jargon

geriatrico (*pl* -ci) geriatric; **istituto** *m* **~** old people's home

Germania *f* Germany

germe *m* germ; *fig* (*principio*) seeds *pl*; **in ~** in embryo

germinare <1l & b> germinate

germogliare <1g & c> sprout

germoglio *m* (*pl* -gli) shoot

geroglifico *m* (*pl* -ci) hieroglyph

gerundio *m* (*pl* -di) gerund

gesso *m* MIN gypsum; MED, *scultura* plaster cast; *per scrivere* chalk

gesticolare <1m> gesticulate

gestione *f* management

gestire <4d> manage

gesto *m* con il braccio, la mano gesture; *con la testa* nod

gestore *m* manager

Gesù *m* Jesus; **~ bambino** baby Jesus

gettare <1b> throw; *fondamenta* lay; *grido* give, let out; **~ fuori** throw out; **~ via** throw away

gettarsi throw o.s.; *di fiume* flow, empty (**in** into)

getto *m* jet; **di ~** in one go; **a ~ continuo** continuously

gettone *m* token; *per giochi* counter; *per giochi d'azzardo* chip; **~ (telefonico)** (telephone) token; **~ di presenza** (*indennità*) attendance fee; **telefono** *m* **a ~** phone taking tokens

ghetto *m* ghetto

ghiacciaio *m* (*pl* -ai) glacier

ghiacciare <1f> *v/t & v/i* freeze

ghiacciato *lago, stagno* frozen; *bibita*

ice-cold; **tè** *m* ~ iced tea

ghiaccio *m* (*pl* -cci) ice; *sulla strada* black ice

ghiacciolo *m* icicle; (*gelato*) ice lolly

ghiaia *f* gravel

ghianda *f* acorn

ghiandola *f* gland

ghigliottina *f* guillotine

ghignare <1a> sneer

ghigno *m* sneer

ghiotto *persona* greedy; *fig: di notizie ecc* avid (**di** for); (*appetitoso*) appetizing

ghiottoneria *f difetto* gluttony; *cibo* delicacy

ghirigoro *m* doodle

ghirlanda *f* garland

ghiro *m* dormouse; **dormire come un** ~ sleep like a log

ghisa *f* cast iron

già already; (*ex*) formerly; **~!** of course!

giacca *f* (*pl* -cche) jacket; *di abito maschile* jacket; **~ a vento** windproof jacket, windcheater; **~ di pelle** leather jacket

giacché since

giacenza *f* (*pl* -ze) (*merce per la vendita*) stock; (*merce invenduta*) unsold goods *pl*; *periodo* stock time; **~ di cassa** cash in *or* on hand; **-e** *pl di magazzino* stock in hand

giacere <2k> lie

giacimento *m* MIN deposit

giacinto *m* hyacinth

giada *f* jade

giaggiolo *m* iris

giaguaro *m* jaguar

giallo 1 *agg* yellow; *libro m* **~**, *film m* **~** thriller **2** *m* yellow; (*libro*, *film*) thriller

Giappone *m* Japan

giapponese *agg*, *m/f* Japanese

giardinaggio *m* gardening

giardiniera *f donna* gardener; *mobile* plant stand; GASTR (mixed) pickles

giardiniere *m* gardener

giardino *m* garden; **~ botanico** botanical gardens *pl*; **~ d'infanzia** kindergarten; **~ pubblico** park

giarrettiera *f* garter

giavellotto *m* javelin

gigante 1 *agg* gigantic, giant *attr* **2** *m* giant

gigantesco (*pl* -chi) gigantic

giglio *m* (*pl* -gli) lily

gilè *m inv* waistcoat, *Am* vest

gin *m inv* gin

ginecologo *m* (*pl* -gi), **-a** *f* gyn(a)ecologist

ginepro *m* juniper

ginestra *f* broom

gingillarsi <1a> fiddle; (*perder tempo*) fool around

gingillo *m* plaything; (*ninnolo*) knick-knack

ginnastica *f* exercises *pl*; *disciplina sportiva* gymnastics; *in palestra* P.E., physical education; **~ presciistica** warm-up exercises (for skiers); **una ~ mentale** a mental exercise

ginocchio *m* (*pl* -cchi *e le* -cchia) knee; **stare in** ~ be on one's knees, be kneeling

giocare <1o> **1** *v/i* play; *d'azzardo*, *in Borsa* gamble; (*scommettere*) bet; **~ a tennis**, *flipper* play; **~ d'astuzia** use cunning **2** *v/t* play; (*ingannare*) trick

giocarsi (*perdere al gioco*) gamble away; (*beffarsi*) make fun; *carriera* destroy, throw away

giocatore *m*, **-trice** *f* player; *d'azzardo* gambler

giocattolo *m* toy

gioco *m* (*pl* -chi) game; **il** ~ gambling; **~ d'azzardo** game of chance; **~ da bambini** child's play; **~ di prestigio** conjuring trick; **~ elettronico** computer game; **Giochi Olimpici** Olympic Games; **l'ho detto per** ~ **!** I was joking!

giocoliere *m* juggler

gioia *f* joy; (*gioiello*) jewel; *fig* **darsi alla pazza** ~ go wild (with excitement)

gioielleria *f* jeweller's (shop), *Am* jewelry store

gioielliere *m*, **-a** *f* jeweller, *Am* jeweler

gioiello *m* jewel

gioire <4d> rejoice (**di** in)

giornalaio *m* (*pl* -ai), **-a** *f* newsagent

giornale m (news)paper; (*rivista*) magazine; (*registro*) journal; **~ radio** news (bulletin); **~ scandalistico testata** tabloid; *stampa in genere* gutter press

giornaliero 1 agg day; **abbonamento** m ~ day pass; **spese** fpl **-e** day-to-day expenses **2** m day labo(u)rer

giornalino m per ragazzi comic; ~ **aziendale** inhouse newspaper, staff magazine

giornalismo m journalism

giornalista m/f (mpl -sti) journalist, reporter

giornalistico (pl -ci) attività, esperienza journalistic; *agenzia, servizio* news attr

giornalmente daily

giornata f day; ~ (**lavorativa**) **di 8 ore** 8-hour day; **lo finiremo in** ~ we'll finish it today or by the end of the day; **vivere alla** ~ live from day to day

giorno m day; ~ **di arrivo / partenza** arrival / departure date; ~ **di paga** payday; ~ **feriale** weekday, working day; ~ **festivo** (public) holiday; **illuminato a** ~ floodlit; **l'altro** ~ the other day; **ogni** ~ every day; **a -i** (*fra pochi giorni*) in a few days (time); **al** ~ a day; **al** ~ **d'oggi** nowadays; **in pieno** ~ in broad daylight; **di** ~ by day

giostra f merry-go-round, Am carousel

giovane 1 agg young; (*giovanile*) youthful **2** m/f young man, youth; *ragazza* young woman, girl; **i -i** pl young people

giovanile youthful

giovanotto m young man, youth

giovare <1a> (*essere utile*) be useful (**a** to); (*far bene*) be good (**a** for)

giovarsi: ~ **di** make use of; *consigli* take

Giove m Jupiter

giovedì m inv Thursday; **di** ~ on Thursdays

gioventù f youth; (*i giovani*) young people pl

gioviale jovial, jolly

giovinezza f youth

giradischi m record player

giraffa f giraffe

giramondo m/f rolling stone, wanderer

girandola f (*fuoco d'artificio*) Catherine wheel; (*giocattolo*) windmill; (*banderuola*) weather vane

girare <1a> **1** v/t turn; *ostacolo* get round; *posto, città, negozi* go round; *mondo, paese* travel round; *film* shoot; (*mescolare*) mix; FIN endorse **2** v/i turn; *rapidamente* spin; (*andare in giro*) wander or roam around; **con un veicolo** drive around; **mi gira la testa** I feel dizzy, my head is spinning

girarrosto m GASTR spit

girasole m sunflower

girata f turn; (*passeggiata a piedi*) walk, stroll; *in macchina* drive; FIN endorsement; ~ **in bianco** blank endorsement

giravolta f turn; AUTO spin; *fig* U-turn

girevole revolving

girino m tadpole

giro m turn; (*circolo*) circle; (*percorso abituale*) round; (*deviazione*) detour; (*passeggiata a piedi*) walk, stroll; *in macchina* drive; *in bicicletta* ride; *di pista* lap; *di motore* rev(olution); (*viaggio*) tour; ~ **d'affari** turnover; ~ **di capitali** circulation of capital; ~ **turistico della città** city sightseeing tour; **fare il** ~ **dei negozi** go round the shops; **nel** ~ **di una settimana** within a week; **senza tanti -i di parole** without beating about the bush so much; ~ **di prova** test drive; **essere in** ~ (*da qualche parte*) be around (somewhere); (*fuori*) be out; **mettere in** ~ spread; *fig* **prendere in** ~ **qu** pull s.o.'s leg; **a** ~ **di posta** by return of post

girocollo m inv: **maglione** m **a** ~ crewneck (sweater)

gironzolare <1m> hang around; ~ **per negozi** wander about the shops

girovagare <1m, c & e> wander about

girovago (*pl* -ghi) **1** *agg* gente nomadic **2** *m* wanderer; (*ambulante*) itinerant

gita *f* trip, excursion; **andare in ~** go on a trip *or* excursion; **~ domenicale** Sunday outing; **~ in bicicletta** bike ride

gitano *m*, **-a** *f* gypsy

gitante *m*/*f* (day) tripper

giù down; (*sotto*) below; (*da basso*) downstairs; **andar ~** go down; *fig* **non mi va** it sticks in my throat; *fig* **essere ~** be down *or* depressed; *di salute* be run down; **mandar ~** swallow (*anche fig*); **un po' più in ~** a bit lower down; **su e ~** up and down; **da Roma in ~** south of Rome

giubbotto *m* sports jacket; **~ di salvataggio** life jacket

giudicare <1l & d> **1** *v*/*t* judge; (*considerare*) consider, judge; **~ male qu** misjudge s.o.; **lo hanno giudicato colpevole** he has been found guilty. **2** *v*/*i* judge

giudice *m* judge; **~ istruttore** examining magistrate; **~ di gara** referee

giudiziario (*pl* -ri) judicial; **vendita *f* -a** sale by order of the court

giudizio *m* (*pl* -zi) judg(e)ment; (*senno*) wisdom; DIR (*causa*) trial; (*sentenza*) verdict; **a mio ~** in my opinion; **~ civile** civil action, lawsuit; **mettere ~** turn over a new leaf

giudizioso sensible

giugno *m* June

giunco *m* (*pl* -chi) reed

giungere <3d> **1** *v*/*t*: **le mani** clasp one's hands **2** *v*/*i* arrive (**a** in, at), reach (**a** sth); **~ a Roma / alla stazione** arrive in Rome / at the station, reach Rome / the station; *fig* **~ in porto** reach one's goal; **questa mi giunge nuova** it's news to me

giungla *f* jungle

giunta *f* addition; POL junta; **~ comunale** town council; **per ~** in addition, moreover

giunto *pp* → **giungere**

giuntura *f* ANAT joint

giuramento *m* oath; **falso ~** perjury; **fare un ~** swear an oath; **prestare ~** take the oath

giurare <1a> swear

giurato 1 *agg* sworn **2** *m* member of the jury

giuria *f* jury

giuridico (*pl* -ci) legal

giurisdizione *f* jurisdiction

giurisprudenza *f* jurisprudence

giurista *m*/*f* (*mpl* -sti) jurist

giustezza *f* accuracy; *di argomentazione* soundness; TIP justification

giustificare <1m & d> justify

giustificazione *f* justification

giustizia *f* justice; **fare ~ sommaria** administer summary justice

giusto 1 *agg* just, fair; (*adatto*) right, appropriate; (*esatto*) correct, right, exact **2** *avv* correctly; *mirare* accurately; (*proprio, per l'appunto*) just; **~!** that's right! **3** *m* (*uomo giusto*) just man; **pretendo solo il ~** I just want what is rightfully mine

glaciale glacial, icy

gladiolo *m* gladiolus

glassa *f* GASTR icing

gli 1 *art mpl* the; **avere gli occhi azzurri** have blue eyes **2** *pron* (*a lui*) (to) him; (*a esso*) (to) it; (*a loro*) (to) them; **dagli i libri** give him / them the books, give the books to him / them

glicemia *f* glyc(a)emia

glicerina *f* glycerine

glicine *m* wisteria

glie-: **~-la, ~-lo, ~-li, ~-le, ~-ne** = *pron* gli *or* le with *pron* la, lo, li, le, ne

globale global

globo *m* globe; **~ oculare** eyeball; **~ terrestre** globe

globulo *m* globule; MED corpuscle; **~ rosso / bianco** red / white blood cell

gloria *f* glory

glorificare <1m & d> glorify

glorioso glorious

glossa *f* gloss

glossario *m* (*pl* -ri) glossary

glucosio *m* glucose

gnocchi *mpl* (*di patate*) gnocchi (*small potato dumplings*)

gnorri *m F*: **fare lo ~** act dumb F

goal *m inv* SP goal

gobba *f* hump

gobbo 1 *agg* hunchbacked **2** *m* hunchback

goccia *f* (*pl* -cce) drop; **a ~ a ~** little by little

gocciolare <1l> drip

gocciolio *m* (*pl* -ii) drip

godere <2a> **1** *v/t* enjoy; **godersela** enjoy o.s. **2** *v/i* (*rallegrarsi*) be delighted (*di* at)

godimento *m* enjoyment

goffo awkward, clumsy

gol *m inv* SP goal

gola *f* throat; (*ingordigia*) greed(iness), gluttony; GEOG gorge; **mal** *m* **di ~** sore throat; **far ~ a** tempt

golf *m inv* golf; (*cardigan*) cardigan; (*maglione*) sweater; **giocatore** *m* **di ~** golf player, golfer

golfista *m/f* golfer

golfo *m* gulf

golosità *f* (*ghiottoneria*) greed(iness), gluttony; (*leccornia*) delicacy

goloso greedy; **essere ~ di dolci** have a sweet tooth

golpe *m inv* coup

gomito *m* elbow; **curva** *f* **a ~** sharp bend; *fig* **alzare il ~** hit the bottle

gomitolo *m* ball (of wool)

gomma *f* rubber; *per cancellare* eraser; (*pneumatico*) tyre, *Am* tire; **~ da masticare** (chewing) gum; AUTO **~ di scorta** spare tyre (*Am* tire); **avere una ~ a terra** have a flat tyre (*Am* tire)

gommapiuma *f* foam rubber

gommato *carta* gummed; *tessuto* rubberized

gommista *m* (*pl* -i) tyre (*Am* tire) specialist

gommone *m* rubber dinghy

gondola *f* gondola

gondoliere *m* gondolier

gonfiare <1k> **1** *v/t con aria* inflate; *le guance* puff out; *fig* (*esagerare*) exaggerate, magnify **2** *v/i e* **gonfiarsi** swell up; *fig* puff up

gonfio (*pl* -fi) swollen; *pneumatico* inflated; *stomaco* bloated; *fig* puffed up (**di** with); *fig* **a -e vele** splendidly

gonfiore *m* swelling

gonna *f* skirt; **~ a pieghe** pleated skirt; **~ pantalone** culottes *pl*

gorgo *m* (*pl* -ghi) whirlpool

gorgogliare <1g> *di stomaco* rumble; *dell'acqua* gurgle

gorilla *m inv* gorilla; F (*guardia del corpo*) bodyguard, gorilla F

gotico (*pl* -ci) *m/agg* Gothic

gotta *f* MED gout

governante 1 *f* housekeeper **2** *m* ruler

governare <1b> POL govern, rule; MAR steer

governativo government *attr*; *scuola* state *attr*

governatore *m* governor

governo *m* government; MAR steering; **~ di coalizione** coalition government; **~ di minoranza** minority government

gozzo *m* MED goitre, *Am* goiter

gozzovigliare <1g> make merry

gracchiare <1k> *di corvo* caw; *di rane* croak; *di persona* squawk

gracidare <1l> croak

gracile (*debole*) delicate

gradasso *m* boaster

gradazione *f* gradation; (*sfumatura*) shade; **~ alcolica** alcohol(ic) content

gradevole pleasant, agreeable

gradimento *m* liking

gradinata *f* flight of steps; *stadio* stand; *a teatro* gallery, balcony

gradino *m* step

gradire <4d> like; (*desiderare*) wish; **gradirei sapere** I would like to know; **gradisce un po' di vino?** would you like some wine?

gradito pleasant; (*bene accetto*) welcome

grado[1] *m* degree; *in una gerarchia*, MIL rank; **30 -i all'ombra** 30 degrees in the shade; **in ~ di lavorare** capable of working, fit for work; **essere in ~ di** be in a position to; **per -i** by degrees

grado[2] *m*: **di buon ~** willingly

graduale gradual

graduare <1l> graduate

graduatoria f list

graduazione f graduation

graffa f TIP brace

graffiare <1k> scratch

graffio m (pl -ffi) scratch

graffiti mpl graffiti

grafia f (hand)writing

grafica f graphics pl

grafico (pl -ci) **1** agg graphic **2** m (diagramma) graph; (disegnatore) graphic artist

grafite f graphite

grafologia f handwriting analysis

grammatica f grammar

grammaticale grammatical

grammo m gram(me)

gran → **grande**

grana 1 f grain; F (seccatura) trouble; F soldi dough F, cash; F **piantare una ~** stir up trouble; F **pieni di ~** rolling in money F **2** m inv cheese similar to Parmesan

granaio m (pl -ai) barn

granata f MIL grenade; BOT pomegranate

Gran Bretagna f Great Britain

granchio m (pl -chi) crab; fig blunder; fig **prendere un ~** make a blunder

grandangolare m FOT wide-angle lens

grande big, large; (alto) big, tall; (largo) wide; fig (intenso, notevole) great; (adulto) grown-up, big; (vecchio) old; FERR **~ velocità** high speed; **non è un gran che** it's nothing special

grandezza f (dimensione) size; (larghezza) width; (ampiezza) breadth; (altezza) height; fig (eccellenza) greatness; (grandiosità) grandeur

grandinare <1l> hail

grandinata f hailstorm

grandine f hail

grandioso grand

granduca m (pl -chi) grand duke

granducato m grand duchy

granduchessa f grand duchess

granello m grain; **~ di pepe** peppercorn; **~ di polvere** speck of dust; **~ di sabbia** grain of sand

granita f type of ice made of frozen crystals of coffee or fruit syrup

granito m granite

grano m (chicco) grain; (frumento) wheat; fig grain, ounce

granturco m maize, corn

grappa f grappa, brandy made from the remains of the grapes used in wine-making

grappolo m bunch

grassetto m TIP bold (type)

grasso 1 agg fat; (unto) greasy; cibo fatty **2** m fat; di bue, pecora suet; **macchia f di ~** grease stain; **~ lubrificante** grease; **privo di -i** fat-free

grassoccio (pl -cci) plump

grata f grating

gratella f, **graticola** f GASTR grill

gratifica f bonus

gratin m: **al ~** au gratin

gratinato → **al gratin**

gratis free (of charge)

gratitudine f gratitude

grato grateful; (gradito) welcome; **vi sarei grato se …** I would be grateful if …, I would appreciate it if …

grattacapo m problem, headache F

grattacielo m skyscraper

grattare <1a> scratch; (raschiare) scrape; (grattugiare) grate; F swipe F, pinch F

grattugia f (pl -ge) grater

grattugiare <1f> grate; **pane m grattugiato** breadcrumbs pl

gratuito free (of charge); (infondato) gratuitous

gravare <1a> **1** v/t burden **2** v/i weigh (su on)

grave (pesante) heavy; (serio) serious; (difficile) hard

gravidanza f pregnancy

gravità f seriousness, gravity; FIS (forza f di) ~ (force of) gravity

gravoso onerous

grazia f grace; (gentilezza) favo(u)r; REL grace; DIR pardon; **in ~ di** thanks to; **con ~** gracefully; **colpo m di ~** coup de grâce

graziare <1g> pardon

G

grazie *int* thank you, thanks; *tante ~* thank you so much; *~ a* thanks to; *~ a Dio!* thank goodness!

grazioso charming; (*carino*) pretty

Grecia *f* Greece

greco (*pl* -ci) **1** *agg* Greek **2** *m*, **-a** *f* Greek

gregge *m* (*pl* le -ggi) flock

greggio (*pl* -ggi) **1** *agg* (*non lavorato*) raw, crude **2** *m* crude (*petroleum*)

grembiule *m* apron

grembo *m* lap; (*materno*) womb; *fig* bosom

gremito crowded

gretto (*avaro*) mean; (*di mente ristretta*) narrow-minded

gridare <1a> **1** *v/t* shout, yell; *~ aiuto* shout for help **2** *v/i* shout, yell; (*strillare*) scream

grido *m* (*pl gen* le -da) shout, cry

grigio (*pl* -gi) grey, *Am* gray; *fig* (*triste*) sad; (*scialbo*) dull, dreary

grigiore *m* greyness, *Am* grayness; *fig* (*monotonia*) dullness, dreariness

griglia *f* (*grata*) grating; GASTR grill; *alla ~* grilled

grilletto *m* trigger

grillo *m* cricket; *fig* (*capriccio*) fancy, whim

grimaldello *m* device for picking locks

grinfie *fpl fig* clutches

grinta *f* grit; *fig* determination

grinza *f* di stoffa crease

grinzoso *viso* wrinkled; (*spiegazzato*) creased

grissino *m* bread stick

grondaia *f* gutter

grondare <1a> **1** *v/i* (*colare*) pour; (*gocciolare*) drip; *~ di sudore* be dripping with sweat **2** *v/t* drip with

groppa *f* back

groppo *m*: *avere un ~ alla gola* have a lump in one's throat

grossezza *f* (*dimensione*) size; (*spessore*) thickness; (*l'essere grosso*) largeness

grossista *m/f* (*mpl* -i) wholesaler

grosso 1 *agg* big, large; (*spesso*) thick; *mare* rough; *sale, ghiaia* coarse; *F pezzo m ~* big shot F; *questa è -a!* this is too much!; *sbagliarsi di ~* make a big mistake; *farla -a* make a fine mess **2** *m* bulk

grossolano coarse; *errore* serious

grossomodo roughly

grotta *f* cave; *artificiale* grotto

grottesco (*pl* -chi) grotesque

groviglio *m* (*pl* -gli) tangle; *fig* muddle

gru *f inv* crane

gruccia *f* (*pl* -cce) crutch; *per vestiti* hanger

grumo *m* clot; *di farina* lump

gruppo *m* group; *~ sanguigno* blood group; *~ di lavoro* working group; *a -i* in groups

guadagnare <1a> earn; (*ottenere*) gain

guadagno *m* gain; (*profitto*) profit; (*entrate*) earnings *pl*; *margine m di ~* profit margin

guaina *f* sheath; (*busto*) corset, girdle

guaio *m* (*pl* -ai) trouble; (*danno*) damage; *-ai a te se lo fai!* woe betide you if you do!; *essere nei -ai* be in trouble

guancia *f* (*pl* -ce) cheek

guanciale *m* pillow

guanto *m* glove

guantone *m*: *~ da boxe* boxing glove

guardaboschi *m inv* forest ranger

guardacaccia *m inv* gamekeeper

guardacoste *m inv* MAR coastguard

guardalinee *m inv* SP assistant referee, linesman

guardamacchine *m* car park (*Am* parking lot) attendant

guardare <1a> **1** *v/t* look at; (*osservare, stare a vedere*) watch; (*custodire*) watch, look after; (*esaminare*) check **2** *v/i* look; (*controllare*) check; *di finestra* overlook (*su* sth); *di porta* lead (*su* to); *~ a sud* face south

guardarsi look at o.s.; *~ da* beware of; (*astenersi*) refrain from

guardaroba *m inv* cloakroom, *Am* checkroom; *armadio* wardrobe

guardarobiere *m*, **-a** *f* cloakroom attendant

guardia f guard; ~ **forestale** forest ranger; ~ **di finanza** Customs and Excise officer; ~ **di pubblica sicurezza** policeman; ~ **del corpo** bodyguard; ~ **medica, medico** m **di** ~ doctor on duty; **fare la** ~ keep guard; **stare in** ~ be on one's guard

guardiano m **-a** f (custode) warden; (portiere) caretaker; (guardia) guard; di parco keeper; ~ **notturno** night watchman

guardone m voyeur

guardrail m inv guardrail

guarigione f recovery; **in via di** ~ on the mend

guarire <4d> **1** v/t cure **2** v/i recover; di ferita heal

guarnire <4d> decorate; abiti trim; GASTR garnish

guarnizione f (abbellimento) trimming; GASTR garnish; di rubinetto washer; AUTO ~ **del freno** brake lining

guastafeste m/f inv spoilsport

guastare <1a> spoil, ruin; meccanismo break

guastarsi break down; di tempo change for the worse; di cibi go bad, spoil

guasto 1 agg broken; telefono, ascensore out of order; AUTO broken down; cibi bad, off F; dente rotten, decayed **2** m fault, failure; AUTO breakdown

guerra f war; ~ **civile** civil war; ~ **lampo** blitz; ~ **fredda** Cold War

guerrafondaio m (pl -ai) warmonger

guerriglia f guerrilla warfare

guerrigliero m, **-a** f guerrilla

gufo m owl

guida f guidance; (persona, libro) guide; AUTO driving; ~ **alpina** mountain guide; ~ **telefonica** phone book; ~ **turistica** tourist guide; AUTO ~ **a destra / a sinistra** right-hand / left-hand drive

guidare <1a> guide; AUTO drive

guidatore m, **-trice** f driver

guinzaglio m (pl -gli) lead, leash

guizzare <1a> dart

guscio m (pl -sci) shell

gustare <1a> taste; fig enjoy

gusto m taste; (sapore) flavo(u)r; fig (piacere) pleasure; **buon / cattivo** ~ good / bad taste; **senza** ~ tasteless

gustoso tasty; fig delightful

H

h abbr (= **ora**) h (= hour)

ha abbr (= **ettaro**) ha (= hectare)

ha, hai, hanno → **avere**

habitat m inv BIO habitat

habitué m/f inv regular customer

hacker m/f INFOR inv hacker

hall f inv foyer

hamburger m inv hamburger

handicap m inv handicap

handicappato 1 agg disabled, handicapped **2** m, **-a** f disabled or handicapped person

hard disk m inv INFOR hard disk

hardware m inv INFOR hardware

harem m inv harem

hashish m inv hashish

henné m inv henna

herpes m inv herpes

hg abbr (= **ettogrammo**) hg (= hectogram)

hinterland m inv hinterland

hit parade f inv hit parade

hl abbr (= **ettolitro**) hl (= hectolitre)

hm abbr (= **ettometro**) hm (= hectometre)

ho → **avere**

hobby *m inv* hobby
hockey *m inv* hockey; **~ su ghiaccio** ice hockey
holding *f inv* holding

hostess *f inv* hostess; **~ di terra** (*guida*) member of ground staff
hotel *m inv* hotel
hot dog *m inv* hot dog

I

i *art mpl* the
iberico (*pl* -ci) Iberian
iceberg *m inv* iceberg
icona *f* icon
iconografia *f* iconography
Iddio *m* God
idea *f* idea; (*opinione*) opinion; **~ fissa** obsession, idée fixe; **cambiare ~** change one's mind; **non avere la minima ~ di qc** not have the slightest idea about sth; **scambio m di -e** exchange of views; **neanche per ~!** of course not!
ideale *m/agg* ideal
idealizzare <1a> idealize
ideare <1b> *scherzo, scusa* think up; *metodo, oggetto nuovo* invent; *piano, progetto* devise
ideatore *m*, **-trice** *f* originator; *di metodo, oggetto nuovo* inventor
idem ditto
identico (*pl* -ci) identical
identificare <1n & d> identify
identificazione *f* identification
identikit® *m inv* Identikit
identità *f inv* identity
ideologia *f* ideology
ideologico (*pl* -ci) ideological
idioma *m* (*pl* -i) idiom
idiomatico (*pl* -ci) idiomatic
idiota 1 *agg* idiotic, stupid **2** *m/f* (*mpl* -i) idiot, fool
idiozia *f* stupidity, idiocy; (*assurdità*) nonsense; **un'~** a stupid *or* idiotic thing to do / say
idolo *m* idol
idoneità *f* suitability; *qualifica* qualification

idoneo suitable (*a* for)
idrante *m* hydrant
idratante *della pelle* moisturizing
idratare <1a> *la pelle* moisturize
idraulico 1 *agg* hydraulic; **impianto m ~** plumbing **2** *m* (*pl* -ci) plumber
idrico water *attr*
idromassaggio *m* Jacuzzi®, whirlpool bath
idroelettrico hydroelectric
idrofilo: cotone m ~ cotton wool, *Am* absorbent cotton
idrofobo ZO rabid; (*furioso*) foaming at the mouth
idrogeno *m* hydrogen
idroplano *m* hydroplane
iena *f* hyena
ieri yesterday; **~ l'altro, l'altro ~** the day before yesterday; **~ mattina** yesterday morning
igiene *f* hygiene; **~ del corpo** personal hygiene; **ufficio m d'~** public health office
igienico (*pl* -ci) hygienic; **carta f -a** toilet paper
ignaro unaware (*di* of)
ignorante (*non informato*) ignorant; (*incolto*) uneducated; (*maleducato*) rude
ignoranza *f* ignorance
ignorare <1a> (*non considerare*) ignore; (*non sapere*) not know; **lo ignoro** I don't know
ignoto unknown
il *art m sg* the; **~ signor Conte** Mr Conte; **~ martedì** on Tuesdays; **3000 lire ~ chilo** 3000 lire a kilo; **mi piace il caffè** I like coffee

illecito illicit

illegale illegal

illegalità f illegality

illeggibile illegible

illegittimo illegitimate

illeso unhurt

illimitato unlimited

ill.mo *abbr* (= ***illustrissimo***) *formal style of address in correspondence*

illogico (*pl* -ci) illogical

illudere <3q> deceive

illudersi delude o.s.

illuminare <1m> light up; *fig* enlighten

illuminazione f lighting; *fig* flash of inspiration; ~ **stradale** street lighting

illusione f illusion

illuso 1 *pp* → ***illudere*** 2 *m/f* (*sognatore*) dreamer

illusorio (*pl* -ri) illusory

illustrare <1a> illustrate

illustratore *m*, **-trice** *f* illustrator

illustrazione f illustration

illustre illustrious

imballaggio *m* (*pl* -ggi) *operazione* packing; (*involucro*) package

imballare <1a> pack; AUTO ~ **il motore** race the engine

imballo *m* → ***imballaggio***

imbalsamare <1a> embalm; *animale* stuff

imbambolato *occhi, sguardo* blank; *dal sonno* bleary-eyed; **non star lí fermo ~!** don't stand there gawping!

imbarazzante embarrassing

imbarazzare <1a> embarrass

imbarazzato embarrassed

imbarazzo *m* embarrassment; (*disturbo*) trouble; **non avere che l'~ della scelta** be spoilt for choice; ~ **di stomaco** upset stomach; **mettere in ~ qu** embarrass s.o.

imbarcadero *m* landing stage

imbarcare <1d> embark; *carico* load

imbarcarsi go on board, embark; ~ **in un'impresa** embark on an undertaking

imbarcazione f boat; ~ **da diporto** pleasure boat

imbarco *m* (*pl* -chi) *di passeggeri* boarding, embarkation; *di carico* loading; (*banchina*) landing stage

imbattersi <3a> : ~ **in qu** bump into s.o.

imbattibile unbeatable

imbecille **1** *agg* idiotic, stupid **2** *m/f* imbecile, fool

imbiancare <1d> **1** *v/t* whiten; *con pitture* paint; *tessuti* bleach **2** *v/i e* **imbiancarsi** go white

imbianchino *m* (house) painter

imboccare <1d> *persona* feed; *fig* prompt; ~ **una strada** turn into a road

imboccatura f (*apertura*) opening; (*ingresso*) entrance; MUS mouthpiece

imbocco *m* entrance

imboscata f ambush

imbottigliamento *m* bottling; AUTO traffic jam

imbottigliare <1g> bottle; *di veicoli* hold up; **sono rimasto imbottigliato nel traffico** I was stuck in a traffic jam

imbottire <4d> stuff; *giacca* pad; *fig* (*riempire*) cram, stuff

imbottito stuffed; *panino* filled

imbottitura f stuffing; *di giacca* padding

imbranato clumsy

imbrattare <1a> soil; (*macchiare*) stain

imbrattatele *m/f inv* dauber

imbrogliare <1g & c> **1** *v/t* (*raggirare*) take in; (*truffare*) cheat, swindle; *fig* confuse **2** *v/i* cheat

imbroglio *m* (*pl* -gli) (*truffa*) trick; *fig* (*pasticcio*) mess

imbroglione *m*, **-a** *f* cheat, swindler

imbronciato sulky

imbrunire <4d> get dark

imbruttire <4d> **1** *v/t* make ugly **2** *v/i* become ugly

imbucare <1d> *posta* post, *Am* mail

imburrare <1a> butter

imbuto *m* funnel

imitare <1a or 1l> imitate

imitazione f imitation

immagazzinare <1a> store

immaginare <1m> imagine; (*supporre*) suppose; **s'immagini!** not at all!

immaginario (*pl* -ri) imaginary

immaginazione *f* imagination

immagine *f* image

immancabile *cortesia, sorriso* unfailing; *persona* ever present; *macchina fotografica* inevitable

immangiabile inedible

immatricolare <1n> register

immatricolarsi enrol, *Am* enroll; *all'università* matriculate, enrol

immatricolazione *f* registration; *all'università* matriculation, enrol(l)ment

immaturità *f* immaturity

immaturo *persona* immature; (*precoce*) premature; *frutto* unripe

immedesimarsi <1n> identify (**in** with)

immediatamente immediately

immediato immediate; (*pronto*) prompt

immenso immense

immergere <3uu> immerse, dip; (*lasciare immerso*) soak

immergersi plunge; *di subacqueo, sottomarino* dive; *fig* immerse o.s. (**in** in)

immeritato undeserved

immersione *f* immersion; *di subacqueo, sottomarino* dive

immerso 1 *pp* → **immergere 2** *agg* immersed

immettere <3ee> introduce (**in** into); INFOR *dati* enter; (*portare*) lead (**in** into)

immettersi: ~ **in** get into

immigrante *m/f* immigrant

immigrare <1a> immigrate

immigrato *m*, **-a** *f* immigrant

immigrazione *f* immigration; (*immigrati*) immigrants *pl*; FIN inflow

imminente imminent; *pericolo* impending; *pubblicazione* forthcoming

imminenza *f* imminence

immischiare <1k> involve

immischiarsi meddle (**in** with), interfere (**in** in)

immissione *f* introduction; *di manodopera* intake; INFOR *di dati* entry

immobile 1 *agg* motionless, still **2** *mpl*: **-i** real estate *sg*

immobiliare: **agente** *m/f* ~ estate agent, *Am* realtor; **società** *f* ~ *di compravendita* property company; *di costruzione* construction company

immobilismo *m* inactivity; POL opposition to progress

immobilità *f* immobility; POL, FIN inactivity

immobilizzare <1a> immobilize; FIN *capitali* tie up

immondizia *f* (*gen pl*) rubbish, refuse, *Am* trash

immorale immoral

immoralità *f* immorality

immortale immortal

immortalità *f* immortality

immune MED immune (**a** to); (*esente*) free (**da** from)

immunità *f* immunity

immunitario: **sistema** *m* ~ immune system

immunizzare <1a> immunize

immunodeficienza *f* immunodeficiency

immutabile *decisione, legge* unchangeable; *principi, tradizioni* unchanging

immutato unchanged

impacchettare <1a> (*confezionare*) wrap (up); (*mettere in pacchetti*) package

impacciare <1f> *movimenti* hamper; *persona* hinder

impacciato (*imbarazzato*) embarrassed; (*goffo*) awkward, clumsy

impaccio *m* (*pl* -cci) (*ostacolo*) hindrance; (*situazione difficile*) awkward situation; (*imbarazzo*) awkwardness

impacco *m* (*pl* -cchi) MED compress

impadronirsi <4d>: ~ **di qc** take possession of sth, seize sth; *fig* master sth

impagabile priceless

impaginare <1m> TIP paginate

impaginazione *f* pagination

impalcatura f temporanea scaffolding; fig framework, structure

impallidire <4d> di persona turn pale

impanare <1a> GASTR coat with breadcrumbs

impanato in breadcrumbs, breaded

impantanarsi <1a> get bogged down

impaperarsi <1m> falter

imparare <1a> learn (**a** to)

imparentarsi <1b>: **~ con qu** become related to s.o.

impari unequal; MAT odd

impartire <4d> give

imparziale impartial

imparzialità f impartiality

impassibile impassive

impastare <1a> mix; pane knead

impasto m GASTR dough; (mescolanza) mixture

impatto m impact

impaurire <4d> frighten

impaurirsi become frightened

impaziente impatient

impazienza f impatience

impazzata: **all'~** correre at breakneck speed; colpire wildly

impazzire <4d> go mad or crazy; **far ~ qu** drive s.o. mad or crazy

impeccabile impeccable

impedimento m hindrance; (ostacolo) obstacle; DIR impediment; **essere d'~** be a hindrance

impedire <4d> prevent; (ostruire) block, obstruct; (impacciare) hinder; **~ a qu di fare qc** prevent s.o. or keep s.o. from doing sth

impegnare <1a> (dare come pegno) pawn; (riservare) reserve, book; spazio, corsia occupy, take up; SP avversario keep under pressure; (costringere) oblige; **~ qu di lavoro** keep s.o. busy or occupied; **~ qu per contratto** bind s.o. by contract

impegnarsi (prendersi l'impegno) commit o.s., undertake (**a** to); (concentrarsi) apply o.s. (**in** to); **mi sono impegnata a farlo** I've committed myself to doing it, I've undertaken to do it

impegnativo (che richiede impegno) demanding; pranzo, serata, abito formal; (vincolante) binding

impegnato (occupato) busy; fig (politically) committed; **sono già ~** I've made other arrangements, I'm doing something else

impegno m commitment; (appuntamento) engagement; (zelo) zeal, care; COM **senza ~** with no commitment

impensabile unthinkable

impensato unexpected

imperante (dominante) prevailing

imperare <1b> rule (**su** over)

imperativo m/agg imperative

imperatore m, **-trice** f emperor; donna empress

impercettibile imperceptible

imperdonabile unforgivable

imperfetto m/agg imperfect

imperfezione f imperfection

impermeabile 1 agg waterproof **2** m raincoat

impermeabilità f impermeability

impermeabilizzare <1a> waterproof

impero m empire; (potere) rule

impersonale impersonal

impersonare <1a> personify; (interpretare) play (the part of)

impertinente impertinent

impertinenza f impertinence

imperturbabile imperturbable

imperturbabilità f imperturbability

imperversare <1b> rage; fig di moda be all the rage

impeto m impetus, force; (accesso) outburst; (slancio) passion, heat; **parlare con ~** speak forcefully

impetuoso impetuous

impiantare <1a> azienda, ufficio set up; congegno, apparecchiatura install; MED implant

impianto m operazione installation; (apparecchiature) plant; (sistema) system; MED implant; **~ elettrico** wiring; **~ di risalita** ski lift; **~ di riscaldamento** heating system; **~ stereo** stereo (system); **-i pl sanitari** bathroom fixtures and fittings

impiastro *m* poultice; *fig* pain in the neck

impiccare <1d> hang

impiccarsi hang o.s.

impicciare <1f> be in the way

impicciarsi: ~ *di o in qc* interfere *or* meddle in sth

impiccio *m* (*pl* -cci) (*ostacolo*) hindrance; (*seccatura*) bother; *essere d'~* be in the way; *essere in un* ~ be in trouble

impiegare <1b & e> (*usare*) use; *tempo*, *soldi* spend; (*metterci*) take; (*assumere*) employ; *ho impiegato un'ora* it took me an hour

impiegato *m*, **-a** *f* employee; ~ *di banca* bank clerk; ~ *di ruolo* permanent employee

impiego *m* (*pl* -ghi) (*uso*) use; (*occupazione*) employment; (*posto*) job; FIN investment; *domanda f d'~* job application; *offerta f d'~* job offer

impietosire <4d> move to pity

impietosirsi be moved to pity

impigliare <1g> entangle

impigliarsi get entangled

impigrire <4d> **1** *v/t* make lazy **2** *v/i e* **impigrirsi** get lazy

implacabile implacable

implicare <1l & d> (*coinvolgere*) implicate; (*comportare*) imply

implicito implicit

implorare <1c> implore

impolverato dusty, covered with *or* in dust

imponente imposing, impressive

imponibile 1 *agg* taxable **2** *m* taxable income

impopolare unpopular

impopolarità *f* unpopularity

imporre <3ll> impose; *prezzo* fix

imporsi (*farsi valere*) assert o.s.; (*avere successo*) be successful, become established; (*essere necessario*) be necessary

importante important

importanza *f* importance; *darsi* ~ give o.s. airs; *senza* ~ not important, unimportant

importare <1c> **1** *v/t* FIN, INFOR import **2** *v/i* matter, be important; (*essere necessario*) be necessary; *e a te che te ne importa?* what's it to you?; *non importa* it doesn't matter; *non gliene importa niente* he couldn't care less

importatore *m*, **-trice** *f* importer

importazione *f* import; ~ *clandestina* smuggling; *permesso m d'~* import permit

importo *m* amount

importunare <1a> (*assillare*) pester; (*disturbare*) bother

importuno troublesome; *domanda*, *osservazione* ill-timed

imposizione *f* imposition; (*tassazione*) taxation; (*tassa*) tax

impossessarsi <1b>: ~ *di* seize

impossibile impossible

impossibilità *f* impossibility

imposta[1] *f* tax; ~ *di consumo* excise duty; ~ *diretta* / *indiretta* direct / indirect tax; ~ *sul reddito* income tax; ~ *sul valore aggiunto* value added tax; ~ *sul fatturato* sales tax; *ufficio m delle -e* tax office

imposta[2] *f di finestra* shutter

impostare <1c> *lavoro* plan; *problema* set out; *lettera* post, *Am* mail

imposto *pp* → *imporre*

impostore *m* impostor

impotente powerless; (*inefficace*) ineffectual; MED impotent

impotenza *f* powerlessness; MED impotence

impraticabile *strada* impassable

impratichirsi <4d> get practice (*in* in)

imprecare <1d & b> curse, swear (*contro* at)

imprecazione *f* curse

imprecisato *numero*, *quantità* indeterminate; *motivi*, *circostanze* not clear

imprecisione *f* inaccuracy

impreciso inaccurate

impregnare <1a> impregnate; (*imbevere*) soak

impregnarsi become impregnated (*di* with)

imprenditore *m*, **-trice** *f* entrepreneur

imprenditoriale entrepreneurial

impreparato unprepared

impresa f (*iniziativa*) enterprise, undertaking; (*azienda*) business, firm; **~ familiare** family business; **piccola ~** small business; **~ di servizi pubblici** utility company

impresario m (*pl* -ri) contractor; TEA impresario

impressionabile impressionable; FOT sensitive

impressionante impressive; (*spaventoso*) frightening; (*sconvolgente*) upsetting, shocking

impressionare <1a> (*turbare*) upset, shock; (*spaventare*) frighten; (*colpire*) impress; FOT expose

impressionato FOT exposed; **~ favorevolmente** (favourably) impressed

impressione f impression; (*turbamento*) shock; (*paura*) fright; TIP printing

impresso pp → **imprimere**

imprevedibile unforeseeable; *persona* unpredictable

imprevisto 1 *agg* unexpected **2** *m* unforeseen event; **salvo imprevisti** all being well

imprigionare <1a> imprison

imprimere <3r> impress; *fig nella mente* fix firmly, imprint; *movimento* impart; TIP print

improbabile unlikely, improbable

improbabilità f unlikelihood, improbability

improduttivo unproductive

impronta f impression, mark; (*orma*) footprint; (*traccia*) track; *fig* mark; **-e** *pl* **digitali** fingerprints

improprio (*pl* -ri) improper

improvvisamente suddenly

improvvisare <1a> improvize

improvvisarsi take on the role of

improvvisata f surprise

improvvisato improvized, impromptu

improvviso sudden; (*inaspettato*) unexpected; **all'~** suddenly; (*inaspettatamente*) unexpectedly

imprudente careless; (*non saggio*)

imprudent, rash

imprudenza f carelessness; (*mancanza di saggezza*) imprudence, rashness

impugnare <1a> grasp; DIR contest

impugnatura f grip; (*manico*) handle

impulsivo impulsive

impulso m impulse

impunità f impunity

impunito unpunished

impuntarsi (*ostinarsi*) dig one's heels in

imputato m, **-a** f accused

imputazione f charge

imputridire rot

in *prp* in; *moto a luogo* to; **~ casa** at home; **è ~ Scozia** he is in Scotland; **va ~ Inghilterra** he is going to England; **~ italiano** in Italian; **~ campagna** in the country; **essere ~ viaggio** be travelling; **viaggiare ~ macchina** travel by car; **nel 1999** in 1999; **una giacca ~ pelle** a leather jacket; **~ vacanza** on holiday; **se fossi ~ te** if I were you, if I were in your place

inabile unfit (**a** for); (*disabile*) disabled

inabitabile uninhabitable

inabitato uninhabited

inaccessibile inaccessible, out of reach; *fig persona* unapproachable; *prezzi* exorbitant

inaccettabile unacceptable

inacidire <4d>, **inacidirsi** turn sour

inadatto unsuitable (**a** for), unsuited (**a** to)

inadeguato inadequate

inafferrabile elusive; (*incomprensibile*) incomprehensible

inalare <1a> inhale

inalatore m inhaler, puffer F

inalazione f inhalation

inalterabile *sentimento* unchangeable; *colore* fast; *metallo* non-tarnish

inalterato unchanged

inamidare <1m> starch

inammissibile inadmissible

inanimato inanimate; (*senza vita*) lifeless

inappellabile final, irrevocable

inappetenza f lack of appetite

inarcare <1d> *schiena* arch; *sopracciglia* raise

inaridire <4d> **1** v/t *parch* **2** v/i dry up

inaspettato unexpected

inasprimento m (*intensificazione*) worsening; *di carattere* embitterment

inasprire <4d> exacerbate, make worse; *carattere* embitter

inasprirsi get worse; *di persona* become embittered

inattaccabile unassailable

inattendibile unreliable

inatteso unexpected

inattività f inactivity

inattivo *persona, capitale* idle; *vulcano* dormant

inattuabile (*non fattibile*) impracticable; (*non realistico*) unrealistic

inaugurare <1m> *mostra* (officially) open, inaugurate; *lapide, monumento* unveil; F *oggetto nuovo* christen F

inaugurazione f *di mostra* (official) opening, inauguration; *di lapide* unveiling; F *di oggetto nuovo* christening F

inavvertenza f inadvertence

inavvertito unnoticed

incagliarsi <1g> MAR run aground

incalcolabile incalculable

incalzante *pericolo* imminent; *richieste* pressing

incalzare <1a> pursue; *fig con richieste* ply

incamminarsi <1m> set out

incandescente incandescent; *fig* heated

incantare <1a> enchant

incantarsi (*restare affascinato*) be spellbound; (*sognare a occhi aperti*) be in a daze; TEC jam

incantato *per effetto di magia* enchanted; (*trasognato*) in a daze; (*affascinato*) spellbound

incantesimo m spell

incantevole delightful, charming

incanto[1] m (*incantesimo*) spell; **come per ~** as if by magic

incanto[2] m COM auction; **mettere es-**

all'~ sell at auction, put up for auction

incapace **1** agg incapable (**di** of); (*incompetente*) incompetent **2** m/f incompetent person

incapacità f (*inabilità*) inability; (*incompetenza*) incompetence

incappare <1a>: **~ in** nebbia, difficoltà run into

incapricciarsi <1f>: **~ di qu** take a liking to s.o.

incarcerare <1m> imprison

incaricare <1m & d> (*dare istruzioni a*) instruct; **~ qu di fare qc** tell or instruct s.o. to do sth

incaricarsi: **~ di qc** (*occuparsi di*) see to sth, deal with sth

incaricato m, **-a** f (*responsabile*) person in charge; (*funzionario*) official, representative

incarico m (pl -chi) (*compito*) task, assignment; (*nomina*) appointment; **per ~ di** on behalf of

incarnare <1a> embody

incarnazione f incarnation

incartamento m file, dossier

incartare <1a> wrap (up) (in paper)

incarto m wrapping; (*incartamento*) file, dossier

incassare <1a> COM (*riscuotere*) cash; *fig colpi, insulti ecc* take

incasso m (*riscossione*) collection; (*somma incassata*) takings pl

incastonare <1a> set

incastonatura f setting

incastrare <1a> fit in; F *fig* (*far apparire colpevole*) frame F; (*mettere in una posizione difficile*) corner F

incastro m joint

incatenare <1a> chain

incavato hollow; *occhi* deep-set

incendiare <1b & k> set fire to

incendiario m (pl m -ri), **-a** f arsonist, firebug F

incendio m (pl -di) fire; **~ doloso** arson

incenerimento m incineration

incenerire <4d> reduce to ashes

inceneritore m incinerator

incenso m incense

incensurato irreproachable; DIR **es-**

sere ~ have a clean record
incentivare <1a> (*incrementare*) boost
incentivo *m* incentive
incerata *f* oilcloth
incertezza *f* uncertainty
incerto 1 *agg* uncertain **2** *m* uncertainty
incessante incessant
incetta *f:* **fare** ~ **di qc** stockpile sth
inchiesta *f* investigation; FIN ~ **di mercato** market survey; **commissione** *f* **d'**~ committee *or* board of inquiry
inchinare <1a> bow
inchinarsi bow
inchino *m* bow; *di donna* curtsy
inchiodare <1c> **1** *v/t* nail; *coperchio* nail down; *fig* **essere inchiodato in un luogo** be stuck in a place **2** *v/i* AUTO jam on the brakes
inchiostro *m* ink; ~ **di china** Indian ink
inciampare <1a> trip (**in** over); ~ **in qu** run into s.o.
incidentale (*casuale*) accidental; (*secondario*) incidental
incidente *m* (*episodio*) incident; ~ **aereo** plane crash; ~ **stradale** road accident
incidere[1] <3q> *v/i* affect (**su** sth)
incidere[2] <3q> *v/t* engrave; (*tagliare*) cut; (*registrare*) record
incidersi *fig* (*restare impresso*) be engraved (**in** on)
incinta pregnant
incirca: **all'**~ more or less
incisione *f* engraving; (*acquaforte*) etching; (*taglio*) cut; MED incision; (*registrazione*) recording
incisivo 1 *agg* incisive **2** *m* (*dente*) incisor
incitare <1l> incite
incivile uncivilized; (*villano*) rude, impolite
inclinare <1a> **1** *v/t* tilt **2** *v/i:* ~ **a** (*tendere a*) be inclined to
inclinato tilted
inclinazione *f* inclination
incline inclined (**a** to)
includere <3q> include; (*allegare*)

enclose, inclose; **incluso il servizio** service included
inclusivo inclusive
incluso 1 *pp* → **includere 2** *agg* included; (*compreso*) inclusive; (*allegato*) enclosed
incoerente (*incongruente*) inconsistent
incoerenza *f* inconsistency
incognita *f* unknown quantity
incognito *m:* **in** ~ incognito
incollare <1c> stick; *con colla liquida* glue
incollarsi stick (**a** to)
incolonnare <1a> *numeri ecc* put in a column; *persone* line up
incolore colo(u)rless
incolpare <1a> blame
incolparsi: ~ **a vicenda** blame each other
incolto uneducated; (*trascurato*) unkempt; AGR uncultivated
incolume unharmed
incolumità *f* safety
incombente *pericolo* impending
incombenza *f* task
incominciare <1f> start, begin (**a** to)
incomodare <1m & c> inconvenience
incomodarsi put o.s. out; **non si incomodi!** don't put yourself out!, please don't go to any trouble!
incomodo 1 *agg* (*inopportuno*) inconvenient; (*scomodo*) uncomfortable **2** *m* inconvenience
incompatibile incompatible; (*intollerabile*) unacceptable
incompatibilità *f* incompatibility
incompetente incompetent; **sono** ~ **in materia** I'm no expert
incompetenza *f* incompetence
incompiuto unfinished
incompleto incomplete
incomprensibile incomprehensible, impossible to understand
incomprensione *f* lack of understanding; (*malinteso*) misunderstanding
incompreso misunderstood
inconcepibile inconceivable

inconciliabile irreconcilable
inconcludente inconclusive; *persona* ineffectual
incondizionato unconditional
inconfondibile unmistakable
inconfutabile indisputable
inconsapevole (*ignaro*) unaware
inconsapevolezza *f* lack of awareness
inconscio *m/agg* unconscious
inconsistente insubstantial; *fig* (*infondato*) unfounded; (*vago*) vague
inconsistenza *f* flimsiness
inconsolabile inconsolable
inconsueto unusual
incontentabile hard to please, very demanding; (*perfezionista*) perfectionist
incontestato undisputed
incontrare <1a> **1** *v/t* meet; *difficoltà* come up against, encounter **2** *v/i e* **incontrarsi** meet (*con* s.o.)
incontrario: *all'~* the other way round; (*nel modo sbagliato*) the wrong way round
incontrastato undisputed
incontro **1** *m* meeting; ~ *di calcio* football match; POL ~ *al vertice* summit (meeting) **2** *prp*: ~ *a* towards; *andare* ~ *a qu* go and meet s.o.; *fig* meet s.o. halfway
inconveniente *m* (*svantaggio*) drawback; (*ostacolo*) hitch
incoraggiamento *m* encouragement
incoraggiante encouraging
incoraggiare <1f> encourage
incorniciare <1f> frame
incoronare <1a> crown
incoronazione *f* coronation
incorporare <1m & c> incorporate
incorreggibile incorrigible
incorrere <3o> ~ *in sanzioni* incur; *errore* make
incorruttibile incorruptible
incosciente unconscious; (*irresponsabile*) reckless
incoscienza *f* unconsciousness; (*insensatezza*) recklessness
incostante changeable; *negli affetti* fickle

incostanza *f* changeableness; *negli affetti* fickleness
incostituzionale unconstitutional
incostituzionalità *f* unconstitutionality
incredibile incredible
incredulo incredulous, disbelieving
incrementare <1a> increase
incremento *m* increase, growth; ~ *demografico* population growth
increspare <1a> *acque* ripple; *capelli* frizz; *tessuto* gather
incriminare <1m> indict
incrociare <1f> **1** *v/t* cross **2** *v/i* MAR, AVIA cruise
incrocio *m* (*pl* -ci) (*intersezione*) crossing; (*crocevia*) crossroads; *di razze animali* cross(-breed)
incrollabile indestructible; *fig* unshakeable
incubatrice *f* incubator
incubazione *f* incubation
incubo *m* nightmare
incudine *f* anvil
incurabile incurable
incurante heedless (*di* of)
incuria *f* negligence
incuriosire <4d>: ~ *qu* make s.o. curious, arouse s.o.'s curiosity
incuriosirsi become curious
incursione *f* raid; ~ *aerea* air raid
incurvare <1a> bend
incustodito unattended, unguarded; *passaggio a livello* unmanned
indaco *m/agg* indigo
indaffarato busy
indagare <1e> **1** *v/t cause, fenomeni* investigate **2** *v/i* investigate (*su, intorno a* sth)
indagine *f* (*ricerca, studio*) research; *della polizia* investigation; ~ *di mercato* market survey; ~ *demoscopica* (public) opinion poll
indebitare <1m>, **indebitarsi** get into debt
indebitato in debt
indebolimento *m* weakening
indebolire <4d> *v/t & v/i* weaken
indecente indecent
indecenza *f* (*vergogna*) disgrace,

outrage; (*mancanza di pudore*) indecency

indecisione *f* indecision; *abituale* indecisiveness

indeciso undecided; *abitualmente* indecisive

indefinito indefinite

indegno unworthy

indelebile indelible; *colore* fast

indenne *persona* uninjured; *cosa* undamaged

indennità *f inv* (*gratifica*) allowance, benefit; (*risarcimento*) compensation; ~ **di trasferta** travel allowance; ~ **parlamentare** MP's allowance

indennizzare <1a> compensate (**per** for)

indennizzo *m* (*compenso*) compensation

indescrivibile indescribable

indesiderato unwanted

indeterminato *tempo* unspecified, indefinite; *quantità* indeterminate

India *f* India

indiano 1 *agg* Indian; *in fila -a* in single file **2** *m*, *-a f* Indian

indicare <1l & d> show, indicate; *col dito* point at *or* to; (*consigliare*) suggest, recommend; (*significare*) mean

indicativo *m* GRAM indicative

indicato (*consigliabile*) advisable; (*adatto*) suitable

indicatore 1 *agg* indicative; *cartello m* ~ road sign **2** *m* indicator; (*strumento*) gauge, indicator; ~ **del livello di carburante** fuel gauge; AUTO ~ **di direzione** indicator

indicazione *f* indication; (*direttiva*) direction; (*informazione*) piece of information; MED *-i pl* directions (for use); *-i pl* **stradali** road signs

indice *m* index; ANAT index finger, forefinger; TV ~ **di ascolto** ratings *pl*

indicibile indescribable

indietreggiare <1f> draw back; *camminando all'indietro* step back; MIL retreat

indietro behind; *tornare, girarsi* back; **essere** ~ *con il lavoro* be behind; *mentalmente* be backward; *nei*

pagamenti be in arrears; *di orologio* be slow; **dare** ~ (*restituire*) give back; **tirarsi** ~ draw back; *fig* back out; **all'**~ backwards; AUTO **fare marcia** ~ reverse; *fig* back-pedal

indifeso undefended; (*inerme*) defenceless, helpless

indifferente indifferent; **lasciare qu** ~ leave s.o. cold, cut no ice with s.o.; **non** ~ appreciable, considerable; **per me è** ~ it's all the same to me

indifferenza *f* indifference

indigeno 1 *agg* native, indigenous **2** *m*, **-a** *f* native

indigestione *f* indigestion

indigesto indigestible

indignare <1a> ~ **qu** make s.o. indignant, arouse s.o.'s indignation

indignarsi get indignant (**per** about)

indignazione *f* indignation

indimenticabile unforgettable

indipendente independent (**da** of); ~ **dalla mia volontà** outside my control

indipendentemente independently; ~ **dall'età** regardless of age, whatever the age

indipendenza *f* independence

indire <3t> *conferenza, elezioni, sciopero* call; *concorso* announce

indiretto indirect

indirizzare <1a> direct; *lettera* address; (*spedire*) send

indirizzario *m* address book; *per spedizione* mailing list

indirizzo *m* address; (*direzione*) direction

indisciplina *f* lack of discipline, indiscipline

indisciplinato undisciplined

indiscreto indiscreet

indiscrezione *f* indiscretion

indiscriminato indiscriminate

indiscusso unquestioned

indiscutibile unquestionable

indispensabile 1 *agg* indispensable, essential **2** *m* essentials *pl*

indispettire <4d> irritate

indispettirsi get irritated

indispettito irritated

indisporre <3ll> irritate
indisposizione f indisposition
indisposto (*ammalato*) indisposed
indistinto indistinct, faint
indistruttibile indestructible
indivia f endive
individuale individual
individualismo m individualism
individualista m/f (mpl -i) individualist
individualità f individuality
individuo m individual
indivisibile indivisible
indiviso undivided
indizio m (pl -zi) clue; (*segno*) sign; (*sintomo*) symptom; DIR **-i** pl circumstantial evidence sg
indole f nature
indolente indolent
indolenza f indolence
indolore painless
indomani m: *l'*~ the next day
indossare <1c> (*mettersi*) put on; (*portare*) wear
indossatore m, **-trice** f model
indotto pp → **indurre**
indovinare <1a> guess; *futuro* predict
indovinato (*ben riuscito*) successful; (*ben scelto*) well chosen
indovinello m riddle
indovino m, **-a** f fortune-teller
indubbiamente undoubtedly
indugiare <1f> **1** v/t *partenza* delay **2** v/i (*tardare*) delay; (*esitare*) hesitate; (*attardarsi*) linger
indugiarsi linger
indugio m (pl -gi) delay; **senza ~** without delay
indulgente indulgent; *giudice, sentenza* lenient
indulgenza f indulgence; *di giudice, sentenza* leniency
indumento m garment, item of clothing; **gli -i** pl clothes
indurire <4d> **1** v/t harden; *fig cuore* harden; *corpo* toughen (up) **2** v/i e **indurirsi** go hard, harden
indurito hardened
indurre <3e> induce
industria f industry; (*operosità*) industriousness; ~ **automobilistica** car industry; ~ **dei servizi** service industry, services; ~ **pesante** heavy industry
industriale **1** agg industrial **2** m industrialist
industrializzare <1a> industrialize
industrializzazione f industrialization
ineccepibile irreproachable; *ragionamento* faultless
inedito unpublished; *fig* novel
inefficace ineffective
inefficacia f ineffectiveness
inefficiente inefficient
inefficienza f inefficiency
ineguagliabile (*senza rivali*) unrivalled; (*senza confronto*) incomparable, beyond compare
ineguaglianza f inequality
ineguale (*non uguale*) unequal; (*discontinuo*) uneven
inequivocabile unequivocal
inerte (*inoperoso*) idle; (*immobile*) inert, motionless; (*senza vita*) lifeless; FIS inert
inerzia f inertia; (*inattività*) inactivity; **forza** f **d'**~ force of inertia
inesattezza f inaccuracy
inesatto inaccurate
inesauribile inexhaustible
inesorabile inexorable
inesperienza f inexperience, lack of experience
inesperto inexperienced
inesplicabile inexplicable
inesplorato unexplored
inesploso unexploded
inesprimibile (*indicibile*) indescribable
inestimabile inestimable; **bene** invaluable
inetto inept
inevaso pending
inevitabile inevitable
inezia f trifle
infallibile infallible
infame **1** agg (*turpe*) infamous, foul; *spir* horrible, terrible **2** m/f P (*delatore*) grass P
infantile *letteratura, giochi* children's;

malattie childhood; *(immaturo)* childish, infantile

infanzia *f* childhood; *(primi mesi)* infancy *(anche fig)*; *(bambini)* children

infarinare <1a> (dust with) flour

infarinatura *f* fig smattering

infarto *m* cardiaco heart attack

infastidire <4d> annoy, irritate

infaticabile tireless

infatti in fact

infatuarsi <1m>: ~ *di qu* become infatuated with s.o.

infedele 1 *agg* unfaithful; *traduzione* inaccurate **2** *m/f* REL infidel

infedeltà *f inv* unfaithfulness

infelice unhappy; *(inopportuno)* unfortunate; *(malriuscito)* bad

infelicità *f* unhappiness

inferiore 1 *agg* lower; *fig* inferior (*a* to); *di qualità* ~ of inferior quality; *essere ~ a qu* be inferior to s.o., be s.o.'s inferior; ~ *alla media* below average **2** *m/f* inferior; *(subalterno)* subordinate

inferiorità *f* inferiority; *complesso m d'~* inferiority complex

infermeria *f* infirmary

infermiere *m*, **-a** *f* nurse

infermità *f inv* illness

infermo 1 *agg (ammalato)* ill; *(invalido)* invalid **2** *m*, **-a** *f* invalid

infernale infernal

inferno *m* hell

inferriata *f* grating; *(cancellata)* railings *pl*

infertilità *f* infertility

infestare <1b> infest

infettare <1b> infect

infettarsi become infected

infettivo infectious

infetto infected

infezione *f* infection

infiammabile flammable

infiammare <1a> *fig*, MED inflame

infiammarsi become inflamed

infiammazione *f* inflammation; ~ *alla gola* inflammation of the throat

inferire <4d> *di maltempo, malattie* rage; ~ *su* o *contro* savagely attack

infilare <1a> *fili, corde, ago* thread;

(inserire) insert, put in; *(indossare)* put on; *strada* take; ~ *le mani in tasca* put one's hands in one's pockets; ~ *la porta* uscendo / entrando slip out / in

infilarsi *indumento* slip on; *(conficcarsi)* stick; *(introdursi)* slip (*in* into); *(stiparsi)* squeeze (*in* into)

infiltrare <1a> infiltrate

infiltrarsi seep; *fig* infiltrate

infiltrazione *f* infiltration; *di liquidi* seepage

infilzare <1a> pierce; *perle* thread; *fig* string together

infimo lowest

infine *(alla fine)* finally, eventually; *(insomma)* in short

infinità *f* infinity; *ho un'~ di cose da fare* I've got no end of things to do

infinito 1 *agg* infinite **2** *m* infinity; GRAM infinitive; *ripetere all'~* say over and over again

infischiarsi <1k> F: ~ *di* not give a hoot about F; *me ne infischio* I couldn't care less F

infittire *v/t & v/i* <4d> thicken

inflazione *f* inflation; *tasso m d'~* (rate of) inflation

inflessibile inflexible

inflessibilità *f* inflexibility

inflessione *f* inflection

infliggere <3cc> inflict

inflitto *pp* → **infliggere**

influente influential

influenza *f* influence; MED flu, influenza

influenzabile easily influenced, impressionable

influenzare <1b> influence

influire <4d>: ~ *su* influence, have an effect on

influsso *m* influence

infondato unfounded, without foundation

infondere <3bb> *fig* instil

inforcare <1d> *occhiali* put on; *bicicletta* get on, mount

informale informal

informare <1a> inform (*di* of)

informarsi find out (*di*, *su* about)

informatica *f scienza* information

technology, computer science

informatico (pl -ci) **1** agg computer attr **2** m, **-a** f computer scientist

informato informed

informatore m, **-trice** f informant; della polizia informer

informazione f piece of information; **ufficio** m **-i** information office

informe shapeless

informicolirsi <4d> have pins and needles

infortunio m (pl -ni) accident; **~ sul lavoro** accident at work, industrial accident; **assicurazione** f **contro gli -i** accident insurance

infossato occhi deep-set, sunken

infrangere <3d> break

infrangibile unbreakable; **vetro** m **~** shatterproof glass

infranto pp → **infrangere**

infrarosso infrared

infrasettimanale midweek

infrastruttura f infrastructure

infrazione f offence, Am offense; **~ al codice stradale** traffic offence (Am offense)

infreddatura f cold

infruttuoso fruitless

infuocare fig inflame

infuocato (caldissimo) scorching, blistering; discorso, tramonto fiery

infuori: **all'~** outwards; **all'~ di** except

infuriare <1k> **1** v/t infuriate, enrage **2** v/i rage

infuriarsi fly into a rage

infuriato furious

infusione f, **infuso** m infusion; (tisana) herbal tea

ingaggiare <1f> (reclutare) recruit; attore, cantante lirico engage; SP sign (up); (iniziare) start, begin

ingaggio m (pl -ggi) (reclutamento) recruitment; SP signing; (somma) fee

ingannare <1a> deceive; **~ il tempo** kill time

ingannarsi deceive o.s.

inganno m deception, deceit

ingarbugliare <1g> tangle; fig confuse, muddle

ingarbugliarsi get entangled; fig get confused

ingegnarsi <1a> do one's utmost (**a**, **per** to)

ingegnere m engineer

ingegneria f engineering; **~ genetica** genetic engineering; **~ meccanica** mechanical engineering

ingegno m (mente) mind; (intelligenza) brains pl; (genio) genius; (inventiva) ingenuity

ingegnoso ingenious

ingelosire <4d> **1** v/t make jealous **2** v/i be jealous

ingente enormous

ingenuità f ingenuousness

ingenuo ingenuous

ingerenza f interference

ingerire <4d> swallow

ingerirsi interfere

ingessare <1b> put in plaster

ingessatura f plaster

Inghilterra f England

inghiottire <4d> swallow

ingiallire <4d> v/t & v/i yellow, turn yellow

ingiallito yellowed

inginocchiarsi <1k> kneel (down)

ingiù: **all'~** down(wards)

ingiungere <3d>: **~ a qu di fare qc** order s.o. to do sth

ingiunzione f injunction; **~ di pagamento** final demand

ingiuria f insult

ingiuriare <1k> insult

ingiustificato unjustified

ingiustizia f injustice

ingiusto unjust, unfair

inglese **1** m/agg English **2** m/f Englishman; donna Englishwoman f

ingoiare <1i> swallow

ingolfare <1a>, **ingolfarsi** flood

ingombrante cumbersome, bulky

ingombrare <1a> passaggio block (up); stanza, mente clutter (up)

ingombro **1** agg passaggio blocked; stanza, mente cluttered (up) **2** m hindrance, obstacle; **essere d'~** be in the way

ingordo greedy

ingorgare <1e> block

ingorgarsi get blocked

ingorgo *m* (*pl* -ghi) blockage; ~ **stradale** traffic jam

ingovernabile ungovernable

ingozzare <1a> *cibo* devour, gobble up; *persona* stuff (**di** with)

ingozzarsi stuff o.s (**di** with)

ingranaggio *m* (*pl* -ggi) gear; *fig* machine;

ingranare <1a> engage; *fig* F **le cose cominciano a ~** things are beginning to work out

ingrandimento *m* enlargement; *di azienda, città* expansion, growth

ingrandire <4d> enlarge; *azienda, città* expand, develop; (*esagerare*) exaggerate

ingrandirsi grow

ingrassare <1a> **1** *v/t animali* fatten (up); (*lubrificare*) grease **2** *v/i* get fat, put on weight; *di birra, burro ecc* be fattening

ingratitudine *f* ingratitude

ingrato ungrateful; *lavoro, compito* thankless

ingrediente *m* ingredient

ingresso *m* entrance; (*atrio*) hall; (*accesso*) admittance; INFOR input; ~ **libero** admission free; *vietato l'~* no entry, no admittance

ingrossare <1c> **1** *v/t* make bigger; (*gonfiare, accrescere*) swell **2** *v/i e* **ingrossarsi** get bigger; (*gonfiarsi*) swell

ingrossato swollen

ingrosso: **all'~** (*all'incirca*) roughly, about; COM wholesale; **commercio** *m* **all'~** wholesale (trade)

ingualcibile crease-resistant

inguaribile incurable

inguinale groin *attr*; **ernia** *f* ~ hernia

inguine *m* ANAT groin

ingurgitare <1m> gulp down

inibire <4d> prohibit, forbid; PSI inhibit

inibito inhibited

inibizione *f* PSI inhibition

iniettare <1b> inject; ~ **qc a qu** inject s.o. with sth; **occhi** *mpl* **iniettati di sangue** bloodshot eyes

iniettarsi: ~ **qc** inject o.s. with sth

iniezione *f* injection; **motore** *m* **a ~** fuel-injection engine

inimicarsi <1d> fall out (**con** with)

inimicizia *f* enmity

inimitabile inimitable

inimmaginabile unimaginable

ininterrotto continuous

iniziale **1** *agg* initial; **stipendio** *m* ~ starting salary **2** *f* initial

inizializzare <1a> INFOR initialize

iniziare <1g> **1** *v/t* begin, start; *ostilità, dibattito* open; *fig* initiate **2** *v/i* begin, start; *di ostilità, dibattito* open; ~ **a fare qc** begin or start doing sth, begin or start to do sth

iniziativa *f* initiative; ~ **privata** private enterprise; **di mia** ~ on my own initiative; **spirito** *m* **d'~** initiative

inizio *m* (*pl* -zi) start, beginning; **avere** ~ start, begin; **dare** ~ **a qc** start sth

in loco on the premises

innaffiare <1k> water

innaffiatoio *m* (*pl* -oi) watering can

innalzare <1a> raise; (*erigere*) erect

innalzarsi rise

innamorarsi <1a> fall in love (**di** with)

innamorato **1** *agg* in love (**di** with) **2** *m*, **-a** *f* boyfriend; *donna* girlfriend

innanzi **1** *prp* before; ~ **a** in front of; ~ **tutto** first of all; (*soprattutto*) above all **2** *avv stato in luogo* in front; (*avanti*) forward; (*prima*) before; **d'ora** ~ from now on

innato innate, inborn

innaturale unnatural

innervosire <4d>: ~ **qu** make s.o. nervous; (*irritare*) get on s.o.'s nerves

innervosirsi get nervous; (*irritarsi*) get irritated

innestare <1b> BOT, MED graft; EL *spina* insert; AUTO *marcia* engage

innesto *m* BOT, MED graft; AUTO clutch; EL connection

inno *m* hymn; ~ **nazionale** national anthem

innocente innocent

innocenza *f* innocence

innocuo innocuous, harmless

innovativo innovative
innovazione f innovation
innumerevole innumerable
inodore odo(u)rless
inoffensivo harmless, inoffensive
inoltrare <1a> forward
inoltrarsi advance, penetrate (**in** into)
inoltrato late
inoltre besides
inondare <1a> flood
inondazione f flood
inoperoso idle
inopportuno (*inadatto*) inappropriate; (*intempestivo*) untimely; *persona* tactless
inorridire <4d> **1** v/t horrify **2** v/i be horrified
inorridito horrified
inospitale inhospitable, unwelcoming
inosservato unobserved, unnoticed; (*non rispettato*) disregarded; **passare ~** go unnoticed
inossidabile stainless
inquadrare <1a> *dipinto, fotografia* frame; *fig* put into context
inquadrarsi be part of
inquadratura f frame
inqualificabile *fig* unspeakable
inquietante *che preoccupa* worrying; *che turba* disturbing
inquietare <1b> (*preoccupare*) worry; (*turbare*) disturb; **fare ~ qu** make s.o. cross
inquietarsi (*preoccuparsi*) get worried; (*impazientirsi*) get cross
inquieto restless; (*preoccupato*) worried, anxious; (*adirato*) angry
inquietudine f anxiety
inquilino m, **-a** f tenant
inquinamento m pollution; *da sostanze radioattive* contamination; **~ acustico** noise pollution; **~ atmosferico** air pollution; **~ dell'ambiente** pollution
inquinante 1 *agg* polluting; **non ~** environmentally friendly; **sostanza** f **~** pollutant **2** m pollutant
inquinare <1a> pollute; *fig* (*corrompere*) corrupt; DIR *prove* tamper with
insabbiamento m *di porto* silting up *fig* shelving
insabbiare <1k> *fig* shelve
insabbiarsi *di porto* get silted up; *fig* grind to a halt
insaccare <1d> put in bags
insaccati mpl sausages
insalata f salad; **~ mista** mixed salad **~ verde** green salad
insalatiera f salad bowl
insanabile (*incurabile*) incurable; *fig* (*irrimediabile*) irreparable
insanguinato bloodstained
insaponare <1a> soap
insapore tasteless
insaporire <4d> flavo(u)r
insaputa: **all'~ di qu** unknown to s.o.
insaziabile insatiable
inscatolare <1m> tin, can
inscenare <1a> stage
inscindibile inseparable
insegna f sign; (*bandiera*) flag; (*stemma*) symbol; (*decorazione*) decoration
insegnamento m teaching
insegnante 1 *agg* teaching; **corpo** m **~** staff **2** m/f teacher
insegnare <1a> teach; **~ qc a qu** teach s.o. sth
inseguimento m chase, pursuit
inseguire <4b> chase, pursue
inseminazione f insemination; **~ artificiale** artificial insemination
insenatura f inlet
insensato 1 *agg* senseless, idiotic **2** m, **-a** f fool, idiot
insensibile insensitive (**a** to); *parte del corpo* numb
insensibilità f insensitivity; *di parte del corpo* numbness
inseparabile inseparable
inserire <4d> insert; (*collegare: in elettrotecnica*) connect; *annuncio* put in, place
inserirsi fit in; *in una conversazione* join in
inserto m (*pubblicazione*) supplement; (*insieme di documenti*) file
inservibile unusable

inserviente *m/f* attendant

inserzione *f* insertion; *sul giornale* ad(vert), advertisement

insetticida *m* (*pl* -i) insecticide

insettifugo *m* (*pl* -ghi) insect repellant

insetto *m* insect

insicurezza *f* insecurity, lack of security

insicuro insecure

insidia *f* (*tranello*) snare; (*inganno*) trick

insidioso insidious

insieme 1 *avv* together; (*contemporaneamente*) at the same time 2 *prp*: **~ a**, **~ con** together with 3 *m* whole; *di abiti* outfit; **nell'~** on the whole

insignificante insignificant

insinuare <1m> insert; *fig dubbio*, *sospetto* sow the seeds of; **~ che** insinuate that

insinuarsi penetrate; *fig* **~ in** creep into

insinuazione *f* insinuation

insipido insipid

insistente insistent

insistenza *f* insistence

insistere <3f> insist; (*perseverare*) persevere; **~ a fare qc** insist on doing sth

insoddisfacente unsatisfactory

insoddisfatto unsatisfied; (*scontento*) dissatisfied

insoddisfazione *f* dissatisfaction

insofferente intolerant

insofferenza *f* intolerance

insolazione *f* sunstroke

insolente insolent

insolenza *f* insolence; *espressione* insolent remark

insolito unusual

insolubile insoluble

insoluto unsolved; *debito* unpaid, outstanding

insolvente insolvent

insolvenza *f* insolvency

insolvibile insolvent

insomma (*in breve*) briefly, in short; **~!** well, really!

insonne sleepless

insonnia *f* insomnia

insonnolito sleepy

insonorizzazione *f* soundproofing

insopportabile unbearable, intolerable

insorgere <3d> rise (up) (**contro** against); *di difficoltà* come up, crop up

insormontabile insurmountable

insorto 1 *pp* → **insorgere** 2 *m* rebel

insospettabile above suspicion; (*impensato*) unsuspected

insospettato unsuspected

insospettire <4d> 1 *v/t*: **~ qu** make s.o. suspicious, arouse s.o.'s suspicion 2 *v/i e* **insospettirsi** become suspicious

insostenibile untenable; (*insopportabile*) unbearable

insostituibile irreplaceable

insperato unhoped for; (*inatteso*) unexpected

inspiegabile inexplicable

inspirare <1a> breathe in, inhale

instabile unstable; *tempo* changeable

instabilità *f* instability; *del tempo* changeability

installare <1a> install

installazione *f* installation

instancabile tireless, untiring

insù: **all'~** upwards

insubordinato insubordinate

insubordinazione *f* insubordination

insuccesso *m* failure

insufficiente insufficient; (*inadeguato*) inadequate

insufficienza *f* (*scarsità*) insufficiency; (*inadeguatezza*) inadequacy; **~ cardiaca** cardiac insufficiency

insulare *popolazione*, *flora ecc* island attr

insulina *f* insulin

insulso *fig* (*privo di vivacità*) dull; (*vacuo*) inane; (*sciocco*) silly

insultare <1a> insult

insulto *m* insult

insuperabile unsuperable; (*ineguagliabile*) incomparable

insuperato unsurpassed

insurrezione *f* insurrection

intaccare <1d> (*corrodere*) corrode;

fig (*danneggiare*) damage; *scorte, capitale* make inroads into

intagliare <1g> carve

intaglio *m* carving

intanto (*nel frattempo*) meanwhile; (*per ora*) for the time being; (*invece*) yet; **~ che** while

intarsio *m* (*pl* -si) inlay

intasamento *m* blockage; **~ del traffico** traffic jam

intasare <1a> block

intasarsi get blocked

intasato blocked

intascare <1d> pocket

intatto intact

integrale 1 *agg* whole; MAT integral; *edizione* unabridged; **pane** *m* **~** wholemeal bread **2** *m* MAT integral

integrare <1l> integrate; (*aumentare*) supplement

integrarsi integrate

integrazione *f* integration; **cassa** *f* **~** form of income support

integrità *f* integrity

intelaiatura *f* framework

intelletto *m* intellect

intellettuale *agg*, *m/f* intellectual

intelligente intelligent

intelligenza *f* intelligence; **~ artificiale** artificial intelligence, AI

intendere <3c> (*comprendere*) understand; (*udire*) hear; (*voler dire*) mean; (*avere intenzione*) intend; (*pretendere*) want; **s'intende!** naturally!, of course!

intendersi (*capirsi*) understand each other; (*accordarsi*) agree; **~ di qc** know a lot about sth; **intendersela** have an affair (**con** with)

intenditore *m*, **-trice** *f* connoisseur, expert

intensificare <1n & d> intensify

intensificarsi intensify

intensità *f* intensity; EL strength

intensivo intensive

intenso intense

intento 1 *agg* engrossed (**a** in), intent (**a** on) **2** *m* aim, purpose

intenzionale intentional, deliberate

intenzione *f* intention; **avere l'~ di fare qc** intend to do sth; **con ~ in-**tentionally; **senza ~** uninentionally

interamente entirely, wholly

interagire <4d> interact

interattivo interactive

interazione *f* interaction

intercalare 1 *v/t* insert **2** *m* stock phrase

intercambiabile interchangeable

intercapedine *f* cavity

intercedere <3a> intercede (**presso** with; **per** on behalf of)

intercettare <1b> intercept

intercettazione *f* interception; **-i** *pl* **telefoniche** phone tapping *sg*

intercontinentale intercontinental

intercorrere <3o> *di tempo* elapse; (*esserci*) exist, be

interdentale: filo *m* **~** (dental) floss

interdetto 1 *pp* → **interdire 2** *agg* (*sbalordito*) astonished; (*sconcertato*) puzzled **3** *m*, **-a** *f* F idiot F

interdire <3t> forbid; **~ a qu di fare qc** forbid s.o. to do sth; DIR **~ qu** deprive s.o. of his / her civil rights

interdizione *f* ban

interessamento *m* interest; (*intervento*) intervention

interessante interesting; **in stato ~** pregnant

interessare <1b> **1** *v/t* interest; (*riguardare*) concern **2** *v/i* matter

interessarsi be interested, take an interest (**a, di** in); (*occuparsi*) take care (**di** of)

interessato 1 *agg* interested (**a** in); (*implicato*) involved (**a** in); *spreg parere, opinione* biased; *persona* self-interested **2** *m*, **-a** *f* person concerned

interesse *m* interest; (*tornaconto*) benefit; **tasso** *m* **d'~** interest rate; **~ composto** compound interest; **per ~** out of self-interest; **senza ~** of no interest; FIN **senza -i** interest-free

interfaccia *f* (*pl* -cce) INFOR interface

interferenza *f* interference

interferire <4d> interfere

interfono *m* intercom

interiezione *f* interjection

interiora *fpl* entrails

interiore *m/agg* interior

interlocutore *m*, **-trice** *f*: **la sua -trice** the woman he was in conversation with

interludio *m* interlude

intermediario *m* (*pl* -ri), **-a** *f* intermediary

intermedio (*pl* -di) intermediate; *bilancio, relazione* interim

intermezzo *m* intermezzo

interminabile interminable

intermittente intermittent

internamento *m* internment; *in manicomio* committal

internare <1b> intern; *in manicomio* commit

internazionale international

internet *m* Internet; **navigare nell'~** surf the Net

internista *m/f* (*pl* -i) internist

interno **1** *agg* internal, inside *attr*; GEOG inland; POL, FIN domestic; *fig* inner; **alunno** *m* ~ boarder **2** *m* (*parte interna*) inside, interior; GEOG interior; TELEC extension; **via Dante n. 6 ~ 9** 6 via Dante, Flat 9; **ministero** *m* **dell'Interno** *o* **degli Interni** Home Office, *Am* Department of the Interior; **all'~** inside; SP ~ **destro / sinistro** inside right / left

intero whole, entire; (*completo*) complete; **latte** *m* ~ whole milk; MAT **numero** *m* ~ integer; **l'-a somma** the full amount

interpellare <1b> consult

interporre <3ll> *autorità, influenza* bring to bear

interporsi intervene

interpretare <1m & b> interpret; *personnagio* play; MUS play, perform

interpretazione *f* interpretation; TEA, MUS, *film* performance

interprete *m/f* interpreter; *attore, musicista* performer; ~ **simultaneo** (**-a**) interpreter; **fare da** ~ interpret, act as interpreter

interpunzione *f* punctuation

interrogare <1m, b & e> question; EDU test

interrogativo **1** *agg* GRAM interrogative; *occhiata* questioning; **pun-** **to** *m* ~ question mark **2** *m* (*domanda*) question; (*dubbio*) doubt

interrogatorio *m* (*pl* -ri) questioning

interrogazione *f* questioning; *domanda* question; EDU oral test

interrompere <3rr> interrupt; (*sospendere*) break off, stop; *comunicazioni, forniture* cut off

interrotto *pp* → **interrompere**

interruttore *m* EL switch

interruzione *f* interruption

intersecare <1m, b & d> intersect

intersezione *f* intersection

interurbana *f* long-distance (phone) call

interurbano intercity; **comunicazione** *f* **-a** long-distance (phone) call

intervallo *m* interval; *di scuola, lavoro* break

intervenire <4p> intervene; (*partecipare*) take part, participate (**a** in); MED operate

intervento *m* intervention; (*partecipazione*) participation; MED operation; **pronto** ~ emergency services

intervista *f* interview

intervistare <1a> interview

intervistatore *m*, **-trice** *f* interviewer

intesa *f* (*accordo*) understanding; (*patto*) agreement; SP team work

inteso **1** *pp* → **intendere 2** *agg* (*capito*) understood; (*destinato*) intended, meant (**a** to); **siamo -i?** agreed?; **ben** ~ needless to say, of course

intestare <1b> *assegno* make out (**a** to); *proprietà* register (**a** in the name of); **carta** *f* **intestata** letterhead, letterheaded notepaper

intestatario *m* (*pl* -ri), **-a** *f* di assegno payee; *di proprietà* registered owner

intestazione *f* heading; *su carta da lettere* letterhead

intestinale intestinal

intestino *m* intestine, gut

intimare <1l or 1a> order

intimazione *f* order

intimidazione *f* intimidation

intimidire <4d> intimidate

intimità f privacy; *di un rapporto* intimacy

intimo 1 *agg* intimate; (*segreto*) private; (*accogliente*) cosy, *Am* cozy; *amico* close, intimate 2 *m persona* close friend, intimate; (*abbigliamento*) underwear

intimorire <4d> frighten

intingere <3d> dip

intingolo *m* sauce

intitolare <1m> (*dare il titolo a*) call, entitle; (*dedicare*) dedicate (**a** to)

intitolarsi be called

intollerabile intolerable

intollerante intolerant

intolleranza f intolerance

intonacare <1m, c & d> plaster

intonaco *m* (*pl* -chi) plaster

intonare <1c> *strumento* tune; *colori* co-ordinate

intonarsi (*armonizzare*) go well (**a, con** with)

intonato MUS in tune; *colori pl* -i colours that go well together

intontire <4d> daze

intontito dazed

intoppo *m* (*ostacolo*) hindrance; (*contrattempo*) snag

intorno 1 *prp*: ~ **a** around; (*circa*) (round) about, around; (*riguardo a*) about 2 *avv* around; **tutt'**~ all around; **guardarsi** ~ look around

intossicare <1m, c & d> poison

intossicazione f poisoning; ~ **alimentare** food poisoning

intralciare <1f> hinder, hamper

intralcio *m* (*pl* -ci) hindrance

intramuscolare MED intramuscular

intransigente intransigent

intransitivo intransitive

intraprendente enterprising

intrapresa f enterprise

intraprendere <3c> undertake

intrattabile intractable; *prezzo* fixed, non-negotiable

intrattenere <2q> entertain; ~ **buoni rapporti con qu** be on good terms with s.o.

intrattenersi dwell (**su** on)

intravedere <2s> glimpse, catch a glimpse of; *fig* (*presagire*) anticipate, see

intravisto *pp* → **intravedere**

intrecciare <1f> plait, braid; (*intessere*) weave

intrecciarsi intertwine

intreccio *m* (*pl* -cci) *fig* (*trama*) plot

intricato tangled; *disegno* intricate; *fig* complicated

intrigante scheming; (*affascinante*) intriguing

intrigo *m* (*pl* -ghi) plot

intrinseco (*pl* -ci) intrinsic

introdurre <3e> introduce; (*inserire*) insert

introdursi get in

introduzione f introduction

introito *m* income; (*incasso*) takings *pl*

intromettersi <3ee> interfere; (*interporsi*) intervene

intromissione f interference; (*intervento*) intervention

introvabile impossible to find

introverso 1 *agg* introverted 2 *m*, -a f introvert

intrufolarsi <1m> sneak in

intruglio *m* (*pl* -gli) concoction

intrusione f intrusion

intruso *m*, -a f intruder

intuire <4d> know instinctively

intuito *m* intuition

intuizione f intuition

inumano inhuman

inumidire <4d> dampen, moisten

inumidirsi get damp

inutile useless; (*superfluo*) unnecessary, pointless

inutilità f uselessness

inutilizzabile unusable

inutilizzato unused

inutilmente pointlessly, needlessly

invadente 1 *agg* nosy 2 *m/f* busybody

invadenza f nosiness

invadere <3q> invade; (*occupare*) occupy; (*inondare*) flood

invaghirsi <4d>: ~ **di** take a fancy to

invalidare <1m> invalidate

invalidità f disability

invalido 1 *agg* disabled; DIR invalid

2 *m*, **-a** *f* disabled person

invano in vain

invariabile invariable

invariabilità *f* unchanging nature

invariato unchanged

invasione *f* invasion (**di** of)

invasore *m* invader

invecchiare <1k> **1** *v/t* age **2** *v/i* age, get older; *di vini, cibi* mature; *fig* (*cadere in disuso*) date

invece instead; (*ma*) but; **~ di fare** instead of doing

inveire <4d>: **~ contro** inveigh against

invenduto unsold

inventare <1b> invent

inventario *m* (*pl* -ri) inventory

inventore *m*, **-trice** *f* inventor

invenzione *f* invention

invernale winter *attr*; **sport** *mpl* **-i** winter sports

inverno *m* winter; **d'~** in winter

inverosimile improbable, unlikely

inversione *f* (*scambio*) reversal; AUTO **~ di marcia** U-turn

inverso 1 *agg* reverse **2** *m* opposite

invertire <4b or 4d> reverse; (*capovolgere*) turn upside down; CHIM, EL invert; **~ la marcia** turn round; **~ le parti** exchange roles

investigare <1m, b & e> investigate

investigatore *m*, **-trice** *f* investigator

investigazione *f* investigation

investimento *m* investment; *di veicolo* crash; *di pedone* running over; **~ di capitali** capital investment

investire <4d or 4b> *pedone* run over; *veicolo* smash into, collide with; FIN, *fig* invest

inviare <1h> send

inviato *m*, **-a** *f* envoy; *di giornale* correspondent

invidia *f* envy

invidiare <1k> envy

invidioso envious

invincibile invincible

invio *m* (*pl* -vii) dispatch; INFO **tasto** *m* **d'~** enter key

inviolabile inviolable

invisibile invisible

invitante *profumo* enticing; *offerta* tempting

invitare <1a> invite

invitato *m*, **-a** *f* guest

invito *m* invitation; **~ a presentarsi** summons *sg*

invocare <1c & d> invoke; (*implorare*) plead for, beg for

invocazione *f* invocation; (*richiesta*) plea

invogliare <1g & c> induce

involontario (*pl* -ri) involuntary

involtini *mpl* GASTR rolled stuffed slices of meat

involto *m* bundle; (*pacco*) parcel

involucro *m* wrapping

inzaccherare <1m> spatter with mud

inzuppare <1a> soak; (*intingere*) dip

inzuppato soaked

io 1 *pron* I; **~ stesso** myself; **sono ~!** it's me! **2** *m inv* ego

iodio *m* iodine

ionico (*pl* -ci) ARCHI Ionic

iosa: a ~ in abundance, aplenty

iperalimentazione *f* overfeeding

iperattivo hyperactive

iperbole *f figura retorica* hyperbole; MAT hyperbola

ipermercato *m* hypermarket

ipersensibile hypersensitive

ipertensione *f* high blood pressure

ipnosi *f* hypnosis

ipnotizzare <1a> hypnotize

ipocalorico (*pl* -ci) low in calories

ipocrisia *f* hypocrisy

ipocrita 1 *agg* hypocritical **2** *m/f* (*mpl* -i) hypocrite

ipoteca *f* (*pl* -che) mortgage; **accendere un'~** take out a mortgage

ipotecare <1b & d> mortgage

ipotesi *f* hypothesis

ipotetico (*pl* -ci) hypothetical

ipotizzare <1a> hypothesize

ippica *f* (horse) riding

ippocastano *m* horse chestnut

ippodromo *m* race-course

ippopotamo *m* hippo(potamus)

ira *f* anger; **avere uno scatto d'~** fly into a rage

iracheno 1 *agg* Iraqi **2** *m*, **-a** *f* Iraqi

Iran *m* Iran

iraniano **1** *agg* Iranian **2** *m*, **-a** *f* Iranian

Iraq *m* Iraq

irascibile irritable, irascible

iride *f* (*arcobaleno*) rainbow; ANAT, BOT iris

Irlanda *f* Ireland

irlandese **1** *agg* Irish **2** *m* Irish Gaelic **3** *m/f* Irishman; *donna* Irishwoman

ironia *f* irony

ironico (*pl* -ci) ironic(al)

ironizzare <1a> be ironic

IRPEF *abbr* (= **Imposta sul Reddito delle Persone Fisiche**) income tax

irradiare <1k> *v/t & v/i* radiate

irradiazione *f* radiation

irraggiungibile unattainable

irragionevole unreasonable

irrazionale irrational

irreale unreal

irrealizzabile unattainable

irrefrenabile uncontrollable

irregolare irregular

irregolarità *f inv* irregularity

irreparabile irreparable

irreperibile impossible to find

irreprensibile irreproachable

irreprimibile irrepressible

irrequietezza *f* restlessness

irrequieto restless

irresistibile irresistible

irresponsabile irresponsible

irresponsabilità *f* irresponsibility

irrestringibile non-shrink; *parzialmente* shrink-resistant

irrevocabile irrevocable

irriconoscibile unrecognizable

irrigare <1e> irrigate

irrigazione *f* irrigation

irrigidire <4d> stiffen; *fig disciplina* tighten

irrigidirsi stiffen

irrigidito stiff

irrilevante irrelevant

irrimediabile irremediable

irrinunciabile *diritto* inalienable

irripetibile unrepeatable

irrisorio (*pl* -ri) derisive; *quantità, somma di denaro* derisory; *prezzo*

ridiculously low

irritabile irritable

irritabilità *f* irritability

irritante irritating

irritare <1l or 1a> irritate

irritarsi become irritated

irrobustire <4d> strengthen, build up

irrompere <3rr> burst (*in* into)

irruzione *f*: **fare ~ in** burst into; *di polizia* raid

iscritto **1** *pp* → **iscrivere 2** *m*, **-a** *f* member; *a gare, concorsi* entrant; EDU pupil, student **3** *m*: **per ~ in** writing

iscrivere <3tt> register; *a gare, concorsi* enter (**a** for, in); EDU enrol(l) (**a** at)

iscriversi *in un elenco* register; **~ a** *partito, associazione* join; *gara* enter; EDU enrol(l) at

iscrizione *f* inscription

islamico (*pl* -ci) Islamic

Islanda *f* Iceland

islandese **1** *m/agg* Icelandic **2** *m/f* Icelander

isola *f* island; **~ pedonale** pedestrian precinct; **~ spartitraffico** traffic island

isolamento *m* isolation; TEC insulation; **~ acustico** soundproofing

isolano *m*, **-a** *f* islander

isolante **1** *agg* insulating **2** *m* insulator

isolare <1l> isolate; TECH insulate

isolarsi isolate o.s., cut o.s. off

isolato **1** *agg* isolated; TECH insulated **2** *m* outsider; *di case* block

ispettore *m*, **-trice** *f* inspector

ispezionare <1a> inspect

ispezione *f* inspection

ispirare <1a> inspire

ispirarsi *di artista* get inspiration (**a** from)

ispirazione *f* inspiration; (*impulso*) impulse; (*idea*) idea

Israele *m* Israel

israeliano *m*, **-a** *f* Israeli

issare <1a> hoist

istallare <1a> → **installare**

istantanea *f* snap

istantaneo instantaneous
istante *m* instant; **all'~** instantly
istanza *f* (*esigenza*) need; (*domanda*) application; DIR petition
ISTAT *abbr* (= **Istituto Centrale di Statistica**) central statistics office
isterico <*pl* -ci> hysterical
istigare <11 & e> instigate
istintivo instinctive
istinto *m* instinct
istituire <4d> establish
istituto *m* institute; *assistenziale* institution, home; **~ di bellezza** beauty salon; **~ di credito** bank
istituzione *f* institution
istmo *m* isthmus
istruire <4d> educate, teach; (*dare istruzioni a, addestrare*) instruct
istruirsi educate o.s.
istruito educated
istruttivo instructive
istruttore *m*, **-trice** *f* instructor
istruzione *f* education; (*direttiva*) instruction; **-i** *pl* **per l'uso** instructions (for use)
Italia *f* Italy
italiano **1** *m/agg* Italian; **parla ~?** do you speak Italian? **2** *m*, **-a** *f* Italian
itinerario *m* (*pl* -ri) route, itinerary
ittico <*pl* -ci> fish
iugoslavo → **yugoslavo**
iuta *f* jute
IVA *abbr* (= **Imposta sul Valore Aggiunto**) VAT (= value-added tax)

J

jazz *m* jazz
jazzista *m/f* (*mpl* -i) jazz musician
jeans *mpl* jeans
jeep *f inv* jeep
jet *m inv* jet
jet-lag *m inv* jet lag
jet-set *m inv* jet set
jockey *m inv* jockey
jogging *m* jogging; **fare ~** jog, go for a jog
joint-venture *f inv* joint venture
jolly *m inv* joker
joule *m inv* joule
joy-stick *m inv* joystick
judo *m* judo
juke-box *m inv* jukebox
jumbo *m* jumbo
junior *m/agg* (*pl* juniores) junior

K

karatè *m* karate
kg *abbr* (= **chilogrammo**) kg (= kilogram)
killer *m inv* killer
kit *m inv* kit
kitsch *agg inv*, *m* kitsch
kiwi *m inv* BOT kiwi (fruit)
km *abbr* (= **chilometro**) km (= kilometre)
km/h *abbr* (= **chilometri all'ora**) km/h (= kilometres per hour)
kmq *abbr* (= **chilometri quadrati**) km^2 (= square kilometres)
knock-out knock-out

k.o.: *mettere qu ~* knock s.o. out; *fig* trounce s.o.

kolossal *m inv* epic

krapfen *m inv* GASTR doughnut

kümmel *m* kümmel

kV *abbr* (= *chilovolt*) kV (= kilovolt)

kW *abbr* (= *chilowatt*) kW (= kilowatt)

kWh *abbr* (= *chilowattora*) kWh (= kilowatt hour)

L

L *abbr* (= *lira*) L (= lire)

l *abbr* (= *litro*) l (= litre)

l' = *lo, la*

la¹ *art fsg* the; *~ signora Rossi* Mrs Rossi; *~ domenica* on Sundays; *mi piace la birra* I like beer

la² *pron* **1** *sg* (*persona*) her; (*cosa, animale*) it; *~ prenderò* I'll take it **2** *anche La sg* you

la³ *m* MUS A; *nel solfeggio della scala* la(h)

là there; *di ~* that way; (*in quel luogo*) in there; *di ~ di* on the other side of; *più in ~* further on; *nel tempo* later on

labbro *m* (*pl* le -a) lip

labile (*passeggero*) fleeting, short-lived

labirinto *m* labyrinth

laboratorio *m* (*pl* -ri) lab, laboratory; (*officina*) workshop

laboriosità *f* laboriousness; *di persona* industriousness

laborioso laborious; *persona* hard-working, industrious

laburista **1** *agg* Labo(u)r **2** *m/f* Labo(u)r Party member; *elettore* Labo(u)r supporter

lacca *f* (*pl* -cche) lacquer; *per capelli* hair spray, lacquer

laccare <1d> lacquer

laccio *m* (*pl* -cci) tie, (draw)string; *-cci pl delle scarpe* shoe laces

lacerante *dolore, grido* piercing

lacero tattered, in tatters

lacrima *f* tear

lacrimare <1l> water

lacrimevole heart-rending; *film m ~* tear-jerker

lacrimogeno: *gas m ~* tear gas

lacuna *f* gap

lacunoso incomplete

ladino 1 *agg* South Tyrolean **2** *m*, **-a** *f* South Tyrolean

ladro *m*, **-a** *f* thief

laggiù down there; *distante* over there

laghetto *m* pond

lagna *f* (*lamentela*) whining; *persona* whiner; (*cosa noiosa*) bore

lagnanza *f* complaint

lagnarsi <1a> complain (*di* about)

lago *m* (*pl* -ghi) lake; *~ artificiale* reservoir; *~ di Garda* Lake Garda

laguna *f* lagoon

laico (*pl* -ci) **1** *agg scuola, stato* secular **2** *m*, **-a** *f* member of the laity

lama *f* blade; *~ di coltello* knife blade

lamentare <1a> lament, deplore

lamentarsi complain (*di* about)

lamentela *f* complaint

lamento *m* whimper

lamentoso whining

lametta *f*: *~ (da barba)* razor blade

lamiera *f* metal sheet; *~ ondulata* corrugated iron

lamina *f* foil; *~ d'oro* gold leaf

lampada *f* lamp; *~ alogena* halogen lamp; *~ a stelo* floor lamp, *Br* standard lamp; *~ al neon* neon light

lampadario *m* (*pl* -ri) chandelier

lampadina *f* light bulb; *~ tascabile*

torch, *Am* flashlight

lampante blindingly obvious

lampeggiare <1f> flash

lampeggiatore *m* AUTO indicator; FOT flashlight

lampione *m* streetlight

lampo *m* lightning; *in un* ~ in a flash

lampone *m* raspberry

lana *f* wool; *pura* ~ *vergine* pure new wool

lancetta *f* needle, indicator; *di orologio* hand

lancia *f* (*pl* -ce) spear; MAR launch; ~ *di salvataggio* lifeboat

lanciare <1f> throw; *prodotto* launch; ~ *un'occhiata* glance, take a quick look; ~ *un urlo* give a shout, shout

lanciarsi rush; ~ *contro* throw o.s at, attack; F ~ *in un' impresa* embark on a venture; F *mi lancio* I'll go for it F, I'll take the plunge F

lancinante *dolore* piercing

lancio *m* (*pl* -ci) throwing; *di prodotto* launch; ~ *del disco* discus; ~ *del giavellotto* javelin; ~ *del peso* putting the shot

languire <4a or 4d> languish

languore *m* lang(u)or; *ho un* ~ *allo stomaco* I'm feeling peckish

lanificio *m* (*pl* -ci) wool mill

lanterna *f* lantern; (*faro*) lighthouse

lapide *f* gravestone; *su monumento* plaque

lapis *m inv* pencil

lardo *m* lard

larghezza *f* width, breadth; ~ *di vedute* broad-mindedness

largo (*pl* -ghi) **1** *agg* wide, broad; *indumento* loose, big; (*abbondante*) large, generous; ~ *di manica* generous **2** *m* width; (*piazza*) square; *andare al* ~ head for the open sea; *al* ~ *di* off the coast of; *farsi* ~ elbow one's way through; *stare alla* -*a da* steer clear of, keep away from

larice *m* larch

laringe *f* larynx

laringite *f* laryngitis

larva *f* ZO larva

lasagne *fpl* lasagne *sg*

lasciapassare *m inv* pass

lasciare <1f> leave; (*abbandonare*) give up; (*concedere*) let; (*smettere di tenere*) let go; *lascia andare!, lascia perdere!* forget it!

lasciarsi separate, leave each other; ~ *andare* let o.s. go

lascito *m* legacy

lascivo lascivious

laser *m inv*, *agg inv* laser

lassativo *m/agg* laxative

lasso *m*: ~ *di tempo* period of time

lassù up there

lastra *f di pietra* slab; *di metallo, ghiaccio, vetro* sheet; MED x-ray

lastrico *m* (*pl* -chi o -ci): *fig ridursi sul* ~ lose everything

latente latent

laterale lateral

laterizio *m* (*mpl* -zi) bricks and tiles *pl*

latino **1** *agg* Latin; ~-*americano* Latin-American **2** *m* Latin; ~-*americano, -a* Latin-American

latitante *m/f* fugitive

latitudine *f* latitude

lato *m* side; *a* ~ *di, di* ~ *a* beside; *d'altro* ~ on the other hand

latrare <1a> bark

latrato *m* barking

latrina *f* latrine

latta *f* can, tin; ~ *di benzina* petrol can, *Am* gas can

lattaio *m* (*pl* -ai), -*a* *f* milkman; *donna* milkwoman

lattante *m* infant, small baby

latte *m* milk; ~ *a lunga conservazione* long-life milk; ~ *intero* whole milk; ~ *materno* mother's milk; ~ *scremato* skim(med) milk

latteo milk *attr*; *Via f Lattea* Milky Way

latteria *f* dairy

lattice *m* latex

latticinio *m* (*pl* -ni) dairy product

lattina *f* can, tin

lattuga *f* (*pl* -ghe) lettuce

laurea *f* degree

laurearsi <1l> graduate

laureato *m*, -*a* *f* graduate

lava *f* lava

lavabile washable; **~ in lavatrice** machine-washable

lavabo m basin

lavacristallo m AUTO windscreen (Am) windshield) washer

lavaggio m (pl -ggi) washing; **~ a secco** dry-cleaning; **~ del cervello** brainwashing

lavagna f blackboard; GEOL slate; **~ luminosa** overhead projector

lavanda f BOT lavender

lavanderia f laundry; **~ a gettone** laundrette

lavandino m basin; *nella cucina* sink

lavapiatti m/f inv dishwasher

lavare <1a> wash; **~ i panni** do the washing

lavarsi wash; **~ le mani** wash one's hands; **~ i denti** brush or clean one's teth

lavastoviglie f inv dishwasher

lavatoio m (pl m -oi) laundry; *di casa* laundry (room), utility room

lavatrice f washing machine

lavello m basin; *nella cucina* sink

lavina f avalanche

lavorare <1a> **1** v/i work **2** v/t *materia prima* process; *legno* carve; *terra* work

lavorativo: giorno m **~** working day

lavorato *legno* carved

lavoratore m, **-trice** f worker; **~ autonomo** self-employed person; **~ dipendente** employee

lavorazione f *di materia prima* processing; *di legno* carving

lavoro m work; *(impiego)* job; **~ di gruppo** teamwork; **~ malfatto** botched job; **~ nero** moonlighting; **-i** pl **occasionali** o **saltuari** odd jobs; **per ~** on business; **condizioni** fpl **di ~** working conditions; **permesso** m **di ~** work permit; **posto** m **di ~** place of work, workplace; **-i in corso** roadworks, work in progress; **senza ~** unemployed

le[1] art fpl the

le[2] pron fsg to her; fpl them; *anche* **Le** you

leader m/f inv leader

leale loyal

lealtà f loyalty

lebbra f leprosy

lebbroso m, **-a** f leper

lecca-lecca m inv lollipop

leccare <1d> lick; F **~ qu** suck up to s.o. F, lick s.o.'s boots F

leccio m (pl -cci) holm oak

leccornia f appetizing dish, delicacy

lecito legal, permissible; **se mi è ~** if I may

lega f (pl -ghe) league; METAL alloy

legale 1 agg legal **2** m/f lawyer

legalità f legality

legalizzare <1a> legalize

legame m tie, relationship; *(nesso)* link, connection

legamento m ANAT ligament

legare <1e> tie; *persona* tie up; *(collegare)* link; *fig di lavoro* tie down

legarsi *fig* tie o.s. down

legazione f legation

legge f law; **studiare ~** study or read law; **a norma di ~** up to standard; **a norma di ~ ...** complies with ...; **fuori ~** illegal, unlawful

leggenda f legend; *di carta geografica ecc* key

leggendario (pl -ri) legendary

leggere <3cc> read; **~ le labbra** lipread; **~ nel pensiero a qu** read s.o.'s mind

leggerezza f lightness; *fig* casualness; **con ~** thoughtlessly, unthinkingly

leggero light; *(lieve, di poca importanza)* slight; *(superficiale)* thoughtless; *caffè* weak; **alla -a** lightly, light-heartedly

leggibile legible

leggio m (pl -ii) lectern; MUS music stand

legislativo legislative

legislatore m legislator

legislatura f *periodo* term of parliament

legislazione f legislation

legittimare <1m> approve

legittimazione f approval

legittimo legitimate

legna *f* (fire)wood; *far ~* collect firewood

legname *m* timber; *~ da costruzione* lumber

legno *m* (*pl* i -i) wood; *di ~* wooden

legumi *mpl* peas and beans; *secchi* pulses

lei *pron fsg soggetto* she; *oggetto, con preposizione* her; *~ stessa* herself; *anche Lei* you; *dare del ~ a qu* address s.o. as 'lei'

lembo *m* di gonna hem, bottom; *di terra* stip

lente *f* lens; *-i pl* glasses, spectacles, specs F; *-i pl* (*a contatto*) contact lenses, contacts F; *~ d'ingrandimento* magnifying glass

lentezza *f* slowness

lenticchia *f* lentil

lentiggine *f* freckle

lento slow; (*allentato*) slack; *abito* loose

lenza *f* fishing rod

lenzuolo *m* (*pl* i -i *e* le -a) sheet

leone *m* lion; ASTR **Leone** Leo

leonessa *f* lioness

leopardo *m* leopard

lepre *f* hare

lercio filthy

lesbica *f* lesbian

lesionare damage

lesione *f* MED injury

lessare <1a> boil

lessico *m* (*pl* -ci) vocabulary; (*dizionario*) glossary

lesso **1** *agg* boiled **2** *m* boiled beef

letale lethal

letame *m* manure, dung

letargo *m* (*pl* -ghi) lethargy

lettera *f* letter; *alla ~* to the letter; *~ assicurata* registered letter; *~ commerciale* business letter; *~ di accompagnamento* covering letter; FIN *~ di cambio* bill of exchange; *~ espresso* (letter sent) express delivery; *~ raccomandata* recorded delivery letter

letterale literal

letterario (*pl* -ri) literary

letterato *m*, **-a** *f* man / woman of letters

letteratura *f* literature

lettino *m* cot; *dal medico* bed; *dallo psicologo* couch; *~ solare* sunbed

letto[1] *m* bed; *~ a una piazza* single bed; *~ matrimoniale* double bed; *andare a ~* go to bed; *essere a ~* be in bed

letto[2] *pp* → **leggere**

lettore *m*, **-trice** *f* reader; *all'università* lecturer in a foreign language; INFOR disk drive; *~ compact disc* CD player; *~ ottico* optical character reader

lettura *f* reading

leucemia *f* leuk(a)emia

leva *f* lever; MIL call-up, *Am* draft; AUTO *~ del cambio* gear lever

levante *m* east

levare <1b> (*alzare*) raise, lift; (*togliere*) take, (re)move; (*rimuovere*) take out, remove; *macchia* remove, get out; *dente* take out, extract; *~ l'ancora* weigh anchor

levarsi get up, rise; *di sole* rise, come up; *indumento* take off; *~ il vizio di fare qc* get out of the habit of doing sth; *levatelo dalla testa!* you can get that idea out of your head!

levata *f* di posta collection

levatrice *f* midwife

levigare <1l, b & e> smooth down

levigato smooth

lezione *f* lesson; *all'università* lecture; *fig dare una ~ a qu* teach s.o. a lesson

li *pron mpl* them

lì there; *~ per ~* there and then; *giù di ~* thereabouts; *di ~ a pochi giorni* a few days later

libanese *agg*, *m/f* Lebanese

Libano *m* (the) Lebanon

libbra *f* pound

libellula *f* dragon-fly

liberale **1** *agg* generous; POL liberal **2** *m/f* liberal

liberalità *f* generosity

liberalizzare <1a> liberalize

liberalizzazione *f* liberalization

liberamente freely

liberare <1l> release, free;

(*sgomberare*) empty; *stanza* vacate

liberarsi: ~ *di* get rid of

liberazione *f* release; *di nazione* liberation

libero free; *camera d'albergo* vacant, free

libertà *f inv* freedom, liberty; **mettersi in** ~ change into more comfortable clothes; ~ *di stampa* freedom of the press; **prendersi la ~ di fare qc** take the liberty of doing sth; ~ **provvisoria** bail

Libia *f* Libya

libico (*pl* -ci) **1** *agg* Libyan **2** *m*, -a *f* Libyan

libraio (*pl* -ai) bookseller

librario (*pl* -ri) book *attr*

libreria *f* bookstore, *Br* -shop; (*biblioteca*) book collection, library; *mobile* bookcase

libretto *m* booklet; MUS libretto; ~ *di assegni* cheque book, *Am* check book; AUTO ~ *di circolazione* registration document; ~ *di risparmio* bank book

libro *m* book; ~ *di testo* textbook; ~ *illustrato* picture book

licenza *f* FIN licence, *Am* license, permit; MIL leave; EDU school leaving certificate; ~ *di costruzione* building *or* construction permit; ~ *di esercizio* trading licence (*Am* license)

licenziamento *m* dismissal; *per motivi economici* dismissal, *Br* redundancy

licenziare <1g> dismiss; *per motivi economici* dismiss, lay off, *Br* make redundant; ~ *alle stampe* pass for press

licenziarsi resign

liceo *m* high school; ~ *classico* (*scientifico*) high school that *specializes in arts* (*science*) *subjects*

lido *m* beach

lieto happy; ~ *di conoscerla* nice *or* pleased to meet you

lieve light; (*di poca gravità*) slight, minor; *sorriso, rumore* faint

lievitare <1l & b> rise; *fig* rise, be on the increase

lievito *m* yeast; ~ *in polvere* baking powder

lilla *m/agg* lilac

lillà *m* lilac (tree)

lima *f* file

limare <1a> file

limetta *f* emery board; *di metallo* nail file

limitare <1l> limit, restrict (**a** to); (*contenere*) limit, contain

limitato limited; FIN **società** *f* **a responsabilità -a** limited company; **è** ~ *di persona* he's got his limitations

limitazione *f* limitation; ~ *delle nascite* birth control; *senza -i* without restriction

limite *m* limit; (*confine*) boundary; ~ *di età* age limit; ~ *di velocità* speed limit; *al* ~ at most, at the outside; *nei -i del possibile* to the best of one's ability

limitrofo bordering, neighbo(u)ring

limonata *f* lemonade

limone *m* lemon; (*albero*) lemon tree

limpidezza *f* cleanness

limpido clear; *acqua* crystal-clear, limpid

lince *f* lynx

linciare <1f> lynch

linea *f* line; ~ *dell'autobus* bus route; **mantenere la ~** keep one's figure; TELEC **restare in** ~ stay on the line, not hang up

lineamenti *mpl* (*fisionomia*) features

lineare linear

lineetta *f* dash

linfonodo *m* lymph node

lingotto *m* ingot

lingua *f* tongue; (*linguaggio*) language; ~ *madre* mother tongue; ~ *parlata* colloquial language; ~ *straniera* foreign language; ~ *nazionale* official language

linguaggio *m* (*pl* -ggi) language; ~ *tecnico* technical language, jargon; INFOR ~ *di programmazione* programming language

linguistica *f* linguistics

lino *m* BOT flax; *tessuto* linen

liofilizzato freeze-dried

liquidare <1l> (*pagare*) pay; *merci* clear; *azienda* liquidate; *fig questione* settle; *problema* dispose of; *persona* F liquidate F, dispose of F

liquidazione *f* liquidation; **~ totale** clearance sale

liquidità *f* liquid assets *pl*, liquidity

liquido *m/agg* liquid

liquirizia *f* liquorice

liquore *m* liqueur

lira *f* lira

lirica *f* (*pl* -che) lyric poem; MUS **la ~** opera

lirico (*pl* -ci) lyric; *cantante* opera *attr*; **teatro** *m* **~** opera house

lisca *f* (*pl* -che) fishbone

lisciare <1f> smooth (down); (*accarezzare*) stroke; *capelli* straighten

liscio (*pl* -sci) smooth; *bevanda* straight, neat; *fig* **passarla -a** get away with it

liso worn

lista *f* (*elenco*) list; (*striscia*) strip; **~ d'attesa** waiting list; **in ~ d'attesa** on the waiting list, wait-listed; AVIA on standby; **~ dei vini** wine list

listino *m*: **~ di borsa** share index; **~ prezzi** price list

Lit. *abbr* (= *lire italiane*) L (= lire)

lite *f* quarrel, argument; JUR lawsuit; **~ coniugale** marital dispute

litigare <1l & e> quarrel, argue

litigio *m* (*pl* -gi) quarrel, argument

litigioso argumentative, quarrelsome

litografia *f* lithography

litografo *m* lithograph

litorale 1 *agg* coastal **2** *m* coast

litoranea *f* coast road

litoraneo coast *attr*, coastal

litro *m* litre, *Am* liter

Lituania *f* Lithuania

lituano 1 *agg* Lithuanian **2** *m*, **-a** *f* Lithuanian

liturgia *f* liturgy

liturgico (*pl* -ci) liturgical

liutaio *m* (*pl* -ai) lute maker

liuto *m* lute

livella *f* level

livellamento *m* levelling

livellare <1b> level

livello *m* level; AUTO **~ dell'olio** oil level; *fig* **ad altissimo ~** first-class, first-rate; **sopra il ~ del mare** above sea level; **~ di vita** standard of living

livido 1 *agg* livid; *braccio*, *viso* black and blue; *occhio* black; *per il freddo* blue **2** *m* bruise

lo 1 *art m/sg* the **2** *pron m/sg* him; *cosa*, *animale* it; **non ~ so** I don't know

lobo *m* lobe

locale 1 *agg* local; MED **anestesia** *f* **~** local an(a)esthetic **2** *m* room; *luogo pubblico* place; FERR local train

località *f inv* town; **~ balneare** seaside resort; **~ turistica** tourist resort

localizzare <1a> locate; (*delimitare*) localize

locandina *f* TEA bill

locatario *m* (*pl* -ri), **-a** *f* tenant

locatore *m*, **-trice** *f* landlord; *donna* landlady

locazione *f* rental

locomotiva *f* locomotive

locomozione *f* locomotion; **mezzo** *m* **di ~** means of transport

locuzione *f* fixed expression

lodare <1c> praise

lode *f* praise

lodevole praiseworthy, laudable

loggia *f* (*pl* -gge) loggia

loggione *m* TEA gallery

logica *f* logic

logico (*pl* -ci) logical

logorare <1l> wear out

logorio *m* wear and tear

logoro *indumento* worn (out), threadbare

lombaggine *f* lumbago

Lombardia *f* Lombardy

lombardo 1 *agg* of Lombardy **2** *m*, **-a** *f* native of Lombardy

lombata *f* loin

lombo *m* loin

lombrico *m* (*pl* -chi) earthworm

Londra *f* London

longevo longlived

longitudine *f* GEOG longitude

lontananza *f* distance; *tra persone* separation

lontano 1 *agg* far; *nel tempo* far-off;

passato, futuro, parente distant; **alla -a** *concoscere* vaguely, slightly; **siamo cugini alla -a** we're distant cousins **2** *avv* far (away); **da ~** from a distance; **abita molto ~?** do you live very far away?

lontra *f* otter

loquace talkative

lordo dirty; *peso, reddito ecc* gross

loro 1 *pron soggetto* they; *oggetto* them; *forma di cortesia, anche* **Loro** you **2** *possessivo* their; *forma di cortesia, anche* **Loro** your; **il ~ amico** their / your friend; **i ~ genitori** their / your parents **3** *pron*: **il ~** theirs; *forma di cortesia, anche* **Loro** yours

lotta *f* struggle; SP wrestling; *fig* fight

lottare <1c> wrestle, struggle (**con** with); *fig* fight (**contro** against; **per** for)

lottatore *m* wrestler

lotteria *f* lottery; **biglietto** *m* **della ~** lottery ticket

lotto *m* lottery; *di terreno* plot

lozione *f* lotion; **~ dopobarba** aftershave

L.st. *abbr* (= **lira sterlina**) £ (= pound)

lubrificante *m* lubricant; AUTO lubricating oil

lubrificare <1m & d> lubricate

lucchetto *m* padlock

luccicare <1l & d> sparkle

luccio *m* (*pl* -cci) pike

lucciola *f* glowworm

luce *f* light; **~ al neon** neon light; **dare alla ~ un figlio** give birth to a son; *fig* **far ~ su qc** shed light on sth; AUTO **-i pl di posizione** side lights; **-i pl posteriori** rear lights

lucente shining, gleaming

lucentezza *f* shininess

lucertola *f* lizard

lucidare <1l> polish; *disegno* trace

lucidatrice *f* floor polisher

lucido 1 *agg superficie, scarpe* shiny; FOT glossy; *persona* lucid **2** *m* polish; *disegno* transparency; **~ da scarpe** shoe polish

lucrativo lucrative

lucro *m*: **a scopo di ~** profit-making;

senza fini di ~ non-profit-making

luglio *m* July

lugubre sombre, *Am* somber, lugubrious

lui *pron msg soggetto* he; *oggetto* him; **a ~** to him; *oggetto* **stesso** himself

lumaca *f* (*pl* -che) slug

lume *m* (*lampada*) lamp; *luce* light; *fig* **perdere il ~ della ragione** lose one's mind

luminosità *f* luminosity; FOT speed

luminoso luminous; *stanza* bright, full of light; **sorgente** *f* **-a** light source

luna *f* moon; *fig* **avere la ~ storta** be in a mood; **~ crescente / calante** crescent / waning moon; **~ piena** full moon; **~ di miele** honeymoon

luna-park *m inv* amusement park, *Br* funfair

lunario *m*: **sbarcare il ~** make ends meet

lunatico (*pl* -ci) moody

lunedì *m inv* Monday; **il o di ~** on Mondays

lunetta *f* ARCHI lunette

lunghezza *f* length

lungo (*pl* -ghi) **1** *agg* long; *caffè* weak; **non essere ~!** don't be long!, don't take forever!; **a ~** at length, for a long time; *fig* **alla -a** in the long run; **andare per le -ghe** drag on; **di gran -a** by far **2** *prp* along; (*durante*) throughout

lungolago *m* (*pl* -ghi) lakeside, lakeshore

lungomare *m inv* sea front

lunotto *m* AUTO rear window

luogo *m* (*pl* -ghi) place; **~ di nascita** birthplace, place of birth; **avere ~** take place, be held; **fuori ~** out of place; **in primo ~** in the first place; **in qualche ~** somewhere, someplace; **in nessun ~** nowhere

lupo *m* wolf

lurido filthy

lusinga *f* (*pl* -ghe) flattery

lusingare <1e> flatter

lusinghiero flattering

lussazione *f* dislocation

lusso *m* luxury; **albergo** *m* **di ~**

luxury hotel
lussuoso luxurious
lustrare <1a> polish

lustro *m* shine, lustre, *Am* luster; *fig* prestige; (*periodo*) five-year period
lutto *m* mourning

M

m *abbr* (= **metro**) m (= metre)
ma but; (*eppure*) and yet; ~ **cosa dici?** what are you talking about?; ~ **va!** nonsense!; ~ **no!** not at all!, of course not!
maccheroni *mpl* macaroni *sg*
macchia *f* spot; *di sporco* stain; (*bosco*) scrub; **allargarsi a ~ d'olio** spread like wildfire
macchiare <1k> stain, mark
macchiato stained; **caffè** *m* ~ *espresso with a splash of milk*
macchina *f* machine; (*auto*) car; *fig* machinery; ~ **fotografica** camera; ~ **da cucire** sewing machine; ~ **da presa** cine camera; ~ **da scrivere** typewriter; ~ **sportiva** sports car; ~ **a noleggio** hire car, rental car; **fatto a** ~ machine made
macchinario *m* (*pl* -ri) machinery
macchinista *m* (*pl* -i) FERR train driver
macedonia *f:* ~ (**di frutta**) fruit salad
macellaio *m* (*pl* -ai), **-a** *f* butcher
macellare <1b> butcher
macelleria *f* butcher's
macerie *fpl* rubble *sg*
macigno *m* boulder
macinacaffè *m inv* coffee mill, coffee grinder
macinapepe *m inv* pepper mill, pepper grinder
macinare <1l> grind
macinino *m* mill; *spir* old banger
macrobiotica *f* health food; **negozio** *m di* ~ health food shop
macrobiotico (*mpl* -ci) macrobiotic
macroscopico (*pl* -ci) *fig* huge,

enormous; *errore* monumental, colossal
Madonna *f* Madonna, Our Lady; PITT ~ **con bambino** Madonna and Child
madonnaro *m pavement artist specializing in sacred images*
madre *f* mother
madrelingua **1** *f* mother tongue **2** *m/f* native speaker
madrepatria *f* native land, mother country
madreperla *f* mother-of-pearl
madrevite *f* nut
madrina *f* godmother
maestà *f* majesty
maestoso majestic
maestrale *m* north-west wind
maestranze *fpl* workers
maestria *f* mastery
maestro **1** *agg* (*principale*) main; MAR **albero** *m* ~ main mast; **muro** *m* ~ loadbearing wall **2** *m* master; MUS, PITT maestro, master; **colpo** *m* **da** ~ masterstroke **3** *m*, **-a** *f* teacher; ~ **di nuoto** swimming teacher *or* instructor; ~ **di sci** ski instructor
mafia *f* Mafia
maga *f* witch
magari **1** *avv* maybe, perhaps **2** *int* ~**!** if only! **3** *cong* ~ **venisse** if only he would come
magazzinaggio *m* storage
magazzino *m* warehouse; *di negozio* stock room; (*emporio*) factory shop; **grandi -i** *pl* department stores
maggio *m* May
maggiolino *m* June bug, May beetle
maggiorana *f* marjoram

maggioranza *f* majority; **~ azionaria** majority shareholding

maggiorare <1a> increase

maggiore 1 *agg* bigger; (*più vecchio*) older; MUS major; **il ~** the biggest; *figlio* the oldest; *artista* the greatest; *azionista* the major, the largest; **la maggior parte del tempo / di noi** most of the time / of us, the majority of the time / of us; **andare per la ~** be a crowd pleaser **2** *m* MIL major

maggiorenne adult *attr*

maggioritario (*pl* -ri) majority; **sistema** *m* **~** first-past-the-post system

magia *f* magic

magico (*pl* -ci) magic(al)

magistrale (*eccellente*) masterful; **istituto** *m* **~** teacher training college

magistrato DIR *m* magistrate

maglia *f* top; (*maglione*) sweater; SP shirt, jersey; *ai ferri* stitch; **lavorare a ~** knit; SP **~ gialla** yellow jersey

maglieria *f* knitwear

maglietta *f* tee-shirt

maglione *m* sweater

magnanimo magnanimous

magnesia *f* magnesia

magnesio *m* magnesium

magnete *m* magnet

magnetico (*pl* -ci) magnetic

magnifico (*pl* -ci) magnificent

magnolia *f* magnolia

mago *m* **1** (*pl* -ghi) wizard **2** (*pl* -gi) **i re -gi** the Three Wise Men, the Magi

magro thin; *cibo* low in fat; *fig consolazione* small; *guadagno* meagre, *Am* meager

mai never; (*qualche volta*) ever; **~ più** never again; **più che ~** more than ever; **non accetterò e poi ~** I will never agree, never; **chi ha ~ detto che ...** who said that ...; **come ~?** how come?; **se ~** if ever; **meglio tardi che ~** better late than never; **dove / perché ~?** where / why on earth?

maiale *m* pig; (*carne f di*) **~** pork

maiolica *f* (*pl* -che) majolica

maionese *f* mayonnaise

mais *m* maize

maiuscola *f* capital (letter)

maiuscolo capital

mal → **male**

malandato *vestito, divano, macchina* dilapidated; *persona* poorly, not very well

malanno *m* misfortune; (*malattia*) illness

malapena: **a ~** hardly, barely

malaria *f* malaria

malaticcio (*pl* -cci) sickly

malato 1 *agg* ill; **essere ~ di cuore** have heart problems; **~ di mente** mentally ill **2** *m*, **-a** *f* ill person

malattia *f* illness; **essere / mettersi in ~** be / go on sick leave; **~ infettiva** infectious disease; **-e** *pl* **della pelle** skin diseases; **-e** *pl* **veneree** sexually transmitted diseases

malavita *f* underworld

malavoglia *f* unwillingness, reluctance; **di ~** unwillingly, grudgingly, reluctantly

malconcio (*pl* -ci) *vestito, divano, macchina* dilapidated, the worse for wear; *persona* poorly, not very well

malcontento 1 *agg* discontented, dissatisfied **2** *m* discontent

malcostume *m* immorality

maldestro awkward, clumsy

male 1 *m* evil; **che c'è di ~?** where's the harm in it?; **andare a ~** go off, go bad; **aversela** *o* **prendersela a ~** take it the wrong way; MED **mal di gola** sore throat; **mal di testa / di denti** headache / toothache; **mal di mare** seasickness; **far ~ a qu** hurt s.o.; **mi fa ~ il braccio** my arm hurts; **il cioccolato mi fa ~** chocolate doesn't agree with me; **fare ~ alla salute** be bad for you; **farsi ~** hurt o.s. **2** *avv* badly; **capire ~** misunderstand; **di ~ in peggio** from bad to worse; **meno ~!** thank goodness!; **stare ~** (*essere malato*) be ill; (*essere giù*) be depressed; **il giallo mi sta ~** yellow doesn't suit me, I don't suit yellow; **il divano sta ~ qui** the couch doesn't look right here; **sta ~ ...** it's not done to ...; **mi ha**

risposto ~ he gave me a rude answer

maledetto 1 *pp* → **maledire 2** *agg* dratted, damn(ed)

maledire <3t> curse

maledizione *f* curse; ~*!* damn!

maleducato bad-mannered, uncouth

malessere *m* indisposition; *fig* malaise

malfamato disreputable

malfatto *cosa* badly made

malfattore *m* criminal

malformazione *f* MED, BIO malformation

malgoverno *m* POL misgovernment

malgrado 1 *prp* in spite of, despite **2** *avv mio/tuo* ~ against my/your will **3** *cong* although

maligno malicious, spiteful; MED malignant

malinconia *f* melancholy

malinconico (*pl* -ci) melancholic

malincuore: *a* ~ reluctantly, unwilling

malintenzionato 1 *agg* shady, suspicious **2** *m*, -**a** *f* shady character

malinteso *m* misunderstanding

malizia *f* (*cattiveria*) malice, spite; (*astuzia*) trick; *con* ~ maliciously, spitefully

malizioso malicious, spiteful; *sorriso* mischievous

malloppo *m* (*refurtiva*) loot

malmenare <1a> mistreat

malmesso *vestito, divano, macchina* the worse for wear; *sono un po'* ~ I'm a bit hard up

malnutrito under-nourished

malnutrizione *f* malnutrition

malore *m*: *è stato colto da un* ~ he was suddenly taken ill

malsano unhealthy

malsicuro unsafe

malta *f* mortar

maltempo *m* bad weather

malto *m* malt

maltrattare <1a> mistreat, ill-treat

malumore *m* bad mood; *essere di* ~ be in a bad mood

malvagio (*pl* -gi) evil, wicked

malvisto unpopular

malvivente *m* lout

malvolentieri unwillingly, reluctantly

mamma *f* mother, mum; ~ *mia!* goodness!

mammella *f* breast

mammifero *m* mammal

mammografia *f* mammography

manager *m/f* manager

manageriale managerial, management *attr*

mancanza *f* lack (*di* of); (*errore*) oversight; ~ *di abitazioni* housing shortage; ~ *di corrente* power failure; ~ *di personale* lack of staff, staff shortage; *per* ~ *di tempo* for lack of time

mancare <1d> **1** *v/i* be missing; (*venire meno*) fail; (*morire*) pass away; *a qu manca qc* s.o. lacks sth; *mi mancano le forze* I don't have the strength; *mi manca la casa* I miss home; *mi mancano 5000 lire* I'm 5000 lire short; *manca la benzina nella macchina* the car needs filling up; *mancano tre mesi a Natale* it's three months to Christmas; *sentirsi* ~ feel faint; *non mancherò* I'll do that, I'll be sure to do it; *c'è mancato poco che cadesse* he almost fell; *ci mancherebbe altro!* no way!, you must be joking!; ~ *di qc* (*non avere*) lack sth, be lacking in sth; ~ *di fare qc* fail *or* omit to do sth; ~ *di parola* break one's promise **2** *v/t* miss

mancato *occasione* missed, lost; *tentativo* unsuccessful; *è un poeta* ~ he should have been a poet; ~ *pagamento* non-payment

manchevole faulty, defective

mancia *f* (*pl* -ce) tip

manciata *f* handful

mancino 1 *agg* left-handed; *fig colpo m* ~ blow beneath the belt, dirty trick **2** *m*, -**a** *f* left-hander

mandante *m/f* DIR client; F *person who hires a contract killer*

mandare <1a> send; ~ *qu a prendere qc* send s.o. for sth; ~ *a monte*

M

ruin, send up in smoke F; *fig* **~ giù** digest, take in

mandarino *m* BOT mandarin (orange)

mandato *m* POL mandate; DIR warrant; **~ bancario** banker's order; **~ di pagamento** payment order; **~ d'arresto** arrest warrant

mandibola *f* jaw

mandolino *m* mandolin

mandorla *f* almond

mandorlo *m* almond tree

mandria *f* herd

maneggevole easy to handle, manageable

maneggiare <1f> handle (*anche fig*)

maneggio *m* (*pl* -ggi) handling; *per cavalli* riding school

manesco (*pl* -chi) a bit too ready with one's fists

manette *fpl* handcuffs

manganello *m* truncheon

mangereccio (*pl* -ci) edible

mangiabile edible

mangiacassette *m* *inv*, **mangianastri** *m inv* cassette player

mangiare 1 *v/t* <1f> eat; *fig* squander; **mangiarsi le parole** mumble; **mangiarsi un'occasione** throw away *or* waste an opportunity **2** *m* food

mangime *m* fodder

mangiucchiare <1g> snack, eat between meals

mango *m* (*pl* -ghi) mango

mania *f* mania

Manica *f*: **la ~** the (English) Channel

manica *f* (*pl* -che) sleeve; **senza -che** sleeveless; **è un altro paio di -che!** that's another kettle of fish

manicaretto *m* delicacy

manichino *m* dummy

manico *m* (*pl* -chi *o* -ci) handle; *di violino* neck

manicomio *m* (*pl* -mi) mental home

manicotto *m* TEC sleeve

manicure *f inv* manicure; (*persona*) manicurist

maniera *f* (*modo*) way, manner; (*stile*) manner; **-e** *pl* manners

manifattura *f* manufacture; (*stabili-*

mento) factory

manifestante *m/f* demonstrator

manifestare <1b> **1** *v/t* (*esprimere*) express; (*mostrare*) show, demonstrate **2** *v/i* demonstrate

manifestarsi appear, show up; *di malattia* manifest itself

manifestazione *f* expression; *il mostrare* show, demonstration; **~ di protesta** demonstration, demo F; **~ sportiva** sporting event

manifesto 1 *agg* obvious **2** *m* poster

maniglia *f* handle; *di autobus, metro* strap

manipolare <1m> manipulate; *vino* adulterate

manipolazione *f* manipulation; *di vino* adulteration

mano *f* (*pl* -i) hand; **fuori ~** out of the way, not easy to get at; *fig* **alla ~** approachable; **di seconda ~** second-hand; **dare una ~ a qu** give s.o. a hand; **mettere ~ a qc** start sth; **lavo le pentole che sporco a ~ a ~** I wash the dirty pots as I go along; **tenersi per ~** hold hands; **man ~ che** as (and when); **-i in alto!** hands up!

manodopera *f* labo(u)r

manomettere <3ee> tamper with

manopola *f* knob

manoscritto *m* manuscript

manovale *m* hod carrier

manovella *f* starting handle; TEC crank

manovra *f* manoeuvre, *Am* maneuver

manovrare <1c> **1** *v/t* TEC operate; FERR shunt; *fig* manipulate **2** *v/i* manoeuvre, *Am* maneuver

mansarda *f* (*locale*) attic

mansueto docile

mantello *m* (*cappa*) cloak; *di animale* coat; (*strato*) covering, layer

mantenere <2q> keep, maintain; *famiglia* keep, maintain; *in buono stato* maintain; **mantenersi in forma** keep in shape

mantenimento *m* maintenance; *di famiglia* keep

manto *m* cloak; *di animale* coat; *fig* **~**

di neve mantle of snow

Mantova *f* Mantua

mantovano 1 *agg* Mantuan **2** *m*, **-a** *f* native of Mantua

manuale 1 *agg* manual **2** *m* manual, handbook

manubrio *m* (*pl* -ri) handlebars *pl*

manutenzione *f* maintenance

manzo *m* steer, bullock; *carne* beef

mappa *f* map

mappamondo *m* globe

maratona *f* marathon

maratoneta *m/f* (*mpl* -i) marathon runner

marca *f* (*pl* -che) brand, make; (*etichetta*) label; ~ *da bollo* revenue stamp

marcare <1d> mark; *goal* score

marcato *accento, lineamenti* strong

marchiare <1k> brand (*anche fig*)

marchio *m* (*pl* -chi) FIN brand; ~ *depositato* registered trademark

marcia *f* (*pl* -ce) march; SP walk; TEC AUTO gear; ~ *indietro* reverse; *mettersi in* ~ set off

marciapiede *m* pavement, *Am* sidewalk; FERR platform

marciare <1f> march

marcio (*pl* -ci) bad, rotten; (*corrotto*) corrupt, rotten to the core; *avere torto* ~ be totally wrong

marcire <4d> go bad, rot; *fig* rot

marco *m* (*pl* -chi) mark

mare *m* sea; *in alto* ~ on the high seas

marea *f* tide; *fig una* ~ *di* loads of; *alta* ~ high tide; *bassa* ~ low tide; ~ *nera* oil slick

mareggiata *f* storm

maremoto *m* tidal wave

margarina *f* margarine

margherita *f* marguerite

margheritina *f* daisy

margine *m* margin; (*orlo*) edge, brink; *vivere ai -i della società* live on the fringes of society

marina *f* coast(line); MAR navy; PITT seascape

marinaio *m* (*pl* -ai) sailor

marinare <1a> GASTR marinate; F ~ *la scuola* play truant, *Br* bunk off school F

marinato GASTR marinated

marino sea, marine

marionetta *f* puppet, marionette

marito *m* husband

marittimo maritime

marmellata *f* jam; ~ *di arance* marmalade

marmitta *f* AUTO silencer, *Am* muffler; ~ *catalitica* catalytic converter

marmo *m* marble

marmotta *f* marmot; *dormire come una* ~ sleep like a log

marocchino 1 *agg* Moroccan **2** *m*, **-a** *f* Moroccan

Marocco *m* Morocco

marrone 1 *agg* (chestnut) brown **2** *m colore* (chestnut) brown; (*castagno*) chestnut

marsala *m* Marsala, *dessert wine*

marsina *f* tails

Marte *m* Mars

martedì *m inv* Tuesday; ~ *grasso* Shrove Tuesday, *Br* Pancake Day F

martello *m* hammer; ~ *pneumatico* pneumatic drill

martire *m/f* martyr

martirio *m* (*pl* -ri) martyrdom

martora *f* marten

marxismo *m* Marxism

marxista *m/f* (*mpl* -i) Marxist

marzapane *m* marzipan

marziano *m* Martian

marzo *m* March

mascalzone *m* rogue, rascal

mascara *m inv* mascara

mascarpone *m* mascarpone

mascella *f* jaw

maschera *f* mask; *in cinema, teatro* usher; *donna* usherette; ~ *antigas* gas mask; ~ *subacquea* face mask; *ballo m in* ~ masked ball

mascherare <1l> mask; *fig* camouflage, conceal

mascherarsi put on a mask; (*travestirsi*) dress up (*da* as)

maschile *spogliatoio, abito* men's; *caratteristica* male; GRAM masculine

maschilista (*pl* -i) **1** *m* male chauvinist, sexist **2** *agg* chauvinistic, sexist

maschio (*pl* -chi) **1** *agg* male; *hanno*

tre figli -i they have three sons or boys **2** m (*ragazzo*) boy; (*uomo*) man; ZO male

mascolino masculine

mascotte f inv mascot

massa f mass; EL earth; F **una ~ di cosa da fare** masses of things to do F

massacrare <1a> massacre

massacro m massacre

massaggiare <1f> massage

massaggiatore m, **-trice** f masseur; *donna* masseuse

massaggio m (pl -ggi) massage

massaia f housewife

massiccio (pl -cci) **1** agg massive; *oro, noce ecc* solid **2** m massif

massima f saying, maxim; (*temperatura*) maximum; **di ~** *progetto, accordo* preliminary; **in linea di ~** generally speaking, on the whole

massimale m maximum

massimo 1 agg greatest, maximum **2** m maximum; **al ~** at most

mass media mpl mass media

masso m rock

masticare <1l & d> chew

mastice m mastic; (*stucco*) putty

mastino m mastiff

mastodontico (pl -ci) gigantic, enormous

masturbarsi <1a>, gen **masturbarsi** masturbate

masturbazione f masturbation

matassa f skein

matematica f mathematics, maths F, Am math F

matematico (pl -ci) **1** agg mathematical **2** m, **-a** f mathematician

materassino m airbed, lilo®

materasso m mattress

materia f matter; (*materiale*) material; (*disciplina*) subject; **~ facoltativa** optional subject; **~ obbligatoria** compulsory subject; **~ prima** raw material; **~ sintetica** synthetic (material)

materiale 1 agg material; (*rozzo*) coarse, rough **2** m material; TEC equipment

materialista (mpl -i) **1** agg materialistic **2** m/f materialist

maternità f inv motherhood; *in ospedale* maternity

materno maternal; **scuola** f **-a** nursery school

matita f pencil; **~ colorata** colo(u)red pencil; **~ per gli occhi** eye pencil; **~ per sopracciglia** eyebrow pencil

matrice f matrix

matricola f register; *all'università* first-year student

matrigna f stepmother

matrimoniale matrimonial

matrimonio m (pl -ni) marriage; *rito* wedding

mattina f morning; **di ~** in the morning; **questa ~** this morning; **domani ~** tomorrow morning

mattinata f morning; TEA matinee

mattiniero: essere ~ be an early bird

mattino m morning; **di buon ~** early in the morning

matto 1 agg mad, crazy, insane (**per** about); **avere una voglia -a di qc** be dying for sth; **essere ~ da legare** be insane, be mad as a hatter **2** m, **-a** f madman, lunatic; *donna* madwoman, lunatic; **mi piace da -i andare al cinema** I'm mad about the cinema

mattone m brick; *fig* **che ~!** what a turgid piece of writing!

mattonella f tile

mattutino morning attr

maturare <1a> *interessi* accrue; **~ una decisione** reach a decision

maturità f maturity; (*diploma*) A level

maturo *frutto* ripe; *persona* mature; **i tempi sono -i** the time is ripe

mausoleo m mausoleum

mazza f club; (*martello*) sledgehammer; *da baseball* bat; **~ da golf** golf club

mazzo m bunch, bundle; **~ di fiori** bunch of flowers, bouquet; **~ di chiavi** bunch of keys; **~ di carte** pack or deck of cards

mc *abbr* (= **metro cubo**) m³ (= cubic metre)

me (= **mi** before **lo, la, li, le, ne**) me; **dammelo** give me it, give it to me; **come** ~ like me; **fai come** ~ do what I do; **per** ~ for me; **secondo** ~ in my opinion

meccanica *f* mechanics; *di orologio* mechanism; **la ~ di un incidente** how an accident happened; **~ di precisione** precision engineering

meccanicamente mechanically

meccanico (*pl* -ci) **1** *agg* mechanical **2** *m* mechanic

meccanismo *m* mechanism

mecenate *m/f* sponsor

mèche *f inv* streak

medaglia *f* medal

medesimo (very) same; **il** ~ the (very) same; **la** -a the (very) same

media *f* average; **in** ~ on average; **superiore** (**inferiore**) **alla** ~ above (below) average; **~ oraria** average speed

mediano **1** *agg* central, middle **2** *m* SP half-back

mediante by (means of)

mediatore *m*, **-trice** *f* mediator

mediazione *f* mediation

medicamento *m* medicine

medicare <1l, b & d> *persona* treat; *ferita* clean, disinfect

medicazione *f* treatment; (*bende*) dressing

medicina *f* medicine; **~ interna** internal medicine; **~ legale** forensic medicine; **~ sportiva** sports medicine

medicinale **1** *agg* medicinal **2** *m* medicine

medico (*pl* -ci) **1** *agg* medical; **visita** *f* -**a** medical examination, physical F **2** *m* doctor; **~ generico** general practitioner, *Br* GP; **~ di famiglia** family doctor; **~ di guardia** duty doctor

medievale medi(a)eval

medio (*pl* -di) **1** *agg* *età, classe ecc* middle *attr*; *guadagno, statura, rendimento* average **2** *m* middle finger

mediocre mediocre

mediocrità *f* mediocrity

medioevo *m* Middle Ages

meditare <1l & b> **1** *v/t* think about; (*progettare*) plan **2** *v/i* meditate; (*riflettere*) think; **~ su qc** think about sth

meditazione *f* meditation; (*riflessione*) consideration, reflection

mediterraneo **1** *agg* Mediterranean **2** *m* **Mediterraneo** Mediterranean (Sea)

medium *m/f inv* medium

medusa *f* ZO jellyfish

megalomania *m* megalomania

meglio **1** *avv* better; **~!, tanto ~!** so much the better!; **alla** ~ to the best of one's ability; **di bene in** ~ better and better **2** *agg* better; *superlativo* best **3** *m* best; **fare del proprio** ~ do one's best **4** *f* **avere la** ~ **su** get the better of

mela *f* apple

melagrana *f* pomegranate

melanzana *f* aubergine, *Am* eggplant

melma *f* mud

melo *m* apple (tree)

melodia *f* melody

melodico (*pl* -ci) melodic

melodramma *m* (*pl* -i) melodrama

melodrammatico melodramatic

melograno *m* pomegranate tree

melone *m* melon

membrana *f* membrane; **~ del timpano** eardrum

membro *m* (*pl* le membra) ANAT limb; *persona* (*pl* i -i) member

memorabile memorable

memorandum *m inv* memo(random); (*promemoria*) memo

memoria *f* memory; INFOR storage capacity; **a** ~ by heart; **in** ~ **di** in memory of; **~ centrale** main memory; **questo nome non ti richiama alla** ~ **niente** doesn't that name remind you of anything?; **-e** *pl* memoirs

memorizzare <1a> memorize; INFOR save

menare <1a> lead; F (*picchiare*) hit

mendicante *m/f* beggar

mendicare <1l, d or 1d> **1** *v/t* beg (for); *aiuto*, *lavoro ecc* beg for, plead for **2** *v/i* beg

menefreghismo *m* couldn't-careless attitude

meninge *f*: F **spremersi le -e** rack one's brains F

meningite *f* meningitis

meno 1 *avv* least; *superlativo* least; MATH minus; *il ~ possibile* as little as possible; *di ~* at least; *a ~ che* unless; *per lo ~* at least; *sono le sei ~ un quarto* it's a quarter to six; *sempre ~* less and less; *fare a ~ di qc* do without sth; *venir ~ a qcno* forze desert s.o.; *venir ~ alla parola data* not keep one's word **2** *prp* except

menomato damaged; (*handicappato*) disabled

menomazioni *fpl* damage *sg*

mensa *f di fabbrica* canteen; MIL mess; *~ universitaria* refectory

mensile 1 *agg* monthly; *tessera f ~ per treno, autobus* monthly season ticket **2** *m* (*periodico*) monthly

mensilità *f inv* salary

mensola *f* bracket

menta *f* mint; *~ piperita* peppermint

mentale mental

mentalità *f inv* mentality

mentalmente mentally

mente *f* mind; *malato di ~* mentally ill; *avere in ~ di fare qc* be planning to do sth, be thinking about doing sth; *tenere a ~ qc* bear sth in mind; *non mi viene in ~ il nome di ...* I can't remember the name of ...; *mi è uscito di ~* it slipped my mind

mentire <4d or b> lie

mento *m* chin

mentre while

menù *m inv* menu *anche* INFOR

menzionare <1a> mention

menzogna *f* lie

meraviglia *f* wonder; *a ~* marvel(l)ously, wonderfully

meravigliare <1g> astonish

meravigliarsi: *~ di* be astonished by;

mi meraviglio di te you astonish me

meravigliato astonished

meraviglioso marvel(l)ous, wonderful

mercante *m* merchant

mercanteggiare <1f> bargain, haggle

mercantile 1 *agg* nave cargo *attr*; *porto* commercial **2** *m* cargo ship

mercanzia *f* merchandise

mercato *m* market; *~ coperto* covered market, indoor market; *~ estero* foreign market; *~ mondiale* world market; *~ interno* domestic market; *~ unico europeo* single European market; *~ nero* black market; *~ delle pulci* flea market; *a buon ~* cheap, inexpensive

merce *f* goods; *~ di contrabbando* contraband

merceria *f* (*pl* -ie) haberdashery

mercoledì *m inv* Wednesday; *~ delle Ceneri* Ash Wednesday

mercurio *m* mercury; AST **Mercurio** Mercury

merda P shit P

merenda *f* snack

meridiana *f* sundial

meridiano 1 *agg* midday *attr* **2** *m* meridian

meridionale 1 *agg* southern; *Italia f ~* southern Italy **2** *m/f* southerner

meridione *m* south; *il Meridione* southern Italy

meringa *f* (*pl* -ghe) meringue

meritare <1l & b> **1** *v/t* deserve; *non merita un prezzo così alto* it's not worth that much **2** *v/i*: *un libro che merita* a worthwhile book; *non ti arrabbiare, non merita* don't get angry, it's/he's not worth it

meritevole worthy (*di* of)

merito *m* merit; *in ~ a* as regards; *per ~ suo* thanks to him

merletto *m* lace

merlo *m* ZO blackbird; ARCHI *-i pl* battlements

merluzzo *m* cod

meschino mean, petty; (*infelice*) wretched

mescolanza f mixture

mescolare <1l> mix; *insalata* toss; *caffè* stir

mescolarsi mix, blend

mese m month; *una volta al* ~ once a month; *ai primi del* ~ on the first of every month

messa[1]: ~ *in piega* set; ~ *in scena* production; AUTO ~ *in marcia* starting; ~ *in moto* start-up; FOT ~ *a fuoco* focussing; ~ *a punto di meccanismo* adjustment; *di motore* (fine-)tuning; *di testo* finalization

messa[2] f REL mass; ~ *solenne* high mass

messaggero m messenger

messaggio m (pl -ggi) message

messale m missal

messicano 1 agg Mexican **2** m, **-a** f Mexican

Messico m Mexico

messinscena f production; *fig* act

messo pp → **mettere**

mestiere m trade; (*professione*) profession; *essere del* ~ be a professional *or* an expert

mestolo m ladle

mestruazione f menstruation

meta f destination; SP try; *fig* goal, aim

metà f inv half; *punto centrale* middle, centre; *siamo a* ~ *del viaggio* we're half-way there; *a* ~ *prezzo* half price; *a* ~ *strada* halfway; *fare a* ~ go halves (*di* on)

metabolico metabolic

metabolismo m metabolism

metadone m methadone

metafora f metaphor

metaforico (pl -ci) metaphorical

metallico (pl -ci) metallic

metallizzato metallic

metallo m metal; ~ *prezioso* precious metal

metallurgia f metallurgy

metamorfosi f inv metamorphosis

metano m methane

metanodotto m gas pipeline

meteora f meteor

meteorite m o f meteorite

meteorologico (pl -ci) meteoro-logical, weather *attr*; **bollettino** m ~ weather forecast; **servizio** m ~ weather service

meticoloso meticulous

metodico (pl -ci) methodical

metodo m method

metrica f metrics

metrico (pl -ci) metric

metro[1] m metre, *Am* meter; ~ *quadrato* square metre (*Am* meter); ~ *cubo* cubic metre (*Am* meter)

metrò[2] m inv (*metropolitana*) underground, *Am* subway

metronotte m inv night watchman

metropoli f inv metropolis

metropolitana f underground, *Am* subway

mettere <3ee> put; *vestito* put on; ~ *a punto meccanismo* adjust; *motore* (fine-)tune; ~ *in moto* start (up); ~ *in ordine* tidy up; ~ *al sicuro* put away safely; ~ *su casa* set up house; **mettiamo che** let's assume that

mettersi *abito, cappello ecc* put on; ~ *a letto* go to bed, take to one's bed; ~ *a sedere* sit down; AVIA, AUTO ~ *la cintura* fasten one's seat belt; ~ *a fare qc* start to do sth; ~ *in cammino* set out, get going

mezzaluna f (pl mezzelune) half moon, crescent; GASTR two-handled chopper

mezzanino m mezzanine

mezzanotte f midnight

mezzo 1 agg half; *uno e* ~ one and a half; *mezz'ora* half-hour; *le sei e* ~ half-past six; ~ *chilo* a half kilo; *a -a strada* halfway; *di -a età* middle-aged **2** avv half **3** m (*parte centrale*) middle; (*metà*) half; (*strumento*) means sg; (*veicolo*) means sg of transport; *prendere un* ~ *pubblico* use public transport; *-i pl di comunicazione di massa* mass media; *-i pl di pagamento* means of payment; *a* ~ by means of; *a* ~ *posta* by post,; *in* ~ *a due persone, due libri* between; *in* ~ *a quei documenti* in the middle of *or* among those papers; *in* ~ *alla stanza* in the middle of the room;

M

nel ~ di in the middle of; *giusto ~* happy medium

mezzobusto *m* (*pl* mezzibusti) half-length photograph / portrait

mezzofondo *m* middle distance

mezzogiorno *m* midday; GEOG **Mezzogiorno** south (of Italy), southern Italy

mezzoservizio *m*: *lavorare a ~* work part-time

mg *abbr* (= *milligrammo*) mg (= milligram)

mi¹ *m* MUS E; *nel solfeggio della scala* me, mi

mi² *pron* me; *riflessivo* myself; *eccomi* here I am

miagolare <11> miaow, mew

miagolio *m* miaowing, mewing

mica: *non ho ~ finito* I'm nowhere near finished; *non è ~ vero* there's not the slightest bit of truth in it; *~ male* not bad at all

miccia *f* fuse

micidiale *veleno*, *clima* deadly; *fatica*, *sforza* exhausting, killing

micio F *m* (*pl* -ci) (pussy) cat

micosi *f inv* mycosis

microbiologia *f* microbiology

microbo *m* microbe

microcamera *f* miniature camera

microchirurgia *f* microsurgery

microclima *m* microclimate

microcomputer *m inv* microcomputer

microcosmo *m* microcosm

microfilm *m inv* microfilm

microfono *m* microphone, mike F

microonda *f* microwave; *forno m a -e* microwave (oven)

microprocessore *m* microprocessor

microrganismo *m* microorganism

microscopico (*pl* -ci) microscopic

microscopio *m* (*pl* -pi) microscope

midollo *m* marrow; *~ osseo* bone marrow; *~ spinale* spinal cord

miei *mpl* di *mio* my

miele *m* honey

mietere <3a> harvest

migliaio *m* (*pl* -aia *f*) thousand; *un ~* a *or* one thousand; *fig un ~ di per-*

sone thousands of people; *a migliaia* in their thousands

miglio¹ *m* (*pl* -glia *f*) *misura* mile; *~ marino* nautical mile

miglio² *m grano* millet

miglioramento *m* improvement

migliorare <1a> **1** *v/t* improve **2** *v/i e* migliorarsi improve, get better

migliore better; *il ~* the best

mignolo *m* (*o dito ~*) little finger; *del piede* little toe

migrare <1a> migrate

migrazione *f* migration

-mila thousand; *due~* two thousand

milanese **1** *agg* of Milan **2** *m/f* inhabitant of Milan

Milano *f* Milan

miliardario *m* (*pl* -ri), **-a** *f* billionaire, multimillionaire

miliardo *m* billion

milionario *m* (*pl* -ri), **-a** *f* millionaire; *donna* millionairess

milione *m* million

militare <11> fight, militate (*contro* against; *per* for); *~ in un partito* be a member of a party **2** *agg* military **3** *m* soldier; *fare il ~* do one's military service

militarismo *m* militarism

militarista *m/f* (*mpl* -i) militarist

militarizzare <1a> hand over to the military; *partito* structure like the army

milite *m* soldier; *il ~ ignoto* the Unknown Soldier

militesente exempt from military service

milizia *f* militia

mille (*pl* mila) a thousand

millefoglie *m inv* vanilla slice

millennio *m* (*pl* -nni) millennium

millepiedi *m inv* millipede

millesimo *m/agg* thousandth

milligrammo *m* milligram(me)

millimetro *m* millimetre, *Am* -meter

milza *f* spleen

mimetizzare <1a> MIL camouflage

mimetizzarsi camouflage o.s.; *fig ~ tra la folla* get lost in the crowd

mimica *f* mime

mimo *m* mime

mimosa *f* mimosa

mina *f* mine; *di matita* lead

minaccia *f* (*pl* -cce) threat

minacciare <1f> threaten

minaccioso threatening

minare <1a> mine; *fig* undermine

minato: *campo m ~* minefield

minareto *m* minaret

minatore *m* miner

minatorio (*pl* -ri) threatening

minerale *m/agg* mineral

minestra *f* soup; *~ di fagioli* bean soup; *~ di verdura* vegetable soup

minestrina *f* clear soup, broth

minestrone *m* minestrone

miniatura *f* miniature

miniera *f* mine (*anche fig*)

minigolf *m inv* miniature golf

minigonna *f* mini(skirt)

minimizzare <1a> minimize

minimo **1** *agg* least, slightest; *prezzo, offerta* lowest; *salario, temperatura* minimum **2** *m* minimum; *come ~, dovresti ...* you should at least ...

ministero *m* ministry; (*gabinetto*) government, ministry; *pubblico ~* state prosecutor

ministro *m* minister; *~ degli Esteri* Foreign Secretary, *Am* Secretary of State; *~ degli Interni* Home Secretary, *Am* Secretary of the Interior; *primo ~* Prime Minister; *consiglio m dei -i* Cabinet

minoranza *f* minority

minorato **1** *agg* severely handicapped **2** *m*, *-a f* severely handicapped person

minore **1** *agg* minor; *di età* younger; *distanza* shorter; *più piccolo* smaller; **2** *m/f*: *vietato ai -i di 18 anni* no admittance to those under 18 years of age; *film* X-rated

minorenne **1** *agg* under-age **2** *m/f* minor

minuscola *f* small letter, lower case letter

minuscolo tiny, miniscule

minuto **1** *agg persona* tiny; *oggetto* minute; *descrizione, indagine* detailed; *commercio m al ~* retail trade **2** *m* minute; *60 pulsazioni al*

~ 60 beats a minute; *ho i -i contati* I don't have a minute to spare

minuzioso *descrizione* detailed; *ricerca* meticulous

mio (*pl* miei) **1** *agg* my; *un ~ amico* a friend of mine, one of my friends; *i miei amici* my friends **2** *pron*: *il ~* mine; *questo libro è ~* this book is mine, this is my book; *i miei* my parents

miope short-sighted

miopia *f* short-sightedness, myopia

mira *f* aim; (*obiettivo*) target; *prendere la ~* take aim; *prendere di ~* aim at; *fig prendere di ~ qu* have it in for s.o.

miracolo *m* miracle; *per ~* by a miracle, miraculously

miraggio *m* (*pl* -ggi) mirage

mirare <1a> aim (*a* at)

mirino *m* MIL sight; FOT viewfinder

mirtillo *m* bilberry

mirto *m* myrtle

miscela *f* mixture; *di caffè, tabacco* blend

miscelatore *m* GASTR mixer; *rubinetto* mixer tap

mischia *f* (*rissa*) scuffle; SP, (*folla*) scrum

mischiare <1k> mix; *carte* shuffle

mischiarsi mix

miscuglio *m* (*pl* -gli) mixture

miserabile wretched, miserable

miserevole pitiful

miseria *f* (*povertà*) poverty; (*infelicità*) misery; *costare una ~* cost next to nothing; F *porca ~!* damn and blast! F

misericordia *f* mercy; *avere ~ di qu* have pity on s.o.

misero wretched

misfatto *m* misdeed

missaggio *m* (*pl* -ggi) → **mixaggio**

missare → **mixare**

missile *m* missile; *~ a lunga gittata* long-range missile

missionario *m* (*pl* -ri), *-a f* missionary

missione *f* mission

misterioso mysterious

mistero *m* mystery

mistico (*pl* -ci) mystic(al)

misto **1** *agg* mixed **2** *m* mixture; ~ **lana** wool mix

misura *f* measurement; (*taglia*) size; (*provvedimento*), *fig* measure; MUS bar; **-e** *pl* **preventive** preventive measures; **unità** *f* **di** ~ unit of measurement; **con** ~ in moderation; **su** ~ made to measure

misurabile measurable, which can be measured

misurare <1a> measure; *vestito* try on; ~ **le spese** limit one's spending

misurarsi *in una gara* compete; ~ **con** compete with

misurato restrained

misurino *m* measuring spoon

mite *persona*, *inverno* mild; *condanna* light

mitigare <1l & e> lessen; *dolore* ease, lessen

mito *m* myth

mitologia *f* mythology

mitologico (*pl* -ci) mythological

mitra *m inv*, **mitragliatrice** *f* machine gun

mitt. *abbr* (= **mittente**) from

mittente *m/f* sender

mixaggio *m* mixing

mixare <1k> mix

ml *abbr* (= **millilitro**) ml (= millilitre)

M.M. *abbr* (= **Marina Militare**) Italian navy

mm *abbr* (= **millimetro**) mm (= millimetre)

mobile **1** *agg* mobile; *ripiano, pannello* removeable; **squadra** *f* ~ flying squad **2** *m* piece of furniture; **-i** *pl* furniture

mobilia *f* furnishings

mobilificio *m* furniture-making factory

mobilio *m* → **mobilia**

mobilità *f* mobility

mobilitare <1m> mobilize

moca *f* mocha

mocassino *m* moccasin

moda *f* fashion; **alla** ~ fashionable, in fashion; *vestirsi* fashionably; **di** ~ fashionable, in fashion; **fuori** ~ out of fashion, unfashionable

modalità *f inv* method

modella *f* model

modellare <1b> model

modello **1** *agg* model **2** *m* model; (*indossatore*) male model; *di vestito* style; (*formulario*) form

modem *m inv* INFOR modem

moderare <1l & c> moderate

moderato moderate

moderatore *m*, **-trice** *f* moderator

moderazione *f* moderation

modernizzare <1a> modernize

moderno modern

modestia *f* modesty

modesto modest; *prezzo* very reasonable

modico (*pl* -ci) reasonable

modifica *f* (*pl* -che) modification

modificare <1m & d> modify

modo *m* (*maniera*) way, manner; (*mezzo*) way; MUS mode; GRAM mood; ~ **di dire** expression; ~ **di vedere** way of looking at things; **per** ~ **di dire** so to speak; **se hai** ~ **di passare da me** if you could drop by; **a** ~ **mio** in my own way; **ad ogni** ~ anyway, anyhow; **di** ~ **che** so that; **in che** ~**?** how?; **in special** ~ especially

modulo *m* form; (*elemento*) module; ~ **di domanda** application form; ~ **d'iscrizione** registration form; ~ **di versamento** *banca* pay-in slip

mogano *m* mahogany

moglie *f* (*pl* -gli) wife

mola *f* grindstone; *di mulino* millstone

molare **1** *v/t* <1c> grind **2** *m* molar

mole *f* (*grandezza*) size

molecola *f* molecule

molestare <1b> bother, trouble; *sessualmente* sexually harass

molestia *f* bother, nuisance; ~ **sessuale** sexual harassment

molesto annoying

molla *f* spring; *fig* spur; **-e** *pl* tongs

mollare <1c> *corda* release, let go; F *schiaffo, ceffone* give; F *fidanzato* dump; ~ **la presa** let go

molle soft; (*bagnato*) wet

molleggiare <1f> be springy

molleggio *m* springs

molletta *f* hairgrip; *da bucato* clothes peg *or* pin

mollica *f* (*pl* -che) crumb

mollusco *m* (*pl* -chi) mollusc, *Am* mollusk

molo *m* pier

molotov *f inv* Molotov cocktail

molteplice multifaceted

moltiplicare <1m & d> **1** *v/t* multiply (*per* by) **2** *v/i e* **moltiplicarsi** multiply

moltitudine *f* multitude, host

molto 1 *agg* a lot of; *con nomi plurali* a lot of, many **2** *avv* a lot; *con aggettivi* very; ~ **meglio** much better, a lot better; *da* ~for a long time; *fra non* ~ before long

momentaneo momentary, temporary

momento *m* moment; *dal* ~ *che* from the moment that; *causale* since; *a -i* sometimes, at moments; *per il* ~ for the moment; *del* ~ short-lived; *sul* ~ at the time

monaca *f* (*pl* -che) nun

monaco *m* (*pl* -ci) monk

monarca *m* (*pl* -chi) monarch

monarchia *f* monarchy

monarchico (*pl* -ci) **1** *agg* monarchical **2** *m*, **-a** *f* monarchist

monastero *m* monastery; *di monache* convent

mondano society; (*terreno*) worldly; *fare vita -a* go out

mondare <1a> *frutta* peel

mondiale 1 *agg* world *attr*; *economia* world *attr*, global; *fenomeno, scala* worldwide; *di fama* ~ world-famous **2** *m*: *i -i di calcio* the World Cup

mondo *m* world; *giro m del* ~ world tour, tour round the world; *l'altro* ~ the next world; *il più bello del* ~ the most beautiful in the world; *di-vertirsi un* ~ enjoy o.s. enormously *or* a lot

monello *m*, **-a** *f* imp, little devil

moneta *f* coin; (*valuta*) currency; (*denaro*) money; (*spiccioli*) change; ~ *d'oro* gold coin

monetario (*pl* -ri) monetary; **Fondo** *m* ~ **internazionale** International Monetary Fund

mongolfiera *m* hot-air balloon

monito *m* reprimand

monografia *f* monograph

monogramma *m* (*pl* -i) monogram

monolocale *m* bedsit

monologo *m* (*pl* -ghi) monolog(ue)

monopattino *m* child's scooter

monopolio *m* (*pl* -li) monopoly

monopolizzare <1a> monopolize

monoposto *m* single-seater

monotonia *f* monotony

monotono monotonous

monouso disposable, throwaway

montacarichi *m inv* hoist

montaggio *m* (*pl* -ggi) TECH assembly; *di film* editing

montagna *f* mountain; *fig* **-e** *pl* **russe** rollercoaster *sg*

montagnoso mountainous

montanaro *m*, **-a** *f* person who lives in the mountains

montare <1a> **1** *v/t* go up, climb; *cavallo* get onto, mount; TEC assemble; *film* edit; GASTR whip; ~ *la* **guardia** mount guard **2** *v/i* go up; *venire* come up; ~ *in macchina* get into; ~ *su scala* climb; *pullman* get on

montarsi: ~ *la testa* get a swollen head, get bigheaded

montatura *f* *di occhiali* frame; *di gioiello* mount; *fig* set-up F, frame-up F

monte *m* mountain; *fig* mountain, pile; *a* ~ upstream; *fig* **mandare a** ~ ruin, mess up F

montone *m* ram; *pelle, giacca* sheepskin

montuoso mountainous

monumento *m* monument

moquette *f inv* fitted carpet

mora *f* BOT *del gelso* mulberry; *del rovo* blackberry

morale 1 *agg* moral **2** *f* morals *pl*; *di favola ecc* moral **3** *m* morale; *essere giù di* ~ be feeling a bit down; *tirare su il* ~ *a qu* cheer s.o. up, lift s.o.'s spirits

moralista *m/f* (*mpl* -i) moralist

M

morbidezza f softness
morbido soft
morbillo m measles sg
morbo m disease
morboso fig unhealthy, unnatural; curiosità morbid
mordace fig biting, mordant
mordere <3uu> bite
morena f moraine
morfina f morphine
moribondo dying
morire <4k> die; fig ~ **di paura** be scared to death; **muoio dalla voglia di una birra** I could murder a pint F, I'm dying for a beer F
mormorare <1l> murmur; (bisbigliare, lamentarsi) mutter
mormorio m murmuring; (brontolio) muttering
morsetto m TEC clamp; EL terminal
morsicare <1l, c & d> bite
morso 1 pp → **mordere 2** m bite; di cibo bit, mouthful; per cavallo bit; **i -i pl della fame** the pangs of hunger
mortale ferita, malattia fatal; offesa, nemico deadly; uomo mortal
mortalità f mortality
morte f death
mortificare <1m & d> mortify
mortificazione f mortification

M

morto 1 pp → **morire 2** agg dead; **stanco** ~ dead tired **3** m, **-a** f dead man; donna dead woman; **i -i pl** the dead
mortorio m: F **essere un** ~ be deadly dull or boring
mortuario (pl -ri) death; **camera** f **-a** chapel
mosaico m (pl -ci) mosaic
mosca f (pl -che) fly; **peso** m ~ flyweight; ~ **cieca** blindman's buff; **restare con un pugno di -e** come away empty-handed
moscatello m muscatel
moscato 1 agg muscat; **noce** f **-a** nutmeg **2** m muscatel
moscerino m gnat, midge
moschea f mosque
moscio (pl -sci) thin, flimsy; fig limp, washed out
moscone m ZO bluebottle; (imbar-

cazione) pedalo
mossa f movement; fig e di judo, karate move
mosso 1 pp → **muovere 2** agg mare rough
mostarda f mustard
mosto m must, unfermented grape juice
mostra f show; (esposizione) exhibition; fig **mettere in** ~ show off
mostrare <1a> show; (indicare) point out
mostrarsi appear
mostro m monster
mostruoso monstrous
motel m inv motel
motivare <1a> cause; personale motivate; (spiegare) explain, give reasons for
motivazione f (spiegazione) explanation; (stimolo) motivation
motivo m reason; MUS theme, motif; su tessuto pattern; **per quale ~?** for what reason?, why?
moto[1] m movement; **fare** ~ get some exercise; **mettere in** ~ motore start (up); fig set in motion
moto[2] f (motor)bike
motocicletta f motorcycle
motociclista m/f (mpl -i) motorcyclist
motociclo m motorcycling
motore m engine; ~ **Diesel** diesel engine; ~ **a due tempi** two-stroke engine; ~ **a quattro tempi** four-stroke engine; ~ **a combustione** internal combustion engine; INFOR ~ **di ricerca** search engine; ~ **fuoribordo** outboard (motor or engine); **veicolo** m **a** ~ motor vehicle; **accendere il** ~ start (up) the engine, turn the key in the ignition; **fermare il** ~ turn off the engine
motorino m moped; ~ **d'avviamento** starter
motorizzato motorized; F **sei** ~ have you got wheels? F
motoscafo m motorboat
motoscooter m inv (motor) scooter
motrice f FERR railcar
motteggio m (pl -ggi) joke

motto *m* motto

mouse *m inv* INFOR mouse

movente *m* motive

movimento *m* movement; (*vita*) life, bustle

mozione *m* motion; **~ di fiducia** vote of confidence

mozzarella *f* mozzarella, *buffalo-milk cheese*

mozzicone *m* cigarette end, (cigarette) stub

mozzo *m* TEC hub

mq *abbr* (= **metro quadrato**) sq m (= square metre)

mucca *f* (*pl* -cche) cow

mucchio *m* (*pl* -chi) pile, heap

muco *m* (*pl* -chi) mucus

mucosa *f* mucous membrane

muffa *f* mo(u)ld; **sapere di ~** taste mo(u)ldy; **fare la ~** go mo(u)ldy

mughetto *m* lily-of-the-valley

mugolare <1l> *di cane* whine; (*gemere*) moan, whine

mugolio *m* whining

mugugnare <1a> grumble

mulattiera *f* mule track

mulatto *m*, **-a** *f* mulatto

mulinello *m su canna da pesca* reel; *vortice d'acqua* eddy

mulino *m* mill; **~ a vento** windmill

mulo *m* mule

multa *f* fine

multare <1a> fine

multicolore multicolo(u)red

multiculturale multicultural

multimediale multimedia

multinazionale *f* agg multinational

multiplo multiple

multiuso multipurpose

mungere <3d> milk

municipale municipal; **consiglio** *m* **~** town council

municipio *m* (*pl* -pi) town council, municipality; *edificio* town hall

munire <4d>: **~ di** supply with, provide with

munizioni *fpl* ammunition

muovere <3ff> 1 *v/t* move 2 *v/i partire* move off (*da* from); **~ incontro a qu** move towards s.o.

muoversi move; F (*sbrigarsi*) get a

move on F

muraglia *f* wall

murale 1 *agg* wall *attr* 2 *m* PITT mural

murare <1a> (*chiudere*) wall up

muratore *m* bricklayer

muratura *f* brickwork

murena *f* moray (eel)

muro *m* (*pl anche* le mura) wall; **~ del suono** sound barrier; *fig* **mi ha messo con le spalle al ~** he'd got my back against the wall; **le -a** *fpl* (city) walls

muschio *m* (*pl* -chi) BOT moss

muscolare muscular; **strappo** *m* **~** strained muscle

muscolatura *f* muscles *pl*

muscolo *m* muscle

muscoloso muscular

museo *m* museum; **~ etnologico** folk museum; **~ d'arte** museum

museruola *f* muzzle

musica *f* music; **~ da camera** chamber music; **~ leggera** light music, easy-listening music

musicale musical; **strumento** *m* **~** musical instrument

musicassetta *f* (music) tape

musicista *m/f* (*mpl* -i) musician

muso *m di animale* muzzle; **tenere il ~ a qu** be in a huff with s.o.

musone *m* sulker

musulmano 1 *agg* Muslim, Moslem 2 *m*, **-a** *f* Muslim, Moslem

muta *f di cani* pack; SP wetsuit

mutabile changeable

mutamento *m* change

mutande *fpl di donna* knickers; *di uomo* (under)pants

mutandine *fpl* knickers; **~ (da bagno)** (swimming) trunks

mutare <1a> *v/t & v/i* change

mutevole → **mutabile**

mutilare <1l> mutilate

mutilato *m* disabled ex-serviceman

mutilazione *f* mutilation

muto 1 *agg* dumb; (*silenzioso*) silent, dumb; **essere ~ dallo stupore** be struck dumb with astonishment; **film ~** silent movie 2 *m*, **-a** *f* mute

mutua *f* fund *that pays out sickness benefit*; **medico** *m* **della -a** doctor

M

recognized by the mutua

mutuato *m*, **-a** *f* person entitled to

sickness benefit

mutuo 1 *agg* mutual **2** *m* mortgage

N

N *abbr* (= **nord**) N (= north)

n. *abbr* (= **numero**) No. (= number)

nacchere *fpl* castanets

nafta *f* naphtha

nano 1 *agg* dwarf **2** *m*, **-a** *f* dwarf

napoletano 1 *agg* Neapolitan **2** *m*, **-a** *f* Neapolitan

Napoli *f* Naples

nappa *f* tassel; (*pelle*) nappa (*type of soft leather*)

narciso *m* BOT narcissus

narcosi *f inv* narcosis

narcotico *m* (*pl* -ci) narcotic

narcotizzare <1a> drug

narice *f* nostril

narrare <1a> tell, narrate

narratore, **-trice** *f* narrator

nascere <3gg> be born; BOT come up; *fig* develop, grow up; *di sole* rise, come up; **sono nato a Roma** I was born in Rome; **le è nata una figlia** she's had a little girl

nascita *f* birth; **fin dalla ~** from birth

nascondere <3hh> hide, conceal

nascondersi hide

nascondiglio *m* (*pl* -gli) hiding place

nascosto 1 *pp* → **nascondere 2** *avv*: **di ~** in secret; **di ~ a qu** unbeknownst to s.o.

nasello *m* (*pesce*) hake

naso *m* nose

nastro *m* tape; *per capelli*, *di decorazione* ribbon; **~ adesivo** adhesive tape, Sellotape®, *Am* Scotch tape®; **~ isolante** insulating tape, *Am* friction tape; **~ magnetico** magnetic tape

Natale *m* Christmas; **vigilia** *f* **di ~** Christmas Eve; **buon ~!** Merry Christmas!

natale *agg* of one's birth

natalità *f* birth rate, number of births

natalizio (*pl* -zi) Christmas

natante 1 *agg* floating **2** *m* boat

nativo 1 *agg* native **2** *m*, **-a** *f* native

NATO *abbr* (= **Organizzazione del Trattato nord-atlantico**) NATO (= North Atlantic Treaty Organization

nato → **nascere**

natura *f* nature; PITT **~ morta** still life; **contro ~** unnatural; **essere paziente per ~** be patient by nature, be naturally patient; **secondo ~** in harmony with nature

naturale natural; **scienze** *fpl* **-i** natural sciences

naturalezza *f* naturalness; **con ~** naturally

naturalizzare <1a>: **è naturalizzato americano** he's a naturalized American

naturalmente naturally, of course; *comportarsi* naturally

naufragare <1l & e> *di nave* be wrecked; *di persona* be shipwrecked; *fig* be ruined, come to grief

naufragio *m* (*pl* -gi) shipwreck; *fig* ruin; **fare ~** *di nave* be wrecked; *di persona* be shipwrecked

naufrago *m* (*pl* -ghi), **-a** *f* survivor of a shipwreck

nausea *f* nausea; **avere la ~** feel sick, *Am* feel nauseous; **dare la ~ a qu** make s.o. feel sick, nauseate s.o. (*anche fig*)

nauseare <1l> nauseate (*anche fig*)

nautica *f* seamanship

nautico (*pl* -ci) nautical

navale naval; *cantiere m* ~ shipyard

navata *f* ARCHI: ~ *centrale* nave; ~ *laterale* aisle

nave *f* ship; ~ *da carico* cargo ship *or* vessel; ~ *passeggeri* passenger ship; ~ *traghetto* ferry

navetta **1** *agg inv*: *bus m* ~ shuttle bus **2** *f* shuttle; ~ *spaziale* space shuttle

navicella *f di astronave* nose cone

navigabile navigable

navigare <11 & e> sail; INFOR navigate

navigatore *m* navigator

navigazione *f* navigation

nazionale **1** *agg* national **2** *f* national team; *la ~ italiana* the Italian team

nazionalismo *m* nationalism

nazionalista *m/f* (*mpl* -i) nationalist

nazionalistico (*pl* -ci) nationalistic

nazionalità *f inv* nationality

nazionalizzare <1a> nationalize

nazione *f* nation

N.B. *abbr* (= *nota bene*) NB (= nota bene)

N.d.A. *abbr* (= *nota dell'autore*) author's note

N.d.E. *abbr* (= *nota dell'editore*) publisher's note

N.d.T. *abbr* (= *nota del traduttore*) translator's note

NE *abbr* (= *nord-est*) NE (= northeast)

ne **1** *pron* (*di lui*) about him; (*di lei*) about her; (*di loro*) about them; (*di ciò*) about it; ~ *sono contento* I'm happy about it; ~ *ho abbastanza* I have enough **2** *avv* from there; ~ *vengo adesso* I've just come back from there

né: ~ ... ~ neither ... nor; *non l'ho trovato ~ a casa ~ in ufficio* I couldn't find him either at home or in the office

neanche neither; *io non vado – neanch'io* I'm not going – neither am I *or* me neither F; *non l'ho ~ visto* I didn't even see him; ~ *per sogno!* in your dreams!

nebbia *f* fog

nebbioso foggy

nebulosa *f* AST nebula

nebuloso *fig* vague, hazy

necessaire *m inv*: ~ (*da viaggio*) beauty case

necessario (*pl* -ri) **1** *agg* necessary **2** *m*: *il ~ per vivere* the basic necessities *pl*

necessità *f inv* need; *ho ~ di parlarti* I need to talk to you; *articolo m di prima* ~ essential; *in caso di ~* if necessary, if need be; *fare qc senza* ~ do sth needlessly; *per ~* out of necessity

nefrite *f* MED nephritis

negare <1e> deny; (*rifiutare*) refuse

negativa *f* negative

negativo *m/agg* negative

negato: *essere ~ per qc* be hopeless at sth

negazione *f* denial; GRAM negative

negli *prp* in and *art* gli

negligente careless, negligent

negligenza *f* carelessness, negligence

negoziante *m/f* shopkeeper

negoziare <1g & c> **1** *v/t* negotiate **2** *v/i* negotiate, bargain; FIN ~ *in* trade in, deal in

negoziato *m* negotiation; *-i pl di pace* peace negotiations

negoziazione *f* negotiation

negozio *m* (*pl* -zi) shop; (*affare*) deal; ~ *di generi alimentari* food shop; ~ *specializzato* specialist shop

negro **1** *agg* black **2** *m*, *-a f* black (man / woman)

nei, nel, nell', nella, nelle, nello *prp* in and *art* i, il, l', la, le, lo

nemico (*pl* -ci) **1** *agg* enemy *attr* **2** *m*, *-a f* enemy

nemmeno neither; ~ *io* me neither; ~ *per idea!* don't even think about it!

neo *m* mole; *fig* flaw

neonato *m*, *-a f* infant, newborn baby

neppure not even; *non ci vado – ~ io* I'm not going – neither am I *or* me neither F

N

nero 1 *agg* black; *fig giornata, periodo* black; *umore* awful, filthy F **2** *m* black; *di seppia* ink **3** *m*, **-a** *f* black (man / woman)

nerofumo *m* lampblack

nervo *m* nerve; **dare sui** (*o ai*) **-i a qu** get on s.o.'s nerves

nervosismo *m* nervousness

nervoso 1 *agg* nervous; (*irritabile*) edgy; (*asciutto*) sinewy; **esaurimento** *m* ~ nervous breakdown **2** *m* F: **il** ~ irritation; **mi viene il** ~ I'm beginning to get really irritated, this is getting on my nerves

nespola *f* medlar

nespolo *m* medlar (tree)

nessuno 1 *agg* no; **non chiamare in nessun caso** don't call in any circumstances; **c'è –a notizia?** is there any news? **2** *pron* nobody, no one; **hai visto ~?** did you see anyone *or* anybody?

nettezza *f* cleanliness; ~ **urbana** cleansing department

netto clean; (*chiaro*) clear; *reddito, peso* net; **interrompere qu di** ~ break in on s.o.

netturbino *m*, **-a** *f* dustman

neurologia *f* neurology

neurologico neurological

neurologo *m* (*pl* -gi), **-a** *f* neurologist

neutrale neutral

neutralità *f* neutrality

neutralizzare <1a> neutralize

neutro neutral; GRAM neuter

neve *f* snow

nevicare <1l & d> snow

nevicata *f* snowfall

nevoso snowy

nevralgia *f* neuralgia

nevralgico (*pl* -ci) neuralgic; **punto** *m* ~ specially painful point; *fig* weak point

nevrosi *f* neurosis

nevrotico (*pl* -ci) **1** *agg* neurotic; F short-tempered, quick to fly off the handle F **2** *m*, **-a** *f* neurotic

nicchia *f* niche

nichel *m* nickel

nicotina *f* nicotine

nido *m* nest

niente 1 *pron m* nothing **2** *avv* nothing; **non ho** ~ I don't have anything, I have nothing; **lo fai tu?** – ~ **affatto!** are you going to do it? – no, I am not!; **tu hai detto che … –** ~ **affatto!** you said that … – no, I did not!; **non ho per – fame** I'm not at all hungry; **non ho capito per** ~ I didn't understand a thing

niente(di)meno no less; ~**!** that's incredible! you don't say!

ninfea *f* water-lily

nipote *m/f di zio* nephew; *donna, ragazza* niece *f*; *di nonno* grandson; *donna, ragazza* granddaughter *f*

nitidezza *f* clarity, clearness; FOT sharpness

nitido clear; FOT sharp

nitrire <4d> neigh

NO *abbr* (= *nord-ovest*) NW (= northwest)

no no; ~ **e poi** ~ absolutely not!, no and that's final!; **come** ~**!** of course!, naturally!; **se** ~ otherwise; **dire di** ~ say no; **credo di** ~ I don't think so

nobile 1 *agg* noble **2** *m/f* aristocrat

nobiltà *f* nobility

nocca *f* (*pl* -cche) knuckle

nocciola *f* hazelnut; **color** *m* ~ hazel

nocciolina *f*: ~ (**americana**) peanut, ground-nut, monkey-nut

nocciolo¹ *m* (*albero*) hazel (tree)

nocciolo² *m di frutto* stone; *di questione* heart, kernel

noce 1 *m* walnut (tree); (*legno*) walnut **2** *f* walnut; ~ **di cocco** coconut; ~ **moscata** nutmeg

nocepesca *f* nectarine

nocivo harmful

nodo *m* knot; *fig* crux; FERR junction; **avere un** ~ **in gola** have a lump in one's throat

noi *pron soggetto* we; *con prp* us; **a** ~ to us; **con** ~ with us; **senza di** ~ without us

noia *f* boredom; **-e** *pl* trouble *sg*; **dar** ~ **a qu** annoy s.o.; **venire a** ~ **a qu** start to bore s.o.

noioso boring; (*molesto*) annoying

noleggiare <1f> hire; MAR, AVIA charter

noleggio *m* hire; MAR, AVIA charter; **~ (di) biciclette** bike hire

nolo *m* hire; **prendere a ~** hire; **dare a ~** hire out

nome *m* name; GRAM noun; **~ di battesimo** Christian name; **~ e cognome** full name; **conoscere qu di ~** know s.o. by name; **in ~ di** in the name of

nomignolo *m* nickname

nomina *f* appointment

nominare <1l & c> (*menzionare*) mention; *a un incarico* appoint (**a** to)

non not; **~ ho fratelli** I don't have any brothers, I have no brothers; **~ ancora** not yet; **~ che io non voglia** not that I don't want to; **~ cedibile** not transferable, non-transferable; **nonché** let alone; (*e anche*) as well as

noncurante nonchalant, casual; **~ di** mindless of, heedless of

noncuranza *f* nonchalance, casualness

nondimeno nevertheless

nonno *m*, **-a** *f* grandfather; *donna* grandmother; **-i** *pl* grandparents

nonnulla *m inv* trifle

nono *m/agg* ninth

nonostante despite; **ciò ~** however

nonsenso *m* nonsense

non stop *agg inv* nonstop

nontiscordardimé *m inv* forget-me-not

non vedente *m/f* blind person

nord *m* north; **mare *m* del ~** North Sea; **a(l) ~ di** (to the) north of

nordest *m* north-east

nordico (*pl* -ci) northern; *lingue* Nordic

nordovest *m* north-west

norma *f* (*precetto*) rule, precept; TEC standard; **-e per l'uso** instructions (for use); **a ~ di legge** up to standard; **a ~ di legge ...** complies with ...

normale normal

normalità *f* normality

normalizzare <1a> normalize;

(*uniformare*) standardize

norvegese *agg, m/f* Norwegian

Norvegia *f* Norway

nostalgia *f* nostalgia; **avere ~ di casa** feel homesick; **avere ~ di qu** miss s.o.

nostrale local, home *attr*

nostrano local, home *attr*

nostro 1 *agg* our; **i -i genitori** *pl* our parents; **un ~ amico** a friend of ours 2 *pron*: **il ~** ours

nota *f* note; FIN bill; **degno di ~** noteworthy; **~ spese** expense account; **prendere ~ di qc** make a note of sth; *situazione, comportamento* take note of sth

notaio *m* (*pl* -ai) notary (public)

notare <1c> (*osservare*) notice; (*annotare*) make a note of, note down; *con segni* mark; **è da ~ che** please note that; **ti faccio ~ che** I'll have you know that

notariato *m* notaryship

notarile notarial

notevole *degno di nota* notable, noteworthy; *grande* considerable, substantial

notificare <1m & d> serve (**a** on)

notizia *f* piece *or* bit *or* item of news; **avere ~ di qu** have news of s.o., hear from s.o.; **-e** *pl* **sportive** sports news; **le ultime -e** *pl* the latest news

notiziario *m* (*pl* -ri) RAD, TV news item

noto well-known; **rendere ~** announce

notorietà *f* fame; *spreg* notoriety

notorio (*pl* -ri) well-known; *spreg* notorious

nottambulo *m*, **-a** *f* night owl

nottata *f* night; **fare la ~** stay up all night

notte *f* night; **di ~** at night; **buona ~!** good night!; **nel cuore della ~** in the middle of the night

notturno night(-time) *attr*; *animale* nocturnal; **ore** *fpl* **-e** hours of darkness

novanta ninety

novantesimo *m/agg* ninetieth

nove nine

novecento 1 *agg* nine hundred 2 *m*:

il Novecento the twentieth century

novella f short story

novembre m November

novità f inv novelty; (notizia) piece or item of news; **essere una ~ sul mercato** be new on the market

novizio (pl -zi) **1** agg novice **2** m, -a f beginner, novice; REL novice

nozione f notion, idea; **-i** pl **di base** rudiments

nozionistico (pl -ci) superficial

nozze fpl wedding sg; **~ d'argento** silver wedding (anniversary); **sposarsi in seconde ~** get married for the second time, remarry

ns. abbr (= **nostro**) our(s), used in correspondence

NU abbr (= **Nazioni Unite**) UN (= **United Nations**); (= **nettezza urbana**) cleansing department

nube f cloud

nubifragio m (pl -gi) cloudburst

nubile donna single, unmarried

nuca f (pl -che) nape of the neck

nucleare nuclear

nucleo m FIS nucleus (anche fig); **~ urbano** urban centre

nudismo m naturism, nudism

nudista m/f (mpl -i) naturist, nudist

nudità f nudity, nakedness

nudo 1 agg nude, naked; (spoglio) bare; **a occhio ~** to the naked eye **2** m PITT nude

nulla 1 avv nothing; **è solo una cosa da ~** it's nothing; **per ~** for nothing; **non per ~** not for nothing **2** m nothing; **non ti ho portato un bel ~** I haven't brought you anything at all

nullaosta m: fig **ottenere il ~** get the green light or go-ahead

nullo invalid; gol disallowed; voto spoiled; **dichiarare ~** declare null and void

numerale m numeral

numerare <1l> number

numerato numbered

numerico (pl -ci) numerical

numero m number; arabo, romano numeral; di scarpa size; **~ di casa** home (tele)phone number; **~ di targa** registration number, Am license number; **~ di telefono** phone number; **~ di volo** flight number; TELEC **sbagliare ~** dial the wrong number; **~ verde** 0800 number, Am toll-free number; **~ legale** quorum; EDU **~ chiuso** restricted enrol(l)ment; **sono venuti in gran ~** lots of them came; F **dare i -i** talk nonsense

numeroso numerous; famiglia, classe large

nuocere <3ii> **~ a** harm; **il fumo nuoce alla salute** smoking is bad for you

nuora f daughter-in-law

nuotare <1c> swim

nuotata f swim

nuotatore m, **-trice** f swimmer

nuoto m swimming; **attraversare la Manica a ~** swim across the Channel

nuovamente again

nuovo 1 agg new; **di ~** again; **essere ~ in una città** be new to a town; **~ fiammante** brand new **2** m: **che c'è di ~?** what's new?

nutriente nourishing

nutrimento m food

nutrire <4d or 4a> feed

nutrirsi: **~ di** live on

nutritivo nutritious

nutrizione f nutrition

nuvola f cloud; fig **cadere dalle -e** be taken aback

nuvoloso cloudy

nylon m nylon

O

O *abbr* (= **ovest**) W (= west)

o *cong* or; **~ ... ~** either ... or

oasi *f inv* oasis

obbedire → **ubbidire**

obbligare <1l, c & e>: **~ qu a fare qc** oblige *or* compel s.o. to do sth

obbligarsi commit o.s. (**a fare** to doing), undertake (**a fare** to do)

obbligatorio (*pl* -ri) obligatory, compulsory

obbligazione *f* obligation; FIN bond

obbligo *m* (*pl* -ghi) obligation; **d'~** obligatory

obesità *f* obesity

obeso obese

obiettare <1b> object, say (**a** to)

obiettivo 1 *agg* objective **2** *m* aim, objective; FOT lens

obiettore *m*: **~ di coscienza** conscientious objector

obiezione *f* objection; **fare ~ di coscienza** be a conscientious objector

obliquo oblique

obliterare <1m> *biglietto* punch

oblò *m inv* MAR porthole

oca *f* (*pl* -che) *f* goose; *fig* silly woman

occasionale casual; **i rapporti** *mpl* **-i** casual sex

occasionalmente occasionally

occasione *f* (*opportunità*) opportunity, chance; (*evento*) occasion; (*affare*) bargain; **automobile** *f* **d'~** second-hand *or* used car; **cogliere l'~** seize the opportunity, jump at the chance F; **all'~** if necessary; **in ~ di** on the occasion of

occhiaie *fpl* MAR bags under the eyes

occhiali *mpl* glasses, specs *Br* F; **~ da sole** sunglasses

occhiata *f* look, glance; **dare un'~** have a look at, glance at; (*sorvegliare*) keep an eye on

occhiello *m* buttonhole

occhio *m* (*pl* -cchi) eye; **a ~ nudo** to the naked eye; **a ~ e croce** roughly; **dare nell'~** attract attention, be noticed; **a quattr' -i** in private

occidentale western; **Europa** *f* **~** Western Europe

occidente *m* west; **a ~ di** (to the) west of

occorrente 1 *agg* necessary **2** *m* necessary materials *pl*

occorrenza *f*: **all'~** if necessary, if need be

occorrere <3o> be necessary; (*accadere*) occur; **mi occorre** I need; **Le occorre altro?** (do you need) anything else?; **occorre programmare le cose** we / you need to plan things; **non occorre!** there's no need!

occupare <1l & c> *spazio* take up, occupy; *tempo* occupy, fill; *posto* have, hold; *persona* keep busy; *di esercizio* occupy

occuparsi take care (**di** of), deal (**di** with); **occupati degli affari tuoi!** mind your own business!; **~ di qu** look after s.o., take care of s.o.

occupato TELEC engaged, *Am* busy; *posto, appartamento* taken; *gabinetto* engaged; *persona* busy; *città, nazione* occupied

occupazione *f di città, paese* occupation; (*attività*) pastime; (*impiego*) job

oceano *m* ocean; **Oceano Atlantico** Atlantic Ocean; **Oceano Pacifico** Pacific Ocean

OCSE *abbr* (= **Organizzazione per la Cooperazione e lo Sviluppo Economico**) OECD (= Organization for Economic Co-operation and Development)

oculista *m/f* (*pl* -i) ophthalmologist

od = **o** (*before a vowel*)

O

odiare <1k> hate, detest

odierno modern-day *attr*, of today, today's

odio *m* hatred

odioso hateful, odious

odontotecnico *m*, **-a** *f* dental technician

odorare <1a> **1** *v/t* smell **2** *v/i* smell (**di** of)

odorato *m* sense of smell

odore *m* smell, odo(u)r; **-i** *pl* GASTR herbs

odoroso fragrant, sweet-smelling

offendere <3c> offend

offendersi take offence, *Am* offense

offensiva *f* offensive

offensivo offensive

offerente *m* bidder; **maggior ~** highest bidder

offerta *f* offer; FIN supply; REL offering; (*dono*) donation; **in asta** bid; **~ d'impiego** job offer; **~ pubblica di acquisto** takeover bid; **~ speciale** special offer

offesa *f* offence, *Am* offense

offeso *pp* → **offendere**

officina *f* workshop; **per macchine** garage

offrire <4f & c> offer; **ti offro da bere** I'll buy *or* stand F you a drink; **posso offrirti qualcosa?** can I get you anything?

oggettivo objective

oggetto *m* object; **-i** *pl* **di valore** valuables

oggi today; **d'~** of today, today's; **da ~ a domani** overnight; **da ~ in poi** from now on; **~ stesso** today, this very day; **~ come ~** at the moment; **~ pomeriggio** this afternoon

oggigiorno nowadays

ogni every; **~ tanto** every so often; **~ sei giorni** every six days

Ognissanti *m inv* All Saints Day

ognuno everyone, everybody

Olanda *f* Holland

olandese 1 *agg m* Dutch **2** *m/f* Dutchman; *donna* Dutchwoman

oleandro *m* oleander

oleoso oily

olfatto *m* sense of smell

oliare <1k> oil

oliera *f type of cruet for oil and vinegar bottles*

Olimpiadi *fpl* Olympic Games, Olympics; **~ invernali** Winter Olympics

olimpionico (*pl* -ci) **1** *agg* Olympic *attr* **2** *m*, **-a** *f* Olympic contestant

olio *m* (*pl* -li) oil; **~ dei freni** brake fluid; **~ lubrificante** lubricating oil, lube; **~ per il cambio** gearbox oil; **~ extra-vergine d'oliva** extra-virgin olive oil; **~ solare** suntan oil

oliva *f* olive

olivo *m* olive (tree)

olmo *m* elm (tree)

OLP *abbr* (= **Organizzazione per la Liberazione della Palestina**) PLO (= Palestine Liberation Organization)

oltraggiare <1f> offend, outrage

oltraggio *m* (*pl* -ggi) offence, *Am* offense, outrage

oltre 1 *prp* in spazio, tempo after, past; (*più di*) over; **vai ~ il semaforo** go past the traffic lights; **aspetto da ~ un'ora** I've been waiting for more than *or* over an hour; **~ a** apart from **2** *avv* nello spazio further; *nel tempo* longer

oltremare overseas

omaggio *m* (*pl* -ggi) homage; (*dono*) gift; **copia (in) ~** free *or* complimentary copy; **~ pubblicitario** (free) gift; **essere in ~ con** come free with

ombelico *m* (*pl* -chi) navel

ombra *f* shadow; *zona non illuminata* shade; *fig* **un'~ di tristezza** a touch of sadness; **all'~** in the shade

ombrello *m* umbrella

ombrellone *m* parasol; *sulla spiaggia* beach umbrella

ombretto *m* eye shadow

ombroso shady; *fig persona* touchy

omelette *f inv* omelette, *Am* omelet

omeopatia *f* homeopathy

omeopatico (*pl* -ci) **1** *agg* homeopathic **2** *m*, **-a** *f* homeopath

omero *m* humerus

omesso *pp* → **omettere**

omettere <3ee> omit, leave out

omicida (*mpl* -di) **1** *agg* murderous **2** *m/f* murderer

omicidio *m* (*pl* -di) murder; **~ colposo** manslaughter; **tentato ~** attempted murder

omogeneizzato homogenized

omogeneo homogenous

omologare <1m, c & e> approve

omonimo 1 *agg* of the same name **2** *m* homonym **3** *m*, **-a** *f* namesake

omosessuale *agg*, *m/f* homosexual

omosessualità *f* homosexuality

OMS *abbr* (= **Organizzazione Mondiale della Sanità**) WHO (= World Health Organization)

on. *abbr* (= **onorevole**) Hon (= honourable)

oncologia *f* oncology

oncologo *m*, **-a** *f* oncologist

onda *f* wave; **-e** *pl* **corte** short wave; **-e** *pl* **lunghe** long wave; **-e** *pl* **medie** medium wave; RAD **andare in ~** go on the air

ondata *f* wave; **~ di caldo** heat wave; **~ di freddo** cold spell

ondeggiare <1f> *di barca* rock; *di bandiera* flutter

ondulato *capelli* wavy; *superficie* uneven; *cartone*, *lamiera* corrugated

onestà *f* honesty

onesto honest; *prezzo*, *critica* fair

onice *m* onyx

onnipotente omnipotent

onnipotenza *f* omnipotence

onnipresente ubiquitous

onnisciente omniscient

onniscienza *f* omniscience

onnivoro 1 *agg* omnivorous **2** *m*, **–a** *f* omnivore

onomastico *m* (*pl* -ci) name day

onorare <1a> be a credit to; **~ qu di qc** hono(u)r s.o. with sth

onorario (*pl* -ri) **1** *agg* honorary **2** *m* fee

onorato respected, hono(u)red

onore *m* hono(u)r; **in ~ di** in hono(u)r of

onorevole   1 *agg*   hono(u)rable **2 Onorevole** *m/f* Member of Parliament

onorificenza *f* hono(u)r

ONU *abbr* (= **Organizzazione delle Nazioni Unite**) UN (= United Nations)

OPA *abbr* (= **Offerta Pubblica di Acquisto (di azioni di società)**) takeover bid

opacità *f di vetro* opaqueness; *di colore, foto* darkness

opaco (*pl* -chi) *vetro* opaque; *calze, rossetto* dark

opera *f* work; MUS opera; **~ d'arte** work of art; **~ buona** good deed; **mettersi all'~** set to work

operaio (*pl* -ai) **1** *agg* working **2** *m*, **-a** *f* worker; **~ specializzato** skilled worker

operare <1l & c> **1** *v/t cambiamento* make; *miracoli* work; MED operate on **2** *v/i* act

operativo operational; *ricerca* applied; *ordine* operative; **piano** *m* **~** plan of operations

operatore *m*, **-trice** *f* operator; *televisivo, cinematografico* cameraman; **~ di Borsa** market trader; **~ sociale** social worker; **~ turistico** tour operator

operazione *f* operation; **~ finanziaria** transaction

operetta *f* operetta

operoso hard-working, industrious

opinione *f* opinion; **secondo la tua ~** in your opinion

oppio *m* opium

opporre <3ll> put forward, offer; *scuse, resistenza* offer

opporsi be opposed

opportunista *m/f* opportunist

opportunità *f inv* opportunity; *di decisione* timeliness; **pari ~** *pl* equal opportunities

opportuno suitable, appropriate; **al momento ~** at a suitable time, at the opportune moment

opposizione *f* opposition; POL **all'~** in opposition

opposto 1 *pp* → **opporre 2** *agg* opposite **3** *m* POL opposition

oppressione *f* oppression

oppressore *m* oppressor

opprimente oppressive

O

opprimere <3r> oppress

oppure or (else)

optare <1c>: ~ **per** choose, opt for

opuscolo m brochure

opzione f option

ora [1] f time; *unità di misura* hour; *che ~ è?, che -e sono?* what time is it?, what's the time?; ~ **legale** daylight saving time; ~ **locale** local time; **-e** pl **straordinarie** overtime sg; ~ **di punta** rush hour; TELEC peak time; *di buon'*~ early

ora [2] 1 avv now; *sono rientrato or ~* I've only just got back; *per ~* for the moment, for the time being; ~ **come** ~ at the moment; *d'*~ **in poi** from now on 2 cong now

orafo m, **-a** f goldsmith

orale 1 agg oral 2 m oral (exam)

orario (pl -ri) 1 agg *tariffa*, hourly; *velocità* per hour; RAD **segnale** ~ time signal; *in senso* ~ clockwise 2 m *di treno, bus, aeroplano* timetable, *Am* schedule; *di negozio* hours of business; *al lavoro* hours of work; ~ **di apertura/chiusura** opening/closing time; ~ **di sportello** banking hours; ~ **flessibile** flexitime; *in* ~ on time

orata f gilthead bream

oratore m, **-trice** f speaker

oratorio 1 agg (pl -ri) as an orator 2 m oratory

orbita f; AST orbit; ANAT eye-socket; *in* ~ in orbit

orchestra f orchestra; (*luogo*) (orchestra) pit

orchestrale 1 agg orchestral 2 m/f member of an orchestra

orchestrare <1b> orchestrate (*anche fig*)

orchestrazione f orchestration

orchidea f orchid

ordigno m device; ~ **esplosivo** explosive device

ordinale m/agg ordinal

ordinamento m rules and regulations; ~ **sociale** rules governing society

ordinare <1l> order; *stanza* tidy up; MED prescribe; REL ordain

ordinario (pl -ri) ordinary; *mediocre* pretty average

ordinato tidy

ordinazione f order; REL ordination

ordine m order; *mettere in* ~ tidy up; ~ **alfabetico** alphabetical order; ~ **di pagamento** payment order; *d'*~ *prim'*~ first-rate, first-class; ~ **del giorno** agenda; *l'*~ **dei medici** the medical association; ~ **permanente** FIN standing order

orecchino m earring

orecchio m (pl -cchi) ear; MUS **a** ~ by ear

orecchioni mpl mumps sg

orefice m/f goldsmith

oreficeria f goldsmithing; (*gioielleria*) jewel(l)er's

orfano 1 agg orphan 2 m, **-a** f orphan

orfanotrofio m orphanage

organico (pl -ci) organic

organismo m organism; *fig* body

organista m/f (mpl -i) organist

organizzare <1a> organize

organizzazione f organization

organo m organ

orgasmo m orgasm

orgoglio m pride

orgoglioso proud

orientabile adjustable, swivelling

orientale 1 agg eastern; (*dell'Oriente*) Oriental; *Europa* f ~ Eastern Europe 2 m/f Oriental

orientamento m: *senso* m *d'*~ sense of direction; ~ **professionale** professional advice

orientare <1b> *antenna, schermo* turn; ~ **qu verso una carriera** guide or steer s.o. towards a career

orientarsi get one's bearings

oriente m east; *l'Oriente* the Orient *Medio Oriente* Middle East; *Estremo Oriente* Far East; *ad* ~ *di* (to the) east of

origano m oregano

originale m/agg original

originalità f originality

originalmente originally

originario (pl -ri) original; *essere* ~ *di* come from, be a native of

popolo originate in
origine *f* origin; **in ~** originally
origliare <1g> eavesdrop
orizzontale horizontal
orizzonte *m* horizon
orlare <1a> hem
orlo *m* edge; *di vestito* hem
orma *f* footprint; *fig* **seguire le -e di qu** follow in s.o.'s footsteps
ormai by now
ormonale hormonal
ormone *m* hormone
ornamentale ornamental
ornamento *m* ornament
ornare <1a> decorate
ornitologia *f* ornithology
ornitologico ornithological
ornitologo *m*, **-a** *f* ornithologist
oro *m* gold; **d'~** (made of) gold
orologeria *f* clock- and watch-making; *negozio* watchmaker's
orologiaio *m* (*pl* -ai) (clock- and) watch-maker
orologio *m* (*pl* -gi) clock; *portatile* watch; **~ a cucù** cuckoo clock; **~ da polso** wristwatch; **~ da tasca** pocket watch; **~ subacqueo** waterproof watch
oroscopo *m* horoscope
orrendo horrendous
orribile horrible
orrore *m* horror (**di** of); **avere qc in ~** hate sth
Orsa *f:* **~ maggiore / minore** Ursa Major / Minor, the Great / Little Bear
orsacchiotto *m* bear cub; (*giocattolo*) teddy (bear)
orso *m* bear; *fig* hermit; **~ bianco** polar bear
ortaggio *m* (*pl* -ggi) vegetable
ortica *f* (*pl* -che) nettle
orticaria *f* nettle rash
orticoltura *f* horticulture
orto *m* vegetable garden, kitchen garden; **~ botanico** botanical gardens
ortodossia *f* orthodoxy
ortodosso orthodox
ortografia *f* spelling
ortolano *m*, **-a** *f* market gardener

ortopedia *f* orthop(a)edics
ortopedico (*pl* -ci) **1** *agg* orthop(a)edic **2** *m*, **-a** *f* orthop(a)edist
orzaiolo *m* stye
orzata *f* *drink made from crushed almonds, sugar and water*
orzo *m* barley; **~ perlato** pearl barley
osare <1c> dare
oscenità *f inv* obscenity
osceno obscene
oscillare <1a> *di corda* sway, swing; *di barca* rock; FIS oscillate; *fig di persona* waver, hesitate; *di prezzi* fluctuate
oscillazione *f di barca* rocking; **~ dei prezzi** price fluctuations *pl*
oscurare <1a> obscure; *luce* block out
oscurità *f* darkness; *fig* obscurity; **nell'~** in the dark
oscuro **1** *agg* dark; (*sconosciuto*) obscure **2** *m* dark; **essere all'~ di qc** be in the dark about sth
ospedale *m* hospital
ospitale hospitable
ospitalità *f* hospitality
ospitare <1l & c> put up; SP be at home to
ospite *m/f* guest; *chi ospita* host; *donna* hostess
ospizio *m* (*pl* -zi) old folk's home
ossatura *f* bone structure; *fig*, ARCHI structure
osseo bone *attr*
osservare <1b> (*guardare*) look at, observe; (*notare*) see, notice, observe; (*far notare*) point out, remark; (*seguire*) abide by, obey; **~ una dieta** keep to a diet, follow a diet; **le faccio ~ che** I'll have you know that
osservatore *m*, **-trice** *f* observer, watcher
osservatorio *m* (*pl* -ri) AST observatory; **~ meteorologico** *f* weather station
osservazione *f* observation; (*affermazione*) remark, observation
ossessione *f* obsession (**di** with); **avere l'~ di** be obsessed with
ossessivo obsessive

ossia or rather

ossidabile liable to tarnish

ossidare <1l & c> tarnish

ossidazione f tarnish

ossigeno m oxygen; **tenda** f ~ oxygen tent

osso m (ANAT pl le ossa) bone; **di ~** bone attr, made of bone; **~ sacro** sacrum; **in carne e -a** in the flesh

ossobuco m (pl ossibuchi) marrowbone; GASTR ossobuco, stew made with knuckle of veal

ostacolare <1m> hinder

ostacolo m obstacle; nell'atletica hurdle; nell'equitazione fence, jump; fig stumbling block, obstacle

ostaggio m (pl -ggi) hostage; **prendere qu in ~** take s.o. hostage

ostello m: **~ della gioventù** youth hostel

osteoporosi f osteoporosis

osteria f inn

ostetrica f obstetrician; (levatrice) midwife

ostetricia f obstetrics

ostetrico (pl -ci) **1** agg obstetric(al) **2** m obstetrician

ostia f Host

ostile hostile

ostilità f inv hostility

ostinarsi <1a> dig one's heels in; **~ a fare qc** persist in doing sth

ostinato obstinate

ostinazione f obstinacy

ostrica f (pl -che) oyster

ostruire <4d> block, obstruct

ostruito blocked

ostruzione f (ostacolo) obstruction, blockage

otite f ear infection

otorinolaringoiatra m/f (pl -i) ear, nose and throat specialist, ENT specialist

ottagonale octagonal

ottagono octagon

ottano m octane; **numero m di -i** octane rating or number

ottanta eighty

ottantesimo m/agg eightieth

ottava f MUS octave

ottavo m/agg eighth

ottenere <2q> get, obtain

ottengo → **ottenere**

ottenibile obtainable

ottica f optics; fig viewpoint, point of view

ottico (pl -ci) **1** agg optical **2** m optician

ottimale optimum

ottimismo m optimism

ottimista m/f (mpl -i) optimist

ottimistico (pl -ci) optimistic

ottimizzare <1a> optimize

ottimo excellent, extremely good

otto 1 agg eight; **oggi a ~** a week today **2** m eight; **~ volante** big dipper

ottobre m October

ottocento 1 agg eight hundred **2** m: **il Ottocento** the nineteenth century

ottone m brass; MUS **-i** pl brass (instruments)

otturare <1a> block; dente fill

otturatore m FOT shutter

otturazione f blocking; di dente filling

ottuso obtuse

ovaia f ANAT ovary

ovale m/agg oval

ovazione f ovation

overdose f inv overdose

ovest m west

ovile m sheep pen; fig fold

ovini mpl sheep

ovunque everywhere

ovvero or rather; (cioè) that is

ovvio (pl -vvi) obvious

oziare <1g> laze around, be idle

ozio m (pl -zi) laziness, idleness

ozioso lazy, idle

ozono m ozone; **buco** m **nell'~** hole in the ozone layer; **strato** m **d' ~** ozone layer

p. *abbr* (= *pagina*) p (= page)

pacato calm, unhurried

pacchetto *m* package, small parcel; *di sigarette, biscotti* packet; **~ azionario** block of shares; **~ turistico** package holiday

pacchiano vulgar, in bad taste

pacco *m* (*pl* -cchi) parcel, package; **~ bomba** parcel bomb; **~ postale** parcel

pace *f* peace; *lasciare in ~ qu* leave s.o. alone *or* in peace

pacifico (*pl* -ci) **1** *agg* peaceful **2** *m*: *il Pacifico* the Pacific

pacifismo *m* pacifism

pacifista *m/f* (*mpl* -i) pacifist

padano *agg* of the Po; *pianura f -a* Po Valley

padella *f di cucina* frying pan

padiglione *m* pavilion; **~ auricolare** auricle

Padova *f* Padua

padovano 1 *agg* Paduan **2** *m*, -a native of Padua

padre *m* father

padrino *m* godfather

padronanza *f* (*controllo*) control; (*conoscenza*) mastery; **~ di sé** self-control

padrone *m*, -a *f* boss; (*proprietario*) owner; *di cane* master; *donna* mistress; **~ di casa** man/lady of the house; *per inquilino* landlord; *donna* landlady

paesaggio *m* (*pl* -ggi) scenery; PITT, GEOG landscape

paesaggista *m/f* PITT landscape painter *or* artist

paesano 1 *agg* country *attr* **2** *m*, -a *f* person from the country; *spreg* country bumpkin

paese *m* country; (*villaggio*) village; (*territorio*) region, area; *i Paesi Bassi pl* the Netherlands; **~ d'origi-**ne country of origin; **-i** *pl* **in via di sviluppo** developing countries; **~ membro** member state

paga *f* (*pl* -ghe) pay

pagabile payable; **~ a vista** payable at sight

pagamento *m* payment; **~ anticipato** payment in advance; **~ alla consegna** cash on delivery; **~ in contanti** payment in cash, cash payment; **~ a rate** payment in insta(l)lments; *altre sono a ~* others you have to pay for

pagare <1e> **1** *v/t acquisto* pay for; *conto, fattura, debito* pay; *ti pago qualcosa da bere* I'll buy you *or* stand you a drink; *gliela faccio ~* he'll pay for this **2** *v/i* pay; **~ anticipatamente** pay in advance; **~ in contanti** pay (in) cash; **~ a rate** pay in instal(l)ments

pagella *f* report, *Am* report card

paghetta *f* pocket money

pagina *f* page; *a ~ 10* on page 10; *-e gialle* Yellow Pages; **~ elettronica** screen page; **~ Web** Web site

paglia *f* straw

paio *m* (*pl* le paia): *un ~ di scarpe, guanti ecc* a pair of; *un ~ di volte* a couple of times

pala *f* shovel; *di elica, turbina, remo* blade; **~ d'altare** altarpiece

palasport *m inv* indoor sports arena

palato *m* palate

palazzina *f* luxury home

palazzo *m* palace; (*edificio*) building; *con appartamenti* block of flats, *Am* apartment block; **~ comunale** town hall; **~ di giustizia** courthouse; **~ dello sport** indoor sports arena

palco *m* (*pl* -chi) dais; TEA stage

palcoscenico *m* (*pl* -ci) stage

palese obvious

Palestina *f* Palestine

palestinese *agg, m/f* Palestinian

palestra *f* gym

paletta *f* shovel; *per la spiaggia* spade; FERR signal(l)ing paddle

paletto *m* tent peg

palla *f* ball; ~ *di neve* snowball; *fig* **cogliere la ~ al balzo** jump at the chance

pallacanestro *f* basketball

pallanuoto *f* water polo

pallavolo *f* volley ball

palliativo *m* palliative

pallido pale

pallina *f* ~ *di vetro* marble; ~ *da golf* golf ball; ~ *da tennis* tennis ball

pallino *m* nel biliardo cue ball; *nelle bocce* jack; *munizione* pellet; *fig* **avere il ~ della pesca** be mad about fishing, be fishing mad; *a -i pl* with spots, spotted

palloncino *m* balloon

pallone *m* ball; *calcio* football, soccer; AVIA balloon; ~ *sonda* weather balloon

pallore *m* paleness, pallor

pallottola *f* pellet; *di pistola* bullet

palma *f* palm

palmo *m* hand's breadth; ANAT palm; *a ~ a ~* gradually, bit by bit, inch by inch

palo *m* pole; *nel calcio* (goal)post

palombaro *m* diver

palpabile *fig* palpable

palpare <1a> feel; MED palpate

palpebra *f* eyelid

palpitare <11> *del cuore* pound

palpitazione *f* palpitation

palpito *m* del cuore beat

paltò *m inv* overcoat, heavy coat

palude *f* marsh

paludoso marshy

palustre marshy; *pianta* marsh

panacea *f* panacea

panca *f* (*pl* -che) bench; *in chiesa* pew

pancarré *m* sliced loaf

pancetta *f* pancetta, *cured belly of pork*

panchetto *m* footstool

panchina *f* bench

pancia *f* (*pl* -ce) *m* stomach, belly F;

di animale belly; *mal m di* ~ stomach-ache, belly-ache F; *mettere su* ~ develop a paunch

panciotto *m* waistcoat, *Am* vest

panciuto big-bellied

pancreas *m inv* pancreas

pane *m* bread; ~ *bianco* white bread *~ nero* (*o di segala*) black *or* rye bread; ~ *integrale* wholewheat bread

panetteria *f* bakery

panettiere *m/f* baker

panettone *m* panettone, *cake made with candied fruit*

panfilo *m* yacht; ~ *a motore* motor yacht

pangrattato *m* breadcrumbs *pl*

panico (*pl* -ci) *m* panic

paniere *m* basket

panificio *m* (*pl* -ci) bakery

panino *m* roll; ~ *imbottito* filled roll

paninoteca *f* sandwich shop

panna *f* cream; ~ *montata* whipped cream

panne *f*: *essere in* ~ have broken down, have had a breakdown

pannello *m* panel; ~ *solare* solar panel

panno *m* pezzo di stoffa cloth; *-i pl* clothes; *se fossi nei tuoi -i* if I were in your shoes

pannocchia *f* cob

pannolino *m* nappy; *per donne* sanitary towel

panorama *m* (*pl* -i) panorama; *fig* overview

panoramica *f* FOT panorama, panoramic view; *fig* overview

pantaloncini *mpl* shorts

pantaloni *mpl* trousers, *Am* pants

pantera *f* ZO panther

pantofola *f* slipper

pantomima *f* pantomime

paonazzo purple

papà *m inv* daddy, dad

papa *m* Pope

papale papal

paparazzo *m*: *i -i pl* the paparazzi

papavero *m* poppy

papera *f* fig (*errore*) slip of the tongue

papero *m*, **-a** *f* gosling

papillon *m inv* bow tie

papiro *m* papyrus

pappa *f* food

pappagallo *m* parrot

paprica *f* paprika

par. *abbr* (= **paragrafo**) para (= paragraph)

parabrezza *m inv* windscreen, *Am* windshield

paracadutare <1a> parachute in

paracadute *m inv* parachute

paracadutista *m/f* (*mpl* -i) parachutist

paracarro *m* post

paradiso *m* heaven, paradise; ~ **terrestre** heaven on earth, Eden

paradossale paradoxical

paradosso *m* paradox

parafango *m* (*pl* -ghi) mudguard, *Am* fender

parafulmine *m* lightning rod

paraggi *mpl* neighbo(u)rhood *sg*; **nei ~ di** (somewhere) near

paragonabile comparable

paragonare <1a> compare

paragone *m* comparison; **a ~ di** compared with, in *or* by comparison with; **senza ~** incomparable

paragrafo *m* paragraph

paralisi *f* paralysis

paralitico *m*, **-a** *f* (*mpl* -ci) paralyzed person

paralizzare <1a> paralyze

parallela *f* parallel line; **-e** *pl* parallel bars

parallelo *m/agg* parallel

paraluce *m inv* FOT lens hood

paralume *m* lampshade

parametro *m* parameter

paranoia *f* paranoia

paranoico (*pl* -ci) **1** *agg* paranoid **2** *m*, **-a** *f* person with paranoia

paranormale *m/agg* paranormal

paraocchi *mpl* blinkers (*anche fig*)

parapetto *m* parapet; MAR rail

paraplegico **1** *agg* paraplegic **2** *m*, **-a** *f* paraplegic

parare <1a> **1** *v/t ornare* decorate; *proteggere* shelter; *occhi* shield; *scansare* parry **2** *v/i* save

parasole *m* parasol; FOT lens hood

parassita *m/f* (*mpl* -i) parasite (*anche fig*)

parata *f* parade

paraurti *m inv* bumper

parcheggiare <1f> *v/t* & *v/i* park

parcheggio *m* parking; *luogo* car park, *Am* parking lot; ~ **sotterraneo** underground car park; **divieto di ~** no parking

parchimetro *m* parking meter

parco[1] (*pl* -chi) *agg*: **essere ~ nel mangiare** eat sparingly

parco[2] *m* (*pl* -chi) park; ~ **dei divertimenti** amusement park; ~ **naturale** nature reserve; ~ **nazionale** national park; ~ **macchine** fleet (of vehicles)

parecchio **1** *agg* a lot of **2** *pron* **parecchi** *mpl*, **parecchie** *fpl* quite a few **3** *avv* quite a lot

pareggiare <1f> **1** *v/t* even up; (*uguagliare*) match, equal; *conto* balance **2** *v/i* SP draw

pareggio *m* (*pl* -ggi) SP draw

parente *m/f* relative

parentela *f* relationship; *parenti* relatives, relations

parentesi *f* bracket; (*detto*) **fra ~** by the by; *fig* **aprire una ~** digress slightly

parere **1** *v/i* <2h> seem, appear; **pare che** it seems that, it would appear that; **che te ne pare?** what do you think (of it)?; **non ti pare?** don't you think?; **a quanto pare** by all accounts; **non mi pare vero!** I can't believe it! **2** *m* opinion; **a mio ~** in my opinion, to my way of thinking

parete *f* wall; ~ **divisoria** partition wall

pari **1** *agg* equal; *numero* even; **essere di ~ altezza** be the same height; **al ~ di** like; **alla ~ the** same; SP **finire alla ~** end in a draw; **senza ~** unrivalled, unequalled **2** *m* (social) equal, peer; **da ~ a ~** as an equal

Parigi Paris

parigino (of) Paris, Parisian

parità *f* equality, parity; ~ **di diritti** equal rights; **a ~ di condizioni** all things being equal

parka *m inv* parka

parlamentare 1 *agg* Parliamentary **2** *v/i* <1a> negotiate **3** *m/f* (*pl* -ri) Member of Parliament, MP

parlamento *m* Parliament; **Parlamento europeo** European Parliament

parlare <1a> talk, speak (*a qu* to s.o.; *di qc* about sth); ~ **del più e del meno** make small talk; **parla inglese?** do you speak English?

parmigiano *m* (*formaggio*) Parmesan

parodia *f* parody

parola *f* word; (*facoltà*) speech; ~ **d'ordine** password; **-e** *pl* **crociate** crossword (puzzle) *sg*; **essere di** ~ keep one's word; **chiedere la** ~ ask for the floor; ~ **per** ~ word for word

parolaccia *f* swear word

parquet *m* parquet floor

parrocchia *f* parish

parrochiale parish *attr*

parroco *m* (*pl* -ci) parish priest

parrucca *f* (*pl* -cche) wig

parrucchiere *m*, **-a** *f* hairdresser; ~ **per signora** ladies' hairdresser

parte *f* part; (*porzione*) portion; (*lato*) side; DIR party; ~ **civile** plaintiff; **far** ~ **di una società** belong to a society, be a member of a society; **prendere** ~ **a** take part in; **a** ~ separate; **scherzi a** ~ joking apart; **mettere da** ~ **qc** put sth aside; **dall'altra** ~ **della strada** on the other side of the street; **da nessuna** ~ nowhere; **da tutte le -i** everywhere; **da** ~ **mia** for my part, as far as I'm concerned; **regalo ecc from me**; **in** ~ in part, partly; **in gran** ~ largely

partecipante *m/f* participant

partecipare <1m> **1** *v/t* announce **2** *v/i*: ~ **a gara** take part in; *dolore, gioia* share

partecipazione *f* (*intervento*) participation; (*annunzio*) announcement; FIN holding; ~ **agli utili** profit-sharing

parteggiare <1f>: ~ **per** support

partenza *f* departure; SP start; INFOR ~ **a freddo** cold start; **essere di** ~ be just about to leave, be on the point of leaving; *fig* **punto** *m* **di** ~ starting point, point of departure

participio *m* (*pl* -pi) participle

particolare 1 *agg* particular; *segretario* private; **in** ~ in particular **2** *m* particular, detail

particolareggiato detailed

particolarità *f inv* special nature

partigiano *m*, **-a** *f* partisan

partire <4a> leave; AUTO, SP start; ~ **per** leave for; ~ **per l'estero** go abroad

partita *f* SP match; *di carte* game; *di merce* shipment; ~ **IVA** VAT registration number; ~ **amichevole** friendly (match); ~ **di calcio** football match

partito *m* POL party; ~ **d'opposizione** opposition (party); **prendere** ~ make up one's mind; **essere ridotto a mal** ~ be in a bad way

partitura *f* score

partner *m/f inv* partner

parto *m* birth; ~ **cesareo** C(a)esarean (section)

partorire <4d> give birth to

part time 1 *agg* part-time **2** *avv* part time

parziale partial; *fig* biased

pascolo *m* pasture

Pasqua *f* Easter

pasquale Easter *attr*

Pasquetta *f* Easter Monday

passaggio *m* (*pl* -ggi) passage; *in macchina* lift, *Am* ride; *atto* passing; SP pass; **essere di** ~ be passing through; ~ **pedonale** pedestrian crossing, *Br* zebra crossing; ~ **a livello** level crossing, *Am* grade crossing; **dare un** ~ **a qu** give s.o. a lift (*Am* ride)

passante *m/f* passer-by

passaporto *m* passport; **controllo** *m* **dei -i** passport control

passare <1a> **1** *v/i* (*trasferirsi*) go (*in* into); SP pass; *di legge* be passed, pass; *di tempo* go by *or* past, pass; ~ **attraverso delle difficoltà** have a difficult time; **~ da / per Milano** go through Milan; **~ dal panettiere** drop by the baker's; **mi è passato di mente** it slipped my mind; **~ di moda** go out of fashion; **~ inosservato** go unnoticed; **~ per imbecille** be taken for a fool **2** v/t *confine* cross; (*sorpassare*) overstep; (*porgere*) pass; (*trascorrere*) spend; TELEC **ti passo Claudio** here's Claudio

passata f quick wipe; GASTR **~ (di pomodoro)** passata, *sieved tomato pulp*

passatempo m pastime, hobby

passato 1 pp → **passare 2** agg past; *alimento* pureed; **l'anno ~** last year **3** m past; GASTR puree

passatoia f runner

passaverdura m inv food mill

passeggero 1 agg passing, short-lived **2** m, **-a** f passenger

passeggiare <1f> stroll, walk

passeggiata f stroll, walk; (*percorso*) walk

passeggino m pushchair

passeggio m (*pl* -ggi): **andare a ~** go for a walk

passe-partout m inv (*chiave*) master key

passerella f (foot)bridge; MAR gangway; AVIA ramp; *per sfilate* catwalk

passero m sparrow

passionale passionate; *delitto* of passion

passione f passion; REL Passion

passivo 1 agg passive; **fumo ~** second-hand smoke **2** m GRAM passive; FIN liabilities pl

passo m step; (*impronta*) footprint; *di libro* passage; GEOG pass; **a ~ di lumaca** at a snail's pace; **~ falso** false move; AUTO **avanzare a ~ d'uomo** crawl; **~ carrabile** driveway; **fare due -i** go for a walk *or* a stroll; *fig* **fare il primo ~** take the first step

pasta f paste; (*pastasciutta*) pasta; (*impasto*) dough; (*dolce*) pastry; **~ dentifricia** toothpaste; **~ frolla** shortcrust pastry; **~ sfoglia** puff pastry

pastasciutta f pasta

pastella f batter

pastello m pastel

pasticca f (*pl* -cche) pastille

pasticceria f pastries pl, cakes pl; *negozio* cake shop

pasticciere m, **-a** f confectioner

pasticcino m pastry

pasticcio m (*pl* -cci) GASTR pie; *fig* mess; **~ di fegato d'oca** pâté de foie gras; **essere nei -i** be in a mess

pastiglia f MED tablet, pill

pastina f *small pasta shapes for soup*

pasto m meal

pastorale 1 m bishop's staff, crozier **2** f REL pastoral letter

pastore 1 m, **-a** f shepherd **2** m REL: **~ (evangelico)** pastor

pastorizzato pasteurized

patata f potato; **-e pl fritte** (French) fries, *Br* chips; **-e pl lesse** boiled potatoes; **-e pl arrosto** roast potatoes

patatine fpl crisps, *Am* chips; (*fritte*) French fries, *Br* chips

patente f: **~ (di guida)** driving licence, *Am* driver's license

paternalismo m paternalism

paternità f paternity

paterno paternal, fatherly

patetico (*pl* -ci) pathetic

patire <4d> **1** v/i suffer (**di** from) **2** v/t suffer (from)

patito 1 agg of suffering **2** m, **-a** f fan; **~ del jazz** jazz fan

patologia f pathology

patologico pathological

patria f homeland

patrigno m stepfather

patrimonio m (*pl* -ni) estate; **~ artistico** artistic heritage; **~ ereditario** genetic inheritance; *fig* **un ~** a fortune

patriota m/f (*mpl* -i) patriot

patriottico patriotic

patriottismo m patriotism

patrocinio m support, patronage

patrono m, **-a** f REL patron saint

patteggiare <1f> negotiate

pattinaggio m (pl -ggi) skating; ~ **artistico** figure skating; ~ **su ghiaccio** ice skating; ~ **a rotelle** roller skating

pattinare <1l> skate; AUTO skid

pattinatore m, **-trice** f skater

pattino m SP skate; ~ **a rotelle** roller skate; ~ **in linea** roller blade

patto m pact; **a** ~ **che** on condition that; **venire a -i** come to terms

pattuglia f patrol

pattumiera f dustbin

paura f fear; **avere** ~ **di** be frightened of; **mettere** (o **fare**) ~ **a qu** frighten s.o.

pauroso fearful; **che fa paura** frightening

pausa f pause; **durante il lavoro** break

pavimento m floor

pavone m peacock

pazientare <1b> be patient

paziente agg, m/f patient

pazienza f patience

pazzesco (pl -chi) crazy

pazzia f madness

pazzo 1 agg mad, crazy; **è** ~ **da legare** he's off his head; **andare** ~ **per** be mad or crazy about 2 m, **-a** f madman; donna madwoman

p.c. abbr (= **per conoscenza**) cc (= carbon copy)

p.e. abbr (= **per esempio**) eg (= for example)

pecca f (pl -cche) fault

peccare <1b & d> sin; ~ **di** be guilty of

peccato m sin; (**che**) ~ **!** what a pity!

pecora f sheep

pecorino m/agg: (**formaggio** m) ~ pecorino (ewe's milk cheese)

peculiarità f inv special feature, peculiarity

pedaggio m (pl -ggi) toll

pedalare <1a> pedal

pedale m pedal; ~ **dell'acceleratore** accelerator

pedalò m inv pedalo

pedana f footrest; SP springboard

pedante pedantic

pedata f kick; (**impronta**) footprint

pediatra m/f (mpl -i) p(a)ediatrician

pediatria f p(a)ediatrics

pedicure 1 m/f chiropodist, Am podiatrist 2 m inv pedicure

pedina f draughtsman; fig cog in the wheel

pedinare <1a> shadow, follow

pedofilia f p(a)edophilia

pedofilo m, **-a** f p(a)edophile

pedonale pedestrian; **zona** f ~ pedestrian precinct; **strisce** fpl **-i** pedestrian crossing sg

pedone m pedestrian

peggio 1 avv worse 2 m: **il** ~ **è che** the worst of it is that; **avere la** ~ get the worst of it; **di male in** ~ from bad to worse

peggioramento m deterioration, worsening

peggiorare <1a> 1 v/t make worse, worsen 2 v/i get worse, worsen

peggiore worse; superlativo worst; **il** ~ the worst; **nel** ~ **dei casi** if the worst comes to the worst

pegno m d'amore, respetto ecc token; **dare qc in** ~ pawn sth

pelare <1a> peel; pollo pluck; fig F fleece F

pellame m skin, pelt

pelle f skin; ~ **scamosciata** suede; **avere la** ~ **d'oca** have gooseflesh; fig **essere** ~ **e ossa** be nothing but skin and bones

pellegrinaggio m (pl -ggi) pilgrimage

pellegrino m, **-a** f pilgrim

pelletteria f leatherwork; **-e** p leather goods

pellicano m pelican

pelliccia f (pl -cce) fur; cappotto fur coat

pellicola f film; ~ **a colori** colo(u)r film; ~ **trasparente** cling film

pelo m hair, coat; (**pelliccia**) coat; **a** ~ **dell'acqua** on the surface of the water; fig **per un** ~ by the skin of one's teeth

peluria f down

pena f (**sofferenza**) pain, suffering; (**punizione**) punishment; ~ **di morte** death penalty; **stare in** ~ **per qu**

worry about s.o.; *vale la ~ soffrire tanto?* is it worth suffering so much?; *non ne vale la ~* it's not worth it; *mi fa ~* I feel sorry for him / her; *a mala ~* hardly

penale 1 *agg* criminal; *codice* penal **2** *f* penalty

penalista *m/f* (*mpl* -i) criminal lawyer

penalità *f inv* penalty

penalizzare <1a> penalize

pendenza *f* slope

pendere <3a> hang; (*essere inclinato*) slope; *fig ~ dalle labbra di qu* hang on s.o.'s every word

pendio *m* slope

pendolare *m/f* commuter

pendolo *m* pendulum

pene *m* penis

penetrante *dolore, freddo* piercing; *fig sguardo* piercing, penetrating; *analisi* penetrating

penetrare <1l & b> **1** *v/t* penetrate **2** *v/i*: *~ in* enter

penicillina *f* penicillin

peninsulare peninsular

penisola *f* peninsula; *~ iberica* Iberian peninsula

penitenza *f* REL penance; *in gioco* forfeit

penitenziario *m* (*pl* -ri) prison

penna *f* pen; *di uccello* feather; *~ biro®* ballpoint (pen), biro; *~ stilografica* fountain pen; *~ a feltro* felt-tip (pen)

pennarello *m* felt-tip (pen)

pennello *m* brush

penombra *f* half-light

penoso painful

pensare <1b> think; *~ a* think about or of; *~ a fare qc* (*ricordarsi di*) remember to do sth; *~ di fare qc* think of doing sth; *che ne pensa?* what do you think?; *cosa stai pensando?* what are you thinking about?; *ci penso io* I'll take care of it; *senza ~* without thinking

pensiero *m* thought; (*preoccupazione*) worry; *stare in ~* be worried or anxious (*per* about); *un piccolo ~* (*regalo*) a little something

pensieroso pensive

pensile hanging

pensilina *f* shelter

pensionamento *m* retirement

pensionato *m*, **-a** *f* pensioner, retired person; (*alloggio*) boarding house

pensione *f* pension; (*albergo*) boarding house; *~ completa* full board; *mezza ~* half board; *andare in ~* retire

pensoso pensive, thoughtful

pentagono *m* pentagon

Pentecoste *f* Whitsun

pentimento *m* remorse

pentirsi <4b or 4d> *di peccato* repent; *~ di aver fatto qc* be sorry for doing sth

pentola *f* pot, pan; *~ a pressione* pressure cooker

penultimo last but one, penultimate

penuria *f* shortage (*di* of); *~ di alloggi* housing shortage

penzolare <1l> dangle

penzoloni dangling

peonia *f* peony

pepare <1a> pepper

pepato peppered

pepe *m* pepper

peperone *m* pepper

per 1 *prp* for; *mezzo* by; *~ qualche giorno* for a few days; *~ questa ragione* for that reason; *~ tutta la notte* throughout the night; *~ iscritto* in writing; *~ esempio* for example; *dieci ~ cento* ten per cent; *uno ~ uno* one by one **2** *cong*: *~ fare qc* (in order) to do sth; *stare ~* be about to

pera *f* pear

peraltro however

perbene 1 *agg* respectable **2** *avv* properly

percento 1 *m* percentage **2** *avv* per cent

percentuale *f agg* percentage

percepire <4d> perceive; (*riscuotere*) cash

percezione *f* perception

perché because; (*affinché*) so that; *~?* why?

P

perciò so, therefore

percorrere <3o> *distanza* cover; *strada, fiume* travel along

percorso 1 pp → **percorrere** 2 m *(tragitto)* route

percossa f blow

percosso → **percuotere**

percuotere <3ff> strike

percussione f percussion; MUS **-i** pl percussion

perdere <3b & 3uu> 1 v/t lose; *treno, occasione* miss; ~ **tempo** waste time; ~ **di vista** lose sight of; *fig* lose touch with 2 v/i lose; *di rubinetto, tubo* leak; **a ~** disposable

perdersi get lost; ~ **d'animo** lose heart

perdita f loss; *di gas, di acqua* leak; **essere in ~** be making a loss; ~ **di tempo** waste of time; **si estendeva a ~ d'occhio** it stretched as far as the eye could see

perditempo 1 m/f inv idler 2 m inv waste of time

perdonare <1a> forgive

perdono m forgiveness; **ti chiedo ~** please forgive me

perenne eternal, never-ending; BOT perennial

perfettamente perfectly

perfetto 1 agg perfect 2 m GRAM perfect (tense)

perfezionamento m adjustment, further improvement; **corso** m **di ~** further training

perfezionare <1a> perfect, further improve

perfezione f perfection; **a ~** to perfection, perfectly

perfezionista m/f perfectionist

perfido treacherous

perfino even

perforare <1c> drill through

perforazione f perforation

pergola f pergola

pergolato m pergola

pericolante on the verge of collapse

pericolo m danger; *(rischio)* risk; **fuori ~** out of danger; **mettere in ~** endanger, put at risk

pericoloso dangerous

periferia f periphery; *di città* outskirts

periferico (pl -ci) peripheral; *quartiere* outlying; INFOR **unità** f **-a** peripheral

perifrasi f inv circumlocution

periodico (pl -ci) 1 agg periodic 2 m periodical; ~ **mensile** monthly

periodo m period; ~ **di transizione** transition period

peripezia f misadventure

perito 1 agg expert 2 m, **-a** f expert

peritonite f peritonitis

perizia f skill, expertise; *esame* examination (by an expert)

perla f pearl; ~ **coltivata** cultured pearl; **collana** f **di -e** pearl necklace

perlina f bead

perlomeno at least

perlopiù usually

perlustrare <1a> patrol

permaloso easily offended, touchy

permanente 1 agg permanent 2 f perm

permanenza f permanence; **in un luogo** stay

permesso 1 pp → **permettere** 2 m permission; *(breve licenza)* permit; MIL leave; ~ **d'atterraggio** permission to land; ~ **di lavoro** work permit; ~ **di soggiorno** residence permit; **(è) ~?** may I?; **con ~** excuse me

permettere <3ee> allow, permit

permettersi afford

pernacchia f F raspberry F

pernice f partridge

perno m pivot

pernottamento m night, overnight stay

pernottare <1c> spend the night, stay overnight

pero m pear (tree)

però but

perpendicolare f/agg perpendicular

perpetuo perpetual

perplesso perplexed

perquisire <4d> search

perquisizione f search; ~ **personale** body search; **mandato** m **di ~** search warrant

persecuzione f persecution; **mania**

f di ~ persecution complex

perseguitare <1m> persecute

perseguitato *m*: ~ *politico* person being persecuted for their political views

perseverante persevering

perseveranza *f* perseverance

perseverare <1m & b> persevere

persiana *f* shutter

persiano Persian

persino → **perfino**

persistente persistent

persistenza *f* persistence

persistere <3f> persist

perso *pp* → **perdere**

persona *f* person; *a* (*o per*) ~ a head, each; *in* ~, *di* ~ in person, personally

personaggio *m* (*pl* -ggi) character; (*celebrità*) personality

personale 1 *agg* personal **2** *m* staff, personnel; AVIA ~ *di terra* ground staff *or* crew; *riduzione f del* ~ cuts in staff, personnel cutbacks

personalità *f inv* personality

personalmente personally

personificare <1n & d> personify

perspicace shrewd

perspicacia *f* shrewdness

persuadere <2i> convince; ~ *qu a fare qc* persuade s.o. to do sth

persuasione *f* persuasion

persuasivo persuasive

persuaso *pp* → **persuadere**

pertanto and so, therefore

pertinente relevant, pertinent

pertinenza *f* relevance, pertinence

perturbazione *f* disturbance; ~ *atmosferica* atmospheric disturbance

peruviano 1 *agg* Peruvian **2** *m*, -a *f* Peruvian

pervenire <4p> arrive; *far* ~ send

perverso perverse

pervertito *m*, -a *f* pervert

p.es. *abbr* (= *per esempio*) eg (= for example)

pesante heavy; *fig libro, film* boring

pesantezza *f* heaviness; ~ *di stomaco* indigestion

pesapersone *f inv* scales; *in negozio ecc* weighing machine

pesare <1a> **1** *v/t* weigh; *ingredienti* weigh out **2** *v/i* weigh

pesca[1] *f* (*pl* -che) (*frutto*) peach

pesca[2] *f* fishing; ~ *con la lenza* angling

pescare <1d> fish for; (*prendere*) catch; *fig* dig up; *ladro, svaligiatore ecc* catch (red-handed)

pescatore *m* fisherman

pesce *m* fish; ~ *spada* swordfish; ~ *d'aprile* April Fool; ASTR *Pesci pl* Pisces

pescecane *m* (*pl* pescicani) shark

peschereccio *m* (*pl* -cci) fishing boat

pescheria *f* fishmonger's

pescivendolo *m*, -a *f* fishmonger

pesco *m* (*pl* -chi) peach (tree)

pescoso with abundant supplies of fish

peso *m* weight; ~ *netto* net weight; *di nessun* ~ of no importance, unimportant; *a* ~ by weight; *fig non voglio essere un* ~ *per te* I don't want to be a burden to you

pessimismo *m* pessimism

pessimista 1 *agg* pessimistic **2** *m/f* (*mpl* -i) pessimist

pessimistico (*pl* -ci) pessimistic

pessimo very bad, terrible

pestaggio *m* (*pl* -ggi) F going-over F

pestare <1a> *carne, prezzemolo* pound; *con piede* step on; (*picchiare*) beat up

peste *f* plague; *persona* pest

pesticida *m* (*pl* -i) pesticide

pesto *m* pesto, *paste of basil, olive oil and pine nuts*

petalo *m* petal

petardo *m* banger

petizione *f* petition

peto *m* F fart F

petroliera *f* (oil) tanker

petrolifero oil *attr*

petrolio *m* oil, petroleum, ~ *greggio* crude

pettegolare <1m> gossip

pettegolezzo *m* piece *or* item of gossip

pettegolo 1 *agg* gossipy **2** *m*, -a *f* gossip

pettinare <11 & b> comb

pettinarsi comb one's hair

pettinatura f hairstyle, hairdo

pettine m comb

pettirosso m robin

petto m chest; (seno) breast; ~ di pollo chicken breast; a doppio ~ double-breasted

pezza f cloth; (toppa) patch

pezzo m piece; di motore part; da/ per un ~ for a long time; due -i bikini; ~ di ricambio spare (part); fig ~ grosso big shot; andare in -i break into pieces; in -i da cento mila lire in denominations of one hundred thousand lira

ph m pH

piacente attractive

piacere 1 v/i <2k>: le piace il vino? do you like wine?; non mi piace il cioccolato I don't like chocolate; non mi piacciono i tuoi amici I don't like your friends; mi piacerebbe saperlo I'd really like to know; faccio come mi pare e piace I do as I please 2 m pleasure; (favore) favo(u)r; ~! pleased to meet you!; viaggio m di ~ pleasure trip; aver ~ di be delighted to; mi fa ~ I'm happy to; con ~ with pleasure; per ~ please; serviti a ~ take as much as you like

piacevole pleasant

piacimento m: a ~ as much as you like

piaga f (pl -ghe) (ferita) wound; fig scourge; agitare il coltello nella ~ rub salt into the wound

pialla f plane

piallare <1a> plane

piana f plain

pianerottolo m landing

pianeta m planet

piangere <3d> 1 v/i cry, weep 2 v/t mourn

pianificare <1m & d> plan

pianificazione f planning

pianista m/f (mpl -i) pianist

piano 1 agg flat 2 avv (adagio) slowly; (a voce bassa) quietly, in a low voice 3 m plan; (pianura) plane; di edificio floor; MUS piano; ~ rialzato mezzanine (floor); primo ~ foreground; PHOT close-up

pianoforte m piano; ~ a coda grand piano

pianta f plant; di città map; del piede sole; ~ di appartamento house plant; ~ medicinale medicinal plant; di sana ~ from start to finish

piantare <1a> plant; chiodo hammer in; F piantala! cut that out! F; F ~ qu dump s.o. F; ~ grane make difficulties

piantarsi F: si sono piantati they've split up F

pianterreno m ground floor, Am first floor

pianto 1 pp → piangere 2 m crying, weeping; (lacrime) tears

pianura f plain

piastra f plate

piastrella f tile

piattaforma f platform; ~ di lancio launch pad

piattino m saucer

piatto 1 agg flat 2 m plate; GASTR dish; MUS -i pl cymbals; ~ forte main course; ~ fondo soup plate; ~ nazionale national dish; ~ piano flat plate; primo ~ first course; ~ del giorno day's special

piazza f square; COM market(place); fig fare ~ pulita make a clean sweep

piazzale m large square; in autostrada toll-booth area

piazzare <1a> place, put; (vendere) sell

piazzista m/f salesman; donna saleswoman

piazzola f small square; ~ di sosta layby

piccante spicy, hot

picchiare <1a> beat

picchiata f AVIA nosedive

picchio m (pl -cchi); ZO woodpecker

piccionaia f TEA gods

piccione m pigeon; ~ viaggiatore carrier pigeon; prendere due ~ con una fava kill two birds with one stone

picco m (pl -cchi) peak; MAR colare

a ~ sink

piccolezza f smallness; (*inezia*) trifle; *fig* pettiness, small-mindedness

piccolo 1 agg small, little; *di statura* short; *meschino* petty **2** m, **-a** f child; **la gatta con i suoi -i** the cat and her young; **da ~** as a child; **fin da ~** since I/he was a child

piccozza f ice ax(e)

picnic m inv picnic; **fare un ~** have a picnic, picnic

pidocchio m (pl -cchi) louse

piede m foot; **-i piatti** flat feet; P cops P, flatfoots P; **a -i** on foot; **su due -i** suddenly; **stare in -i** stand; **a ~ libero** at large; **a -i nudi** barefoot, with bare feet

piedistallo m pedestal

piega f (pl -ghe) wrinkle; *di pantaloni* crease; *di gonna* pleat; **a -ghe** gonna pleated

piegare <1b & e> **1** v/t bend; (*ripiegare*) fold **2** v/i bend

piegarsi bend; *fig* **~ a** comply with

pieghevole sedia folding

Piemonte m Piedmont

piemontese agg, m/f Piedmontese

piena f flood; **a teatro** full house

pienezza f fullness

pieno 1 agg full (**di** of); (*non cavo*) solid; **in ~ giorno** in broad daylight; **in -a notte** in the middle of the night **2** m: **nel ~ dell'inverno** in the depths of winter; AUTO **fare il ~** fill up

pietà f pity (**di** for); PITT pietà; **avere ~ di qu** take pity on s.o.; **senza ~** pitiless, merciless

pietanza f dish

pietoso pitiful; (*compassionevole*) merciful

pietra f stone; **~ focaia** flint; **~ preziosa** precious stone; **~ miliare** milestone (*anche fig*)

pietrina f flint

pietroso stony

pigiama m pyjamas pl, PJs F

pigiare <1f> crush

pigione f rent

pigliare <1g> catch; **~ fiato** catch

one's breath

pigmeo m, **-a** f pygmy

pigna f pinecone

pignolo pedantic, nit-picking F

pignoramento m distraint

pignorare <1a> distrain

pigrizia f laziness

pigro lazy

PIL abbr (= **prodotto interno lordo**) GDP (= gross domestic product)

pila f EL battery; (*catasta*) pile, heap

pilastro m pillar

pillola f pill; **~ (anticoncezionale)** pill; **prendere la ~** be on the pill

pilone m pier; EL pylon

pilota (pl -i) **1** m/f AVIA, MAR pilot; AUTO driver; **~ automatico** automatic pilot **2** agg pilot attr

pilotare <1c> pilot; AUTO drive

pinacoteca f (pl -che) art gallery

pineta f pine forest

ping-pong m table tennis, ping-pong

pinna f di pesce fin; SP flipper

pino m pine

pinolo m pine nut

pinza f pliers pl; MED forceps pl

pinzare <1a> staple

pinzatrice f stapler

pinzette fpl tweezers

pio pious

pioggerella f drizzle

pioggia f (pl -gge) rain; **~ acida** acid rain

piombare <1a> **1** v/t dente fill **2** v/i fall; *precipitarsi* rush (**su** at); **mi è piombato in casa** he dropped in unexpectedly

piombatura f di dente filling

piombino m sinker

piombo m lead; **a ~** plumb; **con/senza ~** benzina leaded/unleaded; *fig* **andare con i piedi di ~** tread carefully

pioniere m, **-a** f pioneer

pioppo m poplar

piovere <3kk> rain; **piove a dirotto** it's raining cats and dogs

piovigginare <1m> drizzle

piovigginoso drizzly

piovoso rainy

piovra f octopus

pipa f pipe; **fumare la ~** smoke a pipe

pipì f F pee F; F **fare la ~** go for a pee F

pipistrello m bat

piramide f pyramid

pirata m (pl -i) pirate; **~ dell'aria** hijacker; **~ della strada** hit-and-run driver; (guidatore spericolato) roadhog

pirofila f oven-proof dish

piroscafo m steamer, steamship

pirotecnica f fireworks pl

pirotecnico (pl -ci) fireworks attr

pisciare <1f> P piss P

piscina f (swimming) pool; **~ coperta** indoor pool

pisello m pea

pisolino m nap

pista f di atletica track; di circo ring; (traccia) trail; di autostrada toll-lane; **~ d'atterraggio** runway; **~ da ballo** dance floor; **~ da sci** ski slope; **~ da sci da fondo** cross country ski trail; **~ ciclabile** bike path

pistacchio m (pl -cchi) pistachio

pistola f pistol; **~ ad acqua** water pistol; **~ automatica** automatic (pistol); **~ a spruzzo** spray gun

pistone m piston

pittore m, **-trice** f painter

pittoresco (pl -chi) picturesque

pittura f painting

pitturare <1a> paint

più 1 avv more (**di, che** than); superlativo most; MAT plus; **~ grande** bigger; **il ~ grande** the biggest; **di ~** more; **non ~** no more; tempo no longer; **~ o meno** more or less; **per di ~** what's more; **mai ~** never again; **al ~ presto** as soon as possible; **al ~ tardi** at the latest **2** agg more; superlativo most; **~ volte** several times **3** m most; MAT plus sign; **per lo ~** mainly; **i ~, le ~** the majority

piuma f feather

piumaggio m plumage

piumino m down; giacca down jacket

piumone m Continental quilt, duvet

piuttosto rather

pizza f pizza

pizzaiolo m pizza maker

pizzeria f pizzeria, pizza parlo(u)r

pizzicare <1l & d> **1** v/t braccio, persona pinch; F ladro catch (redhanded), nick F **2** v/i pinch

pizzico m (pl -chi) pinch

pizzicotto m pinch

pizzo m (merletto) lace

placare <1d> placate; dolore ease

placca f (pl -cche) plate; (targhetta) plaque; **~ dentaria** plaque

placcare <1d> plate; nel rugby tackle; **placcato d'oro** gold-plated

placido placid

planare <1a> glide

planata f: **fare una ~** glide

plancia f bridge; (passerella) gangway, gangplank

planetario (pl -ri) **1** agg planetary **2** m planetarium

plasma m plasma; **~ sanguigno** blood plasma

plasmabile malleable

plasmare <1a> mo(u)ld

plastica f plastic; MED plastic surgery; **posate** fpl **di ~** plastic cutlery

plastico (pl -ci) **1** agg plastic **2** m ARCHI scale model; **esplosivo m al ~** plastic bomb

plastilina® f Plasticine®

platano m plane (tree)

platea f TEA stalls

platino m platinum

plausibile plausible

plenilunio m (pl -ni) full moon

pletora f fig plethora

plettro m plectrum

pleurite f pleurisy

plico m (pl -chi) envelope; **in ~ separato** under separate cover

plurale m/agg plural

pluripartitico (pl -ci) multiparty

plusvalore m capital gains; **tassa f sul ~** capital gains tax

plutonio m plutonium

pneumatico (pl -ci) **1** agg pneumatic **2** m tyre, Am tire; **-i da neve** pl snow tyres (Am tires)

PNL abbr (= **prodotto nazionale lordo**) GNP (= gross national product)

po¹: **un ~** a little (**di** sth), a little bit (**di** of); **un bel ~** quite a lot

poco (pl -chi) **1** agg little; con nomi plurali few **2** avv not much; con aggettivi not very, not greatly; **senti un po'!** just listen!; **a ~ a ~** little by little, gradually; **~ fa** a little while ago; **fra ~** in a little while, soon; **~ dopo** a little while later, soon after; **per ~** cheap; (quasi) almost, nearly

podere m farm

podio m (pl -di) podium, dais; MUS podium

podismo m walking

poesia f poetry; componimento poem

poeta m (pl -i), -essa f poet

poetico (pl -ci) poetic

poggiare <1f & c> lean; (posare) put, place

poggiarsi **~ a** lean on

poggiatesta m inv head rest

poggio m (pl -ggi) mound

poi avv then; **d'ora in ~** from now on; **questa ~!** well I'm blowed!; **dalle 6 in ~** from 6 o'clock on(wards); **prima o ~** sooner or later

poiché since

poker m poker

polacco (pl -cchi) **1** m/agg Polish **2** m, -a f Pole

polare Polar; **circolo m ~ artico / antartico** Arctic / Antarctic circle

polarizzare <1a> polarize

polemica f (pl -che) argument; **fare -che** argue

polemico (pl -ci) argumentative

polemizzare <1a> argue

polenta f polenta, kind of porridge made from cornmeal

policlinico m (pl -ci) general hospital

poliglotta **1** agg multilingual **2** m/f polyglot

poligono m MAT polygon; MIL **~ di tiro** firing range

polio f F polio F

poliomielite f poliomyelitis

polipo m polyp

politica f politics; (strategia) policy; **~ estera** foreign policy; **~ interna** domestic policy; **~ sanitaria** health policy

politico (pl -ci) **1** agg political **2** m, -a f politician

polizia f police; **~ ferroviaria** transport police; **~ stradale** (o **della strada**) traffic police, Am highway patrol; **agente m di ~** police officer

poliziesco (pl -chi) police attr; **romanzo m ~** detective story

poliziotto **1** m policeman **2** agg: **donna f -a** policewoman; **cane m ~** police dog

polizza f policy; **~ di assicurazione** insurance policy

pollame m poultry

pollice m thumb; unità di misura inch

polline m pollen

pollo m chicken; **~ arrosto** roast chicken

polmonare pulmonary

polmone m lung

polmonite f pneumonia

polo¹ m GEOG pole; **~ nord** North Pole; **~ sud** South Pole

polo² **1** m SP polo **2** f inv polo shirt

Polonia f Poland

polpa f flesh; di manzo, vitello meat

polpaccio m (pl -cci) calf

polpastrello m fingertip

polpetta f di carne meatball

polpettone m meat loaf

polpo m octopus

polposo fleshy

polsino m cuff

polso m ANAT wrist; di camicia cuff; pulsazione pulse; **tastare il ~ a qu** take s.o.'s pulse

poltiglia f mush

poltrire <4d> laze around

poltrona f armchair; TEA stall (seat)

poltrone m, -a f lazybones

polvere f dust; (sostanza polverizzata) powder; **caffè m in ~** instant coffee; **latte m in ~** powdered milk

polverina f powder

polverizzare <1a> crush, pulverize; fig pulverize

polveroso dusty

pomata f cream

pomello m cheek; di porta knob

P

pomeridiano afternoon *attr*; **alle tre -e** at three in the afternoon, at three pm

pomeriggio *m* (*pl* -ggi) afternoon; **di ~, nel** ~ in the afternoon; **domani** ~ tomorrow afternoon

pomice *f* agg: (*pietra f*) ~ pumice (stone)

pomo *m* knob; ~ **d'Adamo** Adam's apple

pomodoro *m* tomato

pompa[1] *f* pomp; **impresa f di -e funebri** undertaker's, *Am* mortician

pompa[2] *f* TEC pump

pompelmo *m* grapefruit

pompiere *m* firefighter, *Br* fireman; **-i** *pl* firefighters, *Br* fire brigade

pomposo pompous

ponderare <1l & c> ponder

ponderato *decisione*, *scelta* carefully considered; *persona* reflective

pone → **porre**

ponente *m* west

pongo → **porre**

ponte *m* bridge; ARCHI scaffolding; MAR deck; ~ **girevole** swing bridge; ~ **sospeso** suspension bridge; ~ **radio** radio link; ~ **aereo** airlift; **fare il** ~ have a four-day weekend

pontefice *m* pontiff

ponteggio *m* scaffolding

ponticello *m* MUS bridge

pontificio (*pl* -ci) papal; **Stato m ~** Papal States *pl*

pontile *m* jetty

pop: **musica f ~** pop (music)

popolamento *m di città, Stato* population

popolare 1 *agg* popular; *quartiere* working-class; **ballo m ~** folk dance **2** *v/t* <1l>populate

popolarità *f* popularity

popolato populated; (*abitato*) inhabited; (*pieno*) crowded

popolazione *f* population

popolo *m* people

poppa *f* MAR stern

porcellana *f* porcelain, china

porcellino *m* piglet; ~ **d'India** guinea-pig

porcheria *f* disgusting thing; *fig* **una**

~ filth; **mangiare -e** eat junk food

porchetta *f* suckling pig roasted whole in the oven

porcile *m* pigsty, *Am* pigpen

porcino *m* cep

porco *m* (*pl* -chi) pig

porcospino *m* porcupine

porgere <3d> *mano*, *oggetto* hold out; *aiuto*, *saluto ecc* proffer

porno F 1 *agg* porn(o) F **2** *m* porn F

pornografia *f* pornography

pornografico (*pl* -ci) pornographic

poro *m* pore

poroso porous

porre <3ll> place, put; ~ **una domanda** ask a question; **poniamo che ...** let's suppose (that) ...

porro *m* leek; MED wart

porta *f* door; ~ **scorrevole** sliding door; **a -e chiuse** behind closed doors

portabagagli *m inv* luggage rack; AUTO roof rack

portacenere *m inv* ashtray

portachiavi *m inv* keyring

portacipria *m inv* powder compact

portafinestra *f* (*pl* portefinestre) French window

portafoglio *m* (*pl* -gli) wallet

portafortuna *m inv* good luck charm, talisman

portale *m* door

portalettere *m/f inv* → **postino**

portamento *m* bearing

portamonete *m inv* purse

portaombrelli *m inv* umbrella stand

portapacchi *m inv di macchina* roof rack; *di bicicletta* carrier

portapenne *m inv* pencil case

portare <1c> (*trasportare*) carry; (*accompagnare*) take; (*avere adosso*) wear; (*condurre*) lead; ~ **via** take away; **mi ha portato un regalo** he brought me a present; **portale un regalo** take her a present; ~ **in tavola** serve; **essere portato per qc / per fare qc** have a gift for sth / for doing sth; ~ **fortuna** be lucky; **porta bene i propri anni** he doesn't look his age

portasci *m inv* AUTO ski rack

portasigarette *m inv* cigarette case

portata *f* GASTR course; *di danni* extent; TEC *di camion* load capacity; *di cannocchiale* range; **alla ~ di** *film, libro ecc* suitable for; **a ~ di mano** within reach

portatile portable; **computer** *m* ~ portable (computer); **radio** *f* ~ portable (radio); **telefono** *m* ~ mobile (phone), *Am* cell(ular) phone; **farmacia** *f* ~ first-aid kit

portatore *m*, **-trice** *f* bearer; *di malattia* carrier

portauovo *m inv* eggcup

portavoce *m/f inv* spokesperson

portico *m* (*pl* -ci) porch; **-i** *pl* arcades

portiera *f* door

portiere *m* doorman; (*portinaio*) caretaker; (SP) goalkeeper, goalie F

portinaio *m* (*pl* -ai), **-a** *f* caretaker

portineria *f* caretaker's flat (*Am* apartment)

porto¹ *pp* → **porgere**

porto² *m* *posta* postage; **~ d'armi** gun licence (*Am* license)

porto³ *m* MAR port; **~ d'imbarco** port of embarkation

Portogallo *m* Portugal

portoghese *agg*, *m/f* Portuguese

portone *m* main entrance

porzione *f* share; GASTR portion

posa *f* *di cavi, tubi* laying; FOT exposure; FOT **mettersi in ~** pose

posacenere *m inv* ashtray

posare <1c> **1** *v/t* put, place **2** *v/i* (*stare in posa*) pose; **~ su** rest on; *fig* **~ da intellettuale** pose as an intellectual

posarsi alight

posate *fpl* cutlery *sg*

posato composed

positivo positive

posizione *f* position; **~ chiave** key position

possedere <2o> own, possess

possedimento *m* possession

possessivo possessive

possesso *m* possession

possessore *m* owner, possessor

possiamo → **potere**

possibile **1** *agg* possible; **il più**

presto ~ as soon as possible **2** *m*: **fare il ~** do everything one can, do one's best

possibilità *f inv* possibility; (*occasione*) opportunity, chance; **~ di guadagno** earning potential

possibilmente if possible, if I/you *etc* can

posso → **potere**

posta *f* mail, *Br* post; (*ufficio postale*) post office; **~ aerea** airmail; **per ~** by post; **a giro di ~** by return of post; INFOR **~ elettronica** e-mail; **fermo ~** poste restante

postale postal; **servizio** *m* ~ postal service; **cartolina** *f* ~ postcard

postdatare <1a> postdate

posteggiare <1f> park

posteggio *m* (*pl* -ggi) carpark; **~ dei taxi** taxi rank

posteriore back *attr*, rear *attr*; (*successivo*) later; **sedile** *m* ~ back seat

posticipare <1m> postpone

posticipato: **pagamento** *m* ~ payment in arrears

postino *m*, **-a** *f* postman, *Am* mailman; **donna** postwoman, *Am* mailwoman

posto¹ *pp* → **porre**; **~ che** supposing that

posto² *m* place; (*lavoro*) job, position; **mettere a ~** *stanza* tidy (up); **la tua camera è a ~?** is your room tidy?; **~ macchina** parking space; **~ finestrino / corridoio** window / aisle seat; **ho trovato solo un ~ in piedi** I had to stand; **~ a sedere** seat; **~ di guardia** guard post; INFOR **~ di lavoro** workstation; **~ di polizia** police station; **~ di pronto soccorso** first aid post; **~ di villeggiatura** holiday resort; **vado io al ~ tuo** I'll go in your place, I'll go instead of you; **fuori** ~ out of place

postoperatorio (*pl* -ri) postoperative

postumo posthumous

potabile fit to drink; **acqua** *f* ~ drinking water

potare <1a> prune

potassio *m* potassium

potente powerful; (*efficace*) potent

potenza *f* power; ~ **mondiale** world power; ~ **del motore** engine power

potenziare <1a> strengthen

potere 1 *v/i* <2l> can, be able to; **non posso andare** I can't go; **non ho potuto farlo** I couldn't do it, I was unable to do it; **posso fumare?** do you mind if I smoke?; *formale* may I smoke?; **può essere** perhaps, maybe; ~**può darsi** perhaps, maybe **2** *m* power; ~ **d'acquisto** purchasing power; **essere al** ~ be in power

poveraccio *m* (*pl* -cci), **-a** *f* poor thing, poor creature

poveretto *m*, **poverino** *m* poor man

povero 1 *agg* poor **2** *m*, **-a** *f* poor man; **donna** poor woman; **i -i** *pl* the poor

povertà *f* poverty

pozzanghera *f* puddle

pozzo *m* well; ~ **petrolifero** oil well

pp. *abbr* (= **pagine**) pp (= pages)

p.p. *abbr* (= **per procura**) pp (= for, on behalf of); (= **pacco postale**) small parcel

PP.TT. *abbr* (= **Poste e Telecomunicazioni**) Italian Post Office

pranzare <1a> *a mezzogiorno* have lunch; *la sera* have dinner

pranzo *m a mezzogiorno* lunch; *la sera* dinner

prassi *f inv* standard procedure

prataiolo *m* field mushroom

pratica *f* (*pl* -che) practice; (*esperienza*) experience; (*atto*) file; **mettere in** ~ put into practice; **fare** ~ gain experience, become more experienced; **-che** *pl* papers, documents; **fare le -che necessarie per qc** take the necessary steps for sth; **fare le -che per** *passaporto* gather together the necessary documentation for; **in** ~ in practice; **avere** ~ **di qc** have experience of sth

praticabile *sport* which can be practised; *strada* passable

praticantato *m* apprenticeship

praticare <1l & d> *virtù, pazienza* show; *professione, sport* practise; *locale* frequent; ~ **molto sport** do a lot of sport

pratico (*pl* -ci) practical; **essere** ~ **di** *conoscere bene* know a lot about

prato *m* meadow

preavviso *m* notice

precario (*pl* -ri) precarious

precauzione *f* caution; **-i** *pl* precautions

precedente 1 *agg* preceding **2** *m* precedent; **avere dei -i penali** have a record

precedenza *f* precedence; AUTO **diritto** *m* **di** ~ right of way; **avere la** ~ have precedence; AUTO have right of way; **dare la** ~ give priority; AUTO give way

precedere <3a> precede

precipitare <1m> **1** *v/t* throw; *fig* rush **2** *v/i* fall, plunge

precipitarsi (*affrettarsi*) rush

precipitazione *f* (*fretta*) haste, hurry; **-i** *pl* **atmosferiche** atmospheric precipitation *sg*

precipitoso hasty

precipizio *m* (*pl* -zi) precipice

precisamente precisely

precisare <1a> specify

precisione *f* precision, accuracy; **con** ~ precisely

preciso accurate; *persona* precise; **alle tre -e** at three o'clock exactly *o* precisely, at three o'clock sharp

precoce precocious; *pianta* early

precotto *m* ready-made, pre-cooked

preda *f* prey; **in** ~ **alla disperazione** in despair

predecessore *m*, **-a** *f* predecessor

predestinare <1a> predestine

predica *f* (*pl* -che) sermon

predicare <1l, b & d> preach

prediletto 1 *pp* → **prediligere 2** *agg* favo(u)rite

predilezione *f* predilection

prediligere <3u> prefer

predire <3t> predict

predisporre <3ll> draw up in advance; ~ **a** encourage, promote

predisposto *pp* → **predisporre**

predominare <1m & c> predominate

predominio m (pl -ni) predominance

prefabbricato 1 agg prefabricated **2** m prefabricated building

prefazione f preface

preferenza f preference

preferenziale preferential

preferire <4d> prefer

preferito favo(u)rite

prefetto m prefect

prefettura f prefecture

prefiggersi <3mm> set o.s.

prefisso 1 pp → **prefiggersi 2** m TELEC code

pregare <1b & e> beg (di fare to do); divinità pray to; ti prego di ascoltarmi please listen to me; farsi ~ be coaxed; prego please; prego? I'm sorry (what did you say)?; grazie! – prego! thank you! – you're welcome! or not at all!

preghiera f request; REL prayer

pregiato metallo, pietra precious

pregio m (qualità) good point

pregiudicato m, **-a** f previous offender

pregiudizio m (pl -zi) prejudice

preg.mo abbr (= **pregiatissimo**) formal style of address used in correspondence

pregustare <1a> look forward to

preistoria f prehistory

preistorico (pl -ci) prehistoric

prelato m REL prelate

prelavaggio m pre-wash

prelevamento m di sangue, campione taking; FIN withdrawal; ~ in contanti cash withdrawal

prelevare <1b> sangue, campione take; denaro withdraw

prelibato exquisite

prelievo m (prelevamento) taking; FIN withdrawal; ~ del sangue blood sample

pre-maman 1 agg maternity attr **2** m inv maternity dress

prematrimoniale premarital

prematuro premature

premeditato premeditated

premere <3a> **1** v/t press **2** v/i press (su on); mi preme che it is

important to me that

premessa f introduction

premesso pp → **premettere**

premettere <3ee> say first

premiare <1k & b> give an award or prize to; onestà, coraggio reward

premiato prize-winning, award-winning

premiazione f award ceremony

premio m (pl -mi) prize, award; FIN premium; ~ Nobel per la pace Nobel peace prize; assegnare un ~ award a prize

premura f (fretta) hurry, rush; essere pieno di -e nei confronti di qu be very attentive to s.o.; mettere ~ a qu hurry s.o. along; non c'è ~ there's no hurry o rush

premuroso attentive

prenatale prenatal

prendere <3c> **1** v/t take; malattia, treno catch; cosa prendi? what will you have?; ~ qu per un italiano take or mistake s.o. for an Italian; andare / venire a ~ qu fetch s.o.; ~ fuoco catch fire; ~ il sole sunbathe; ~ paura take fright, get frightened; AVIA ~ quota gain height; ~ in giro qu pull s.o.'s leg; prendersela get upset (per about; con with); che ti prende? what's got into you? **2** v/i turn right ~ a destra turn right

prendisole m inv sundress

prenotare <1c> book, reserve

prenotato booked, reserved

prenotazione f booking, reservation

preoccupare <1m & c> worry, preoccupy

preoccuparsi worry

preoccupato worried, preoccupied

preoccupazione f worry

preparare <1a> prepare

prepararsi get ready (a to), prepare (a to)

preparativi mpl preparations

preparato 1 agg ready, prepared **2** m preparation

preparazione f preparation

preposizione f preposition

prepotente domineering; bisogno pressing

prepotenza f di persona domineering nature; di bisogno pressing nature

presa f grip, hold; abbandonare la ~ let go; fare una ~ presso corriere call a courier; EL ~ di corrente socket; fig ~ di possesso conquest, capture; essere alle -e con qc be grappling with sth

presagio m (pl -gi) omen, sign

presalario m scholarship

presbite far-sighted, long-sighted

prescindere <3v>: ~ da have nothing to do with, not be connected with

prescritto pp → **prescrivere**

prescrivere <3tt> prescribe

prescrizione f prescription

presentare <1b> documenti, biglietto show, present; domanda submit; scuse make; TEA present; (contenere) contain; (far conoscere) introduce (a to)

presentarsi look; (esporre) show itself; occasione present itself, occur

presentatore m, **-trice** f presenter

presentazione f presentation; di richiesta submission; fare le -i make the introductions

presente 1 agg present; hai ~ il negozio ... ? do you know the shop ... ? 2 m present; GRAM present (tense); i -i pl those present, those in attendance

presentimento m premonition

presenza f presence; alla (o in) ~ di in the presence of; di bella ~ fine-looking

presepe m

presepio m (pl -pi) crèche

preservare <1b> protect, keep (da from)

preservativo m condom

presidente m/f chairman; POL **Presidente dello Stato** President; ~ **del Consiglio (dei ministri)** Prime Minister

presidenza f chairmanship; POL presidency

preso pp → **prendere**

pressappoco more or less

pressare <1b> crush; TEC press

pressione f pressure; ~ **atmosferica** atmospheric pressure; ~ **delle gomme** tyre pressure; ~ **sanguigna** blood pressure; fig far ~ su put pressure on, pressure

presso 1 prp (vicino a) near; nella sede di on the premises of; posta care of; vive ~ i genitori he lives with his parents; lavoro ~ la FIAT I work for Fiat 2 m: nei -i di in the vicinity of, in the neighbo(u)rhood of

pressoché almost

prestare <1b> lend; ~ **ascolto** / **aiuto a qu** listen to / help s.o.; ~ **un servizio** provide a service

prestarsi offer one's services; (essere adatto) lend itself (a to)

prestatore m di servizio provider

prestazione f service

prestigio m prestige

prestito m loan; in ~ on loan; dare in ~ lend; prendere in ~ borrow

presto (fra poco) soon; (in fretta) quickly; (di buon'ora) early; a ~! see you soon!; far ~ be quick

presumere <3h> presume

presuntuoso presumptuous

presunzione f presumption

prete m priest

pretendente m/f claimant

pretendere <3c> claim

pretensioso pretentious

pretesa f pretension; avanzare -e put forward claims; senza -e unpretentious

pretesto m pretext

pretore m magistrate

pretura f magistrates' court

prevalenza f prevalence; in ~ prevalently

prevalere <2r> prevail

prevedere <2s> foresee, predict; tempo forecast; di legge provide for

prevedibile predictable

prevendita f advance sale

prevenire <4p> domanda, desiderio anticipate; (evitare) prevent

preventivo 1 agg preventive 2 m estimate

prevenzione f prevention

previdente foresighted

previdenza f foresight; ~ **sociale** social security, Am welfare

previsione f forecast; -**i** pl **del tempo** weather forecast sg

previsto pp → **prevedere**

prezioso precious

prezzemolo m parsley

prezzo m price; ~ **di listino** recommended retail price; ~ **promozionale** special introductory price; **aumento** m **del** ~ price increase; **a buon** ~ cheap; fig **a caro** ~ dearly; **a metà** ~ half-price; **a qualunque** ~ at any cost; ~ **netto** net price

prigione f prison

prigionia f imprisonment

prigioniero m, -**a** f prisoner; **fare** ~ take prisoner

prima¹ avv before; (in primo luogo) first; ~ **di fare qc** before doing sth; ~ **o poi** sooner or later; ~ **che** before; **quanto** ~ as soon as possible

prima² f FERR first class; AUTO first gear; TEA first night

primario (pl -ri) prime

primavera f spring

primaverile spring attr

primitivo primitive; (iniziale) original

primizia f early crop

primo 1 agg first; ~ **piano** m first floor; **in** -**a visione** film just out 2 m, -**a** f first; **ai** -**i del mese** at the beginning of the month; **sulle** -**e** in the beginning, at first 3 m GASTR first course, starter

primogenito 1 agg first-born 2 m, -**a** f first-born

principale 1 agg main 2 m boss

principato m principality

principe m prince

principessa f princess

principiante m/f beginner

principio m (pl -pi) (inizio) start, beginning; (norma) principle; **al** ~ at the start, in the beginning; **da** ~ from the start or beginning or outset; **per** ~ as a matter of principle; **in**

linea di ~ in theory

privare <1a> deprive (**di** of)

privarsi deprive o.s. (**di** of)

privatizzare <1a> privatize

privato 1 agg private; **in** ~ in private 2 m private citizen

privazione f deprivation; (sacrificio) privation

privilegiare <1f> favo(u)r, prefer

privilegiato privileged

privilegio m (pl -gi) privilege

privo : ~ **di** lacking in, devoid of; ~ **di sensi** unconscious

pro 1 m inv: **i** ~ **e i contro** the pros and cons; **a che** ~**?** what's the point or use? 2 prp for; ~ **capite** per capita, each

probabile probable

probabilità f inv probability

problema m (pl -i) problem

problematico (pl -ci) problematic

proboscide f trunk

procedere <3a> carry on; fig (agire) proceed; DIR ~ **contro qu** take legal proceedings against s.o.

procedimento m process

procedura f procedure; DIR proceedings pl

processare <1b> try

processione f procession

processo m process; DIR trial; ~ **civile** civil proceedings; ~ **di fabbricazione** manufacturing process; ~ **verbale** minutes pl; **essere sotto** ~ be on trial

processuale DIR trial attr

procinto m: **essere in** ~ **di** be about to, be on the point of

proclamare <1a> proclaim

proclamazione f proclamation

procura f power of attorney; **Procura di Stato** public prosecutor's office; **per** ~ by proxy

procurare <1a> (causare) cause; ~ **qc a qu** cause s.o. sth

procurarsi get hold of, obtain

procuratore m, -**trice** f person with power of attorney; DIR lawyer for the prosecution; ~ **generale** Attorney General

prodigio m (pl -gi) prodigy

P

prodigioso tremendous, prodigious

prodotto **1** pp → **produrre** **2** m product; **-i** pl **alimentari** foodstuffs; **-i** pl **farmaceutici** pharmaceuticals; **~ finito** finished product; **~ interno / nazionale lordo** gross domestic / national product; **-i** pl **di bellezza** cosmetics

produco → **produrre**

produrre <3e> produce; danni cause

produttività f productivity

produttivo productive

produttore m, **-trice** f producer

produzione f production; **~ giornaliera** daily production or output; **~ in serie** mass production

prof. abbr (= **professore**) Prof. (= Professor)

profanare <1a> desecrate

profano **1** agg profane **2** m fig: **sono un ~ di** I know nothing about

professionale esperienza, impegno professional; scuola, corso vocational

professione f profession; **~ di fede** profession of faith; **calciatore** m **di ~** professional footballer

professionista m/f (mpl -i) professional, pro F; **libero ~** self-employed person

professore m, **-essa** f teacher; d'università professor

profeta m (pl -i) prophet

profezia f prophecy

proficuo profitable

profilassi f inv prophylaxis

profilattico (pl -ci) prophylactic

profilo m profile

profitto m (vantaggio) advantage; FIN **conto -i e perdite** profit and loss account

profondità f inv depth; FOT **~ di campo** depth of field

profondo deep

prof. ssa abbr (= **professoressa**) Prof. (= Professor)

profugo m (pl -ghi), **-a** f refugee

profumare <1a> perfume, scent

profumatamente **pagare ~** pay through the nose, pay a fortune

profumeria f perfume shop

profumo m perfume

progettare <1b> plan

progettazione f design

progetto m design; di costruzione project; **~ pilota** pilot project; **~ di legge** bill

prognosi f inv prognosis

programma m (pl -i) programme, Am program; INFOR program; **~ applicativo** application; **~ di scrittura** word processor; **~ televisivo** TV program(me); **fuori ~** unscheduled; **avere in ~ qualcosa** have something planned

programmare <1a> plan; INFOR program

programmatore m, **-trice** f programmer

programmazione f programming; FIN **~ economica** economic planning; INFOR **linguaggio** m **di ~** programming language

progredire <4d> progress

progredito advanced

progressione f progression

progressivo progressive

progresso m progress; **fare -i** make progress

proibire <4d> ban, prohibit; **~ a qu di fare qc** forbid s.o. to do sth

proibizione f ban

proiettare <1b> throw; film screen, show; fig project

proiettile m projectile

proiettore m projector; **~ per diapositive** slide projector

proiezione f projection; di film screening, showing

prole f children, offspring

proletario (pl -ri) **1** agg proletariat **2** m proletarian

pro loco f inv local tourist board

prologo m (pl -ghi) prolog(ue)

prolunga f EL extension cord

prolungamento m extension

prolungare <1e> nel spazio extend; nel tempo prolong, extend

prolungarsi di strada extend; di riunione go on, continue

promemoria m inv memo

promessa f promise

promesso *pp* → **promettere**

promettente promising

promettere <3ee> promise; ~ **bene** look promising

promontorio *m* (*pl* -ri) promontory, headland

promosso *pp* → **promuovere**

promozione *f* promotion; EDU year; ~ **delle vendite** sales promotion

promuovere <3ff> promote; EDU move up

pronipote *m/f di nonni* great-grandson; *donna, ragazza* great-granddaughter; *di zii* great-nephew; *donna, ragazza* great-niece

pronome *m* pronoun

prontezza *f* readiness, promptness; (*rapidità*) speediness, promptness; ~ **di spirito** quick thinking

pronto (*preparato*) ready (*a fare qc* to do sth; *per qc* for sth); (*rapido*) speedy, prompt; TELEC ~! hello!; **pagamento** *m* -**a cassa** payment in cash, cash payment; ~ **soccorso** first aid; *in ospedale* accident and emergency, A&E; ~ **per l'uso** ready to use

pronuncia *f* pronunciation

pronunciare <1f> pronounce; **non ha pronunciato una parola** he didn't say a word

pronunciarsi give an opinion (*su* on)

pronunciato *fig* definite, pronounced

propaganda *f* propaganda; POL ~ **elettorale** electioneering

propagare <1e> propagate; *fig* spread

propagarsi spread (*anche fig*)

propano *m* propane

propenso inclined (*a fare qc* to do sth)

propizio (*pl* -zi) suitable

propongo → **proporre**

proponimento *m* resolution; **fare** ~ **di fare qc** decide *or* make up one's mind to do sth

proporre <3ll> propose

proporsi stand (**come** as); ~ **di fare qc** intend to do sth

proporzionale proportional

proporzionato in proportion (*a* to)

proporzione *f* proportion; **in** ~ in proportion (*a, con* to)

proposito *m* intention; **a che** ~? what about?; **a** ~ by the way; **a** ~ **di** about, with reference to; **di** ~ deliberately, on purpose; **capitare a** ~ turn up at just the right moment

proposizione *f* GRAM sentence

proposta *f* proposal

proposto *pp* → **proporre**

propriamente really

proprietà *f inv* property; *diritto* ownership; ~ **privata** private property; **essere di** ~ **di qu** belong to s.o., be s.o.'s property

proprietario *m* (*pl* -ri), -**a** *f* owner

proprio (*pl* -ri) **1** *agg* own; (*caratteristico*) typical; (*adatto*) proper; **nome** *m* ~ proper noun; **amor** *m* ~ pride; **a** -**e spese** at one's own expense **2** *avv* (*davvero*) really; **è** ~ **lui che me l'ha chiesto** he's the one who asked me!; **è** ~ **impossibile** that is quite impossible **3** *m* (*beni*) personal property; **lavorare in** ~ be self-employed

propulsione *f* propulsion

propulsore *m* propeller

prora *f* prow

proroga *f* (*pl* -ghe) postponement; (*prolungamento*) extension

prorogare <1l, e & c> (*rinviare*) postpone; (*prolungare*) extend

prosa *f* prose

prosciogliere <3ss> release; DIR acquit

prosciugare <1e> drain; *di sole* dry up

prosciutto *m* ham, prosciutto; ~ **cotto** cooked ham; ~ **crudo** salted airdried ham

proseguimento *m* continuation

proseguire <4a> **1** *v/t* continue **2** *v/i* continue, carry on, go on

prosperare <1l & c> prosper

prosperità *f* prosperity

prospero prosperous

prospettiva *f* perspective; (*panorama*) view; *fig* point of view;

P

senza -e without prospects

prospetto *m disegno* elevation; (*facciata*) facade; (*tabella*) table; ~ **pubblicitario** brochure

prossimamente shortly, soon

prossimità *f inv* proximity; **in ~ di** near, close to

prossimo 1 *agg* close; **la -a volta** the next time; **il lavoro è ~ alla fine** the work is nearly finished **2** *m* fellow human being, neighbo(u)r

prostituta *f* prostitute

prostituzione *f* prostitution

protagonista *m/f* (*mpl* -i) protagonist

proteggere <3cc> protect (**da** from)

proteico protein *attr*

proteina *f* protein

protesi *f inv* prosthesis; ~ **dentaria** false teeth, dentures

protesta *f* protest

protestante *agg*, *m/f* Protestant

protestare <1b> *v/t* & *v/i* protest

protettivo protective

protetto *pp* → **proteggere**

protezione *f* protection; ~ **degli animali** prevention of cruelty to animals; ~ **dell'ambiente** environment protection, protection of the environment; ~ **del paesaggio** nature conservation; ~ **delle acque** prevention of water pollution; INFOR ~ **dati** data protection

protocollare 1 *agg* official **2** *v/t* <1c> register

protocollo *m* protocol; (*registro*) register; TEC standard; **foglio** *m* ~ foolscap; **mettere a** ~ register

prototipo *m* prototype

prova *f* (*esame*) test; (*tentativo*) attempt; (*testimonianza*) proof; *di abito* fitting; SP heat; TEA **-e** *pl* rehearsal *sg*; TEA **-e** *pl* **generali** dress rehearsal *sg*; ~ **di laboratorio** lab test; **banco** *m* **di** ~ test bench; **a ~ di bomba** bombproof; **salvo ~ contraria** unless otherwise stated; **per insufficienza di -e** for lack of evidence; **mettere alla** ~ put to the test

provare <1c> test, try out; *vestito* try (on); (*dimostrare*) prove; TEA re-

hearse; ~ **a fare qc** try to do sth

provato proven; *fig* marked (**da** by)

provengo → **provenire**

provenienza *f* origin

provenire <4p> come (**da** from)

proventi *mpl* income *sg*

proverbio *m* (*pl* -i) proverb

provetta *f* test-tube; **bambino** *m* **in** ~ test-tube baby

provincia *f* (*pl* -ce) province

provinciale 1 *agg* provincial; **strada** *f* ~ B road **2** *m/f* provincial **3** *f* B road

provino *m* screen-test; (*campione*) sample

provocante provocative

provocare <1l, c & d> (*causare*) cause; (*sfidare*) provoke; *invidia* arouse

provvedere <2s> **1** *v/t* provide (**di** with) **2** *v/i* ~ **a** take care of

provvedimento *m* measure; ~ **d'urgenza** emergency measure

provvidenza *f* providence

provvigione *f* commission

provvisorio (*pl* -ri) provisional

provvista *f*: **fare -e** go (food) shopping; **far ~ di qc** stock up on sth

provvisto 1 *pp* → **provvedere 2** *agg*: **essere ~ di** be provided with, have; **essere ben ~ di qc** have lots of sth

prozio *m*, **-a** *f* great-uncle; *donna* great-aunt

prua *f* prow

prudente careful, cautious

prudenza *f* care, caution

prudere <3a>: **mi prude la mano** my hand itches

prugna *f* plum; ~ **secca** prune

prurito *m* itch

P.S. *abbr* (= **Pubblica Sicurezza**) police; (= **post scriptum**) PS (= post scriptum)

pseudo ... pseudo ...

pseudonimo *m* pseudonym

psicanalisi *f* psychoanalysis

psicanalista *m/f* (*mpl* -i) psychoanalyst

psiche *f* psyche

psichiatra *m/f* (*mpl* -i) psychiatrist

psichiatria *f* psychiatry

psichiatrico (*pl* -ci) psychiatric

psicologia *f* psychology

psicologico (*pl* -ci) psychological

psicologo *m* (*pl* -gi), **-a** *f* psychologist

psicosi *f inv* psychosis

psicoterapia *f* psychotherapy

P.T.P. *abbr* (= *Posto Telefonico Pubblico*) public telephone

pubblicare <1l & d> publish

pubblicazione *f* publication; **-i** *pl* **matrimoniali** banns

pubblicità *f inv* publicity, advertising; *annuncio* ad(vert); ~ **televisiva** TV ad, *Br* commercial; **fare** ~ **a** *evento* publicize; *prodotto* advertise

pubblicitario 1 *agg* advertising **2** *m*, **-a** *f* publicist

pubblico (*pl* -ci) **1** *agg* public; **Pubblico Ministero** public prosecutor **2** *m* public; (*spettatori*) audience; **in** ~ in public

pube *m* pubis

pubertà *f* puberty

pudore *m* modesty; **senza** ~ shameless, immodest

pugilato *m* boxing; **incontro** *m* **di** ~ boxing match

pugile *m* boxer

pugnalare <1a> stab

pugnale *m* dagger

pugno *m* fist; (*colpo*) punch; *quantità* handful; **di proprio** ~ in one's own handwriting; **avere in** ~ **qc** have sth in one's grasp; **ti ho in** ~ I've got you now; **rimanere con un** ~ **di mosche** come away empty-handed; **fare a -i** fight, come to blows

pulce *f* flea

pulcino *m* chick

puledro *m*, **-a** *f* colt; (*femmina*) filly

pulire <4d> clean

pulito clean; *fig* cleaned-out

pulitura *f* cleaning; ~ **a secco** dry cleaning

pulizia *f* cleanliness; *fig* ~ **etnica** ethnic cleansing; **donna** *f* **delle -e** cleaner; **fare le -e** do the cleaning, clean

pullman *m inv* coach, bus

pullover *m inv* pullover

pullulare <1l>: ~ **di** be teeming or swarming with

pulpito *m* pulpit

pulsante *m* button

pulsare <1a> pulsate

pulsazione *f* pulsation

pulviscolo *m* dust

pungente *foglia* prickly; *freddo, parola* sharp, biting; *desiderio* sharp

pungere <3d> prick; *di ape, vespa* sting; ~ **qu sul vivo** cut s.o. to the quick

pungiglione *m* sting

punibile punishable (**con** by)

punire <4d> punish

punizione *f* punishment; SP **calcio** *m* **di** ~ free kick

punta *f* di *spillo, coltello* point; *di dita, lingua* tip; GEOG peak; *fig* touch, trace; **ora** *f* **di** ~ peak hour; **ce l'ho sulla** ~ **della lingua** it's on the tip of my tongue; *fig* **prendere qc di** ~ face sth head-on

puntare <1a> **1** *v/t* pin (**su** to); (*dirigere*) point (**verso** at); (*scommettere*) bet (**su** on); *fig* ~ **i piedi** dig one's heels in **2** *v/i* (*dirigersi*) head (**verso** for); ~ **a successo, matrimonio** aspire to, set one's sights on; ~ **su contare su** rely on

puntata *f* instal(l)ment; (*scommessa*) bet

punteggiatura *f* punctuation

punteggio *m* score

puntiglio *m* obstinacy

puntiglioso punctilious

puntina *f*; *di giradischi* stylus; ~ (**da disegno**) drawing pin, *Am* thumbtack

puntino *m* dot; **a** ~ perfectly, to perfection

punto 1 *pp* → **pungere 2** *m* point; MED, (*maglia*) stitch; ~ **di vista** point of view, viewpoint; ~ **cardinale** point of the compass; ~ **culminante** height; ~ **di partenza** starting point; ~ **di fusione** melting point; **fino a che** ~ **sei arrivato?** how far have you got?; **alle dieci in** ~ at ten o'clock exactly *or* on the dot; ~ **fermo** full stop, *Am* period; **due -i** colon; ~ **e virgola** semi-colon;

~ esclamativo exclamation mark; **~ interrogativo** question mark; **di ~ in bianco** suddenly, without warning; **essere sul ~ di fare qc** be on the point of doing sth, be about to do sth
puntuale punctual
puntualità f punctuality
puntualizzare <1a> make clear
puntura f di ape, vespa sting; di ago prick; MED injection; **~ d'insetto** insect bite
punzecchiare <1k> prick; fig (provocare) tease
può, puoi → **potere**
pupazzo m puppet; **~ di neve** snowman
pupilla f pupil
purché provided, on condition that

pure 1 cong even if; (tuttavia) (and) yet **2** avv too, as well; **pur di** in order to; **venga ~ avanti !** do come in!
purè m puree
purezza f purity
purga f (pl -ghe) purge
purgante m laxative
puro pure
purtroppo unfortunately
pus m pus
pustola f pimple
putrefare <3aa> rot, putrefy
puttana f P whore P
puzza f stink
puzzare <1a> stink (**di** of)
puzzo m stink
puzzola f ZO polecat
puzzolente stinking, evil-smelling
p.v. abbr (= **prossimo venturo**) next

Q

q abbr (= **quintale**) 100 kilograms
qua here; **passa di ~** come this way; **al di ~ di** on this side of
quaderno m exercise book
quadrangolare four-sided
quadrangolo m quadrangle
quadrante m quadrant; di orologio dial
quadrare <1a> **1** v/t MAT square; conti balance **2** v/i di conti balance, square F; fig **i conti non quadrano** there's something fishy going on
quadrato 1 agg square; fig persona rational **2** m square; tabella ecc list
quadrifoglio m (pl -gli) four-leaf clover
quadro 1 agg square **2** m painting, picture; MAT square; fig **nel ~ di** as part of; **~ (sinottico)** table; **-i pl direttivi** senior executives, senior management sg; **~ di comando** control panel; **~ a olio** oil painting; **a -i** check attr

quadruplo m/agg quadruple
quaggiù down here
quaglia f quail
qualche a few; (un certo) some; interrogativo any; **~ giorno** I'm staying for a few days; **~ giorno usciamo insieme** we'll go out some day; **~ cosa** something; **~ volta** sometime; alcune volte a few times; a volte sometimes; **in ~ luogo** somewhere; **~ mese fa** a few months ago; **in ~ modo** somehow
qualcheduno someone, somebody
qualcosa something; interrogativo anything, something; **qualcos'altro** something else; **~ da mangiare** something to eat; **~ di bello** something beautiful
qualcuno someone, somebody; in interrogazioni anche anyone, anybody; **qualcun'altro** someone or somebody else; **c'è ~?** (is) anybody or anyone home?

quale 1 *agg* what; **~ *libro vuoi?*** which book do you want?; ***città ~ Roma*** cities like Rome **2** *pron*: ***prendi un libro – ~?*** take a book – which one?; ***il / la ~ persona*** who, that; *cosa* which, that; ***la persona della ~ stai parlando*** the person you're talking about **3** *avv* as

qualifica *f* (*pl* -che) qualification; **~ *professionale*** profession

qualificare <1m & d> qualify; (*definire*) describe

qualificarsi give one's name (***come*** as); *a esame, gara* qualify

qualificato qualified

qualificazione *f* qualification

qualità *f inv* quality; ***merce f di prima ~*** top quality goods; **~ *della vita*** quality of life

qualora in the event that

qualsiasi any; *non importa quale* whatever; **~ *persona*** anyone; **~ *cosa faccia*** whatever I do

qualunque any; ***uno ~*** any one; **~ *cosa*** anything; **~ *cosa faccia*** whatever I do; **~ *stagione*** whatever the season; ***l'uomo ~*** the man in the street

qualvolta *ogni ~* every time that

quando when; *per ~?* when?; *da ~?* how long?; **~ *vengo*** when I come; *ogni volta che* whenever I come; *di ~ in ~* now and then, from time to time

quantità *f inv* quantity, amount

quantitativo *m* quantity, amount

quanto 1 *agg* how much; *con nomi plurali* how many; ***tutto ~ il libro*** the whole book; ***tutti -i*** *pl* every single one *sg*; **-*i ne abbiamo oggi?*** what is the date today?, what is today's date? **2** *avv*: **~ *dura ancora?*** how long will it go on for?; **~ *a me*** as for me; **~ *costa?*** how much is it?; **~ *prima*** as soon as possible; *in ~* since, because; *per ~ ne sappia* as far as I know **3** *m*: *teoria f dei -i* quantum theory

quaranta forty

quarantena *f* quarantine

quarantenne 1 *agg* forty or so **2** *m/f*

person in his / her forties

quarantesimo *m/agg* fortieth

quaresima *f* Lent

quarta *f* AUTO fourth (gear)

quartiere *m* district; MIL quarters *pl*; **~ *generale*** headquarters

quarto 1 *agg* fourth **2** *m* fourth; (*quarta parte*) quarter; **~ *d'ora*** quarter of an hour; ***sono le due e un ~*** it's (a) quarter past two; ***un ~ di rosso*** a quarter-litre (*Am* liter) of red; **-*i di finale*** quarter-finals

quarzo *m* quartz; ***orologio m al ~*** quartz watch

quasi almost; **~ *mai*** hardly ever

quassù up here

quattordicesimo *m/agg* fourteenth

quattordici fourteen

quattrini *mpl* money *sg*, cash *sg*

quattro four; *al ~ per cento* at four per cent; *fare ~ passi* go for a stroll; *farsi in ~ per fare qc* go to a lot of trouble to do sth

quattrocchi *m inv*: *a ~* in private

quattrocento 1 *agg* four hundred **2** *m*: *il Quattrocento* the fifteenth century

quattromila four thousand

quegli, quei → **quello**

quello 1 *agg* that, *pl* those **2** *pron* that (one), *pl* those (ones); **~ *che*** the one that; *tutto ~ che* all (that), everything (that)

quercia *f* (*pl* -ce) oak

querela *f* legal action; *sporgere ~ contro qc* take legal action against s.o., sue s.o.; **~ *per diffamazione*** action for slander

quesito *m* question

questi → **questo**

questionario *m* (*pl* -ri) questionnaire

questione *f* question; **~ *di fiducia*** question *or* matter of trust; *qui non è ~ di* it is not a question *or* matter of; *è ~ di fortuna* it's a matter of luck; *è fuori ~* it is out of the question; *mettere qc in ~* cast doubt on sth

questo 1 *agg* this, *pl* these; *quest'oggi* today **2** *pron* this (one), *pl* these (ones); **~ qui** this one here; **con ~** with that; **per ~** for that reason; **quest'oggi** today; **-a poi!** well I'm blowed!; **ci mancherebbe anche -a!** that's all we'd need!; **-a non me l'aspettavo** I wasn't expecting this

questore *m* chief of police

questura *f* offices of the chief of police

qui here; **~ vicino** near here; **fin ~** up to here; **passa di ~!** come this way!; **voglio uscire di ~** I want to get out of here; **di ~ a un mese** a month from now, in a month's time

quietanza *f* receipt

quiete *f* peace and quiet

quieto quiet

quindecismo *m/agg* fifteenth

quindi 1 *avv* then **2** *cong* therefore

quindici fifteen; **tra ~ giorni** in two weeks (time), *Br* in a fortnight('s time)

quindicina *f*: **una ~** about fifteen; *una ~ di giorni* about two weeks, *Br* about a fortnight

quinta *f* AUTO fifth (gear); TEA **le -e** the wings; *fig* **dietro le -e** behind the scenes

quintale *m* hundred kilos; **mezzo ~** fifty kilos

quinto *m/agg* fifth

quota *f* (*parte*) share, quota; (*altitudine*) altitude; **perdere ~** lose altitude; **prendere ~** gain altitude

quotare <1c> (*valutare*) value; FIN **azioni** *pl* **quotate in borsa** shares listed *or* quoted on the Stock Exchange

quotato respected

quotazione *f di azioni* value, price; **~ d'acquisto** bid price; **~ di vendita** offer price

quotidianamente daily

quotidiano 1 *agg* daily **2** *m* daily (newspaper)

quoziente *m*: **~ d'intelligenza** IQ

R

R. *abbr* (= **raccomandata**) recorded delivery, *Am* certified mail

rabarbaro *m* rhubarb

rabbia *f* rage; (*stizza*) anger; MED rabies; **accesso** *m* **di ~** fit of rage; **fare ~ a qu** make s.o. cross

rabbino *m* rabbi

rabbioso *gesto, sguardo* of rage; *cane* rabid

rabbrividire <4d> shudder; *per paura* shiver

rabbuiarsi <1i> get dark, darken; *fig* darken

racc. *abbr* (= **raccomandata**) recorded delivery, *Am* certified mail

raccapricciante appalling, sickening

raccattare <1a> (*tirar su*) pick up

racchetta *f* racquet; **~ da sci** ski pole

racchiudere <3b> contain

raccogliere <3ss> (*tirar su*) pick up; (*radunare*) gather, collect; AGR harvest; **~ i frutti di qc** reap the benefits of sth

raccoglitore *m* ring binder; **~ del vetro** bottle bank

raccolgo → **raccogliere**

raccolta *f* collection; AGR harvest; **fare ~ di francobolli** collect stamps

raccolto 1 *pp* → **raccogliere 2** *m* harvest

raccomandabile: **un tipo poco ~** a shady character

raccomandare <1a> **1** *v/t* recommend **2** *v/i*: **~ a qu di fare qc** tell s.o. to do sth

raccomandata *f* recorded delivery (letter), *Am* certified mail raccomandazione *f* recommendation

raccontare <1a> tell; **~ per filo e per segno** tell in great detail

racconto *m* story

raccordo *m* TEC connection; *strada* slip road; **~ anulare** ring road; **~ autostradale** junction

rada *f* roads *pl*, roadstead

radar *m inv* radar; **impianto** *m* ~ radar installation; **uomini** *pl* ~ air traffic controllers

raddolcire <4d> sweeten; *fig* soften

raddolcirsi *di aria* grow milder; *di carattere* mellow

raddoppiare <1k> double; *sforzi* redouble

raddrizzare <1a> straighten

raddrizzarsi straighten up

radere <3b> shave; *sfiorare* skim; **~ al suolo** raze (to the ground)

radersi shave

radiare <1k> strike off

radiatore *m* radiator

radiazione *f* radiation

radicale radical

radice *f* root; **~ quadrata** square root; **mettere -i** put down roots

radio *f inv* radio; *(stazione)* radio station; **giornale** *m* ~ (radio) news; **via ~** by radio; **ascoltare la ~** listen to the radio

radioascoltatore *m*, **-trice** *f* (radio) listener

radioattività *f* radioactivity

radioattivo radioactive

radiocronaca *f* (radio) commentary

radiocronista *m/f* (*pl* -i) (radio) commentator

radiodramma *m* (*pl* -i) (radio) play

radiofonico radio *attr*

radiografia *f* x-ray

radiografico (*pl* -ci): **esame** *m* ~ x-ray

radioregistratore *m* radio cassette recorder

radioso radiant

radiosveglia *f* clock radio

radiotaxi *m inv* taxi, cab

radiotelefono *m* radio

radioterapia *f* radiation treatment

radiotrasmittente *f apparecchio* radio transmitter; *stazione* radio station

rado *pettine* wide-toothed; *alberi, capelli* sparse; **di ~** seldom

radunare <1a> collect, gather

radunarsi collect, gather

raduno *m* rally

rafano *m* horseradish

raffermo *pane* stale

raffica *f* (*pl* -che) gust; *di mitragliatrice* burst

raffigurare <1a> represent

raffinare <1a> refine

raffinatezza *f* refinement; **gli piacciono le -e** he likes the finer things in life

raffinato *fig* refined

raffineria *f* refinery

rafforzare <1c> strengthen

raffreddamento *m* cooling; **~ ad acqua** water cooling

raffreddare <1a> cool

raffreddarsi cool down; MED catch cold

raffreddato *fig*: **essere molto ~** have a very bad cold

raffreddore *m* cold; **~ da fieno** hay fever

rag. *abbr* (= **ragioniere**) accountant

ragazza *f* girl; **la mia ~** my girlfriend; **~ alla pari** au pair; **nome** *m* **da ~** maiden name

ragazzo *m* boy; **il mio ~** my boyfriend

raggio *m* (*pl* -ggi) ray; MAT radius; **~ d'azione** range; *fig* duties, responsibilities; **~ di sole** ray of sunshine; **-i** *pl* **X** x-rays; **-i** *pl* **infrarossi / ultravioletti** infrared / ultraviolet rays

raggirare <1a> fool, take in

raggiro *m* trick

raggiungere <3d> *luogo* reach, get to; *persona* join; *scopo* achieve

raggomitolare <1n> wind *or* roll into a ball

raggomitolarsi curl up

raggrinzito wrinkled

ragionamento *m* reasoning

ragionare <1a> reason; **~ di** talk about, discuss

R

ragione f reason; (diritto) right; ~ **sociale** company name; **per -i di salute** for health reasons; **aver ~** be right; **dare ~ a qu** admit that s.o. is right; **a ~, con ~** rightly; **senza ~** for no reason

ragioneria f book-keeping; EDU high school specializing in business studies

ragionevole reasonable

ragioniere m, **-a** f accountant

ragnatela f spider's web

ragno m spider

ragù m inv meat sauce for pasta

RAI-TV abbr (= **Radio Televisione Italiana**) Italian state radio and television

rallegramenti mpl congratulations

rallegrare <1a> cheer up, brighten up

rallegrarsi cheer up, brighten up; ~ **con qu di qc** congratulate s.o. on sth

rallentare <1b> slow down; fig ~ **il lavoro** ease off in one's work

rallentatore m: **al ~** in slow motion

ramanzina f lecture

rame m copper

ramificarsi <1m & d> di fiume branch

ramificazione f ramification

ramino m (gioco) rummy

rammaricare <1m & d> disappoint

rammaricarsi be disappointed (di at)

rammarico m (pl -chi) regret

rammendare <1a> darn

rammendo m darn

rammollire <4d> v/t & v/i soften

ramo m branch

ramoscello m twig

rampa f flight; ~ **di carico** loading ramp; ~ **d'accesso** slip road; ~ **di lancio** launch(ing) pad

rampicante 1 agg climbing; **pianta** f ~ climber **2** m climber

rampone m crampon

rana f frog; **uomo** m ~ frogman

rancido rancid

rancore m ranco(u)r

randagio (pl -gi) stray

randello m club

rango m (pl -ghi) rank

rannicchiarsi <1k> huddle up

rannuvolamento m clouding over

rannuvolarsi <1m> cloud over

ranocchio m (pl -cchi) frog

rapa f turnip

rapace 1 m bird of prey **2** agg fig predatory; **uccello** m ~ bird of prey

rapida f rapids pl

rapidità f speed, rapidity

rapido 1 agg quick, fast; crescita, aumento rapid **2** m (**treno** m) ~ intercity train

rapimento m abduction, kidnap-(p)ing

rapina f robbery

rapinare <1a> rob

rapinatore m, **-trice** f robber

rapire <4d> abduct, kidnap

rapitore m, **-trice** f abductor, kidnap(p)er

rappacificare <1n & d> reconcile

rappacificazione f reconciliation

rappezzare <1b> patch; fig discorso, articolo cobble together

rappezzo m patch

rapporto m resoconto report; relazione relationship; nesso connection, link; **-i pl interpersonali** personal relationships; **avere -i pl di lavoro con qu** be a colleague of s.o., work with s.o.; **in ~ a** in connection with; **le due cose sono in ~** the two things are related or connected

rappresentante m/f representative

rappresentanza f agency; ~ **esclusiva** sole agency

rappresentare <1b> represent; TEA perform

rappresentazione f representation; TEA performance

rarità f inv rarity

raro rare

rasare <1a> shave

rasatura f shaving

raschiare <1k> scrape; ruggine, sporco scrape off

raschiarsi ~ **la gola** clear one's throat

rasentare <1b> (sfiorare) scrape; fig (avvicinarsi) verge on; ~ **il muro** hug the wall

rasente: **~ a** very close to

rasoio m (pl -oi) razor; **~ di sicurezza** safety razor; **~ elettrico** electric razor

raspo m cluster

rassegna f festival; di pittura ecc exhibition; **passare in ~** review

rassegnarsi <1a> resign o.s (**a** to)

rassegnato resigned

rassegnazione f resignation

rasserenare <1a> calm down

rasserenarsi di cielo, tempo clear up

rassicurare <1a> reassure

rassicurarsi feel reassured

rassomigliante similar

rassomiglianza f resemblance

rassomigliare <1g> **~ a** look like, resemble

rassomigliarsi look like or resemble each other

rastrellare <1b> rake; fig comb

rastrelliera f rack; **~ per biciclette** bike rack

rastrello m rake

rata f instal(l)ment; **a -e** in instalments; **~ qc a rate** buy sth on hire purchase or Am the installment plan

rateale: **pagamento** m **~** payment in insta(l)lments; **vendita** f **~** hire purchase, Am installment plan

ratificare <1m & d> ratify

ratto m ZO rat

rattoppare <1c> patch

rattoppo m patch

rattrappire <4d>, **rattrappirsi** go stiff

rattrappito stiff

rattristare <1a> sadden, make sad

rattristarsi become sad

raucedine f hoarseness

rauco (pl -chi) hoarse

ravanello m radish

ravioli mpl ravioli sg

ravvicinamento m approach; fig reconciliation

ravvicinare <1a> move closer; fig (confrontare) compare; (riappacificare) reconcile

ravvivare <1a> revive

razionale rational

razionalizzare <1a> rationalize

razionare <1a> ration

razione f ration

razza f race; fig sort, kind; ZO breed

razzia f raid

razziale racial

razzismo m racism

razzista agg, m/f (mpl -i) racist

razzo m rocket; **come un ~** like greased lightning, like a bat out of hell

re m inv king; MUS D

reagire <4d> react (**a** to)

reale vero real; regale royal

realismo m realism

realista m/f (mpl -i) realist

realistico (pl -ci) realistic

realizzabile feasible

realizzare <1a> realize; piano, progetto carry out

realizzarsi di sogno come true; di persona find o.s., find fulfilment

realizzazione f fulfilment; (cosa realizzata) achievement

realmente really

realtà f reality; **in ~** in fact, actually; **~ virtuale** virtual reality

reato m (criminal) offence (Am offense); **-i pl minori** minor offences

reattore m AVIA jet engine; aereo jet; **~ nucleare** nuclear reactor

reazionario (pl -ri) **1** agg reactionary **2** m, **-a** f reactionary

reazione f reaction

recapitare <1m> deliver

recapito m delivery; (indirizzo) address; **~ telefonico** phone number

recare <1d> portare bring; arrecare cause

recarsi go

recensione f review

recensire <4d> review

recensore m reviewer, critic

recente recent

recentemente recently

recintare <1a> enclose

recinto m enclosure; per animali pen, enclosure; steccato fence

recipiente m container, recipient

reciproco (pl -ci) mutual, reciprocal

R

recita *f* performance

recitare <1l & b> **1** *v/t* recite; TEA play (the part of); *preghiera* say **2** *v/i* act

reclamare <1a> **1** *v/i* complain **2** *v/t* claim

réclame *f inv* advert

reclamizzare <1a> advertise

reclamo *m* complaint

reclusione *f* seclusion

recluso *m* prisoner

recluta *f* recruit

record *m inv* record; **stabilire il ~** set the record; **a tempo di ~** in record time

recuperare → **ricuperare**

recupero → **ricupero**

redatto *pp* → **redigere**

redattore *m*, **-trice** *f* editor; *di articolo* writer; **~ capo** editor-in-chief

redazione *f* editorial staff; *di articolo* writing

redditizio (*pl* -zi) profitable

reddito *m* income; **~ annuo** annual income

Redentore *m* REL Redeemer

redigere <3oo> *testo, articolo* write; *lista* draw up

redini *fpl* reins

reduce *m/f* ex-serviceman

referendum *m inv* referendum

referenza *f* reference

referto *m* (official) report

refettorio *m* (*pl* -ri) refectory

refill *m inv* refill

refrigerante cooling

refrigerare <1m> refrigerate

refrigerio *m* (*pl* -ri) coolness

refurtiva *f* stolen property

regalare <1a> give; **regalarsi qc** treat o.s. to sth

regale regal

regalino *m* gift, present, little something F

regalo *m* gift, present; **articolo m da ~** gift

regata *f* (boat) race

reggere <3cc> **1** *v/t* (*sostenere*) support; (*tenere in mano*) hold; (*sopportare*) bear; GRAM take **2** *v/i di tempo* last; *di ragionamento* stand up; fig

non reggo più I can't take any more

reggersi stand

reggia *f* (*pl* -gge) palace

reggicalze *m inv* suspender belt

reggipetto *m*, **reggiseno** *m* bra, *Am* brassiere

regia *f* production; *di film* direction

regime *m* régime; MED diet; MED **essere a ~** be on a diet

regina *f* queen

regionale regional

regione *f* region

regista *m/f* director; TEA producer

registrare <1a> *in un registro* enter, record, register; *rilevare* show, register; *canzone, messaggio* record

registratore *m*: **~ (a cassetta)** cassette recorder; **~ a nastro** tape recorder; **~ di cassa** cash register

registrazione *f* recording

registro *m* register

regnare <1a> reign

regno *m* kingdom; *periodo* reign

regola *f* rule; **in ~** in order; **di ~** as a rule

regolabile adjustable

regolamento *m* regulation; **~ dei conti** settling of accounts

regolare **1** *v/t* <1l & b> regulate; *spese, consumo* cut down on; TEC adjust; *questione* sort out, settle; *conto, debito* settle **2** *agg* regular

regolarità *f* regularity

regolarizzare <1a> *situazione* sort out, put in order

regredire <4d> regress

regressione *f* regression

regressivo regressive

regresso *m* regression

reimpiego *m* (*pl* -ghi) *di capitali* reinvestment; *di personale* re-employment

relatività *f* relativity; **teoria f della ~** theory of relativity

relativo relative (**a** to); (*corrispondente*) relevant

relatore *m*, **-trice** *f* speaker

relazione *f* legame relationship; *esposizione* report; **avere una ~ con qu** have an affair *or* a relationship with s.o.; *in ~ a* with reference to; *-i pubbliche* public relations, PR

religione *f* religion

religiosa *f* nun

religiosità *f* religion

religioso 1 *agg* religious **2** *m* monk

relitto *m* wreck

remare <1b> row

rematore *m* rower

remo *m* oar

remoto remote

remunerare <1m> pay

remunerativo remunerative, well-paid; *non ~* unpaid

remunerazione *f* payment, remuneration

rendere <3c> *restituire* give back, return; *fruttare* yield; *senso, idea* render; *~ un servizio a qu* do s.o. a favo(u)r; *~ conto a qu di qc* account to s.o. for sth; *~ felice* make happy

rendimento *m di macchina, impiegato* performance; *~ giornaliero* daily output *or* production

rendita *f income*; *~ vitalizia* annuity; *vivere di ~* have private means

rene *m* kidney

reparto *m* department

repentaglio *m*: *mettere a ~* risk, endanger

reperibile available; *difficilmente ~* difficult to find

reperire <4d> find

reperto *m* find; DIR exhibit

repertorio *m* (*pl* -ri) TEA, MUS repertory

replica *f* (*pl* -che) (*copia*) replica; TV repeat; TEA repeat performance; (*risposta*) answer, response; *il suo tono non ammette -e* his tone of voice leaves no room for discussion

replicare <1l, b & d> *ripetere* repeat; *ribattere* reply, answer

reportage *m inv* report

reporter *m/f inv* reporter, journalist

repressione *f* repression

repressivo repressive

represso *pp* → **reprimere**

reprimere <3r> repress

repubblica *f* (*pl* -che) republic

repubblicano republican

repulsione *f* repulsion

reputare <1l & b> consider, deem

reputarsi consider o.s.

reputazione *f* reputation

requisire <4d> requisition

requisito *m* requirement

resa *f* surrender; *restituzione* return; *~ dei conti* settling of accounts

residence *m inv* block of service flats (*Am* apartments)

residente resident

residenza *f* (official) address; *sede* seat; *soggiorno* stay

residenziale residential; *zona f ~* residential area

residuo *m* remainder

resina *f* resin

resistente sturdy, strong; *~ al fuoco* fire-resistant

resistenza *f* resistance; *instancabilità* stamina

resistere <3f> *al freddo ecc* stand up to; *opporsi* resist; *non resisto più* I can't take any more

reso *pp* → **rendere**

resoconto *m* report

respingere <3d> *richiesta, pretendente* reject, turn down; *nemico, attacco* repel

respinto *pp* → **respingere**

respirare <1a> **1** *v/t* breathe (in) **2** *v/i* breathe; *fig* draw breath

respiratore *m* respirator; *per apnea* snorkel

respirazione *f* breathing; *~ artificiale* artificial respiration

respiro *m* breathing; *trattenere il ~* hold one's breath; *fig un attimo di ~* a moment's rest

responsabile responsible (*di* for); DIR liable (*di* for)

responsabilità *f inv* responsibility; DIR liability; *~ civile* civil liability; *~ limitata* limited liability

ressa *f* crowd

restare <1b> stay, remain; *avanzare* be left; *~ indietro* stay behind; *~ perplesso / vedovo* be puzzled / widowed; *restarci male* be hurt

restaurare <1a> restore

R

restauratore *m*, **-trice** *f* restorer

restauro *m* restoration; **chiuso per -i** closed for restoration

restituire <4d> return; *saluto* restore

restituzione *f* return

resto *m* rest, remainder; (*soldi*) change; **-i** *pl* remains; **del ~** anyway, besides

restringere <3d> narrow; *vestito, giacca* take in

restringersi *di strada* narrow; *di stoffa* shrink

restrizione *f* restriction

rete *f per pescare ecc* net; SP goal; INFOR, TELEC, FERR network; **~ autostradale** road network; **~ metallica** wire netting

retina *f* ANAT retina

retribuire <4d> pay

retribuzione *f* payment

retroattivo retroactive

retrobottega *m inv* back shop

retrocedere <3l> retreat; *fig* lose ground

retrodatare <1a> backdate

retrogrado reactionary

retromarcia *f* (*pl* -ce) AUTO reverse (gear)

retroscena *mpl fig* background *sg*

retrospettivo *mostra* retrospective

retroterra *m inv* hinterland

retrovisivo: **specchietto** *m* **~** rearview mirror

retta¹ *f somma* fee

retta² *f* MAT straight line

retta³ *f*: **dare ~ a qu** listen to s.o.

rettangolare rectangular

rettangolo *m* rectangle

rettifica *f* (*pl* -che) correction

rettificare <1m & d> correct

rettile *m* reptile

rettilineo straight

rettorato *m* rectorship

rettore *m* rector

reumatico (*pl* -ci) rheumatic

reumatismo *m* rheumatism

revisionare <1a> *conti* audit; AUTO MOT, put through the MOT test; *testo* revise

revisione *f di conti* audit; AUTO MOT; *di testo* revision

revoca *f* (*pl* -che) repeal

revocare <1l, b & d> repeal, revoke

R.I. *abbr* (= **Repubblica Italiana**) Italian Republic

ri- *prefisso* re-.

riabilitare <1n> rehabilitate

riabilitazione *f* rehabilitation

riacquistare <1a> get back, regain; *casa* buy back

riagganciare <1f> TELEC hang up

riallacciare <1f> refasten; TELEC reconnect

rialzare <1a> *alzare di nuovo* pick up; *aumentare* raise, increase

rialzo *m* rise, increase

rianimare <1m> *speranze, entusiasmo* revive; (*rallegrare*) cheer up; MED resuscitate

rianimarsi revive

rianimazione *f* resuscitation; **centro** *m* **di ~** intensive care unit, ICU

riapertura *f* reopening

riaprire <4f> reopen

riarmare <1a> rearm

riarmo *m* rearmament

riassettare <1b> tidy up

riassetto *m* tidy-up

riassumere <3h> re-employ; (*riepilogare*) summarize

riassunto **1** *pp* → **riassumere 2** *m* summary

riavere <2b> get back, regain; **ho riavuto il raffreddore** I've got another cold

riaversi recover (**da** from), get over (**da** sth)

ribaltabile folding

ribaltare <1a> **1** *v/t* overturn **2** *v/i di macchina, barca* turn over

ribassare <1a> **1** *v/t* lower **2** *v/i* fall, drop

ribasso *m* fall, drop; *sconto* discount; **essere in ~** be falling *or* dropping

ribattere <3a> **1** *v/t argomento* refute **2** *v/i* (*replicare*) answer back; (*insistere*) insist; **~ a un'accusa** deny an accusation

ribellarsi <1b> rebel (**a** against)

ribelle **1** *agg* rebellious **2** *m/f* rebel

ribellione *f* rebellion

ribes *m inv* currant; **~ nero**

blackcurrant; **~ rosso** redcurrant

ribrezzo *m* horror; **fare ~ a** disgust

ricadere <2c> fall; *cadere di nuovo* fall back; *fig* relapse

ricaduta *f* relapse

ricamare <1a> embroider

ricambiare <1k> change; *contraccambiare* return, reciprocate

ricambio *m* change; *(sostituzione)* replacement; *pezzo* (spare) part; **pezzo** *m* **di ~** spare part

ricamo *m* embroidery

ricapitolare <1n> sum up, recapitulate

ricaricare <1m & d> *batteria* recharge

ricattare <1a> blackmail

ricattatore *m*, **-trice** *f* blackmailer

ricatto *m* blackmail

ricavare <1a> derive; *denaro* get

ricavato *m* **di vendita** proceeds

ricchezza *f* wealth

riccio[1] *m* (*pl* -cci) ZO hedgehog; BOT *spiny outer casing of the chestnut*, **~ di mare** sea urchin

riccio[2] (*pl* -cci) **1** *agg* curly **2** *m* curl

ricciolo *m* curl

ricco (*pl* -cchi) **1** *agg* rich, wealthy; **~ di** rich in **2** **-a** *f* rich or wealthy man / woman; **i -i pl** the rich

ricerca *f* (*pl* -che) research; *di persona scomparsa, informazione ecc* search (**di** for); EDU project; **alla ~ di** in search of

ricercare <1d> *(cercare di nuovo)* look again for; *(cercare con cura)* search *or* look for

ricercato **1** *agg oggetto, artista* sought-after **2** *m* man wanted by the police

ricercatore *m*, **-trice** *f* researcher

ricetta *f* prescription; GASTR recipe

ricevere <3a> receive; *di medico* see patients; **~ gente** have guests

ricevimento *m* receipt; *festa* reception

ricevitore *m* receiver

ricevuta *f* receipt; **accusare ~** acknowledge receipt

richiamare <1a> *(chiamare di nuovo)* call again; *(chiamare indietro)* call back; *attirare* draw; *fig rimproverare* rebuke, reprimand; **~ l'attenzione di qu** draw s.o.'s attention (**su** to); **~ qu all'ordine** call s.o. to order

richiamarsi ~ a refer to

richiedente *m/f* applicant

richiedere <3k> ask for again; *(necessitare di)* take, require; *documento* apply for

richiesta *f* request (**di qc** for sth); FIN demand; **a** (*o* **su**) **~ di** at the request of; **più informazioni saranno disponibili su ~** further information on request

richiesto 1 *pp* → **richiedere 2** *agg:* **molto ~** much in demand, much sought after

riciclaggio *m* (*pl* -ggi) recycling

riciclare <1a> recycle

ricompensa *f* reward

ricompensare <1b> reward (**qu di qc** s.o. for sth)

riconciliare <1g> reconcile

riconciliazione *f* reconciliation

ricondurre <3e> *(riportare)* take back (**a** to); *(imputare)* attribute (**a** to)

riconoscente grateful; **mostrarsi ~** show one's gratitude

riconoscenza *f* gratitude; **per ~** out of gratitude

riconoscere <3n> recognise; *ammettere* acknowledge; **riconosco che** I admit that; **non si riconosce più** he's unrecognisable

riconoscibile recognizable

riconoscimento *m* recognition

riconquistare <1a> reconquer

ricordare <1c> remember; *(menzionare)* mention; **~ qc a qu** remind s.o. of sth

ricordarsi remember (**di qc** sth; **di fare qc** to do sth)

ricordo *m* memory; *oggetto* memento; **~ di viaggio** souvenir

ricorrente recurrent, recurring

ricorrenza *f* recurrence; *di evento* anniversary

ricorrere <3o> *di date, di festa* take place, happen; **~ a qu** turn to s.o.; **~ a qc** have recourse to sth; **oggi**

R

ricorre l'aniversario del nostro matrimonio today is our wedding anniversary

ricorso 1 *pp* → **ricorrere 2** *m* DIR appeal; *avere ~ a avvocato, medico* see; *avere ~ all'aiuto di qu* ask for s.o.'s help; *presentare ~* appeal

ricostruire <4d> rebuild; *fig* reconstruct

ricostruzione *f* rebuilding; *fig* reconstruction

ricotta *f* ricotta, *soft cheese made from ewe's milk*

ricoverare <1m & c> admit

ricoverato 1 *agg* admitted **2** *m*, **-a** *f in ospedale* admission; *(refugio)* shelter

ricovero *m in ospedale* admission; *(refugio)* shelter

ricreazione *f* recreation; *nelle scuole* break, recreation, *Am* recess

ricredersi <3a> change one's mind

ricuperare <1m> **1** *v/t* get back, recover; *libertà, fiducia* regain; *spazio* gain; *tempo* make up; *~ il tempo perso* make up for lost time **2** *v/i* catch up

ricupero *m* recovery; *~ del centro storico* development of the old part of town; EDU *corso m di ~* remedial course; *materiale m di ~* scrap; SP *partita f di ~* rescheduled match

ricurvo bent, crooked

ridare <1r> *restituire* give back, return; *fiducia, forze* restore

ridere <3b> laugh *(di* at); *far ~ di sé* make a fool of o.s.; *se la ride del parere degli altri* he couldn't care less what people think

ridicolizzare <1a> ridicule

ridicolo 1 *agg* ridiculous **2** *m* ridicule; *mettere qu in ~, gettare il ~ su qu* ridicule s.o.

ridimensionare <1a> downsize; *fig* get into perspective

ridotto 1 *pp* → **ridurre 2** *agg*: *a prezzi -i* at reduced prices

riduco → **ridurre**

ridurre <3e> reduce *(a* to); *prezzi, sprechi* reduce, cut; *personale*

reduce, cut back; *~ al silenzio* reduce to silence

ridursi decrease, diminish; *~ a fare qc* be reduced to doing sth; *~ male* be in a bad way; *~ in miseria* ruin o.s.

riduzione *f* reduction, cut; *~ del personale* staff cutbacks

riempire <4g> fill (up); *formulario* fill in

rientrare <1a> come back; *a casa* come home; *questo non rientrava nei miei piani* that was not part of the plan

rientro *m* return; *al tuo ~* when you get back

rifare <3aa> do again; *(rinnovare)* do up; *stanza* tidy (up); *letto* make

rifarsi *vita* rebuild; *casa* renovate; *guardaroba* replace; *~ di qc* make up for sth

riferimento *m* reference; *punto m di ~* point of reference; *con ~ a* with reference to

riferire <4d> report

riferirsi: *~ a* refer to

rifiutare <1a> *e* **rifiutarsi** refuse

rifiuto *m* refusal; *-i pl* waste *sg*, refuse *sg*; *(spazzatura)* rubbish *sg*; *-i tossici* toxic waste

riflessione *f* thought, reflection; FIS reflection

riflessivo thoughtful; GRAM reflexive

riflesso 1 *pp* → **riflettere 2** *m* reflection; *(gesto istintivo)* reflex *(movement)*; *ho agito di ~* it was a reflex action, I did it automatically

riflettere <3qq> **1** *v/t* reflect **2** *v/i* think; *~ su qc* think about sth, reflect on sth

riflettersi be reflected

riflettore *m* floodlight

riflusso *m* ebb

riforma *f* reform; REL Reformation; *~ monetaria* monetary reform

riformare <1a> *(rifare)* re-shape, reform; *(cambiare)* reform; MIL declare unfit

riformato REL Reformed; MIL declared unfit

rifornimento m AVIA refuelling; **-i** pl supplies, provisions; **fare ~ di cibo** stock up on food; **fare ~ di benzina** fill up

rifornire <4d> macchina fill (up); frigo restock, fill (**di** with); **~ il magazzino** restock

rifornirsi stock up (**di** on)

rifugiarsi <1f> take refuge

rifugiato m, **-a** f refugee; **~ politico** political refugee

rifugio m (pl -gi) shelter; **~ alpino** mountain hut; **~ antiaereo** air-raid shelter

riga f (pl -ghe) f line; (fila) row; (regolo) rule; **in stoffa** stripe; **nei capelli** parting, Am part; **stoffa f a -ghe** striped fabric

rigatoni mpl rigatoni sg

rigenerare <1m & b> regenerate

rigenerazione f regeneration

rigetto m MED rejection; fig mental block

rigido (duro) rigid; muscolo, articolazione stiff; clima harsh; fig: severo strict

rigirare <1a> **1** v/i walk around **2** v/t turn over and over; denaro launder; **~ il discorso** change the subject

rigirarsi turn round; nel letto toss and turn

rigo m (pl -ghi) line; **~ musicale** staff, stave

rigoglioso lush, luxuriant

rigore m di clima harshness; (severità) strictness; SP (anche calcio m di ~) penalty (kick); **area f di ~** penalty area; **di ~** compulsory

rigoroso rigorous

riguardante about, regarding

riguardare <1a> look at again; (rivedere) review, look at; (riferirsi) be about, concern; **per quanto riguarda ...** as far as ... is concerned; **non ti riguarda** it's none of your business, it doesn't concern you

riguardarsi take care of o.s.

riguardo m (attenzione) care; (rispetto) respect; **mancanza f di ~** lack of respect; **di ~** important; **~ a**

as regards, about; **senza ~** carelessly

rilasciare <1f> release; documento issue

rilascio m release; di passaporto issue

rilassamento m relaxation

rilassare <1a> e **rilassarsi** relax

rilassato relaxed

rilegare <1e> libro bind

rilegatore m bookbinder

rilegatura f binding

rilevare <1b> (ricavare) find; (osservare) note, notice; ditta acquire, buy up; **da quanto è successo si rileva che ...** from what has happened, we can gather that ...

rilievo m relief; fig **dare ~ a qc, mettere qc in ~** emphasize or highlight sth; **di ~** important; **di nessun ~** of no importance

rima f rhyme; **far ~** rhyme

rimandare <1a> send again; (restituire) send back, return; palla return; (rinviare) postpone

rimanente 1 agg remaining **2** m rest, balance

rimanenza f remainder

rimanere <2m> stay, remain; (avanzare) be left (over); **rimanerci male** be hurt; **come siete rimasti per stasera?** what arrangements did you make for this evening?

rimango → **rimanere**

rimarginare <1m> e **rimarginarsi** heal

rimasto pp → **rimanere**

rimbalzare <1a> bounce

rimbalzo m bounce

rimboccare <1d> coperte tuck in; **rimboccarsi le maniche** roll up one's sleeves

rimborsare <1a> reimburse, refund, pay back

rimborso m reimbursement, repayment; **~ spese** reimbursement of expenses; **contro ~** COD, cash on delivery

rimboschimento m reforestation

rimboschire <4d> reforest

rimediare <1k & b> **1** v/i **~ a** make

R

up for, remedy; **come posso ~?** how can I put things right? **2** *v/t* find, scrape together

rimedio *m* (*pl* -di) remedy; MED medicine; **senza ~** hopeless

rimescolare <1m> mix again; *più volte* mix thoroughly; *caffè* stir again

rimessa *f di auto* garage; *degli autobus* depot; FIN remittance; SP **~ laterale** throw-in

rimettere <3ee> put back, return; (*affidare*) refer; *vomitare* bring up; **~ a posto** put back; **~ in ordine** tidy up; *ci ho rimesso molti soldi* I lost a lot of money

rimettersi *di tempo* improve; **~ da qc** get over sth; **~ a qu** put o.s. in s.o.'s hands

rimmel® *m inv* mascara

rimodernare <1b> modernize

rimorchiare <1k & c> AUTO tow (away)

rimorchiatore *m* tug

rimorchio *m* AUTO tow; *veicolo* trailer

rimorso *m* remorse

rimozione *f* removal

rimpatriare <1k & m> **1** *v/t* repatriate **2** *v/i* return *or* go home

rimpatrio *m* (*pl* -ri) repatriation

rimpiangere <3d> regret (**di avere fatto qc** doing sth); *tempi passati, giovinezza* miss

rimpianto 1 *pp* → **rimpiangere 2** *m* regret

rimpiazzare <1a> replace

rimpicciolire <4d> **1** *v/t* make smaller **2** *v/i* become smaller, shrink

rimproverare <1m & c> scold; *impiegato* reprimand; **~ qc a qu** reproach s.o. for sth

rimprovero *m* scolding; *dal capo* reprimand; **-i** *pl* reproaches

rimuovere <3ff> remove; *muovere di nuovo* move again

rinascere <3gg> be born again; *di passione, speranza* be revived; *fig* **sentirsi ~** feel rejuvenated

Rinascimento *m* Renaissance

rincarare <1a> **1** *v/t* increase, put up; **~ la dose** make matters worse **2** *v/i*

increase in price

rincaro *m* increase in price

rinchiudere <3b> shut up

rinchiudersi shut o.s. up

rincorrere <3o> run *or* chase after

rincorsa *f* run-up

rincorso *pp* → **rincorrere**

rincrescere <3n>: *mi rincresce* I'm sorry; *se non ti rincresce* if you don't mind

rincrescimento *m* regret

rinfacciare <1f>: **~ qc a qu** cast sth up to s.o.

rinforzare <1c> strengthen

rinforzarsi get stronger

rinforzo *m* reinforcement; MIL **-i** *pl* reinforcements

rinfrescare <1d> **1** *v/t* cool down, make cooler; (*ristorare*) refresh; (*rinnovare*) freshen up; **~ la memoria a qu** refresh s.o.'s memory **2** *v/i* cool down

rinfrescarsi freshen up

rinfresco *m* (*pl* -chi) buffet (party)

rinfusa: *alla* **~** any which way, all higgledy-piggledy

ringhiare <1k> growl

ringhiera *f* railing

ringiovanire <4d> **1** *v/t* make feel younger; *di aspetto* make look younger **2** *v/i* feel younger; *di aspetto* look younger

ringraziamento: *un* **~** a word of thanks; *lettera f di* **~** thank you letter, letter of thanks; *i miei* **-i** *pl* my thanks

ringraziare <1g> thank (**di** for)

rinnovamento *m* change; *di contratto, tessera* renewal

rinnovare <1c> renovate; *guardaroba* replace; *abbonamento* renew; (*ripetere*) renew, repeat

rinnovarsi renew itself; (*ripetersi*) be repeated, happen again

rinnovo *m* renovation; *di guardaroba* replacement; *di abbonamento* renewal; *di richiesta* repetition

rinsavire <4d> **1** *v/t*: **~ qu** bring s.o. back to his / her senses **2** *v/i* come to one's senses

rintanarsi <1a> hide, go to earth

rintracciare <1f> track down

rinuncia f (pl -ce) renunciation (**a** of)

rinunciare <1f> give up (**a** sth)

rinunzia → **rinuncia**

rinvenimento m recovery; di resti discovery

rinvenire <4p> **1** v/t recover; resti discover **2** v/i regain consciousness, come round

rinviare <1h> (mandare indietro) return; (posticipare) postpone, put off; a letteratura refer

rinvio m (pl -vii) return; di riunione postponement; in un testo cross-reference

rione m district

riordinare <1m> tidy up; **~ le idee** set one's ideas in order

riorganizzare <1a> reorganize

riorganizzazione f reorganization

riparare <1a> **1** v/t (proteggere) protect (**da** from); (aggiustare) repair; un torto make up for **2** v/i escape

ripararsi dalla pioggia shelter, take shelter (**da** from)

riparato sheltered

riparazione f repair; fig di torta, ingiustizia putting right, reparation; **officina** f **-i** garage

riparo m shelter; **mettersi al ~** take shelter

ripartire[1] v/i <4a> leave again

ripartire[2] v/t <4d> divide (up)

ripartizione f division

ripassare <1a> **1** v/i → **passare** **2** v/t col ferro iron; lezione revise, Am review

ripensamento m: **avere un ~** have second thoughts

ripensare <1b> riflettere think; **~ a qc** think about sth again; **ci ho ripensato** I've changed my mind

ripetere <3a> repeat; **ti ho ripetuto mille volte la stessa cosa** I've told you the same thing a thousand times

ripetizione f repetition; **dare -i a qu** tutor s.o.

ripetuto repeated

ripido steep

ripiegare <1b & e> **1** v/t fold (up) again **2** v/i fall back

ripiego m (pl -ghi) makeshift (solution)

ripieno 1 agg full; GASTR stuffed **2** m stuffing

riporre <3ll> put away; speranze place

riportare <1c> take back; (riferire) report; vittoria, successo achieve; MAT carry over; tasche sew on; danni, ferite sustain

riporto m amount carried over

riposare <1c> v/t & v/i rest

riposarsi rest

riposato: **a mente -a** once I've / you've had some rest

riposo m rest; **giorno** m **di ~** day off; **collocare a ~** retire; **senza ~** nonstop

ripostiglio m (pl -gli) boxroom, storeroom

riprendere <3c> take again; (prendere indietro) take back; lavoro go back to; FOT record; **~ coscienza** regain consciousness; **~ a fare qc** start doing sth again

riprendersi ~ da qc get over sth

ripresa f resumption; di vestito alteration; film shot; AUTO acceleration; RAD, TV **in ~ diretta** (broadcast) live; **a più -e** several times, on several occasions

riproduco → **riprodurre**

riprodurre <3e> reproduce

riprodursi di animali breed, reproduce; di situazione happen again

riproduzione f reproduction; **~ vietata** copyright

riprovare <1c> **1** v/t feel again; vestito try on again **2** v/i try again

ripugnante disgusting, repugnant

ripugnanza f disgust, repugnance

ripugnare <1a>: **~ a qu** disgust s.o.

ripulire <4d> clean again; (rimettere in ordine) tidy (up); spir empty, clean out

risa fpl laughter sg

risaia f rice field

risalire <4m> **1** v/t *scale* go back up
2 v/i (*rincarare*) go up again; **~ alle
origini** go back to source
risalita f ascent; **impianti** mpl **di ~** ski
lifts
risaltare <1a> stand out
risalto m: **fare ~** stand out; **mettere
in ~, dare ~ a** highlight
risanamento m redevelopment; FIN
improvement; **~ del deficit pubblico** reduction in the public deficit
risanare <1a> redevelop; FIN improve
risarcimento m compensation
risarcire <4d> *persona* compensate
(**di** for); *danno* compensate for
risata f laugh
riscaldamento m heating; **~ centrale** central heating system (*for a
block of flats*)
riscaldare <1a> heat *or* warm up
riscaldarsi warm o.s.
rischiararsi <1a> clear (up); *cielo*
clear (up); **~ in volto** cheer up
rischiare <1k> **1** v/t risk **2** v/i: **~ di
sbagliare** risk making a mistake
rischio m (pl -chi) risk; **a ~ della propria vita** risking one's own life;
mettere a ~ put at risk
rischioso risky
riscontrare <1a> (*confrontare*) compare; (*controllare*) check; (*incontrare*) come up against; *errori* come
across
riscontro m comparison; check; **in ~
alla Vostra** in response to yours
riscuotere <3ff> FIN *soldi* draw;
assegno cash; *fig* earn
risentimento m resentment
risentire <4b> **1** v/t hear again **2** v/i
feel the effects (**di** of)
risentirsi TELEC talk again; (*offendersi*) take offence (*Am* offense)
riserbo m reserve; **senza ~** openly
riserva f reserve; (*scorta*) stock, reserve; *fig* reservation; AUTO **essere
in ~** be running out of fuel; **fondo** m
di ~ reserve stock; **avere delle -e** pl
su qc have reservations about sth;
senza -e without reservation,
wholeheartedly; **~ naturale** nature

reserve; **fare ~ di** stock up on
riservare <1b> keep; (*prenotare*)
book, reserve
riservarsi reserve; **mi riservo di non
accettare** I reserve the right not to
accept
riservatezza f reserve
riservato reserved; (*confidenziale*)
confidential
risiedere <3a> be resident, reside
riso¹ 1 pp → **ridere 2** m laughing
riso² m rice
risolto pp → **risolvere**
risolutezza f determination, resolution; **con ~** with determination
risoluto determined
risoluzione f resolution; (*soluzione*)
solution; **~ d'un contratto** cancellation of a contract; **prendere una ~**
make a decision
risolvere <3g> solve; (*decidere*) resolve
risolversi be solved; (*decidersi*) decide, resolve; **~ in nulla** come to
nothing
risonanza f MUS resonance; *fig*: **di
scandalo** reverberations pl
risorgere <3d> rise; *fig*: **di industria**
ecc experience a rebirth
Risorgimento m Risorgimento, *the
reunification of Italy*
risorsa f resource
risotto m risotto
risparmiare <1k> save; *fig* spare
risparmiarsi conserve one's energy
risparmiatore m saver
risparmio m (pl -mi) saving; **-i** pl savings; **cassa** f **di ~** savings bank
rispecchiare <1k> reflect
rispettare <1b> respect; *legge, contratto* abide by
rispettivo respective
rispetto 1 m respect **2** prp: **~ a** (*confronto a*) compared with; (*in relazione a*) as regards
risplendere <3a> shine, glitter
rispondere <3hh> answer (**a** sth),
reply (**a** to); (*reagire*) respond; *saluto* acknowledge; **~ alle speranze**
come up to expectations; **~ di qc** be
accountable for sth (**a** to); **~ male**

answer back; TELEC **non risponde** there's no answer

risposta *f* answer, reply; (*reazione*) response; **~ pagata** reply paid

rissa *f* brawl

ristabilimento *m di ordine* restoration; *di regolamento* re-introduction; (*guarigione*) recovery

ristabilire <4d> *ordine* restore; *regolamento* re-introduce; **~ la verità** set the record straight

ristabilirsi recover

ristampa *f* reprint

ristampare <1a> reprint

ristorante *m* restaurant

ristrettezza *f di idee* narrowness; **vivere nelle -e** live in straitened circumstances

ristretto: **caffè** *m inv* **~** very strong coffee

ristrutturare <1a> *azienda* restructure

ristrutturazione *f* restructuring

risultare <1a> (*derivare*) result; (*rivelarsi*) turn out; **mi risulta che ...** as far as I know ...

risultato *m* result; **senza ~** unsuccessfully

risurrezione *f* REL Resurrection

risvegliare <1g>, **risvegliarsi** *fig* reawaken

risveglio *m* (*pl* -gli) awakening; *fig* reawakening; **al mio ~** when I woke

ritardare <1a> **1** *v/t* delay **2** *v/i* be late; *orologio* be slow

ritardatario *m* (*pl* -ri), **-a** *f* latecomer

ritardo *m* delay; **senza ~** without delay; **essere in ~** be late

ritenere <2q> (*credere*) believe

ritenersi: **si ritiene molto intelligente** he thinks he is very intelligent

ritenuta *f* deduction (*su* from); **~ alla fonte** deduction at source

ritirare <1a> withdraw, pull back; (*tirare di nuovo*) throw again; *proposta* withdraw; (*prelevare*) collect, pick up

ritirarsi (*restringersi*) shrink; **~ a vita privata** retire into private life; **~ da**

gara, *esame ecc* withdraw from

ritiro *m* withdrawal

ritmo *m* rhythm

rito *m* ceremony; **essere di ~** be customary

ritoccare <1d> touch up

ritornare <1a> **1** *v/i venire* get back, come back, return; *andare* go back, return; *su argomento* go back (*su* over); **~ verde** turn green again; **~ in sé** come to one's senses **2** *v/t* return

ritornello *m* refrain

ritorno *m* return; **far ~** come back, return; **essere di ~** be back; **viaggio** *m di* **~** return trip

ritrarre <3xx> pull away; PITT paint; (*rappresentare*) depict

ritrattare <1a> retract

ritrattazione *f* retraction

ritratto *m* portrait; *fig il* **~ di qu** the spitting image of s.o.

ritrovare <1c> find; (*riacquistare*) regain

ritrovarsi meet again; (*capitare*) find o.s.; (*orientarsi*) get one's bearings

ritrovo *m* meeting; *luogo* meeting place; **~ notturno** nightclub

ritto straight

riunificazione *f* reunification

riunione *f* meeting; *di amici, famiglia* reunion

riunire <4d> gather

riunirsi meet

riuscire <4o> succeed; (*essere capace*) manage; **non riesco a capire** I can't understand; **~ bene / male** be a success / a failure; *di foto* come out well / badly; **~ in qc** be successful in sth

riuscita *f* success

riuscito successful

riutilizzare <1a> re-use

riutilizzazione *f* re-use

riva *f* shore

rivale 1 *agg* rival *attr* **2** *m/f* rival

rivaleggiare <1f> compete

rivalità *f* rivalry

rivalutare <1a> revalue; *persona* change one's mind about

rivalutazione *f* revaluation

R

rivedere <2s> see again; (*ripassare*) review, look at again; (*verificare*) check

rivelare <1a> reveal

rivelazione *f* revelation

rivendere <3a> resell

rivendicare <1m & d> demand

rivendicazione *f* demand; *-i pl salariali* wage demands

rivendita *f negozio* retail outlet

rivenditore *m*, **-trice** *f* retailer; ~ *specializzato* dealer

rivestimento *m* covering

rivestire <4b> (*foderare*) cover; *ruolo* play; *carica* fill

rivestirsi get dressed again

rivincita *f* return match; *prendersi la* ~ get one's revenge

rivista *f* magazine; TEA revue; MIL review; ~ *di moda* fashion magazine

rivolgere <3d> turn; *domanda* address (*a qu* to s.o.); *non mi rivolge mai il saluto* he never acknowledges me; ~ *la parola a qu* speak to s.o., address s.o.; ~ *l'attenzione a qc* turn one's attention to sth

rivolgersi ~ *a qu* apply to s.o. (*per* for)

rivolgimento *m fig* upheaval

rivolta *f* revolt

rivoltare <1c> turn; (*mettere sottosopra*) turn upside down; (*disgustare*) revolt

rivoltella *f* revolver

rivoluzionario (*pl* -ri) revolutionary

rivoluzione *f* revolution

rizzare <1a> put up; *bandiera* raise; *orecchie* prick up

rizzarsi straighten up; *mi si sono rizzati i capelli in testa* my hair stood on end

roba *f* things *pl*, stuff; ~ *da mangiare* food, things *or* stuff to eat; ~ *da matti!* would you believe it!

robot *m inv* robot; *da cucina* food processor

robustezza *f* sturdiness

robusto sturdy

rocca *f* (*pl* -cche) fortress

roccia *f* (*pl* -cce) rock

rocciatore *m* rock climber

roccioso rocky

rock *m inv* MUS rock; *concerto* *m* ~ rock concert

rockettaro *m*, **-a** *f* rocker

roco (*pl* -chi) hoarse

rodaggio *m* running in; *fig* *sono ancora in* ~ I'm still finding my feet; *in* ~ running in

rodere <3b> gnaw at

rodersi ~ *dalla gelosia* be eaten up with jealousy

roditore *m* rodent

rogna *f* F *di cane* mange; *problema* hassle

rognone *m di animale* kidney

Roma *f* Rome

romanico (*pl* -ci) Romanesque

romano 1 *agg* Roman; *fare alla* *-a* go Dutch **2** *m*, **-a** *f* Roman

romanticismo *m* Romanticism

romantico (*pl* -ci) **1** *agg* romantic **2** *m*, **-a** *f* romantic

romanziere *m* novelist

romanzo 1 *agg* Romance **2** *m* novel; ~ *giallo* thriller

rombare <1a> rumble

rombo[1] *m* rumble

rombo[2] *m* ZO turbot

rombo[3] *m* MAT rhombus

romeno 1 *agg* Romanian **2** *m*, **-a** *f* Romanian

rompere <3rr> **1** *v/t* break; F ~ *le scatole a qu* get on s.o.'s nerves F **2** *v/i* F be a pain F; *fig* ~ *con qu* break it off with s.o.

rompersi break; ~ *un braccio* break one's arm

rompicapo *m inv* puzzle; (*problema*) headache

rompighiaccio *m inv* ice-breaker; ALP ice-pick

rondine *f* swallow

ronzare <1a> buzz

ronzio *m* buzzing

rosa 1 *f* rose; ~ *dei venti* wind rose **2** *m/agg inv* pink

rosaio *m* (*pl* -ai) *pianta* rosebush

rosario *m* (*pl* -ri) REL rosary

rosato *m* rosé

rosbif *m inv* roast beef

roseo pink; *avvenire* rosy

roseto *m* rose garden

rosmarino *m* rosemary

rosolare <1l & c> brown

rosolia *f* German measles *sg*

rosone *m* ARCHI rose window

rospo *m* toad; *fig* F **ingoiare il ~** lump it F

rossastro reddish

rossetto *m* lipstick

rossiccio (*pl* -cci) reddish

rosso 1 *agg* red **2** *m* red; **~ d'uovo** egg yolk; **fermarsi al ~** stop at a red light; **passare col ~** go through a red light

rossore *m* red patch

rosticceria *f* rotisserie (*shop selling roast meat*)

rotaia *f* rail

rotare <1o> rotate

rotatoria *f* roundabout, *Am* traffic circle

rotazione *f* rotation

rotella *f* castor

rotocalco *m* (*pl* -chi) magazine

rotolare <1l & c> *v/t & v/i* roll

rotolarsi roll (around)

rotolino *m* FOTO film

rotolo *m* roll; FOTO film; **andare a -i** go to rack and ruin; **mandare a -i** ruin

rotondo round

rotta *f* MAR, AVIA course; *fig* (*giusta direzione*) straight and narrow; **cambiare ~** change course; **a ~ di collo** at breakneck speed

rottame *m* wreck

rotto 1 *pp* → **rompere 2** *agg* broken

rottura *f* breaking; F **tra innamorati** break-up; F **che ~!** what a pain! F

rotula *f* kneecap

roulotte *f inv* caravan

routine *f* routine

rovesciare <1f & b> *liquidi* spill; *oggetto* knock over; (*capovolgere*) overturn, upset; *fig* turn upside down

rovesciarsi overturn, capsize

rovesciata *f calcio* bicycle kick

rovescio (*pl* -sci) reverse; *in tennis* backhand; *fig* **~ d'acqua** downpour, cloudburst; **~ di fortuna** reversal of fortune; **il ~ della medaglia** the other side of the coin; **mettersi una maglia al ~** put a sweater on inside out

rovina *f* ruin; **andare in -e** go to rack and ruin; **mandare in -e** ruin; **-e** *pl* ruins

rovinare <1a> ruin

rovinarsi ruin o.s.

rovo *m* bramble

rozzo rough and ready

RSM *abbr* (= **Repubblica di San Marino**) Republic of San Marino

R.U. *abbr* (= **Regno Unito**) UK (= United Kingdom)

ruba *f*: **andare a ~** sell like hot cakes, walk out the door

rubare <1a> steal

rubinetto *m* tap; **~ dell'acqua calda** hot water tap

rubino *m* ruby

rubrica *f* (*pl* -che) *di libro* table of contents; *quaderno* address book; *di giornale* column; TV report

rude rough and ready

rudere *m* ruin; **-i** *pl* ruins

rudimentale rudimentary, basic

rudimenti *mpl* basics, rudiments

ruga *f* (*pl* -ghe) wrinkle, line

ruggine *f* rust

ruggire <4d> roar

ruggito *m* roar

rugiada *f* dew

rugoso rough; *pelle* wrinkled; *albero* gnarled

rullare <1a> MAR roll; AVIA taxi

rullino *m* FOTO film

rullio *m* roll

rullo *m* roll; **~ compressore** steam roller

rum *m* rum

ruminare <1a> chew the cud; *fig* ruminate

rumore *m* noise; **far ~** make a noise, be noisy

rumoreggiare <1f> be noisy; *di tuono* growl, rumble; *di folla* mutter

rumoroso noisy

ruolo *m* role; **personale** *m* **di ~** (permanent) members of staff

ruota *f* wheel; **~ anteriore** front

R

wheel; **~ dentata** cog; **~ posteriore** back wheel; **~ motrice** drive wheel; **~ di scorta** spare wheel; *fig* **mettere i bastoni tra le -e a qu** put a spoke in s.o.'s wheel

rupe *f* cliff

rupestre *inv* rock *attr*; **arte** *f* **~** wall painting

ruscello *m* stream

russare <1a> snore

Russia *f* Russia

russo 1 *agg* Russian **2** *m*, **-a** *f* Russian

rustico (*pl* -ci) rural, rustic; *fig* unsophisticated

ruttare <1a> belch; *di bambino* burp

ruttino *m* burp

rutto *m* belch

ruvidezza *f* roughness

ruvido rough

ruzzolare <1l> fall

ruzzolone *m* fall; **fare un ~** fall

S

S *abbr* (= **sud**) S (= south)

S. *abbr* (= **santo**) St (= Saint)

s *abbr* (= **secondo**) s, sec (= second)

S.A. *abbr* (= **Società Anonima**) Ltd (= Limited)

sa → **sapere**

sabato *m* Saturday; **di ~** on Saturdays; **è meglio uscire di ~** it's better to go out on a Saturday

sabbia *f* sand

sabbioso sandy

sabotaggio *m* sabotage

sabotare <1a> sabotage

sabotatore *m*, **-trice** *f* saboteur

sacca *f* (*pl* -cche) bag; ANAT, BIO sac

saccarina *f* saccharin

saccheggiare <1f> sack; *spir* raid

saccheggio *m* (*pl* -ggi) sack, sacking

sacchetto *m* bag

sacco *m* (*pl* -cchi) sack; *fig* F **un ~ di** piles of F; **costa un ~** it costs a fortune; **~ a pelo** sleeping bag; **~ da montagna** backpack, rucksack; *fig* **vuotare il ~** spill the beans; *confidarsi* pour one's heart out

saccopelista *m/f* backpacker, hiker

sacerdote *m* priest

sacramento *m* sacrament

sacrificare <1m & d> sacrifice

sacrificarsi sacrifice o.s.

sacrificio *m* (*pl* -ci) sacrifice

sacrilegio *m* sacrilege

sacro sacred; **osso** *m* **~** sacrum

sadico (*pl* -ci) **1** *agg* sadistic **2** *m*, **-a** *f* sadist

sadismo *m* sadism

safari *m* *inv* safari; **~ fotografico** photo safari

saggezza *f* wisdom

saggiare <1f> test

saggio[1] (*pl* -ggi) **1** *agg* wise **2** *m* wise man, sage

saggio[2] *m* (*pl* -ggi) test; (*campione*) sample; *scritto* essay; *di danza, musica* end of term show; **~ d'interesse** interest rate, rate of interest; **~ di sconto** discount rate

saggista *m/f* essayist

saggistica *f* essay-writing

Sagittario *m* ASTR Sagittarius

sahariana *f* safari jacket

sala *f* room; (*soggiorno*) living room; **~ da pranzo** dining room; **~ di lettura** reading room; **~ giochi** amusement arcade; **~ operatoria** (operating) theatre, *Am* operating room

salamandra *f* salamander

salame *m* salami

salamoia *f*: **in ~** in brine

salare <1a> salt

salariale pay *attr*

salariato *m* employee

salario *m* (*pl* -ri) salary, wages; ~ **base** basic salary *or* wage

salatino *m* savo(u)ry

salato savo(u)ry; *acqua* salt; *cibo* salted; F (*caro*) steep F; **troppo ~** salty

saldare <1a> weld; *ossa* set; *fattura* pay (off)

saldatura *f* welding; **una ~** a weld

saldo 1 *agg* steady, secure; *fig* **essere ~ nelle proprie convizioni** be unshakeable in one's beliefs; **tenersi ~** hold on tight **2** *m* payment; *in svendita* sale item; (*resto*) balance; **-i** *pl* **di fine stagione** end-of-season sales; **articolo in ~** sale item; **~ attivo** net assets; **~ passivo** net liabilities

sale *m* salt; **ha poco ~ in zucca** he's not very bright

salgo → **salire**

salice *m* willow; **~ piangente** weeping willow

saliera *f* salt cellar

salina *f* salt works

salire <4m> **1** *v/i* climb; *di livello, prezzi, temperatura*, rise; **~ in macchina** get in; **~ su scala** climb; *treno, autobus* get on **2** *v/t*: **~ le scale** go up, climb; *venire* come up, climb

saliscendi *m inv*: **finestra f a ~** sash window

salita *f* climb; *strada* slope; **strada f in ~** steep street

saliva *f* saliva

salma *f* corpse, body

salmastro 1 *agg* briny **2** *m* salt

salmone *m* salmon; **~ affumicato** smoked salmon

salmonella *f* salmonella (poisoning)

salone *m* living room; (*esposizione*) show; **~ dell'automobile** motor show; **~ di bellezza** beauty salon

salotto *m* lounge

salpare <1a> sail

salsa *f* sauce; **~ di pomodoro** tomato sauce

salsiccia *f* (*pl* -cce) sausage

saltare <1a> **1** *v/t* jump; (*omettere*) skip; **~ (in padella)** sauté **2** *v/i* jump; *di bottone* come off; *di fusibile* blow;

F *di impegno* be cancelled; **~ (giù) dal letto** jump out of bed; **~ dalla gioia** jump for joy; **è saltata la corrente** there's been a power cut; **~/ far ~ in aria** blow up; **~ fuori** turn up

saltellare <1b> hop

saltimbocca *m inv* fried veal topped with prosciutto and a sage leaf

salto *m* jump; (*dislivello*) change in level; **~ mortale** somersault; **~ in alto** high jump; **~ in lungo** long jump; *fig* **~ nel buio** leap in the dark; **faccio un ~ da te** I'll drop by *or* in

saltuariamente occasionally

saltuario (*pl* -ri) occasional; **lavoro m ~** casual work

salubre healthy

salumeria *f* shop that sells salumi

salumi *mpl* cold meat *sg*

salutare 1 *agg* healthy; *fig discussione* helpful **2** *v/t* <1a> say hello to, greet; **salutami la tua famiglia** say hello to the family for me

salute *f* health; **~!** cheers!; **alla tua ~!** cheers!, here's to you!

salutista *m/f* (*mpl* -i) health fanatic

saluto *m* wave; **tanti -i** greetings

salvagente *m inv* lifebelt; *giubbotto* life jacket; *per bambini* ring; (*isola spartitraffico*) traffic island

salvaguardare <1a> protect, safeguard

salvaguardia *f* protection

salvare <1a> save, rescue

salvataggio *m* (*pl* -ggi) salvage; **barca f di ~** lifeboat

salve! hello!

salvezza *f* salvation

salvia *f* sage

salvietta *f* napkin, *Br* serviette

salvo 1 *agg* safe **2** *prp* except; **~ che** unless; **~ imprevisti** barring accidents, all being well **3** *m*: **mettersi in ~** take shelter

sambuco *m* (*pl* -chi) elder

San = **Santo**

sanare <1a> heal; FIN, ARCHI restore

sanatorio *m* (*pl* -ri) sanatorium, *Am* sanitarium

sandalo *m* sandal; BOT sandalwood

sangue *m* blood; **a ~ freddo** in cold

S

blood; **donare il ~** give blood; GASTR **al ~** rare

sanguigno: gruppo m ~ blood group; **vaso** m ~ blood vessel

sanguinare <1l> bleed; **mi sangui- na il naso** my nose is bleeding

sanguinoso bloody

sanguisuga f (pl -ghe) leech

sanità f health; **amministrazione** health care

sanitario (pl -ri) health attr; **assi- stenza** f **-a** health care

sanno → **sapere**

sano healthy; **~ e salvo** safe and sound

santo 1 agg holy; **acqua** f **-a** holy water; **tutto il ~ giorno** the whole blessed day **2** m, **-a** f saint; **davanti al nome** St

santuario m (pl -ri) sanctuary

sanzione f sanction

sapere <2n> **1** v/t know; (essere capa- ce di) be able to; (venire a) ~ hear; **sai nuotare?** can you swim?; **lo so** I know **2** v/i: **far ~ qc a qu** let s.o. know sth; **saperla lunga** know all about it; **non si sa mai** you never know; **per quel che ne so** as far as I know; **~ di** (avere sapore di) taste of; **non sa di nulla** it doesn't taste of anything **3** m knowledge

sapiente 1 agg wise **2** m/f (scienzato) scientist

sapienza f wisdom

sapone m soap

saponetta f toilet soap

sapore m taste (di of); **-i** pl aromatic herbs; **avere ~ di qc** taste of sth; **senza ~** tasteless

saporito tasty

saracinesca f (pl -sche) roller shut- ter

sarcasmo m sarcasm; **non fare ~!** don't be sarcastic!

sarcastico (pl -ci) sarcastic

sarcofago m (pl -gi e -ghi) sar- cophagus

Sardegna f Sardinia

sardina f sardine

sardo 1 agg Sardinian **2** m, **-a** f Sardinian

sarò → **essere**

sarto m, **-a** f tailor; per donne dress- maker

sartoria f tailor's; per donne dressmaker's

sasso m stone; **restare di ~** be thunderstruck

sassofonista m/f (mpl -i) saxo- phone player, saxophonist

sassofono m saxophone

satellite 1 m satellite **2** agg satellite attr; **città** f ~ satellite town

satira f satire

satirico (pl -ci) satirical

saturare <1l> saturate (di with)

saturazione f saturation

saturo saturated

sauna f sauna

saziare <1g> satiate

saziarsi eat one's fill; **non ~ mai di fare qc** never get tired of doing sth

sazietà f: **mangiare a ~** eat one's fill

sazio (pl -zi) full (up)

sbadato absent-minded

sbadigliare <1g> yawn

sbadiglio m (pl -gli) yawn

sbagliare <1g> **1** v/i e **sbagliarsi** make a mistake; **hai sbagliato a dirle la verità** you were wrong to tell her the truth **2** v/t make a mis- take in; **~ persona** have the wrong person; **~ strada** go the wrong way

sbagliato wrong

sbaglio m (pl -gli) mistake; **per ~** by mistake; **senza -i** flawless

sbalordimento m amazement, stu- pefaction

sbalordire <4d> stun, amaze

sbalorditivo amazing, incredible

sbalzare <1a> throw; temperatura change

sbalzo m jump; **~ di temperatura** change in temperature

sbandare <1a> AUTO skid; FERR, fig go off the rails

sbandata f AUTO skid; F **prendersi una ~ per qu** develop a crush on s.o.

sbarazzare <1a> clear

sbarazzarsi: ~ di get rid of

sbarcare <1d> **1** v/t merci unload; persone disembark; fig **~ il lunario**

make ends meet **2** *v/i* disembark

sbarco *m* (*pl* -chi) *di merce* unloading; *di persone* disembarkation

sbarra *f* bar; **essere alla ~** be on trial

sbarramento *m* fence; (*ostacolo*) barrier

sbarrare <1a> bar; *assegno* cross; *occhi* open wide

sbarrato *assegno* crossed; *occhi* wide open

sbattere <3a> **1** *v/t porta* slam, bang; (*urtare*) bang; GASTR beat; **~ la porta in faccia a qu** close the door in s.o.'s face **2** *v/i* bang

sbattitore *m* hand mixer

sbendare <1b> take the bandage(s) off

sberla *f* F slap

sbiadire <4d> fade

sbiadito faded; *stile* colo(u)rless

sbiancare <1d> **1** *v/t* bleach **2** *v/i* turn pale

sbilanciare <1f> unbalance, throw off balance

sbilanciarsi lose one's balance; *fig* commit o.s.

sbizzarrirsi <4d> indulge o.s.

sbloccare <1c & d> clear; *macchina* unblock; *prezzi* deregulate

sblocco *m* (*pl* -chi) *f* clearing; *di macchina* unblocking; *di prezzi* deregulation

sboccare <1d> **~ in** *di fiume* flow into; *di strada* lead to

sbocciare <1f & c> open (out)

sbocco *m* (*pl* -chi) FIN outlet; *di situazione* way out; **strada** *f* **senza ~** dead end, cul-de-sac

sbornia *f* F hangover; **prendersi una ~** get drunk

sborsare <1a> F cough up F

sbottonare <1a> unbutton

sbottonarsi *fig* open up (**con** to); **~ la giacca** unbutton one's jacket

sbozzare <1c> draft, rough out

sbraitare <1a> shout, yell

sbranare <1a> tear apart

sbriciolare <1l> spread crumbs

sbrigare <1e> attend to

sbrigarsi hurry up

sbrigativo (*rapido*) hurried, rushed; (*brusco*) brusque

sbrinare <1a> *frigorifero* defrost

sbrinatore *m* defrost control

sbrogliare <1g & c> untangle, disentangle; **sbrogliarsela** sort things out

sbronza *f* F hangover

sbronzarsi <1a> F get drunk

sbronzo F tight F, sloshed F

sbucare <1d> emerge; **da dove sei sbucato?** where did you spring from?

sbucciare <1f> *frutta, patate* peel; **sbucciarsi le ginocchia** skin one's knees

sbucciato peeled; *ginocchio* skinned

sbucciatura *f* graze

s.c. *abbr* (= **sopra citato**) above-mentioned

scabroso rough, uneven; *fig* offensive

scacchiera *f* chessboard

scacciare <1f> chase away

scacco *m* (*pl* -chi) (chess) piece; *fig* setback; **~ matto** checkmate; **-cchi** *pl* chess *sg*; **giocare a -cchi** play chess; **a -cchi** checked

scadente 1 → **scadere 2** *agg* second-rate

scadenza *f* deadline; *su alimento* best before date; **~ del termine** deadline, last date; **a breve ~** short-term; **a lunga ~** long-term

scadere <2c> *di passaporto* expire; *di cambiale* fall due; (*perdere valore*) decline (in quality)

scaduto expired; *alimento* past its sell-by date

scaffale *m* shelves *pl*

scaglia *f* flake; *di legno* chip; *di pesce* scale

scagliare <1g> hurl

scagliarsi ~ contro attack

scala *f* staircase; GEOG scale; **~ (a pioli)** ladder; **~ mobile** escalator; FIN sliding scale; **~ musicale** (musical) scale; **disegno** *m* **in ~** scale drawing; **su larga ~** on a large scale; **su ~ nazionale** country-wide; **fare le -e** climb the stairs

scalare <1a> climb

S

scalata f climb; ~ *al successo* rise to fame

scalatore m, **-trice** f climber

scaldabagno m water heater

scaldare <1a> heat (up); fig ~ *la testa a qu* get s.o. worked up

scaldarsi warm up; fig get worked up, get excited

scaldavivande m inv food warmer

scalinata f steps pl

scalino m step

scalo m AVIA stop; MAR port of call; *volo* m *senza* ~ nonstop flight; *fare* ~ *a* call at

scalogna f bad luck; *portare* ~ be unlucky

scalognato unlucky

scaloppina f escalope

scalpello m chisel

scaltro shrewd

scalzo barefoot

scambiare <1k> (*confondere*) mistake (*per* for); (*barattare*) exchange, swap F (*con* for)

scambio m (pl -bi) exchange; *di persona* mistake; FERR points pl; **-i** pl *commerciali* trade sg; ~ *di lettere* exchange of letters; ~ *d'opinioni* exchange of views; **-i** pl *culturali* cultural exchange sg; *libero* ~ free trade

scampagnata f day out in the country

scampanellare <1b> ring

scampanellata f ring

scampi mpl ZO scampi

scampo m escape, way out

scampolo m remnant

scandagliare <1g> sound; fig sound out

scandalistico (pl -ci) scandal-mongering

scandalizzare <1a> scandalize, shock

scandalizzarsi be scandalized or shocked (*di* by)

scandalizzato scandalized

scandalo m scandal

scandaloso scandalous

scandinavo **1** agg Scandinavian **2** m, **-a** f Scandinavian

scanner m inv INFOR scanner

scannerizzare <1a> INFOR scan

scansafatiche m/f inv lazybones

scansare <1a> (*allontanare*) move; (*evitare*) avoid

scansarsi move out of the way

scansia f bookcase

scantinato m cellar

scapito m: *a* ~ *di* to the detriment of

scapola f shoulder blade, ANAT scapula

scapolo **1** agg single, unmarried **2** m bachelor

scappamento m TEC exhaust

scappare <1a> (*fuggire*) run away; (*affrettarsi*) rush, run; *lasciarsi* ~ *l'occasione* let the opportunity slip; *mi è scappata la pazienza* I lost patience

scappatella f di bambino escapade; *fare delle -lle* get into mischief

scappatoia f way out

scarabocchiare <1k & c> scribble

scarabocchio m (pl -cchi) scribble

scarafaggio m (pl -ggi) cockroach

scaraventare <1b> throw, hurl

scaraventarsi throw or hurl o.s. (*contro* at)

scarcerare <1l> release

scarcerazione f release

scardinare <1l> take off the hinges

scarica f (pl -che) discharge

scaricare <1l & d> unload; batteria run down; rifiuti, sostanze nocive dump; responsabilità offload, get rid of; ~ *arsi la coscienza* ease one's conscience; F ~ *qu* get rid of s.o.; INFOR ~ *dalla rete* download; INFOR ~ *su dischetto* download to disk

scaricarsi relax, unwind F; di batteria run down

scarico (pl -chi) **1** agg camion empty; batteria run-down **2** m di merce unloading; luogo dump; di responsabilità offloading; *gas* m *di* ~ exhaust (fumes); *tubo* m *di* ~ exhaust (pipe); *divieto di* ~ no dumping; **-chi** pl *industriali* industrial waste sg

scarlattina f scarlet fever

scarpa f shoe; **-e** pl *da uomo* / *da*

donna men's/women's shoes

scarpata *f* (*burrone*) escarpment

scarpetta *f* shoe; **-e** *pl* **da ginnastica** trainers

scarpinare <1a> trek

scarpinata *f* trek

scarpone *m* (heavy) boot; **~ da sci** ski boot

scarseggiare <1f> become scarce; **~ di qc** not have much of sth, be short of sth

scarsezza *f*, **scarsità** *f* shortage, scarcity; **~ di viveri** food shortage

scarso scarce, in short supply; **essere ~ di qc** be lacking in sth; **quattro chilometri -si** barely four kilometres

scartare <1a> (*svolgere*) unwrap; (*eliminare*) reject

scarto *m* rejection; (*cosa scartata*) reject; **merce** *f* **di ~** imperfect goods

scassare <1a> F ruin, wreck

scassarsi F give up the ghost F

scassato F done for F

scassinare <1a> force open

scassinatore *m*, **-trice** *f* burglar

scasso *m* forced entry; **furto** *m* **con ~** breaking and entering, burglary

scatenare <1a> *fig* unleash

scatenarsi *fig*: *di tempesta* break; *di collera* break out; *di persona* let one's hair down

scatenato unrestrained

scatola *f* box; *di tonno, piselli* tin, can; **in ~** *cibo* tinned, canned; AVIA **~ nera** black box

scattare <1a> **1** *v/t* FOT take **2** *v/i* go off; *di serratura* catch; (*arrabbiarsi*) lose one's temper; *di atleta* put on a spurt; **~ in piedi** jump up; **far ~** activate

scatto *m* click; SP spurt; FOTO exposure; *di foto* taking; TELEC unit; FOTO **~ automatico** automatic timer; **uno ~ di rabbia** an angry gesture; **~ di stipendio** automatic raise

scavalcare <1d> *muro* climb (over)

scavare <1a> *con pala* dig; *con trivella* excavate

scavi *mpl* archeologici dig *sg*

scegliere <3ss> choose, pick, select

scelgo → **scegliere**

scelta *f* choice, selection; **di prima ~** first-rate; **prendine uno a ~** take your pick

scelto 1 *pp* → **scegliere 2** *agg* handpicked; *merce, pubblico* (specially) selected

scemo 1 *agg* stupid, idiotic **2** *m*, **-a** *f* idiot

scena theatre, *Am* theater; (*scenata*) scene; *fig* **colpo** *m* **di ~** coup de théâtre; **mettere in ~** produce; *fig* **fare ~ muta** be struck dumb

scenario *m* (*pl* -ri) screenplay; *fig* scenery

scenata *f* scene; **fare una ~ (a qu)** make a scene

scendere <3c> **1** *v/i andare* go down, descend; *venire* come down, descend; *da cavallo* get down, dismount; *dal treno, dall' autobus* get off; *dalla macchina* get out; *di temperatura, prezzi* go down, drop; **~ a terra** come (back) down to earth **2** *v/t*: **~ le scale** *andare* go down the stairs; *venire* come down the stairs

scendiletto *m* bedside rug

sceneggiatura *f* screenplay

scenografia *f* sets *pl*

scenografo *m*, **-a** *f* set designer

scetticismo *m* scepticism, *Am* skepticism

scettico 1 *agg* sceptical, *Am* skeptical **2** *m*, **-a** *f* sceptic, *Am* skeptic

scheda *f* card; (*formulario*) form; **~ elettorale** ballot (paper); INFOR **~ grafica** graphics card; **~ telefonica** phonecard

schedario *m* (*pl* -ri) file

schedina *f* pools coupon

scheggia *f* (*pl* -gge) sliver

scheletro *m* skeleton

schema *m* (*pl* -i) diagram; (*abbozzo*) outline

schematico (*pl* -ci) general; *disegno* schematic

schematizzare <1a> outline

scherma *f* fencing; **tirare di ~** fence

schermo *m* screen; (*riparo*) shield

scherzare <1a> play; (*burlare*) joke

scherzo *m* joke; MUS scherzo;

S

essere uno ~ (*facile*) be child's play; **-i a parte** joking aside; **per ~ fare**, **dire qc** as a joke

scherzoso playful

schiaccianoci *m inv* pair of nutcrackers, nutcrackers *pl*

schiacciare <1f> **1** *v/t* crush; *noce* crack; **~ un piede a qu** step on s.o.'s toes; F **~ un sonnellino** have a snooze F, have forty winks F **2** *v/i* SP smash

schiacciato crushed, squashed

schiaffeggiare <1f> slap

schiaffo *m* slap

schiamazzare <1a> make a din

schiamazzo *m* yell, scream

schiantare <1a> **1** *v/t* crash, smash **2** *v/i e* **schiantarsi** crash

schianto *m* crash

schiarire <4d> lighten

schiarirsi brighten up

schiarita *f* bright spell

schiavitù *f* slavery

schiavo 1 *agg*: **essere ~ di** be a slave to **2** *m*, **-a** *f* slave

schiena *f* back; **mal di ~** back ache

schienale *m di sedile* back

schiera *f* group; **a ~** in ranks

schierare <1b> line up

schierarsi **~ in favore di qu** come out in favo(u)r of s.o.

schietto pure; *fig* frank

schifezza *f*: **che ~!** how disgusting!

schifo *m* disgust; **fare ~ a qu** disgust s.o.

schifoso disgusting; (*pessimo*) dreadful

schioppo *m* shotgun

schiuma *f* foam; **~ da bagno** bubble bath; **~ da barba** shaving foam

schiumoso foamy

schivare <1a> avoid, dodge F

schivo shy

schizzare <1a> **1** *v/t* (*spruzzare*) squirt; (*abbozzare*) sketch **2** *v/i* squirt; (*saltare*) jump

schizzinoso fussy

schizzo *m* squirt; (*abbozzo*) (*lightning*) sketch

sci *m inv* ski; *attività* skiing; **~ acquatico** water ski/skiing; **~ di fondo** cross-country ski/skiing

sciacquare <1a> rinse

sciacquatura *f* rinse

sciagura *f* disaster

sciagurato *giorno*, *evento* unfortunate

scialle *m* shawl

scialuppa *f* dinghy; **~ di salvataggio** lifeboat

sciame *m* swarm

sciare <1h> ski

sciarpa *f* scarf

sciatica *f* sciatica

sciatore *m*, **-trice** *f* skier

sciatteria *f* untidiness, sloppiness F

sciatto untidy, sloppy F

scientifico (*pl* -ci) scientific

scienza *f* science; **-e** *pl* **naturali** natural science

scienziato *m*, **-a** *f* scientist

scimmia *f* monkey

scimmiottare <1c> ape

scimpanzè *m inv* chimpanzee, chimp F

scintilla *f* spark

scintillante sparkling

scintillare <1a> sparkle

scintillio *m* sparkle

sciocchezza *f* (*idiozia*) stupidity; **è solo una ~** it's nothing

sciocco (*pl* -cchi) **1** *agg* silly **2** *m*, **-a** *f* silly thing

sciogliere <3ss> untie; *capelli* undo, let down; *matrimonio* dissolve; *neve* melt; *dubbio*, *problema* clear up

sciogliersi *di corda*, *nodo* come undone; *di burro*, *neve* melt; *di questione*, *problema* resolve itself

scioglilingua *m inv* tongue-twister

scioltezza *f* nimbleness; *fisica* agility

sciolto 1 *pp* → **sciogliere 2** *agg neve*, *ghiaccio* melted; *matrimonio* dissolved; **a briglia -a** at breakneck speed

scioperante *m/f* striker

scioperare <1l & c> strike

sciopero *m* strike; **fare ~** go on strike; **~ bianco** work-to-rule; **~ generale** general strike; **~ della fame** hunger strike

sciovia *f* ski-lift

sciovinismo *m* chauvinism

sciovinista *m/f* (*mpl* -i) chauvinist

scipito bland

scippatore *m*, **-trice** *f* bag-snatcher

scippo *m* bag-snatching

scirocco *m* sirocco

sciroppo *m* syrup

scissione *f* splitting

scisto *m* GEOL schist

sciupare <1a> (*logorare*) wear out; *salute* ruin; *tempo, denaro* waste, fritter away

sciupato *persona* drawn; *cosa* worn out

scivolare <1l> slide; (*cadere*) slip

scivolo *m* slide; (*caduta*) slip; *gioco* chute; ~ **d'emergenza** escape chute

scivoloso slippery

sclerosi *f* inv MED sclerosis; ~ **multipla** multiple sclerosis, MS

scocciare F <1f> bother, annoy, hassle F

scocciatore F *m*, **-trice** *f* pest F, nuisance F

scocciatura F *f* nuisance F

scodella *f* bowl

scogliera *f* cliff

scoglio *m* (*pl* -gli) rock; *fig* stumbling block

scoiattolo *m* squirrel

scolapasta *m* inv colander

scolare <1a> drain

scolaro *m*, **-a** *f* schoolboy; *ragazza* schoolgirl

scolastico (*pl* -ci) school *attr*

scoliosi *f* inv curvature of the spine

scollato low-necked; *donna* wearing a low neck

scollatura *f* neck(line)

scollo *m* neck

scolo *m* drainage

scolorire <4d> **1** *v/t* fade **2** *v/i e* **scolorirsi** fade

scolorito faded

scolpire <4d> *marmo, statua* sculpt; *legno* carve; *fig* engrave

scommessa *f* bet

scommesso *pp* → **scommettere**

scommettere <3ee> bet

scomodare <1l & c> disturb

scomodarsi put o.s. out; **non si sco-**

modi please don't go to any bother

scomodo uncomfortable; (*non pratico*) inconvenient

scomparire <4e> disappear

scomparsa *f* disappearance

scomparso *pp* → **scomparire**

scompartimento *m* compartment; FERR ~ **per** (**non**) **fumatori** (non-)smoking compartment

scompenso *m* imbalance; ~ **cardiaco** cardiac insufficiency

scompigliare <1g> *persona* ruffle the hair of; *capelli* ruffle

scompiglio *m* (*pl* -gli) confusion

scomponibile flat pack *attr*, modular

scomporre <3ll> break down

scomporsi **senza** ~ without showing any emotion

sconcertante disconcerting

sconcio (*pl* -ci) indecent; *parola* disgusting, filthy

sconclusionato incoherent

sconfiggere <3cc> defeat

sconfinare <1a> trespass; MIL cross the border

sconfinato vast, boundless

sconfitta *f* defeat

sconfitto *pp* → **sconfiggere**

sconfortante discouraging, disheartening

sconfortare <1c> discourage, dishearten

sconforto *m* discouragement

scongelare <1b> thaw

scongiurare <1a> beg; *pericolo* avert

sconosciuto **1** *agg* unknown **2** *m*, **-a** *f* stranger

sconsigliare <1g> advise against; ~ **qc a qu** advise s.o. against sth

sconsolato disconsolate

scontare <1a> FIN deduct, discount; *pena* serve

scontato discounted; (*previsto*) expected; ~ **del 30%** 30% discount or deduction

scontento **1** *agg* unhappy, not satisfied (*di* with) **2** *m* unhappiness, dissatisfaction

sconto *m* discount; **praticare uno ~**

give a discount

scontrarsi <1a> collide (**con** with); *fig* clash (**con** with)

scontrino *m* receipt; **fare lo ~ alla cassa** please pay at the cash desk before ordering

scontro *m* AUTO collision; *fig* clash

scontroso unpleasant, disagreeable

sconveniente inappropriate, unacceptable

sconvolgente upsetting, distressing; **di un'intelligenza ~** incredibly intelligent

sconvolgere <3d> upset

sconvolto 1 *pp* → **sconvolgere 2** *agg paese* in upheaval

scopa *f* broom

scopare <1a> sweep; P shag P

scoperchiare <1k> *pentola* take the lid off

scoperta *f* discovery

scoperto 1 *pp* → **scoprire 2** *agg pentola* uncovered; **a capo ~** bareheaded; **assegno** *m* **~** bad cheque, rubber cheque F **3** *m* FIN overdraft; **allo ~** in the open

scopo *m* aim, purpose; **allo ~ di fare qc** in order to do sth; **senza ~** aimlessly

scoppiare <1k & c> *di bomba, petardo* explode; *di palloncino, pneumatico* burst; **~ in lacrime** burst into tears; **~ a ridere** burst out laughing; **~ di caldo** be boiling hot

scoppio *m* (*pl* -ppi) explosion; *di palloncino* bursting; *fig* outbreak

scoprire <4f> *contenitore* take the lid off; (*denudare*) uncover; *piani, verità* discover, find out

scoraggiare <1f> discourage, dishearten

scoraggiarsi become discouraged, lose heart

scoraggiato discouraged, disheartened

scorciatoia *f* short cut

scordare <1c>, **scordarsi di** forget

scordato MUS out of tune

scoreggia *f* (*pl* -gge) F fart F

scoreggiare <1f> F fart F

scorgere <3d> see, make out; **non**

farsi ~ not let o.s. be seen

scoria *f* waste

scorpione *m* scorpion; ASTR **Scorpione** Scorpio

scorrere <3o> **1** *v/i* flow, run; *di tempo* go past, pass **2** *v/t giornale* skim

scorretto (*errato*) incorrect; (*non onesto*) unfair

scorrevole *porta* sliding; *stile* flowing

scorso 1 *pp* → **scorrere 2** *agg l'anno* **~** last year

scorta *f* escort; (*provvista*) supply, stock

scortare <1c> escort

scortese rude, discourteous

scortesia *f* rudeness, lack of courtesy

scorto *pp* → **scorgere**

scorza *f* peel; *fig* exterior

scossa *f* shake; **~ di terremoto** (earth) tremor; **~ elettrica** electric shock

scosso *pp* → **scuotere**

scostare <1c> move away (**da** from)

scostarsi move (aside); *fig* **~ dalla retta via** leave the straight and narrow

scottante delicate

scottare <1c> **1** *v/t* burn; GASTR *verdure* blanch; **mi sono scottato le dita** I burned my fingers **2** *v/i* burn; **scotta!** it's hot!

scottato *verdure* blanched

scottatura *f* burn; **ho già avuto troppe -e** I've had my fingers burned once too often

Scozia *f* Scotland

scozzese 1 *agg* Scottish **2** *m/f* Scot

screditare <1l> discredit

scremato skimmed; **parzialmente ~** semi-skimmed

screpolare <1l & b> e **screpolarsi** crack

screpolatura *f* crack

scricchiolare <1l> creak

scricchiolio *m* (*pl* -ii) creak

scricciolo *m* ZO wren

scritta *f* inscription

scritto 1 *pp* → **scrivere 2** *m* writing; **per ~** in writing

scrittore *m*, **-trice** *f* writer

scrittura f writing; REL scripture

scritturare <1a> engage, sign F

scrivania f desk

scrivere <3tt> write; (*annotare*) write down; **come si scrive ... ?** how do you spell ... ?

scroccare <1c & d> F scrounge F

scrollare <1c> shake; **~ le spalle** shrug (one's shoulders)

scrosciare <1f & c> *di pioggia* fall in torrents

scrupolo m scruple; **senza -i** unscrupulous

scrupolosità f scrupulousness

scrupoloso scrupulous

scrutare <1a> look at intently; *orizzonte* scan

scrutatore m, **-trice** f POL person counting votes

scrutinio m (pl -ni) POL counting; EDU *teachers' meeting to discuss pupils' performance*

scucire <4a> unpick; F **scuci i soldi!** cough up! F

scucirsi come apart at the seams

scuderia f stable

scudetto m SP championship

scudo m shield

sculacciare <1f> spank

scultore m, **-trice** f sculptor

scultura f sculpture

scuola f school; **~ di lingue** language school; **~ elementare** primary school; **~ media** secondary school; **~ parificata** private school officially recognized by the state; **~ serale** evening classes pl; **~ superiore** high school; **~ guida** driving school; **andare a ~** go to school

scuotere <3ff> shake

scuotersi shake off

scure f ax(e)

scurire <4d> v/t & v/i darken

scuro 1 agg dark **2** m darkness; **essere allo ~ di qc** be in the dark about sth

scusa f excuse; **chiedere ~** apologize

scusare <1a> forgive; (*giustificare*) excuse; **mi scusi** I'm sorry; **scusi, scusa** excuse me

scusarsi apologize

S.C.V. abbr (= **Stato della Città del Vaticano**) Vatican City

s.d. abbr (= **senza data**) undated

sdebitarsi <1b> pay one's debts

sdegnare <1a> (*disprezzare*) despise; (*fare arrabbiare*) incense

sdegnarsi get angry (**con** with)

sdegno m moral indignation

sdentato toothless

sdoganamento m customs clearance

sdoganare <1a> clear through customs

sdolcinato sloppy

sdraiare <1i> lay

sdraiarsi lie down

sdraiato lying down

sdraio m: (*sedia f a*) **~** deck chair

se[1] cong if; **~ mai** if need be; **~ mai arrivasse ...** should he arrive ...; **come ~** as if; **~ no** if not

se[2] pron = **si** in front of **lo, la, li, le, ne**

sé oneself; *lui* himself; *lei* herself; *loro* themselves; *esso, essa* itself; **da ~** (by) himself / herself / themselves

sebbene even though, although; **~ abbia detto la verità** even though he told the truth

secca f (pl -cche) shallows

seccante fig annoying

seccare <1d> **1** v/t dry; fig annoy **2** v/i e **seccarsi** dry; fig get annoyed

seccatore m, **-trice** f nuisance, pest

seccatura f nuisance

secchio m (pl -cchi) bucket, pail

secco (pl -cchi) **1** agg dry; *fiori, pomodori* dried; *risposta, tono* curt; *frutta f -a* dried fruit; (*noci*) nuts pl **2** m: **rimanere a ~** run out of petrol; fig run out of money; **pulire a ~** dryclean

secolare *albero, tradizione* hundred-year old

secolo m century; **ti ho aspettato un ~!** I waited hours for you!

seconda f AUTO second (gear); FERR second class; EDU second year

secondario (pl -ri) secondary

secondo 1 agg second; **di -a mano** second-hand; **~ fine** ulterior motive,

S

hidden agenda **2** *prp* according to; **~ me** in my opinion; **~ le istruzioni** as per instructions **3** *m* second; GASTR main course

secrétaire *m inv mobile* writing desk

sedano *m* celery

sedare <1b> calm (down)

sedativo *m* sedative

sede *f* headquarters; **la Santa Sede** the Holy See

sedentario (*pl* -ri) sedentary

sedere 1 *m* F rear end F **2** *v/i* <2o> e **sedersi** sit down

sedia *f* chair; **~ a sdraio** deck chair; **~ a dondolo** rocking chair; **~ a rotelle** wheelchair

sedicesimo *m/agg* sixteenth

sedicente so-called, self-styled

sedici sixteen

sedile *m* seat; AUTO **~ posteriore** back seat

seducente attractive

sedurre <3e> seduce; (*attrarre*) attract

seduta *f* session; (*posa*) sitting; **~ plenaria** plenary session

seduto seated

seduttore *m*, **-trice** *f* seducer; *donna* seductress

seduzione *f* seduction

S.E. e O. *abbr* (= **salvo errori e omissioni**) E & OE (= errors and omissions excepted)

seg. *abbr* (= **seguente**) foll. (= following)

sega *f* (*pl* -ghe) saw

segale *f* rye; **pane** *m* **di ~** rye bread

segare <1e> saw

segatura f sawdust

seggio *m* (*pl* -ggi) seat; **~ (elettorale)** polling station

seggiola *f* chair

seggiolino *m di macchina, bicicletta* child's seat

seggiolone *m* high chair

seggiovia *f* chair lift

seggo → **sedere**

segnalare <1a> signal; (*annunciare*) report

segnale *m* signal; (*segno*) sign; **~ d'allarme** alarm; **~ orario** (*alla ra-*

dio) time signal; **~ stradale** roa sign

segnaletica *f* signs *pl*; **~ strada** road signs *pl*

segnalibro *m* bookmark

segnare <1a> (*marcare*) mark; (*an notare*) note down; SP score; **~ a di qu** point s.o. out, point to s.o. **sentirsi segnato a dita** feel the fin ger pointed at you; **ha segnato du gol** he scored two goals

segno *m* sign; (*traccia*) mark, trac (*cenno*) gesture, sign; **-i** *pl* **caratter stici** distinguishing marks; *fig* **no dar -i di vita** not get in touch; **co gliere nel ~** hit the nail on the hea **~ zodiacale** sign of the zodiac; *far il ~ della croce* cross o.s.; *lasciare ~* leave a mark

segretaria *f* secretary; **~ di direzion** executive secretary

segretariato *m* secretariat

segretario *m* (*pl* -ri) secretary; POL **di partito** party leader

segreteria *f carica* secretaryshi *ufficio* administrative office; *attivi* secretarial duties *pl*; **~ telefonic** answering machine, answerphone

segreto 1 *agg* secret **2** *m* secret; **professionale** confidentiality

seguace *m/f* disciple, follower

seguente next, following

seguire <4a> **1** *v/t* follow; *corso* tak **2** *v/i* follow (**a qc** sth); *come segu* as follows

seguitare <1l>: **~ a fare qc** carry o doing sth

seguito *m persone* retinue; (*sostenit ri*) followers; *di film* sequel; *di ~* on after the other, in succession; *in* after that; *in ~ a* following, in th wake of

sei¹ → **essere**

sei² six

seicento 1 *agg* six hundred **2** *m:* **Seicento** the seventeenth century

selciato *m* paving

selezione *f* selection

self-service *m inv* self-service

sella *f* saddle

sellino *m* saddle

seltz m: **acqua** f **di ~** soda (water)

selva f forest

selvaggina f game

selvaggio (pl -ggi) **1** agg animale, fiori wild; tribù, omicidio savage **2** m, **-a** f savage

selvatico (pl -ci) wild

semaforo m traffic lights

sembrare <1a> seem; (assomigliare a) resemble, look like

seme m seed

semestre m six months; EDU term

semicerchio m (pl -chi) semi-circle, half-moon

semicircolare semi-circular

semiconduttore m EL semi-conductor

semifinale f semi-final

semifreddo m soft icecream

semilavorato m semi-finished

semina f sowing

seminare <1l> sow

seminario m (pl -ri) seminar

seminudo half-naked

seminuovo practically new

semisfera f hemisphere

semolino m semolina

semplice simple; (non doppio) single; (spontaneo) natural

semplicità f simplicity

semplificare <1m & d> simplify

semplificazione f simplification

sempre always; **ci conosciamo da ~** we've known each other practically for ever; **è quello di ~** he's the same as always; **per ~** for ever; **~ più** more and more; **~ più vecchio** older and older; **piove ~ di più** the rain's getting heavier and heavier; **~ che** as long as, on condition that

sen. abbr (= **senatore**) Sen (= senator)

senape f mustard

senato m senate

senatore m, **-trice** f senator

senile senile

senno m common sense; **uscire di ~** lose one's mind; (arrabbiarsi) lose control

seno m breast; GEOG inlet; MAT sine; **in ~ a** in

sensato sensible

sensazionale sensational

sensazione f sensation, feeling; (impressione) feeling; **fare ~** cause a sensation; **ho la ~ che** I have a feeling that

sensibile sensitive; (evidente) significant, substantial

sensibilità f sensitivity

sensibilizzare <1a> make more aware (**a** of)

senso m sense; (significato) meaning; (direzione) direction; **buon ~** common sense; **~ unico** one way; **~ vietato** no entry; **in ~ orario** clockwise; **privo di -i** unconscious; **perdere i -i** faint

sensore m TEC sensor

sensuale sensual

sensualità f sensuality

sentenza f DIR verdict; **~ di morte** death sentence

sentenziare <1g> fig pass judgment

sentiero m path

sentimentale sentimental

sentimento m feeling, sentiment

sentinella f sentry

sentire <4b> feel; (udire) hear; (ascoltare) listen to; odore smell; cibo taste

sentirsi feel; **sentirsela di fare qc** feel up to doing sth

senza without; **senz'altro** definitely; **~ dubbio** more than likely, probably; **~ impegno** (with) no obligation or commitment; **~ di me** without me

senzatetto m/f inv homeless person; **i -i** pl the homeless

separare <1a or 1l & b> separate

separarsi separate, split up F

separazione f separation; **~ dei beni** division of property

sepolto pp → **seppellire**

sepoltura f burial

seppellire <4d> bury

seppia f cuttle fish

seppure even if

sequestrare <1b> confiscate; DIR impound, seize; (rapire) kidnap

sequestro m kidnap(ping); DIR

impounding, seizure

sera f evening; **di ~** in the evenings; **questa ~** this evening; **verso ~** towards evening

serale evening attr

serata f evening; (festa) party; **~ danzante** dance; **~ di gala** gala (evening)

serbatoio m (pl -oi) tank; **~ di riserva** reserve tank

serbo[1] **1** agg Serbian **2** m, **-a** f Serb

serbo[2] m: **tenere in ~** keep; **avere qc in ~** have sth in store

serenata f serenade

serenità f serenity

sereno serene; fig relaxed, calm

serial m inv serial

seriale INFOR serial; **porta** f **~** serial port

sericoltura f silk-worm farming

serie f inv series; **articolo** m **di ~** mass produced item; **produzione** f **in ~** mass production

serietà f seriousness

serigrafia f silk-screen printing

serio (pl -ri) **1** agg serious; (affidabile) reliable **2** m: **sul ~** seriously

sermone m sermon

serpe f grass snake

serpeggiare <1f> wind

serpente m snake

serpentina f linea wavy line; strada winding street

serra f greenhouse

serramanico m: **coltello** m **a ~** flick knife

serranda f shutter

serrare <1b> close; denti, pugni clench; **~ il ritmo** step up the pace

serrata f lock-out

serratura f lock; **~ a combinazione** combination lock

servire <4b> **1** v/i be useful; **non mi serve** I don't need it; **a che serve questo?** what's this for?; **~ da bere a qu** pour s.o. a drink **2** v/t serve; **mi serve aiuto** I need help

servirsi (usare) use (di sth); **prego, si serva!** a tavola please help yourself!

servitù f slavery, servitude; (personale) servants pl

servizio m (pl -zi) service; (favore) favo(u)r; (dipartimento) department; in giornale feature (story); **lavorare a mezzo ~** work part-time; **~ assistenza tecnica** after-sales service; **~ civile** community service in lieu of military service; **~ militare** military service; **~ d'emergenza** emergency service; **~ da tavola** dinner service; **di ~** on duty; **fuori ~** out of order; **in ~** on duty; **-zi** pl services

servofreno m servo brake

servosterzo m power steering

sesamo m sesame

sessanta sixty

sessantenne sixty-year-old

sessantesimo m/agg sixtieth

sessantina f: **una ~** about sixty (di sth); **sulla ~** about sixty

sesso m sex

sessuale sexual

sessualità f sexuality

sesto m/agg sixth

seta f silk; **~ artificiale** artificial silk

sete f thirst; **aver ~** be thirsty

setola f bristle

setta f sect

settanta seventy

settantenne seventy-year-old

settantesimo m/agg seventieth

settantina f: **una ~** about seventy (di sth); **sulla ~** about seventy

settare <1a> macchina, computer set up

sette seven

settecento **1** agg seven hundred **2** m: **il Settecento** the eighteenth century

settembre m September

settentrionale **1** agg northern **2** m northerner

settentrione m north

setticemia f septic(a)emia

settimana f week; **~ corta** five-day week; **~ santa** Easter week

settimanale m/agg weekly

settimo m/agg seventh

settore m sector

severità f severity

severo severe

sezione *f* section

sfaccendato idle

sfacchinata *f* backbreaking job

sfacciato cheeky

sfacelo *m* ruin

sfamare <1a> feed

sfarfallio *m* flicker

sfarzo *m* splendo(u)r

sfarzoso magnificent

sfasciare <1f> smash; MED unbandage

sfasciarsi smash

sfaticato *m*, **-a** *f* idler

sfavillare <1a> *di occhi* sparkle; *di fuoco* flicker

sfavillio *m di occhi* sparkle

sfavore *m* disadvantage

sfavorevole unfavourable

sfera *f* sphere; **~ d'azione** responsibilities, duties; **~ di competenza** area of expertise

sferico (*pl* -ci) spherical

sfida *f* challenge

sfidare <1a> challenge

sfiducia *f* distrust, mistrust; **voto *m* di ~** vote of no confidence

sfiduciato discouraged, disheartened

sfigurare <1a> **1** *v/t* disfigure **2** *v/i* look out of place

sfigurato disfigured

sfilare <1a> **1** *v/t* unthread; (*togliere*) take off **2** *v/i* parade

sfilata *f*: **~ di moda** fashion show

sfinimento *m* exhaustion

sfinito exhausted

sfiorare <1a> brush; *argomento* touch on

sfiorire <4d> fade, wither

sfitto empty, not let

sfocato *foto* blurred

sfociare <1f> flow

sfogare <1e> *rabbia, frustrazione* vent, get rid of (**con, su** on)

sfogarsi vent one's feelings; **non ti sfogare su di me** don't take it out on me; **~ con qu** confide in s.o., pour one's heart out to s.o.

sfoglia : **pasta *f* ~** puff pastry

sfogliare <1g & c> *libro* leaf through

sfogo *m* (*pl* -ghi) outlet; MED rash

sfoltire <4d> thin

sfondare <1a> break; *porta* break down; *muro* knock down; *pavimento* break through

sfondo *m* background

sformare <1a> stretch out of shape

sformato *m* GASTR soufflé

sfornito : **essere ~ di qc** be out of sth

sfortuna *f* bad luck, misfortune

sfortunatamente unfortunately

sfortunato unlucky, unfortunate

sforzare <1c> strain

sforzarsi try very hard, make every effort

sforzo *m* effort; *fisico* strain; **fare uno ~** make an effort; *fisicamente* strain o.s.; **senza ~** effortlessly

sfracellarsi <1b> break into pieces, shatter

sfrattare <1a> evict

sfratto *m* eviction; *avviso* notice to quit

sfregare <1e> rub

sfrenato unrestrained

sfrontato insolent

sfruttamento *m* exploitation

sfruttare <1a> exploit

sfuggevole fleeting

sfuggire <4a> (*scampare*) escape (**a** from); **mi è sfuggito di mente** it slipped my mind

sfuggita *f*: **di ~** in passing

sfumatura *f* nuance; *di colore* shade

sfuriata *f* (angry) tirade

sfuso loose; *burro* melted; *vino* in bulk

sgabello *m* stool

sgabuzzino *m* cupboard

sgambetto *m*: **fare lo ~ a qu** trip s.o. up

sganciare <1f> unhook; FERR uncouple; F *soldi* fork out F

sganciarsi become unhooked; *di persona* release o.s.; *fig* free o.s.

sgarbato rude

sgarbo *m* discourtesy

sgelare <1b> thaw

sgelo *m* thaw

sghembo crooked; **di ~** crookedly, not in a straight line

S

sgobbare <1c> slave

sgobbone *m*, **-a** *f* F swot F

sgocciolare <1l> *v/t* & *v/i* drip

sgomberare <1l> → **sgombrare**

sgombero *m di strada* clearing; (*trasloco*) removal

sgombrare <1a> *strada, stanza* clear; *ostacolo* remove; *appartamento* clear out, empty

sgombro[1] *agg strada, stanza* empty

sgombro[2] *m* mackerel

sgomentare <1a> frighten

sgomentarsi be frightened

sgomento *m* fear

sgonfiare <1k> **1** *v/t* let the air out of **2** *v/i* e **sgonfiarsi** become deflated; **il braccio si è sgonfiato** the swelling in the arm has gone down

sgonfio (*pl* -fi) flat; MED not swollen

sgradevole unpleasant

sgradito unwelcome

sgranchire <4d>, **sgranchirsi**: ~ **le gambe** stretch one's legs

sgraziato awkward

sgridare <1a> scold, tell off F

sgridata *f* scolding, telling off F

sguaiato raucous

sgualdrina *f* tart

sguardo *m* look; (*occhiata*) glance; **al primo** ~ at first glance

sguazzare <1a> splash about; *fig* F ~ **nei soldi** be rolling (in it) F

shampoo *m inv* shampoo

shock *m inv* shock; ~ **culturale** culture shock

si[1] *pron* oneself; *lui* himself; *lei* herself; *esso, essa* itself; *loro* themselves; *reciproco* each other; **spazzolarsi i capelli** brush one's hair; ~ **è spazzolato i capelli** he brushed his hair; ~ **dice** they say; **cosa ~ può dire?** what can one say?, what can I say?; ~ **capisce da sé** it's self-evident

si[2] *m* MUS B

sì *avv* yes; **dire di** ~ say yes; ~ **e no** yes and no; **penso di** ~ I think so

sia ~ ... ~ ... both ... and ...; (*o l'uno*

o l'altro) either ... or ...; ~ **che ...** ~ **che ...** whether ... or whether ...

siamo → **essere**

sibilare <1l> hiss; *di vento* whistle

sibilo *m* hiss; *di vento* whistle

sicario *m* hired killer, hit man F

sicché (and) so

siccità *f* drought

siccome since

Sicilia *f* Sicily

siciliano **1** *agg* Sicilian **2** *m*, **-a** *f* Sicilian

sicura *f* safety catch

sicurezza *f* security; (*protezione*) safety; (*certezza*) certainty; **pubblica** ~ police; **cintura** *f* **di** ~ seat belt; **misure** *fpl* **di** ~ safety measures

sicuro **1** *agg luogo* safe; *investimento* sound, safe; (*certo*) sure; ~ **di sé** self confident, sure of o.s.; **di** ~ definitely **2** *m*: **essere al** ~ **da qc** be safe from sth; **mettere al** ~ put in a safe place

siderurgia *f* iron and steel industry

sidro *m* cider

siedo → **sedere**

siepe *f* hedge

siero *m* MED serum

sieropositivo HIV positive

siesta *f* siesta

siete → **essere**

sifilide *f* MED syphilis

sig. *abbr* (= **signore**) Mr (= mister)

sigaretta *f* cigarette; ~ **col filtro** filter tip

sigaro *m* cigar

sigg. *abbr* (= **signori**) Messrs

sigillare <1a> seal

sigillo *m* seal

sigla *f* initials *pl*; *musicale* theme (tune)

sig.na *abbr* (= **signorina**) Miss, Ms

significare <1m & d> mean

significativo significant

significato *m* meaning

signora *f* lady; **mi scusi,** ~! excuse me!; **la** ~ **Rossi** Mrs Rossi; **-e e signori** ladies and gentlemen

signore *m* gentleman; **mi scusi,** ~! excuse me!; **il signor Rossi** Mr Rossi; **i -i Rossi** Mr and Mrs Rossi signorile *appartamento* luxury; *modi* gentlemanly

signorina *f* young lady; **è ancora ~** she's not married; **la ~ Rossi** Miss Rossi

sig.ra *abbr* (= **signora**) Mrs

silenziatore *m* silencer, *Am* muffler

silenzio *m* silence; **fare ~** be quiet; **~!** silence!, quiet!

silenzioso silent

sillaba *f* syllable

sillabare <1l> split into syllables

silo *m* silo

siluro *m* MAR torpedo

simboleggiare <1f> symbolize

simbolico (*pl* -ci) symbolic

simbolismo *m* symbolism

simbolo *m* symbol

simile similar

simmetria *f* symmetry

simmetrico (*pl* -ci) symmetric(al)

simpatia *f* liking; (*affinità*) sympathy; **avere ~ per qu** like s.o.

simpatico (*pl* -ci) likeable

simpatizzare <1a> become friends

simposio *m* (*pl* -si) symposium

simulare <1l> feign; TEC simulate

simulazione *f* pretence, *Am* pretense; TECH simulation; **~ elettronica** electronic simulation

sinagoga *f* (*pl* -ghe) synagogue

sinceramente sincerely; (*in verità*) honestly

sincerarsi <1b> make sure

sincerità *f* sincerity

sincero sincere

sincronizzare <1a> synchronize

sindacalista *m/f* (*mpl* -i) trade unionist

sindacato *m* trade union

sindaco *m* (*pl* -ci) mayor

sinfonia *f* symphony

sinfonico (*pl* -ci) symphonic

singhiozzare <1a> sob

singhiozzo *m*: **avere il ~** have hiccups; **-zi** *pl* sobs

single *m/f inv* single

singolare **1** *agg* singular; (*insolito*) unusual; (*strano*) strange **2** *m* singular; SP singles

singolo **1** *agg* individual; *camera,* *letto* single **2** *m* individual; SP singles

sinistra *f* left; **a ~** on the left; **andare a ~** to the left

sinistro **1** *agg* left, left-hand; *fig* sinister **2** *m* accident

sino → **fino**

sinonimo **1** *agg* synonymous **2** *m* synonym

sintesi *f inv* synthesis; (*riassunto*) summary

sintetico (*pl* -ci) synthetic; (*riassunto*) brief; **materiale *m* ~** synthetic (material)

sintetizzare <1a> synthesize; (*riassumere*) summarize, sum up

sintomo *m* symptom

sintonia *f* RAD tuning; *fig* **essere in ~** be on the same wavelength (**con** as)

sintonizzare <1a> RAD tune

sintonizzarsi tune in (**su** to)

sinusite *f* sinusitis

sipario *m* (*pl* -ri) curtain

sirena *f* siren; *mitologica* mermaid; **~ d'allarme** alarm

siringa *f* (*pl* -ghe) MED syringe; **~ monouso** disposable syringe

sismico (*pl* -ci) seismic

sistema *m* (*pl* -i) system; **~ antibloccaggio** anti-lock braking system; **~ elettorale proporzionale** proportional representation; **~ immunitario** immune system; **~ monetario** monetary system; INFOR **~ operativo** operating system

sistemare <1b> put; (*mettere in ordine*) arrange; *casa* do up

sistemarsi tidy o.s. up; (*trovare casa, sposarsi*) settle down

sistematico (*pl* -ci) systematic

sistemazione *f* place; (*lavoro*) job; *in albergo* accommodation

sito site; **in ~** on the premises

situare <1l> locate, find

situato: **essere ~** be situated

situazione *f* situation

slacciare <1f> undo

slalom *m* slalom

slanciato slender

slancio *m* (*pl* -ci) impulse

slavo **1** *agg* Slav, Slavonic **2** *m*, **-a** *f* Slav

sleale disloyal

slealtà f disloyalty

slegare <1e> untie

slegarsi free o.s.

slegato fig incoherent, disjointed

slip m inv underpants; da donna knickers; ~ da bagno bathing trunks

slitta f sledge

slittino m sled; SP bobsleigh

s.l.m. abbr (= sul livello del mare) above sea level

slogan m inv slogan

slogare <1e> dislocate

slogarsi : ~ una caviglia sprain one's ankle

slogatura f sprain

sloggiare <1f> move out

smacchiare <1k> take the stains out of

smacchiatore m stain remover

smagliatura f ladder, Am run; MED stretch mark

smaltare <1a> enamel

smaltimento m FIN disposal of stock; di rifiuti tossici disposal

smaltire <4d> dispose of

smalto m enamel; per ceramiche glaze; ~ per unghie nail varnish or polish

smantellamento m dismantling

smantellare <1b> dismantle

smarrimento m loss

smarrire <4d> lose

smarrirsi get lost

smarrito 1 pp → smarrire 2 agg lost

smascherare <1l> unmask

Sme abbr (= Sistema monetario europeo) EMS (= European Monetary System)

smemorato forgetful

smentire <4d> prove to be wrong; non si smentisce mai! he doesn't change!

smentita f denial

smeraldo 1 m emerald 2 agg emerald (green)

smercio m (pl -ci) sale

smesso pp → smettere

smettere <3ee> 1 v/t stop; abiti stop wearing 2 v/i stop (di fare qc doing sth)

smilitarizzare <1a> demilitarize

smilitarizzazione f demilitarization

sminuire <4d> problema downplay; persona belittle

smistamento m FERR shunting

smistare <1a> FERR shunt

smisurato boundless

smodato excessive

smog m smog

smontabile which can be taken apart, Am knockdown

smontaggio m dismantling

smontare <1a> 1 v/i (da cavallo) dismount 2 v/t dismantle; persona deflate

smorfia f grimace

smorfioso affected, simpering

smorto persona deathly pale; colore dull

smorzare <1c> colore tone down; luce dim; entusiasmo dampen

smuovere <3ff> shift, move

snellezza f slenderness

snellire <4d> slim down; fig pare down

snello slim, slender

snervante irritating, wearing on the nerves

snob 1 agg snobbish 2 m/f inv snob

SO abbr (= sud-ovest) SW (= southwest)

so → sapere

sobborgo m (pl -ghi) suburb

sobrietà f sobriety

sobrio (pl -ri) sober

Soc. abbr (= società) Co (= company); soc. (= society)

socchiudere <3b> half-close

socchiuso 1 pp → socchiudere 2 agg half-closed; porta ajar

soccombere <3a> succumb

soccorrere <3o> help

soccorritore m rescue worker

soccorso 1 pp → soccorrere 2 m rescue; venire in ~ a qu come to s.o.'s rescue; pronto ~ first aid; ~ stradale breakdown service, Am wrecking service; segnale m di ~ distress signal

sociale social
socialismo *m* socialism
socialista (*mpl* -i) *agg*, *m/f* socialist
socializzare <1a> socialize
società *f inv* company; (*associazione*) society; ~ **a responsabilità limitata** limited liability company; ~ **in nome collettivo** general partnership; ~ **per azioni** joint stock company; ~ **del benessere** welfare society; ~ **dei consumi** consumer society
socievole sociable
socio *m* (*pl* -ci), **-a** *f* member; FIN partner
sociologia *f* sociology
sociologo *m* (*pl* -gi), **-a** *f* sociologist
soddisfacente satisfying
soddisfare <3aa> satisfy
soddisfatto **1** *pp* → **soddisfare**
2 *agg* satisfied; **essere ~ di qu** be satisfied with s.o.
soddisfazione *f* satisfaction
sodio *m* sodium
sodo *uovo* hard-boiled; *fig* **venire al ~** get down to brass tacks
sofà *m inv* sofa
sofferente suffering
sofferenza *f* suffering
soffermare <1a> *attenzione* turn
soffermarsi dwell (**su** on)
sofferto *pp* → **soffrire**
soffiare <1k> blow; F swipe F; **~arsi il naso** blow one's nose
soffice soft
soffio *m* puff
soffitta *f* attic
soffitto *m* ceiling
soffocante suffocating
soffocare <1l, c & d> suffocate
soffriggere <3cc> fry gently
soffrire <4f> **1** *v/t* suffer; *persone* bear, stand **2** *v/i* suffer (**di** from)
sofisticato sophisticated
software *m inv* software
softwarista *m/f* software engineer
soggettivo subjective
soggetto **1** *agg* subject; ~ **a tassa** subject to tax; **andare ~ a qc** suffer from sth **2** *m* GRAM subject
soggezione *f* subjection

soggiornare <1a> stay
soggiorno *m* stay; **permesso *m* di ~** residence permit
soglia *f* threshold
sogliola *f* sole
sognare <1a> e **sognarsi** dream (**di** about, of)
sognatore *m*, **-trice** *f* dreamer
sogno *m* dream; **neppure per ~!** in your dreams!
soia *f* soya
sol *m inv* MUS G
solaio *m* (*pl* -ai) attic, loft
solamente only; ~ **ieri** just yesterday
solare solar
solarium *m inv* solarium
solco *m* (*pl* -chi) furrow
soldato *m* soldier
soldi *mpl* money *sg*
sole *m* sun; **c'è il ~** it's sunny; **colpo *m* di ~** sunstroke; **prendere il ~** sunbathe
soleggiare <1f> dry in the sun
soleggiato sun-dried
solenne solemn
solennità *f inv* solemnity
solere <2p>: ~ **fare** be in the habit of doing
soletta *f* insole
solforico (*pl* -ci) sulphur, *Am* sulfur *attr*; **acido *m* ~** sulphuric, *Am* sulfuric acid
solidale *fig* in agreement
solidarietà *f* solidarity
solidarizzare <1a> agree, be in agreement
solidità *f* solidity
solido solid; (*robusto*) sturdy
solista *m/f* (*mpl* -i) soloist
solitario (*pl* -ri) **1** *agg* solitary; *luogo* lonely; *navigatore* solo **2** *m* solitaire; *gioco* patience
solito usual, same; **al** *o* **di ~** usually; **come al ~** as usual; **più del ~** more than usual
solitudine *f* solitude, being alone
sollecitare <1m> (*stimolare*) urge; *risposta* ask (again) for
sollecito **1** *agg persona* diligent; *risposta, reazione* prompt; **lettera *f* di ~** reminder **2** *m* reminder

S

sollecitudine f di persona diligence; di risposta promptness

solleticare <1m & d> tickle; appetito whet

solletico m tickling; fare il ~ a qu tickle s.o.; soffrire il ~ be ticklish

sollevamento m lifting; (insurrezione) rising; ~ pesi weightlifting

sollevare <1b> lift; problema, obiezione bring up

sollevarsi di popolo rise up; AVIA climb, rise

sollievo m relief

solo 1 agg lonely; (non accompagnato) alone; (unico) only; MUS solo; da ~ by myself/yourself etc, on my/your etc own **2** avv only **3** m MUS solo

solstizio m (pl -zi) solstice

soltanto only; ~ ieri only yesterday

solubile soluble

soluzione f solution; ~ provvisoria stopgap

solvente 1 agg FIN solvent **2** m CHIM solvent

somigliante similar

somiglianza f resemblance

somigliare <1g>: ~ a qu resemble s.o.

somma f (addizione) addition; risultato sum; (importo) amount (of money), sum; fare la ~ di add (up); fig tirare le -e sum up

sommare <1a> add; ~ a total, come to

sommario (pl -ri) **1** agg summary **2** m summary; di libro table of contents

sommato: tutto ~ all things considered, on the whole

sommergere <3uu> submerge; fig overwhelm (di with)

sommergersi submerge, dive

sommergibile m submarine

sommerso città submerged; strade inches deep in water

sommesso voce quiet

somministrare <1a> MED administer

sommo 1 agg supreme **2** m summit; fig height

sommossa f uprising

sondaggio m (pl -ggi): ~ (d'opinione) (opinion) poll

sondare <1a> sound; fig test

sonnambulo m, **-a** f sleepwalker

sonnecchiare <1k> doze

sonnifero m sleeping tablet

sonno m sleep; aver ~ be sleepy; prendere ~ fall asleep

sonnolento drowsy

sonnolenza f drowsiness

sono → essere

sonorità f inv sonority

sonoro sound attr; risa, applausi loud; colonna f -a sound-track

sontuosità f magnificence

sontuoso sumptuous, magnificent

soppesare <1a> weigh; fig weigh up

sopportabile bearable, tolerable

sopportare <1c> peso bear; fig bear, stand F

soppressione f deletion; di regola abolition

soppresso pp → sopprimere

sopprimere <3r> delete; regola abolish

sopra 1 prp on; (più in alto di) above; (riguardo a) about, on; ~ il tavolo on the table; l'uno ~ l'altro one on top of the other; i bambini ~ cinque anni children over five; 5 gradi ~ zero 5 degrees above zero; al di ~ di qc over sth **2** avv on top; (al piano superiore) upstairs; dormirci ~ sleep on it; vedi ~ see above; la parte di ~ the top or upper part

soprabito m (over)coat

sopracciglio m (fpl -a) eyebrow

sopraccoperta f di letto bedspread; di libro dustjacket

sopraffare <3aa> overwhelm

sopraggiungere <3d> di persona turn up, arrive on the scene; di difficoltà arise, come up F

sopralluogo m (pl -ghi) inspection (of the site)

soprammobile m ornament

soprannaturale supernatural

soprannome m nickname

soprannumero m: in ~ overcrowded

soprano m soprano; mezzo ~

mezzo(-soprano)

soprappensiero → **sovrapensiero**

soprassalto: *di* ~ with a start

soprattassa *f* surcharge

soprattutto particularly, (e)specially, above all

sopravvalutare <1a> overvalue; *fig* overestimate

sopravvenire <4p> turn up, appear

sopravvento *m*: *avere o prendere il* ~ have the upper hand

sopravvissuto 1 *agg* surviving 2 *m*, -a *f* survivor

sopravvivenza *f* survival

sopravvivere <3zz> survive, outlive (*a qu* s.o.)

soprintendente *m/f* supervisor

sopruso *m* abuse of power

soqquadro *m*: *mettere a* ~ turn upside down

sorbetto *m* sorbet

sorbire <4d> sip

sorbirsi put up with

sorcio *m* (*pl* -ci) mouse

sordina *f* mute; *in* ~ in secret, on the quiet

sordità *f* deafness

sordo deaf

sordomuto deaf and dumb

sorella *f* sister

sorellastra *f* stepsister

sorgente *f* spring; *fig* source

sorgere <3d> *di sole* rise, come up; *fig* arise, come up

sormontare <1a> *difficoltà* overcome, surmount

sorpassare <1a> go past; AUTO pass, overtake; *fig* exceed

sorpassato out of date

sorpasso *m*: *divieto di* ~ no passing, no overtaking; *fare un* ~ pass, overtake

sorprendente surprising

sorprendere <3c> surprise; (*cogliere sul fatto*) catch

sorpresa *f* surprise

sorpreso *pp* → **sorprendere**

sorridere <3b> smile

sorriso 1 *pp* → **sorridere** 2 *m* smile

sorseggiare <1f> sip

sorso *m* mouthful

sorta *f* sort, kind

sorte *f* fate; *tirare a* ~ draw lots

sorteggiare <1f> draw

sorteggio *m* (*pl* -ggi) draw

sorto *pp* → **sorgere**

sorveglianza *f* supervision; *di edificio* security

sorvegliare <1g> supervise; *edificio* provide security for; *bagagli ecc* look after, take care of

sorvolare <1a> 1 *v/t* AVIA fly over 2 *v/i fig*: ~ *su* skim over, skip

sosia *m inv* double

sospendere <3c> suspend; (*appendere*) hang

sospensione *f* suspension

sospeso 1 *pp* → **sospendere** 2 *agg* hanging; *fig questione* pending; *tenere in* ~ *persona* keep in suspense

sospettare <1b> suspect; ~ *qu o di qu* suspect s.o.

sospetto 1 *agg* suspicious 2 *m*, -a *f* suspect

sospettoso suspicious

sospirare <1a> 1 *v/i* sigh 2 *v/t* long for

sospiro *m* sigh

sosta *f* stop; (*pausa*) break, pause; *senza* ~ nonstop; *divieto di* ~ no parking

sostantivo *m* noun

sostanza *f* substance; *in* ~ in short, to sum up

sostare <1c> stop

sostegno *m* support; *a* ~ *di* in support of

sostenere <2q> support; (*affermare*) maintain

sostengo → **sostenere**

sostenitore *m*, -trice *f* supporter

sostentamento *m* support

sostenuto *stile* formal; *velocità* high

sostituibile which can be replaced, replaceable

sostituire <4d> : ~ *X con Y* replace X with Y, substitute Y for X

sostituto *m*, -a *f* substitute, replacement

sostituzione *f* substitution, replacement

sottaceti *mpl* pickles

sottana *f* slip, underskirt; (*gonna*) skirt; REL cassock

sotterranea *f* underground

sotterraneo 1 *agg* underground *attr* **2** *m* cellar

sotterrare <1b> bury

sottile fine; *fig* subtle; *udito* keen

sottintendere <3c> imply

sottinteso 1 *pp* → **sottintendere** **2** *m* allusion

sotto 1 *prp* under; *i bambini ~ cinque anni* children under five; *5 gradi ~ zero* 5 degrees below (zero); *~ la pioggia* in the rain; *al di ~ di qc* under sth **2** *avv* below; (*più in basso*) lower down; (*al di sotto*) underneath; (*al piano di ~*) downstairs

sottobanco under the counter

sottobraccio: *camminare ~* walk arm-in-arm; *prendere qu ~* take s.o.'s arm

sottocchio: *tenere ~ qc* keep an eye on sth

sottochiave under lock and key

sottocosto at less than cost price

sottoesposto FOT underexposed

sottofondo *m* background

sottolineare <1n> *anche fig* underline

sottomarino 1 *agg* underwater *attr* **2** *m* submarine

sottomesso 1 *pp* → **sottomettere** **2** *agg* submissive; *popolo* subject *attr*

sottomettere <3ee> submit; *popolo* subdue

sottomissione *f* submission

sottopassaggio *m* (*pl* -ggi) underpass

sottoporre <3ll> submit

sottoporsi: *~ a* undergo

sottoscritto 1 *pp* → **sottoscrivere** **2** *m* undersigned

sottoscrivere <3tt> *documento* sign; *teoria* subscribe to; *abbonamento* take out

sottoscrizione *f* signing; (*abbonamento*) subscription

sottosopra *fig* upside-down

sottosuolo *m* subsoil; *ricchezze fpl*

del ~ mineral wealth; *nel ~* under ground

sottosviluppato underdeveloped

sottovalutare <1a> undervalue; *per sona* underestimate

sottoveste *f* slip, underskirt

sottovoce quietly, sotto voce

sottrarre <3xx> MAT subtract; *dena ro* embezzle

sottrarsi: *~ a qc* avoid sth

sottratto *pp* → **sottrarre**

sottrazione *f* MAT subtraction; *di de naro* embezzlement

sottufficiale *m* non-commissione officer, NCO

souvenir *m inv* souvenir

sovietico (*pl* -ci) Soviet

sovrabbondante overabundant

sovrabbondanza *f* overabundance

sovrabbondare <1a> be overabun dant; *~ di* have an overabundance of

sovraccarico 1 *agg* overloaded (*d* with) **2** *m* overload

sovrano 1 *agg* sovereign **2** *m, -a* sovereign

sovrappensiero: *essere ~* be lost in thought

sovrappeso 1 *agg* overweight **2** *m* excess weight

sovrappopolato overpopulated

sovrapporre <3ll> overlap

sovrapposizione *f* overlapping

sovrapproduzione *f* overproduc tion

sovrastare <1a> overlook, domi nate

sovrintendente *m/f* → **soprinten dente**

sovrumano superhuman

sovvenzionare <1a> give a grant t

sovvenzione *f* grant

sovversivo subversive

S.P. *abbr* (= **Strada Provinciale**) E road

S.p.A. *abbr* (= **Società per Azioni** joint stock company

spaccare <1d> break in two; *legn* split, chop

spaccarsi break in two

spaccatura *f* crevice

spacciare <1f> *droga* deal in, push F; *siamo spacciati!* we've had it!

spacciarsi: ~ *per* pass o.s. off as

spacciatore *m*, **-trice** *f di droga* dealer

spaccio *m* (*pl* -cci) *di droga* dealing; *negozio* general store

spacco *m* (*pl* -cchi) *m in gonna* slit; *in giacca* vent

spaccone *m*, **-a** *f* braggart

spada *f* sword

spadroneggiare <1f> throw one's weight around

spaesato disorient(at)ed, confused

spaghetti *mpl* spaghetti *sg*

Spagna *f* Spain

spagnolo 1 *m/agg* Spanish **2** *m*, **-a** *f* Spaniard

spago *m* (*pl* -ghi) string

spalancare <1d> open wide

spalla *f* shoulder; *girare le* -*e a qu* turn one's back on s.o.; *era di* -*e* he had his back to me; *stringersi nelle* -*e* shrug; *vivere alle* -*e di qu* live off s.o.

spalleggiare <1f> support, back up

spalliera *f* wallbars

spallina *f* shoulder pad

spalmare <1a> spread

spalti *mpl* terraces

spandere <3a> spread

spandersi spread

spanto *pp* → **spandere**

sparare <1a> **1** *v/i* shoot (*a* at) **2** *v/t*: ~ *un colpo* fire a shot

sparatoria *f* gunfire, series of shots

sparecchiare <1k> clear

spareggio *m* SP play-off

spargere <3uu> spread; *lagrime*, *sangue* shed

sparire <4d *or* 4e> disappear

sparizione *f* disappearance

sparo *m* (gun)shot

sparpagliare <1g> scatter

sparso 1 *pp* → **spargere 2** *agg* scattered

spartiacque *m inv* watershed

spartire <4d> divide (up), split F

spartito *m* score

spartitraffico *m* (*pl* -ci) traffic island

spartizione *f* division

spasimante *m/f* admirer

spasimo *m* agony

spasmo *m* MED spasm

spasso *m* fun; *andare a* ~ go for a walk; *fig essere a* ~ be out of work, be unemployed; *è uno* ~ he / it's a good laugh; *per* ~ as a joke, for fun

spassoso very funny

spastico (*pl* -ci) spastic

spaurito frightened

spavaldo cocky, over-confident

spaventapasseri *m inv* scarecrow

spaventare <1b> frighten, scare

spaventarsi be frightened, be scared

spavento *m* fright; *mi sono preso uno* ~ I got a fright

spaventoso frightening

spaziale space *attr*

spazientirsi <4d> get impatient, lose one's patience

spazio *m* (*pl* -zi) space; ~ *aereo* airspace

spazioso spacious

spazzacamino *m* chimney sweep

spazzaneve *m inv* snowplough, *Am* -plow

spazzare <1a> sweep

spazzatura *f* rubbish, garbage

spazzino *m*, **-a** *f* street sweeper

spazzola *f* brush

spazzolare <1l> brush

spazzolino *m* brush; ~ *da denti* toothbrush

specchiarsi <1k> look at o.s.; (*riflettersi*) be mirrored, be reflected

specchietto *m* mirror; (*prospetto*) table; AUTO ~ *retrovisore* rear-view mirror

specchio *m* (*pl* -cchi) mirror

speciale special

specialista *m/f* (*mpl* -i) specialist

specialità *f inv* special(i)ty

specializzarsi <1a> specialize

specialmente especially

specie 1 *f inv* species; *una* ~ *di* a sort or kind of **2** *avv* especially

specificare <1m & d> specify

specifico (*pl* -ci) specific

speculare <1l & b> speculate (*in* in, *su* on)

S

speculativo speculative

speculatore *m*, **-trice** *f* speculator

speculazione *f* speculation

spedire <4d> send

spedito fast

spedizione *f* dispatch, sending; *di merce* shipping; (*viaggio*) expedition; **agenzia** *f* **di ~** shipping agency; **spese** *pl* **di ~** shipping costs

spedizioniere *m* courier

spegnere <3vv> put out; *luce, motore, radio* turn off, switch off

spegnersi *di fuoco* go out; *di motore* stop, die F

spellare <1a> skin

spellarsi peel

spelonca *f* (*pl* -che) cave

spendere <3c> spend; *fig* invest

spennare <1a> *pollo* pluck

spensierato carefree

spento *pp* → **spegnere**

speranza *f* hope; **senza ~** hopeless

sperare <1b> **1** *v/t* hope for **2** *v/i* trust (**in** in)

sperduto lost; *luogo* remote, isolated

spergiuro **1** *m* perjury **2** *m*, **-a** *f* perjurer

sperimentale experimental

sperimentare <1a> try; *in laboratorio* test; *fig: fatica, dolore* feel; *droga* experiment with

sperma *m* sperm

sperperare <1l & b> fritter away, squander

sperpero *m* frittering away, squandering

spesa *f* expense; **fare la ~** do the shopping; **fare -e** go shopping; **-e** *pl* **di produzione** production costs; **-e** *pl* **di pubblicità** advertising costs; **-e** *pl* **vive** incidental expenses; **a proprie -e** at one's own expense

spesso **1** *agg* thick; **-e volte** many times, often **2** *avv* often, frequently

spessore *m* thickness

spett. *abbr* (= **spettabile**) Messrs; *in lettera* **Spett. Ditta** Dear Sirs

spettacolare spectacular

spettacolo *m* show; (*panorama*) spectacle, sight; **~ teatrale** show

spettare <1b>: **questo spetta a te**

this is yours; **non spetta a te giudicare** it's not up to you to judge

spettatore *m*, **-trice** *f* spectator; TEA member of the audience

spettinare <1l & b>: **~ qu** ruffle s.o.'s hair

spettro *m* ghost; FIS spectrum

spezie *fpl* spices

spezzare <1b> break in two

spezzarsi break

spezzatino *m* stew

spezzato **1** *agg* broken (in two) **2** *m* co-ordinated two-piece suit

spezzettare <1a> break up

spia *f* spy; TEC pilot light; **fare la ~** tell, sneak

spiacente: **essere ~** be sorry; **sono molto ~** I am very sorry

spiacere <2k>: **mi spiace** I am sorry

spiacevole unpleasant

spiaggia *f* (*pl* -gge) beach

spianare <1a> roll

spiare <1h> spy on

spiazzo *m* empty space; *in bosco* clearing

spiccato strong

spicchio *m* (*pl* -cchi) *di frutto* section; **~ d'aglio** clove of garlic

spicciarsi <1f> hurry up

spiccioli *mpl* (small) change *sg*

spiedo *m* spit; **allo ~** spit-roasted

spiegabile possible to explain

spiegare <1b & e> (*stendere*) spread, (*chiarire*) explain

spiegarsi explain what one means; **mi spiego?** have I made myself clear?; **non so se mi spiego** I don't know if I make myself clear

spiegazione *f* explanation

spiegazzare <1a> crease

spietato merciless, pitiless

spiga *f* (*pl* -ghe) *di grano* ear

spigato herring-bone *attr*

spigliato confident

spigola *f* sea bass

spigolo *m* corner

spilla *f* *gioiello* brooch; **~ da balia** safety pin

spillo *m* pin; **~ di sicurezza** safety pin

spina *f* BOT thorn; ZO spine; *di pesce*

bone; EL plug; ANAT **~ dorsale** spine; **parcheggio m a ~ di pesce** angle parking; **birra f alla ~** draught beer, beer on tap; *fig* **stare sulle -e** be on tenterhooks

spinaci *mpl* spinach *sg*

spinale spinal

spinello Ⓕ *m* joint Ⓕ

spingere <3d> push; *fig* drive

spino *m* thorn

spinoso thorny

spinta *f* push

spinterogeno *m* AUTO distributor

spinto *pp* → **spingere**

spionaggio *m* (*pl* -ggi) espionage

spiraglio *m* (*pl* -gli) crack; *di luce, speranza* gleam, glimmer

spirale *f* spiral; *contraccettivo* coil

spirare <1a> blow; *fig* die

spirito *m* spirit; *(disposizione)* mind; *(umorismo)* wit; **avere ~ d'osservazione** be observant; **fare dello ~** be witty

spiritoso witty

spirituale spiritual

splendere <3a> shine

splendente bright

splendido wonderful, splendid

splendore *m* splendo(u)r

spogliare <1g> undress; *(rubare)* rob

spogliarsi undress, strip; **~ di qc** give sth up

spogliarello *m* striptease

spogliatoio *m* (*pl* -oi) dressing room, locker room

spoglio (*pl* -gli) bare

spola *f:* **fare la ~ da un posto all'altro** shuttle backwards and forwards between two places

spolverare <1l> dust

spolverizzare <1a> dust (**di** with)

sponda *f di letto* edge, side; *di fiume* bank; *nel biliardo* cushion

sponsor *m inv* sponsor

sponsorizzare <1a> sponsor

spontaneità *f* spontaneity

spontaneo spontaneous

sporadico (*pl* -ci) sporadic

sporcare <1c & d> dirty

sporcarsi get dirty

sporcizia *f* dirt

sporco (*pl* -chi) **1** *agg* dirty **2** *m* dirt

sporgere <3d> **1** *v/t* hold out; *denuncia* make **2** *v/i* jut out

sporgersi lean out

sport *m inv* sport; **~pl invernali** winter sports; **fare dello ~** do sport; **per ~** for fun

sporta *f* shopping bag; *di vimini* shopping basket

sportello *m* door; **~ automatico** automatic teller machine, cash dispenser

sportivo **1** *agg* sports *attr*; *persona* sporty; **campo m ~** playing field **2** *m*, **-a** *f* sportsman; *donna* sportswoman

sporto *pp* → **sporgere**

sposa *f* bride; **abito m da ~** wedding dress

sposare <1c> marry

sposarsi get married

sposato married

sposo *m* bridegroom; **-i** *pl* newlyweds

spostare <1a> *(trasferire)* move, shift; *(rimandare)* postpone

spostarsi move

S.P.Q.R. *abbr* (= **Senatus Populusque Romanus**) the Senate and People of Rome

spranga *f* (*pl* -ghe) bar

sprangare <1e> bar

sprecare <1b & d> waste, squander

spreco *m* (*pl* -chi) waste

spregevole contemptible, despicable

spregiudicato unprejudiced, unbiased; *spreg* unscrupulous

spremere <3a> squeeze

spremilimoni *m inv* lemon squeezer

spremuta *f* juice; **~ di limone** lemon juice; **~ d'arancia** orange juice

sprizzare <1a> spurt; *fig* exude

sprofondare <1a> sink; *fig* **~ dalla vergogna** be overcome with embarrassment

spronare <1a> spur on

sprone *m* spur

sproporzionato disproportionate (**a** to), out of proportion (**a** to)

sproposito *m* blunder; **fare uno ~**

do something silly; **costare uno ~**
cost a fortune; **a ~** out of turn
sprovveduto inexperienced
sprovvisto: **~ di** lacking; **sono ~ di ...**
I don't have any ...; **alla -a** unexpectedly
spruzzare <1a> spray
spruzzatore *m* spray
spruzzo *m* spray; *fango* splatter
spudorato shameless
spugna *f* sponge
spuma *f* foam
spumante: (**vino** *m*) **~** sparkling wine
spumeggiante frothy; *persona* bubbly
spuntare <1a> stick out; BOT come up; *di sole* appear; *di giorno* break;
gli è spuntato un dente he has cut a tooth
spuntino *m* snack
spunto *m* suggestion; **prendere ~ da** be inspired by
sputare <1a> **1** *v/i* spit **2** *v/t* spit out
sputo *m* spittle
squadra *f strumento* set square;
(*gruppo*) squad; SP team; **~ volante** flying squad
squalifica *f* (*pl* -che) disqualification
squalificare <1m & d> disqualify
squallido squallid
squallore *m* squalor
squalo *m* shark
squama *f* flake; *di pesce* scale
squarcio *m* (*pl* -ci) *in stoffa* rip, tear;
in nuvole break
squilibrato **1** *agg* insane **2** *m*, **-a** *f* lunatic
squilibrio *m* (*pl* -ri) imbalance
squillare <1a> ring
squillo *m* ring; **ragazza** *f* **~** callgirl
squisito *cibo* delicious
sradicare <1l & d> uproot; *fig* (*eliminare*) eradicate, uproot
S.r.l. *abbr* (= **Società a responsabilità limitata**) Ltd (= limited)
SS. *abbr* (= **santi**) Saints
S.S. *abbr* (= **Sua Santità**) His Holiness (the Pope); (= **Strada Statale**) A road

stabile **1** *agg* steady; (*duraturo*)
stable; *tempo* settled **2** *m* building
stabilimento *m* (*fabbrica*) plant, B
factory; **~ balneare** lido
stabilire <4d> *data, obiettivi, recor*
set; (*decidere*) decide, settle
stabilirsi settle
stabilità *f* steadiness; *di relazione*
moneta stability
stabilizzare <1a> stabilize
staccare <1d> remove, detach; E
unplug; TELEC **~ il ricevitore** lift th
receiver
stadio *m* (*pl* -di) stage; SP stadium
staffa *f* stirrup; **perdere le -e** blow
one's top
staffetta *f* SP relay; **corsa** *f* **a ~** rela
race
stage *m inv* training period
stagionale seasonal
stagionare <1a> age, mature; *legn*
season
stagionato aged, mature; *legno* sea
soned
stagione *f* season; **alta ~** high sea
son; **bassa ~** low season; **~ morta**
off-season; **frutta** *f* **di ~** fruit in sea
son, seasonal fruit
stagnare <1a> *dell'acqua* grow stag
nant; FIN stagnate
stagnante stagnant
stagno **1** *m* pond; TEC tin **2** *agg* wa
tertight
stalla *f per bovini* cowshed; *per caval*
stable
stamani, stamattina this morning
stambecco *m* (*pl* -cchi) ibex
stampa *f* press; *tecnica* printing; FO
print; *posta* **-e** *pl* printed matter
libro *m* **in corso di ~** book that ha
gone to press; **~ locale** local press
~ scandalistica tabloids, gutte
press; **libertà** *f* **di ~** freedom of the
press
stampante *f* INFOR printer; **~ a gette**
di inchiostro ink-jet printer; **~ lase**
laser printer
stampare <1a> print
stampatello *m* block letters *pl*
stampato *m* INFOR printout, hard
copy

stampella *f* crutch

stampo *m* mo(u)ld

stancare <1d> tire (out)

stancarsi get tired, tire

stanchezza *f* tiredness, fatigue

stanco (*pl* -chi) tired; ~ *morto* dead beat

stand *m inv* stand

standard *m/agg inv* standard

standardizzare <1a> standardize

standardizzazione *f* standardization

stanga *f* (*pl* -ghe) bar

stanghetta *f* leg

stanotte tonight; (*la notte scorsa*) last night

stantuffo *m* piston

stanza *f* room

stanziare <1g> *somma di denaro* allocate, earmark

stanzino *m* boxroom

stappare <1a> take the top off

star *f inv* star

stare <1q> be; (*restare*) stay; (*abitare*) live; ~ *in piedi* stand; ~ *bene* be well; *di vestiti* suit; ~ *per fare qc* be about to do sth; *stammi a sentire* listen to me; *lascialo* ~ leave him alone, let him be; ~ *telefonando* be on the phone, be making a phonecall; *come sta?* how are you?, how are things?; *ben ti sta!* serves you right!; *ci sto!* here I am!; *sta bene* all right, ok

starnutire <4d> sneeze

starnuto *m* sneeze

start *m inv* off

starter *m inv* SP starter; AUTO choke

stasera this evening, tonight

statale 1 *agg* state *attr* **2** *m/f* (*gen pl* -i) civil servant **3** *f* main road

statistica *f* (*pl* -che) statistics

Stati Uniti d'America *mpl* United States of America, USA

statizzare <1a> nationalize

stato 1 *pp* → *essere* e *stare* **2** *m* *anche* POL state; ~ *assistenziale* Welfare State; ~ *civile* marital status; ~ *maggiore* general staff; ~ *di salute* state of health, condition; *essere in* ~ *di fare* be in a position

to do; *essere in* ~ *interessante* be pregnant

statua *f* statue

statunitense 1 *agg* US *attr*, American **2** *m/f* US citizen, citizen of the United States

statura *f* height; *fig* stature

statuto *m* statute

stavolta this time

stazionamento *m* parking

stazionare <1a> be parked

stazionario (*pl* -ri) stationary

stazione *f* station; ~ *di servizio* service station; ~ *balneare* seaside resort; ~ *centrale* main station; ~ *climatica* health resort; ~ *termale* spa; ~ *trasmittente* radio station

stecca *f* (*pl* -cche) *di biliardo* cue; *di sigarette* carton; MED splint; MUS wrong note

stecchino *m* toothpick

stella *f* star; ~ *alpina* edelweiss; ~ *polare* North Star, Pole Star; ~ *cadente* shooting star; ~ *di mare* starfish; *fig vedere le* -e see stars

stelo *m* stem, stalk

stemma *m* (*pl* -i) coat of arms

stendere <3c> spread; *braccio* stretch out; *biancheria* hang out, hang up; *verbale* draw up

stendersi stretch out

stendibiancheria *m inv* clothes dryer

stenodattilografa *f* shorthand typist

stenodattilografia *f* shorthand typing

stenografare <1m & c> take down in shorthand

stenografia *f* shorthand

stentare <1b>: ~ *a fare qc* find it hard to do sth, have difficulty doing sth

stento *m*: *a* ~ with difficulty; -*i pl* hardship

stereo *m inv* stereo

stereotipo 1 *agg* stereotypical **2** *m* stereotype

sterile sterile

sterilità *f* sterility

sterilizzare <1a> sterilize

sterilizzazione f sterilization
sterlina f sterling
sterminare <1l & b> exterminate
sterminato vast
sterminio m (pl -ni) extermination
sterno m breastbone, ANAT sternum
sterzare <1b> steer; **~ a sinistra** turn left
sterzata f swerve
sterzo m AUTO steering
steso pp → **stendere**
stesso same; **lo ~, la stessa** the same one; **è lo ~** it's all the same; **oggi ~** this very day; **io ~** myself; **se ~** himself; **l'ho visto coi miei stessi occhi** I saw it with my very own eyes
stile m style; SP **~ libero** freestyle
stilografica f fountain pen
stima f (ammirazione) esteem; (valutazione) estimate
stimare <1a> persona esteem; oggetto value, estimate (the value of); (ritenere) think, consider
stimarsi think or consider o.s.
stimato respected
stimolante **1** agg stimulating **2** m stimulant
stimolare <1l> stimulate
stimolo m stimulus
stinco m (pl -chi) shin
stingere <3d> **1** v/t fade **2** v/i e **stingersi** fade
stinto pp → **stingere**
stipare <1a> cram
stipato crammed (di with)
stipendiato m, **-a** f person on a salary
stipendio m (pl -di) salary
stipulare <1l> stipulate
stipulazione f stipulation
stiramento m MED pulled muscle
stirare <1a> iron; **non si stira** it's non-iron
stirarsi pull
stiratura f ironing
stiro m: **ferro m da ~** iron; **non ~** non-iron
stirpe f (origine) birth
stitichezza f constipation
stivale m boots; **-i** pl **di gomma** rubber boots, Br wellingtons
sto → **stare**
stoccafisso m stockfish (air-dried cod)
stoccaggio m (pl -ggi) stocking
stoffa f material; fig **avere ~** be talented
stomaco m (pl -chi) stomach; **dolori** mpl **di ~** stomach pains; **mi sono tolto un peso dallo ~** I got it off my chest
stonare <1c> di cantante sing out of tune; fig be out of place; di colori clash
stonato persona tone deaf; nota false; strumento out of tune
stop m inv AUTO brake light; cartello stop sign
stoppare <1c> stop
storcere <3d> twist; **~ il naso** make a face
storcersi bend; **~ un piede** twist one's ankle
stordimento m dizziness
stordire <4d> stun
stordito stunned
storia f history; (narrazione) story; **~ dell'arte** history of art; **non far -e!** don't make a fuss or scene!
storico (pl -ci) **1** agg historical; (memorabile) historic **2** m, **-a** f historian
storiografia f historiography
storiografo m, **-a** f historiographer
storione m sturgeon
stormo m di uccelli flock
stornare <1a> pericolo avert
storno m uccello starling
storpio (pl -pi) **1** agg crippled **2** m **-a** f cripple
storta f: **prendere una ~ al piede** twist one's ankle
storto crooked
stoviglie fpl dishes
strabico (pl -ci) cross-eyed
strabismo m strabismus
stracarico (pl -chi) overloaded
stracaro exceedingly expensive
stracciare <1f> tear up
stracciatella f type of soup; gelato chocolate chip
stracciato in shreds

straccio (*pl* -cci) **1** *m per pulire* cloth; *per spolverare* duster **2** *agg:* **carta** *f* **-a** waste paper

strada *f* road; **per ~** down the road; **sono** (**già**) **per ~** I'm coming, I'm on my way; **~ provinciale** B road; **~ a senso unico** one-way street; **~ statale** A road; **farsi ~** push one's way through; **nella vita** get on in life; **a mezza** ~ half-way

stradale road *attr*; **incidente** *m* ~ road accident; **polizia** *f* ~ traffic police; **regolamento** *m* ~ rule of the road; **rete** *f* ~ road network

stradario *m* street-finder, street map

strafare <3aa> exaggerate

strage *f* slaughter; **fare ~ di cuori** be a heartbreaker

stragrande: **la ~ maggioranza** the vast majority

stranezza *f* strangeness

strangolare <1l> strangle

straniero **1** *agg* foreign **2** *m,* **-a** *f* foreigner

strano strange

straordinario (*pl* -ri) **1** *agg* special; *eccezionale* extraordinary **2** *m* overtime

strapazzare <1a> treat badly; **uova** *fpl* **strapazzate** scrambled eggs

strapazzarsi overdo it

strapazzo *m* strain; **essere uno ~** be exhausting; **da ~** third-rate

strapieno crowded

strapiombo *m*: **a ~** overhanging

strappare <1a> tear, rip; (*staccare*) tear down; (*togliere*) grab, snatch (**a qu** out of s.o.'s hands)

strappo *m* tear, rip; MED torn ligament; *fig* **uno ~ alla regola** an exception to the rule

straricco (*pl* -cchi) extremely rich

straripare <1a> flood, overflow its banks

strascico *m* (*pl* -chi) train; *fig* aftereffects

stratagemma *m* (*pl* -i) stratagem

strategia *f* strategy

strategico (*pl* -ci) strategic

strato *m* layer; **~ d'ozono** ozone layer; **~ protettivo** protective coating; **~ sociale** social stratum

stravagante extravagant

stravaganza *f* extravagance

stravecchio (*pl* -cchi) ancient

stravedere <2s>: **~ per qu** worship s.o.

stravincere <3d> win by a mile

stravolgere <3d> change radically; (*travisare*) twist; (*stancare*) exhaust

stravolto **1** *pp* → **stravolgere** **2** *agg* (*stanco*) exhausted

strazio *m* (*pl* -zi): **era uno ~** it was painful

strega *f* (*pl* -ghe) witch

stregare <1e> bewitch

stregone *m* wizard

stremare <1b> exhaust

stremato exhausted

stress *m inv* stress

stressante stressful

stressare <1b> stress

stretta *f* hold; **~ di mano** handshake; **mettere qu alle -e** put s.o. in a tight corner

strettamente closely; **tenere qc ~** (**in mano**) clutch sth (in one's hand)

strettezza *f* narrowness

stretto **1** *pp* → **stringere** **2** *agg* narrow; *vestito, scarpe* too tight; **lo ~ necessario** the bare minimum **3** *m* GEOG strait

strettoia *f* bottleneck

stridere <3a> *di porta* squeak; *di colori* clash

stridulo shrill

strillare <1a> scream

strillo *m* scream

striminzito skimpy

strimpellare <1b> strum

stringa *f* (*pl* -ghe) lace

stringere <3d> **1** *v/t* make narrower; *abito* take in; *vite* tighten; **~ amicizia** become friends **2** *v/i di tempo* press up

stringersi *intorno a tavolo* squeeze up

striscia *f* (*pl* -sce) strip; *dipinta* stripe; **-sce** *pl* **pedonali** pedestrian crossing *sg*, *Br* zebra crossing *sg*; **a -sce** striped

strisciare <1f> **1** *v/t piedi* scrape; (*sfiorare*) brush, smear (**contro**

against) **2** v/i crawl

striscio m MED smear

striscione m banner

strizzare <1a> wring; **~ l'occhio a qu** wink at s.o.

strofa f verse

strofinaccio m (pl -cci) dish towel

strofinare <1a> rub

stroncare <1d> albero knock down; vita snuff out; F idea shoot down

stropicciare <1f> crush, wrinkle

strozzare <1c> strangle

strozzatura f narrowing

strozzino m, **-a** f loan shark F

struggente all-consuming

struggere <3cc> consume

strumentalizzare make use of

strumento m instrument; **~ musicale** musical instrument; **~ ad arco / a fiato** string / wind instrument

strutto m lard

struttura f structure

strutturale structural

strutturare <1a> structure

struzzo m ZO ostrich

stuccare <1d> plaster

stucco m (pl -cchi) plaster; **rimanere di ~** be thunderstruck, Br be gobsmacked F

studente m, **-essa** f student; **casa f dello ~** hall of residence

studiare <1k> study

studio m (pl -di) study; di artista, RAD, TV studio; di professionista office; di medico surgery; **borsa f di ~** bursary

studioso 1 agg studious **2** m, **-a** f scholar

stufa f stove; **~ elettrica / a gas** electric / gas fire

stufare <1a> GASTR stew; fig bore

stufarsi get bored (**di** with)

stufato m stew

stufo: essere ~ di qc be bored with sth

stuolo m host

stupefacente 1 agg amazing, stupefying **2** m narcotic

stupefatto amazed, stupefied

stupendo stupendous

stupidaggine f stupidity; **è una ~**

(cosa senza importanza) it's nothing

stupidità f stupidity

stupido 1 agg stupid **2** m, **-a** f idiot

stupire <4d> **1** v/t amaze **2** v/i e **stupirsi** be amazed

stupore m amazement

stuprare <1a> rape

stupratore m rapist

stupro m rape

sturare <1a> clear, unblock

stuzzicadenti m inv toothpick

stuzzicare <1l & d> tease; **~ l'appetito** whet the appetite

su 1 prp on; argomento about; (circa) (round) about; **sul tavolo** on the table; **sul mare** by the sea; **sulle tremila lire** round about three thousand lire; **~ misura** made to measure; **nove volte ~ dieci** nine times out of ten **2** avv up; (al piano di sopra) upstairs; **~!** come on!; **avere ~** vestito have on; **guardare in ~** look up

sub m/f inv skin diver

subacqueo 1 agg underwater **2** m, **-a** f skin diver

subaffittare <1a> sublet

subaffitto m sublet

subdolo underhand

subentrare <1a>: **~ a qu** replace s.o., take s.o.'s place

subire <4d> danni, perdita suffer

subito immediately

subordinare <1m> subordinate

suburbano suburban

succedere <3a o 3l> (accadere) happen; **~ a** in carica succeed; **che succede?** what's going on?

successione f succession

successivo successive

successo 1 pp → **succedere 2** m success; **di ~** successful

successore m successor

succhiare <1k> suck

succo m (pl -cchi) juice; **~ d'arancia** orange juice

succoso juicy

succursale f branch

sud m south; **~ ovest** south-west; **~ est** south-east; **al ~ di** (to the) south of sudare <1a> perspire, sweat

sudata *f* perspiration, sweat

sudato sweaty

suddividere <3q> subdivide

suddivisione *f* subdivision

sudicio (*pl* -ci) **1** *agg* dirty **2** *m* dirt

sudiciume *m* dirt

sudore *m* perspiration, sweat

sufficiente sufficient

sufficienza *f* sufficiency; *a* ~ enough

suffragio *m* (*pl* -gi) suffrage; ~ *universale* universal suffrage

suggerimento *m* suggestion

suggerire <4d> suggest; TEA prompt

suggeritore *m* TEA prompter

suggestionare <1a> influence

suggestione *f* influence

suggestivo picturesque

sughero *m* cork

sugli *prp* **su** and *art* **gli**

sugo *m* (*pl* -ghi) sauce; *di arrosto* juice; *al* ~ with sauce

sui *prp* **su** and *art* **i**

suicida *m/f* suicide (victim)

suicidarsi <1a> commit suicide, kill o.s.

suicidio *m* (*pl* -di) suicide

suino pork *attr*

sul *prp* **su** and *art* **il**

sull', sulla, sulle, sullo *prp* **su** and *art* **l', la, le, lo**

suo **1** *agg* his; *di cosa* its; *-a f* her; *di cosa* its; *il* ~ *maestro* his teacher; *i suoi amici* his friends; *questo libro è* ~ this is his book; *Suo* your **2** *pron*: *il* ~ his; *di cosa* its; *la -a f* hers; *di cosa* its

suocera *f* mother-in-law

suocero *m* father-in-law; *-i pl* mother- and father-in-law, in-laws F

suola *f* sole

suolo *m* ground; (*terreno*) soil

suonare <1o> **1** *v/t* play; *campanello* ring **2** *v/i* play; *alla porta* ring

suono *m* sound

suora *f* REL nun

super *f* inv F 4-star

superare <1l> go past; *fig* overcome; *esame* pass

superato out of date

superbia *f* haughtiness

superbo haughty

superficiale superficial

superficie *f* surface; *in* ~ on the surface

superfluo superfluous

superiora *f* Mother Superior

superiore **1** *agg* top; *qualità* superior; ~ *alla media* better than average **2** *m* superior

superiorità *f* superiority

superlativo *m/agg* superlative

supermarket *m inv*, **supermercato** *m* supermarket

superstite **1** *agg* surviving **2** *m/f* survivor

superstizione *f* superstition

superstizioso superstitious

superstrada *f* motorway, *Am* highway (*with no tolls*)

superuomo *m* (*pl* -uomini) superman

suppergiù about

supplementare additional, supplementary

supplemento *m* supplement; ~ *intercity* intercity supplement; FERR *fare il* ~ pay a supplement

supplente *m/f* replacement; EDU supply teacher

supplenza *f* supply teaching

supplicare <1l & d> beg

supplizio *m* (*pl* -zi) torture

suppongo → **supporre**

supporre <3ll> suppose

supporto *m* TEC support; INFOR ~ *dati* data support

supposizione *f* supposition

supposta *f* MED suppository

supposto *pp* → **supporre**

suppurare <1a> MED suppurate

suppurazione *f* suppuration

supremazia *f* supremacy

supremo supreme

surf *m inv* surfboard; *fare* ~ surf, go surfing

surfista *m/f* (*mpl* -i) surfer

surgelare <1b> freeze

surgelato **1** *agg* frozen **2** *m*: *-i pl* frozen food *sg*

surriscaldare <1a> overheat

surrogato *m* substitute

S

suscettibile touchy; *è ~ di miglioramento* it's likely to improve
suscettibilità *f* touchiness
suscitare <1l> arouse
susina *f* plum
susino *m* plum (tree)
sussidio *m* (*pl* -di) grant, allowance; *~ di disoccupazione* unemployment benefit
sussultare <1a> start, jump
sussulto *m* start, jump
sussurrare <1a> *v/t & v/i* whisper
sussurro *m* whisper
sutura *f* MED stitches *pl*
svagarsi <1e> take one's mind off things
svago *m* (*pl* -ghi) distraction; *per ~* to take one's mind off things
svaligiare <1f> burgle, *Am* burglarize
svalutare <1a> devalue
svalutazione *f* devaluation
svanire <4d> vanish
svantaggio *m* (*pl* -ggi) disadvantage
svantaggioso disadvantageous
svariato varied
svedese 1 *m/agg* Swedish **2** *m/f* Swede
sveglia *f* alarm clock
svegliare <1g> waken (up)
svegliarsi waken up
sveglio awake; *fig* alert
svelare <1a> *segreto* reveal
svelto quick; *alla -a* quickly
svendere <3a> sell at a reduced price
svendita *f* clearance

svenimento *m* fainting fit
svenire <4p> faint
sventolare <1l & b> *v/t & v/i* wave
sventura *f* misfortune
sventurato unfortunate
svenuto *pp* → **svenire**
svergognato shameless
svernare <1b> spend the winter in
svestire <4b> undress
svestirsi get undressed, undress
Svezia *f* Sweden
sviare <1h> deflect; *fig* divert
svignarsela <1a> slip away
sviluppare <1a> develop
svilupparsi develop
sviluppato developed
sviluppo *m* development
svincolo *m* di strada junction
svista *f* oversight; *per ~* by some oversight
svitare <1a> unscrew
svitato unscrewed; *fig* essere *~* have a screw loose
Svizzera *f* Switzerland
svizzero 1 *agg* Swiss **2** *m*, **-a** *f* Swiss
svogliatezza *f* laziness
svogliato lazy
svolazzare <1a> flutter
svolgere <3d> *rotolo* unwrap; *tema* develop; *attività* carry out
svolgersi happen; *di film* be set
svolgimento *m* course; *di tema* development
svolta *f* turning; *fig* turning point
svoltare <1c>: *~ a destra* turn right
svolto *pp* → **svolgere**
svuotare <1c> empty

T

t *abbr* (= **tonnellata**) t (= tonne)
tabaccaio *m* (*pl* -ai), **-a** *f* tobacconist
tabaccheria *f* tobacconist's
tabacco *m* (*pl* -cchi) tobacco

tabagismo *m* smoking
tabella *f* table; *~ dei prezzi* price list; *fig ~ di marcia* schedule
tabellina *f* multiplication table

tabellone *m* board; *per avvisi* notice board; *~ pubblicitario* billboard

tabernacolo *m* tabernacle

tabù *m*/*agg inv* taboo

tabulato *m* printout

TAC *abbr* (= *Tomografia Assiale Computerizzata*) CAT (= computerized axial tomography)

taccagno mean, stingy F

taccheggio *m* shoplifting

tacchino *m* turkey

tacco *m* (*pl* -cchi) heel

taccuino *m* notebook

tacere <2k> **1** *v/t* keep quiet about, say nothing about **2** *v/i* not say anything, be silent

tachicardia *f* tachycardia

tachimetro *m* speedometer

tacitare <11> *scandalo* hush up

tacito tacit

taciturno taciturn

tafano *m* ZO horsefly

tafferuglio *m* (*pl* -gli) scuffle

taglia *f* (*misura*) size; *di ~ media* medium; *~ forte* outsize; *~ unica* one size

tagliacarte *m inv* paper-knife

tagliando *m* coupon; AUTO service; *fare il ~* have the vehicle serviced

tagliare <1g> cut; *albero* cut down; *legna* chop; *~ i capelli* have one's hair cut; *fig ~ la strada a qu* cut in front of s.o.

tagliarsi cut o.s.; *mi sono tagliata un dito* I've cut my finger

tagliatelle *fpl* tagliatelle *sg*

tagliente sharp

tagliere *m* chopping board

taglierini *mpl type of* noodles

taglio *m* (*pl* -gli) cut; *~ cesareo* C(a)esarean (section)

tailleur *m inv* suit

talco *m* (*pl* -chi) talc, talcum powder

tale such a; *-i pl* such; *~ e quale* just like; *un ~* someone; *il signor tal dei -i* Mr So-and-so

talento *m* talent

tallonare <1a> *persona* follow close behind; *nel rugby* heel

talloncino *m* coupon

tallone *m* heel

talmente so

talora sometimes

talpa *f* mole

talvolta sometimes

tamburo *m* drum

tamponamento *m* AUTO collision; *~ a catena* multi-vehicle pile-up

tamponare <1a> *falla* plug; AUTO collide with, crash into

tampone *m* MED swab; *per donne* tampon; *per timbri* (ink) pad; INFOR buffer

tana *f* den

tandem *m inv* tandem

tangente *f* MAT tangent; F (*percentuale illecita*) kickback F; F (*bustarella*) bribe; F (*pizzo*) protection money

tangenziale *f* ring road

tanica *f* container; MAR *per fuoribordo* tank

tanto 1 *agg* so much; *-i p*l so many; *-i saluti* best wishes; *-e grazie* thank you so much, many thanks **2** *pron* much; *-i pl* many **3** *avv* (*così*) so; *con verbi* so much; *di ~ in ~* from time to time; *~ quanto* as much as; *è da ~* (*tempo*) *che non lo vedo* I haven't seen him for a long time; *~ per cambiare* for a change

tappa *f* stop; *di viaggio* stage

tappare <1a> plug; *bottiglia* put the cork in

tapparella *f* rolling shutter

tappeto *m* carpet

tappezzare <1a> (*wall*)paper

tappezzeria *f di pareti* wallpaper; *di sedili* upholstery

tappo *m* cap, top; *di sughero* cork; *di lavandini, vasche* plug

tarare <1a> TEC calibrate

tarchiato stocky

tardare <1a> **1** *v/t* delay **2** *v/i* be late

tardi late; *più ~* later (on); *al più ~* at the latest; *a più ~!* see you!; *far ~* (*arrivare in ritardo*) be late; (*stare alzato*) stay up late; *in ufficio* work late

tardivo late; *fig* retarded, slow

tardo late

targa *f* (*pl* -ghe) nameplate; AUTO numberplate

targhetta f tag; *su porta* nameplate
tariffa f rate; *nei trasporti* fare; *doganale* tariff
tarlato worm-eaten
tarlo m woodworm
tarma f (clothes) moth
tartaro m tartar
tartaruga f (pl -ghe) *terrestre* tortoise; *aquatica* turtle
tartina f canapé
tartufo m truffle
tasca f (pl -che) pocket; *ne ho piene le -che* I'm fed up with this
tascabile 1 agg pocket attr **2** m paperback
tassa f tax; ~ *di circolazione* road tax; ~ *di soggiorno* visitor tax; *esente da* ~ tax free; *soggetto a* ~ subject to tax
tassametro m meter, clock F
tassare <1a> tax
tassello m *nel muro* plug
tassista m/f (mpl -i) taxi driver
tasso¹ m FIN rate; ~ *d'inflazione* inflation rate, rate of inflation; ~ *d'interesse* interest rate; ~ *di sconto* discount rate
tasso² m ZO badger
tasso³ m BOT yew
tastare <1a> feel; *fig ~ il terreno* test the water, see how the land lies
tastiera f keyboard
tastierista m/f (mpl -i) keyboarder
tasto m key; INFOR ~ *operativo* function key
tattica f (pl -che) tactics pl
tattico (pl -ci) tactical
tatto m (senso) touch; *fig* tact; *mancanza f di* ~ tactlessness, lack of tact
tatuaggio m (pl -ggi) tattoo
tatuare <1l> tattoo
taverna f country-style restaurant
tavola f table; (asse) plank, board; *in libro* plate; ~ *calda* snackbar; ~ *rotonda* round table; SP ~ *a vela* sailboard; *mettersi a* ~ sit down to eat; *a ~!* lunch/dinner is ready!, come and get it! F
tavoletta f: ~ *di cioccolata* bar of chocolate
tavolo m table

taxi m inv taxi
tazza f cup
tazzina f espresso cup
tbc, TBC abbr (= **tubercolosi**) TB (= tuberculosis)
TCI abbr (= **Touring Club Italiano**) Italian motoring organization
te you; ~ *l'ho venduto* I sold it to you
tè m tea; ~ *freddo* iced tea; *sala f da* ~ tearoom; *tazza f da* ~ teacup
teatrale theatre, Am theater; *fig* theatrical; *rappresentazione f* ~ play
teatro m theatre, Am theater; *fig* (luogo) scene; ~ *all'aperto* open air theatre (Am theater); ~ *lirico* opera (house)
tecnica f (pl -che) technique; (tecnologia) technology
tecnico (pl -ci) **1** agg technical **2** m technician
tecnologia f technology; *alta* ~ high technology, high tech F
tecnologico (pl -ci) technological
tedesco (pl -chi) **1** m/agg German **2** m, **-a** f German
tegame m (sauce)pan
teglia f baking tin
tegola f tile
teiera f teapot
tel. abbr (= **telefono**) tel (= telephone)
tela f cloth; PITT canvas; ~ *cerata* oilcloth
telaio m (pl -ai) loom; *di automobile* chassis; *di bicicletta, finestra* frame
telecamera f television camera
telecomando m remote control
telecomunicazioni fpl telecommunications, telecomms
telefax m inv fax
teleferica f (pl -che) cableway
telefilm m inv film made for television
telefonare <1m & b> (tele)phone, ring (*a qu* s.o.)
telefonata f (tele)phone call; ~ *interurbana* long-distance (phone) call; ~ *urbana* local call; *fare una* ~ *a qu* ring *or* phone s.o.
telefonico (pl -ci) (tele)phone attr
telefonista m/f (mpl -i) (switch-

board) operator

telefonino *m* mobile (phone), *Am* cell(ular) phone

telefono *m* (tele)phone; **~ a gettoni** *telephone that takes tokens*; **~ a scheda** (*magnetica*) cardphone; **~ a tastiera** push-button (tele)phone; **~ cellulare** cellphone, cellular (tele)phone; *dare un colpo di ~ a qu* give s.o. a ring

telegiornale *m* news *sg*

telegrafare <1m & b> telegraph

telegrafico (*pl* -ci) *stile* telegraphic; *risposta* very brief

telegrafo *m* telegraph

telegramma *m* (*pl* -i) telegram

teleguidato remote controlled

telelavoro *m* teleworking

teleobiettivo *m* telephoto lens

telepatia *f* telepathy

teleschermo *m* TV screen

telescopio *m* (*pl* -pi) telescope

teleselezione *f* STD

telespettatore *m*, **-trice** *f* TV viewer

televisione *f* television, TV; **~ via cavo** cable television or TV; **~ via satellite** satellite television or TV

televisivo television *attr*, TV *attr*

televisore *m* television (set), TV (set); **~ a colori** colo(u)r TV

telex *m inv* telex

telone *m* tarpaulin; TEA curtain

tema *m* theme, subject

temerario (*pl* -ri) reckless

temere <2a> be afraid *or* frightened of

temperamatite *m inv* pencil sharpener

temperamento *m* temperament

temperare <1l & b> *acciaio* temper; *matita* sharpen

temperato *acciaio* tempered; *matita* sharp; *clima* temperate

temperatura *f* temperature; **~ ambiente** room temperature

tempesta *f* storm

tempestoso stormy

tempia *f* temple

tempio *m* (*pl* -pli) temple

tempo *m* time; METEO weather; **~ libero** free time; *a ~ parziale* part-

time; *a ~ perso* in one's spare time; *a ~ pieno* full-time; SP *-i pl* **supplementari** extra time *sg*, *Am* overtime *sg*; *a ~, in ~* in time; *col ~* in time, eventually; *un ~* once, long ago; *per ~ (presto)* in good time; (*di buon'ora*) early; *non ho ~* I don't have (the) time; *lavora da molto ~* he has been working for a long time; *fa bel / brutto ~* the weather is lovely / nasty

temporale *m* thunderstorm

temporaneo temporary

tenace *materiali, sostanze* strong; *fig* tenacious

tenacia *f fig* tenacity

tenaglie *fpl* pincers *pl*

tenda *f* curtain; *da campeggio* tent

tendenza *f* tendency

tendere <3c> **1** *v/t molla, elastico, muscoli* stretch; *corde del violino* tighten; *mano* hold out, stretch out; *fig trappola* lay; **~ un braccio per fare qc** reach out to do sth; **~ le braccia a qu** hold one's arms out to s.o. **2** *v/i:* **~ a** (*aspirare a*) aim at; (*essere portati a*) tend to; (*avvicinarsi a*) verge on

tendina *f* net curtain

tendine *m* tendon

tenebre *fpl* darkness *sg*

tenente *m* lieutenant

tenere <2q> **1** *v/t* hold; (*conservare, mantenere*) keep; (*gestire*) run; *spazio* take up; *conferenza* give; **~ d'occhio** keep an eye on, watch **2** *v/i* hold (on); **~ a** (*dare importanza a*) care about; SP support

tenerezza *f* tenderness

tenero tender; *pietra, legno* soft

tenersi (*reggersi*) hold on (*a* to); (*mantenersi*) keep o.s.; **~ in piedi** stand (up)

tengo → **tenere**

tennis *m* tennis; **~ da tavolo** table tennis

tennista *m/f* (*mpl* -i) tennis player

tenore *m* MUS tenor; **~ di vita** standard of living

tensione *f* voltage; *fig* tension

tentare <1b> try, attempt; (*allettare*)

T

tempt; **~ tutto il possibile** do everything possible

tentativo *m* attempt

tentazione *f* temptation

tenue *colore* pale; *luce, speranza* faint

tenuta *f (capacità)* capacity; *(resistenza)* stamina; *(divisa)* uniform; *(abbigliamento)* outfit; AGR estate; **a ~ d'aria** airtight; AUTO **~ di strada** roadholding ability

teologia *f* theology

teologico (*pl* -ci) theological

teologo *m* (*pl* -gi), **-a** *f* theologian

teorema *m* (*pl* -i) theorem

teoria *f* theory

teorico (*pl* -ci) theoretical

tepore *m* warmth

teppista *m/f* (*pl* -i) hooligan

terapia *f* therapy

tergicristallo *m* AUTO windscreen (*Am* windshield) wiper

termale thermal; **stazione** *f* **~** spa; **stabilimento** *m* **~** baths *pl*

terme *fpl* baths

terminal *m inv* AVIA air terminal, terminal building

terminale 1 *agg* terminal; **stazione** *f* **~** terminus **2** *m* INFOR, EL terminal

terminare <11 & b> *v/t & v/i* end, finish, terminate

termine *m* end; *(confine)* limit; FIN *(scadenza)* deadline; *(parola)* term; **-i di consegna** terms of delivery; **~ tecnico** technical term; **a breve / lungo ~** in the short / long term; **in altri -i** in other words; **volgere al ~** come to an end

termocoperta *f* electric blanket

termometro *m* thermometer

termos *m inv* thermos®

termosifone *m* radiator

termostato *m* thermostat

terra *f* earth; *(regione, proprietà, terreno agricolo)* land; *(superficie del suolo)* ground; *(pavimento)* floor; **a ~** on the ground; AVIA, MAR **scendere a ~** get off; TEC **mettere a ~** earth; **cadere a o per ~** fall (down)

terracotta *f* (*pl* terrecotte) terracotta

terraferma *f* dry land, terra firma

terrapieno *m* embankment

terrazza *f*, **terrazzo** *m* balcony, terrace

terremoto *m* earthquake

terreno 1 *agg* earthly; *piano* ground, *Am* first **2** *m* *(superficie)* ground; *(suolo, materiale)* soil; *(appezzamento)* plot of land; *fig* *(settore, tema)* field, area; **perdere / guadagnare ~** lose / gain ground; **~ fabbricabile** land that may be built on

terrestre land *attr*, terrestrial; *della Terra* of the Earth; **globo** *m* **~** globe

terribile terrible

terrina *f* bowl

territoriale territorial

territorio *m* (*pl* -ri) territory

terrore *m* terror

terrorismo *m* terrorism

terrorista *m/f* (*mpl* -i) terrorist

terrorizzare <1a> terrorize

terza *f* AUTO third (gear)

terziario *m* (*pl* -ri) tertiary sector, services *pl*

terzino *m* SP back

terzo 1 *agg* third; **il ~ mondo** the Third World; **-a pagina** arts page **2** *m* third

teschio *m* (*pl* -chi) skull

tesi *f inv* ~ (**di laurea**) thesis

teso 1 *pp* → **tendere 2** *agg* taut; *fig* tense

tesoro *m* treasure; *(tesoreria)* treasury

tessera *f* card; **~ d'abbonamento** season ticket

tessile 1 *agg* textile **2** *-i mpl* textiles

tessuto *m* fabric, material; **~ di lana** wool; **-i** *pl* fabrics, material *sg*

test *m inv* test

testa *f* head; **a ~** each, a head; **alla ~ di** at the head of; **essere in ~** lead

testamento *m* will

testardaggine *f* stubbornness

testardo stubborn

testata *f* *(giornale)* newspaper; *di letto* headboard; AUTO cylinder head; **~ nucleare** nuclear warhead

teste *m/f* witness

testicolo *m* testicle

testimone *m/f* witness; **~ oculare**

eyewitness; **Testimoni** pl **di Geova** Jehovah's Witnesses

testimonianza f testimony; (*prova*) proof

testimoniare <1k & c> **1** v/i testify, give evidence **2** v/t fig testify to; DIR ~ **il falso** commit perjury

testo m text

tetano m tetanus

tetro gloomy

tetto m roof

tettoia f roof

Tevere m Tiber

TG abbr (= **Telegiornale**) TV news

thermos → **termos**

ti you; *riflessivo* yourself

tibia f shinbone, tibia

tic m inv di orologio tick; MED tic

ticchettio m di orologio ticking; di pioggia patter

ticket m inv MED charge

tiene → **tenere**

tiepido lukewarm, tepid; fig half-hearted, lukewarm

tifo m MED typhus; fig **fare il ~ per una squadra** be a fan or supporter of a team

tifoso m, **-a** f fan, supporter

tiglio m (pl -gli) lime tree

tigre f tiger

timbrare <1a> stamp

timbro m stamp; MUS timbre; ~ **postale** postage stamp

timidezza f shyness, timidity

timido shy, timid

timo m BOT thyme

timone m MAR, AVIA rudder; fig helm

timoniere m helmsman

timore m fear

timoroso timorous

timpano m MUS kettledrum; ANAT eardrum

tingere <3d> dye

tinta f (colorante) dye; (colore) colo(u)r

tintarella f (sun)tan

tinto pp → **tingere**

tintoria f dry-cleaner's

tintura f dyeing; (colorante) dye; ~ **di iodio** iodine

tipico (pl -ci) typical

tipo m sort, kind, type; F fig guy

tipografia f printing; stabilimento printer's

tipografo m printer

tipografico typographical

tir m heavy goods vehicle, HGV

tiranneggiare <1f> tyrannize

tirannia f tyranny

tiranno 1 agg tyrannical **2** m tyrant

tirare <1a> **1** v/t pull; (tendere) stretch; (lanciare) throw; (sparare) fire; (tracciare) draw; ~ **fuori** take out; ~ **su** da terra pick up; bambino bring up; ~ **giù** take down **2** v/i pull; di abito be too tight; di vento blow; (sparare) shoot; ~ **avanti** (arrangiarsi) get by, manage; (continuare) keep going; ~ **dritto** go straight on; ~ **a sorte** draw lots

tirarsi: ~ **indietro** back off; fig back out

tiratore m, **-trice** f shot

tiratura f di libro print run; di giornale circulation

tirchio (pl -chi) **1** agg mean, stingy F **2** m, **-a** f miser, skinflint F

tiro m (lancio) throw; (sparo) shot; ~ **con l'arco** archery; fig **un brutto ~** a nasty trick; **essere a ~** be within range

tirocinante m/f trainee

tirocinio m (pl -ni) training

tiroide f thyroid

tirolese agg, m/f Tyrolean, Tyrolese

Tirolo m Tyrol

tisana f herbal tea, tisane

titolare m/f owner

titolo m title; dei giornali headline; FIN security; ~ **a reddito fisso** fixed income security; ~ **di** as; ~ **di studio** qualification

titubare <1l> hesitate

tizio m, **-a** f: **un ~** somebody, some man; **una -a** somebody, some woman

toccare <1d> **1** v/t touch; (riguardare) concern, be about **2** v/i happen (a to); **gli tocca metà dell'eredità** half the estate is going to him; **tocca a me** it's my turn; **mi tocca partire** I must go, I have to go

tocco m (pl -cchi) touch
togliere <3ss> take (away), remove; (eliminare) take off; (tirare fuori) take out, remove; (revocare) lift, raise; dente take out, extract; ~ **di mezzo** get rid of; **ciò non toglie che** the fact remains that
togliersi giacca take off, remove; (spostarsi) take o.s. off; ~ **dai piedi** get out of the way
tolgo → **togliere**
tollerante tolerant
tolleranza f tolerance
tollerare <1l & c> tolerate
tolto pp → **togliere**
tomba f grave
tombola f bingo
tomografia f MED tomography; ~ **assiale computerizzata** computerized axial tomography
tonaca f (pl -che) habit
tonalità f inv tonality
tondeggiante roundish
tondo round; (grassoccio) plump; **chiaro e ~** quite clearly
tonfo m in acqua splash
tonico m (pl -ci) tonic
tonificare <1m & d> tone up
tonnellata f tonne
tonno m tuna
tono m tone; **rispondere a ~** (a proposito) answer to the point; per le rime answer back
tonsille fpl ANAT tonsils
tonsillite f tonsillitis
topazio m (pl -zi) topaz
topo m mouse
topografia f topography
Topolino m Mickey Mouse
toppa f (serratura) keyhole; (rattoppo) patch
torace m chest
torbido liquid cloudy
torcere <3d> twist; biancheria wring
torchio m (pl -chi) press
torcia f (pl -ce) f torch
torcicollo m stiff neck
tordo m thrush
torinese of Turin
Torino f Turin
tormenta f snowstorm

tormentare <1a> torment
tormentarsi torment o.s.
tormento m torment
tornaconto m benefit
tornante m hairpin bend
tornare <1a> venire come back, return; andare go back, return; (quadrare) balance; ~ **utile** prove useful; ~ **a fare / dire qc** do / say sth again; **ben tornato!** welcome back!; ~ **in sé** come to one's senses
torneo m tournament; **Torneo delle Sei Nazioni** Six Nations Cup
tornio m (pl -ni) lathe
toro m bull; ASTR **Toro** Taurus
torpedine f ZO electric ray
torpore m torpor
torre f tower
torrefare <3aa> roast
torrefazione f roasting
torreggiare <1f> tower (su over)
torrente m stream
torrido torrid
torrone m nougat
torsione f twisting; TEC torsion
torso m torso
torsolo m core
torta f cake
tortellini mpl tortellini sg
torto m wrong; **aver ~** be wrong; **a ~** wrongly
tortora f turtledove
tortuoso (sinuoso) winding; (ambiguo) devious
tortura f torture
torturare <1a> torture
torvo sguardo dark, black
tosaerba f e m lawnmower
tosare <1a> pecore shear
Toscana f Tuscany
toscano Tuscan
tosse f cough; ~ **canina** whooping cough; **aver la ~** have a cough
tossico (pl -ci) **1** agg toxic **2** m, **-a** f F druggie F
tossicodipendente m/f drug addict
tossicodipendenza f drug addiction
tossicomane m/f drug addict
tossire <4a & d> cough
tostapane m toaster

tostare <1c> *pane* toast; *caffè* roast
tot 1 *agg* so many **2** *pron* so much
totale *m/agg* total
totalità *f* (*interezza*) entirety, totality; **nella ~ dei casi** in all cases
totip *m* competition similar to football pools, based on horse racing
totocalcio *m* competition similar to football pools
tovaglia *f* tablecloth
tovagliolo *m* napkin, serviette
tozzo 1 *agg* stocky **2** *m di pane* crust
tra → **fra**
traballare <1a> stagger; *mobile* wobble
traboccare <1d> overflow (*anche fig*)
traccia *f* (*pl* -cce) (*orma*) footprint; *di veicolo* track; (*indizio*) clue; (*segno*) trace; (*abbozzo*) sketch
tracciare <1f> *linea* draw; (*delineare*) outline; (*abbozzare*) sketch
trachea *f* windpipe
tracolla *f* (shoulder) strap; **a ~** slung over one's shoulder; **borsa f a ~** shoulder bag
tracollo *m* collapse
tradimento *m* betrayal; POL treason; **a ~** treacherously
tradire <4d> betray; *coniuge* be unfaithful to
tradirsi give o.s. away
traditore 1 *agg* (*infedele*) unfaithful **2** *m*, **-trice** *f* traitor
tradizionale traditional
tradizione *f* tradition
tradotto *pp* → **tradurre**
tradurre <3e> translate; **~ in inglese** translate into English
traduttore *m*, **-trice** *f* translator
traduzione *f* translation
trafficante *m/f spreg* dealer; **~ di droga** drug dealer
trafficare <1l & d> deal, trade (**in** in); *spreg* traffic (**in** in); (*armeggiare*) tinker; (*affaccendarsi*) bustle about
traffico *m* (*pl* -chi e -ci) traffic; **~ aereo** air traffic; **~ stradale** road traffic; **densità f del ~** volume of traffic
traforo *m* tunnel

tragedia *f* tragedy
traghettare <1a> ferry
traghetto *m* ferry
tragico (*pl* -ci) tragic
tragitto *m* journey
traguardo *m* finishing line
traiettoria *f* trajectory
trainare <1l> (*rimorchiare*) tow; *di animali* pull, draw
traino *m* towing; *veicolo* vehicle on tow; **a ~** on tow
tralasciare <1f> (*omettere*) omit, leave out; (*interrompere*) interrupt
traliccio *m* (*pl* -cci) EL pylon; TEC trellis
tram *m inv* tram
trama *f fig* plot
tramandare <1a> hand down
tramare <1a> *fig* plot
trambusto *m* (*confusione*) bustle; (*tumulto*) uproar, commotion
tramezzino *m* sandwich
tramezzo *m* partition
tramite 1 *m* (*collegamento*) link; (*intermediario*) go-between **2** *prep* through
tramontana *f* north wind
tramontare <1a> set
tramonto *m* sunset; *fig* decline
trampolino *m* diving board; SCI ski jump
tranello *m* trap
tranne except
tranquillante *m* tranquil(l)izer
tranquillità *f* peacefulness, tranquillity
tranquillizzare <1a>: **~ qu** set s.o.'s mind at rest
tranquillo calm, peaceful
transatlantico (*pl* -ci) **1** *agg* transatlantic **2** *m* liner
transazione *f* DIR settlement; FIN transaction
transenna *f* barrier
transistor *m inv* transistor
transitabile *strada* passable
transitare <1l> pass
transitivo GRAM transitive
transito *m* transit; **divieto di ~** no thoroughfare
transitorio (*pl* -ri) transitory

transizione f transition

transoceanico (pl -ci) ocean attr

trantran m F routine

tranviere m (manovratore) tram driver; (controllore) tram conductor

trapanare <1l> drill

trapano m drill; **~ a percussione** percussion drill

trapezio m (pl -zi) trapeze; MAT trapezium

trapezista m/f (mpl -i) trapeze artist

trapiantare <1a> transplant

trapianto m transplant

trappola f trap

trapunta f quilt

trarre <3xx> conclusioni draw; vantaggio derive; **tratto da un libro di** taken from a book by

trasalire <4m> jump

trasandato scruffy; lavoro slipshod

trasbordare <1a> transfer

trasbordo m transfer

trascinare <1a> drag; (travolgere) sweep away; fig (entusiasmare) carry away

trascorrere <3o> **1** v/t spend **2** v/i pass, go by

trascorso pp → trascorrere

trascrivere <3tt> transcribe

trascrizione f transcription

trascurabile unimportant

trascurare <1a> neglect; (tralasciare) ignore; **~ di fare qc** fail to do sth

trascuratezza f negligence

trascurato careless, negligent; (trasandato) slovenly; (ignorato) neglected

trasferibile transferable

trasferimento m transfer

trasferire <4d> transfer

trasferirsi move

trasferta f transfer; SP away game

trasformare <1a> transform; TEC process; nel rugby convert

trasformarsi change, turn (**in** into)

trasformatore m transformer

trasformazione f transformation

trasfusione f transfusion

trasgredire <4d> disobey

trasgressione f disobedience

trasgressore m transgressor

traslocare <1c & d> v/t & v/i move

trasloco m (pl -chi) move

trasmettere <3ee> pass on; RAD, TV broadcast, transmit; DIR diritti transfer

trasmissibile transmissible

trasmissione f transmission; RAD, TV broadcast, transmission; (programma) programme, Am program; RAD, TV **~ in diretta** live broadcast; INFOR **~ dati** data transmission

trasognato dreamy

trasparente 1 agg transparent **2** m transparency

trasparenza f transparency

trasportare <1c> transport

trasporto m transport; **~ combinato rotaia-strada** piggyback transport; **-i pubblici** public transport sg

trasversale 1 agg transverse **2** f MAT transversal

tratta f trade; FIN draft

trattamento m treatment

trattare <1a> **1** v/t treat; TEC treat, process; FIN deal in; (negoziare) negotiate **2** v/i deal; **~ di** be about; FIN **~ in** deal in

trattarsi: di che si tratta? what's it about?

trattative fpl negotiations, talks

trattato m treatise; DIR, POL treaty; **~ di pace** peace treaty

trattenere <2q> (far restare) keep, hold; (far perder tempo) hold up; (frenare) restrain; fiato, respiro hold; lacrime hold back; somma withhold

trattenersi (rimanere) stay; (frenarsi) restrain o.s.; **~ dal fare qc** refrain from doing sth

trattenuta f deduction

trattino m dash; in parole composte hyphen

tratto 1 pp → trarre **2** m di spazio, tempo stretch; di penna stroke; (linea) line; **a un ~** all of a sudden; **-i** pl (lineamenti) features; **a -i** at intervals

trattore m tractor

trattoria f restaurant

trauma m (pl -i) trauma

traumatico (*pl* -ci) traumatic

travaglio *m*: MED ~ *di parto* labo(u)r

travasare <1a> decant

trave *f* beam

traversa *f* crossbeam

traversare <1b> cross

traversata *f* crossing

traverso: *flauto m* ~ flute; *andare di ~ di cibi* go down the wrong way; *per vie -e* by devious means

travestimento *m* disguise

travestire <4b> disguise

travestirsi disguise o.s., dress up (*da* as)

travestito *m* transvestite

travolgere <3d> carry away (*anche fig*); *con un veicolo* run over

travolto *pp* → *travolgere*

trazione *f* TEC traction; AUTO ~ *anteriore/posteriore* front-/rear-wheel drive

tre three

trebbiare <1k> AGR thresh

treccia *f* (*pl* -cce) plait

trecento 1 *agg* three hundred 2 *m*: *il Trecento* the fourteenth century

tredicesimo *m/agg* thirteenth

tredici thirteen

tregua *f* truce; *fig* break, let-up

trekking *m* hiking

tremante trembling, shaking

tremare <1b> tremble, shake (*di*, *per* with)

tremendo terrible, tremendous

tremila three thousand

treno *m* train; ~ *intercity* intercity train; ~ *merci* goods train; *in* ~ by train

trenta thirty

trentenne *agg*, *m/f* thirty-year-old

trentesimo *m/agg* thirtieth

trentina: *una* ~ about thirty; *essere sulla* ~ be about thirty, be in one's thirties

treppiedi *m inv* tripod

treruote *m inv* three-wheeler

triangolare triangular

triangolo *m* triangle; AUTO warning triangle

tribù *f inv* tribe

tribuna *f* platform

tribunale *m* court; ~ *per i minorenni* juvenile court

tributario (*pl* -ri) tax

tributo *m* tax; *fig* tribute

tricheco *m* (*pl* -chi) walrus

triciclo *m* tricycle

tricolore 1 *agg* tricolo(u)r(ed) 2 *m* tricolo(u)r

triennale *contratto*, *progetto* three-year; *mostra*, *festival* three-yearly

triennio *m* (*pl* -nni) three-year period

triestino of Trieste

trifoglio *m* (*pl* -gli) clover

triglia *f* red mullet

trilaterale trilateral

trillare <1a> trill

trillo *m* trill

trim. *abbr* (= *trimestre*) term

trimestrale quarterly

trimestre *m* quarter; EDU term

trincea *f* trench

trincerare <1b> entrench

trincerarsi entrench o.s.

trinchetto *m* foremast

trinciare <1f> cut up, chop

Trinità *f* Trinity

trio *m* trio

trionfare <1a> triumph (*su* over)

trionfo *m* triumph

triplicare <1l & d> triple

triplice triple

triplo 1 *agg* triple 2 *m*: *il* ~ three times as much (*di* as)

trippa *f* tripe

triste sad

tristezza *f* sadness

tritacarne *m inv* mincer

tritare <1a> mince

tritatutto *m inv* mincer

trito minced; *fig* ~ *e ritrito* rehashed

trittico *m* (*pl* -ci) triptych

triturare <1a> grind

trivellare <1b> drill

trivella *f* drill

triviale trivial

trofeo *m* trophy

tromba *f* MUS trumpet; AUTO horn; ~ *d'aria* whirlwind; ~ *delle scale* stairwell

trombone *m* trombone

trombosi f thrombosis

troncare <1d> cut off; fig break off

tronchese m wire cutters pl

tronco m (pl -chi) ANAT, BOT trunk; FERR section; **licenziare in ~** fire on the spot or there and then

trono m throne

tropicale tropical

tropici mpl tropics

troppo 1 agg too much; **-i** pl too many 2 avv too much; **non ~** not too much; **è ~ tardi** it's too late

trota f trout

trottare <1c> trot

trotto m trot

trottola f (spinning) top

trovare <1c> find; (inventare) find, come up with; **andare a ~ qu** (go and) see s.o.

trovarsi be; **~ bene** be happy

trovata f good idea

truccare <1d> make up; motore soup up; partita, elezioni fix

truccarsi put on one's make-up

truccatore m, **-trice** f make-up artist

trucco m (pl -cchi) make-up; (inganno, astuzia) trick

truce fierce; (crudele) cruel

truffa f fraud

truffare <1a> defraud (**di** of)

truffatore m, **-trice** f trickster, con artist F

truppa f troops pl; fig horde

tu you; **dammi del tu** call me 'tu'; **sei ~?** is that you?

tuba f tuba

tubatura f, **tubazione** f pipes pl, piping

tubercolosi f tuberculosis

tubero m tuber

tubetto m tube

tubo m pipe; flessibile hose; AUTO **~ di scappamento** exhaust (pipe); **~ fluorescente** fluorescent light

tuffare <1a> dip

tuffarsi (immergersi) dive; (buttarsi dentro) throw o.s. (anche fig)

tuffo m dip; SP dive

tugurio m (pl -ri) hovel

tulipano m tulip

tumore m tumo(u)r

tumulto m riot

tumultuoso tumultuous

tunica f (pl -che) tunic

Tunisia f Tunisia

tunisino 1 agg Tunisian 2 m, **-a** f Tunisian

tunnel m inv tunnel; **~ dell'orrore** ghost train

tuo (pl tuoi) 1 agg your; **il ~ amico** your friend; **un ~ amico** a friend of yours 2 pron: **il ~** yours

tuonare <1c> thunder

tuono m thunder

tuorlo m yolk

turare <1a> stop; bottiglia put the top on

turbamento m perturbation

turbante m turban

turbare <1a> upset, disturb

turbina f turbine

turbine m whirlwind

turbolenza f turbulence

turboreattore m turbojet

turchese m/agg turquoise

Turchia f Turkey

turco (pl -chi) 1 m/agg Turkish 2 m, **-a** f Turk

turismo m tourism; **~ di massa** mass tourism

turista m/f (mpl -i) tourist

turistico (pl -ci) tourist; **assegno** m **~ turistico** traveller's cheque, Am traveler's check

turno m turn; di lavoro shift; **a ~** in turn; **di ~** on duty; **è il mio ~** it's my turn; **~ di riposo** rest day; **darsi il ~** take turns

tuta f da lavoro boiler suit, overalls; **~ da ginnastica** track suit; **~ da sci** salopettes

tutela f protection; DIR guardianship

tutelare <1b> protect

tutore m, **-trice** f guardian

tuttavia still

tutto 1 agg whole; **-i, -e** pl all; **~ il libro** the whole book; **-i i giorni** every day; **-i e tre** all three; **noi -i** all of us 2 avv all; **era ~ solo** he was all alone; **del ~** quite; **in ~** altogether, in all 3 pron all; gente everybody, everyone; cose everything; **lo ha**

mangiato ~ he ate it all
tuttora still

TV *abbr* (= **televisione**) TV (= television)

U

ubbidiente obedient
ubbidienza *f* obedience
ubbidire <4d> obey; ~ **ai genitori** obey one's parents
ubriacare <1d>: ~ **qu** get s.o. drunk
ubriacarsi get drunk
ubriachezza *f* drunkenness
ubriaco (*pl* -chi) **1** *agg* drunk **2** *m*, **-a** *f* drunk
uccello *m* bird; ~ **rapace** bird of prey
uccidere <3q> kill
uccidersi kill o.s.
ucciso *pp* → **uccidere**
uccisione *f* killing
udienza *f* (audience) audience; DIR hearing
udire <4n> hear
udito *m* hearing
uditorio *m* (*pl* -ri) audience
Ue *abbr* (= **Unione europea**) EU (= European Union)
Uem *abbr* (= **Unione economica e monetaria europea**) EMU (= Economic and Monetary Union)
ufficiale **1** *agg* official; **non** ~ unofficial **2** *m* official; MIL officer
ufficio *m* (*pl* -ci) office; ~ **cambi** bureau de change; ~ **oggetti smarriti** lost property; ~ **postale** post office; ~ **stampa** press office; ~ **di collocamento** Jobcentre; ~ **turistico** tourist information office
ufficioso unofficial
ufo¹ *m*: **a** ~ at other people's expense, free (of charge)
ufo² *m* UFO
uguaglianza *f* equality
uguagliare <1g> make equal; (*livellare*) level; (*essere pari a*) equal
uguale equal; *lo stesso* the same;

terreno level
UIL *abbr* (= **Unione Italiana del Lavoro**) Italian trade union organization
ulcera *f* ulcer; ~ **gastrica** gastric ulcer
ulteriore further
ultimamente recently
ultimare <1l> complete
ultimatum *m inv* ultimatum
ultimo **1** *agg* last; *più recente* latest; ~ **piano** top floor **2** *m*, **-a** *f* last; *fino all'*- till the end
ultracorto: **onde** *fpl* **-e** ultrashort waves
ultrasuono *m* ultrasound
ultravioletto ultraviolet
ululare <1l> howl
ululato *m* howl
umanità *f* humanity
umanitario (*pl* -ri) humanitarian
umano human; *trattamento ecc* humane
Ume *abbr* (= **unione monetaria (europea)**) EMU (= European Monetary Union)
umidificatore *m* humidifier
umidità *f* dampness
umido **1** *agg* damp **2** *m* dampness; GASTR **in** ~ stewed
umile (*modesto*) humble; *mestiere* menial
umiliante humiliating
umiliare <1g> humiliate
umiliazione *f* humiliation
umiltà *f* humility
umore *m* mood; **di buon** ~ in a good mood; **di cattivo** ~ in a bad mood
umorismo *m* humo(u)r
umorista *m/f* (*mpl* -i) humorist

un, una → uno
unanime unanimous
unanimità f unanimity; all'~ unanimously
uncinetto m crochet hook; lavorare all'~ crochet
uncino m hook
undicesimo m/agg eleventh
undici eleven
ungere <3d> grease
ungherese agg, m/f Hungarian
Ungheria f Hungary
unghia f nail
unguento m ointment, cream
unico (pl -ci) only; (senza uguali) unique; moneta f single currency
unifamiliare: casa f ~ detached house
unificare <1m & d> unify
unificazione f unification
uniformare <1a> standardize
uniformarsi: ~ a conform to; regole, direttive comply with
uniforme f/agg uniform
uniformità f uniformity
unione f union; fig unity; Unione economica e monetaria Economic and Monetary Union; Unione europea European Union; Unione monetaria (europea) (European) Monetary Union
unire <4d> unite; congiungere join
unirsi unite; ~ in matrimonio marry
unità f inv unit; ~ monetaria monetary unit; ~ di misura unit of measurement; INFOR ~ a dischi flessibili disk drive; ~ pl periferiche peripherals
unito united
universale universal
università f inv university
universitario (pl -ri) 1 agg university attr 2 m, -a f university student; (professore) university lecturer
universo m universe
uno 1 art a; before a vowel or silent h an; un' uovo an egg 2 agg a, one 3 m one; ~ e mezzo one and a half 4 pron one; a ~ a ~ one by one; l'~ dopo l'altro one after the other; l'un l'altro each other, one another

unto 1 pp → ungere 2 agg greasy 3 m grease
unzione f: estrema ~ last rites
uomo m (pl uomini) man; ~ d'affari businessman; ~ di fiducia right-hand man; ~ qualunque man in the street; da ~ abbigliamento ecc for men, men's
uovo m (pl le -a) egg; ~ alla coque soft-boiled egg; ~ di Pasqua Easter egg; ~ al tegame fried egg; -a pl strapazzate scrambled eggs
uragano m hurricane
uranio m uranium
urbanistica f town planning
urbano urban; fig urbane
uretra f urethra
urgente urgent
urgenza f urgency; in caso d'~ in an emergency
urina f urine
urlare <1a> scream
urlo m (pl anche le -a) scream
urna f urn; elettorale ballot box
urologo m (pl -gi), -a f urologist
urrà! hooray!
urtare <1a> bump into, collide with; con un veicolo hit; fig offend; ~ i nervi a qu get on s.o.'s nerves
urto m bump; (scontro) collision
u.s. abbr (= ultimo scorso) last, ult.
USA abbr (= Stati uniti d'America) USA (= United States of America)
usa: ~ e getta disposable
usanza f custom, tradition
usare <1a> 1 v/t use 2 v/i use; (essere di moda) be in fashion
usato used; (di seconda mano) second-hand
uscire <4o> come out; (andare fuori) go out
uscita f exit, way out; INFOR output; ~ di sicurezza emergency exit; via d'~ way out
usignolo m nightingale
uso m use; (abitudine) custom; pronto per l'~ ready to use; fuori ~ out of use; ~ indebito misuse; per ~ interno for internal use; per ~ esterno not to be taken internally
US(S)L, Us(s)l abbr (= Unità

(*Socio-*)*sanitaria Locale*) local health authority

ustionarsi <1a> burn o.s.

ustione *f* burn

usuale usual

usufruire <4d>: ~ *di qc* have the use of sth

usura *f di denaro* illegal money lending; (*logorio*) wear and tear

usuraio *m* (*pl* -i) loan shark

utensile 1 *agg*: *macchina f* ~ machine tool **2** *m* utensil

utente *m/f* user; ~ *della strada* road user

utero *m* womb

utile 1 *agg* useful; *in tempo* ~ within the time limit **2** *m* FIN profit; *unire l'*~ *al dilettevole* combine business with pleasure; ~ *netto* net profit; ~ *d'esercizio* operating profit

utilità *f* usefulness

utilitaria *f* economy car

utilizzare <1a> use

utilizzazione *f* use

utopia *f* utopia

utopista *m/f* (*mpl* -i) dreamer

uva *f* grapes *pl*; ~ *passa* raisins *pl*; ~ *spina* gooseberry

---

V

V *abbr* (= *volt*) V (= volt)

V. *abbr* (= *via*) St (= street)

v. *abbr* (= *vedi*) see

va → *andare*

vacante vacant

vacanza *f* holiday; *-e pl estive* summer holiday(s); *andare in* ~ go on holiday

vacca *f* (*pl* -cche) cow

vaccinare <1a> vaccinate

vaccinazione *f* vaccination; ~ *antitetanica* tetanus injection *or* shot

vaccino *m* vaccine

vado → *andare*

vagabondare <1a> wander

vagabondo 1 *agg* (*girovago*) wandering; (*fannullone*) idle **2** *m*, *-a f* (*giramondo*) wanderer; (*fannullone*) idler, layabout F; (*barbone*) tramp

vagare <1e> wander (aimlessly)

vagina *f* ANAT vagina

vaglia *m inv*: ~ (*postale*) postal order; ~ *bancario* bill of exchange, draft

vago (*pl* -ghi) vague

vagone *m* carriage; ~ *letto* sleeper; ~ *merci* goods wagon; ~ *ristorante* dining car

vai → *andare*

vaiolo *m* smallpox

valanga *f* (*pl* -ghe) avalanche

valere <2r> be worth; (*essere valido*) be valid; *non vale nulla* it's worthless, it isn't worth anything; *far* ~ *diritti, autorità* assert; *non vale!* that's not fair!

valersi: ~ *di qc* avail o.s. of sth

valeriana *f* valerian

valevole valid

valgo → *valere*

valico *m* (*pl* -chi) pass

validità *f* validity

valido valid; *persona* fit; *non* ~ invalid

valigia *f* (*pl* -gie) suitcase; *fare le -e* pack

valle *f* valley

valore *m* value; (*coraggio*) bravery, valo(u)r; ~ *aggiunto* added value; ~ *commerciale* market value; ~ *corrente* current value; ~ *energetico* energy value; *-i pl* securities; *di* ~ valuable; *senza* ~ worthless

valorizzare <1a> increase the value of; (*far risaltare*) show off

V

valoroso courageous

valuta f currency; **stabilità f della ~** monetary stability

valutare <1a> value

valutario monetary

valutazione f valuation

valvola f valve; EL fuse; **~ dell'aria** air valve

valzer m inv waltz

vandalismo m vandalism

vandalo m vandal

vanga f (pl -ghe) spade

vangelo m gospel

vaniglia f vanilla

vanità f vanity

vanitoso vain

vanno → **andare**

vano 1 agg minacce, promesse empty; (inutile) vain 2 m (spazio vuoto) hollow; (stanza) room; AUTO **~ portaoggetti** glove compartment

vantaggio m (pl -ggi) advantage; **in gara** lead

vantaggioso advantageous

vantare <1a> speak highly of; possedere boast

vantarsi boast (**di** of)

vanto m boast

vapore m vapo(u)r; MAR steamer; **~ (d'acqua)** steam

vaporetto m water bus

vaporizzare <1a> (nebulizzare) spray

vaporoso floaty; (vago) woolly

variabile 1 agg changeable 2 f MAT variable

variare <1k> v/t & v/i vary

variazione f variation

varice f varicose vein

varicella f chickenpox

varietà 1 f inv variety 2 m inv variety, Am vaudeville; (**spettacolo m di**) ~ variety (Am vaudeville) show

vario (pl -ri) varied; **-ri** pl various

variopinto multicolo(u)red

vasca f (pl -che) (serbatoio, cisterna) tank; (lunghezza di piscina) length; di fontana basin; **~ (da bagno)** bath, (bath)tub

vaselina f vaseline

vasellame m dishes

vaso m pot; ANAT vessel

vassoio m (pl -oi) tray

vasto vast

V.d.F. abbr (= **vigili del fuoco**) fire brigade, Am fire department

ve = **vi** (before **lo, la, li, le, ne**)

vecchiaia f old age

vecchio (pl -cchi) 1 agg old 2 m, **-a** f old man; donna old woman

vece f: **in ~ di** instead of; **fare le -i di qu** take s.o.'s place

vedere <2s> see; **far ~** show; **stare a ~** watch

vedovo 1 agg widowed 2 m, **-a** f widower; donna widow

veduta f view (**su** of); **~ aerea** aerial view; fig **larghezza f di -e** broadmindedness

vegetale 1 agg vegetable attr; regno, vita plant attr 2 m plant

vegetare <1l & b> vegetate

vegetariano 1 agg vegetarian attr 2 m, **-a** f vegetarian

vegetazione f vegetation

vegeto vecchio spry; **vivo e ~** hale and hearty

veggente m/f (chiaroveggente) clairvoyant

veglia f (l'essere svegli) wakefulness; (il vegliare) vigil; **essere tra la ~ e il sonno** be half asleep

vegliare <1g> 1 v/i keep watch 2 v/t: **~ qu** watch over s.o.

veicolo m vehicle; **~ spaziale** spaceship

vela f sail; attività sailing; **fare ~** set sail; **tutto è andato a gonfie -e** everything went swimmingly

veleggiare <1f> sail

veleno m poison; di animali venom (anche fig)

velenoso poisonous; fig venomous

veliero m sailing ship

velina: **carta f ~ per imballaggio** tissue paper

velismo m sailing

velista m/f sailor

velivolo m aircraft

velluto m velvet; **~ a coste** corduroy

velo m veil

veloce fast, quick

velocemente quickly

velocità f inv speed; **limite** m **di ~** speed limit; **eccesso** m **di ~** speeding; **~ della luce** speed of light; **~ di crociera** cruising speed

velodromo m velodrome

vena f vein; **essere in ~** be in the mood

vendemmia f (grape) harvest

vendemmiare <1k> v/t v/i harvest

vendere <3a> sell; **~ all'ingrosso** sell wholesale; **~ al minuto** retail

vendetta f revenge

vendicare <1f & d> avenge

vendicarsi get one's revenge (**di qu** on s.o.; **di qc** for sth)

vendita f sale; **~ di fine stagione** end-of-season sale; **~ diretta** direct selling

venditore m, **-trice** f salesman; donna saleswoman

venerare <1l & b> revere

venerazione f veneration

venerdì m inv Friday; **Venerdì Santo** Good Friday

Venere f Venus

Venezia f Venice

veneziano 1 agg of Venice, Venetian 2 m, **-a** f Venetian

vengo → **venire**

venire <4p> come; (riuscire) turn out; come ausiliare be; **i suoi disegni vengono ammirati da tutti** his drawings are admired by all; **~ a costare** total, work out at; **~ a sapere** qc learn sth, find sth out; **~ al dunque** get to the point; **mi sta venendo fame** I'm getting hungry

ventaglio m (pl -gli) fan

ventenne agg, m/f twenty-year-old

ventesimo m/agg twentieth

venti twenty

ventilatore m fan

ventilazione f ventilation

ventina f: **una ~** about twenty

ventiquattrore f inv (valigetta) overnight bag

vento m wind; **c'è ~** it's windy

ventoso windy

ventre m stomach; **basso ~** lower abdomen

venturo next

venuta f arrival

venuto 1 pp → **venire** 2 m, **-a** f: **il primo ~** just anyone; **non è certo il primo ~** he's not just anyone

veramente really

veranda f veranda

verbale 1 agg verbal 2 m record; di riunione minutes pl

verbalizzare <1a> record (in writing), take down; riunione take the minutes of; (esprimere a parole) verbalize

verbalmente verbally

verbo m GRAM verb

verde 1 agg green; benzina unleaded; **numero ~** freephone number; **essere al ~** be broke 2 m green; POL **i -i** pl the Greens

verdetto m verdict

verdura f vegetables pl

vergine 1 agg virgin attr 2 f: virgin; ASTR **Vergine** Virgo

verginità f virginity

vergogna f shame; (timidezza) shyness

vergognarsi <1a> be ashamed; (essere timido) be shy

vergognoso ashamed; (timido) shy; azione shameful

verifica f (pl -che) check

verificare <1m & d> check

verificarsi (accadere) occur, take place; (avverarsi) come true

verità f truth

verme m worm; **~ solitario** tapeworm

vermut m vermouth

vernice f paint; trasparente varnish; pelle patent leather; fig veneer; **~ antiruggine** rust-proofing paint; **~ fresca** wet paint; **~ protettiva** protective coating

verniciare <1f> paint; con vernice trasparente varnish; **verniciato di fresco** wet paint

verniciatura f painting; con vernice trasparente varnishing; fig veneer

vero 1 agg (rispondente a verità) true; (autentico) real; **sei contento, ~?** you're happy, aren't you?; **ti piace il**

V

gelato, ~? you like icecream, don't you?; **fosse ~!** if only (it were true!) **2** *m* truth; PITT **dal ~** from life

veronese 1 *agg* of Verona **2** *m/f* inhabitant of Verona

verosimile likely

verruca *f* (*pl* -che) wart

versamento *m* payment; **ricevuta** *f* **di ~** receipt for payment

versante *m* slope

versare <1b> **1** *v/t vino* pour; *denaro* pay; (*rovesciare*) spill **2** *v/i* (*trovarsi, essere*) be

versione *f* version; (*traduzione*) translation; **in ~ originale** original language version

verso 1 *prp* towards; **andare ~ casa** head for home; **~ le otto** about eight o'clock **2** *m di poesie* verse; (*modo*) manner; **non c'è ~** there is no way

vertebra *f* vertebra

vertebrale: **colonna** *f* **~** spinal column

verticale 1 *agg* vertical **2** *f* vertical (line); *in ginnastica* handstand

vertice *m* summit; **incontro** *m* **al ~** summit (meeting)

vertigine *f* vertigo, dizziness; **ho le -i** I feel dizzy

vertiginoso *altezza* dizzy; *prezzi* staggering, sky-high; *velocità* breakneck

verza *f* savoy (cabbage)

vescica *f* (*pl* -che) ANAT bladder

vescovo *m* bishop

vespa *f* ZO wasp

vespaio *m* (*pl* -ai) wasps' nest; *fig* hornets' nest

vestaglia *f* dressing gown, *Am* robe

veste *f fig* (*capacità, funzione*) capacity; **in ~ ufficiale** in an offical capacity

vestiario *m* wardrobe

vestire <4b> dress; (*portare*) wear

vestirsi get dressed; *in un certo modo* dress; **~irsi da** (*travestirsi*) dress up as

vestito *m da uomo* suit; *da donna* dress; (*capo di vestiario*) item of clothing, garment; **-i** *pl* clothes; **-i** *pl* **da uomo** men's wear

veterinario *m* (*pl* -ri), **-a** *f* veterinary surgeon, vet F

veto *m* veto; **porre il ~ a** veto

vetraio *m* (*pl* -i), (*installatore*) glazier

vetrata *f finestra* large window; *porta* glass door; *di chiesa* stained-glass window

vetreria *f* (*fabbrica*) glass works; (*negozio*) glazier's

vetrina *f* (*shop*) window; *mobile* display cabinet; *di museo, fig* showcase

vetrinista *m/f* (*mpl* -i) window dresser

vetro *m* glass; *di finestra, porta* pane; **di ~** glass *attr*; **~ armato** reinforced glass; **~ smerigliato** frosted glass

vetta *f* top; *di montagna* peak

vettura *f* AUTO car; FERR carriage; **~ da corsa** racing car; **in ~!** all aboard!

vi 1 *pron* you; *riflessivo* yourselves; *reciproco* each other **2** *avv* → **ci**

via 1 *f* street, road; *fig* way; **~ Marconi** Marconi St; **lettera** *f* (**per**) **~ aerea** airmail letter; **Via lattea** Milky Way; **ricorrere alle -e legali** take legal action; **in ~ eccezionale** as an exception; **per ~ di** by; (*a causa di*) because of **2** *m* off, starting signal; SP **dare il ~** give the off; *fig* **dare il ~ a qc** get sth under way **3** *avv* away; **andar ~** go away, leave; **~ ~** (*gradualmente*) little by little, gradually; (*man mano*) as (and when); **e così ~** and so on; **~!** *per scacciare* go away!, scram! F; (*suvvia*) come on! **4** *prp* via, by way of

viabilità *f* road conditions *pl*; (*rete stradale*) road network; (*traffico stradale*) road traffic

viadotto *m* viaduct

viaggiare <1f> travel; **~ per affari** travel on business

viaggiatore *m*, **-trice** *f* travel(l)er

viaggio *m* (*pl* -ggi) journey; **~ aereo** flight; **~ per mare** voyage; **~ di nozze** honeymoon; **~ in comitiva** group travel; **~ in treno** train journey; **~ d'affari** business trip; **~ di studio** study trip; **cestino** *m* **da ~** packed meal; **mettersi in ~** set out;

essere in ~ be away, be travelling
viale *m* avenue
viavai *m inv* coming and going
vibrare <1a> vibrate
vibrazione *f* vibration
vice- *prefisso* vice-
vice *m/f inv* deputy
vicedirettore *m* assistant manager
vicenda *f* (*episodio*) event; (*storia*) story; *alterne ~e* changing fortunes; *a ~* (*a turno*) in turn; (*scambievolmente*) each other, one another
viceversa vice versa
vicinanza *f* nearness, proximity; *-e pl* neighbo(u)rhood *sg*, vicinity *sg*
vicinato *m* neighbo(u)rhood; (*persone*) neighbo(u)rs *pl*
vicino 1 *agg* near, close; *~ a* near, close to; (*accanto a*) next to; *da ~ esaminare* closely; *visto* close up 2 *avv* nearby, close by 3 *m*, *-a f* neighbo(u)r
vicolo *m* lane; *~ cieco* dead end
videata *f* INFOR display
video *m* video; F (*schermo*) screen
videocamera *f* videocamera
videocassetta *f* video (cassette)
videocontrollo *m* video surveillance
videogioco *m* video game
videoregistratore *m* video (recorder)
videoteca *f* video library; (*negozio*) video shop
videotel *m inv* Italian Videotex®
videotelefono *m* videophone, viewphone
vietare <1b> forbid; *~ a qu di fare qc* forbid s.o. to do sth
vietato: *~ fumare* no smoking
vigente in force
vigilante *m* security guard
vigilanza *f* vigilance; *sotto ~* under surveillance
vigilare <1l> *persone* watch (over); (*pattugliare*) patrol
vigile 1 *agg* watchful 2 *m/f*: *~ (urbano)* local police officer; *~ del fuoco* firefighter
vigilia *f* night before, eve; *~ di Natale* Christmas Eve
vigliacco (*pl* -cchi) 1 *agg* cowardly

2 *m*, *-a f* coward
vigna *f* (small) vineyard
vigneto *m* vineyard
vignetta *f* cartoon
vigore *m* vigo(u)r
vigoroso vigorous
vile 1 *agg* vile; (*codardo*) cowardly 2 *m* coward
villa *f* villa
villaggio *m* (*pl* -ggi) village; *~ turistico* holiday village
villeggiatura *f* holiday
villino *m* house
vincere <3d> 1 *v/t* win; *avversario, nemico* defeat, beat; *difficoltà* overcome 2 *v/i* win
vincersi (*dominarsi*) control o.s.
vincita *f* win
vincitore *m*, *-trice f* winner
vincolare <1l> bind; *capitale* tie up
vincolo *m* bond
vino *m* wine; *~ bianco* white wine; *~ rosso* red wine; *~ da pasto* table wine
vinto *pp* → **vincere**
viola *f* MUS viola; BOT violet; *~ del pensiero* pansy
violare <1l> violate; *legge* break
violazione *f* violation; *di leggi, patti, accordi* breach; *~ di domicilio* unlawful entry
violentare <1b> rape
violentatore *m* rapist
violento violent
violenza *f* violence
violinista *m/f* (*mpl* -i) violinist
violino *m* violin
violoncello *m* cello
vipera *f* viper
virgola *f* comma; MAT decimal point
virile manly, virile
virtù *f inv* virtue
virtuoso 1 *agg* virtuous 2 *m* virtuoso
virus *m inv* virus
viscere *fpl* insides; *fig: della terra* bowels
vischio *m* (*pl* -chi) mistletoe
viscido slimy
viscosa *f* viscose
viscoso viscous
visibile visible

visibilità f visibility

visiera f di berretto peak; di casco visor

visione f sight, vision; **prendere ~ di qc** have a look at sth; **in ~** for examination

visita f visit; ~ **medica** medical (examination); **far ~ a qu** visit s.o.

visitare <1l> visit; MED examine

visitatore m, -trice f visitor

visivo visual

viso m face

visone m mink

vissuto pp → vivere

vista f (senso) sight; (capacità visiva) eyesight; (veduta) view; **a prima ~** at first sight; MUS at sight; **in ~ di** in sight of; fig in view of; **conoscere qu di ~** know s.o. by sight; fig **perdere qu di ~** lose touch with s.o.

visto 1 pp → vedere; ~ **che** seeing that 2 m visa; ~ **d'entrata** entry visa; ~ **di transito** transit visa; ~ **d'uscita** exit visa

vistoso eye-catching

visuale 1 agg visual 2 f (veduta) view

vita f life; (durata della vita) lifetime; ANAT waist; **a ~** for life; **costo m della ~** cost of living; **senza ~** lifeless

vitale vital; persona lively, full of life

vitalità f inv vitality

vitamina f vitamin

vite¹ f TEC screw

vite² f AGR vine

vitello m calf; GASTR veal

viticoltore m vinegrower

viticoltura f vinegrowing

vitreo fig: sguardo, occhio glazed, glassy

vittima f victim

vitto m diet food; ~ **e alloggio** bed and board

vittoria f victory

vittorioso victorious

vivace lively; colore bright

vivacità f liveliness; di colori brightness

vivaio m di pesci tank; di piante nursery; fig breeding ground

vivanda f food

viva voce m inv speakerphone

vivente living

vivere <3zz> 1 v/i live (**di** on) 2 v/t (passare, provare) experience; ~ **una vita tranquilla** live quietly, lead a quiet life

viveri mpl food (supplies)

vivisezione f vivisection

vivo 1 agg (in vita) alive; (vivente) living; colore bright; **farsi ~** get in touch; (arrivare) turn up; ~ **e vegeto** hale and hearty 2 m: **dal ~** trasmissione, concerto live; **entrare nel ~ della questione** get to the heart of the matter; **i ~ i** pl the living

viziare <1g> persona spoil

viziato persona spoiled; aria f **-a** stale air

vizio m (pl -zi) vice; (cattiva abitudine) (bad) habit; (dipendenza) addiction; ~ **cardiaco** heart defect

vizioso persona dissolute; **circolo m ~** vicious circle

v.le abbr (= viale) St (= street)

vocabolario m (pl -ri) (lessico) vocabulary; (dizionario) dictionary

vocabolo m word

vocale 1 agg vocal 2 f vowel

vocazione f vocation

voce f voice; fig rumo(u)r; in dizionario, elenco entry; **ad alta ~** in a loud voice, loudly; **a bassa ~** in a low voice, quietly; **spargere la ~** spread rumo(u)rs

voglia f (desiderio) wish, desire; (volontà) will; sulla pelle birthmark; **avere ~ di fare qc** feel like doing sth; **morire dalla ~ di fare qc** be dying to do sth; **contro ~, di mala ~** unwillingly, reluctantly

voglio → volere

voi you; riflessivo yourselves; reciproco each other; **a ~** to you; **senza di ~** without you

vol. abbr (= volume) vol (= volume)

volano m shuttlecock

volante 1 agg flying 2 m AUTO (steering) wheel 3 f flying squad

volantino m leaflet

volare <1a> fly

volata f SP final sprint; **di ~** in a rush

volenteroso willing

volentieri willingly; **~!** with pleasure!

volere **1** <2t> *v/t & v/i* want; ***vorrei …*** I would *or* I'd like …; ***vorrei partire*** I'd like to leave; **~ dire** mean; **~ bene a qu** (*amare*) love s.o.; **ci vogliono dieci mesi** it takes ten months; **senza ~** without meaning to **2** *m* will

volgare vulgar

volgarità *f* vulgarity

volgere <3d> **1** *v/t:* **~ le spalle** turn one's back **2** *v/i:* **~ al termine** draw to a close; **il tempo volge al brutto** the weather is getting worse; **~ al peggio** take a turn for the worse

volo *m* flight; (*caduta*) fall; **prendere il ~** *di uccello* fly away; *di persona* run away; **~ a vela** gliding; **~ diretto** direct flight; **~ di linea** scheduled flight; **~ internazionale** international flight; **~ nazionale** domestic flight; **~ senza scalo** nonstop flight; *fig* **afferrare qc al ~** be quick to grasp sth

volontà *f* will; **a ~** as much as you like; **buona ~** goodwill

volontariato *m* voluntary work

volontario (*pl* -ri) **1** *agg* voluntary **2** *m*, **-a** *f* volunteer

volpe *f* fox; *femmina* vixen

volt *m inv* volt

volta *f* time; (*turno*) turn; ARCHI vault; **una ~** once; **due -e** twice; **qualche ~** sometimes; **questa ~** this time; **ogni ~** every time; **una ~ per sempre** once and for all; **poco per ~** little by little; **un'altra ~ ancora** una volta one more time; **lo faremo un'altra ~** we'll do it some other time; **molte -e** many times, often

voltaggio *m* (*pl* -ggi) voltage

voltare <1c> **1** *v/t* turn; *pagina* turn (over); **~ le spalle a qu** *azione* turn one's back on s.o.; *posizione* have one's back to s.o. **2** *v/i* turn; **~ a destra** turn right

voltarsi turn (round)

volto[1] *m* face

volto[2] *pp* → **volgere**

volume *m* volume

voluminoso bulky

voluttà *f* voluptuousness

vomitare <1l & c> vomit, throw up F; *fig* **mi fa ~** it makes me sick

vomito *m* vomit

vongola *f* ZO, GASTR clam

voragine *f* chasm, abyss

vortice *m* whirl; *in acqua* whirlpool; *di vento* whirlwind

vostro **1** *agg* your; **i -i amici** your friends **2** *pron:* **il ~** yours; **questi libri sono -i** these books are yours

votare <1a> vote

votazione *f* vote

voto *m* POL vote; EDU mark; REL, *fig* vow; **mettere qc ai -i** put sth to the vote, take a vote on sth

v.r. *abbr* (= **vedi retro**) see over

Vs. *abbr* (= **vostro**) your

v.s. *abbr* (= **vedi sopra**) see above

V.U. *abbr* (= **Vigili Urbani**) police

vulcanico (*pl* -ci) volcanic

vulcano *m* volcano

vulnerabile vulnerable

vuole → **volere**

vuotare <1c> empty

vuotarsi empty

vuoto **1** *agg* empty; (*non occupato*) vacant; (*privo*) devoid (*di* of) **2** *m* (*spazio*) empty space; (*recipiente*) empty; FIS vacuum; *fig* void; **~ d'aria** air pocket; **~ a perdere** non-returnable container; **~ a rendere** returnable container; **andare a ~** fall through; (*confezionato*) **sotto ~** vacuum-packed

V

W

W *abbr* (= **watt**) W (= watt); (= **viva**) long live
walkman *m inv* Walkman®
watt *m inv* watt
WC *abbr* (= **gabinetto**) WC (= water closet)
week-end *m inv* weekend

western *m inv* Western; **~ all'italiana** spaghetti Western
whisky *m inv* whisky
windsurf *m inv* (*tavola*) sailboard; *attività* windsurfing; **fare ~** go windsurfing
W.L. *abbr* (= **vagone letto**) sleeper

XY

X, x *f* x; **raggi** *mpl* **~** X-rays
xenofobia *f* xenophobia
xenofobo 1 *agg* xenophobic **2** *m*, **-a** *f* xenophobe
xilofono *m* xylophone

yacht *m inv* yacht
yoga *m* yoga
yogurt *m inv* yoghurt
yugoslavo 1 *agg* Yugoslav(ian) **2** *m*, **-a** *f* Yugoslav(ian)

Z

zabaione *m* zabaglione
zafferano *m* saffron
zaffiro *m* sapphire
zagara *f* orange blossom
zaino *m* rucksack
zampa *f* ZO (*piede*) paw; *di uccello* claw; (*zoccolo*) hoof; (*arto*) leg; GASTR *di maiale* trotter; *fig* **giù le -e!** hands off!; **a ~ di elefante** flared
zampillare <1a> gush
zampillo *m* spurt
zampone *m* GASTR stuffed pig's trotter
zanzara *f* mosquito

zanzariera *f* mosquito net; *su finestre* insect screen
zappa *f* hoe
zappare <1a> hoe
zapping *m inv*: **fare lo ~** zap
zattera *f* raft
zavorra *f* ballast
zebra *f* zebra
zecca[1] *f* (*pl* -cche) ZO tick
zecca[2] *f* (*pl* -cche) Mint; **nuovo di ~** brand-new
zelante zealous
zelo *m* zeal
zenit *m* zenith

zenzero *m* ginger

zeppo: **pieno ~** crammed (**di** with)

zerbino *m* doormat

zero *m* zero; *nel tennis* love; *nel calcio* nil; *fig* **partire da ~** start from scratch; **2 gradi sotto ~** 2 degrees below zero

zigomo *m* cheekbone

zigzag *m inv* zigzag

zimbello *m* decoy; *fig* laughing stock

zinco *m* zinc

zingaro m, **-a** *f* gipsy

zio *m*, **-a** *f* uncle; *donna* aunt

zitto quiet; **sta ~!** be quiet!; *in tono minaccioso* keep your mouth shut! F

zoccolo *m* clog; ZO hoof; ARCHI base

zodiacale: **segni** *mpl* **-i** signs of the Zodiac

zodiaco *m* Zodiac

zolfo *m* sulphur, *Am* sulfur

zona *f* zone, area; **~ di libero scambio** free trade area; **~ disco** short-stay parking area; **~ industriale** industrial area; **~ pedonale** pedestrian precinct; **~ residenziale** residential area; **~ verde** green belt

zonzo: **andare a ~** wander around

zoo *m inv* zoo

zoppicare <1l, c & d> limp; *di mobile* wobble

zoppo lame; (*zoppicante*) limping; *mobile* wobbly

zucca *f* (*pl* -cche) marrow; *fig* F (*testa*) bonce F, nut F

zuccherare <1l> sugar

zuccheriera *f* sugar bowl

zucchero *m* sugar; **~ greggio** brown sugar; **~ vanigliato** vanilla sugar; **~ in zollette** sugar cubes

zucchini *mpl* courgettes, *Am* zucchini(s)

zuffa *f* scuffle

zuppa *f* soup; **~ di verdura** vegetable soup; **~ di pesce** fish soup; **~ inglese** trifle

zuppiera *f* tureen

zuppo soaked, wet through

A

a [ə] *stressed* [eɪ] *art* un *m*, una *f*; *masculine before s + consonant, gn, ps, z* uno; *feminine before vowel* un'; **~ cat** un gatto; **~ joke** uno scherzo; **~ girl** una ragazza; **an island** un'isola; **£5 ~ ride** una corsa 5 sterline; **£2 ~ litre** 2 sterline al litro; **five flights ~ day** cinque voli al giorno

a·back [ə'bæk] *adv*: **taken ~** preso alla sprovvista

a·ban·don [ə'bændən] *v/t* abbandonare; *hope, scheme* rinunciare a

a·bashed [ə'bæʃt] *adj* imbarazzato

a·bate [ə'beɪt] *v/i of storm, flood waters* calmarsi

ab·at·toir ['æbətwɑː(r)] mattatoio *m*

ab·bey ['æbɪ] abbazia *f*

ab·bre·vi·ate [ə'briːvɪeɪt] *v/t* abbreviare

ab·bre·vi·a·tion [əbriːvɪ'eɪʃn] abbreviazione *f*

ab·di·cate ['æbdɪkeɪt] *v/i* abdicare

ab·di·ca·tion [æbdɪ'keɪʃn] abdicazione *f*

ab·do·men ['æbdəmən] addome *m*

ab·dom·i·nal [æb'dɒmɪnl] *adj* addominale

ab·duct [əb'dʌkt] *v/t* sequestrare, rapire

ab·duc·tion [əb'dʌkʃn] sequestro *m*, rapimento *m*

ab·hor·rence [əb'hɒrəns] *fml* orrore *m*

ab·hor·rent [əb'hɒrənt] *adj fml* ripugnante

♦ **abide** [ə'baɪd] *v/t* attenersi a

a·bil·i·ty [ə'bɪlətɪ] abilità *f inv*

a·blaze [ə'bleɪz] *adj* in fiamme

a·ble ['eɪbl] *adj* (*skilful*) capace; **be ~ to** essere capace a; **I wasn't ~ to see / hear** non ero in grado di vedere / sentire

a·ble-bod·ied [eɪbl'bɒdiːd] *adj* robusto; MIL abile

ab·nor·mal [æb'nɔːml] *adj* anormale

ab·nor·mal·ly [æb'nɔːməlɪ] *adv* in modo anomalo

a·board [ə'bɔːd] **1** *prep* a bordo di **2** *adv*: **be ~** essere a bordo; **go ~** salire a bordo

a·bol·ish [ə'bɒlɪʃ] *v/t* abolire

ab·o·li·tion [æbə'lɪʃn] abolizione *f*

a·bort [ə'bɔːt] *v/t mission, rocket launch* annullare; COMPUT: *program* interrompere

a·bor·tion [ə'bɔːʃn] aborto *m*; **have an ~** abortire

a·bor·tive [ə'bɔːtɪv] *adj* fallito; **the plan proved ~** il piano si è rivelato un fallimento

a·bout [ə'baʊt] **1** *prep* (*concerning*) su; **I'll tell you all ~ it** ti dirò tutto al riguardo; **talk ~ sth** parlare di qc; **be angry ~ sth** essere arrabbiato per qc; **there's nothing you can do ~ it** non ci puoi fare niente; **what's it ~?** *of book, film* di cosa parla?; *of complaint, problem* di cosa si tratta? **2** *adv* (*roughly*) intorno a, verso; (*nearly*) quasi; **it's ~ ready** è quasi pronto; **be ~ to ...** (*be going to*) essere sul punto di ...; **be ~** (*somewhere near*) essere nei paraggi; **there are a lot of people ~** c'è un sacco di gente qui

a·bove [ə'bʌv] **1** *prep* (*higher than*) sopra; (*more than*) sopra, oltre; **~ all** soprattutto **2** *adv* sopra; **on the floor ~** al piano di sopra

a·bove-men·tioned [əbʌv'menʃnd] *adj* suddetto

ab·ra·sion [ə'breɪʒn] abrasione *f*

ab·ra·sive [ə'breɪsɪv] *adj personality* ruvido

a·breast [ə'brest] *adv* fianco a fianco; **keep ~ of** tenere al corrente di

a·bridge [ə'brɪdʒ] *v/t* ridurre

a·broad [ə'brɔːd] *adv* all'estero

a·brupt [əˈbrʌpt] *adj departure* improvviso; *manner* brusco

a·brupt·ly [əˈbrʌptlɪ] *adv leave* improvvisamente; *say* bruscamente

ab·scess [ˈæbsɪs] accesso *m*

ab·sence [ˈæbsəns] assenza *f*

ab·sent [ˈæbsənt] *adj* assente

ab·sen·tee [æbsənˈtiː] *n* assente *m/f*

ab·sen·tee·ism [æbsənˈtiːɪzm] assenteismo *m*

ab·sent-mind·ed [æbsəntˈmaɪndɪd] *adj* distratto

ab·sent-mind·ed·ly [æbsəntˈmaɪndɪdlɪ] *adv* distrattamente

ab·so·lute [ˈæbsəluːt] *adj power* assoluto; *idiot* totale

ab·so·lute·ly [ˈæbsəluːtlɪ] *adv* (*completely*) assolutamente; **~ not!** assolutamente no!; **do you agree? – ~** sei d'accordo? – assolutamente sì

ab·so·lu·tion [æbsəˈluːʃn] REL assoluzione *f*

ab·solve [əbˈzɒlv] *v/t* assolvere

ab·sorb [əbˈsɔːb] *v/t* assorbire; **~ed in ...** assorto in ...

ab·sorb·en·cy [əbˈsɔːbənsɪ] assorbenza *f*

ab·sorb·ent [əbˈsɔːbənt] *adj* assorbente

ab·sorb·ing [əbˈsɔːbɪŋ] *adj* avvincente

ab·stain [əbˈsteɪn] *v/i from voting* astenersi

ab·sten·tion [əbˈstenʃn] *in voting* astensione *f*

ab·sti·nence [ˈæbstɪnəns] astinenza *f*

ab·stract [ˈæbstrækt] *adj* astratto

ab·struse [əbˈstruːs] *adj* astruso

ab·surd [əbˈsɜːd] *adj* assurdo

ab·surd·i·ty [əbˈsɜːdətɪ] assurdità *f*

ab·surd·ly [əbˈsɜːdlɪ] *adv* in modo assurdo

a·bun·dance [əˈbʌndəns] abbondanza *f*

a·bun·dant [əˈbʌndənt] *adj* abbondante

a·buse¹ [əˈbjuːs] *n* abuso *m*; (*ill treatment*) maltrattamento *m*; (*insults*) insulti *mpl*

a·buse² [əˈbjuːz] *v/t* abusare di; (*treat*

badly) maltrattare; (*insult*) insultare

a·bu·sive [əˈbjuːsɪv] *adj language* offensivo; **become ~** diventare aggressivo

a·bys·mal [əˈbɪzml] *adj* F (*very bad*) pessimo

a·byss [əˈbɪs] abisso *m*

AC [ˈeɪsiː] *abbr* (= **alternating current**) c.a. (corrente *f* alternata)

ac·a·dem·ic [ækəˈdemɪk] **1** *n* docente *m/f* universitario, -a **2** *adj* accademico; *person* portato per lo studio

a·cad·e·my [əˈkædəmɪ] accademia *f*

ac·cede [əkˈsiːd] *v/i:* **~ to throne** salire a

ac·cel·e·rate [əkˈseləreɪt] *v/t & v/i* accelerare

ac·cel·e·ra·tion [əkseləˈreɪʃn] *of car* accelerazione *f*

ac·cel·e·ra·tor [əkˈseləreɪtə(r)] *of car* acceleratore *m*

ac·cent [ˈæksənt] accento *m*

ac·cen·tu·ate [əkˈsentjueɪt] *v/t* accentuare

ac·cept [əkˈsept] *v/t* accettare

ac·cept·a·ble [əkˈseptəbl] *adj* accettabile

ac·cept·ance [əkˈseptəns] accettazione *f*

ac·cess [ˈækses] **1** *n* accesso *m*; **have ~ to** *computer* avere accesso a; *child* avere il permesso di vedere **2** *v/t* accedere a

'ac·cess code COMPUT codice *m* di accesso

ac·ces·si·ble [əkˈsesəbl] *adj* accessibile

ac·ces·sion [əkˈseʃn] ascesa *f*

ac·ces·so·ry [əkˈsesərɪ] *for wearing* accessorio *m*; LAW complice *m/f*

'ac·cess road svincolo *m*

'ac·cess time COMPUT tempo *m* di accesso

ac·ci·dent [ˈæksɪdənt] incidente *m*; **by ~** per caso

ac·ci·den·tal [æksɪˈdentl] *adj* accidentale

ac·ci·den·tal·ly [æksɪˈdentlɪ] *adv* accidentalmente

ac·claim [əˈkleɪm] **1** *n* consenso *m* **2** *v/t* acclamare

ac·cla·ma·tion [æklə'meɪʃn] acclamazioni *fpl*

ac·cli·mate, ac·cli·ma·tize [ə'klaɪmət, ə'klaɪmətaɪz] **1** *v/t* acclimatare **2** *v/i* acclimatarsi

ac·com·mo·date [ə'kɒmədeɪt] *v/t* ospitare; *special requirements* tenere conto di

ac·com·mo·da·tion [əkɒmə'deɪʃn] sistemazione *f*

ac·com·pa·ni·ment [ə'kʌmpənɪmənt] MUS accompagnamento *m*

ac·com·pa·nist [ə'kʌmpənɪst] MUS: *with Gerald Moore as his ~* con l'accompagnamento di Gerald Moore

ac·com·pa·ny [ə'kʌmpənɪ] *v/t* (*pret & pp -ied*) accompagnare

ac·com·plice [ə'kʌmplɪs] complice *m/f*

ac·com·plish [ə'kʌmplɪʃ] *v/t task* compiere; *goal* conseguire

ac·com·plished [ə'kʌmplɪʃt] *adj* dotato

ac·com·plish·ment [ə'kʌmplɪʃmənt] *of a task* realizzazione *f*; (*talent*) talento *m*; (*achievement*) risultato *m*

ac·cord [ə'kɔːd] accordo *m*; *of his / my own ~* di sua / mia spontanea volontà

ac·cord·ance [ə'kɔːdəns]: *in ~ with* conformemente a

ac·cord·ing [ə'kɔːdɪŋ] *adv*: *~ to* secondo

ac·cord·ing·ly [ə'kɔːdɪŋlɪ] *adv* di conseguenza

ac·cor·di·on [ə'kɔːdɪən] fisarmonica *f*

ac·cor·di·on·ist [ə'kɔːdɪənɪst] fisarmonicista *m/f*

ac·count [ə'kaʊnt] *financial* conto *m*; (*report, description*) resoconto *m*; *give an ~ of* fare un resoconto di; *on no ~* per nessuna ragione; *on ~ of* a causa di; *take ... into ~, take ~ of ...* tenere conto di ...

♦ account for *v/t* (*explain*) giustificare; (*make up, constitute*) ammontare a

ac·count·abil·i·ty [əkaʊntə'bɪlətɪ] responsabilità *f*

ac·coun·ta·ble [ə'kaʊntəbl] *adj* responsabile; *be held ~* essere considerato responsabile

ac·coun·tant [ə'kaʊntənt] contabile *m/f*; *running own business* commercialista *m/f*

ac'count hol·der titolare *m/f* di conto; *of current account* correntista *m/f*

ac'count num·ber numero *m* di conto

ac·counts [ə'kaʊnts] *npl* contabilità *f*

ac·cu·mu·late [ə'kjuːmjʊleɪt] **1** *v/t* accumulare **2** *v/i* accumularsi

ac·cu·mu·la·tion [əkjuːmjʊ'leɪʃn] accumulazione *f*

ac·cu·ra·cy ['ækjʊrəsɪ] precisione *f*

ac·cu·rate ['ækjʊrət] *adj* preciso

ac·cu·rate·ly ['ækjʊrətlɪ] *adv* con precisione

ac·cu·sa·tion [ækjuː'zeɪʃn] accusa *f*

ac·cuse [ə'kjuːz] *v/t* accusare; *he ~d me of lying* mi ha accusato di mentire; *be ~d of ...* LAW essere accusato di ...

ac·cused [ə'kjuːzd] *n* LAW accusato *m*, -a *f*

ac'cus·ing [ə'kjuːzɪŋ] *adj* accusatorio

ac'cus·ing·ly [ə'kjuːzɪŋlɪ] *adv look, point* con aria accusatoria; *say* con tono accusatorio

ac·cus·tom [ə'kʌstəm] *v/t*: *get ~ed to* abituarsi; *be ~ed to* essere abituato a

ace [eɪs] *in cards* asso *m*; (*in tennis: shot*) ace *m* inv

ache [eɪk] **1** *n* dolore *m* **2** *v/i* fare male; *my head ~s* mi fa male la testa

a·chieve [ə'tʃiːv] *v/t* realizzare; *success, fame* ottenere

a·chieve·ment [ə'tʃiːvmənt] *of ambition* realizzazione *f*; (*thing achieved*) successo *m*

ac·id ['æsɪd] *n* acido *m*

a·cid·i·ty [ə'sɪdətɪ] *also fig* acidità *f*

ac·id 'rain pioggia *f* acida

'ac·id test *fig* prova *f* della verità

ac·knowl·edge [ək'nɒlɪdʒ] v/t riconoscere; *by smile, nod* far capire di aver notato; *he ~d the applause with a smile* ha risposto all'applauso con un sorriso; *~ (receipt of) a letter* accusare ricezione di una lettera

ac·knowl·edg(e)·ment [ək'nɒlɪdʒmənt] riconoscimento m; (*smile, nod*) cenno m; (*letter*) lettera f di accusata ricezione; *in ~ of thanking* come pegno di riconoscenza di; *~s* (*in book*) ringraziamenti mpl

ac·ne ['æknɪ] MED acne m

a·corn ['eɪkɔːn] BOT ghianda f

a·cous·tics [ə'kuːstɪks] acustica f

ac·quaint [ə'kweɪnt] v/t: *be ~ed with* fml conoscere

ac·quaint·ance [ə'kweɪntəns] *person* conoscenza f

ac·qui·esce [ækwɪ'es] v/i fml acconsentire

ac·qui·es·cence [ækwɪ'esns] fml consentimento m

ac·quire [ə'kwaɪə(r)] v/t acquisire

ac·qui·si·tion [ækwɪ'zɪʃn] acquisizione f

ac·quis·i·tive [ə'kwɪzətɪv] adj avido

ac·quit [ə'kwɪt] v/t LAW assolvere

ac·quit·tal [ə'kwɪtl] LAW assoluzione f

a·cre ['eɪkə(r)] acro m

a·cre·age ['eɪkrɪdʒ] estensione f in acri

ac·rid ['ækrɪd] adj smell acre

ac·ri·mo·ni·ous [ækrɪ'məʊnɪəs] adj aspro

ac·ro·bat ['ækrəbæt] acrobata m/f

ac·ro·bat·ic [ækrə'bætɪk] adj acrobatico

ac·ro·bat·ics [ækrə'bætɪks] npl acrobazie fpl

ac·ro·nym ['ækrənɪm] acronimo m

a·cross [ə'krɒs] 1 prep on other side of dall'altro lato di; *sail ~ the Atlantic* attraversare l'Atlantico in barca a vela; *walk ~ the street* attraversare la strada; *a bridge ~ the river* un ponte sul fiume; *~ Europe* all over in tutta Europa 2 adv to other side dall'altro lato; *10 m ~* largo 10 m; *they*

came to the river and swam ~ sono arrivati al fiume e l'hanno attraversato a nuoto

a·cryl·ic [ə'krɪlɪk] adj acrilico

act [ækt] 1 v/i agire; THEA recitare; (*pretend*) fare finta; *~ as* fare le funzioni di 2 n (*deed*) atto m; *of play* atto m; *in variety show* numero m; (*pretence*) finta f; (*law*) atto m; *~ of God* causa f di forza maggiore

act·ing ['æktɪŋ] 1 n recitazione f; *she went into ~* si è data alla recitazione 2 adj (*temporary*) facente funzione; *the ~ president* il facente funzione di presidente

ac·tion ['ækʃn] azione f; *out of ~* (*not functioning*) fuori uso; *take ~* agire; *bring an ~ against* LAW fare causa a

ac·tion 're·play TV replay m inv

ac·tive ['æktɪv] adj attivo; GRAM attivo

ac·tiv·ist ['æktɪvɪst] POL attivista m/f

ac·tiv·i·ty [æk'tɪvətɪ] attività f

ac·tor ['æktə(r)] attore m

ac·tress ['æktrɪs] attrice f

ac·tu·al ['æktʃʊəl] adj reale; *cost* effettivo; *the ~ ceremony starts at 10* la cerimonia vera e propria comincia alle 10

ac·tu·al·ly ['æktʃʊəlɪ] adv (*in fact, to tell the truth*) in realtà; *expressing surprise* veramente; *~ I do know him* stressing the converse a dire il vero, lo conosco

ac·u·punc·ture ['ækjʊpʌŋktʃə(r)] agopuntura f

a·cute [ə'kjuːt] adj pain, sense acuto; *shortage* estremo

a·cute·ly [ə'kjuːtlɪ] adv (*extremely*) estremamente

AD [eɪ'diː] abbr (= *anno domini*) d.C. (= dopo Cristo)

ad [æd] → *advertisement*

ad·a·mant ['ædəmənt] adj categorico

ad·a·mant·ly ['ædəməntlɪ] adv categoricamente

Ad·am's ap·ple [ædəmz'æpəl] pomo m di Adamo

a·dapt [ə'dæpt] 1 v/t adattare 2 v/i of

person adattarsi

a·dapt·a·bil·i·ty [ədæptə'bɪlɪtɪ] adattabilità *f*

a·dap·ta·ble [ə'dæptəbl] *adj* adatta·bile

a·dap·ta·tion [ædæp'teɪʃn] *of play etc* adattamento *m*

a·dapt·or [ə'dæptə(r)] *electrical* adattatore *m*

add [æd] **1** *v/t* aggiungere; MATH ad·dizionare **2** *v/i of person* fare le som·me

♦ add on *v/t 15% etc* aggiungere

♦ add up **1** *v/t* sommare **2** *v/i fig* qua·drare

ad·der ['ædə(r)] vipera *f* rossa

ad·dict ['ædɪkt] *to football, chess* ma·niaco *m*, -a *f*; *drug* ~ tossicomane *m/f*, tossicodipendente *m/f*; *heroin* ~ eroinomane *m/f*; *TV* ~ teledipen·dente *m/f*

ad·dict·ed [ə'dɪktɪd] *adj* dipendente; *be* ~ *to drugs, alcohol* essere dedito a; *football, computer games etc* essere un maniaco di

ad·dic·tion [ə'dɪkʃn] *to drugs* dipen·denza *f*, assuefazione *f*; *to TV, choco·late etc* dipendenza *f*

ad·dic·tive [ə'dɪktɪv] *adj*: *be* ~ *of drugs* provocare dipendenza *o* as·suefazione; *of TV, chocolate etc* pro·vocare dipendenza

ad·di·tion [ə'dɪʃn] MATH addizione *f*; *to list, company etc* aggiunta *f*; *in* ~ *to* in aggiunta a

ad·di·tion·al [ə'dɪʃnl] *adj* aggiuntivo

ad·di·tive ['ædɪtɪv] additivo *m*

add-on ['ædɒn] complemento *m*

ad·dress [ə'dres] **1** *n* indirizzo *m*; *form of* ~ appellativo *m* **2** *v/t letter* indirizzare; *audience* tenere un di·scorso a; *person* rivolgersi a

ad·dress book indirizzario *m*

ad·dress·ee [ædre'si:] destinatario *m*, -a *f*

ad·ept [ə'dept] *adj* esperto; *be* ~ *at* essere esperto in

ad·e·quate ['ædɪkwət] *adj* adeguato

ad·e·quate·ly ['ædɪkwətlɪ] *adv* ade·guatamente

ad·here [əd'hɪə(r)] *v/i* aderire

♦ adhere to *v/t surface* aderire a; *rules* attenersi a

ad·he·sive [əd'hi:sɪv] *n* adesivo *m*

ad·he·sive 'plas·ter cerotto *m*

ad·he·sive 'tape nastro *m* adesivo

ad·ja·cent [ə'dʒeɪsnt] *adj* adiacente

ad·jec·tive ['ædʒɪktɪv] aggettivo *m*

ad·join [ə'dʒɔɪn] *v/t* essere adiacente a

ad·join·ing [ə'dʒɔɪnɪŋ] *adj* adiacente

ad·journ [ə'dʒɜ:n] *v/i* aggiornare

ad·journ·ment [ə'dʒɜ:nmənt] ag·giornamento *m*

ad·just [ə'dʒʌst] *v/t* regolare; ~ *o.s. to* adattarsi a

ad·just·a·ble [ə'dʒʌstəbl] *adj* rego·labile

ad·just·ment [ə'dʒʌstmənt] regola·zione *f*; *psychological* adattamento *m*

ad lib [æd'lɪb] **1** *adj & adv* a braccio F **2** *v/i (pret & pp* -*bed)* improvvisare

ad·min·is·ter [əd'mɪnɪstə(r)] *v/t me·dicine* somministrare; *company* am·ministrare; *country* governare

ad·min·is·tra·tion [ədmɪnɪ'streɪʃn] amministrazione *f*; *(government)* governo *m*

ad·min·is·tra·tive [ədmɪnɪ'strətɪv] *adj* amministrativo

ad·min·is·tra·tor [əd'mɪnɪstreɪtə(r)] amministratore *m*, -trice *f*

ad·mi·ra·ble ['ædmərəbl] *adj* ammi·revole

ad·mi·ra·bly ['ædmərəblɪ] *adv* am·mirevolmente

ad·mi·ral ['ædmərəl] ammiraglio *m*

ad·mi·ra·tion [ædmə'reɪʃn] ammira·zione *f*

ad·mire [əd'maɪə(r)] *v/t* ammirare

ad·mir·er [əd'maɪərə(r)] ammiratore *m*, -trice *f*

ad·mir·ing [əd'maɪərɪŋ] *adj* ammira·tivo

ad·mir·ing·ly [əd'maɪərɪŋlɪ] *adv* con ammirazione

ad·mis·si·ble [əd'mɪsəbl] *adj* ammis·sibile

ad·mis·sion [əd'mɪʃn] *(confession)* ammissione *f*; ~ *free* entrata *f* libera

ad·mit [əd'mɪt] *v/t (pret & pp* -*ted)*

ammettere; *to a place* lasciare entrare; *to school, club etc* ammettere; *to hospital* ricoverare

ad·mit·tance [əd'mɪtəns]: **no** ~ vietato l'accesso

ad·mit·ted·ly [əd'mɪtedlɪ] *adv* effettivamente

ad·mon·ish [əd'mɒnɪʃ] *v/t fml* ammonire

a·do [ə'duː]: **without further** ~ senza ulteriori indugi

ad·o·les·cence [ædə'lesns] adolescenza *f*

ad·o·les·cent [ædə'lesnt] **1** *n* adolescente *m/f* **2** *adj* adolescenziale

a·dopt [ə'dɒpt] *v/t* adottare

a·dop·tion [ə'dɒpʃn] adozione *f*

adop·tive par·ents [ədɒptɪv 'peərənts] *npl* genitori *mpl* adottivi

a·dor·a·ble [ə'dɔːrəbl] *adj* adorabile

ad·o·ra·tion [ædə'reɪʃn] adorazione *f*

a·dore [ə'dɔː(r)] *v/t* adorare

a·dor·ing [ə'dɔːrɪŋ] *adj* in adorazione

ad·ren·al·in [ə'drenəlɪn] adrenalina *f*

a·drift [ə'drɪft] *adj* alla deriva; *fig* sbandato

a·u·la·tion [ædjʊ'leɪʃn] adulazione *f*

ad·ult ['ædʌlt] **1** *n* adulto *m*, -a *f* **2** *adj* adulto

ad·ult ed·u·ca·tion corsi *mpl* per adulti

a·dul·ter·ous [ə'dʌltərəs] *adj* *relationship* extraconiugale

a·dul·ter·y [ə'dʌltərɪ] adulterio *m*

'adult film *euph* film *m inv* per adulti

ad·vance [əd'vɑːns] **1** *n (money)* anticipo *m*; *in science etc* progresso *m*; MIL avanzata *f*; **in** ~ in anticipo; **make ~s** (*progress*) fare progressi; *sexually* fare delle avances **2** *v/i* MIL avanzare; (*make progress*) fare progressi **3** *v/t theory* avanzare; *sum of money* anticipare; *human knowledge, a cause* fare progredire

ad·vance 'book·ing prenotazione *f*

ad·vanced [əd'vɑːnst] *adj country, level* avanzato; *learner* di livello avanzato

ad·vance 'no·tice preavviso *m*

ad·vance 'pay·ment pagamento *m* anticipato

ad·van·tage [əd'vɑːntɪdʒ] vantaggio *m*; **it's to your** ~ è a tuo vantaggio; **take** ~ **of** *opportunity* approfittare di

ad·van·ta·geous [ædvən'teɪdʒəs] *adj* vantaggioso

ad·vent ['ædvent] *fig* avvento *m*

'ad·vent cal·en·dar *calendario m dell'Avvento con finestrelle numerate che i bambini aprono giorno per giorno*

ad·ven·ture [əd'ventʃə(r)] avventura *f*

ad·ven·tur·ous [əd'ventʃərəs] *adj* avventuroso

ad·verb ['ædvɜːb] avverbio *m*

ad·ver·sa·ry ['ædvəsərɪ] avversario *m*, -a *f*

ad·verse ['ædvɜːs] *adj* avverso

ad·vert ['ædvɜːt] → **advertisement**

ad·ver·tise ['ædvətaɪz] **1** *v/t job* mettere un annuncio per; *product* reclamizzare **2** *v/i for job* mettere un annuncio; *for product* fare pubblicità

ad·ver·tise·ment [əd'vɜːtɪsmənt] annuncio *m*, inserzione *f*; *for product* pubblicità *f inv*

ad·ver·tis·er ['ædvətaɪzə(r)] acquirente *m/f* di uno spazio pubblicitario; *in magazine, newspaper* inserzionista *m/f*

ad·ver·tis·ing ['ædvətaɪzɪŋ] pubblicità *f inv*

'ad·ver·tis·ing a·gen·cy agenzia *f* pubblicitaria; 'ad·ver·tis·ing budg·et budget *m inv* per la pubblicità; 'ad·ver·tis·ing cam·paign campagna *f* pubblicitaria; 'ad·ver·tis·ing rev·e·nue proventi *mpl* della pubblicità

ad·vice [əd'vaɪs] consigli *mpl*; *legal, financial* consulenza *f*; **a bit of** ~ un consiglio; **take s.o.'s** ~ seguire il consiglio di qu

ad·vis·a·ble [əd'vaɪzəbl] *adj* consigliabile

ad·vise [əd'vaɪz] *v/t person* consigliare a; *caution etc* consigliare; ~ **s.o. to ...** consigliare a qd di ...

ad·vis·er [əd'vaɪzə(r)] consulente *m/f*

ad·vo·cate ['ædvəkeɪt] *v/t* propugnare

aer·i·al ['eərɪəl] *n* antenna *f*

aer·i·al 'pho·to·graph fotografia *f* aerea

aer·o·bics [eə'rəʊbɪks] *nsg* aerobica *f*

aer·o·dy·nam·ic [eərəʊdaɪ'næmɪk] *adj* aerodinamico

aer·o·nau·ti·cal [eərəʊ'nɔːtɪkl] *adj* aeronautico

aer·o·plane ['eərəpleɪn] aeroplano *m*

aer·o·sol ['eərəsɒl] spray *m inv*

aer·o·space in·dus·try ['eərəspeɪs ɪndʌstrɪ] industria *f* aerospaziale

aes·thet·ic [iːs'θetɪk] *adj* estetico

af·fa·ble ['æfəbl] *adj* affabile

af·fair [ə'feə(r)] (*matter*) affare *m*; (*event*) caso *m*; (*business*) affare *m*; (*love*) relazione *f*, **foreign ~s** affari *mpl* esteri; **have an ~ with** avere una relazione con

affect [ə'fekt] *v/t* MED colpire; (*influence*) influire su; (*concern*) riguardare; (*cause feelings to*) colpire

af·fec·tion [ə'fekʃn] affetto *m*

af·fec·tion·ate [ə'fekʃnət] *adj* affettuoso

af·fec·tion·ate·ly [ə'fekʃnətlɪ] *adv* affettuosamente

af·fin·i·ty [ə'fɪnɪtɪ] affinità *f inv*

af·fir·ma·tive [ə'fɜːmətɪv] *adj* affermativo; **answer in the ~** rispondere affermativamente

af·flict [ə'flɪkt] *v/t* tormentare; **be ~ed with** soffrire di

af·flu·ence ['æfluəns] benessere *m*

af·flu·ent ['æfluənt] *adj* benestante; **~ society** società *f inv* del benessere

af·ford [ə'fɔːd] *v/t*: **be able to ~ sth** *financially* potersi permettere qc; **I can't ~ the time** non ne ho il tempo; **it's a risk we can't ~ to take** è un rischio che non possiamo permetterci di correre

af·ford·a·ble [ə'fɔːdəbl] *adj* abbordabile

af·front [ə'frʌnt] *n* affronto *m*

a·float [ə'fləʊt] *adj boat* a galla; **keep the company ~** tenere a galla l'azienda

a·fraid [ə'freɪd] *adj*: **be ~** avere paura; **be ~ of** avere paura di; **I'm ~** *expressing regret* sono spiacente; **I'm ~ so** temo che sia così; **I'm ~ not** purtroppo no

a·fresh [ə'freʃ] *adv* da capo

Af·ri·ca ['æfrɪkə] Africa *f*

Af·ri·can ['æfrɪkən] **1** *n* africano *m*, -a *f* **2** *adj* africano

af·ter ['ɑːftə(r)] **1** *prep* dopo; **~ her/ me/you** dopo di lei/me/te; **~ all** dopo tutto; **~ that** dopo; **the day ~ tomorrow** dopodomani **2** *adv* dopo; **the day ~** il giorno dopo

af·ter·math ['ɑːftəmæθ]: **the ~ of war** il dopoguerra; **in the ~ of** nel periodo immediatamente successivo a

afternoon [ɑːftə'nuːn] pomeriggio *m*; **in the ~** nel pomeriggio; **this ~** oggi pomeriggio; **good ~** buon giorno

'af·ter sales serv·ice servizio *m* dopovendita; **'af·ter·shave** dopobarba *m inv*; **'af·ter·taste** retrogusto *m*

af·ter·wards ['ɑːftəwədz] *adv* dopo

a·gain [ə'geɪn] *adv* di nuovo; **I never saw him ~** non l'ho mai più visto

a·gainst [ə'geɪnst] *prep lean* contro; **America ~ Brazil** SP America contro Brasile; **I'm ~ the idea** sono contrario all'idea; **what do you have ~ her?** cos'hai contro di lei?; **~ the law** contro la legge

age [eɪdʒ] **1** *n* (*also era*) età *f inv*; **at the ~ of** all'età di; **under ~** minorenne; **she's five years of ~** ha cinque anni; **I've been waiting for ~s** F ho aspettato un secolo **F 2** *v/i* invecchiare

aged¹ [eɪdʒd] *adj*: **a boy ~ 16** un ragazzo di 16 anni; **he was ~ 16** aveva 16 anni

aged² ['eɪdʒɪd] **1** *adj*: **her ~ parents** i

suoi anziani genitori **2** n: **the ~** gli anziani

'**age group** fascia f d'età

'**age lim·it** limite m d'età

a·gen·cy ['eɪdʒənsɪ] agenzia f

a·gen·da [ə'dʒendə] ordine m del giorno; **on the ~** all'ordine del giorno

a·gent ['eɪdʒənt] agente m/f

ag·gra·vate ['ægrəveɪt] v/t aggravare; (annoy) seccare

ag·gre·gate ['ægrɪgət] n insieme m; **in (the)** ~ nel complesso; **win on ~** SP vincere ai punti

ag·gres·sion [ə'greʃn] aggressione f

ag·gres·sive [ə'gresɪv] adj (also dynamic) aggressivo

ag·gres·sive·ly [ə'gresɪvlɪ] adv con aggressività

ag·gro ['ægrəʊ] P grane fpl

a·ghast [ə'gɑːst] adj inorridito

a·gile ['ædʒaɪl] adj agile

a·gil·i·ty [ə'dʒɪlətɪ] agilità f

ag·i·tate ['ædʒɪteɪt] v/i: ~ **for** / **against** mobilitarsi per / contro

ag·i·tat·ed ['ædʒɪteɪtɪd] adj agitato

ag·i·ta·tion [ædʒɪ'teɪʃn] agitazione f

ag·i·ta·tor [ædʒɪ'teɪtə(r)] agitatore m, -trice f

AGM [eɪdʒiː'em] abbr (= **annual general meeting**) assemblea f annuale

ag·nos·tic [æg'nɒstɪk] n agnostico m, -a f

a·go [ə'gəʊ] adv: **2 days** ~ due giorni fa; **long** ~ molto tempo fa; **how long ~?** quanto tempo fa?

ag·o·nize ['ægənaɪz] v/i angosciarsi; ~ **over** angosciarsi per

ag·o·niz·ing ['ægənaɪzɪŋ] adj angosciante

ag·o·ny ['ægənɪ] agonia f; mental angoscia f

a·gree [ə'griː] **1** v/i essere d'accordo; of figures, accounts quadrare; (reach agreement) mettersi d'accordo; **I** ~ sono d'accordo; **it doesn't ~ with me** of food mi fa male **2** v/t price concordare; ~ **that sth should be done** concordare che si dovrebbe fare qc

a·gree·a·ble [ə'griːəbl] adj (pleasant) piacevole; **be ~** (in agreement) essere d'accordo

a·gree·ment [ə'griːmənt] (consent, contract) accordo m; **reach ~ on** trovare un accordo su

ag·ri·cul·tur·al [ægrɪ'kʌltʃərəl] adj agricolo

ag·ri·cul·ture ['ægrɪkʌltʃə(r)] agricoltura f

a·head [ə'hed] adv davanti; (in advance) avanti; **200 m** ~ 200 m più avanti; **be ~ of** essere davanti a; **plan / think** ~ programmare per tempo; **arrive ~ of the others** arrivare prima degli altri

aid [eɪd] **1** n aiuto m **2** v/t aiutare

aide [eɪd] assistente m/f

Aids [eɪdz] Aids m

ail·ing ['eɪlɪŋ] adj economy malato

ail·ment ['eɪlmənt] disturbo m

aim [eɪm] **1** n in shooting mira f; (objective) obiettivo m; **take** ~ prendere la mira; **2** v/i in shooting mirare; ~ **at doing sth, ~ to do sth** aspirare a fare qc **3** v/t: **be ~ed at** of remark etc essere rivolto a; of guns essere puntato contro

aim·less ['eɪmlɪs] adj senza obiettivi; wandering senza meta

air [eə(r)] **1** n aria f; **by ~ travel** in aereo; send mail per via aerea; **in the open** ~ all'aperto; **on the ~** RAD, TV in onda **2** v/t room arieggiare; fig: views rendere noto

'**air·bag** airbag m inv; '**air·base** base f aerea; '**air-con·di·tioned** adj con aria condizionata; '**air-con·di·tion·ing** aria f condizionata; '**air·craft** aereo m; '**air·craft car·ri·er** portaerei f inv; '**air fare** tariffa f aerea; '**air·field** campo m d'aviazione; '**air force** aeronautica f militare; '**air host·ess** hostess f inv; '**air let·ter** aerogramma m; '**air·lift 1** n ponte m aereo **2** v/t trasportare per via aerea; '**air·line** compagnia f aerea; '**air·lin·er** aereo m di linea; '**air·mail: by** ~ per via aerea; '**air·plane** aeroplano m; '**air·pock·et** vuoto m d'aria; '**air pol·lu·tion** inquinamento *m* atmosferico; **'air·port** aeroporto *m*; **'air·sick: get ~** soffrire il mal d'aereo *o* l'aereo; **'air·space** spazio *m* aereo; **'air ter·mi·nal** terminale *m*; **'air·tight** *adj container* ermetico; **'air traf·fic** traffico *m* aereo; **'air-traf·fic con·trol** controllo *m* del traffico aereo; **air-traf·fic con'trol·ler** controllore *m* di volo

air·y ['eərɪ] *adj room* arieggiato; *attitude* noncurante

aisle [aɪl] corridoio *m*; *in supermarket* corsia *f*; *in church* navata *f* laterale

aisle seat posto *m* corridoio

a·jar [ə'dʒɑː(r)] *adj*: **be ~** essere socchiuso

a·lac·ri·ty [ə'lækrɪtɪ] alacrità *f*

a·larm [ə'lɑːm] **1** *n* allarme *m*; **raise the ~** dare l'allarme **2** *v/t* allarmare

a'larm clock sveglia *f*

a·larm·ing [ə'lɑːmɪŋ] *adj* allarmante

a·larm·ing·ly [ə'lɑːmɪŋlɪ] *adv* in modo allarmante

al·bum ['ælbəm] *for photographs*, *(record)* album *m inv*

al·co·hol ['ælkəhɒl] alcol *m*; **~-free** analcolico

al·co·hol·ic [ælkə'hɒlɪk] **1** *n* alcolizzato *m*, -a *f* **2** *adj* alcolico

a·lert [ə'lɜːt] **1** *n (signal)* allarme *m*; **be on the ~** stare all'erta; *of troops*, *police* essere in stato di allerta **2** *v/t* mettere in guardia **3** *adj* all'erta *inv*

A-lev·el ['eɪlevl] diploma *f* di scuola media superiore in Gran Bretagna che permettere di accedere all'università

al·ge·bra ['ældʒɪbrə] algebra *f*

al·i·bi ['ælɪbaɪ] alibi *m inv*

a·li·en ['eɪlɪən] **1** *n (foreigner)* straniero *m*, -a *f*; *from space* alieno *m*, -a *f* **2** *adj* estraneo; **be ~ to s.o.** essere estraneo a qu

a·li·en·ate ['eɪlɪəneɪt] *v/t* alienarsi

a·light [ə'laɪt] *adj*: **be ~** essere in fiamme; **set sth ~** dare fuoco a qc

a·lign [ə'laɪn] *v/t* allineare

a·like [ə'laɪk] **1** *adj* simile; **be ~** assomigliarsi **2** *adv*: **it appeals to old and young ~** attira vecchi e giovani allo stesso tempo

al·i·mo·ny ['ælɪmənɪ] alimenti *mpl*

a·live [ə'laɪv] *adj*: **be ~** essere vivo; **~ and kicking** vivo e vegeto

all [ɔːl] **1** *adj* tutto; *(any whatever)* qualsiasi; **~ day/month** tutto il giorno/mese; **beyond ~ doubt** al di là di qualsiasi dubbio **2** *pron* tutto; **~ of us/them** tutti noi/loro; **he ate ~ of it** lo ha mangiato tutto; **that's ~, thanks** è tutto, grazie; **for ~ I care** per quello che me ne importa; **for ~ I know** per quel che ne so; **~ at once** tutto in una volta; *(suddenly)* tutt'a un tratto; **~ but** *(nearly)* quasi; **~ but John agreed** *(except)* erano tutti d'accordo tranne John; **~ the better** molto meglio; **~ the time** tutto il tempo; **they're not at ~ alike** non si assomigliano affatto; **not at ~!** niente affatto!; **two ~** SP due pari; **~ right** → **alright**

al·lay [ə'leɪ] *v/t* attenuare

al·le·ga·tion [ælɪ'geɪʃn] accusa *f*

al·lege [ə'ledʒ] *v/t* dichiarare

al·leged [ə'ledʒd] *adj* presunto

al·leg·ed·ly [ə'ledʒɪdlɪ] *adv* a quanto si suppone

al·le·giance [ə'liːdʒəns] fedeltà *f*

al·ler·gic [ə'lɜːdʒɪk] *adj* allergico; **be ~ to** essere allergico a

al·ler·gy ['ælədʒɪ] allergia *f*

al·le·vi·ate [ə'liːvɪeɪt] *v/t* alleviare

al·ley ['ælɪ] vicolo *m*

al·li·ance [ə'laɪəns] alleanza *f*

al·lied ['ælaɪd] MIL alleato

al·lo·cate ['æləkeɪt] *v/t* assegnare

al·lo·ca·tion [ælə'keɪʃn] assegnazione *f*; *(amount)* parte *f*

al·lot [ə'lɒt] *v/t (pret & pp -ted)* assegnare

al·lot·ment [ə'lɒtmənt] *Br* lotto *m* da coltivare

al·low [ə'laʊ] *v/t (permit)* permettere; *(calculate for)* calcolare; **be ~ed** essere autorizzato; **it's not ~ed** è vietato; **passengers are not ~ed to smoke** è vietato ai passeggeri fumare; **dogs not ~ed** vietato l'ingresso ai cani; **~ s.o. to ...** permettere a qu di ...

♦ **allow for** *v/t* tenere conto di

al·low·ance [ə'lauəns] (*money*) sussidio *m*; (*pocket money*) paghetta *f*; **make ~s for sth** tenere conto di qc; **make ~s for s.o.** essere indulgente con qu

al·loy ['ælɔɪ] lega *m*

'all-pur·pose *adj* multiuso *inv*; 'all-round *adj improvement* generale; *person* eclettico; 'all-time: **be at an ~ low** *of* inflation, unemployment aver raggiunto il minimo storico

♦ allude to [ə'lu:d] *v/t* alludere a

al·lur·ing [ə'lu:rɪŋ] *adj* attraente

al·lu·sion [ə'lu:ʒn] allusione *f*

al·ly ['ælaɪ] *n* alleato *m*, -a *f*

Al·might·y [ɔːl'maɪtɪ]: **the ~** l'Onnipotente

al·mond ['ɑːmənd] mandorla *f*

al·most ['ɔːlməʊst] *adv* quasi

a·lone [ə'ləʊn] *adj* solo

a·long [ə'lɒŋ] **1** *prep* lungo; **walk ~ the street** camminare lungo la strada **2** *adv*: **~ with** insieme con; *all* (*all the time*) per tutto il tempo; **we're going, would you like to come ~?** noi andiamo, vuoi venire con noi?

a·long·side [əlɒŋ'saɪd] *prep* di fianco a; *person* al fianco di; **draw up ~** accostare; **draw up ~ s.o.** accostare vicino a qu; **~ him** al suo fianco

a·loof [ə'lu:f] *adj* in disparte

a·loud [ə'laʊd] *adv* ad alta voce; *laugh, call* forte

al·pha·bet ['ælfəbet] alfabeto *m*

al·pha·bet·i·cal [ælfə'betɪkl] *adj* alfabetico

al·pine ['ælpaɪn] *adj* alpino

Alps [ælps] *npl* Alpi *fpl*

al·read·y [ɔːl'redɪ] *adv* già

al·right [ɔːl'raɪt] *adj*: **it's ~** va bene; **are you ~?** (*not hurt*) stai bene?; **I'm ~** (*not hurt*) sto bene; (*have got enough*) va bene così; **is the monitor ~?** (*in working order*) funziona il monitor?; **is it ~ with you if I ...?** ti va bene se ...?; **~, you can have one!** va bene, puoi averne uno!; **~, I heard you!** sì, ti ho sentito!; **everything is ~ now between them** adesso va tutto bene tra di loro;

that's ~ (*don't mention it*) non c'è di che; (*I don't mind*) non fa niente; **~, that's enough!** basta così!

Al·sa·tian [æl'seɪʃn] *Br* pastore *m* tedesco

al·so ['ɔːlsəʊ] *adv* anche

al·tar ['ɒltə(r)] REL altare *m*

al·ter ['ɒltə(r)] *v/t* modificare; *clothes* aggiustare

al·ter·a·tion [ɒltə'reɪʃn] modifica *f*

al·ter·nate ['ɒltəneɪt] **1** *v/i* alternare **2** *adj* ['ɒltənət] alternato; **on ~ days** a giorni alterni; **on ~ Mondays** un lunedì su due

al·ter·nat·ing 'cur·rent ['ɒltəneɪtɪŋ] corrente *f* alternata

al·ter·na·tive [ɒl'tɜːnətɪv] **1** *n* alternativa *f* **2** *adj* alternativo

al·ter·na·tive·ly [ɒl'tɜːnətɪvlɪ] *adv* alternativamente

al·though [ɔːl'ðəʊ] *conj* benché, sebbene

al·ti·tude ['æltɪtjuːd] altitudine *f*

al·to·geth·er [ɔːltə'geðə(r)] *adv* (*completely*) completamente; (*in all*) complessivamente

al·tru·ism ['æltruːɪzm] altruismo *m*

al·tru·is·tic [æltruː'ɪstɪk] *adj* altruistico

a·lu·min·i·um [æljʊ'mɪnɪəm], *Am* a·lu·mi·num [ə'luːmɪnəm] alluminio *m*

al·ways ['ɔːlweɪz] *adv* sempre

a.m. [eɪ'em] *abbr* (= **ante meridiem**) di mattina

a·mal·gam·ate [ə'mælgəmeɪt] *v/i* of *companies* fondersi

a·mass [ə'mæs] *v/t* accumulare

am·a·teur ['æmətə(r)] *n* (*unskilled*) dilettante *m/f*; SP non professionista *m/f*

am·a·teur·ish ['æmətərɪʃ] *adj pej* dilettantesco

a·maze [ə'meɪz] *v/t* stupire

a·mazed [ə'meɪzd] *adj* stupito

a·maze·ment [ə'meɪzmənt] stupore *m*

a·maz·ing [ə'meɪzɪŋ] *adj* (*surprising*) sorprendente; F (*good*) incredibile

a·maz·ing·ly [ə'meɪzɪŋlɪ] *adv* incredibilmente

am·bas·sa·dor [æm'bæsədə(r)] ambasciatore *m*, -trice *f*

am·ber ['æmbə(r)] *n* ambra *f*; **at ~** giallo

am·bi·dex·trous [æmbɪ'dekstrəs] *adj* ambidestro

am·bi·ence ['æmbɪəns] atmosfera *f*

am·bi·gu·i·ty [æmbɪ'gjuːətɪ] ambiguità *f*

am·big·u·ous [æm'bɪgjʊəs] *adj* ambiguo

am·bi·tion [æm'bɪʃn] ambizione *f*

am·bi·tious [æm'bɪʃəs] *adj* ambizioso

am·biv·a·lent [æm'bɪvələnt] *adj* ambiguo

am·ble ['æmbl] *v/i* camminare con calma; **we were ambling along the riverbank** stavamo passeggiando lungo il fiume

am·bu·lance ['æmbjʊləns] ambulanza *f*

am·bush ['æmbʊʃ] **1** *n* agguato *m* **2** *v/t* tendere un agguato a; **be ~ed by** subire un agguato da parte di

a·mend [ə'mend] *v/t* emendare

a·mend·ment [ə'mendmənt] emendamento *m*

a·mends [ə'mendz]: **make ~** fare ammenda

a·men·i·ties [ə'miːnətɪz] *npl* comodità *fpl*

A·mer·i·ca [ə'merɪkə] America *f*

A·mer·i·can [ə'merɪkən] **1** *n* americano *m*, -a *f* **2** *adj* americano

a·mi·a·ble ['eɪmɪəbl] *adj* amichevole

a·mi·ca·ble ['æmɪkəbl] *adj* amichevole

a·mi·ca·bly ['æmɪkəblɪ] *adv* amichevolmente

am·mu·ni·tion [æmjʊ'nɪʃn] munizioni *fpl*; *fig* arma *f*

am·ne·sia [æm'niːzɪə] amnesia *f*

am·nes·ty ['æmnəstɪ] amnistia *f*

a·mong(st) [ə'mʌŋ(st)] *prep* tra

a·mor·al [eɪ'mɒrəl] *adj* amorale

a·mount [ə'maʊnt] quantità *f inv*; (*sum of money*) importo *m*

♦ **amount to** *v/t of income, sum* ammontare a; (*be equal to*) equivalere a

am·phib·i·an [æm'fɪbɪən] anfibio *m*

am·phib·i·ous [æm'fɪbɪəs] *adj animal* anfibio; *vehicle* anfibio

am·phi·the·a·ter *Am*, **am·phi·the·a·tre** ['æmfɪθɪɑːtə(r)] anfiteatro *m*

am·ple ['æmpl] *adj* abbondante; (*more than enough*) in abbondanza

am·pli·fi·er ['æmplɪfaɪə(r)] amplificatore *m*

am·pli·fy ['æmplɪfaɪ] *v/t (pret & pp -ied)* sound amplificare

am·pu·tate ['æmpjuːteɪt] *v/t* amputare

am·pu·ta·tion [æmpjʊ'teɪʃn] amputazione *f*

a·muse [ə'mjuːz] *v/t (make laugh etc)* divertire; (*entertain*) intrattenere

a·muse·ment [ə'mjuːzmənt] (*merriment*) divertimento *m*; (*entertainment*) intrattenimento *m*; **~s** (*games*) divertimenti *mpl*; **to our great ~** con nostro grande divertimento

a'muse·ment ar·cade sala *f* giochi

a'muse·ment park parco *m* giochi

a·mus·ing [ə'mjuːzɪŋ] *adj* divertente

an [æn] → **a**

an·a·bol·ic 'ster·oid [ænə'bɒlɪk] anabolizzante *m*

an·ae·mi·a [ə'niːmɪə] anemia *f*

an·aem·ic [ə'niːmɪk] *adj* anemico

an·aes·thet·ic [ænəs'θetɪk] *n* anestetico *m*

an·aes·the·tist [ə'niːsθətɪst] anestesista *m/f*

an·a·log ['ænəlɒg] *adj* COMPUT analogico

a·nal·o·gy [ə'nælədʒɪ] analogia *f*

an·a·lyse ['ænəlaɪz] *v/t* analizzare; (*psychoanalyse*) psicanalizzare

a·nal·y·sis [ə'næləsɪs] (*pl* **analyses** [ə'næləsiːz]) analisi *f inv*

an·a·lyst ['ænəlɪst] *also* PSYCH analista *m/f*

an·a·lyt·i·cal [ænə'lɪtɪkl] *adj* analitico

an·a·lyze *Am* → **analyse**

an·arch·y ['ænəkɪ] anarchia *f*

a·nat·o·my [ə'nætəmɪ] anatomia *f*

an·ces·tor ['ænsestə(r)] antenato *m*, -a *f*

an·chor ['æŋkə(r)] **1** *n* NAUT ancora *f* **2** *v/i* NAUT gettare l'ancora

'an·chor·man TV presentatore *m*, anchorman *m inv*

an·cient ['eɪnʃənt] *adj* antico

an·cil·lar·y [æn'sɪlərɪ] *adj staff* ausiliario

and [ənd] *stressed* [ænd] *conj* e; **5 ~ 5 makes 10** 5 più 5 fa 10; **three hundred ~ sixty** trecentosessanta; **worse ~ worse** sempre peggio; **I'll come ~ pick you up** vengo a prenderti

an·ec·dote ['ænɪkdəʊt] aneddoto *m*

a·ne·mi·a etc Am → **anaemia** etc

an·es·thet·ic etc Am → **anaesthetic** etc

an·gel ['eɪndʒl] REL, *fig* angelo *m*

an·ger ['æŋgə(r)] **1** *n* rabbia *f* **2** *v/t* fare arrabbiare

an·gi·na [æn'dʒaɪnə] angina *f* (pectoris)

an·gle ['æŋgl] *n* angolo *m*; (*position, fig*) angolazione *f*

an·gler ['æŋglə(r)] pescatore *m*, -trice *f* (con amo e lenza)

An·gli·can ['æŋglɪkən] REL **1** *adj* anglicano **2** *n* anglicano *m*, -a *f*

An·glo-Sax·on [æŋgləʊ'sæksn] **1** *adj* anglosassone **2** *n person* anglosassone *m/f*

an·gry ['æŋgrɪ] *adj* arrabbiato; **be ~ with s.o.** essere arrabbiato con qu

an·guish ['æŋgwɪʃ] angoscia *f*

an·gu·lar ['æŋgjʊlə(r)] *adj face, shape* spigoloso

an·i·mal ['ænɪml] animale *m*

an·i·mated ['ænɪmeɪtɪd] *adj* animato

an·i·ma·ted car'toon cartone *m* animato

an·i·ma·tion [ænɪ'meɪʃn] animazione *f*

an·i·mos·i·ty [ænɪ'mɒsɪtɪ] animosità *f*

an·kle ['æŋkl] caviglia *f*

an·nex [ə'neks] *v/t state* annettere

an·nexe ['æneks] *n* (*building*) edificio *m* annesso; *to document* annesso *m*

an·ni·hi·late [ə'naɪəleɪt] *v/t* annientare

an·ni·hi·la·tion [ənaɪə'leɪʃn] annientamento *m*

an·ni·ver·sa·ry [ænɪ'vɜːsərɪ] (*wedding ~*) anniversario *m*

an·no·tate ['ænəteɪt] *v/t report* annotare

an·nounce [ə'naʊns] *v/t* annunciare

an·nounce·ment [ə'naʊnsmənt] annuncio *m*

an·nounc·er [ə'naʊnsə(r)] TV, *Radio* annunciatore *m*, -trice *f*

an·noy [ə'nɔɪ] *v/t* infastidire; **be ~ed** essere infastidito

an·noy·ance [ə'nɔɪəns] (*anger*) irritazione *f*, (*nuisance*) fastidio *m*

an·noy·ing [ə'nɔɪɪŋ] *adj* irritante

an·nu·al ['ænjʊəl] *adj* annuale

an·nu·al gen·er·al 'meet·ing assemblea *f* annuale

an·nu·i·ty [ə'njuːɪtɪ] rendita *f* annuale

an·nul [ə'nʌl] *v/t* (*pret & pp* **-led**) *marriage* annullare

an·nul·ment [ə'nʌlmənt] annullamento *m*

a·non·y·mous [ə'nɒnɪməs] *adj* anonimo

an·o·rak ['ænəræk] *Br* giacca *f* a vento

an·o·rex·i·a [ænə'reksɪə] anoressia *f*

an·o·rex·ic [ænə'reksɪk] *adj* anoressico

an·oth·er [ə'nʌðə(r)] **1** *adj* un altro *m*, un'altra *f* **2** *pron* un altro *m*, un'altra *f*; **one ~** l'un l'altro; **do they know one ~ ?** si conoscono?

an·swer ['ɑːnsə(r)] **1** *n to letter, person, problem* risposta *f* **2** *v/t letter, person* rispondere a; **~ the door** aprire la porta; **~ the telephone** rispondere al telefono

♦ answer back **1** *v/t person* ribattere a **2** *v/i* ribattere

♦ answer for *v/t* rispondere di

an·swer·ing ma·chine ['ɑːnsərɪŋ] TELEC segreteria *f* telefonica

ans·wer·phone ['ɑːnsəfəʊn] segreteria *f* telefonica

ant [ænt] formica *f*

an·tag·o·nis·m [æn'tægənɪzm] antagonismo *m*

an·tag·o·nis·tic [æntægə'nɪstɪk] *adj* ostile

an·tag·o·nize [æn'tægənaɪz] *v/t* contrariare

Ant·arc·tic [ænt'ɑ:ktɪk] *n* Antartico *m*

an·te·na·tal [æntɪ'neɪtl] *adj* durante la gravidanza; **~ classes** corso *m* di preparazione al parto; **~ clinic** clinica *f* per gestanti

an·ten·na [æn'tenə] antenna *f*

an·thol·o·gy [æn'θɒlədʒɪ] antologia *f*

an·thro·pol·o·gy [ænθrə'pɒlədʒɪ] antropologia *f*

an·ti·bi·ot·ic [æntɪbaɪ'ɒtɪk] *n* antibiotico *m*

an·ti·bod·y ['æntɪbɒdɪ] anticorpo *m*

an·tic·i·pate [æn'tɪsɪpeɪt] *v/t* prevedere

an·tic·i·pa·tion [æntɪsɪ'peɪʃn] previsione *f*

an·ti·clock·wise ['æntɪklɒkwaɪz] *Br* **1** *adj* antiorario **2** *adv* in senso antiorario

an·tics ['æntɪks] *npl* buffonate *fpl*

an·ti·dote ['æntɪdəʊt] antidoto *m*

an·ti·freeze ['æntɪfri:z] antigelo *m inv*

an·tip·a·thy [æn'tɪpəθɪ] antipatia *f*

an·ti·quat·ed ['æntɪkweɪtɪd] *adj* antiquato

an·tique [æn'ti:k] *n* pezzo *m* d'antiquariato

an'tique dealer antiquario *m*, -a *f*

an·tiq·ui·ty [æn'tɪkwətɪ] antichità *f inv*

an·ti·sep·tic [æntɪ'septɪk] **1** *adj* antisettico **2** *n* antisettico *m*

an·ti·so·cial [æntɪ'səʊʃl] *adj* asociale

an·ti·vi·rus pro·gram [æntɪ'vaɪrəs] COMPUT programma *m* antivirus

anx·i·e·ty [æŋ'zaɪətɪ] ansia *f*

anx·ious ['æŋkʃəs] *adj* ansioso; **be ~ for ...** *for news etc* essere ansioso di avere ...

an·y ['enɪ] **1** *adj* qualche; **are there ~ diskettes / glasses?** ci sono dei dischetti / bicchieri?; **is there ~ bread?** c'è del pane?; **is there ~ improvement?** c'è qualche miglioramento?; **there aren't ~ diskettes / glasses** non ci sono dischetti / bicchieri; **there isn't ~ bread** non c'è pane; **there isn't ~ improvement** non c'è nessun miglioramento; **have you ~ idea at all?** hai qualche idea?; **take ~ one you like** prendi quello che vuoi **2** *pron*: **do you have ~?** ne hai?; **there aren't ~ left** non ce ne sono più; **there isn't ~ left** non ce n'è più; **~ of them could be guilty** chiunque di loro potrebbe essere colpevole **3** *adv* un po'; **is that ~ better / easier?** è un po' meglio / più facile?; **I don't like it ~ more** non mi piace più

an·y·bod·y ['enɪbɒdɪ] *pron* qualcuno; *with negative* nessuno; *(whoever)* chiunque; **is there ~ there?** c'è qualcuno?; **there wasn't ~ there** non c'era nessuno; **~ could do it** lo potrebbe fare chiunque

an·y·how ['enɪhaʊ] comunque; **if I can help you ~, let me know** se ti posso aiutare in qualsiasi modo, fammi sapere

an·y·one ['enɪwʌn] → **anybody**

an·y·thing ['enɪθɪŋ] *pron* qualcosa; *with negatives* niente, nulla; **I didn't hear** ~ non ho sentito niente *o* nulla; **~ but** per niente; **she was ~ but helpful** non è stata per niente d'aiuto; **~ else?** qualcos'altro?

an·y·way ['enɪweɪ] → **anyhow**

an·y·where ['enɪweə(r)] *adv* da qualche parte; *with negative* da nessuna parte; *(wherever)* dovunque; **I can't find it ~** non riesco a trovarlo da nessuna parte

a·part [ə'pɑ:t] *adv in distance* distante; **the two cities are 250 miles ~** le due città distano 250 miglia l'una dall'altra; **live ~** *of people* vivere separati; **~ from** *(excepting)* a parte, tranne; *(in addition to)* oltre a

a·part·ment [ə'pɑ:tmənt] appartamento *m*

a'part·ment block *Am* palazzo *m* (d'appartamenti)

ap·a·thet·ic [æpə'θetɪk] *adj* apatico

ap·a·thy ['æpəθɪ] apatia *f*

ape [eɪp] scimmia *f*

a·pe·ri·tif [ə'perɪtiːf] aperitivo *m*

ap·er·ture ['æpətʃə(r)] PHOT apertura *f*

a·piece [ə'piːs] *adv* l'uno *m*, l'una *f*; **you can have one ~** potete averne uno a testa

a·pol·o·get·ic [əpɒlə'dʒetɪk] *adj letter, smile* di scuse; **he was very ~ for being late** si è scusato molto di essere in ritardo

a·pol·o·gize [ə'pɒlədʒaɪz] *v/i* scusarsi; **~ to s.o.** scusarsi con qu

a·pol·o·gy [ə'pɒlədʒɪ] scusa *f*; **make an ~ to s.o.** fare le proprie scuse a qu

a·pos·tle [ə'pɒsl] REL apostolo *m*

a·pos·tro·phe [ə'pɒstrəfɪ] GRAM apostrofo *m*

ap·pal [ə'pɔːl] *v/t* sconvolgere

ap·pal·ling [ə'pɔːlɪŋ] *adj* sconvolgente; *language* scioccante

ap·pa·ra·tus [æpə'reɪtəs] apparecchio *m*

ap·par·ent [ə'pærənt] *adj* evidente; (*seeming real*) apparente; **become ~ that ...** diventare evidente che ...

ap·par·ent·ly [ə'pærəntlɪ] *adv* apparentemente

ap·pa·ri·tion [æpə'rɪʃn] (*ghost*) apparizione

ap·peal [ə'piːl] **1** *n* (*charm*) attrattiva *f*; *for funds etc*, LAW appello *m* **2** *v/i* LAW fare appello

♦ **appeal to** (*be attractive to*) attirare

♦ **appeal for** *v/t blood, help* fare un appello per ottenere; **the President / appealed for calm** il Presidente ha fatto appello alla calma

ap·peal·ing [ə'piːlɪŋ] *adj idea, offer* allettante; *glance* supplichevole

ap·pear [ə'pɪə(r)] *v/i* apparire, comparire; *in film etc* apparire; *of new product* comparire; *in court* comparire; (*look, seem*) apparire; **it ~s that ...** sembra che ...

ap·pear·ance [ə'pɪərəns] (*arrival*) apparizione *f*, comparsa *f*; *in film etc*

apparizione *f*; *in court* comparizione *f*; (*look*) aspetto *m*; **put in an ~** fare un salto; **judge by ~s** giudicare dalle apparenze

ap·pease [ə'piːz] *v/t gods, anger* placare; *tyrant* compiacere

ap·pen·di·ci·tis [əpendɪ'saɪtɪs] appendicite *f*

ap·pen·dix [ə'pendɪks] MED, *of book etc* appendice *f*

ap·pe·tite ['æpɪtaɪt] appetito *m*; **~ for sth** *fig* sete *f* di qc

ap·pe·tiz·er ['æpɪtaɪzə(r)] *food* stuzzichino *m*; *drink* aperitivo *m*

ap·pe·tiz·ing ['æpɪtaɪzɪŋ] *adj* appetitoso

ap·plaud [ə'plɔːd] **1** *v/i* applaudire **2** *v/t also fig* applaudire

ap·plause [ə'plɔːz] applauso *m*; (*praise*) approvazione *f*

ap·ple ['æpl] mela *f*

ap·ple 'pie torta *f* di mele

ap·ple 'sauce composta *f* di mele

ap·pli·ance [ə'plaɪəns] apparecchio *m*; *household* elettrodomestico *m*

ap·pli·ca·ble [ə'plɪkəbl] *adj* applicabile

ap·pli·cant ['æplɪkənt] candidato *m*, -a *f*

ap·pli·ca·tion [æplɪ'keɪʃn] *for job etc* candidatura *f*; *for passport, visa* domanda *f*, richiesta *f*; *for university* domanda *f* di iscrizione

ap·pli·ca·tion form modulo *m* di richiesta; *for passport, visa* modulo *f* di richiesta; *for university* modulo *f* di richiesta di iscrizione

ap·ply [ə'plaɪ] (*pret & pp -ied*) **1** *v/t* applicare **2** *v/i of rule, law* applicarsi

♦ **apply for** *v/t job, passport* fare domanda per; *university* fare domanda di iscrizione a

♦ **apply to** *v/t* (*contact*) rivolgersi a; (*affect*) applicarsi a

ap·point [ə'pɔɪnt] *v/t to position* nominare

ap·point·ment [ə'pɔɪntmənt] *to position* nomina *f*; (*meeting*) appuntamento *m*

ap'point·ments di·a·ry agenda *f* degli appuntamenti

ap·prais·al [əˈpreɪz(ə)l] valutazione *f*

ap·pre·cia·ble [əˈpriːʃəbl] *adj* notevole

ap·pre·ci·ate [əˈpriːʃɪeɪt] **1** *v/t* apprezzare; (*acknowledge*) rendersi conto di; *thanks, I ~ it* grazie, te ne sono grato; *I ~ that ...* mi rendo conto che ... **2** *v/i* FIN rivalutarsi

ap·pre·ci·a·tion [əpriːʃɪˈeɪʃn] *of kindness etc* riconoscenza *f*, *of music etc* apprezzamento *m*

ap·pre·ci·a·tive [əˈpriːʃətɪv] *adj* (*showing gratitude*) riconoscente; (*showing pleasure*) soddisfatto

ap·pre·hen·sion [æprɪˈhenʃn] apprensione *f*

ap·pre·hen·sive [æprɪˈhensɪv] *adj* apprensivo

ap·pren·tice [əˈprentɪs] apprendista *m/f*

ap·pren·tice·ship [əˈprentɪsʃɪp] apprendistato *m*

ap·proach [əˈprəʊtʃ] **1** *n* avvicinamento *m*; (*proposal*) contatto *m*; *to problem* approccio *m* **2** *v/t* (*get near to*) avvicinarsi a; (*contact*) contattare; *problem* abbordare

ap·proach·a·ble [əˈprəʊtʃəbl] *adj person* abbordabile

ap·pro·pri·ate¹ [əˈprəʊprɪət] *adj* appropriato

ap·pro·pri·ate² [əˈprəʊprɪeɪt] *v/t also euph* appropriarsi di

ap·prov·al [əˈpruːvl] approvazione *f*

ap·prove [əˈpruːv] *v/t & v/i* approvare

♦ **approve of** *v/t* approvare

ap·prox·i·mate [əˈprɒksɪmət] *adj* approssimativo

ap·prox·i·mate·ly [əˈprɒksɪmətlɪ] *adv* approssimativamente

ap·prox·i·ma·tion [əprɒksɪˈmeɪʃn] approssimazione *f*

APR [eɪpiːˈɑː] *abbr* (= *annual percentage rate*) tasso *m* di interesse annuo

a·pri·cot [ˈeɪprɪkɒt] albicocca *f*

A·pril [ˈeɪprəl] aprile *m*

a·pron [ˈeɪprən] grembiule *m*

apt [æpt] *adj pupil* portato; *remark* appropriato; *be ~ to ...* avere tendenza a ...

ap·ti·tude [ˈæptɪtjuːd] attitudine *f*

'ap·ti·tude test test *m inv* attitudinale

aq·ua·lung [ˈækwəlʌŋ] autorespiratore *m*

a·quar·i·um [əˈkweərɪəm] acquario *m*

A·quar·i·us [əˈkweərɪəs] ASTR Acquario *m*

a·quat·ic [əˈkwætɪk] *adj* acquatico

Ar·ab [ˈærəb] **1** *n* arabo *m*, -a *f* **2** *adj* arabo

Ar·a·bic [ˈærəbɪk] **1** *n* arabo *m* **2** *adj* arabo

ar·a·ble [ˈærəbl] *adj* coltivabile

ar·bi·tra·ry [ˈɑːbɪtrərɪ] *adj* arbitrario

ar·bi·trate [ˈɑːbɪtreɪt] *v/i* arbitrare

ar·bi·tra·tion [ɑːbɪˈtreɪʃn] arbitrato *m*

ar·bi·tra·tor [ˈɑːbɪtreɪtə(r)] arbitro *m*

ar·cade [ɑːˈkeɪd] (*games ~*) sala *f* giochi

arch [ɑːtʃ] *n* arco *m*

ar·chae·o·log·i·cal [ɑːkɪəˈlɒdʒɪkl] *adj* archeologico

ar·chae·ol·o·gist [ɑːkɪˈɒlədʒɪst] archeologo *m*, -a *f*

ar·chae·ol·o·gy [ɑːkɪˈɒlədʒɪ] archeologia *f*

ar·cha·ic [ɑːˈkeɪɪk] *adj* arcaico

arch·bish·op [ɑːtʃˈbɪʃəp] arcivescovo *m*

ar·che·ol·o·gy *etc Am* → **archaeology** *etc*

ar·cher [ˈɑːtʃə(r)] arciere *m*, -a *f*

ar·chi·tec·t [ˈɑːkɪtekt] architetto *m*

ar·chi·tec·tur·al [ɑːkɪˈtektʃərəl] *adj* architettonico

ar·chi·tec·ture [ˈɑːkɪtektʃə(r)] architettura *f*

ar·chives [ˈɑːkaɪvz] *npl* archivi *mpl*

arch·way [ˈɑːtʃweɪ] arco *m*

Arc·tic [ˈɑːktɪk] *n* Artico *m*

ar·dent [ˈɑːdənt] *adj* ardente

ar·du·ous [ˈɑːdjʊəs] *adj* arduo

ar·e·a [ˈeərɪə] area *f*; (*region*) zona *f*

'ar·e·a code *Am* TELEC prefisso *m*

telefonico; *official name* indicativo *m* distrettuale

a·re·na [ə'ri:nə] SP arena *f*

Ar·gen·ti·na [ɑ:dʒən'ti:nə] Argentina *f*

Ar·gen·tin·i·an [ɑ:dʒən'tɪnɪən] **1** *adj* argentino **2** *n* argentino *m*, -a *f*

ar·gu·a·bly ['ɑ:gjʊəblɪ] *adv* probabilmente; **he's ~ the best** si può dire che è il migliore

ar·gue ['ɑ:gju:] **1** *v/i* (*quarrel*) litigare; (*reason*) sostenere **2** *v/t*: **~ that ...** sostenere che ...

ar·gu·ment ['ɑ:gjʊmənt] (*quarrel*) litigio *m*; (*reasoning*) argomento *m*

ar·gu·ment·a·tive [ɑ:gjʊ'mentətɪv] *adj* polemico

a·ri·a ['ɑ:rɪə] MUS aria *f*

ar·id ['ærɪd] *adj land* arido

Ar·i·es ['eərɪ:z] ASTR Ariete *m*

a·rise [ə'raɪz] *v/i* (*pret* **arose**, *pp* **arisen**) *of situation, problem* emergere

a·ris·en [ə'rɪzn] *pp* → **arise**

ar·is·toc·ra·cy [ærɪ'stɒkrəsɪ] aristocrazia *f*

ar·is·to·crat ['ærɪstəkræt] aristocratico *m*, -a *f*

ar·is·to·crat·ic [ærɪstə'krætɪk] *adj* aristocratico

a·rith·me·tic [ə'rɪθmətɪk] aritmetica *f*

arm[1] [ɑ:m] *n of person* braccio *m*; *of chair* bracciolo *m*

arm[2] [ɑ:m] *v/t* armare; **~ s.o. / sth with sth** armare qu / qc di qc

ar·ma·ments ['ɑ:məmənts] *npl* armamenti *mpl*

arm·chair ['ɑ:mtʃeə(r)] poltrona *f*

armed [ɑ:md] *adj* armato

armed 'forc·es *npl* forze *fpl* armate

armed 'rob·ber·y rapina *f* a mano armata

ar·mor *Am*, ar·mour ['ɑ:mə(r)] armatura *f*; (*metal plates*) blindatura *f*

ar·mored ve·hi·cle *Am*, ar·moured ve·hi·cle [ɑ:məd'vi:ɪkl] veicolo *m* blindato

arm·pit ['ɑ:mpɪt] ascella *f*

arms [ɑ:mz] *npl* (*weapons*) armi *fpl*

ar·my ['ɑ:mɪ] esercito *m*

a·ro·ma [ə'rəʊmə] aroma *m*

a·rose [ə'rəʊz] *pret* → **arise**

a·round [ə'raʊnd] **1** *prep* (*in circle, roughly*) intorno a; *room, world* attraverso; **it's ~ the corner** è dietro l'angolo **2** *adv* (*in the area*) qui intorno; (*encircling*) intorno; **he lives ~ here** abita da queste parti; **walk ~** andare in giro; **she has been ~** (*has travelled, is experienced*) ha girato; **he's still ~** F (*alive*) è ancora in circolazione

a·rouse [ə'raʊz] *v/t* suscitare; (*sexually*) eccitare

ar·range [ə'reɪndʒ] *v/t* (*put in order*) sistemare; *music* arrangiare; *meeting, party etc* organizzare; *time and place* combinare; **I've ~d to meet her** ho combinato di incontrarla

♦ arrange for *v/t* provvedere a; **I've arranged for him to meet us** ho provveduto affinché ci incontrasse

ar·range·ment [ə'reɪndʒmənt] (*agreement*) accordo *m*; *of party, meeting* organizzazione *f*; (*layout: of furniture etc*) disposizione *f*; *of music* arrangiamento *m*; **~s** *for party, meeting* preparativi *mpl*; **make ~s** prendere disposizioni

ar·rears [ə'rɪəz] *npl* arretrati *mpl*; **be in ~** *of person* essere in arretrato; **be paid in ~** *for job* essere pagato a lavoro effettuato

ar·rest [ə'rest] **1** *n* arresto *m*; **be under ~** essere in arresto **2** *v/t* arrestare

ar·riv·al [ə'raɪvl] arrivo *m*; **~s** *at airport* arrivi *mpl*

ar·rive [ə'raɪv] *v/i* arrivare

♦ arrive at *v/t place, decision* arrivare a

ar·ro·gance ['ærəgəns] arroganza *f*

ar·ro·gant ['ærəgənt] *adj* arrogante

ar·ro·gant·ly ['ærəgəntlɪ] *adv* con arroganza

ar·row ['ærəʊ] freccia *f*

arse [ɑ:s] ∨ culo *m* ∨

ar·se·nic ['ɑ:sənɪk] arsenico *m*

ar·son ['ɑ:sn] incendio *m* doloso

ar·son·ist ['ɑ:sənɪst] piromane *m/f*

art [ɑːt] arte f; **the ~s** l'arte

ar·te·ry ['ɑːtərɪ] MED arteria f

'**art gal·ler·y** galleria f d'arte

ar·thri·tis [ɑː'θraɪtɪs] artrite f

ar·ti·choke ['ɑːtɪʃəʊk] carciofo m

ar·ti·cle ['ɑːtɪkl] articolo m

ar·tic·u·late [ɑː'tɪkjʊlət] adj speech chiaro; **be ~ of person** esprimersi bene

ar·tic·u·lat·ed 'lor·ry [ɑːtɪkjʊleɪtɪd] Br autoarticolato m

ar·ti·fi·cial [ɑːtɪ'fɪʃl] adj artificiale; (not sincere) finto

ar·ti·fi·cial in'tel·li·gence intelligenza f artificiale

ar·til·le·ry [ɑː'tɪlərɪ] artiglieria f

ar·ti·san ['ɑːtɪzæn] artigiano m, -a f

ar·tist ['ɑːtɪst] artista m/f

ar·tis·tic [ɑː'tɪstɪk] adj artistico

'**arts de·gree** laurea f in discipline umanistiche

as [æz] **1** conj (while, when) mentre; (because) dato che; (like) come; **~ he grew older, ...** diventando più vecchio, ...; **~ if** come se; **~ usual** come al solito; **~ necessary** in base alla necessità; **2** adv: **~ high / pretty / ...** alto / carino come ...; **~ much ~ that?** così tanto?; **run ~ fast ~ you can** corri più veloce che puoi **3** prep come; **~ a child** da bambino; **~ a schoolgirl** quando andava a scuola; **I'm talking to you ~ a friend** ti parlo come amico; **dressed ~ a policeman** vestito da poliziotto; **work ~ a teacher / translator** essere insegnante / traduttore; **~ for** quanto a; **~ Hamlet** nel ruolo di Amleto

asap ['eɪzæp] abbr (= **as soon as possible**) quanto prima

as·bes·tos [æz'bestɒs] amianto m

As·cen·sion [ə'senʃn] REL Ascensione f

as·cent [ə'sent] path salita f; of mountain ascensione f; fig ascesa f

ash [æʃ] cenere f; **~es** ceneri fpl

a·shamed [ə'ʃeɪmd] adj: **be ~ of** vergognarsi di; **you should be ~ of yourself** dovresti vergognarti

a·shore [ə'ʃɔː(r)] adv a terra; **go ~** sbarcare

ash·tray ['æʃtreɪ] posacenere m, portacenere m

Ash 'Wednes·day mercoledì m inv delle Ceneri

A·sia ['eɪʒə] Asia f

A·sian ['eɪʒən] **1** n asiatico m, -a f; (Indian, Pakistani) indiano m, -a f **2** adj asiatico; (Indian, Pakistani) indiano

a·side [ə'saɪd] adv da parte; **take s.o. ~** prendere a parte qu; **joking ~** scherzi a parte; **~ from** a parte

ask [ɑːsk] **1** v/t person chiedere a; (invite) invitare; question fare; favour chiedere; **can I ~ you something?** posso chiederti una cosa?; **~ s.o. about sth** chiedere a qu di qc; **~ s.o. for ...** chiedere a qu ...; **~ s.o. to ...** chiedere a qu di ... **2** v/i chiedere

♦ **ask after** v/t person chiedere di

♦ **ask for** v/t chiedere; person chiedere di

♦ **ask out** v/t for a drink, night out chiedere di uscire a

ask·ing price ['ɑːskɪŋpraɪs] prezzo m di domanda

a·sleep [ə'sliːp] adj: **he's (fast) ~** sta dormendo (profondamente); **fall ~** addormentarsi

as·par·a·gus [ə'spærəgəs] asparagi mpl

as·pect ['æspekt] aspetto m

as·phalt ['æsfælt] n asfalto m

as·phyx·i·ate [æ'sfɪksɪeɪt] v/t asfissiare

as·phyx·i·a·tion [əsfɪksɪ'eɪʃn] asfissia f

as·pi·ra·tion [æspə'reɪʃn] aspirazione f

as·pi·rin ['æsprɪn] aspirina f

ass [æs] F (idiot) cretino m, -a; Am P (backside) culo m P

as·sai·lant [ə'seɪlənt] assalitore m, -trice f

as·sas·sin [ə'sæsɪn] assassino m, -a f

as·sas·sin·ate [ə'sæsɪneɪt] v/t assassinare

as·sas·sin·a·tion [əsæsɪ'neɪʃn] assassinio m

as·sault [ə'sɒlt] **1** n assalto m; LAW aggressione f **2** v/t aggredire

as·sem·ble [ə'sembl] **1** v/t parts assemblare, montare **2** v/i of people radunarsi

as·sem·bly [ə'semblɪ] assemblea f; of parts assemblaggio m

as·sem·bly line catena f di montaggio

as·sem·bly plant officina f di montaggio

as·sent [ə'sent] v/i acconsentire

as·sert [ə'sɜːt]: v/t: ~ o.s. farsi valere

as·ser·tive [ə'sɜːtɪv] adj person sicuro di sé

as·sess [ə'ses] v/t valutare

as·sess·ment [ə'sesmənt] valutazione f

as·set ['æset] FIN attivo m; fig: thing vantaggio m; person elemento m prezioso

as·sign [ə'saɪn] v/t: person destinare; thing assegnare

as·sign·ment [ə'saɪnmənt] (task, study) compito m

as·sim·i·late [ə'sɪmɪleɪt] v/t information assimilare; person into group integrare

as·sist [ə'sɪst] v/t assistere

as·sis·tance [ə'sɪstəns] assistenza f

as·sis·tant [ə'sɪstənt] assistente m/f; in shop commesso m, -a f

as·sis·tant di'rec·tor vice-direttore m; of film aiuto-regista m/f

as·sis·tant 'man·ag·er of business vice-responsabile m/f; of hotel, restaurant vice-direttore m

as·so·ci·ate [ə'səʊʃɪeɪt] **1** v/t associare **2** v/i: ~ with frequentare **3** n [ə'səʊʃɪət] socio m, -a f

as·so·ci·ate pro'fes·sor professore m associato, professoressa f associata

as·so·ci·a·tion [əsəʊsɪ'eɪʃn] associazione f; in ~ with in associazione con

as·sort·ed [ə'sɔːtɪd] adj assortito

as·sort·ment [ə'sɔːtmənt] assortimento m; there was a whole ~ of people c'era gente di tutti i tipi

as·sume [ə'sjuːm] v/t (suppose) supporre

as·sump·tion [ə'sʌmpʃn] supposizione f; The Assumption REL l'Assunzione f

as·sur·ance [ə'ʃʊərəns] assicurazione f, garanzia f; (confidence) sicurezza f; he gave me his personal ~ that ... mi ha assicurato personalmente che ...

as·sure [ə'ʃʊə(r)] v/t (reassure): ~ s.o. of sth assicurare qc a qu

as·sured [ə'ʃʊəd] adj (confident) sicuro

as·ter·isk ['æstərɪsk] asterisco m

asth·ma ['æsmə] asma f

asth·mat·ic [æs'mætɪk] adj asmatico

as·ton·ish [ə'stɒnɪʃ] v/t sbalordire; be ~ed essere sbalordito

as·ton·ish·ing [ə'stɒnɪʃɪŋ] adj sbalorditivo

as·ton·ish·ing·ly [ə'stɒnɪʃɪŋlɪ] adv in modo sbalorditivo

as·ton·ish·ment [ə'stɒnɪʃmənt] stupore m

as·tound [ə'staʊnd] v/t stupefare

as·tound·ing [ə'staʊndɪŋ] adj stupefacente

a·stray [ə'streɪ] adv: go ~ smarrirsi; morally uscire dalla retta via

a·stride [ə'straɪd] **1** adv a cavalcioni **2** prep a cavalcioni di

as·trol·o·ger [ə'strɒlədʒə(r)] astrologo m, -a f

as·trol·o·gy [ə'strɒlədʒɪ] astrologia f

as·tro·naut ['æstrənɔːt] astronauta m/f

as·tron·o·mer [ə'strɒnəmə(r)] astronomo m, -a f

as·tro·nom·i·cal [æstrə'nɒmɪkl] adj price etc astronomico

as·tron·o·my [ə'strɒnəmɪ] astronomia f

as·tute [ə'stjuːt] adj astuto

a·sy·lum [ə'saɪləm] mental manicomio m; political asilo m

at [ət] stressed [æt] prep (with places) a; he works ~ the hospital lavora in ospedale; ~ the baker's dal panettiere o in panetteria; ~ Joe's da Joe; ~ the door alla porta; ~ 10 pounds a 10 sterline; ~ the age of 18 all'età di 18 anni; ~ 5 o'clock alle cinque; ~ war in guerra; ~ night di notte; ~

the moment you called nel momento in cui hai chiamato; **~ 150 km/h** a 150 km/h; **be good / bad ~ sth** essere / non essere bravo in qc

ate [eɪt] *pret of* **eat**

a·the·is·m ['eɪθɪɪzm] ateismo *m*

a·the·ist ['eɪθɪɪst] ateo *m*, -a *f*

ath·lete ['æθliːt] atleta *m/f*

ath·let·ic [æθ'letɪk] *adj* atletico

ath·let·ics [æθ'letɪks] *nsg* atletica *f*

At·lan·tic [ət'læntɪk] *n* Atlantico *m*

at·las ['ætləs] atlante *m*

at·mos·phere ['ætməsfɪə(r)] *of earth, mood* atmosfera *f*

at·mos·pher·ic pol·lu·tion [ætməs'ferɪk] inquinamento *m* atmosferico

at·om ['ætəm] atomo *m*

'at·om bomb bomba *f* atomica

a·tom·ic [ə'tɒmɪk] *adj* atomico

a·tom·ic 'en·er·gy energia *f* nucleare

a·tom·ic 'waste scorie *fpl* nucleari

a·tom·iz·er ['ætəmaɪzə(r)] vaporizzatore *m*

a·tone [ə'təʊn] *v/i:* **~ for** scontare

a·tro·cious [ə'trəʊʃəs] *adj* atroce

a·troc·i·ty [ə'trɒsətɪ] atrocità *f inv*

at·tach [ə'tætʃ] *v/t* attaccare; *importance* attribuire; *document, file* allegare; **be ~ed to** (*fond of*) essere attaccato a

at·tach·ment [ə'tætʃmənt] (*fondness*) attaccamento *m*; **to email** allegato *m*

at·tack [ə'tæk] **1** *n* aggressione *f*; MIL attacco *m* **2** *v/t* aggredire; MIL attaccare

at·tempt [ə'tempt] **1** *n* tentativo *m* **2** *v/t* tentare; **~ to do sth**

at·tend [ə'tend] *v/t wedding, funeral* partecipare a; *school, classes* frequentare

♦ **attend to** *v/t* (*deal with*) sbrigare; *customer* servire; *patient* assistere

at·tend·ance [ə'tendəns] partecipazione *f*; *at school* frequenza *f*

at·tend·ant [ə'tendənt] *in museum etc* sorvegliante *m/f*

at·ten·tion [ə'tenʃn] attenzione *f*; **bring sth to s.o.'s ~** informare qu di qc; *your ~* **please** attenzione; *pay ~*

fare attenzione; **for the ~ of** *in faxes etc* alla cortese attenzione di

at·ten·tive [ə'tentɪv] *adj listener* attento

at·tic ['ætɪk] soffitta *f*

at·ti·tude ['ætɪtjuːd] atteggiamento *m*

attn *abbr* (= **attention**) c.a. (= alla cortese attenzione di)

at·tor·ney [ə'tɜːnɪ] avvocato *m*; **power of ~** delega *f*

at·tract [ə'trækt] *v/t* attirare; **be ~ed to s.o.** essere attirato da qu

at·trac·tion [ə'trækʃn] attrazione *f*

at·trac·tive [ə'træktɪv] *adj* attrattivo; *person* attraente

at·trib·ute¹ [ə'trɪbjuːt] *v/t* attribuire; **~ sth to ...** attribuire qc a ...

at·trib·ute² ['ætrɪbjuːt] *n* attributo *m*

au·ber·gine ['əʊbəʒiːn] melanzana *f*

auc·tion ['ɔːkʃn] **1** *n* asta *f* **2** *v/t* mettere all'asta

♦ **auction off** *v/t* vendere all'asta

auc·tio·neer [ɔːkʃə'nɪə(r)] banditore *m*, -trice *f*

au·da·cious [ɔː'deɪʃəs] *adj* audace

au·dac·i·ty [ɔː'dæsətɪ] audacia *f*

au·di·ble ['ɔːdəbl] *adj* udibile

au·di·ence ['ɔːdɪəns] pubblico *m*; TV telespettatori *mpl*; *with the Pope etc* udienza *f*

au·di·o ['ɔːdɪəʊ] *adj* audio *inv*

au·di·o·vi·su·al [ɔːdɪəʊ'vɪʒʊəl] *adj* audiovisivo

au·dit ['ɔːdɪt] **1** *n of accounts* revisione *f o* verifica *f* contabile; *software* **~** inventario *m* dei software **2** *v/t* verificare

au·di·tion [ɔː'dɪʃn] **1** *n* audizione *f* **2** *v/i* fare un'audizione

au·di·tor ['ɔːdɪtə(r)] revisore *m* contabile

au·di·to·ri·um [ɔːdɪ'tɔːrɪəm] *of theatre etc* sala *f*

Au·gust ['ɔːɡəst] agosto *m*

aunt [ɑːnt] zia *f*

au pair (girl) [əʊ'peə(r)] ragazza *f* alla pari

au·ra ['ɔːrə]: **she has an ~ of confidence** emana sicurezza

aus·pic·es ['ɔːspɪsɪz]: **under the ~**

of sotto l'egida di

aus·pi·cious [ɔːˈspɪʃəs] *adj* propizio

aus·tere [ɔːˈstɪə(r)] *adj* austero

aus·ter·i·ty [ɒsˈterətɪ] *economic* austerità *f*

Aus·tra·li·a [ɒˈstreɪlɪə] Australia *f*

Aus·tra·li·an [ɒˈstreɪlɪən] **1** *adj* australiano **2** *n* australiano *m*, -a *f*

Aus·tri·a [ˈɒstrɪə] Austria *f*

Aus·tri·an [ˈɒstrɪən] **1** *adj* austriaco **2** *n* austriaco *m*, -a *f*

au·then·tic [ɔːˈθentɪk] *adj* autentico

au·then·tic·i·ty [ɔːθenˈtɪsətɪ] autenticità *f*

au·thor [ˈɔːθə(r)] autore *m*, autrice *f*

au·thor·i·tar·i·an [ɔːθɒrɪˈteərɪən] *adj* autoritario

au·thor·i·ta·tive [ɔːˈθɒrɪtətɪv] *adj* autoritario; *information* autorevole

au·thor·i·ty [ɔːˈθɒrətɪ] autorità *f inv*; (*permission*) autorizzazione *f*; **be in ~** avere l'autorità; **be an ~ on** essere un'autorità in materia di; **the authorities** le autorità

au·thor·i·za·tion [ɔːθəraɪˈzeɪʃn] autorizzazione *f*

au·thor·ize [ˈɔːθəraɪz] *v/t* autorizzare; **be ~d to …** essere autorizzato a …

au·tis·tic [ɔːˈtɪstɪk] *adj* autistico

au·to·bi·og·ra·phy [ɔːtəbaɪˈɒɡrəfɪ] autobiografia *f*

au·to·crat·ic [ɔːtəˈkrætɪk] *adj* autocratico

au·to·graph [ˈɔːtəɡrɑːf] autografo *m*

au·to·mate [ˈɔːtəmeɪt] *v/t* automatizzare

au·to·mat·ic [ɔːtəˈmætɪk] **1** *adj* automatico **2** *n car* macchina *f* con il cambio automatico; *gun* pistola *f* automatica; *washing machine* lavatrice *f* automatica

au·to·mat·i·cal·ly [ɔːtəˈmætɪklɪ] *adv* automaticamente

au·to·ma·tion [ɔːtəˈmeɪʃn] automazione *f*

au·to·mo·bile [ˈɔːtəməbiːl] automobile *f*

au·ton·o·mous [ɔːˈtɒnəməs] *adj* autonomo

au·ton·o·my [ɔːˈtɒnəmɪ] autonomia *f*

au·to·pi·lot [ˈɔːtəʊpaɪlət] pilota *m* automatico

au·top·sy [ˈɔːtɒpsɪ] autopsia *f*

au·tumn [ˈɔːtəm] autunno *m*

aux·il·ia·ry [ɔːɡˈzɪlɪərɪ] *adj* ausiliario

a·vail [əˈveɪl] **1** *n*: **to no ~** invano **2** *v/t*: **~ o.s. of** avvalersi di

a·vai·la·ble [əˈveɪləbl] *adj* disponibile

av·a·lanche [ˈævəlɑːnʃ] valanga *f*

av·a·rice [ˈævərɪs] avarizia *f*

a·venge [əˈvendʒ] *v/t* vendicare

av·e·nue [ˈævənjuː] corso *m*; *fig* strada *f*

av·e·rage [ˈævərɪdʒ] **1** *adj* medio; (*of mediocre quality*) mediocre **2** *n* media *f*; **above** / **below ~** sopra / sotto la media; **on ~** in media, mediamente **3** *v/t* raggiungere in media

◆ **average out** *v/t* fare la media di

◆ **average out at** *v/t* risultare in media a

a·verse [əˈvɜːs] *adj*: **not be ~ to** non avere niente contro

a·ver·sion [əˈvɜːʃn] avversione *f*; **have an ~ to** avere un'avversione per

a·vert [əˈvɜːt] *v/t one's eyes* distogliere; *crisis* evitare

a·vi·a·ry [ˈeɪvɪərɪ] voliera *f*

a·vi·a·tion [eɪvɪˈeɪʃn] aviazione *f*; **~ industry** industria *f* aeronautica

av·id [ˈævɪd] *adj* avido

av·o·ca·do [ævəˈkɑːdəʊ] avocado *m inv*

a·void [əˈvɔɪd] *v/t* evitare

a·void·a·ble [əˈvɔɪdəbl] *adj* evitabile

a·wait [əˈweɪt] *v/t* attendere

a·wake [əˈweɪk] *adj* sveglio; **it's keeping me ~** mi impedisce di dormire

a·ward [əˈwɔːd] **1** *n* (*prize*) premio *m* **2** *v/t* assegnare; *damages* riconoscere; **she was ~ed the Nobel Prize for …** le hanno assegnato il premio Nobel per …

a·ware [əˈweə(r)] *adj* conscio, consapevole; **be ~ of sth** essere conscio o consapevole di qc; **become ~ of sth**

rendersi conto di qc

a·ware·ness [ə'weənɪs] consapevolezza f

a·way [ə'weɪ] adv via; SP fuori casa; **be** ~ *travelling, sick etc* essere via; **go/run** ~ andare/correre via; **look** ~ guardare da un'altra parte; **it's 2 miles** ~ dista 2 miglia; **Christmas is still six weeks** ~ mancano ancora sei settimane a Natale; **take sth** ~ **from s.o.** togliere qc a qu; **put sth** ~ mettere via qc

a'way match SP partita f fuori casa

awe [ɔː] soggezione f

awe·some ['ɔːsm] adj F (terrific) fantastico

aw·ful ['ɔːfl] adj tremendo, terribile; **I feel** ~ F sto da cani F

aw·ful·ly ['ɔːflɪ] adv F (very) da matti F

awk·ward ['ɔːkwəd] adj (clumsy) goffo; (difficult) difficile; (embarrassing) scomodo; **feel** ~ sentirsi a disagio

awn·ing ['ɔːnɪŋ] tenda f

ax Am, **axe** [æks] **1** n scure f, accetta f **2** v/t project, job sopprimere

ax·le ['æksl] asse f

B

BA [biː'eɪ] abbr (= **Bachelor of Arts**) (degree) laurea f in lettere; (person) laureato m, -a f in lettere

ba·by ['beɪbɪ] n bambino m, -a f

'**baby boom** baby boom m inv

ba·by·ish ['beɪbɪɪʃ] adj infantile

'**ba·by-sit·ter** baby-sitter m/f inv

bach·e·lor ['bætʃələ(r)] scapolo m

back [bæk] **1** n of person schiena f; of animal, hand dorso m; of car, bus parte f posteriore; of book, house retro m; of clothes rovescio m; of drawer fondo m; of chair schienale m; SP terzino m; **in the** ~ (**of the car**) (nei sedili) di dietro; **at the** ~ **of the bus** in fondo all'autobus; ~ **to front** al contrario; **at the** ~ **of beyond** in capo al mondo **2** adj door, steps di dietro; wheels, legs posteriore; garden, room sul retro; payment, issue arretrato; ~ **road** strada secondaria **3** adv: **please move/stand** ~ indietro, per favore; **2 metres** ~ **from the edge** a 2 metri dal bordo; ~ **in 1935** nel 1935; **give sth** ~ **to s.o.** restituire qc a qu; **she'll be** ~

tomorrow sarà di ritorno domani; **when are you coming** ~? quando torni?; **take sth** ~ **to the store** because unsatisfactory riportare qc indietro al negozio; **they wrote/ phoned** ~ hanno risposto alla lettera/telefonata; **he hit me** ~ mi ha restituito il colpo **4** v/t (support) appoggiare; car guidare in retromarcia; horse puntare su; ~ **the car into the garage** mettere la macchina in garage in retromarcia **5** v/i of driver fare retromarcia

♦**back away** v/i indietreggiare

♦**back down** v/i fig fare marcia indietro

♦**back off** v/i spostarsi indietro; from danger tirarsi indietro

♦**back onto** v/t dare su

♦**back out** v/i fig tirarsi indietro

♦**back up 1** v/t (support) confermare; claim, argument supportare; file fare un backup di; **back s.o. up** spalleggiare qu; **be backed up of** traffic essere congestionato **2** v/i in car fare retromarcia

'**back·ache** mal m inv di schiena; **back·bench·er** [bæk'bentʃə(r)]

B

parlamentare *m/f* ordinario, -a; 'back·bit·ing maldicenze *fpl*; 'back·bone *also fig* spina *f* dorsale; 'back·break·ing *adj* massacrante; back 'burn·er: put sth on the ~ accantonare qc; 'back·date *v/t* retrodatare; 'back·door porta *f* di dietro

back·er ['bækə(r)] FIN finanziatore *m*, -trice *f*

back'fire *v/i fig* avere effetto contrario; ~ on s.o. ritorcersi contro qu; 'back·ground *n* sfondo *m*; *fig:* of person background *m inv*; of story, event retroscena *mpl*; 'back·hand *n* in tennis rovescio *m*; back·hand·er ['bækhændə(r)] F bustarella *f* F

'back·ing ['bækɪŋ] *n* moral appoggio *m*; financial finanziamento *m*; MUS accompagnamento *m*

'back·ing group MUS gruppo *m* d'accompagnamento

'back·lash reazione *f* violenta; 'back·log: ~ of work lavoro *m* arretrato; ~ of unanswered letters corrispondenza *f* arretrata; 'back·pack *n* zaino *m*; 'back·pack·er saccopelista *m/f*, 'back·pack·ing il viaggiare con zaino e sacco a pelo; 'back·ped·al *v/i fig* fare marcia indietro; 'back seat of car sedile *m* posteriore; back-seat 'driv·er: you're a terrible ~! smettila di dire come si deve guidare!; 'back·side F sedere *m*; 'back·space (key) (tasto di) ritorno *m*; 'back·stairs scala *f* di servizio; 'back streets npl vicoli *mpl*; 'back·stroke SP dorso *m*; 'back·track *v/i* tornare indietro; 'back·up (support) rinforzi *mpl*; COMPUT backup *m inv*; 'back·up disk COMPUT disco *m* di backup

back·ward ['bækwəd] *adj child* tardivo; *society* arretrato; *glance* all'indietro

backwards ['bækwədz] *adv* indietro

back'yard cortile *m*; not in my ~ *fig* non in casa mia

ba·con ['beɪkn] pancetta *f*

bac·te·ri·a [bæk'tɪərɪə] npl batteri *mpl*

bad [bæd] *adj news, manners* cattivo; *weather, cold, headache* brutto; *mistake, accident* grave; *egg, food* guasto; smoking is ~ for you il fumo fa male; it's not ~ non è male; that's too ~ shame peccato!; feel ~ about sth (guilty) sentirsi in colpa per qc; be ~ at essere negato per; Friday's ~, how about Thursday? venerdì non posso, che ne dici di giovedì?

bad 'debt debito *m* insoluto

badge [bædʒ] distintivo *m*

bad·ger ['bædʒə(r)] *v/t* tasso *m*

bad 'lan·guage parolacce *fpl*

bad·ly ['bædlɪ] *adv* male; *injured, damaged* gravemente; he ~ needs a haircut/rest ha urgente bisogno di tagliarsi i capelli/riposare; he is ~ off (poor) è povero

bad-man·nered [bæd'mænəd] *adj* maleducato

bad·min·ton ['bædmɪntən] badminton *m inv*

bad-tem·pered [bæd'tempəd] *adj* irascibile

baf·fle ['bæfl] *v/t*: be ~d essere perplesso

baf·fling ['bæflɪŋ] *adj* sconcertante

bag [bæg] borsa *f*; *plastic, paper* busta *f*

bag·gage ['bægɪdʒ] bagagli *mpl*

bag·gage re·claim ['riːkleɪm] ritiro *m* bagagli

'bag·gage trol·ley carrello *m*

bag·gy ['bægɪ] *adj* senza forma

'bag·pipes npl cornamusa *fsg*

bail [beɪl] *n* LAW cauzione *f*; on ~ su cauzione

♦ bail out 1 *v/t* LAW scarcerare su cauzione; *fig* tirare fuori dai guai 2 *v/i* of aeroplane lanciarsi col paracadute

bai·liff ['beɪlɪf] ufficiale *m* giudiziario

bait [beɪt] *n* esca *f*

bake [beɪk] *v/t* cuocere al forno

baked 'beans [beɪkt] npl fagioli *mpl* in salsa rossa

baked po'ta·toes npl patate *fpl* cotte al forno con la buccia

bak·er ['beɪkə(r)] fornaio *m*, -a *f*

bak·er's ['beɪkəz] panetteria f
bak·er·y ['beɪkərɪ] panetteria f
bak·ing pow·der ['beɪkɪŋ] lievito m
bal·ance ['bæləns] **1** n equilibrio m; (*remainder*) resto m; *of bank account* saldo m **2** v/t tenere in equilibrio; ~ **the books** fare il bilancio **3** v/i stare in equilibrio; *of accounts* quadrare
bal·anced ['bælənst] adj (*fair*) obiettivo; *diet, personality* equilibrato
bal·ance of 'pay·ments bilancia f dei pagamenti
bal·ance of 'trade bilancia f commerciale
'bal·ance sheet bilancio m (di esercizio)
bal·co·ny ['bælkənɪ] *of house* balcone m; *in theatre* prima galleria f
bald [bɔːld] adj *man* calvo; **he's going** ~ sta perdendo i capelli
bald·ing ['bɔːldɪŋ] adj stempiato
Bal·kan ['bɔːlkən] adj balcanico
Bal·kans ['bɔːlkənz] npl: **the** ~ i Balcani mpl
ball[1] [bɔːl] palla f; *football* pallone m; **be on the** ~ essere sveglio; **play** ~ fig collaborare; **the ~'s in his court** la prossima mossa è sua
ball[2] [bɔːl] (*dance*) ballo m
bal·lad ['bæləd] ballata f
ball 'bear·ing cuscinetto m a sfere
bal·le·ri·na [bælə'riːnə] ballerina f
bal·let ['bæleɪ] *art* danza f classica; *dance* balletto m
'bal·let danc·er ballerino m classico, ballerina f classica
'ball game F: **that's a different** ~ è un altro paio di maniche
bal·lis·tic mis·sile [bə'lɪstɪk] missile m balistico
bal·loon [bə'luːn] *child's* palloncino m; *for flight* mongolfiera f
bal·loon·ist [bə'luːnɪst] aeronauta m/f
bal·lot ['bælət] **1** n votazione f **2** v/t *members* consultare tramite votazione
'bal·lot box urna f elettorale
'bal·lot pa·per scheda f elettorale
'ball·park F: **be in the right** ~ essere nell'ordine corretto di cifre; **'ball-**

park fig·ure F cifra f approssimativa
'ball·point (pen) penna f a sfera
balls [bɔːlz] npl V (*also courage*) palle fpl V
bam·boo [bæm'buː] n bambù m inv
ban [bæn] **1** n divieto m (**on** di) **2** v/t (*pret & pp* **-ned**) proibire
ba·nal [bə'nɑːl] adj banale
ba·na·na [bə'nɑːnə] banana f
band [bænd] banda f; *pop* gruppo m; *of material* nastro m
ban·dage ['bændɪdʒ] **1** n benda f **2** v/t bendare
B&B [biː'n'biː] abbr (= **bed and breakfast**) pensione f familiare, bed and breakfast m inv
ban·dit ['bændɪt] brigante m
'band·wag·on n: **jump on the** ~ seguire la corrente
ban·dy ['bændɪ] adj *legs* storto
bang [bæŋ] **1** n colpo m **2** v/t *door* chiudere violentemente; (*hit*) sbattere; **I –ed my knee on the table** ho battuto il ginocchio contro il tavolo **3** v/i sbattere; **the door ~ed shut** la porta si è chiusa con un colpo
bang·er ['bæŋə(r)] F (*sausage*) salamino m; **an old** ~ (*car*) una vecchia carretta
ban·gle ['bæŋgl] braccialetto m
ban·is·ters ['bænɪstəz] npl ringhiera fsg
ban·jo ['bændʒəʊ] banjo m inv
bank[1] [bæŋk] *of river* riva f
bank[2] [bæŋk] **1** n FIN banca f **2** v/i: ~ **with** avere un conto presso **3** v/t *money* mettere in banca
♦ **bank on** v/t contare su; **don't bank on it** non ci contare; **bank on s.o. doing sth** dare per scontato che qu faccia qc
'bank ac·count conto m bancario
'bank bal·ance saldo m
bank·er ['bæŋkə(r)] banchiere m
'bank·er's card carta f assegni
'bank·er's 'or·der ordine m di pagamento
bank 'hol·i·day giorno m festivo
bank·ing ['bæŋkɪŋ] professione f bancaria

B

'bank loan prestito *m* bancario; 'bank man·ag·er direttore *m* di banca; 'bank note banconota *f*; 'bank rate tasso *m* ufficiale di sconto; 'bank·roll *v/t* finanziare

bank·rupt ['bæŋkrʌpt] 1 *adj* fallito; **go ~** fallire 2 *v/t* portare al fallimento

bank·rupt·cy ['bæŋkrʌpsɪ] bancarotta *f*

'bank state·ment estratto *m* conto

ban·ner ['bænə(r)] *n* striscione *m*

banns [bænz] *npl* pubblicazioni *mpl* (matrimoniali)

ban·quet ['bæŋkwɪt] *n* banchetto *m*

ban·ter ['bæntə(r)] *n* scambio *m* di battute

bap·tis·m ['bæptɪzm] *n* battesimo *m*

bap·tize [bæp'taɪz] *v/t* battezzare

bar¹ [bɑː(r)] *n* of iron sparanga *f*; of chocolate tavoletta *f*; for drinks bar *m inv*; (counter) bancone *m*; **a ~ of soap** una saponetta; **be behind ~s** (in prison) essere dietro le sbarre

bar² [bɑː(r)] *v/t* (pret & pp **-red**) vietare l'ingresso a; **he's been ~red from the club** gli hanno vietato l'ingresso al club

bar³ [bɑː(r)] *prep* (except) tranne

bar·bar·i·an [bɑː'beərɪən] barbaro *m*, -a *f*

bar·bar·ic [bɑː'bærɪk] *adj* barbaro

bar·be·cue ['bɑːbɪkjuː] 1 *n* barbecue *m inv* 2 *v/t* cuocere al barbecue

barbed 'wire [bɑːbd] filo *m* spinato

bar·ber ['bɑːbə(r)] barbiere *m*

bar·bi·tu·rate [bɑː'bɪtjʊrət] barbiturico *m*

'bar code codice *m* a barre

bare [beə(r)] *adj* (naked) nudo; (empty: room) spoglio; mountainside brullo

'bare·foot *adj*: **be ~** essere scalzo

bare-head·ed [beə'hedɪd] *adj* senza cappello

'bare·ly ['beəlɪ] *adv* appena

bar·gain ['bɑːgɪn] 1 *n* (deal) patto *m*; (good buy) affare *m*; **it's a ~!** (deal) è un affarone!; **into the ~** per giunta 2 *v/i* tirare sul prezzo

♦ bargain for *v/t* (expect) aspettarsi;

he got more than he bargained for non se l'aspettava

barge [bɑːdʒ] *n* NAUT chiatta *f*

♦ barge into *v/t* piombare su

bar·i·tone ['bærɪtəʊn] *n* baritono *m*

bark¹ [bɑːk] 1 *n* of dog abbaiare *m* 2 *v/i* abbaiare

bark² [bɑːk] of tree corteccia *f*

bar·ley ['bɑːlɪ] orzo *m*

'bar·maid barista *f*

'bar·man barista *m*

barm·y ['bɑːmɪ] *adj* F pazzoide F

barn [bɑːn] granaio *m*

ba·rom·e·ter [bə'rɒmɪtə(r)] also fig barometro *m*

Ba·roque [bə'rɒk] *adj* barocco

bar·racks ['bærəks] *npl* MIL caserma *fsg*

bar·rage ['bærɑːʒ] MIL sbarramento *m*; fig raffica *f*

bar·rel ['bærəl] (container) barile *m*

bar·ren ['bærən] *adj* land arido

bar·ri·cade [bærɪ'keɪd] *n* barricata *f*

bar·ri·er ['bærɪə(r)] barriera *f*; **language ~** l'ostacolo *m* della lingua

bar·ring ['bɑːrɪŋ] *prep*: **~ accidents** salvo imprevisti

bar·ris·ter ['bærɪstə(r)] avvocato *m*

bar·row ['bærəʊ] carriola *f*

'bar ten·der barista *m/f*

bar·ter ['bɑːtə(r)] 1 *n* baratto *m* 2 *v/i* barattare

base [beɪs] 1 *n* base *f* 2 *v/t* basare; **~ sth on sth** basare qc su qc; **be ~d in** in city, country essere di base a; **be ~d on** essere basato su

'base·ball baseball *m inv*

'base·ball bat mazza *f* da baseball

'base·ball cap berretto *m* da baseball

base·less ['beɪslɪs] *adj* infondato

base·ment ['beɪsmənt] seminterrato *m*

'base rate FIN tasso *m* base

bash [bæʃ] 1 *n* F colpo *m* 2 *v/t* F sbattere

ba·sic ['beɪsɪk] *adj* knowledge, equipment rudimentale; salary di base; beliefs fondamentale

ba·sic·al·ly ['beɪsɪklɪ] *adv* essenzialmente

ba·sics ['beɪsɪks] *npl:* **the ~** i rudimenti *mpl;* **get down to ~** venire al sodo

bas·il ['bæzɪl] basilico *m*

ba·sil·i·ca [bə'zɪlɪkə] basilica *f*

ba·sin ['beɪsn] *for washing* lavandino *m*

ba·sis ['beɪsɪs] (*pl* **bases** ['beɪsiːz]) base *f*

bask [bɑːsk] *v/i* crogiolarsi

bas·ket ['bɑːskɪt] cestino *m; in basketball* cesto *m*

'bas·ket·ball basket *m inv,* pallacanestro *f*

bass [beɪs] **1** *n* (*part*) voce *f* di basso; (*singer*) basso *m;* (*double bass*) contrabbasso *m;* (*guitar*) basso *m* **2** *adj* di basso

bas·tard ['bɑːstəd] F bastardo *m,* -a *f* F

bat¹ [bæt] **1** *n* mazza *f; for table tennis* racchetta *f* **2** *v/i* (*pret & pp* **-ted**) SP battere

bat² [bæt] *v/t* (*pret & pp* **-ted**): **he didn't ~ an eyelid** non ha battuto ciglio

bat³ [bæt] (*animal*) pipistrello *m*

batch [bætʃ] *n of students* gruppo *m; of goods* lotto *m; of bread* infornata *f*

ba·ted ['beɪtɪd] *adj:* **with ~ breath** col fiato sospeso

bath [bɑːθ] bagno *m;* **have a ~, take a ~** fare il bagno

bathe [beɪð] *v/i* (*swim, have bath*) fare il bagno

'bath·ing cost·ume, 'bath·ing suit costume *m* da bagno

'bath mat tappetino *m* da bagno; **'bath·robe** accappatoio *m;* **'bath·room** (*stanza f da*) bagno *m*

baths [bɑːðz] *npl* Br bagni *mpl* pubblici

'bath tow·el asciugamano *m* da bagno

'bath·tub vasca *f* da bagno

bat·on ['bætən] *of conductor* bacchetta *f*

bat·tal·i·on [bə'tælɪən] MIL battaglione *m*

bat·ter ['bætə(r)] *n* pastella *f*

bat·tered ['bætəd] *adj* maltrattato;

old hat, suitcase etc malridotto

bat·ter·y ['bætrɪ] pila *f;* MOT batteria *f*

'bat·ter·y charg·er caricabatterie *m inv*

bat·ter·y-op·e·rat·ed [bætrɪ'ppəreɪtɪd] *adj* a pile

bat·tle ['bætl] **1** *n also fig* battaglia *f* **2** *v/i against illness etc* lottare

'bat·tle·field, 'bat·tle·ground campo *m* di battaglia

'bat·tle·ship corazzata *f*

bawd·y ['bɔːdɪ] *adj* spinto

bawl [bɔːl] *v/i* (*shout*) urlare; (*weep*) strillare

♦ **bawl out** *v/t* F fare una lavata di capo a

bay [beɪ] (*inlet*) baia *f*

bay·o·net ['beɪənet] *n* baionetta *f*

bay 'win·dow bovindo *m*

BBC [biːbiː'siː] *abbr* (= **British Broadcasting Corporation**) BBC *f inv*

BC [biː'siː] *abbr* (= **before Christ**) a. C. (= avanti Cristo)

be [biː] *v/i* (*pret* **was** / **were**, *pp* **been**) essere; *it's me* sono io; *was she there?* era lì?; *how much is* / *are ...?* quant'è / quanto sono ...?; *there is, there are* c'è, ci sono; *~ careful* sta' attento; *don't ~ sad* non essere triste; *how are you?* come stai?; *he's very well* sta bene; *I'm hot* / *cold* ho freddo / caldo; *it's hot* / *cold* fa freddo / caldo; *he's seven* ha sette anni ◊ *has the postman been?* è passato il postino?; *I've never been to Japan* non sono mai stato in Giappone; *I've been here for hours* sono qui da tanto ◊ *tags: that's right, isn't it?* giusto, no?; *she's American, isn't she?* è americana, vero? ◊ *v aux:* **I am thinking**, sto pensando; *he was running* stava correndo; *you're ~ing silly* stai facendo lo sciocco; *he's working in London* lavora a Londra; *I'll be waiting for an answer* aspetterò una risposta ◊ *obligation:* **you are to do what I tell you** devi fare quello che ti dico; *I*

B

was to tell you this dovevo dirtelo; **you were not to tell anyone** non dovevi dirlo a nessuno ◊ *passive* essere, venire (*not with past tenses*); **he was killed** è stato ucciso; **they have been sold** sono stati venduti; **it will ~ sold for £100** sarà *o* verrà venduto a 100 sterline

♦ **be in for** *v/t* doversi aspettare; **you're in for a disappointment** resterai deluso

beach [biːtʃ] *n* spiaggia *f*

'**beach ball** pallone *m* da spiaggia

'**beach•wear** abbigliamento *m* da spiaggia

beads [biːdz] *npl* perline *fpl*

beak [biːk] becco *m*

bea•ker ['biːkə(r)] bicchiere *m*

'**be-all**: **the ~ and end-all** la cosa più importante

beam [biːm] **1** *n in ceiling etc* trave *f* **2** *v/i* (*smile*) fare un sorriso radioso **3** *v/t* (*transmit*) trasmettere

bean [biːn] (*vegetable*) fagiolo *m*; *of coffee* chicco *m*; **be full of ~s** F essere particolarmente vivace

'**bean•bag** *seat* poltrona *f* sacco

bear¹ [beə(r)] *animal* orso *m*

bear² [beə(r)] (*pret* **bore**, *pp* **borne**) **1** *v/t weight* portare; *costs* sostenere; (*tolerate*) sopportare; *child* dare alla luce **2** *v/i*: **bring pressure to ~ on** fare pressione su

♦ **bear out** *v/t* (*confirm*) confermare; **bear s.o. out** appoggiare qu

bear•a•ble ['beərəbl] *adj* sopportabile

beard [bɪəd] barba *f*

beard•ed ['bɪədɪd] *adj* con la barba

bear•ing ['beərɪŋ] *in machine* cuscinetto *m*; **that has no ~ on the case** ciò non ha alcuna attinenza col caso

'**bear mar•ket** FIN mercato *m* cedente

beast [biːst] bestia *f*

beat [biːt] **1** *n of heart* battito *m*; *of music* ritmo *m* **2** *v/i* (*pret* **beat**, *pp* **beaten**) *of heart* battere; *of rain* picchiettare; **~ about the bush** menar il can per l'aia **3** *v/t* (*pret* **beat**, *pp* **beaten**) *in competition* battere; (*hit*)

picchiare; *drum* suonare; **~ it!** F fila!; **it ~s me** non capisco

♦ **beat up** *v/t* picchiare

beat•en ['biːtən] **1** *adj*: **off the ~ track** fuori mano **2** *pp* → **beat**

beat•ing ['biːtɪŋ] (*physical*) botte *fpl*

beat-up *adj* F malconcio

beau•ti•cian [bjuː'tɪʃn] estetista *m/f*

beau•ti•ful ['bjuːtɪful] *adj* bello; **thanks, that's just ~!** grazie, così va bene

beau•ti•ful•ly ['bjuːtɪflɪ] *adv* stupendamente

beau•ty ['bjuːtɪ] *of woman, sunset* bellezza *f*

'**beau•ty sal•on** istituto *m* di bellezza

♦ **beaver away** *v/i* F sgobbare F

be•came [bɪ'keɪm] *pret* → **become**

be•cause [bɪ'kɒz] *conj* perché; **~ of** a causa di

beck•on ['bekn] *v/i* fare cenno

be•come [bɪ'kʌm] *v/i* (*pret* **became**, *pp* **become**) diventare; **what's ~ of her?** che ne è stato di lei?

be•com•ing [bɪ'kʌmɪŋ] *adj* grazioso

bed [bed] *n* letto *m*; **~ of flowers** aiuola *f*; **go to ~** andare a letto; **he's still in ~** è ancora a letto; **go to ~ with** andare a letto con

bed and 'breakfast pensione *f* familiare, bed and breakfast *m inv*

'**bed•clothes** *npl* coperte e lenzuola *fpl*

bed•ding ['bedɪŋ] materasso *m* e lenzuola *fpl*

bed•lam ['bedləm] F manicomio *m*

bed•rid•den ['bedrɪdən] *adj* costretto a letto; '**bed•room** camera *f* da letto; '**bed•side**: **be at the ~ of** essere al capezzale di; **bed•side 'lamp** lampada *f* da comodino; **bed•side 'ta•ble** comodino *m*; '**bed-sit, bed-sit•ter** monolocale *m*; '**bed•spread** copriletto *m*; '**bed•time** ora *f* di andare a letto

bee [biː] ape *f*

beech [biːtʃ] faggio *m*

beef [biːf] **1** *n* manzo *m*; F (*complaint*) problema *m* **2** *v/i* F (*complain*) lagnarsi

♦ **beef up** *v/t* rinforzare

'beef·bur·ger hamburger *m inv*

'bee·hive alveare *m*

'bee·line: **make a ~ for** andare diritto a

been [biːn] *pp* → **be**

beep [biːp] **1** *n* bip *m inv* **2** *v/i* suonare **3** *v/t* (*call on pager*) chiamare sul cercapersone

beep·er ['biːpə(r)] (*pager*) cercapersone *m inv*

beer [bɪə(r)] birra *f*

bee·tle ['biːtl] coleottero *m*

beet·root ['biːtruːt] barbabietola *f*; **as red as a ~** rosso come un peperone

be·fore [bɪ'fɔː(r)] **1** *prep* prima di; ~ **eight o'clock** prima delle otto **2** *adv* prima; **have you been to England ~?** sei già stato in Inghilterra?; **I've seen this film ~** questo film l'ho già visto **3** *conj* prima che; **I saw him ~ he left** l'ho visto prima che partisse; **I saw him ~ I left** l'ho visto prima di partire

be·fore·hand *adv* prima

be·friend [bɪ'frend] *v/t* fare amicizia con

beg [beg] (*pret & pp* **-ged**) **1** *v/i* mendicare **2** *v/t*: ~ *s.o. to ...* pregare qu di ...

be·gan [bɪ'gæn] *pret* → **begin**

beg·gar ['begə(r)] *n* mendicante *m/f*

be·gin [bɪ'gɪn] *v/t & v/i* (*pret* **began**, *pp* **begun**) cominciare; **to ~ with** per cominciare

be·gin·ner [bɪ'gɪnə(r)] principiante *m/f*

be·gin·ning [bɪ'gɪnɪŋ] inizio *m*; (*origin*) origine *f*

be·grudge [bɪ'grʌdʒ] *v/t* (*envy*) invidiare; (*give reluctantly*) dare malvolentieri

be·gun [bɪ'gʌn] *pp* → **begin**

be·half: **on ~ of** a nome di; **on my / his ~** a nome mio / suo

be·have [bɪ'heɪv] *v/i* comportarsi; ~ (*o.s.*) comportarsi bene; ~ (**yourself**)**!** comportati bene!

be·hav·iour [bɪ'heɪvjə(r)] comportamento *m*

be·hind [bɪ'haɪnd] **1** *prep in position* dietro; *in progress* indietro rispetto a; *in order* dietro a; **be ~** (*responsible for*) essere dietro a; (*support*) appoggiare **2** *adv* (*at the back*) dietro; **she had to stay ~** è dovuta rimanere; **be ~ in match** essere in svantaggio; **be ~ with sth** essere indietro con qc

beige [beɪʒ] *adj* beige *inv*

be·ing ['biːɪŋ] (*existence*) esistenza *f*; (*creature*) essere *m*

be·lat·ed [bɪ'leɪtɪd] *adj* in ritardo

belch [beltʃ] **1** *n* rutto *m* **2** *v/i* ruttare

Bel·gian ['beldʒən] **1** *adj* belga **2** *n* belga *m/f*

Bel·gium ['beldʒəm] Belgio *m*

be·lief [bɪ'liːf] convinzione *f*; *in God* fede *f*; **your ~ in me** il fatto che tu creda in me

be·lieve [bɪ'liːv] *v/t* credere

♦ **believe in** *v/t God, person* credere in; *ghost, person* credere a

be·liev·er [bɪ'liːvə(r)] REL credente *m/f*; **I'm a great ~ in ...** credo fermamente in ...

be·lit·tle [bɪ'lɪtl] *v/t* sminuire

bell [bel] *in church, school* campana *f*; *on door* campanello *m*

bel·lig·er·ent [bɪ'lɪdʒərənt] *adj* bellicoso

bel·low ['beləʊ] **1** *n* urlo *m*; *of bull* muggito *m* **2** *v/i* urlare; *of bull* muggire

bel·ly ['belɪ] pancia *f*

'bel·ly·ache *v/i* F brontolare F

be·long [bɪ'lɒŋ] *v/i*: **where does this ~?** dove va questo?; **I don't ~ here** mi sento un estraneo; **at last he found a place where he ~ed** finalmente ha trovato un posto adatto a lui

♦ **belong to** *v/t* appartenere a

be·long·ings [bɪ'lɒŋɪŋz] *npl* cose *fpl*

be·lov·ed [bɪ'lʌvɪd] *adj* adorato

be·low [bɪ'ləʊ] **1** *prep* sotto **2** *adv* di sotto; *in text* sotto; **see** ~ vedi sotto; **10 degrees** ~ 10 gradi sotto zero

belt [belt] *n* cintura *f*; **tighten one's ~** *fig* stringere la cinghia

♦ **belt up** *v/i* (*fasten seat belt*) allaccia-

B

re la cintura (di sicurezza); **belt up!** F sta' zitto!

be·moan [bɪ'məʊn] v/t lamentarsi di

bench [bentʃ] (seat) panchina f; (work~) banco m

'bench·mark punto m di riferimento

bend [bend] **1** n curva f **2** v/t (pret & pp **bent**) piegare **3** v/i (pret & pp **bent**) curvarsi; of person inchinarsi
♦ bend down v/i chinarsi

bend·er ['bendə(r)] F sbronza f F

be·neath [bɪ'niːθ] **1** prep sotto **2** adv di sotto; **they think he's ~ her** lo considerano inferiore a lei

ben·e·dic·tion [benɪ'dɪkʃn] benedizione f

ben·e·fac·tor ['benɪfæktə(r)] benefattore m, -trice f

ben·e·fi·cial [benɪ'fɪʃl] adj vantaggioso

ben·e·fit ['benɪfɪt] **1** n (advantage) vantaggio m; payment indennità f inv **2** v/t andare a vantaggio di **3** v/i trarre vantaggio (**from** da)

be·nev·o·lence [bɪ'nevələns] benevolenza f

be·nev·o·lent [bɪ'nevələnt] adj benevolo

be·nign [bɪ'naɪn] adj benevolo; MED benigno

bent [bent] **1** adj F corrotto **2** pret & pp → **bend**

be·queath [bɪ'kwiːð] v/t also fig lasciare in eredità

be·quest [bɪ'kwest] lascito m

be·reaved [bɪ'riːvd] **1** adj addolorato **2** n: **the ~** i familiari mpl del defunto

be·ret ['bereɪ] berretto m

ber·ry ['berɪ] bacca f

ber·serk [bə'zɜːk] adv: **go ~** dare in escandescenze

berth [bɜːθ] on ship, train cuccetta f; **give s.o. a wide ~** stare alla larga da qu

be·seech [bɪ'siːtʃ] v/t: **~ s.o. to do sth** implorare qu di fare qc

be·side [bɪ'saɪd] prep accanto a; **be ~ o.s.** essere fuori di sé; **that's ~ the point** questo non c'entra

be·sides [bɪ'saɪdz] **1** adv inoltre **2** prep (apart from) oltre a

be·siege [bɪ'siːdʒ] v/t also fig assediare

best [best] **1** adj migliore **2** adv meglio; **it would be ~ if ...** sarebbe meglio se ...; **I like her ~** lei è quella che mi piace di più **3** n: **do one's ~** fare del proprio meglio; **the ~** il meglio; (outstanding thing or person) il/la migliore; **they've done the ~ they can** hanno fatto tutto il possibile; **make the ~ of** cogliere il lato buono di; **all the ~!** tanti auguri!

best be'fore date scadenza f; **best 'man** at wedding testimone m dello sposo; '**best-sell·er** bestseller m inv

bet [bet] **1** n scommessa f **2** v/i scommettere; **you ~!** ci puoi scommettere!

be·tray [bɪ'treɪ] v/t tradire

be·tray·al [bɪ'treɪəl] tradimento m

bet·ter ['betə(r)] **1** adj migliore; **get ~** migliorare **2** adv meglio; **you'd ~ ask permission** faresti meglio a chiedere il permesso; **I'd really ~ not** sarebbe meglio di no; **all the ~ for us** tanto meglio per noi; **I like her ~** lei mi piace di più

bet·ter 'off adj: **be ~** stare meglio finanziariamente; **the ~** la classe abbiente

be·tween [bɪ'twiːn] prep tra; **~ you and me** tra me e te

bev·er·age ['bevərɪdʒ] fml bevanda f

be·ware [bɪ'weə(r)] v/t: **~ of ...!** (stai) attento a ...!

be·wil·der [bɪ'wɪldə(r)] v/t sconcertare

be·wil·der·ment [bɪ'wɪldəmənt] perplessità f inv

be·yond [bɪ'jɒnd] **1** prep oltre, al di là di; **it's ~ me** (don't understand) non capisco; (can't do it) va oltre le mie capacità **2** adv più in là

bi·as ['baɪəs] n against pregiudizio m; in favour of preferenza f

bi·as(s)ed ['baɪəst] adj parziale

bib [bɪb] for baby bavaglino m

B

Bible ['baɪbl] bibbia f
bib·li·cal ['bɪblɪkl] adj biblico
bib·li·og·ra·phy [bɪblɪ'ɒgrəfɪ] bibliografia f
bi·car·bon·ate of so·da [baɪˈkɑːbəneɪt] bicarbonato m di sodio
bi·cen·te·na·ry [baɪsenˈtiːnərɪ] bicentenario m
bi·ceps ['baɪseps] npl bicipiti mpl
bick·er ['bɪkə(r)] v/i bisticciare
bi·cy·cle ['baɪsɪkl] n bicicletta f
bid [bɪd] 1 n at auction offerta f; (attempt) tentativo m 2 v/t & v/i (pret & pp **bid**) at auction offrire
bid·der ['bɪdə(r)] offerente m/f
bi·en·ni·al [baɪˈenɪəl] adj biennale
bi·fo·cals [baɪˈfəʊkəlz] npl occhiali mpl bifocali
big [bɪg] 1 adj grande; **my ~ brother / sister** mio fratello / mia sorella maggiore; **~ name** nome importante 2 adv: **talk ~** spararle grosse
big·a·mist ['bɪgəmɪst] bigamo m, -a f
big·a·mous ['bɪgəməs] adj bigamo
big·a·my ['bɪgəmɪ] bigamia f
'big·head F pallone m gonfiato F
big·head·ed [bɪg'hedɪd] adj F presuntuoso
big·ot ['bɪgət] fanatico m, -a f
bike [baɪk] 1 n F bici f inv F 2 v/i andare in bici; **I ~d here** sono venuto in bici
bik·er ['baɪkə(r)] motociclista m/f; (courier) corriere m
bi·ki·ni [bɪ'kiːnɪ] bikini m inv
bi·lat·er·al [baɪ'lætərəl] adj bilaterale
bi·lin·gual [baɪ'lɪŋgwəl] adj bilingue
bill [bɪl] 1 n in hotel, restaurant conto m; (gas / electricity ~) bolletta f; (invoice) fattura f; Am: money banconota f; POL disegno m di legge; (poster) avviso m 2 v/t (invoice) mandare la fattura a
'bill·fold Am portafoglio m
bil·li·ards ['bɪljədz] nsg biliardo m
bil·li·on ['bɪljən] (1,000,000,000) miliardo m
bill of ex'change FIN cambiale f
bill of 'sale atto m di vendita
bin [bɪn] n bidone m

bi·na·ry ['baɪnərɪ] adj binario
bind [baɪnd] v/t (pret & pp **bound**) also fig legare; (LAW: oblige) obbligare
bind·ing ['baɪndɪŋ] 1 adj agreement, promise vincolante 2 n of book rilegatura f; of ski attacco m
bin·go ['bɪŋgəʊ] tombola f
bi·noc·u·lars [bɪˈnɒkjʊləz] npl binocolo msg
bi·o·chem·ist [baɪəʊ'kemɪst] biochimico m, -a f
bi·o·chem·is·try [baɪəʊ'kemɪstrɪ] biochimica f
bi·o·de·grad·a·bil·i·ty [baɪəʊdɪgreɪdə'bɪlətɪ] biodegradabilità f inv
bi·o·de·gra·da·ble [baɪəʊdɪ'greɪdəbl] adj biodegradabile
bi·og·ra·pher [baɪˈɒgrəfə(r)] biografo m, -a f
bi·og·ra·phy [baɪ'ɒgrəfɪ] biografia f
bi·o·log·i·cal [baɪə'lɒdʒɪkl] adj biologico
bi·ol·o·gist [baɪ'ɒlədʒɪst] biologo m, -a f
bi·ol·o·gy [baɪ'ɒlədʒɪ] biologia f
bi·o·tech·nol·o·gy [baɪəʊtek'nɒlədʒɪ] biotecnologia f
bird [bɜːd] uccello m
'bird·cage gabbia f per uccelli; **bird of 'prey** (uccello m) rapace m; **'bird sanc·tu·a·ry** rifugio m per uccelli; **bird's eye 'view** vista f a volo d'uccello
bi·ro® ['baɪrəʊ] biro f
birth [bɜːθ] also fig nascita f; (labour) parto m; **give ~ to** child partorire; **date of ~** data di nascita
'birth cer·tif·i·cate certificato m di nascita; **'birth con·trol** controllo m delle nascite; **'birth·day** compleanno m; **happy ~!** buon compleanno!; **'birth·mark** voglia f; **'birth·place** luogo m di nascita; **'birth·rate** tasso m di nascita
bis·cuit ['bɪskɪt] biscotto m
bi·sex·u·al ['baɪseksjʊəl] 1 adj bisessuale 2 n bisessuale m/f
bish·op ['bɪʃəp] vescovo m
bit¹ [bɪt] n (piece) pezzo m; (part) parte f; COMPUT bit m inv; **a ~ (a**

B

little) un po'; *a ~ of* (*a little*) un po' di; *a ~ of news / advice* una notizia / un consiglio; *~ by ~* poco a poco; *I'll be there in a ~* (*in a little while*) sarò lì tra poco

bit² [bɪt] *for a horse* morso *m*

bit³ [bɪt] *pret* → **bite**

bitch [bɪtʃ] **1** *n dog* cagna *f*; F *woman* bastarda *f*, F, stronza *f* V **2** *v/i* F (*complain*) lamentarsi

bitch·y ['bɪtʃɪ] *adj* F *person, remark* velenoso

bite [baɪt] **1** *n* morso *m*; *let's have a ~* (*to eat*) mangiamo un boccone; *he didn't get a ~ of angler* non ha abboccato neanche un pesce **2** *v/t* (*pret* **bit**, *pp* **bitten**) mordere; *one's nails* mangiarsi **3** *v/i* (*pret* **bit**, *pp* **bitten**) mordere; *of fish* abboccare

bit·ten ['bɪtn] *pp* → **bite**

bit·ter ['bɪtə(r)] **1** *adj taste* amaro; *person* amareggiato; *weather* gelido; *argument* aspro **2** *n beer* birra *f* amara

bit·ter·ly ['bɪtəlɪ] *adv resent* profondamente; *~ cold* gelido

bi·zarre [bɪ'zɑː(r)] *adj* bizzarro

blab [blæb] *v/i* (*pret & pp* **-bed**) F spifferare F

blab·ber·mouth ['blæbəmaʊθ] F spione *m*, -a *f*

black [blæk] **1** *adj also fig* nero; *person* negro, nero; *tea* senza latte **2** *n* (*colour*) nero *m*; (*person*) nero *m*, -a *f*; *in the ~* FIN in attivo; *in ~ and white fig* nero su bianco

♦**black out** *v/i* svenire

'**black·ber·ry** mora *f* di rovo; '**black·bird** merlo *m*; '**black·board** lavagna *f*; **black 'box** scatola *f* nera; **black e'con·o·my** economia *f* sommersa

black·en ['blækn] *v/t fig: person's name* infangare

black 'eye occhio *m* nero; '**black·head** punto *m* nero, comedone *m*; **black 'ice** ghiaccio *m* (sulla strada); '**black·list 1** *n* lista *f* nera **2** *v/t* mettere sulla lista nera; '**black·mail 1** *n also fig* ricatto *m* **2** *v/t* ricattare; '**black·mail·er** ricattatore *m*, -trice

f; **black 'mar·ket** mercato *m* nero

black·ness ['blæknɪs] *of night* oscurità *f inv*

'**black·out** ELEC black-out *m inv*; MED svenimento *m*

black 'pud·ding sanguinaccio *m*

'**black·smith** fabbro *m* ferraio

blad·der ['blædə(r)] vescica *f*

blade [bleɪd] *of knife, sword* lama *f*; *of helicopter* pala *f*; *of grass* filo *m*

blame [bleɪm] **1** *n* colpa *f*; (*responsibility*) responsabilità *f inv* **2** *v/t* biasimare; *~ s.o. for sth* ritenere qu responsabile di qc

bland [blænd] *adj smile, answer* insulso; *food* insipido

blank [blæŋk] **1** *adj* (*not written on*) bianco; *tape* vergine; *look* vuoto **2** *n* (*empty space*) spazio *m*; *my mind's a ~* ho la testa vuota

blank 'check *Am*, **blank 'cheque** assegno *m* in bianco

blan·ket ['blæŋkɪt] *n also fig* coperta *f*

blare [bleə(r)] *v/i* suonare a tutto volume

♦**blare out 1** *v/i* strepitare **2** *v/t* fare rimbombare

blas·pheme [blæs'fiːm] *v/i* bestemmiare

blas·phe·my ['blæsfəmɪ] bestemmia *f*

blast [blɑːst] **1** *n* (*explosion*) esplosione *f*; (*gust*) raffica *f* **2** *v/t* far esplodere; *~!* accidenti!

♦**blast off** *v/i of rocket* essere lanciato

blast fur·nace altoforno *m*

'**blast-off** lancio *m*

bla·tant ['bleɪtənt] *adj* palese

blaze [bleɪz] **1** *n* (*fire*) incendio *m*; *a ~ of colour* un'esplosione di colore **2** *v/i of fire* ardere

♦**blaze away** *v/i with gun* sparare a raffica

blaz·er ['bleɪzə(r)] blazer *m inv*

bleach [bliːtʃ] **1** *n for clothes* varechina *f*; *for hair* acqua *f* ossigenata **2** *v/t hair* ossigenarsi

bleak [bliːk] *adj countryside* desolato; *weather* cupo; *future* deprimente

blear·y-eyed ['blɪərɪaɪd] *adj*: **be ~** avere lo sguardo appannato

bleat [bli:t] *v/i of sheep* belare

bled [bled] *pret & pp* → **bleed**

bleed [bli:d] (*pret & pp* **bled**) **1** *v/i* sanguinare **2** *v/t fig* dissanguare

bleed·ing ['bli:dɪŋ] *n* emorragia *f*

bleep [bli:p] **1** *n* blip *m inv* **2** *v/i* suonare **3** *v/t* (*call on pager*) chiamare sul cercapersone

bleep·er ['bli:pə(r)] (*pager*) cercapersone *m inv*

blem·ish ['blemɪʃ] **1** *n on skin* imperfezione *f*; *on fruit* ammaccatura *f* **2** *v/t reputation* infangare

blend [blend] **1** *n* miscela *f* **2** *v/t* miscelare

♦ **blend in 1** *v/i* inserirsi; (*look good*) armonizzare **2** *v/t in cooking* incorporare

blend·er ['blendə(r)] *machine* frullatore *m*

bless [bles] *v/t* benedire; (**God**) **~ you!** Dio ti benedica!; **~ you!** (*in response to sneeze*) salute!; **~ me!**, **~ my soul!** santo cielo!; **be ~ed with** godere di

bless·ing ['blesɪŋ] *also fig* benedizione *f*

blew [blu:] *pret* → **blow**

blind [blaɪnd] **1** *adj* cieco; **be ~ to** *fig* non vedere **2** *n*: **the ~** i ciechi **3** *v/t* accecare

blind 'al·ley vicolo *m* cieco; **blind 'date** appuntamento *m* al buio; **'blind·fold 1** *n* benda *f* **2** *v/t* bendare (gli occhi a) **3** *adv* con gli occhi bendati

blind·ing ['blaɪndɪŋ] *adj* atroce; *light* accecante, abbagliante

blind·ly ['blaɪndlɪ] *adv feel*, *grope* a tastoni; *fig* ciecamente

'blind spot *in road* punto *m* cieco; (*ability that is lacking*) punto *m* debole

blink [blɪŋk] *v/i of person* sbattere le palpebre; *of light* tremolare

blink·ered ['blɪŋkəd] *adj fig* ottuso

blip [blɪp] *on radar screen* segnale *m*; *fig* battuta *f* d'arresto

bliss [blɪs] felicità *f inv*

blis·ter ['blɪstə(r)] **1** *n* vescichetta *f* **2** *v/i* formare una vescichetta; *of paint* formare delle bolle

blis·ter pack blister *m inv*

bliz·zard ['blɪzəd] bufera *f* di neve

bloat·ed ['bləʊtɪd] *adj* gonfio

blob [blɒb] *of liquid* goccia *f*

bloc [blɒk] POL blocco *m*

block [blɒk] **1** *n* blocco *m*; *in town* isolato *m*; *of shares* pacchetto *m*; (*blockage*) blocco *m*; **~ of flats** palazzo *m* (d'appartamenti) **2** *v/t* bloccare

♦ **block in** *v/t with vehicle* bloccare macchina di; **somebody's car was blocking me in** qualcuno ha bloccato la mia macchina parcheggiando la sua

♦ **block out** *v/t light* impedire

♦ **block up** *v/t sink etc* otturare

block·ade [blɒ'keɪd] **1** *n* blocco *m* **2** *v/t* bloccare

block·age ['blɒkɪdʒ] ingorgo *m*

block·bust·er ['blɒkbʌstə(r)] successone *m*

block 'let·ters *npl* maiuscole *fpl*

bloke [bləʊk] F tipo *m* F

blond [blɒnd] *adj* biondo

blonde [blɒnd] *n* (*woman*) bionda *f*

blood [blʌd] sangue *m*; **in cold ~** a sangue freddo

'blood al·co·hol lev·el concentrazione *f* di alcol etilico nel sangue; **'blood bank** banca *f* del sangue; **'blood bath** bagno *m* di sangue; **'blood do·nor** donatore *m*, -trice *f* di sangue; **'blood group** gruppo *m* sanguigno

blood·less ['blʌdlɪs] *adj coup* senza spargimento di sangue

'blood poi·son·ing setticemia *f*; **'blood pres·sure** pressione *f* del sangue; **'blood re·la·tion**, **'blood rel·a·tive** consanguineo *m*, -a *f*; **'blood sam·ple** prelievo *m* di sangue; **'blood·shed** spargimento *m* di sangue; **'blood·shot** *adj* iniettato di sangue; **'blood·stain** macchia *f* di sangue; **'blood·stain·ed** *adj* macchiato di sangue; **'blood·stream** circolazione *f* (del sangue); **'blood**

test analisi *f inv* del sangue; **'blood-thirst·y** *adj* assetato di sangue; **'blood trans·fu·sion** trasfusione *f* di sangue; **'blood ves·sel** vaso *m* sanguigno

blood·y ['blʌdɪ] **1** *adj hands etc* insanguinato; *battle* sanguinoso; F maledetto; *~ hell!* porca miseria! F; *it's a ~ nuisance* è una gran rottura F; *you're a ~ genius!* sei un geniaccio! F **2** *adv: that's ~ difficult / easy!* è facile / difficile da morire!; *I'm ~ tired* sono stanco morto!; *you'll ~ well do it!* eccome se lo farai!

blood·y-mind·ed [blʌdɪ'maɪndɪd] *adj* F ostinato

bloom [bluːm] **1** *n* fiore *m*; *in full ~* in piena fioritura **2** *v/i also fig* fiorire

blos·som ['blɒsəm] **1** *n* fiori *mpl* **2** *v/i also fig* fiorire

blot [blɒt] **1** *n* macchia *f* **2** *v/t* (*pret & pp -ted*) (*dry*) asciugare
♦ **blot out** *v/t memory* cancellare; *view* nascondere

blotch [blɒtʃ] chiazza *f*

blotch·y ['blɒtʃɪ] *adj* coperto di chiazze

blouse [blaʊz] camicetta *f*

blow [bləʊ] **1** *n* colpo *m* **2** *v/t* (*pret blew*, *pp blown*) *of wind* soffiare; *smoke* soffiare; F (*spend*) sperperare; F *opportunity* mandare all'aria; *~ a whistle* fischiare; *~ one's nose* soffiarsi il naso **3** *v/i* (*pret blew*, *pp blown*) *of wind, person* soffiare; *of fuse* saltare; *of tyre* scoppiare; *the whistle blew for half-time* è stato fischiato l'intervallo
♦ **blow off 1** *v/t* portar via **2** *v/i* volar via
♦ **blow out 1** *v/t candle* spegnere **2** *v/i of candle* spegnersi
♦ **blow over 1** *v/t* abbattere **2** *v/i* rovesciarsi; *of storm, upset* calmarsi
♦ **blow up 1** *v/t with explosives* far saltare; *balloon* gonfiare; *photograph* ingrandire **2** *v/i also fig* esplodere

'blow-dry *v/t* (*pret & pp -ied*) asciugare col phon

'blow job ∨ pompino *m* ∨

blown [bləʊn] *pp → blow*

'blow-out *of tyre* scoppio *m*; F (*big meal*) abbuffata *f*

'blow-up *of photo* ingrandimento *m*

blue [bluː] **1** *adj* blu; F *film* porno **2** *n* blu *m inv*

blue 'chip *adj* sicuro; *company* di alto livello; **blue-'col·lar work·er** operaio *m*, -a *f*; **'blue·print** cianografia *f*, (*fig: plan*) programma *m*

blues [bluːz] *npl* MUS blues *m inv*; *have the ~* essere giù

'blues sing·er cantante *m/f* blues

bluff [blʌf] **1** *n* (*deception*) bluff *m inv* **2** *v/i* bluffare

blun·der ['blʌndə(r)] **1** *n* errore *m* **2** *v/i* fare un errore

blunt [blʌnt] *adj* spuntato; *person* diretto

blunt·ly ['blʌntlɪ] *adv speak* senza mezzi termini

blur [blɜː(r)] **1** *n* massa *f* indistinta **2** *v/t* (*pret & pp -red*) offuscare

blurb [blɜːb] *on book* note *fpl* di copertina
♦ **blurt out** [blɜːt] *v/t* spiattellare

blush [blʌʃ] **1** *n* rossore *m* **2** *v/i* arrossire

blush·er ['blʌʃə(r)] *cosmetic* fard *m inv*

blus·ter ['blʌstə(r)] *v/i* protestare

blus·ter·y ['blʌstərɪ] *adj* ventoso

BO [biːˈəʊ] *abbr* (= *body odour*) odori *mpl* corporei

board [bɔːd] **1** *n* asse *f*; *for game* scacchiera *f*; *for notices* tabellone *m*; *~ (of directors)* consiglio *m* (d'amministrazione); *on ~ (plane, train, boat)* a bordo; *take on ~ comments etc* prendere in esame; (*fully realize truth of*) accettare; *across the ~* a tutti i livelli **2** *v/t aeroplane etc* salire a bordo di **3** *v/i of passengers* salire a bordo
♦ **board up** *v/t* chiudere con assi
♦ **board with** *v/t* essere a pensione da

board and 'lodg·ing vitto e alloggio *m*

board·er ['bɔːdə(r)] pensionante *m/f*; EDU convittore *m* , -trice *f*

'board game gioco *m* da tavolo

'board·ing card carta *f* d'imbarco;

'**board·ing house** pensione *f*;
'**board·ing pass** carta *f* d'imbarco;
'**board·ing school** collegio *m*

'**board meet·ing** riunione *f* di consiglio

'**board room** sala *f* del consiglio

boast [bəʊst] **1** *n* vanteria *f* **2** *v/i* vantarsi

boat [bəʊt] (*small, for leisure*) barca *f*; (*ship*) nave *f*; **go by ~** andare in nave

bob¹ [bɒb] (*haircut*) caschetto *m*

bob² [bɒb] *v/i* (*pret & pp -bed*) *of boat etc* andare su e giù

♦ **bob up** *v/i* spuntare

'**bob·sleigh**, '**bob·sled** bob *m inv*

bod·ice ['bɒdɪs] corpetto *m*

bod·i·ly ['bɒdɪlɪ] **1** *adj* corporale **2** *adv eject* di peso

bod·y ['bɒdɪ] corpo *m*; *dead* cadavere *m*; **~ of water** massa *f* d'acqua; **~** (*suit*) (*undergarment*) body *m inv*

'**bod·y ar·mour** giubbotto *m* antiproiettile; '**body·guard** guardia *f* del corpo; '**body lan·guage** linguaggio *m* del corpo; '**bod·y o·dour** odori *mpl* corporei; '**bod·y pierc·ing** piercing *m inv*; '**body shop** MOT carrozzeria *f*; '**body·stock·ing** body *m inv*; '**body·work** MOT carrozzeria *f*

bog palude *f*

bog·gle ['bɒgl] *v/i*: **the mind ~s!** è incredibile!

bo·gus ['bəʊgəs] *adj* fasullo

boil¹ [bɔɪl] *n* (*swelling*) foruncolo *m*

boil² [bɔɪl] **1** *v/t* far bollire **2** *v/i* bollire

♦ **boil down to** *v/t* ridursi a

♦ **boil over** *v/i of milk etc* traboccare bollendo

boil·er ['bɔɪlə(r)] caldaia *f*

boil·ing point ['bɔɪlɪŋ] *of liquid* punto *m* d'ebollizione; **reach ~** *fig* perdere le staffe

bois·ter·ous ['bɔɪstərəs] *adj* turbolento

bold [bəʊld] **1** *adj* (*brave*) audace **2** *n print* neretto *m*; **in ~** in neretto

bol·ster ['bəʊlstə(r)] *v/t confidence* rafforzare

bolt [bəʊlt] **1** *n on door* catenaccio *m*; (*metal pin*) bullone *m*; *of lightning* fulmine *m*; **like a ~ from the blue** come un fulmine a ciel sereno **2** *adv*: **~ upright** diritto come un fuso **3** *v/t* (*fix with bolts*) fissare con bulloni; (*close*) chiudere col catenaccio **4** *v/i* (*run off*) scappare via

bomb [bɒm] **1** *n* bomba *f* **2** *v/t* bombardare; (*blow up*) fare esplodere una bomba in, far saltare

bom·bard [bɒm'bɑːd] *v/t* (*attack*) bombardare; **~ with questions** bombardare di domande

'**bomb attack** attacco *m* dinamitardo

bomb·er ['bɒmə(r)] (*aeroplane*) bombardiere *m*; (*terrorist*) dinamitardo *m*, -a *f*

'**bomb·er jack·et** bomber *m inv*

'**bomb·proof** *adj* a prova di bomba;
'**bomb scare** allarme-bomba *m*;
'**bomb·shell** *fig*: *news* bomba *f*

bond [bɒnd] **1** *n* (*tie*) legame *m*; FIN obbligazione *f*; **government ~s** titoli *mpl* di Stato **2** *v/i* aderire

bone [bəʊn] **1** *n* osso *m* **2** *v/t meat* disossare; *fish* togliere la lisca a

bon·fire ['bɒnfaɪə(r)] falò *m inv*

bonk [bɒŋk] *v/t & v/i* P scopare P

bon·net ['bɒnɪt] *of car* cofano *m*

bo·nus ['bəʊnəs] (*money*) gratifica *f*; (*something extra*) vantaggio *m* in più

boo [buː] **1** *n* fischio *m* **2** *v/t & v/i actor, speaker* fischiare

boob¹ [buːb] *n* F (*breast*) tetta *f* P

boob² [buːb] *n* F (*mistake*) errore *m* **2** *v/i* F (*make a mistake*) fare un errore

boob² [buːb] *n* F (*breast*) tetta *f* P

boo·boo ['buːbuː] *n* F → **boob¹**

book [bʊk] **1** *n* libro *m*; **~ of matches** bustina *f* di fiammiferi **2** *v/t* (*reserve*) prenotare; *of policeman* multare; SP ammonire **3** *v/i* (*reserve*) prenotare

♦ **book in 1** *v/i* prenotare una camera; (*check in*) registrarsi **2** *v/t* prenotare una camera per

'**book·case** scaffale *m*

booked up [bʊkt'ʌp] *adj* tutto esaurito; *person* occupatissimo

book·ie ['bʊkɪ] F allibratore *m*

book·ing ['bʊkɪŋ] (*reservation*) prenotazione *f*

'**book·ing clerk** impiegato *m* della biglietteria

'**book·ing of·fice** biglietteria *f*

'**book·keep·er** contabile *m/f*

'**book·keep·ing** contabilità *f inv*

book·let ['bʊklɪt] libretto *m*

'**book·mak·er** allibratore *m*

books [bʊks] *npl* (*accounts*) libri *mpl* contabili; *do the* ~ tenere la contabilità; *cook the* ~*s* falsificare i libri contabili

'**book·sell·er** libraio *m*, -a *f*; '**book·shelf** mensola *f*; '**book·shop** libreria *f*; '**book·stall** edicola *f*; '**book to·ken** buono *m* libro

boom[1] [buːm] **1** *n* boom *m inv* **2** *v/i of business* andare a gonfie vele

boom[2] [buːm] **1** *n* (*bang*) rimbombo *m* **2** *v/i* rimbombare

boor [bɔː(r)] *n* zotico *m*

boor·ish ['bɔːrɪʃ] *adj* da zotico

boost [buːst] **1** *n* spinta *f* **2** *v/t production, sales* incrementare; *confidence* aumentare

boot[1] [buːt] *n* stivale *m*; (*climbing* ~) scarpone *m*; *for football* scarpetta *m*

boot[2] [buːt] *of car* bagagliaio *m*

♦ **boot out** *v/t* F sbattere fuori F

♦ **boot up** *v/t & v/i* COMPUT inizializzare

booth [buːð] *at market, fair* bancarella *f*; (*telephone* ~) cabina *f*

booze [buːz] *n* F alcolici *mpl*

booz·er ['buːzə(r)] F (*pub*) pub *m inv*; (*person*) beone *m*, -a *f* F

'**booze-up** F bevuta *f*

bor·der ['bɔːdə(r)] **1** *n between countries* confine *m*; (*edge*) bordo *m* **2** *v/t country* confinare con

♦ **border on** *country* confinare con; (*be almost*) rasentare

'**bor·der·line** *adj* al limite; *a* ~ *case* un caso limite

bore[1] [bɔː(r)] *v/t hole* praticare

bore[2] [bɔː(r)] **1** *n* (*person*) persona *f* noiosa; *it's such a* ~ è una seccatura **2** *v/t* annoiare

bore[3] [bɔː(r)] *pret* → **bear**[2]

bored [bɔːd] *adj* annoiato; *I'm* ~ mi sto annoiando

bore·dom ['bɔːdəm] noia *f*

bor·ing ['bɔːrɪŋ] *adj* noioso

born [bɔːn] *adj*: *be* ~ essere nato; *where were you* ~? dove sei nato?; *be a* ~ ... essere un ... nato

borne [bɔːn] *pp* → **bear**[2]

bor·row ['bɒrəʊ] *v/t* prendere in prestito

bos·om ['bʊzm] *of woman* seno *m*

boss [bɒs] boss *m inv*

♦ **boss about** *v/t* dare ordini a

boss·y ['bɒsɪ] *adj* prepotente

bo·tan·i·cal [bə'tænɪkl] *adj* botanico

bo·tan·ic(·al) gar·dens *npl* orto *m* botanico

bot·a·nist ['bɒtənɪst] botanico *m*, -a *f*

bot·a·ny ['bɒtənɪ] botanica *f*

botch [bɒtʃ] *v/t* fare un pasticcio con

both [bəʊθ] **1** *adj pron* entrambi, tutti *mpl* e due, tutte *fpl* e due, tutt'e due; *I know* ~ *(of the) brothers* conosco tutt'e due i fratelli; ~ *(of the) brothers were there* tutt'e due i fratelli erano lì; ~ *of them* entrambi *2 adv*: ~ *my mother and I* sia mia madre che io; *is it business or pleasure?* – ~ per piacere o per affari? – tutt'e due

both·er ['bɒðə(r)] **1** *n* disturbo *m*; *it's no* ~ non c'è problema **2** *v/t* (*disturb*) disturbare; (*worry*) preoccupare **3** *v/i*: *don't* ~ (*you needn't do it*) non preoccuparti; *you needn't have* ~*ed!* non dovevi!

bot·tle ['bɒtl] **1** *n* bottiglia *f*; *for baby* biberon *m* **2** *v/t* imbottigliare

♦ **bottle out** *v/i* P tirarsi indietro

♦ **bottle up** *v/t feelings* reprimere

'**bot·tle bank** contenitore *m* per la raccolta del vetro

bot·tled wa·ter ['bɒtld] acqua *f* in bottiglia

'**bot·tle·neck** *n* ingorgo *m*

'**bot·tle-o·pen·er** apribottiglie *m inv*

bot·tom ['bɒtəm] **1** *adj* più basso **2** *n* fondo *m*; (*buttocks*) sedere *m*; *at the* ~ *of the screen* in basso sullo schermo; *at the* ~ *of the page* / *street* in fondo alla pagina/strada; *she* *started at the ~ and she's a manager now* ha cominciato dal basso e ora è dirigente

♦ **bottom out** v/i toccare il fondo

bot·tom 'line (*fig: financial outcome*) risultato *m* finanziario; *the ~* (*the real issue*) l'essenziale *m*

bought [bɔːt] *pret & pp* → **buy**

boul·der ['bəʊldə(r)] macigno *m*

bounce [baʊns] **1** v/t ball far rimbalzare **2** v/i of ball rimbalzare; *on sofa etc* saltare; *of cheque* essere protestato

bounc·er ['baʊnsə(r)] buttafuori *m inv*

bouncy ['baʊnsɪ] *adj* ball che rimbalza bene; *chair* molleggiato

bound¹ [baʊnd] *adj*: *be ~ to do sth* (*sure to*) dover per forza qc; (*obliged to*) essere obbligato a fare qc; *the train is ~ to be late* il treno sarà senz'altro in ritardo

bound² [baʊnd] *adj*: *be ~ for* of ship essere diretto a

bound³ [baʊnd] **1** n (*jump*) balzo *m* **2** v/i saltellare

bound⁴ [baʊnd] *pret & pp* → **bind**

bound·a·ry ['baʊndərɪ] confine *m*

bound·less ['baʊndlɪs] *adj* illimitato

bou·quet [buˈkeɪ] bouquet *m inv*

bour·bon ['bɜːbən] bourbon *m inv*

bout [baʊt] MED attacco *m*; *in boxing* incontro *m*

bou·tique [buːˈtiːk] boutique *f inv*

bo·vine spon·gi·form en·ceph·a·lo·pa·thy [bəʊvaɪnspʌdʒɪfɔːmensefəˈlɒpəθɪ] encefalite *f* spongiforme bovina

bow¹ [baʊ] **1** n as greeting inchino *m* **2** v/i inchinarsi **3** v/t head chinare

bow² [bəʊ] (*knot*) fiocco *m*; MUS archetto *m*

bow³ [baʊ] of ship prua *f*

bow·els ['baʊəlz] npl intestino msg

bowl¹ [bəʊl] (*container*) bacinella *f*; for soup, cereal ciotola *f*; for cooking, salad terrina *f*; plastic contenitore *m* di plastica

bowl² [bəʊl] **1** n ball boccia *f* **2** v/i in bowling lanciare

♦ **bowl over** v/t (*fig: astonish*) strabiliare

bowl·er ['bəʊlə(r)] (*hat*) bombetta *f*; *in cricket* lanciatore *m*

bowl·ing ['bəʊlɪŋ] bowling *m inv*

'bowl·ing al·ley pista *f* da bowling

bowls [bəʊlz] nsg (*game*) bocce *fpl*

bow 'tie (cravatta *f* a) farfalla *f*

box¹ [bɒks] n container scatola *f*; on form casella *f*

box² [bɒks] v/i do boxing fare pugilato; *he ~ed well* ha combattuto bene

box·er ['bɒksə(r)] pugile *m*

'box·er shorts npl boxer *mpl*

box·ing ['bɒksɪŋ] pugilato *m*, boxe *f inv*

'Box·ing Day Br Santo Stefano; **'box·ing glove** guantone *m* da pugile; **'box·ing match** incontro *m* di pugilato; **'box·ing ring** quadrato *m*, ring *m inv*

'box num·ber at post office casella *f*

'box of·fice botteghino *m*

boy [bɔɪ] child bambino *m*; youth ragazzo *m*; son figlio *m*

boy·cott ['bɔɪkɒt] **1** n boicottaggio *m* **2** v/t boicottare

'boy·friend ragazzo *m*

boy·ish ['bɔɪʃ] adj da ragazzo

boy'scout boy-scout *m inv*

bra [brɑː] reggiseno *m*

brace [breɪs] on teeth apparecchio *m* (ai denti)

brace·let ['breɪslɪt] braccialetto *m*

brac·es ['breɪsɪz] npl bretelle *fpl*

brack·et ['brækɪt] for shelf staffa *f*; in text parentesi *f inv*

brag [bræg] v/i (*pret & pp* **-ged**) vantarsi

braid [breɪd] (*trimming*) passamaneria *f*

braille [breɪl] braille *m*

brain [breɪn] cervello *m*; *use your ~* usa il cervello

'brain dead adj MED cerebralmente morto

brain·less ['breɪnlɪs] adj F deficiente

brains [breɪnz] npl (*intelligence*) cervello msg

'brain·storm Br attacco *m* di follia; **brain·storm·ing** ['breɪnstɔːmɪŋ]

B

brain-storming *m inv*; '**brain surgeon** neurochirurgo *m*; '**brain surgery** neurochirurgia *f*; '**brain tumour** tumore *m* al cervello; '**brainwash** *v/t* fare il lavaggio del cervello a; *we've been ~ed into believing that ...* ci hanno fatto il lavaggio del cervello per convincerci che ...; '**brain-wave** (*brilliant idea*) lampo *m* di genio

brain-y ['breɪnɪ] *adj* F geniale

brake [breɪk] **1** *n* freno *m* **2** *v/i* frenare

'brake flu-id MOT liquido *m* dei freni; '**brake light** MOT fanalino *m* d'arresto; '**brake ped-al** MOT pedale *m* del freno

branch [brɑːntʃ] *n of tree* ramo *m*; *of bank, company* filiale *f*
♦ branch off *v/i of road* diramarsi
♦ branch out *v/i* diversificarsi

brand [brænd] **1** *n* marca *f*; **2** *v/t*: *be ~ed a traitor* essere tacciato di tradimento

brand 'im-age brand image *f inv*
bran-dish ['brændɪʃ] *v/t* brandire
brand 'lead-er marca *f* leader di mercato; **brand 'loy-al-ty** fedeltà *f inv* alla marca; '**brand name** marca *f*

brand-'new *adj* nuovo di zecca
bran-dy ['brændɪ] brandy *m inv*
brass [brɑːs] (*alloy*) ottone *m*; *the ~* MUS gli ottoni
brass 'band fanfara *f*
bras-sière [brə'zɪə(r)] *Am* reggiseno *m*
brat [bræt] *pej* marmocchio *m*
bra-va-do [brə'vɑːdəʊ] spavalderia *f*
brave [breɪv] *adj* coraggioso
brave-ly ['breɪvlɪ] *adv* coraggiosamente
brav-er-y ['breɪvərɪ] coraggio *m*
brawl [brɔːl] **1** *n* rissa *f* **2** *v/i* azzuffarsi
brawn-y ['brɔːnɪ] *adj* muscoloso
Bra-zil [brə'zɪl] Brasile *m*
Bra-zil-ian [brə'zɪlɪən] **1** *adj* brasiliano **2** *n* brasiliano *m*, -a *f*
breach [briːtʃ] *n* (*violation*) violazione *f*; *in party* rottura *f*

breach of 'con-tract LAW inadempienza *f* di contratto
bread [bred] *n* pane *m*
'bread-crumbs *npl for cooking* pane *msg* grattato; *for bird* briciole *fpl*
'bread knife coltello *m* per il pane
breadth [bredθ] larghezza *f*
'bread-win-ner: *be the ~* mantenere la famiglia
break [breɪk] **1** *n also fig* rottura *f*; (*rest*) pausa *f*; *give s.o. a ~* F (*opportunity*) dare un'opportunità a qu; *take a ~* fare una pausa; *without a ~ work, travel* senza sosta; *lucky ~* colpo di fortuna **2** *v/t* (*pret broke, pp broken*) *china, egg, bone* rompere; *rules, law* violare; *promise non* mantenere; *news* comunicare; *record* battere **3** *v/i* (*pret broke, pp broken*) *of china, egg, toy* rompersi; *of news* diffondersi; *of storm* scoppiare; *of boy's voice* cambiare
♦ break away *v/i* scappare; *from organization, tradition* staccarsi
♦ break down **1** *v/i of vehicle, machine* avere un guasto; *of talks* arenarsi; *in tears* scoppiare in lacrime; (*mentally*) avere un esaurimento **2** *v/t door* buttare giù; *figures* analizzare
♦ break even *v/i* COM coprire le spese
♦ break in *v/i* (*interrupt*) interrompere; *of burglar* entrare con la forza
♦ break off **1** *v/t* staccare; *engagement* rompere; *they've broken it off* si sono lasciati **2** *v/i* (*stop talking*) interrompersi
♦ break out *v/i* (*start up*) scoppiare; *of prisoners* evadere; *he broke out in a rash* gli è venuta l'orticaria
♦ break up **1** *v/t* (*into component parts*) scomporre; *fight* far cessare **2** *v/i of ice* spaccarsi; *of couple* separarsi; *of band, meeting* sciogliersi
break-a-ble ['breɪkəbl] *adj* fragile
break-age ['breɪkɪdʒ] danni *mpl*
'break-down *of vehicle, machine* guasto *m*; *of talks* rottura *f*; (*nervous ~*) esaurimento *m* (nervoso); *of figures* analisi *f inv*

'break·down ser·vice servizio *m* di soccorso stradale

'break·down truck carro *m* attrezzi

break-'e·ven point punto *m* di rottura di pareggio

break·fast ['brekfəst] *n* colazione *f*; **have ~** fare colazione

'break·fast tel·e·vi·sion programmi *mpl* televisivi del mattino

'break-in furto *m* (con scasso)

'**break·through** *in plan, negotiations* passo *m* avanti; *of science, technology* scoperta *f*; '**break·up** *of marriage, partnership* rottura *f*

breast [brest] *of woman* seno *m*

'breast·feed *v/t* (*pret & pp* **breastfed**) allattare

'breast·stroke nuoto *m* a rana

breath [breθ] respiro *m*; **there wasn't a ~ of air** non c'era un filo d'aria; **be out of ~** essere senza fiato; **take a deep ~** fai un respiro profondo

breath·a·lyse ['breθəlaɪz] *v/t* sottoporre ad alcoltest

breath·a·lys·er® ['breθəlaɪzə(r)] alcoltest *m inv*

breathe [briːð] *v/t & v/i* respirare

♦ breathe in 1 *v/i* inspirare 2 *v/t* respirare

♦ breathe out *v/i* espirare

breath·ing ['briːðɪŋ] *n* respiro *m*

breath·less ['breθlɪs] *adj* senza fiato

breath·less·ness ['breθlɪsnɪs] fiato *m* corto

breath·tak·ing ['breθteɪkɪŋ] *adj* mozzafiato

bred [bred] *pret & pp* → **breed**

breed [briːd] 1 *n* razza *f* 2 *v/t* (*pret & pp* **bred**) allevare; *fig* generare 3 *v/i* (*pret & pp* **bred**) *of animals* riprodursi

breed·er ['briːdə(r)] allevatore *m*, -trice *f*

breed·ing ['briːdɪŋ] allevamento *m*; *of person* educazione *f*

'breed·ing ground *fig* terreno *m* fertile

breeze [briːz] brezza *f*

breez·i·ly ['briːzɪlɪ] *adv fig* con disinvoltura

breez·y ['briːzɪ] *adj* ventoso; *fig* brioso

brew [bruː] 1 *v/t beer* produrre; *tea* fare 2 *v/i of storm* prepararsi; **there's trouble ~ing** ci sono guai in vista

brew·er ['bruːə(r)] produttore *m* di birra

brew·er·y ['bruːərɪ] fabbrica *f* di birra

bribe [braɪb] 1 *n* bustarella *f* 2 *v/t* corrompere

brib·er·y ['braɪbərɪ] corruzione *f*

brick [brɪk] mattone *m*

'brick·lay·er muratore *m*

brid·al suite ['braɪdl] suite *f inv* nuziale

bride [braɪd] sposa *f*

'bride·groom sposo *m*

'brides·maid damigella *f* d'onore

bridge¹ [brɪdʒ] 1 *n* ponte *m*; *of ship* ponte *m* di comando; **~ of the nose** setto *m* nasale; 2 *v/t gap* colmare

bridge² [brɪdʒ] (*card game*) bridge *m inv*

bri·dle ['braɪdl] briglia *f*

brief¹ [briːf] *adj* breve

brief² [briːf] 1 *n* (*mission*) missione *f*; (P: *lawyer*) avvocato *m* 2 *v/t*: **~ s.o. on sth** *instruct* dare istruzioni a qu su qc; *inform* mettere qu al corrente di qc

'brief·case valigetta *f*

brief·ing ['briːfɪŋ] briefing *m inv*

brief·ly ['briːflɪ] *adv* (*for a short period of time*) brevemente; (*in a few words, to sum up*) in breve

briefs [briːfs] *npl* slip *m inv*

bright [braɪt] *adj colour* vivace; *smile, future* radioso; (*sunny*) luminoso; (*intelligent*) intelligente; **~ red** rosso vivo

♦ brighten up ['braɪtn] 1 *v/t* ravvivare; 2 *v/i of weather* schiarirsi; *of face, person* rallegrarsi

bright·ly ['braɪtlɪ] *adv smile* in modo radioso; *shine, lit* intensamente; *coloured* in modo sgargiante

bright·ness ['braɪtnɪs] luminosità *f inv*

bril·liance ['brɪljəns] *of person*

genialità *f inv*; *of colour* vivacità *f inv*

bril·liant ['brɪljənt] *adj sunshine etc* sfolgorante; (*very good*) eccezionale; (*very intelligent*) brillante

brim [brɪm] *of container* orlo *m*; *of hat* falda *f*

brim·ful ['brɪmfʊl] *adj* colmo

bring [brɪŋ] *v/t* (*pret & pp* **brought**) portare; **~ it here, will you** portalo qui, per favore; **can I ~ a friend?** posso portare un amico?

♦ **bring about** *v/t* causare

♦ **bring around** *v/t from a faint* far rinvenire; (*persuade*) convincere

♦ **bring back** *v/t* restituire; (*re-introduce*) reintrodurre; *memories* risvegliare

♦ **bring down** *v/t tree, government, aeroplane* abbattere; *rates, inflation, price* far scendere

♦ **bring in** *v/t interest, income* rendere; *legislation* introdurre; *verdict* emettere; (*involve*) coinvolgere

♦ **bring on** *v/t illness* provocare

♦ **bring out** *v/t* (*produce: book*) pubblicare; *new product* lanciare

♦ **bring to** *v/t from a faint* far rinvenire

♦ **bring up** *v/t child* allevare; *subject* sollevare; (*vomit*) vomitare

brink [brɪŋk] *also fig* orlo *m*

brisk [brɪsk] *adj person, tone* spiccio; *walk* svelto; *trade* vivace

brist·les ['brɪslz] *npl* peli *mpl*

brist·ling ['brɪslɪŋ] *adj*: **be ~ with** brulicare di

Brit [brɪt] F britannico *m*, -a *f*

Brit·ain ['brɪtn] Gran Bretagna *f*

Brit·ish ['brɪtɪʃ] **1** *adj* britannico **2** *n*: **the ~** i britannici

Brit·on ['brɪtn] britannico *m*, -a *f*

brit·tle ['brɪtl] *adj* fragile

broach [brəʊtʃ] *v/t subject* affrontare

broad [brɔːd] *adj* largo; (*general*) generale; **in ~ daylight** in pieno giorno

'broad·cast 1 *n* trasmissione *f* **2** *v/t* trasmettere

'broad·cast·er giornalista *m/f* radiotelevisivo, -a

'broad·cast·ing diffusione *f* radiotelevisiva

broad·en ['brɔːdn] **1** *v/i* allargarsi **2** *v/t* allargare

broad·ly ['brɔːdlɪ] *adv*: **~ speaking** parlando in senso lato

broad·mind·ed [brɔːd'maɪndɪd] *adj* di larghe vedute

broad·mind·ed·ness [brɔːd'maɪndɪdnɪs] larghezza *f* di vedute

broc·co·li ['brɒkəlɪ] broccoli *mpl*

bro·chure ['brəʊʃə(r)] dépliant *m inv*, opuscolo *m*

broke [brəʊk] **1** *adj* al verde; **go ~** (*go bankrupt*) andare sul lastrico **2** *pret* → **break**

bro·ken ['brəʊkn] **1** *adj* rotto; *English* stentato; *marriage* fallito; **she's from a ~ home** i suoi sono separati **2** *pp* → **break**

bro·ken-heart·ed [brəʊkn'hɑːtɪd] *adj* col cuore spezzato

bro·ker ['brəʊkə(r)] mediatore *m*, -trice *f*

brol·ly ['brɒlɪ] F ombrello *m*

bron·chi·tis [brɒŋ'kaɪtɪs] bronchite *f*

bronze [brɒnz] *n* bronzo *m*

brooch [brəʊtʃ] spilla *f*

brood [bruːd] *v/i of person* rimuginare

broom [bruːm] scopa *f*

broth [brɒθ] (*soup*) minestra *f*; (*stock*) brodo *m*

broth·el ['brɒθl] bordello *m*

broth·er ['brʌðə(r)] fratello *m*; **they're ~s** sono fratelli; **~s and sisters** fratelli e sorelle

'broth·er-in-law (*pl* **brothers-in-law**) cognato *m*

broth·er·ly ['brʌðəlɪ] *adj* fraterno

brought [brɔːt] *pret & pp* → **bring**

brow [braʊ] (*forehead*) fronte *f*; *of hill* cima *f*

brown [braʊn] **1** *n* marrone *m*; *eyes, hair* castano **2** *adj* marrone; (*tanned*) abbronzato **3** *v/t in cooking* rosolare **4** *v/i in cooking* rosolarsi

Brown·ie ['braʊnɪ] giovane esploratrice *f*

brown 'pa·per carta *f* da pacchi;

brown pa·per 'bag sacchetto *m* di carta; **'brown 'sug·ar** zucchero *m* non raffinato

browse [braʊz] *v/i in shop* curiosare; **~ through a book** sfogliare un libro

brows·er ['braʊzə(r)] COMPUT browser *m inv*

bruise [bruːz] **1** *n* livido *m*; *on fruit* ammaccatura *f* **2** *v/t person* fare un livido a; *fruit* ammaccare **3** *v/i of person* coprirsi di lividi; *of fruit* ammaccarsi

bruis·ing ['bruːzɪŋ] *adj fig* doloroso

brunch [brʌnʃ] brunch *m inv*

bru·nette [bruː'net] *n* brunetta *f*

brunt [brʌnt] *n*: **bear the ~ of ...** subire il peggio di ...

brush [brʌʃ] **1** *n* spazzola *f*; (*paint~*) pennello *m*; (*tooth~*) spazzolino *m* da denti; (*conflict*) scontro *m* **2** *v/t* spazzolare; (*touch lightly*) sfiorare; (*move away*) spostare; **~ your teeth** lavati i denti

♦ **brush against** *v/t* sfiorare

♦ **brush aside** *v/t* ignorare

♦ **brush off** *v/t* spazzolare via; *criticism* ignorare

♦ **brush up** *v/t* ripassare

'brush-off: **give s.o. the ~** F rispondere picche a qu F

'brush·work PAINT pennellata *f*

brusque [brʊsk] *adj* brusco

Brus·sels ['brʌslz] Bruxelles *f inv*

Brus·sels 'sprout cavolino *m* di Bruxelles

bru·tal ['bruːtl] *adj* brutale

bru·tal·i·ty [bruː'tælətɪ] brutalità *f inv*

bru·tal·ly ['bruːtəlɪ] *adv* brutalmente

brute [bruːt] bruto *m*

'brute force forza *f* bruta

BSE [biːesˈiː] *abbr* (= **bovine spongiform encephalopathy**)

bub·ble ['bʌbl] *n* bolla *f*

'bub·ble bath bagnoschiuma *m inv*; **'bub·ble gum** gomma *f* da masticare; **'bub·ble wrap** *n* involucro *m* a bolle

bub·bly ['bʌblɪ] *n* F (*champagne*) champagne *m inv*

buck¹ [bʌk] *n Am* F (*dollar*) dollaro *m*

buck² [bʌk] *v/i of horse* sgroppare

buck³ [bʌk] *n*: **pass the ~** scaricare la responsabilità

buck·et ['bʌkɪt] *n* secchio *m*

'buck·et shop *agenzia f di viaggi che pratica forti sconti*

buck·le¹ ['bʌkl] **1** *n* fibbia *f* **2** *v/t belt* allacciare

buck·le² ['bʌkl] *v/i of wood, metal* piegarsi

♦ **buck·le down** *v/i* mettersi a lavorare

bud [bʌd] *n* BOT bocciolo *m*

bud·dy ['bʌdɪ] F amico *m*, -a *f*

budge [bʌdʒ] **1** *v/t* smuovere; (*make reconsider*) far cambiare idea a **2** *v/i* muoversi; (*change one's mind*) cambiare idea

bud·ger·i·gar ['bʌdʒərɪgɑː(r)] pappagallino *m*

bud·get ['bʌdʒɪt] **1** *n* budget *m inv*; *of company* bilancio *m* preventivo; *of state* bilancio *m* dello Stato; **I'm on a ~** devo stare attento ai soldi **2** *v/i* prevedere le spese

♦ **budget for** *v/t* preventivare

bud·gie ['bʌdʒɪ] F pappagallino *m*

buff¹ [bʌf] *adj* (*colour*) beige *inv*

buff² [bʌf] *n* appassionato *m*, -a *f*

buf·fa·lo ['bʌfələʊ] bufalo *m*

buff·er ['bʌfə(r)] RAIL respingente *m*; COMPUT buffer *m inv*; *fig* cuscinetto *m*

buf·fet¹ ['bʊfeɪ] *n* (*meal*) buffet *m inv*

buf·fet² ['bʌfɪt] *v/t of wind* sballottare

bug [bʌg] **1** *n* (*insect*) insetto *m*; (*virus*) virus *m inv*; (*spying device*) microspia *f*; COMPUT bug *m inv* **2** *v/t* (*pret & pp -ged*) *room* installare microspie in; *telephone* mettere sotto controllo; F (*annoy*) seccare

bug·gy ['bʌgɪ] *for baby* passeggino *m*

build [bɪld] **1** *n of person* corporatura *f* **2** *v/t* (*pret & pp **built***) costruire

♦ **build up 1** *v/t relationship* consolidare; *collection* mettere insieme **2** *v/i of tension, traffic* aumentare; **build up one's strength** rimettersi in forze

'build·er ['bɪldə(r)] *person* muratore

m; *company* impresario m edile
'build·ing ['bɪldɪŋ] edificio m, palazzo m; (*activity*) costruzione f
'build·ing blocks *npl for child* mattoncini *mpl*; 'build·ing site cantiere m edile; 'build·ing so·ci·e·ty *Br* istituto m di credito immobiliare; 'build·ing trade edilizia f
'build-up *of traffic, pressure* aumento m; *of arms, forces* ammassamento m; (*publicity*) pubblicità f *inv*
built [bɪlt] *pret & pp* → **build**
built-in ['bɪltɪn] *adj wardrobe* a muro; *flash* incorporato
built-up 'ar·e·a abitato m
bulb [bʌlb] BOT bulbo m; (*light ~*) lampadina f
bulge [bʌldʒ] **1** n rigonfiamento m **2** v/i sporgere
bu·lim·i·a [buˈlɪmɪə] bulimia f
bulk [bʌlk] grosso m; **in ~** in grande quantità; *wholesale* all'ingrosso
'bulk·y ['bʌlkɪ] *adj* voluminoso
bull [bʊl] toro m
bull·doze ['bʊldəʊz] v/t (*demolish*) abbattere con il bulldozer; **~ into sth** *fig* costringere qu a fare qc
bull·doz·er ['bʊldəʊzə(r)] bulldozer m *inv*
bul·let ['bʊlɪt] proiettile m, pallottola f
bul·le·tin ['bʊlɪtɪn] bollettino m
'bul·le·tin board COMPUT bulletin board m *inv*; *Am: on wall* bacheca f
'bul·let-proof *adj* a prova di proiettile
'bull mar·ket FIN mercato m in ascesa
'bull's-eye centro m del bersaglio; **hit the ~** fare centro
'bull·shit **1** n V stronzate *fpl* V **2** v/i (*pret & pp* **-ted**) V dire stronzate V
bul·ly ['bʊlɪ] **1** n prepotente m/f **2** v/t (*pret & pp* **-ied**) tiranneggiare
'bul·ly·ing ['bʊlɪŋ] n prepotenze *fpl*
bum [bʌm] **1** n F *worthless person* mezza calzetta f F; (*Br: bottom*) sedere m; (*Am: tramp*) barbone m **2** *adj* F (*useless*) del piffero **3** v/t (*pret & pp* **-med**) F *cigarette etc* scroccare

♦ **bum around, bum about** v/i F (*travel*) vagabondare; (*be lazy*) oziare
'bum-bag F marsupio m
bum·ble·bee ['bʌmblbɪ] bombo m
bump [bʌmp] **1** n (*swelling*) gonfiore m; (*lump*) bernoccolo m; *on road* cunetta f; **get a ~ on the head** prendere un colpo in testa **2** v/t battere
♦ **bump into** v/t *table* battere contro; (*meet*) incontrare
♦ **bump off** v/t F (*murder*) far fuori F
♦ **bump up** v/t F (*prices*) aumentare
bump·er ['bʌmpə(r)] **1** n MOT paraurti m *inv*; **the traffic was ~ to ~** c'era una coda di macchine **2** *adj* (*extremely good*) eccezionale
bumph [bʌmf] *Br* F scartoffie *fpl*
'bump-start v/t car mettere in moto a spinte; (*fig: economy*) dare una spinta a
bump·y ['bʌmpɪ] *adj road* accidentato; *flight* movimentato
bun [bʌn] *hairstyle* chignon m *inv*; *for eating* panino m dolce
bunch [bʌntʃ] *of people* gruppo m; *of keys, flowers* mazzo m; **a ~ of grapes** un grappolo d'uva
bun·dle ['bʌndl] *of clothes* fagotto m; *of wood* fascina f
♦ **bundle up** v/t fare un fagotto di; (*dress warmly*) coprire bene
bung [bʌŋ] v/t F buttare
bun·ga·low ['bʌŋgələʊ] bungalow m *inv*
bun·gee jump·ing ['bʌndʒɪdʒʌmpɪŋ] salto m con l'elastico
bun·gle ['bʌŋgl] v/t pasticciare
bunk [bʌŋk] cuccetta f
'bunk beds *npl* letti *mpl* a castello
buoy [bɔɪ] n NAUT boa f
buoy·ant ['bɔɪənt] *adj* (*cheerful*) allegro; *fig: economy* sostenuto
bur·den ['bɜːdn] **1** n *also fig* peso m **2** v/t: **~ s.o. with sth** *fig* opprimere qu con qc
bu·reau ['bjʊərəʊ] (*office*) ufficio m
bu·reauc·ra·cy [bjʊəˈrɒkrəsɪ] burocrazia f
bu·reau·crat ['bjʊərəkræt] burocrate m/f

bu·reau·crat·ic [bjʊərə'krætɪk] *adj* burocratico

burg·er ['bɜːgə(r)] hamburger *m inv*

bur·glar ['bɜːglə(r)] ladro *m*

'**bur·glar a·larm** antifurto *m*

bur·glar·ize ['bɜːgləraɪz] *v/t Am* svaligiare

bur·glar·y ['bɜːglərɪ] furto *m* (con scasso)

bur·gle ['bɜːgl] *v/t* svaligiare

bur·i·al ['berɪəl] sepoltura *f*

bur·ly ['bɜːlɪ] *adj* robusto

burn [bɜːn] **1** *n* bruciatura *f*; *superficial* scottatura *f*; *very serious* ustione *f* **2** *v/t* (*pret & pp* **burnt**) bruciare; *of sun* scottare **3** *v/i* (*pret & pp* **burnt**) ardere; *of house* bruciare; *of toast* bruciarsi; (*get sunburnt*) scottarsi, bruciarsi; *~ to death* morire carbonizzato

♦ **burn down 1** *v/t* dare alle fiamme **2** *v/i* essere distrutto dal fuoco

♦ **burn out** *v/t*: **burn o.s. out** esaurirsi; *a burned-out car* un'auto bruciata

burnt [bɜːnt] *pret & pp* → **burn**

burp [bɜːp] **1** *n* rutto *m* **2** *v/i* ruttare **3** *v/t baby* far fare il ruttino a

burst [bɜːst] **1** *n in water pipe* rottura *f*; *of gunfire* raffica *f*; *a ~ of energy* un'esplosione d'energia **2** *adj* bucato **3** *v/t* (*pret & pp* **burst**) *balloon* far scoppiare **4** *v/i* (*pret & pp* **burst**) *of balloon, tyre* scoppiare; *~ into a room* irrompere in una stanza; *~ into tears* scoppiare in lacrime; *~ out laughing* scoppiare a ridere

bur·y ['berɪ] *v/t* (*pret & pp* **-ied**) seppellire; *hide* nascondere; *~ o.s. in work* immergersi nel lavoro

bus [bʌs] **1** *n* autobus *m inv*; (*long distance*) pullman *m inv* **2** *v/t* (*pret & pp* **-sed**) trasportare in autobus

'**bus driv·er** autista *m/f* di autobus

bush [bʊʃ] (*plant*) cespuglio *m*; (*land*) boscaglia *f*

bushed [bʊʃt] *adj* F (*tired*) distrutto

bush·y ['bʊʃɪ] *adj eyebrows* irsuto

busi·ness ['bɪznɪs] (*trade*) affari *mpl*; (*company*) impresa *f*; (*work*) lavoro

m; (*affair, matter*) faccenda *f*; (*as subject of study*) economia *f* aziendale; *in the insurance ~* (*sector*) nel campo delle assicurazioni; *on ~* per affari; *that's none of your ~!, mind your own ~!* fatti gli affari tuoi!

'**busi·ness card** biglietto *m* da visita (della ditta); '**busi·ness class** business class *f inv*; '**busi·ness hours** *npl* orario *msg* di apertura; **busi·ness·like** ['bɪznɪslaɪk] *adj* efficiente; '**busi·ness lunch** pranzo *m* d'affari; '**busi·ness·man** uomo *m* d'affari; '**busi·ness meet·ing** riunione *f* d'affari; '**busi·ness school** istituto *m* commerciale; '**busi·ness stud·ies** *nsg* (*course*) economia *f* aziendale; '**busi·ness trip** viaggio *m* d'affari; '**busi·ness·wom·an** donna *f* d'affari

busk·er ['bʌskə(r)] musicista *m/f* ambulante

'**bus lane** corsia *f* riservata (ai mezzi pubblici); '**bus shel·ter** pensilina *f* (dell'autobus); '**bus sta·tion** autostazione *f*; '**bus stop** fermata *f* dell'autobus

bust[1] [bʌst] *n of woman* petto *m*

bust[2] [bʌst] **1** *adj* F (*broken*) scassato; *go ~* fallire **2** *v/t* scassare

'**bus tick·et** biglietto *m* dell'autobus

♦ **bus·tle about** ['bʌsl] *v/i* affaccendarsi

'**bust-up** F rottura *f*

bust·y ['bʌstɪ] *adj* prosperoso

bus·y ['bɪzɪ] **1** *adj* occupato; *day* intenso; *street* animato; *shop, restaurant* affollato; TELEC occupato; *be ~ doing sth* essere occupato a fare qc; *I'm ~ talking to Gran* sto parlando con la nonna **2** *v/t* (*pret & pp* **-ied**): *~ o.s. with* tenersi occupato con

'**bus·y·bod·y** impiccione *m*, -a *f*

but [bʌt] *unstressed* [bət] **1** *conj* ma; *~ then* (*again*) d'altra parte **2** *prep*: *all ~ him* tutti tranne lui; *the last ~ one* il penultimo; *the next ~ one* il secondo; *~ for you* se non fosse per te; *nothing ~ the best* solo il meglio

butch·er ['bʊtʃə(r)] macellaio *m*, -a *f*

butch·er's ['bʊtʃəz] macelleria *f*

B

butt [bʌt] **1** *n* *of cigarette* mozzicone *m*; *of joke* bersaglio *m*; *Am* P (*backside*) culo *m* P **2** *v/t* dare una testata a; *of goat, bull* dare una cornata a
♦ **butt in** *v/i* interrompere
but·ter ['bʌtə(r)] **1** *n* burro *m* **2** *v/t* imburrare
♦ **butter up** *v/t* F arruffianarsi F
'**but·ter·cup** ranuncolo *m*
'**but·ter·fly** *also swimming* farfalla *f*
but·tocks ['bʌtəks] *npl* natiche *fpl*
but·ton ['bʌtn] **1** *n* bottone *m*; *on machine* pulsante *m* **2** *v/t* abbotto-nare
♦ **button up** → **button**
'**but·ton·hole 1** *n* *in suit* occhiello *m* **2** *v/t* attaccare un bottone a
but·tress ['bʌtrəs] contrafforte *m*
bux·om ['bʌksəm] *adj* formoso
buy [baɪ] **1** *n* acquisto *m* **2** *v/t* (*pret & pp* **bought**) comprare; *can I ~ you a drink?* posso offrirti da bere?; *£5 doesn't ~ much* con 5 sterline non si compra granché
♦ **buy off** *v/t* (*bribe*) comprare
♦ **buy out** *v/t* COM rilevare
♦ **buy up** *v/t* accaparrarsi
buy·er ['baɪə(r)] acquirente *m/f*; *for department store, supermarket* buyer *m inv*
buzz [bʌz] **1** *n* ronzio *m*; F (*thrill*) emozione *f* **2** *v/i* *of insect* ronzare; *with buzzer* suonare **3** *v/t* with

buzzer chiamare
♦ **buzz off** *v/i* F levarsi di torno F
buzz·er ['bʌzə(r)] cicalino *m*
by [baɪ] **1** *prep* agency da; (*near, next to*) vicino a, accanto a; (*no later than*) entro, per; (*past*) davanti a; (*mode of transport*) in; *side ~ side* fianco a fianco; *~ day/night* di giorno/notte; *~ bus/train* in autobus/treno; *~ the hour/ton* a ore/tonnellate; *~ my watch* secondo il mio orologio; *a book ~ ...* un libro di ...; *murdered ~ her husband* assassinata dal marito; *~ o.s.* da solo; *pay ~ cheque* pagare con un assegno; *~ a couple of minutes* per pochi minuti; *2 ~ 4* (*measurement*) 2 per 4; *~ this time tomorrow* domani a quest'ora **2** *adv*: *~ and ~* (*soon*) tra breve
bye(-bye) [baɪ] ciao
'**by-e·lec·tion** elezione *f* straordinaria di un parlamentare; **by·gone** ['baɪ-gɒn] **1** *n*: *let ~s be ~s* metterci una pietra sopra **2** *adj*: *in ~ days* nei giorni andati; '**by·pass 1** *n* (*road*) circonvallazione *f*; MED by-pass *m inv* **2** *v/t* aggirare; '**by-prod·uct** sottoprodotto *m*; **by·stand·er** ['baɪstændə(r)] astante *m/f*
byte [baɪt] byte *m inv*
'**by·word** *n*: *be a ~ for* essere sinonimo di

C

cab [kæb] (*taxi*) taxi *m inv*; *of truck* cabina *f*; *~ driver* tassista *m/f*
cab·a·ret ['kæbəreɪ] spettacolo *m* di cabaret
cab·bage ['kæbɪdʒ] cavolo *m*
cab·in ['kæbɪn] *of plane, ship* cabina *f*
'**cab·in at·tend·ant** assistente *m/f* di volo
'**cab·in crew** equipaggio *m* di volo

cab·i·net ['kæbɪnɪt] armadietto *m*; POL Consiglio *m* dei ministri; *display ~* vetrina *f*; *drinks ~* mobile *m* bar
'**cab·i·net mak·er** ebanista *m/f*; '**cab·i·net meet·ing** riunione *f* del Consiglio dei ministri; '**cab·i·net min·is·ter** membro *m* del Consiglio dei ministri; '**cab·i·net re·shuf·fle**

rimpasto *m* del governo

ca·ble ['keɪbl] ELEC, *for securing* cavo *m*; ~ *(TV)* tv *f* via cavo

'**ca·ble car** cabina *f* (di funivia)

'**ca·ble tel·e·vi·sion** televisione *f* via cavo

cac·tus ['kæktəs] cactus *m inv*

CAD-CAM ['kædkæm] *abbr* (= *computer assisted design-computer assisted manufacture*) CAD-CAM *m*

cad·die ['kædɪ] **1** *n in golf* portamazze *m inv* **2** *v/i* portare le mazze

ca·det [kə'det] cadetto *m*

cadge [kædʒ] *v/t*: ~ *sth from s.o.* scroccare qc a qu

Cae·sar·e·an [sɪ'zeərɪən] *n* parto *m* cesareo

caf·é ['kæfeɪ] caffè *m inv*, bar *m*

caf·e·te·ri·a [kæfə'tɪərɪə] tavola *f* calda

caf·feine ['kæfiːn] caffeina *f*

cage [keɪdʒ] gabbia *f*

ca·gey ['keɪdʒɪ] *adj* evasivo

ca·hoots [kə'huːts] F: *be in ~ with* essere in combutta con

ca·jole [kə'dʒəʊl] *v/t* convincere con le lusinghe

cake [keɪk] **1** *n* dolce *m*, torta *f*; *be a piece of ~* F essere un gioco da ragazzi **2** *v/i of mud, blood* indurirsi

ca·lam·i·ty [kə'læmətɪ] calamità *f inv*

cal·ci·um ['kælsɪəm] calcio *m*

cal·cu·late ['kælkjʊleɪt] *v/t* calcolare

cal·cu·lat·ing ['kælkjʊleɪtɪŋ] *adj* calcolatore

cal·cu·la·tion [kælkjʊ'leɪʃn] calcolo *m*

cal·cu·la·tor ['kælkjʊleɪtə(r)] calcolatrice *f*

cal·en·dar ['kælɪndə(r)] calendario *m*

calf[1] [kɑːf] (*pl calves* [kɑːvz]) *young cow* vitello *m*

calf[2] [kɑːf] (*pl calves* [kɑːvz]) *of leg* polpaccio *m*

'**calf·skin** *n* vitello *m*

cal·i·ber *Am*, **cal·i·bre** ['kælɪbə(r)] *of gun* calibro *m*; *a man of his ~* un uomo del suo calibro

call [kɔːl] **1** *n* (*phone ~*) telefonata *f*; (*shout*) grido *m*; (*demand*) richiesta *f*; (*visit*) visita *f*; *be on ~ of doctor* essere di guardia; *pay s.o. a ~* far visita a qu **2** *v/t on phone* chiamare; (*summon*) chiamare; (*shout*) gridare; (*describe as*) definire; *meeting, election* indire, convocare; *what have they ~ed the baby?* come hanno chiamato il bambino?; *~ s.o. as a witness* citare qu a testimoniare; *~ a flight* annunciare un volo; *s.o. names* dare dei titoli a qu **3** *v/i on phone* chiamare; (*shout*) gridare; (*visit*) passare

◆ **call at** (*stop at*) passare da

◆ **call back 1** *v/t also* TELEC richiamare **2** *v/i on phone* richiamare; (*make another visit*) ripassare

◆ **call for** *v/t* (*collect*) passare a prendere; (*demand*) reclamare; (*require*) richiedere

◆ **call in 1** *v/t* (*summon*) far venire **2** *v/i on phone* chiamare; *call in sick* chiamare per dire di essere ammalato

◆ **call off** *v/t strike* revocare; *wedding, appointment* disdire

◆ **call on** *v/t* (*urge*) sollecitare; (*visit*) visitare

◆ **call out** *v/t* (*shout*) chiamare ad alta voce; (*summon*) chiamare

◆ **call up** *v/t on phone* chiamare; COMPUT aprire

'**call box** cabina *f* telefonica

'**call cen·tre** centro *m* chiamate

call·er ['kɔːlə(r)] *on phone* persona *f* che ha chiamato; (*visitor*) visitatore *m*, -trice *f*

'**call girl** squillo *f inv*

cal·lous ['kæləs] *adj* freddo, insensibile

cal·lous·ly ['kæləslɪ] *adv* freddamente, insensibilmente

cal·lous·ness ['kæləsnɪs] freddezza *f*, insensibilità *f*

calm [kɑːm] **1** *adj* calmo **2** *n* calma *f*

◆ **calm down 1** *v/t* calmare **2** *v/i* calmarsi

calm·ly ['kɑːmlɪ] *adv* con calma

cal·o·rie ['kælərɪ] caloria *f*

cam·cor·der ['kæmkɔːdə(r)] video-camera f

came [keɪm] pret → **come**

cam·e·ra ['kæmərə] macchina f fotografica; (video ~) videocamera f; (television ~) telecamera f

'cam·e·ra·man cameraman m inv

cam·ou·flage ['kæməflɑːʒ] **1** n mimetizzazione f; of soldiers tuta f mimetica **2** v/t mimetizzare; fig mascherare

camp [kæmp] **1** n campo m; **make ~** accamparsi **2** v/i accamparsi

cam·paign [kæm'peɪn] **1** n campagna f **2** v/i militare

cam·paign·er [kæm'peɪnə(r)] militante m/f

camp·er ['kæmpə(r)] person campeggiatore m, -trice f; vehicle camper m inv

camp·ing ['kæmpɪŋ] campeggio m; **go ~** andare in campeggio

'camp·site camping m inv, campeggio m

cam·pus ['kæmpəs] campus m inv

can[1] [kæn] unstressed [kən] v/aux (pret **could**) ◊ (ability) potere; **~ you hear me?** mi senti?; **I can't see** non vedo; **~ you speak French?** sai parlare francese?; **~ he call me back?** mi può richiamare?; **as fast as you ~** più veloce che puoi; **as well as you ~** meglio che puoi ◊ (permission) potere; **~ I help you?** posso aiutarla?; **~ you help me?** mi può aiutare?; **~ I have a beer/ coffee?** posso avere una birra/ un caffè?; **that can't be right** non può essere giusto

can[2] [kæn] **1** n for drinks lattina f; for food scatola f **2** v/t (pret & pp **-ned**) inscatolare

Can·a·da ['kænədə] Canada m

Ca·na·di·an [kə'neɪdɪən] **1** adj canadese **2** n canadese m/f

ca·nal [kə'næl] (waterway) canale m

ca·nar·y [kə'neərɪ] canarino m

can·cel ['kænsl] v/t annullare

can·cel·la·tion [kænsə'leɪʃn] annullamento m

can·cel·la·tion fee penalità f (per annullamento)

can·cer ['kænsə(r)] cancro m

Can·cer ['kænsə(r)] ASTR Cancro m

can·cer·ous ['kænsərəs] adj canceroso

c&f abbr (= **cost and freight**) c&f

can·did ['kændɪd] adj franco

can·di·da·cy ['kændɪdəsɪ] candidatura f

can·di·date ['kændɪdət] candidato m, -a f

can·did·ly ['kændɪdlɪ] adv francamente

can·died ['kændiːd] adj candito

can·dle ['kændl] candela f

'can·dle·stick portacandele m inv

can·dor Am, **can·dour** ['kændə(r)] franchezza f

can·dy ['kændɪ] Am (sweet) caramella f; (sweets) dolciumi mpl

can·dy·floss ['kændɪflɒs] zucchero m filato

cane [keɪn] canna f; for walking bastone m

can·is·ter ['kænɪstə(r)] barattolo m; spray bombola f

can·na·bis ['kænəbɪs] hashish m

canned [kænd] adj fruit, tomatoes in scatola; (recorded) registrato

can·ni·bal·ize ['kænɪbəlaɪz] v/t riciclare parti di

can·not ['kænɒt] → **can**[1]

can·ny ['kænɪ] adj (astute) arguto

ca·noe [kə'nuː] canoa f

'can o·pen·er apriscatole m inv

can't [kɑːnt] → **can**[1]

can·tan·ker·ous [kæn'tæŋkərəs] adj irascibile

can·teen [kæn'tiːn] in factory mensa f

can·vas ['kænvəs] tela f

can·vass ['kænvəs] **1** v/t (seek opinion of) fare un sondaggio tra **2** v/i POL fare propaganda elettorale

can·yon ['kænjən] canyon m inv

cap [kæp] (hat) berretto m; of bottle, jar tappo m; of pen cappuccio m; of lens coperchio m

ca·pa·bil·i·ty [keɪpə'bɪlətɪ] of person capacità f inv; MIL potenziale m

ca·pa·ble ['keɪpəbl] *adj* (*efficient*) capace; **be ~ of** essere capace di

ca·pac·i·ty [kə'pæsətɪ] capacità *f inv*; *of car engine* potenza *f*; *of factory* capacità *f inv* produttiva; **in my ~ as ...** in qualità di ...

cap·i·tal ['kæpɪtl] *n of country* capitale *f*; (*capital letter*) maiuscola *f*; *money* capitale *m*

cap·i·tal ex'pend·i·ture spese *fpl* in conto capitale

cap·i·tal 'gains tax imposta *f* sui redditi di capitale

cap·i·tal 'growth aumento *m* del capitale

cap·i·tal·is·m ['kæpɪtəlɪzm] capitalismo *m*

'cap·i·tal·ist ['kæpɪtəlɪst] **1** *adj* capitalista **2** *n* capitalista *m/f*

♦ **cap·i·tal·ize on** ['kæpɪtəlaɪz] *v/t* trarre vantaggio da

cap·i·tal 'let·ter lettera *f* maiuscola

cap·i·tal 'pun·ish·ment pena *f* capitale

ca·pit·u·late [kə'pɪtjuleɪt] *v/i* capitolare

ca·pit·u·la·tion [kæpɪtju'leɪʃn] capitolazione *f*

Cap·ri·corn ['kæprɪkɔːn] ASTR Capricorno *m*

cap·size [kæp'saɪz] **1** *v/i* ribaltarsi **2** *v/t* far ribaltare

cap·sule ['kæpsjul] *of medicine* cachet *m inv*; (*space ~*) capsula *f*

cap·tain ['kæptɪn] *n* capitano *m*

cap·tion ['kæpʃn] *n* didascalia *f*

cap·ti·vate ['kæptɪveɪt] *v/t* affascinare

cap·tive ['kæptɪv] *adj* prigioniero

cap·tiv·i·ty [kæp'tɪvətɪ] cattività *f*

cap·ture ['kæptʃə(r)] **1** *n of building, city* occupazione *f*; *of city* presa *f*; *of criminal, animal* cattura *f* **2** *v/t person, animal* catturare; *city, building* occupare; *city* prendere; *market share* conquistare; (*portray*) cogliere

car [kɑː(r)] macchina *f*, auto *f inv*; *of train* vagone *m*; **by ~** in macchina

ca·rafe [kə'ræf] caraffa *f*

car·a·mel ['kærəmel] *sweet* caramel-

la *f* morbida

car·at ['kærət] carato *m*

car·a·van ['kærəvæn] roulotte *f inv*

'car·a·van site campeggio *m* per roulotte

car·bo·hy·drate [kɑːbə'haɪdreɪt] carboidrato *m*

'car bomb autobomba *f*

car·bon mon·ox·ide [kɑːbənmɒn-'ɒksaɪd] monossido *m* di carbonio

car·bu·ret·or [kɑːbju'retə(r)] carburatore *m*

car·cass ['kɑːkəs] carcassa *f*

car·cin·o·gen ['kɑːsɪnədʒen] cancerogeno *m*

car·cin·o·genic [kɑːsɪnə'dʒenɪk] *adj* cancerogeno

card [kɑːd] *to mark special occasion* biglietto *m*; (*post~*) cartolina *f*; (*business ~*) biglietto *m* (da visita); (*playing ~*) carta *f*; COMPUT scheda *f*; *material* cartoncino *m*

'card·board cartone *m*

card·board 'box scatola *f* di cartone

car·di·ac ['kɑːdɪæk] *adj* cardiaco

car·di·ac ar'rest arresto *m* cardiaco

car·di·gan ['kɑːdɪgən] cardigan *m inv*

car·di·nal ['kɑːdɪnl] *n* REL cardinale *m*

'card in·dex schedario *m*; **'card key** tessera *f* magnetica; **'card phone** telefono *m* a scheda

care [keə(r)] **1** *n of baby, pet* cure *fpl*; *of the elderly* assistenza *f*; *of the sick* cura *f*; (*worry*) preoccupazione *f*; **take ~** (*be cautious*) fare attenzione; **take ~** (**of yourself**)! (*goodbye*) stammi bene; **take ~ of** (*look after: baby, dog*) prendersi cura di; *tool, house, garden* tenere bene; (*deal with*) occuparsi di; (*handle*) **with ~!** *on label* maneggiare con cura **2** *v/i* interessarsi; **I don't ~!** non mi importa; **I couldn't ~ less** non potrebbe importarmene di meno

care of → **c/o**

♦ **care about** *v/t* interessarsi a

♦ **care for** *v/t* (*look after*) prendersi cura di; **I don't care for your tone** non mi piace il tuo tono; **would you**

care for a tea? *fml* gradirebbe un tè?

ca·reer [kəˈrɪə(r)] (*profession*) carriera *f*; (*path through life*) vita *f*

ca·reers of·fi·cer consulente *m/f* professionale

'care·free *adj* spensierato

care·ful ['keəfʊl] *adj* (*cautious*) attento; (*thorough*) attento; (**be**) **~!** (stai) attento!

care·ful·ly ['keəfʊlɪ] *adv* con cautela

care·less ['keəlɪs] *adj* incurante; *driver*, *worker* sbadato; *work* fatto senza attenzione; *error* di disattenzione; **you are so ~!** sei così sbadato!

care·less·ly ['keəlɪslɪ] *adv* senza cura

carer ['keərə(r)] accompagnatore *m*, -trice *f*

ca·ress [kəˈres] **1** *n* carezza *f* **2** *v/t* accarezzare

care·tak·er ['keəteɪkə(r)] custode *m/f*

'care·worn *adj* provato

'car fer·ry traghetto *m* (per le macchine)

car·go ['kɑːgəʊ] carico *m*

'car hire autonoleggio *m*

'car hire com·pa·ny compagnia *f* di autonoleggio

car·i·ca·ture ['kærɪkətjʊə(r)] *n* caricatura *f*

car·ing ['keərɪŋ] *adj* premuroso

'car me·chan·ic meccanico *m* per auto

car·nage ['kɑːnɪdʒ] carneficina *f*

car·na·tion [kɑːˈneɪʃn] garofano *m*

car·ni·val ['kɑːnɪvl] carnevale *m*

car·ol ['kærəl] *n* canzone *f* di Natale

car·ou·sel [kærəˈsel] *at airport* nastro *m* trasportatore; *for slide projector* carrello *m*

'car park parcheggio *m*

'car park at·tend·ant parcheggiatore *m*, -trice *f*

car·pen·ter ['kɑːpɪntə(r)] falegname *m*

car·pet ['kɑːpɪt] tappeto *m*; (*fitted ~*) moquette *f inv*

'car phone telefono *m* da automobi-

le; 'car·pool *n* uso *m* condiviso della macchina dell'uno o dell'altro tra un gruppo di persone; 'car·port posto *m* auto coperto; **car 'ra·di·o** autoradio *f inv*

car·riage ['kærɪdʒ] carrozza *f*; COM trasporto *m*

car·ri·er ['kærɪə(r)] (*company*) compagnia *f* di trasporto; *of disease* portatore *m* sano, portatrice *f* sana

'car·ri·er bag sacchetto *m*

car·rot ['kærət] carota *f*

car·ry ['kærɪ] (*pret & pp* **-ied**) **1** *v/t* portare; *of pregnant woman* portare in grembo; *of ship, plane, bus etc* trasportare; *proposal* approvare; **get carried away** farsi prendere dall'entusiasmo **2** *v/i of sound* sentirsi

♦ **carry on 1** *v/i* (*continue*) andare avanti, continuare; (*make a fuss*) fare storie; (*have an affair*) avere una storia **2** *v/t* (*conduct*) portare avanti

♦ **carry out** *v/t survey etc* effettuare; *orders etc* eseguire

'car·ry·cot porte-enfant *m inv*

'car seat *for child* seggiolino *m* per auto

cart [kɑːt] carretto *m*

car·tel [kɑːˈtel] cartello *m*

car·ton ['kɑːtn] *for storage, transport* cartone *m*; *of cigarettes* stecca *f*

car·toon [kɑːˈtuːn] *in newspaper, magazine* fumetto *m*; *on TV, film* cartone *m* animato

car·toon·ist [kɑːˈtuːnɪst] *for newspaper etc* vignettista *m/f*

car·tridge ['kɑːtrɪdʒ] *for gun, printer* cartuccia *f*

carve [kɑːv] *v/t meat* tagliare; *wood* intagliare

carv·ing ['kɑːvɪŋ] *figure* scultura *f*

'car wash lavaggio *m* per auto

case[1] [keɪs] *for glasses, pen* astuccio *m*; *of whisky, wine* cassa *f*; (*suitcase*) valigia *f*; **glass ~** teca *f*

case[2] [keɪs] *n* (*instance, for police*), MED caso *m*; (*argument*) argomentazione *f*; LAW causa *f*; **in ~ ...** in caso ...; **take an umbrella in ~ it rains** prendi un ombrello in caso piovesse; *in any* ~ in ogni caso; *in that* ~ in questo caso

'case his·to·ry MED cartella *f* clinica

'case·load numero *m* di assistiti; *my doctor's* ~ il numero dei pazienti del mio dottore

cash [kæʃ] **1** *n* contanti *mpl*; F (*money*) soldi *mpl*; ~ *down* in contanti; *pay (in)* ~ pagare in contanti; ~ *in advance* pagamento *m* anticipato; ~ *on delivery* → COD **2** *v/t cheque* incassare

♦ cash in on *v/t* guadagnare su

'cash card carta *f* per prelievi; 'cash cow vacca *f* da mungere; 'cash desk cassa *f*; cash 'dis·count sconto *m* su pagamento in contanti; 'cash di·spens·er (sportello *m*) Bancomat® *m*; 'cash flow flusso *m* di cassa

cash·ier [kæˈʃɪə(r)] *n in shop etc* cassiere *m*, -a *f*

'cash ma·chine (sportello *m*) Bancomat® *m*

'cash·mere ['kæʃmɪər] *adj* cashemere *m inv*

'cash·point (sportello *m*) Bancomat® *m*

'cash re·gis·ter cassa *f*

ca·si·no [kəˈsiːnəʊ] casinò *m inv*

cas·ket ['kɑːskɪt] *Am* (*coffin*) bara *f*

cas·se·role ['kæsərəʊl] *n meal* stufato *m*; *container* casseruola *f*

cas·sette [kəˈset] cassetta *f*

cas·sette play·er mangiacassette *m inv*

cas·sette re·cord·er registratore *m* (a cassette)

cast [kɑːst] **1** *n of play* cast *m inv*; (*mould*) stampo *m* **2** *v/t* (*pret & pp* cast) *doubt, suspicion* far sorgere (*on* su); *shadow* proiettare; *metal* colare (in uno stampo); *play* assegnare le parti per; ~ *s.o. as ... for play* far fare a qu il ruolo di ...; *he was* ~ *as Romeo* gli è stata assegnata la parte di Romeo; ~ *a glance at s.o./sth* gettare uno sguardo su qu/qc

♦ cast off *v/i of ship* sciogliere gli ormeggi

caste [kɑːst] casta *f*

cast·er ['kɑːstə(r)] *on chair etc* rotella *f*

cast·er sug·ar zucchero *m* raffinato

cast 'iron ghisa *f*

cast-'iron *adj* di ghisa

cas·tle ['kɑːsl] castello *m*

'cast·or ['kɑːstə(r)] → caster

cas·trate [kæˈstreɪt] *v/t* castrare

cas·tra·tion [kæˈstreɪʃn] castrazione *f*

cas·u·al ['kæʒʊəl] *adj* (*chance*) casuale; (*offhand*) disinvolto; (*irresponsible*) noncurante; *remark* poco importante; *clothes* casual *inv*; (*not permanent*) occasionale; ~ *sex* rapporti *mpl* occasionali

cas·u·al·ly ['kæʒʊəlɪ] *adv dressed* (in modo) casual; *say* con disinvoltura

cas·u·al·ty ['kæʒʊəltɪ] *dead person* vittima *f*; *injured* ferito *m*

'cas·u·al wear abbigliamento *m* casual

cat [kæt] gatto *m*; *wild* felino *m*

cat·a·log *Am*, cat·a·logue ['kætəlɒg] *n* catalogo *m*

cat·a·lyst ['kætəlɪst] catalizzatore *m*

cat·a·lyt·ic con·vert·er [kætəˈlɪtɪk] marmitta *f* catalitica

cat·a·pult ['kætəpʌlt] **1** *v/t fig: to fame, stardom* catapultare **2** *n* catapulta *f*; *toy* fionda *f*

cat·a·ract ['kætərækt] MED cataratta *f*

ca·tas·tro·phe [kəˈtæstrəfɪ] catastrofe *f*

cat·a·stroph·ic [kætəˈstrɒfɪk] *adj* catastrofico

catch [kætʃ] **1** *n* presa *f*; *of fish* pesca *f*; *on handbag, box* chiusura *f*; *on door, window* fermo *m*; *on brooch* fermaglio *m*; (*problem*) inghippo *m* **2** *v/t* (*pret & pp* caught) *ball, escaped prisoner* prendere; *bus, train* prendere; *fish* prendere; (*in order to speak to*) trovare; (*hear*) afferrare; *illness* prendere; ~ *(a) cold* prendere un raffreddore; ~ *s.o.'s eye of person, object* attirare l'attenzione di qu; ~ *sight of*, ~ *a glimpse of* intravedere; ~ *s.o. doing sth* sorpren-

dere qu a fare qc
♦ **catch on** *v/i* (*become popular*) fare presa; (*understand*) afferrare
♦ **catch up** *v/i* recuperare; **catch up with s.o.** raggiungere qu; **catch up with sth** *work*, *studies* mettersi in pari con qc
♦ **catch up on** *v/t* recuperare
catch-22 [kætʃtwentɪ'tuː]: **it's a ~ situation** è una situazione senza via d'uscita
catch·ing ['kætʃɪŋ] *adj also fig* contagioso
catch·y ['kætʃɪ] *adj tune* orecchiabile
cat·e·gor·ic [kætə'gɒrɪk] *adj* categorico
cat·e·gor·i·cal·ly [kætə'gɒrɪklɪ] *adv* categoricamente
cat·e·go·ry ['kætɪgɒrɪ] categoria *f*
♦ **cater for** ['keɪtə(r)] *v/t* (*meet the needs of*) rispondere alle esigenze di; (*provide food for*) organizzare rinfreschi per
ca·ter·er ['keɪtərə(r)] ristoratore *m*, -trice *f*
ca·ter·pil·lar ['kætəpɪlə(r)] bruco *m*
ca·the·dral [kə'θiːdrl] cattedrale *f*, duomo *m*
Cath·o·lic ['kæθəlɪk] **1** *adj* cattolico **2** *n* cattolico *m*, -a *f*
Ca·thol·i·cism [kə'θɒlɪsɪzm] cattolicesimo *m*
'**cat·nap 1** *n* pisolino *m* **2** *v/i* (*pret & pp* **-ped**) schiacciare un pisolino
'**cat's eye** *on road* catarifrangente *m*
cat·tle ['kætl] *npl* bestiame *m*
cat·ty ['kætɪ] *adj* maligno
'**cat·walk** passerella *f*
caught [kɔːt] *pret & pp* → **catch**
cau·li·flow·er ['kɒlɪflaʊə(r)] cavolfiore *m*
cause [kɔːz] **1** *n* causa *f*, (*grounds*) motivo *m*; (*objective*) causa *f* **2** *v/t* causare; **what ~d you to leave so early?** perché sei andato via così presto?
caus·tic ['kɔːstɪk] *adj fig* caustico
cau·tion ['kɔːʃn] **1** *n* (*carefulness*) cautela *f*, prudenza *f*; ~ **is advised** si raccomanda la prudenza **2** *v/t* (*warn*) mettere in guardia

cau·tious ['kɔːʃəs] *adj* cauto, prudente
cau·tious·ly ['kɔːʃəslɪ] *adv* con cautela
cave [keɪv] caverna *f*, grotta *f*
♦ **cave in** *v/i of roof* crollare
cav·i·ar ['kævɪɑː(r)] caviale *m*
cav·i·ty ['kævətɪ] cavità *f inv*; *in tooth* carie *f inv*
cc [siː'siː] **1** *abbr* (= **carbon copy**) cc (= copia *f* carbone); (= **cubic centimetres**) cc *m inv* (= centimetri cubici); MOT cilindrata *f* **2** *v/t memo* fare una copia di; *person* mandare una copia per conoscenza a
CD [siː'diː] *abbr* (= **compact disc**) CD *m inv*
CD play·er lettore *m* CD; **CD-ROM** [siːdiː'rɒm] CD-ROM *m inv*; **CD-ROM drive** drive *m inv* per CD-ROM
cease [siːs] *v/t & v/i* cessare
'**cease-fire** cessate il fuoco *m inv*
cei·ling ['siːlɪŋ] *of room* soffitto *m*; (*limit*) tetto *m*, plafond *m inv*
cel·e·brate ['selɪbreɪt] **1** *v/i* festeggiare **2** *v/t* celebrare, festeggiare; (*observe*) festeggiare
cel·e·brat·ed ['selɪbreɪtɪd] *adj* acclamato; **be ~ for** essere famoso per
cel·e·bra·tion [selɪ'breɪʃn] celebrazione *f*, festeggiamento *m*
ce·leb·ri·ty [sɪ'lebrətɪ] celebrità *f inv*
cel·e·ry ['selərɪ] sedano *m*
cel·i·ba·cy ['selɪbəsɪ] celibato *m*
cel·i·bate ['selɪbət] *adj man* celibe; *woman* nubile
cell [sel] *for prisoner* cella *f*; BIO cellula *f*; *in spreadsheet* casella *f*, cella *f*
cel·lar ['selə(r)] *of house* cantina *f*; *of wine* collezione *f* di vini
cel·list ['tʃelɪst] violoncellista *m/f*
cel·lo ['tʃeləʊ] violoncello *m*
cel·lo·phane ['seləfeɪn] cellofan *m inv*
cel·lu·lar phone [seljuːlər'fəʊn] telefono *m* cellulare, cellulare *m*
cel·lu·lite ['seljuːlaɪt] cellulite *f*
ce·ment [sɪ'ment] **1** *n* cemento *m*; (*adhesive*) mastice *m* **2** *v/t* cementare; *friendship* consolidare

cem·e·tery ['semətrɪ] cimitero *m*

cen·sor ['sensə(r)] *v/t* censurare

cen·sor·ship ['sensəʃɪp] censura *f*

cen·sus ['sensəs] censimento *m*

cent [sent] centesimo *m*

cen·te·na·ry [sen'tiːnərɪ] centenario *m*

cen·ter *Am* → **centre**

cen·ti·grade ['sentɪgreɪd] *adj* centigrado; *10 degrees* ~ 10 gradi centigradi

cen·ti·me·ter *Am*, **cen·ti·me·tre** ['sentɪmiːtə(r)] centimetro *m*

cen·tral ['sentrəl] *adj location, flat* centrale; *(main)* principale, centrale; ~ *London / France* il centro di Londra / della Francia; *be* ~ *to sth* essere fondamentale per qc

cen·tral 'heat·ing riscaldamento *m* autonomo

cen·tral·ize ['sentrəlaɪz] *v/t decision making* accentrare

cen·tral 'lock·ing MOT chiusura *f* centralizzata

cen·tral 'pro·ces·sing u·nit unità *f* *inv* centrale

cen·tral res·er·va·tion MOT banchina *f* spartitraffico

cen·tre ['sentə(r)] **1** *n* centro *m*; *in the* ~ *of* al centro di **2** *v/t* centrare

♦ centre on *v/t* essere incentrato su

cen·tre of 'grav·i·ty centro *m* di gravità

cen·tu·ry ['sentʃərɪ] secolo *m*

CEO [siːiːˈəʊ] *abbr* (= *Chief Executive Officer*) direttore *m* generale

ce·ram·ic [sɪˈræmɪk] *adj* ceramico

ce·ram·ics [sɪˈræmɪks] (*pl: objects*) ceramiche *fpl*; (*sg: art*) ceramica *f*

ce·re·al ['sɪərɪəl] (*grain*) cereale *m*; (*breakfast* ~) cereali *mpl*

cer·e·mo·ni·al [serɪˈməʊnɪəl] **1** *adj* da cerimonia **2** *n* cerimoniale *m*

cer·e·mo·ny ['serɪmənɪ] (*event*) cerimonia *f*; (*ritual*) cerimonie *fpl*

cer·tain ['sɜːtn] *adj* (*sure, particular*) certo; *it's* ~ *that ...* è certo che ...; *a* ~ *Mr S.* un certo Sig S.; *make* ~ accertarsi; *know / say for* ~ sapere / dire con certezza

cer·tain·ly ['sɜːtnlɪ] *adv* certamente; ~ *not!* certo che no!

cer·tain·ty ['sɜːtntɪ]) certezza *f*; *it's a* ~ è una cosa certa; *he's a* ~ *to win* vincerà di certo

cer·tif·i·cate [səˈtɪfɪkət] *qualification* certificazione *f*; *official paper* certificato *m*

cer·ti·fy ['sɜːtɪfaɪ] *v/t* (*pret & pp -ied*) dichiarare ufficialmente

Ce·sar·e·an *Am* → **Caesarean**

ces·sa·tion [seˈseɪʃn] cessazione *f*

c/f *abbr* (= **cost and freight**) c/f

CFC [siːefˈsiː] *abbr* (= **chlorofluorocarbon**) CFC *m inv* (= clorofluorocarburi *mpl*)

chain [tʃeɪn] **1** *n* catena *f* **2** *v/t*: ~ *sth / s.o. to sth* incatenare qc / qu a qc

chain re'ac·tion reazione *f* a catena; **'chain smoke** *v/i* fumare una sigaretta dopo l'altra; **'chain smok·er** fumatore *m*, -trice *f* incallito; **'chain store** *store* negozio *m* di una catena; *company* catena *f* di negozi

chair [tʃeə(r)] **1** *n* sedia *f*; (*arm* ~) poltrona *f*; *at university* cattedra *f*; *the* ~ (*electric* ~) la sedia elettrica; *at meeting* presidente *m/f*; *take the* ~ presiedere **2** *v/t meeting* presiedere

'chair lift seggiovia *f*

'chair·man presidente *m*

chair·man·ship ['tʃeəmənʃɪp] presidenza *f*

'chair·per·son presidente *m/f*

'chair·wom·an presidente *f*

cha·let ['ʃæleɪ] chalet *m inv*

chal·ice ['tʃælɪs] REL calice *m*

chalk [tʃɔːk] gesso *m*

chal·lenge ['tʃælɪndʒ] **1** *n* sfida *f* **2** *v/t* sfidare; (*call into question*) mettere alla prova

chal·len·ger ['tʃælɪndʒə(r)] sfidante *m/f*

chal·len·ging ['tʃælɪndʒɪŋ] *adj job, undertaking* stimolante

'cham·ber·maid ['tʃeɪmbəmeɪd] cameriera *f*; **'cham·ber mu·sic** musica *f* da camera; **Cham·ber of 'Com·merce** Camera *f* di Commercio

cham·ois (leather) [ˈʃæmɪ] camoscio *m*

cham·pagne [ʃæmˈpeɪn] champagne *m inv*

cham·pi·on [ˈʃæmpɪən] **1** *n* SP campione *m*, -essa *f*; *of cause* difensore *m*, -a *f* **2** *v/t* (*cause*) difendere

cham·pi·on·ship [ˈʃæmpɪənʃɪp] *event* campionato *m*; *title* titolo *m* di campione; *of cause* difesa *f*

chance [tʃɑːns] (*possibility*) probabilità *f inv*; (*opportunity*) opportunità *f inv*, occasione *f*; (*risk*) rischio *m*; (*luck*) caso *m*; **by ~** per caso; **take a ~** correre un rischio; *I'm not taking any ~s* non voglio correre nessun rischio; *you don't stand a ~* non hai nessuna possibilità

Chan·cel·lor [ˈtʃɑːnsələr] *in Germany* cancelliere *f*; **~ (of the Exchequer)** *in Britain* ministro *m* del tesoro

chan·de·lier [ʃændəˈlɪər] lampadario *m*

change [tʃeɪndʒ] **1** *n* cambiamento *m*; *small coins* moneta *f*; *from purchase* resto *m*; **for a ~** per cambiare; **a ~ of clothes** un ricambio di vestiti **2** *v/t* (*alter*) cambiare; *one's clothes* cambiarsi **3** *v/i* cambiare; (*put on different clothes*) cambiarsi; *you ~ at Crewe* devi cambiare a Crewe

change·a·ble [ˈtʃeɪndʒəbl] *adj* incostante; *weather* variabile

change·o·ver passaggio *m*; *period* fase *f* di transizione; *in relay race* passaggio *m* del testimone

chang·ing room [ˈtʃeɪndʒɪŋ] SP spogliatoio *m*; *in shop* camerino *m*

chan·nel [ˈtʃænl] *on TV, in water* canale *m*

Chan·nel 'Tun·nel tunnel *m* della Manica

chant [tʃɑːnt] **1** *n* slogan *m inv*; REL canto *m* **2** *v/i* gridare; *of demonstrators* gridare slogan; REL cantare

cha·os [ˈkeɪɒs] caos *m inv*

cha·ot·ic [keɪˈɒtɪk] *adj* caotico

chap [tʃæp] *n* F tipo *m* F

chap·el [ˈtʃæpl] cappella *f*

chapped [tʃæpt] *adj* screpolato

chap·ter [ˈtʃæptər] *of book* capitolo *m*; *of organization* filiale *f*

char·ac·ter [ˈkærɪktər] (*nature*) carattere *m*; (*person*) tipo *m*; *in book, play* personaggio *m*; *in writing* carattere *m*; *he's a real ~* è un tipo speciale

char·ac·ter·is·tic [kærɪktəˈrɪstɪk] **1** *n* caratteristica *f* **2** *adj* caratteristico

char·ac·ter·is·ti·cal·ly [kærɪktəˈrɪstɪklɪ] *adv* in modo caratteristico; *he was ~ rude* era maleducato, come al solito

char·ac·ter·ize [ˈkærɪktəraɪz] *v/t* caratterizzare

cha·rade [ʃəˈrɑːd] *fig* farsa *f*

char·coal [ˈtʃɑːkəʊl] *for barbecue* carbonella *f*; *for drawing* carboncino *m*

charge [tʃɑːdʒ] **1** *n* (*fee*) costo *m*; LAW accusa *f*; *free of ~* gratis; *be in ~* essere responsabile; *take ~* assumersi l'incombenza; *take ~ of sth* farsi carico di qc **2** *v/t* *sum of money* far pagare; *person* far pagare a; (*put on account*) addebitare; LAW accusare; *battery* caricare; *how much do you ~ for …?* quanto prende per …? **3** *v/i* (*attack*) attaccare

'charge ac·count conto *m* (spese)

'charge card carta *f* di addebito

cha·ris·ma [kəˈrɪzmə] carisma *m*

char·is·mat·ic [kærɪzˈmætɪk] *adj* carismatico

char·i·ta·ble [ˈtʃærɪtəbl] *adj* *institution* di beneficenza; *donation* in beneficenza; *person* caritatevole

char·i·ty [ˈtʃærətɪ] *assistance* carità *f*; *organization* associazione *f* di beneficenza

char·la·tan [ˈʃɑːlətən] ciarlatano *m*, -a *f*

charm [tʃɑːm] **1** *n* *appealing quality* fascino *m*; *on bracelet etc* ciondolo *m* **2** *v/t* (*delight*) conquistare

charm·ing [ˈtʃɑːmɪŋ] *adj* affascinante; *house, village* incantevole

charred [tʃɑːd] *adj* carbonizzato

chart [tʃɑːt] *diagram* diagramma *m*; *for ship* carta *f* nautica; *for aeroplane* carta f aeronautica; **the ~s** MUS l'hit parade f inv

char·ter ['tʃɑːtə(r)] v/t plane, boat noleggiare

'**char·ter flight** volo m charter inv

chase [tʃeɪs] **1** n inseguimento m **2** v/t inseguire

♦ **chase away** v/t cacciare (via)

chas·er ['tʃeɪsə(r)] alcolico bevuto dopo un altro di diverso tipo

chas·sis ['tʃæsɪ] of car telaio m

chat [tʃæt] **1** n chiacchierata f; useless talk chiacchiere fpl **2** v/i (pret & pp -ted) chiacchierare

♦ **chat up** v/t F abbordare F

'**chat show** talk show m inv

'**chat show host** conduttore m, -trice f di un talk show

chat·ter ['tʃætə(r)] **1** n parlantina f **2** v/i talk fare chiacchiere; of teeth battere

'**chat·ter·box** chiacchierone m, -a f

chat·ty ['tʃætɪ] adj person chiacchierone; letter familiare

chauf·feur ['ʃəʊfə(r)] n autista m/f

'**chauf·feur-driv·en** adj con autista

chau·vin·ist ['ʃəʊvɪnɪst] n sciovinista m/f; (male ~) maschilista m

chau·vin·ist·ic [ʃəʊvɪˈnɪstɪk] adj sciovinista

cheap [tʃiːp] adj (inexpensive) economico; (nasty) cattivo; (mean) tirchio

cheat [tʃiːt] **1** n person imbroglione m, -a f; in cards baro m; (deception) truffa f **2** v/t imbrogliare; **~ s.o. out of sth** estorcere qc a qu con l'inganno **3** v/i imbrogliare; in cards barare; **~ on one's wife** tradire la propria moglie

check¹ [tʃek] **1** adj shirt a quadri **2** n quadro m

check² [tʃek] **1** n to verify sth verifica f; **keep in ~**, **hold in ~** tenere sotto controllo; **keep a ~ on** tenere sotto controllo **2** v/t (verify) verificare; (restrain) controllare; (stop) bloccare; with a tick marcare **3** v/i verificare; **did you ~ check for signs of forced entry?** hai guardato se c'erano segni di infrazione?

♦ **check in** v/i registrarsi

♦ **check off** v/t segnare

♦ **check on** v/t controllare

♦ **check out 1** v/i of hotel saldare il conto **2** v/t (look into) verificare; club, restaurant etc provare

♦ **check up on** v/t fare dei controlli su

♦ **check with** v/i of person verificare con; (tally: of information) combaciare con

check³ [tʃek] Am → **cheque**

checked [tʃekt] adj material a quadri

checkers ['tʃekəz] nsg Am: game dama f

'**check-in (coun·ter)** banco m dell'accettazione

'**check·ing ac·count** Am conto m corrente

'**check-in time** check in m inv; '**check·list** lista f di verifica; '**check·mark** Am segno m; '**check·mate** n scacco m matto; '**check·out** cassa f; '**check-out time** from hotel ora f di check-out; '**check·point** military, police posto m di blocco; '**check·room** Am for coats guardaroba m inv; '**check·up** medical check up m inv; dental visita f di controllo

cheek [tʃiːk] guancia f; (impudence) sfacciataggine f

'**cheek·bone** zigomo m

cheek·i·ly ['tʃiːkɪlɪ] adv sfacciatamente

cheek·y ['tʃiːkɪ] adj sfacciato

cheer [tʃɪə(r)] **1** n acclamazione f; **three ~s for …** hip, hip, hurrà per …; **~!** (toast) salute!; **~s!** F (thanks) grazie! **2** v/t acclamare **3** v/i fare acclamazioni

♦ **cheer on** v/t incitare

♦ **cheer up 1** v/i consolarsi; **cheer up!** su con la vita! **2** v/t tirare su

cheer·ful ['tʃɪəfʊl] adj allegro

cheer·ing ['tʃɪərɪŋ] n acclamazioni fpl

cheer·i·o [tʃɪərɪˈəʊ] F ciao F

cheer·y ['tʃɪərɪ] adj → **cheerful**

cheese [tʃiːz] formaggio m

'**cheese·burg·er** cheeseburger m inv

'cheese·cake dolce *m* al formaggio

chef [ʃef] chef *m/f inv*

chem·i·cal ['kemɪkl] **1** *adj* chimico **2** *n* sostanza *f* chimica

chem·i·cal 'war·fare guerra *f* chimica

chemist ['kemɪst] *in laboratory* chimico *m*, -a *f; who dispenses medicine* farmacista *m/f*

chem·is·try ['kemɪstrɪ] chimica *f*, *fig* alchimia *f*

'chem·ist's (shop) farmacia *f*

chem·o·ther·a·py [ki:məʊ'θerəpɪ] chemioterapia *f*

cheque [tʃek] assegno *m*

'cheque·book libretto *m* degli assegni

cheque (guar·an'tee) card carta *f* assegni

cher·ish ['tʃerɪʃ] *v/t* avere a cuore

cher·ry ['tʃerɪ] *fruit* ciliegia *f; tree* ciliegio *m*

cher·ub ['tʃerəb] cherubino *m*

chess [tʃes] scacchi *mpl*

'chess·board scacchiera *f*

'chess·man, chess·piece pezzo *m* degli scacchi

chest [tʃest] *of person* petto *m;* (*box*) cassa *f; I'm glad I've got that off my ~* sono contento di essermi tolto questo peso dallo stomaco

chest·nut ['tʃesnʌt] castagna *f; tree* castagno *m*

chest of 'drawers comò *m inv*, cassettone *m*

chew [tʃu:] *v/t* masticare; *of dog, rats* rosicchiare

chew·ing gum ['tʃu:ɪŋ] gomma *f* da masticare

chic [ʃi:k] *adj* chic *inv*

chick [tʃɪk] pulcino *m;* F (*girl*) ragazza *f*

chick·en ['tʃɪkɪn] **1** *n* pollo *m;* F fifone *m*, -a *f* F **2** *adj* F (*cowardly*) fifone *m*

♦ chicken out *v/i* F tirarsi indietro per la fifa F

'chick·en·feed F una bazzecola

'chick·en·pox varicella *f*

chief [tʃi:f] **1** *n* (*head*) principale *m/f; of tribe* capo *m* **2** *adj* principale

chief·ly ['tʃi:flɪ] *adv* principalmente

chil·blain ['tʃɪlbleɪn] gelone *m*

child [tʃaɪld] (*pl children* ['tʃɪldrən]) *also pej* bambino *m*, -a *f; they have two children* hanno due figli

'child a·buse violenza *f* sui minori; 'child·birth parto *m;* child·hood ['tʃaɪldhʊd] infanzia *f*

child·ish ['tʃaɪldɪʃ] *adj pej* infantile, puerile

child·ish·ly ['tʃaɪldɪʃlɪ] *adv pej* puerilmente

child·ish·ness ['tʃaɪldɪʃnɪs] *pej* puerilità *f inv*

child·less ['tʃaɪldlɪs] *adj* senza figli

child·like ['tʃaɪldlaɪk] *adj* innocente

'child·mind·er baby-sitter *m/f inv*

'child·ren ['tʃɪldrən] *pl* → child

Chil·e ['tʃɪlɪ] Cile *m*

Chil·e·an ['tʃɪlɪən] **1** *adj* cileno **2** *n* cileno *m*, -a *f*

chill [tʃɪl] **1** *n in air* freddo *m; illness* colpo *m* di freddo; *there's a ~ in the air* l'aria è fredda **2** *v/t wine* mettere in fresco

♦ chill out *v/i* P rilassarsi

chilli (pepper) ['tʃɪlɪ] peperoncino *m*

chil·ly ['tʃɪlɪ] *adj weather, welcome* freddo; *I'm feeling a bit ~* ho un po' freddo; *it's a bit ~ this morning* sta freddino stamattina

chime [tʃaɪm] *v/i* suonare

chim·ney ['tʃɪmnɪ] camino *m*

chim·pan·zee [tʃɪmpæn'zi:] scimpanzé *m inv*

chin [tʃɪn] mento *m*

Chi·na ['tʃaɪnə] Cina *f*

chi·na ['tʃaɪnə] porcellana *f*

Chi·nese [tʃaɪ'ni:z] **1** *adj* cinese **2** *n language* cinese *m; person* cinese *m/f*

chink [tʃɪŋk] *gap* fessura *f; sound* tintinnio *m*

chip [tʃɪp] **1** *n fragment* scheggia *f; damage* scheggiatura *f, in gambling* fiche *f inv;* COMPUT chip *m; ~s* patate *fpl* fritte; *Am* patatine *fpl* **2** *v/t* (*pret & pp -ped*) *damage* scheggiare

♦ chip in *v/i* (*interrupt*) intervenire; *with money* contribuire chi·rop·o·dist [kɪ'rɒpədɪst] pedicure m/f inv

chi·ro·prac·tor ['kaɪrəʊpræktə(r)] chiroterapeuta m/f

chirp [tʃɜːp] v/i cinguettare

chis·el ['tʃɪzl] n scalpello m

chit-chat ['tʃɪtʃæt] chiacchiere fpl

chiv·al·rous ['ʃɪvlrəs] adj cavalleresco

chive [tʃaɪv] erba f cipollina

chlo·rine ['klɔːriːn] cloro m

chlor·o·form ['klɒrəfɔːm] cloroformio m

choc·a·hol·ic [tʃɒkə'hɒlɪk] n F fanatico m, -a f del cioccolato

chock-a-block [tʃɒkə'blɒk] adj F pieno zeppo

chock-full [tʃɒk'fʊl] adj F strapieno

choc·o·late ['tʃɒkələt] cioccolato m; in box cioccolatino m; hot ~ cioccolata f calda

'choc·o·late cake dolce m al cioccolato

choice [tʃɔɪs] 1 n scelta f; I had no ~ non avevo scelta 2 adj (top quality) di prima scelta

choir ['kwaɪə(r)] coro m

'choir·boy corista m

choke [tʃəʊk] 1 n MOT starter m inv 2 v/i soffocare; he ~d on a bone si è strozzato con un osso 3 v/t soffocare

cho·les·te·rol [kə'lestərɒl] colesterolo m

choose [tʃuːz] v/t & v/i (pret chose, pp chosen) scegliere

choos·ey ['tʃuːzɪ] adj F selettivo

chop [tʃɒp] 1 n action colpo m; meat braciola f 2 v/t (pret & pp -ped) wood spaccare; meat, vegetables tagliare a pezzi

♦ chop down v/t tree abbattere

chop·per ['tʃɒpə(r)] tool accetta f; F (helicopter) elicottero m

'chop·ping board ['tʃɒpɪŋ] tagliere m

'chop·sticks npl bastoncini mpl (cinesi)

cho·ral ['kɔːrəl] adj corale

chord [kɔːd] MUS accordo m

chore [tʃɔː(r)] household faccenda f domestica

chor·e·o·graph ['kɒrɪəgrɑːf] v/t coreografare

chor·e·og·ra·pher [kɒrɪ'ɒgrəfə(r)] coreografo m, -a f

chor·e·og·ra·phy [kɒrɪ'ɒgrəfɪ] coreografia f

cho·rus ['kɔːrəs] singers, of song coro m

chose [tʃəʊz] pret → choose

cho·sen ['tʃəʊzn] pp → choose

Christ [kraɪst] Cristo m; ~! Cristo!

chris·ten ['krɪsn] v/t battezzare

chris·ten·ing ['krɪsnɪŋ] battesimo m

Chris·tian ['krɪstʃən] 1 n cristiano m, -a f 2 adj cristiano; attitude da cristiano

Chris·ti·an·i·ty [krɪstɪ'ænətɪ] cristianesimo m

'Chris·tian name nome m di battesimo

Christ·mas ['krɪsməs] Natale m; at ~ a Natale; Merry ~! Buon Natale!

'Christ·mas card biglietto m di auguri natalizi; Christ·mas 'Day giorno m di Natale; Christ·mas 'Eve vigilia f di Natale; 'Christ·mas present regalo m di Natale; 'Christ·mas tree albero m di Natale

chrome, chro·mi·um [krəʊm, 'krəʊmɪəm] cromo m

chro·mo·some ['krəʊməsəʊm] cromosoma m

chron·ic ['krɒnɪk] adj cronico

chron·o·log·i·cal [krɒnə'lɒdʒɪkl] adj cronologico; in ~ order in ordine cronologico

chrys·an·the·mum [krɪ'sænθəməm] crisantemo m

chub·by ['tʃʌbɪ] adj paffuto

chuck [tʃʌk] v/t F buttare

♦ chuck out v/t F object buttare via; person buttare fuori

chuck·ing-out time ['tʃʌkɪŋ'aʊt] F ora f di chiusura

chuck·le ['tʃʌkl] 1 n risatina f 2 v/i ridacchiare

chum [tʃʌm] amico m, -a f

chum·my ['tʃʌmɪ] adj F pappa e ciccia F; be ~ with essere pappa e ciccia con chunk [tʃʌŋk] pezzo *m*

chunk·y ['tʃʌŋkɪ] *adj sweater* spesso; *tumbler* tozzo; *person, build* tarchiato

church [tʃɜːtʃ] chiesa *f*

church 'hall sala *f* parrocchiale; **church 'serv·ice** funzione *f* religiosa; **'church·yard** cimitero *m* (di una chiesa)

churl·ish ['tʃɜːlɪʃ] *adj* sgarbato

chute [ʃuːt] scivolo *m*; *for waste disposal* canale *m* di scarico

CIA [siːaɪ'eɪ] *abbr* (= *Central Intelligence Agency*) CIA *f*

ci·der ['saɪdə(r)] sidro *m*

CIF [siːaɪ'ef] *abbr* (= *cost insurance freight*) CIF

ci·gar [sɪ'gɑː(r)] sigaro *m*

cig·a·rette [sɪgə'ret] sigaretta *f*

cig·a·rette end mozzicone *m* di sigaretta; **cig·a·rette light·er** accendino *m*; **cig·a·rette pa·per** carta *f* per sigarette

cin·e·ma ['sɪnɪmə] cinema *m*

cin·na·mon ['sɪnəmən] canella *f*

cir·cle ['sɜːkl] **1** *n* cerchio *m*; (*group*) cerchia *f* **2** *v/t* (*draw circle around*) cerchiare **3** *v/i of plane* girare in tondo; *of bird* volteggiare

cir·cuit ['sɜːkɪt] ELEC circuito *m*; (*lap*) giro *m*

'cir·cuit board COMPUT circuito *m* stampato; **'cir·cuit break·er** ELEC interruttore *m* automatico; **'cir·cuit train·ing** SP percorso *m* ginnico

cir·cu·lar ['sɜːkjʊlə(r)] **1** *n giving information* circolare *f* **2** *adj* circolare

cir·cu·late ['sɜːkjʊleɪt] **1** *v/i* circolare **2** *v/t memo* far circolare

cir·cu·la·tion [sɜːkjʊ'leɪʃn] BIO circolazione *f*; *of newspaper, magazine* tiratura *f*

cir·cum·fer·ence [sə'kʌmfərəns] circonferenza *f*

cir·cum·stan·ces ['sɜːkəmstənsɪs] *npl* circostanze *fpl*; (*financial*) situazione *fsg* (economica); **under no ~** in nessuna circostanza; **under the ~** date le circostanze

cir·cus ['sɜːkəs] circo *m*

cir·rho·sis (of the liv·er) [sɪ'rəʊsɪs] cirrosi *f* (epatica)

cis·tern ['sɪstən] cisterna *f*; *of WC* serbatoio *m*

cite [saɪt] *v/t* citare

cit·i·zen ['sɪtɪzn] cittadino *m*, -a *f*

cit·i·zen·ship ['sɪtɪznʃɪp] cittadinanza *f*

citr·us fruit ['sɪtrəs] agrume *m*

cit·y ['sɪtɪ] città *f inv*

city 'centre centro *m* (della città)

city 'hall sala *f* municipale

civ·ic ['sɪvɪk] *adj* civico

civ·il ['sɪvl] *adj* civile

civ·il en·gi·neer ingegnere *m* civile

ci·vil·i·an [sɪ'vɪljən] **1** *n* civile *m/f* **2** *adj clothes* civile

ci·vil·i·ty [sɪ'vɪlɪtɪ] civiltà *f*

civ·i·li·za·tion [sɪvəlaɪ'zeɪʃn] civilizzazione *f*

civ·i·lize ['sɪvəlaɪz] *v/t person* civilizzare

civ·il 'rights *npl* diritti *mpl* civili; **civ·il 'ser·vant** impiegato *m*, -a *f* statale; **civ·il 'ser·vice** pubblica amministrazione *f*; **civ·il 'war** guerra *f* civile

claim [kleɪm] **1** *n* (*request*) richiesta *f*; (*right*) diritto *m*; (*assertion*) affermazione *f* **2** *v/t* (*ask for as a right*) rivendicare; *damages* richiedere; (*assert*) affermare; *lost property* reclamare; **they have ~ed responsibility for the attack** hanno rivendicato l'attentato

claim·ant ['kleɪmənt] richiedente *m/f*

clair·voy·ant [kleə'vɔɪənt] *n* chiaroveggente *m/f*

clam [klæm] vongola *f*

♦ clam up *v/i* (*pret & pp -med*) F chiudersi come un riccio

clam·ber ['klæmbə(r)] *v/i* arrampicarsi

clam·my ['klæmɪ] *adj hands* appiccicaticcio; *weather* afoso

clam·or *Am*, clam·our ['klæmə(r)] *noise* clamore *m*; (*outcry*) protesta *f*

♦ clamour for *v/t* chiedere a gran voce

clamp [klæmp] **1** *n fastener* morsa *f*;

for wheel ceppo *m* (bloccaruote) **2** *v/t fasten* bloccare (con una morsa); *fig: hand etc* stringere; *car* mettere i ceppi a

♦ **clamp down** *v/i* usare il pugno di ferro

♦ **clamp down on** *v/t* mettere un freno a

clan [klæn] clan *m inv*

clan·des·tine [klæn'destɪn] *adj* clandestino

clang [klæŋ] **1** *n* suono *m* metallico **2** *v/i*: ~ **shut** chiudersi con un suono metallico

clang·er ['klæŋə(r)] F gaffe *f inv*; **drop a** ~ fare una gaffe

clap [klæp] *v/t & v/i* (*pret & pp* **-ped**) (*applaud*) applaudire

clar·et ['klærɪt] *wine* claret *m inv*

clar·i·fi·ca·tion [klærɪfɪ'keɪʃn] chiarimento *m*

clar·i·fy ['klærɪfaɪ] *v/t* (*pret & pp* **-ied**) chiarire

clar·i·net [klærɪ'net] clarinetto *m*

clar·i·ty ['klærətɪ] chiarezza *f*

clash [klæʃ] **1** *n* scontro *m* **2** *v/i* scontrarsi; *of opinions* essere in contrasto; *of colours* stonare; *of events* coincidere

clasp [klɑːsp] **1** *n fastener* chiusura *f* **2** *v/t in hand* stringere

class [klɑːs] **1** *n* (*lesson*) lezione *f*; (*group of people, category*) classe *f*; **social** ~ classe *f* sociale **2** *v/t* classificare

clas·sic ['klæsɪk] **1** *adj* (*typical*) classico; (*definitive*) eccellente; **she wrote the** ~ **biography of ...** la sua biografia di ... è un classico **2** *n* classico *m*

clas·si·cal ['klæsɪkl] *adj* classico

clas·si·fi·ca·tion [klæsɪfɪ'keɪʃn] classificazione *f*

clas·si·fied ['klæsɪfaɪd] *adj information* riservato

'**clas·si·fied ad**(**·ver·tise·ment**) inserzione *f*, annuncio *m*

clas·si·fy ['klæsɪfaɪ] *v/t* (*pret & pp* **-ied**) (*categorize*) classificare

'**class·mate** compagno *m*, -a *f* di classe; '**class·room** aula *f*; '**class**

'**war·fare** lotta *f* di classe

classy ['klɑːsɪ] *adj* F d'alta classe

clat·ter ['klætə(r)] **1** *n* frastuono *m* **2** *v/i* fare baccano; ~ **down the stairs** scendere rumorosamente le scale

clause [klɔːz] *in agreement* articolo *m*; GRAM proposizione *f*

claus·tro·pho·bi·a [klɔːstrə'fəʊbɪə] claustrofobia *f*

claw [klɔː] **1** *n* artiglio *m*; *of lobster* chela *m* **2** *v/t* (*scratch*) graffiare

clay [kleɪ] argilla *f*

clean [kliːn] **1** *adj* pulito **2** *adv* F (*completely*) completamente **3** *v/t* pulire; *teeth* lavarsi; *car, hands, face* lavare; *clothes* lavare o pulire a secco

♦ **clean out** *v/t room, cupboard* pulire a fondo; *fig* ripulire

♦ **clean up 1** *v/t also fig* ripulire **2** *v/i* pulire; (*wash*) ripulirsi; *on stock market etc* fare fortuna

clean·er ['kliːnə(r)] *male* uomo *m* delle pulizie; *female* donna *f* delle pulizie; (*dry* ~) lavanderia *f*, tintoria *f*

'**clean·ing wom·an** donna *f* delle pulizie

cleanse [klenz] *v/t skin* detergere

cleans·er ['klenzə(r)] *for skin* detergente *m*

cleans·ing cream ['klenzɪŋ] latte *f* detergente

clear [klɪə(r)] **1** *adj* chiaro; *weather, sky* sereno; *water, eyes* limpido; *skin* uniforme; *conscience* pulito; **I'm not** ~ **about it** non l'ho capito bene; **I didn't make myself** ~ non mi sono spiegato bene; **I made it** ~ **to him** gliel'ho fatto capire **2** *adv*: **loud and** ~ forte e chiaro; **stand** ~ **of** stare lontano da; **steer** ~ **of** stare alla larga da **3** *v/t roads etc* sgomb(e)rare; (*acquit*) scagionare; (*authorize*) autorizzare; (*earn*) guadagnare al netto; *fence* scavalcare con un salto; *debt* saldare; ~ **one's throat** schiarirsi la gola; ~ **the table** sparecchiare (la tavola) **4** *v/i of sky* schiarirsi; *of mist* diradarsi

C

◆ **clear away** v/t mettere via

◆ **clear off** v/i F filarsela F

◆ **clear out 1** v/t *cupboard* sgomb(e)rare **2** v/i sparire

◆ **clear up 1** v/i *(tidy up)* mettere in ordine; *of weather* schiarirsi; *of illness, rash* sparire **2** v/t *(tidy)* mettere in ordine; *mystery, problem* risolvere

clear·ance ['klɪərəns] *space* spazio *m* libero; *(authorization)* autorizzazione *f*

clear·ance sale liquidazione *f*

clear·ing ['klɪərɪŋ] *in woods* radura *f*

clear·ly ['klɪəlɪ] *adv* chiaramente

cleav·age ['kliːvɪdʒ] décolleté *m inv*

cleav·er ['kliːvə(r)] mannaia *f*

clem·en·cy ['klemənsɪ] clemenza *f*

clench [klenʃ] v/t serrare

cler·gy ['klɜːdʒɪ] clero *m*

cler·gy·man ['klɜːdʒɪmæn] ecclesiastico *m*

clerk [klɑːk, *Am* klɜːrk] impiegato *m*, -a *f*; *Am: in shop* commesso *m*, -a *f*

clev·er ['klevə(r)] *adj* intelligente; *gadget, device* ingegnoso; **don't get ~ with me** non fare il furbo con me

clev·er·ly ['klevəlɪ] *adv* intelligentemente

cli·ché ['kliːʃeɪ] frase *f* stereotipata

cli·chéd ['kliːʃeɪd] *adj* stereotipato

click [klɪk] **1** *n* COMPUT click *m inv* **2** v/i *of camera etc* scattare

◆ **click on** v/t COMPUT cliccare su

cli·ent ['klaɪənt] cliente *m/f*

cli·en·tele [kliːən'tel] clientela *f*

cliff [klɪf] scogliera *f*

cli·mate ['klaɪmət] clima *m*

'cli·mate change mutazione *f* climatica

cli·mat·ic [klaɪ'mætɪk] *adj* climatico

cli·max ['klaɪmæks] *n* punto *m* culminante

climb [klaɪm] **1** *n up mountain* scalata *f*, arrampicata *f* **2** v/t salire su; *clamber up* arrampicarsi su; *mountaineering* scalare **3** v/i *of plane, road, inflation* salire; *clamber* arrampicarsi

◆ **climb down** v/i scendere; *fig* fare marcia indietro

climb·er ['klaɪmə(r)] *person* alpinista *m/f*

climb·ing ['klaɪmɪŋ] alpinismo *m*

climb·ing wall parete *f* artificiale per esercitarsi nella scalata

clinch [klɪntʃ] v/t *deal* concludere; **that ~es it** questo risolve la questione

cling [klɪŋ] v/i (*pret* & *pp* **clung**) *of clothes* essere attillato

◆ **cling to** v/t *of child* avvinghiarsi a; *ideas, tradition* aggrapparsi a

'cling·film pellicola *f* trasparente

cling·y ['klɪŋɪ] *adj child, boyfriend* appiccicoso

clin·ic ['klɪnɪk] clinica *f*

clin·i·cal ['klɪnɪkl] *adj* clinico

clink [klɪŋk] **1** *n noise* tintinnio *m* **2** v/i tintinnare

clip¹ [klɪp] **1** *n fastener* fermaglio *m*; *for hair* molletta *f*; *for paper* graffetta *f* **2** v/t (*pret* & *pp* **-ped**): **~ sth to sth** attaccare qc a qc

clip² [klɪp] **1** *n from film* spezzone *f* **2** v/t (*pret* & *pp* **-ped**) *hair, hedge, grass* tagliare

'clip·board fermablocco *m inv*

clip·pers ['klɪpəz] *npl for hair* rasoio *m*; *for nails* tronchesina *f*; *for gardening* tosasiepi *fpl*

clip·ping ['klɪpɪŋ] *from newspaper* ritaglio *m*

clique [kliːk] combriccola *f*

cloak *n* cappa *f*

'cloak·room guardaroba *m inv*; *(euph: toilet)* servizi *mpl*

clock [klɒk] orologio *m*; F *(speedometer)* contachilometri *m inv*

'clock ra·di·o radiosveglia *f*; **'clockwise** *adv* in senso orario; **'clockwork** meccanismo *m* di orologio; *it went like ~* è andato liscio come l'olio

◆ **clog up** [klɒg] (*pret* & *pp* **-ged**) **1** v/i intasarsi **2** v/t intasare

clone [kləʊn] **1** *n* clone *m* **2** v/t clonare

close¹ [kləʊs] **1** *adj family, friend* intimo; *resemblance* stretto; **we are very ~** siamo molto uniti; **be ~ to s.o.** *emotionally* essere vicino a qu

2 *adv* vicino; **~ at hand** a portata di mano; **~ by** nella vicinanze

close² [kləʊz] **1** *v/t* chiudere **2** *v/i* of *door, eyes* chiudersi; *of shop* chiudere

◆ **close down** *v/t & v/i* chiudere

◆ **close in** *v/i* circondare; *of fog, night* calare

◆ **close up 1** *v/t building* chiudere **2** *v/i* (*move closer*) avvicinarsi

closed [kləʊzd] *adj* chiuso

closed-cir·cuit 'tel·e·vi·sion televisione *f* a circuito chiuso

'close-knit *adj* affiatato

close·ly ['kləʊslɪ] *adv listen, watch* attentamente; *cooperate* fianco a fianco

clos·et ['klɒzɪt] *Am* armadio *m*

close-up ['kləʊsʌp] primo piano *m*

clos·ing date ['kləʊzɪŋ] termine *m*

clos·ing time ['kləʊzɪŋ] ora *f* di chiusura

clo·sure ['kləʊʒə(r)] chiusura *f*

clot [klɒt] **1** *n of blood* grumo *m* **2** *v/i* (*pret & pp* **-ted**) *of blood* coagularsi

cloth [klɒθ] (*fabric*) tessuto *m*; *for cleaning* straccio *m*

clothes [kləʊðz] *npl* vestiti *mpl*

'clothes brush spazzola *f* per vestiti; **'clothes hang·er** attaccapanni *m inv*; **'clothes·horse** stendibiancheria *m inv*; **'clothes·line** filo *m* stendibiancheria *inv*; **'clothes peg** molletta *f* per i panni

cloth·ing ['kləʊðɪŋ] abbigliamento *m*

cloud [klaʊd] *n* nuvola *f*; **a ~ of smoke / dust** una nuvola di fumo / polvere

◆ **cloud over** *v/i of sky* rannuvolarsi

'cloud·burst temporale *m*

cloud·less ['klaʊdlɪs] *adj sky* sereno

cloud·y ['klaʊdɪ] *adj* nuvoloso

clout [klaʊt] F (*blow*) botta *f*; (*fig: influence*) impatto *m*

clove of **'gar·lic** [kləʊv] spicchio *m* d'aglio

clown [klaʊn] *in circus* pagliaccio *m*; (*joker, also pej*) pagliaccio *m*

club [klʌb] *n weapon* clava *f*; *in golf* mazza *f*; *organization* club *m inv*

clue [kluː] indizio *m*; **I haven't a ~** F non ne ho la minima idea; **he hasn't a ~** (*is useless*) non ci capisce niente

clued-up [kluːd'ʌp] *adj* F beninformato

clump [klʌmp] *n of earth* zolla *f*; *group* gruppo *m*

clum·si·ness ['klʌmzɪnɪs] goffaggine *f*

clum·sy ['klʌmzɪ] *adj person* goffo, maldestro

clung [klʌŋ] *pret & pp* → **cling**

clus·ter ['klʌstə(r)] **1** *n* gruppo *m* **2** *v/i of people* raggrupparsi; *of houses* essere raggruppato

clutch [klʌtʃ] **1** *n* MOT frizione *f* **2** *v/t* stringere

◆ **clutch at** *v/t* cercare di afferrare

clut·ter ['klʌtə(r)] **1** *n* oggetti *mpl* alla rinfusa **2** *v/t* (*also:* **~ up**) ingombrare

Co. *abbr* (= **Company**) C.ia (= compagnia)

c/o *abbr* (= **care of**) presso

coach [kəʊtʃ] **1** *n* (*trainer*) allenatore *m*, -trice *f*; *of singer etc* maestro *m*, -a *f*; *on train* vagone *m*; (*Br: bus*) pullman *m inv* **2** *v/t* allenare; *singer, actor* dare lezioni a

coach·ing ['kəʊtʃɪŋ] allenamento *m*; *of singer, actor* lezioni *fpl*

'coach par·ty gruppo *m* di turisti; **'coach sta·tion** stazione *f* dei pullman; **'coach tour** viaggio *m* turistico in pullman

co·ag·u·late [kəʊ'æɡjʊleɪt] *v/i of blood* coagularsi

coal [kəʊl] carbone *m*

co·a·li·tion [kəʊə'lɪʃn] coalizione *f*

'coal·mine miniera *f* di carbone

coarse [kɔːs] *adj skin, fabric* ruvido; *hair* spesso; (*vulgar*) grossolano

coarse·ly ['kɔːslɪ] *adv* (*vulgarly*) grossolanamente; *ground* a grani grossi

coast [kəʊst] *n* costa *f*; **at the ~** sulla costa

coast·al ['kəʊstl] *adj* costiero

coast·er ['kəʊstə(r)] *for glass* sottobicchiere *m*; *for bottle* sottobottiglia *m*

C

'**coast·guard** *organization, person* guardia *f* costiera

'**coast·line** costa *f*, litorale *m*

coat [kəʊt] **1** *n* (*over~*) cappotto *m*; *of animal* pelliccia *f*; *of paint etc* mano *f* **2** *v/t* (*cover*) ricoprire

'**coat·hang·er** attaccapanni *m inv*, gruccia *f*

coat·ing ['kəʊtɪŋ] strato *m*

co·au·thor ['kəʊːθə(r)] **1** *n* co-autore *m*, -trice *f* **2** *v/t* scrivere insieme

coax [kəʊks] *v/t* convincere con le moine; ~ **sth out of s.o.** ottenere qc da qu con le moine

cob·bled ['kɒbld] *adj* lastricato (a ciottoli)

cob·ble·stone ['kɒblstəʊn] ciottolo *m*

cob·web ['kɒbweb] ragnatela *f*

co·caine [kə'keɪn] cocaina *f*

cock [kɒk] *n chicken* gallo *m*; *any male bird* maschio *m* (di uccelli); V (*penis*) cazzo *m* V

cock·eyed [kɒk'aɪd] *adj* F *idea etc* strampalato

'**cock·pit** *of plane* cabina *f* (di pilotaggio)

cock·roach ['kɒkrəʊtʃ] scarafaggio *m*

'**cock·tail** cocktail *m inv*

'**cock·tail par·ty** cocktail party *m inv*

'**cock·tail shak·er** shaker *m inv*

cock·y ['kɒkɪ] *adj* F arrogante

co·coa ['kəʊkəʊ] *drink* cioccolata *f* calda

co·co·nut ['kəʊkənʌt] cocco *m*

co·co·nut palm palma *f* di cocco

COD [siːəʊ'diː] *abbr* (= **cash on delivery**) pagamento *m* contrassegno

cod·dle ['kɒdl] *v/t sick person* coccolare; *pej: child* viziare

code [kəʊd] *n* codice *m*

co·ed·u·ca·tion·al [kəʊedjʊ'keɪʃnl] *adj* misto

co·erce [kəʊ'ɜːs] *v/t* costringere

co·ex·ist [kəʊɪg'zɪst] *v/i* coesistere

co·ex·ist·ence [kəʊɪg'zɪstəns] coesistenza *f*

cof·fee ['kɒfɪ] caffè *m inv*

'**cof·fee bar** caffè *m inv*; '**cof·fee bean** chicco *m* di caffè; '**cof·fee**

break pausa *f* per il caffè; '**cof·fee cup** tazza *f* da caffè; '**cof·fee grind·er** ['graɪndə(r)] macinacaffè *m inv*; '**cof·fee mak·er** caffettiera *f*; '**cof·fee pot** caffettiera *f*; '**cof·fee shop** caffetteria *f*; '**cof·fee ta·ble** tavolino *m*

cof·fin ['kɒfɪn] bara *f*

cog [kɒg] dente *m*

co·gnac ['kɒnjæk] cognac *m inv*

'**cog·wheel** ruota *f* dentata

co·hab·it [kəʊ'hæbɪt] *v/i* convivere

co·her·ent [kəʊ'hɪərənt] *adj* coerente

coil [kɔɪl] **1** *n of rope* rotolo *m* **2** *v/t*: ~ (**up**) avvolgere

coin [kɔɪn] *n* moneta *f*

co·in·cide [kəʊɪn'saɪd] *v/i* coincidere

co·in·ci·dence [kəʊ'ɪnsɪdəns] coincidenza *f*

coke [kəʊk] P (*cocaine*) coca *f*

Coke® [kəʊk] Coca® *f*

cold [kəʊld] **1** *adj* freddo; *I'm* (*feeling*) ~ ho freddo; *it's* ~ *of weather* fa freddo; *in* ~ *blood* a sangue freddo; *get* ~ *feet* F farsi prendere dalla fifa F **2** *n* freddo *m*; MED raffreddore *m*; *I have a* ~ ho il raffreddore

cold-blood·ed [kəʊld'blʌdɪd] *adj also murder* a sangue freddo; *person* spietato

cold 'call·ing porta-a-porta *m*; *by phone* televendite *fpl*

'**cold cuts** *npl* affettati *mpl*

cold·ly ['kəʊldlɪ] *adv* freddamente

cold 'meat affettati *mpl*

cold·ness ['kəʊldnɪs] *fig* freddezza *f*

'**cold sore** febbre *f* del labbro

cole·slaw ['kəʊlslɔː] *insalata f di cavolo, carote, cipolle tritati e maionese*

col·ic ['kɒlɪk] colica *f*

col·lab·o·rate [kə'læbəreɪt] *v/i* collaborare

col·lab·o·ra·tion [kəlæbə'reɪʃn] collaborazione *f*; *with enemy* collaborazionismo *m*

col·lab·o·ra·tor [kə'læbəreɪtə(r)] collaboratore *m*, -trice *f*; *with enemy* collaborazionista *m/f*

col·lapse [kə'læps] *v/i* crollare; *of*

person accasciarsi

col·lap·si·ble [kəˈlæpsəbl] *adj* pieghevole

col·lar [ˈkɒlə(r)] collo *m*, colletto *m*; *of dog, cat* collare *m*

ˈcol·lar·bone clavicola *f*

col·league [ˈkɒliːg] collega *m/f*

col·lect [kəˈlekt] **1** *v/t person*: go andare a prendere; *person*: come venire a prendere; *tickets, cleaning etc* ritirare; *as hobby* collezionare; (*gather*) raccogliere **2** *v/i* (*gather together*) radunarsi **3** *adv Am*: *call* ~ telefonare a carico del destinatario

col·lect·ed [kəˈlektɪd] *adj person* controllato; *the ~ works of ...* l'opera omnia di ...

col·lec·tion [kəˈlekʃn] collezione *f*; *in church* colletta *f*; *of poems, stories* raccolta *f*

col·lec·tive [kəˈlektɪv] *adj* collettivo

col·lec·tive ˈbar·gain·ing trattative *fpl* sindacali

col·lec·tor [kəˈlektə(r)] collezionista *m/f*

col·lege [ˈkɒlɪdʒ] istituto *m* parauniversitario; *at Oxford and Cambridge* college *m inv*

col·lide [kəˈlaɪd] *v/i* scontrarsi

col·li·sion [kəˈlɪʒn] collisione *f*, scontro *m*

col·lo·qui·al [kəˈləʊkwɪəl] *adj* colloquiale

co·lon [ˈkəʊlən] *punctuation* due punti *mpl*; ANAT colon *m inv*

colo·nel [ˈkɜːnl] colonnello *m*

co·lo·ni·al [kəˈləʊnɪəl] *adj* coloniale

co·lo·nize [ˈkɒlənaɪz] *v/t country* colonizzare

co·lo·ny [ˈkɒlənɪ] colonia *f*

co·lor *etc Am* → **colour** *etc*

co·los·sal [kəˈlɒsl] *adj* colossale

col·our [ˈkʌlə(r)] **1** *n* colore *m*; *in cheeks* colorito *m*; *in* ~ *film etc* a colori; *~s* MIL bandiera *f* **2** *v/t* colorare; *one's hair* tingere **3** *v/i* (*blush*) diventare rosso

ˈcol·our-blind *adj* daltonico

col·oured [ˈkʌləd] *adj person* di colore

ˈcol·our fast *adj* con colori resistenti

col·our·ful [ˈkʌləfʊl] *adj* pieno di colori; *account* pittoresco

col·our·ing [ˈkʌlərɪŋ] colorito *m*

ˈcol·our pho·to·graph fotografia *f* a colori

ˈcol·our scheme abbinamento *m* dei colori

ˈcol·our TV tv *f inv* a colori

colt [kəʊlt] puledro *m*

col·umn [ˈkɒləm] colonna *f*; (*newspaper feature*) rubrica *f*

col·umn·ist [ˈkɒləm(n)ɪst] giornalista *m/f* che cura una rubrica

co·ma [ˈkəʊmə] coma *m inv*

comb [kəʊm] **1** *n* pettine *m* **2** *v/t* pettinare; *area* rastrellare

com·bat [ˈkɒmbæt] **1** *n* combattimento *m* **2** *v/t* combattere

com·bi·na·tion [kɒmbɪˈneɪʃn] combinazione *f*

com·bine [kəmˈbaɪn] **1** *v/t* unire; *ingredients* mescolare **2** *v/i of chemical elements* combinarsi

com·bine har·vest·er [kɒmbaɪn-ˈhɑːvɪstə(r)] mietitrebbia *f*

com·bus·ti·ble [kəmˈbʌstɪbl] *adj* combustibile

com·bus·tion [kəmˈbʌstʃn] combustione *f*

come [kʌm] *v/i* (*pret* **came**, *pp* **come**) venire; *of train, bus* arrivare; *you'll* ~ *to like it* finirà per piacerti; *how* ~? F come mai? F

♦ **come about** *v/i* (*happen*) succedere

♦ **come across** *v/t* (*find*) trovare **2** *v/i of idea, humour* essere capito; *she comes across as ...* dà l'impressione di essere ...

♦ **come along** *v/i* (*come too*) venire; (*turn up*) presentarsi; (*progress*) fare progressi; *how is it coming along?* come sta andando?; *your Italian has come along a lot* il tuo italiano è migliorato molto

♦ **come apart** *v/i* smontarsi; (*break*) andare in pezzi

♦ **come away** *v/i of person, button* venire via

♦ **come back** *v/i* ritornare; *it came back to me* mi è tornato in mente

◆ **come by 1** *v/i* passare **2** *v/t* (*acquire*) ottenere

◆ **come down** *v/i* venire giù; *in price, amount etc* scendere; *of rain, snow* cadere; *he came down the stairs* è sceso dalle scale

◆ **come for** *v/t* (*attack*) assalire; (*collect*) venire a prendere

◆ **come forward** *v/i* (*present o.s.*) farsi avanti

◆ **come from** *v/t* venire da; *where do you come from?* di dove sei?

◆ **come in** *v/i* entrare; *of train, in race* arrivare; *of tide* salire; *come in!* entra!

◆ **come in for** *v/t* attirare; *come in for criticism* attirare delle critiche

◆ **come in on** *v/t* partecipare a; *come in on a deal* stare a un accordo

◆ **come off** *v/i of handle etc* staccarsi

◆ **come on** *v/i* (*progress*) fare progressi; *how's the work coming on?* come sta venendo il lavoro?; *come on!* dai!; *in disbelief* ma dai!

◆ **come out** *v/i of person, book, sun* uscire; *of results, product* venir fuori; *of stain* venire via; *of gay* rendere nota la propria omosessualità

◆ **come round** *v/i to s.o.'s home* passare; (*regain consciousness*) rivenire

◆ **come to 1** *v/t place, position* arrivare a; *that comes to £70* fanno 70 sterline **2** *v/i* (*regain consciousness*) rinvenire

◆ **come up** *v/i* salire; *of sun* sorgere; *something has come up* si è presentato qualcosa

◆ **come up with** *v/t new idea etc* venir fuori con

'**come·back** ritorno *m*; *make a ~* tornare alla ribalta

co·me·di·an [kə'miːdɪən] comico *m*, -a *f*; *pej* buffone *m*

'**come·down** passo *m* indietro

com·e·dy ['kɒmədɪ] commedia *f*

com·et ['kɒmɪt] cometa *f*

come·up·pance [kʌm'ʌpəns] *n* F: *he'll get his ~* avrà quello che si merita

com·fort ['kʌmfət] **1** *n* comodità *f inv*; (*consolation*) conforto *m* **2** *v/t* confortare

'**com·for·ta·ble** ['kʌmfətəbl] *adj chair, room* comodo; *be ~ in chair* stare comodo; *in situation* essere a proprio agio; (*financially*) essere agiato

com·fy ['kʌmfɪ] *adj* F → **comfortable**

com·ic ['kɒmɪk] **1** *n to read* fumetto *m*; (*comedian*) comico *m*, -a *f* **2** *adj* comico

com·i·cal ['kɒmɪkl] *adj* comico

com·ic book fumetto *m*

com·ic strip striscia *f* (di fumetti)

com·ma ['kɒmə] virgola *f*

com·mand [kə'mɑːnd] **1** *n* comando *m* **2** *v/t person* comandare a

com·man·deer [kɒmən'dɪə(r)] *v/t* appropriarsi di

com·mand·er [kə'mɑːndə(r)] comandante *m*

com·mand·er·in·'chief comandante *m* in capo

com·mand·ing of·fi·cer [kə'mɑːndɪŋ] ufficiale *m* comandante

com·mand·ment [kə'mɑːndmənt]: *the Ten Commandments* REL i Dieci Comandamenti

com·mem·o·rate [kə'meməreɪt] *v/t* commemorare

com·mem·o·ra·tion [kəmemə'reɪʃn]: *in ~ of* in commemorazione di

com·mence [kə'mens] *v/t & v/i* cominciare

com·mend [kə'mend] *v/t* (*praise*) lodare; (*recommend*) raccomandare

com·mend·a·ble [kə'mendəbl] *adj* lodevole

com·men·da·tion [kɒmen'deɪʃn] *for bravery* riconoscimento *m*

com·men·su·rate [kə'menʃərət] *adj*: *~ with* commisurato a

com·ment ['kɒment] **1** *n* commento *m*; *no ~!* no comment! **2** *v/i* fare commenti

com·men·ta·ry ['kɒməntrɪ] cronaca *f*

com·men·tate ['kɒməntett] *v/i* commentare

com·men·ta·tor [ˈkɒmənteɪtə(r)] *on TV* telecronista *m/f; on radio* radiocronista *m/f*

com·merce [ˈkɒmɜːs] commercio *m*

com·mer·cial [kəˈmɜːʃl] **1** *adj* commerciale **2** *n* (*advert*) pubblicità *f inv*

com·mer·cial 'break interruzione *f* pubblicitaria

com·mer·cial·ize [kəˈmɜːʃlaɪz] *v/t Christmas etc* commercializzare

com·mer·cial 'tel·e·vi·sion televisione *f* privata

com·mer·cial 'trav·el·ler rappresentante *m/f*

com·mis·e·rate [kəˈmɪzəreɪt] *v/i* esprimere rincrescimento (**with** a)

com·mis·sion [kəˈmɪʃn] **1** *n* (*payment, committee*) commissione *f*; (*job*) incarico *m* **2** *v/t for a job* incaricare

com·mis·sion·aire [kəmɪʃəˈneə(r)] portiere *m*

Com·mis·sion·er [kəˈmɪʃənə(r)] *in European Union* Commissario *m*, -a *f*

com·mit [kəˈmɪt] *v/t* (*pret & pp* **-ted**) *crime* commettere; *money* assegnare; *~ o.s.* impegnarsi

com·mit·ment [kəˈmɪtmənt] impegno *m*

com·mit·tee [kəˈmɪtɪ] comitato *m*

com·mod·i·ty [kəˈmɒdətɪ] prodotto *m*

com·mon [ˈkɒmən] *adj* comune; *in ~* in comune; **have sth in ~ with s.o.** avere qc in comune con qu

com·mon·er [ˈkɒmənə(r)] persona *f* non nobile

com·mon 'law husband/ wife *convivente al quale spettano legalmente i diritti di una moglie / un marito*

com·mon·ly [ˈkɒmənlɪ] *adv* comunemente

Com·mon 'Mar·ket Mercato *m* Comune

com·mon·place *adj* luogo *m* comune

Com·mons [ˈkɒmənz] *npl*: **the ~** la Camera dei Comuni

com·mon 'sense buon senso *m*

com·mo·tion [kəˈməʊʃn] confusione *f*

com·mu·nal [ˈkɒmjʊnl] *adj* comune

com·mu·nal·ly [ˈkɒmjʊnəlɪ] *adv* in comune

com·mu·ni·cate [kəˈmjuːnɪkeɪt] *v/t & v/i* comunicare

com·mu·ni·ca·tion [kəmjuːnɪˈkeɪʃn] comunicazione *f*

com·mu·ni·ca·tions *npl* comunicazioni *fpl*

com·mu·ni·ca·tions sat·el·lite satellite *m* per telecomunicazioni

com·mu·ni·ca·tive [kəˈmjuːnɪkətɪv] *adj person* comunicativo

Com·mu·nion [kəˈmjuːnɪən] REL comunione *f*

com·mu·ni·qué [kəˈmjuːnɪkeɪ] comunicato *m* ufficiale

Com·mu·nis·m [ˈkɒmjʊnɪzm] comunismo *m*

Com·mu·nist [ˈkɒmjʊnɪst] **1** *adj* comunista **2** *n* comunista *m/f*

com·mu·ni·ty [kəˈmjuːnətɪ] comunità *f inv*

com·mu·ni·ty cen·tre centro *m* comunitario

com·mu·ni·ty serv·ice servizio *m* civile (come pena per reati minori)

com·mute [kəˈmjuːt] **1** *v/i* fare il/la pendolare **2** *v/t* LAW commutare

com·mut·er [kəˈmjuːtə(r)] pendolare *m/f*

com·mut·er traf·fic traffico *m* dei pendolari

com·mut·er train treno *m* dei pendolari

com·pact [kəmˈpækt] **1** *adj* compatto **2** *n* [ˈkɒmpækt] *for powder* portacipria *m inv*

com·pact 'disc → **CD**

com·pan·ion [kəmˈpænjən] compagno *m*, -a *f*

com·pan·ion·ship [kəmˈpænjənʃɪp] compagnia *f*

com·pa·ny [ˈkʌmpənɪ] COM società *f inv*; (*ballet ~, theatre ~*) compagnia *f*; (*companionship, guests*) compagnia *f*

com·pa·ny: **keep s.o. ~** fare compagnia a qu

com·pa·ny 'car auto *f inv* della ditta

com·pa·ny 'law diritto *m* societario

com·pa·ra·ble ['kɒmpərəbl] *adj* paragonabile; (*similar*) simile

com·par·a·tive [kəm'pærətɪv] **1** *adj* (*relative*) relativo; *study, method* comparato; GRAM comparativo **2** *n* GRAM comparativo *m*

com·par·a·tive·ly [kəm'pærətɪvlɪ] *adv* relativamente

com·pare [kəm'peə(r)] **1** *v/t* paragonare; **~ sth with sth / s.o. with s.o.** paragonare qc a qc/qu a qu; **~d with ...** rispetto a ... **2** *v/i* reggere il confronto; **how did he ~?** com'era rispetto gli altri?

com·pa·ri·son [kəm'pærɪsn] paragone *m*, confronto *m*; **in ~ with** in confronto a; **there's no ~** non c'è paragone

com·part·ment [kəm'pɑːtmənt] scomparto *m*; RAIL scompartimento *m*

com·pass ['kʌmpəs] bussola *f*; (*pair of*) **~es** for geometry compasso *m*

com·pas·sion [kəm'pæʃn] compassione *f*

com·pas·sion·ate [kəm'pæʃənət] *adj* compassionevole

com·pas·sion·ate leave congedo *m* per motivi familiari

com·pat·i·bil·i·ty [kəmpætə'bɪlɪtɪ] compatibilità *f inv*

com·pat·i·ble [kəm'pætəbl] *adj also* COMPUT compatibile; **we're not ~** siamo incompatibili

com·pel [kəm'pel] *v/t* (*pret & pp* **-led**) costringere

com·pel·ling [kəm'pelɪŋ] *adj argument* convincente; *film, book* avvincente

com·pen·sate ['kɒmpənseɪt] **1** *v/t* **with money** risarcire **2** *v/i*: **~ for** compensare

com·pen·sa·tion [kɒmpən'seɪʃn] *money* risarcimento *m*; *reward* vantaggio *m*; *comfort* consolazione *f*

com·père ['kɒmpeə(r)] presentatore *m*, -trice *f*

com·pete [kəm'piːt] *v/i* competere;

(*take part*) gareggiare; **~ for** contendersi

com·pe·tence ['kɒmpɪtəns] competenza *f*

com·pe·tent ['kɒmpɪtənt] *adj* competente

com·pe·tent·ly ['kɒmpɪtəntlɪ] *adv* con competenza

com·pe·ti·tion [kɒmpə'tɪʃn] (*contest*) concorso *m*; SP gara *f*; (*competing, competitors*) concorrenza *f*

com·pet·i·tive [kəm'petɪtɪv] *adj* competitivo; *sport* agonistico; *price, offer* concorrenziale

com·pet·i·tive·ly [kəm'petɪtɪvlɪ] *adv*: **~ priced** a prezzi concorrenziali

com·pet·i·tive·ness competitività *f inv*

com·pet·i·tor [kəm'petɪtə(r)] *in contest* concorrente *m/f*; **our ~s** COM la concorrenza

com·pile [kəm'paɪl] *v/t* compilare

com·pla·cen·cy [kəm'pleɪsənsɪ] autocompiacimento *m*

com·pla·cent [kəm'pleɪsənt] *adj* compiaciuto; **be ~ about sth** compiacersi di qc

com·plain [kəm'pleɪn] *v/i* lamentarsi; *to shop, manager* reclamare; **~ of** MED accusare

com·plaint [kəm'pleɪnt] lamentela *f*; *to shop* reclamo *m*; MED disturbo *m*

com·ple·ment ['kɒmplɪmənt] *v/t* completare; **they ~ each other** si completano bene

com·ple·men·ta·ry [kɒmplɪ'mentərɪ] *adj* complementare

com·plete [kəm'pliːt] **1** *adj* (*total*) completo; (*finished*) terminato; **I made a ~ fool of myself** mi sono comportato da perfetto idiota **2** *v/t task, building etc* completare; *form* compilare

com·plete·ly [kəm'pliːtlɪ] *adv* completamente

com·ple·tion [kəm'pliːʃn] completamento *m*; **payment on ~** pagamento a conclusione lavori

com·plex ['kɒmpleks] **1** *adj* complesso **2** *n also* PSYCH complesso *m*

com·plex·ion [kəm'plekʃn] *facial* carnagione *f*

com·plex·i·ty [kəm'pleksɪtɪ] complessità *f inv*

com·pli·ance [kəm'plaɪəns] conformità *f inv*

com·pli·cate ['komplɪkeɪt] *v/t* complicare

com·pli·cat·ed ['komplɪkeɪtɪd] *adj* complicato

com·pli·ca·tion [komplɪ'keɪʃn] complicazione *f*; **~s** MED complicazioni

com·pli·ment ['komplɪmənt] **1** *n* complimento *m* **2** *v/t* fare i complimenti a

com·pli·men·ta·ry [komplɪ'mentərɪ] *adj* lusinghiero; (*free*) in omaggio

com·pli·ments slip ['komplɪmənts] biglietto *m* intestato della ditta

com·ply [kəm'plaɪ] *v/i* (*pret & pp* **-ied**) ubbidire; **~ with** osservare; *of products, equipment* essere conforme a

com·po·nent [kəm'pəʊnənt] componente *m*

com·pose [kəm'pəʊz] *v/t also* MUS comporre; **be ~d of** essere composto da; **~ o.s.** ricomporsi

com·posed [kəm'pəʊzd] *adj* (*calm*) calmo

com·pos·er [kəm'pəʊzə(r)] MUS compositore *m*, -trice *f*

com·po·si·tion [kompə'zɪʃn] *also* MUS composizione *f*; (*essay*) tema *m*

com·po·sure [kəm'pəʊʒə(r)] calma *f*

com·pound ['kompaʊnd] *n* CHEM composto *m*

com·pound 'in·ter·est interesse *m* composto

com·pre·hend [komprɪ'hend] *v/t* (*understand*) capire

com·pre·hen·sion [komprɪ'henʃn] comprensione *f*

com·pre·hen·sive [komprɪ'hensɪv] *adj* esauriente

com·pre·hen·sive in·sur·ance polizza *f* casco

com·pre·hen·sive·ly [komprɪ'hensɪvlɪ] *adv* in modo esauriente

com·pre·hen·sive school scuola *f* secondaria

com·press ['kompres] **1** *n* MED impacco *m* **2** *v/t* [kəm'pres] *air, gas* comprimere; *information* condensare

com·prise [kəm'praɪz] *v/t* comprendere; (*make-up*) costituire; **be ~d of** essere composto da

com·pro·mise ['komprəmaɪz] **1** *n* compromesso *m* **2** *v/i* arrivare a un compromesso **3** *v/t* (*jeopardize*) compromettere; **~ o.s.** compromettersi

com·pul·sion [kəm'pʌlʃn] PSYCH coazione *f*

com·pul·sive [kəm'pʌlsɪv] *adj* *behaviour* patologico; *reading, viewing* avvincente

com·pul·so·ry [kəm'pʌlsərɪ] *adj* obbligatorio; **~ education** scuola *f* dell'obbligo

com·put·er [kəm'pjuːtə(r)] computer *m inv*; **have sth on ~** avere qc sul computer

com·put·er-aid·ed de'sign progettazione *f* assistita dall'elaboratore; **com·put·er-aid·ed man·u'fac·ture** produzione *f* computerizzata; **com·put·er-con'trolled** *adj* controllato dal computer; **com'puter game** computer game *m inv*

com·put·er·ize [kəm'pjuːtəraɪz] *v/t* computerizzare

com·put·er 'lit·er·ate *adj* che ha dimestichezza con il computer; **com·put·er 'sci·ence** informatica *f*; **com·put·er 'sci·en·tist** informatico *m*, -a *f*

com·put·ing [kəm'pjuːtɪŋ] *n* informatica *f*

com·rade ['komreɪd] *also* POL compagno *m*, -a *f*

com·rade·ship ['komreɪdʃɪp] cameratismo *m*

con [kon] **1** *n* F truffa *f* **2** *v/t* (*pret & pp* **-ned**) F truffare; **~ s.o. into doing sth** far fare qc a qu con l'inganno

con·ceal [kən'siːl] *v/t* nascondere

con·ceal·ment [kən'siːlmənt] occultazione *f*

con·cede [kən'siːd] *v/t* (*admit*) am-

mettere; *goal* concedere
con·ceit [kən'siːt] presunzione *f*
con·ceit·ed [kən'siːtɪd] *adj* presuntuoso
con·cei·va·ble [kən'siːvəbl] *adj* concepibile
con·ceive [kən'siːv] *v/i of woman* concepire; **~ of** (*imagine*) immaginare
con·cen·trate ['kɒnsəntreɪt] **1** *v/i* concentrarsi **2** *v/t one's attention, energies* concentrare
con·cen·trat·ed ['kɒnsəntreɪtɪd] *adj juice etc* concentrato
con·cen·tra·tion [kɒnsən'treɪʃn] concentrazione *f*
con·cept ['kɒnsept] concetto *m*
con·cep·tion [kən'sepʃn] *of child* concepimento *m*
con·cern [kən'sɜːn] **1** *n* (*anxiety*) preoccupazione *f*; (*care*) interesse *m*; (*business*) affare *m*; (*company*) impresa *f*; **there's no cause for ~** non c'è motivo di preoccuparsi; **it's none of your ~** non sono affari tuoi **2** *v/t* (*involve*) riguardare; (*worry*) preoccupare; **~ o.s. with** preoccuparsi di
con·cerned [kən'sɜːnd] *adj* (*anxious*) preoccupato; (*caring*) interessato; (*involved*) in questione; **as far as I'm ~** per quanto mi riguarda
con·cern·ing [kən'sɜːnɪŋ] *prep* riguardo a
con·cert ['kɒnsət] concerto *m*
con·cert·ed [kən'sɜːtɪd] *adj* (*joint*) congiunto
con·cer·to [kən'tʃeətəʊ] concerto *m*
con·ces·sion [kən'seʃn] (*compromise*) concessione *f*
con·cil·i·a·to·ry [kənsɪlɪ'eɪtərɪ] *adj* conciliatorio
con·cise [kən'saɪs] *adj* conciso
con·clude [kən'kluːd] **1** *v/t* concludere; **~ sth from sth** concludere qc da qc **2** *v/i* concludere
con·clu·sion [kən'kluːʒn] conclusione *f*; **in ~** in conclusione
con·clu·sive [kən'kluːsɪv] *adj* conclusivo

con·coct [kən'kɒkt] *v/t meal, drink* mettere insieme; *excuse, story* inventare
con·coc·tion [kən'kɒkʃn] *food, drink* intruglio *m*
con·crete[1] ['kɒŋkriːt] *adj* concreto
con·crete[2] ['kɒŋkriːt] *n* calcestruzzo *m*; **~ jungle** giungla *f* di cemento
con·cur [kən'kɜː(r)] *v/i* (*pret & pp* **-red**) essere d'accordo
con·cus·sion [kən'kʌʃn] commozione *f* cerebrale
con·demn [kən'dem] *v/t action* condannare; *building* dichiarare inagibile; (*doom*) condannare
con·dem·na·tion [kɒndəm'neɪʃn] *of action* condanna *f*
con·den·sa·tion [kɒnden'seɪʃn] *on walls, windows* condensa *f*
con·dense [kən'dens] **1** *v/t* (*make shorter*) condensare **2** *v/i of steam* condensarsi
con·densed 'milk [kən'densd] latte *m* condensato
con·de·scend [kɒndɪ'send] *v/i*: **he ~ed to speak to me** si è degnato di rivolgermi la parola
con·de·scend·ing [kɒndɪ'sendɪŋ] *adj* (*patronizing*) borioso
con·di·tion [kən'dɪʃn] **1** *n* condizione *f*; MED malattia *f*; **~s** (*circumstances*) condizioni; **on / that** a condizione che; **in / out of ~** in / fuori forma **2** *v/t* PSYCH condizionare
con·di·tion·al [kən'dɪʃnl] **1** *adj acceptance* condizionale **2** *n* GRAM condizionale *m*
con·di·tion·er [kən'dɪʃnə(r)] *for hair* balsamo *m*; *for fabric* ammorbidente *m*
con·di·tion·ing [kən'dɪʃnɪŋ] PSYCH condizionamento *m*
con·do·lences [kən'dəʊlənsɪz] *npl* condoglianze *fpl*
con·dom ['kɒndəm] preservativo *m*
con·done [kən'dəʊn] *v/t actions* scusare
con·du·cive [kən'djuːsɪv] *adj*: **be ~ to** favorire
con·duct ['kɒndʌkt] **1** *n* (*behaviour*)

condotta *f* **2** *v/t* [kən'dʌkt] (*carry out*) condurre; ELEC condurre; MUS dirigere; **~ o.s.** comportarsi

con·duct·ed tour [kən'dʌktɪd] visita *f* guidata

con·duc·tor [kən'dʌktə(r)] MUS direttore *m* d'orchestra; *on bus* bigliettaio *m*; PHYS conduttore *m*

con·duc·tress [kən'dʌktrɪs] bigliettaia *f*

cone [kəʊn] cono *m*; *of pine tree* pigna *f*; *on motorway* birillo *m*

♦ **cone off** *v/t* chiudere al traffico

con·fec·tion·er [kən'fekʃənə(r)] pasticciere *m*, -a *f*

con·fec·tion·e·ry [kən'fekʃənərɪ] dolciumi *mpl*

con·fed·e·ra·tion [kənfedə'reɪʃn] confederazione *f*

con·fer [kən'fɜ:(r)] (*pret & pp* **-red**) **1** *v/t* (*bestow*) conferire **2** *v/i* (*discuss*) confabulare

con·fe·rence ['kɒnfərəns] congresso *m*; **family ~** consiglio *m* di famiglia

con·fe·rence cen·tre centro *m* congressi

con·fe·rence room sala *f* riunioni

con·fess [kən'fes] **1** *v/t* *sin*, *crime* confessare **2** *v/i* confessare; REL confessarsi; **~ to sth** confessare qc; **~ to a weakness for sth** confessare di avere un debole per qc

con·fes·sion [kən'feʃn] confessione *f*

con·fes·sion·al [kən'feʃnl] REL confessionale *m*

con·fes·sor [kən'fesə(r)] REL confessore *m*

con·fide [kən'faɪd] **1** *v/t* confidare **2** *v/i*: **~ in s.o.** confidarsi con qu

con·fi·dence ['kɒnfɪdəns] (*assurance*) sicurezza *f* (di sé); (*trust*) fiducia *f*; **in ~** in confidenza

con·fi·dent ['kɒnfɪdənt] *adj* sicuro; *person* sicuro di sé

con·fi·den·tial [kɒnfɪ'denʃl] *adj* riservato, confidenziale; *adviser* di fiducia

con·fi·den·tial·ly [kɒnfɪ'denʃlɪ] *adv* in confidenza

con·fi·dent·ly ['kɒnfɪdəntlɪ] *adv* con sicurezza

con·fine [kən'faɪn] *v/t* (*imprison*) richiudere; (*restrict*) limitare; **be ~d to one's bed** essere costretto a letto

con·fined [kən'faɪnd] *adj space* ristretto

con·fine·ment [kən'faɪnmənt] (*imprisonment*) reclusione *f*; MED parto *m*

con·firm [kən'fɜ:m] *v/t* confermare

con·fir·ma·tion [kɒnfə'meɪʃn] conferma *f*

con·firmed [kɒn'fɜ:md] *adj bachelor* incallito

con·fis·cate ['kɒnfɪskeɪt] *v/t* sequestrare

con·flict ['kɒnflɪkt] **1** *n* conflitto *m* **2** *v/i* [kən'flɪkt] *of statements*, *accounts* essere in conflitto; *of dates* coincidere

con·form [kən'fɔ:m] *v/i* conformarsi; **~ to** *of products, acts etc* essere conforme a

con·form·ist [kən'fɔ:mɪst] *n* conformista *m/f*

con·front [kən'frʌnt] *v/t* (*face*) affrontare; **~ s.o. with sth** mettere qc di fronte a qc; **the problems ~ing us** i problemi che dobbiamo affrontare

con·fron·ta·tion [kɒnfrən'teɪʃn] scontro *m*

con·fuse [kən'fju:z] *v/t*) confondere; **~ s.o. with s.o.** confondere qu con qu

con·fused [kən'fju:zd] *adj* confuso

con·fus·ing [kən'fju:zɪŋ] *adj* che confonde

con·fu·sion [kən'fju:ʒn] confusione *f*

con·geal [kən'dʒi:l] *v/i of blood*, *fat* rapprendersi

con·gen·ial [kən'dʒi:nɪəl] *adj* (*pleasant*) simpatico

con·gen·i·tal [kən'dʒenɪtl] *adj* MED congenito

con·gest·ed [kən'dʒestɪd] *adj* congestionato

con·ges·tion [kən'dʒestʃn] congestione f; **traffic** ~ la congestione del traffico

con·grat·u·late [kənˈgrætjʊleɪt] v/t congratularsi con

con·grat·u·la·tions [kəngrætjʊˈleɪʃnz] npl congratulazioni fpl; **~ on ...** congratulaizioni per ...

con·grat·u·la·to·ry [kəngrætjʊˈleɪtəri] adj di congratulazioni

con·gre·gate [ˈkɒŋgrɪgeɪt] v/i (gather) riunirsi

con·gre·ga·tion [kɒŋgrɪˈgeɪʃn] REL fedeli mpl

con·gress [ˈkɒŋgres] (conference) congresso m; **Congress** in US il Congresso

Con·gres·sion·al [kənˈgreʃnl] adj del Congresso

Con·gress·man [ˈkɒŋgresmən] membro m del Congresso

co·ni·fer [ˈkɒnɪfə(r)] conifera f

con·jec·ture [kənˈdʒektʃə(r)] n (speculation) congettura f

con·ju·gate [ˈkɒndʒʊgeɪt] v/t GRAM coniugare

con·junc·tion [kənˈdʒʌŋkʃn] GRAM congiunzione f; **in ~ with** insieme a

con·junc·ti·vi·tis [kəndʒʌŋktɪˈvaɪtɪs] congiuntivite f

♦ con·jure up [ˈkʌndʒə(r)] v/t (produce) far apparire (come) per magia; (evoke) evocare

con·jur·er, con·jur·or [ˈkʌndʒərə(r)] (magician) prestigiatore m, -trice f

'con·jur·ing tricks [ˈkʌndʒərɪŋ] npl giochi mpl di prestigio

con man [ˈkɒnmæn] F truffatore m

con·nect [kəˈnekt] v/t (join, link) collegare; to power supply allacciare; ~ **s.o. with s.o.** TELEC mettere in comunicazione qu con qu

con·nect·ed [kəˈnektɪd] adj: **be well-~** avere conoscenze influenti; **be ~ with ...** essere collegato con; **by marriage** essere imparentato con

con·nect·ing flight [kəˈnektɪŋ] coincidenza f (volo)

con·nec·tion [kəˈnekʃn] (link) collegamento m; when travelling coinci-

denza f; (personal contact) conoscenza f; **in ~ with** a proposito di

con·nois·seur [kɒnəˈsɜː(r)] intenditore m, -trice f

con·quer [ˈkɒŋkə(r)] v/t conquistare; fig: fear etc vincere

con·quer·or [ˈkɒŋkərə(r)] conquistatore m, -trice f

con·quest [ˈkɒŋkwest] conquista f

con·science [ˈkɒnʃəns] coscienza f; **have a guilty/clear ~** avere la coscienza sporca/a posto; **on one's ~** sulla coscienza

con·sci·en·tious [kɒnʃɪˈenʃəs] adj coscienzioso

con·sci·en·tious·ness [kɒnʃɪˈenʃəsnəs] coscienziosità f inv

con·sci·en·tious ob'ject·or obiettore m di coscienza

con·scious [ˈkɒnʃəs] adj (aware) consapevole; (deliberate) conscio; MED cosciente; **be/become ~ of** rendersi conto di

con·scious·ly [ˈkɒnʃəslɪ] adv consapevolmente

con·scious·ness [ˈkɒnʃəsnɪs] (awareness) consapevolezza f; MED conoscenza f; **lose/regain ~** perdere/riprendere conoscenza

con·sec·u·tive [kənˈsekjʊtɪv] adj consecutivo

con·sen·sus [kənˈsensəs] consenso m

con·sent [kənˈsent] **1** n consenso m **2** v/i acconsentire

con·se·quence [ˈkɒnsɪkwəns] (result) conseguenza f

con·se·quent·ly [ˈkɒnsɪkwəntlɪ] adv (therefore) di conseguenza

con·ser·va·tion [kɒnsəˈveɪʃn] (preservation) tutela f

con·ser'va·tion area f soggetta a vincoli urbanistici e ambientali

con·ser·va·tion·ist [kɒnsəˈveɪʃnɪst] ambientalista m/f

con·ser·va·tive [kənˈsɜːvətɪv] **1** adj (conventional) conservatore; clothes tradizionale; estimate cauto; **Conservative** Br POL conservatore **2** n Br POL **Conservative** conservatore m, -trice f con·ser·va·to·ry [kən'sɜːvətrɪ] veranda f; MUS conservatorio m

con·serve ['kɒnsɜːv] **1** n (jam) marmellata f **2** v/t [kən'sɜːv] energy, strength risparmiare

con·sid·er [kən'sɪdə(r)] v/t (regard) considerare; (show regard for) tener conto di; (think about) pensare a; ~ **doing sth** prendere in considerazione la possibilità di fare qc; **it is ~ed to be his best work** è considerata la sua opera migliore

con·sid·er·a·ble [kən'sɪdrəbl] adj considerevole

con·sid·er·a·bly [kən'sɪdrəblɪ] adv considerevolmente

con·sid·er·ate [kən'sɪdərət] adj person, attitude premuroso; **be ~ of** avere riguardo per

con·sid·er·ate·ly [kən'sɪdərətlɪ] adv premurosamente

con·sid·er·a·tion [kənsɪdə'reɪʃn] (thought) considerazione f; (thoughtfulness, concern) riguardo m; (factor) fattore m; **take sth into ~** prendere in considerazione qc; **under ~** in esame

con·sign·ment [kən'saɪnmənt] COM consegna f

♦ con·sist of [kən'sɪst] v/t consistere in

con·sis·ten·cy [kən'sɪstənsɪ] (texture) consistenza f; (unchangingness) coerenza f

con·sis·tent [kən'sɪstənt] adj (unchanging) coerente

con·sis·tent·ly [kən'sɪstəntlɪ] adv in modo coerente; always costantemente

con·so·la·tion [kɒnsə'leɪʃn] consolazione f

con·sole [kən'səʊl] v/t consolare

con·sol·i·date [kən'sɒlɪdeɪt] v/t consolidare

con·so·nant ['kɒnsənənt] n GRAM consonante f

con·sor·ti·um [kən'sɔːtɪəm] consorzio m

con·spic·u·ous [kən'spɪkjʊəs] adj: **be** / **look** ~ spiccare; **feel** ~ sentirsi fuori posto

con·spir·a·cy [kən'spɪrəsɪ] cospirazione f

con·spir·a·tor [kən'spɪrətə(r)] cospiratore m, -trice f

con·spire [kən'spaɪə(r)] v/i cospirare

con·stant ['kɒnstənt] adj (continuous) costante

con·stant·ly ['kɒnstəntlɪ] adv costantemente

con·ster·na·tion [kɒnstə'neɪʃn] costernazione f

con·sti·pat·ed ['kɒnstɪpeɪtɪd] adj stitico

con·sti·pa·tion [kɒnstɪ'peɪʃn] stitichezza f

con·stit·u·en·cy [kən'stɪtjʊənsɪ] Br POL circoscrizione f elettorale

con·stit·u·ent [kən'stɪtjʊənt] n (component) componente m; Br POL elettore m, -trice f

con·sti·tute ['kɒnstɪtjuːt] v/t costituire

con·sti·tu·tion [kɒnstɪ'tjuːʃn] also POL costituzione f

con·sti·tu·tion·al [kɒnstɪ'tjuːʃənl] adj POL costituzionale

con·straint [kən'streɪnt] (restriction) restrizione f

con·struct [kən'strʌkt] v/t building etc costruire

con·struc·tion [kən'strʌkʃn] costruzione f; **under ~** in costruzione

con·struc·tion in·dus·try edilizia f; **con'struc·tion site** cantiere m edile; **con'struc·tion work·er** operaio m edile

con·struc·tive [kən'strʌktɪv] adj costruttivo

con·sul ['kɒnsl] console m

con·su·late ['kɒnsjʊlət] consolato m

con·sult [kən'sʌlt] v/t (seek the advice of) consultare

con·sul·tan·cy [kən'sʌltənsɪ] (company) società f inv di consulenza; (advice) consulenza f

con·sul·tant [kən'sʌltənt] n (adviser) consulente m/f

con·sul·ta·tion [kɒnsəl'teɪʃn] consultazione f

con·sult·ing hours orario m di visita

con·sult·ing room ambulatorio *m*
con·sume [kən'sjuːm] *v/t* consumare
con·sum·er [kən'sjuːmə(r)] (*purchaser*) consumatore *m*, -trice *f*
con·sum·er 'con·fi·dence fiducia *f* dei consumatori; **con'sum·er goods** *npl* beni *mpl* di consumo; **con'sum·er so·ci·e·ty** società *f inv* dei consumi
con·sump·tion [kən'sʌmpʃn] consumo *m*
con·tact ['kɒntækt] **1** *n* contatto *m*; (*person*) conoscenza *f*; **keep in ~ with s.o.** mantenere i contatti con qu **2** *v/t* mettersi in contatto con
'con·tact lens lente *f* a contatto
'con·tact num·ber numero *m* presso cui si è reperibili
con·ta·gious [kən'teɪdʒəs] *adj also fig* contagioso
con·tain [kən'teɪn] *v/t* (*hold*) contenere; *flood, disease, revolt* contenere; **~ o.s.** contenersi
con·tain·er [kən'teɪnə(r)] (*recipient*) contenitore *m*; COM container *m inv*
con'tain·er ship nave *f* portacontainer
con·tam·i·nate [kən'tæmɪneɪt] *v/t* contaminare
con·tam·i·na·tion [kəntæmɪ'neɪʃn] contaminazione *f*
con·tem·plate ['kɒntəmpleɪt] *v/t* (*look at*) contemplare; (*think about*) considerare; **~ doing sth** considerare la possibilità di fare qc
con·tem·po·ra·ry [kən'tempərərɪ] **1** *adj* contemporaneo **2** *n* coetaneo *m*, -a *f*
con·tempt [kən'tempt] disprezzo *m*; **be beneath ~** essere spregevole
con·temp·ti·ble [kən'temptəbl] *adj* spregevole
con·temp·tu·ous [kən'temptjʊəs] *adj* sprezzante
con·tend [kən'tend] *v/i*: **~ for sth** contendersi qc; **~ with s.o. / sth** confrontarsi con qc / qu
con·tend·er [kən'tendə(r)] *in sport, competition* concorrente *m/f*; *against*

champion sfidante *m/f*; POL candidato *m*, -a *f*
con·tent[1] ['kɒntent] *n* contenuto *m*
con·tent[2] [kən'tent] **1** *adj* contento **2** *v/t*: **~ o.s. with** accontentarsi di
con·tent·ed [kən'tentɪd] *adj* contento
con·ten·tion [kən'tenʃn] (*assertion*) opinione *f*; **be in ~ for** essere in lizza per
con·ten·tious [kən'tenʃəs] *adj* polemico
con·tent·ment [kən'tentmənt] soddisfazione *f*
con·tents ['kɒntents] *npl of house, letter, bag etc* contenuto *m*
con·test[1] ['kɒntest] *n* (*competition*) concorso *m*; (*struggle, for power*) lotta *f*
con·test[2] [kən'test] *v/t leadership etc* essere in lizza per; *will* impugnare
con·tes·tant [kən'testənt] concorrente *m/f*
con·text ['kɒntekst] contesto *m*; **look at sth in ~ / out of ~** considerare qc in / fuori contesto
con·ti·nent ['kɒntɪnənt] *n* continente *m*; **the ~** l'Europa continentale
con·ti·nen·tal [kɒntɪ'nentl] *adj* continentale
con·ti·nen·tal 'break·fast *colazione f a base di caffè, pane, burro e marmellata*
con·tin·gen·cy [kən'tɪndʒənsɪ] eventualità *f inv*
con·tin·u·al [kən'tɪnjʊəl] *adj* continuo
con·tin·u·al·ly [kən'tɪnjʊəlɪ] *adv* continuamente
con·tin·u·a·tion [kəntɪnjʊ'eɪʃn] seguito *m*
con·tin·ue [kən'tɪnjuː] **1** *v/t* continuare; **~ doing sth** continuare a fare qc; **to be ~d** continua ... **2** *v/i* continuare
con·ti·nu·i·ty [kɒntɪ'njuːətɪ] continuità *f inv*; *in films* ordine *m* della sceneggiatura
con·tin·u·ous [kən'tɪnjʊəs] *adj* ininterrotto

con·tin·u·ous·ly [kən'tɪnjʊəslɪ] *adv* ininterrottamente

con·tort [kən'tɔːt] *v/t* contorcere

con·tour ['kɒntʊə(r)] profilo *m*; *on map* curva *f* di livello

con·tra·cep·tion [kɒntrə'sepʃn] contraccezione *f*

con·tra·cep·tive [kɒntrə'septɪv] *n* anticoncezionale *m*, contraccettivo *m*

con·tract[1] ['kɒntrækt] *n* contratto *m*

con·tract[2] [kən'trækt] **1** *v/i* (*shrink*) contrarsi **2** *v/t illness* contrarre

con·trac·tor [kən'træktə(r)] appaltatore *m*, -trice *f*; **building ~** ditta *f* di appalti (edili)

con·trac·tu·al [kən'træktjʊəl] *adj* contrattuale

con·tra·dict [kɒntrə'dɪkt] *v/t* contraddire

con·tra·dic·tion [kɒntrə'dɪkʃn] contraddizione *f*

con·tra·dic·to·ry [kɒntrə'dɪktrɪ] *adj account* contraddittorio

con·trap·tion [kən'træpʃn] F aggeggio *m*

con·tra·ry[1] ['kɒntrərɪ] **1** *adj* contrario; **~ to** contrariamente a **2** *n*: **on the ~** al contrario

con·tra·ry[2] [kən'treərɪ] *adj*: **be ~** (*perverse*) essere un bastian contrario

con·trast ['kɒntrɑːst] **1** *n* contrasto *m*; **by ~** invece **2** *v/t* [kən'trɑːst] confrontare **3** *v/i* contrastare

con·trast·ing [kən'trɑːstɪŋ] *adj* contrastante

con·tra·vene [kɒntrə'viːn] *v/t* contravvenire a

con·trib·ute [kən'trɪbjuːt] **1** *v/i with money, material, time* contribuire; *to magazine, paper* collaborare (**to** con); *to discussion* intervenire (**to** in); (*help to cause*) contribuire a creare **2** *v/t money* contribuire con

con·tri·bu·tion [kɒntrɪ'bjuːʃn] *money* offerta *f*; *to political party, church* donazione *f*; *of time, effort* contributo *m*; *to debate* intervento *m*; *to magazine* collaborazione *f*

con·trib·u·tor [kən'trɪbjʊtə(r)] *of money* finanziatore *m*, -trice *f*; *to magazine* collaboratore *m*, -trice *f*

con·trol [kən'trəʊl] **1** *n* controllo *m*; **take ~ of** assumere il controllo di; **lose ~ of** perdere il controllo di; **lose ~ of o.s.** perdere il controllo; **circumstances beyond our ~** cause indipendenti dalla nostra volontà; **be in ~ of sth** tenere qc sotto controllo; **get out of ~** diventare incontrollabile; **the situation is under ~** la situazione è sotto controllo; **bring a blaze under ~** circoscrivere un incendio; **~s** *of aircraft, vehicle* comandi *m*; **~s** (*restrictions*) restrizioni **2** *v/t* (*pret & pp* **-led**) (*govern*) controllare; *traffic* dirigere; (*restrict*) contenere; (*regulate*) regolare; **~ o.s.** controllarsi

con'trol cen·ter *Am*, **con'trol cen·tre** centro *m* di controllo

con'trol freak F *persona f che vuole avere tutto e tutti sotto controllo*

con·trolled 'sub·stance [kən'trəʊld] sostanza *f* stupefacente

con·trol·ling 'in·ter·est [kən'trəʊlɪŋ] FIN maggioranza *f* delle azioni

con'trol pan·el quadro *m* dei comandi

con'trol tow·er torre *f* di controllo

con·tro·ver·sial [kɒntrə'vɜːʃl] *adj* controverso

con·tro·ver·sy ['kɒntrəvɜːsɪ] polemica *f*

con·va·lesce [kɒnvə'les] *v/i* rimettersi (in salute)

con·va·les·cence [kɒnvə'lesns] convalescenza *f*

con·vene [kən'viːn] *v/t* indire

con·ve·ni·ence [kən'viːnɪəns] *of having sth, location* comodità *f inv*; **at my / your ~** a mio/tuo comodo; **all** (**modern**) **~s** tutti i comfort

con've·ni·ence food scatolame *m*, *cibi precotti ecc*

con've·ni·ence store negozio *m* alimentari

con·ve·ni·ent [kən'viːnɪənt] *adj location, device* comodo; **whenever**

it's ~ quando ti va bene

con·ve·ni·ent·ly [kən'vi:nɪəntlɪ] *adv* comodamente

con·vent ['kɒnvənt] convento *m*

con·ven·tion [kən'venʃn] *(tradition)* convenzione *f*; *(conference)* congresso *m*

con·ven·tion·al [kən'venʃnl] *adj person, ideas* convenzionale; *method* tradizionale

♦ con·verge on [kən'vɜːdʒ] *v/t* convergere su

con·ver·sant [kən'vɜːsənt] *adj*: *be ~ with* essere pratico di

con·ver·sa·tion [kɒnvə'seɪʃn] conversazione *f*

con·ver·sa·tion·al [kɒnvə'seɪʃnl] *adj* colloquiale

con·verse ['kɒnvɜːs] *n (opposite)* contrario *m*

con·verse·ly [kən'vɜːslɪ] *adv* per contro

con·ver·sion [kən'vɜːʃn] conversione *f*; *of house* trasformazione *f*

con'ver·sion ta·ble tabella *f* di conversione

con·vert ['kɒnvɜːt] **1** *n* convertito *m*, -a *f* **2** *v/t* [kən'vɜːt] convertire **3** *v/i* trasformarsi (*into* in); *house, room* trasformare

con·ver·ti·ble [kən'vɜːtəbl] *n car* cabriolet *f inv*, decappottabile *f*

con·vey [kən'veɪ] *v/t (transmit)* comunicare; *(carry)* trasportare

con'vey·or belt [kən'veɪə(r)] nastro *m* trasportatore

con·vict ['kɒnvɪkt] **1** *n* carcerato *m*, -a *f* **2** *v/t* [kən'vɪkt] LAW condannare; *~ s.o. of sth* condannare qu per qc

con·vic·tion [kən'vɪkʃn] LAW condanna *f*; *(belief)* convinzione *f*

con·vince [kən'vɪns] *v/t* convincere

con·vinc·ing [kən'vɪnsɪŋ] *adj* convincente

con·viv·i·al [kən'vɪvɪəl] *adj (friendly)* gioviale

con·voy ['kɒnvɔɪ] convoglio *m*

con·vul·sion [kən'vʌlʃn] MED convulsione *f*

cook [kʊk] **1** *n* cuoco *m*, -a *f*; *I'm a*

good ~ cucino bene **2** *v/t vegetables, meat* cucinare; *meal, dinner* preparare; *a ~ed meal* un pasto caldo; ~ *the books* F falsificare i registri **3** *v/i of person* cucinare; *of vegetables, meat* cuocere

'cook·book ricettario *m*

cook·er ['kʊkə(r)] cucina *f*

cook·e·ry ['kʊkərɪ] cucina *f*

'cook·e·ry book ricettario *m*

cook·ie ['kʊkɪ] *Am* biscotto *m*

cook·ing ['kʊkɪŋ] *food* cucina *f*; *he does all the* ~ è lui che cucina

cool [ku:l] **1** *n* F: *keep / lose one's* ~ conservare / perdere la calma **2** *adj weather, breeze, drink* fresco; *(calm)* calmo; *(unfriendly)* freddo **3** *v/i of food* raffreddarsi; *of tempers* calmarsi; *of interest* raffreddarsi **4** *v/t* F: ~ *it!* calma!

♦ cool down **1** *v/i* raffreddarsi; *of weather* rinfrescare; *fig: of tempers* calmarsi **2** *v/t food* raffreddare; *fig* calmare

cool·ing-'off pe·ri·od periodo *m* di riflessione

co·op·e·rate [kəʊ'ɒpəreɪt] *v/i* cooperare

co·op·e·ra·tion [kəʊɒpə'reɪʃn] cooperazione *f*

co·op·e·ra·tive [kəʊ'ɒpərətɪv] **1** *n* COM cooperativa *f* **2** *adj* COM cooperativo; *(helpful)* disponibile (a collaborare)

co·or·di·nate [kəʊ'ɔːdɪneɪt] *v/t* coordinare

co·or·di·na·tion [kəʊɔːdɪ'neɪʃn] *of activities* coordinamento *m*; *of body* coordinazione *f*

cop [kɒp] *n* F poliziotto *m*

cope [kəʊp] *v/i* farcela; ~ *with* farcela con

cop·i·er ['kɒpɪə(r)] *machine* fotocopiatrice *f*

co·pi·lot ['kəʊpaɪlət] secondo pilota *m*

co·pi·ous ['kəʊpɪəs] *adj* abbondante

cop·per ['kɒpə(r)] *n metal* rame *m*

cop·y ['kɒpɪ] **1** *n* copia *f*; *written material* materiale *m*; *fair* ~ bella copia *f*; *rough* ~ brutta copia *f*;

make a ~ **of a file** fare una copia di un file **2** v/t (pret & pp **-ied**) copiare

'cop·y·cat F copiare m, -a f F; **cop·y·cat 'crime** reato m a imitazione di un altro; 'cop·y·right n diritti mpl d'autore, copyright m inv; 'cop·y·writ·er in advertising copywriter m

cor·al ['kɔrəl] corallo m

cord [kɔːd] (string) corda f; (cable) filo m

cor·di·al ['kɔːdɪəl] adj cordiale

cord·less 'phone ['kɔːdlɪs] cordless m inv

cor·don ['kɔːdn] cordone m

♦ cor·don off v/t transennare; put cordon around recintare

cords [kɔːdz] npl trousers pantaloni mpl di velluto a coste

cor·du·roy ['kɔːdərɔɪ] velluto m a coste

core [kɔː(r)] **1** n of fruit torsolo m; of problem nocciolo m; of organization, party cuore m **2** v/t fruit togliere il torsolo a **3** adj issue, meaning essenziale

cork [kɔːk] in bottle tappo m di sughero; (material) sughero m

'cork·screw n cavatappi m inv

corn [kɔːn] grain frumento m; Am (maize) granturco m

cor·ner ['kɔːnə(r)] **1** n of page, room, street angolo m; of table spigolo m; in football calcio m d'angolo, corner m inv; **in the ~** nell'angolo; **on the ~** of street all'angolo; **around the ~** dietro l'angolo **2** v/t person bloccare; ~ **a market** prendersi il monopolio di un mercato **3** v/i of driver, car affrontare una curva

'cor·ner kick in football calcio m d'angolo

'cor·ner shop piccola drogheria f

'corn·flakes npl fiocchi mpl di granturco, cornflakes mpl

'corn·flour farina f di granturco

corn·y ['kɔːnɪ] adj F scontato; sentimental sdolcinato

cor·o·na·ry ['kɔrənərɪ] **1** adj coronario **2** n infarto m

cor·o·ner ['kɔrənə(r)] ufficiale m pubblico che indaga sui casi di morte sospetta

cor·po·ral ['kɔːpərəl] n caporale m maggiore

cor·po·ral 'pun·ish·ment punizione f corporale

cor·po·rate ['kɔːpərət] adj COM aziendale; ~ **image** corporate image f inv; **sense of ~ loyalty** corporativismo m

cor·po·ra·tion [kɔːpə'reɪʃn] (business) corporation f inv

corps [kɔː(r)] nsg corpo m

corpse [kɔːps] cadavere m

cor·pu·lent ['kɔːpjʊlənt] adj corpulento

cor·pus·cle ['kɔːpʌsl] globulo m

cor·rect [kə'rekt] **1** adj giusto; behaviour corretto; **she's ~** ha ragione **2** v/t correggere

cor·rec·tion [kə'rekʃn] correzione f

cor·rect·ly [kə'rektlɪ] adv giustamente; behave correttamente

cor·re·spond [kɔrɪ'spɒnd] v/i (match, write) corrispondere; ~ **to** corrispondere a; ~ **with** corrispondere con

cor·re·spon·dence [kɔrɪ'spɒndəns] (agreement, letters) corrispondenza f

cor·re·spon·dent [kɔrɪ'spɒndənt] corrispondente m/f

cor·re·spon·ding [kɔrɪ'spɒndɪŋ] adj (equivalent) corrispondente

cor·ri·dor ['kɔrɪdɔː(r)] in building corridoio m

cor·rob·o·rate [kə'rɒbəreɪt] v/t corroborare

cor·rode [kə'rəʊd] v/t & v/i corrodere

cor·ro·sion [kə'rəʊʒn] corrosione f

cor·ru·gated 'card·board ['kɒrəgeɪtɪd] cartone m ondulato

cor·ru·gated 'i·ron lamiera f (di ferro) ondulata

cor·rupt [kə'rʌpt] **1** adj also COMPUT corrotto; v/t morals, youth traviare; (bribe) corrompere

cor·rup·tion [kə'rʌpʃn] corruzione f

Cor·si·ca ['kɔːsɪkə] Corsica f

Cor·si·can ['kɔːsɪkən] **1** adj corso **2** n corso m, -a f

cos·met·ic [koz'metɪk] *adj* cosmetico; *surgery* estetico; *fig* di facciata
cos·met·ics [koz'metɪks] *npl* cosmetici *mpl*
cos·met·ic 'sur·geon chirurgo *m* estetico
cos·met·ic 'sur·ger·y chirurgia *f* estetica
cos·mo·naut ['kozmənɔːt] cosmonauta *m/f*
cos·mo·pol·i·tan [kozmə'polɪtən] *adj city* cosmopolitano
cost¹ [kost] **1** *n also fig* costo *m*; *at all ~s* a ogni costo; *I've learnt to my ~* l'ho imparato a mie spese; *~s* LAW spese **2** *v/t* (*pret & pp* **cost**) costare; FIN: *proposal, project* fare il preventivo di; *how much does it ~?* quanto costa?; *it ~ me my health* ci ho rimesso la salute
cost² [kost] *v/t* (*pret & pp* **costed**) FIN: *proposal, project* fare il preventivo di
cost and 'freight COM costo e nolo; **'cost-con·scious** *adj*: *be ~* fare attenzione ai consumi; **'cost-ef·fec·tive** *adj* conveniente; **'cost, insurance and freight** COM costo, assicurazione e nolo
cost·ly ['kostlɪ] *adj mistake* costoso; *it would be a ~ mistake* potresti pagarla cara
cost of 'liv·ing costo *m* della vita
cost 'price prezzo *m* di costo
cos·tume ['kostjuːm] *for actor* costume *m*
cos·tume 'jew·el·lery, *Am* **cos·tume 'jew·el·ry** bigiotteria *f*
co·sy *adj* (*comfortable*) gradevole; (*intimate and friendly*) intimo; *be nice and ~ in bed* starsene al calduccio a letto; *a nice ~ little job* un lavoretto tranquillo
cot [kot] *for child* lettino *m*
cot·tage ['kotɪdʒ] cottage *m inv*
cot·tage 'cheese fiocchi *mpl* di latte
cot·ton ['kotn] **1** *n* cotone *m* **2** *adj* di cotone
♦ **cotton on** *v/i* F afferrare F
♦ **cotton on to** *v/t* F afferrare F
cot·ton 'wool ovatta *f*

couch [kautʃ] *n* divano *m*
'couch po·ta·to F teledipendente *m/f*
cou·chette [kuː'ʃet] cuccetta *f*
cough [kof] **1** *n* tosse *f*; *to get attention* colpetto *m* di tosse **2** *v/i* tossire; *to get attention* tossicchiare
♦ **cough up 1** *v/t blood etc* sputare; F *money* cacciar fuori F **2** *v/i* F (*pay*) cacciare i soldi F
'cough medicine, 'cough syrup sciroppo *m* per la tosse
could¹ [kud] *v/aux*: *~ I have my key?* mi dà la chiave?; *~ you help me?* mi puoi dare una mano?; *this ~ be our bus* questo potrebbe essere il nostro autobus; *you ~ be right* magari hai ragione; *I ~n't say for sure* non potrei giurarci; *he ~ have got lost* può darsi che si sia smarrito; *you ~ have warned me!* in indignation avresti potuto avvisarmi!
could² [kud] *pret* → **can**
coun·cil ['kaunsl] *n* (*assembly*) consiglio *m*; (*city* ~) comune *m*
'coun·cil house casa *f* popolare
coun·cil·lor ['kaunsələ(r)] consigliere *m*, -a *f* (comunale)
'coun·cil tax imposta *f* comunale sugli immobili
coun·sel ['kaunsl] **1** *n* (*advice*) consiglio *m*; (*lawyer*) avvocato *m* **2** *v/t course of action* consigliare; *person* offrire consulenza a
coun·sel·ing *Am*, **coun·sel·ling** ['kaunslɪŋ] terapia *f*
coun·sel·or, *Am* **coun·sel·or** ['kaunslə(r)] (*adviser*) consulente *m/f*
count¹ [kaunt] *aristrocrat* conte *m*
count² [kaunt] **1** *n* conteggio *m*; *keep/lose ~ of* tenere/perdere il conto di; *what's your ~?* quanti ne hai contati? **2** *v/i* contare; *that doesn't ~* questo non conta **3** *v/t* contare; *~ yourself lucky* considerati fortunato
♦ **count on** *v/t* contare su
'count·down conto *m* alla rovescia
coun·te·nance ['kauntənəns] *v/t* approvare

coun·ter[1] ['kaʊntə(r)] *in shop, café* banco *m; in game* segnalino *m*

coun·ter[2] ['kaʊntə(r)] **1** *v/t* neutralizzare **2** *v/i (retaliate)* rispondere

coun·ter[3] ['kaʊntə(r)] *adv:* **run ~ to** andare contro

'**coun·ter·act** *v/t* neutralizzare

coun·ter-at·tack 1 *n* contrattacco *m* **2** *v/i* contrattaccare

'**coun·ter·bal·ance 1** *n* contrappeso *m* **2** *v/t* fare da contrappeso a

coun·ter'es·pi·o·nage controspionaggio *m*

coun·ter·feit ['kaʊntəfɪt] **1** *v/t* falsificare **2** *adj* falso

coun·ter·foil ['kaʊntəfɔɪl] matrice *f*

'**coun·ter·part** *person* omologo *m*, -a *f*

coun·ter·pro'duc·tive *adj* controproducente

'**coun·ter·sign** *v/t* controfirmare

coun·tess ['kaʊntɪs] contessa *f*

count·less ['kaʊntlɪs] *adj* innumerevole

coun·try ['kʌntrɪ] **1** *n (nation)* paese *m; as opposed to town* campagna *f; in the ~* in campagna **2** *adj* **roads, life** di campagna

coun·try and 'west·ern MUS country and western *m inv;* '**coun·try·man** (*fellow ~*) connazionale *m;* '**coun·try·side** campagna *f*

coun·ty ['kaʊntɪ] contea *f*

coup [kuː] POL colpo *m* di stato, golpe *m inv; fig* colpo *m*

cou·ple ['kʌpl] *n* coppia *f; just a ~* solo un paio; *a ~ of* un paio di

cou·pon ['kuːpɒn] buono *m*

cour·age ['kʌrɪdʒ] coraggio *m*

cou·ra·geous [kə'reɪdʒəs] *adj* coraggioso

cou·ri·er ['kʊrɪə(r)] *(messenger)* corriere *m; with tourist party* accompagnatore *m* turistico, accompagnatrice *f* turistica

course [kɔːs] *n series of lessons* corso *m; part of meal* portata *f; of ship, plane* rotta *f; for golf* campo *m; for race, skiing* pista *f; of ~ (certainly)* certo; *(naturally)* ovviamente; *of ~ not* certo che no; *first ~* primo *m;*

second ~ secondo *m; ~ of action* linea *f* di condotta; *~ of treatment* cura *f; in the ~ of* nel corso di

court [kɔːt] *n* LAW corte *f; (courthouse)* tribunale *m;* SP campo *m; take s.o. to ~* fare causa a qu; *out of ~* in via amichevole

'**court case** caso *m* (giudiziario)

cour·te·ous ['kɜːtɪəs] *adj* cortese

cour·te·sy ['kɜːtəsɪ] cortesia *f*

'**court·house** tribunale *m*, palazzo *m* di giustizia; **court 'mar·tial 1** *n* corte *f* marziale **2** *v/t* processare in corte marziale; '**court or·der** ingiunzione *f* del tribunale; '**court·room** aula *f* del tribunale; '**court·yard** cortile *m*

cous·in ['kʌzn] cugino *m*, -a *f*

cove [kəʊv] *small bay* cala *f*

cov·er ['kʌvə(r)] **1** *n protective* fodera *f; of book, magazine* copertina *f; (shelter)* riparo *m; insurance* copertura *f; ~s for bed* coperte *fpl; take ~* ripararsi **2** *v/t* coprire; *distance* percorrere; *of journalist* fare un servizio su; *we're not ~ed for theft* non siamo coperti contro i furti

◆ **cover up 1** *v/t* coprire; *fig* insabbiare **2** *v/i:* **cover up for s.o.** *fig* coprire qu

cov·er·age ['kʌvərɪdʒ] *by media* copertura *f; the trial got a lot of ~* il processo ha avuto molta risonanza

cov·er·ing let·ter ['kʌvrɪŋ] lettera *f* d'accompagnamento

cov·ert [kəʊ'vɜːt] *adj* segreto

'**cov·er-up** insabbiamento *m; it looks like a ~* sembra che qualcuno stia cercando di insabbiare le prove

cow [kaʊ] mucca *f*

cow·ard ['kaʊəd] vigliacco *m*, -a *f*

cow·ard·ice ['kaʊədɪs] vigliaccheria *f*

cow·ard·ly ['kaʊədlɪ] *adj* vile

'**cow·boy** cow-boy *m inv*

cow·er ['kaʊə(r)] *v/i* rannicchiarsi

coy [kɔɪ] *adj (evasive)* evasivo; *(flirtatious)* civettuolo

'**coz·y** *Am* → **cosy**

CPU [siːpiː'juː] *abbr* (= *central*

processing unit) unità *f* centrale di elaborazione

crab [kræb] *n* granchio *m*

crack [kræk] **1** *n* crepa *f*; (*joke*) battuta *f* **2** *v/t cup, glass* incrinare; *nut* schiacciare; *code* decifrare; F (*solve*) risolvere; **~ a joke** fare una battuta **3** *v/i* incrinarsi; **get ~ing** F darsi una mossa F

♦ **crack down on** *v/t* prendere serie misure contro

♦ **crack up** *v/i* (*have breakdown*) avere un esaurimento; F (*laugh*) scoppiare a ridere

'crack·brained *adj* F pazzoide *f*

'crack·down intensificazione *f* dei controlli (**on** su)

cracked [krækt] *adj cup, glass* incrinato; F (*crazy*) tocco F

crack·er ['krækə(r)] *to eat* cracker *m inv*

crack·le ['krækl] *v/i of fire* schioppettare

cra·dle ['kreɪdl] *n for baby* culla *f*

craft[1] [krɑːft] NAUT imbarcazione *f*

craft[2] [krɑːft] (*skill*) abilità *f inv* artigiana; (*trade*) mestiere *m*

crafts·man ['krɑːftsmən] artigiano *m*

craft·y ['krɑːftɪ] *adj* astuto

crag [kræg] *rock* rupe *f*

cram [kræm] *v/t papers, food* infilare; *people* stipare

cramp [kræmp] *n* crampo *m*

cramped [kræmpt] *adj room, flat* esiguo

cran·ber·ry ['krænbərɪ] mirtillo *m*

crane [kreɪn] **1** *n machine* gru *f inv* **2** *v/t:* **~ one's neck** allungare il collo

crank [kræŋk] *n strange person* tipo *m* strambo

'crank·shaft albero *m* a gomiti

crash [kræʃ] **1** *n noise* fragore *m*; *accident* incidente *m*; COM crollo *m*; COMPUT crash *m inv* **2** *v/i fall noisily* fracassarsi; *of thunder* rombare; *of car* schiantarsi; *of two cars* scontrarsi, schiantarsi; *of plane* precipitare; COM: *of market* crollare; COMPUT fare un crash; F (*sleep*) dormire **3** *v/t car* avere un incidente con

♦ **crash out** *v/i* F (*fall asleep*) addormentarsi; *without meaning to* crollare F

'crash bar·ri·er barriera *f* protettiva; **'crash course** corso *m* intensivo; **'crash di·et** dieta *f* lampo; **'crash hel·met** casco *m* (di protezione); **'crash-land** *v/i* fare un atterraggio di fortuna; **'crash land·ing** atterraggio *m* di fortuna

crate [kreɪt] (*packing case*) cassetta *f*

cra·ter ['kreɪtə(r)] *of volcano* cratere *m*

crave [kreɪv] *v/t* smaniare dalla voglia di

crav·ing ['kreɪvɪŋ] voglia *f*; *pej* smania *f*

crawl [krɔːl] **1** *n in swimming* crawl *m*, stile *m* libero; *at a ~* (*very slowly*) a passo d'uomo **2** *v/i on floor* andare (a) carponi; (*move slowly*) avanzare lentamente

♦ **crawl with** *v/t* brulicare di

cray·on ['kreɪən] *n* matita *f* colorata; *wax* pastello *m* a cera

craze [kreɪz] moda *f*

cra·zy ['kreɪzɪ] *adj* pazzo; **be ~ about s.o.** essere pazzo di qu; **be ~ about sth** andare matto per qc

creak [kriːk] **1** *n* scricchiolio *m* **2** *v/i* scricchiolare

creak·y ['kriːkɪ] *adj* che scricchiola

cream [kriːm] **1** *n for skin* crema *f*; *for coffee, cake* panna *f*; *colour* color *m* panna **2** *adj* color panna

cream 'cheese formaggio *m* fresco da spalmare

cream·er ['kriːmə(r)] *for coffee* panna *f* liofilizzata

cream·y ['kriːmɪ] *adj* (*with lots of cream*) cremoso

crease [kriːs] **1** *n accidental* grinza *f*; *deliberate* piega *f* **2** *v/t accidentally* sgualcire

cre·ate [kriː'eɪt] *v/t* creare

cre·a·tion [kriː'eɪʃn] creazione *f*

cre·a·tive [kriː'eɪtɪv] *adj* creativo

cre·a·tor [kriː'eɪtə(r)] creatore *m*, -trice *f*; **the Creator** REL il Creatore

crea·ture ['kriːtʃə(r)] creatura *f*

crèche [kreʃ] *for children* asilo *m* nido; REL presepe *m*

cred·i·bil·i·ty [kredə'bılətı] credibilità *f inv*

cred·i·ble ['kredəbl] *adj* credibile

cred·it ['kredıt] **1** *n* FIN credito *m*; (*honour*) merito *m*; *be in ~* avere un saldo attivo; *get the ~ for sth* prendersi il merito di qc **2** *v/t* (*believe*) credere; *~ an amount to an account* accreditare una cifra su un conto

cred·i·ta·ble ['kredıtəbl] *adj* lodevole

'cred·it card carta *f* di credito

'cred·it lim·it limite *m* di credito

cred·i·tor ['kredıtə(r)] creditore *m*, -trice *f*

'cred·it·wor·thy *adj* solvibile

cred·u·lous ['kredjʊləs] *adj* credulo

creed [kri:d] credo *m inv*

creep [kri:p] **1** *n pej* tipo *m* odioso **2** *v/i* (*pret & pp* **crept**) *quietly* avanzare quatto quatto; *slowly* avanzare lentamente

creep·er ['kri:pə(r)] BOT rampicante *m*

creeps [kri:ps] *npl* F: *the house / he gives me the ~* la casa / lui mi fa venire la pelle d'oca

creep·y ['kri:pı] *adj* F che dà i brividi; *be ~* F far paura

cre·mate [krı'meıt] *v/t* cremare

cre·ma·tion [krı'meıʃn] cremazione *f*

cre·ma·to·ri·um [kremə'tɔ:rıəm] crematorio *m*

crept [krept] *pret & pp* → **creep**

cres·cent ['kresənt] *n shape* mezzaluna *f*

crest [krest] *of hill, bird* cresta *f*

crest·fal·len *adj* abbattuto

cre·vasse [krə'væs] voraggine *f*

crev·ice ['krevıs] crepa *f*

crew [kru:] *n of ship, plane* equipaggio *m*; *of workers etc* squadra *f*; (*film ~*) troupe *f inv*; (*crowd, group*) ghenga *f*

'crew cut taglio *m* a spazzola

'crew neck girocollo *m*

crick [krık] *n*: *~ in the neck* torcicollo *m*

crick·et ['krıkıt] *insect* grillo *m*; *game* cricket *m inv*

crime [kraım] (*offence*) reato *m*; (*criminality*) criminalità *f inv*; (*shameful act*) crimine *m*

crim·i·nal ['krımınl] **1** *n* delinquente *m/f* **2** *adj* LAW penale; (*shameful*) vergognoso; *a ~ offence* un reato

crim·son ['krımzn] *adj* cremisi *inv*

cringe [krındʒ] *v/i* morire di vergogna

crip·ple ['krıpl] **1** *n* (*disabled person*) invalido *m*, -a *f* **2** *v/t person* rendere invalido; *fig* paralizzare

cri·sis ['kraısıs] (*pl* **crises** ['kraısı:z]) crisi *f inv*

crisp [krısp] *adj weather, air, lettuce, new shirt* fresco; *bacon, toast* croccante; *bank notes* nuovo di zecca

crisps [krısps] *npl Br* patatine *fpl*

cri·te·ri·on [kraı'tıərıən] criterio *m*

crit·ic ['krıtık] critico *m*, -a *f*

crit·i·cal ['krıtıkl] *adj* critico

crit·i·cal·ly ['krıtıklı] *adv speak etc* criticamente; *~ ill* gravemente malato

crit·i·cis·m ['krıtısızm] critica *f*

crit·i·cize ['krıtısaız] *v/t* criticare

croak [krəʊk] **1** *n of frog* gracidio *m*; *of person* rantolo *m* **2** *v/i of frog* gracidare; *of person* parlare con voce rauca

cro·chet ['krəʊʃeı] **1** *n* lavoro *m* all'uncinetto **2** *v/t* lavorare all'uncinetto

crock·e·ry ['krɒkərı] stoviglie *fpl*

croc·o·dile ['krɒkədaıl] coccodrillo *m*

cro·cus ['krəʊkəs] croco *m*

cro·ny ['krəʊnı] F amico *m*, -a *f*

crook [krʊk] *n* truffatore *m*, -trice *f*

crook·ed ['krʊkıd] *adj streets* tortuoso; *picture* storto; (*dishonest*) disonesto

crop [krɒp] **1** *n* raccolto *m*; *type of grain etc* coltura *f*; *fig* scaglione *m* **2** *v/t* (*pret & pp* **-ped**) *hair, photo* tagliare

♦ **crop up** *v/i* venir fuori

cross [krɒs] **1** adj (angry) arrabbiato **2** n croce f **3** v/t (go across) attraversare; ~ **o.s.** REL farsi il segno della croce; ~ **one's legs** accavallare le gambe; **keep one's fingers** ~ed fare gli scongiuri; **it never** ~ed **my mind** non mi è passato per la testa **4** v/i (go across) attraversare; of lines intersecarsi

♦ **cross off, cross out** v/t depennare

'**cross·bar** of goal traversa f; of bicycle canna f; in high jump asticella f

'**cross·check 1** n controllo m incrociato **2** v/t fare un controllo incrociato su

cross-'coun·try corsa f campestre

cross-coun·try ('skiing) sci m inv di fondo

crossed 'check Am, **crossed 'cheque** [krɒst] assegno m sbarrato

cross-ex·am·i·na·tion LAW interrogatorio m in contraddittorio

cross-ex·am·ine v/t LAW interrogare in contraddittorio

cross-eyed ['krɒsaɪd] adj strabico

cross·ing ['krɒsɪŋ] NAUT traversata f; for pedestrians attraversamento m pedonale

'**cross·roads** nsg incrocio m; fig bivio m; '**cross-sec·tion** of people campione m rappresentativo; '**cross-walk** Am passaggio m pedonale; '**cross·word** (**puz·zle**) cruciverba m inv

crotch [krɒtʃ] of person inguine m; of trousers cavallo m

crouch [kraʊtʃ] v/i accovacciarsi

crow [krəʊ] n bird corvo m; **as the** ~ **flies** in linea d'aria

'**crow·bar** piede m di porco

crowd [kraʊd] n folla f

crowd·ed ['kraʊdɪd] adj affollato

crown [kraʊn] **1** n corona f; on tooth capsula f **2** v/t king incoronare; tooth incapsulare

cru·cial ['kruːʃl] adj essenziale

cru·ci·fix ['kruːsɪfɪks] crocifisso m

cru·ci·fix·ion [kruːsɪ'fɪkʃn] crocifissione f

cru·ci·fy ['kruːsɪfaɪ] v/t (pret & pp -ied) REL crocifiggere; fig fare a pezzi

crude [kruːd] **1** adj (vulgar) volgare; (unsophisticated) rudimentale **2** n: ~ (oil) (petrolio m) greggio m

crude·ly ['kruːdlɪ] adv speak volgarmente; made rozzamente

cru·el ['kruːəl] adj crudele

cru·el·ty ['kruːəltɪ] crudeltà f inv

cruise [kruːz] **1** n crociera f **2** v/i of people fare una crociera; of car, plane viaggiare a velocità di crociera

'**cruise lin·er** nave f da crociera

cruis·ing speed ['kruːzɪŋ] also fig velocità f inv di crociera

crumb [krʌm] briciola f

crum·ble ['krʌmbl] **1** v/t sbriciolare **2** v/i of bread sbriciolarsi; of stonework sgretolarsi; fig: of opposition etc crollare

crum·bly ['krʌmblɪ] adj friabile

crum·ple ['krʌmpl] **1** v/t (crease) sgualcire **2** v/i (collapse) accasciarsi

crunch [krʌntʃ] **1** n F: **when it comes to the** ~ al momento cruciale **2** v/i of snow, gravel scricchiolare

cru·sade [kruː'seɪd] n also fig crociata f

crush [krʌʃ] **1** n crowd ressa f; **have a** ~ **on** avere una cotta per **2** v/t schiacciare; (crease) sgualcire; **they were** ~ed **to death** sono morti schiacciati **3** v/i (crease) sgualcire

crust [krʌst] on bread crosta f

crust·y ['krʌstɪ] adj bread croccante

crutch [krʌtʃ] for injured person stampella f

cry [kraɪ] **1** n (call) grido m; **have a** ~ piangere **2** v/t (pret & pp -ied) (call) gridare **3** v/i (pret & pp -ied) (weep) piangere

♦ **cry out** v/t & v/i gridare

♦ **cry out for** v/t (need) aver fortemente bisogno di

cryp·tic ['krɪptɪk] adj sibillino

crys·tal ['krɪstl] **1** n mineral cristallo m; glass cristalli mpl **2** adj di cristallo

crys·tal·lize ['krɪstlaɪz] **1** v/t concre-

tizzare **2** v/i of thoughts etc
concretizzarsi

cub [kʌb] cucciolo m

Cu·ba ['kju:bə] Cuba f

Cu·ban ['kju:bən] **1** adj cubano **2** n
cubano m, -a f

cube [kju:b] shape cubo m

cu·bic ['kju:bɪk] adj cubico

cu·bic ca'pac·i·ty TECH cilindrata f

cu·bi·cle ['kju:bɪkl] (changing room)
cabina f

cu·cum·ber ['kju:kʌmbə(r)] cetriolo m

cud·dle ['kʌdl] **1** n coccole fpl **2** v/t
coccolare

cud·dly ['kʌdlɪ] adj kitten etc tenero;
liking cuddles coccolone

cue [kju:] n for actor etc imbeccata f;
for billiards stecca f

cuff [kʌf] **1** n of shirt polsino m;
(blow) schiaffo m; Am (of trousers)
risvolto m; **off the ~** improvvisando
2 v/t hit dare uno schiaffo a

'cuff link gemello m

'cul-de-sac ['kʌldəsæk] vicolo m
cieco

cu·li·nar·y ['kʌlɪnərɪ] adj culinario

cul·mi·nate ['kʌlmɪneɪt] v/i culminare; **~ in** culminare in

cul·mi·na·tion [kʌlmɪ'neɪʃn] culmine m

cu·lottes ['kju:lɒt] npl gonna f
pantalone

cul·prit ['kʌlprɪt] colpevole m/f

cult [kʌlt] culto m

cul·ti·vate ['kʌltɪveɪt] v/t land coltivare; person coltivarsi

cul·ti·vat·ed ['kʌltɪveɪtɪd] adj person
colto

cul·ti·va·tion [kʌltɪ'veɪʃn] of land
coltivazione f

cul·tu·ral ['kʌltʃərəl] adj culturale

cul·ture ['kʌltʃə(r)] n cultura f

cul·tured ['kʌltʃəd] adj (cultivated)
colto

'cul·ture shock shock m inv culturale

cum·ber·some ['kʌmbəsəm] adj ingombrante; procedure macchinoso

cu·mu·la·tive ['kju:mjʊlətɪv] adj cumulativo

cun·ning ['kʌnɪŋ] **1** n astuzia f **2** adj
astuto

cup [kʌp] n tazza f; (trophy) coppa f; **a
~ of tea** una tazza di tè

cup·board ['kʌbəd] armadio m

'cup fi·nal finale f di coppa

cu·po·la ['kju:pələ] cupola f

'cup tie partita f di coppa

cu·ra·ble ['kjʊərəbl] adj curabile

cu·ra·tor [kjʊə'reɪtə(r)] direttore m,
-trice di museo

curb [kɜ:b] **1** n on powers etc freno m
2 v/t tenere a freno

cur·dle ['kɜ:dl] v/i of milk cagliare

cure [kjʊə(r)] **1** n MED cura f **2** v/t
MED guarire; by drying essiccare; by
salting salare; by smoking affumicare

cur·few ['kɜ:fju:] coprifuoco m

cu·ri·os·i·ty [kjʊərɪ'ɒsətɪ] curiosità f
inv

cu·ri·ous ['kjʊərɪəs] adj (inquisitive)
curioso; (strange) strano

cu·ri·ous·ly ['kjʊərɪəslɪ] adv (inquisi-
tively) con curiosità; (strangely) stranamente; **~ enough ...** sembrerà
strano ma ...

curl [kɜ:l] **1** n in hair ricciolo m; of
smoke spirale f **2** v/t arricciare **3** v/i
of hair arricciarsi; of leaf, paper etc
accartocciarsi

♦ curl up v/i acciambellarsi

curl·y ['kɜ:lɪ] adj hair riccio; tail a ricciolo

cur·rant ['kʌrənt] (dried fruit) uva f
passa

cur·ren·cy ['kʌrənsɪ] money valuta f;
foreign ~ valuta estera

cur·rent ['kʌrənt] **1** n corrente f **2** adj
(present) attuale

'cur·rent ac·count conto m corrente

cur·rent af'fairs, cur·rent e'vents
npl attualità f inv

cur·rent af'fairs pro·gramme programma m di attualità

cur·rent·ly ['kʌrəntlɪ] adv attualmente

cur·ric·u·lum [kə'rɪkjʊləm] programma m (scolastico)

cur·ric·u·lum vi·tae ['vi:taɪ]

curriculum *m inv* vitae

cur·ry ['kʌrɪ] *dish* piatto *m* al curry; *spice* curry *m inv*

curse [kɜːs] **1** *n spell* maledizione *f*; *(swearword)* imprecazione *f* **2** *v/t maledire*; *(swear at)* imprecare contro **3** *v/i (swear)* imprecare

cur·sor ['kɜːsə(r)] COMPUT cursore *m*

cur·so·ry ['kɜːsərɪ] *adj* di sfuggita

curt [kɜːt] *adj* brusco

cur·tail [kɜː'teɪl] *v/t trip etc* accorciare

cur·tain ['kɜːtn] tenda *f*; THEA sipario *m*

curve [kɜːv] **1** *n* curva *f* **2** *v/i (bend)* fare una curva

cush·ion ['kʊʃn] **1** *n for couch etc* cuscino *m* **2** *v/t blow, fall* attutire

cus·tard ['kʌstəd] crema *f* (pasticcera)

cus·to·dy ['kʌstədɪ] *of children* custodia *f*; **in ~** LAW in detenzione preventiva

cus·tom ['kʌstəm] *(tradition)* usanza *f*; COM clientela *f*; **as was his ~** com'era suo solito

cus·tom·a·ry ['kʌstəmərɪ] *adj* consueto; **it is ~ to …** è consuetudine …

cus·tom·er ['kʌstəmə(r)] cliente *m/f*

cus·tom·er re'la·tions *npl* relazione *f* clienti

cus·tom·er 'ser·vice servizio *m* assistenza al cliente

cus·toms ['kʌstəmz] *npl* dogana *f*

Cus·toms and 'Ex·cise Ufficio *m* Dazi e Dogane; **'cus·toms clear·ance** sdoganamento *m*; **'cus·toms in·spec·tion** controllo *m* doganale; **'cus·toms of·fi·cer** doganiere *m*, -a *f*

cut [kʌt] **1** *n with knife, of hair, clothes* taglio *m*; *(reduction)* riduzione *f*; *in public spending* taglio *m*; **my hair needs a ~** devo tagliarmi i capelli **2** *v/t (pret & pp cut)* tagliare; *(reduce)* ridurre; **get one's hair ~** tagliarsi i capelli; **I ~ my finger** mi sono tagliato un dito

♦ **cut back 1** *v/i in costs* limitare le spese **2** *v/t employees* ridurre

♦ **cut down 1** *v/t tree* abbattere **2** *v/i in smoking etc* limitarsi

♦ **cut down on** *v/t cigarettes, chocolate* ridurre la quantità di; **cut down on smoking** fumare di meno

♦ **cut off** *v/t with knife, scissors etc* tagliare; *(isolate)* isolare; **I've been cut off** TELEC è caduta la linea

♦ **cut out** *v/t with scissors* ritagliare; *(eliminate)* eliminare; **cut that out!** F smettila!; **be cut out for sth** essere tagliato per qc

♦ **cut up** *v/t meat etc* sminuzzare

cut·back *in production* riduzione *f*; *in public spending* taglio *m*

cute [kjuːt] *adj (pretty)* carino; *(smart, clever)* furbo

cu·ti·cle ['kjuːtɪkl] pellicina *f*

cut·le·ry ['kʌtlərɪ] posate *fpl*

'cut-off date scadenza *f*

cut-'price *adj goods* a prezzo ridotto; *store* di articoli scontati

'cut-throat *adj competition* spietato

cut·ting ['kʌtɪŋ] **1** *n from newspaper etc* ritaglio *m* **2** *adj remark* tagliente

CV [siː'viː] *abbr* (= **curriculum vitae**) CV *m inv* (= *curriculum m inv* vitae)

cy·ber·space ['saɪbəspeɪs] ciberspazio *m*

cy·cle ['saɪkl] **1** *n (bicycle)* bicicletta *f*; *of events* ciclo *m* **2** *v/i to work* andare in bicicletta

'cy·cle path pista *f* ciclabile

cy·cling ['saɪklɪŋ] ciclismo *m*; **he's taken up ~** ha cominciato ad andare in bicicletta

cy·clist ['saɪklɪst] ciclista *m/f*

cyl·in·der ['sɪlɪndə(r)] cilindro *m*

cy·lin·dri·cal [sɪ'lɪndrɪkl] *adj* cilindrico

cyn·ic ['sɪnɪk] cinico *m*, -a *f*

cyn·i·cal ['sɪnɪkl] *adj* cinico

cyn·i·cal·ly ['sɪnɪklɪ] *adv* cinicamente

cyn·i·cism ['sɪnɪsɪzm] cinismo *m*

cy·press ['saɪprəs] cipresso *m*

cyst [sɪst] cisti *f inv*

Czech [tʃek] **1** *adj* ceco; **the ~ Republic** la Repubblica Ceca **2** *n person* ceco *m*, -a *f*; *language* ceco *m*

dab [dæb] **1** n (*small amount*) tocco m, pochino m **2** v/t (*remove*) (*pret & pp -bed*) tamponare; (*apply*) applicare; **~ a cut with ointment** applicare una pomata sul taglio
♦ **dabble in** v/t dilettarsi di
dad [dæd] papà m inv
dad·dy ['dædɪ] papà m inv
dad·dy long·legs zanzarone m
daf·fo·dil ['dæfədɪl] trombone m
daft [dɑːft] adj stupido
dag·ger ['dægə(r)] pugnale m
dai·ly ['deɪlɪ] **1** n (*paper*) quotidiano m; (*cleaning woman*) domestica f **2** adj quotidiano
dain·ty ['deɪntɪ] adj aggraziato
dair·y cat·tle ['deərɪ] vacche fpl da latte; **'dair·y farm·ing** produzione f di latticini; **'dair·y prod·ucts** npl latticini mpl
dais ['deɪɪs] palco m
dai·sy ['deɪzɪ] margherita f
dam [dæm] **1** n for water diga f **2** v/t (*pret & pp -med*) river costruire una diga su
dam·age ['dæmɪdʒ] **1** n also fig danno m **2** v/t danneggiare; fig: reputation etc compromettere
dam·ages ['dæmɪdʒɪz] npl LAW risarcimento msg
dam·ag·ing ['dæmɪdʒɪŋ] adj nocivo
dame [deɪm] Am F (*woman*) tizia fF; **she's quite a ~!** che donna!
damn [dæm] **1** int F accidenti **2** n: F **I don't give a ~!** non me ne frega niente! F **3** adj F maledetto **4** adv F incredibilmente **5** v/t (*condemn*) maledire; **~ it!** F accidenti!; **~ ed if I will** F non me lo sogno nemmeno
damned [dæmd] → **damn** adj & adv
damn·ing ['dæmɪŋ] adj evidence schiacciante; report incriminante
damp [dæmp] adj umido
damp·en ['dæmpən] v/t inumidire

dance [dɑːns] **1** n ballo m **2** v/i ballare; of ballerina danzare; **would you like to ~?** ti va di ballare?; fml posso invitarla a ballare?
danc·er ['dɑːnsə(r)] (*performer*) ballerino m, -a f; **be a good ~** ballare bene
danc·ing ['dɑːnsɪŋ] ballo m, danza f
dan·de·lion ['dændɪlaɪən] dente m di leone
dan·druff ['dændrʌf] forfora f
dan·druff sham·poo shampoo m inv antiforfora inv
Dane [deɪn] danese m/f
dan·ger ['deɪndʒə(r)] pericolo m; **be in ~** essere in pericolo; **out of ~** of patient fuori pericolo
dan·ger·ous ['deɪndʒərəs] adj pericoloso
dan·ger·ous 'driv·ing guida f pericolosa
dan·ger·ous·ly ['deɪndʒərəslɪ] adv drive spericolatamente; **~ ill** gravemente malato
dan·gle ['dæŋgl] **1** v/t dondolare **2** v/i pendere
Da·nish ['deɪnɪʃ] **1** adj danese **2** n (*language*) danese m
Da·nish ('pastry) dolcetto m ripieno
dare [deə(r)] **1** v/i osare; **~ to do sth** osare fare qc; **how ~ you!** come osi! **2** v/t: **~ s.o. to do sth** sfidare qu a fare qc
dare·dev·il ['deədevɪl] scavezzacollo m
dar·ing ['deərɪŋ] adj audace
dark [dɑːk] **1** n buio m, oscurità f; **after ~** dopo il calare della notte; **keep s.o. in the ~** fig tenere qu all'oscuro **2** adj room, night buio; hair, eyes, colour scuro; **~ green / blue** verde / blu scuro
dark·en ['dɑːkn] v/i of sky oscurarsi
dark 'glasses npl occhiali mpl scuri

dark·ness ['dɑːknɪs] oscurità *f*

'dark·room PHOT camera *f* oscura

dar·ling ['dɑːlɪŋ] **1** *n* tesoro *m*; *be ~ and ...* sii carino e ... **2** *adj* caro

darn [dɑːn] **1** *n* (*mend*) rammendo *m* **2** *v/t* (*mend*) rammendare

dart [dɑːt] **1** *n for throwing* freccetta *f* **2** *v/i* scagliarsi

darts [dɑːts] *nsg* (*game*) freccette *fpl*

'dart(s)·board tabellone *m* delle freccette

dash [dæʃ] **1** *n in punctuation* trattino *m*, lineetta *f*; *of whisky, milk* goccio *m*; *of salt* pizzico *m*; (MOT: *dashboard*) cruscotto *m*; *make a ~ for* precipitarsi su **2** *v/i* precipitarsi; *I must ~* devo scappare **3** *v/t hopes* stroncare

♦ **dash off 1** *v/i* scappare **2** *v/t* (*write quickly*) buttare giù

'dash·board cruscotto *m*

data ['deɪtə] *dati mpl*

'data·base base *f* dati; **da·ta 'cap·ture** inserimento *f* dati; **da·ta 'pro·cess·ing** elaborazione *f* dati; **da·ta pro'tec·tion** protezione *f* dati; **da·ta 'stor·age** memorizzazione *f* dati, archiviazione *f* dati

date¹ [deɪt] (*fruit*) dattero *m*

date² [deɪt] **1** *n* data *f*; (*meeting*) appuntamento *m*; *your ~ is here* è arrivato il tuo ragazzo, è arrivata la tua ragazza; *what's the ~ today?* quanti ne abbiamo oggi?; *out of ~ clothes* fuori moda; *passport* scaduto; *up to ~* aggiornato; (*fashionable*) attuale **2** *v/t letter, cheque* datare; (*go out with*) uscire con; *that ~s you* (*shows your age*) quanto sei vecchio

dat·ed ['deɪtɪd] *adj* superato

daub [dɔːb] *v/t*: *~ paint on a wall* imbrattare il muro di vernice

daugh·ter ['dɔːtə(r)] figlia *f*

'daugh·ter-in-law (*pl daughters-in-law*) nuora *f*

daunt [dɔːnt] *v/t* scoraggiare

daw·dle ['dɔːdl] *v/i* ciondolare

dawn [dɔːn] **1** *n* alba *f*; *fig: of new age* albori *mpl* **2** *v/i*: *it ~ed on me that ...* mi sono reso conto che ...

day [deɪ] giorno *m*; *what ~ is it today?* che giorno è oggi?; *~ off* giorno *m* di ferie; *by ~* di giorno; *~ by ~* giorno per giorno; *the ~ after* il giorno dopo; *the ~ after tomorrow* dopodomani; *the ~ before* il giorno prima; *the ~ before yesterday* l'altro ieri; *~ in ~ out* senza tregua; *in those ~s* a quei tempi; *one ~* un giorno; *the other ~* (*recently*) l'altro giorno; *let's call it a ~!* lasciamo perdere!

'day boy alunno *m* esterno; **'day·break**: *at ~* allo spuntare del giorno; **'day care** asilo *m*; **'day·dream 1** *n* sogno *m* ad occhi aperti **2** *v/i* essere sovrappensiero; **'day dream·er** sognatore *m*, -trice *f*; **'day girl** alunna *f* esterna; **day re'turn** biglietto *m* di andata e ritorno in giornata; **'day·time**: *in the ~* durante il giorno; **day·light 'sav·ing time** ora *f* legale; **'day·trip** gita *f* di un giorno

daze [deɪz] *n*: *in a ~* sbalordito

dazed [deɪzd] *adj by good / bad news* sbalordito; *by a blow* stordito

daz·zle ['dæzl] *v/t of light, fig* abbagliare

DC [diː'siː] *abbr* (= *direct current*) c.c.; (=corrente *f* continua); *District of Columbia*) DC

dead [ded] **1** *adj person, plant* morto; *battery* scarica; *phone* muto; *light bulb* bruciato; *be ~ F of place* essere un mortorio F **2** *adv* F (*very*) da matti F; *~ beat, ~ tired* stanco morto; *that's ~ right* è assolutamente vero; *it's ~ interesting* è interessante da matti F **3** *n: the ~* (*dead people*) i morti; *in the ~ of night* nel cuore della notte

dead·en ['dedn] *v/t pain* attenuare; *sound* attutire

dead 'end (*street*) vicolo *m* cieco; **dead-'end job** lavoro *m* senza prospettive; **dead 'heat** pareggio *m*; **'dead·line** scadenza *f*; *for newspaper, magazine* termine *m* per l'invio in stampa; **'dead·lock** *n in talks* punto *m* morto

dead·ly ['dedlɪ] *adj* (*fatal*) mortale; F

(*boring*) di una noia mortale F

deaf [def] *adj* sordo

deaf-and-'dumb *adj* sordomuto

deaf·en ['defn] *v/t* assordare

deaf·en·ing ['defnɪŋ] *adj* assordante

deaf·ness ['defnɪs] sordità *f inv*

deal [diːl] **1** *n* accordo *m*; *it's a ~!* affare fatto!; *(a good ~ (bargain)* un affare; *(a lot)* molto; *a great ~ of (lots)* un bel po' di; *it's your ~ in games* tocca a te **2** *v/t* (*pret & pp dealt*) cards distribuire; *~ a blow to* inferire un duro colpo a

♦ **deal in** *v/t* (*trade in*) trattare; *drugs* trafficare

♦ **deal out** *v/t* cards distribuire

♦ **deal with** *v/t* (*handle*) occuparsi di; *situation* gestire; *(do business with)* trattare con

deal·er ['diːlə(r)] *(merchant)* commerciante *m/f*; *(drug ~)* spacciatore *m*, -trice *f*

deal·ing ['diːlɪŋ] *(drug ~)* spaccio *m*

deal·ings ['diːlɪŋz] *npl (business)* rapporti *mpl*

dealt [delt] *pret & pp → deal*

dean [diːn] *of college* preside *m*

dear [dɪə(r)] *adj* caro; *Dear Sir* Egregio Signore; *Dear Richard/Dear Margaret* caro Richard/cara Margareth; *(oh) ~!, ~ me!* povero/a me!

dear·ly ['dɪəlɪ] *adv love* teneramente

death [deθ] morte *f*

'death cer·tif·i·cate certificato *m* di decesso; **'death pen·al·ty** pena *f* di morte; **'death toll** numero *m* delle vittime

de·ba·ta·ble [dɪ'beɪtəbl] *adj* discutibile

de·bate [dɪ'beɪt] **1** *n* dibattimento *m*, POL dibattito *m*; *after much ~* dopo molto dibattere **2** *v/i* dibattere; *~ with o.s. whether ...* considerare se ... **3** *v/t* dibattere su

de·bauch·er·y [dɪ'bɔːtʃərɪ] depravazione *f*

deb·it ['debɪt] **1** *n* addebito *m* **2** *v/t*: ~ *£150 to s.o.'s account* addebitare £ 150 a qu; *~ an account with £ 150*

addebitare £ 150 su un conto

'deb·it card carta *f* di debito

deb·ris ['debriː] *of plane* rottami *mpl*; *of building* macerie *fpl*

debt [det] debito *m*; *be in ~ (financially)* avere dei debiti

debt·or ['detə(r)] debitore *m*, -trice *f*

de·bug [diː'bʌg] *v/t (pret & pp -ged) room* togliere le microspie da; COMPUT togliere gli errori da

dé·but ['deɪbjuː] *n* debutto *m*

dec·ade ['dekeɪd] decennio *m*, decade *f*

dec·a·dence ['dekədəns] decadenza *f*

dec·a·dent ['dekədənt] *adj* decadente

de·caf·fein·at·ed [dɪ'kæfɪneɪtɪd] *adj* decaffeinato

de·cant·er [dɪ'kæntə(r)] caraffa *f*

de·cap·i·tate [dɪ'kæpɪteɪt] *v/t* decapitare

de·cay [dɪ'keɪ] **1** *n of organic matter* decomposizione *f*; *of civilization* declino *m*; *(decayed matter)* marciume *m*; *in teeth* carie *f inv* **2** *v/i of organic matter* decomporsi; *of civilization* declinare; *of teeth* cariarsi

de·ceased [dɪ'siːst]: *the ~* il defunto *m*, la defunta *f*

de·ceit [dɪ'siːt] falsità *f*, disonestà *f*

de·ceit·ful [dɪ'siːtful] *adj* falso, disonesto

de·ceive [dɪ'siːv] *v/t* ingannare

De·cem·ber [dɪ'sembə(r)] dicembre *m*

de·cen·cy ['diːsənsɪ] decenza *f*; *he had the ~ to ...* ha avuto la decenza di ...

de·cent ['diːsənt] *adj price, proposition* corretto; *meal, sleep* decente; *(adequately dressed)* presentabile; *a ~ guy* un uomo per bene; *that's very ~ of you* è molto gentile da parte tua

de·cen·tral·ize [diː'sentrəlaɪz] *v/t* decentralizzare

de·cep·tion [dɪ'sepʃn] inganno *m*

de·cep·tive [dɪ'septɪv] *adj* ingannevole

de·cep·tive·ly [dɪ'septɪvlɪ] *adv*: *it*

looks ~ simple sembra semplice solo all'apparenza

dec·i·bel ['desɪbel] decibel *m inv*

de·cide [dɪ'saɪd] **1** *v/t (make up one's mind)* decidere; *(conclude, settle)* risolvere **2** *v/i* decidere; *you ~* decidi tu

de·cid·ed [dɪ'saɪdɪd] *adj (definite)* deciso

de·cid·er [dɪ'saɪdə(r)]: *be the ~ of match etc* essere decisivo

de·ci·du·ous [dɪ'sɪdjuəs] *adj* che perde le foglie in inverno

dec·i·mal ['desɪml] *n* decimale

dec·i·mal 'point *punto m che separa i decimali; in Italy* virgola *f*

dec·i·mate ['desɪmeɪt] *v/t* decimare

de·ci·pher [dɪ'saɪfə(r)] *v/t* decifrare

de·ci·sion [dɪ'sɪʒn] decisione *f; (conclusion)* risoluzione *f;* **come to a ~** prendere una decisione

de'ci·sion-mak·er responsabile *m/f;* **be a ~** *(be able to make decisions)* saper prendere delle decisioni

de·ci·sive [dɪ'saɪsɪv] *adj* risoluto; *(crucial)* decisivo

deck [dek] *of ship* ponte *m; of bus* piano *m; of cards* mazzo *m*

'deck·chair sedia *f* a sdraio, sdraio *f inv*

dec·la·ra·tion [deklə'reɪʃn] dichiarazione *f*

de·clare [dɪ'kleə(r)] *v/t* dichiarare

de·cline [dɪ'klaɪn] **1** *n in number, standards* calo *m; in health* peggioramento *m* **2** *v/t invitation* declinare; *~ to comment / accept* esimersi dal commentare / accettare **3** *v/i (refuse)* declinare; *(decrease)* diminuire; *of health* peggiorare

de·clutch [diː'klʌtʃ] *v/i* lasciare andare la frizione

de·code [diː'kəʊd] *v/t* decodificare

de·com·pose [diːkəm'pəʊz] *v/i* decomporsi

déc·or ['deɪkɔː(r)] arredamento *m*

dec·o·rate ['dekəreɪt] *v/t with paint* imbiancare; *with paper* tappezzare; *(adorn),* MIL decorare

dec·o·ra·tion [dekə'reɪʃn] *paint* vernice *f; paper* tappezzeria *f;*

(ornament) addobbi *mpl;* MIL decorazione *f*

dec·o·ra·tive ['dekərətɪv] *adj* decorativo

dec·o·ra·tor ['dekəreɪtə(r)] *(interior ~)* imbianchino *m*

de·co·rum [dɪ'kɔːrəm] decoro *m*

de·coy ['diːkɔɪ] *n* esca *f*

de·crease ['diːkriːs] **1** *n* diminuzione *f* **2** *v/t* ridurre **3** *v/i* ridursi

de·crep·it [dɪ'krepɪt] *adj* decrepito

ded·i·cate ['dedɪkeɪt] *v/t book etc* dedicare; *~ o.s. to ...* consacrarsi a ...

ded·i·cat·ed ['dedɪkeɪtɪd] *adj* dedito

ded·i·ca·tion [dedɪ'keɪʃn] *in book* dedica *f; to cause, work* dedizione *f*

de·duce [dɪ'djuːs] *v/t* dedurre

de·duct [dɪ'dʌkt] *v/t* detrarre; *~ sth from sth* detrarre qc da qc

de·duc·tion [dɪ'dʌkʃn] *from salary* trattenuta *f; (conclusion)* deduzione *f;* ~ *at source* ritenuta *f* alla fonte

dee·jay ['diːdʒeɪ] F dj *m/f inv*

deed [diːd] *n (act)* azione *f;* LAW atto *m*

deem [diːm] *v/t* ritenere

deep [diːp] *adj hole, water, voice, thinker* profondo; *colour* intenso; *you're in ~ trouble* sei davvero nei guai

deep·en ['diːpən] **1** *v/t* rendere più profondo **2** *v/i* diventare più profondo; *of crisis* aggravarsi; *of mystery* infittirsi

'deep freeze *n* congelatore *m;* **'deep-froz·en food** surgelati *mpl;* **'deep-fry** *v/t (pret & pp -ied)* friggere (immergendo nell'olio); **deep 'fry·er** padella *f* (per friggere); *electric* friggitrice *f*

deer [dɪə(r)] *(pl deer)* cervo *m*

de·face [dɪ'feɪs] *v/t* vandalizzare

def·a·ma·tion [defə'meɪʃn] diffamazione *f*

de·fam·a·to·ry [dɪ'fæmətərɪ] *adj* diffamatorio

de·fault ['diːfɒlt] *adj* COMPUT di default

de·feat [dɪ'fiːt] **1** *n* sconfitta *f* **2** *v/t* sconfiggere; *this problem ~s me* questo problema è troppo grande per me

defeatist [dɪˈfiːtɪst] *adj attitude* disfattista

de·fect [ˈdiːfekt] *n* difetto *m*

de·fec·tive [dɪˈfektɪv] *adj* difettoso

de·fend [dɪˈfend] *v/t* difendere

de·fend·ant [dɪˈfendənt] accusato *m*, -a *f*; *in criminal case* imputato *m*, -a *f*

de·fence [dɪˈfens] difesa *f*; **come to s.o.'s ~** venire in aiuto a qu

de·fence budg·et POL budget *m inv* della difesa

de·fence law·yer avvocato *m* difensore

de·fence·less [dɪˈfenslɪs] *adj* indifeso

de·fence play·er SP difensore *m*

de·fence wit·ness LAW testimone *m/f* della difesa

de·fense *etc Am* → **defence** *etc*

de·fen·sive [dɪˈfensɪv] **1** *n*: **on the ~** sulla difensiva; **go on the ~** mettersi sulla difensiva **2** *adj weaponry* difensivo; *person* sulla difensiva

de·fen·sive·ly [dɪˈfensɪvlɪ] *adv* sulla difensiva; **play ~** SP ritirarsi in difesa

de·fer [dɪˈfɜː(r)] *v/t* (*pret & pp* **-red**) (*postpone*) rinviare

def·er·ence [ˈdefərəns] deferenza *f*

def·er·en·tial [defəˈrenʃl] *adj* deferente

de·fi·ance [dɪˈfaɪəns] sfida *f*; **in ~ of** a dispetto di

de·fi·ant [dɪˈfaɪənt] *adj* provocatorio

de·fi·cien·cy [dɪˈfɪʃənsɪ] (*lack*) carenza *f*

de·fi·cient [dɪˈfɪʃənt] *adj* carente; **be ~ in …** essere carente di …

def·i·cit [ˈdefɪsɪt] deficit *m inv*

de·fine [dɪˈfaɪn] *v/t* definire

def·i·nite [ˈdefɪnɪt] *adj date, time, answer* preciso; *improvement* netto; (*certain*) certo; **are you ~ about that?** ne sei sicuro?; **nothing ~ has been arranged** non è stato previsto niente di preciso

def·i·nite 'ar·ti·cle GRAM articolo *m* determinativo

def·i·nite·ly [ˈdefɪnɪtlɪ] *adv* senza dubbio; *smell, hear* distintamente

def·i·ni·tion [defɪˈnɪʃn] definizione *f*

de·fin·i·tive [dɪˈfɪnɪtɪv] *adj biography* più completo; *performance* migliore

de·flect [dɪˈflekt] *v/t ball, blow* deviare; sviare; **be ~ed from** essere sviato da

de·for·est·a·tion [diːfɒrɪsˈteɪʃn] disboscamento *m*

de·form [dɪˈfɔːm] *v/t* deformare

de·for·mi·ty [dɪˈfɔːmɪtɪ] deformità *f inv*

de·fraud [dɪˈfrɔːd] *v/t* defraudare; *Inland Revenue* frodare

de·frost [diːˈfrɒst] *v/t food* scongelare; *fridge* sbrinare

deft [deft] *adj* agile

de·fuse [diːˈfjuːz] *v/t bomb* disinnescare; *situation* placare

de·fy [dɪˈfaɪ] *v/t* (*pret & pp* **-ied**) (*disobey*) disobbedire a

de·gen·e·rate [dɪˈdʒenəreɪt] *v/i* degenerare; **~ into** degenerare in

de·grade [dɪˈgreɪd] *v/t* degradare

de·grad·ing [dɪˈgreɪdɪŋ] *adj position, work* degradante

de·gree [dɪˈgriː] *from university* laurea *f*; *of temperature, angle, latitude* grado *m*; **a ~ of** (*amount*) un po' di; **by ~s** per gradi; **to a certain ~** fino a un certo punto; **there is a ~ of truth in that** c'è del vero in questo; **get one's ~** prendere la laurea

de·hy·drat·ed [diːhaɪˈdreɪtɪd] *adj* disidratato

de-ice [diːˈaɪs] *v/t* togliere il ghiaccio da

de-ic·er [diːˈaɪsə(r)] (*spray*) antigelo *m inv*

deign [deɪn] *v/i*: **~ to …** degnarsi di …

de·i·ty [ˈdiːɪtɪ] divinità *f inv*

de·ject·ed [dɪˈdʒektɪd] *adj* sconfortato

de·lay [dɪˈleɪ] **1** *n* ritardo **2** *v/t* ritardare; **be ~ed** (*be late*) essere in ritardo; **~ doing sth** tardare a fare qc; **sorry, I've been ~ed** scusa, sono stato trattenuto **3** *v/i* tardare

del·e·gate [ˈdelɪgət] **1** *n* delegato *m*,

-a f **2** v/t ['delɪgeɪt] task, person delegare

del·e·ga·tion [delɪ'geɪʃn] of task delega f; (people) delegazione f

de·lete [dɪ'liːt] v/t cancellare

de·lete key COMPUT tasto m 'cancella'

de·le·tion [dɪ'liːʃn] act cancellazione f; that deleted cancellatura f

del·i ['delɪ] → delicatessen

de·lib·e·rate [dɪ'lɪbərət] **1** adj deliberato **2** v/i [dɪ'lɪbəreɪt] riflettere

de·lib·e·rate·ly [dɪ'lɪbərətlɪ] adv deliberatamente

del·i·ca·cy ['delɪkəsɪ] delicatezza f; (food) prelibatezza f

del·i·cate ['delɪkət] adj delicato

del·i·ca·tes·sen [delɪkə'tesn] gastronomia f

del·i·cious [dɪ'lɪʃəs] adj delizioso, ottimo

de·light [dɪ'laɪt] n gioia f; **to my great ~** con mio grande piacere

de·light·ed [dɪ'laɪtɪd] adj lieto

de·light·ful [dɪ'laɪtfʊl] adj molto piacevole

de·lim·it [diː'lɪmɪt] v/t delimitare

de·lin·quen·cy [dɪ'lɪŋkwənsɪ] delinquenza f (minorile)

de·lin·quent [dɪ'lɪŋkwənt] n delinquente m/f

de·lir·i·ous [dɪ'lɪrɪəs] adj MED delirante; (ecstatic) in delirio

de·liv·er [dɪ'lɪvə(r)] v/t consegnare; message trasmettere; baby far nascere; **~ a speech** tenere un discorso

de·liv·er·y [dɪ'lɪvərɪ] of goods, mail consegna f; of baby parto m

de·liv·er·y charge: **there is no ~** la consegna è gratuita; **de·liv·er·y date** termine m di consegna; **de·liv·er·y man** fattorino m; **de·liv·er·y note** bolla f, documento m di trasporto; **de·liv·er·y serv·ice** consegna f a domicilio; **de·liv·er·y van** furgone m delle consegne

de·lude [dɪ'luːd] v/t ingannare; **~ s.o. into believing sth** far credere qc a qu; **you're deluding yourself** ti sbagli

de·luge ['deljuːdʒ] **1** n temporale m; fig valanga f **2** v/t fig sommergere

de·lu·sion [dɪ'luːʒn] illusione f; of others inganno m

de luxe [də'lʌks] adj di lusso

♦ delve into [delv] v/t addentrarsi in; s.o.'s past scavare in

de·mand [dɪ'mɑːnd] **1** n rivendicazione f; COM domanda f; **in ~** richiesto **2** v/t esigere; (require) richiedere

de·mand·ing [dɪ'mɑːndɪŋ] adj job impegnativo; person esigente

de·mean·ing [dɪ'miːnɪŋ] adj avvilente

de·ment·ed [dɪ'mentɪd] adj demente

de·mise [dɪ'maɪz] scomparsa f

dem·o ['deməʊ] (protest) manifestazione f; of video etc dimostrazione f

de·moc·ra·cy [dɪ'mɒkrəsɪ] democrazia f

dem·o·crat ['deməkræt] democratico m, -a f; **Democrat** POL democratico m, -a f

dem·o·crat·ic [demə'krætɪk] adj democratico

dem·o·crat·ic·al·ly [demə'krætɪklɪ] adv democraticamente

'dem·o disk disco m dimostrativo

de·mo·graph·ic [deməʊ'græfɪk] adj demografico

de·mol·ish [dɪ'mɒlɪʃ] v/t demolire

dem·o·li·tion [demə'lɪʃn] demolizione f

de·mon ['diːmən] demone m

dem·on·strate ['demənstreɪt] **1** v/t (prove) dimostrare; machine fare una dimostrazione di **2** v/i politically manifestare

dem·on·stra·tion [demən'streɪʃn] dimostrazione f; (protest) manifestazione f

de·mon·stra·tive [dɪ'mɒnstrətɪv] adj espansivo

de·mon·stra·tor ['demənstreɪtə(r)] (protester) manifestante m/f

de·mor·al·ized [dɪ'mɒrəlaɪzd] adj demoralizzato

de·mor·al·iz·ing [dɪ'mɒrəlaɪzɪŋ] adj demoralizzante

de·mote [diː'məʊt] v/t retrocedere;

MIL degradare

de·mure [dɪ'mjʊə(r)] *adj* contegnoso

den [den] (*study*) studio *m*

de·ni·al [dɪ'naɪəl] *of rumour, accusation* negazione *f; of request, right* negazione *f,* rifiuto *m*

den·im ['denɪm] denim *m inv*

den·ims ['denɪmz] *npl* (*jeans*) jeans *m inv*

Den·mark ['denmɑːk] Danimarca *f*

de·nom·i·na·tion [dɪnɒmɪ'neɪʃn] *of money* banconota *f;* REL confessione *f; money in small ~s* denaro *m* in banconote di piccolo taglio

de·nounce [dɪ'naʊns] *v/t* denunciare

dense [dens] *adj* fitto; (*stupid*) ottuso

dense·ly ['densli] *adv:* ~ *populated* densamente popolato

den·si·ty ['densɪtɪ] *of population* densità *f inv*

dent [dent] **1** *n* ammaccatura *f* **2** *v/t* ammaccare

den·tal ['dentl] *adj treatment* dentario, dentale; *hospital* dentistico

den·ted ['dentɪd] *adj* ammaccato

den·tist ['dentɪst] dentista *m/f*

den·tist·ry ['dentɪstrɪ] odontoiatria *f*

den·tures ['dentʃəz] *npl* dentiera *f*

de·ny [dɪ'naɪ] *v/t* (*pret & pp -ied*) negare; *rumour* smentire; *I was denied the right to ...* mi è stato negato il diritto di ...

de·o·do·rant [diː'əʊdərənt] deodorante *m*

de·part [dɪ'pɑːt] *v/i* partire; ~ *from* (*deviate from*) allontanarsi da

de·part·ment [dɪ'pɑːtmənt] *of university* dipartimento *m; of government* ministero *m; of store, company* reparto *m*

de·part·ment store grande magazzino *m*

de·par·ture [dɪ'pɑːtʃə(r)] partenza *f;* (*deviation*) allontanamento *m; a new ~ for government, organization* una svolta

de·par·ture lounge sala *f* partenze

de·par·ture time ora *f* di partenza

de·pend [dɪ'pend] *v/i: that ~s* dipen-

de; *it ~s on the weather* dipende dal tempo; *I am ~ing on you* conto su di te

de·pen·da·ble [dɪ'pendəbl] *adj* affidabile

de·pen·dant [dɪ'pendənt] → **dependent**

de·pen·dence, de·pen·den·cy [dɪ'pendəns, dɪ'pendənsɪ] dipendenza *f*

de·pen·dent [dɪ'pendənt] **1** *n* persona *f* a carico; *a married man with ~s* un uomo sposato con famiglia a carico **2** *adj* dipendente; ~ *children* figli *mpl* a carico

de·pict [dɪ'pɪkt] *v/t in painting, writing* raffigurare

de·plete [dɪ'pliːt] *v/t* intaccare

de·plor·a·ble [dɪ'plɔːrəbl] *adj* deplorevole

de·plore [dɪ'plɔː(r)] *v/t* deplorare, lamentarsi di

de·ploy [dɪ'plɔɪ] *v/t* (*use*) spiegare; (*position*) schierare

de·pop·u·la·tion [diːpɒpjʊ'leɪʃn] spopolamento *m*

de·port [dɪ'pɔːt] *v/t* deportare

de·por·ta·tion [diːpɔː'teɪʃn] deportazione *f*

de·por'ta·tion or·der ordine *m* di deportazione

de·pose [dɪ'pəʊz] *v/t* deporre

de·pos·it [dɪ'pɒzɪt] **1** *n in bank* versamento *m,* deposito *m; of mineral* deposito *m; on purchase* acconto *m;* (*against loss, damage*) cauzione *f* **2** *v/t money* versare, depositare; (*put down*) lasciare; *silt, mud* depositare

de·pos·it ac·count libretto *m* di risparmio

dep·ot ['depəʊ] (*train station*) stazione *f* ferroviaria; (*bus station*) rimessa *f* degli autobus; *for storage* magazzino *m*

de·praved [dɪ'preɪvd] *adj* depravato

de·pre·ci·ate [dɪ'priːʃɪeɪt] *v/i* FIN svalutarsi

de·pre·ci·a·tion [dɪpriːʃɪ'eɪʃn] FIN svalutazione *f*

de·press [dɪ'pres] v/t person deprimere

de·pressed [dɪ'prest] adj person depresso

de·press·ing [dɪ'presɪŋ] adj deprimente

de·pres·sion [dɪ'preʃn] depressione f

dep·ri·va·tion [deprɪ'veɪʃn] privazione f; (lack: of sleep, food) carenza f

de·prive [dɪ'praɪv] v/t: ~ **s.o. of sth** privare qu di qc

de·prived [dɪ'praɪvd] adj socialmente svantaggiato

depth [depθ] profondità f inv; **in ~** (thoroughly) a fondo; **in the ~s of winter** in pieno inverno; **be out of one's ~** in water non toccare (il fondo); **when they talk about politics I'm out of my ~** la politica va al di là della mia comprensione

dep·u·ta·tion [depjʊ'teɪʃn] deputazione f

♦ **deputize for** ['depjʊtaɪz] v/t fare le veci di

dep·u·ty ['depjʊtɪ] vice m/f inv

'**dep·u·ty lead·er** of party vice segretario m

de·rail [dɪ'reɪl] v/t: **be ~ed** of train essere deragliato

de·ranged [dɪ'reɪndʒd] adj squilibrato

de·reg·u·late [dɪ'regjʊleɪt] v/t deregolamentare

de·reg·u·la·tion [dɪregjʊ'leɪʃn] deregolamentazione f

der·e·lict ['derəlɪkt] adj desolato

de·ride [dɪ'raɪd] v/t deridere

de·ri·sion [dɪ'rɪʒn] derisione f

de·ri·sive [dɪ'raɪsɪv] adj remarks, laughter derisorio

de·ri·sive·ly [dɪ'raɪsɪvlɪ] adv con aria derisoria

de·ri·so·ry [dɪ'raɪsərɪ] adj amount, salary irrisorio

de·riv·a·tive [dɪ'rɪvətɪv] adj (not original) derivato

de·rive [dɪ'raɪv] v/t trarre; **be ~d from** of word derivare da

der·ma·tol·o·gist [dɜːmə'tɒlədʒɪst]

dermatologo m, -a f

de·rog·a·to·ry [dɪ'rɒgətrɪ] adj peggiorativo

de·scend [dɪ'send] **1** v/t scendere; **be ~ed from** discendere da **2** v/i scendere; of mood, darkness calare

de·scen·dant [dɪ'sendənt] discendente m/f

de·scent [dɪ'sent] discesa f; (ancestry) discendenza f; **of Chinese ~** di origini cinesi

de·scribe [dɪ'skraɪb] v/t descrivere; ~ **sth as sth** descrivere qc come qc

de·scrip·tion [dɪ'skrɪpʃn] descrizione f

des·e·crate ['desɪkreɪt] v/t profanare

des·e·cra·tion [desɪ'kreɪʃn] profanazione f

de·seg·re·gate [diː'segrəgeɪt] eliminare la segregazione in

des·ert[1] ['dezət] n also fig deserto m

des·ert[2] [dɪ'zɜːt] **1** v/t (abandon) abbandonare **2** v/i of soldier disertare

de·sert·ed [dɪ'zɜːtɪd] adj deserto

de·sert·er [dɪ'zɜːtə(r)] MIL disertore m

de·ser·ti·fi·ca·tion [dɪzɜːtɪfɪ'keɪʃn] desertificazione f

de·ser·tion [dɪ'zɜːʃn] (abandoning) abbandono m; MIL diserzione f

des·ert 'is·land isola f deserta

de·serve [dɪ'zɜːv] v/t meritare

de·sign [dɪ'zaɪn] **1** n design m; technical progettazione f; (drawing) progetto m, disegno m; (pattern) motivo m; **the machine's unique ~** la concezione unica della macchina **2** v/t house, car progettare; clothes disegnare; **this machine is not ~ed for ...** questa macchina non è stata concepita per ...

des·ig·nate ['dezɪgneɪt] v/t person designare; **it has been ~d a no smoking area** quest'area è riservata ai non fumatori

de·sign·er [dɪ'zaɪnə(r)] designer m/f inv; of building, car, ship progettista m/f; **costume ~** costumista m/f; **fashion ~** stilista m/f; **interior ~** arredatore m, -trice f

de'sign·er clothes *npl* abiti *mpl* firmati

de'sign fault difetto *m* di concezione

de'sign school scuola *f* di design

de·sir·a·ble [dɪ'zaɪrəbl] *adj* desiderabile; (*advisable*) preferibile

de·sire [dɪ'zaɪə(r)] *n* desiderio *m*

desk [desk] scrivania *f*; *in hotel* reception *f inv*

'desk clerk *Am* receptionist *m/f inv*; 'desk di·a·ry agenda *f* da tavolo; 'desk·top scrivania *f*, (*computer*) computer *m inv* da tavolo; (*screen*) desktop *m inv*; desk·top 'pub·lish·ing editoria *f* elettronica

des·o·late ['desələt] *adj place* desolato

de·spair [dɪ'speə(r)] **1** *n* disperazione *f*; *in ~* disperato **2** *v/i* disperare; *~ of sth / s.o.* aver perso la fiducia in qc/qu; *~ of doing sth* disperare di fare qc

des·per·ate ['despərət] *adj* disperato; *be ~ for a cigarette / drink* morire dalla voglia di una sigaretta / bere qualcosa

des·per·a·tion [despə'reɪʃn] disperazione *f*

des·pic·a·ble [dɪs'pɪkəbl] *adj* deplorevole

de·spise [dɪ'spaɪz] *v/t* disprezzare

de·spite [dɪ'spaɪt] *prep* malgrado, nonostante

de·spon·dent [dɪ'spɒndənt] *adj* abbattuto

des·pot ['despɒt] despota *m*

des·sert [dɪ'zɜːt] dolce *m*, dessert *m inv*

des·ti·na·tion [destɪ'neɪʃn] destinazione *f*

des·tined ['destɪnd] *adj*: *be ~ for fig* essere destinato a

des·ti·ny ['destɪnɪ] destino *m*

des·ti·tute ['destɪtjuːt] *adj* indigente

de·stroy [dɪ'strɔɪ] *v/t* distruggere

de·stroy·er [dɪ'strɔɪə(r)] NAUT cacciatorpediniere *m*

de·struc·tion [dɪ'strʌkʃn] distruzione *f*

de·struc·tive [dɪ'strʌktɪv] *adj* distruttivo; *child* scalmanato

de·tach [dɪ'tætʃ] *v/t* staccare

de·tach·a·ble [dɪ'tætʃəbl] *adj* staccabile

de·tached [dɪ'tætʃt] *adj* (*objective*) distaccato

de'tached house villetta *f*

de·tach·ment [dɪ'tætʃmənt] (*objectivity*) distacco *m*

de·tail ['diːteɪl] *n* dettaglio *m*; *in ~* dettagliatamente

de·tailed ['diːteɪld] *adj* dettagliato

de·tain [dɪ'teɪn] *v/t* (*hold back*) trattenere; *as prisoner* trattenere

de·tain·ee [diːteɪn'iː] detenuto *m*, -a *f*

de·tect [dɪ'tekt] *v/t* rilevare; *anxiety, irony* cogliere

de·tec·tion [dɪ'tekʃn] *of criminal, crime* investigazione *f*; *of smoke etc* rilevamento *m*

de·tec·tive [dɪ'tektɪv] (*policeman*) agente *m/f* investigativo

de'tec·tive nov·el romanzo *m* giallo, giallo *m*

de·tec·tor [dɪ'tektə(r)] rilevatore *m*

dé·tente ['deɪtɒnt] POL distensione *f*

de·ten·tion [dɪ'tenʃn] (*imprisonment*) detenzione *f*

de·ter [dɪ'tɜː(r)] *v/t* (*pret & pp* **-red**) dissuadere; *~ s.o. from doing sth* dissuadere qu dal fare qc

de·ter·gent [dɪ'tɜːdʒənt] detergente *m*

de·te·ri·o·rate [dɪ'tɪərɪəreɪt] *v/i* deteriorarsi

de·te·ri·o·ra·tion [dɪtɪərɪə'reɪʃn] deterioramento *m*

de·ter·mi·na·tion [dɪtɜːmɪ'neɪʃn] (*resolution*) determinazione *f*

de·ter·mine [dɪ'tɜːmɪn] *v/t* (*establish*) determinare

de·ter·mined [dɪ'tɜːmɪnd] *adj* determinato, deciso

de·ter·rent [dɪ'terənt] *n* deterrente *m*

de·test [dɪ'test] *v/t* detestare

de·test·a·ble [dɪ'testəbl] *adj* detestabile

de·to·nate ['detəneɪt] **1** *v/t* fare detonare **2** *v/i* detonare

de·to·na·tion [detə'neɪʃn] detonazione f

de·tour ['di:tʊə(r)] n deviazione f

♦ **de·tract from** [dɪ'trækt] v/t merit, value sminuire; enjoyment rovinare; room, décor rovinare l'effetto di

de·tri·ment ['detrɪmənt]: **to the ~ of** a scapito di

de·tri·men·tal [detrɪ'mentl] adj nocivo

deuce [dju:s] in tennis 40 pari m inv

de·val·u·a·tion [di:vælju'eɪʃn] of currency svalutazione f

de·val·ue [di:'vælju:] v/t currency svalutare

dev·a·state ['devəsteɪt] v/t also fig devastare

dev·a·stat·ing ['devəsteɪtɪŋ] adj devastante

de·vel·op [dɪ'veləp] **1** v/t film, business sviluppare; land, site valorizzare; (originate) scoprire; illness, cold contrarre **2** v/i (grow) svilupparsi; ~ **into** diventare

de·vel·op·er [dɪ'veləpə(r)] of property impresario m, a f edile

de·vel·op·ing coun·try paese m in via di sviluppo

de·vel·op·ment [dɪ'veləpmənt] sviluppo m; of land, site valorizzazione f; (origination) scoperta f

de·vice [dɪ'vaɪs] (tool) dispositivo m

dev·il ['devl] diavolo m

de·vi·ous ['di:vɪəs] (sly) subdolo

de·vise [dɪ'vaɪz] v/t escogitare

de·void [dɪ'vɔɪd] adj: **be ~ of** essere privo di

dev·o·lu·tion [di:və'lu:ʃn] POL decentramento m

de·vote [dɪ'vəʊt] v/t time, effort, money dedicare

de·vot·ed [dɪ'vəʊtɪd] adj son etc devoto; **be ~ to a person** essere molto attaccato a una persona

dev·o·tee [dɪvəʊ'ti:] appassionato m, -a f

de·vo·tion [dɪ'vəʊʃn] to a person attaccamento m; to one's job dedizione f

de·vour [dɪ'vaʊə(r)] v/t food, book divorare

de·vout [dɪ'vaʊt] adj devoto; **a ~ Catholic** un cattolico fervente

dew [dju:] rugiada f

dex·ter·i·ty [dek'sterətɪ] destrezza f

di·a·be·tes [daɪə'bi:ti:z] nsg diabete m

di·a·bet·ic [daɪə'betɪk] **1** n diabetico m, -a f **2** adj diabetico; foods per diabetici

di·a·bol·i·cal [daɪə'bɒlɪkl] adj P (very bad) penoso

di·ag·nose ['daɪəgnəʊz] v/t diagnosticare

di·ag·no·sis [daɪəg'nəʊsɪs] (pl diagnoses [daɪəg'nəʊsi:z]) diagnosi f inv

di·ag·o·nal [daɪ'ægənl] adj diagonale

di·ag·o·nal·ly [daɪ'ægənlɪ] adv diagonalmente

di·a·gram ['daɪəgræm] diagramma m

di·al ['daɪəl] **1** n of clock, meter quadrante m; TELEC disco m combinatore **2** v/i (pret & pp **-led**, Am **-ed**) TELEC comporre il numero **3** v/t (pret & pp **-led**, Am **-ed**) TELEC number comporre

di·a·lect ['daɪəlekt] dialetto m

di·al·ling code ['daɪlɪŋ] prefisso m

'di·al·ling tone, Am **'dial tone** segnale m di linea libera

di·a·log Am, **di·a·logue** ['daɪəlɒg] dialogo m

di·a·logue box COMPUT riquadro m di dialogo

di·am·e·ter [daɪ'æmɪtə(r)] diametro m

di·a·met·ri·cal·ly [daɪə'metrɪkəlɪ] adv: ~ **opposed** diametricamente opposto

di·a·mond ['daɪəmənd] (jewel) diamante m; (shape) losanga f; ~**s** in cards quadri mpl

di·a·per ['daɪəpər] Am pannolino m

di·a·phragm ['daɪəfræm] diaframma m

di·ar·rhe·a Am, **di·ar·rhoe·a** [daɪə'ri:ə] diarrea f

di·a·ry ['daɪərɪ] for thoughts diario m; for appointments agenda f

dice [daɪs] **1** n dado m **2** v/t (cut) tagliare a dadini

di·chot·o·my [daɪ'kɒtəmɪ] dicotomia f

dic·tate [dɪk'teɪt] v/t letter, novel dettare; course of action imporre

dic·ta·tion [dɪk'teɪʃn] dettatura f

dic·ta·tor [dɪk'teɪtə(r)] POL dittatore m

dic·ta·tori·al [dɪktə'tɔ:rɪəl] adj dittatoriale

dic·ta·tor·ship [dɪk'teɪtəʃɪp] dittatura f

dic·tion·a·ry ['dɪkʃənrɪ] dizionario m

did [dɪd] pret → **do**

die [daɪ] v/i morire; ~ of cancer/Aids morire di cancro/AIDS; I'm dying to know/leave muoio dalla voglia di sapere/andare via

♦ **die away** v/i of noise estinguersi

♦ **die down** v/i of noise, fire estinguersi; of storm, excitement placarsi

♦ **die out** v/i of custom scomparire; of species estinguersi

die·sel ['di:zl] (fuel) diesel m

di·et ['daɪət] **1** n dieta f **2** v/i to lose weight essere a dieta

di·e·ti·tian [daɪə'tɪʃn] dietologo m, -a f

dif·fer ['dɪfə(r)] v/i (be different) differire, essere differente; (disagree) non essere d'accordo

dif·fe·rence ['dɪfrəns] differenza f; (disagreement) divergenza f; it doesn't make any ~ non fa nessuna differenza

dif·fe·rent ['dɪfrənt] adj diverso, differente

dif·fe·ren·ti·ate [dɪfə'renʃɪeɪt]: v/i distinguere; ~ **between** things distinguere tra; people fare distinzioni tra

dif·fe·rent·ly ['dɪfrəntlɪ] adv diversamente, differentemente

dif·fi·cult ['dɪfɪkəlt] adj difficile

dif·fi·cul·ty ['dɪfɪkəltɪ] difficoltà f inv; with ~ a fatica

dif·fi·dence ['dɪfɪdəns] diffidenza f

dif·fi·dent ['dɪfɪdənt] adj diffidente

dig [dɪg] (pret & pp **dug**) **1** v/t scava-

re **2** v/i: it was ~ging into me mi si stava conficcando dentro

♦ **dig out** v/t tirar fuori

♦ **dig up** v/t garden scavare; buried object dissotterrare; tree sradicare; information scovare

di·gest [daɪ'dʒest] v/t also fig digerire

di·gest·i·ble [daɪ'dʒestəbl] adj food digeribile

di·ges·tion [daɪ'dʒestʃn] digestione f

di·ges·tive [daɪ'dʒestɪv] adj digestivo; ~ juices succhi mpl gastrici; ~ **system** apparato m digerente

dig·ger ['dɪgə(r)] (machine) scavatrice f

di·git ['dɪdʒɪt] (number) cifra f; a 4 ~ number un numero di 4 cifre

di·gi·tal ['dɪdʒɪtl] adj digitale

dig·ni·fied ['dɪgnɪfaɪd] adj dignitoso

dig·ni·ta·ry ['dɪgnɪtərɪ] dignitario m

dig·ni·ty ['dɪgnɪtɪ] dignità f

di·gress [daɪ'gres] v/i fare una digressione

di·gres·sion [daɪ'greʃn] digressione f

digs [dɪgz] npl camera f in affitto

dike [daɪk] along a river argine m; across a river diga f

di·lap·i·dat·ed [dɪ'læpɪdeɪtɪd] adj rovinato; house cadente

di·late [daɪ'leɪt] v/i of pupils dilatarsi

di·lem·ma [dɪ'lemə] dilemma m; be in a ~ trovarsi in un dilemma

dil·et·tante [dɪle'tæntɪ] dilettante m/f

dil·i·gent ['dɪlɪdʒənt] adj diligente

di·lute [daɪ'lu:t] v/t diluire

dim [dɪm] **1** adj room buio; light fioco; outline indistinto; (stupid) idiota; prospects vago **2** v/t (pret & pp **-med**): ~ **the headlights** abbassare le luci **3** v/i (pret & pp **-med**) of lights abbassarsi

di·men·sion [daɪ'menʃn] (measurement) dimensione f

di·min·ish [dɪ'mɪnɪʃ] v/t & v/i diminuire

di·min·u·tive [dɪ'mɪnjʊtɪv] **1** n diminutivo m **2** adj minuscolo

dim·ple ['dɪmpl] fossetta f

din [dɪn] n baccano m

dine [daɪn] *v/i fml* cenare

din·ner ['daɪnə(r)] *in a restaurant* cliente *m/f*; **fellow ~** commensale *m/f*

din·ghy ['dɪŋgɪ] *small yacht* dinghy *m*; *rubber boat* gommone *m*

din·gy ['dɪndʒɪ] *adj atmosphere* offuscato; *(dirty)* sporco

din·ing car ['daɪnɪŋ] RAIL vagone *m* ristorante; **'din·ing room** *in house* sala *f* da pranzo; *in hotel* sala *f* ristorante; **'din·ing ta·ble** tavolo *m* da pranzo

din·ner ['dɪnə(r)] *in the evening* cena *f*; *at midday* pranzo *m*; *formal gathering* ricevimento *m*

'din·ner guest invitato *m*, -a; **'dinner jack·et** smoking *m inv*; **'dinner par·ty** cena *f*; **'din·ner serv·ice** servizio *m* (di piatti)

di·no·saur ['daɪnəsɔ:(r)] dinosauro *m*

dip [dɪp] **1** *n (swim)* tuffo *m*; *for food* salsa *f*; *in road* pendenza *f* **2** *v/t (pret & pp -ped)* immergere; **~ the headlights** abbassare le luci **3** *v/i (pret & pp -ped) of road* scendere

di·plo·ma [dɪ'pləʊmə] diploma *m*

di·plo·ma·cy [dɪ'pləʊməsɪ] diplomazia *f*

di·plo·mat ['dɪpləmæt] diplomatico *m*, -a *f*

di·plo·mat·ic [dɪplə'mætɪk] *adj* diplomatico

dip·lo·mat·i·cal·ly [dɪplə'mætɪklɪ] *adv* con diplomazia

dip·lo·mat·ic im·mu·ni·ty immunità *f* diplomatica

dire ['daɪə(r)] *adj* tremendo

di·rect [daɪ'rekt] **1** *adj* diretto **2** *v/t play* mettere in scena; *film* curare la regia di; *attention* dirigere; *could you please ~ me to …?* mi può per favore indicare la strada per …?

di·rect 'cur·rent ELEC corrente *f* continua

di·rect 'deb·it FIN ordine *m* di addebito automatico

di·rec·tion [dɪ'rekʃn] direzione *f*; *of film, play* regia *f*; **~s** *(instructions)*, *to a place* indicazioni *fpl*; *for use* istruzioni *fpl*

di·rec·tion 'in·di·ca·tor MOT freccia *f*

di·rec·tive [dɪ'rektɪv] *of EU etc* direttiva *f*

di·rect·ly [dɪ'rektlɪ] **1** *adv (straight)* direttamente; *(soon, immediately)* immediatamente **2** *conj* (non) appena; **I'll do it ~ I've finished this** lo faccio (non) appena ho finito questo

di·rec·tor [dɪ'rektə(r)] *of company* direttore *m*, -trice *f*; *of play, film* regista *m/f*

di·rec·to·ry [dɪ'rektərɪ] elenco *m*; TELEC guida *f* telefonica

dirt [dɜːt] sporco *m*, sporcizia *f*

'dirt cheap *adj* F a un prezzo stracciato

dirt·y ['dɜːtɪ] **1** *adj* sporco; *(pornographic)* sconcio **2** *v/t (pret & pp -ied)* sporcare

dirt·y 'trick tiro *m* mancino

dis·a·bil·i·ty [dɪsə'bɪlətɪ] handicap *m inv*, invalidità *f inv*

dis·a·bled [dɪs'eɪbld] **1** *n* handicappato *m*, -a *f*; **the ~** i disabili **2** *adj* handicappato

dis·ad·van·tage [dɪsəd'vɑːntɪdʒ] *(drawback)* svantaggio *m*; **be at a ~** essere svantaggiato

dis·ad·van·taged [dɪsəd'vɑːntɪdʒd] *adj* penalizzato

dis·ad·van·ta·geous [dɪsədvən'teɪdʒəs] *adj* svantaggioso

dis·a·gree [dɪsə'griː] *v/i of person* non essere d'accordo

♦ **disagree with** *v/t of person* non essere d'accordo con; *of food* fare male a

dis·a·gree·a·ble [dɪsə'griːəbl] *adj* sgradevole

dis·a·gree·ment [dɪsə'griːmənt] disaccordo *m*; *(argument)* discussione *f*

dis·al·low [dɪsə'laʊ] *v/t goal* annullare

dis·ap·pear [dɪsə'pɪə(r)] *v/i* sparire, scomparire

dis·ap·pear·ance [dɪsə'pɪərəns] sparizione *f*, scomparsa *f*

D

dis·ap·point [dɪsə'pɔɪnt] *v/t* deludere

dis·ap·point·ed [dɪsə'pɔɪntɪd] *adj* deluso

dis·ap·point·ing [dɪsə'pɔɪntɪŋ] *adj* deludente

dis·ap·point·ment [dɪsə'pɔɪntmənt] delusione *f*

dis·ap·prov·al [dɪsə'pruːvl] disapprovazione *f*

dis·ap·prove [dɪsə'pruːv] *v/i* disapprovare; **~ of** disapprovare

dis·ap·prov·ing [dɪsə'pruːvɪŋ] *adj look* di disapprovazione

dis·ap·prov·ing·ly [dɪsə'pruːvɪŋlɪ] *adv* con disapprovazione

dis·arm [dɪs'ɑːm] **1** *v/t* disarmare **2** *v/i* disarmarsi

dis·ar·ma·ment [dɪs'ɑːməmənt] disarmo *m*

dis·arm·ing [dɪs'ɑːmɪŋ] *adj* disarmante

dis·as·ter [dɪ'zɑːstə(r)] disastro *m*

di'sas·ter ar·e·a area *f* disastrata; (*fig: person*) disastro *m*

di·sas·trous [dɪ'zɑːstrəs] *adj* disastroso

dis·band [dɪs'bænd] **1** *v/t* sciogliere **2** *v/i* sciogliersi

dis·be·lief [dɪsbə'liːf] incredulità *f*; **in ~** con incredulità

disc [dɪsk] disco *m*

dis·card [dɪ'skɑːd] *v/t* sbarazzarsi di

dis·cern [dɪ'sɜːn] *v/t improvement, intentions* percepire; *outline* distinguere

dis·cern·i·ble [dɪ'sɜːnəbl] *adj improvement* percepibile; *outline* distinguibile

dis·cern·ing [dɪ'sɜːnɪŋ] *adj person* perspicace; **the car for the ~ driver** la macchina per i guidatori che sanno fare la differenza

dis·charge ['dɪstʃɑːdʒ] **1** *n from hospital* dimissione *f; from army* congedo *m* **2** *v/t* [dɪs'tʃɑːdʒ] *from hospital* dimettere; *from army* congedare; *from job* licenziare; LAW prosciogliere

di·sci·ple [dɪ'saɪpl] discepolo *m*, -a *f*

dis·ci·pli·nar·y [dɪsɪ'plɪnərɪ] *adj* disciplinare

dis·ci·pline ['dɪsɪplɪn] **1** *n* disciplina *f* **2** *v/t child, dog* imporre disciplina a; *employee* applicare provvedimenti disciplinari a

'**disc jock·ey** disc jockey *m/f inv*

dis·claim [dɪs'kleɪm] *v/t* negare; *responsibility* declinare

dis·close [dɪs'kləʊs] *v/t* svelare, rivelare

dis·clo·sure [dɪs'kləʊʒə(r)] rivelazione *f*

dis·co ['dɪskəʊ] discoteca *f*

dis·col·or *Am,* **dis·col·our** [dɪs'kʌlə(r)] *v/i* scolorire

dis·com·fort [dɪs'kʌmfət] *n* disagio *m*; (*pain*) fastidio *m*

dis·con·cert [dɪskən'sɜːt] *v/t* sconcertare

dis·con·cert·ed [dɪskən'sɜːtɪd] *adj* sconcertato

dis·con·nect [dɪskə'nekt] *v/t* (*detach*) sconnettere; *supply, telephones* staccare; **they'll ~ you if you don't pay your phone bill** ti staccheranno il telefono se non paghi la bolletta; **I was ~ed** TELEC è caduta la linea

dis·con·so·late [dɪs'kɒnsələt] *adj* sconsolato

dis·con·tent [dɪskən'tent] malcontento *m*

dis·con·tent·ed [dɪskən'tentɪd] *adj* scontento

dis·con·tin·ue [dɪskən'tɪnjuː] *v/t* interrompere; **be a ~d line** essere fuori produzione

dis·cord ['dɪskɔːd] MUS dissonanza *f; in relations* contrasto *m*

dis·co·theque ['dɪskətek] discoteca *f*

dis·count ['dɪskaʊnt] **1** *n* sconto *m; a 10% ~* uno sconto del 10% **2** *v/t* [dɪs'kaʊnt] *goods* scontare; *theory* trascurare

dis·cour·age [dɪs'kʌrɪdʒ] *v/t* (*dissuade*) scoraggiare

dis·cour·age·ment [dɪs'kʌrɪdʒmənt] *being disheartened* scoraggiamento *m*; **meet with ~** non avere incoraggiamento

dis·cov·er [dɪˈskʌvə(r)] *v/t* scoprire

dis·cov·er·er [dɪˈskʌvərə(r)] scopritore *m*, -trice *f*

dis·cov·e·ry [dɪˈskʌvərɪ] scoperta *f*

dis·cred·it [dɪsˈkredɪt] *v/t* screditare

di·screet [dɪˈskriːt] *adj* discreto

di·screet·ly [dɪˈskriːtlɪ] *adv* discretamente

di·screp·an·cy [dɪˈskrepənsɪ] incongruenza *f*

di·scre·tion [dɪˈskreʃn] discrezione *f*; *at your* ~ a tua discrezione

di·scrim·i·nate [dɪˈskrɪmɪneɪt] *v/i*: ~ *against* discriminare; ~ *between* (*distinguish between*) distinguere tra

di·scrim·i·nat·ing [dɪˈskrɪmɪneɪtɪŋ] *adj* esigente

di·scrim·i·na·tion [dɪˈskrɪmɪneɪʃn] *sexual, racial etc* discriminazione *f*

dis·cus [ˈdɪskəs] SP: *object* disco *m*; SP: *event* lancio *m* del disco

di·scuss [dɪˈskʌs] *v/t* discutere; *of article* trattare di; *the article ~es whether ...* l'articolo esamina se ...

di·scus·sion [dɪˈskʌʃn] discussione *f*

'dis·cus throw·er lanciatore *m*, -trice *f* di disco

dis·dain [dɪsˈdeɪn] *n* sdegno *m*

dis·ease [dɪˈziːz] malattia *f*

dis·em·bark [dɪsəmˈbɑːk] *v/i* sbarcare

dis·en·chant·ed [dɪsənˈtʃɑːntɪd] *adj* disincantato; ~ *with* disilluso di

dis·en·gage [dɪsənˈgeɪdʒ] *v/t* svincolare

dis·en·tan·gle [dɪsənˈtæŋgl] *v/t* districare

dis·fig·ure [dɪsˈfɪgə(r)] *v/t* sfigurare; *fig* deturpare

dis·grace [dɪsˈgreɪs] 1 *n* vergogna *f*; *it's a* ~ è una vergogna; *in* ~ in disgrazia 2 *v/t* disonorare

dis·grace·ful [dɪsˈgreɪsful] *adj behaviour, situation* vergognoso

dis·grun·tled [dɪsˈgrʌntld] *adj* scontento

dis·guise [dɪsˈgaɪz] 1 *n* travestimento *m*; *be in* ~ essere travestito 2 *v/t one's voice, handwriting* camuffare; *fear, anxiety* dissimulare; ~ *o.s. as*

travestirsi da; *he was ~d as a woman* era travestito da donna

dis·gust [dɪsˈgʌst] 1 *n* disgusto *m*; *in* ~ disgustato 2 *v/t* disgustare

dis·gust·ing [dɪsˈgʌstɪŋ] *adj* disgustoso

dish [dɪʃ] *part of meal* piatto *m*; *for serving* piatto *m*; *for cooking* recipiente *m*

'dish·cloth strofinaccio *m*

dis·heart·en·ed [dɪsˈhɑːtnd] *adj* demoralizzato

dis·heart·en·ing [dɪsˈhɑːtnɪŋ] *adj* demoralizzante

di·shev·eled [dɪˈʃevld] *adj person, appearance* arruffato; *after effort* scompigliato

dis·hon·est [dɪsˈɒnɪst] *adj* disonesto

dis·hon·es·ty [dɪsˈɒnɪstɪ] disonestà *f*

dis·hon·or *etc Am* → **dishonour** *etc*

dis·hon·our [dɪsˈɒnə(r)] *n* disonore *m*; *bring* ~ *on* coprire di disonore

dis·hon·our·a·ble [dɪsˈɒnərəbl] *adj* disdicevole

'dish·wash·er *machine* lavastoviglie *f inv*; *person* lavapiatti *m/f inv*

'dish·wash·ing liq·uid *Am* detersivo *m* per i piatti

'dish·wa·ter acqua *f* dei piatti

dis·il·lu·sion [dɪsɪˈluːʒn] *v/t* disilludere

dis·il·lu·sion·ment [dɪsɪˈluːʒnmənt] disillusione *f*

dis·in·clined [dɪsɪnˈklaɪnd] *adj* restio (*to* a)

dis·in·fect [dɪsɪnˈfekt] *v/t* disinfettare

dis·in·fec·tant [dɪsɪnˈfektənt] disinfettante *m*

dis·in·her·it [dɪsɪnˈherɪt] *v/t* diseredare

dis·in·te·grate [dɪsˈɪntɪgreɪt] *v/i* disintegrarsi; *of marriage, building* andare in pezzi

dis·in·ter·est·ed [dɪsˈɪntərɪstɪd] *adj* (*unbiased*) disinteressato

dis·joint·ed [dɪsˈdʒɔɪntɪd] *adj* sconnesso

disk [dɪsk] disco *m*; (*diskette*) dischetto *m*; *on* ~ su dischetto *m* 'disk drive COMPUT lettore *m o* drive *m inv* di dischetti

disk·ette [dɪsˈket] dischetto *m*

dis·like [dɪsˈlaɪk] **1** *n* antipatia *f*; **take a ~ to s.o.** prendere qu in antipatia **2** *v/t: I ~ cats* non mi piacciono i gatti; *I ~ watching TV* non mi piace guardare la TV

dis·lo·cate ['dɪsləkeɪt] *v/t shoulder* lussare

dis·lodge [dɪsˈlɒdʒ] *v/t* rimuovere

dis·loy·al [dɪsˈlɔɪəl] *adj* sleale

dis·loy·al·ty [dɪsˈlɔɪəltɪ] slealtà *f*

dis·mal ['dɪzməl] *adj weather, news* deprimente; *person (sad), failure* triste; *person (negative)* ombroso

dis·man·tle [dɪsˈmæntl] *v/t* smontare; *organization* demolire

dis·may [dɪsˈmeɪ] **1** *n* costernazione *f* **2** *v/t* costernare

dis·miss [dɪsˈmɪs] *v/t employee* licenziare; *suggestion, possibility* scartare; *idea, thought* accantonare

dis·miss·al [dɪsˈmɪsl] *of employee* licenziamento *m*

dis·mount [dɪsˈmaʊnt] *v/i* smontare

dis·o·be·di·ence [dɪsəˈbiːdɪəns] disobbidienza *f*

dis·o·be·di·ent [dɪsəˈbiːdɪənt] *adj* disobbidiente

dis·o·bey [dɪsəˈbeɪ] *v/t* disobbedire a

dis·or·der [dɪsˈɔːdə(r)] *(untidiness)* disordine *m*; *(unrest)* disordini *mpl*; MED disturbo *m*

dis·or·der·ly [dɪsˈɔːdəlɪ] *adj room, desk* in disordine; *mob* turbolento

dis·or·gan·ized [dɪsˈɔːgənaɪzd] *adj* disorganizzato

dis·o·ri·ent·ed [dɪsˈɔːrɪəntɪd], dis·o·ri·en·tat·ed [dɪsˈɔːrɪənteɪtɪd] *adj* disorientato

dis·own [dɪsˈəʊn] *v/t* disconoscere

dis·par·ag·ing [dɪˈspærɪdʒɪŋ] *adj* dispregiativo

dis·par·i·ty [dɪˈspærətɪ] disparità *f inv*

dis·pas·sion·ate [dɪˈspæʃənət] *adj (objective)* spassionato

dis·patch [dɪˈspætʃ] *v/t (send)* spedire

dis·pen·sa·ry [dɪˈspensərɪ] *in phar-*

macy dispensario *m*

◆di·spense with [dɪˈspens] *v/t* fare a meno di

di·sperse [dɪˈspɜːs] **1** *v/t* dissipare **2** *v/i of crowd* disperdersi; *of mist* dissiparsi

dis·pir·it·ed [dɪˈspɪrɪtɪd] *adj* abbattuto

dis·place [dɪsˈpleɪs] *v/t (supplant)* rimpiazzare

dis·play [dɪˈspleɪ] **1** *n* esposizione *f*, mostra *f*; *in shop window* articoli *mpl* in esposizione; COMPUT visualizzazione *f*; **be on ~** *at exhibition* essere in esposizione *o* mostra; *(be for sale)* essere esposto in vendita **2** *v/t emotion* manifestare; *at exhibition* esporre; *(for sale)* esporre in vendita; COMPUT visualizzare

di·splay cab·i·net *in museum* teca *f*; *in shop* vetrinetta *f*

dis·please [dɪsˈpliːz] *v/t* contrariare; **they were ~d with her** erano contrariati con lei

dis·plea·sure [dɪsˈpleʒə(r)] disappunto *m*

dis·po·sa·ble [dɪˈspəʊzəbl] *adj* usa e getta *inv*

dis·po·sa·ble 'in·come reddito *m* disponibile

dis·pos·al [dɪˈspəʊzl] *(getting rid of)* eliminazione *f*; *of pollutants, nuclear waste* smaltimento *m*; *I am at your ~* sono a tua disposizione; *put sth at s.o.'s ~* mettere qc a disposizione di qu

◆dis·pose of [dɪˈspəʊz] *v/t (get rid of)* sbarazzarsi di

dis·posed [dɪˈspəʊzd] *adj:* **be ~ to do sth** *(willing)* essere disposto a fare qc; **be well ~ towards** essere ben disposto verso

dis·po·si·tion [dɪspəˈzɪʃn] *(nature)* indole *f*

dis·pro·por·tion·ate [dɪsprəˈpɔːʃənət] *adj* sproporzionato

dis·prove [dɪsˈpruːv] *v/t* smentire

dis·pute [dɪˈspjuːt] **1** *n* controversia *f*; *(industrial)* contestazione *f*; **be in ~** essere controverso **2** *v/t* contestare; *(fight over)* contendersi

dis·qual·i·fi·ca·tion [dɪskwɒlɪfɪˈkeɪ-ʃn] squalifica f; *it's a ~* è penalizzante

dis·qual·i·fy [dɪsˈkwɒlɪfaɪ] v/t (*pret & pp -ied*) squalificare

dis·re·gard [dɪsrəˈgɑːd] **1** n mancanza f di considerazione **2** v/t ignorare

dis·re·pair [dɪsrəˈpeə(r)]: *in a state of ~* in cattivo stato

dis·rep·u·ta·ble [dɪsˈrepjʊtəbl] adj depravato; *area* malfamato

dis·re·spect [dɪsrəˈspekt] mancanza f di rispetto

dis·re·spect·ful [dɪsrəˈspektfʊl] adj irriverente

dis·rupt [dɪsˈrʌpt] v/t *train service* creare disagi a; *meeting, class* disturbare; (*intentionally*) creare scompiglio in

dis·rup·tion [dɪsˈrʌpʃn] *of train service* disagio m; *of meeting, class* disturbo m; (*intentional*) scompiglio m

dis·rup·tive [dɪsˈrʌptɪv] adj *influence* deleterio; *he's very ~ in class* è un elemento di disturbo nella classe

dis·sat·is·fac·tion [dɪssætɪsˈfækʃn] insoddisfazione f

dis·sat·is·fied [dɪsˈsætɪsfaɪd] adj insoddisfatto

dis·sen·sion [dɪˈsenʃn] dissenso m

dis·sent [dɪˈsent] **1** n dissenso m **2** v/i *~ from* dissentire da

dis·si·dent [ˈdɪsɪdənt] n dissidente m/f

dis·sim·i·lar [dɪsˈsɪmɪlə(r)] adj dissimile

dis·so·ci·ate [dɪˈsəʊʃɪeɪt] v/t: *~ o.s. from* dissociarsi da

dis·so·lute [ˈdɪsəluːt] adj dissoluto

dis·so·lu·tion [ˈdɪsəluːʃn] POL scioglimento m

dis·solve [dɪˈsɒlv] **1** v/t *substance* sciogliere **2** v/i *of substance* sciogliersi

dis·suade [dɪˈsweɪd] v/t dissuadere; *~ s.o. from doing sth* dissuadere qu dal fare qc

dis·tance [ˈdɪstəns] **1** n distanza f; *in the ~* in lontananza **2** v/t: *~ o.s. from* prendere le distanze da

dis·tant [ˈdɪstənt] adj lontano

dis·taste [dɪsˈteɪst] avversione f

dis·taste·ful [dɪsˈteɪstfʊl] adj spiacevole

dis·till·er·y [dɪsˈtɪlərɪ] distilleria f

dis·tinct [dɪˈstɪŋkt] adj (*clear*) netto; (*different*) distinto; *as ~ from* contrariamente a

dis·tinc·tion [dɪˈstɪŋkʃn] (*differentiation*) distinzione f; *hotel / product of ~* hotel / prodotto d'eccezione

dis·tinc·tive [dɪˈstɪŋktɪv] adj caratteristico

dis·tinct·ly [dɪˈstɪŋktlɪ] adv distintamente; (*decidedly*) decisamente

dis·tin·guish [dɪˈstɪŋgwɪʃ] v/t (*see*) distinguere; *~ between X and Y* distinguere tra X e Y

dis·tin·guished [dɪˈstɪŋgwɪʃt] adj (*famous*) insigne; (*dignified*) distinto

dis·tort [dɪˈstɔːt] v/t distorcere

dis·tract [dɪˈstrækt] v/t *person* distrarre; *attention* distogliere

dis·tract·ed [dɪˈstræktɪd] adj assente

dis·trac·tion [dɪˈstrækʃn] *of attention* distrazione f; *drive s.o. to ~* fare impazzire qu

dis·traught [dɪˈstrɔːt] adj affranto

dis·tress [dɪˈstres] **1** n sofferenza f; *in ~ of ship, aircraft* in difficoltà **2** v/t (*upset*) angosciare

dis·tress·ing [dɪˈstresɪŋ] adj sconvolgente

dis·tress sig·nal segnale m di pericolo

dis·trib·ute [dɪˈstrɪbjuːt] v/t distribuire

dis·tri·bu·tion [dɪstrɪˈbjuːʃn] distribuzione f

dis·trib·u·tor [dɪsˈtrɪbjutə(r)] COM distributore m

dis·trict [ˈdɪstrɪkt] quartiere m

dis·trust [dɪsˈtrʌst] **1** n diffidenza f **2** v/t non fidarsi di

dis·turb [dɪˈstɜːb] v/t disturbare; *do not ~* non disturbare

dis·turb·ance [dɪˈstɜːbəns] (*interruption*) fastidio m; *~s* (*civil unrest*) disordini mpl

dis·turbed [dɪ'stɜːbd] *adj* (*concerned, worried*) turbato; *psychologically* malato di mente

dis·turb·ing [dɪ'stɜːbɪŋ] *adj* inquietante

dis·used [dɪs'juːzd] *adj* inutilizzato

ditch [dɪtʃ] **1** *n* fosso *m* **2** *v/t* F *boyfriend* scaricare F; F *car* sbarazzarsi di

dith·er ['dɪθə(r)] *v/i* titubare

di·van [dɪ'væn] (*bed*) divano *m*

dive [daɪv] **1** *n* tuffo *m*; (*underwater*) immersione *f*; *of plane* picchiata *f*; F (*bar etc*) bettola *f* F; **take a ~** F *of sterling etc* crollare **2** *v/i* tuffarsi; (*underwater*) fare immersione; *of submarine* immergersi; *of plane* scendere in picchiata; **the goalie ~d for the ball** il portiere si è tuffato per prendere la palla

div·er ['daɪvə(r)] *off board* tuffatore *m*, -trice *f*; (*underwater*) sub *m/f inv*, sommozzatore *m*, -trice *f*

di·verge [daɪ'vɜːdʒ] *v/i* divergere

di·verse [daɪ'vɜːs] *adj* svariato

di·ver·si·fi·ca·tion [daɪvɜːsɪfɪ'keɪʃn] COM diversificazione *f*

di·ver·si·fy [daɪ'vɜːsɪfaɪ] *v/i* (*pret & pp -ied*) COM diversificare

di·ver·sion [daɪ'vɜːʃn] *for traffic* deviazione *f*; *to distract attention* diversivo *m*

di·ver·si·ty [daɪ'vɜːsətɪ] varietà *f inv*

di·vert [daɪ'vɜːt] *v/t traffic* deviare; *attention* sviare, distogliere

di·vest [daɪ'vest] *v/t*: **~ s.o. of sth** privare qu di qc

di·vide [dɪ'vaɪd] *v/t* dividere

div·i·dend ['dɪvɪdend] FIN dividendo *m*; **pay ~s** *fig* dare i suoi frutti

di·vine [dɪ'vaɪn] *adj* REL, F divino

div·ing ['daɪvɪŋ] *from board* tuffi *mpl*; (*scuba ~*) immersione *f*

'**div·ing board** trampolino *m*

di·vis·i·ble [dɪ'vɪzəbl] *adj* divisibile

di·vi·sion [dɪ'vɪʒn] divisione *f*; *of company* sezione *f*

di·vorce [dɪ'vɔːs] **1** *n* divorzio *m*; **get a ~** divorziare; **get ~d** divorziare **3** *v/i* divorziare

di·vorced [dɪ'vɔːst] *adj* divorziato

di·vor·cee [dɪvɔː'siː] divorziato *m*, -a *f*

di·vulge [daɪ'vʌldʒ] *v/t* divulgare

DIY [diːaɪ'waɪ] *abbr* (= *do it yourself*) fai da te *m inv*, bricolage *m*

DI'Y store negozio *m* di bricolage; *smaller shop* ferramenta *f*

diz·zi·ness ['dɪzɪnəs] giramento *m* di testa, vertigini *fpl*

diz·zy ['dɪzɪ] *adj* stordito; **I feel ~** mi gira la testa

DJ [diː'dʒeɪ] *abbr* (= *disc jockey*) dj *m/f inv*; (= *dinner jacket*) smoking *m inv*

DNA [diːen'eɪ] *abbr* (= *deoxyribonucleic acid*) DNA *m inv* (= acido *m* deossiribonucleico)

do [duː] (*pret did, pp done*) **1** *v/t* fare; *one's hair* farsi; *100mph etc* andare a; **~ the ironing / cooking** stirare / cucinare; **what are you ~ing tonight?** cosa fai stasera?; **I don't know what to ~** non so cosa fare; **no, I'll ~ it** no, lo faccio; *stress on I* no, lo faccio io; **~ it right now!** fallo subito!; **have you done this before?** lo hai già fatto?; **have one's hair done** farsi fare i capelli **2** *v/i* (*be suitable, enough*) andare bene; **that will ~!** basta così!; **~ well** (*do a good job*) essere bravo; (*be in good health*) stare bene; *of business* andare bene; **well done!** (*congratulations!*) bravo!; **how ~ you ~?** molto piacere **3** *v/aux*: **~ you know him?** lo conosci?; **I ~n't know** non (lo) so; **~ be quick** sii veloce; **you like London? – yes I ~** ti piace Londra? – sì (mi piace); **he works hard, doesn't he?** lavora sodo, no?; **~n't you believe me?** non mi credi?; **you ~ believe me, ~n't you?** mi credi, non è vero?; **you ~n't know the answer, ~ you? – no I ~n't** non sai la risposta, vero? – no, non la so

♦**do away with** *v/t* (*abolish*) abolire

♦**do in** *v/t* F (*exhaust*) stravolgere F; **I'm done in** sono stravolto

♦**do out of** *v/t*: **do s.o. out of sth** F fregare qc a qu F

♦**do up** *v/t* (*renovate*) restaurare;

(*fasten*) allacciare; **do up your buttons** abbottonati; **do up your shoe-laces** allacciati le scarpe

♦ **do with** *v/t*: **I could do with ...** mi ci vorrebbe ...; **he won't have anything to do with it** (*won't get involved*) non vuole averci niente a che fare

♦ **do without 1** *v/i* farne a meno **2** *v/t* fare a meno di

do·cile ['dəʊsaɪl] *adj* docile

dock¹ [dɒk] **1** *n* NAUT bacino *m* **2** *v/i* *of ship* entrare in porto; *of spaceship* agganciarsi

dock² [dɒk] LAW banco *m* degli imputati

dock·er ['dɒkə(r)] portuale *m*

'**dock·yard** cantiere *m* navale

doc·tor ['dɒktə(r)] *n* MED dottore *m*, -essa *f*

doc·tor·ate ['dɒktərət] dottorato *m*

doc·trine ['dɒktrɪn] dottrina *f*

doc·u·dra·ma ['dɒkjʊdrɑːmə] ricostruzione *f* filmata

doc·u·ment ['dɒkjʊmənt] *n* documento *m*

doc·u·men·ta·ry [dɒkjʊ'mentərɪ] *n* *programme* documentario *m*

doc·u·men·ta·tion [dɒkjʊmen'teɪʃn] documentazione *f*

dodge [dɒdʒ] *v/t* *blow* schivare; *person, issue* evitare; *question* aggirare

dodg·ems ['dɒdʒəms] *npl* autoscontro *m*

dog [dɒg] **1** *n* cane *m* **2** *v/t* (*pret & pp -ged*) *of bad luck* perseguitare

'**dog catch·er** accalappiacani *m inv*

dog-eared ['dɒgɪəd] *adj* *book* con le orecchie

dog·ged ['dɒgɪd] *adj* accanito

dog·gie ['dɒgɪ] *in children's language* cagnolino *m*

dog·gy bag ['dɒgɪbæg] *pacchetto m con gli avanzi di una cena al ristorante per l'asporto*

'**dog·house: be in the ~** F essere nei casini F

dog·ma ['dɒgmə] dogma *m*

dog·mat·ic [dɒg'mætɪk] *adj* dogmatico

do-good·er [duː'gʊdə(r)] *pej* impiccione *m*, -a *f*

dogs·body ['dɒgzbɒdɪ] F bestia *m* da soma

'**dog-tired** *adj* F stravolto

do-it-your·self [duːɪtjə'self] fai da te *m inv*

dol·drums ['dɒldrəmz]: **be in the ~** *of economy* essere in stallo; *of person* essere giù di corda

dole [dəʊl] Br F assegno *m* di disoccupazione; **be on the ~** ricevere l'assegno di disoccupazione

'**dole money** Br F assegni *mpl* di disoccupazione

♦ **dole out** *v/t* distribuire

doll [dɒl] *toy*, F *woman* bambola *f*

♦ **doll up** *v/t*: **get dolled up** mettersi in ghingheri

dol·lar ['dɒlə(r)] dollaro *m*

dol·lop ['dɒləp] *n* F cucchiaiata *f*

dol·phin ['dɒlfɪn] delfino *m*

dome [dəʊm] *of building* cupola *f*

do·mes·tic [də'mestɪk] *adj* domestico; *news, policy* interno

do·mes·tic 'an·i·mal animale *m* domestico

do·mes·ti·cate [də'mestɪkeɪt] *v/t* *animal* addomesticare; **be ~d** *of person* essere incline a fare i lavori di casa

do·mes·tic flight volo *m* nazionale

dom·i·nant ['dɒmɪnənt] *adj* dominante; *member* principale

dom·i·nate ['dɒmɪneɪt] *v/t* dominare

dom·i·na·tion [dɒmɪ'neɪʃn] dominio *m*

dom·i·neer·ing [dɒmɪ'nɪərɪŋ] *adj* autoritario

dom·i·no ['dɒmɪnəʊ] domino *m*; **play ~s** giocare a domino

do·nate [dəʊ'neɪt] *v/t* donare

do·na·tion [dəʊ'neɪʃn] donazione *f*

done [dʌn] *pp* → **do**

don·key ['dɒŋkɪ] asino *m*

do·nor ['dəʊnə(r)] donatore *m*, -trice *f*

do·nut ['dəʊnʌt] *Am* → **doughnut**

doo·dle ['duːdl] *v/i* scarabocchiare

doom [duːm] *n* (*fate*) destino *f*; (*ruin*) rovina *f*

doomed [duːmd] *adj project* condannato al fallimento; *we are* ~ siamo condannati; *the* ~ *ship* la nave destinata ad affondare; *the* ~ *plane* l'aereo destinato a cadere

door [dɔː(r)] porta *f*; *of car* portiera *f*; *there's someone at the* ~ stanno suonando alla porta

'**door·bell** campanello *m*; '**door·knob** pomello *m* della porta; '**door·man** usciere *m*; '**door·mat** zerbino *m*; '**door·step** gradino *m* della porta; '**door·way** vano *m* della porta

dope [dəʊp] **1** *n* (*drugs*) droga *f* leggera; *in sport* doping *m inv*; F (*idiot*) cretino *m*, -a *f*; F (*information*) soffiata *f* **2** *v/t* dopare

dor·mant [ˈdɔːmənt] *adj*: ~ *volcano* vulcano *m* inattivo; *lie* ~ *of plant* rimanere latente

dor·mi·to·ry [ˈdɔːmɪtrɪ] dormitorio *m*

dos·age [ˈdəʊsɪdʒ] dosaggio *m*

dose [dəʊs] *n* dose *f*

dot [dɒt] *n* puntino *m*; *in email address* punto *m*; *on the* ~ (*exactly*) in punto

♦ **dote on** [dəʊt] *v/t* stravedere per

dot·ing [ˈdəʊtɪŋ] *adj* adorante

dot·ted line [ˈdɒtɪd] linea *f* tratteggiata

dot·ty [ˈdɒtɪ] *adj* F svitato

dou·ble [ˈdʌbl] **1** *n* (*amount*) doppio *m*; (*person*) sosia *m inv*; *of film star* controfigura *f*; (*room with two beds*) doppio; (*room with double bed*) matrimoniale **2** *adj* doppio; *in* ~ *fig·ures* a due cifre **3** *adv*: ~ *the amount* il doppio della quantità **4** *v/t* raddoppiare **5** *v/i* raddoppiare

♦ **double back** *v/i* (*go back*) fare dietrofront

♦ **double up** *v/i in pain* piegarsi in due; (*share a room*) dividere la stanza

dou·ble-'bass contrabbasso *m*; **dou·ble 'bed** letto *m* matrimoniale; **dou·ble-'breast·ed** *adj* a doppio petto; **dou·ble'check** *v/t & v/i* ricontrollare; **dou·ble 'chin** doppio mento *m*; **dou·ble'cross** *v/t* fare il

doppio gioco con; **doub·le deck·er** '**bus** autobus *m inv* a due piani; **doub·le 'glaz·ing** doppi vetri *mpl*; **dou·ble'park** *v/i* parcheggiare in doppia fila; '**dou·ble-quick** *adj*: *in* ~ *time* in un batter d'occhio; '**dou·ble room** *with two beds* camera *f* doppia; *with double bed* camera *f* matrimoniale

doub·les [ˈdʌblz] *npl in tennis* doppio *msg*

doubt [daʊt] **1** *n* dubbio *m*; *be in* ~ essere in dubbio; *no* ~ (*probably*) senz'altro **2** *v/t*: ~ *s.o. / sth* dubitare di qu/qc; ~ *that* ... dubitare che ...

doubt·ful [ˈdaʊtfʊl] *adj remark, look* dubbio; *be* ~ *of person* essere dubbioso; *it is* ~ *whether* ... è in dubbio se ...

doubt·ful·ly [ˈdaʊtflɪ] *adv* con aria dubbiosa

doubt·less [ˈdaʊtlɪs] *adj* senza dubbio

dough [dəʊ] impasto *m*; F (*money*) quattrini *mpl*

dough·nut [ˈdəʊnʌt] bombolone *m*, krapfen *m inv*

dove [dʌv] colomba *f*; *fig* pacifista *m/f*

dow·dy [ˈdaʊdɪ] *adj* scialbo

down¹ [daʊn] *n* (*feathers*) piuma *f*, piumino *m*

down² [daʊn] **1** *adv* (*downwards*) giù; ~ *there* laggiù; *fall* ~ cadere giù; *die* ~ calmarsi; *£200* ~ (*as deposit*) un acconto di £200; ~ *south* a sud; *be* ~ *of price, rate* essere diminuito; (*not working*) non funzionare; F (*depressed*) essere giù **2** *prep* giù da; (*along*) lungo; *I looked* ~ *the list* ho scorso la lista; *the third door* ~ *this corridor* la terza porta lungo questo corridoio; *walk* ~ *a street* percorrere una strada **3** *v/t* (*swallow*) buttare giù; (*destroy*) abbattere

'**down-and-out** *n* senza tetto *m/f inv*; '**down·cast** *adj* (*dejected*) abbattuto; '**down·fall** rovina *f*; *of politician, government* caduta *f*; '**down·grade** *v/t* ridimensionare; *employee* retrocedere di livello; **down·heart·ed** [daʊn'hɑːtɪd] *adj* abbattuto; **down·'hill** *adv* in discesa; **go ~** *fig* peggiorare; **'down·hill ski·ing** discesa *f* libera; **'down·load** *v/t* COMPUT scaricare; **'down·mark·et** *adj* di fascia medio-bassa; **'down pay·ment** deposito *m*, acconto *m*; **'down·play** *v/t* minimizzare; **'down·pour** acquazzone *m*; **'down·right 1** *adj*: **it's a ~ lie** è una bugia bella e buona; **he's a ~ idiot** è un perfetto idiota **2** *adv* dangerous, stupid etc assolutamente; **'downside** (disadvantage) contropartita *f*; **'down·size 1** *v/t*: company ridimensionare; **the ~ed version** of car la versione ridotta **2** *v/i* of company ridimensionarsi; **'down·stairs** *adj & adv* al piano di sotto; **down-to-'earth** *adj* approach pratico; **she's very ~ about it** ha i piedi molto per terra al riguardo; **'down·town** *adj & adv* in centro; **'down·turn** in economy flessione *f* **'down·wards** *adj & adv* verso il basso

doze [dəʊz] **1** *n* sonnellino *m* **2** *v/i* fare un sonnellino
♦ **doze off** *v/i* assopirsi
doz·en ['dʌzn] dozzina *f*; **~s of ...** F un sacco di ... F
drab [dræb] *adj* scialbo
draft [drɑːft] of document bozza *f*; Am MIL leva *f*; Am → **draught 2** *v/t* document fare una bozza di; Am MIL arruolare
'draft dodg·er Am MIL renitente *f* alla leva
drag [dræg] **1** *n*: **it's a ~ having to ...** F è una rottura dover ... F; **he's a ~** F è una pizza F; **the main ~** P il corso principale; **in ~** vestito da donna; **a man in ~** un travestito **2** *v/t* (pret & pp **-ged**) (pull) trascinare; (search) dragare **3** *v/i* (pret & pp **-ged**) of time non passare mai; of show, film trascinarsi; **~ s.o. into sth** (involve) tirare in ballo qu in qc; **~ sth out of s.o.** (get information from) tirare fuori qc da qu
♦ **drag away**: *v/t*: **drag o.s. away**

from the TV staccarsi dalla TV
♦ **drag in** *v/t into conversation* tirare fuori
♦ **drag on** *v/i* (last long time) trascinarsi
♦ **drag out** *v/t* (prolong) tirare per le lunghe
♦ **drag up** *v/t* F (mention) rivangare
drag·on ['drægn] drago *m*; *fig* strega *f*
drain [dreɪn] **1** *n* (pipe) tubo *m* di scarico; under street tombino *m*; **a ~ on resources** un salasso per le risorse **2** *v/t* water fare colare; oil fare uscire; vegetables scolare; land drenare; glass, tank svuotare; (exhaust: person) svuotare **3** *v/i* of dishes scolare
♦ **drain away** *v/i* of liquid defluire
♦ **drain off** *v/t* water fare defluire
drain·age ['dreɪnɪdʒ] (drains) fognatura *f*; of water from soil drenaggio *m*
'drain·pipe tubo *m* di scarico
dra·ma ['drɑːmə] (art form) arte *f* drammatica; (acting) recitazione *f*; (excitement) dramma *m*; (play: on TV) sceneggiato *m*; **~ classes** corso *m* di recitazione
dra·mat·ic [drə'mætɪk] *adj* drammatico; (exciting) sorprendente; gesture teatrale
dra·mat·i·cal·ly [drə'mætɪklɪ] *adv* say drammaticamente; decline, rise, change etc drasticamente
dram·a·tist ['dræmətɪst] drammaturgo *m*, -a *f*
dram·a·ti·za·tion [dræmətaɪ'zeɪʃn] (play) adattamento *m* teatrale
dram·a·tize ['dræmətaɪz] *v/t* story adattare; *fig* drammatizzare
drank [dræŋk] *pret* → **drink**
drape [dreɪp] *v/t* cloth, coat appoggiare; **~d in** (covered with) avvolto in
drap·er·y ['dreɪpərɪ] drappeggio *m*
drapes [dreɪps] *npl* Am tende *fpl*
dras·tic ['dræstɪk] *adj* drastico
draught [drɑːft] **1** *n* of air corrente *f* (d'aria); **~ (beer), beer on ~** birra *f* alla spina
draughts [drɑːfts] *nsg game* dama *f*
draughts·man ['drɑːftsmən] disegnatore *m* industriale; of plan

disegnatore m, -trice f

draught·y ['drɑːftɪ] adj pieno di correnti d'aria

draw [drɔː] **1** n in match, competition pareggio m; in lottery estrazione f, sorteggio m; (attraction) attrazione f **2** v/t t (pret **drew**, pp **drawn**) picture, map disegnare; cart, curtain, tirare; in lottery, gun, knife estrarre; (attract) attirare; (lead) tirare; from bank account ritirare **3** v/i t (pret **drew**, pp **drawn**) disegnare; in match, competition pareggiare; ~ **near** avvicinarsi

♦ **draw back 1** v/i (recoil) tirarsi indietro **2** v/t hand ritirare; curtains aprire

♦ **draw on 1** v/i (approach) avvicinarsi **2** v/t (make use of) attingere a

♦ **draw out** v/t wallet etc estrarre; money from bank ritirare

♦ **draw up 1** v/t document redigere; chair accostare **2** v/i of vehicle fermarsi; **draw up alongside s.o.** accostarsi a qu

'**draw·back** inconveniente m

draw·er[1] [drɔː(r)] of desk etc cassetto m

draw·er[2] [drɔː(r)] (person) disegnatore m, -trice f; **she's a good ~** disegna bene

'**draw·ing** ['drɔːɪŋ] disegno m

'**draw·ing board** tecnigrafo m; **go back to the ~** fig ricominciare da capo

'**draw·ing pin** puntina f

drawl [drɔːl] n pronuncia f strascicata

drawn [drɔːn] pp → **draw**

dread [dred] v/t aver il terrore di; **I ~ him finding it out** ho il terrore che lo scopra

dread·ful ['dredful] adj terribile

dread·ful·ly ['dredflɪ] adv F (extremely) terribilmente; behave malissimo

dream [driːm] **1** n sogno m **2** adj F house etc dei sogni **3** v/t sognare **4** v/i sognare; **I ~t about you** ti ho sognato

♦ **dream up** v/t sognare

dream·er ['driːmə(r)] (daydreamer)

sognatore m, -trice f

dream·y ['driːmɪ] adj voice, look sognante

drear·y ['drɪərɪ] adj deprimente; (boring) noioso

dredge [dredʒ] v/t harbour, canal dragare

♦ **dredge up** v/t fig scovare

dregs [dregz] npl of coffee fondi mpl; **the ~ of society** la feccia della società

drench [drentʃ] v/t inzuppare; **get ~ed** inzupparsi; **I'm ~ed** sono fradicio

dress [dres] **1** n for woman vestito m; (clothing) abbigliamento m **2** v/t person vestire; wound medicare; salad condire; **get ~ed** vestirsi **3** v/i vestirsi; ~ **in red** vestirsi di rosso

♦ **dress up** v/i vestirsi elegante; (wear a disguise) travestirsi; **dress up as a ghost** travestirsi da fantasma

'**dress cir·cle** prima galleria f

dress·er ['dresə(r)] in kitchen credenza f

dress·ing ['dresɪŋ] for salad condimento m; for wound medicazione f

dress·ing 'down sgridata f; '**dress·ing gown** vestaglia f; '**dress·ing room** in theatre spogliatoio m; '**dress·ing ta·ble** toilette f inv

'**dress·mak·er** sarto m, -a f

'**dress re·hears·al** prova f generale

dress·y ['dresɪ] adj F sull'elegante F

drew [druː] pret → **draw**

drib·ble ['drɪbl] v/i of person sbavare; of water gocciolare; SP dribblare

dried [draɪd] adj fruit etc essicato

dri·er ['draɪə(r)] → **dryer**

drift [drɪft] **1** n of snow cumulo m **2** v/i of snow accumularsi; of ship andare alla deriva; (go off course) uscire dalla rotta; of person vagabondare

♦ **drift apart** v/i of couple allontanarsi (l'uno dall'altro)

drift·er ['drɪftə(r)] vagabondo m, -a f

drill [drɪl] **1** n (tool) trapano m; (exercise), MIL esercitazione f **2** v/t tunnel scavare; ~ **a hole** fare un foro col trapano 3 *v/i*: *for oil* trivellare; MIL addestrarsi

dril·ling rig ['drɪlɪŋrɪg] (*platform*) sonda *f*

dri·ly ['draɪlɪ] *adv remark* ironicamente

drink [drɪŋk] **1** *n* bevanda *f*; **non-alcoholic ~** bibita *f* (analcolica); **a ~ of ...** un bicchiere di ...; **go for a ~** andare a bere qualcosa **2** *v/t & v/i* (*pret* **drank**, *pp* **drunk**) bere; **I don't ~** non bevo

♦ **drink up 1** *v/i* (*finish drink*) finire il bicchiere **2** *v/t* (*drink completely*) finire di bere

drink·a·ble ['drɪŋkəbl] *adj* potabile

drink 'driv·ing guida *f* in stato di ebbrezza

drink·er ['drɪŋkə(r)] bevitore *m*, -trice *f*

drink·ing ['drɪŋkɪŋ] *of alcohol* consumo *m* di alcolici; **he has a ~ problem** beve troppi alcolici

'drink·ing wa·ter acqua *f* potabile

'drinks ma·chine distributore *m* di bevande

drip [drɪp] **1** *n action* gocciolamento *m*; *amount* goccia *f*; MED flebo *f inv* **2** *v/i* (*pret & pp* **-ped**) gocciolare

'drip-dry *adj* non-stiro

drip·ping ['drɪpɪŋ] *adv*: **~ wet** fradicio

drive [draɪv] **1** *n* percorso *m* in macchina; (*outing*) giro *m* in macchina; (*driveway*) viale *m*; (*energy*) grinta *f*; COMPUT lettore *m*; (*campaign*) campagna *f*; **left-/right-hand ~** MOT guida *f* a sinistra/destra **2** *v/t* (*pret* **drove**, *pp* **driven**) *vehicle* guidare; (*take in car*) portare (in macchina); TECH azionare; **that noise/this man is driving me mad** questo rumore/quest'uomo mi fa diventare matto **3** *v/i* (*pret* **drove**, *pp* **driven**) guidare; **I ~ to work** vado al lavoro in macchina

♦ **drive at** *v/t*: **what are you driving at?** dove vuoi andare a parare?

♦ **drive away 1** *v/t* portare via (in macchina); (*chase off*) cacciare **2** *v/i* andare via (in macchina)

♦ **drive in** *v/t nail* piantare

♦ **drive off** → **drive away**

driv·el ['drɪvl] *n* sciocchezze *fpl*

driv·en ['drɪvn] *pp* → **drive**

driv·er ['draɪvə(r)] guidatore *m*, -trice *f*, conducente *m/f*; *of train* macchinista *m/f*; COMPUT driver *m inv*

'driv·er's li·cence *Am* patente *f* (di guida)

'drive·way viale *m*

driv·ing ['draɪvɪŋ] **1** *n* guida *f* **2** *adj rain* violento

driv·ing 'force elemento *m* motore; **'driv·ing in·struct·or** istruttore *m*, -trice *f* di guida; **'driv·ing les·son** lezione *f* di guida; **'driv·ing li·cence** patente *f* (di guida); **'driv·ing school** scuola *f* guida; **'driv·ing test** esame *m* di guida

driz·zle ['drɪzl] **1** *n* pioggerella *f* **2** *v/i* piovvigginare

drone [drəʊn] *n* (*noise*) ronzio *m*

droop [druːp] *v/i* abbassarsi; *of plant* afflosciarsi

drop [drɒp] **1** *n of rain* goccia *f*; (*small amount*) goccio *m*; *in price, temperature* calo *m*; *in number* calo *m* **2** *v/t* (*pret & pp* **-ped**) far cadere; *from plane* sganciare; *person from car* lasciare; *person from team* scartare; (*stop seeing*) smettere di frequentare; *charges, demand etc* abbandonare; (*give up*) lasciare perdere; **~ a line to** scrivere due righe a **3** *v/i* (*pret & pp* **-ped**) cadere; (*decline*) calare

♦ **drop in** *v/i* (*visit*) passare

♦ **drop off 1** *v/t person, goods* lasciare **2** *v/i* (*fall asleep*) addormentarsi; (*decline*) calare

♦ **drop out** *v/i from competition, school* ritirarsi

'drop·out (*from school*) persona *f* che ha abbandonato gli studi; (*from society*) emarginato *m*, -a *f*

drops [drɒps] *npl for eyes* collirio *m*

drought [draʊt] siccità *f*

drove [drəʊv] *pret* → **drive**

drown [draʊn] **1** *v/i* annegare **2** *v/t person* annegare; *sound* coprire; **be ~ed** annegare

drow·sy ['drauzɪ] *adj* sonnolento

drudg·e·ry ['drʌdʒərɪ] lavoro *m* ingrato

drug [drʌg] **1** *n* droga *f*; **be on ~s** drogarsi **2** *v/t* (*pret & pp* **-ged**) drogare

'**drug addict** tossicodipendente *m/f*

'**drug deal·er** spacciatore *m*, -trice *f* (di droga)

'**drug·store** *esp Am* negozio-bar *m* che vende articoli vari, inclusi medicinali

'**drug traf·fick·ing** traffico *m* di droga

drum [drʌm] *n* MUS tamburo *m*; (*container*) bidone *m*; **~s** *in pop music* batteria *f*

♦ **drum into** *v/t* (*pret & pp* **-med**): **drum sth into s.o.** inculcare qc in qu

♦ **drum up** *v/t*: **drum up support** cercare supporto

drum·mer [drʌmə(r)] batterista *m/f*; *in brass band* percussionista *m/f*

'**drum·stick** MUS bacchetta *f*; *of poultry* coscia *f*

drunk [drʌŋk] **1** *n* ubriacone *m*, -a *f* **2** *adj* ubriaco; **get ~** ubriacarsi **3** *pp* → **drink**

drunk·en [drʌŋkn] *voices, laughter* da ubriaco; **~ party** festa *f* in cui si beve molto

drunk 'driv·ing guida *f* in stato di ebbrezza

dry [draɪ] **1** *adj* secco; (*ironic*) ironico; *clothes* asciutto; (*where alcohol is banned*) dove la vendita e il consumo di alcolici sono illegali **2** *v/t & v/i* (*pret & pp* **-ied**) asciugare

♦ **dry out** *v/i* asciugare; *of alcoholic* disintossicarsi

♦ **dry up** *v/i* *of river* prosciugarsi; F (*be quiet*) stare zitto

'**dry-clean** *v/t* pulire *o* lavare a secco; '**dry clean·er** tintoria *f*; '**dry-clean·ing** (*clothes*) abiti *mpl* portati in tintoria

dry·er ['draɪə(r)] (*machine*) asciugatrice *f*

DTP [di:ti:'pi:] *abbr* (= **desktop publishing**) desk-top publishing *m*, impaginazione *f* elettronica

du·al ['dju:əl] *adj* doppio

du·al 'car·riage·way *Br* carreggiata *f* a due corsie

dub [dʌb] *v/t* (*pret & pp* **-bed**) *film* doppiare

du·bi·ous ['dju:bɪəs] *adj* equivoco; (*having doubts*) dubbioso

duch·ess duchessa *f*

duck [dʌk] **1** *n* anatra *f* **2** *v/i* piegarsi **3** *v/t* one's head piegare; *question* aggirare

dud [dʌd] *n* F (*false note*) falso *m*

due [dju:] *adj* (*owed, proper*) dovuto; **be ~** *of train, baby etc* essere previsto; **I'm ~ to meet him** dovrei incontrarlo; **~ to** (*because of*) a causa di; **be ~ to** (*be caused by*) essere dovuto a; **in ~ course** a tempo debito

dues [dju:z] *npl* quota *fsg*

du·et [dju:'et] MUS duetto *m*

dug [dʌg] *pret & pp* → **dig**

duke [dju:k] duca *m*

dull [dʌl] *adj* *weather* grigio; *sound, pain* sordo; (*boring*) noioso

du·ly ['dju:lɪ] *adv* (*as expected*) come previsto; (*properly*) debitamente

dumb [dʌm] *adj* (*mute*) muto; F (*stupid*) stupido

dumb·found·ed [dʌm'faʊndɪd] *adj* ammutolito

dum·my ['dʌmɪ] *for clothes* manichino *m*; *for baby* succhiotto *m*

dump [dʌmp] **1** *n for rubbish* discarica *f*; (*unpleasant place*) postaccio *m* **2** *v/t* (*deposit*) lasciare; (*dispose of*) scaricare; *toxic waste etc* sbarazzarsi di

dump·ling ['dʌmplɪŋ] *fagotto m di pasta ripieno, sia dolce che salato*

dune [dju:n] duna *f*

dung [dʌŋ] sterco *m*

dun·ga·rees [dʌŋgə'ri:z] *npl* salopette *f inv*

dunk [dʌŋk] *v/t in coffee etc* inzuppare

du·o ['dju:əʊ] MUS duo *m inv*

du·pli·cate ['dju:plɪkət] **1** *n* duplicato *m*; **in ~** in duplicato **2** *v/t* ['dju:plɪkeɪt] (*copy*) duplicare; (*repeat*) rifare

du·pli·cate 'key chiave *f* di scorta

du·ra·ble ['djʊərəbl] *adj material* resistente; *relationship* durevole

du·ra·tion [djʊə'reɪʃn] durata *f*

du·ress [djʊə'res]: **under ~** sotto costrizione

dur·ing ['djʊərɪŋ] *prep* durante

dusk [dʌsk] crepuscolo *m*

dust [dʌst] **1** *n* polvere *f* **2** *v/t* spolverare; **~ sth with sth** (*sprinkle*) spolverare qc con qc

'**dust·bin** bidone *m* della spazzatura

'**dust cov·er** *for book* sopraccoperta *f*

duster ['dʌstə(r)] (*cloth*) straccio *m* (per spolverare)

'**dust jack·et** *of book* sopraccoperta *f*; '**dust·man** spazzino *m*; '**dust·pan** paletta *f*

dust·y ['dʌstɪ] *adj table* impolverato; *road* polveroso

Dutch [dʌtʃ] **1** *adj* olandese; **go ~** F fare alla romana F **2** *n language* olandese *m*; **the ~** gli Olandesi

du·ty ['djuːtɪ] dovere *m*; *on goods* tassa *f* doganale, dazio *m*; **be on ~** essere di servizio; **be off ~** essere fuori servizio

du·ty 'free 1 *adj* duty free *inv* **2** *n* acquisto *m* fatto in un duty free

du·ty free al'low·ance limite *m* di acquisto in un duty free

du·ty'free shop duty free *m inv*

dwarf [dwɔːf] **1** *n* nano *m*, -a *f* **2** *v/t* fare scomparire

♦ **dwell on** [dwel] *v/t* rimuginare

dwin·dle ['dwɪndl] *v/i* diminuire

dye [daɪ] **1** *n* tintura *f*; *for food* colorante *m* **2** *v/t* colorare, tingere

dy·ing ['daɪɪŋ] *adj person* morente; *industry*, *tradition* in via di disparizione; **his ~ day** il giorno della sua morte

dy·nam·ic [daɪ'næmɪk] *adj person* dinamico

dy·na·mism ['daɪnəmɪzm] dinamismo *m*

dy·na·mite ['daɪnəmaɪt] *n* dinamite *f*

dy·na·mo ['daɪnəməʊ] TECH dinamo *f inv*

dy·nas·ty ['dɪnəstɪ] dinastia *f*

dys·lex·i·a [dɪs'leksɪə] dislessia *f*

dys·lex·ic [dɪs'leksɪk] **1** *adj* dislessico **2** *n* dislessico *m*, -a *f*

E

each [iːtʃ] **1** *adj* ogni **2** *adv* ciascuno; **they're £1.50 ~** costano £1,50 ciascuno **3** *pron* ciascuno *m*, -a *f*, ognino *m*, -a *f*; **~ other** l'un l'altro *m*, l'una l'altra *f*; **we know ~ other** ci conosciamo; **we drive ~ other's car** guidiamo l'uno la macchina dell'altro

ea·ger ['iːgə(r)] *adj* entusiasta; **be ~ to do sth** essere ansioso di fare qc; **be ~ for** essere desideroso di

ea·ger 'bea·ver F fanatico *m*, -a *f* F

ea·ger·ly ['iːgəlɪ] *adv* ansiosamente

ea·ger·ness ['iːgənɪs] smania *f*

ea·gle ['iːgl] aquila *f*

ea·gle-eyed [iːgl'aɪd] *adj*: **be ~ eyed** avere l'occhio di falco

ear¹ [ɪə(r)] *of person*, *animal* orecchio *m*

ear² [ɪə(r)] *of corn* spiga *f*

'**ear·ache** mal *m* d'orecchi

'**ear·drum** timpano *m*

earl [ɜːl] conte *m*

'**ear·lobe** lobo *m* dell'orecchio

ear·ly ['ɜːlɪ] **1** *adj* (*not late*) primo; *arrival* anticipato; (*farther back in time*) antico; **in the ~ hours** nelle prime ore; **in the ~ stages** nelle fasi iniziali; **in ~ spring** all'inizio della primavera; **~ October** inizio ottobre; *at an ~ age* in giovane età; *I'm an ~ riser* mi alzo sempre presto; *let's have an ~ supper* ceniamo presto; *an ~ Picasso* un Picasso primo periodo; *the ~ Romans* gli antichi Romani; *~ music* musica *f* primitiva; *I look forward to an ~ reply* resto in attesa di una sollecita risposta 2 *adv* (*not late*) presto; (*ahead of time*) in anticipo; *it's too ~* è troppo presto; *you're a bit ~* sei un po' in anticipo

'ear·ly bird persona *f* mattiniera; *planning ahead* persona *f* previdente

ear·mark ['ɪəmɑːk] *v/t* riservare; *~ sth for sth* riservare qc a qc

earn [ɜːn] *v/t* guadagnare; *of interest* fruttare; *holiday, drink etc* guadagnarsi; *~ one's living* guadagnarsi da vivere; *his honesty ~ed him everybody's respect* la sua onestà gli è valsa il rispetto di tutti

ear·nest ['ɜːnɪst] serio; *in ~* sul serio

earn·ings ['ɜːnɪŋz] *npl* guadagno *m*

'ear·phones *npl* cuffie *fpl* (d'ascolto); 'ear·pierc·ing *adj* perforante; 'ear·ring orecchino *m*; 'ear·shot: *within ~* a portata d'orecchio; *out of ~* fuori dalla portata d'orecchio

earth [ɜːθ] (*soil, planet*) terra *f*; *where on ~ have you been?* F dove cavolo sei stato? F

earth·en·ware ['ɜːθənweə(r)] *n* terracotta *f*

earth·ly ['ɜːθlɪ] *adj* terreno; *it's no use ...* F è perfettamente inutile ...

earth·quake ['ɜːθkweɪk] terremoto *m*

earth-shat·ter·ing ['ɜːθʃætərɪŋ] *adj* sconvolgente

ease [iːz] 1 *n* facilità *f*; *be at* (*one's*) *~, feel at ~* essere *o* sentirsi a proprio agio; *be or feel ill at ~* essere *o* sentirsi a disagio 2 *v/t* (*relieve*) alleviare; *it will ~ my mind* mi darà sollievo 3 *v/i of pain* alleviarsi

♦ ease off 1 *v/t* (*remove*) togliere con cautela 2 *v/i of pain, rain* diminuire

ea·sel ['iːzl] cavalletto *m*

eas·i·ly ['iːzəlɪ] *adv* (*with ease*) facilmente; (*by far*) di gran lunga

east [iːst] 1 *n* est *m* 2 *adj* orientale 3 *adv travel* a est

Eas·ter ['iːstə(r)] Pasqua *f*

Eas·ter 'Day il giorno *o* la domenica di Pasqua

'Eas·ter egg uovo *m* di Pasqua

eas·ter·ly ['iːstəlɪ] *adj*: *~ wind* vento *m* dell'est; *in an ~ direction* verso est

Eas·ter 'Mon·day lunedì *m inv* di Pasqua, Pasquetta *f*

east·ern ['iːstən] *adj* orientale

east·ward(s) ['iːstwəd(z)] *adv* verso est

eas·y ['iːzɪ] *adj* facile; (*relaxed*) tranquillo; *take things ~* (*slow down*) prendersela con calma; *take it ~!* (*calm down*) calma!; *I've had it ~* ho avuto una vita facile

'eas·y chair poltrona *f*

eas·y-go·ing ['iːzɪgəʊɪŋ] *adj*: *he's very ~* gli va bene quasi tutto

eat [iːt] *v/t & v/i* (*pret ate*, *pp eaten*) mangiare

♦ eat out *v/i* mangiare fuori

♦ eat up *v/t finish* finire di mangiare; *fig* mangiare; *with jealousy* consumare; *eat up your beans* eat them all mangia tutti i fagioli

eat·a·ble ['iːtəbl] *adj* commestibile; *lunch, dish* mangiabile

eat·en ['iːtn] *pp → eat*

eau de Co·logne [əʊdəkə'ləʊn] acqua *f* di Colonia

eaves [iːvz] *npl* cornicione *m*

eaves·drop ['iːvzdrɒp] *v/i* (*pret & pp -ped*) origliare; *~ on s.o. / sth* origliare qu / qc

ebb [eb] *v/i of tide* rifluire

♦ ebb away *v/i fig*: *of courage, strength* venire meno

ec·cen·tric [ɪk'sentrɪk] 1 *adj* eccentrico 2 *n* eccentrico *m*, -a *f*

ec·cen·tric·i·ty [ɪksen'trɪsɪtɪ] eccentricità *f inv*

ech·o ['ekəʊ] 1 *n* eco *f* 2 *v/i* risuonare 3 *v/t words* ripetere; *views* condividere

e·clipse [ɪ'klɪps] 1 *n* eclissi *f inv* 2 *v/t*

fig eclissare

e·co·lo·gi·cal [iːkəˈlɒdʒɪkl] *adj* ecologico; **~ balance** equilibrio *m* ecologico

e·co·lo·gi·cal·ly [iːkəˈlɒdʒɪklɪ] *adv* ecologicamente

e·co·lo·gi·cal·ly 'friend·ly *adj* ecologico

e·col·o·gist [ɪˈkɒlədʒɪst] ecologista *m/f*

e·col·o·gy [ɪˈkɒlədʒɪ] ecologia *f*

ec·o·nom·ic [iːkəˈnɒmɪk] *adj* economico

ec·o·nom·i·cal [iːkəˈnɒmɪkl] *adj* (*cheap*) economico; (*thrifty*) parsimonioso

ec·o·nom·i·cal·ly [iːkəˈnɒmɪklɪ] *adv* (*in terms of economics*) economicamente; (*thriftily*) con parsimonia

ec·o·nom·ics [iːkəˈnɒmɪks] *science* economia *f; financial aspects* aspetti *mpl* economici

e·con·o·mist [ɪˈkɒnəmɪst] economista *m/f*

e·con·o·mize [ɪˈkɒnəmaɪz] *v/i* risparmiare, fare economie

♦ **economize on** *v/t* risparmiare su

e·con·o·my [ɪˈkɒnəmɪ] *of a country* economia *f;* (*saving*) risparmio *m*, economia *f*

e'con·o·my class classe *f* economica; **e'con·o·my drive** regime *m* di risparmio; **e'con·o·my size** confezione *f* famiglia

e·co·sys·tem [ˈiːkəʊsɪstm] ecosistema *m*

e·co·tour·ism [ˈiːkəʊtʊərɪzm] agriturismo *m*

ec·sta·sy [ˈekstəsɪ] estasi *f*

ec·sta·t·ic [ɪkˈstætɪk] *adj* in estasi

ec·ze·ma [ˈeksmə] eczema *m*

edge [edʒ] **1** *n of knife* filo *m; of table, seat, lawn* bordo *m; of road* ciglio *m; of cliff* orlo *m; in voice* sfumatura *f* tagliente; **there's an ~ of cynicism in his voice** c'è una punta di cinismo nella sua voce; **on ~** → **edgy 2** *v/t* profilare **3** *v/i* (*move slowly*) muoversi con cautela

edge·ways [ˈedʒweɪz] *adv:* **I couldn't get a word in ~** non sono

riuscito a piazzare una parola

edg·y [ˈedʒɪ] *adj* teso

ed·i·ble [ˈedɪbl] *adj* commestibile

ed·it [ˈedɪt] *v/t text* rivedere; *prepare for publication* curare; *newspaper* dirigere; *TV program, film* montare; COMPUT editare

e·di·tion [ɪˈdɪʃn] edizione *f*

ed·i·tor [ˈedɪtə(r)] *of text* revisore *m; of publication* curatore *m,* -trice *f; of newspaper* direttore *m,* -trice; *of TV program* responsabile *m/f* del montaggio; *of film* tecnico *m* del montaggio; **sports ~** redattore *m,* -trice sportivo, -a; *in charge* caporedattore *m,* -trice *f* sportivo, -a

ed·i·to·ri·al [edɪˈtɔːrɪəl] **1** *adj* editoriale; **the ~ staff** la redazione **2** *n* editoriale *m,* articolo *m* di fondo

EDP [iːdiːˈpiː] *abbr* (= **electronic data processing**) EDP (= elaborazione *f* elettronica dei dati)

ed·u·cate [ˈedjʊkeɪt] *v/t child* istruire; *consumers* educare; **he was ~d at Cambridge** ha studiato a Cambridge

ed·u·cat·ed [ˈedjʊkeɪtɪd] *adj person* istruito

ed·u·ca·tion [edjʊˈkeɪʃn] istruzione *f;* **the ~ system** la pubblica istruzione

ed·u·ca·tion·al [edjʊˈkeɪʃnl] *adj* didattico; (*informative*) istruttivo

eel [iːl] anguilla *f*

ee·rie [ˈɪərɪ] *adj* inquietante

ef·fect [ɪˈfekt] effetto *m;* **take ~** *of medicine, drug* fare effetto; **come into ~** *of law* entrare in vigore

ef·fec·tive [ɪˈfektɪv] *adj* (*efficient*) efficace; (*striking*) d'effetto; **~ May 1** con decorrenza dal 1 maggio; **a very ~ combination** un abbinamento di grande effetto

ef·fem·i·nate [ɪˈfemɪnət] *adj* effeminato

ef·fer·ves·cent [efəˈvesnt] *adj also fig* effervescente

ef·fi·cien·cy [ɪˈfɪʃnsɪ] efficienza *f; of machine* rendimento *m*

ef·fi·cient [ɪˈfɪʃənt] *adj* efficiente; *machine* ad alto rendimento

ef·fi·cient·ly [ɪˈfɪʃəntlɪ] *adv* con efficienza

ef·flu·ent [ˈefluənt] scarichi *mpl*

ef·fort [ˈefət] sforzo *m*; **make an ~ to do sth** fare uno sforzo per fare qc

ef·fort·less [ˈefətlɪs] *adj* facile

ef·fron·te·ry [ɪˈfrʌntərɪ] sfrontatezza *f*, sfacciataggine *f*

ef·fu·sive [ɪˈfjuːsɪv] *adj* thanks, welcome caloroso

e.g. [iːˈdʒiː] *ad o* per esempio

e·gal·i·tar·i·an [ɪgælɪˈteərɪən] *adj* egualitario

egg [eg] uovo *m*; *of woman* ovulo *m*

♦ **egg on** *v/t* istigare

'egg·cup portauovo *m inv*; **'egg·head** F intellettualoide *m/f*; **'egg·plant** Am melanzana *f*; **'egg·shell** guscio *m* d'uovo; **'egg tim·er** timer *m* per misurare il *tempo di cottura delle uova*

e·go [ˈiːgəʊ] ego *m*

e·go·cen·tric [iːgəʊˈsentrɪk] *adj* egocentrico

e·go·ism [ˈiːgəʊɪzm] egoismo *m*

e·go·ist [ˈiːgəʊɪst] egoista *m/f*

E·gypt [ˈiːdʒɪpt] Egitto *m*

E·gyp·tian [ɪˈdʒɪpʃn] **1** *adj* egiziano **2** *n* egiziano *m*, -a *f*

ei·der·down [ˈaɪdədaʊn] (*quilt*) piumino *m*

eight [eɪt] otto

eigh·teen [eɪˈtiːn] diciotto

eigh·teenth [eɪˈtiːnθ] *n & adj* diciottesimo, -a

eighth [eɪtθ] *n & adj* ottavo, -a

eigh·ti·eth [ˈeɪtɪɪθ] *n & adj* ottantesimo, -a

eigh·ty [ˈeɪtɪ] ottanta

ei·ther [ˈaɪðə(r)] **1** *adj* l'uno o l'altro; (*both*) entrambi *pl*; **at ~ side of the street** da entrambi i lati della strada **2** *pron* l'uno o l'altro *m*, l'una o l'altra *f* **3** *adv* nemmeno, neppure; **I won't go** ~ non vado nemmeno *o* neppure io **4** *conj*: **~ my mother or my sister** mia madre o mia sorella; **he doesn't like ~ wine or beer** non gli piacciono né il vino, né la birra; **~ you write or phone** o scrivi, o telefoni

e·ject [ɪˈdʒekt] **1** *v/t* espellere **2** *v/i from plane* eiettarsi

♦ **eke out** [iːk] *v/t* usare con parsimonia; *grant etc* arrotondare

elaborate [ɪˈlæbərət] **1** *adj* elaborato **2** *v/i* [ɪˈlæbəreɪt] fornire particolari

e·lab·o·rate·ly [ɪˈlæbəreɪtlɪ] *adv* in modo elaborato

e·lapse [ɪˈlæps] *v/i* trascorrere

e·las·tic [ɪˈlæstɪk] **1** *adj* elastico **2** *n* elastico *m*

e·las·ti·ca·ted [ɪˈlæstɪkeɪtɪd] *adj* elasticizzato

e·las·tic 'band elastico *m*

e·las·tic·i·ty [ɪlæsˈtɪsətɪ] elasticità *f*

E·las·to·plast® [ɪˈlæstəplɑːst] cerotto *m*

e·lat·ed [ɪˈleɪtɪd] *adj* esultante

el·a·tion [ɪˈleɪʃn] esultanza *f*

el·bow [ˈelbəʊ] **1** *n* gomito *m* **2** *v/t*: **~ out of the way** allontanare a spintoni

el·der [ˈeldə(r)] **1** *adj* maggiore **2** *n* maggiore *m/f*; **she's two years my ~** è più vecchia di me di due anni

el·der·ly [ˈeldəlɪ] *adj* anziano

el·dest [ˈeldəst] **1** *adj* maggiore **2** *n* maggiore *m/f*; **the ~** il/la maggiore

e·lect [ɪˈlekt] **1** *v/t* eleggere; **~ to ...** decidere di ... **2** *adj*: **the president ~** il futuro presidente

e·lec·tion [ɪˈlekʃn] elezione *f*

e·lec·tion cam·paign campagna *f* elettorale

e·lec·tion day giorno *m* delle elezioni

e·lec·tive [ɪˈlektɪv] *adj* facoltativo

e·lec·tor [ɪˈlektə(r)] elettore *m*, -trice *f*

e·lec·to·ral sys·tem [ɪˈlektərəlsɪstm] sistema *m* elettorale

e·lec·to·rate [ɪˈlektərət] elettorato *m*

e·lec·tric [ɪˈlektrɪk] *adj also fig* elettrico

e·lec·tri·cal [ɪˈlektrɪkl] *adj* elettrico

e·lec·tri·cal en·gi'neer ingegnere *m* elettrico

e·lec·tri·cal en·gi'neer·ing ingegneria *f* elettrica

e·lec·tric 'blan·ket coperta *f* elettrica

e·lec·tric 'chair sedia *f* elettrica

e·lec·tri·cian [ɪlek'trɪʃn] elettricista *m/f*

e·lec·tri·ci·ty [ɪlek'trɪsətɪ] elettricità *f*

e·lec·tric 'ra·zor rasoio *m* elettrico

e·lec·tri·fy [ɪ'lektrɪfaɪ] *v/t* (*pret & pp* **-ied**) elettrificare; *fig* elettrizzare

e·lec·tro·cute [ɪ'lektrəkjuːt] *v/t* fulminare

e·lec·trode [ɪ'lektrəʊd] elettrodo *m*

e·lec·tron [ɪ'lektrɒn] elettrone *m*

e·lec·tron·ic [ɪlek'trɒnɪk] *adj* elettronico

e·lec·tron·ic da·ta 'pro·ces·sing elaborazione *f* elettronica dei dati

e·lec·tron·ic 'mail posta *f* elettronica

e·lec·tron·ics [ɪlek'trɒnɪks] elettronica *f*

el·e·gance ['elɪgəns] eleganza *f*

el·e·gant ['elɪgənt] *adj* elegante

el·e·gant·ly ['elɪgəntlɪ] *adv* elegantemente

el·e·ment ['elɪmənt] elemento *m*

el·e·men·ta·ry [elɪ'mentərɪ] *adj* (*rudimentary*) elementare

el·e·men·ta·ry school *Am* scuola *f* elementare

el·e·men·ta·ry teacher maestro *m*, -a *f* elementare

el·e·phant ['elɪfənt] elefante *m*

el·e·vate ['elɪveɪt] *v/t* elevare

el·e·va·tion [elɪ'veɪʃn] (*altitude*) altitudine *f*

el·e·va·tor ['elɪveɪtə(r)] *Am* ascensore *m*

el·e·ven [ɪ'levn] undici

el·e·venth [ɪ'levnθ] *n & adj* undicesimo, -a; *at the ~ hour* all'ultima ora, all'ultimo momento

el·i·gi·ble ['elɪdʒəbl] *adj*: *be ~ to do sth* avere il diritto di fare qc; *be ~ for sth* aver diritto a qc

el·i·gi·ble 'bach·e·lor buon partito *m*

e·lim·i·nate [ɪ'lɪmɪneɪt] *v/t* eliminare; *be ~d from competition* essere eliminato

e·lim·i·na·tion [ɪ'lɪmɪneɪʃn] eliminazione *f*

e·lite [eɪ'liːt] **1** *n* elite *f inv* **2** *adj* elitario

el·lipse [ɪ'lɪps] ellisse *f*

elm [elm] olmo *m*

e·lope [ɪ'ləʊp] *v/i* scappare (per sposarsi)

el·o·quence ['eləkwəns] eloquenza *f*

el·o·quent ['eləkwənt] *adj* eloquente

el·o·quent·ly ['eləkwəntlɪ] *adv* con eloquenza

else [els] *adv*: *anything ~* qualcos'altro; *anything ~? in shop* (desidera) altro?; *nothing ~* nient'altro; *if you've got nothing ~ to do* se non hai altro da fare; *nobody ~* nessun altro; *everyone ~ is going* tutti gli altri vanno; *who ~ was there?* chi altro c'era?; *someone ~* qualcun altro; *something ~* qualcos'altro; *let's go somewhere ~* andiamo da qualche altra parte; *or ~* altrimenti

else·where ['elsweə(r)] *adv* altrove

e·lude [ɪ'luːd] *v/t* (*escape from*) sfuggire a; (*avoid*) sfuggire a; *the name ~s me* il nome mi sfugge

e·lu·sive [ɪ'luːsɪv] *adj person* difficile da trovare; *quality* raro; *criminal* inafferrabile

e·ma·ci·at·ed [ɪ'meɪsɪeɪtɪd] *adj* emaciato

e-mail ['iːmeɪl] **1** *n* e-mail *m inv* **2** *v/t person* mandare un e-mail a; *text* mandare per e-mail

'e-mail ad·dress indirizzo *m* e-mail

e·man·ci·pat·ed [ɪ'mænsɪpeɪtɪd] *adj woman* emancipato

e·man·ci·pa·tion [ɪmænsɪ'peɪʃn] emancipazione *f*

em·balm [ɪm'bɑːm] *v/t* imbalsamare

em·bank·ment [ɪm'bæŋkmənt] *of river* argine *m*; RAIL massicciata *f*

em·bar·go [em'bɑːgəʊ] embargo *m inv*

em·bark [ɪm'bɑːk] *v/i* imbarcarsi

♦ embark on *v/i* imbarcarsi in

em·bar·rass [ɪm'bærəs] *v/t* imbarazzare

em·bar·rassed [ɪm'bærəst] *adj* imbarazzato

em·bar·rass·ing [ɪm'bærəsɪŋ] *adj* imbarazzante

em·bar·rass·ment [ɪm'bærəsmənt] imbarazzo *m*

em·bas·sy ['embəsɪ] ambasciata *f*

em·bel·lish [ɪm'belɪʃ] *v/t* ornare; *story* ricamare su

em·bers ['embəz] *npl* brace *fsg*

em·bez·zle [ɪm'bezl] *v/t* appropriarsi indebitamente di

em·bez·zle·ment [ɪm'bezlmənt] appropriazione *f* indebita

em·bez·zler [ɪm'bezlə(r)] malversatore *m*, -trice *f*

em·bit·ter [ɪm'bɪtə(r)] *v/t* amareggiare

em·blem ['embləm] emblema *f*

em·bod·i·ment [ɪm'bɒdɪmənt] incarnazione *f*

em·bod·y [ɪm'bɒdɪ] *v/t* (*pret & pp* **-ied**) incarnare

em·bo·lis·m ['embəlɪzm] embolia *f*

em·boss [ɪm'bɒs] *v/t metal* lavorare a sbalzo; *paper, fabric* stampare in rilievo

em·brace [ɪm'breɪs] **1** *n* abbraccio *m* **2** *v/t* (*hug, include*) abbracciare **3** *v/i of two people* abbracciarsi

em·broi·der [ɪm'brɔɪdə(r)] *v/t* ricamare; *fig* ricamare su

em·broi·der·y [ɪm'brɔɪdərɪ] ricamo *m*

em·bry·o ['embrɪəʊ] embrione *m*

em·bry·on·ic [embrɪ'ɒnɪk] *adj fig* embrionale

em·e·rald ['emərəld] *precious stone* smeraldo *m*; *colour* verde *m* smeraldo

e·merge [ɪ'mɜːdʒ] *v/i* (*appear*) emergere; *it has ~d that ...* è emerso che ...

e·mer·gen·cy [ɪ'mɜːdʒənsɪ] emergenza *f*; *in an ~* in caso di emergenza; **emer·gen·cy 'ex·it** uscita *f* di sicurezza; **e'mer·gen·cy land·ing** atterraggio *m* di fortuna; **e'mer·gen·cy serv·ices** *npl* servizi *mpl* di soccorso

em·er·y board ['emərɪbɔːd] limetta *f* (da unghie)

em·i·grant ['emɪgrənt] emigrante *m/f*

em·i·grate ['emɪgreɪt] *v/i* emigrare

em·i·gra·tion [emɪ'greɪʃn] emigrazione *f*

Em·i·nence ['emɪnəns]: REL *His ~* Sua Eminenza

em·i·nent ['emɪnənt] *adj* eminente

em·i·nent·ly ['emɪnəntlɪ] *adv* decisamente

e·mis·sion [ɪ'mɪʃn] *of gases* emanazione *f*

e·mit [ɪ'mɪt] *v/t* (*pret & pp* **-ted**) *heat, gases* emanare; *light, smoke* emettere; *smell* esalare

e·mo·tion [ɪ'məʊʃn] emozione *f*

e·mo·tion·al [ɪ'məʊʃnl] *adj problems, development* emozionale; (*causing emotion*) commovente; (*showing emotion*) commosso

em·pa·thize ['empəθaɪz] *v/i* immedesimarsi; *~ with s.o.* immedesimarsi con qu; *~ with sth* capire qc

em·per·or ['empərə(r)] imperatore *m*

em·pha·sis ['emfəsɪs] enfasi *f*; *on word* rilievo *m*

em·pha·size ['emfəsaɪz] *v/t* enfatizzare; *word* dare rilievo a

em·phat·ic [ɪm'fætɪk] *adj* enfatico

em·pire ['empaɪə(r)] impero *m*

em·ploy [ɪm'plɔɪ] *v/t* dare lavoro a; (*take on*) assumere; (*use*) impiegare; *she's ~ed as a secretary* lavora come segretaria; *he hasn't been ~ed for six months* non lavora da sei mesi

em·ploy·ee [emplɔɪ'iː] dipendente *m/f*

em·ploy·er [em plɔɪ'ə(r)] datore *m*, -trice *f* di lavoro

em·ploy·ment [em plɔɪmənt] occupazione *f*; (*work*) impiego *m*; *be seeking ~* essere in cerca di occupazione

em'ploy·ment a·gen·cy agenzia *f* di collocamento

em·press ['emprɪs] imperatrice *f*

emp·ti·ness ['emptɪnɪs] vuoto *m*

emp·ty ['emptɪ] **1** *adj* vuoto **2** *v/t*

E

(*pret & pp* **-ied**) vuotare **3** *v/i* (*pret & pp* **-ied**) *of room, street* svuotarsi

em·u·late ['emjʊleɪt] *v/t* emulare

e·mul·sion [ɪ'mʌlʃn] *n paint* emulsione *f*

en·a·ble [ɪ'neɪbl] *v/t person* permettere a; *thing* permettere; ~ *s.o. to do sth* permettere a qu di fare qc

en·act [ɪ'nækt] *v/t law* emanare; THEA rappresentare

e·nam·el [ɪ'næml] smalto *m*

enc abbr (= **enclosure(s)**) all. (= allegato *m*)

en·chant [ɪn'tʃɑːnt] *v/t* (*delight*) incantare

en·chant·ing [ɪn'tʃɑːntɪŋ] *adj smile, village, person* incantevole

en·cir·cle [ɪn'sɜːkl] *v/t* circondare

encl abbr (= **enclosure(s)**) all. (= allegato *m*)

en·close [ɪn'kləʊz] *v/t in letter* allegare; *please find ~d ...* in allegato, ...; *area* recintare

en·clo·sure [ɪn'kləʊʒə(r)] *with letter* allegato *m*

en·core ['ɒŋkɔː(r)] bis *m inv*

en·coun·ter [ɪn'kaʊntə(r)] **1** *n* incontro *m* **2** *v/t* incontrare

en·cour·age [ɪn'kʌrɪdʒ] *v/t* incoraggiare

en·cour·age·ment [ɪn'kʌrɪdʒmənt] incoraggiamento *m*

en·cour·ag·ing [ɪn'kʌrɪdʒɪŋ] *adj* incoraggiante

♦encroach on [ɪn'krəʊtʃ] *v/t land, time* invadere; *rights* violare

en·cy·clo·pe·di·a [ɪnsaɪklə'piːdɪə] enciclopedia *f*

end [end] **1** *n* (*extremity*) estremità *f inv*; (*conclusion*) fine *f*; (*purpose*) fine *m*; *in the ~* alla fine; *for hours on ~* senza sosta; *stand sth on ~* mettere qc verticale; *at the ~ of July* alla fine di luglio; *put an ~ to* mettere fine a **2** *v/t* terminare **3** *v/i* finire

♦end up *v/i* finire; *I'll end up doing it myself* finirò per farlo io stesso

en·dan·ger [ɪn'deɪndʒə(r)] *v/t* mettere in pericolo

en'dan·gered spe·cies specie *f in*

via d'estinzione

en·dear·ing [ɪn'dɪərɪŋ] *adj* accattivante

en·deav·our [ɪn'devə(r)] **1** *n* tentativo *m* **2** *v/t* tentare

en·dem·ic [ɪn'demɪk] *adj* endemico

end·ing ['endɪŋ] finale *m*; GRAM desinenza *f*

end·less ['endlɪs] *adj* interminabile

en·dorse [en'dɔːs] *v/t cheque* girare; *candidacy* appoggiare; *product* fare pubblicità a

en·dorse·ment [en'dɔːsmənt] *of cheque* girata *f*; *of candidacy* appoggio *m*; *of product* pubblicità *f*

end 'prod·uct prodotto *m* finale

end re'sult risultato *m* finale

en·dur·ance [ɪn'djʊrəns] resistenza *f*

en·dure [ɪn'djʊə(r)] **1** *v/t* sopportare **2** *v/i* (*last*) resistere

en·dur·ing [ɪn'djʊərɪŋ] *adj* durevole

end-us·er [end'juːzə(r)] utilizzatore *m* finale

en·e·my ['enəmɪ] nemico *m*, -a *f*

en·er·get·ic [enə'dʒetɪk] *adj* energico

en·er·get·ic·al·ly [enə'dʒetɪklɪ] *adv* con energia

en·er·gy ['enədʒɪ] energia *f*

en·er·gy-sav·ing ['enədʒɪseɪvɪŋ] *adj device* per risparmiare energia

'en·er·gy sup·ply rifornimento *m* di energia elettrica

en·force [ɪn'fɔːs] *v/t* far rispettare

en·gage [ɪn'geɪdʒ] **1** *v/t* (*hire*) ingaggiare **2** *v/i* TECH ingranare

♦engage in *v/t* occuparsi di; *conversation* coinvolgere in

en·gaged [ɪn'geɪdʒd] *adj to be married* fidanzato; *get ~* fidanzarsi

en'gaged tone *Br* TELEC segnale *m* d'occupato

en·gage·ment [ɪn'geɪdʒmənt] (*appointment*) impegno *m*; *to be married* fidanzamento *m*; MIL scontro *m*

en'gage·ment ring anello *m* di fidanzamento

en·gag·ing [ɪn'geɪdʒɪŋ] *adj smile, person* accattivante

en·gine ['endʒɪn] motore *m*

en·gi·neer [endʒɪ'nɪə(r)] **1** *n* ingegnere *m*; *for sound, software* tecnico *m*; NAUT macchinista *m* **2** *v/t fig*: *meeting etc* macchinare, architettare

en·gi·neer·ing [endʒɪ'nɪərɪŋ] ingegneria *f*

En·gland ['ɪŋglənd] Inghilterra *f*

En·glish ['ɪŋglɪʃ] **1** *adj* inglese **2** *n* (*language*) inglese *m*; **the ~** gli inglesi

En·glish 'Chan·nel Manica *f*

En·glish·man inglese *m*

En·glish·wom·an inglese *f*

en·grave [ɪn'greɪv] *v/t* incidere

en·grav·ing [ɪn'greɪvɪŋ] (*drawing*) stampa *f*, (*design*) incisione *f*

en·grossed [ɪn'grəʊst] *adj*: **~ in** assorto in

en·gulf [ɪn'gʌlf] *v/t* avvolgere

en·hance [ɪn'hɑːns] *v/t* accrescere; *performance*, *reputation* migliorare

e·nig·ma [ɪ'nɪgmə] enigma *m*

e·nig·mat·ic [enɪg'mætɪk] *adj* enigmatico

en·joy [ɪn'dʒɔɪ] *v/t*: **did you ~ the film?** ti è piaciuto il film?; **I ~ reading** mi piace leggere; **~ your meal!** buon appetito!; **~ o.s.** divertirsi

en·joy·a·ble [ɪn'dʒɔɪəbl] *adj* piacevole

en·joy·ment [ɪn'dʒɔɪmənt] piacere *m*, divertimento *m*

en·large [ɪn'lɑːdʒ] *v/t* ingrandire

en·large·ment [ɪn'lɑːdʒmənt] ingrandimento *m*

en·light·en [ɪn'laɪtn] *v/t* illuminare

en·list [ɪn'lɪst] **1** *v/i* MIL arruolarsi **2** *v/t*: **~ the help of ...** ottenere l'appoggio di ...

en·liv·en [ɪn'laɪvn] *v/t* animare

en·mi·ty ['enmətɪ] inimicizia *f*

e·nor·mi·ty [ɪ'nɔːmətɪ] enormità *f inv*

e·nor·mous [ɪ'nɔːməs] *adj* enorme

e·nor·mous·ly [ɪ'nɔːməslɪ] *adv* enormemente

e·nough [ɪ'nʌf] **1** *adj* sufficiente, abbastanza *inv* **2** *pron* abbastanza; **will £50 be ~?** saranno sufficienti £50?;

I've had ~! ne ho abbastanza!; **thanks, I've had ~** *food*, *drinks* grazie, basta così; **that's ~, calm down!** adesso basta, calmati! **3** *adv* abbastanza; **strangely ~** per quanto strano

en·quire [ɪn'kwaɪə(r)] *v/i* chiedere informazioni, informarsi; **~ about** *sth* chiedere informazioni su qc; **~ into sth** fare delle ricerche su qc

en·quir·ing [ɪn'kwaɪrɪŋ] *adj*: **have an ~ mind** avere una mente curiosa

en·quir·y [ɪn'kwaɪrɪ] richiesta *f* di informazioni; (*public ~*) indagine *f*

en·raged [ɪn'reɪdʒd] *adj* arrabbiato

en·rich [ɪn'rɪtʃ] *v/t* arricchire

en·roll [ɪn'rəʊl] *v/i* iscriversi

en·rol·ment [ɪn'rəʊlmənt] iscrizione *f*

en·sue [ɪn'sjuː] *v/i* seguire

en suite (bath·room) ['ɒnswiːt] bagno *m* in camera

en·sure [ɪn'ʃʊə(r)] *v/t* assicurare

en·tail [ɪn'teɪl] *v/t* comportare

en·tan·gle [ɪn'tæŋgl] *v/t in rope* impigliare; **become ~d in** impigliarsi in; *in love affair* invischiarsi in

en·ter ['entə(r)] **1** *v/t room*, *house* entrare in; *competition* inscriversi a; *person*, *horse in race* iscrivere; (*write down*) registrare; COMPUT inserire **2** *v/i* entrare; THEA entrare in scena; *in competition* iscriversi **3** *n* COMPUT invio *m*

en·ter·prise ['entəpraɪz] (*initiative*) intraprendenza *f*, (*venture*) impresa *f*

en·ter·pris·ing ['entəpraɪzɪŋ] *adj* intraprendente

en·ter·tain [entə'teɪn] **1** *v/t* (*amuse*) intrattenere; (*consider: idea*) considerare **2** *v/i* (*have guests*) ricevere

en·ter·tain·er [entə'teɪnə(r)] artista *m/f*

en·ter·tain·ing [entə'teɪnɪŋ] *adj* divertente

en·ter·tain·ment [entə'teɪnmənt] *adj* divertimento *m*

en·thrall [ɪn'θrɔːl] *v/t* affascinare

en·thu·si·as·m [ɪn'θjuːzɪæzm] entusiasmo *m*

en·thu·si·ast [ɪn'θjuːzɪˈæst] appassionato m, -a f

en·thu·si·as·tic [ɪnθjuːzɪˈæstɪk] adj entusiasta

en·thu·si·as·tic·al·ly [ɪnθjuːzɪˈæstɪklɪ] adv con entusiasmo

en·tice [ɪnˈtaɪs] v/t attirare

en·tire [ɪnˈtaɪə(r)] adj intero

en·tire·ly [ɪnˈtaɪəlɪ] adv interamente

en·ti·tle [ɪnˈtaɪtl] v/t dare il diritto a; **be ~d to do sth** avere il diritto di fare qc

en·ti·tled [ɪnˈtaɪtld] adj book intitolato

en·trance [ˈentrəns] entrata f, ingresso m; THEA entrata f in scena; (admission) ammissione f

en·tranced [ɪnˈtrɑːnst] adj incantato

'en·trance ex·am·(i·na·tion) esame m di ammissione

'en·trance fee quota f di ingresso

en·trant [ˈentrənt] concorrente m/f

en·treat [ɪnˈtriːt] v/t supplicare; **~ s.o. to do sth** supplicare qu di fare qc

en·trenched [ɪnˈtrentʃt] adj attitudes radicato

en·tre·pre·neur [ɒntrəprəˈnɜː] imprenditore m, -trice f

en·tre·pre·neur·i·al [ɒntrəprəˈnɜːrɪəl] adj imprenditoriale

en·trust [ɪnˈtrʌst] v/t affidare; **~ s.o. with sth, ~ sth to s.o.** affidare qc a qu

en·try [ˈentrɪ] (way in) entrata f; (admission) ingresso m; in diary annotazione f; in accounts, dictionary voce f

'en·try form modulo m d'iscrizione; 'en·try·phone citofono m; 'en·try vi·sa visto m d'ingresso

e·nu·me·rate [ɪˈnjuːməreɪt] v/t enumerare

en·vel·op [ɪnˈveləp] v/t avviluppare

en·ve·lope [ˈenvələup] busta f

en·vi·a·ble [ˈenvɪəbl] adj invidiabile

en·vi·ous [ˈenvɪəs] adj invidioso; **be ~ of s.o.** essere invidioso di qu

en·vi·ron·ment [ɪnˈvaɪərənmənt] ambiente m

en·vi·ron·men·tal [ɪnvaɪərənˈmentl]

adj ambientale

en·vi·ron·men·tal·ist [ɪnvaɪərən-ˈmentəlɪst] ambientalista m/f

en·vi·ron·men·tal·ly friend·ly [ɪnvaɪərənˈmentəlɪ] adj ecologico

en·vi·ron·men·tal pol·lu·tion inquinamento m ambientale

en·vi·ron·men·tal pro·tec·tion tutela f dell'ambiente

en·vi·rons [ɪnˈvaɪərənz] npl dintorni mpl

en·vis·age [ɪnˈvɪzɪdʒ] v/t prevedere

en·voy [ˈenvɔɪ] inviato m, -a f

en·vy [ˈenvɪ] **1** n invidia f; **be the ~ of** essere invidiato da **2** v/t (pret & pp **-ied**): **~ s.o. sth** invidiare qc a qu

e·phem·er·al adj effimero

ep·ic [ˈepɪk] **1** n epopea f **2** adj journey mitico; **a task of ~ proportions** un'impresa titanica

ep·i·cen·tre [ˈepɪsentr] epicentro m

ep·i·dem·ic [epɪˈdemɪk] epidemia f

ep·i·lep·sy [ˈepɪlepsɪ] epilessia f

ep·i·lep·tic [epɪˈleptɪk] epilettico m, -a f

ep·i·lep·tic 'fit attacco m epilettico

ep·i·log Am, ep·i·logue [ˈepɪlɒg] epilogo m

ep·i·sode [ˈepɪsəud] episodio m

ep·i·taph [ˈepɪtɑːf] epitaffio m

e·poch [ˈiːpɒk] epoca f

e·poch-mak·ing [ˈiːpɒkmeɪkɪŋ] adj che fa epoca

e·qual [ˈiːkwl] **1** adj uguale, pari inv; **be ~ to** task essere all'altezza di **2** n: **be the ~ of** essere equivalente a; **treat s.o. as his ~** trattare qualcuno alla pari **3** v/t (pret & pp **-led**, Am **-ed**) (be as good as) uguagliare; **4 times 12 ~s 48** 4 per 12 fa 48

e·qual·i·ty [ɪˈkwɒlətɪ] uguaglianza f, parità f

e·qual·ize [ˈiːkwəlaɪz] **1** v/t uniformare **2** v/i Br SP pareggiare

e·qual·iz·er [ˈiːkwəlaɪzə(r)] Br SP goal m inv del pareggio

e·qual·ly [ˈiːkwəlɪ] adv ugualmente; **~, ...** allo stesso modo, ...

e·qual 'rights npl parità f di diritti

e·quate [ɪˈkweɪt] v/t equiparare; **~ sth with sth** equiparare qc e qc e·qua·tion [ɪˈkweɪʒn] MATH equazione f

e·qua·tor [ɪˈkweɪtə(r)] equatore m

e·qui·lib·ri·um [iːkwɪˈlɪbrɪəm] equilibrio m

e·qui·nox [ˈiːkwɪnɒks] equinozio m

e·quip [ɪˈkwɪp] v/t (pret & pp -ped) equipaggiare; ~ s.o. / sth with sth equipaggiare qu / qc di qc; he's not ~ped to handle it fig non ha la capacità di gestirlo

e·quip·ment equipaggiamento m; electrical, electronic apparecchiature fpl

eq·ui·ty [ˈekwətɪ] FIN capitale m azionario

e·quiv·a·lent [ɪˈkwɪvələnt] 1 adj equivalente; be ~ to essere equivalente a 2 n equivalente m

e·ra [ˈɪərə] era f

e·rad·i·cate [ɪˈrædɪkeɪt] v/t sradicare

e·rase [ɪˈreɪz] v/t cancellare

e·ras·er [ɪˈreɪzə(r)] gomma f (da cancellare)

e·rect [ɪˈrekt] 1 adj eretto

e·rect 2 v/t erigere

e·rec·tion [ɪˈrekʃn] erezione f

er·go·nom·ic [ɜːgəʊˈnɒmɪk] adj furniture ergonomico

e·rode [ɪˈrəʊd] v/t erodere; of acid corrodere; fig: rights, power eliminare

e·ro·sion [ɪˈrəʊʒn] erosione f; of acid corrosione f; fig eliminazione f

e·rot·ic [ɪˈrɒtɪk] adj erotico

e·rot·i·cism [ɪˈrɒtɪsɪzm] erotismo m

er·rand [ˈerənd] commissione f; run ~s fare commissioni

er·rat·ic [ɪˈrætɪk] adj irregolare

er·ror [ˈerə(r)] errore m

'er·ror mes·sage COMPUT messaggio m di errore

e·rupt [ɪˈrʌpt] v/i of volcano eruttare; of violence esplodere; of person dare in escandescenze

e·rup·tion [ɪˈrʌpʃn] of volcano eruzione f; of violence esplosione f

es·ca·late [ˈeskəleɪt] v/i of costs aumentare; of war intensificarsi

es·ca·la·tion [eskəˈleɪʃn] escalation f inv

es·ca·la·tor [ˈeskəleɪtə(r)] scala f mobile

es·cape [ɪˈskeɪp] 1 n of prisoner, animal, gas fuga f; have a narrow ~ scamparla per un pelo 2 v/i of prisoner, animal scappare, fuggire; of gas fuoriuscire 3 v/t: the word ~s me la parola mi sfugge

es·cape chute AVIA scivolo m

es·cort [ˈeskɔːt] 1 n accompagnatore m, -trice f; (guard) scorta f 2 v/t [ɪˈskɔːt] socially accompagnare; act as guard to scortare

es·pe·cial [ɪˈspeʃl] → special

es·pe·cial·ly [ɪˈspeʃlɪ] adv specialmente

es·pi·o·nage [ˈespɪɒnɑːʒ] spionaggio m

es·pres·so (cof·fee) [esˈpresəʊ] espresso m

es·say [ˈeseɪ] n saggio m; in school tema m

es·sen·tial [ɪˈsenʃl] adj essenziale

es·sen·tial·ly [ɪˈsenʃlɪ] adv essenzialmente

es·tab·lish [ɪˈstæblɪʃ] v/t company fondare; (create, determine) stabilire; ~ o.s. as imporsi come

es·tab·lish·ment [ɪˈstæblɪʃmənt] firm azienda f; hotel, restaurant struttura f; the Establishment la classe dirigente

es·tate [ɪˈsteɪt] (area of land) tenuta f; (possessions of dead person) patrimonio m

es'tate a·gen·cy agenzia f immobiliare; es'tate a·gent agente m/f immobiliare; es'tate car giardiniera f

es·thet·ic etc Am → aesthetic etc

es·ti·mate [ˈestɪmət] 1 n stima f, valutazione f; COM preventivo m 2 v/t stimare

es·ti·ma·tion [estɪˈmeɪʃn] stima f; he has gone up / down in my ~ è salito / sceso nella mia stima; in my ~ (opinion) a mio giudizio

es·tranged [ɪsˈtreɪndʒd] adj wife, husband separato

es·tu·a·ry [ˈestjʊərɪ] estuario m

ETA [iːtiːˈeɪ] abbr (= estimated time of arrival) ora f d'arrivo prevista

etc [et'setrə] *abbr* (= *et cetera*) ecc.
(= eccetera)

etch·ing ['etʃɪŋ] acquaforte *f*

e·ter·nal [ɪ'tɜːnl] *adj* eterno

e·ter·ni·ty [ɪ'tɜːnətɪ] eternità *f*

eth·i·cal ['eθɪkl] *adj* etico

eth·ics ['eθɪks] etica *f*

eth·nic ['eθnɪk] *adj* etnico

eth·nic 'group gruppo *m* etnico, etnia *f*

eth·nic mi'nor·i·ty minoranza *f* etnica

EU [iː'juː] *abbr* (= *European Union*)
UE *f* (= Unione *f* europea)

eu·phe·mism ['juːfəmɪzm] eufemismo *m*

eu·pho·ri·a [juː'fɔːrɪə] euforia *f*

eu·ro ['juərəu] euro *m inv*; **'Eu·ro·cheque** Eurocheque *m inv*; **Eu·ro·crat** ['juərəukræt] funzionario *m*, -a *f* della Commissione europea; **'Eu·ro MP** eurodeputato *m*, -a *f*

Eu·rope ['juərəp] Europa *f*

Eu·ro·pe·an [juərə'pɪən] **1** *adj* europeo **2** *n* europeo *m*, -a *f*; **Eu·ro·pe·an Com'mis·sion** Commissione *f* europea; **Eu·ro·pe·an Com'mis·sion·er** Commissario *m* europeo; **Eu·ro·pe·an 'Par·lia·ment** Parlamento *m* europeo; **Eu·ro·pe·an 'Un·ion** Unione *f* europea

eu·tha·na·si·a [juːθə'neɪzɪə] eutanasia *f*

e·vac·u·ate [ɪ'vækjueɪt] *v/t* evacuare

e·vade [ɪ'veɪd] *v/t* eludere; *taxes* evadere

e·val·u·ate [ɪ'væljueɪt] *v/t* valutare

e·val·u·a·tion [ɪvæljʊ'eɪʃn] valutazione *f*

e·van·gel·ist [ɪ'vændʒəlɪst] evangelizzatore *m*, -trice *f*

e·vap·o·rate [ɪ'væpəreɪt] *v/i of water* evaporare; *of confidence* svanire

e·vap·o·ra·tion [ɪvæpə'reɪʃn] *of water* evaporazione *f*

e·va·sion [ɪ'veɪʒn] elusione *f*; *of taxes* evasione *f*

e·va·sive [ɪ'veɪsɪv] *adj* evasivo

eve [iːv] vigilia *f*

e·ven ['iːvn] **1** *adj* (*regular*) omogeneo; *breathing* regolare; *surface* piano; *hem* diritto; (*number*) pari *inv*; *players, game* alla pari; **get ~ with …** farla pagare a … **2** *adv* persino; **the car ~ has a CD player** la macchina ha persino un lettore CD; **~ bigger** ancora più grande; **~ better / worse** ancora meglio / peggio; **not ~** nemmeno, neppure; **~ so** nonostante questo; **~ if** anche se **3** *v/t*: **~ the score** pareggiare

eve·ning ['iːvnɪŋ] sera *f*; **in the ~** di sera; **this ~** stasera; **good ~** buona sera

'eve·ning class corso *m* serale; **'eve·ning dress** *for woman* vestito *m* da sera; *for man* abito *m* scuro; **eve·ning 'pa·per** giornale *m* della sera

e·ven·ly ['iːvnlɪ] *adv* (*regularly*) in modo omogeneo; *breathe* regolarmente

e·vent [ɪ'vent] evento *m*, avvenimento *m*; *social* manifestazione *f*; SP prova *f*; **at all ~s** ad ogni modo

e·vent·ful [ɪ'ventfʊl] *adj* movimentato

e·ven·tu·al [ɪ'ventjʊəl] *adj* finale

e·ven·tu·al·ly [ɪ'ventjʊəlɪ] *adv* finalmente, alla fine

ev·er ['evə(r)] *adv* mai; **have you ~ been to …?** sei mai stato in …?; **for ~** per sempre; **as ~** come sempre; **~ more** sempre di più; **~ since he left I have been worried** da quando è partito sono preoccupato; **~ since his sister's death** dalla morte di sua sorella; **he's been depressed ~ since** è depresso da allora

ev·er·green ['evəgriːn] *n* sempreverde *m*

ev·er·last·ing [evə'lɑːstɪŋ] *adj* eterno

ev·ery ['evrɪ] *adj* ogni; **one in ~ ten houses** una casa su dieci; **~ other day** un giorno sì, uno no; **~ now and then** ogni tanto

ev·ery·bod·y ['evrɪbɒdɪ] → **everyone**

ev·ery·day ['evrɪdeɪ] *adj* di tutti i giorni

ev·ery·one ['evrɪwʌn] *pron* tutti *pl*

ev·ery·thing ['evrɪθɪŋ] *pron* tutto

ev·ery·where ['evrɪweə(r)] *adv* dovunque, dappertutto; (*wherever*) dovunque

e·vict [ɪ'vɪkt] *v/t* sfrattare

ev·i·dence ['evɪdəns] prova *f*; **give ~** testimoniare

ev·i·dent ['evɪdənt] *adj* evidente

ev·i·dent·ly ['evɪdəntlɪ] *adv* evidentemente

e·vil ['iːvl] **1** *adj* cattivo **2** *n* male *m*

e·voke [ɪ'vəʊk] *v/t image* evocare

ev·o·lu·tion [iːvə'luːʃn] evoluzione *f*

e·volve [ɪ'vɒlv] *v/i* evolvere

ewe [juː] pecora *f* femmina

ex- [eks] *pref* ex-

ex [eks] F (*former wife*) ex *f inv* F; (*former husband*) ex *m inv* F

ex·act [ɪg'zækt] *adj* esatto

ex·act·ing [ɪg'zæktɪŋ] *adj task* impegnativo; *employer* esigente; *standards* rigido

ex·act·ly [ɪg'zæktlɪ] *adv* esattamente; **~!** esatto!, esattamente!; **not ~** non esattamente

ex·ag·ge·rate [ɪg'zædʒəreɪt] *v/t & v/i* esagerare

ex·ag·ge·ra·tion [ɪgzædʒə'reɪʃn] esagerazione *f*

ex·am [ɪg'zæm] esame *m*; **sit an ~** dare *o* sostenere un esame; **pass an ~** passare *o* superare un esame; **fail an ~** essere bocciato a un esame

ex·am·i·na·tion [ɪgzæmɪ'neɪʃn] esame *m*; *of patient* visita *f*

ex·am·ine [ɪg'zæmɪn] *v/t* esaminare; *patient* visitare

ex·am·in·er [ɪg'zæmɪnə(r)] EDU esaminatore *m*, -trice *f*

ex·am·ple [ɪg'zɑːmpl] esempio *m*; **for ~** ad *o* per esempio; **set a good / bad ~** dare il buon / cattivo esempio

ex·as·pe·rat·ed [ɪg'zæspəreɪt] *adj* esasperato

ex·as·pe·rat·ing [ɪg'zæspəreɪtɪŋ] *adj* esasperante

ex·ca·vate ['ekskəveɪt] *v/t* (*dig*) scavare; *of archaeologist* riportare alla luce

ex·ca·va·tion [ekskə'veɪʃn] scavo *m*

ex·ca·va·tor ['ekskəveɪtə(r)] escavatrice *f*

ex·ceed [ɪk'siːd] *v/t* (*be more than*) eccedere, superare; (*go beyond*) oltrepassare, superare

ex·ceed·ing·ly [ɪk'siːdɪŋlɪ] *adj* estremamente

ex·cel [ɪk'sel] (*pret & pp* -**led**) **1** *v/i* eccellere; **~ at** eccellere in **2** *v/t*: **~ o.s.** superare se stesso

ex·cel·lence ['eksələns] eccellenza *f*

ex·cel·lent ['eksələnt] *adj* eccellente

ex·cept [ɪk'sept] *prep* eccetto; **~ for** fatta eccezione per; **~ that ...** eccetto che ...

ex·cep·tion [ɪk'sepʃn] eccezione *f*; **with the ~ of** con l'eccezione di; **take ~ to** avere da ridire su; (*be offended by*) risentirsi per

ex·cep·tion·al [ɪk'sepʃnl] *adj* eccezionale

ex·cep·tion·al·ly [ɪk'sepʃnlɪ] *adv* (*extremely*) eccezionalmente

ex·cerpt ['eksɜːpt] estratto *m*

ex·cess [ɪk'ses] **1** *n* eccesso *m*; **eat / drink to ~** mangiare / bere all'eccesso; **be in ~ of** eccedere **2** *adj* in eccesso

ex·cess 'bag·gage eccedenza *f* di bagaglio

ex·cess 'fare supplemento *m* tariffa

ex·ces·sive [ɪk'sesɪv] *adj* eccessivo

ex·change [ɪks'tʃeɪndʒ] **1** *n of views, information* scambio *m*; *between schools* scambio *m* culturale; **in ~ (for)** in cambio (di) **2** *v/t* cambiare; **~ sth for sth** cambiare qc con qc

ex'change rate FIN tasso *m* di cambio

ex·ci·ta·ble [ɪk'saɪtəbl] *adj* eccitabile

ex·cite [ɪk'saɪt] *v/t* (*make enthusiastic*) eccitare

ex·cit·ed [ɪk'saɪtɪd] *adj* eccitato; **get ~** eccitarsi; **get ~ about sth** eccitarsi per qc

ex·cite·ment [ɪk'saɪtmənt] eccitazione *f*

ex·cit·ing [ɪk'saɪtɪŋ] *adj* eccitante, emozionante

ex·claim [ɪkˈskleɪm] *v/t* esclamare

ex·cla·ma·tion [ekskləˈmeɪʃn] esclamazione *f*

ex·cla·ma·tion mark punto *m* esclamativo

ex·clude [ɪkˈskluːd] *v/t* escludere

ex·clud·ing [ɪkˈskluːdɪŋ] *prep* ad esclusione di

ex·clu·sive [ɪkˈskluːsɪv] *adj* esclusivo

ex·com·mu·ni·cate [ekskəˈmjuːnɪkeɪt] *v/t* REL scomunicare

ex·cru·ci·a·ting [ɪkˈskruːʃɪeɪtɪŋ] *adj pain* lancinante

ex·cur·sion [ɪkˈskɜːʃn] escursione *f*, gita *f*

ex·cuse [ɪkˈskjuːs] **1** *n* scusa *f* **2** *v/t* [ɪkˈskjuːz] scusare; **~ s.o. from sth** dispensare qu da qc; **~ me** *to get attention, interrupting* scusami, mi scusi *fml; to get past* permesso

ex·di·rec·to·ry: *Br be* ~ non comparire sull'elenco telefonico

e·x·e·cute [ˈeksɪkjuːt] *v/t criminal* giustiziare; *plan* attuare

ex·e·cu·tion [eksɪˈkjuːʃn] *of criminal* esecuzione *f; of plan* attuazione *f*

ex·e·cu·tion·er [eksɪˈkjuːʃnə(r)] carnefice *m*

ex·ec·u·tive [ɪgˈzekjʊtɪv] dirigente *m/f*

ex·ec·u·tive ˈbrief·case ventiquattrore *f inv*

ex·ec·u·tive ˈwash·room bagno *m* della direzione

ex·em·pla·ry [ɪgˈzemplərɪ] *adj* esemplare

ex·empt [ɪgˈzempt] *adj:* **be ~ from** essere esente da

ex·er·cise [ˈeksəsaɪz] **1** *n (physical)*, EDU esercizio *m;* MIL esercitazione *f;* **take ~** fare esercizio **2** *v/t muscle* fare esercizio con; *dog* far fare esercizio a; *caution, restraint* adoperare **3** *v/i* fare esercizio

ˈex·er·cise bike cyclette *f inv;* **ˈex·er·cise book** EDU quaderno *m* di esercizi; **ˈex·er·cise class** esercitazione *f*

ex·ert [ɪgˈzɜːt] *v/t authority* esercitare; **~ o.s.** sforzarsi

ex·er·tion [ɪgˈzɜːʃn] sforzo *m*

ex·hale [eksˈheɪl] *v/t* esalare

ex·haust [ɪgˈzɔːst] **1** *n fumes* gas *mpl* di scarico; *pipe* tubo *m* di scappamento **2** *v/t (tire)* estenuare; *(use up)* esaurire

ex·haust·ed [ɪgˈzɔːstɪd] *adj (tired)* esausto

exˈhaust fumes *npl* gas *mpl* di scarico

ex·haust·ing [ɪgˈzɔːstɪŋ] *adj* estenuante

ex·haus·tion [ɪgˈzɔːstʃn] spossatezza *f*

ex·haus·tive [ɪgˈzɔːstɪv] *adj* esauriente

exˈhaust pipe tubo *m* di scappamento

ex·hib·it [ɪgˈzɪbɪt] **1** *n in exhibition* oggetto *m* esposto; LAW prova *f* **2** *v/t of gallery, artist* esporre; *(give evidence of)* manifestare

exhibition [eksɪˈbɪʃn] esposizione *f; of bad behaviour* manifestazione *f; of skill* dimostrazione *f*

ex·hi·bi·tion·ist [eksɪˈbɪʃnɪst] esibizionista *m/f*

ex·hil·a·rat·ing [ɪgˈzɪləreɪtɪŋ] *adj* emozionante

ex·ile [ˈeksaɪl] **1** *n* esilio *m; person* esiliato *m,* -a *f* **2** *v/t* esiliare

ex·ist [ɪgˈzɪst] *v/i* esistere; **~ on** vivere di

ex·ist·ence [ɪgˈzɪstəns] esistenza *f;* **in ~** esistente; **come into ~** nascere

ex·ist·ing [ɪgˈzɪstɪŋ] *adj* attuale

ex·it [ˈeksɪt] **1** *n* uscita *f* **2** *v/i* COMPUT uscire

ex·on·e·rate [ɪgˈzɒnəreɪt] *v/t* scagionare

ex·or·bi·tant [ɪgˈzɔːbɪtənt] *adj* esorbitante

ex·ot·ic [ɪgˈzɒtɪk] *adj* esotico

ex·pand [ɪkˈspænd] **1** *v/t* espandere **2** *v/i* espandersi; *of metal* dilatarsi

♦ expand on *v/t* dilungarsi su

ex·panse [ɪkˈspæns] distesa *f*

ex·pan·sion [ɪkˈspænʃn] espansione *f; of metal* dilatazione *f*

ex·pat·ri·ate [eksˈpætrɪət] **1** *adj*

resitente all'estero **2** *n* residente *m/f* all'estero

ex·pect [ɪk'spekt] **1** *v/t* aspettare; (*suppose, demand*) aspettarsi **2** *v/i*: **be ~ing** aspettare un bambino; *I ~ so* immagino di sì

ex·pec·tant [ɪk'spektənt] *adj* pieno di aspettativa

ex·pec·tant 'moth·er donna *f* in stato interessante

ex·pec·ta·tion [ekspek'teɪʃn] aspettativa *f*; **~s** (*demands*) aspettative *fpl*

ex·pe·dient [ɪk'spiːdɪənt] *n* espediente *m*

ex·pe·di·tion [ekspɪ'dɪʃn] spedizione *f*; *go on a shopping/sightseeing ~* andare a fare spese/in giro a visitare

ex·pel [ɪk'spel] *v/t* (*pret & pp* **-led**) espellere

ex·pend [ɪk'spend] *v/t energy* spendere

ex·pend·a·ble [ɪk'spendəbl] *adj person* sacrificabile

ex·pen·di·ture [ɪk'spendɪtʃə(r)] spesa *f*

ex·pense [ɪk'spens] spesa *f*; *at the company's ~* a spese della società; *a joke at my ~* uno scherzo a mie spese; *at the ~ of his health* a spese della sua salute

ex'pense ac·count nota *f* spese

ex·pen·ses [ɪk'spensɪz] *npl* spese *fpl*

ex·pen·sive [ɪk'spensɪv] *adj* caro

ex·pe·ri·ence [ɪk'spɪərɪəns] **1** *n* esperienza *f* **2** *v/t pain, pleasure* provare; *problem, difficulty* incontrare

ex·pe·ri·enced [ɪk'spɪərɪənst] *adj* con esperienza; *he's ~ in teaching* ha esperienza nell'insegnamento

ex·per·i·ment [ɪk'sperɪmənt] **1** *n* esperimento *m* **2** *v/i* fare esperimenti; *~ on animals* sperimentare su; *~ with* (*try out*) sperimentare

ex·per·i·men·tal [ɪksperɪ'mentl] *adj* sperimentale

ex·pert ['ekspɜːt] **1** *adj* esperto **2** *n* esperto *m*, -a *f*

ex·pert ad'vice parere *m* di un esperto

ex·pert·ise [ekspɜː'tiːz] competenza *f*

ex·pire [ɪk'spaɪə(r)] *v/i* scadere

ex·pi·ry [ɪk'spaɪərɪ] scadenza *f*

ex'pi·ry date data *f* di scadenza

ex·plain [ɪk'spleɪn] **1** *v/t* spiegare **2** *v/i* spiegarsi

ex·pla·na·tion [eksplə'neɪʃn] spiegazione *f*

ex·plic·it [ɪk'splɪsɪt] *adj instructions* esplicito

ex·plic·it·ly [ɪk'splɪsɪtlɪ] *adv state, forbid* esplicitamente

ex·plode [ɪk'spləʊd] **1** *v/i of bomb* esplodere **2** *v/t bomb* fare esplodere

ex·ploit[1] ['eksplɔɪt] *n* exploit *m inv*

ex·ploit[2] [ɪk'splɔɪt] *v/t person, resources* sfruttare

ex·ploi·ta·tion [eksplɔɪ'teɪʃn] sfruttamento *m*

ex·plo·ra·tion [eksplə'reɪʃn] esplorazione *f*

ex·plor·a·to·ry [ɪk'splɒrətərɪ] *adj surgery* esplorativo

ex·plore [ɪk'splɔː(r)] *v/t country, possibility etc* esplorare

ex·plor·er [ɪk'splɔːrə(r)] esploratore *m*, -trice *f*

ex·plo·sion [ɪk'spləʊʒn] esplosione *f*; *a population ~* un'esplosione demografica

ex·plo·sive [ɪk'spləʊsɪv] *n* esplosivo *m*

ex·port ['ekspɔːt] **1** *n action* esportazione *f*; *item* prodotto *m* di esportazione **2** *v/t goods*, COMPUT esportare

'ex·port cam·paign campagna *f* per l'esportazione

ex·port·er ['ekspɔːtə(r)] esportatore *m*, -trice *f*

ex·pose [ɪk'spəʊz] *v/t* (*uncover*) scoprire; *scandal, person* denunciare; *~ sth to sth* esporre qc a qc

ex·po·sure [ɪk'spəʊʒə(r)] esposizione *f*; *to cold weather* esposizione *f* prolungata al freddo; *of dishonest behaviour* denuncia *f*; PHOT posa *f*

ex·press [ɪk'spres] **1** *adj* (*fast, explicit*) espresso **2** *n* (*train*) espresso *m*

3 v/t (speak of, voice) esprimere; ~ **o.s. well / clearly** esprimersi bene / chiaramente; ~ **o.s.** (emotionally) esprimersi

ex·pres·sion [ɪkˈspreʃn] espressione f; (expressiveness) espressività f

ex·pres·sive [ɪkˈspresɪv] adj espressivo

ex·press·ly [ɪkˈspreslɪ] adv espressamente

ex·press·way [ɪkˈspresweɪ] autostrada f

ex·pul·sion [ɪkˈspʌlʃn] espulsione f

ex·qui·site [ekˈskwɪzɪt] adj (beautiful) squisito

ex·tend [ɪkˈstend] **1** v/t estendere; house, repertoire ampliare; runway, path prolungare; contract, visa prorogare; thanks, congratulations porgere **2** v/i of garden etc estendersi

ex·ten·sion [ɪkˈstenʃn] to house annesso m; of contract, visa proroga f; TELEC interno m

ex·ten·sion ca·ble prolunga f

ex·ten·sive [ɪkˈstensɪv] adj ampio

ex·tent [ɪkˈstent] ampiezza f, portata f; **to such an ~ that** a un punto tale che; **to a certain ~** fino a un certo punto

ex·ten·u·at·ing cir·cum·stanc·es [ɪkˈstenjʊeɪtɪŋ] npl circostanze fpl attenuanti

ex·te·ri·or [ɪkˈstɪərɪə(r)] **1** adj esterno **2** n of building esterno m; of person aspetto m esteriore

ex·ter·mi·nate [ɪkˈstɜːmɪneɪt] v/t sterminare

ex·ter·nal [ɪkˈstɜːnl] adj (outside) esterno

ex·tinct [ɪkˈstɪŋkt] adj species estinto

ex·tinc·tion [ɪkˈstɪŋkʃn] of species estinzione f

ex·tin·guish [ɪkˈstɪŋgwɪʃ] v/t spegnere

ex·tin·guish·er [ɪkˈstɪŋgwɪʃə(r)] estintore m

ex·tort [ɪkˈstɔːt] v/t estorcere; ~ **money from ...** estorcere denaro da ...

ex·tor·tion [ɪkˈstɔːʃn] estorsione f

ex·tor·tion·ate [ɪkˈstɔːʃənət] adj prices esorbitante; **that's ~!** è un furto!

ex·tra [ˈekstrə] **1** n extra m inv **2** adj in più; **be ~** (cost more) essere a parte **3** adv particolarmente; **an ~ special day** un giorno particolarmente speciale

ex·tra 'charge costo m aggiuntivo

ex·tract¹ [ˈekstrækt] n estratto m

ex·tract² [ɪkˈstrækt] v/t estrarre; information estorcere

ex·trac·tion [ɪkˈstrækʃn] estrazione f

ex·tra·dite [ˈekstrədaɪt] v/t estradare

ex·tra·di·tion [ekstrəˈdɪʃn] estradizione f

ex·tra·di·tion trea·ty accordo m di estradizione

ex·tra·mar·i·tal [ekstrəˈmærɪtl] adj extraconiugale

ex·tra·or·di·nar·i·ly [ekstrəːdɪnˈeərɪlɪ] adv eccezionalmente

ex·tra·or·di·na·ry [ɪkˈstrɔːdɪnərɪ] adj straordinario

ex·tra 'time SP tempi mpl supplementari

ex·trav·a·gance [ɪkˈstrævəgəns] stravaganza f

ex·trav·a·gant [ɪkˈstrævəgənt] adj with money stravagante

ex·treme [ɪkˈstriːm] **1** n estremo m **2** adj estremo

ex·treme·ly [ɪkˈstriːmlɪ] adv estremamente

ex·trem·ist [ɪkˈstriːmɪst] estremista m/f

ex·tri·cate [ˈekstrɪkeɪt] v/t districare

ex·tro·vert [ˈekstrəvɜːt] n / adj estroverso m, -a f

ex·u·be·rant [ɪgˈzjuːbərənt] adj esuberante

ex·ult [ɪgˈzʌlt] v/i esultare

eye [aɪ] **1** n occhio m; of needle cruna f; **keep an ~ on** tenere d'occhio **2** v/t scrutare

'eye·ball bulbo m oculare; 'eye·brow sopracciglio m; 'eye·catch·ing adj appariscente; 'eye·lash ciglio m; 'eye·lid palpebra f; 'eye·lin·er eyeliner m inv; 'eye·sha·dow ombretto m; 'eye·sight vista f; **'eye·sore** pugno m in un occhio; **'eye strain** affaticamento m

della vista; **'eye·wit·ness** testimone m/f oculare

F

F abbr (= **Fahrenheit**) F (= Fahrenheit)

fab·ric ['fæbrɪk] (material) tessuto m

fab·u·lous ['fæbjʊləs] adj fantastico

fab·u·lous·ly ['fæbjʊləslɪ] adv incredibile

fa·çade [fə'sɑːd] of building, person facciata f

face [feɪs] **1** n viso m, faccia f; ~ **to** ~ faccia a faccia; **lose** ~ perdere la faccia **2** v/t person, the sea etc essere di fronte a; facts, truth affrontare
♦ **face up to** v/t affrontare

'face·cloth guanto m di spugna; **'face·lift** lifting m inv del viso; **'face pack** maschera f di bellezza; **'face 'val·ue** valore m nominale; **take sth at** ~ giudicare qc dalle apparenze

fa·cial ['feɪʃl] n pulizia f del viso

fa·cil·i·tate [fə'sɪlɪteɪt] v/t facilitare

fa·cil·i·ties [fə'sɪlətɪz] npl strutture fpl

fact [fækt] fatto m; **in ~, as a matter of** ~ in realtà

fac·tion ['fækʃn] fazione f

fac·tor ['fæktə(r)] fattore m

fac·to·ry ['fæktərɪ] fabbrica f

fac·ul·ty ['fækəltɪ] facoltà f inv

fad [fæd] mania f passeggera

fade [feɪd] v/i of colours sbiadire; of light smorzarsi; of memories svanire

fad·ed ['feɪdɪd] adj colour, jeans sbiadito

fag [fæg] F (cigarette) sigaretta f

fag end F (cigarette end) mozzicone m di sigaretta

Fahr·en·heit ['færənhaɪt] adj Fahrenheit

fail [feɪl] **1** v/i fallire **2** v/t test, exam

essere bocciato a; **he ~ed to arrive in time** non è riuscito ad arrivare in tempo; **he never ~s to write** non manca mai di scrivere **2** n: **without** ~ con certezza

fail·ing ['feɪlɪŋ] n difetto m

fail·ure ['feɪljə(r)] fallimento m

faint [feɪnt] **1** adj vago **2** v/i svenire

faint·ly ['feɪntlɪ] adv vagamente

fair[1] [feə(r)] n (fun ~) luna park m inv; COM fiera f

fair[2] [feə(r)] adj hair biondo; complexion chiaro; (just) giusto; **it's not** ~ non è giusto adv: ~ **enough** e va bene

fair·ly ['feəlɪ] adv treat giustamente; (quite) piuttosto

fair·ness ['feənɪs] of treatment giustizia f

fai·ry ['feərɪ] fata f

'fai·ry tale fiaba f, favola f

faith [feɪθ] fede f

faith·ful ['feɪθfl] adj fedele; **be ~ to one's partner** essere fedeli al proprio compagno

faith·ful·ly ['feɪθflɪ] adv fedelmente; **Yours** ~ distinti saluti

fake [feɪk] **1** n falso m **2** adj falso **3** v/t (forge) falsificare; (feign) simulare

fall[1] [fɔːl] n Am autunno m

fall[2] [fɔːl] **1** v/i (pret **fell**, pp **fallen**) of person, government, night cadere; of prices, temperature calare; **it ~s on a Tuesday** cade di martedì; ~ **ill** ammalarsi **2** n of person, government caduta f; in price, temperature calo m
♦ **fall back on** v/t ricorrere a
♦ **fall behind** v/i with work, studies rimanere indietro

- ◆**fall down** v/i cadere
- ◆**fall for** v/t (*fall in love with*) innamorarsi di; (*be deceived by*) abboccare a
- ◆**fall out** v/i of hair cadere; (*argue*) litigare
- ◆**fall over** v/i cadere
- ◆**fall through** v/i of plans andare a monte

fal·len ['fɔːlən] pp → **fall**

fal·li·ble ['fæləbl] adj fallibile

'**fallout** precipitazione f

false [fɔːls] adj falso

false a'larm falso allarme m

false·ly ['fɔːlslɪ] adv: **be ~ accused of sth** essere ingiustamente accusato di qc

false 'start in race falsa partenza f

false 'teeth npl dentiera f

fal·si·fy ['fɔːlsɪfaɪ] v/t (*pret & pp -ied*) falsificare

fame [feɪm] fama f

fa·mil·i·ar [fə'mɪljə(r)] adj (*intimate*) intimo; form of address, (*well-known*) familiare; **be ~ with sth** conoscere bene qc; **that looks / sounds ~** ha un'aria familiare

fa·mil·i·ar·i·ty [fəmɪlɪ'jærɪtɪ] with subject and course conoscenza f

fa·mil·i·ar·ize [fəm'ɪljəraɪz] v/t familiarizzare; **~ o.s. with ...** familiarizzarsi con ...

fam·i·ly ['fæməlɪ] famiglia f

fam·i·ly 'doc·tor medico m di famiglia; **fam·i·ly 'name** cognome m; **fam·i·ly 'plan·ning** pianificazione f familiare; **fam·i·ly 'plan·ning clin·ic** consultorio m per la pianificazione familiare; **fam·i·ly 'tree** albero m genealogico

fam·ine ['fæmɪn] fame f

fam·ished ['fæmɪʃt] adj F affamato

fa·mous ['feɪməs] adj famoso; **be ~ for ...** essere noto per ...

fan¹ [fæn] n (*supporter*) fan m/f

fan² [fæn] n for cooling: electric ventilatore m; handheld ventaglio m **2** v/t (*pret & pp -ned*): **~ o.s.** farsi aria

fa·nat·ic [fə'nætɪk] n fanatico m, -a f

fa·nat·i·cal [fə'nætɪkl] adj fanatico

fa·nat·i·cism [fə'nætɪsɪzm] fanatismo m

'**fan belt** MOT cinghia f della ventola

'**fan club** fan club m inv

fan·cy ['fænsɪ] **1** adj design stravagante **2** n: **as the ~ takes you** quanto ti va; **take a ~ to s.o.** prendere a benvolere qu **3** v/t (*pret & pp -ied*) F avere voglia di; **I'm sure he fancies you** sono sicuro che gli piaci

fan·cy 'dress costume m

fan·cy-'dress par·ty festa f in maschera

fang [fæŋ] dente m aguzzo

'**fan mail** lettere fpl dei fans

fan·ta·size ['fæntəsaɪz] v/i fantasticare

fan·tas·tic [fæn'tæstɪk] adj (*very good*) fantastico; (*very big*) enorme

fan·tas·ti·cal·ly [fæn'tæstɪklɪ] adv (*extremely*) incredibilmente

fan·ta·sy ['fæntəsɪ] fantasia f

far [fɑː(r)] adv lontano; (*much*) molto; **~ away** lontano; **how ~ is it to ...?** quanto dista ...?; **as ~ as the corner / hotel** fino all'angolo / hotel; **as ~ as I can see** per quanto posso vedere; **as ~ as I know** per quanto ne so; **you've gone too ~** in behaviour sei andato troppo oltre; **so ~ so good** fin qui tutto bene

farce [fɑːs] farsa f

fare [feə(r)] n for travel tariffa f

Far 'East Estremo Oriente m

fare·well [feə'wel] n addio m

fare'well par·ty festa f d'addio

far-fetched [fɑː'fetʃt] adj inverosimile

farm [fɑːm] n fattoria f

farm·er ['fɑːmə(r)] agricoltore m, -trice f

'**farm·house** cascina f

farm·ing ['fɑːmɪŋ] n agricoltura f

'**farm·work·er** bracciante m/f

'**farm·yard** cortile m di una cascina

far-'off adj lontano

far·sight·ed [fɑː'saɪtɪd] adj previdente; Am OPT presbite

fart [fɑːt] **1** n F scoreggia f F, peto m

2 v/i F scoreggiare F, petare

far·ther ['fɑːðə(r)] adv più lontano

far·thest ['fɑːðəst] adv travel etc più lontano

fas·ci·nate ['fæsɪneɪt] v/t affascinare; **I always was ~d by the idea of ...** mi ha sempre affascinato l'idea di ...

fas·ci·nat·ing ['fæsɪneɪtɪŋ] adj affascinante

fas·ci·na·tion [fæsɪ'neɪʃn] with subject fascino m

fas·cis·m ['fæʃɪzm] fascismo m

fas·cist ['fæʃɪst] **1** n fascista m/f **2** adj fascista

fash·ion ['fæʃn] n moda f; (manner) maniera f, modo m; **in ~** alla moda; **out of ~** fuori moda

fash·ion·a·ble ['fæʃnəbl] adj alla moda

fash·ion·a·bly ['fæʃnəblɪ] adv dressed alla moda

'**fash·ion-con·scious** adj fanatico della moda; '**fash·ion de·sign·er** stilista m/f; '**fash·ion mag·a·zine** rivista f di moda; '**fash·ion show** sfilata f di moda

fast[1] [fɑːst] **1** adj veloce, rapido; **be ~** of clock essere avanti **2** adv velocemente; **stuck ~** fissato saldamente; **~ asleep** profondamente addormentato

fast[2] [fɑːst] n not eating digiuno m

fas·ten ['fɑːsn] **1** v/t chiudere; dress, seat-belt allacciare; **~ sth onto sth** attaccare qc a qc; brooch appuntare qc su qc **2** v/i of dress etc allacciarsi

fas·ten·er ['fɑːsnə(r)] chiusura f

fast 'food fast food m; **fast·food 'res·tau·rant** fast food m inv; **fast 'for·ward 1** n on video etc riavvolgimento m rapido **2** v/i riavvolgere rapidamente; '**fast lane** on road corsia f di sorpasso; **in the ~** fig: of life a cento all'ora; '**fast train** rapido m

fat [fæt] **1** adj grasso **2** n grasso m

fa·tal ['feɪtl] adj fatale

fa·tal·i·ty [fə'tælətɪ] fatalità f inv

fa·tal·ly ['feɪtəlɪ] adv: **~ injured** ferito a morte

fate [feɪt] fato m

fat·ed ['feɪtɪd] adj: **be ~ to do sth** essere destinato a fare qc

fa·ther ['fɑːðə(r)] n padre m; **Father Martin** REL padre Martin

Fa·ther 'Christ·mas Babbo m Natale

fa·ther·hood ['fɑːðəhʊd] paternità f

'**fa·ther-in-law** (pl **fathers-in-law**) suocero m

fa·ther·ly ['fɑːðəlɪ] adj paterno

fath·om ['fæðəm] n NAUT fathom m inv

♦**fathom out** v/t fig spiegarsi; **I just can't fathom you out** proprio non ti capisco

fa·tigue [fə'tiːg] n stanchezza f

fat·so ['fætsəʊ] n F ciccione m, -a f F

fat·ten ['fætn] v/t animal ingrassare

fat·ty ['fætɪ] **1** adj grasso **2** n F person ciccione m, -a f F

fau·cet ['fɔːsɪt] Am rubinetto m

fault [fɔːlt] n (defect) difetto m; **it's your / my ~** è colpa tua / mia; **find ~ with** criticare

fault·less ['fɔːltlɪs] adj person, performance impeccabile

fault·y ['fɔːltɪ] adj goods difettoso

fa·vor etc Am → **favour** etc

fa·vour ['feɪvə(r)] **1** n favore m; **do s.o. a ~** fare un favore a qu; **do me a ~!** (don't be stupid) fammi il piacere!; **in ~ of ...** a favore di ...; **be in ~ of ...** essere a favore di ... **2** v/t (prefer) preferire, prediligere

fa·vou·ra·ble ['feɪvərəbl] adj reply etc favorevole

fa·vou·rite ['feɪvərɪt] **1** n prediletto m, -a f; (food) piatto m preferito; in race, competition favorito m, -a f **2** adj preferito

fa·vou·rit·ism ['feɪvrɪtɪzm] favoritismo m

fax [fæks] **1** n fax m inv; **send sth by ~** inviare qc per fax **2** v/t inviare per fax; **~ sth to s.o.** inviare qc per fax a qc

FBI abbr (= **Federal Bureau of Investigation**) FBI f

fear [fɪə(r)] **1** n paura f **2** v/t avere paura di

fear·less ['fɪəlɪs] *adj* intrepido

fear·less·ly ['fɪəlɪslɪ] *adv* intrepidamente

fea·si·bil·i·ty stud·y [fiːzə'bɪlətɪ] studio *m* di fattibilità

fea·si·ble ['fiːzəbl] *adj* fattibile

feast [fiːst] *n* banchetto *m*

feat [fiːt] *n* prodezza *f*

feath·er ['feðə(r)] piuma *f*

fea·ture ['fiːtʃə(r)] **1** *n on face* tratto *m*; *of city, building, plan, style* caratteristica *f*; *in paper* servizio *m*; *(film)* lungometraggio *m*; *make a ~ of ...* mettere l'accento su ... **2** *v/t of film* avere come protagonista

'fea·ture film lungometraggio *m*

Feb·ru·a·ry ['februərɪ] febbraio *m*

fed [fed] *pret & pp* → **feed**

fed·e·ral ['fedərəl] *adj* federale

fed·e·ra·tion [fedə'reɪʃn] federazione *f*

fed 'up *adj* F stufo F; *be ~ with ...* essere stufo di ...

fee [fiː] tariffa *f*; *of lawyer, doctor etc* onorario *m*

fee·ble ['fiːbl] *adj* debole

feed [fiːd] *v/t (pret & pp fed)* nutrire; *family* mantenere; *baby* dare da mangiare a

'feed·back *n* riscontro *m*, feedback *m inv*

feel [fiːl] *(pret & pp felt)* **1** *v/t (touch)* toccare; *(sense)* sentire; *pain, pleasure, sensation* sentire; *(think)* pensare **2** *v/i* sentirsi; *it ~s like silk / cotton* sembra seta / cotone al tatto; *your hand ~s hot / cold* la tua mano è calda / fredda; *I ~ hungry* ho fame; *I ~ tired* sono stanco; *how are you ~ing today?* come ti senti oggi?; *how does it ~ to be rich?* che sensazione fa essere ricchi?; *do you ~ like a drink / meal?* hai voglia di bere / mangiare qualcosa?; *I ~ like going / staying* ho voglia di andare / rimanere; *I don't ~ like it* non ne ho voglia

♦ **feel up to** *v/t* sentirsi in grado di

feel·er ['fiːlə(r)] *of insect* antenna *f*

'feel·good fac·tor fattore *m* tranquillizzante

feel·ing ['fiːlɪŋ] sentimento *m*; *(emotion)* sensazione *f*; *(sensation)* sensibilità *f*; *what are your ~s about it?* quali sono le tue impressioni in proposito?; *I have mixed ~s about him* ho sensazioni contrastanti nei suoi riguardi; *I have this ~ that ...* ho la sensazione che ...

feet [fiːt] *pl* → **foot**

fe·line ['fiːlaɪn] *adj* felino

fell [fel] *pret* → **fall**

fel·low ['feləʊ] *n (man)* tipo *m*

fel·low 'cit·i·zen concittadino *m*, -a *f*; **fel·low 'coun·try·man** compatriota *m*/*f*; **fel·low 'man** prossimo *m*

fel·o·ny ['felənɪ] *Am* delitto *m*

felt¹ [felt] *n* feltro *m*

felt² [felt] *pret & pp* → **feel**

felt 'tip, felt-tip(·ped) 'pen pennarello *m*

fe·male ['fiːmeɪl] **1** *adj* femmina; *typical of women* femminile **2** *n* femmina *f*; F *(woman)* donna *f*

fem·i·nine ['femɪnɪn] **1** *adj* femminile **2** *n* GRAM femminile *m*

fem·i·nis·m ['femɪnɪzm] femminismo *m*

fem·i·nist ['femɪnɪst] **1** *n* femminista *f* **2** *adj* femminista

fence [fens] *n round garden etc* recinto *m*; F *criminal* ricettatore *m*, -trice *f*; *sit on the ~* non prendere partito

♦ **fence in** *v/t land* recintare

fenc·ing ['fensɪŋ] SP scherma *f*

fend [fend] *v/i: ~ for o.s.* badare a se stesso

fer·ment¹ [fə'ment] *v/i of liquid* fermentare

fer·ment² ['fɜːment] *n (unrest)* fermento *m*

fer·men·ta·tion [fɜːmen'teɪʃn] fermentazione *f*

fern [fɜːn] felce *f*

fe·ro·cious [fə'rəʊʃəs] *adj* feroce

fer·ry ['ferɪ] *n* traghetto *m*

fer·tile ['fɜːtaɪl] *adj* fertile

fer·til·i·ty [fɜː'tɪlətɪ] fertilità *f*

fer'til·i·ty drug cura *f* per sviluppare la fertilità

fer·ti·lize ['fɜːtəlaɪz] *v/t ovum* fecondare

fer·ti·liz·er ['fɜːtəlaɪzə(r)] *for soil* fertilizzante *m*

fer·vent ['fɜːvənt] *adj admirer* fervente

fer·vent·ly ['fɜːvəntlɪ] *adv* ardentemente

fes·ter ['festə(r)] *v/i of wound* fare infezione

fes·ti·val ['festɪvl] festival *m inv*

fes·tive ['festɪv] *adj* festivo; **the ~ season** le festività

fes·tiv·i·ties [fe'stɪvətɪz] *npl* festeggiamenti *mpl*

fe·tal ['fiːtl] *adj* fetale

fetch [fetʃ] *v/t (go and ~)* andare a prendere; *(come and ~)* venire a prendere; *thing* prendere; *price* rendere

fe·tus ['fiːtəs] feto *m*

feud [fjuːd] **1** *n* faida *f* **2** *v/i* litigare

fe·ver ['fiːvə(r)] febbre *f*

fe·ver·ish ['fiːvərɪʃ] *adj also fig* febbrile; *I'm feeling* ~ mi sento la febbre

few [fjuː] **1** *adj (not many)* pochi; *a* ~ ... alcuni ...; *a* ~ **people** alcune persone, qualche persona; *a* ~ **books** alcuni libri, qualche libro; *quite a* ~, *a good* ~ *(a lot)* parecchi **2** *pron* *(not many)* pochi; *a* ~ *(some)* alcuni; *quite a* ~, *a good* ~ *(a lot)* parecchi

fewer ['fjuːə(r)] *adj* meno; ~ *than* ... meno di ...

fi·an·cé [fɪ'ɒnseɪ] fidanzato *m*

fi·an·cée [fɪ'ɒnseɪ] fidanzata *f*

fi·as·co [fɪ'æskəʊ] fiasco *m*

fib [fɪb] *n* frottola *f*

fi·ber *Am* → **fibre**

fi·bre ['faɪbə(r)] *n* fibra *f*

'fi·bre·glass *n* fibra *f* di vetro; **fi·bre 'op·tic** *adj* fibra *f* ottica; **fi·bre 'op·tics** tecnologia *f* delle fibre ottiche

fick·le ['fɪkl] *adj* incostante

fic·tion ['fɪkʃn] *n (novels)* narrativa *f*; *(made-up story)* storia *f*

fic·tion·al ['fɪkʃnl] *adj* immaginario

fic·ti·tious [fɪk'tɪʃəs] *adj* fittizio

fid·dle ['fɪdl] **1** *n* F *(violin)* violino *m*; *it's a* ~ F *(cheat)* è una fregatura F **2** *v/i:* ~ *with* ... giocherellare con ...;

~ *around with* ... trafficare con ... **3** *v/t accounts, results* truccare

fi·del·i·ty [fɪ'delətɪ] fedeltà *f*

fid·get ['fɪdʒɪt] *v/i* agitarsi

fid·get·y ['fɪdʒɪtɪ] *adj* in agitazione; **get** ~ mettersi in agitazione

field [fiːld] campo *m*; *(competitors in race)* formazione *f*; *that's not my* ~ non è il mio campo

field·er ['fiːldə(r)] *in cricket* esterno *m*

'field e·vents *npl* atletica *f* leggera (escluse le specialità su pista)

fierce [fɪəs] *adj animal* feroce; *wind, storm* violento

fierce·ly ['fɪəslɪ] *adv* ferocemente; *say sth* ~ dire qc in tono aggressivo

fi·er·y ['faɪərɪ] *adj personality, temper* focoso

fif·teen [fɪf'tiːn] quindici

fif·teenth [fɪf'tiːnθ] *n & adj* quindicesimo, -a

fifth [fɪfθ] *n & adj* quinto, -a

fifth·ly ['fɪfθlɪ] *adv* al quinto posto

fif·ti·eth ['fɪftɪɪθ] *n & adj* cinquantesimo, -a

fif·ty ['fɪftɪ] cinquanta

fif·ty-'fif·ty *adv* metà e metà; *go* ~ *with s.o.* fare a metà con qu

fig [fɪg] fico *m*

fight [faɪt] **1** *n* lotta *f*; *in war* combattimento *m*; *(argument)* litigio *m*; *in boxing* incontro *m* **2** *v/t (pret & pp* **fought)** *(brawl)* azzuffare; *in war* combattere; *in boxing* battersi contro; *disease, injustice* combattere **3** *v/i (pret & pp* **fought)** *in war* combattere; *of drunks, schoolkids* azzuffarsi; *(argue)* litigare

♦ **fight for** *v/t one's rights, a cause* lottare per

fight·er ['faɪtə(r)] combattente *m/f*; *aeroplane* caccia *m inv*; *(boxer)* pugile *m*; *she's a* ~ è combattiva

fight·ing ['faɪtɪŋ] *n* risse *fpl*; *he's always in trouble for* ~ è sempre nei guai perché scatena risse

fig·u·ra·tive ['fɪgjərətɪv] *adj use of word* figurato; *art* figurativo

fig·ure ['fɪgə(r)] *n (digit)* cifra *f*; *of person* linea *f*; *(form, shape)* figura *f*

♦ **figure out** v/t (*understand*) capire; *calculation* calcolare

'**fig·ure skat·er** pattinatore m, -trice f artistico, -a

'**fig·ure skat·ing** pattinaggio m artistico

file[1] [faɪl] **1** n for papers raccoglitore m; *contents* dossier m inv, pratica f; COMPUT file m inv; **on ~** in archivio **2** v/t documents schedare

♦ **file away** v/t documents archiviare

file[2] [faɪl] n for wood, fingernails lima f

'**file man·ag·er** COMPUT file manager m inv

fi·li·al ['fɪlɪəl] adj filiale

fil·ing cab·i·net ['faɪlɪŋkæbɪnət] schedario m

fill [fɪl] **1** v/t riempire; tooth otturare **2** n: **eat one's ~** mangiare a sazietà

♦ **fill in** v/t form compilare; hole riempire; **fill s.o. in** mettere al corrente qu

♦ **fill in for** v/t sostituire temporaneamente

♦ **fill out 1** v/t form compilare **2** v/i (get fatter) arrotondarsi

♦ **fill up 1** v/t riempire **2** v/i of stadium, theatre riempirsi

fil·let ['fɪlɪt] n filetto m

fil·let '**steak** filetto m

fill·ing ['fɪlɪŋ] **1** n in sandwich ripieno m; in tooth otturazione f **2** adj food pesante

'**fill·ing sta·tion** stazione f di rifornimento

film [fɪlm] **1** n for camera pellicola f; at cinema film m inv **2** v/t person, event riprendere, filmare; scene girare

'**film-mak·er** regista m/f

'**film star** stella f del cinema

fil·ter ['fɪltə(r)] **1** n filtro m **2** v/t coffee, liquid filtrare

♦ **filter through** v/i of news, reports diffondersi

'**fil·ter pa·per** carta f filtrante

'**fil·ter tip** (cigarette) filtro m

filth [fɪlθ] sporcizia f; (obscenities) sconcezze fpl

filth·y ['fɪlθɪ] adj sporco; language etc volgare

fin [fɪn] of fish pinna f

fi·nal ['faɪnl] **1** adj finale **2** n SP finale f

fi·na·le [fɪ'nɑːlɪ] finale m

fi·nal·ist ['faɪnəlɪst] finalista m/f

fi·nal·ize ['faɪnəlaɪz] v/t plans, design mettere a punto

fi·nal·ly ['faɪnəlɪ] adv infine; (at last) finalmente

fi·nals ['faɪnəlz] npl EDU esami mpl finali

fi·nance ['faɪnæns] **1** n finanza f **2** v/t finanziare

fi·nan·ces ['faɪnænsɪz] npl finanze fpl

fi·nan·cial [faɪ'nænʃl] adj finanziario

fi·nan·cial·ly [faɪ'nænʃəlɪ] adv finanziariamente

fi·nan·cial '**year** esercizio m (finanziario)

fi·nan·cier [faɪ'nænsɪə(r)] n finanziatore m, -trice f

find [faɪnd] v/t (pret & pp found) trovare; **if you ~ it too hot / cold** se lo trovi troppo caldo / freddo; **~ a person innocent / guilty** LAW giudicare una persona innocente / colpevole

♦ **find out** v/t & v/i scoprire

find·ings ['faɪndɪŋz] npl of report conclusioni fpl

fine[1] [faɪn] adj day, weather, city bello; wine, performance buono; distinction, line sottile; **how's that? – that's ~** com'è? – va benissimo; **that's ~ by me** a me sta bene; **how are you? –** ~ come stai? – bene

fine[2] [faɪn] **1** n penalty multa f **2** v/t multare

fine-'tooth comb: go through sth with a ~ passare qc al setaccio

fine-'tune v/t also fig mettere a punto

fin·ger ['fɪŋgə(r)] **1** n dito m **2** v/t passare le dita su

'**fin·ger·nail** unghia f; '**fin·ger·print 1** n impronta f digitale **2** v/t prendere le impronte digitali di; '**fin·ger·tip** punta f del dito; **have sth at one's ~s** knowledge sapere qc a menadito

fin·i·cky ['fɪnɪkɪ] adj person pignolo; design, pattern complicato

fin·ish ['fɪnɪʃ] **1** *v/t* finire; **~ doing sth** finire di fare qc **2** *v/i* finire **3** *n of product* finitura *f*; *finishing line* traguardo *m*

♦ **finish off** *v/t* finire

♦ **finish up** *v/t food* finire; **he finished up liking London** Londra ha finito per piacergli

♦ **finish with** *v/t boyfriend etc* lasciare

fin·ish·ing line ['fɪnɪʃɪŋ] traguardo *m*

Fin·land ['fɪnlənd] Finlandia *f*

Finn [fɪn] finlandese *m/f*

Finn·ish ['fɪnɪʃ] **1** *adj* finlandese, finnico **2** *language* finlandese *m*

fir [fɜːr(r)] abete *m*

fire ['faɪə(r)] **1** *n* fuoco *m*; (*blaze*) incendio *m*; (*bonfire, campfire etc*) falò *m inv*; **be on ~** essere in fiamme; **catch ~** prendere fuoco; **set sth on ~**, **set ~ to sth** dare fuoco a qc **2** *v/i* (*shoot*) sparare **3** *v/t* F (*dismiss*) licenziare

'**fire a·larm** allarme *m* antincendio; '**fire·arm** arma *f* da fuoco; '**fire bri·gade** vigili *mpl* del fuoco; '**fire·crack·er** petardo *m*; '**fire door** porta *f* taglia-fuoco; '**fire drill** esercitazione *f* antincendio; '**fire en·gine** autopompa *f*; '**fire es·cape** scala *f* antincendio; '**fire ex·tin·guish·er** ['faɪərɪkstɪŋgwɪʃə(r)] estintore *m*; '**fire fight·er** pompiere *m*; '**fire·guard** parafuoco *m inv*; '**fire·man** pompiere *m*; '**fire·place** camino *m*; '**fire sta·tion** caserma *f* dei pompieri; '**fire truck** *Am* autopompa *f*; '**fire·wood** legna *f* da ardere; '**fire·works** *npl* fuochi *mpl* d'artificio

firm[^1] [fɜːm] *adj grip, handshake* energico; *flesh, muscles* sodo; *voice, parents* deciso; *decision* risoluto; *date, offer* definitivo; *control* rigido; *foundations* solido; *believer* convinto; **a ~ deal** un accordo definito

firm[^2] [fɜːm] *n* COM azienda *f*

first [fɜːst] **1** *adj* primo; **who's ~ please?** chi è il primo, per favore? **2** *n* primo *m*, -a *f* **3** *adv arrive, finish* per primo; (*beforehand*) prima; **~ of**

all (*for one reason*) innanzitutto; **at ~** in un primo tempo, al principio

first 'aid pronto soccorso *m*; **first-'aid box**, **first-'aid kit** cassetta *f* del pronto soccorso; '**first·born** *adj* primogenito; '**first class 1** *adj* di prima classe **2** *adv travel* in prima classe; **first 'floor** primo piano *m*; *Am* piano *m* terra; **first'hand** *adj* diretto; **First 'La·dy** *of US* First Lady *f inv*

first·ly ['fɜːstlɪ] *adv* in primo luogo

first 'name nome *m* di battesimo; **first 'night** prima serata *f*; **first of'fend·er** delinquente *m/f* non pregiudicato, -a; **first-'rate** *adj* di prima qualità

fis·cal ['fɪskl] *adj* fiscale

fish [fɪʃ] **1** *n* (*pl fish*) pesce *m*; **drink like a ~** F bere come una spugna F; **feel like a ~ out of water** sentirsi come un pesce fuor d'acqua **2** *v/i* pescare

fish and 'chips *npl* pesce e patate fritte

'**fish·bone** lisca *f*

fish·er·man ['fɪʃəmən] pescatore *m*

fish 'fin·ger bastoncino *m* di pesce

fish·ing ['fɪʃɪŋ] pesca *f*

'**fish·ing boat** peschereccio *m*; '**fish·ing line** lenza *f*; '**fish·ing rod** canna *f* da pesca

fish·mon·ger ['fɪʃmʌŋgə(r)] pescivendolo *m*

fish·y ['fɪʃɪ] *adj* F (*suspicious*) sospetto

fist [fɪst] pugno *m*

fit[^1] [fɪt] *n* MED attacco *m*; **a ~ of rage / jealousy** un accesso di rabbia / gelosia

fit[^2] [fɪt] *adj physically* in forma; *morally* adatto; **keep ~** tenersi in forma

fit[^3] [fɪt] **1** *v/t* (*pret & pp* **-ted**) *of clothes* andare bene a; (*attach*) installare **2** *v/i* (*pret & pp* **-ted**) *of clothes* andare bene; *of piece of furniture etc* starci **3** *n*: **it is a good ~** *of piece of furniture etc* ci sta perfettamente; *of clothes* calza a pennello; **it's a tight ~** *of piece of furniture etc* ci sta appena; *of clothes* va giusto giusto

♦ **fit in 1** *v/i of person in group* integrarsi; *it fits in with our plans* si concilia con i nostri programmi **2** *v/t*: *fit s.o. into schedule* fissare un appuntamento a qu

fit·ful ['fɪtfʊl] *adj sleep* a tratti

fit·ness ['fɪtnɪs] *physical* forma *f*

'fit·ness cen·ter *Am*, 'fit·ness cen·tre palestra *f*

fit·ted 'car·pet ['fɪtɪd] moquette *f inv*; fit·ted 'kitch·en cucina *f* componibile; fit·ted 'sheet lenzuolo *m* con gli angoli

fit·ter ['fɪtə(r)] *n* assemblatore *m*, -trice *f*

fit·ting ['fɪtɪŋ] *adj* appropriato

fit·tings ['fɪtɪŋz] *npl* equipaggiamento *msg*

five [faɪv] cinque

fiv·er ['faɪvə(r)] F banconota *f* da cinque sterline

fix [fɪks] **1** *n* (*solution*) soluzione *f*; *be in a ~* F essere nei casini F **2** *v/t* (*attach*) fissare; (*repair*) aggiustare; (*arrange: meeting etc*) fissare; *lunch* preparare; *dishonestly: match etc* manipolare; ~ *sth onto sth* attaccare qc a qc; *I'll ~ you a drink* ti preparo da bere

♦ **fix up** *v/t meeting* fissare; *it's all fixed up* è tutto stabilito

fixed [fɪkst] *adj in one position* fisso; *timescale, exchange rate* stabilito

fix·tures ['fɪkstʃəz] *npl in room* installazioni *fpl* fisse; SP incontro *m*

♦ **fiz·zle out** ['fɪzl] *v/i* F sfumare F

fiz·zy ['fɪzɪ] *adj drink* gassato

flab [flæb] *on body* ciccia *f*

flab·ber·gast ['flæbəgɑːst] *v/t* F: *be ~ed* cadere dalle nuvole

flab·by ['flæbɪ] *adj muscles, stomach* flaccido

flag¹ [flæg] *n* bandiera *f*

flag² [flæg] *v/i* (*pret & pp -ged*) (*tire*) soccombere

'flag·pole asta *f*

fla·grant ['fleɪgrənt] *adj* flagrante

'flag·ship *fig* cavallo *m* di battaglia

'flag·staff asta *f*

'flag·stone lastra *f* di pietra

flair [fleə(r)] *n* (*talent*) talento *m*; (*style*) stile *m*

flake [fleɪk] *n of snow* fiocco *m*; *of paint, plaster* scaglia *f*

♦ **flake off** *v/i* squamarsi

flak·y ['fleɪkɪ] *adj* squamato

flak·y 'pas·try pasta *f* sfoglia

flam·boy·ant [flæm'bɔɪənt] *adj personality* esuberante

flam·boy·ant·ly [flæm'bɔɪəntlɪ] *adv dressed* in modo vistoso

flame [fleɪm] *n* fiamma *f*; *go up in ~s* incendiarsi

flam·ma·ble ['flæməbl] *adj* infiammabile

flan [flæn] sformato *m*

flank [flæŋk] **1** *n* fianco *m* **2** *v/t*: *be ~ed by* essere affiancato da

flan·nel ['flænl] *n for washing* guanto *m* di spugna

flap [flæp] **1** *n of envelope, pocket* falda *f*; *of table* ribalta *f*; *be in a ~* F essere in fibrillazione F **2** *v/t* (*pret & pp -ped*) *wings* sbattere **3** *v/i* (*pret & pp -ped*) *of flag etc* sventolare; (*panic*) andare in fibrillazione F

flare [fleə(r)] **1** *n* (*distress signal*) razzo *m*; *in dress* svasatura *f*; ~*s trousers* pantaloni *mpl* a zampa di elefante **2** *v/t nostrils* allargare

♦ **flare up** *v/i of violence, illness, temper* esplodere; *of fire* divampare

flash [flæʃ] **1** *n of light* lampo *m*; PHOT flash *m inv*; *in a ~* F in un istante; *have a ~ of inspiration* avere un lampo di genio; ~ *of lightning* lampo *m* **2** *v/i of light* lampeggiare **3** *v/t*: ~ *one's headlights* lampeggiare

'flash·back *in film* flashback *m inv*

flash·er ['flæʃə(r)] MOT freccia *f*; F *person* esibizionista *m*

'flash·light *esp Am* pila *f*; PHOT flash *m inv*

flash·y ['flæʃɪ] *adj pej* appariscente

flask [flɑːsk] (*vacuum ~*) termos *m inv*

flat¹ [flæt] **1** *adj surface, land, tone* piatto; *beer* sgassato; *battery, tyre* a terra; *shoes* basso; *A/B ~* MUS la/si bemolle; *and that's ~* F punto e

basta F **2** *adv* MUS sotto tonalità; *~ out* work, run, *drive* a tutto gas **3** *n* gomma *f* a terra

flat² [flæt] *n* Br (*apartment*) appartamento *m*

flat-chest·ed [flæˈtʃestɪd] *adj* piatto

flat·ly [ˈflætlɪ] *adv* refuse, *deny* risolutamente

'**flat·mate** persona *f* con cui si divide la casa

'**flat rate** tariffa *f* forfettaria

flat·ten [ˈflætn] *v/t* land, *road* livellare; *by bombing, demolition* radere al suolo

flat·ter [ˈflætə(r)] *v/t* adulare

flat·ter·er [ˈflætərə(r)] adulatore *m*, -trice *f*

flat·ter·ing [ˈflætərɪŋ] *adj* comments lusinghiero; *Jane's dress is very ~* il vestito di Jane le dona molto

flat·ter·y [ˈflætərɪ] adulazione *f*

flat·u·lence [ˈflætjʊləns] flatulenza *f*

flat·ware [ˈflætweər] Am stoviglie *fpl*

flau·tist [ˈflɔːtɪst] flautista *m/f*

fla·vor *etc* Am → **flavour** *etc*

fla·vour [ˈfleɪvə(r)] **1** *n* gusto *m* **2** *v/t* food insaporire

fla·vour·ing [ˈfleɪvərɪŋ] *n* aroma *m*

flaw [flɔː] *n* difetto *m*

flaw·less [ˈflɔːlɪs] *adj* perfetto

flea [fliː] *n* pulce *f*

fleck [flek] puntino *m*

fled [fled] *pret & pp* → **flee**

flee [fliː] *v/i* (*pret & pp* **fled**) scappare

fleece [fliːs] *v/t* F fregare F

fleet [fliːt] *n* NAUT flotta *f*; *of taxis, trucks* parco *m* macchine

fleet·ing [ˈfliːtɪŋ] *adj* visit *etc* di sfuggita; *catch a ~ glimpse of* vedere di sfuggita

flesh [fleʃ] carne *f*; *of fruit* polpa *f*; *meet / see a person in the ~* incontrare / vedere una persona in carne e ossa

flex [fleks] **1** *v/t* muscles flettere **2** *n* ELEC cavo *m*

flex·i·bil·i·ty [fleksəˈbɪlətɪ] flessibilità *f*

flex·i·ble [ˈfleksəbl] *adj* flessibile; *I'm quite ~ about arrangements, timing* sono abbastanza flessibile

flex·(i)·time [ˈfleks(ɪ)taɪm] orario *m* flessibile

flew [fluː] *pret* → **fly**

flick [flɪk] *v/t* tail agitare; *he ~ed a fly off his hand* ha cacciato via una mosca dalla mano; *she ~ed her hair out of her eyes* si è tolta i capelli dagli occhi con un gesto

♦ **flick through** *v/t* book, *magazine* sfogliare

flick·er [ˈflɪkə(r)] *v/i* of light tremolare

'**flick-knife** coltello *m* a scatto

fli·er [ˈflaɪə(r)] (*circular*) volantino *m*

flies [flaɪz] *npl* on *trousers* patta *f*

flight [flaɪt] volo *m*; (*fleeing*) fuga *f*; *~ (of stairs)* rampa *f* (di scale)

'**flight at·tend·ant** assistente *m/f* di volo; '**flight crew** equipaggio *m* di volo; '**flight deck** in aeroplane cabina *f* di pilotaggio; *of aircraft carrier* ponte *m* di decollo; '**flight num·ber** numero *m* di volo; '**flight path** rotta *f* (di volo); '**flight re·cord·er** registratore *m* di volo; '**flight time** departure orario *m* di volo; *duration* durata *f* di volo

flight·y [ˈflaɪtɪ] *adj* volubile

flim·sy [ˈflɪmzɪ] *adj* structure, *furniture* leggero; *dress, material* sottile; *excuse* debole

flinch [flɪntʃ] *v/i* sobbalzare

fling [flɪŋ] **1** *v/t* (*pret & pp* **flung**) scagliare; *~ o.s. into a chair* buttarsi su una sedia **2** *n* F (*affair*) avventura *f*

♦ **flip through** [flɪp] *v/t* (*pret & pp* **-ped**) book, *magazine* sfogliare

flip·per [ˈflɪpə(r)] for *swimming* pinna *f*

flirt [flɜːt] **1** *v/i* flirtare **2** *n* flirt *m inv*

flir·ta·tious [flɜːˈteɪʃəs] *adj* civettuolo

float [fləʊt] *v/i* galleggiare; FIN fluttuare

float·ing vot·er [ˈfləʊtɪŋ] elettore che cambia spesso opinione

flock [flɒk] **1** *n* of *sheep* gregge *m* **2** *v/i* accorrere in massa

flog [flɒg] *v/t* (*pret & pp* **-ged**) (*whip*) fustigare; F (*sell*) vendere

flood [flʌd] **1** *n* inondazione *f* **2** *v/t of river* inondare; **~ its banks** *of river* straripare

♦ **flood in** *v/i* affluire

flood·ing ['flʌdɪŋ] inondazione *f*

'**flood·light** *n* riflettore *m*

flood·lit ['flʌdlɪt] *adj match* illuminato da riflettori

flood wa·ters ['flʌdwɔːtəz] *npl* acque *fpl* di inondazione

floor [flɔː(r)] *n* pavimento *m*; (*storey*) piano *m*

'**floor·board** asse *f* del pavimento; '**floor cloth** straccio *m* per lavare per terra; '**floor·lamp** *Am* lampada *f* a stelo

flop [flɒp] **1** *v/i* (*pret & pp* **-ped**) crollare; F (*fail*) fare fiasco **2** *n* F (*failure*) fiasco *m*

flop·py ['flɒpɪ] *adj not stiff* floscio; (*weak*) moscio

flop·py (**disk**) floppy *m inv*, floppy disk *m inv*

Flor·ence ['flɒrəns] Firenze

Flor·en·tine ['flɒrəntaɪn] **1** *adj* fiorentino **2** *n* fiorentino *m*, -a *f*

flor·ist ['flɒrɪst] fiorista *m/f*

floss [flɒs] **1** *n for teeth* filo *m* interdentale **2** *v/t*: **~ one's teeth** passare il filo interdentale

flour ['flaʊə(r)] farina *f*

flour·ish ['flʌrɪʃ] *v/i* fiorire; *of business, civilization* prosperare

flour·ish·ing ['flʌrɪʃɪŋ] *adj business, trade* prospero

flow [fləʊ] **1** *v/i of river, traffic, current* scorrere; *of work* procedere **2** *n of river, ideas* flusso *m*

'**flow·chart** diagramma *m* (di flusso)

flow·er ['flaʊə(r)] **1** *n* fiore *m* **2** *v/i* fiorire

'**flow·er·bed** aiuola *f*; '**flow·er·pot** vaso *m* per fiori; '**flow·er show** esposizione *f* floreale

flow·er·y ['flaʊərɪ] *adj pattern* a fiori; *style of writing* fiorito

flown [fləʊn] *pp* → **fly**

flu [fluː] influenza *f*

fluc·tu·ate ['flʌktjʊeɪt] *v/i* oscillare

fluc·tu·a·tion [flʌktjʊ'eɪʃn] oscillazione *f*

flu·en·cy ['fluːənsɪ] *in a language* scioltezza *f*

flu·ent ['fluːənt] *adj* fluente; **he speaks ~ Spanish** parla correntemente lo spagnolo

flu·ent·ly ['fluːəntlɪ] *adv speak, write* correntemente

fluff [flʌf] *material* lanugine *f*; **a bit of ~** un po' di lanugine

fluff·y ['flʌfɪ] *adj material, hair* lanuginoso; *clouds* soffice; **~ toy** peluche *m inv*

fluid ['fluːɪd] *n* fluido *m*

flung [flʌŋ] *pret & pp* → **fling**

flunk [flʌŋk] *v/t Am* F essere bocciato a

flu·o·res·cent [fluə'resnt] *adj light* fluorescente

flur·ry ['flʌrɪ] *of snow* raffica *f*

flush [flʌʃ] **1** *v/t toilet* tirare l'acqua di; **~ sth down the toilet** buttare qc giù dal water **2** *v/i* (*go red in the face*) diventare rosso; **the toilet won't ~** lo sciacquone del bagno non funziona **3** *adj* (*level*) a filo; **be ~ with ...** a filo con ...

♦ **flush away** *v/t down toilet* buttare giù dal water

♦ **flush out** *v/t rebels etc* scovare

flus·ter ['flʌstə(r)] *v/t* mettere in agitazione; **get ~ed** mettersi in agitazione

flute [fluːt] MUS flauto *m* traverso; *glass* flute *m inv*

flut·ter ['flʌtə(r)] **1** *v/i of bird* sbattere le ali; *of wings* sbattere; *of flag* sventolare; *of heart* battere forte **2** *n* F (*bet*) piccola scommessa *f*

fly[1] [flaɪ] *n insect* mosca *f*

fly[2] [flaɪ] *n on trousers* patta *f*

fly[3] [flaɪ] (*pret* **flew**, *pp* **flown**) **1** *v/i* volare; *of flag* sventolare; (*rush*) precipitarsi; **~ into a rage** perdere le staffe **2** *v/t aeroplane* pilotare; *airline* volare con; (*transport by air*) spedire per via aerea

♦ **fly away** *v/i of bird, plane* volare via

♦ **fly back** *v/i* (*travel back*) ritornare (in aereo)

♦ **fly in** *v/i of plane, passengers* arrivare **2** *v/t supplies etc* mandare per via aerea

♦ **fly off** v/i of hat etc volare via

♦ **fly out** v/i partire in aereo

♦ **fly past** v/i in formation volare in formazione; of time volare

fly·ing ['flaɪɪŋ] n volare m

fly·ing 'sau·cer disco m volante

'**fly·o·ver** MOT cavalcavia m inv

foam [fəʊm] n on liquid schiuma f

foam 'rub·ber gommapiuma® f

FOB [efəʊ'bi:] abbr (= **free on board**) FOB

fo·cus ['fəʊkəs] **1** n of attention centro m; PHOT fuoco m; **be in ~ / be out of ~** PHOT essere a fuoco / non essere a fuoco **2** v/t: ~ **one's attention on** focalizzare l'attenzione su **3** v/i mettere a fuoco

♦ **focus on** v/t problem, issue focalizzare l'attenzione su; PHOT mettere a fuoco

fod·der ['fɒdə(r)] foraggio m

foe·tal ['fi:tl] adj → **fetal**

foe·tus ['fi:təs] → **fetus**

fog [fɒg] nebbia f

♦ **fog up** v/i (pret & pp **-ged**) appannarsi

'**fog·bound** adj bloccato dalla nebbia

fog·gy ['fɒgɪ] adj nebbioso; **I haven't the foggiest (idea)** non ne ho la più pallida idea

foi·ble ['fɔɪbl] fisima f

foil[1] [fɔɪl] n carta f stagnola

foil[2] [fɔɪl] v/t (thwart) sventare

fold[1] [fəʊld] **1** v/t paper etc piegare; ~ **one's arms** incrociare le braccia **2** v/i of business chiudere i battenti **3** n in cloth etc piega f

♦ **fold up 1** v/t chairs etc chiudere; clothes piegare **2** v/i of chair, table chiudere

fold[2] [fəʊld] n for sheep etc ovile m

fold·er ['fəʊldə(r)] for documents cartellina f; COMPUT directory f inv

fold·ing ['fəʊldɪŋ] adj pieghevole; ~ **chair** sedia f pieghevole

fo·li·age ['fəʊlɪɪdʒ] fogliame m

folk [fəʊk] (people) gente f; **my ~** (family) i miei parenti; **come in, my ~s** F entrate, gente F

'**folk dance** danza f popolare; '**folk mu·sic** musica f folk; '**folk sing·er** cantante m/f folk; '**folk song** canzone f popolare

fol·low ['fɒləʊ] **1** v/t (also understand) seguire **2** v/i seguire; logically quadrare; **it ~s from this that ...** ne consegue che ...; **as ~s** quanto segue

♦ **follow up** v/t letter, inquiry dare seguito a

fol·low·er ['fɒləʊə(r)] of politician etc seguace m/f; of football team tifoso m, -a f; **are you a ~ of ...?** of TV programme segui ...?

fol·low·ing ['fɒləʊɪŋ] **1** adj seguente **2** n people seguito m; **the ~** quanto segue

'**fol·low-up meet·ing** riunione f ulteriore

'**fol·low-up vis·it** to doctor etc visita f successiva

fol·ly ['fɒlɪ] (madness) follia f

fond [fɒnd] adj (loving) affezionato; memory caro; **he is ~ of travel** gli piace viaggiare

fon·dle ['fɒndl] v/t accarezzare

fond·ness ['fɒndnɪs] for person affetto m; for wine, food gusto m

font [fɒnt] for printing carattere m; in church fonte f battesimale

food [fu:d] cibo m; **I like Italian ~** mi piace la cucina italiana; **there's no ~ in the house** non c'è niente da mangiare in casa

'**food chain** catena f alimentare

food·ie ['fu:dɪ] F buongustaio m, -a f

'**food mix·er** mixer m inv

food poi·son·ing ['fu:dpɔɪznɪŋ] intossicazione f alimentare

fool [fu:l] **1** n pazzo m, -a f; **make a ~ of o.s.** rendersi ridicolo **2** v/t ingannare; ~ **s.o. into believing that ...** far credere a qu che ...

♦ **fool about, fool around** v/i fare lo sciocco; sexually avere l'amante

♦ **fool around with** v/t knife, drill etc trastullarsi con; s.o.'s wife avere una relazione con

'**fool·har·dy** adj temerario

fool·ish ['fu:lɪʃ] adj sciocco

fool·ish·ly ['fuːlɪʃlɪ] *adv* scioccamente

'fool·proof *adj* a prova di idiota

foot [fʊt] (*pl* **feet** [fiːt])*also measurement* piede *m*; **on** ~ a piedi; *I've been on my feet all day* sono stato in piedi tutto il giorno; *be back on one's feet* essere di nuovo in piedi; *at the* ~ *of the page* a piè di pagina; *at the* ~ *of the hill* ai piedi della collina; *put one's* ~ *in it* F fare una gaffe

foot·age ['fʊtɪdʒ] pellicola *f* cinematografica

'foot·ball (*soccer*) calcio *m*; *American style* football *m* americano; (*ball*) pallone *m* da calcio; *for American football* pallone *m* da football americano

foot·bal·ler ['fʊtbɔːlə(r)] calciatore *m*, -trice *f*

'foot·ball hoo·li·gan teppista *m* del calcio; **'foot·ball pitch** campo *m* da calcio; **'foot·ball play·er** *soccer* calciatore *m*, -trice *f*; *American style* giocatore *m* di football americano; **'foot·bridge** passerella *f*

foot·er ['fʊtə(r)] COMPUT piè *m* di pagina

foot·hills ['fʊthɪlz] *npl* colline *fpl* pedemontane

'foot·hold in *climbing* punto *m* d'appoggio; *gain a* ~ *fig* conquistarsi uno spazio

foot·ing ['fʊtɪŋ] (*basis*) presupposti *mpl*; *lose one's* ~ perdere il punto d'appoggio; *be on the same* ~ /a *different* ~ essere sullo stesso piano/su un piano diverso; *be on a friendly* ~ *with* ... avere rapporti amichevoli con ...

foot·lights ['fʊtlaɪts] *npl* luci *fpl* della ribalta; **'foot·mark** impronta *f* di piede; **'foot·note** nota *f* a piè di pagina; **'foot·path** sentiero *m*; **'foot·print** impronta *f* di piede; **'foot·step** passo *m*; *follow in s.o.'s* ~*s* seguire i passi di qu; **'foot·stool** sgabello *m* per i piedi; **'foot·wear** calzatura *f*

for [fə(r)], [fɔː(r)] *prep* ◊ *purpose, destination etc* per; *a train* ~ ... un treno per ...; *clothes* ~ *children* abbigliamento *m* per bambini; *it's too big/small* ~ *you* è troppo grande/piccolo per te; *here's a letter* ~ *you* c'è una lettera per te; *this is* ~ *you* questo è per te; *what is there* ~ *lunch?* cosa c'è per pranzo?; *the steak is* ~ *me* la bistecca è per me; *what is this* ~? a cosa serve?; *what* ~? a che scopo?, perché?; ◊ *time* per; ~ *three days/two hours* per tre giorni/due ore; *I have been waiting* ~ *an hour* ho aspettato (per) un'ora; *please get it done* ~ *Monday* per favore, fallo per lunedì; ◊ *distance* per; *I walked* ~ *a mile* ho camminato per un miglio; *it stretches* ~ *100 miles* si estende per 100 miglia; ◊ (*in favour of*) per; ~ *campaign* ~ fare una campagna per; *I am* ~ *the idea* sono a favore dell'idea; ◊ (*instead of, on behalf of*) per; *let me do that* ~ *you* lascia che te lo faccia io, lascia che faccia questo per te; *we are agents* ~ ... siamo rappresentanti di ...; ◊ (*in exchange for*) per; *I bought it* ~ £25 l'ho comprato per 25 sterline; *how much did you sell it* ~? a quanto l'hai venduto?

for·bade [fə'bæd] *pret* → **forbid**

for·bid [fə'bɪd] *v/t* (*pret* **forbade**, *pp* **forbidden**) vietare, proibire; ~ *s.o. to do sth* vietare *o* proibire a qu di fare qc

for·bid·den [fə'bɪdn] **1** *adj* vietato, proibito; *smok·ing* ~ vietato fumare; *park·ing* ~ divieto di sosta **2** *pp* → **forbid**

for·bid·ding [fə'bɪdɪŋ] *adj* ostile

force [fɔːs] **1** *n* (*violence*) forza *f*; *come into* ~ *of law etc* entrare in vigore; *the* ~*s* MIL le forze armate **2** *v/t door, lock* forzare; ~ *s.o. to do sth* forzare *o* costringere qu a fare qc; ~ *sth open* aprire qc con la forza ♦ **force back** *v/t tears etc* trattenere

forced [fɔːst] *adj laugh, smile* forzato

forced 'land·ing atterraggio *m* d'emergenza

force·ful ['fɔːsful] *adj* argument, speaker convincente; character energico

force·ful·ly ['fɔːsflɪ] *adv* in modo energico

for·ceps ['fɔːseps] *npl* MED forcipe *f*

for·ci·ble ['fɔːsəbl] *adj* entry forzato; argument convincente

for·ci·bly ['fɔːsəblɪ] *adv* restrain con la forza

ford [fɔːd] *n* guado *m*

fore [fɔː(r)] *n*: **come to the ~** salire alla ribalta

fore·arm avanbraccio *m*; **fore·bears** ['fɔːbeəz] *npl* antenati *mpl*; **fore·bod·ing** [fəˈbəʊdɪŋ] presentimento *m*; **'fore·cast 1** *n* previsione *f* **2** *v/t* (*pret & pp* **forecast**) prevedere; **'fore·court** of garage area *f* di rifornimento; **fore·fa·thers** ['fɔːfɑːðəz] *npl* antenati *mpl*; **'fore·fin·ger** indice *m*; **'fore·front**: **be in the ~ of** essere all'avanguardia in; **'fore·gone** *adj*: **that's a ~ conclusion** è una conclusione scontata; **'fore·ground** primo piano *m*; **'fore·hand** in tennis diritto *m*; **'fore·head** fronte *f*

for·eign ['fɒrən] *adj* straniero; trade, policy estero

for·eign af·fairs *npl* affari *mpl* esteri; **for·eign 'aid** aiuti *mpl* ad altri paesi; **for·eign 'bod·y** corpo *m* estraneo; **for·eign 'cur·ren·cy** valuta *f* estera

for·eign·er ['fɒrənə(r)] straniero *m*, -a *f*

for·eign ex'change cambio *m* valutario; **for·eign 'lan·guage** lingua *f* straniera; **'For·eign Of·fice** in UK Ministero *m* degli esteri; **for·eign 'pol·i·cy** politica *f* estera; **For·eign 'Sec·re·ta·ry** in UK ministro *m* degli esteri

'fore·man caposquadra *m*

fore·most 1 *adv* (uppermost) soprattutto **2** *adj* (leading) principale

fo·ren·sic 'medi·cine [fəˈrenzɪk] medicina *f* legale

fo·ren·sic 'scien·tist medico *m* legale

'fore·run·ner precursore *m*; **fore·'saw** *pret* → **foresee**; **fore·'see** *v/t* (*pret* **foresaw**, *pp* **foreseen**) prevedere; **fore·'see·a·ble** [fəˈsiːəbl] *adj* prevedibile; **in the ~ future** per quanto si possa prevedere in futuro; **fore'seen** *pp* → **foresee**; **'fore·sight** lungimiranza *f*

for·est ['fɒrɪst] foresta *f*

for·est·er ['fɒrɪstə(r)] guardaboschi *m/f*

for·est·ry ['fɒrɪstrɪ] scienze *fpl* forestali

'fore·taste anteprima *m*, assaggio *m*

fore'tell *v/t* (*pret & pp* **foretold**) predire

fore'told *pret & pp* → **foretell**

for·ev·er [fəˈrevə(r)] *adv* per sempre; **it is ~ raining here** piova continuamente qui

for·gave [fəˈgeɪv] *pret* → **forgive**

fore·word ['fɔːwɜːd] prefazione *f*

for·feit ['fɔːfɪt] *v/t* right, privilege etc perdere

forge [fɔːdʒ] *v/t* (counterfeit) contraffare; signature falsificare

♦forge ahead *v/i* prendere il sopravvento

forg·er ['fɔːdʒə(r)] falsario *m*, -a *f*

forg·er·y ['fɔːdʒərɪ] (banknote) falsificazione *f*; (document) falso *m*

for·get [fəˈget] *v/t* (*pret* **forgot**, *pp* **forgotten**) dimenticare; **~ it** lasciala perdere, ti fa solo perdere tempo

for·get·ful [fəˈgetful] *adj* smemorato

for'get-me-not non-ti-scordar-di-me *m inv*

for·give [fəˈgɪv] *v/t & v/i* (*pret* **forgave**, *pp* **forgiven**) perdonare

for·given [fəˈgɪvn] *pp* → **forgive**

for·give·ness [fəˈgɪvnɪs] perdono *m*

for·got [fəˈgɒt] *pret* → **forget**

for·got·ten [fəˈgɒtn] *pp* → **forget**

fork [fɔːk] *n* for eating forchetta *f*; for gardening forca *f*; in road biforcazione *f*

♦fork out *v/t & v/i* F (pay) sborsare F

fork·lift 'truck muletto *m*

form [fɔːm] **1** *n* (shape) forma *f*; (document) modulo *m*; in school classe *f*; **be on / off ~** essere in / fuori forma; **in the ~ of** sotto forma di 2 *v/t* in clay etc modellare; *friendship* creare; *opinion* formarsi; *past tense etc* formare; (*constitute*) costituire 3 *v/i* (*take shape, develop*) formarsi

form·al ['fɔːml] *adj* formale

for·mal·i·ty [fə'mælətɪ] formalità *f inv*; **it's just a ~** è solo una formalità; **the formalities** le formalità

for·mal·ly ['fɔːməlɪ] *adv* formalmente

for·mat ['fɔːmæt] **1** *v/t* (*pret & pp* **-ted**) *diskette* formattare; *document* impaginare **2** *n* (*size: of magazine etc*) formato *m*; (*makeup: of programme*) formula *f*

for·ma·tion [fɔː'meɪʃn] formazione *f*

for·ma·tive ['fɔːmətɪv] *adj* formativo; **in his ~ years** nei suoi anni formativi

for·mer ['fɔːmə(r)] *adj* wife, president ex *inv*; *statement, arrangement* precedente; **the ~** quest'ultimo

for·mer·ly ['fɔːməlɪ] *adv* precedentemente

for·mi·da·ble ['fɔːmɪdəbl] *adj* imponente

for·mu·la ['fɔːmjʊlə] formula *f*

for·mu·late ['fɔːmjʊleɪt] *v/t* (*express*) formulare

for·ni·cate ['fɔːnɪkeɪt] *v/i fml* fornicare

for·ni·ca·tion [fɔːnɪ'keɪʃn] *fml* fornicazione *f*

fort [fɔːt] MIL forte *m*

forth [fɔːθ] *adv*: **back and ~** avanti e indietro; **and so ~** eccetera; **from that day** da quel giorno in poi

forth·com·ing ['fɔːθkʌmɪŋ] *adj* (*future*) prossimo; *personality* comunicativo

'**forth·right** *adj* schietto

for·ti·eth ['fɔːtɪəθ] *n & adj* quarantesimo, -a

fort·night ['fɔːtnaɪt] due settimane

for·tress ['fɔːtrɪs] MIL fortezza *f*

for·tu·nate ['fɔːtʃənət] *adj* fortunato

for·tu·nate·ly ['fɔːtʃənətlɪ] *adv* fortunatamente

for·tune ['fɔːtʃuːn] sorte *f*; (*lot of money*) fortuna *f*; **tell s.o.'s ~** predire il futuro a qu

'**for·tune-tell·er** chiromante *m/f*

for·ty ['fɔːtɪ] quaranta; **have ~ winks** F fare un pisolino F

Fo·rum ['fɔːrəm] *Roman* foro *m*

fo·rum ['fɔːrəm] *fig* foro *m*

for·ward ['fɔːwəd] **1** *adv* avanti **2** *adj pej: person* diretto **3** *n* SP attaccante *m* **4** *v/t letter* inoltrare

'**for·ward·ing ad·dress** ['fɔːwədɪŋ] recapito *m*

'**for·ward·ing a·gent** COM spedizioniere *m*

'**for·ward-look·ing** *adj* progressista

fos·sil ['fɒsəl] fossile *m*

fos·sil·ized ['fɒsəlaɪzd] *adj* fossilizzato

fos·ter ['fɒstə(r)] *v/t child* avere in affidamento; *attitude, belief* incoraggiare

'**fos·ter child** figlio *m*, -a *f* in affidamento

'**fos·ter home** famiglia *f* di accoglienza

'**fos·ter par·ents** *npl* genitori *mpl* con affidamento

fought [fɔːt] *pret & pp* → **fight**

foul [faʊl] **1** *n* SP fallo *m* **2** *adj smell, taste* pessimo; *weather* orribile **3** *v/t* SP fare un fallo contro

found[1] [faʊnd] *v/t school etc* fondare

found[2] [faʊnd] *pret & pp* → **find**

foun·da·tion [faʊn'deɪʃn] *of theory etc* fondamenta *fpl*; (*organization*) fondazione *f*; *make-up* fondotinta *m*

foun·da·tions [faʊn'deɪʃnz] *npl of building* fondamenta *fpl*

found·er ['faʊndə(r)] *n* fondatore *m*, -trice *f*

found·ing ['faʊndɪŋ] *n* fondazione *f*

foun·dry ['faʊndrɪ] fonderia *f*

foun·tain ['faʊntɪn] fontana *f*

'**foun·tain pen** penna *f* stilografica

four [fɔː(r)] **1** *adj* quattro **2** *n*: **on all ~s** a quattro zampe

'**four-let·ter** '**word** parolaccia *f*; '**four-post·er** ('**bed**) letto *m* a baldacchino; '**four-star** *adj hotel etc* a quattro stelle; **four-star** (**'pet·rol**) super f

four-teen [fɔːˈtiːn] quattordici

four-teenth [ˈfɔːtiːnθ] n & adj quattordicesimo, -a

fourth [fɔːθ] n & adj quarto, -a

four-wheel 'drive MOT quattro per quattro m inv

fowl [faul] pollame m

fox [fɒks] **1** n volpe f **2** v/t (puzzle) mettere in difficoltà

foy·er [ˈfɔɪeɪ] atrio m

frac·tion [ˈfrækʃn] frazione f

frac·tion·al·ly [ˈfrækʃnəlɪ] adv lievemente

frac·ture [ˈfræktʃə(r)] **1** n frattura f **2** v/t fratturare

fra·gile [ˈfrædʒaɪl] adj fragile

frag·ment [ˈfrægmənt] n frammento m

frag·men·ta·ry [frægˈmentərɪ] adj frammentario

fra·grance [ˈfreɪgrəns] fragranza f

fra·grant [ˈfreɪgrənt] adj profumato

frail [freɪl] adj gracile

frame [freɪm] **1** n of picture, window cornice f; of glasses montatura f; of bicycle telaio m; ~ **of mind** stato m d'animo **2** v/t picture incorniciare; F person incastrare F

'frame-up F montatura f

'frame·work struttura f

France [frɑːns] Francia f

fran·chise [ˈfræntʃaɪz] n for business concessione f

frank [fræŋk] adj franco

frank·furt·er [ˈfræŋkfɜːtə(r)] wurstel m inv

frank·ly [ˈfræŋklɪ] adv francamente

frank·ness [ˈfræŋknɪs] franchezza f

fran·tic [ˈfræntɪk] adj search, attempt frenetico; (worried) agitatissimo

fran·ti·cal·ly [ˈfræntɪklɪ] adv freneticamente

fra·ter·nal [frəˈtɜːnl] adj fraterno

fraud [frɔːd] frode f; person impostore m, -trice f

fraud·u·lent [ˈfrɔːdjʊlənt] adj fraudolento

fraud·u·lent·ly [ˈfrɔːdjʊləntlɪ] adv in modo fraudolento

frayed [freɪd] adj cuffs liso

freak [friːk] **1** n unusual event fenomeno m anomalo; two-headed person, animal etc scherzo m di natura; F strange person tipo m, -a f strambo, -a; movie /**jazz** ~ F (fanatic) fanatico m, -a f del cinema / del jazz **2** adj wind, storm etc violento

freck·le [ˈfrekl] lentiggine f

free [friː] **1** adj (at liberty, not occupied) libero; (no cost) gratuito; **are you ~ this afternoon?** sei libero oggi pomeriggio?; ~ **and easy** spensierato; **for ~** travel, get sth gratis **2** v/t prisoners liberare

free·bie [ˈfriːbɪ] F omaggio m

free·dom [ˈfriːdəm] libertà f

free·dom of 'speech libertà f di parola

free·dom of the 'press libertà f di stampa

free 'en·ter·prise liberalismo m economico; **free 'kick** in soccer calcio m di punizione; **free·lance** [ˈfriːlɑːns] **1** adj free lance inv **2** adv work free lance inv; **free·lanc·er** [ˈfriːlɑːnsə(r)] free lance m/f inv

free mar·ket e'con·o·my economia f del libero mercato; **free-range 'chick·en** pollo m ruspante; **free-range 'eggs** npl uova fpl di galline ruspanti; **free 'sam·ple** campione m gratuito; **free 'speech** libertà f di espressione; **'free·way** Am autostrada f; **free'wheel** v/i on bicycle andare a ruota libera

freeze [friːz] (pret **froze**, pp **frozen**) **1** v/t food, river gelare; wages, account congelare; video bloccare **2** v/i of water gelare

♦ **freeze over** v/i of river gelare

'freeze-dried adj liofilizzato

freez·er [ˈfriːzə(r)] freezer m inv, congelatore m

freez·ing [ˈfriːzɪŋ] **1** adj gelato; **it's ~ out here** si gela qui fuori; **it's ~** (**cold**) of weather si gela; of water è gelata; **I'm ~** (**cold**) sono congelato **2** n: **10 below ~** 10 gradi sotto zero 'freez·ing com·part·ment freezer *m inv*

'freez·ing point punto *m* di congelamento

freight [freɪt] *n* carico *m*; *costs* trasporto *m*

freight·er ['freɪtə(r)] *ship* nave *f* da carico; *aeroplane* aereo *f* da carico

French [frentʃ] **1** *adj* francese **2** *n* (*language*) francese *m*; *the ~* i francesi

French 'bread baguette *fpl*; 'French fries *npl* patate *fpl* fritte; 'Frenchman francese *m*; French 'stick baguette *f inv*; French 'win·dows *npl* vetrata *f*; 'French·wom·an francese *f*

fren·zied ['frenzɪd] *adj attack, activity* frenetico; *mob* impazzito

fren·zy ['frenzɪ] frenesia *f*

fre·quen·cy ['friːkwənsɪ] frequenza *f*

fre·quent[1] ['friːkwənt] *adj* frequente

fre·quent[2] [frɪ'kwent] *v/t bar etc* frequentare

fre·quent·ly ['friːkwentlɪ] *adv* frequentemente

fres·co ['freskəʊ] affresco *m*

fresh [freʃ] *adj fruit, meat etc*, (*cold*) fresco; (*new: start*) nuovo

fresh 'air aria *f* fresca

fresh·en ['freʃn] *v/i of wind* rinfrescare

♦freshen up **1** *v/i* rinfrescarsi **2** *v/t room, paintwork* rinfrescare

'fresh·er ['freʃə(r)] matricola *f*

fresh·ly ['freʃlɪ] *adv* appena

fresh·ness ['freʃnɪs] *of fruit, meat, climate* freschezza *f*; *of style, approach* novità *f*

fresh 'or·ange spremuta *f* d'arancia

'fresh·wa·ter *adj* d'acqua dolce

fret [fret] *v/i* (*pret & pp* -*ted*) agitarsi

Freud·i·an ['frɔɪdɪən] *adj* freudiano

fric·tion ['frɪkʃn] PHYS frizione *f*; *between people* attrito *m*

Fri·day ['fraɪdeɪ] venerdì *m inv*

fridge [frɪdʒ] frigo *m*

fried 'egg [fraɪd] uovo *m* fritto

fried po'ta·toes *npl* patate *fpl* saltate

friend [frend] amico *m*, -a *f*; *make ~s* fare amicizia; *make ~s with s.o.* fare amicizia con qu

friend·li·ness ['frendlɪnɪs] amichevolezza *f*

friend·ly ['frendlɪ] **1** *adj* amichevole; (*easy to use*) facile da usare; *be ~ with s.o.* (*be friends*) essere in rapporti d'amicizia con qu; *they're very ~ with each other* sono molto in confidenza; *he started getting too ~* ha cominciato a prendersi troppa confidenza **2** *n* SP amichevole *f*

'friend·ship ['frendʃɪp] amicizia *f*

fries [fraɪz] *npl* patate *fpl* fritte

fright [fraɪt] paura *f*; *give s.o. a ~* far paura a qu

fright·en ['fraɪtn] *v/t* spaventare; *be ~ed (of)* aver paura (di); *don't be ~ed* non aver paura

♦frighten away *v/t* far scappare

fright·en·ing ['fraɪtnɪŋ] *adj* spaventoso

fri·gid ['frɪdʒɪd] *adj sexually* frigido

frill [frɪl] *on dress etc* volant *m inv*; *~s* (*fancy extras*) fronzoli *mpl*

frill·y ['frɪlɪ] *adj* pieno di volant

fringe [frɪndʒ] frangia *f*; (*edge*) margini *mpl*

fringe ben·e·fits *npl* benefici *mpl* accessori

frisk [frɪsk] *v/t* frugare F

frisk·y ['frɪskɪ] *adj puppy etc* vivace

♦fritter away ['frɪtə(r)] *v/t time, fortune* sprecare

fri·vol·i·ty [frɪ'vɒlətɪ] frivolezza *f*

friv·o·lous ['frɪvələs] *adj person, pleasures* frivolo

frizz·y ['frɪzɪ] *adj hair* crespo

frog [frɒg] rana *f*

'frog·man sommozzatore *m*, -trice *f*

from [frɒm] *prep* ◊ *in time* da; *~ 9 to 5* (*o'clock*) dalle 9 alle 5; *~ the 18th century* dal XVIII secolo; *~ today on* da oggi in poi; *~ next Tuesday* da martedì della prossima settimana ◊ *in space* da; *~ here to there* da qui a lì; *we drove here ~ Paris* siamo venuti qui in macchina da Parigi ◊ *origin* di; *a letter ~ Jo* una lettera di Jo; *a gift ~ the management* un regalo della direzione; *it doesn't say who it's* ~ non c'è scritto di chi è; *I am* ~ *Liverpool* sono di Liverpool; *made* ~ *bananas* fatto di banane ◊ (*because of*) di; *tired* ~ *the journey* stanco del viaggio; *it's* ~ *overeating* è a causa del troppo mangiare

front [frʌnt] **1** *n of building* lato *m* principale; *of car, statue* davanti *m inv*; *of book* copertina *f*; (*cover organization*) facciata *f*; MIL, *of weather* fronte *m*; *in* ~ davanti; *in* ~ *of* davanti a; *at the* ~ davanti; *at the* ~ *of* of bus etc nella parte anteriore di **2** *adj wheel, seat* anteriore **3** *v/t TV programme* presentare

front 'bench POL principali esponenti *mpl* del governo e dell'opposizione nel Parlamento; **front 'cov·er** copertina *f*; **front 'door** porta *f* principale; **front 'en·trance** entrata *f* principale

fron·tier ['frʌntɪə(r)] *also fig* frontiera *f*

front 'line MIL fronte *m*; **front 'page** *of newspaper* prima pagina *f*; **front page 'news** *nsg* notizia *f* di prima pagina; **front 'row** prima fila *f*; **front seat 'pas·sen·ger** *in car* passeggero *m* davanti; **front-wheel 'drive** trazione *f* anteriore

frost [frɒst] *n* brina *f*

'frost·bite congelamento *m*

'frost·bit·ten *adj* congelato

frosted glass ['frɒstɪd] vetro *m* smerigliato

'frost·y ['frɒstɪ] *adj also fig* gelido

froth [frɒθ] *n* spuma *f*

froth·y ['frɒθɪ] *adj cream etc* spumoso

frown [fraʊn] **1** *n* cipiglio *m* **2** *v/i* aggrottare le sopracciglia

froze [frəʊz] *pret* → **freeze**

fro·zen ['frəʊzn] **1** *adj* gelato; *wastes* gelido; *food* surgelato; *I'm* ~ F sono congelato F **2** *pp* → **freeze**

fro·zen 'food cibi *mpl* surgelati

fruit [fruːt] *n* frutto *m*; *collective* frutta *f*

'fruit cake dolce *f* con frutta candita

'fruit·ful ['fruːtfʊl] *adj discussions etc* fruttuoso

'**fruit juice** succo *m* di frutta; '**fruit ma·chine** slot machine *f inv*; **fruit 'sal·ad** macedonia *f*

frus·trate [frʌ'streɪt] *v/t person* frustrare; *plans* scombussolare

frus·trat·ed [frʌ'streɪtɪd] *adj look, sigh* frustrato

frus·trat·ing [frʌ'streɪtɪŋ] *adj* frustrante

frus·trat·ing·ly [frʌ'streɪtɪŋlɪ] *adv slow, hard* in modo frustrante

frus·tra·tion [frʌ'streɪʃn] frustrazione *f*; *sexual* ~ insoddisfazione *f* sessuale; *the* ~*s of modern life* le frustrazioni della vita moderna

fry [fraɪ] *v/t* (*pret & pp* -**ied**) friggere

'fry·ing pan ['fraɪɪŋ] padella *f*

fuck [fʌk] *v/t* V scopare V; ~! cazzo!

♦ **fuck off** *v/i* V andare affanculo V; *fuck off!* vaffanculo!

fuck·ing ['fʌkɪŋ] **1** *adj* V del cazzo V **2** *adv* V; *I'm* ~ *late!* V sono in ritardo, cazzo!; *I'm* ~ *tired* cazzo, come sono stanco

fu·el ['fjuːəl] **1** *n* carburante *m* **2** *v/t fig* alimentare

fu·gi·tive ['fjuːdʒətɪv] *n* fuggiasco *m*, -a *f*

ful·fil, *Am* **ful·fill** [fʊl'fɪl] *v/t* (*pret & pp* -**led**) *dreams* realizzare; *needs, expectations* soddisfare; *contract* eseguire; *requirements* corrispondere a; *feel* ~*led in job, life* sentirsi soddisfatto

ful·fil·ment, *Am* **ful·fill·ment** [fʊl'fɪlmənt] *of contract* esecuzione *f*; *of dreams* realizzazione *f*; *moral, spiritual* soddisfazione *f*

full [fʊl] *adj* pieno (*of* di); *account, report* esauriente; *life* intenso; ~ *up hotel, with food* pieno; *in* ~ *write* per intero; *pay in* ~ saldare il conto

full 'board pensione *f* completa; '**full-grown** *adj* adulto; ~ *adult per·son* adulto in età matura; *animal* adulto completamente sviluppato; '**full-length** *adj dress* lungo; ~ *film* lungometraggio *m*; **full 'moon** luna *f* piena; **full 'stop** punto *m* fermo; **full-'time** *adj & adv worker, job* a tempo pieno

ful·ly ['fʊlɪ] *adv booked, recovered* completamente; *understand, explain* perfettamente; *describe* ampiamente

fum·ble ['fʌmbl] *v/t catch* farsi sfuggire

♦ **fumble about** *v/i in bags, pockets* frugare; *move in the dark* andare a tastoni; *search in the dark* cercare a tastoni

fume [fjuːm] *v/i:* **be fuming** F (*be very angry*) essere nero F

fumes [fjuːmz] *npl* esalazioni *fpl*

fun [fʌn] divertimento *m;* **it was great** → era molto divertente; **bye, have** ~! ciao, divertiti!; **for** ~ per divertirsi; (*joking*) per scherzo; **make** ~ **of** prendere in giro

func·tion ['fʌŋkʃn] **1** *n* (*purpose*) funzione *f*; (*reception etc*) cerimonia *f* **2** *v/i* funzionare; ~ **as** servire da

func·tion·al ['fʌŋkʃnl] *adj* funzionale

fund [fʌnd] **1** *n* fondo *m* **2** *v/t project etc* finanziare

fun·da·men·tal [fʌndə'mentl] *adj* fondamentale

fun·da·men·tal·ist [fʌndə'mentlɪst] *n* fondamentalista *m/f*

fun·da·men·tal·ly [fʌndə'mentlɪ] *adv* fondamentalmente

fund·ing ['fʌndɪŋ] *money* fondi *mpl*

fu·ne·ral ['fjuːnərəl] funerale *m*

'**fu·ne·ral di·rec·tor** impresario *m* delle pompe funebri

'**fu·ne·ral home** *Am,* '**fu·ne·ral par·lour** obitorio *m*

'**fun·fair** luna park *m inv*

fun·gus ['fʌŋgəs] fungo *m*

fu·nic·u·lar ('**rail·way**) [fjuː'nɪkjʊlə(r)] funicolare *f*

fun·nel ['fʌnl] *n of ship* imbuto *m*

fun·ni·ly ['fʌnɪlɪ] *adv* (*oddly*) stranamente; (*comically*) in modo divertente; ~ **enough** per quanto strano

fun·ny ['fʌnɪ] *adj* (*comical*) divertente; (*odd*) strano

'**fun·ny bone** osso *m* del gomito

fur [fɜː(r)] pelliccia *f*; *on animal* pelo *m*

fu·ri·ous ['fjʊərɪəs] *adj* (*angry*) furioso; (*intense*) spaventoso; **at a** ~ **pace** a tutta velocità

fur·nace ['fɜːnɪs] forno *m*

fur·nish ['fɜːnɪʃ] *v/t room* arredare; (*supply*) fornire

fur·ni·ture ['fɜːnɪtʃə(r)] mobili *mpl*; **a piece of** ~ un mobile

fur·ry ['fɜːrɪ] *adj animal* coperto di pelliccia

fur·ther ['fɜːðə(r)] **1** *adj* (*additional*) ulteriore; (*more distant*) più lontano; **until** ~ **notice** fino a nuovo avviso; **have you anything** ~ **to say?** ha qualcosa da aggiungere? **2** *adv walk, drive* oltre; ~, **I want to say ...** inoltre, volevo dire ...; **two miles** ~ (**on**) due miglia più avanti **3** *v/t cause etc* favorire

fur·ther ed·u·ca·tion istruzione *f* universitaria o para-universitaria

fur·ther·more *adv* inoltre

fur·thest ['fɜːðɪst] **1** *adj* più lontano **2** *adv:* **this is the** ~ **north** è il punto più a nord; **the** ~ **man has travelled in space** l'uomo più lontano che si è raggiunto nello spazio

fur·tive ['fɜːtɪv] *adj glance* furtivo

fur·tive·ly ['fɜːtɪvlɪ] *adv* furtivamente

fu·ry ['fjʊərɪ] (*anger*) furore *m*

fuse [fjuːz] **1** *n* ELEC fusibile *m* **2** *v/i* ELEC bruciarsi **3** *v/t* ELEC bruciare

'**fuse·box** scatola *f* dei fusibili

fu·se·lage ['fjuːzəlaːʒ] fusoliera *f*

'**fuse wire** filo *m* per fusibili

fu·sion ['fjuːʒn] fusione *f*

fuss [fʌs] *n* agitazione *f*; *about film, event* scalpore *m*; **make a** ~ *complain* fare storie; *behave in exaggerated way* agitarsi; **make a** ~ **of** be very attentive to colmare qu di attenzioni

fuss·y ['fʌsɪ] *adj person* difficile; *design etc* complicato; **be a** ~ **eater** essere schizzinoso nel mangiare

fu·tile ['fjuːtaɪl] *adj* futile

fu·til·i·ty [fjuː'tɪlɪtɪ] futilità *f inv*

fu·ture ['fjuːtʃə(r)] **1** *n* futuro *m*; **in** ~ in futuro **2** *adj* futuro

fu·tures ['fju:tʃəz] *npl* FIN titoli *mpl* a termine

'fu·tures mar·ket FIN mercato *m* dei titoli a termine

fu·tur·is·tic [fju:tʃə'rɪstɪk] *adj* design futuristico

fuzz·y ['fʌzɪ] *adj* hair crespo; (*out of focus*) sfuocato

G

gab [gæb] *n*: **have the gift of the ~** F avere la parlantina F

gab·ble ['gæbl] *v/i* parlare troppo in fretta

♦ gad about [gæd] *v/i* (*pret & pp* **-ded**) andarsene in giro

gad·get ['gædʒɪt] congegno *m*

Gael·ic ['geɪlɪk] *n* language gaelico *m*

gaffe [gæf] gaffe *f inv*

gag [gæg] **1** *n* bavaglio *m*; (*joke*) battuta *f* **2** *v/t* (*pret & pp* **-ged**) person imbavagliare; *the press* azzittire

gai·ly ['geɪlɪ] *adv* (*blythely*) allegramente

gain [geɪn] *v/t* (*acquire*) acquisire, acquistare; **~ speed** acquistare velocità; **~ 10 pounds** aumentare di 10 libbre

ga·la ['gɑːlə] *concert etc* serata *f* di gala

gal·ax·y ['gæləksɪ] AST galassia *f*

gale [geɪl] bufera *f*

gal·lant ['gælənt] *adj* galante

gall blad·der ['gɔːlblædə(r)] cistifellea *f*

gal·le·ry ['gælərɪ] galleria *f*

gal·ley ['gælɪ] *on ship* cambusa *f*

♦ gal·li·vant around ['gælɪvænt] *v/i* andarsene a spasso

gal·lon ['gælən] gallone *m*; **~s of tea** F litri *mpl* di tè

gal·lop ['gæləp] *v/i* galoppare

gal·lows ['gæləʊz] *npl* forca *fsg*

gall·stone ['gɔːlstəʊn] calcolo *m* biliare

gal·lore [gə'lɔː(r)] *adj*: **apples / novels ~** mele / romanzi a iosa

gal·va·nize ['gælvənaɪz] *v/t* TECH galvanizzare; *fig* stimolare

gam·ble ['gæmbl] *v/i* giocare (d'azzardo)

gam·bler ['gæmblə r)] giocatore *m*, -trice *f* (d'azzardo)

gam·bling ['gæmblɪŋ] *n* gioco *m* (d'azzardo)

game [geɪm] *n* gioco *m*; (*match, in tennis*) partita *f*

'game·keep·er guardacaccia *m/f inv*

'game re·serve riserva *f* di caccia

gam·mon ['gæmən] coscia *f* di maiale affumicata

gang [gæŋ] banda *f*

♦ gang up on *v/t* mettersi contro

'gang rape **1** *n* stupro *m* collettivo **2** *v/t* stuprare in massa

gan·grene ['gæŋgriːn] MED cancrena *f*

gang·ster ['gæŋstə(r)] malvivente *m*, gangster *m inv*

'gang war·fare guerra *f* tra bande

'gang·way passaggio *m*; *for ship* passerella *f*

gaol [dʒeɪl] → **jail**

gap [gæp] *in wall, for parking* buco *m*; *in conversation, life* vuoto *m*; *in time* intervallo *m*; *in story, education* lacuna *f*; *between two people's characters* scarto *m*

gape [geɪp] *v/i of person* rimanere a bocca aperta; *of hole* spalancarsi

♦ gape at *v/t* guardare a bocca aperta

gap·ing ['geɪpɪŋ] *adj* hole spalancato

'gap year anno *m* tra la fine del liceo e l'inizio dell'università dedicato ad altre attività

G

gar·age ['gærɪdʒ] n for parking garage m inv; for petrol stazione f di servizio; for repairs officina f

gar·bage ['gɑːbɪdʒ] rifiuti mpl; (fig: nonsense) idiozie fpl

gar·bled ['gɑːbld] adj message ingarbugliato

gar·den ['gɑːdn] giardino m; for vegetables orto m

'gar·den cen·ter Am, **'gar·den cen·tre** centro m per il giardinaggio

gar·den·er ['gɑːdnə(r)] giardiniere m, -a f

gar·den·ing ['gɑːdnɪŋ] giardinaggio m

gar·gle ['gɑːgl] v/i fare i gargarismi

gar·goyle ['gɑːgɔɪl] ARCHI gargouille f inv

gar·ish ['geərɪʃ] adj sgargiante

gar·land ['gɑːlənd] n ghirlanda f

gar·lic ['gɑːlɪk] aglio m

gar·lic 'bread pane m all'aglio

gar·ment ['gɑːmənt] capo m d'abbigliamento

gar·nish ['gɑːnɪʃ] v/t guarnire

gar·ret ['gærɪt] soffitta f

gar·ri·son ['gærɪsn] n guarnigione f

gar·ter ['gɑːtə(r)] giarrettiera f

gas [gæs] n gas m inv; (esp Am: gasoline) benzina f

'gas bill bolletta f del gas

gash [gæʃ] n taglio m

gas·ket ['gæskɪt] guarnizione f

'gas man impiegato m del gas

'gas me·ter contatore m del gas

gas·o·line ['gæsəliːn] Am benzina f

gasp [gɑːsp] **1** n sussulto m **2** v/i rimanere senza fiato; **~ for breath** essere senza fiato; **he collapsed ~ing for breath** si è accasciato senza fiato

'gas ped·al Am acceleratore m; **'gas pipe·line** gasdotto m; **'gas sta·tion** Am stazione f di rifornimento; **'gas stove** cucina f a gas

gas·tric ['gæstrɪk] adj MED gastrico; **gas·tric 'flu** MED influenza f intestinale; **gas·tric 'juices** npl succhi mpl gastrici; **gas·tric 'ul·cer** MED ulcera f gastrica

gate [geɪt] cancello m; of city, castle, at airport porta f

ga·teau ['gætəʊ] torta f

'gate·crash v/t intrufolarsi in

'gate·way ingresso m; fig via f d'accesso

gath·er ['gæðə(r)] **1** v/t facts, information raccogliere; **~ speed** acquistare velocità; **am I to ~ that ...?** devo dedurre che ...? **2** v/i (understand) dedurre

♦ **gather up** v/t possessions radunare

gath·er·ing ['gæðərɪŋ] n (group of people) raduno m

gau·dy ['gɔːdɪ] adj pacchiano

gauge [geɪdʒ] **1** n indicatore m **2** v/t pressure misurare; opinion valutare

gaunt [gɔːnt] adj smunto

gauze [gɔːz] garza f

gave [geɪv] pret → **give**

gaw·ky ['gɔːkɪ] adj impacciato

gawp [gɔːp] v/i F rimanere come un ebete F; **~ at sth** fissare qc con aria inebetita

gay [geɪ] **1** n (homosexual) omosessuale m/f **2** adj omosessuale; club gay inv

gaze [geɪz] **1** n sguardo m **2** v/i fissare

♦ **gaze at** v/t fissare

GB [dʒiː'biː] abbr (= **Great Britain**) GB (= Gran Bretagna f)

GDP [dʒiːdiː'piː] abbr (= **gross domestic product**) PIL m (= prodotto m interno lordo)

gear [gɪə(r)] n (equipment) equipaggiamento m; in vehicles marcia f

'gear·box MOT scatola f del cambio

'gear le·ver, **'gear shift** MOT leva f del cambio

geese [giːs] pl → **goose**

gel [dʒel] for hair, shower gel m inv

gel·a·tine ['dʒeləti:n] gelatina f

gel·ig·nite ['dʒelɪgnaɪt] gelignite f

gem [dʒem] gemma f; fig: book etc capolavoro m; person perla f rara

Gem·i·ni ['dʒeminaɪ] ASTR Gemelli mpl

gen·der ['dʒendə(r)] genere m

gene [dʒiːn] gene m; **it's in his ~s** è una sua caratteristica innata

gen·e·ral ['dʒenrəl] **1** n MIL generale m; **in ~** in generale **2** adj generale

gen·e·ral e'lec·tion elezioni fpl politiche

gen·er·al·i·za·tion [dʒenrələ'zeɪʃn] generalizzazione f

gen·e·ral·ize ['dʒenrəlaɪz] v/i generalizzare

gen·e·ral·ly ['dʒenrəlɪ] adv generalmente; **~ speaking** in generale

gen·e·ral prac'ti·tion·er medico m generico

gen·e·rate ['dʒenəreɪt] v/t generare; **in linguistics** formare

gen·e'ra·tion [dʒenə'reɪʃn] generazione f

gen·e'ra·tion gap scarto m generazionale

gen·e·ra·tor ['dʒenəreɪtə(r)] ELEC generatore m

ge·ner·ic drug [dʒə'nerɪk] MED medicina f senza una marca specifica

gen·e·ros·i·ty [dʒenə'rɒsɪtɪ] generosità f

gen·e·rous ['dʒenərəs] adj generoso

ge·net·ic [dʒɪ'netɪk] adj genetico

ge·net·i·cal·ly [dʒɪ'netɪklɪ] adv geneticamente; **~ modified** transgenico

ge·net·ic 'code codice m genetico; **ge·net·ic en·gi'neer·ing** ingegneria f genetica; **ge·net·ic 'fin·ger·print** esame m del DNA

ge·net·i·cist [dʒɪ'netɪsɪst] genetista m/f

ge·net·ics [dʒɪ'netɪks] genetica f

ge·ni·al ['dʒi:nɪəl] adj person, company gioviale

gen·i·tals ['dʒenɪtlz] npl genitali mpl

ge·ni·us ['dʒi:nɪəs] genio m

Gen·o·a ['dʒenəʊə] Genova f

gen·o·cide ['dʒenəsaɪd] genocidio m

gen·tle ['dʒentl] adj delicato; breeze, slope dolce

gen·tle·man ['dʒentlmən] signore m; **he's a real ~** è un vero gentleman

gen·tle·ness ['dʒentlnɪs] delicatezza f; of breeze, slope dolcezza f

gen·tly ['dʒentlɪ] adv delicatamente; blow, slope dolcemente

gents [dʒents] toilet bagno m degli uomini

gen·u·ine ['dʒenjʊɪn] adj autentico; (sincere) sincero

gen·u·ine·ly ['dʒenjʊɪnlɪ] adv sinceramente

ge·o·graph·i·cal [dʒɪə'græfɪkl] adj geografico

ge·og·ra·phy [dʒɪ'ɒgrəfɪ] geografia f

ge·o·log·i·cal [dʒɪə'lɒdʒɪkl] adj geologico

ge·ol·o·gist [dʒɪ'ɒlədʒɪst] geologo m, -a f

ge·ol·o·gy [dʒɪ'ɒlədʒɪ] geologia f

ge·o·met·ric, ge·o·met·ri·cal [dʒɪə-'metrɪk(l)] adj geometrico

ge·om·e·try [dʒɪ'ɒmɪtrɪ] geometria f

ge·ra·ni·um [dʒə'reɪnɪəm] geranio m

ger·i·at·ric [dʒerɪ'ætrɪk] **1** adj geriatrico **2** n anziano m, -a f

germ [dʒɜ:m] also fig germe m

Ger·man ['dʒɜ:mən] **1** adj tedesco **2** n person tedesco m, -a f; language tedesco m

Ger·man 'mea·sles nsg rosolia f

Ger·man 'shep·herd pastore m tedesco

Ger·ma·ny ['dʒɜ:mənɪ] Germania f

ger·mi·nate ['dʒɜ:mɪneɪt] v/i of seed germogliare

germ 'war·fare guerra f batteriologica

ges·tic·u·late [dʒe'stɪkjʊleɪt] v/i gesticolare

ges·ture ['dʒestʃə(r)] n also fig gesto m

get [get] v/t (pret & pp **got**) (obtain) prendere; (fetch) andare a prendere; (receive: letter) ricevere; (receive: knowledge, respect etc) ottenere; (catch: bus, train, flu) prendere; (become) diventare; (arrive) arrivare; (understand) afferrare; **~ sth done** causative farsi fare qc; **~ s.o. to do sth** far fare qc a qu; **I'll ~ him to do it** glielo faccio fare; **~ to do sth** have opportunity avere occasione di fare qc; **~ one's hair cut** tagliarsi i capelli; **~ sth ready** preparare qc; **~**

going (*leave*) andare via; *have got* avere; *I have got to study* / *see him* devo studiare / vederlo; *I don't want to, but I've got to* non voglio, ma devo; *~ to know* venire a sapere

♦ **get about** v/i (*travel*) andare in giro; (*be mobile*) muoversi

♦ **get along** v/i (*progress*) procedere; *how is he getting along at school?* come se la cava a scuola?; *come to party etc* venire; *with s.o.* andare d'accordo

♦ **get at** v/t (*criticize*) prendersela con; (*imply, mean*) volere arrivare a; *I don't understand what you're getting at* non capisco dove vuoi arrivare

♦ **get away 1** v/i (*leave*) andare via **2** v/t: *get sth away from s.o.* togliere qc a qu

♦ **get away with** v/t cavarsela per

♦ **get back 1** v/i (*return*) ritornare; *I'll get back to you on that* ti faccio sapere **2** v/t (*obtain again*) recuperare

♦ **get by** v/i (*pass*) passare; *financially* tirare avanti

♦ **get down 1** v/i *from ladder etc* scendere; (*duck etc*) abbassarsi **2** v/t (*depress*) buttare giù

♦ **get down to** v/t (*start: work*) mettersi a; (*reach: real facts*) arrivare a; *let's get down to business* parliamo d'affari

♦ **get in 1** v/i (*arrive: of train, plane*) arrivare; (*come home*) arrivare a casa; *to car* salire; *how did they get in?* of thieves, mice etc come sono entrati? **2** v/t *to suitcase etc* far entrare

♦ **get off 1** v/i *from bus etc* scendere; (*finish work*) finire; (*not be punished*) cavarsela **2** v/t (*remove*) togliere; *clothes, hat, footgear* togliersi; *get off the grass!* togliti dal prato!

♦ **get off with** v/t F *sexually* rimorchiare F; *get off with a small fine* cavarsela con una piccola multa

♦ **get on 1** v/i *to bike, bus, train* salire; (*be friendly*) andare d'accordo; (*advance: of time*) farsi tardi; (*become*

old) invecchiare; (*make progress*) procedere; *he's getting on well at school* se la sta cavando bene a scuola; *it's getting on* getting late si sta facendo tardi; *he's getting on* getting old sta invecchiando; *he's getting on for 50* va per i 50 anni **2** v/t: *get on the bus* / *one's bike* salire sull'autobus / sulla bici; *get one's hat on* mettersi il cappello; *I can't get these trousers on* non riesco a mettermi questi pantaloni

♦ **get out 1** v/i *of car etc* scendere; *of prison* uscire; *get out!* fuori!; *let's get out of here* usciamo da qui; *I don't get out much these days* non esco molto in questi giorni **2** v/t (*extract: nail, something jammed*) tirare fuori; (*remove: stain*) mandare via; (*pull out: gun, pen*) tirare fuori

♦ **get over** v/t *fence, disappointment etc* superare; *lover etc* dimenticare

♦ **get over with** v/t togliersi; *let's get it over with* togliamocelo

♦ **get through** v/i *on telephone* prendere la linea; (*make self understood*) farsi capire; *get through to s.o.* (*make self understood*) farsi capire da qu; *I called you all day but I didn't manage to get through* ti ho chiamato tutto il giorno, ma era sempre occupato

♦ **get up 1** v/i *of person, wind* alzarsi **2** v/t (*climb: hill*) salire su

'get·a·way *from robbery* fuga *f*

'get·a·way car macchina *f* per la fuga

'get-to·geth·er ritrovo *m*

ghast·ly ['gɑːstlɪ] *adj colour, experience, person etc* orrendo; *you look ~* hai un aspetto orribile

gher·kin ['gɜːkɪn] cetriolino *m* sotto aceto

ghet·to ['getəʊ] ghetto *m*

ghost [gəʊst] fantasma *m*, spettro *m*

ghost·ly ['gəʊstlɪ] *adj* spettrale

'ghost town città *f inv* fantasma

ghoul [guːl] persona *f* morbosa

ghoul·ish ['guːlɪʃ] *adj* macabro

gi·ant ['dʒaɪənt] **1** *n* gigante *m* **2** *adj* gigante

gib·ber·ish ['dʒɪbərɪʃ] F bestialità *fpl* F

gibe [dʒaɪb] *n* frecciatina *f*

gib·lets ['dʒɪblɪts] *npl* frattaglie *fpl* (di volatili)

gid·di·ness ['gɪdɪnɪs] giramenti *mpl* di testa

gid·dy ['gɪdɪ] *adj*: *I feel ~* mi gira la testa

gift [gɪft] regalo *m*

gift·ed ['gɪftɪd] *adj* dotato

'**gift to·ken**, '**gift voucher** buono *m* d'acquisto

'**gift-wrap 1** *n* carta *f* da regalo **2** *v/t* (*pret & pp -ped*) *would you like it ~ped?* le faccio un pacco regalo?

gig [gɪg] F concerto *m*

gi·ga·byte ['gɪgəbaɪt] COMPUT gigabyte *m inv*

gi·gan·tic [dʒaɪˈgæntɪk] *adj* gigante

gig·gle ['gɪgl] **1** *v/i* ridacchiare **2** *n* risatina *f*

gig·gly ['gɪglɪ] *adj* ridacchiante

gill [gɪl] *of fish* branchia *f*

gilt [gɪlt] *n* doratura *f*; *~s* FIN titoli *mpl* obbligazionari

gim·mick ['gɪmɪk] trovata *f*

gim·mick·y ['gɪmɪkɪ] *adj* appariscente

gin [dʒɪn] gin *m inv*; *~ and tonic* gin and tonic *m inv*

gin·ger ['dʒɪndʒə(r)] **1** *n spice* zenzero *m* **2** *adj hair* rosso carota; *cat* rosso

gin·ger 'beer bibita *f* allo zenzero

'**gin·ger·bread** pan *m* di zenzero

gin·ger·ly ['dʒɪndʒəlɪ] *adv* con cautela

gip·sy ['dʒɪpsɪ] zingaro *m*, -a *f*

gi·raffe [dʒɪˈrɑːf] giraffa *f*

gir·der ['gɜːdə(r)] *n* trave *f*

girl [gɜːl] ragazza *f*

'**girl·friend** *of boy* ragazza *f*; *of girl* amica *f*

'**girl 'guide** giovane esploratrice *f*

girl·ie ['gɜːlɪ] *adj* F da femminuccia *f*

'**girl·ie mag·a·zine** *pornographic* rivista *f* per soli uomini

girl·ish ['gɜːlɪʃ] *adj* tipicamente femminile

gi·ro ['dʒaɪərəʊ] bonifico *m*

gist [dʒɪst] sostanza *f*

give [gɪv] *v/t* (*pret gave*, *pp given*) dare; *present* fare; (*supply: electricity etc*) fornire; *talk, groan* fare; *party* dare; *pain, appetite* far venire; *~ her my love* salutala da parte mia

♦**give away** *v/t as present* regalare; (*betray*) tradire; *give o.s. away* tradirsi

♦**give back** *v/t* restituire

♦**give in 1** *v/i surrender* arrendersi **2** *v/t* (*hand in*) consegnare

♦**give off** *v/t smell, fumes* emettere

♦**give onto** *v/t* (*open onto*) dare su

♦**give out 1** *v/t leaflets etc* distribuire **2** *v/i of supplies, strength* esaurirsi

♦**give up 1** *v/t smoking etc* rinunciare a; *he gave up smoking* ha smesso di fumare; *give o.s. up to the police* consegnarsi alla polizia **2** *v/i* (*cease habit*) smettere; (*stop making effort*) lasciar perdere

♦**give way** *v/i of bridge etc* cedere; MOT dare la precedenza

give-and-'take concessioni *fpl* reciproche

giv·en ['gɪvn] *pp* → **give**

'**giv·en name** nome *m* di battesimo

gla·ci·er ['glæsɪə(r)] ghiacciaio *m*

glad [glæd] *adj* contento

glad·ly ['glædlɪ] *adv* volentieri

glam·or *Am* → **glamour**

glam·or·ize ['glæməraɪz] *v/t* esaltare

glam·or·ous ['glæmərəs] *adj* affascinante

glam·our ['glæmə(r)] fascino *m*

glance [glɑːns] **1** *n* sguardo *m*; *at first ~* a prima vista **2** *v/i* dare un'occhiata *o* uno sguardo

♦**glance at** *v/t* dare un'occhiata *o* uno sguardo a

gland [glænd] ghiandola *f*

glan·du·lar fe·ver ['glændjʊlə(r)] mononucleosi *f*

glare [gleə(r)] **1** *n of sun, headlights* luce *f* abbagliante **2** *v/i of sun, headlights* splendere di luce abbagliante

♦**glare at** *v/t* guardare di storto

glar·ing ['gleərɪŋ] *adj mistake* lampante

glar·ing·ly ['gleərɪŋlɪ] *adv*: **be ~ obvious** essere più che ovvio

glass [glɑːs] *material* vetro *m*; *for drink* bicchiere *m*

glass 'case teca *f*

glasses *npl* occhiali *mpl*

'glass·house serra *f*

glaze [gleɪz] *n* smalto *m* trasparente

♦ **glaze over** *v/i of eyes* appannarsi

glazed [gleɪzd] *adj expression* assente

gla·zi·er ['gleɪzɪə(r)] *n* vetraio *m*

glaz·ing ['gleɪzɪŋ] vetri *mpl*

gleam [gliːm] **1** *n* luccichio *m* **2** *v/i* luccicare

glee [gliː] allegria *f*

glee·ful ['gliːfʊl] *adj* allegro

glib [glɪb] *adj* poco convincente

glib·ly ['glɪblɪ] *adv* in modo poco convincente

glide [glaɪd] *v/i of skier, boat* scivolare; *of bird, plane* planare

glid·er ['glaɪdə(r)] aliante *m*

glid·ing ['glaɪdɪŋ] *n* SP volo *m* planato

glim·mer ['glɪmə(r)] **1** *n of light* barlume *m*; **~ of hope** barlume *m* di speranza **2** *v/i* emettere un barlume

glimpse [glɪmps] **1** *n* occhiata *f*; **catch a ~ of** intravedere **2** *v/t* intravedere

glint [glɪnt] **1** *n* luccichio *m* **2** *v/i of light, eyes* luccicare

glis·ten ['glɪsn] *v/i* scintillare

glit·ter ['glɪtə(r)] *v/i* brillare

glit·ter·ati *npl*: **the ~** il bel mondo

gloat [gləʊt] *v/i* gongolare

♦ **gloat over** *v/t* compiacersi di

glo·bal ['gləʊbl] *adj* (*worldwide*) mondiale; *without exceptions* globale

glo·bal e'con·o·my economia *f* mondiale

glo·bal 'mar·ket mercato *m* mondiale

glo·bal 'war·ming effetto *m* serra

globe [gləʊb] globo *m*; *model of earth* mappamondo *m*

gloom [gluːm] (*darkness*) penombra

f; mood tristezza *f*

gloom·i·ly ['gluːmɪlɪ] *adv* tristemente

gloom·y ['gluːmɪ] *adj room* buio; *mood, person* triste; *day* grigio

glo·ri·ous ['glɔːrɪəs] *adj weather, day* splendido; *victory* glorioso

glo·ry ['glɔːrɪ] *n* gloria *f*; (*beauty*) splendore *m*

gloss [glɒs] *n* (*shine*) lucido *m*; (*general explanation*) glossa *f*

♦ **gloss over** *v/t* sorvolare su

glos·sa·ry ['glɒsərɪ] glossario *m*

'gloss paint vernice *f* lucida

gloss·y ['glɒsɪ] **1** *adj paper* patinato **2** *n magazine* rivista *f* femminile

glove [glʌv] guanto *m*

'glove com·part·ment *in car* cruscotto *m*

'glove pup·pet burattino *m*

glow [gləʊ] **1** *n of light, fire* bagliore *m*; *in cheeks* colorito *m* vivo; *of candle* luce *f* fioca **2** *v/i of light* brillare; **her cheeks ~ed** è diventata rossa

glow·er ['glaʊə(r)] *v/i*: **~ at s.o.** guardare qu in cagnesco

glow·ing ['gləʊɪŋ] *adj description* entusiastico

glu·cose ['gluːkəʊs] glucosio *m*

glue [gluː] **1** *n* colla *f* **2** *v/t*: **~ sth to sth** incollare qc a qc; **be ~d to the TV** F essere incollato alla TV F

glum [glʌm] *adj* triste

glum·ly ['glʌmlɪ] *adv* tristemente

glut [glʌt] *n* eccesso *m*

glut·ton ['glʌtən] ghiottone *m*, -a *f*

glut·ton·y ['glʌtənɪ] ghiottoneria *f*

GMT [dʒiːem'tiː] *abbr* (= **Greenwich Mean Time**) ora *f* di Greenwich

gnarled [nɑːld] *adj branch, hands* nodoso

gnat [næt] moscerino *m*

gnaw [nɔː] *v/t bone* rosicchiare

GNP [dʒiːen'piː] *abbr* (= **gross national product**) PNL *m* (= prodotto *m* nazionale lordo)

go [gəʊ] **1** *n* (*try*) tentativo *m*; **it's my ~** tocca a me, è il mio turno; **have a ~ at sth** (*try*) fare un tentativo in qc; (*complain about*) lamentarsi di qc;

be on the ~ essere indaffarato; *in one ~* drink, write etc tutto in una volta **2** *v/i* ◊ (pret **went**, pp **gone**) andare; (leave: of train, plane) partire; (leave: of people) andare via; (work, function) funzionare; (become) diventare; (come out: of stain etc) andare via; (cease: of pain etc) sparire; (match: of colours etc) stare bene insieme; **~ shopping / ~ jogging** andare a fare spese / andare a correre; *I must be ~ing* devo andare; *let's ~!* andiamo!; **~ for a walk** andare a fare una passeggiata; **~ to bed** andare a letto; **~ to school** andare a scuola; *how's the work ~ing?* come va il lavoro?; *they're ~ing for £50* (being sold at) li vendono a £50; *be all gone* (finished) essere finito; *I've gone 15 miles* ho fatto 15 miglia; *there are two days to ~ before ...* mancano due giorni a ...; *the story ~es that ...* la storia dice che ...; *to ~ Am food* da asporto ◊ future *I'm ~ing to meet him tomorrow* lo incontrerò domani; *it's ~ing to snow* sta per nevicare
♦ **go ahead** *v/i and do sth* andare avanti; *go ahead!* (on you go) fai pure!
♦ **go ahead with** *v/t* plans etc andare avanti con
♦ **go along with** *v/t* suggestion concordare con
♦ **go at** *v/t* (attack) scagliarsi contro
♦ **go away** *v/i* of person, pain andare via; of rain smettere
♦ **go back** *v/i* (return) ritornare; (date back) rimontare; *we go back a long way* ci conosciamo da una vita; *go back to sleep* tornare a dormire
♦ **go by** *v/i* of car, people, time passare
♦ **go down** *v/i* scendere; of sun, ship tramontare; of ship affondare; of swelling diminuire; *will it go down well with them?* la prenderanno bene?
♦ **go for** *v/t* (attack) attaccare; *I don't much go for gin* non vado matto per il gin; *she really goes for him* le

piace davvero
♦ **go in** *v/i* to room, house entrare; of sun andare via; (fit: of part etc) andare
♦ **go in for** *v/t* competition, race iscriversi a; (like, take part in) dedicarsi a
♦ **go off 1** *v/i* (leave) andarsene; of bomb esplodere; of gun sparare; of alarm scattare; of light spegnersi; of milk etc andare a male **2** *v/t* (stop liking) stufarsi di
♦ **go on** *v/i* (continue) andare avanti; (happen) succedere; *go on, do it!* encouraging dai, fallo!; *what's going on?* cosa sta succedendo?
♦ **go on at** *v/t* (nag) sgridare
♦ **go out** *v/i* of person uscire; of light, fire spegnersi
♦ **go out with** *v/t* romantically uscire con
♦ **go over** *v/t* (check) esaminare; (do again) rifare
♦ **go through** *v/t* illness, hard times passare; (check) controllare; (read through) leggere
♦ **go under** *v/i* (sink) affondare; of company fallire
♦ **go up** *v/i* salire
♦ **go without 1** *v/t* food etc fare a meno di **2** *v/i* farne a meno
goad [gəʊd] *v/t* spronare
'**go-a-head 1** *n* via libera *m*; *get the ~* avere il via libera **2** *adj* (enterprising, dynamic) intraprendente
goal [gəʊl] (sport: target) rete *f*; (sport: points) gol *m* inv; (objective) obiettivo *m*
goal·ie ['gəʊlɪ] F portiere *m*
'**goal·keep·er** portiere *m*; '**goal kick** rimessa *f*; '**goal·mouth** area *f* di porta; '**goal·post** palo *m*
goat [gəʊt] capra *f*
gob·ble ['gɒbl] *v/t* tranguigiare
♦ **gobble up** *v/t* tranguigiare
gob·ble·dy·gook ['gɒbldɪguːk] F linguaggio *m* incomprensibile
'**go-be·tween** mediatore *m*, -trice *f*
gob·smacked ['gɒbsmækt] *adj* P sbigottito
god [gɒd] dio *m*; *thank God!* grazie a Dio!; *oh God!* Dio mio!

'god·child figlioccio *m*, -a *f*
'god·daugh·ter figliaccia *f*
god·dess ['gɒdɪs] dea *f*
'god·fa·ther *also in mafia* padrino *m*; 'god·for·sak·en ['gɒdfəseɪkən] *adj place, town* dimenticato da Dio; 'god·moth·er madrina *f*; 'god·pa·rent *man* padrino *m*; *woman* madrina *f*; 'god·send benedizione *f*; 'god·son figlioccio *m*
go·fer ['gəʊfə(r)] F galoppino *m*, -a *f* F
gog·gles ['gɒglz] *npl* occhiali *mpl*
go·ing ['gəʊɪŋ] *adj price etc* corrente; ~ *concern* azienda *f* florida
go·ings-on [gəʊɪŋz'ɒn] *npl* vicende *fpl*
gold [gəʊld] 1 *n* oro *m* 2 *adj* d'oro
gold·en [gəʊldn] *adj sky, hair* dorato
gold·en 'hand·shake buonuscita *f*
gold·en 'wed·ding (an·ni·ver·sa·ry) nozze *fpl* d'oro
'gold·fish pesce *m* rosso; 'gold mine *fig* miniera *f* d'oro; 'gold·smith orefice *m/f*
golf [gɒlf] golf *m*
'golf ball palla *f* da golf; 'golf club *organization* club *m inv* di golf; *stick* mazza *f* da golf; 'golf course campo *m* di golf
golf·er ['gɒlfə(r)] giocatore *m*, -trice *f* di golf
gon·do·la ['gɒndələ] gondola *f*
gon·do·lier [gɒndə'lɪə(r)] gondoliere *m*
gone [gɒn] *pp* → **go**
gong [gɒŋ] gong *m inv*
good [gʊd] 1 *adj* buono; *weather, film* bello; *actor, child* bravo; *a* ~ **many** un bel po' (di); *be* ~ *at* essere bravo in; *be* ~ *for s.o.* fare bene a qu; *be* ~ *for sth* andare bene per qc; ~! bene!; *it's* ~ *to see you* è bello vederti 2 *n* bene *m*; *it did him no* ~ non gli ha fatto bene; *it did him a lot of* ~ gli ha fatto molto bene; *what* ~ *is that to me?* a che cosa mi serve?; *the* ~ il buono; *people* i buoni
good·bye [gʊd'baɪ] arrivederci; *say*

~ *to s.o., wish s.o.* ~ salutare qu
'good-for-nothing *n* buono *m*, -a *f* nulla; **Good 'Fri·day** venerdì *m inv* santo; **good-hu·mored** *Am*, **good-hu·moured** [gʊd'hju:məd] *adj* di buon umore; **good-'look·ing** [gʊd'lʊkɪŋ] *adj* attraente; **good-na·tured** [gʊd'neɪt͡ʃəd] di buon cuore
good·ness ['gʊdnɪs] *adj* bontà *f*; *thank* ~! grazie al cielo
goods [gʊdz] *npl* COM merce *fsg*
good·will buona volontà *f*
good·y-good·y ['gʊdɪgʊdɪ] *n* F santarellino *m*, -a *f*
goo·ey ['gu:ɪ] *adj* appiccicoso
goof [gu:f] *v/i* F fare una gaffe
goose [gu:s] (*pl geese* [gi:s])oca *f*
goose·ber·ry ['gʊzbərɪ] uva *f* spina
'goose pim·ples *npl* pelle *f* d'oca
gorge [gɔ:dʒ] 1 *n* gola *f* 2 *v/t*: ~ *o.s. on sth* strafogarsi di qc
gor·geous ['gɔ:dʒəs] *adj* stupendo; *smell* ottimo
go·ril·la [gə'rɪlə] gorilla *m*
gosh [gɒʃ] *int* caspita
go-'slow sciopero *m* bianco
Gos·pel ['gɒspl] *in Bible* vangelo *m*
'gos·pel truth sacrosanta verità *f inv*
gos·sip ['gɒsɪp] 1 *n* pettegolezzo *m*; *person* pettegolo *m*, -a *f* 2 *v/i* spettegolare
'gos·sip col·umn cronaca *f* rosa
'gos·sip col·um·nist giornalista *m/f* di cronaca rosa
gossipy ['gɒsɪpɪ] *adj letter* pieno di chiacchiere
got [gɒt] *pret & pp* → **get**
gour·met ['gʊəmeɪ] *n* buongustaio *m*, -a *f*
gov·ern ['gʌvn] *v/t country* governare
gov·ern·ment ['gʌvnmənt] governo *m*
gov·er·nor ['gʌvənə(r)] governatore *m*
gown [gaʊn] (*long dress*) abito *m* lungo; (*wedding dress*) abito *m* da sposa; *of academic, judge* toga *f*; *of surgeon* camice *m*

GP [dʒi:'pi:] *abbr* (= *General Practitioner*) medico *m* generico

grab [græb] *v/t* (*pret & pp* **-bed**) afferrare; ~ *a bite to eat* fare uno spuntino rapido; ~ *some sleep* farsi una dormita

grace [greɪs] *of dancer etc* grazia *f*; *before meals* preghiera *f* (prima di un pasto)

grace·ful ['greɪsfʊl] *adj* aggraziato

grace·ful·ly ['greɪsfʊlɪ] *adv* move con grazia

gra·cious ['greɪʃəs] *adj person* cortese; *style* elegante; *living* agiato; *good ~!* santo cielo!

grade [greɪd] **1** *n* (*quality*) qualità *f inv*; EDU voto *m* **2** *v/t* classificare

'grade school *Am* scuola *f* elementare

gra·di·ent ['greɪdɪənt] pendenza *f*

grad·u·al ['grædʒʊəl] *adj* graduale

grad·u·al·ly ['grædʒʊəlɪ] *adv* gradualmente

grad·u·ate ['grædʒʊət] **1** *n* laureato *m*, -a *f* **2** *v/i from university* laurearsi

grad·u·a·tion [grædʒʊ'eɪʃn] laurea *f*; *ceremony* cerimonia *f* di laurea

graf·fi·ti [grə'fi:ti:] graffiti *mpl*

graft [grɑ:ft] **1** *n* BOT innesto *m*; MED trapianto *m*; F (*hard work*) duro lavoro *m* **2** *v/t* BOT innestare; MED trapiantare

grain [greɪn] cereali *mpl*; *seed* granello *m*; *of rice, wheat* chicco *m*; *in wood* venatura *f*; *go against the ~* essere contro natura

gram [græm] grammo *m*

gram·mar ['græmə(r)] grammatica *f*

'gram·mar school liceo *m*

gram·mat·i·cal [grə'mætɪkl] *adj* grammaticale

gram·mat·i·cal·ly *adv* grammaticalmente

grand [grænd] **1** *adj* grandioso; F (*very good*) eccezionale **2** *n* F (*£1000*) mille sterline *fpl*

'grand·dad ['grændæd] nonno *m*

'grand·child nipote *m/f*

'grand·daugh·ter nipote *f*

gran·deur ['grændʒə(r)] grandiosità *f*

'grand·fa·ther nonno *m*

'grand·fa·ther clock pendolo *m*

gran·di·ose ['grændɪəʊs] *adj* grandioso

'grand·ma F nonna *f*; **'grandmoth·er** nonna *f*; **'grand·pa** F nonno *m*; **'grand·par·ents** *npl* nonni *mpl*; **grand pi'an·o** pianoforte *m* a coda; **grand 'slam** grande slam *m inv*; **'grand·son** nipote *m*; **'grandstand** tribuna *f*

gran·ite ['grænɪt] granito *m*

gran·ny ['grænɪ] F nonna *f*

'gran·ny flat appartamento *m* annesso

grant [grɑ:nt] **1** *n money* sussidio *m*; *for university* borsa *f* di studio **2** *v/t visa* assegnare; *permission* concedere; *request, wish* esaudire; *take sth for ~ed* dare qc per scontato; *he takes his wife for ~ed* considera quello che fa sua moglie come dovuto

gran·ule ['grænju:l] granello *m*

grape [greɪp] acino *m* d'uva; ~*s* uva *fsg*

'grape·fruit pompelmo *m*; **'grapefruit juice** succo *m* di pompelmo; **'grape·vine** *I heard on the ~ that …* ho sentito dire che …

graph [grɑ:f] grafico *m*

graph·ic ['græfɪk] **1** *adj* grafico; (*vivid*) vivido **2** *n* COMPUT grafico *m*; ~*s* grafica *f*

graph·i·cal·ly ['græfɪklɪ] *adv describe* in modo vivido

graph·ic de'sign·er grafico *m*, -a *f*

♦ **grap·ple with** ['græpl] *v/t attacker* lottare con; *problem etc* essere alle prese con

grasp [grɑ:sp] **1** *n physical* presa *f*; *mental* comprensione *f* **2** *v/t physically, mentally* afferrare

grass [grɑ:s] *n* erba *f*

'grass·hop·per cavalletta *f*; **grass roots** *npl people* massa *f* popolare; **grass 'wid·ow** donna *f* il cui marito è spesso assente; **grass 'wid·ow·er** uomo *m* la cui moglie è spesso assente

gras·sy ['grɑ:sɪ] *adj* erboso

grate¹ [greɪt] *n metal* grata *f*

grate² [greɪt] **1** v/t in cooking grattugiare **2** v/i of sounds stridere

grate·ful ['greɪtfʊl] adj grato; **be ~ to s.o.** essere grato a qu

grate·ful·ly ['greɪtfʊlɪ] adv con gratitudine

grat·er ['greɪtə(r)] grattugia f

grat·i·fy ['grætɪfaɪ] v/t (pret & pp **-ied**) soddisfare

grat·ing ['greɪtɪŋ] **1** n grata f **2** adj sound, voice stridente

grat·i·tude ['grætɪtjuːd] gratitudine f

gra·tu·i·tous [grə'tjuːɪtəs] adj gratuito

gra·tu·i·ty [grə'tjuːətɪ] (tip) mancia f

grave¹ [greɪv] n tomba f

grave² [greɪv] adj (serious) grave

grav·el ['grævl] n ghiaia f

'grave·stone lapide f

'grave·yard cimitero m

♦ grav·i·tate towards ['grævɪteɪt] v/t gravitare intorno a

grav·i·ty ['grævətɪ] PHYS forza f di gravità

gra·vy ['greɪvɪ] sugo m della carne

gray Am → **grey**

graze¹ [greɪz] v/i of cow, horse brucare

graze² [greɪz] **1** v/t arm etc graffiare **2** n graffio m

grease [griːs] n grasso m

grease-proof 'pa·per carta f oleata

greas·y ['griːsɪ] adj food, hair, skin grasso; hands, plate unto

great [greɪt] adj grande; F (very good) fantastico; **~ to see you!** sono contento di vederti!

Great 'Brit·ain Gran Bretagna f; **great-'grand·child** pronipote m/f; **great-'grand·daugh·ter** pronipote f; **great-'grand·moth·er** bisnonna f; **great-'grand·fa·ther** bisnonno m; **great-'grand·par·ents** npl bisnonni mpl; **great-'grand·son** pronipote m

great·ly ['greɪtlɪ] adv molto

great·ness ['greɪtnɪs] grandezza f

Greece [griːs] Grecia f

greed [griːd] avidità f; for food ingordigia f

greed·i·ly ['griːdɪlɪ] adv con avidità; eat con ingordigia

greed·y ['griːdɪ] adj avido; for food ingordo

Greek [griːk] **1** n greco m, -a f; language greco m **2** adj greco

green [griːn] adj verde; environmentally ecologico; **the Greens** POL i verdi

green 'beans npl fagiolini mpl; **'green belt** zona f verde tutt'intorno ad una città; **green card** driving insurance carta f verde; **green 'fin·gers: have ~** avere il pollice verde; **'green·gro·cer** fruttivendolo m, -a f; **'green·horn** F pivello m, -a f; **'green·house** serra f; **'green·house ef·fect** effetto m serra; **'green·house gas** gas m inv inquinante; **green 'pep·per** vegetable peperone m

greens [griːnz] npl verdura f

greet [griːt] v/t salutare

greet·ing ['griːtɪŋ] saluto m

'greet·ings card biglietto m d'auguri

gre·gar·i·ous [grɪ'geərɪəs] adj person socievole

gre·nade [grɪ'neɪd] granata f

grew [gruː] pret → **grow**

grey [greɪ] adj grigio; hair bianco; **be going ~** cominciare ad avere i capelli bianchi

grey-haired [greɪ'heəd] adj con i capelli bianchi

'grey·hound levriero m

grid [grɪd] grata f; on map reticolato m

'grid·lock in traffic ingorgo m

grief [griːf] dolore m

grief-strick·en ['griːfstrɪkn] adj addolorato

griev·ance ['griːvəns] rimostranza f

grieve [griːv] v/i essere addolorato; **~ for s.o.** essere addolorato per qu

grill [grɪl] **1** n for cooking grill m inv; metal frame griglia f; dish grigliata f; on window grata f **2** v/t food fare alla griglia; (interrogate) mettere sotto torchio

grille [grɪl] grata f

grim [grɪm] *adj* cupo; *determination* accanito

gri·mace ['grɪməs] *n* smorfia *f*

grime [graɪm] sporcizia *f*

grim·ly ['grɪmlɪ] *adv* con aria grave

grim·y ['graɪmɪ] *adj* sudicio

grin [grɪn] **1** *n* sorriso *m* **2** *v/i* (*pret* & *pp* -ned) sorridere

grind [graɪnd] *v/t* (*pret* & *pp* ground) *coffee, meat* macinare; ~ one's teeth digrignare i denti

grip [grɪp] **1** *n* on rope etc presa *f*; **he's losing his ~** losing skills sta perdendo dei colpi; **get to ~s with sth** affrontare qc **2** *v/t* (*pret* & *pp* -ped) afferrare; *of brakes* fare presa su; **be ~ped by sth** by panic essere preso da qc

gripe [graɪp] **1** *n* lamentela *f* **2** *v/i* lamentarsi

grip·ping ['grɪpɪŋ] *adj* avvincente

gris·tle ['grɪsl] cartilagine *f*

grit [grɪt] **1** *n* (*dirt*) granelli *mpl*; *for roads* sabbia *f* **2** *v/t* (*pret* & *pp* -ted): ~ one's teeth stringere i denti

grit·ty ['grɪtɪ] *adj* F *book, film etc* realistico

groan [grəʊn] **1** *n* gemito *m* **2** *v/i* gemere

gro·cer ['grəʊsə(r)] droghiere *m*; **at the ~'s** (**shop**) dal droghiere

gro·cer·ies ['grəʊsərɪz] *npl* generi *mpl* alimentari

gro·cer·y store ['grəʊsərɪ] drogheria *f*

grog·gy ['grɒgɪ] *adj* F intontito

groin [grɔɪn] ANAT inguine *m*

groom [gruːm] **1** *n* for bride sposo *m*; *for horse* stalliere *m* **2** *v/t* horse strigliare; (*train, prepare*) preparare; **well ~ed** in appearance ben curato

groove [gruːv] scanalatura *f*

grope [grəʊp] **1** *v/i* in the dark brancolare **2** *v/t* sexually palpeggiare

♦ grope for *v/t* door handle cercare a tastoni; *the right word* cercare di trovare

gross [grəʊs] *adj* (*coarse, vulgar*) volgare; *exaggeration* madornale; FIN lordo

gross do·mes·tic 'prod·uct prodotto *m* interno lordo

gross na·tion·al 'prod·uct prodotto *m* nazionale lordo

grot·ty ['grɒtɪ] *adj* F *street, flat* squallido; **I feel** ~ sto da schifo F

ground¹ [graʊnd] **1** *n* suolo *m*; (*area, for sport*) terreno *m*; (*reason*) motivo *m*, ragione *f*; ELEC terra *f*; **on the** ~ per terra; **on the ~s of** a causa di **2** *v/t* ELEC mettere a terra

ground² [graʊnd] *pret* & *pp* → **grind**

'ground con·trol controllo *m* da terra; **'ground crew** personale *m* di terra; **'ground floor** pianoterra *m inv*

ground·ing ['graʊndɪŋ] *in subject* basi *fpl*; **have a good ~ in** avere delle buoni basi di

ground·less ['graʊndlɪs] *adj* infondato; **'ground plan** pianta *f* del piano terra; **'ground staff** SP personale *m* addetto alla manutenzione dei campi sportivi; *at airport* personale *m* di terra; **'ground·work** lavoro *m* di preparazione

group [gruːp] **1** *n* gruppo *m* **2** *v/t* raggruppare

group·ie ['gruːpɪ] F ragazza *f* che segue un gruppo o cantante rock in tutti i concerti

group 'ther·a·py terapia *f* di gruppo

grouse¹ [graʊs] (*pl* grouse) *bird* gallo *m* cedrone

grouse² [graʊs] **1** *n* F lamentela *f* **2** *v/i* F brontolare

grov·el ['grɒvl] *v/i* fig umiliarsi

grow [grəʊ] (*pret* grew, *pp* grown) **1** *v/i* of child, animal, plant crescere; *of number, amount* aumentare; *of business* svilupparsi; **let one's hair ~** farsi crescere i capelli; ~ old / tired invecchiare / stancarsi; ~ into sth diventare qc **2** *v/t* flowers coltivare

♦ grow up *of person* crescere; *of city* svilupparsi; **grow up!** comportati da adulto!

growl [graʊl] **1** *n* grugnito *m* **2** *v/i* ringhiare

grown [grəʊn] *pp* → **grow**

grown-up ['grəʊnʌp] **1** *n* adulto *m*, -a *f* **2** *adj* adulto

growth [grəʊθ] *of person* crescita *f; of company* sviluppo *m;* (*increase*) aumento *m;* MED tumore *m*

grub[1] [grʌb] *of insect* larva *f*

grub[2] [grʌb] F (*food*) mangiare *m*

grub·by ['grʌbɪ] *adj* sporco

grudge [grʌdʒ] **1** *n* rancore *m;* **bear s.o. a ~** portare rancore a qu **2** *v/t* dare a malincuore; **~ s.o. sth** invidiare qc a qu

grudg·ing ['grʌdʒɪŋ] *adj* riluttante

grudg·ing·ly ['grʌdʒɪŋlɪ] *adv* a malincuore

gru·el·ing *Am*, **gru·el·ling** ['gruːəlɪŋ] *adj climb, task* estenuante

gruff [grʌf] *adj* burbero

grum·ble ['grʌmbl] *v/i* brontolare

grum·bler ['grʌmblə(r)] brontolone *m, -a f*

grump·y ['grʌmpɪ] *adj* scontroso

grunt [grʌnt] **1** *n* grugnito *m* **2** *v/i* grugnire

guar·an·tee [gærən'tiː] **1** *n* garanzia *f;* **~ period** periodo *m* di garanzia **2** *v/t* garantire

guar·an·tor [gærən'tɔː(r)] garante *m*

guard [gɑːd] **1** *n* guardia *m;* **be on one's ~ against** stare in guardia contro **2** *v/t* fare la guardia a

♦ **guard against** *v/t* guardarsi da

'guard dog cane *m* da guardia

guard·ed ['gɑːdɪd] *adj reply* cauto

guard·i·an ['gɑːdɪən] LAW tutore *m, -trice f*

guard·i·an 'an·gel angelo *m* custode

guer·ril·la [gə'rɪlə] guerrigliero *m, -a f*

guer·ril·la 'war·fare guerriglia *f*

guess [ges] **1** *n* supposizione *f;* **I give you three ~es** ti do tre possibilità di indovinare **2** *v/t the answer* indovinare; **I ~ so** suppongo di sì; **I ~ not** suppongo di no **3** *v/i correctly* indovinare; **I was just ~ing** ho tirato a indovinare

'guess·work congettura *f*

guest [gest] ospite *m/f*

'guest·house pensione *f*

'guest·room camera *f* degli ospiti

guf·faw [gʌ'fɔː] **1** *n* sghignazzata *f* **2** *v/i* sghignazzare

guid·ance ['gaɪdəns] consigli *mpl*

guide [gaɪd] **1** *n person, book* guida *f* **2** *v/t* guidare

'guide·book guida *f* turistica

guid·ed mis·sile ['gaɪdɪd] missile *m* guidato

'guide dog cane *m* per ciechi

guid·ed 'tour visita *f* guidata

guide·lines ['gaɪdlaɪnz] *npl* direttive *fpl*

guilt [gɪlt] colpa *f;* LAW colpevolezza *f*

guilt·y ['gɪltɪ] *adj also* LAW colpevole; **have a ~ conscience** avere la coscienza sporca

guin·ea pig ['gɪnɪpɪg] porcellino *m* d'india; *for experiments, fig* cavia *f*

guise [gaɪz]: **under the ~ of** dietro la maschera di

gui·tar [gɪ'tɑː(r)] chitarra *f*

gui·tar case custodia *f* della chitarra

gui·tar·ist [gɪ'tɑːrɪst] chitarrista *m/f*

gui·tar play·er chitarrista *m/f*

gulf [gʌlf] golfo *m; fig* divario *m;* **the Gulf** il Golfo

gull [gʌl] *n bird* gabbiano *m*

gul·let ['gʌlɪt] ANAT esofago *m*

gul·li·ble ['gʌlɪbl] *adj* credulone

gulp [gʌlp] **1** *n of water* sorso *m; of air* boccata *f* **2** *v/i in surprise* deglutire

♦ **gulp down** *v/t drink* ingoiare; *food* trangugiare

gum[1] [gʌm] *in mouth* gengiva *f*

gum[2] [gʌm] *n* (*glue*) colla *f;* (*chewing gum*) gomma *f*

gump·tion ['gʌmpʃn] F sale *m* in zucca F

gun [gʌn] *pistol, revolver, rifle* arma *f* da fuoco; (*cannon*) cannone *m*

♦ **gun down** *v/t* (*pret & pp* **-ned**) sparare a morte a

'gun·fire spari *mpl;* **'gun·man** uomo *m* armato; *robber* rapinatore *m;* **'gun·point: at ~** con un'arma puntata addosso; **'gun·shot** sparo *m;* **'gun·shot wound** ferita *f* da arma da fuoco

gur·gle ['gɜːgl] *v/i of baby, drain* gorgogliare

gu·ru ['guru] *fig* guru *m inv*

gush [gʌʃ] *v/i of liquid* sgorgare

gush·y ['gʌʃɪ] *adj* F (*enthusiastic*)

iper-entusiastico
gust [gʌst] raffica *f*
gus·to ['gʌstəʊ]: **with ~** con slancio
gust·y ['gʌstɪ] *of weather* ventoso; **~ wind** vento a raffiche
gut [gʌt] **1** *n* intestino *m*; F (*stomach*) pancia *f* **2** *v/t* (*pret & pp* **-ted**) (*destroy*) sventrare
guts [gʌts] *npl* F (*courage*) fegato *m* F
guts·y ['gʌtsɪ] *adj* F *person* che ha fegato; F *thing to do* che richiede fegato
gut·ter ['gʌtə(r)] *on pavement* canaletto *m* di scolo; *on roof* grondaia *f*
'**gutter·press** *pej* stampa *f* scandalistica
guv [gʌv] F capo *m*, -a *f* F
guy [gaɪ] F tipo *m* F; **hey, you ~s** ei, gente

guz·zle ['gʌzl] *v/t* ingozzarsi di
gym [dʒɪm] palestra *f*; (*activity*) ginnastica *f*
'**gym class** educazione *f* fisica
gym·na·si·um [dʒɪm'neɪzɪəm] palestra *f*
gym·nast ['dʒɪmnæst] ginnasta *m/f*
gym·nas·tics [dʒɪm'næstɪks] *nsg* ginnastica *f*
'**gym shoes** *npl* scarpe *fpl* da ginnastica
'**gym teacher** insegnante *m/f* di educazione fisica
gy·ne·col·o·gy *etc Am* → **gynaecology** *etc*
gy·nae·col·o·gy [gaɪnɪ'kɒlədʒɪ] ginecologia *f*
gy·nae·col·o·gist [gaɪnɪ'kɒlədʒɪst] ginecologo *m*, -a *f*
gyp·sy ['dʒɪpsɪ] zingaro *m*, -a *f*

H

hab·it ['hæbɪt] abitudine *f*; **get into the ~ of doing sth** prendere l'abitudine di fare qc
hab·it·a·ble ['hæbɪtəbl] *adj* abitabile
hab·i·tat ['hæbɪtæt] habitat *m inv*
ha·bit·u·al [hə'bɪtjʊəl] *adj* solito; *smoker, drinker* incallito
hack [hæk] *n* (*poor writer*) scribacchino *m*
hack·er ['hækə(r)] COMPUT hacker *m/f inv*
hack·neyed ['hæknɪd] *adj* trito
had [hæd] *pret & pp* → **have**
had·dock ['hædək] haddock *m inv*
haem·or·rhage ['hemərɪdʒ] **1** *n* emorragia *f* **2** *v/i* avere un'emorragia
hag·gard ['hægəd] *adj* tirato
hag·gle ['hægl] *v/i* contrattare
hail [heɪl] *n* grandine *f*
'**hail·stone** chicco *m* di grandine
'**hail·storm** grandinata *f*

hair [heə(r)] capelli *mpl*; *single* capello *m*; *on body, of animal* pelo *m*
'**hair·brush** spazzola *f* per capelli; '**hair·cut** taglio *m* di capelli; '**hair·do** F pettinatura *f*; '**hair·dress·er** parrucchiere *m*, -a *f*; **at the ~'s** dal parrucchiere; '**hair·dri·er**, '**hair·dry·er** fon *m inv*
hair·less ['heəlɪs] *adj* glabro
'**hair·pin** forcina *f*; **hair·pin 'bend** tornante *m*; **hair·rais·ing** ['heəreɪzɪŋ] *adj* terrificante; **hair re·mov·er** [heərɪ'mu:və(r)] crema *f* depilatoria
'**hair's breadth** *fig*: **by a ~** per un pelo
hair-split·ting ['heəsplɪtɪŋ] *n* pedanteria *f*; '**hair spray** lacca *f* per capelli; '**hair·style** acconciatura *f*; '**hair·styl·ist** parrucchiere *m*, -a *f*
hair·y ['heərɪ] *adj arm, animal* peloso; F (*frightening*) preoccupante
half [hɑːf] **1** *n* (*pl* **halves** [hɑːvz])

metà *f inv*, mezzo *m*; **~** *past ten* le dieci e mezza; **~** *an hour* mezz'ora; **~** *a pound* mezza libbra; *go halves with s.o. on sth* fare a metà di qc con qu **2** *adj* mezzo **3** *adv* a metà

half-heart·ed [hɑːfˈhɑːtɪd] *adj* poco convinto; **half 'term** *vacanza f a metà trimestre*; **half 'time 1** *n* SP intervallo *m* **2** *adj*: **~** *job* lavoro a metà giornata; **~** *score* risultato alla fine del primo tempo; **half'way 1** *adj* *stage, point* intermedio **2** *adv also fig* a metà strada; **~** *finished* fatto a metà

hall [hɔːl] *large room* sala *f*; *hallway in house* ingresso *m*

Hal·low·e·en [hæləʊˈiːn] vigilia *f* d'Ognissanti

halo [ˈheɪləʊ] aureola *f*

halt [hɔːlt] **1** *v/i* fermarsi **2** *v/t* fermare **3** *n*: *come to a* **~** arrestarsi

halve [hɑːv] *v/t* dimezzare

ham [hæm] prosciutto *m*

ham·burg·er [ˈhæmbɜːgə(r)] hamburger *m inv*

ham·mer [ˈhæmə(r)] **1** *n* martello *m* **2** *v/i* martellare; **~** *at the door* picchiare alla porta

ham·mock [ˈhæmək] amaca *f*

ham·per[1] [ˈhæmpə(r)] *n for food* cestino *m*

ham·per[2] [ˈhæmpə(r)] *v/t* (*obstruct*) ostacolare

ham·ster [ˈhæmstə(r)] criceto *m*

hand [hænd] *n* mano *m*; *of clock* lancetta *f*; (*worker*) operaio *m*; *at* **~,** *to* **~** a portata di mano; *at first* **~** di prima mano; *by* **~** a mano; *on the one* **~** *...,* *on the other* **~** *...* da un lato ..., dall'altro ...; *in* **~** (*being done*) in corso; *on your right* **~** sulla tua destra; **~s off!** giù le mani!; **~s up!** mani in alto!; *change* **~s** cambiare di mano; *give s.o. a* **~** dare una mano a qu

♦ **hand down** *v/t* passare
♦ **hand in** *v/t* consegnare
♦ **hand on** *v/t* passare
♦ **hand out** *v/t* distribuire
♦ **hand over** *v/t* consegnare; *child to parent etc* dare

hand·bag borsetta *f*; **hand·book** manuale *m*; **hand·brake** freno *m* a mano; **hand·cuff** *v/t* ammanettare; **hand·cuffs** [ˈhæn(d)kʌfs] *npl* manette *fpl*

hand·i·cap [ˈhændɪkæp] handicap *m inv*

hand·i·capped [ˈhændɪkæpt] *adj also fig* handicappato

hand·i·craft [ˈhændɪkrɑːft] artigianato *m*

hand·i·work [ˈhændɪwɜːk] opera *f*

hand·ker·chief [ˈhæŋkətʃɪf] fazzoletto *m*

han·dle [ˈhændl] **1** *n* maniglia *f* **2** *v/t goods* maneggiare; *case, deal* trattare; *difficult person* prendere; *let me* **~** *this* lascia fare a me; *be able to* **~** *s.o.* saperci fare con qu

han·dle·bars [ˈhændlbɑːz] *npl* manubrio *msg*

hand lug·gage bagaglio *m* a mano; **hand·made** [hæn(d)ˈmeɪd] *adj* fatto a mano; **hand·rail** corrimano *m inv*; **hand·shake** stretta *f* di mano

hands-off [hændzˈɒf] *adj approach* teorico; *he has a* **~** *style of management* non partecipa direttamente agli aspetti pratici della gestione

hand·some [ˈhænsəm] *adj* bello

hands-on [hændzˈɒn] *adj experience* pratico; *he has a* **~** *style of management* partecipa direttamente agli aspetti pratici della gestione

hand·writ·ing calligrafia *f*

hand·writ·ten [ˈhændrɪtn] *adj* scritto a mano

hand·y [ˈhændɪ] *adj tool, device* pratico; *it's* **~** *for the shops* è comodo per i negozi; *it might come in* **~** potrebbe tornare utile

hang [hæŋ] **1** *v/t* (*pret & pp* **hung**) *picture* appendere; *person* (*pret & pp* **hanged**) impiccare **2** *v/i* (*pret & pp* **hung**) *of dress, hair* cadere; *his coat was* **~***ing behind the door* il suo cappotto era appeso dietro la porta **3** *n*: *get the* **~** *of* F capire

♦ **hang about** *v/i on streets* gironzolare; *hang about a minute!* F un attimo!

◆ **hang on** v/i (wait) aspettare

◆ **hang on to** v/t (keep) tenere

◆ **hang up** v/i TELEC riattaccare

han·gar ['hæŋə(r)] hangar m inv

hang·er ['hæŋə(r)] for clothes gruccia f

hang glid·er ['hæŋglaɪdə(r)] deltaplano m

hang glid·ing ['hæŋglaɪdɪŋ] deltaplano m

'**hang·o·ver** postumi mpl della sbornia

◆ **hanker after** ['hæŋkə(r)] v/t desiderare

han·kie, **han·ky** ['hæŋkɪ] F fazzoletto m

hap·haz·ard [hæp'hæzəd] adj a casaccio

hap·pen ['hæpn] v/i succedere; **if you ~ to see him** se ti capita di vederlo; **what has ~ed to you?** cosa ti è successo?

◆ **happen across** v/t trovare per caso

hap·pen·ing ['hæpnɪŋ] avvenimento m

hap·pi·ly ['hæpɪlɪ] adv allegramente; (gladly) volentieri; (luckily) per fortuna

hap·pi·ness ['hæpɪnɪs] felicità f inv

hap·py ['hæpɪ] adj felice

hap·py-go-'luck·y adj spensierato

'**hap·py hour** orario m in cui le consumazioni costano meno

har·ass [hə'ræs] v/t tormentare; sexually molestare

har·assed [hər'æst] adj stressato

har·ass·ment [hə'ræsmənt] persecuzione f; **sexual ~** molestie fpl sessuali

har·bor Am, **har·bour** ['ha:bə(r)] 1 n porto m 2 v/t criminal dar rifugio a; grudge covare

hard [ha:d] adj duro; (difficult) difficile; facts, evidence concreto; drug pesante; **~ of hearing** duro d'orecchio

'**hard·back** n libro m con copertina rigida; **hard-boiled** [ha:d'bɔɪld] adj egg sodo; '**hard cop·y** copia f stampata; '**hard core** n (pornography)

pornografia f hard-core; **hard 'cur·ren·cy** valuta f forte; **hard 'disk** hard disk m inv

hard·en ['ha:dn] 1 v/t indurire 2 v/i of glue indurirsi; of attitude irrigidirsi

'**hard hat** casco m; (construction worker) muratore m; **hard-head·ed** [ha:d'hedɪd] adj pratico; **hard-heart·ed** [ha:d'ha:tɪd] adj dal cuore duro; **hard 'line** linea f dura; **hard-'lin·er** sostenitore m, -trice f della linea dura

hard·ly ['ha:dlɪ] adv a malapena; **~ ever** quasi mai; **you can ~ expect him to ...** non puoi certo aspettarti che lui ...; **~! ci** mancherebbe!

hard·ness ['ha:dnɪs] durezza f; (difficulty) difficoltà f inv

hard·'sell tecnica f aggressiva di vendita

hard·ship ['ha:dʃɪp] difficoltà fpl economiche

hard 'shoul·der corsia f di emergenza; **hard 'up** adj al verde; '**hard·ware** ferramenta fpl; COMPUT hardware m inv; '**hard·ware store** negozio m di ferramenta; **hard-work·ing** [ha:d'wə:kɪŋ] adj che lavora duro

har·dy ['ha:dɪ] adj resistente

hare [heə(r)] lepre f

hare-brained ['heəbreɪnd] adj pazzo

harm [ha:m] 1 n danno m; **it wouldn't do any ~ to ...** non sarebbe una cattiva idea ... 2 v/t danneggiare

harm·ful ['ha:mful] adj dannoso

harm·less ['ha:mlɪs] adj innocuo

har·mo·ni·ous [ha:'məʊnɪəs] adj armonioso

har·mo·nize ['ha:mənaɪz] v/i armonizzare

har·mo·ny ['ha:mənɪ] armonia f

harp [ha:p] n arpa f

◆ **harp on about** v/t F menarsela su F

har·poon [ha:'pu:n] n arpione m

harsh [ha:ʃ] adj criticism, words duro; colour, light troppo forte

harsh·ly ['ha:ʃlɪ] adv duramente

har·vest ['ha:vɪst] n raccolto m

H

hash [hæʃ] n F: **make a ~ of** fare un pasticcio di

hash·ish ['hæʃiʃ] hashish *m inv*

'hash mark cancelletto *m*

haste [heɪst] *n* fretta *f*

has·ten ['heɪsn] *v/i*: **~ to do sth** affrettarsi a fare qc

hast·i·ly ['heɪstɪlɪ] *adv* in fretta

hast·y ['heɪstɪ] *adj* frettoloso

hat [hæt] cappello *m*

hatch [hætʃ] *n for serving food* passavivande *m inv*; *on ship* boccaporto *m*

♦ hatch out *v/i of eggs* schiudersi

hatch·et ['hætʃɪt] ascia *f*; **bury the ~** seppellire l'ascia di guerra

hate [heɪt] **1** *n* odio *m* **2** *v/t* odiare

ha·tred ['heɪtrɪd] odio *m*

haugh·ty ['hɔːtɪ] *adj* altezzoso

haul [hɔːl] **1** *n of fish* pescata *f* **2** *v/t* (*pull*) trascinare

haul·age ['hɔːlɪdʒ] autotrasporto *m*

'haul·age com·pa·ny impresa *f* di autotrasporto

haul·i·er ['hɔːlɪə(r)] autotrasportatore *m*

haunch [hɔːntʃ] anca *f*

haunt [hɔːnt] **1** *v/t*: **this place is ~ed** questo posto è infestato dai fantasmi **2** *n* ritrovo *m*

haunt·ing ['hɔːntɪŋ] *adj tune* indimenticabile

have [hæv] (*pret & pp had*) **1** *v/t* ◊ avere; *breakfast, shower* fare; **can I ~ ...?** posso avere ...?; **I'll ~ a coffee** prendo un caffè; **~ lunch / dinner** pranzare / cenare; **do you ~ ...?** ha ...? ◊ *must*: **~ (got) to** dovere; **I ~ (got) to go** devo andare ◊ *causative*: **~ sth done** far fare qc; **I had the printer fixed** ho fatto riparare la stampante; **I had my hair cut** mi sono tagliata i capelli **2** *v/aux* avere; *with verbs of motion* essere; **~ you seen her?** l'hai vista?; **I ~ come** sono venuto

♦ have back *v/t*: **when can I have it back?** quando posso riaverlo?

♦ have on *v/t* (*wear*) portare, indossare; **do you have anything on tonight?** (*have planned*) hai programmi per stasera?

ha·ven ['heɪvn] *fig* oasi *f inv*

hav·oc ['hævək] caos *m inv*; **play ~ with** scombussolare

hawk [hɔːk] *also fig* falco *m*

hay [heɪ] fieno *m*

'hay fe·ver raffreddore *m* da fieno

'hay·stack pagliaio *m*

haz·ard ['hæzəd] *n* rischio *m*

'haz·ard lights *npl* MOT luci *fpl* di emergenza

haz·ard·ous ['hæzədəs] *adj* rischioso

haze [heɪz] foschia *f*

ha·zel ['heɪzl] *n* (*tree*) nocciolo *m*

'ha·zel·nut nocciola *f*

haz·y ['heɪzɪ] *adj view, image* indistinto; *memories* vago; **I'm a bit ~ about it** non ne sono certo

he [hiː] *pron* lui; **~'s French** è francese; **you're funny, ~'s not** tu sei spiritoso, lui no; **there ~ is** eccolo

head [hed] **1** *n* testa *f*; (*boss, leader*) capo *m*; *of primary school* direttore *m*, -trice *f*; *of secondary school* preside *m/f*; *on beer* schiuma *f*; *of nail* capocchia *f*; *of queue, line* inizio *m*; *of tape recorder* testina *f*; **£15 a ~** 15 sterline a testa; **~s or tails?** testa o croce?; **at the ~ of the list** in cima alla lista; **~ over heels** *fall* a capofitto; **~ over heels in love** pazzamente innamorato; **lose one's ~** (*go crazy*) perdere la testa **2** *v/t* (*lead*) essere a capo di; *ball* colpire di testa

'head·ache mal *m* di testa

'head·band fascia *f* per i capelli

head·er ['hedə(r)] *in soccer* colpo *m* di testa; *in document* intestazione *f*

'head·hunt *v/t* COM: **be ~ed** essere selezionato da un cacciatore di teste

'head·hunt·er COM cacciatore *m* di teste

head·ing ['hedɪŋ] *in list* titolo *m*

'head·lamp fanale *m*; 'head·land promontorio *m*; 'head·light fanale *m*; 'head·line *in newspaper* titolo; **make the ~s** fare titolo; 'head·long *adv fall* a testa in giù; 'head·mas·ter *in primary school* direttore *m*; *in secondary school* preside *m*; 'head·mis·tress *in primary* *school* direttrice *f*; *in secondary school* preside *f*; **head 'of·fice** *of company* sede *f* centrale; **head·'on 1** *adv* crash frontalmente **2** *adj* crash frontale; **'head·phones** *npl* cuffie *fpl*; **'head·quar·ters** *npl* sede *fsg*; MIL quartier *msg* generale; **'head·rest** poggiatesta *m inv*; **'head·room** *for vehicle under bridge* altezza *f* utile; *in car* altezza *f* dell'abitacolo; **'head·scarf** foulard *m inv*; **'head·strong** *adj* testardo; **'head 'teach·er** *in primary school* direttore *m*, -trice *f*; *in secondary school* preside *m/f*; **head 'wait·er** capocameriere *m*; **'head·wind** vento *m* di prua

head·y ['hedɪ] *adj drink, wine etc* inebriante

heal [hiːl] *v/t v/i* guarire

♦ **heal up** *v/i* cicatrizzarsi

health [helθ] salute *f*; (*public ~*) sanità *f inv*; **your ~!** (alla) salute!

'health care assistenza *f* sanitaria

'health farm beauty farm *f inv*; **'health food** alimenti *mpl* macrobiotici; **'health food store** negozio *m* di macrobiotica; **'health in·su·rance** assicurazione *f* contro le malattie; **'health re·sort** stazione *f* termale

health·y ['helθɪ] *adj also fig* sano

heap [hiːp] *n* mucchio *m*

♦ **heap up** *v/t* ammucchiare

hear [hɪə(r)] *v/t & v/i* (*pret & pp* **heard**) sentire

♦ **hear about** *v/t* sapere di

♦ **hear from** *v/t* (*have news from*) avere notizie di

heard [hɜːd] *pret & pp* → **hear**

hear·ing ['hɪərɪŋ] udito *m*; LAW udienza *f*; **be within / out of ~** essere / non essere a portata di voce

'hear·ing aid apparecchio *m* acustico

'hear·say diceria *f*; **by ~** per sentito dire

hearse [hɜːs] carro *m* funebre

heart [hɑːt] cuore *m*; *of problem etc* nocciolo *m*; **know sth by ~** sapere qc a memoria

'heart at·tack infarto *m*; **'heart·beat** battito *m* cardiaco; **'heart·break·ing** ['hɑːtbreɪkɪŋ] *adj* straziante; **'heart·brok·en** *adj* affranto; **'heart·burn** bruciore *m* di stomaco; **'heart fail·ure** infarto *m*; **'heart·felt** ['hɑːtfelt] *adj sympathy* sentito

hearth [hɑːθ] focolare *m*

heart·less ['hɑːtlɪs] *adj* spietato

heart·rend·ing ['hɑːtrendɪŋ] *adj plea, sight* straziante

hearts [hɑːts] *npl in cards* cuori *mpl*

'heart throb F idolo *m*

'heart trans·plant trapianto *m* cardiaco

heart·y ['hɑːtɪ] *adj appetite* robusto; *meal* sostanzioso; *person* gioviale

heat [hiːt] calore *m*; (*hot weather*) caldo *m*

♦ **heat up** *v/t* riscaldare

heat·ed ['hiːtɪd] *adj swimming pool* riscaldato; *discussion* animato

heat·er ['hiːtə(r)] *radiator* termosifone *m*; *electric, gas* stufa *f*; *in car* riscaldamento *m*

heath [hiːθ] brughiera *f*

hea·then ['hiːðn] *n* pagano *m*, -a *f*

heath·er ['heðə(r)] erica *f*

heat·ing ['hiːtɪŋ] riscaldamento *m*

'heat·proof, 'heat-re·sis·tant *adj* termoresistente; **'heat·stroke** colpo *m* di calore; **'heat·wave** ondata *f* di caldo

heave [hiːv] *v/t* (*lift*) sollevare

heav·en ['hevn] paradiso *m*; **good ~s!** santo cielo!

heav·en·ly ['hevnlɪ] *adj* F divino

heav·y ['hevɪ] *adj* pesante; *cold, rain, accent* forte; *traffic* intenso; *food* pesante; *smoker* accanito; *drinker* forte; *financial loss, casualties* ingente; **be a ~ sleeper** avere il sonno pesante

heav·y·'du·ty *adj* resistente

'heav·y·weight *adj* SP di pesi massimi

heck·le ['hekl] *v/t* interrompere di continuo

hec·tic ['hektɪk] *adj* frenetico

hedge [hedʒ] *n* siepe *f*

hedge·hog ['hedʒhɒg] riccio *m*

hedge·row ['hedʒrəʊ] siepe *f*

heed [hiːd] *v/t:* **pay ~ to …** ascoltare …

heel [hiːl] *of foot* tallone *m*, calcagno *m*; *of shoe* tacco *m*

'heel bar calzeria *f* istantanea

hef·ty ['heftɪ] *adj* massiccio

height [haɪt] altezza *f*; *of aeroplane* altitudine *f*; **at the ~ of summer** nel pieno dell'estate

height·en ['haɪtn] *v/t effect, tension* aumentare

heir [eə(r)] erede *m*

heir·ess ['eərɪs] ereditiera *f*

held [held] *pret & pp →* **hold**

hel·i·cop·ter ['helɪkɒptə(r)] elicottero *m*

hell [hel] inferno *m*; **what the ~ are you doing / do you want?** F che diavolo fai / vuoi? F; **go to ~!** F va' all'inferno! F; **a ~ of a lot** F un casino F; **one ~ of a nice guy** F un tipo in gambissima

hel·lo [hə'ləʊ] *int informal* ciao; *more formal* buongiorno; buona sera; TELEC pronto; **say ~ to s.o.** salutare qu

helm [helm] NAUT timone *m*

hel·met ['helmɪt] *of motorcyclist* casco *m*; *of soldier* elmetto *m*

help [help] **1** *n* aiuto *m* **2** *v/t* aiutare; **~ o.s.** *to food* servirsi; **I can't ~ it** non ci posso far niente; **I couldn't ~ laughing** non ho potuto fare a meno di ridere

help·er ['helpə(r)] aiutante *m/f*

help·ful ['helpful] *adj person* di aiuto; *advice* utile; **he was very ~** mi è stato di grande aiuto

help·ing ['helpɪŋ] *of food* porzione *f*

help·less ['helplɪs] *adj* (*unable to cope*) indifeso; (*powerless*) impotente

help·less·ly ['helplɪslɪ] *adv:* **we watched ~** guardavamo impotenti

help·less·ness ['helplɪsnɪs] impotenza *f*

'help me·nu COMPUT menu *m inv* della guida in linea

hem [hem] *n of dress etc* orlo *m*

hem·i·sphere ['hemɪsfɪə(r)] emisfero *m*

'hem·line orlo *m*

hen [hen] gallina *f*

hench·man ['hentʃmən] *pej* scagnozzo *m*

'hen par·ty *equivalente m al femminile della festa d'addio al celibato*

hen·pecked ['henpekt] *adj:* **~ husband** marito *m* succube della moglie

hep·a·ti·tis [hepə'taɪtɪs] epatite *f*

her [hɜː(r)] **1** *adj* il suo *m*, la sua *f*, i suoi *mpl*, le sue *fpl*; **~ ticket** il suo biglietto; **~ brother / sister** suo fratello / sua sorella **2** *pron direct object* la; *indirect object* le; *after prep* lei; **I know ~** la conosco; **I gave ~ the keys** le ho dato le chiavi; **this is for ~** questo è per lei; **who? ~ ~** chi? – lei

herb [hɜːb] *for medicines* erba *f* medicinale; *for flavouring* erba *f* aromatica

herb(al) 'tea ['hɜː(əl)] tisana *f*

herd [hɜːd] *n* mandria *f*

here [hɪə(r)] *adv* qui, qua; **~'s to you!** *as toast* salute!; **~ you are** *giving sth* ecco qui; **~!** *in roll-call* presente!

he·red·i·ta·ry [hə'redɪtərɪ] *adj disease* ereditario

he·red·i·ty [hə'redɪtɪ] ereditarietà *f inv*

her·i·tage ['herɪtɪdʒ] patrimonio *m*

her·mit ['hɜːmɪt] eremita *m/f*

her·ni·a ['hɜːnɪə] MED ernia *f*

he·ro ['hɪərəʊ] eroe *m*

he·ro·ic [hɪ'rəʊɪk] *adj* eroico

he·ro·i·cal·ly [hɪ'rəʊɪklɪ] *adv* eroicamente

her·o·in ['herəʊɪn] eroina *f*

'her·o·in ad·dict eroinomane *m/f*

her·o·ine ['herəʊɪn] eroina *f*

her·o·ism ['herəʊɪzm] eroismo *m*

her·on ['herən] airone *m*

her·pes ['hɜːpiːz] MED herpes *m*

her·ring ['herɪŋ] aringa *f*

hers [hɜːz] *pron* il suo *m*, la sua *f*, i suoi *mpl*, le sue *fpl*; **a friend of ~** un suo amico

her·self [hɜː'self] *pron reflexive* si;

emphatic se stessa; *after prep* sé, se stessa; **she must be proud of** ~ deve'essere fiera di sé *o* se stessa; **she hurt** ~ si è fatta male; **she told me so** ~ me l'ha detto lei stessa; **by** ~ da sola

hes·i·tant ['hezɪtənt] *adj* esitante

hes·i·tant·ly ['hezɪtəntlɪ] *adv* con esitazione

hes·i·tate ['hezɪteɪt] *v/i* esitare

hes·i·ta·tion [hezɪ'teɪʃn] esitazione *f*

het·er·o·sex·u·al [hetərəʊ'seksjʊəl] *adj* eterosessuale

hey·day ['heɪdeɪ] tempi *mpl* d'oro

hi [haɪ] *int* ciao

hi·ber·nate ['haɪbəneɪt] *v/i* andare in letargo

hic·cup ['hɪkʌp] *n* singhiozzo *m*; *(minor problem)* intoppo *m*; **have the ~s** avere il singhiozzo

hid [hɪd] *pret* → **hide**

hid·den ['hɪdn] **1** *adj* nascosto **2** *pp* → **hide**

hid·den a'gen·da *fig* secondo fine *m*

hide[1] *(pret* **hid**, *pp* **hidden**) **1** *v/t* nascondere **2** *v/i* nascondersi

hide[2] [haɪd] *n of animal* pelle *f*

hide-and-'seek nascondino *m*

'hide·a·way rifugio *m*

hid·e·ous ['hɪdɪəs] *adj face, weather* orrendo; *crime* atroce

hid·ing[1] *(beating)* batosta *f*

hid·ing[2] ['haɪdɪŋ] *n*: **be in** ~ tenersi nascosto; **go into** ~ darsi alla macchia

'hid·ing place nascondiglio *m*

hi·er·ar·chy ['haɪərɑːkɪ] gerarchia *f*

hi-fi ['haɪfaɪ] hi-fi *m inv*

high [haɪ] **1** *adj building, price, mountain, note, temperature, salary* alto; *wind, speed* forte; *quality, hopes* buono; *(on drugs)* fatto F; ~ **in the sky** in alto nel cielo; **have a very ~ opinion of ...** stimare molto ...; *it is* ~ *time he left* sarebbe ora che se ne andasse **2** *n in statistics* livello *m* record **3** *adv* in alto

'high·brow *adj* intellettuale; **'high·chair** seggiolone *m*; **high·'class** *adj* di (prima) classe; **High 'Court** Corte *f* Suprema; **high 'div·ing** tuffo *m*;

high·'fre·quen·cy *adj* ad alta frequenza; **high·'grade** *adj* di buona qualità; **high-hand·ed** [haɪ'hændɪd] *adj* autoritario; **high-heeled** [haɪ'hiːld] *adj* col tacco alto; **'high jump** salto *m* in alto; **high-'lev·el** *adj* ad alto livello; **'high life** bella vita *f*; **'high·light 1** *n (main event)* clou *m inv*; *in hair* colpo *m* di sole **2** *v/t with pen* evidenziare; COMPUT selezionare; **'high·light·er** *pen* evidenziatore *m*

high·ly ['haɪlɪ] *adv desirable, likely* molto; **be** ~ **paid** essere pagato profumatamente; **think** ~ **of s.o.** stimare molto qu

high·ly 'strung *adj* nervoso

high per'form·ance *adj drill, battery* ad alto rendimento; **high-pitched** [haɪ'pɪtʃt] *adj* acuto; **'high point** clou *m inv*; **high-pow·ered** [haɪ'paʊəd] *adj engine* potente; *intellectual* di prestigio; **high 'pres·sure 1** *n weather* alta pressione *f* **2** *adj* TECH ad alta pressione; *salesman* aggressivo; **high 'priest** gran sacerdote *m*; **'high·rise** palazzone *m*; **'high school** scuola *f* superiore; **high so'ci·e·ty** alta società *f inv*; **high-speed 'train** treno *m* ad alta velocità; **high 'street** via *f* principale; **high 'tech 1** *n* high-tech *m inv* **2** *adj* high tech; **high 'tide** alta marea *f*; **high-'volt·age** alta tensione *f*; **high 'wa·ter** alta marea *f*; **High·way 'Code** Codice *m* stradale

hi·jack ['haɪdʒæk] **1** *v/t* dirottare **2** *n* dirottamento *m*

hi·jack·er ['haɪdʒækə(r)] dirottatore *m*, -trice *f*

hike[1] [haɪk] **1** *n* camminata *f* **2** *v/i* fare camminate

hike[2] [haɪk] *n in prices* aumento *m*

hik·er ['haɪkə(r)] escursionista *m/f*

hik·ing ['haɪkɪŋ] escursionismo *m*

'hik·ing boots *npl* scarponcini *mpl* da camminata

hi·lar·i·ous [hɪ'leərɪəs] *adj* divertentissimo

hill [hɪl] collina *f*; *(slope)* altura *f*

hill·side ['hɪlsaɪd] pendio *m*

hill·top ['hɪltɒp] cima *f* della collina

hill·y ['hɪlɪ] *adj* collinoso

hilt [hɪlt] impugnatura *f*

him [hɪm] *pron direct object* lo; *indirect object* gli; *after prep* lui; *I know ~* lo conosco; *I gave ~ the keys* gli ho dato le chiavi; *this is for ~* questo è per lui; *who? ~ ~* chi? – lui

him·self [hɪm'self] *pron* se stesso; *after prep* sé, se stesso; *he must be proud of ~* dev'essere fiero di sé *o* se stesso; *he hurt ~* si è fatto male; *he told me so ~* me l'ha detto lui stesso; *by ~* da solo

hind [haɪnd] *adj* posteriore

hin·der ['hɪndə(r)] *v/t* intralciare

hin·drance ['hɪndrəns] intralcio *m*

hind·sight ['haɪndsaɪt]: *with ~* con il senno di poi

hinge [hɪndʒ] cardine *m*

♦ **hinge on** *v/t* dipendere da

hint [hɪnt] *n* (*clue*) accenno *m*; (*piece of advice*) consiglio *m*; (*implied suggestion*) allusione *f*; *of red, sadness etc* punta *f*

hip [hɪp] *n* fianco *m*

hip 'pock·et tasca *f* posteriore

hip·po·pot·a·mus [hɪpə'pɒtəməs] ippopotamo *m*

hire ['haɪə(r)] *v/t room, hall* affittare; *workers, staff* assumere; *conjuror etc* ingaggiare

hire 'pur·chase acquisto *m* rateale

his [hɪz] **1** *adj* il suo *m*, la sua *f*, i suoi *mpl*, le sue *fpl*; *~ bag* la sua valigia; *~ brother/sister* suo fratello/sua sorella **2** *pron* il suo *m*, la sua *f*, i suoi *mpl*, le sue *fpl*; *a friend of ~* un suo amico

hiss [hɪs] *v/i* sibilare

his·to·ri·an [hɪ'stɔːrɪən] storico *m*, -a *f*

his·tor·ic [hɪ'stɒrɪk] *adj* storico

his·tor·i·cal [hɪ'stɒrɪkl] *adj* storico

his·to·ry ['hɪstərɪ] storia *f*

hit [hɪt] **1** *v/t* (*pret & pp* **hit**) colpire; (*collide with*) sbattere contro; *I ~ my knee* ho battuto il ginocchio; *he was ~ by a bullet* è stato colpito da

un proiettile; *it suddenly ~ me* (*I realized*) improvvisamente ho realizzato; *~ town* (*arrive*) arrivare (in città) **2** *n* (*blow*) colpo *m*; (*success*) successo *m*

♦ **hit back** *v/i* reagire

♦ **hit on** *v/t idea* trovare

♦ **hit out at** *v/t* (*criticize*) attaccare

hit-and-run *adj*: *~ accident* incidente *m* con omissione di soccorso

hitch [hɪtʃ] **1** *n* (*problem*) contrattempo *m*; *without a ~* senza contrattempi **2** *v/t*: *~ sth to sth* legare qc a qc; *with hook* agganciare qc a qc; *~ a lift* chiedere un passaggio **3** *v/i* (*hitchhike*) fare l'autostop

♦ **hitch up** *v/t wagon, trailer* attaccare

'hitch·hike *v/i* fare l'autostop

'hitch·hik·er autostoppista *m/f*

'hitch·hik·ing autostop *m inv*

hi-'tech 1 *n* high-tech *m inv* **2** *adj* high tech

'hit·list libro *m* nero; **'hit·man** sicario *m*; **hit-or-'miss** *adj*: *on a ~ basis* affidandosi al caso; **'hit squad** commando *m*

HIV [eɪtʃaɪ'viː] *abbr* (= *human immunodeficiency virus*) HIV *m*

hive [haɪv] *for bees* alveare *m*

♦ **hive off** *v/t* (COM: *separate off*) separare

HIV-'pos·i·tive sieropositivo

hoard [hɔːd] **1** *n* provvista *f*; *~ of money* gruzzolo *m* **2** *v/t* accumulare

hoard·er ['hɔːdə(r)] persona *f* che non butta mai niente

hoarse [hɔːs] *adj* rauco

hoax [həʊks] *n* scherzo *m*; *malicious* falso allarme *m*

hob [hɒb] *on cooker* piano *m* di cottura

hob·ble ['hɒbl] *v/i* zoppicare

hob·by ['hɒbɪ] hobby *m inv*

hock·ey ['hɒkɪ] hockey *m* (su prato)

hoist [hɔɪst] **1** *n* montacarichi *m inv* **2** *v/t* (*lift*) sollevare; *flag* issare

hold [həʊld] **1** *v/t* (*pret & pp* **held**) *in hand* tenere; (*support, keep in place*) reggere; *passport, licence* avere; *prisoner, suspect* trattenere; (*contain*) contenere; *job, post* occupare; *course* tenere; **~ hands** tenersi per mano; **~ one's breath** trattenere il fiato; *he can ~ his drink* regge bene l'alcol; **~ s.o. responsible** ritenere qu responsabile; **~ that ...** (*believe, maintain*) sostenere che ...; **~ the line** TELEC resti in linea **2** *n in ship, plane* stiva f; **catch ~ of sth** afferrare qc; *lose one's ~ on sth on rope etc* perdere la presa su qc

♦ **hold against** *v/t*: **hold sth against s.o.** volerne a qu per qc

♦ **hold back 1** *v/t crowds* contenere; *facts* nascondere **2** *v/i* (*hesitate*) esitare; *he's holding back not telling all* non sta dicendo tutta la verità

♦ **hold on** *v/i* (*wait*) attendere; TELEC restare in linea; *hold on a minute!* aspetta un attimo!

♦ **hold on to** *v/t* (*keep*) tenere; *belief* aggrapparsi a

♦ **hold out 1** *v/t hand* tendere; *prospect* offrire **2** *v/i of supplies* durare; *of trapped miners etc* resistere

♦ **hold up 1** *v/t hand* alzare; *bank etc* rapinare; (*make late*) trattenere; *hold sth up as an example* portare qc ad esempio

♦ **hold with** *v/t* (*approve of*) essere d'accordo con

'**hold·all** borsone *m*

hold·er ['həʊldə(r)] (*container*) contenitore *m*; *of passport* titolare *m*; *of ticket* possessore *m*; *of record* detentore *m*, -trice *f*

'**hold·ing com·pa·ny** holding *f inv*

'**hold·up** (*robbery*) rapina *f*; (*delay*) ritardo *m*

hole [həʊl] buco *m*

hol·i·day ['hɒlədeɪ] vacanza *f*; *public* giorno *m* festivo; (*day off*) giorno *m* di ferie; **go on ~** andare in vacanza

hol·i·day·mak·er ['hɒlədeɪmeɪkə(r)] vacanziere *m*, -a *f*

Hol·land ['hɒlənd] Olanda *f*

hol·low ['hɒləʊ] *adj object* cavo, vuoto; *cheeks* infossato

hol·ly ['hɒlɪ] agrifoglio *m*

hol·o·caust ['hɒləkɔːst] olocausto *m*

hol·o·gram ['hɒləgræm] ologramma *m*

hol·ster ['həʊlstə(r)] fondina *f*

ho·ly ['həʊlɪ] *adj* santo

Ho·ly 'Spir·it Spirito *m* Santo

'**Ho·ly Week** settimana *f* santa

home [həʊm] **1** *n* casa *f*; (*native country*) patria *f*; *for old people* casa *f* di riposo; *for children* istituto *m*; *at ~* a casa; **make yourself at ~** fai come a casa tua; *at ~* SP in casa; *work from ~* lavorare da casa **2** *adv* a casa; **go ~** andare a casa; *is she ~ yet?* è tornata?

'**home ad·dress** indirizzo *m* di casa; **home 'bank·ing** home-banking *m inv*; '**home·com·ing** ritorno *m*; **home com'put·er** computer *m inv* (per casa)

home·less ['həʊmlɪs] *adj* senza tetto; *the ~* i senzacasa

'**home·lov·ing** *adj* casalingo

home·ly ['həʊmlɪ] *adj* semplice; (*welcoming*) accogliente

home'made *adj* fatto in casa, casalingo; '**home match** incontro *m* casalingo; **home 'mov·ie** filmino *m* (casalingo); '**Home Of·fice** Ministero *m* degli Interni

'**home page** home page *f*; **Home 'Sec·ret·ar·y** Ministro *m* degli Interni; '**home·sick** *adj*: *be ~* avere nostalgia di casa; '**home town** città *f inv* natale

home·ward ['həʊmwəd] *adv* verso casa

'**home·work** EDU compiti *mpl* a casa

'**home·work·ing** COM telelavoro *m inv*

hom·i·cide ['hɒmɪsaɪd] *crime* omicidio *m*; *Am: police department* (squadra *f*) omicidi *f*

hom·o·graph ['hɒməgræf] omografo *m*

ho·mo·pho·bi·a [həmə'fəʊbɪə] omofobia *f*

ho·mo·sex·u·al [həmə'seksjʊəl] **1** *adj* omosessuale **2** *n* omosessuale *m/f* hon·est ['ɒnɪst] *adj* onesto

hon·est·ly ['ɒnɪstlɪ] *adv* onestamente; *~!* ma insomma!

hon·es·ty ['ɒnɪstɪ] onestà *f inv*

hon·ey ['hʌnɪ] miele *m*; F *(darling)* tesoro *m*

'hon·ey·comb favo *m*

'hon·ey·moon *n* luna *f* di miele

honk [hɒŋk] *v/t horn* suonare

hon·or *etc Am* → **honour** *etc*

hon·our ['ɒnə(r)] **1** *n* onore *m* **2** *v/t* onorare

hon·our·a·ble ['ɒnrəbl] *adj* onorevole

hood [hʊd] *over head* cappuccio *m*; *over cooker* cappa *f*; MOT: *on convertible* capote *f inv*

hood·lum ['huːdləm] gangster *m inv*

hoof [huːf] zoccolo *m*

hook [hʊk] gancio *m*; *for fishing* amo *m*; *off the ~* TELEC staccato

hooked [hʊkt] *adj*: *be ~ on s.o. / sth* essere fanatico di qu / qc; *be ~ on sth on drugs* essere assuefatto a qc

hook·er ['hʊkə(r)] F prostituta *f*; *in rugby* tallonatore *m*

hoo·li·gan ['huːlɪgən] teppista *m/f*

hoo·li·gan·is·m ['huːlɪgənɪzm] teppismo *m*

hoop [huːp] cerchio *m*

hoot [huːt] **1** *v/t horn* suonare **2** *v/i of car* suonare il clacson; *of owl* gufare

hoo·ver® ['huːvə(r)] **1** *n* aspirapolvere *m* **2** *v/t carpets, room* pulire con l'aspirapolvere

hop¹ [hɒp] *n plant* luppolo *m*

hop² [hɒp] *v/i (pret & pp -ped)* saltare

hope [həʊp] **1** *n* speranza *f*; *there's no ~ of that* non farci conto **2** *v/i* sperare; *~ for sth* augurarsi qc; *I ~ so* spero di sì; *I ~ not* spero di no **3** *v/t*: *I ~ you like it* spero che ti piaccia

hope·ful ['həʊpfʊl] *adj person* ottimista; *(promising)* promettente

hope·ful·ly ['həʊpflɪ] *adv say, wait* con ottimismo; *(I / we hope)* si spera

hope·less ['həʊplɪs] *adj position, prospect* senza speranza; *(useless: person)* negato F

ho·ri·zon [həˈraɪzn] orizzonte *m*

hor·i·zon·tal [hɒrɪˈzɒntl] *adj* orizzontale

hor·mone ['hɔːməʊn] ormone *m*

horn [hɔːn] *of animal* corno *m*; MOT clacson *m inv*

hor·net ['hɔːnɪt] calabrone *m*

horn-rimmed 'spec·ta·cles [hɔːnrɪmd] *npl* occhiali *mpl* con montatura di tartaruga

horn·y ['hɔːnɪ] *adj* F *sexually* arrapato P

hor·o·scope ['hɒrəskəʊp] oroscopo *m*

hor·ri·ble ['hɒrɪbl] *adj* orribile

hor·ri·fy ['hɒrɪfaɪ] *v/t (pret & pp -ied)* inorridire; *I was horrified* ero scioccato

hor·ri·fy·ing ['hɒrɪfaɪɪŋ] *adj experience* terrificante; *idea, prices* allucinante

hor·ror ['hɒrə(r)] orrore *m*; *the ~s of war* le atrocità della guerra

'hor·ror mov·ie film *m* dell'orrore

hors d'oeu·vre [ɔːˈdɜːvr] antipasto *m*

horse [hɔːs] cavallo *m*

'horse·back *n*: *on ~* a cavallo; **horse 'chest·nut** ippocastano *m*; **'horse·pow·er** cavallo-vapore *m*; **'horse·shoe** ferro *m* di cavallo

hor·ti·cul·ture ['hɔːtɪkʌltʃə(r)] orticoltura *f*

hose [həʊz] *n* tubo *m* di gomma

hos·pice ['hɒspɪs] ospedale *m* per i malati terminali

hos·pi·ta·ble [hɒˈspɪtəbl] *adj* ospitale

hos·pi·tal ['hɒspɪtl] ospedale *m*; *go into ~* essere ricoverato (in ospedale)

hos·pi·tal·i·ty [hɒspɪˈtælətɪ] ospitalità *f inv*

host [həʊst] *n at party, reception* padrone *m* di casa; *of TV programme* presentatore *m*, -trice *f*

hos·tage ['hɒstɪdʒ] ostaggio *m*; *be taken ~* essere preso in ostaggio

hos·tel ['hɒstl] *for students* pensionato *m*; *(youth ~)* ostello *m* (della gioventù)

hos·tess ['həʊstɪs] *at party, reception*

padrona *f* di casa; *on aeroplane* hostess *f inv*

hos·tile ['hɒstaɪl] *adj* ostile

hos·til·i·ty [hɒ'stɪlətɪ] ostilità *f inv*

hot [hɒt] *adj weather, water* caldo; *(spicy)* piccante; F *(good)* bravo *(at sth* in qc); *it's ~* fa caldo; *I'm ~* ho caldo

'hot dog hot dog *m inv*

ho·tel [həʊ'tel] albergo *m*

'hot·plate piastra *f* riscaldante

'hot spot *military, political* zona *f* calda

hour ['aʊə(r)] ora *f*

hour·ly ['aʊəlɪ] *adj pay, rate* a ora; *at ~ intervals* ad ogni ora

house [haʊs] **1** *n* casa *f*; POL camera *f*; THEA sala *f*; *at your ~* a casa tua, da te **2** *v/t* [haʊz] alloggiare

'house·boat house boat *f inv*;
'house·break·ing furto *m* con scasso; 'house·hold famiglia *f*;
'household 'name nome *m* conosciuto; 'house hus·band casalingo *m*; 'house·keep·er governante *f*;
'house·keep·ing *activity* governo *m* della casa; *money* soldi *mpl* per le spese di casa; **house·warm·ing (party)** ['haʊswɔːmɪŋ] festa *f* per inaugurare la nuova casa; 'house·wife casalinga *f*; 'house·work lavori *mpl* domestici

hous·ing ['haʊzɪŋ] alloggi *mpl*; TECH alloggiamento *m*

hov·el ['hɒvl] tugurio *m*

hov·er ['hɒvə(r)] *v/i* librarsi

'hov·er·craft hovercraft *m inv*

how [haʊ] *adv* come; *~ are you?* come stai?; *~ about …?* che ne dici di …?; *~ much?* quanto?; *~ much is it? of cost* quant'è?; *~ many?* quanti?; *~ often?* ogni quanto?; *~ odd / lovely!* che strano / bello!

how·ev·er *adv* comunque; *~ big / rich they are* per quanto grandi / ricchi siano

howl [haʊl] *v/i of dog* ululare; *of person in pain* urlare; *~ with laughter* sbellicarsi dalle risate

howl·er ['haʊlə(r)] *mistake* strafalcione *m*

hub [hʌb] *of wheel* mozzo *m*

'hub·cap coprimozzo *m*

♦huddle together ['hʌdl] *v/i* stringersi l'un l'altro

hue [hju:] tinta *f*

huff [hʌf]: *be in a ~* essere imbronciato

hug [hʌg] **1** *v/t (pret & pp* **-ged)** abbracciare **2** *n* abbraccio *m*

huge [hju:dʒ] *adj* enorme

hull [hʌl] scafo *m*

hul·la·ba·loo [hʌləbə'lu:] baccano *m*

hum [hʌm] *(pret & pp* **-med) 1** *v/t song, tune* canticchiare **2** *v/i of person* canticchiare; *of machine* ronzare

hu·man ['hju:mən] **1** *n* essere *m* umano **2** *adj* umano; *~ error* errore *m* umano

human 'be·ing essere *m* umano

hu·mane [hju:'meɪn] *adj* umano

hu·man·i·tar·i·an [hju:mænɪ'teərɪən] *adj* umanitario

hu·man·i·ty [hju:'mænətɪ] umanità *f inv*

human 'race genere *m* umano

human re'sources *npl* risorse *fpl* umane

hum·ble ['hʌmbl] *adj origins, person* umile; *house* modesto

hum·drum ['hʌmdrʌm] *adj* monotono

hu·mid ['hju:mɪd] *adj* umido

hu·mid·i·fi·er [hju:'mɪdɪfaɪə(r)] umidificatore *m*

hu·mid·i·ty [hju:'mɪdətɪ] umidità *f inv*

hu·mil·i·ate [hju:'mɪlɪeɪt] *v/t* umiliare

hu·mil·i·at·ing [hju:'mɪlɪeɪtɪŋ] *adj* umiliante

hu·mil·i·a·tion [hju:mɪlɪ'eɪʃn] umiliazione *f*

hu·mil·i·ty [hju:'mɪlətɪ] umiltà *f inv*

hu·mor *Am* → **humour**

hu·mor·ous ['hju:mərəs] *adj person* spiritoso; *story* umoristico

hu·mour ['hju:mə(r)] umorismo *m*; *(mood)* umore *m*; *sense of* ~ senso dell'umorismo

hump [hʌmp] **1** *n of camel, person* gobba *f*; *on road* dosso *m* **2** *v/t* F (*carry*) portare

hunch [hʌntʃ] (*idea*) impressione *f; of detective* intuizione *f*

hun·dred ['hʌndrəd] cento *m; a ~ ...* cento ...

hun·dredth ['hʌndrəθ] *n & adj* centesimo, -a

'**hun·dred·weight** cinquanta chili (*circa*)

hung [hʌŋ] *pret & pp* → **hang**

Hun·gar·i·an [hʌŋ'geəriən] **1** *adj* ungherese **2** *n person* ungherese *m/f; language* ungherese *m*

Hun·ga·ry ['hʌŋɡəri] Ungheria *f*

hun·ger ['hʌŋɡə(r)] fame *f*

hung-o·ver [hʌŋ'əʊvə(r)] *adj:* **feel ~** avere i postumi della s⸱ornia

hun·gry ['hʌŋɡri] *adj* affamato; **I'm ~** ho fame

hunk [hʌŋk] *n* tocco *m;* F (*man*) fusto *m* F

hun·ky-do·ry [hʌŋki'dɔːri] *adj* F: **everything's ~** tutto va a meraviglia

hunt [hʌnt] **1** *n for animals* caccia *f; for job, house, missing child* ricerca *f* **2** *v/t animal* cacciare

♦ **hunt for** *v/t* cercare

hunt·er ['hʌntə(r)] cacciatore *m*, -trice *f*

hunt·ing ['hʌntɪŋ] caccia *f*

hur·dle ['hɜːdl] *also fig* ostacolo *m*

hur·dler ['hɜːdlə(r)] SP ostacolista *m/f*

hur·dles *npl* SP: **100 metres ~** i cento metri a ostacoli

hurl [hɜːl] *v/t* scagliare

hur·ray [hʊ'reɪ] *int* urrà!

hur·ri·cane ['hʌrɪkən] uragano *m*

hur·ried ['hʌrɪd] *adj* frettoloso

hur·ry ['hʌrɪ] **1** *n* fretta *f;* **be in a ~** avere fretta **2** *v/i* (*pret & pp* -**ied**) sbrigarsi

♦ **hurry up** *v/i* sbrigarsi; **hurry up!** sbrigati! **2** *v/t* fare fretta a

hurt [hɜːt] (*pret & pp* **hurt**) **1** *v/i* far male; **does it ~?** ti fa male? **2** *v/t physically* far male a; *emotionally* ferire

hus·band ['hʌzbənd] marito *m*

hush [hʌʃ] *n* silenzio *m;* ~*!* silenzio!

♦ **hush up** *v/t scandal etc* mettere a tacere

husk [hʌsk] pula *m*

hus·ky ['hʌski] *adj voice* roco

hus·tle ['hʌsl] **1** *n:* ~ **and bustle** trambusto *m* **2** *v/t person* spingere

hut [hʌt] capanno *m*

hy·a·cinth ['haɪəsɪnθ] giacinto *m*

hy·brid ['haɪbrɪd] *n plant, animal* ibrido *m*

hy·drant ['haɪdrənt] idrante *m*

hy·drau·lic [haɪ'drɔːlɪk] *adj* idraulico

hy·dro·e·lec·tric [haɪdrəʊɪ'lektrɪk] *adj* idroelettrico

'**hy·dro·foil** ['haɪdrəfɔɪl] *boat* aliscafo *m*

hy·dro·gen ['haɪdrədʒən] idrogeno *m*

'**hy·dro·gen bomb** bomba *f* H

hy·giene ['haɪdʒiːn] igiene *f*

hy·gien·ic [haɪ'dʒiːnɪk] *adj* igienico

hymn [hɪm] inno *m* (sacro)

hype [haɪp] *n* pubblicità *f inv*

hy·per·ac·tive [haɪpər'æktɪv] *adj* iperattivo

hy·per·mar·ket ['haɪpəmɑːkɪt] ipermercato *m*

hy·per·sen·si·tive [haɪpə'sensɪtɪv] *adj* ipersensibile

hy·per·ten·sion [haɪpə'tenʃn] ipertensione *f*

hy·per·text ['haɪpətekst] COMPUT ipertesto *m*

hy·phen ['haɪfn] trattino *m*

hyp·no·sis [hɪp'nəʊsɪs] ipnosi *f*

hyp·no·ther·a·py [hɪpnəʊ'θerəpɪ] ipnoterapia *f*

hyp·no·tize ['hɪpnətaɪz] *v/t* ipnotizzare

hy·po·chon·dri·ac [haɪpə'kɒndriæk] *n* ipocondriaco *m*, -a *f*

hy·poc·ri·sy [hɪ'pɒkrəsɪ] ipocrisia *f*

hyp·o·crite ['hɪpəkrɪt] ipocrita *m/f*

hyp·o·crit·i·cal [hɪpə'krɪtɪkl] *adj* ipocrita

hy·po·ther·mi·a [haɪpəʊ'θɜːmɪə] ipotermia *f*

hy·poth·e·sis [haɪ'pɒθəsɪs] (*pl* **hypotheses** [haɪ'pɒθəsiːz]) ipotesi *f inv*

y·po·thet·i·cal [haɪpə'θetɪkl] *adj* ipotetico

hys·ter·ec·to·my [hɪstə'rektəmɪ] isterectomia *f*

hys·te·ri·a [hɪ'stɪərɪə] isteria *f*

hys·ter·i·cal [hɪ'sterɪkl] *adj person*, *laugh* isterico; F (*very funny*) buffissimo; **become ~** avere una crisi isterica

hys·ter·ics [hɪ'sterɪks] *npl laughter* attacco *m* di risa; MED crisi *f* isterica

---

I

[aɪ] *pron* io; **~ am English** sono inglese; **you're crazy, ~'m not** tu sei pazzo, io no

ce [aɪs] ghiaccio *m*; **break the ~** *fig* rompere il ghiaccio

♦ ice up *v/i of engine, wings* ghiacciarsi

ce·berg ['aɪsbɜːg] iceberg *m inv*; **'ice·box** *Am* frigo *m*; **'ice·break·er** *ship* rompighiaccio *m inv*; **'ice cream** gelato *m*; **'ice cream par·lor** *Am*, **'ice cream par·lour** gelateria *f*; **'ice cube** cubetto *m* di ghiaccio

ced [aɪst] *adj drink* ghiacciato; *cake* glassato

ced 'cof·fee caffè *m inv* freddo

♦ ice hock·ey hockey *m inv* sul ghiaccio; **'ice lol·ly** ghiacciolo *m*; **'ice rink** pista *f* di pattinaggio; **'ice skate** pattinare (sul ghiaccio); **'ice skat·ing** pattinaggio *m* (sul ghiaccio)

♦ci·cle ['aɪsɪkl] ghiacciolo *m*

♦cing ['aɪsɪŋ] glassa *f*

♦con ['aɪkɒn] *cultural* mito *m*; COMPUT icona *f*

♦cy ['aɪsɪ] *adj road, surface* ghiacciato; *welcome* glaciale

ID [aɪ'diː] *abbr* (= *identity*): **have you got any ~ on you?** ha un documento d'identità?

dea [aɪ'dɪə] idea *f*; **good ~!** ottima idea!; **I have no ~** non ne ho la minima idea; **it's not a good ~ to ...** non è una buona idea ...

i·deal [aɪ'dɪəl] *adj* (*perfect*) ideale; **it's not ~ but we'll take it** non è l'ideale ma lo prendiamo lo stesso

i·deal·is·tic [aɪdɪə'lɪstɪk] *adj person* idealista; *views* idealistico

i·deal·ly [aɪ'dɪəlɪ] *adv*: **the hotel is ~ situated** l'albergo si trova in una posizione ideale; **~, we would do it like this** l'ideale sarebbe farlo così

i·den·ti·cal [aɪ'dentɪkl] *adj* identico; **~ twins** gemelli *mpl* monozigotici

i·den·ti·fi·ca·tion [aɪdentɪfɪ'keɪʃn] identificazione *f*, riconoscimento *m*; *papers etc* documento *m* di riconoscimento o d'identità

i·den·ti·fy [aɪ'dentɪfaɪ] *v/t* (*pret & pp* **-ied**) (*recognize*) identificare, riconoscere; (*point out*) individuare

i·den·ti·ty [aɪ'dentətɪ] identità *f inv*; **~ card** carta *f* d'identità; **a case of mistaken ~** uno scambio di persona

i·de·o·log·i·cal [aɪdɪə'lɒdʒɪkl] *adj* ideologico

i·de·ol·o·gy [aɪdɪ'ɒlədʒɪ] ideologia *f*

id·i·om ['ɪdɪəm] (*saying*) locuzione *f* idiomatica

id·i·o·mat·ic [ɪdɪə'mætɪk] *adj* naturale

id·i·o·syn·cra·sy [ɪdɪə'sɪŋkrəsɪ] piccola mania *f*

id·i·ot ['ɪdɪət] idiota *m/f*

id·i·ot·ic [ɪdɪ'ɒtɪk] *adj* idiota

i·dle ['aɪdl] **1** *adj person* disoccupato; *threat* vuoto; *machinery* inattivo; **in an ~ moment** in un momento libero 2 *v/i of engine* girare al minimo

♦ **idle away** *v/t the time etc* trascorrere oziando

i·dol ['aɪdl] *n* idolo *m*

i·dol·ize ['aɪdəlaɪz] *v/t* idolatrare

i·dyl·lic [ɪ'dɪlɪk] *adj* idilli(a)co

if [ɪf] *conj* se; ~ *only you had told me* se (solo) me l'avessi detto

ig·nite [ɪg'naɪt] *v/t* dar fuoco a

ig·ni·tion [ɪg'nɪʃn] *in car* accensione *f*; ~ *key* chiave *f* dell'accensione

ig·no·rance ['ɪgnərəns] ignoranza *f*

ig·no·rant ['ɪgnərənt] *adj (rude)* cafone; *be* ~ *of sth* ignorare qc

ig·nore [ɪg'nɔ:(r)] *v/t* ignorare

ill [ɪl] *adj* ammalato; *fall* ~, *be taken* ~ ammalarsi; *feel* ~ sentirsi male; *look* ~ avere una brutta cera; *feel* ~ *at ease* sentirsi a disagio

il·le·gal [ɪ'li:gl] *adj* illegale

il·le·gi·ble [ɪ'ledʒəbl] *adj* illeggibile

il·le·git·i·mate [ɪlɪ'dʒɪtɪmət] *adj child* illegittimo

ill-fat·ed [ɪl'feɪtɪd] *adj* sfortunato

il·li·cit [ɪ'lɪsɪt] *adj copy, imports* illegale; *pleasure, relationship* illecito

il·lit·e·rate [ɪ'lɪtərət] *adj* analfabeta

ill-man·nered [ɪl'mænəd] *adj* maleducato

ill-na·tured [ɪl'neɪtʃəd] *adj* d'indole cattiva

ill·ness ['ɪlnɪs] malattia *f*

il·log·i·cal [ɪ'lɒdʒɪkl] *adj* illogico

ill-tem·pered [ɪl'tempəd] *adj* irascibile

ill'treat *v/t* maltrattare

il·lu·mi·nate [ɪ'lu:mɪneɪt] *v/t building etc* illuminare

il·lu·mi·nat·ing [ɪ'lu:mɪneɪtɪŋ] *adj remarks etc* chiarificatore

il·lu·sion [ɪ'lu:ʒn] illusione *f*

il·lus·trate ['ɪləstreɪt] *v/t* illustrare

il·lus·tra·tion [ɪlə'streɪʃn] *(picture)* illustrazione *f*; *with examples* esemplificazione *f*

il·lus·tra·tor [ɪlə'streɪtə(r)] illustratore *m*, -trice *f*

ill 'will rancore *m*

im·age ['ɪmɪdʒ] immagine *f*; *(exact likeness)* ritratto *m*

'im·age-con·scious *adj* attento all'immagine

i·ma·gi·na·ble [ɪ'mædʒɪnəbl] *adj* immaginabile; *the biggest / smallest size* ~ la misura più grande / piccola che si possa immaginare

i·ma·gi·na·ry [ɪ'mædʒɪnərɪ] *adj* immaginario

i·ma·gi·na·tion [ɪmædʒɪ'neɪʃn] immaginazione *f*, fantasia *f*; *it's all in your* ~ è tutto frutto della tua immaginazione

i·ma·gi·na·tive [ɪ'mædʒɪnətɪv] *adj* fantasioso

i·ma·gine [ɪ'mædʒɪn] *v/t* immaginare; *I can just* ~ *it* me l'immagino; *you're imagining things* è frutto della tua immaginazione

im·be·cile ['ɪmbəsi:l] ebete *m/f*

IMF [aɪem'ef] *abbr* (= *International Monetary Fund*) FMI *m* (= *Fondo m* Monetario Internazionale)

im·i·tate ['ɪmɪteɪt] *v/t* imitare

im·i·ta·tion [ɪmɪ'teɪʃn] imitazione *f*; *learn by* ~ imparare copiando

im·mac·u·late [ɪ'mækjʊlət] *adj* immacolato

im·ma·te·ri·al [ɪmə'tɪərɪəl] *adj (not relevant)* irrilevante

im·ma·ture [ɪmə'tʃʊə(r)] *adj* immaturo

im·me·di·ate [ɪ'mi:dɪət] *adj* immediato; *the* ~ *family* i familiari più stretti; *the* ~ *problem* il problema più immediato; *in the* ~ *neighbourhood* nelle immediate vicinanze

im·me·di·ate·ly [ɪ'mi:dɪətlɪ] *adv* immediatamente; ~ *after the bank / church* subito dopo la banca / chiesa

im·mense [ɪ'mens] *adj* immenso

im·merse [ɪ'mɜːs] *v/t* immergere; ~ *o.s. in* immergersi in

im·mer·sion heat·er [ɪ'mɜːʃn] scaldabagno *m* elettrico

im·mi·grant ['ɪmɪgrənt] *n* immigrato *m*, -a *f*

im·mi·grate ['ɪmɪgreɪt] *v/i* immigrare

im·mi·gra·tion [ɪmɪ'greɪʃn] *act* immigrazione f; *Immigration government department* ufficio m stranieri

im·mi·nent['ɪmɪnənt] *adj* imminente

im·mo·bi·lize [ɪ'məʊbɪlaɪz] *v/t factory, person, car* immobilizzare

im·mo·bi·liz·er [ɪ'məʊbɪlaɪzə(r)] *on car* immobilizzatore m

im·mod·er·ate [ɪ'mɒdərət] *adj* smodato

im·mor·al [ɪ'mɒrəl] *adj* immorale

im·mo·ral·i·ty [ɪmɒ'rælɪtɪ] immoralità f *inv*

im·mor·tal [ɪ'mɔːtl] *adj* immortale

im·mor·tal·i·ty [ɪmɔː'tælɪtɪ] immortalità f *inv*

im·mune [ɪ'mjuːn] *adj to illness, infection* immune; *from ruling, requirement* esente

im·mune sys·tem MED sistema m immunitario

im·mu·ni·ty [ɪ'mjuːnɪtɪ] *to infection* immunità f *inv*; *from ruling* esenzione f; *diplomatic* ~ immunità f *inv* diplomatica

im·pact ['ɪmpækt] *n of meteorite, vehicle* urto m; *of new manager etc* impatto m; *(effect)* effetto m

im·pair [ɪm'peə(r)] *v/t* danneggiare

im·paired [ɪm'peəd] *adj* danneggiato

im·par·tial [ɪm'pɑːʃl] *adj* imparziale

im·pass·a·ble [ɪm'pɑːsəbl] *adj road* impraticabile

im·passe ['æmpɑːs] *in negotiations etc* impasse m *inv*

im·pas·sioned [ɪm'pæʃnd] *adj speech, plea* appassionato

im·pas·sive [ɪm'pæsɪv] *adj* impassibile

im·pa·tience [ɪm'peɪʃəns] impazienza f

im·pa·tient [ɪm'peɪʃənt] *adj* impaziente

im·pa·tient·ly [ɪm'peɪʃəntlɪ] *adv* con impazienza

im·peach [ɪm'piːtʃ] *v/t President* mettere in stato d'accusa

im·pec·ca·ble [ɪm'pekəbl] *adj* impeccabile

im·pec·ca·bly [ɪm'pekəblɪ] *adv* impeccabilmente

im·pede [ɪm'piːd] *v/t* ostacolare

im·ped·i·ment [ɪm'pedɪmənt] *in speech* difetto m

im·pend·ing [ɪm'pendɪŋ] *adj* imminente

im·pen·e·tra·ble [ɪm'penɪtrəbl] *adj* impenetrabile

im·per·a·tive [ɪm'perətɪv] **1** *adj* essenziale **2** *n* GRAM imperativo m

im·per·cep·ti·ble [ɪmpɜ'septɪbl] *adj* impercettibile

im·per·fect [ɪm'pɜ:fekt] **1** *adj* imperfetto **2** *n* GRAM imperfetto m

im·pe·ri·al [ɪm'pɪərɪəl] *adj* imperiale

im·per·son·al [ɪm'pɜːsənl] *adj* impersonale

im·per·so·nate [ɪm'pɜːsəneɪt] *v/t as a joke* imitare; *illegally* fingersi

im·per·ti·nence [ɪm'pɜːtɪnəns] impertinenza f

im·per·ti·nent [ɪm'pɜːtɪnənt] *adj* impertinente

im·per·tur·ba·ble [ɪmpə'tɜːbəbl] *adj* imperturbabile

im·per·vi·ous [ɪm'pɜːvɪəs] *adj*: ~ *to* indifferente a

im·pe·tu·ous [ɪm'petjʊəs] *adj* impetuoso

im·pe·tus ['ɪmpɪtəs] *of campaign etc* impeto m

im·ple·ment ['ɪmplɪmənt] **1** *n* utensile m **2** *v/t* implementare; *measures* attuare, implementare

im·pli·cate ['ɪmplɪkeɪt] *v/t* implicare; ~ *s.o. in sth* implicare qu in qc

im·pli·ca·tion [ɪmplɪ'keɪʃn] conseguenza f possibile; *by* ~ implicitamente

im·pli·cit [ɪm'plɪsɪt] *adj* implicito; *trust* assoluto

im·plore [ɪm'plɔː(r)] *v/t* implorare

im·ply [ɪm'plaɪ] *v/t* (*pret & pp* *-ied*) implicare; *are you ~ing I was lying?* stai insinuando che ho mentito?

im·po·lite [ɪmpə'laɪt] *adj* maleducato

im·port ['ɪmpɔːt] **1** *n* importazione f; *item* articolo m d'importazione **2** *v/t* importare

im·por·tance [ɪm'pɔːtəns] importanza f

im·por·tant [ɪm'pɔːtənt] adj importante

im·por·ter [ɪm'pɔːtə(r)] importatore m, -trice f

im·pose [ɪm'pəʊz] v/t tax imporre; ~ o.s. on s.o. disturbare qu

im·pos·ing [ɪm'pəʊzɪŋ] adj imponente

im·pos·si·bil·i·ty [ɪmpɒsɪ'bɪlɪtɪ] impossibilità f inv

im·pos·si·ble [ɪm'pɒsɪbəl] adj impossibile

im·pos·tor [ɪm'pɒstə(r)] impostore m, -a f

im·po·tence ['ɪmpətəns] impotenza f

im·po·tent ['ɪmpətənt] adj impotente

im·pov·er·ished [ɪm'pɒvərɪʃt] adj impoverito

im·prac·ti·cal [ɪm'præktɪkəl] adj person senza senso pratico; suggestion poco pratico

im·press [ɪm'pres] v/t fare colpo su; be ~ed by s.o./sth essere colpito da qu/qc; $500 an hour? – I'm ~ed 500 dollari all'ora? – però; terrible work, I'm not ~ed pessimo lavoro, vergogna

im·pres·sion [ɪm'preʃn] impressione f; (impersonation) imitazione f; make a good/bad ~ on s.o. fare buona/cattiva impressione su qu; I get the ~ that ... ho l'impressione che ...

im·pres·sion·a·ble [ɪm'preʃənəbl] adj impressionabile

im·pres·sive [ɪm'presɪv] adj notevole

im·print ['ɪmprɪnt] n of credit card impressione f

im·pris·on [ɪm'prɪzn] v/t incarcerare

im·pris·on·ment [ɪm'prɪznmənt] carcerazione f; 15 years' ~ 15 anni di carcere o reclusione

im·prob·a·ble [ɪm'prɒbəbl] adj improbabile

im·prop·er [ɪm'prɒpə(r)] adj behaviour sconveniente; use improprio

im·prove [ɪm'pruːv] v/t & v/i migliorare

im·prove·ment [ɪm'pruːvmənt] miglioramento m

im·pro·vise ['ɪmprəvaɪz] v/i improvvisare

im·pu·dent ['ɪmpjʊdənt] adj impudente

im·pulse ['ɪmpʌls] impulso m; do sth on an ~ fare qc d'impulso

'impulse buy acquisto m d'impulso

im·pul·sive [ɪm'pʌlsɪv] adj impulsivo

im·pu·ni·ty [ɪm'pjuːnətɪ]: with ~ impunemente

im·pure [ɪm'pjʊə(r)] adj impuro

in [ɪn] 1 prep ◊ ~ Birmingham/Milan a Birmingham/Milano; ~ the street per strada; ~ the box nella scatola; put it ~ your pocket mettilo in tasca; wounded ~ the leg/arm ferito alla gamba/al braccio ◊ ~ 1999 nel 1999; ~ two hours from now tra due ore; over period of in due ore; ~ the morning la mattina; ~ the summer d'estate; ~ September a o in settembre ◊ ~ English/Italian in inglese/italiano; ~ a loud voice a voce alta; ~ his style nel suo stile; ~ yellow di giallo ◊ ~ crossing the road (while) mentre attraversava la strada; ~ agreeing to this (by virtue of) accettando questo ◊ ~ his first novel nel suo primo romanzo; ~ Dante in Dante ◊ three ~ all tre in tutto; one ~ ten uno su dieci 2 adv: be ~ at home essere a casa; in the building etc esserci; arrived: of train essere arrivato; in its position essere dentro; is she ~? c'è?; ~ here/there qui/lì (dentro) 3 adj (fashionable, popular) in, di moda

in·a·bil·i·ty [ɪnə'bɪlɪtɪ] incapacità f inv

in·ac·ces·si·ble [ɪnək'sesɪbl] adj inaccessibile

in·ac·cu·rate [ɪn'ækjʊrət] adj inaccurato

in·ac·tive [ɪn'æktɪv] adj inattivo

in·ad·e·quate [ɪn'ædɪkwət] adj inadeguato

in·ad·vis·a·ble [ɪnəd'vaɪzəbl] adj sconsigliabile

in·an·i·mate [ɪnˈænɪmət] *adj* inanimato

in·ap·pro·pri·ate [ɪnəˈprəuprɪət] *adj* inappropriato

in·ar·tic·u·late [ɪnɑːˈtɪkjulət] *adj* che si esprime male

in·at·ten·tive [ɪnəˈtentɪv] *adj* disattento

in·au·di·ble [ɪnˈɔːdɪbl] *adj* impercettibile

in·au·gu·ral [ɪˈnɔːgjərəl] *adj speech* inaugurale

in·au·gu·rate [ɪˈnɔːgjʊreɪt] *v/t* inaugurare

in·born [ˈɪnbɔːn] *adj* innato

in·breed·ing [ˈɪnbriːdɪŋ] unioni *fpl* tra consanguinei

in·cal·cu·la·ble [ɪnˈkælkjuləbl] *adj damage* incalcolabile

in·ca·pa·ble [ɪnˈkeɪpəbl] *adj* incapace; **be ~ of doing sth** essere incapace di fare qc

in·cen·di·a·ry de·vice [ɪnˈsendɪərɪ] ordigno *m* incendiario

in·cense¹ [ˈɪnsens] *n* incenso *m*

in·cense² [ɪnˈsens] *v/t* fare infuriare

in·cen·tive [ɪnˈsentɪv] incentivo *m*

in·ces·sant [ɪnˈsesnt] *adj* incessante

in·ces·sant·ly [ɪnˈsesntlɪ] *adv* incessantemente

in·cest [ˈɪnsest] incesto *m*

inch [ɪntʃ] pollice *m*

in·ci·dent [ˈɪnsɪdənt] incidente *m*

in·ci·den·tal [ɪnsɪˈdentl] *adj* casuale; **~ expenses** spese accessorie

in·ci·den·tal·ly [ɪnsɪˈdentlɪ] *adv (by the way)* a proposito

in·cin·e·ra·tor [ɪnˈsɪnəreɪtə(r)] inceneritore *m*

in·ci·sion [ɪnˈsɪʒn] incisione *f*

in·ci·sive [ɪnˈsaɪsɪv] *adj mind, analysis* acuto

in·cite [ɪnˈsaɪt] *v/t* incitare; **~ s.o. to do sth** istigare qu a fare qc

in·clem·ent [ɪnˈklemənt] *adj weather* inclemente

in·cli·na·tion [ɪnklɪˈneɪʃn] *tendency, liking* inclinazione *f*

in·cline [ɪnˈklaɪn] *v/t*: **be ~d to believe sth** essere propenso a cre-

dere qc; **be ~d to do sth** avere la tendenza di fare qc

in·close, in·clos·ure → *enclose, enclosure*

in·clude [ɪnˈkluːd] *v/t* includere, comprendere

in·clud·ing [ɪnˈkluːdɪŋ] *prep* compreso, incluso

in·clu·sive [ɪnˈkluːsɪv] **1** *adj price* tutto compreso **2** *prep*: **~ of VAT** IVA compresa **3** *adv*: **from Monday to Thursday ~** dal lunedì al giovedì compreso

in·co·her·ent *adj* incoerente

in·come [ˈɪnkəm] reddito *m*

'in·come tax imposta *f* sul reddito

in·com·ing [ˈɪnkʌmɪŋ] *adj flight, phonecall, mail* in arrivo; *tide* montante; *president* entrante

in·com·pa·ra·ble [ɪnˈkɒmprəbl] *adj* incomparabile

in·com·pat·i·bil·i·ty [ɪnkɒmpætɪˈbɪlɪtɪ] incompatibilità *f inv*

in·com·pat·i·ble [ɪnkəmˈpætɪbl] *adj* incompatibile

in·com·pe·tence [ɪnˈkɒmpɪtəns] incompetenza *f*

in·com·pe·tent [ɪnˈkɒmpɪtənt] *adj* incompetente

in·com·plete [ɪnkəmˈpliːt] *adj* incompleto

in·com·pre·hen·si·ble [ɪnkɒmprɪˈhensɪbl] *adj* incomprensibile

in·con·cei·va·ble [ɪnkənˈsiːvəbl] *adj* inconcepibile

in·con·clu·sive [ɪnkənˈkluːsɪv] *adj* inconcludente

in·con·gru·ous [ɪnˈkɒngruəs] *adj* fuori luogo

in·con·sid·er·ate [ɪnkənˈsɪdərət] *adj* poco gentile

in·con·sis·tent [ɪnkənˈsɪstənt] *adj* incoerente

in·con·so·la·ble [ɪnkənˈsəuləbl] *adj* inconsolabile

in·con·spic·u·ous [ɪnkənˈspɪkjuəs] *adj* poco visibile; **make o.s. ~** passare inosservato

in·con·ve·ni·ence [ɪnkənˈviːnɪəns] *n* inconveniente *m*

in·con·ve·ni·ent [ɪnkənˈviːnɪənt] *adj*

scomodo; *time* poco opportuno

in·cor·po·rate [ɪn'kɔːpəreɪt] *v/t* includere

in·cor·rect [ɪnkə'rekt] *adj answer* errato; *behaviour* scorretto; *am I ~ in thinking …?* sbaglio a pensare che …?

in·cor·rect·ly [ɪnkə'rektlɪ] *adv* in modo errato

in·cor·ri·gi·ble [ɪn'kɒrɪdʒəbl] *adj* incorreggibile

in·crease [ɪn'kriːs] **1** *v/t & v/i* aumentare **2** *n* ['ɪnkriːs] aumento *m*; *on the* ~ in aumento

in·creas·ing [ɪn'kriːsɪŋ] *adj* crescente

in·creas·ing·ly [ɪn'kriːsɪŋlɪ] *adv* sempre più

in·cred·i·ble [ɪn'kredɪbl] *adj* (*amazing*, *very good*) incredibile

in·crim·i·nate [ɪn'krɪmɪneɪt] *v/t* compromettere; ~ *o.s.* compromettersi

in·cu·ba·tor ['ɪŋkjʊbeɪtə(r)] incubatrice *f*

in·cur [ɪn'kɜː(r)] *v/t* (*pret & pp* **-red**) *costs* affrontare; *debts* contrarre; *s.o.'s anger* esporsi a

in·cu·ra·ble [ɪn'kjʊrəbl] *adj* incurabile

in·debt·ed [ɪn'detɪd] *adj*: *be ~ to s.o.* essere (molto) obbligato a qu

in·de·cent [ɪn'diːsnt] *adj* indecente

in·de·ci·sive [ɪndɪ'saɪsɪv] *adj* indeciso

in·de·ci·sive·ness [ɪndɪ'saɪsɪvnɪs] indecisione *f*

in·deed [ɪn'diːd] *adv* (*in fact*) in effetti; (*yes, agreeing*) esatto; *very much ~* moltissimo; *thank you very much ~* grazie mille

in·de·fi·na·ble [ɪndɪ'faɪnəbl] *adj* indefinibile

in·def·i·nite [ɪn'defɪnɪt] *adj* indeterminato; ~ *article* GRAM articolo *m* indeterminativo

in·def·i·nite·ly [ɪn'defɪnɪtlɪ] *adv* a tempo indeterminato

in·del·i·cate [ɪn'delɪkət] *adj* indelicato

in·dent ['ɪndent] **1** *n in text* rientro *m* a margine **2** *v/t* [ɪn'dent] *line*

rientrare il margine di

in·de·pen·dence [ɪndɪ'pendəns] indipendenza *f*

in·de·pen·dent [ɪndɪ'pendənt] *adj* indipendente

in·de·pen·dent·ly [ɪndɪ'pendəntlɪ] *adv* indipendentemente; ~ *of* indipendentemente da

in·de·scri·ba·ble [ɪndɪ'skraɪbəbl] *adj* indescrivibile

in·de·scrib·a·bly [ɪndɪ'skraɪbəblɪ] *adv*: ~ *beautiful* di una bellezza indescrivibile; ~ *bad* pessimo

in·de·struc·ti·ble [ɪndɪ'strʌktəbl] *adj* indistruttibile

in·de·ter·mi·nate [ɪndɪ'tɜːmɪnət] *adj* indeterminato

in·dex ['ɪndeks] indice *m*

'in·dex card scheda *f*; '**in·dex finger** indice *m*; **in·dex-'linked** *adj* indicizzato

In·di·a ['ɪndɪə] India *f*

In·di·an ['ɪndɪən] **1** *adj* indiano **2** *n person* indiano *m*, -a *f*; *American* indiano *m*, -a *f* d'America

In·di·an 'sum·mer estate *f* di San Martino

in·di·cate ['ɪndɪkeɪt] **1** *v/t* indicare **2** *v/i when driving* segnalare (il cambiamento di direzione)

in·di·ca·tion [ɪndɪ'keɪʃn] indicazione *f*

in·di·ca·tor ['ɪndɪkeɪtə(r)] *on car* indicatore *m* di direzione, freccia *f* F

in·dict [ɪn'daɪt] *v/t* incriminare

in·dif·fer·ence [ɪn'dɪfrəns] indifferenza *f*

in·dif·fer·ent [ɪn'dɪfrənt] *adj* indifferente; (*mediocre*) mediocre

in·di·ges·ti·ble [ɪndɪ'dʒestɪbl] *adj* indigesto

in·di·ges·tion [ɪndɪ'dʒestʃn] indigestione *f*

in·dig·nant [ɪn'dɪgnənt] *adj* indignato

in·dig·na·tion [ɪndɪg'neɪʃn] indignazione *f*

in·di·rect [ɪndɪ'rekt] *adj* indiretto

in·di·rect·ly [ɪndɪ'rektlɪ] *adv* indirettamente

in·dis·creet [ɪndɪˈskriːt] *adj* indiscreto

in·dis·cre·tion [ɪndɪˈskreʃn] indiscrezione *f*; *sexual* scappatella *f*

in·dis·crim·i·nate [ɪndɪˈskrɪmɪnət] *adj* indiscriminato

in·dis·pen·sa·ble [ɪndɪˈspensəbl] *adj* indispensabile

in·dis·posed [ɪndɪˈspəʊzd] *adj* (*not well*) indisposto

in·dis·pu·ta·ble [ɪndɪˈspjuːtəbl] *adj* indiscutibile

in·dis·pu·ta·bly [ɪndɪˈspjuːtəblɪ] *adv* indiscutibilmente

in·dis·tinct [ɪndɪˈstɪŋkt] *adj* indistinto

in·dis·tin·guish·a·ble [ɪndɪˈstɪŋgwɪʃəbl] *adj* indistinguibile

in·di·vid·u·al [ɪndɪˈvɪdjʊəl] **1** *n* individuo *m* **2** *adj* (*separate*) singolo; (*personal*) individuale

in·di·vid·u·a·list [ɪndɪˈvɪdjʊəlɪst] *adj* individualista

in·di·vid·u·al·ly [ɪndɪˈvɪdjʊəlɪ] *adv* individualmente

in·di·vis·i·ble [ɪndɪˈvɪzɪbl] *adj* indivisibile

in·doc·tri·nate [ɪnˈdɒktrɪneɪt] *v/t* indottrinare

in·do·lence [ˈɪndələns] indolenza *f*

in·do·lent [ˈɪndələnt] *adj* indolente

In·do·ne·sia [ɪndəˈniːʒə] Indonesia *f*

In·do·ne·sian [ɪndəˈniːʒən] **1** *adj* indonesiano **2** *n person* indonesiano *m*, -a *f*

in·door [ˈɪndɔː(r)] *adj activities, games* al coperto; *arena, swimming pool* coperto

in·doors [ɪnˈdɔːz] *adv in building* all'interno; *at home* in casa

in'duc·tion course [ɪnˈdʌkʃn] corso *m* d'avviamento

in·dulge [ɪnˈdʌldʒ] **1** *v/t o.s., one's tastes* soddisfare **2** *v/i*: ~ **in sth** lasciarsi andare a qc; *in joke* permettersi qc

in·dul·gence [ɪnˈdʌldʒəns] *of tastes, appetite etc* soddisfazione *f*; (*laxity*) indulgenza *f*

in·dul·gent [ɪnˈdʌldʒənt] *adj* (*not strict enough*) indulgente

in·dus·tri·al [ɪnˈdʌstrɪəl] *adj* industriale

in·dus·tri·al 'ac·tion agitazione *f* sindacale

in·dus·tri·al dis'pute vertenza *f* sindacale

in·dus·tri·al es'tate zona *f* industriale

in·dus·tri·al·ist [ɪnˈdʌstrɪəlɪst] industriale *m*

in·dus·tri·al·ize [ɪnˈdʌstrɪəlaɪz] **1** *v/t* industrializzare **2** *v/i* industrializzarsi

in·dus·tri·al 'waste scorie *fpl* industriali

in·dus·tri·ous [ɪnˈdʌstrɪəs] *adj* diligente

in·dus·try [ˈɪndəstrɪ] industria *f*

in·ef·fec·tive [ɪnɪˈfektɪv] *adj* inefficace

in·ef·fec·tu·al [ɪnɪˈfektʃʊəl] *adj person* inetto

in·ef·fi·cient [ɪnɪˈfɪʃənt] *adj* inefficiente

in·el·i·gi·ble [ɪnˈelɪdʒɪbl] *adj*: **be ~ for sth** non avere diritto a qc

in·ept [ɪˈnept] *adj* inetto

in·e·qual·i·ty [ɪnɪˈkwɒlɪtɪ] disuguaglianza *f*

in·es·ca·pa·ble [ɪnɪˈskeɪpəbl] *adj* inevitabile

in·es·ti·ma·ble [ɪnˈestɪməbl] *adj* inestimabile

in·ev·i·ta·ble [ɪnˈevɪtəbl] *adj* inevitabile; *the ~ bottle of ...* l'immancabile bottiglia di ...

in·ev·i·ta·bly [ɪnˈevɪtəblɪ] *adv* inevitabilmente

in·ex·cu·sa·ble [ɪnɪkˈskjuːzəbl] *adj* imperdonabile

in·ex·haus·ti·ble [ɪnɪgˈzɔːstəbl] *adj supply* inesauribile

in·ex·pen·sive [ɪnɪkˈspensɪv] *adj* poco costoso, economico

in·ex·pe·ri·enced [ɪnɪkˈspɪərɪənst] *adj* inesperto

in·ex·plic·a·ble [ɪnɪkˈsplɪkəbl] *adj* inspiegabile

in·ex·pres·si·ble [ɪnɪkˈspresɪbl] *adj* inesprimibile

in·fal·li·ble [ɪnˈfælɪbl] *adj* infallibile

in·fa·mous ['ɪnfəməs] adj famigerato

in·fan·cy ['ɪnfənsɪ] of person infanzia f; of state, institution stadio m iniziale

in·fant ['ɪnfənt] bambino m piccolo, bambina f piccola

in·fan·tile ['ɪnfəntaɪl] adj pej infantile

in·fan·try ['ɪnfəntrɪ] fanteria f

in·fan·try 'sol·dier fante m

'in·fant school scuola f elementare

in·fat·u·at·ed [ɪn'fætʃueɪtɪd] adj: be ~ with s.o. essere infatuato di qu

in·fect [ɪn'fekt] v/t of person contagiare; food, water contaminare; become ~ed of wound infettarsi; of person contagiarsi

in·fec·tion [ɪn'fekʃn] infezione f

in·fec·tious [ɪn'fekʃəs] adj disease infettivo, contagioso; fig: laughter contagioso

in·fer [ɪn'fɜː(r)] v/t (pret & pp -red): ~ sth from sth dedurre qc da qc

in·fe·ri·or [ɪn'fɪərɪə(r)] adj quality, workmanship inferiore; in rank subalterno

in·fe·ri·or·i·ty [ɪnfɪərɪ'ɒrɪtɪ] in quality inferiorità f inv

in·fe·ri·or·i·ty com·plex complesso m d'inferiorità

in·fer·tile [ɪn'fɜːtaɪl] adj sterile

in·fer·til·i·ty [ɪnfə'tɪlɪtɪ] sterilità f inv

in·fi·del·i·ty [ɪnfɪ'delɪtɪ] infedeltà f inv

in·fil·trate ['ɪnfɪltreɪt] v/t infiltrare

in·fi·nite ['ɪnfɪnət] adj infinito

in·fin·i·tive [ɪn'fɪnətɪv] GRAM infinito m

in·fin·i·ty [ɪn'fɪnətɪ] infinito m

in·firm [ɪn'fɜːm] adj infermo

in·fir·ma·ry [ɪn'fɜːmərɪ] infermeria f

in·fir·mi·ty [ɪn'fɜːmətɪ] infermità f inv

in·flame [ɪn'fleɪm] v/t passions accendere

in·flam·ma·ble [ɪn'flæməbl] adj infiammabile

in·flam·ma·tion [ɪnflə'meɪʃn] MED infiammazione f

in·flat·a·ble [ɪn'fleɪtəbl] adj dinghy gonfiabile

in·flate [ɪn'fleɪt] v/t tyre, dinghy gonfiare; economy inflazionare

in·fla·tion [ɪn'fleɪʃn] inflazione f

in·fla·tion·a·ry [ɪn'fleɪʃənərɪ] adj inflazionistico

in·flec·tion [ɪn'flekʃn] of voice intonazione f

in·flex·i·ble [ɪn'fleksɪbl] adj attitude, person inflessibile

in·flict [ɪn'flɪkt] v/t: ~ sth on s.o. punishment infliggere qc a qu; wound, suffering procurare qc a qu

'in·flight adj: ~ entertainment intrattenimento a bordo

in·flu·ence ['ɪnfluəns] 1 n influenza f; be a good / bad ~ on s.o. avere una buona / cattiva influenza su qu; people who have ~ persone influenti; who were your main ~s? chi si è ispirato principalmente? 2 v/t s.o.'s thinking esercitare un'influenza su; decision influenzare

in·flu·en·tial [ɪnflu'enʃl] adj writer, philosopher, film-maker autorevole; she knows ~ people conosce gente influente

in·flu·en·za [ɪnflu'enzə] influenza f

in·form [ɪn'fɔːm] 1 v/t informare; ~ s.o. about sth informare qu di qc; please keep me ~ed tienimi informato 2 v/i denunciare; ~ on s.o. denunciare qu

in·for·mal [ɪn'fɔːml] adj informale

in·for·mal·i·ty [ɪnfɔː'mælɪtɪ] informalità f inv

in·form·ant [ɪn'fɔːmənt] informatore m, -trice f

in·for·ma·tion [ɪnfə'meɪʃn] informazione f; a bit of ~ un'informazione

in·for·ma·tion 'sci·ence informatica f

in·for·ma·tion 'sci·en·tist informatico m, -a f

in·for·ma·tion tech'nol·o·gy informatica f

in·for·ma·tive [ɪn'fɔːmətɪv] adj article etc istruttivo; he wasn't very ~ non è stato di grande aiuto

in·form·er [ɪn'fɔːmə(r)] informatore m, -trice f

in·fra-red [ɪnfrə'red] adj infrarosso

in·fra·struc·ture ['ɪnfrəstrʌktʃə(r)] infrastruttura f

in·fre·quent [ɪn'friːkwənt] adj raro

in·fu·ri·ate [ɪn'fjʊərɪeɪt] v/t far infuriare

in·fu·ri·at·ing [ɪn'fjʊərɪeɪtɪŋ] adj esasperante

in·fuse [ɪn'fjuːz] v/i: let the tea ~ lasciare in infusione il tè

in·fu·sion [ɪn'fjuːʒn] (herb tea) infuso m

in·ge·ni·ous [ɪn'dʒiːnɪəs] adj ingegnoso

in·ge·nu·i·ty [ɪndʒɪ'njuːətɪ] ingegnosità f inv

in·got ['ɪŋgət] lingotto m

in·gra·ti·ate [ɪn'greɪʃɪeɪt] v/t: ~ o.s. with s.o. ingraziarsi qu

in·grat·i·tude [ɪn'grætɪtjuːd] ingratitudine f

in·gre·di·ent [ɪn'griːdɪənt] for cooking ingrediente m; fig: for success elemento m

in·hab·it [ɪn'hæbɪt] v/t abitare

in·hab·it·a·ble [ɪn'hæbɪtəbl] adj abitabile

in·hab·i·tant [ɪn'hæbɪtənt] abitante m/f

in·hale [ɪn'heɪl] 1 v/t inalare 2 v/i when smoking aspirare

in·ha·ler [ɪn'heɪlə(r)] inalatore m

in·her·it [ɪn'herɪt] v/t ereditare

in·her·i·tance [ɪn'herɪtəns] eredità f inv

in·hib·it [ɪn'hɪbɪt] v/t growth, conversation etc inibire

in·hib·it·ed [ɪn'hɪbɪtɪd] adj inibito

in·hi·bi·tion [ɪnhɪ'bɪʃn] inibizione f

in·hos·pi·ta·ble [ɪnhɒ'spɪtəbl] adj inospitale

in-house 1 adj aziendale 2 adv work all'interno dell'azienda

in·hu·man [ɪn'hjuːmən] adj disumano

in·i·tial [ɪ'nɪʃl] 1 adj iniziale 2 n iniziale f 3 v/t (write initials on) siglare (con le iniziali)

in·i·tial·ly [ɪ'nɪʃlɪ] adv inizialmente

in·i·ti·ate [ɪ'nɪʃɪeɪt] v/t avviare

in·i·ti·a·tion [ɪnɪʃɪ'eɪʃn] avviamento m

in·i·tia·tive [ɪ'nɪʃɪtɪv] iniziativa f; do sth on one's own ~ fare qc di propria iniziativa; take the ~ prendere l'iniziativa

in·ject [ɪn'dʒekt] v/t medicine, drug, fuel iniettare; capital investire

in·jec·tion [ɪn'dʒekʃn] MED, of fuel iniezione f; of capital investimento m

'in-joke: it's an ~ è una battuta tra di noi / loro

in·jure ['ɪndʒə(r)] v/t ferire; ~ o.s. ferirsi

in·jured ['ɪndʒəd] 1 adj leg ferito; feelings offeso 2 npl feriti mpl

in·ju·ry ['ɪndʒərɪ] ferita f

'in·ju·ry time SP minuti mpl di recupero

in·jus·tice [ɪn'dʒʌstɪs] ingiustizia f

ink [ɪŋk] inchiostro m

ink·jet ('prin·ter) stampante f a getto d'inchiostro

in·land ['ɪnlənd] adj areas dell'interno; mail nazionale; sea interno

In·land 'Rev·e·nue fisco m

in-laws ['ɪnlɔːz] npl famiglia fsg della moglie / del marito; (wife's / husband's parents) suoceri mpl

in·lay ['ɪnleɪ] n intarsio m

in·let ['ɪnlet] of sea insenatura f; in machine presa f

in·mate ['ɪnmeɪt] of prison detenuto m, -a f; of mental hospital ricoverato m, -a f

inn [ɪn] locanda f

in·nate [ɪ'neɪt] adj innato

in·ner ['ɪnə(r)] adj interno

in·ner 'cit·y centro m in degrado di una zona urbana; ~ decay degrado del centro urbano

'in·ner·most adj thoughts etc più intimo

in·ner 'tube camera f d'aria

in·nings ['ɪnɪŋz] nsg in cricket turno m di battuta

in·no·cence ['ɪnəsəns] innocenza f

in·no·cent ['ɪnəsənt] adj innocente

in·noc·u·ous [ɪ'nɒkjʊəs] adj innocuo

in·no·va·tion [ɪnə'veɪʃn] innovazione f

in·no·va·tive ['ɪnəvətɪv] adj innovativo

in·no·va·tor ['ɪnəveɪtə(r)] innovatore m, -trice f

in·nu·me·ra·ble [ɪ'njuːmərəbl] adj innumerevole

i·noc·u·late [ɪ'nɒkjuleɪt] v/t vaccinare

i·noc·u·la·tion [ɪnɒkju'leɪʃn] vaccinazione f

in·of·fen·sive [ɪnə'fensɪv] adj inoffensivo

in·or·gan·ic [ɪnɔː'gænɪk] adj inorganico

'in·pa·tient degente m/f

in·put ['ɪnput] 1 n contributo m; COMPUT input m inv 2 v/t (pret & pp -ted or input) into project contribuire con; COMPUT inserire

in·quest ['ɪnkwest] inchiesta f giudiziaria

in·quire [ɪn'kwaɪə(r)] v/i domandare; ~ into sth svolgere indagini su qc

in·quir·y [ɪn'kwaɪərɪ] richiesta f di informazioni; (public ~) indagine f

in·quis·i·tive [ɪn'kwɪzətɪv] adj curioso

in·sane [ɪn'seɪn] adj pazzo

in·san·i·ta·ry [ɪn'sænɪtrɪ] adj antigienico

in·san·i·ty [ɪn'sænɪtɪ] infermità f mentale

in·sa·tia·ble [ɪn'seɪʃəbl] adj insaziabile

in·scrip·tion [ɪn'skrɪpʃn] iscrizione f

in·scru·ta·ble [ɪn'skruːtəbl] adj imperscrutabile

in·sect ['ɪnsekt] insetto m

in·sec·ti·cide [ɪn'sektɪsaɪd] insetticida m

'in·sect re·pel·lent insettifugo m

in·se·cure [ɪnsɪ'kjuə(r)] adj insicuro

in·se·cu·ri·ty [ɪnsɪ'kjuərɪtɪ] insicurezza f

in·sen·si·tive [ɪn'sensɪtɪv] adj insensibile

in·sen·si·tiv·i·ty [ɪnsensɪ'tɪvɪtɪ] insensibilità f inv

in·sep·a·ra·ble [ɪn'sepərəbl] adj two issues inscindibile; two people inseparabile

in·sert ['ɪnsɜːt] 1 n in magazine etc inserto m 2 v/t [ɪn'sɜːt] inserire; ~ sth into sth inserire qc in qc

in·ser·tion [ɪn'sɜːʃn] (act) inserimento m

in·side [ɪn'saɪd] 1 n of house, box interno m; of road destra f; sinistra f; someone on the ~ at Lloyds qualcuno che lavora ai Lloyds; ~ out a rovescio; turn sth ~ out rivoltare qc; know sth ~ out sapere qc a menadito 2 prep dentro; ~ of 2 hours in meno di due ore 3 adv stay, remain, go, carry dentro; I've never been ~ non sono mai entrato 4 adj interno; ~ information informazioni riservate; ~ lane SP corsia f interna; on road corsia f di marcia; ~ pocket tasca f interna

in·sid·er [ɪn'saɪdə(r)]: an ~ from the Department ... un impiegato del Ministero ...

in·sid·er 'deal·ing FIN insider trading m inv

in·sides [ɪn'saɪdz] npl pancia fsg; intestines budella fpl

in·sid·i·ous [ɪn'sɪdɪəs] adj insidioso

in·sight ['ɪnsaɪt]: it offers an ~ into ... permette di capire ...; full of ~ molto intuitivo

in·sig·nif·i·cant [ɪnsɪg'nɪfɪkənt] adj insignificante

in·sin·cere [ɪnsɪn'sɪə(r)] adj falso

in·sin·cer·i·ty [ɪnsɪn'serɪtɪ] falsità f inv

in·sin·u·ate [ɪn'sɪnjueɪt] v/t (imply) insinuare

in·sist [ɪn'sɪst] v/i insistere; please keep it, I ~ tienilo, ci tengo!

♦insist on v/t esigere; insist on doing sth insistere per fare qc

in·sis·tent [ɪn'sɪstənt] adj insistente

in·so·lent ['ɪnsələnt] adj insolente

in·sol·u·ble [ɪn'sɒljubl] adj problem insolvibile; substance insolubile

in·sol·vent [ɪn'sɒlvənt] adj insolvente

in·som·ni·a [ɪn'sɒmnɪə] insonnia f

in·som·ni·ac [ɪn'sɒmnɪæk] persona f che soffre di insonnia

in·spect [ɪn'spekt] v/t work, tickets,

baggage controllare; *building, factory, school* ispezionare

in·spec·tion [ɪn'spekʃn] *of work, tickets, baggage* controllo *m*; *of building, factory, school* ispezione *f*

in·spec·tor [ɪn'spektə(r)] *in factory* ispettore *m*, -trice *f*; *on buses* controllore *m*; *of police* ispettore *m*

in·spi·ra·tion [ɪnspə'reɪʃn] ispirazione *f*; (*very good idea*) lampo *m* di genio

in·spire [ɪn'spaɪə(r)] *v/t respect etc* suscitare; *be ~d by s.o./sth* essere ispirato da qu/qc

in·sta·bil·i·ty [ɪnstə'bɪlɪtɪ] *of character, economy* instabilità *f inv*

in·stall [ɪn'stɔːl] *v/t computer, telephones, software* installare

in·stal·la·tion [ɪnstə'leɪʃn] *of new equipment, software* installazione *f*; **military ~** struttura *f* militare

in·stal·ment, in·stall·ment *Am* [ɪn'stɔːlmənt] *of story, TV drama etc* puntata *f*; (*payment*) rata *f*

in·stance ['ɪnstəns] (*example*) esempio *m*; **for ~** per esempio

in·stant ['ɪnstənt] **1** *adj* immediato **2** *n* istante *m*; **in an ~** in un attimo

in·stan·ta·ne·ous [ɪnstən'teɪnɪəs] *adj* immediato

in·stant 'cof·fee caffè *m inv* istantaneo *o* solubile

in·stant·ly ['ɪnstəntlɪ] *adv* istantaneamente

in·stead [ɪn'sted] *adv* invece; **~ of** invece di

in·step ['ɪnstep] collo *m* del piede

in·stinct ['ɪnstɪŋkt] istinto *m*

in·stinc·tive [ɪn'stɪŋktɪv] *adj* istintivo

in·sti·tute ['ɪnstɪtjuːt] **1** *n* istituto *m* **2** *v/t new law* introdurre; *enquiry* avviare

in·sti·tu·tion [ɪnstɪ'tjuːʃn] *governmental* istituto *m*; *sth traditional* istituzione *f*; (*setting up*) avviamento *m*

in·struct [ɪn'strʌkt] *v/t* (*order*) dare istruzioni a; (*teach*) istruire; **~ s.o. to do sth** (*order*) dare istruzioni a qu di fare qc

in·struc·tion [ɪn'strʌkʃn] istruzione

f; **~s for use** istruzioni per l'uso

in·struc·tion man·u·al libretto *m* d'istruzioni

in·struc·tive [ɪn'strʌktɪv] *adj* istruttivo

in·struc·tor [ɪn'strʌktə(r)] istruttore *m*, -trice *f*

in·stru·ment ['ɪnstrəmənt] strumento *m*

in·sub·or·di·nate [ɪnsə'bɔːdɪnət] *adj* insubordinato

in·suf·fi·cient [ɪnsə'fɪʃnt] *adj* insufficiente

in·su·late ['ɪnsjʊleɪt] *v/t* ELEC isolare; *against cold* isolare termicamente

'in·su·lat·ing tape nastro *m* isolante

in·su·la·tion [ɪnsjʊ'leɪʃn] ELEC isolamento *m*; *against cold* isolamento *m* termico

in·su·lin ['ɪnsjʊlɪn] insulina *f*

in·sult ['ɪnsʌlt] **1** *n* insulto *m* **2** *v/t* [ɪn'sʌlt] insultare

in·sur·ance [ɪn'ʃʊərəns] assicurazione *f*

in·sur·ance com·pa·ny compagnia *f* di assicurazioni; **in'sur·ance pol·i·cy** polizza *f* di assicurazione; **in'sur·ance prem·i·um** premio *m* assicurativo

in·sure [ɪn'ʃʊə(r)] *v/t* assicurare

in·sured [ɪn'ʃʊəd] **1** *adj* assicurato; **be ~ed** essere assicurato **2** *n*: **the ~** l'assicurato

in·sur·moun·ta·ble [ɪnsə'maʊntəbl] *adj* insormontabile

in·tact [ɪn'tækt] *adj* (*not damaged*) intatto

in·take ['ɪnteɪk] *of college etc* (numero *m* di) iscrizioni *fpl*

in·te·grate ['ɪntɪgreɪt] *v/t* integrare

in·te·grat·ed 'cir·cuit [ɪntɪgreɪtɪd] *adj* circuito *m* integrato

in·teg·ri·ty [ɪn'tegrətɪ] integrità *f inv*

in·tel·lect ['ɪntəlekt] intelletto *m*

in·tel·lec·tual [ɪntə'lektjʊəl] **1** *adj* intellettuale **2** *n* intellettuale *m/f*

in·tel·li·gence [ɪn'telɪdʒəns] intelligenza *f*; (*information*) informazioni *fpl*

in·tel·li·gence of·fi·cer agente *m/f*

dei servizi segreti

in·tel·li·gence ser·vice servizi *mpl* segreti

in·tel·li·gent [ɪn'telɪdʒənt] *adj* intelligente

in·tel·li·gi·ble [ɪn'telɪdʒəbl] *adj* intelligibile

in·tend [ɪn'tend] *v/i:* ~ **to do sth** (*do on purpose*) volere fare qc; (*plan to do*) avere intenzione di fare qc; **that's not what I ~ed** non è quello che intendevo

in·tense [ɪn'tens] *adj pleasure, heat, pressure* intenso; *concentration* profondo; **he's too** ~ è troppo serio

in·ten·si·fy [ɪn'tensɪfaɪ] (*pret & pp -ied*) **1** *v/t effect, pressure* intensificare **2** *v/i of pain* acuirsi; *of fighting* intensificarsi

in·ten·si·ty [ɪn'tensətɪ] intensità *f inv*

in·ten·sive [ɪn'tensɪv] *adj* intensivo

in·ten·sive 'care (u·nit) MED (*reparto m di*) terapia *f* intensiva

in·ten·sive 'course corso *m* intensivo

in·tent [ɪn'tent] *adj* **be** ~ **on doing sth** (*determined to do*) essere deciso a fare qc; (*concentrating on*) essere intento a fare qc

in·ten·tion [ɪn'tenʃn] intenzione *f*; **I have no** ~ **of** ... (*refuse to*) non ho intenzione di ...

in·ten·tion·al [ɪn'tenʃənl] *adj* intenzionale

in·ten·tion·al·ly [ɪn'tenʃnlɪ] *adv* intenzionalmente

in·ter·ac·tion [ɪntər'ækʃn] interazione *f*

in·ter·ac·tive [ɪntər'æktɪv] *adj* interattivo

in·ter·cede [ɪntə'siːd] *v/i* intercedere

in·ter·cept [ɪntə'sept] *v/t* intercettare

in·ter·change ['ɪntətʃeɪndʒ] *Am* MOT interscambio *m*

in·ter·change·a·ble [ɪntə'tʃeɪndʒəbl] *adj* interscambiabile

in·ter·com ['ɪntəkɒm] citofono *m*

in·ter·course ['ɪntəkɔːs] *sexual* rapporto *m* sessuale

in·ter·de·pend·ent [ɪntədɪ'pendənt] *adj* interdipendente

in·ter·est ['ɪntrəst] **1** *n* interesse *m*; FIN: *rate* interesse *m*; *money paid/received* interessi *mpl*; **take an** ~ **in sth** interessarsi di qc **2** *v/t* interessare; **does that offer** ~ **you?** t'interessa l'offerta?

in·ter·est·ed ['ɪntrəstɪd] *adj* interessato; **be** ~ **in sth** interessarsi di qc; **thanks, but I'm not** ~ grazie, non mi interessa

in·ter·est-free 'loan prestito *m* senza interessi

in·ter·est·ing ['ɪntrəstɪŋ] *adj* interessante

'in·ter·est rate FIN tasso *m* d'interesse

in·ter·face ['ɪntəfeɪs] **1** *n* interfaccia *f* **2** *v/i* interfacciarsi

in·ter·fere [ɪntə'fɪə(r)] *v/i* interferire
♦ **interfere with** *v/t* manomettere; *plans* intralciare

in·ter·fer·ence [ɪntə'fɪərəns] interferenza *f*; *on radio* interferenze *fpl*

in·te·ri·or [ɪn'tɪərɪə(r)] **1** *adj* interno **2** *n of house* interno *m*; *of country* entroterra *m*

in·te·ri·or 'dec·o·ra·tor arredatore *m*, -trice *f*; in·te·ri·or de'sign architettura *f* d'interni; in·te·ri·or de'sign·er architetto *m* d'interni

in·ter·lude ['ɪntəluːd] *at theatre, concert* intervallo *m*; (*period*) parentesi *f*

in·ter·mar·ry [ɪntə'mærɪ] *v/i* (*pret & pp -ied*) fare matrimoni misti

in·ter·me·di·a·ry [ɪntə'miːdɪərɪ] *n* intermediario *m*, -a *f*

in·ter·me·di·ate [ɪntə'miːdɪət] *adj* intermedio

in·ter·mis·sion [ɪntə'mɪʃn] *in theatre, cinema* intervallo *m*

in·tern [ɪn'tɜːn] *v/t* internare

in·ter·nal [ɪn'tɜːnl] *adj* interno

in·ter·nal com'bus·tion en·gine motore *m* a scoppio

in·ter·nal·ly [ɪn'tɜːnəlɪ] *adv:* **he's bleeding** ~ ha un'emorragia interna; **not to be taken** ~ per uso esterno

in·ter·na·tion·al [ɪntə'næʃnl] *adj*

internazionale **2** *n match* partita *f*
internazionale; *player* giocatore *m*, -trice *f* della nazionale

In·ter·na·tion·al Court of 'Jus·tice Corte *f* Internazionale di Giustizia

in·ter·na·tion·al·ly [ɪntəˈnæʃnəlɪ] *adv* a livello internazionale

In·ter·na·tion·al 'Mon·e·tar·y Fund Fondo *m* Monetario Internazionale

In·ter·net [ˈɪntənet] Internet *m inv*; **on the ~** su Internet; **~ service provider** provider *m inv* di servizi Internet

in·ter·pret [ɪnˈtɜːprɪt] **1** *v/t linguistically* tradurre; *piece of music, comment etc* interpretare **2** *v/i* fare da interprete

in·ter·pre·ta·tion [ɪntɜːprɪˈteɪʃn] *linguistic* traduzione *f*; *of piece of music, meaning* interpretazione *f*

in·ter·pret·er [ɪnˈtɜːprɪtə(r)] interprete *m/f*

in·ter·re·lat·ed [ɪntərɪˈleɪtɪd] *adj* correlato

in·ter·ro·gate [ɪnˈterəgeɪt] *v/t* interrogare

in·ter·ro·ga·tion [ɪnterəˈgeɪʃn] interrogatorio *m*

in·ter·rog·a·tive [ɪntəˈrɒgətɪv] *n* GRAM forma *f* interrogativa

in·ter·ro·ga·tor [ɪntərəˈgeɪtə(r)] interrogante *m/f*

in·ter·rupt [ɪntəˈrʌpt] *v/t & v/i* interrompere

in·ter·rup·tion [ɪntəˈrʌpʃn] interruzione *f*

in·ter·sect [ɪntəˈsekt] **1** *v/t* intersecare **2** *v/i* intersecarsi

in·ter·sec·tion [ˈɪntəsekʃn] (*crossroads*) incrocio *m*

in·ter·val [ˈɪntəvəl] intervallo *m*; **sunny ~s** schiarite

in·ter·vene [ɪntəˈviːn] *v/i of person, police etc* intervenire; *of time* trascorrere

in·ter·ven·tion [ɪntəˈvenʃn] intervento *m*

in·ter·view [ˈɪntəvjuː] **1** *n on TV, in paper* intervista *f*; *for job* intervista *f* d'assunzione, colloquio *m* di lavoro **2** *v/t on TV, for paper* intervistare; *for*

job sottoporre a intervista

in·ter·view·ee [ˈɪntəvjuːˈiː] *on TV* intervistato *m*, -a *f*; *for job* candidato *m*, -a *f*

in·ter·view·er [ˈɪntəvjuːə(r)] *on TV, for paper* intervistatore *m*, -trice *f*; (*for job*) persona *f* che conduce un'intervista d'assunzione

in·tes·tine [ɪnˈtestɪn] intestino *m*

in·ti·ma·cy [ˈɪntɪməsɪ] intimità *f inv*

in·ti·mate [ˈɪntɪmət] *adj friend, thoughts* intimo; **be ~ with s.o.** *sexually* avere rapporti intimi con qu

in·tim·i·date [ɪnˈtɪmɪdeɪt] *v/t* intimidire

in·tim·i·da·tion [ɪntɪmɪˈdeɪʃn] intimidazione *f*

in·to [ˈɪntʊ] *prep* in; **he put it ~ his suitcase** l'ha messo in valigia; **translate ~ English** tradurre in inglese; **be ~ sth** F (*like*) amare qc; (*be involved with*) interessarsi di qc; **be ~ drugs** fare uso di droga; **when you're ~ the job** quando sei pratico del lavoro

in·tol·e·ra·ble [ɪnˈtɒlərəbl] *adj* intollerabile

in·tol·e·rant [ɪnˈtɒlərənt] *adj* intollerante

in·tox·i·cat·ed [ɪnˈtɒksɪkeɪtɪd] *adj* ubriaco

in·tran·si·tive [ɪnˈtrænsɪtɪv] *adj* intransitivo

in·tra·ve·nous [ɪntrəˈviːnəs] *adj* endovenoso

in·trep·id [ɪnˈtrepɪd] *adj* intrepido

in·tri·cate [ˈɪntrɪkət] *adj* complicato

in·trigue [ˈɪntriːg] **1** *n* intrigo *m* **2** *v/t* [ɪnˈtriːg] intrigare; **I would be ~d to know …** m'interesserebbe molto sapere …

in·tri·gu·ing [ɪnˈtriːgɪŋ] *adj* intrigante

in·tro·duce [ɪntrəˈdjuːs] *v/t person* presentare; *new technique etc* introdurre; **may I ~ …?** permette che le presenti …?

in·tro·duc·tion [ɪntrəˈdʌkʃn] *to person* presentazione *f*; *to a new food, sport etc* approccio *m*; *in book, of new technique* introduzione *f* in·tro·vert ['ɪntrəvɜːt] introverso m, -a f

in·trude [ɪn'truːd] v/i importunare

in·trud·er [ɪn'truːdə(r)] intruso m, -a f

in·tru·sion [ɪn'truːʒn] intrusione f

in·tu·i·tion [ɪntjuː'ɪʃn] intuito m

in·vade [ɪn'veɪd] v/t invadere

in·val·id¹ [ɪn'vælɪd] adj non valido

in·va·lid² ['ɪnvəlɪd] n MED invalido m, -a f

in·val·i·date [ɪn'vælɪdeɪt] v/t claim, theory invalidare

in·val·u·a·ble [ɪn'væljʊbl] adj help, contributor prezioso

in·var·i·a·bly [ɪn'veɪrɪəblɪ] adv (always) invariabilmente

in·va·sion [ɪn'veɪʒn] invasione f

in·vent [ɪn'vent] v/t inventare

in·ven·tion [ɪn'venʃn] invenzione f

in·ven·tive [ɪn'ventɪv] adj fantasioso

in·ven·tor [ɪn'ventə(r)] inventore m, -trice f

in·ven·to·ry ['ɪnvəntrɪ] inventario m

in·verse [ɪn'vɜːs] adj order inverso

in·vert [ɪn'vɜːt] v/t invertire

in·vert·ed 'com·mas [ɪn'vɜːtɪd] npl virgolette fpl

in·ver·te·brate [ɪn'vɜːtɪbrət] n invertebrato m

invest [ɪn'vest] v/t & v/i investire

in·ves·ti·gate [ɪn'vestɪgeɪt] v/t indagare su

in·ves·ti·ga·tion [ɪnvestɪ'geɪʃn] indagine f

in·ves·ti·ga·tive 'jour·nal·ism [ɪn'vestɪgətɪv] giornalismo m investigativo

in·vest·ment [ɪn'vestmənt] investimento m

in·ves·tor [ɪn'vestə(r)] investitore m, -trice

in·vig·or·at·ing [ɪn'vɪgəreɪtɪŋ] adj climate tonificante

in·vin·ci·ble [ɪn'vɪnsəbl] adj invincibile

in·vis·i·ble [ɪn'vɪzɪbl] adj invisibile

in·vi·ta·tion [ɪnvɪ'teɪʃn] invito m

in·vite [ɪn'vaɪt] v/t invitare; **can I ~ you for a meal?** posso invitarti a pranzo?

♦ invite in v/t invitare a entrare

in·voice ['ɪnvɔɪs] **1** n fattura f **2** v/t customer fatturare

in·vol·un·ta·ry [ɪn'vɒləntrɪ] adj involontario

in·volve [ɪn'vɒlv] v/t hard work, expense comportare; (concern) riguardare; **what does it ~?** che cosa comporta?; **get ~d with sth** entrare a far parte di qc; **get ~d with s.o. emotionally, romantically** legarsi a qu

in·volved [ɪn'vɒlvd] adj (complex) complesso

in·volve·ment [ɪn'vɒlvmənt] in a project etc partecipazione f; in a crime, accident coinvolgimento m

in·vul·ne·ra·ble [ɪn'vʌlnərəbl] adj invulnerabile

in·ward ['ɪnwəd] **1** adj direction verso l'interno; feeling, thoughts intimo **2** adv verso l'interno

in·ward·ly ['ɪnwədlɪ] adv dentro di sé

i·o·dine ['aɪədiːn] iodio m

IOU [aɪəʊ'juː] abbr (= **I owe you**) pagherò m

IQ [aɪ'kjuː] abbr (= **intelligence quotient**) quoziente m d'intelligenza

I·ran [ɪ'rɑːn] Iran m

I·ra·ni·an [ɪ'reɪnɪən] **1** adj iraniano **2** n person iraniano m, -a f

I·raq [ɪ'rækɪ] Iraq m

I·ra·qi [ɪ'rækɪ] **1** adj iracheno **2** n person iracheno m, -a f

Ire·land ['aɪələnd] Irlanda f

i·ris ['aɪərɪs] of eye iride f; flower iris m inv

I·rish ['aɪərɪʃ] adj irlandese

'I·rish·man irlandese m

'I·rish·wom·an irlandese f

i·ron ['aɪən] **1** n substance ferro m; for clothes ferro m da stiro **2** v/t shirts etc stirare

i·ron·ic(al) [aɪ'rɒnɪk(l)] adj ironico

i·ron·ing ['aɪənɪŋ]: **do the ~** stirare

'i·ron·ing board asse m da stiro

'i·ron·works stabilimento m siderurgico

i·ron·y ['aɪərənɪ] ironia f

ir·ra·tion·al [ɪ'ræʃənl] adj irrazionale

ir·rec·on·ci·la·ble [ɪrekən'saɪləbl] *adj* inconciliabile

ir·re·cov·e·ra·ble [ɪrɪ'kʌvərəbl] *adj* irrecuperabile

ir·re·gu·lar [ɪ'regjʊlə(r)] *adj* irregolare

ir·rel·e·vant [ɪ'reləvənt] *adj* non pertinente

ir·rep·a·ra·ble [ɪ'repərəbl] *adj* irreparabile

ir·re·place·a·ble [ɪrɪ'pleɪsəbl] *adj object, person* insostituibile

ir·re·pres·si·ble [ɪrɪ'presəbl] *adj sense of humour* incontenibile; *person* che non si lascia abbattere

ir·re·proa·cha·ble [ɪrɪ'prəʊtʃəbl] *adj* irreprensibile

ir·re·sis·ti·ble [ɪrɪ'zɪstəbl] *adj* irresistibile

ir·re·spec·tive [ɪrɪ'spektɪv] *adj*: ~ **of** a prescindere da

ir·re·spon·si·ble [ɪrɪ'spɒnsəbl] *adj* irresponsabile

ir·re·trie·va·ble [ɪrɪ'triːvəbl] *adj* irrecuperabile

ir·rev·e·rent [ɪ'revərənt] *adj* irriverente

ir·rev·o·ca·ble [ɪ'revəkəbl] *adj* irrevocabile

ir·ri·gate ['ɪrɪgeɪt] *v/t* irrigare

ir·ri·ga·tion [ɪrɪ'geɪʃn] irrigazione *f*

ir·ri·ga·tion ca·nal canale *m* d'irrigazione

ir·ri·ta·ble ['ɪrɪtəbl] *adj* irritabile

ir·ri·tate ['ɪrɪteɪt] *v/t* irritare

ir·ri·tat·ing ['ɪrɪteɪtɪŋ] *adj* irritante

ir·ri·ta·tion [ɪrɪ'teɪʃn] irritazione *f*

Is·lam ['ɪzlɑːm] Islam *m*

Is·lam·ic [ɪz'læmɪk] *adj* islamico

is·land ['aɪlənd] isola *f*; (*traffic*) ~ isola *f* spartitraffico

is·land·er ['aɪləndə(r)] isolano *m*, -a *f*

i·so·late ['aɪsəleɪt] *v/t* isolare

i·so·lat·ed ['aɪsəleɪtɪd] *adj house, occurrence* isolato

i·so·la·tion [aɪsə'leɪʃn] *of a region* isolamento *m*; *in* ~ *taken etc* da solo

i·so·la·tion ward reparto *m* d'isola-mento

ISP [aɪes'piː] *abbr* (= **Internet service provider**) provider *m inv* di servizi Internet

Is·rael ['ɪzreɪl] Israele *m*

Is·rae·li [ɪz'reɪlɪ] **1** *adj* israeliano **2** *n person* israeliano *m*, -a *f*

is·sue ['ɪʃuː] **1** *n* (*matter*) questione *f*; (*result*) risultato *m*; *of magazine* numero *m*; *the point at* ~ il punto in discussione; *take* ~ *with s.o.*/*sth* prendere posizione contro qu/qc **2** *v/t passports, visa* rilasciare; *supplies* distribuire; *coins* emettere; *warning* dare

IT [aɪ'tiː] *abbr* (= **information technology**) IT *f*

it [ɪt] *pron* ◊ *as subject: what colour is* ~? - ~ *is red* di che colore è? – è rosso; ~*'s raining* piove; ~*'s me*/*him* sono io / è lui; ~*'s Charlie here* TELEC sono Charlie; *that's* ~! (*that's right*) proprio così!; (*finished*) finito! ◊ *as object* lo *m*, la *f*; *I broke* ~ l'ho rotto, -a; *I can't eat* ~ *all* non posso mangiarla tutta

I·tal·i·an [ɪ'tæljən] **1** *adj* italiano **2** *n person* italiano *m*, -a *f*; *language* italiano *m*

i·tal·ic [ɪ'tælɪk] *adj* in corsivo

It·a·ly ['ɪtəlɪ] Italia *f*

itch [ɪtʃ] **1** *n* prurito *m* **2** *v/i* prudere

i·tem ['aɪtəm] *on agenda* punto *m* (all'ordine del giorno); *on shopping list* articolo *m*; *in accounts* voce *f*; *news* ~ notizia *f*; ~ *of clothing* capo *m* di vestiario

i·tem·ize ['aɪtəmaɪz] *v/t invoice* dettagliare

i·tin·e·ra·ry [aɪ'tɪnərərɪ] itinerario *m*

its [ɪts] *adj* il suo *m*, la sua *f*, i suoi *mpl*, le sue *fpl*

it's [ɪts] → **it is**; **it has**

it·self [ɪt'self] *pron reflexive* si; *emphatic* di per sé; *by* ~ (*alone*) da solo; (*automatically*) da sé

i·vo·ry ['aɪvərɪ] avorio *m*

i·vy ['aɪvɪ] edera *f*

J

jab [dʒæb] v/t (*pret & pp* **-bed**) conficcare

jab·ber ['dʒæbə(r)] v/i parlare fitto fitto

jack [dʒæk] n MOT cric m *inv; in cards* fante m

♦ jack up v/t MOT sollevare con il cric

jack·et ['dʒækɪt] n giacca f, *of book* copertina f

jack·et po·ta·to patata f al forno con la buccia

'jack-knife 1 n coltello m a serramanico 2 v/i: **the lorry ~d** il rimorchio dell'articolato si è messo di traverso

'jack·pot primo premio m; **hit the ~** vincere il primo premio; *fig* fare un terno al lotto

jade [dʒeɪd] giada f

jad·ed ['dʒeɪdɪd] adj spossato

jag·ged ['dʒægɪd] adj frastagliato

jail [dʒeɪl] n prigione f

jam¹ [dʒæm] *for bread* marmellata f

jam² [dʒæm] 1 n MOT ingorgo m; **be in a ~** F (*difficulty*) essere in difficoltà 2 v/t (*pret & pp* **-med**) (*ram*) ficcare; (*cause to stick*) bloccare; *broadcast* disturbare; **be ~med** *of roads* essere congestionato; *of door, window* essere bloccato 3 v/i (*pret & pp* **-med**) (*stick*) bloccarsi; (*squeeze*) stiparsi

♦ jam on v/t: **jam on the brakes** inchiodare

jam-'packed adj F pieno zeppo

jan·i·tor ['dʒænɪtə(r)] custode m

Jan·u·a·ry ['dʒænjuərɪ] gennaio m

Ja·pan [dʒə'pæn] Giappone m

Jap·a·nese [dʒæpə'niːz] 1 adj giapponese 2 n *person* giapponese m/f; *language* giapponese m

jar¹ [dʒɑː(r)] n *container* barattolo m

jar² [dʒɑː(r)] v/i (*pret & pp* **-red**) *of noise* stridere; **~ on** dar fastidio a

jar·gon ['dʒɑːgən] gergo m

jaun·dice ['dʒɔːndɪs] itterizia f

jaun·diced ['dʒɔːndɪst] adj *fig* cinico

jaunt [dʒɔːnt] gita f

jaun·ty ['dʒɔːntɪ] adj sbarazzino

jav·e·lin ['dʒævlɪn] (*spear*) giavellotto m; *event* lancio m del giavellotto

jaw [dʒɔː] n mascella f

jay·walk·er ['dʒeɪwɔːkə(r)] pedone m indisciplinato

jazz [dʒæz] jazz m inv

♦ jazz up v/t F ravvivare

jeal·ous ['dʒeləs] adj geloso; **be ~ of ...** essere geloso di ...

jeal·ous·ly ['dʒeləslɪ] adv gelosamente

jeal·ous·y ['dʒeləsɪ] gelosia f

jeans [dʒiːnz] npl jeans mpl

jeep [dʒiːp] jeep f inv

jeer [dʒɪə(r)] 1 n scherno m 2 v/i schernire; **~ at** schernire

jel·ly ['dʒelɪ] gelatina f

'jel·ly ba·by bonbon m inv di gelatina; 'jel·ly bean bonbon m inv di gelatina; 'jel·ly·fish medusa f

jeop·ar·dize ['dʒepədaɪz] v/t mettere in pericolo

jeop·ar·dy ['dʒepədɪ]: **be in ~** essere in pericolo

jerk¹ [dʒɜːk] 1 n scossone m 2 v/t dare uno strattone

jerk² [dʒɜːk] F idiota m/f

jerk·y ['dʒɜːkɪ] adj *movement* a scatti

jer·sey ['dʒɜːzɪ] (*sweater*) maglia f; *fabric* jersey m inv

jest [dʒest] 1 n scherzo m; **in ~** per scherzo 2 v/i scherzare

Je·sus ['dʒiːzəs] Gesù m

jet [dʒet] 1 n *of water* zampillo m; (*nozzle*) becco m; *airplane* jet m inv 2 v/i (*pret & pp* **-ted**) *travel* volare

jet-'black adj (nero) corvino; 'jet en·gine motore m a reazione; 'jet-lag jet-lag m inv jet·ti·son ['dʒetɪsn] v/t gettare; fig abbandonare

jet·ty ['dʒetɪ] molo m

Jew [dʒuː] ebreo m, -a f

jew·el ['dʒuːəl] gioiello m; fig: person perla f

jew·el·er Am, jew·el·ler ['dʒuːlə(r)] gioielliere m

jew·el·lery, jew·el·ry Am ['dʒuːlrɪ] gioielli mpl

Jew·ish ['dʒuːɪʃ] adj ebraico; people ebreo

jif·fy ['dʒɪfɪ] F: in a ~ in un batter d'occhio, in un attimo

jig·saw (puzzle) ['dʒɪgsɔː] puzzle m inv

jilt [dʒɪlt] v/t piantare F

jin·gle ['dʒɪŋgl] 1 n song jingle m inv 2 v/i of keys, coins tintinnare

jinx [dʒɪŋks] n person iettatore m, -trice f; (bad luck) there's a ~ on this project questo progetto è iellato

jit·ters ['dʒɪtəz] npl F: get the ~ avere fifa F

jit·ter·y ['dʒɪtərɪ] adj F nervoso

job [dʒɒb] (employment) lavoro m; (task) compito m; out of a ~ senza lavoro; it's a good ~ you ... meno male che tu ...; you'll have a ~ (it'll be difficult) sarà un'impresa

'job cen·tre Br ufficio m di collocamento; 'job de·scrip·tion elenco m delle mansioni; 'job hunt: be ~ing cercare lavoro

job·less ['dʒɒblɪs] adj disoccupato

job sat·is·fac·tion soddisfazione f nel lavoro

jock·ey ['dʒɒkɪ] n fantino m

jog ['dʒɒg] 1 n corsa f; go for a ~ andare a fare footing 2 v/i (pret & pp -ged) as exercise fare footing 3 v/t (pret & pp -ged) elbow etc urtare; ~ s.o.'s memory rinfrescare la memoria a qu

♦ jog along v/i F procedere

jog·ger ['dʒɒgə(r)] person persona f che fa footing; Am shoe scarpa f da ginnastica

jog·ging ['dʒɒgɪŋ] footing m inv; go ~ fare footing

'jog·ging suit tuta f da ginnastica

join [dʒɔɪn] 1 n giuntura f 2 v/i of roads, rivers unirsi; (become a member) iscriversi 3 v/t (connect) unire; person unirsi a; club iscriversi a; (go to work for) entrare in; of road congiungersi a

♦ join in v/i partecipare

♦ join up v/i MIL arruolarsi

join·er ['dʒɔɪnə(r)] n falegname m

joint [dʒɔɪnt] 1 n ANAT articolazione f; in woodwork giunto m; of meat arrosto m; F place locale m; of cannabis spinello m 2 adj (shared) comune

joint ac·count conto m comune

joint 'ven·ture joint venture f inv

joke [dʒəʊk] 1 n story barzelletta f; (practical ~) scherzo m; play a ~ on fare uno scherzo a; it's no ~ non è uno scherzo 2 v/i (pretend) scherzare

jok·er ['dʒəʊkə(r)] in cards jolly m inv; F burlone m, -a f

jok·ing ['dʒəʊkɪŋ]: ~ apart scherzi a parte

jok·ing·ly ['dʒəʊkɪŋlɪ] adv scherzosamente

jol·ly ['dʒɒlɪ] adj allegro; ~ good benissimo

jolt [dʒəʊlt] 1 n (jerk) scossone m 2 v/t (push) urtare

jos·tle ['dʒɒsl] v/t spintonare

♦ jot down [dʒɒt] v/t (pret & pp -ted) annotare

jour·nal ['dʒɜːnl] magazine rivista f; diary diario m

jour·nal·is·m ['dʒɜːnəlɪzm] giornalismo m

jour·nal·ist ['dʒɜːnəlɪst] giornalista m/f

jour·ney ['dʒɜːnɪ] n viaggio m

jo·vi·al ['dʒəʊvɪəl] adj gioviale

joy [dʒɔɪ] gioia f

'joy·stick COMPUT joystick m inv

ju·bi·lant ['dʒuːbɪlənt] adj esultante

ju·bi·la·tion [dʒuːbɪ'leɪʃn] giubilo m

judge [dʒʌdʒ] 1 n giudice m 2 v/t giudicare; competition fare da giudice a 3 v/i giudicare

judg(e)·ment ['dʒʌdʒmənt] n

J

giudizio m; **I agreed, against my better** ~ ho accettato, pur pensando che fosse sbagliato; **an error of** ~ un errore di valutazione

'Judg(e)·ment Day il giorno m del giudizio

ju·di·cial [dʒuː'dɪʃl] adj giudiziario

ju·di·cious [dʒuː'dɪʃəs] adj giudizioso

ju·do ['dʒuːdəʊ] judo m inv

jug [dʒʌg] brocca f

jug·ger·naut ['dʒʌgənɔːt] bisonte m della strada F

jug·gle ['dʒʌgl] v/t fare giochi di destrezza con; fig: conflicting demands destreggiarsi fra; figures manipolare

jug·gler ['dʒʌglə(r)] giocoliere m

juice [dʒuːs] succo m

juic·y ['dʒuːsɪ] adj succoso; news, gossip piccante

juke·box ['dʒuːkbɒks] juke-box m inv

Ju·ly [dʒʊ'laɪ] luglio m

jum·ble ['dʒʌmbl] mucchio m

♦ jumble up v/t mescolare

'jum·ble sale vendita f di beneficenza

jum·bo (jet) ['dʒʌmbəʊ] jumbo m (jet)

'jum·bo-sized adj gigante

jump [dʒʌmp] 1 n salto m; (increase) impennata f; **give a** ~ **of surprise** sobbalzare 2 v/i saltare; (increase) aumentare rapidamente, avere un'impennata; in surprise sobbalzare; **to one's feet** balzare in piedi; ~ **to conclusions** arrivare a conclusioni affrettate 3 v/t fence etc saltare; F (attack) aggredire; ~ **the queue** non rispettare la fila; ~ **the lights** passare col rosso

♦ jump at v/t opportunity prendere al balzo, cogliere al volo

jump·er¹ ['dʒʌmpə(r)] golf m inv

jump·er² ['dʒʌmpə(r)] SP saltatore m, -trice f

jump·y ['dʒʌmpɪ] adj nervoso

junc·tion ['dʒʌŋkʃn] of roads incrocio m

junc·ture ['dʒʌŋktʃə(r)] fml: **at this** ~ in questo frangente

June [dʒuːn] giugno m

jun·gle ['dʒʌŋgl] giungla f

ju·ni·or ['dʒuːnɪə(r)] 1 adj (subordinate) subalterno; (younger) giovane 2 n in rank subalterno m, -a f; **she is ten years my** ~ ha dieci anni meno di me

'ju·ni·or school scuola f elementare

junk [dʒʌŋk] (rubbish) robaccia f

'junk food alimenti mpl poco sani

junk·ie ['dʒʌŋkɪ] n F tossico m, -a f F

'junk mail posta f spazzatura; 'junk shop negozio m di chincaglierie; 'junk·yard deposito m di robivecchi

jur·is·dic·tion [dʒʊərɪs'dɪkʃn] LAW giurisdizione f

ju·ror ['dʒʊərə(r)] n giurato m, -a f

ju·ry ['dʒʊərɪ] n giuria f

just [dʒʌst] 1 adj giusto 2 adv (barely) appena; (exactly) proprio; (only) solo; **I've** ~ **seen her** l'ho appena vista; ~ **about** (almost) quasi; **I was** ~ **about to leave when ...** stavo proprio per andarmene quando ...; **a house** ~ **like that** una casa proprio così; **he left her** ~ **like that** l'ha lasciata così, senza spiegazioni; **he agreed** ~ **like that** ha accettato così, senza pensarci due volte; ~ **now** (a few moments ago) proprio ora; (at the moment) al momento; ~ **you wait!** aspetta un po'!; ~ **be quiet!** fai silenzio!; ~ **as rich** altrettanto ricco

jus·tice ['dʒʌstɪs] giustizia f

jus·ti·fi·a·ble [dʒʌstɪ'faɪəbl] adj giustificabile

jus·ti·fi·a·bly [dʒʌstɪ'faɪəblɪ] adv a ragione

jus·ti·fi·ca·tion [dʒʌstɪfɪ'keɪʃn] giustificazione f

jus·ti·fy ['dʒʌstɪfaɪ] v/t (pret & pp -ied) also text giustificare

just·ly ['dʒʌstlɪ] adv giustamente

♦ jut out [dʒʌt] v/i (pret & pp -ted) sporgere

ju·ve·nile ['dʒuːvənaɪl] 1 adj minorile; pej puerile 2 n fml minore m/f

ju·ve·nile de'lin·quen·cy delinquenza *f* minorile

ju·ve·nile de'lin·quent delinquente *m/f* minorile

K

k [keɪ] *abbr* (= *kilobyte*) k (=kilobyte *m inv*); (= *thousand*) mille; *earn 25K* guadagnare 25 mila sterline

kan·ga·roo [kæŋgə'ruː] canguro *m*

ka·ra·te [kə'rɑːtɪ] karate *m inv*

ka'ra·te chop colpo *m* di karate

ke·bab [kɪ'bæb] spiedino *m* di carne

keel [kiːl] NAUT chiglia *f*

♦**keel over** *v/i of boat* capovolgersi; *of structure* crollare; *of person* cascare per terra; *faint* svenire

keen [kiːn] *adj person* entusiasta; *interest, competition* vivo; *be ~ on sth* essere appassionato di qc; *I'm not ~ on the idea* l'idea non mi va tanto; *he's ~ on her* lei gli piace molto; *be ~ to do sth* aver molta voglia di fare qc

keep [kiːp] **1** *n* (*maintenance*) vitto e alloggio *m*; *for ~s* F per sempre **2** *v/t* (*pret & pp kept*) tenere; (*not lose*) mantenere; (*detain*) trattenere; *family* mantenere; *animals* allevare; *~ a promise* mantenere una promessa; *~ s.o. company* tenere compagnia a qu; *~ s.o. waiting* far aspettare qu; *~ sth to o.s.* (*not tell*) tenere qc per sé; *~ sth from s.o.* nascondere qc a qu; *~ s.o. from doing sth* impedire a qu di fare qc; *~ trying!* continua a provare!; *don't ~ interrupting!* non interrompere in continuazione! **3** *v/i* (*pret & pp kept*) (*remain*) rimanere; *of food, milk* conservarsi; *~ left* tenere la sinistra; *~ straight on* vai sempre dritto; *~ still* stare fermo

♦**keep away 1** *v/i* stare alla larga; *keep away from ...* stai alla larga da ... **2** *v/t* tenere lontano; *keep s.o.*

away from sth tenere qu lontano da qc

♦**keep back** *v/t* (*hold in check*) trattenere; *information* nascondere

♦**keep down** *v/t voice* abbassare; *costs, inflation etc* contenere; *food* trattenere; *keep the noise down, will you?* fate meno rumore!

♦**keep in** *v/t in hospital* trattenere; *keep a pupil in* punire uno studente trattenendolo oltre l'orario scolastico

♦**keep off 1** *v/t* (*avoid*) evitare; *keep off the grass* non calpestare l'erba **2** *v/i*: *if the rain keeps off* se non piove

♦**keep on 1** *v/i* continuare; *keep on doing sth* continuare a fare qc **2** *v/t employee, coat* tenere

♦**keep on at** *v/t* (*nag*) assillare

♦**keep out 1** *v/t the cold* proteggere da; *person* escludere **2** *v/i of room* non entrare (*of* in); *of argument etc* non immischiarsi (*of* in); *keep out as sign* vietato l'ingresso; *you keep out of this!* non immischiarti!

♦**keep to** *v/t path, rules* seguire; *keep to the point* non divagare

♦**keep up 1** *v/i when walking, running etc* tener dietro **2** *v/t pace, payments* stare dietro a; *bridge, pants* reggere

♦**keep up with** *v/t* stare al passo con; (*stay in touch with*) mantenere i rapporti con

keep·ing ['kiːpɪŋ]: *be in ~ with* essere in armonia con

'**keep·sake** ricordo *m*

keg [keg] barilotto *m*

ken·nel ['kenl] canile *m*

ken·nels ['kenlz] *npl* canile *m*

kept [kept] *pret & pp* → **keep**

kerb [kɜ:b] orlo *m* del marciapiede

ker·nel ['kɜ:nl] nocciolo *m*

ketch·up ['ketʃʌp] ketchup *m inv*

ket·tle ['ketl] bollitore *m*

key [ki:] **1** *n to door, drawer,* MUS chiave *f; on keyboard* tasto *m* **2** *adj (vital)* chiave **3** *v/t* COMPUT battere
♦ **key in** *v/t data* immettere

'**key·board** COMPUT, MUS tastiera *f;* '**key·board·er** COMPUT, MUS tastierista *m/f;* '**key·card** tessera *f* magnetica

keyed-up [ki:d'ʌp] *adj* agitato

'**key·hole** buco *m* della serratura; '**key·note** '**speech** discorso *m* programmatico; '**key·ring** portachiavi *m inv*

kha·ki ['kɑ:kɪ] *adj colour* cachi *inv*

kick [kɪk] **1** *n* calcio *m;* F *(thrill)* gusto *m; (just) for* ~**s** F (solo) per il gusto di farlo **2** *v/t* dare un calcio a; F *habit* liberarsi da **3** *v/i* dare calci; SP calciare; *of horse* scalciare
♦ **kick around** *v/t (treat harshly)* maltrattare; F *(discuss)* discutere di; *kick a ball around* giocare a pallone
♦ **kick in** *v/i* P *(start to operate)* entrare in funzione
♦ **kick off** *v/i* F *(start)* iniziare; *of player* dare il calcio d'inizio
♦ **kick out** *v/t* buttar fuori; *be kicked out of the company/army* essere buttato fuori dalla ditta/dall'esercito
♦ **kick up** *v/t: kick up a fuss* fare una scenata

'**kick·back** F *(bribe)* tangente *f*

'**kick·off** SP calcio *m* d'inizio

kid [kɪd] **1** *n* F *(child)* bambino *m*, -a *f;* F *(young person)* ragazzo *m*, -a *f;* ~ *brother/sister* fratello/sorella minore **2** *v/t (pret & pp -ded)* F prendere in giro **3** *v/i (pret & pp -ded)* F scherzare; *I was only ~ding* stavo solo scherzando

kid·der ['kɪdə(r)] F burlone *m*, -a *f*

kid '**gloves**: *handle s.o. with* ~ trattare qu coi guanti

kid·nap ['kɪdnæp] *v/t (pret & pp -ped)* rapire, sequestrare

kid·nap·per ['kɪdnæpə(r)] rapitore *m,*-trice *f*, sequestratore *m,* -trice *f*

'**kid·nap·ping** ['kɪdnæpɪŋ] rapimento *m*, sequestro *m* (di persona)

'**kid·ney** ['kɪdnɪ] ANAT rene *m; in cooking* rognone *m*

'**kid·ney bean** fagiolo *m* comune

'**kid·ney ma·chine** MED rene *m* artificiale

kill [kɪl] *v/t* uccidere; *plant, time* ammazzare; *be* ~**ed** *in an accident* morire in un incidente; ~ *o.s.* suicidarsi; ~ *o.s. laughing* F morire dalle risate

kil·ler ['kɪlə(r)] *(murderer)* assassino *m*, -a *f; (hired* ~*)* killer *m/f inv;* *flu can be a* ~ si può morire d'influenza

kil·ling ['kɪlɪŋ] omicidio *m;* *make a* ~ F *(lots of money)* fare un pacco di soldi F

kil·ling·ly ['kɪlɪŋlɪ] *adv* F: ~ *funny* divertentissimo

kiln [kɪln] fornace *f*

ki·lo ['ki:ləʊ] chilo *m*

ki·lo·byte ['kɪləʊbaɪt] COMPUT kilobyte *m inv*

ki·lo·gram ['kɪləʊgræm] chilogrammo *m*

ki·lo·me·ter *Am*, **ki·lo·me·tre** [kɪ'lɒmɪtə(r)] chilometro *m*

kilt [kɪlt] kilt *m inv*

kind[1] [kaɪnd] *adj* gentile

kind[2] [kaɪnd] *n (sort)* tipo *m; (make, brand)* marca *f; all* ~**s** *of people* gente di tutti i tipi; *nothing of the* ~*!* niente affatto!; ~ *of sad/strange* F un po' triste/strano

kin·der·gar·ten ['kɪndəgɑ:tn] asilo *m*

kind-heart·ed [kaɪnd'hɑ:tɪd] *adj* di buon cuore

kind·ly ['kaɪndlɪ] **1** *adj* gentile **2** *adv* gentilmente; *(please)* per cortesia

kind·ness ['kaɪndnɪs] *n* gentilezza *f*

king [kɪŋ] re *m inv*

king·dom ['kɪŋdəm] regno *m*

'**king-size(d)** *adj bed* matrimoniale grande; *cigarettes* lungo kink [kɪŋk] *in hose etc* attorcigliamento *m*

kink·y ['kɪŋkɪ] *adj* F particolare F

kiosk ['kiːɒsk] edicola *f*

kip [kɪp] P pisolino *m*

kip·per ['kɪpə(r)] aringa *f* affumicata

kiss [kɪs] **1** *n* bacio *m* **2** *v/t* baciare **3** *v/i* baciarsi

kiss of 'life respirazione *f* bocca a bocca

kit [kɪt] *kit m inv*; (*equipment*) attrezzatura *f*; *for assembly* kit *m inv* da montaggio

kitch·en ['kɪtʃɪn] cucina *f*

kitch·en·ette [kɪtʃɪ'net] cucinino *m*

kitch·en 'sink: **she packs every·thing but the ~** F si porta dietro tutta la casa

kite [kaɪt] aquilone *m*

kit·ten ['kɪtn] gattino *m*

kit·ty ['kɪtɪ] *money* cassa *f* comune

knack [næk] capacità *f inv*; **there's a ~ to it** bisogna saperlo fare

knead [niːd] *v/t dough* lavorare

knee [niː] *n* ginocchio *m*

'knee-cap *n* rotula *f*

kneel [niːl] *v/i* (*pret & pp* **knelt**) inginocchiarsi

'knee-length *adj* al ginocchio

knelt [nelt] *pret & pp* → **kneel**

knew [njuː] *pret* → **know**

knick·ers ['nɪkəz] *npl* mutandine *fpl*; **get one's ~ in a twist** P agitarsi

knick-knacks ['nɪknæks] *npl* F ninnoli *mpl*

knife [naɪf] **1** *n* (*pl* **knives** [naɪvz]) coltello *m* **2** *v/t* accoltellare

knight [naɪt] *n* cavaliere *m*

knit [nɪt] (*pret & pp* **-ted**) **1** *v/t* fare a maglia **2** *v/i* lavorare a maglia

♦ knit together *v/i of broken bone* saldarsi

knit·ting ['nɪtɪŋ] *sth being knitted* lavoro *m* a maglia; *activity* il lavorare *m* a maglia

'knit·ting nee·dle ferro *m* (da calza)

'knit·wear maglieria *f*

knob [nɒb] *on door* pomello *m*; *of butter* noce *f*

knock [nɒk] **1** *n on door* colpo *m*;

(*blow*) botta *f* **2** *v/t* (*hit*) colpire; *head, knee* battere; F (*criticize*) criticare **3** *v/i at the door* bussare (*at* a); **I ~ed my head** ho battuto la testa

♦ knock around **1** *v/t* (*beat*) picchiare **2** *v/i* F (*travel*) vagabondare

♦ knock down *v/t of car* investire; *object, building etc* buttar giù; F (*reduce the price of*) scontare

♦ knock off **1** *v/t* P (*steal*) fregare P **2** *v/i* F (*stop work for the day*) smontare F

♦ knock out *v/t* (*make unconscious*) mettere K.O. F; *power lines etc* mettere fuori uso; (*eliminate*) eliminare

♦ knock over *v/t* far cadere; *of car* investire

'knock·down *adj*: **a ~ price** un prezzo stracciato

knock·er ['nɒkə(r)] *on door* battente *m*

knock-kneed [nɒk'niːd] *adj* con le gambe storte

'knock·out *in boxing* K.O. *m inv*

knot [nɒt] **1** *n* nodo *m* **2** *v/t* (*pret & pp* **-ted**) annodare

'knot·ty ['nɒtɪ] *problem* spinoso

know [nəʊ] **1** *v/t* (*pret* **knew**, *pp* **known**) sapere; *person, place* conoscere; (*recognize*) riconoscere; **~ how to waltz** saper ballare il valzer **2** *v/i* (*pret* **knew**, *pp* **known**) sapere; **I don't ~** non so; **yes, I ~** sì, lo so **3** *n*: **be in the ~** F essere beninformato

'know-all F sapientone *m*, -a *f*

'know-how F know-how *m inv*

know·ing ['nəʊɪŋ] *adj* d'intesa

know·ing·ly ['nəʊɪŋlɪ] *adv* (*wittingly*) deliberatamente; *smile etc* con aria d'intesa

knowl·edge ['nɒlɪdʒ] conoscenza *f*; **to the best of my ~** per quanto ne sappia; **have a good ~ of ...** avere una buona conoscenza di ...

knowl·edge·a·ble ['nɒlɪdʒəbl] *adj* ferrato

known [nəʊn] *pp* → **know**

knuck·le ['nʌkl] nocca *f*

♦ knuckle down *v/i* F impegnarsi

♦ knuckle under *v/i* F cedere

KO [keɪ'əʊ] (*knockout*) K.O. *m inv*

K

Ko·ran [kə'rɑːn] Corano *m*
Ko·re·a [kə'riːə] Corea *f*
Ko·re·an [kə'riːən] **1** *adj* coreano **2** *n* coreano *m*, -a *f*; *language* coreano *m*

ko·sher ['kəʊʃə(r)] *adj* REL kasher; F a posto
kow·tow ['kaʊtaʊ] *v/i* F prostrarsi
ku·dos ['kjuːdɒs] gloria *f*

L

lab [læb] laboratorio *m*
la·bel ['leɪbl] **1** *n* etichetta *f* **2** *v/t baggage* mettere l'etichetta su
la·bor·a·to·ry [lə'bɒrətrɪ] laboratorio *m*
la·bor·a·to·ry tech·ni·cian tecnico *m* di laboratorio
la·bor *etc Am* → **labour** *etc*
la·bo·ri·ous [lə'bɔːrɪəs] *adj* laborioso
'la·bor u·ni·on *Am* sindacato *m*
la·bour ['leɪbə(r)] *n* (*work*) lavoro *m*; *in pregnancy* travaglio *m*; **be in ~** avere le doglie *fpl*
la·boured ['leɪbəd] *adj style, speech* pesante
la·bour·er ['leɪbərə(r)] manovale *m*
'La·bour Par·ty partito *m* laburista
'la·bour ward MED sala *f* travaglio
lace [leɪs] *n material* pizzo *m*; *for shoe* laccio *m*
◆ **lace up** *v/t shoes* allacciare
lack [læk] **1** *n* mancanza *f* **2** *v/t* mancare di **3** *v/i*: **be ~ing** mancare
lac·quer ['lækə(r)] *n for hair* lacca *f*
lad [læd] ragazzo *m*
lad·der ['lædə(r)] scala *f* (a pioli); *Br: in tights* sfilatura *f*
'lad·der-proof *adj Br* indemagliabile
la·den ['leɪdn] *adj* carico
la·dies (room) ['leɪdiːz] bagno *m* per donne
la·dle ['leɪdl] *n* mestolo *m*
la·dy ['leɪdɪ] signora *f*
'la·dy·bird coccinella *f*
'la·dy·like da signora; **she's not very ~** non è certo una signora
lag [læg] *v/t* (*pret & pp* **-ged**) *pipes* isolare

◆ **lag behind** *v/i* essere indietro
la·ger ['lɑːgə(r)] birra *f* (bionda)
la·goon [lə'guːn] laguna *f*
laid [leɪd] *pret & pp* → **lay**
laid-back [leɪd'bæk] *adj* rilassato
lain [leɪn] *pp* → **lie**
lake [leɪk] lago *m*
lamb [læm] *animal, meat* agnello *m*
lame [leɪm] *adj person* zoppo; *excuse* zoppicante
la·ment [lə'ment] **1** *n* lamento *m* **2** *v/t* piangere
lam·en·ta·ble ['læməntəbl] *adj* deplorevole
lam·i·nat·ed ['læmɪneɪtɪd] *adj surface* laminato; *paper* plastificato
lam·i·nat·ed 'glass vetro *m* laminato
lamp [læmp] lampada *f*
'lamp·post lampione *m*
'lamp·shade paralume *m*
land [lænd] **1** *n* terreno *m* (*shore*) terra *f* (*country*) paese *m*; **by ~** per via di terra; **on ~** sulla terraferma; **work on the ~** *as farmer* lavorare la terra **2** *v/t aeroplane* far atterrare; *job* accaparrarsi **3** *v/i of aeroplane* atterrare; *of ball, sth thrown* cadere, finire
land·ing ['lændɪŋ] *n of aeroplane* atterraggio *m*; *top of staircase* pianerottolo *m*
'land·ing field terreno *m* d'atterraggio; **'land·ing gear** carrello *m* d'atterraggio; **'land·ing strip** pista *f* d'atterraggio
'land·la·dy *of bar* proprietaria *f*; *of rented room* padrona *f* di casa;
'land·lord *of bar* proprietario *m*; *of*

rented room padrone *m* di casa;
'**land·mark** punto *m* di riferimento;
fig pietra *f* miliare; '**land own·er**
proprietario *m*, -a *f* terriero, -a;
land·scape ['lændskeɪp] **1** *n* paesaggio *m* **2** *adv print* landscape, orizzontale
'**land·slide** frana *f*
land·slide 'vic·to·ry vittoria *f*
schiacciante
lane [leɪn] *in country* viottolo *m*;
(*alley*) vicolo *m*; MOT corsia *f*
lan·guage ['læŋgwɪdʒ] lingua *f*;
(*speech, style*) linguaggio *m*
'**lan·guage lab** laboratorio *m* linguistico
lank [læŋk] *adj pej: hair* diritto
lank·y ['læŋkɪ] *adj person* allampanato
lan·tern ['læntən] lanterna *f*
lap¹ [læp] *n of track* giro *m* (di pista)
lap² [læp] *n of water* sciabordio *m*
♦ **lap up** *v/t* (*pret & pp* **-ped**) *drink,
milk* leccare; *flattery* compiacersi di
lap³ [læp] *n of person* grembo *m*
la·pel [la'pel] bavero *m*
lapse [læps] **1** *n* (*mistake, slip*) mancanza *f*; *of time* intervallo *m*; **~ of
memory** vuoto *m* di memoria; **~ of
taste** caduta *f* di tono **2** *v/i* scadere;
~ into cadere in
'**lap·top** COMPUT laptop *m inv*
lar·ce·ny ['lɑːsənɪ] furto *m*
lard [lɑːd] lardo *m*
'**lar·der** ['lɑːdə(r)] dispensa *f*
large [lɑːdʒ] *adj* grande; **at ~** in libertà
large·ly ['lɑːdʒlɪ] *adv* (*mainly*) in
gran parte
lark [lɑːk] *bird* allodola *f*
lar·va ['lɑːvə] larva *f*
lar·yn·gi·tis [lærɪn'dʒaɪtɪs] laringite *f*
lar·ynx ['lærɪŋks] laringe *f*
la·ser ['leɪzə(r)] laser *m inv*
'**la·ser beam** raggio *m* laser
'**la·ser print·er** stampante *f* laser
lash¹ [læʃ] *v/t with whip* frustare
lash² [læʃ] *n* (*eyelash*) ciglio *m*
♦ **lash down** *v/t with rope* assicurare
♦ **lash out** *v/i with fists, words* menare
colpi

lass [læs] ragazza *f*
last¹ [lɑːst] **1** *adj in series* ultimo;
(*preceding*) precedente; **~ but one**
penultimo; **~ night** ieri sera; **~ year**
l'anno scorso **2** *adv* **he finished ~**
ha finito per ultimo; *in race* è arrivato ultimo; **when I ~ saw him** l'ultima volta che l'ho visto; **~ but not
least** per finire; **at ~** finalmente
last² [lɑːst] *v/i* durare
last·ing ['lɑːstɪŋ] *adj* duraturo
last·ly ['lɑːstlɪ] *adv* per finire
latch [lætʃ] chiavistello *m*
late [leɪt] **1** *adj* (*behind time*) in ritardo; *in day* tardi; **it's getting ~** si sta
facendo tardi; **of ~** recentemente; **
the ~ 19th century** il tardo XIX secolo **2** *adv* tardi
late·ly ['leɪtlɪ] *adv* recentemente
lat·er ['leɪtə(r)] *adv* più tardi; **see
you ~!** a più tardi; **~ on** più tardi
lat·est ['leɪtɪst] **1** *adj* ultimo, più recente **2** *n*: **at the ~** al più tardi
lathe [leɪð] *n* tornio *m*
la·ther ['lɑːðə(r)] *from soap* schiuma
f; **the horse is in a ~** il cavallo è sudato
Lat·in ['lætɪn] **1** *adj* latino **2** *n* latino
m
Lat·in A'mer·i·ca America *f* Latina
Lat·in A'mer·i·can 1 *n* latino-americano *m*, -a *f* **2** *adj* latino-americano
lat·i·tude ['lætɪtjuːd] *geographical* latitudine *f*; (*freedom to act*) libertà *f
inv* d'azione
lat·ter ['lætə(r)] *adj*: **the ~** quest'ultimo
laugh [lɑːf] **1** *n* risata *f*; **it was a ~** F ci
siamo divertiti **2** *v/i* ridere
♦ **laugh at** *v/t* ridere di
'**laugh·ing stock** zimbello *m*; **become a ~** rendersi ridicolo
laugh·ter ['lɑːftə(r)] risata *f*; **sounds
of ~** delle risate
launch [lɔːntʃ] **1** *n boat* lancia *f*; *of
rocket, product* lancio *m*; *of ship* varo
m **2** *v/t rocket, product* lanciare; *ship*
varare
'**launch cer·e·mo·ny** cerimonia *f* di
lancio
launch·(ing) pad rampa *f* di lancio

L

laun·der ['lɔːndə(r)] v/t clothes lavare e stirare; ~ *money* riciclare denaro sporco

laun·derette [lɔːn'dret] lavanderia f automatica

laun·dry ['lɔːndrɪ] place lavanderia f; clothes bucato m

lau·rel ['lɒrəl] alloro m

lav·a·to·ry ['lævətrɪ] gabinetto m

lav·en·der ['lævəndə(r)] lavanda f

lav·ish ['lævɪʃ] adj meal lauto; reception, lifestyle sontuoso

law [lɔː] legge f; *criminal / civil ~* diritto m penale / civile; *against the ~* contro la legge; *forbidden by ~* vietato dalla legge

law-a·bid·ing ['lɔːəbaɪdɪŋ] adj che rispetta la legge

law court tribunale m

law·ful ['lɔːfʊl] adj legale

law·less ['lɔːlɪs] adj senza legge

lawn [lɔːn] prato m all'inglese; *play on the ~* giocare sul prato

lawn mow·er tagliaerba m inv

law·suit azione f legale

law·yer ['lɔːjə(r)] avvocato m

lax [læks] adj permissivo

lax·a·tive ['læksətɪv] n lassativo m

lay¹ [leɪ] pret → lie

lay² [leɪ] v/t (pret & pp laid) (put down) posare; eggs deporre; V (sexually) scopare V

♦ **lay into** v/t (attack) aggredire

♦ **lay off** v/t workers licenziare; temporarily mettere in cassa integrazione

♦ **lay on** v/t (provide) offrire

♦ **lay out** v/t objects disporre; page impaginare

lay·a·bout F scansafatiche m/f inv

lay-by on road piazzola f di sosta

lay·er ['leɪə(r)] strato m

lay·man laico m

lay-off licenziamento m; *there have been 50 ~s temporary* 50 operai sono stati messi in cassa integrazione

♦ **laze around** [leɪz] v/i oziare

la·zy ['leɪzɪ] adj person pigro; day passato a oziare

lb abbr (= *pound*) libbra f

LCD [elsiː'diː] abbr (= *liquid crystal display*) display m inv a cristalli liquidi

lead¹ [liːd] **1** v/t (pret & pp led) procession, race essere in testa a; company, team essere a capo di; (guide, take) condurre **2** v/i (pret & pp led) in race, competition essere in testa; (provide leadership) dirigere; *a street ~ing off the square* una strada che parte dalla piazza; *a street ~ing into the square* una strada che sbocca sulla piazza; *where is this ~ing?* dove vuoi andare a parare? **3** n in race posizione f di testa; *be in the ~* essere in testa; *take the ~* passare in testa

♦ **lead on** v/i (go in front) guidare

♦ **lead up to** v/t preludere

lead² [liːd] for dog guinzaglio m

lead³ [led] substance piombo m

lead·ed ['ledɪd] adj petrol con piombo

lead·er ['liːdə(r)] person capo m; in race, on market leader m/f inv; in newspaper editoriale m

lead·er·ship ['liːdəʃɪp] of party etc direzione f, leadership f inv; *under his ~* sotto la sua direzione; *~ skills* capacità f di comando; *~ contest* lotta f per la direzione

lead-free ['ledfriː] adj petrol senza piombo

lead·ing ['liːdɪŋ] adj runner in testa; company, product leader inv

lead·ing-edge adj company, technology all'avanguardia

leaf [liːf] (pl leaves [liːvz]) foglia f

♦ **leaf through** v/t sfogliare

leaf·let ['liːflət] dépliant m inv

league [liːg] lega f; SP campionato m

leak [liːk] **1** n of water perdita f; of gas fuga f; *there's been a ~ of information* c'è stata una fuga di notizie **2** v/i of pipe perdere; of boat fare acqua

♦ **leak out** v/i of air, gas fuoriuscire; of news trapelare

leak·y ['liːkɪ] adj pipe che perde; boat che fa acqua

lean¹ [liːn] **1** v/i be at an angle pendere; ~ *against sth* appoggiarsi a qc

2 v/t appoggiare; **~ sth against sth** appoggiare qc a qc

lean² [li:n] adj meat magro; style, prose asciutto

leap [li:p] **1** n salto m; **a great ~ forward** un grande balzo in avanti **2** v/i saltare

leap year anno m bisestile

learn [lɜːn] **1** v/t imparare; (hear) apprendere; **~ how to do sth** imparare a fare qc **2** v/i imparare

learn·er ['lɜːnə(r)] principiante m/f

learn·er driv·er principiante m/f (alla guida)

learn·ing ['lɜːnɪŋ] n (knowledge) sapere m; (act) apprendimento m

learn·ing curve processo m di apprendimento; **be constantly on the ~** non finire mai di imparare

lease [liːs] **1** n (contratto m di) affitto m **2** v/t flat, equipment affittare

♦ lease out v/t flat, equipment dare in affitto

lease 'pur·chase acquisto m in leasing

leash [liːʃ] for dog guinzaglio m

least [liːst] **1** adj (slightest) minimo; **I've the ~ debt** io ho il debito minore **2** adv meno **3** n minimo m; **not in the ~ suprised / disappointed** per niente sorpreso / deluso; **at ~** almeno

leath·er ['leðə(r)] **1** n pelle f, cuoio m **2** adj di pelle, di cuoio

leave [liːv] **1** n (holiday) congedo m; MIL licenza f; **on ~** in congedo, in licenza **2** v/t (pret & pp **left**) lasciare; room, house, office uscire da; station, airport partire da; (forget) dimenticare; **~ school** finire gli studi; **let's ~ things as they are** lasciamo le cose come stanno; **how did you ~ things with him?** come sei rimasto d'accordo con lui?; **~ s.o. / sth alone** lasciare stare qu / qc; **be left** rimanere; **there is nothing left** non è rimasto niente **3** v/i (pret & pp **left**) of person, plane, bus partire; **he's just left** è appena uscito

♦ leave behind v/t intentionally lasciare; (forget) dimenticare

♦ leave on v/t hat, coat non togliersi; TV, computer lasciare acceso

♦ leave out v/t word, figure omettere; (not put away) lasciare in giro; **leave me out of this** non mi immischiare in questa faccenda

leav·ing par·ty festa f d'addio

lec·ture ['lektʃə(r)] **1** n lezione f **2** v/i at university insegnare

lec·ture hall aula f magna

lec·tur·er ['lektʃərə(r)] professore m, -essa universitario, -a

LED [eliː'diː] abbr (= **light-emitting diode**) LED m inv

led [led] pret & pp → **lead¹**

ledge [ledʒ] of window davanzale m; on rock face sporgenza f

ledg·er ['ledʒə(r)] COM libro m mastro

leek [liːk] porro m

leer [lɪə(r)] n sexual sguardo m libidinoso; evil sguardo m malvagio

left¹ [left] **1** adj sinistro; POL di sinistra **2** n sinistra f; **on the ~** a sinistra; **on the ~ of sth** a sinistra di qc; **to the ~ turn**, look a sinistra **3** adv turn, look a sinistra

left² [left] pret & pp → **leave**

left-hand adj sinistro; left-hand 'drive guida f a sinistra; left-'handed adj mancino; left 'lug·gage (office) deposito m bagagli; 'left-overs npl food avanzi mpl; 'left-wing adj POL di sinistra

leg [leg] of person gamba f; of animal zampa f; of turkey, chicken coscia f; of lamb cosciotto m; of journey tappa f; of competition girone m; **pull s.o.'s ~** prendere in giro qu

leg·a·cy ['legəsɪ] eredità f inv

le·gal ['liːgl] adj legale

le·gal ad'vis·er consulente m/f legale

le·gal·i·ty [lɪ'gælətɪ] legalità f inv

le·gal·ize ['liːgəlaɪz] v/t legalizzare

le·gend ['ledʒənd] leggenda f

le·gen·da·ry ['ledʒəndrɪ] adj leggendario

le·gi·ble ['ledʒəbl] adj leggibile

le·gis·late ['ledʒɪsleɪt] v/i legiferare

le·gis·la·tion [ledʒɪs'leɪʃn] legislazione *f*

le·gis·la·tive ['ledʒɪslətɪv] *adj* legislativo

le·gis·la·ture ['ledʒɪsləʃə(r)] POL legislatura *f*

le·git·i·mate [lɪ'dʒɪtɪmət] *adj* legittimo

'leg room spazio *m* per le gambe

lei·sure ['leʒə(r)] svago *m*; **at your ~** con comodo

'lei·sure cen·ter *Am*, **'lei·sure cen·tre** centro *m* sportivo e ricreativo

lei·sure·ly ['leʒəlɪ] *adj pace, lifestyle* tranquillo

'lei·sure time tempo *m* libero

le·mon ['lemən] limone *m*

le·mon·ade [lemə'neɪd] *fizzy* gazzosa *f*; *made from lemon juice* limonata *f*

'le·mon juice succo *m* di limone

'le·mon tea tè *m* inv al limone

lend [lend] *v/t* (*pret & pp* **lent**) prestare; **~ s.o. sth** prestare qc a qu

length [leŋθ] lunghezza *f*; *piece: of material* taglio *m*; **at ~** *describe, explain* a lungo; (*eventually*) alla fine

length·en ['leŋθən] *v/t* allungare

length·y ['leŋθɪ] *adj speech, stay* lungo

le·ni·ent ['liːnɪənt] *adj* indulgente

lens [lenz] *of camera* obiettivo *m*; *of spectacles* lente *f*; *of eye* cristallino *m*

'lens cov·er *of camera* copriobiettivo *m*

Lent [lent] REL Quaresima *f*

lent [lent] *pret & pp* → **lend**

len·til ['lentl] lenticchia *f*

len·til 'soup minestra *f* di lenticchie

Leo ['liːəʊ] ASTR Leone *m*

leop·ard ['lepəd] leopardo *m*

le·o·tard ['liːətɑːd] body *m* inv

les·bi·an ['lezbɪən] **1** *n* lesbica *f* **2** *adj* di/per lesbiche

less [les] *adv* (di) meno; *eat/talk* ~ parlare/mangiare (di) meno; **~ interesting/serious** meno interessante/serio; **it costs ~** costa (di) meno; **~ than £200** meno di £200

less·en ['lesn] *v/t & v/i* diminuire

les·son ['lesn] lezione *f*

let [let] *v/t* (*pret & pp* **let**) (*allow*) lasciare; (*rent*) affittare; **~ s.o. do sth** lasciar fare qc a qu; **~ me go!** lasciami andare!; **~ him come in!** fallo entrare!; **~'s go/stay** andiamo/restiamo; **~'s not argue** non litighiamo; **~ alone** tanto meno; **~ go of sth** *of rope, handle* mollare qc

◆ **let down** *v/t hair* sciogliersi; *blinds* abbassare; (*disappoint*) deludere; *dress, trousers* allungare

◆ **let in** *v/t to house* far entrare

◆ **let off** *v/t not punish* perdonare; *from car* far scendere

◆ **let out** *v/t of room, building* far uscire; *jacket etc* allargare; *groan, yell* emettere

◆ **let up** *v/i* (*stop*) smettere

le·thal ['liːθl] mortale

leth·ar·gic [lɪ'θɑːdʒɪk] *adj* fiacco

leth·ar·gy ['leθədʒɪ] fiacchezza *f*

let·ter ['letə(r)] lettera *f*

'let·ter·box *on street* buca *f* delle lettere; *in door* cassetta *f* della posta; **'let·ter·head** *heading* intestazione *f*; (*headed paper*) carta *f* intestata; **let·ter of 'cred·it** COM lettera *f* di credito

let·tuce ['letɪs] lattuga *f*

'let·up: without a ~ senza sosta

leu·ke·mia [luː'kiːmɪə] leucemia *f*

lev·el ['levl] **1** *adj field, surface* piano; *in competition, scores* pari; **draw ~ with s.o.** *in match* pareggiare; **he drew ~ with the leading car** ha raggiunto l'auto in testa **2** *n* livello *m*; **on the ~** F (*honest*) onesto

lev·el 'cross·ing *Br* passaggio *m* a livello

lev·el-head·ed [levl'hedɪd] *adj* posato

le·ver ['liːvə(r)] **1** *n* leva *f* **2** *v/t*: **~ up/off** sollevare/togliere qc con una leva; **~ sth open** aprire qc facendo leva

lev·er·age ['liːvrɪdʒ] forza *f*; (*influence*) influenza *f*

lev·y ['levɪ] *v/t* (*pret & pp* **-ied**) *taxes* imporre

lewd [luːd] *adj* osceno

li·a·bil·i·ty [laɪə'bɪlətɪ] (*responsibility*) responsabilità *f inv*; F *person* peso *m* morto; F *thing* peso *m*

li·a·ble ['laɪəbl] *adj* (*answerable*) responsabile; *it's ~ to break* (*likely*) è probabile che si rompa

♦ liaise with [lɪ'eɪz] *v/t* tenere i contatti con

li·ai·son [lɪ'eɪzɒn] (*contacts*) contatti *mpl*

li·ar ['laɪə(r)] bugiardo *m*, -a *f*

li·bel ['laɪbl] **1** *n* diffamazione *f* **2** *v/t* diffamare

lib·e·ral ['lɪbrəl] *adj* (*broad-minded*), POL liberale; *portion etc* abbondante

lib·e·rate ['lɪbəreɪt] *v/t* liberare

lib·e·rat·ed ['lɪbəreɪtɪd] *adj woman* emancipato

lib·e·ra·tion [lɪbə'reɪʃn] liberazione *f*

lib·er·ty ['lɪbətɪ] libertà *f inv*; *at ~ of prisoner etc* in libertà; *be at ~ to do sth* poter fare qc

Li·bra ['liːbrə] ASTR Bilancia *f*

li·brar·i·an [laɪ'breərɪən] bibliotecario *m*, -a *f*

li·bra·ry ['laɪbrərɪ] biblioteca *f*

Lib·y·a ['lɪbɪə] Libia *f*

Lib·y·an ['lɪbɪən] **1** *adj* libico **2** *n person* libico *m*, -a *f*

lice [laɪs] *pl* → **louse**

li·cence ['laɪsns] (*driving ~*) patente *f*; (*road tax ~*) bollo *m* (auto); *for TV* canone *m* (televisivo); *for gun* porto *m* d'armi; *for imports / exports* licenza *f*; *for dog* tassa *f*

li·cense ['laɪsns] **1** *v/t issue ~* rilasciare la licenza a; *be ~d to sell alcohol* essere autorizzato alla vendita di alcolici; *the car isn't ~d* la macchina non ha il bollo **2** *n Am* → **licence**

'li·cense plate *Am* targa *f*

lick [lɪk] **1** *n* leccata *f*; *a ~ of paint* una passata di vernice **2** *v/t* leccare; *~ one's lips* leccarsi i baffi

lick·ing ['lɪkɪŋ] F (*defeat*): *get a ~* prendere una batosta

lid [lɪd] coperchio *m*

lie¹ [laɪ] **1** *n* bugia *f*; *tell ~s* dire bugie **2** *v/i* mentire

lie² [laɪ] *v/i* (*pret* lay, *pp* lain) *of person* sdraiarsi; *of object* stare; (*be situated*) trovarsi

♦ lie down *v/i* sdraiarsi

'lie-in: *have a ~* restare a letto fino a tardi

lieu [ljuː] *n*: *in ~ of* invece di

lieu·ten·ant [lef'tenənt] tenente *m*

life [laɪf] (*pl* lives [laɪvz]) vita *f*; *of machine* durata *f*; *of battery* autonomia *f*; *all her ~* tutta la vita; *that's ~!* così è la vita!

'life as·sur·ance *Br* assicurazione *f* sulla vita; 'life belt salvagente *m inv*; 'life·boat lancia *f* di salvataggio; 'life ex·pect·an·cy aspettativa *f* di vita; 'life-guard bagnino *m*, -a *f*; 'life his·to·ry ciclo *m* vitale; life im'pris·on·ment ergastolo *m*; 'life in·sur·ance assicurazione *f* sulla vita; 'life jack·et giubbotto *m* di salvataggio

life·less ['laɪflɪs] *adj* senza vita

life·like ['laɪflaɪk] *adj* fedele

'life·long di vecchia data; 'life-sav·ing *adj drug* salvavita; 'life-sized *adj* a grandezza naturale; 'life-threat·en·ing *adj* mortale; 'life·time *n*: *in my ~* in vita mia

lift [lɪft] **1** *v/t* sollevare **2** *v/i of fog* diradarsi **3** *n Br*: *in building* ascensore *m*; *in car* passaggio *m*; *give s.o. a ~* dare un passaggio a qu

♦ lift off *v/i of rocket* decollare

'lift-off *of rocket* decollo *m*

lig·a·ment ['lɪgəmənt] legamento *m*

light¹ [laɪt] **1** *n* luce *f*; *in the ~ of* alla luce di; *have you got a ~?* hai da accendere? **2** *v/t* (*pret & pp* lit) *fire, cigarette* accendere; (*illuminate*) illuminare **3** *adj not dark* chiaro

light² [laɪt] **1** *adj not heavy* leggero **2** *adv*: *travel ~* viaggiare leggero

♦ light up **1** *v/t* (*illuminate*) illuminare **2** *v/i* (*start to smoke*) accendersi una sigaretta

'light bulb lampadina *f*

light·en¹ ['laɪtn] *v/t colour* schiarire

light·en² ['laɪtn] *v/t load* alleggerire

♦ lighten up *v/i of person* rilassarsi

light·er ['laɪtə(r)] *for cigarettes* accendino *m*

L

light-head·ed [laɪt'hedɪd] *adj* (*dizzy*) stordito; **light-'heart·ed** [laɪt'hɑːtɪd] *adj film* leggero; **'light·house** faro *m*

light·ing ['laɪtɪŋ] illuminazione *f*

light·ly ['laɪtlɪ] *adv touch* leggermente; **get off ~** cavarsela con poco

light·ness ['laɪtnɪs] leggerezza *f*

light·ning ['laɪtnɪŋ] fulmine *m*

'light·ning con·duc·tor parafulmine *m*

'light pen penna *f* luminosa

'light·weight *in boxing* peso *m* leggero

'light year anno *m* luce

like¹ [laɪk] **1** *prep* come; **~ this / that** così; **what is she ~?** *in looks, character* com'è?; **it's not ~ him** not his character non è da lui; **look ~ s.o.** assomigliare a qu **2** *conj* F (*as*) come; **~ I said** come ho già detto

like² [laɪk] *v/t*: **I ~ it / her** mi piace; **I would ~ ...** vorrei ...; **I would ~ to ...** vorrei ...; **would you ~ ...?** ti va ...?; **would you ~ to ...?** ti va di ...?; **he ~s swimming** gli piace nuotare; **if you ~** se vuoi

like·a·ble ['laɪkəbl] *adj* simpatico

like·li·hood ['laɪklɪhʊd] probabilità *f inv*; **in all ~** molto probabilmente

like·ly ['laɪklɪ] *adj* (*probable*) probabile; **not ~!** difficile!

like·ness ['laɪknɪs] (*resemblance*) somiglianza *f*

'like·wise ['laɪkwaɪz] *adv* altrettanto

lik·ing ['laɪkɪŋ] predilizione *f*; **is it to your ~?** *fml* è di tuo gradimento?; **take a ~ to s.o.** prendere qu in simpatia

li·lac ['laɪlək] *flower* lillà *m inv*; *colour* lilla *m inv*

li·ly ['lɪlɪ] giglio *m*

li·ly of the 'val·ley mughetto *m*

limb [lɪm] arto *m*

lime¹ [laɪm] *fruit* limetta *f*

lime² [laɪm] *substance* calce *f*

lime'green *adj* verde *m* acido

'lime·light *n*: **be in the ~** essere in vista

lim·it ['lɪmɪt] **1** *n* limite *m*; **within ~s** entro certi limiti; **off ~s** off-limits; **that's the ~!** F è il colmo! **2** *v/t* limitare

lim·i·ta·tion [lɪmɪ'teɪʃn] limite *m*

lim·it·ed 'com·pa·ny società *f inv* a responsabilità limitata

li·mo ['lɪməʊ] F limousine *f inv*

lim·ou·sine ['lɪməziːn] limousine *f inv*

limp¹ [lɪmp] *adj* floscio

limp² [lɪmp] *n*: **he has a ~** zoppica

line¹ [laɪn] *n on paper, road* linea *f*; *of people, trees* fila *f*; *of text* riga *f*; (*cord*) filo *m*; *of business* settore *m*; TELEC linea *f*; **the ~ is busy** è occupato; **hold the ~** rimanga in linea; **draw the ~ at sth** non tollerare qc; **~ of inquiry** pista *f*; **~ of reasoning** filo *m* del ragionamento; **stand in ~** *esp Am* fare la fila; **in ~ with ...** (*conforming with*) in linea con ...

line² [laɪn] *v/t* foderare

♦ **line up** *v/i* mettersi in fila

lin·e·ar ['lɪnɪə(r)] *adj* lineare

lin·en ['lɪnɪn] *material* lino *m*; *sheets etc* biancheria *f*

lin·er ['laɪnə(r)] *ship* transatlantico *m*

lines·man ['laɪnzmən] SP guardalinee *m inv*

lin·ger ['lɪŋgə(r)] *v/i of person* attardarsi; *of smell, pain* persistere

lin·ge·rie ['lænʒərɪ] lingerie *f inv*

lin·guist ['lɪŋgwɪst] *professional* linguista *m/f*; *person good at languages* poliglotta *m/f*

lin·guis·tic [lɪŋ'gwɪstɪk] *adj* linguistico

lin·ing ['laɪnɪŋ] *of clothes* fodera *f*; *of brakes* guarnizione *f*

link [lɪŋk] **1** *n* (*connection*) legame *m*; *in chain* anello *m* **2** *v/t* collegare

♦ **link up** *v/i* riunirsi; TV collegarsi

li·on ['laɪən] leone *m*

li·on·ess ['laɪənes] leonessa *f*

lip [lɪp] labbro *m*; **~s** labbra

'lip·read *v/i* (*pret & pp* **-read** [red]) leggere le labbra

'lip·stick rossetto *m*

li·queur [lɪ'kjʊə(r)] liquore *m*

liq·uid ['lɪkwɪd] **1** *n* liquido *m* **2** *adj* liquido

liq·ui·date ['lɪkwɪdeɪt] *v/t* liquidare

liq·ui·da·tion [lıkwı'deıʃn] liquidazione f; **go into ~** andare in liquidazione

liq·ui·di·ty [lı'kwıdıtı] FIN liquidità f inv

liq·uid·ize ['lıkwıdaız] v/t frullare

liq·uid·iz·er ['lıkwıdaızə(r)] frullatore m

liq·uor ['lıkə(r)] superalcolici mpl

liq·uo·rice ['lıkərıs] liquirizia f

lisp [lısp] **1** n lisca f **2** v/i parlare con la lisca

list [lıst] **1** n elenco m, lista f **2** v/t elencare

lis·ten ['lısn] v/i ascoltare

♦ **listen in** v/i ascoltare (di nascosto)

♦ **listen to** v/t radio, person ascoltare

lis·ten·er ['lısnə(r)] to radio ascoltatore m, -trice f; **he's a good ~** sa ascoltare

list·ings mag·a·zine ['lıstıŋz] guida f dei programmi radio / TV

list·less ['lıstlıs] adj apatico

lit [lıt] pret & pp → **light**

li·ter Am → **litre**

lit·e·ral ['lıtərəl] adj letterale

lit·e·ral·ly ['lıtərəlı] adv letteralmente

lit·e·ra·ry ['lıtərərı] adj letterario

lit·e·rate ['lıtərət] adj: **be ~** saper leggere e scrivere

lit·e·ra·ture ['lıtrətʃə(r)] letteratura f; F (leaflets) opuscoli mpl

li·tre ['li:tə(r)] litro m

lit·ter ['lıtə(r)] rifiuti mpl; of animal cucciolata f

'**lit·ter bas·ket** cestino m dei rifiuti

'**lit·ter bin** bidone m dei rifiuti

lit·tle ['lıtl] **1** adj piccolo; **the ~ ones** i piccoli **2** the **~ I know** il poco che so; **a ~** un po'; **a ~ bread/wine** un po' di pane / vino; **a ~ is better than nothing** meglio poco che niente **3** adv: **~ by ~** (a) poco a poco; **a ~ better/bigger** un po' meglio/più grande; **a ~ before 6** un po' prima delle 6

live¹ [lıv] v/i (reside) abitare; (be alive) vivere

♦ **live on 1** v/t rice, bread vivere di **2** v/i continue living sopravvivere

♦ **live up: live it up** fare la bella vita

♦ **live up to** v/t essere all'altezza di

♦ **live with** v/t vivere con

live² [laıv] **1** adj broadcast dal vivo **2** adv broadcast in diretta; record dal vivo; ammunition carico

live·li·hood ['laıvlıhud] mezzi mpl di sostentamento; **earn one's ~** guadagnarsi da vivere

live·li·ness ['laıvlınıs] vivacità f inv

live·ly ['laıvlı] adj vivace

liv·er ['lıvə(r)] fegato m

live·stock ['laıvstɒk] bestiame m

liv·id ['lıvıd] adj (angry) furibondo

liv·ing ['lıvıŋ] **1** adj in vita **2** n: **earn one's ~** guadagnarsi da vivere; **what do you do for a ~?** che lavoro fai?; **standard of ~** tenore m di vita

'**liv·ing room** salotto m, soggiorno m

liz·ard ['lızəd] lucertola f

load [ləud] **1** n carico m; **~s of** F un sacco di **2** v/t caricare; **~ sth onto sth** caricare qc su qc

load·ed ['ləudıd] adj F (very rich) ricco sfondato

loaf [ləuf] n (pl loaves [ləuvz]): **a ~ of bread** una pagnotta

♦ **loaf about** v/i F oziare

loaf·er ['ləufə(r)] shoe mocassino m

loan [ləun] **1** n prestito m; **on ~** in prestito **2** v/t: **~ s.o. sth** prestare qc a qu

loathe [ləuð] v/t detestare

loath·ing ['ləuðıŋ] disgusto m

lob·by ['lɒbı] in hotel, theatre atrio m; POL lobby f inv

lobe [ləub] of ear lobo m

lob·ster ['lɒbstə(r)] aragosta f

lo·cal ['ləukl] **1** adj people, bar del posto; produce locale; **I'm not ~** non sono del posto **2** n persona f del posto; **are you a ~?** sei del posto?

'**lo·cal call** TELEC telefonata f urbana; **lo·cal e'lec·tions** npl elezioni fpl amministrative; **lo·cal 'gov·ern·ment** amministrazione f locale

lo·cal·i·ty [ləu'kælıtı] località f inv

lo·cal·ly ['ləukəlı] adv live, work nella zona

lo·cal 'pro·duce prodotti mpl locali

'**lo·cal time** ora f locale

L

lo·cate [ləʊ'keɪt] *v/t new factory etc* situare; *identify position of* localizzare; *be ~d* essere situato

lo·ca·tion [ləʊ'keɪʃn] (*siting*) ubicazione *f; identifying position of* localizzazione *f*; **on ~** *film* in esterni; *the film was shot on ~ in ...* gli esterni del film sono stati girati in ...

loch lago *m*

lock¹ [lɒk] *of hair* ciocca *f*

lock² [lɒk] **1** *n on door* serratura *f* **2** *v/t door* chiudere a chiave; *~ sth in position* bloccare qc
♦ **lock away** *v/t* mettere sottochiave
♦ **lock in** *v/t person* chiudere dentro
♦ **lock out** *v/t of house* chiudere fuori
♦ **lock up** *v/t in prison* mettere dentro

lock·er ['lɒkə(r)] armadietto *m*

'lock·er room spogliatoio *m*

lock·et ['lɒkɪt] medaglione *m*

lock·smith ['lɒksmɪθ] fabbro *m* ferraio

lo·cust ['ləʊkəst] locusta *f*

lodge [lɒdʒ] **1** *v/t complaint* presentare **2** *v/i of bullet* conficcarsi

lodg·er ['lɒdʒə(r)] pensionante *m/f*

loft [lɒft] soffitta *f*

loft·y ['lɒftɪ] *adj peak* alto; *ideals* nobile

log [lɒg] *wood* ceppo *m; written record* giornale *m*
♦ **log off** *v/i* (*pret & pp* **-ged**) disconnettersi (*from* da)
♦ **log on** *v/i* connettersi
♦ **log on to** *v/t* connettersi a

'log·book giornale *m* di bordo

log 'cab·in casetta *f* di legno

log·ger·heads ['lɒgəhedz]: *be at ~* essere ai ferri corti

lo·gic ['lɒdʒɪk] logica *f*

lo·gic·al ['lɒdʒɪkl] *adj* logico

lo·gic·al·ly ['lɒdʒɪklɪ] *adv* a rigor di logica; *arrange* in modo logico

lo·gis·tics [lə'dʒɪstɪks] *npl* logistica *f*

lo·go ['ləʊgəʊ] logo *m inv*

loi·ter ['lɔɪtə(r)] *v/i* gironzolare

lol·li·pop ['lɒlɪpɒp] lecca lecca *m inv*

'lol·li·pop man/wo·man *Br* uomo/donna che aiuta i bambini ad attraversare la strada

lol·ly ['lɒlɪ] (*ice lolly*) ghiacciolo *m;* F

(*money*) grana *f* F

Lon·don ['lʌndən] Londra *f*

lone·li·ness ['ləʊnlɪnɪs] solitudine *f*

lone·ly ['ləʊnlɪ] *adj person* solo; *place* isolato

lon·er ['ləʊnə(r)] persona *f* solitaria

long¹ [lɒŋ] **1** *adj* lungo; *it's a ~ way* è lontano **2** *adv*: *don't be ~* torna presto; *5 weeks is too ~* 5 settimane è troppo; *will it take ~?* ci vorrà tanto?; *that was ~ ago* è stato tanto tempo fa; *~ before then* molto prima di allora; *before ~* poco tempo dopo; *we can't wait any ~er* non possiamo attendere oltre; *he no ~er works here* non lavora più qui; *so ~ as* (*provided*) sempre che; *so ~!* arrivederci!

long² [lɒŋ] *v/i*: *~ for sth* desiderare ardentemente qc; *be ~ing to do sth* desiderare ardentemente fare qc

long-'dis·tance *adj phonecall* interurbano; *race* di fondo; *flight* intercontinentale

long·ing ['lɒŋɪŋ] *n* desiderio *m*

lon·gi·tude ['lɒŋgɪtjuːd] longitudine *f*

'long jump salto *m* in lungo; **'long-'life milk** latte *m* a lunga conservazione; **'long-range** *missile* a lunga gittata; *forecast* a lungo termine; **long-sight·ed** [lɒŋ'saɪtɪd] *adj* presbite; **long-sleeved** [lɒŋ'sliːvd] *adj* a maniche lunghe; **long-'stand·ing** *adj* di vecchia data; **'long-term** *adj plans, investment* a lunga scadenza; *relationship* stabile; **'long wave** RAD onde *fpl* lunghe

long-wind·ed [lɒŋ'wɪndɪd] *adj* prolisso

loo [luː] F gabinetto *m*

look [lʊk] **1** *n* (*appearance*) aspetto *m*; (*glance*) sguardo *m; give s.o./sth a ~* dare uno sguardo a qu/qc; *have a ~ at sth* examine un'occhiata a qc; *can I have a ~ around?* in shop etc posso dare un'occhiata?; *~s* (*beauty*) bellezza *f* **2** *v/i* guardare; (*search*) cercare;

(*seem*) sembrare; **you ~ tired /
different** sembri stanco / diverso

♦ **look after** *v/t* badare a

♦ **look ahead** *v/i fig* pensare al futuro

♦ **look around** *v/i in shop etc* dare un'occhiata in giro; (*~ back*) guardarsi indietro

♦ **look at** *v/t* guardare; (*consider*) considerare

♦ **look back** *v/i* guardare indietro

♦ **look down on** *v/t* disprezzare

♦ **look for** *v/t* cercare

♦ **look forward to** *v/t*: **look forward to doing sth** non veder l'ora di fare qc; **I'm looking forward to the holidays** non vedo l'ora che arrivino le vacanze; **I'm not looking forward to it** non ne ho proprio voglia

♦ **look in on** *v/t* (*visit*) passare a trovare

♦ **look into** *v/t* (*investigate*) esaminare

♦ **look on 1** *v/i* (*watch*) rimanere a guardare **2** *v/t*: **I look on you as a friend** (*consider*) ti considero un amico

♦ **look onto** *v/t garden, street* dare su

♦ **look out** *v/i of window etc* guardare fuori; (*pay attention*) fare attenzione; **look out!** attento!

♦ **look out for** *v/t* cercare; (*be on guard against*) fare attenzione a

♦ **look out of** *v/t window* guardare da

♦ **look over** *v/t house, translation* esaminare

♦ **look round** *v/t museum, city* visitare

♦ **look through** *v/t magazine, notes* scorrere

♦ **look to** *v/t* (*rely on*) contare su

♦ **look up 1** *v/i from paper etc* sollevare lo sguardo; (*improve*) migliorare **2** *v/t word, phone number* cercare; (*visit*) andare a trovare

♦ **look up to** *v/t* (*respect*) avere rispetto

lookout *n person* sentinella *f*; *place* posto *m* di guardia; **be on the ~** stare all'erta; **be on the ~ for** *accommodation etc* cercare di trovare; *new staff etc* essere alla ricerca di

♦ **loom up** [lu:m] *v/i* apparire

loon·y ['lu:nɪ] **1** *n* F matto *m*, -a *f* **2** *adj* F matto

loop [lu:p] *n* cappio *m*

'**loop·hole** *in law etc* scappatoia *f*

loose [lu:s] *adj wire, button* allentato; *clothes* ampio; *tooth* che tentenna; *morals* dissoluto; *wording* vago; **~ change** spiccioli *mpl*; **~ ends** *of problem, discussion* aspetti *mpl* da esaminare

loose·ly ['lu:slɪ] *adv tied* senza stringere; *worded* vagamente

loos·en ['lu:sn] *v/t collar, knot* allentare

loot [lu:t] **1** *n* bottino *m* **2** *v/t & v/i* saccheggiare

loot·er ['lu:tə(r)] saccheggiatore *m*, -trice *f*

♦ **lop off** [lɒp] *v/t* (*pret & pp* -**ped**) tagliar via

lop·sid·ed [lɒp'saɪdɪd] *adj* sbilenco

Lord [lɔːd] (*God*) Signore *m*; **the (House of) ~s** la camera dei Lord

Lord's 'Prayer il Padrenostro *m*

lor·ry ['lɒrɪ] *Br* camion *m inv*

lose [lu:z] (*pret & pp* **lost**) **1** *v/t object* perdere **2** *v/i* SP perdere; *of clock* andare indietro; **I'm lost** mi sono perso; **get lost!** F sparisci!

♦ **lose out** *v/i* rimetterci

los·er ['lu:zə(r)] *in contest* perdente *m/f*; F *in life* sfigato *m*, -a *f*

loss [lɒs] perdita *f*; **make a ~** subire una perdita; **be at a ~** essere perplesso

lost [lɒst] **1** *adj* perso **2** *pret & pp* → **lose**

lost and 'found *Am*, **lost 'prop·er·ty of·fice** *Br* ufficio *m* oggetti smarriti

lot [lɒt] *n*: **the ~** tutto; **a ~, ~s** molto; **a ~ of ice cream, ~s of ice cream** molto gelato; **a ~ of ice creams, ~s of ice creams** molti gelati; **a ~ better / easier** molto meglio / più facile

lo·tion ['ləʊʃn] lozione *f*

lot·te·ry ['lɒtərɪ] lotteria *f*

loud [laʊd] *adj music, voice, noise* forte; *colour* sgargiante

loud'speak·er altoparlante *m*; *for stereo* cassa *f* dello stereo

lounge [laʊndʒ] *in house* soggiorno *m*; *in hotel* salone *m*; *at airport* sala *f* partenze

♦ **lounge about** *v/i* poltrire

'lounge suit completo *m* da uomo

louse [laʊs] (*pl* **lice** [laɪs]) pidocchio *m*

lous·y ['laʊzɪ] *adj* F schifoso F; *I feel ~* mi sento uno schifo

lout [laʊt] teppista *m/f*

lov·a·ble ['lʌvəbl] *adj* adorabile

love [lʌv] **1** *n* amore *m*; *in tennis* zero *m*; *be in ~* essere innamorato; *fall in ~* innamorarsi; *make ~* fare l'amore; *make ~ to* fare l'amore con; *yes, my ~* sì, tesoro **2** *v/t person, country, wine* amare; *~ doing sth* amare fare qc

'love af·fair relazione *f*; **'love-life** vita *f* sentimentale; **'love let·ter** lettera *f* d'amore

love·ly ['lʌvlɪ] *adj face, colour, holiday* bello; *meal, smell* buono; *we had a ~ time* siamo stati benissimo

lov·er ['lʌvə(r)] amante *m/f*

lov·ing ['lʌvɪŋ] *adj* affettuoso

lov·ing·ly ['lʌvɪŋlɪ] *adv* amorosamente

low [ləʊ] **1** *adj bridge, price, voice* basso; *quality* scarso; *be feeling ~* sentirsi giù; *be ~ on petrol* avere poca benzina **2** *n in weather* depressione *f*; *in sales, statistics* minimo *m*

'low·brow *adj* di scarso spessore culturale; **low-'cal·o·rie** *adj* ipocalorico; **'low-cut** *adj dress* scollato

low·er ['ləʊə(r)] *v/t boat, sth to the ground* calare; *flag, hemline* ammainare; *pressure, price* abbassare

'low-fat *adj* magro

'low-key *adj* discreto; **'low·lands** *npl* bassopiano *m*; **low-'pres·sure ar·e·a** area *f* di bassa pressione; **'low sea·son** bassa stagione *f*; **'low tide** bassa marea *f*

loy·al ['lɔɪəl] *adj* leale

loy·al·ly ['lɔɪəlɪ] *adv* lealmente

loy·al·ty ['lɔɪəltɪ] lealtà *f inv*

loz·enge ['lɒzɪndʒ] *shape* rombo *m*; *tablet* pastiglia *f*

LP [el'piː] *abbr* (= *long-playing record*) LP *m inv* (= long-playing *m inv*)

Ltd *abbr* (= *limited*) s.r.l. (= società *f inv* a responsabilità limitata)

lu·bri·cant ['luːbrɪkənt] lubrificante *m*

lu·bri·cate ['luːbrɪkeɪt] *v/t* lubrificare

lu·bri·ca·tion [luːbrɪ'keɪʃn] lubrificazione *f*

lu·cid ['luːsɪd] *adj* (*clear*) chiaro; (*sane*) lucido

luck [lʌk] fortuna *f*; *bad ~* sfortuna; *hard ~!* che sfortuna!; *good ~* fortuna *f*; *good ~!* buona fortuna!

luck·i·ly ['lʌkɪlɪ] *adv* fortunatamente

luck·y ['lʌkɪ] *adj* fortunato; *you were ~* hai avuto fortuna; *he's ~ to be alive* è vivo per miracolo; *that's ~!* che fortuna!

lu·cra·tive ['luːkrətɪv] *adj* redditizio

lu·di·crous ['luːdɪkrəs] *adj* ridicolo

lug [lʌg] *v/t* (*pret & pp* **-ged**) F trascinare

lug·gage ['lʌgɪdʒ] bagagli *mpl*

'lug·gage rack *in train* portabagagli *m inv*

luke·warm ['luːkwɔːm] *adj* tiepido

lull [lʌl] **1** *n in fighting* momento *m* di calma; *in conversation* pausa *f* **2** *v/t*: *~ s.o. into a false sense of security* illudersi che tutto vada bene

lul·la·by ['lʌləbaɪ] ninnananna *f*

lum·ba·go [lʌm'beɪgəʊ] lombaggine *f*

lum·ber ['lʌmbə(r)] (*timber*) legname *m*

lu·mi·nous ['luːmɪnəs] *adj* luminoso

lump [lʌmp] *of sugar* zolletta *f*; (*swelling*) nodulo *m*

♦ **lump together** *v/t* mettere insieme

lump 'sum pagamento *m* unico

lump·y ['lʌmpɪ] *adj sauce* grumoso; *mattress* pieno di buchi

lu·na·cy ['luːnəsɪ] pazzia *f*

lu·nar ['luːnə(r)] *adj* lunare

lu·na·tic ['luːnətɪk] *n* pazzo *m*, -a *f*

lunch [lʌntʃ] pranzo *m*; *have ~* pranzare

'**lunch box** cestino *m* del pranzo;
'**lunch break** pausa *f* pranzo;
'**lunch hour** pausa *f* pranzo;
'**lunch‐time** ora *f* di pranzo

lung [lʌŋ] polmone *m*

'**lung can‐cer** cancro *m* al polmone

♦ **lunge at** [lʌndʒ] *v/t* scagliarsi contro

lurch [lɜːtʃ] *v/i* barcollare

lure [luə(r)] **1** *n* attrattiva *f* **2** *v/t* attirare; **~ s.o. into a trap** far cadere qu in trappola

lu‐rid ['luərɪd] *adj colour* sgargiante; *details* scandaloso

lurk [lɜːk] *v/i of person* appostarsi; *of doubt* persistere

lus‐cious ['lʌʃəs] *adj* sensuale

lush [lʌʃ] *adj vegetation* lussureggiante

lust [lʌst] *n* libidine *f*

lux‐u‐ri‐ous [lʌɡ'ʒʊərɪəs] *adj* lussuoso

lux‐u‐ri‐ous‐ly [lʌɡ'ʒʊərɪəslɪ] *adv* lussuosamente

lux‐u‐ry ['lʌkʃərɪ] **1** *n* lusso **m 2** *adj* di lusso

LV *abbr* (= **luncheon voucher**) buono *m* pasto

lymph gland ['lɪmfɡlænd] ghiandola *f* linfatica

lynch [lɪntʃ] *v/t* linciare

lyr‐i‐cist ['lɪrɪsɪst] paroliere *m*

lyr‐ics ['lɪrɪks] *npl* parole *fpl*, testi *mpl*

M

M [em] *abbr* (= **medium**) M (= medio)

MA [em'eɪ] *abbr* (= **Master of Arts**) master *m inv*

ma'am [mæm] *Am* signora *f*

mac [mæk] F (*mackintosh*) impermeabile *m*

ma‐chine [mə'ʃiːn] **1** *n* macchina *f* **2** *v/t with sewing machine* cucire a macchina; TECH lavorare a macchina

ma'chine gun mitragliatrice *f*

ma‐chine‐'read‐a‐ble *adj* leggibile dalla macchina

ma‐chin‐e‐ry [mə'ʃiːnərɪ] (*machines*) macchinario *m*

ma‐chine trans'la‐tion traduzione *f* fatta dal computer

ma‐chis‐mo [mə'kɪzməʊ] machismo *m*

mach‐o ['mætʃəʊ] *adj* macho *m*

mack‐in‐tosh ['mækɪntɒʃ] impermeabile *m*

mac‐ro ['mækrəʊ] COMPUT macro *f*

mad [mæd] *adj* (*insane*) pazzo *m*; F (*angry*) furioso; **be ~ about** F andar matto per; **drive s.o. ~** far impazzire qu; **go ~** (*become insane*) impazzire; F *with enthusiasm* impazzire; **like ~** F *run, work* come un matto

mad‐am ['mædəm] signora *f*

mad 'cow dis‐ease F morbo *m* della mucca pazza

mad‐den ['mædən] *v/t* (*infuriate*) esasperare

mad‐den‐ing ['mædnɪŋ] *adj* esasperante

made [meɪd] *pret & pp* → **make**

made‐to‐'meas‐ure *adj* su misura

'mad‐house *fig* manicomio *m*

mad‐ly ['mædlɪ] *adv* come un matto; **~ in love** pazzamente innamorato

'mad‐man pazzo *m*

mad‐ness ['mædnɪs] pazzia *f*

Ma‐don‐na [mə'dɒnə] Madonna *f*

Ma‐fi‐a ['mæfɪə] Mafia *f*

mag‐a‐zine [mæɡə'ziːn] *printed* rivista *f*

mag‐got ['mæɡət] verme *m*

M

Ma·gi ['meɪdʒaɪ] REL *Re Magi mpl*

ma·gic ['mædʒɪk] **1** *n* magia *f*; *tricks* giochi *mpl* di prestigio; *like* ~ come per magia **2** *adj* magico

mag·i·cal ['mædʒɪkl] *adj powers, moment* magico

ma·gi·cian [mə'dʒɪʃn] *performer* mago *m*, -a *f*

ma·gic '**spell** incantesimo *m*; **ma·gic** '**trick** gioco *m* di prestigio; **mag·ic** '**wand** bacchetta *f* magica

magistrate ['mædʒɪstreɪt] magistrato *m*

mag·nan·i·mous [mæg'nænɪməs] *adj* magnanimo

mag·net ['mægnɪt] calamita *f*, magnete *m*

mag·net·ic [mæg'netɪk] *adj* calamitato; *also fig* magnetico

mag·net·ic '**stripe** striscia *f* magnetizzata

mag·net·ism [mæg'netɪzm] *of person* magnetismo *m*

mag·nif·i·cence [mæg'nɪfɪsəns] magnificenza *f*

mag·nif·i·cent [mæg'nɪfɪsənt] *adj* magnifico

mag·ni·fy ['mægnɪfaɪ] *v/t* (*pret & pp* *-ied*) ingrandire; *difficulties* ingigantire

mag·ni·fy·ing glass lente *f* d'ingrandimento

mag·ni·tude ['mægnɪtjuːd] *of problem* portata *f*; AST magnitudine *f*

ma·hog·a·ny [mə'hɒgənɪ] mogano *m*

maid [meɪd] *servant* domestica *f*; *in hotel* cameriera *f*

maid·en name [meɪdn] *nome m da ragazza*; **maid·en** '**speech** discorso *m* inaugurale; **maid·en** '**voy·age** viaggio *m* inaugurale

mail [meɪl] **1** *n posta f*; *put sth in the* ~ spedire qc **2** *v/t letter* spedire; *person* spedire a

mail·box *Am* buca *f* delle lettere; *Am: of house* cassetta *f* delle lettere; COMPUT casella *f* postale

mail·ing list mailing list *m inv*

mail·man *Am* postino *m*; **mail·'or·der cat·a·log** *Am*, **mail·'or·der**

cat·a·logue catalogo *m* di vendita per corrispondenza; **mail·'or·der firm** ditta *f* di vendita per corrispondenza; '**mail·shot** mailing *m inv*

maim [meɪm] *v/t* mutilare

main [meɪn] *adj* principale

'**main course** piatto *m* principale; **main** '**en·trance** entrata *f* principale; '**main·frame** mainframe *m inv*; '**main·land** terraferma *f*, continente *m*; *on the* ~ sul continente

main·ly ['meɪnlɪ] *adv* principalmente

main '**road** strada *f* principale

'**main street** corso *m*

main·tain [meɪn'teɪn] *v/t* mantenere; *pace, speed; relationship; machine, house; family; innocence, guilt* sostenere; ~ *that* sostenere che

main·te·nance ['meɪntənəns] *of machine, house* manutenzione *f*; *money* alimenti *mpl*; *of law and order* mantenimento *m*

'**main·te·nance costs** *npl* spese *fpl* di manutenzione

'**main·te·nance staff** addetti *mpl* alla manutenzione

ma·jes·tic [mə'dʒestɪk] *adj* maestoso

maj·es·ty ['mædʒəstɪ] *(grandeur)* maestà *f inv*; *Her Majesty* Sua Maestà

ma·jor ['meɪdʒə(r)] **1** *adj* (*significant*) importante, principale; *in C* ~ MUS in Do maggiore **2** *n* MIL maggiore *m*

ma·jor·i·ty [mə'dʒɒrətɪ] *also* POL maggioranza *f*; maggioranza *f*; *be in the* ~ essere in maggioranza

make [meɪk] **1** *n brand* marca *f* **2** *v/t* (*pret & pp* *made*) *decision* prendere; (*earn*) guadagnare; MATH fare; ~ *s.o. do sth* (*force to*) far fare qc a qu; (*cause to*) spingere qu a fare qc; *you can't* ~ *me do it!* non puoi costringermi a farlo!; ~ *s.o. happy / angry* far felice / arrabbiare qu; ~ *s.o. happy / sad* rendere felice / triste qu; ~ *a decision* prendere una decisione; ~ *a telephone call* fare una telefonata; *made in Japan* made in Japan; ~ *it catch bus, train,* *come, succeed, survive* farcela; *what time do you ~ it?* che ore fai?; ~ **believe** far finta; ~ **do with** arrangiarsi con; *what do you ~ of it?* cosa ne pensi?

♦ **make for** *v/t (go towards)* dirigersi verso

♦ **make off** *v/i* svignarsela

♦ **make off with** *v/t (steal)* svignarsela con

♦ **make out** *v/t list* fare; *cheque* compilare; *(see)* distinguere; *(imply)* far capire; *who shall I make the cheque out to?* a chi devo intestare l'assegno?

♦ **make over**: *make sth over to s.o.* cedere qc a qu

♦ **make up** **1** *v/i of woman, actor* truccarsi; *after quarrel* fare la pace **2** *v/t story, excuse* inventare; *face* truccare; *(constitute)* costituire; *be made up of* essere composto da; *make up one's mind* decidersi; *make it up after quarrel* fare la pace

♦ **make up for** *v/t* compensare; *I'll make up for forgetting your birthday* mi farò perdonare di esermi scordato del tuo compleanno

'make-be·lieve *n* finta *f*

mak·er ['meɪkə(r)] *manufacturer* fabbricante *m/f*

make·shift ['meɪkʃɪft] *adj* improvvisato

make-up ['meɪkʌp] *(cosmetics)* trucco *m*

'make-up bag trousse *f inv* da trucco

mal·ad·just·ed [mælə'dʒʌstɪd] *adj* disadattato

male [meɪl] **1** *adj (masculine)* maschile; *animal, bird, fish* maschio **2** *n man* uomo *m*; *animal, bird, fish* maschio *m*

male 'chau·vin·ism maschilismo *m*; **male chau·vin·ist 'pig** maschilista *m*; **male 'nurse** infermiere *m*

ma·lev·o·lent [mə'levələnt] *adj* malevolo

mal·func·tion [mæl'fʌŋkʃn] **1** *n* cattivo *m* funzionamento **2** *v/i* funzionare male

mal·ice ['mælɪs] cattiveria *f*, malvagità *f*

ma·li·cious [mə'lɪʃəs] *adj* cattivo, malvagio

ma·lig·nant [mə'lɪgnənt] *adj tumour* maligno

mall [mæl] *(shopping ~)* centro *m* commerciale

mal·nu·tri·tion [mælnjuː'trɪʃn] denutrizione *f*

mal·prac·tice [mæl'præktɪs] negligenza *f*

malt ('whis·ky) [mɔːlt] whisky *m inv* di malto

mal·treat [mæl'triːt] *v/t* maltrattare

mal·treat·ment [mæl'triːtmənt] maltrattamento *m*

mam·mal ['mæml] mammifero *m*

mam·moth ['mæməθ] *adj (enormous)* colossale

man [mæn] **1** *n (pl men* [men]*) person, human being* uomo *m*; *(human being)* uomo *m*; *humanity* umanità *f inv*; *in draughts* pedina *f* **2** *v/t (pret & pp* **-ned***) telephones, front desk* essere di servizio a; *it was ~ned by a crew of three* aveva un equipaggio di tre uomini

man·age ['mænɪdʒ] **1** *v/t business, money* gestire; *money; suitcase; can you ~ the suitcase?* ce la fai a portare la valigia?; ~ *to ...* riuscire a ... **2** *v/i cope, financially* tirare avanti; *(financially); can you ~?* ce la fai?

man·age·a·ble ['mænɪdʒəbl] *adj suitcase etc* maneggevole; *hair* docile; *able to be done* fattibile

man·age·ment ['mænɪdʒmənt] *(managing)* gestione *f*; *(managers)* direzione *f*; *under his ~* durante la sua gestione

man·age·ment 'buy·out acquisizione *f* di un'impresa da parte dei suoi dirigenti; **man·age·ment con·sult·ant** consulente *m/f* di gestione aziendale; 'man·age·ment stud·ies corso *m* di formazione manageriale; 'man·age·ment team team *m inv* manageriale

man·ag·er ['mænɪdʒə(r)] manager

M

m/f inv, direttore *m*, -trice *f*

man·a·ge·ri·al [mænɪ'dʒɪərɪəl] *adj* manageriale

man·ag·ing di·rec·tor direttore *m* generale

man·da·rin 'or·ange [mændərɪn] mandarino *m*

man·date ['mændeɪt] *(authority, task)* mandato *m*

man·da·to·ry ['mændətrɪ] *adj* obbligatorio

mane [meɪn] *of horse* criniera *f*

ma·neu·ver *Am* → **manoeuvre**

man·gle ['mæŋgl] *v/t (crush)* stritolare

man·han·dle ['mænhændl] *v/t person* malmenare; *object* caricare

man·hood ['mænhʊd] *maturity* età *f inv* adulta; *(virility)* virilità *f inv*

'man-hour ora *f* lavorativa

'man·hunt caccia *f* all'uomo

ma·ni·a ['meɪnɪə] *(craze)* mania *f*

ma·ni·ac ['meɪnɪæk] F pazzo *m*, -a *f*

man·i·cure ['mænɪkjʊə(r)] *n* manicure *f inv*

man·i·fest ['mænɪfest] **1** *adj* palese **2** *v/t* manifestare; **~ itself** manifestarsi

ma·nip·u·late [mə'nɪpjʊleɪt] *v/t person, bones* manipolare; *equipment* maneggiare

ma·nip·u·la·tion [mənɪpjʊ'leɪʃn] *of person, bones* manipolazione *f*; *of bones*

ma·nip·u·la·tive [mə'nɪpjʊlətɪv] *adj* manipolatore

man'kind umanità *f inv*

man·ly ['mænlɪ] *adj* virile

'man-made *adj* sintetico

man·ner ['mænə(r)] *of doing sth* maniera *f*, modo *m*; *(attitude)* modo *m* di fare

man·ners ['mænəz] *npl*: **good / bad ~** buone / cattive maniere *fpl*; **have no ~** essere maleducato

ma·noeu·vre [mə'nu:və(r)] **1** *n* manovra *f* **2** *v/t* manovrare

man·or ['mænə(r)] maniero *m*

'man·pow·er manodopera *f*, personale *m*

man·sion ['mænʃn] villa *f*

'man·slaugh·ter omicidio *m* colposo

'man·tel·piece ['mæntlpi:s] mensola *f* del caminetto

man·u·al ['mænjʊəl] **1** *adj* manuale **2** *n* manuale *m*

man·u·al·ly ['mænjʊəlɪ] *adv* manualmente

man·u·fac·ture [mænjʊ'fæktʃə(r)] **1** *n* manifattura *f* **2** *v/t equipment* fabbricare

man·u·fac·tur·er [mænjʊ'fæktʃər-ə(r)] fabbricante *m/f*

man·u·fac·tur·ing [mænjʊ'fæktʃər-ɪŋ] *adj industry* manifatturiero

ma·nure [mə'njuə(r)] letame *m*

man·u·script ['mænjʊskrɪpt] manoscritto *m*; *typed* dattiloscritto *m*

man·y ['menɪ] **1** *adj* molti; **~ times** molte volte; **not ~ people / taxis** poche persone / pochi taxi; **too ~ problems / beers** troppi problemi / troppe birre **2** *pron* molti *m*, molte *f*; **a great ~, a good ~** moltissimi; **how ~ do you need?** quanti te ne servono?; **as ~ as 200** ben 200

'man-year anno / uomo *m*

map [mæp] *n* cartina *f*; *(street ~)* pianta *f*, piantina *f*

♦ **map out** *v/t (pret & pp **-ped**)* pianificare

ma·ple ['meɪpl] acero *m*

mar [mɑ:(r)] *v/t (pret & pp **-red**)* guastare

mar·a·thon ['mærəθən] *race* maratona *f*

mar·ble ['mɑ:bl] *material* marmo *m*

March [mɑ:tʃ] marzo *m*

march [mɑ:tʃ] **1** *n* marcia *f*; *(demonstration)* dimostrazione *f*, manifestazione *f* **2** *v/i* marciare; *in protest* dimostrare, manifestare; **~ from A to B** *in protest* sfilare in corteo da A a B

march·er ['mɑ:tʃə(r)] dimostrante *m/f*, manifestante *m/f*

mare [meə(r)] cavalla *f*, giumenta *f*

mar·ga·rine [mɑ:dʒə'ri:n] margarina *f*

mar·gin ['mɑ:dʒɪn] *of page* margine *m*; *(COM: profit margin)* margine *m* di guadagno; **by a narrow** ~ di stretta misura

mar·gin·al ['mɑːdʒɪnl] *adj* (*slight*) leggero

mar·gin·al·ly ['mɑːdʒɪnlɪ] *adv* (*slightly*) leggermente

mar·i·hua·na, mar·i·jua·na [mærɪ'hwɑːnə] marijuana *f*

ma·ri·na [mə'riːnə] porticciolo *m*

mar·i·nade [mærɪ'neɪd] *n* marinata *f*

mar·i·nate ['mærɪneɪt] *v/t* marinare

ma·rine [mə'riːn] **1** *adj* marino **2** *n* MIL marina *f* militare

mar·i·tal ['mærɪtl] *adj* coniugale

mar·i·tal 'sta·tus stato *m* civile

mar·i·time ['mærɪtaɪm] *adj* marittimo

mar·jo·ram ['mɑːdʒərəm] maggiorana *f*

mark[1] [mɑːk] FIN marco *m*

mark[2] [mɑːk] **1** *n* (*stain*) macchia *f*; (*sign, token*) segno *m*; (*trace*); EDU voto *m*; **leave one's** ~ lasciare un segno **2** *v/t* (*stain*) macchiare; EDU correggere; (*indicate*) indicare; (*commemorate*) celebrare; **your essays will be ~ed out of ten** ai temi sarà assegnata una votazione da 1 a 10 *v/i* *of fabric* macchiarsi

♦ **mark down** *v/t goods* ribassare

♦ **mark out** *v/t with a line etc* delimitare; (*fig: set apart*) distinguere

♦ **mark up** *v/t price* aumentare; *goods* aumentare il prezzo di

marked [mɑːkt] *adj* (*definite*) spiccato

mark·er ['mɑːkə(r)] (*highlighter*) evidenziatore *m*

mar·ket ['mɑːkɪt] **1** *n* mercato *m*; *for particular commodity*; (*stock* ~) mercato *m* azionario; **on the** ~ sul mercato **2** *v/t* vendere

mar·ket·a·ble ['mɑːkɪtəbl] *adj* commercializzabile

mar·ket e'con·o·my economia *f* di mercato

'mar·ket for·ces *npl* forze *fpl* di mercato

mar·ket·ing ['mɑːkɪtɪŋ] marketing *m inv*

mar·ket·ing cam·paign campagna *f* di marketing; **'mar·ket·ing de·part·ment** reparto *m* marketing; **'mar·ket·ing mix** marketing mix *m inv*; **'mar·ket·ing strat·e·gy** strategia *f* di marketing

mar·ket 'lead·er leader *m inv* del mercato; **'mar·ket-place** *in town* piazza *f* del mercato; *for commodities* piazza *f*, mercato *m*; **mar·ket re'search** ricerca *f* di mercato; **mar·ket 'share** quota *f* di mercato

mark-up ['mɑːkʌp] ricarico *m*

mar·ma·lade ['mɑːməleɪd] marmellata *f* d'arance

mar·quee [mɑː'kiː] padiglione *f*

mar·riage ['mærɪdʒ] matrimonio *m*; *event* nozze *fpl*

'mar·riage cer·tif·i·cate certificato *m* di matrimonio

mar·riage 'guid·ance coun·se·llor consulente *m/f* matrimoniale

mar·ried ['mærɪd] *adj* sposato; **be ~ to ...** essere sposato con ...

mar·ried 'life vita *f* coniugale

mar·ry ['mærɪ] *v/t* (*pret & pp* **-ied**) sposare; *of priest* unire in matrimonio; **get married** sposarsi

marsh [mɑːʃ] palude *f*

mar·shal ['mɑːʃl] *official* membro *m* del servizio d'ordine

marsh·mal·low [mɑːʃ'mæləʊ] caramella *f* soffice e gommosa

marsh·y ['mɑːʃɪ] *adj* paludoso

mar·tial arts [mɑːʃl'ɑːts] *npl* arti *fpl* marziali

mar·tial 'law legge *f* marziale

mar·tyr ['mɑːtə(r)] martire *m/f*

mar·tyred ['mɑːtəd] *adj fig* da martire

mar·vel ['mɑːvl] meraviglia *f*

♦ **marvel at** *v/t* meravigliarsi di

mar·ve·lous *Am*, **mar·vel·lous** ['mɑːvələs] *adj* meraviglioso

Marx·ism ['mɑːksɪzm] marxismo *m*

Marx·ist ['mɑːksɪst] **1** *adj* marxista **2** *n* marxista *m/f*

mar·zi·pan ['mɑːzɪpæn] marzapane *m*

mas·ca·ra [mæ'skɑːrə] mascara *m inv*

mas·cot ['mæskət] mascotte *f inv*

M

mas·cu·line ['mæskjolɪn] *adj* maschile

mas·cu·lin·i·ty [mæskjʊ'lɪnətɪ] (*virility*) virilità *f inv*

mash [mæʃ] *v/t* passare, schiacciare

mashed po·ta·toes [mæʃt] *npl* purè
m inv di patate

mask [mɑːsk] **1** *n* maschera *f* **2** *v/t
feelings* mascherare

'mask·ing tape *nastro m* adesivo di
carta

mas·och·ism ['mæsəkɪzm] maso-
chismo *m*

mas·och·ist ['mæsəkɪst] masochista
m/f

ma·son ['meɪsn] scalpellino *m*

ma·son·ry ['meɪsnrɪ] muratura *f*

mas·que·rade [mæskə'reɪd] **1** *n fig*
messinscena *f* **2** *v/i*: ~ *as* farsi passare per

mass[1] [mæs] **1** *n great amount* massa
f; *the ~es* le masse; *~es of* F un sacco di F **2** *v/i* radunarsi

mass[2] [mæs] REL messa *f*

mas·sa·cre ['mæsəkə(r)] **1** *n also fig*
massacro *m* **2** *v/t also fig* massacrare

mas·sage ['mæsɑːʒ] **1** *n* massaggio
m **2** *v/t* massaggiare; *figures* manipolare

'mas·sage par·lor *Am*, 'mas·sage
par·lour *euph* casa *f* d'appuntamenti

mas·seur [mæ'sɜː(r)] massaggiatore
m

mas·seuse [mæ'sɜːz] massaggiatri-
ce *f*

mas·sive ['mæsɪv] *adj* enorme; *heart
attack* grave

mass 'me·di·a *npl* mass media *mpl*;
mass·pro'duce *v/t* produrre in serie; **mass pro'duc·tion** produzione
f in serie

mast [mɑːst] *of ship* albero *m*; *for radio signal* palo *m* dell'antenna

mas·ter ['mɑːstə(r)] **1** *n of dog* padrone *m*; *of ship* capitano *m*; *be a ~
of* essere un maestro di **2** *v/t skill,
language* avere completa padronanza di; *situation* dominare

'mas·ter bed·room camera *f* da letto principale

'mas·ter key passe-partout *m inv*

mas·ter·ly ['mɑːstəlɪ] *adj* magistrale

'mas·ter·mind **1** *n fig* cervello *m*
2 *v/t* ideare; **Mas·ter of 'Arts**
master *m inv*; **mas·ter of 'cer-
e·mo·nies** maestro *m* di cerimonie;
'mas·ter·piece capolavoro *m*;
'mas·ter's (de·gree) master *m inv*

mas·ter·y ['mɑːstərɪ] padronanza *f*

mas·tur·bate ['mæstəbeɪt] *v/i* masturbarsi

mat [mæt] *for floor* tappetino *m*; SP
tappeto *m*; *for table* tovaglietta *f* al-
l'americana

match[1] [mæʃ] *for cigarette* fiammifero *m*; *wax* cerino *m*

match[2] [mæʃ] **1** *n (competition)* partita *f*; *be no ~ for s.o.* non poter
competere con qu; *meet one's ~*
trovare pane per i propri denti **2** *v/t
(be the same as)* abbinare; *(equal)*
uguagliare **3** *v/i of colours, patterns*
intonarsi

'match·box scatola *f* di fiammiferi

match·ing ['mæʃɪŋ] *adj* abbinato

'match stick fiammifero *m*

mate [meɪt] **1** *n of animal* compagno
m, -a *f*; NAUT secondo *m*; F *friend*
amico *m*, -a *f* **2** *v/i* accoppiarsi

ma·te·ri·al [mə'tɪərɪəl] **1** *n fabric*
stoffa *f*, tessuto *m*; *substance* materia
f; *~s* occorrente *m* **2** *adj* materiale

ma·te·ri·al·ism [mə'tɪərɪəlɪzm] ma-
terialismo *m*

ma·te·ri·al·ist [mətɪərɪə'lɪst] materialista *m/f*

ma·te·ri·al·is·tic [mətɪərɪə'lɪstɪk] *adj*
materialistico

ma·te·ri·al·ize [mə'tɪərɪəlaɪz] *v/i*
materializzarsi

ma·ter·nal [mə'tɜːnl] *adj* materno

ma·ter·ni·ty [mə'tɜːnətɪ] maternità *f
inv*

ma'ter·ni·ty dress vestito *m* pré-
maman; **ma·ter·ni·ty leave** congedo *m* per maternità; **ma·ter·ni·ty
ward** reparto *m* maternità

math *Am* → **maths**

math·e·mat·i·cal [mæθə'mætɪkl] *adj*
matematico

math·e·ma·ti·cian [mæθəmə'tɪʃn]

matematico *m*, -a *f*

math·e·mat·ics [mæθ'mætɪks] matematica *f*

maths [mæθs] matematica *f*

mat·i·née ['mætɪneɪ] matinée *f inv*

ma·tri·arch ['meɪtrɪɑːk] matriarca *f*

ma·tri·arch·al [meɪtrɪ'ɑːkl] *adj* matriarcale

mat·ri·mo·ny ['mætrɪmənɪ] matrimonio *m*

matt [mæt] *adj* opaco

mat·ter ['mætə(r)] **1** *n* (*affair*) questione *f*, faccenda *f*; PHYS materia *f*; **as a ~ of course** per abitudine; **as a ~ of fact** a dir la verità; **what's the ~?** cosa c'è?; **no ~ what she says** qualsiasi cosa dica **2** *v/i* importare; **it doesn't ~** non importa

mat·ter-of-'fact *adj* distaccato

mat·tress ['mætrɪs] materasso *m*

ma·ture [mə'tjʊə(r)] **1** *adj* maturo **2** *v/i* of person, insurance policy etc maturare; of wine invecchiare

ma·tu·ri·ty [mə'tjʊrətɪ] maturità *f inv*

maul [mɔːl] *v/t also fig* sbranare

max·i·mize ['mæksɪmaɪz] *v/t* massimizzare

max·i·mum ['mæksɪməm] **1** *adj* massimo **2** *n* massimo *m*

May [meɪ] maggio *m*

may [meɪ] *v/aux* ◊ (*possibility*): **it ~ rain** potrebbe piovere, può darsi che piova; **you ~ be right** potresti aver ragione, può darsi che abbia ragione; **it ~ not happen** magari non succederà, può darsi che non succeda ◊ (*permission*): **~ I help / smoke?** posso aiutare / fumare?; **you ~ if you like** puoi farlo se vuoi

may·be ['meɪbɪ] *adv* forse

'**May Day** il primo maggio

may·on·naise [meɪə'neɪz] maionese *f*

may·or ['meə(r)] sindaco *m*

maze [meɪz] *also fig* dedalo *m*, labirinto *m*

MB *abbr* (= **megabyte**) MB *m* (= megabyte *m inv*)

MBA [embiː'eɪ] *abbr* (= **master of business administration**) master

m inv in amministraztione aziendale

MBO [embiː'əʊ] *abbr* (= **management buyout**) acquisizione *f* di un'impresa da parte dei suoi dirigenti

MC [em'siː] *abbr* (= **master of ceremonies**) maestro *m* di cerimonie

MD [em'diː] *abbr* (= **Doctor of Medicine**) dottore *m* in medicina

me [miː] *pron direct & indirect object* mi; *after prep, stressed* me; **she knows ~** mi conosce; **she spoke to ~** mi ha parlato; **she spoke to ~ but not to him** ha parlato a me ma non a lui; **without ~** senza di me; **it's ~** sono io; **who? ~?** chi? io?

mead·ow ['medəʊ] prato *m*

mea·ger *Am*, **mea·gre** ['miːgə(r)] *adj* scarso

meal [miːl] pranzo *m*, pasto *m*; **enjoy your ~!** buon appetito!

'**meal·time** ora *f* di pranzo

mean¹ [miːn] *adj with money* avaro; (*nasty*) cattivo

mean² [miːn] (*pret & pp* **meant**) **1** *v/t* (*signify*) significare, voler dire; **do you ~ it?** (*intend*) dici sul serio?; **~ to do sth** avere l'intenzione di fare qc; **be ~t for** essere destinato a; *of remark* essere diretto a; **doesn't it ~ anything to you?** (*doesn't it matter?*) non conta niente per te? **2** *v/i*: **~ well** avere buone intenzioni

mean·ing ['miːnɪŋ] *of word* significato *m*

mean·ing·ful ['miːnɪŋfʊl] *adj* (*comprehensible*) comprensibile; (*constructive*) costruttivo; *glance* eloquente

mean·ing·less ['miːnɪŋlɪs] *adj* sentence etc senza senso; *gesture* vuoto

means [miːnz] *npl financial* mezzi *mpl*; (*nsg: way*) modo *m*; **~ of transport** mezzo *m* di trasporto; **by all ~** (*certainly*) certamente; **by no ~ rich / poor** lungi dall'essere ricco / povero; **by ~ of** per mezzo di

meant [ment] *pret & pp* → **mean²**

mean·time ['miːntaɪm] **1** *adv* intanto **2** *n*: **in the ~** nel frattempo

mean·while ['miːnwaɪl] **1** *adv* intan-

M

to **2** *n*: *in the* ~ nel frattempo

mea·sles ['miːzlz] *nsg* morbillo *m*

mea·sure ['meʒə(r)] **1** *n* (*step*) misura *f*, provvedimento *m*; *a ~ of success certain amount* un certo successo **2** *v/t* prendere le misure di **3** *v/i* misurare

♦ **measure out** *v/t amount* dosare; *area* misurare

♦ **measure up to** *v/t* dimostrarsi all'altezza di

mea·sure·ment ['meʒəmənt] *action* misurazione *f*; (*dimension*) misura *f*; *system of* ~ sistema *m* di misura

meas·ur·ing jug ['meʒərɪŋ] misurino *m*

'**mea·sur·ing tape** metro *m* a nastro

meat [miːt] carne *f*

'**meat·ball** polpetta *f*

'**meat·loaf** polpettone *m*

me·chan·ic [mɪ'kænɪk] meccanico *m*

me·chan·i·cal [mɪ'kænɪkl] *adj also fig* meccanico

me·chan·i·cal en·gi·neer ingegnere *m* meccanico

me·chan·i·cal en·gi·neer·ing ingegneria *f* meccanica

me·chan·i·cal·ly [mɪ'kænɪklɪ] *adv also fig* meccanicamente

mech·a·nism ['mekənɪzm] meccanismo *m*

mech·a·nize ['mekənaɪz] *v/t* meccanizzare

med·al ['medl] medaglia *f*

med·a·list *Am*, **med·al·list** ['medəlɪst] vincitore *m*,-trice *f* di una medaglia

med·dle ['medl] *v/i* (*interfere*) immischiarsi; ~ *with* (*tinker*) mettere le mani in

me·di·a ['miːdɪə] *npl*: *the* ~ i mass media *mpl*

'**me·di·a cov·er·age**: *it was given a lot of* ~ gli è stato dato molto spazio in tv e sui giornali; *an event that got a lot of* ~ un avvenimento di grande risonanza

med·i·ae·val [medɪ'iːvl] → **medieval**

'**me·di·a e·vent** spettacolo *m* sensazionale; **me·di·a 'hype** montatura *f* della stampa; '**me·di·a stud·ies** scienze *fpl* delle comunicazioni

me·di·ate ['miːdɪeɪt] *v/i* fare da mediatore *m*, -trice *f*

me·di·a·tion [miːdɪ'eɪʃn] mediazione *f*

me·di·a·tor ['miːdɪeɪtə(r)] mediatore *m*, -trice *f*

med·i·cal ['medɪkl] **1** *adj* medico **2** *n* visita *f* medica

'**med·i·cal cer·tif·i·cate** certificato *m* medico; '**med·i·cal ex·am·i·na·tion** visita *f* medica; '**med·i·cal his·to·ry** anamnesi *f inv*; '**med·i·cal pro·fes·sion** professione *f* medica; corpo *m* medico; '**med·i·cal re·cord** cartella *f* clinica

med·i·cat·ed ['medɪkeɪtɪd] *adj* medicato

med·i·ca·tion [medɪ'keɪʃn] medicina *f*

me·dic·i·nal [mɪ'dɪsɪnl] *adj* medicinale

med·i·cine ['medsən] medicina *f*

'**med·i·cine cab·i·net** armadietto *m* dei medicinali

me·di·e·val [medɪ'iːvl] *adj* medievale

me·di·o·cre [miːdɪ'əʊkə(r)] *adj* mediocre

me·di·oc·ri·ty [miːdɪ'ɒkrətɪ] mediocrità *f inv*

med·i·tate ['medɪteɪt] *v/i* meditare

med·i·ta·tion [medɪ'teɪʃn] meditazione *f*

Med·i·ter·ra·ne·an [medɪtə'reɪnɪən] **1** *adj* mediterraneo **2** *n*: *the* ~ il Mar Mediterraneo; *area* i paesi mediterranei

me·di·um ['miːdɪəm] **1** *adj* (*average*) medio; *steak* cotto al punto giusto **2** *n in size* media *f*; (*vehicle*) strumento *m*; (*spiritualist*) medium *m/f inv*

me·di·um-sized ['miːdɪəmsaɪzd] *adj* di grandezza media; **me·di·um 'term**: *in the* ~ a medio termine; '**me·di·um wave** RAD onde *fpl* medie

med·ley ['medlɪ] (*assortment*) misto *m*

meek [mi:k] *adj* mite

meet [mi:t] **1** *v/t* (*pret & pp* **met**) incontrare; (*get to know*) conoscere; (*collect*) andare *o* venire a prendere; *in competition* affrontare; *of eyes* incrociare; (*satisfy*) soddisfare; *I'll ~ you there* ci vediamo lì **2** *v/i* (*pret & pp* **met**) incontrarsi; *in competition* affrontarsi; *of eyes* incrociarsi; *of committee etc* riunirsi; *have you two met?* (*do you know each other?*) vi conoscete? **3** *n Am* SP raduno *m* sportivo

♦ **meet with** *v/t person* avere un incontro con; *opposition, approval etc* incontrare; *it met with success/failure* ha avuto successo/è fallito

meet·ing ['mi:tɪŋ] incontro *m*; *of committee, in business* riunione *f*; appuntamento *m*; *he's in a ~* è in riunione

meet·ing place luogo *m* d'incontro

meg·a·byte ['megəbaɪt] COMPUT megabyte *m inv*

mel·an·chol·y ['melənkəlɪ] *adj* malinconia *f*

mel·low ['meləʊ] **1** *adj* maturo **2** *v/i of person* addolcirsi

me·lo·di·ous [mɪ'ləʊdɪəs] *adj* melodioso

mel·o·dra·mat·ic [melədrə'mætɪk] *adj* melodrammatico

mel·o·dy ['melədɪ] melodia *f*

mel·on ['melən] melone *m*

melt [melt] **1** *v/i* sciogliersi **2** *v/t* sciogliere

♦ **melt away** *v/i fig* svanire

♦ **melt down** *v/t metal* fondere

melt·ing pot ['meltɪŋpɒt] *fig* crogiolo *m* di culture

mem·ber ['membə(r)] *of family* componente *m/f*; *of club* socio *m*; *of organization* membro *m*

Mem·ber of 'Par·lia·ment deputato *m*

mem·ber·ship ['membəʃɪp] iscrizione *f*; *number of members* numero *m* dei soci

mem·ber·ship card tessera *f* d'iscrizione

mem·brane ['membreɪn] membrana *f*

me·men·to [me'mentəʊ] souvenir *m inv*

mem·o ['meməʊ] circolare *f*

mem·oirs ['memwɑːz] *npl* memorie *fpl*

'mem·o pad blocco *m* notes

mem·o·ra·ble ['memərəbl] *adj* memorabile

me·mo·ri·al [mɪ'mɔːrɪəl] **1** *adj* commemorativo **2** *n also fig* memorial *m inv*

mem·o·rize ['meməraɪz] *v/t* memorizzare

mem·o·ry ['memərɪ] (*recollection*) ricordo *m*; *power of recollection* memoria *f*; COMPUT memoria *f*; *in ~ of* in memoria di

men [men] *pl* → **man**

men·ace ['menɪs] **1** *n* (*threat*) minaccia *f*; *person* pericolo *m* pubblico; (*nuisance*) peste *f* **2** *v/t* minacciare

men·ac·ing ['menɪsɪŋ] minaccioso

mend [mend] **1** *v/t* riparare **2** *n*: *be on the ~ after illness* essere in via di guarigione

me·ni·al ['mi:nɪəl] *adj* umile

men·in·gi·tis [menɪn'dʒaɪtɪs] meningite *f*

men·o·pause ['menəpɔːz] menopausa *f*

'men's room *Am* bagno *m* (degli uomini)

men·stru·ate ['menstrʊeɪt] *v/i* avere le mestruazioni

men·stru·a·tion [menstrʊ'eɪʃn] mestruazione *f*

men·tal ['mentl] *adj* mentale; F (*crazy*) pazzo

men·tal a'rith·me·tic calcolo *m* mentale; **men·tal 'cru·el·ty** crudeltà *f inv* mentale; **'men·tal hos·pi·tal** ospedale *m* psichiatrico; **men·tal 'ill·ness** malattia *f* mentale

men·tal·i·ty [men'tælətɪ] mentalità *f inv*

men·tal·ly ['mentəlɪ] *adv inwardly* mentalmente; *calculate etc* a mente

M

men·tal·ly 'hand·i·capped adj handicappato mentale

men·tal·ly 'ill adj malato di mente

men·tion ['menʃn] 1 n cenno m; he made no ~ of it non ne ha fatto cenno 2 v/t accennare a; she ~ed that ... ha accennato al fatto che ...; don't ~ it (you're welcome) non c'è di che

men·tor ['mentɔ:(r)] guida f spirituale

men·u ['menju:] also COMPUT menu m inv

MEP [emi:'pi:] abbr (= Member of the European Parliament) eurodeputato m

mer·ce·na·ry ['mɜ:sɪnərɪ] 1 adj mercenario 2 n MIL mercenario m

mer·chan·dise ['mɜ:tʃəndaɪz] merce f

mer·chant ['mɜ:tʃənt] commerciante m/f

mer·chant 'bank banca f d'affari

mer·chant 'bank·er banchiere m d'affari

mer·ci·ful ['mɜ:sɪfʊl] adj misericordioso

mer·ci·ful·ly ['mɜ:sɪflɪ] adv (thankfully) per fortuna

mer·ci·less ['mɜ:sɪlɪs] adj spietato

mer·cu·ry ['mɜ:kjʊrɪ] mercurio m

mer·cy ['mɜ:sɪ] misericordia f; be at s.o.'s ~ essere alla mercé di qu

mere [mɪə(r)] adj semplice; he's a ~ child è solo un bambino

mere·ly ['mɪəlɪ] adv soltanto

merge [mɜ:dʒ] v/i of two lines etc unirsi; of companies fondersi

merg·er ['mɜ:dʒə(r)] COM fusione f

mer·it ['merɪt] 1 n (worth) merito m; (advantage) vantaggio m 2 v/t meritare

mer·ri·ment ['merɪmənt] ilarità f inv

mer·ry ['merɪ] adj allegro; Merry Christmas! Buon Natale!

'mer·ry-go-round giostra f

mesh [meʃ] in net maglia f

mess [mes] (untidiness) disordine m; (trouble) pasticcio m; be a ~ of room, desk, hair essere in disordine; of situation, s.o.'s life essere

un pasticcio

♦ mess about, mess around 1 v/i (waste time) trastullarsi 2 v/t person menare per il naso

♦ mess around with v/i (play with) giocare con; (interfere with) armeggiare con; s.o.'s wife avere una relazione con

♦ mess up v/t room, papers mettere sottosopra; task, plans, marriage rovinare

mes·sage ['mesɪdʒ] also fig messaggio m

mes·sen·ger ['mesɪndʒə(r)] (courier) fattorino m, -a f

Mes·si·ah [me'saɪə] Messia m

mess·y ['mesɪ] adj room in disordine; person disordinato; job sporco; divorce, situation antipatico

met [met] pret & pp → meet

met·a·bol·ic [metə'bɒlɪk] adj metabolico

me·tab·o·lis·m [mə'tæbəlɪzm] metabolismo m

met·al ['metl] 1 adj in o di metallo 2 n metallo m

me·tal·lic [mɪ'tælɪk] adj metallico

met·a·phor ['metəfə(r)] metafora f

me·te·or ['mi:tɪə(r)] meteora f

me·te·or·ic [mi:tɪ'ɒrɪk] adj fig fulmineo

me·te·or·ite ['mi:tɪəraɪt] meteorite m o f

me·te·or·o·log·i·cal [mi:tɪərə'lɒdʒɪkl] adj meteorologico

me·te·or·ol·o·gist [mi:tɪə'rɒlədʒɪst] meteorologo m, -a f

me·te·or·ol·o·gy [mi:tɪə'rɒlədʒɪ] meteorologia f

me·ter ['mi:tə(r)] for gas etc contatore m; (parking ~) parchimetro m; Am: length metro m

'me·ter read·ing lettura f del contatore

meth·od ['meθəd] metodo m

me·thod·i·cal [mɪ'θɒdɪkl] adj metodico

me·thod·i·cal·ly [mɪ'θɒdɪklɪ] adv metodicamente

me·tic·u·lous [mɪ'tɪkjʊləs] adj meticoloso

me·tic·u·lous·ly [mɪˈtɪkjʊləslɪ] *adv* meticolosamente

me·tre [ˈmiːtə(r)] metro *m*

met·ric [ˈmetrɪk] *adj* metrico

me·trop·o·lis [mɪˈtrɒpəlɪs] metropoli *f inv*

met·ro·pol·i·tan [metrəˈpɒlɪtən] *adj* metropolitano

mew [mjuː] *n & v/i → miaow*

Mex·i·can [ˈmeksɪkən] **1** *adj* messicano **2** *n* messicano *m*, -a *f*

Mex·i·co [ˈmeksɪkəʊ] Messico *m*

mez·za·nine (floor) [ˈmezəniːn] mezzanino *m*

mi·aow [mɪaʊ] **1** *n* miao *m* **2** *v/i* miagolare

mice [maɪs] *pl → mouse*

mick·ey mouse [mɪkɪˈmaʊs] *adj* P *course, qualification* del piffero F

mi·cro·bi·ol·o·gy [ˈmaɪkrəʊ] microbiologia *f*; **'mi·cro·chip** microchip *m inv*; **'mi·cro·cli·mate** microclima *m*; **mi·cro·cosm** [ˈmaɪkrəʊkɒzm] microcosmo *m*; **'mi·cro·e·lec·tron·ics** microelettronica *f*; **'mi·cro·film** microfilm *m inv*; **'mi·cro·or·gan·ism** microrganismo *m*; **'mi·cro·phone** microfono *m*; **mi·cro·proces·sor** microprocessore *m*; **'mi·cro·scope** microscopio *m*; **mi·cro·scop·ic** [maɪkrəˈskɒpɪk] *adj* microscopico; **'mi·cro·wave** *oven* forno *m* a microonde

mid·air [mɪdˈeə(r)]: **in ~** a mezz'aria

mid·day [mɪdˈdeɪ] mezzogiorno *m*

mid·dle [ˈmɪdl] **1** *adj* di mezzo **2** *n* mezzo *m*; **in the ~ of** *floor, room* nel centro di, in mezzo a; *of period of time* a metà di; **be in the ~ of doing sth** stare facendo qc

'mid·dle-aged *adj* di mezz'età; **'Mid·dle Ages** *npl* Medioevo *m*; **mid·dle 'class** *adj* borghese; **the ~ class(es)** *npl* la borghesia *f*; **Mid·dle 'East** Medio Oriente *m*; **'mid·dle·man** intermediario *m*; **mid·dle 'man·age·ment** quadri *mpl* intermedi; **mid·dle 'name** secondo nome *m*; **'mid·dle·weight** *boxer* peso *m* medio

mid·dling [ˈmɪdlɪŋ] *adj* medio

mid·field·er [mɪdˈfiːldə(r)] centrocampista *m*

midge [mɪdʒ] moscerino *m*

midg·et [ˈmɪdʒɪt] *adj* di dimensioni ridotte

'Mid·lands *npl* regione *f* nell'Inghilterra centrale

'mid·night [ˈmɪdnaɪt] mezzanotte *f*; **at ~** a mezzanotte; **'mid·sum·mer** piena estate *f*; **'mid·way** *adv* a metà strada; **~ through** a metà di; **'mid·week** *adv* a metà settimana; **'Mid·west** regione *f* medio-occidentale degli USA; **'mid·wife** ostetrica *f*; **'mid·win·ter** pieno inverno *m*

might¹ [maɪt] *v/aux*: **I ~ be late** potrei far tardi; **it ~ rain** magari piove; **it ~ never happen** potrebbe non succedere mai; **I ~ have lost it** perhaps I did forse l'ho perso; **it would have been possible** avrei potuto perderlo; **he ~ have left** forse se n'è andato; **you ~ as well spend the night here** tanto vale che passi la notte qui; **you ~ have told me!** potevi dirmelo!

might² [maɪt] (power) forze *fpl*

might·y [ˈmaɪtɪ] **1** *adj* potente **2** *adv* F (extremely) molto

mi·graine [ˈmiːgreɪn] emicrania *f*

mi·grant work·er [ˈmaɪgrənt] emigrante *m/f*

mi·grate [maɪˈgreɪt] *v/i* emigrare; *of birds* migrare

mi·gra·tion [maɪˈgreɪʃn] emigrazione *f*; *of birds* migrazione *f*

mike [maɪk] F microfono *m*

Milan [mɪˈlæn] Milano *f*

mild [maɪld] *adj weather* mite; *cheese, person* dolce; *curry* poco piccante; *punishment, sedative* leggero

mil·dew [ˈmɪldjuː] muffa *f*

mild·ly [ˈmaɪldlɪ] *adv* gentilmente; (slightly) moderatamente; **to put it ~** a dir poco

mild·ness [ˈmaɪldnɪs] *of weather* mitezza *f*; *of person, voice* dolcezza *f*

mile [maɪl] miglio *m*; **~s better/easier** F molto meglio/più facile

mile·age [ˈmaɪlɪdʒ] chilometraggio *m*

M

'mile·stone *also fig* pietra *f* miliare

mil·i·tant ['mɪlɪtənt] **1** *adj* militante **2** *n* militante *m/f*

mil·i·ta·ry ['mɪlɪtrɪ] **1** *adj* militare **2** *n:* **the ~** l'esercito *m*, le forze *fpl* armate; *it's run by the ~* è in mano ai militari

mil·i·ta·ry a'cad·e·my accademia *f* militare; **mil·i·ta·ry po'lice** polizia *f* militare; **mil·i·tar·y 'serv·ice** servizio *m* militare

mi·li·tia [mɪ'lɪʃə] milizia *f*

milk [mɪlk] **1** *n* latte *m* **2** *v/t* mungere

'milk bot·tle bottiglia *f* del latte; **milk 'choc·o·late** cioccolato *m* al latte; 'milk float furgone *m* del lattaio; 'milk jug bricco *m* del latte; 'milk·man lattaio *m*; milk of mag'ne·sia latte *m* di magnesia; 'milk·shake frappé *m inv*

'milk·y ['mɪlkɪ] *adj* con tanto latte

Milk·y 'Way Via *f* Lattea

mill [mɪl] *for grain* mulino *m*; *for textiles* fabbrica *f*

♦ mill about, mill around *v/i* brulicare

mil·len·ni·um [mɪ'lenɪəm] millennio *m*

mil·li·gram ['mɪlɪgræm] milligrammo *m*

mil·li·me·ter *Am*, mil·li·me·tre ['mɪlɪmɪtə(r)] millimetro *m*

mil·lion ['mɪljən] milione *m*

mil·lion·aire [mɪljə'neə(r)] miliardario *m*, -a *f*

mime [maɪm] *v/t* mimare

mim·ic ['mɪmɪk] **1** *n* imitatore *m*, -trice *f* **2** *v/t* (*pret & pp* -ked) imitare

mince [mɪns] *v/t meat* carne *f* tritata

'mince·meat *frutta f secca tritata*

mince 'pie *pasticcino m ripieno di frutta secca tritata*

mind [maɪnd] **1** *n* mente *f*, cervello *m*; *it's all in your* ~ è solo la tua immaginazione; *be out of one's* ~ essere matto; *keep sth in* ~ tenere presente qc; *I've a good* ~ *to ...* ho proprio voglia di ...; *change one's* ~ cambiare idea; *it didn't enter my* ~ non

mi è passato per la testa; *give s.o. a piece of one's* ~ cantarne quattro a qu; *make up one's* ~ decidersi; *have sth on one's* ~ essere preoccupato per qc; *keep one's* ~ *on sth* concentrarsi su qc **2** *v/t* (*look after*) tenere d'occhio; *children* badare a; (*heed*) fare attenzione a; *I don't* ~ *tea if that's all you've got* (*object to*) il tè va bene se non hai altro; *I don't* ~ *what we do* non importa cosa facciamo; *do you* ~ *if I smoke?, do you* ~ *my smoking?* le dispiace se fumo?; *would you* ~ *opening the window?* le dispiace aprire la finestra?; ~ *the step!* attento al gradino!; ~ *your own business!* fatti gli affari tuoi! **3** *v/i:* ~! (*be careful*) attenzione!; *never* ~! non farci caso!; *I don't* ~ è uguale *o* indifferente

mind-bog·gling ['maɪndbɒglɪŋ] *adj* incredibile

mind·less ['maɪndlɪs] *adj violence* insensato

mine[1] [maɪn] *pron* il mio *m*, la mia *f*, i miei *mpl*, le mie *fpl*; *a cousin of* ~ un mio cugino

mine[2] [maɪn] **1** *n for coal etc* miniera *f* **2** *v/i:* ~ *for* estrarre

mine[3] [maɪn] **1** *n explosive* mina *f* **2** *v/t* minare

'mine·field *also fig* campo *m* minato

min·er ['maɪnə(r)] minatore *m*

min·e·ral ['mɪnərəl] *n* minerale *m*

'min·e·ral wa·ter acqua *f* minerale

'mine·sweep·er NAUT dragamine *m inv*

min·gle ['mɪŋgl] *v/i of sounds, smells* mischiarsi; *at party* mescolarsi

min·i ['mɪnɪ] *skirt* mini *f inv*

min·i·a·ture ['mɪnɪtʃə(r)] *adj* in miniatura

'min·i·bus minibus *m inv*

'min·i·cab radiotaxi *m inv*

min·i·mal ['mɪnɪməl] *adj* minimo

min·i·mal·ism ['mɪnɪməlɪzm] minimalismo *m*

min·i·mize ['mɪnɪmaɪz] *v/t* minimizzare

min·i·mum ['mɪnɪməm] **1** *adj* minimo **2** *n* minimo *m*

min·i·mum 'wage salario *m* minimo garantito

min·ing ['maɪnɪŋ] industria *f* mineraria

'min·i·se·ries TV miniserie *f inv*

'min·i·skirt minigonna *f*

min·is·ter ['mɪnɪstə(r)] POL ministro *m*; REL pastore *m*

min·is·te·ri·al [mɪnɪ'stɪərɪəl] *adj* ministeriale

min·is·try ['mɪnɪstrɪ] POL ministero *m*

mink [mɪŋk] **1** *adj fur* di visone **2** *n coat* visone *m*

mi·nor ['maɪnə(r)] **1** *adj* piccolo; *in D ~* MUS in Re minore **2** *n* LAW minorenne *m/f*

mi·nor·i·ty [maɪ'nɒrətɪ] minoranza *f*; *be in the ~* essere in minoranza

mint [mɪnt] *n herb* menta *f*; *chocolate* cioccolato *m* alla menta; *sweet* mentina *f*

mi·nus ['maɪnəs] **1** *n* (*~ sign*) meno *m* **2** *prep* meno; *~ 10 degrees* 10 gradi sotto zero

mi·nus·cule ['mɪnəskju:l] *adj* minuscolo

min·ute¹ ['mɪnɪt] *of time* minuto *m*; *in a ~* (*soon*) in un attimo; *just a ~* un attimo

mi·nute² [maɪ'nju:t] *adj* (*tiny*) piccolissimo; (*detailed*) minuzioso; *in ~ detail* minuziosamente

'mi·nute hand lancetta *f* dei minuti

mi·nute·ly [maɪ'nju:tlɪ] *adv* (*in detail*) minuziosamente; (*very slightly*) appena

min·utes ['mɪnɪts] *npl of meeting* verbale *m*

mir·a·cle ['mɪrəkl] miracolo *m*

mi·rac·u·lous [mɪ'rækjʊləs] *adj* miracoloso

mi·rac·u·lous·ly [mɪ'rækjʊləslɪ] *adv* miracolosamente

mi·rage ['mɪrɑːʒ] miraggio *m*

mir·ror ['mɪrə(r)] **1** *n* specchio *m*; MOT specchietto *m* **2** *v/t* riflettere; *be ~ed in sth in water etc* specchiarsi in qc; *fig* rispecchiarsi in qc

mirth [mɜːθ] ilarità *f inv*

mis·an·thro·pist [mɪ'zænθrəpɪst] misantropo *m*

mis·ap·pre·hen·sion [mɪsæprɪ'henʃn]: *be under a ~* sbagliarsi

mis·be·have [mɪsbə'heɪv] *v/i* comportarsi male

mis·be·hav·ior *Am*, **mis·be·hav·iour** [mɪsbə'heɪvjə(r)] comportamento *m* scorretto

mis·cal·cu·late [mɪs'kælkjʊleɪt] *v/t & v/i* calcolare male

mis·cal·cu·la·tion [mɪs'kælkjʊleɪʃn] errore *m* di calcolo

mis·car·riage ['mɪskærɪdʒ] MED aborto *m* spontaneo; *~ of justice* errore *m* giudiziario

mis·car·ry ['mɪskærɪ] *v/i* (*pret & pp -ied*) *of plan* fallire

mis·cel·la·ne·ous [mɪsə'leɪnɪəs] *adj* eterogeneo

mis·chief ['mɪstʃɪf] (*naughtiness*) birichinate *fpl*

mis·chie·vous ['mɪstʃɪvəs] *adj* (*naughty*) birichino; (*malicious*) perfido

mis·con·cep·tion [mɪskən'sepʃn] idea *f* sbagliata

mis·con·duct [mɪs'kɒndʌkt] reato *m* professionale

mis·con·strue [mɪskən'struː] *v/t* interpretare male

mis·de·mea·nor *Am*, **mis·de·mea·nour** [mɪsdə'miːnə(r)] infrazione *f*

mi·ser ['maɪzə(r)] avaro *m*, -a *f*

mis·e·ra·ble ['mɪzrəbl] *adj* (*unhappy*) infelice; *weather, performance* deprimente

mi·ser·ly ['maɪzəlɪ] *adj person* avaro; *amount* misero

mis·e·ry ['mɪzərɪ] (*unhappiness*) tristezza *f*; (*wretchedness*) miseria *f*

mis·fire [mɪs'faɪə(r)] *v/i of joke, scheme* far cilecca; *of engine* perdere colpi

mis·fit ['mɪsfɪt] *in society* disadattato *m*, -a *f*

mis·for·tune [mɪs'fɔːtʃən] sfortuna *f*

mis·giv·ings [mɪs'gɪvɪŋz] *npl* dubbi *mpl*

mis·guid·ed [mɪs'gaɪdɪd] *adj at-*

M

tempts, *theory* sbagliato; **he was ~ in maintaining that ...** sbagliava a sostenere che ...

mis·han·dle [mɪsˈhændl] v/t *situation* gestire male

mis·hap [ˈmɪshæp] incidente *m*

mis·in·form [mɪsɪnˈfɔːm] v/t informare male

mis·in·ter·pret [mɪsɪnˈtɜːprɪt] v/t interpretare male

mis·in·ter·pre·ta·tion [mɪsɪntɜːprɪˈteɪʃn] interpretazione *f* errata

mis·judge [mɪsˈdʒʌdʒ] v/t *person, situation* giudicare male

mis·lay [mɪsˈleɪ] v/t (*pret & pp* **-laid**) smarrire

mis·lead [mɪsˈliːd] v/t (*pret & pp* **-led**) trarre in inganno

mis·lead·ing [mɪsˈliːdɪŋ] adj fuorviante

mis·man·age [mɪsˈmænɪdʒ] v/t gestire male

mis·man·age·ment [mɪsˈmænɪdʒmənt] cattiva gestione *f*

mis·match [ˈmɪsmætʃ] discordanza *f*

mis·placed [ˈmɪspleɪst] adj *loyalty, enthusiasm* malriposto

mis·print [ˈmɪsprɪnt] refuso *m*

mis·pro·nounce [mɪsprəˈnaʊns] v/t pronunciare male

mis·pro·nun·ci·a·tion [mɪsprənʌnsɪˈeɪʃn] errore *m* di pronuncia

mis·read [mɪsˈriːd] v/t (*pret & pp* **-read** [red]) *word, figures* leggere male; *situation* interpretare male

mis·rep·re·sent [mɪsreprɪˈzent] v/t *facts, truth* travisare; **I've been ~ed** hanno travisato quello che ho detto

miss[1] [mɪs]: **Miss Smith** signorina Smith; **~!** signorina!

miss[2] [mɪs] **1** *n*: **give the meeting / party a ~** non andare alla riunione / festa **2** v/t (*not hit*) mancare; *emotionally* sentire la mancanza di; *bus, train, plane* perdere; (*not present at*) mancare a; **I ~ you** mi manchi; **you've just ~ed him** he's just gone è appena uscito; **we must have ~ed the turnoff** ci dev'essere

sfuggito lo svincolo **3** v/i fallire

mis·shap·en [mɪsˈʃeɪpən] adj deforme

mis·sile [ˈmɪsaɪl] (*rocket*) missile *m*

miss·ing [ˈmɪsɪŋ] adj scomparso; **be ~** *of person, plane* essere disperso; **there's a piece ~** manca un pezzo

mis·sion [ˈmɪʃn] (*task, people*) missione *f*

mis·sion·a·ry [ˈmɪʃənrɪ] REL missionario *m*, -a *f*

mis·spell [mɪsˈspel] v/t scrivere male

mist [mɪst] foschia *f*

♦ mist over v/i *of eyes* velarsi di lacrime

♦ mist up v/i *of mirror, window* appannarsi

mis·take [mɪˈsteɪk] **1** *n* errore *m*, sbaglio *m*; **make a ~** fare un errore, sbagliarsi; **by ~** per errore **2** v/t (*pret mistook, pp mistaken*) sbagliare; **~ sth for sth** scambiare qc per qc

mis·tak·en [mɪˈsteɪkən] **1** adj sbagliato; **be ~** sbagliarsi **2** pp → **mistake**

mis·ter [ˈmɪstə(r)] → **Mr**

mis·tress [ˈmɪstrɪs] *lover* amante *f*; *of servant, of dog* padrona *f*

mis·trust [mɪsˈtrʌst] **1** *n* diffidenza *f* **2** v/t diffidare di

mist·y [ˈmɪstɪ] adj *weather* nebbioso; *eyes* velato

mis·un·der·stand [mɪsʌndəˈstænd] v/t (*pret & pp* **-stood**) fraintendere

mis·un·der·stand·ing [mɪsʌndəˈstændɪŋ] *mistake* malinteso *m*, equivoco *m*; *argument* dissapore *m*

mis·use [mɪsˈjuːs] **1** *n* uso *m* improprio **2** v/t [mɪsˈjuːz] usare impropriamente

mit·i·ga·ting cir·cum·stances [ˈmɪtɪgeɪtɪŋ] *npl* circostanze *fpl* attenuanti

mit·ten [ˈmɪtən] muffola *f*

mix [mɪks] **1** *n* (*mixture*) mescolanza *f*; *in cooking* miscuglio *m*; *in cooking*: *ready to use* preparato *m* **2** v/t mescolare **3** v/i *socially* socializzare

♦ mix up v/t confondere; **mix sth up with sth** scambiare qc per qc; **be mixed up** *emotionally* avere disturbi emotivi; *of figures, papers* essere in disordine; *be mixed up in* essere coinvolto in; *get mixed up with* avere a che fare con

♦ **mix with** *v/t (associate with)* frequentare

mixed [mɪkst] *adj* misto; *reactions, reviews* contrastante; *I've got ~ feelings* sono combattuto

mixed 'mar·riage matrimonio *m* misto

mix·er ['mɪksə(r)] *for food* mixer *m inv*; *drink* bibita *f* da mischiare a un superalcolico; *she's a good ~* è molto socievole

mix·ture ['mɪkstʃə(r)] miscuglio *m*; *medicine* sciroppo *m*

mix-up ['mɪksʌp] confusione *f*

moan [məʊn] **1** *n of pain* lamento *m*, gemito *m*; *(complaint)* lamentela *f* **2** *v/i in pain* lamentarsi, gemere; *(complain)* lamentarsi

mob [mɒb] **1** *n* folla *f* **2** *v/t (pret & pp -bed)* prendere d'assalto

mo·bile ['məʊbaɪl] **1** *adj that can be moved* mobile; *she's less ~ now* non si può muovere tanto, ora **2** *n for decoration* mobile *m inv*; *phone* telefonino *m*

no·bile 'home casamobile *f*

no·bile 'phone telefono *m* cellulare

no·bil·i·ty [mə'bɪlətɪ] mobilità *f inv*

nob·ster ['mɒbstə(r)] gangster *m inv*

nock [mɒk] **1** *adj* finto; *exam, election* simulato; *a ~-Tudor house* una casa in stile Tudor **2** *v/t* deridere

nock·e·ry ['mɒkərɪ] *(derision)* scherno *m*; *(travesty)* farsa *f*

nock-up ['mɒkʌp] *(model)* modello *m*

nod cons [mɒd'kɒnz] *npl*: *with all ~* con tutti i comfort

node [məʊd] *form* mezzo *m*; COMPUT modalità *f inv*

nod·el ['mɒdl] **1** *adj employee, husband* modello; *boat, plane* in miniatura **2** *n (miniature)* modellino *m*; *(pattern)* modello *m*; *(fashion ~)* indossatrice *f*; *male ~* indossatore *m* **3** *v/t* indossare **4** *v/i for designer* fare

l'indossatore / -trice; *for artist, photographer* posare

mo·dem ['məʊdem] modem *m inv*

mod·e·rate ['mɒdərət] **1** *adj* moderato **2** *n* POL moderato *m*, -a *f* **3** *v/t* ['mɒdəreɪt] moderare **4** *v/i* calmarsi

mod·e·rate·ly ['mɒdərətlɪ] *adv* abbastanza

mod·e·ra·tion [mɒdə'reɪʃn] *(restraint)* moderazione *f*; *in ~* con moderazione

mod·ern ['mɒdn] *adj* moderno

mod·ern·i·za·tion [mɒdənaɪ'zeɪʃn] modernizzazione *f*

mod·ern·ize ['mɒdənaɪz] **1** *v/t* modernizzare **2** *v/i of business, country* modernizzarsi

mod·ern 'lan·guages lingue *fpl* moderne

mod·est ['mɒdɪst] *adj* modesto

mod·es·ty ['mɒdɪstɪ] modestia *f*

mod·i·fi·ca·tion [mɒdɪfɪ'keɪʃn] modifica *f*

mod·i·fy ['mɒdɪfaɪ] *v/t (pret & pp -ied)* modificare

mod·u·lar ['mɒdjʊlə(r)] *adj furniture* modulare

mod·ule ['mɒdjuːl] modulo *m*; *(space ~)* modulo *m* spaziale

moist [mɔɪst] *adj* umido

moist·en ['mɔɪsn] *v/t* inumidire

mois·ture ['mɔɪstʃə(r)] umidità *f inv*

mois·tur·iz·er ['mɔɪstʃəraɪzə(r)] *for skin* idratante *m*

mo·lar ['məʊlə(r)] molare *m*

mold *etc Am* → **mould** *etc*

mole [məʊl] *on skin* neo *m*; *animal, spy* talpa *f*

mo·lec·u·lar [mə'lekjʊlə(r)] *adj* molecolare

mol·e·cule ['mɒlɪkjuːl] molecola *f*

mo·lest [mə'lest] *v/t child, woman* molestare

mol·ly·cod·dle ['mɒlɪkɒdl] *v/t* F coccolare

mol·ten ['məʊltən] *adj* fuso

mo·ment ['məʊmənt] attimo *m*, istante *m*; *at the ~* al momento; *for the ~* per il momento

mo·men·tar·i·ly [məʊmən'teərɪlɪ] *adv (for a moment)* per un momen-

M

to; (*Am: in a moment*) da un momento all'altro

mo·men·ta·ry ['məʊməntrɪ] *adj* momentaneo

mo·men·tous [mə'mentəs] *adj* importante

mo·men·tum [mə'mentəm] impeto *m*

mon·arch ['mɒnək] monarca *m*

mon·ar·chy ['mɒnəkɪ] monarchia *f*

mon·as·tery ['mɒnəstrɪ] monastero *m*

mo·nas·tic [mə'næstɪk] *adj* monastico

Mon·day ['mʌndeɪ] lunedì *m inv*

mon·e·ta·ry ['mʌnɪtrɪ] *adj* monetario

mon·ey ['mʌnɪ] denaro *m*, soldi *mpl*; '**mon·ey belt** marsupio *m*; '**mon·ey mar·ket** mercato *m* monetario; '**mon·ey or·der** vaglia *m*

mon·grel ['mʌngrəl] cane *m* bastardo

mon·i·tor ['mɒnɪtə(r)] **1** *n* COMPUT monitor *m* **2** *v/t* osservare

monk [mʌŋk] frate *m*, monaco *m*

mon·key ['mʌŋkɪ] scimmia *f*; F (*child*) diavoletto *m*

♦ **monkey about with** *v/t* F armeggiare con

'**mon·key wrench** chiave *f* a rullino

mon·o·gram ['mɒnəgræm] monogramma *m*

mon·o·grammed ['mɒnəgræmd] con il monogramma

mon·o·log *Am*, **mon·o·logue** ['mɒnəlɒg] monologo *m*

mo·nop·o·lize [mə'nɒpəlaɪz] *v/t also fig* monopolizzare

mo·nop·o·ly [mə'nɒpəlɪ] monopolio *m*

mo·not·o·nous [mə'nɒtənəs] *adj* monotono

mo·not·o·ny [mə'nɒtənɪ] monotonia *f*

mon·soon [mɒn'suːn] monsone *m*

mon·ster ['mɒnstə(r)] mostro *m*

mon·stros·i·ty [mɒn'strɒsətɪ] obbrobrio *m*

mon·strous ['mɒnstrəs] *adj* mostruoso

month [mʌnθ] mese *m*

month·ly ['mʌnθlɪ] **1** *adj* mensile **2** *adv* mensilmente **3** *n magazine* mensile *m*

mon·u·ment ['mɒnjʊmənt] monumento *m*

mon·u·ment·al [mɒnjʊ'mentl] *adj fig* monumentale

moo [muː] *v/i* muggire

mood [muːd] (*frame of mind*) umore *m*; (*bad ~*) malumore *m*; *of meeting, country* clima *m*; *be in a good / bad ~* essere di cattivo / buon umore; *be in the ~ for* aver voglia di

mood·y ['muːdɪ] *adj* lunatico; (*bad-tempered*) di cattivo umore

moon [muːn] luna *f*

'**moon·light 1** *n* chiaro *m* di luna **2** *v/i* F lavorare in nero; '**moon·lit** *adj night* di luna piena

moor [mʊə(r)] *v/t boat* ormeggiare

moor·ings ['mʊərɪŋz] *npl* ormeggio *m*

moose [muːs] alce *m*

mop [mɒp] **1** *n for floor* mocio® *m*; *for dishes* spazzolino per i piatti **2** *v/t* (*pret & pp* **-ped**) *floor* lavare; *eyes, face* asciugare

♦ **mop up** *v/t* raccogliere; MIL eliminare

mope [məʊp] *v/i* essere depresso

mo·ped ['məʊped] motorino *m*

mor·al ['mɒrəl] **1** *adj* morale; *person* di saldi principi morali **2** *n of story* morale *f*; *~s* principi *mpl* morali

mo·rale [mə'rɑːl] morale *m*

mo·ral·i·ty [mə'rælətɪ] moralità *f inv*

mor·bid ['mɔːbɪd] *adj* morboso

more [mɔː(r)] **1** *adj* più, altro; *some ~ tea?* dell'altro tè?; *a few ~ sandwiches* qualche altro tramezzino; *for ~ information* per maggiori informazioni; *~ and ~ students / time* sempre più studenti / tempo; *there's no ~ …* non c'è più … **2** *adv* più; *with verbs* di più; *~ important* più importante; *~ often* più spesso; *~ and ~* sempre di più; *~ or less* più o meno; *once ~* ancora una volta; *~ than 100* oltre 100; *I don't live* there any ~ non abito più in **3** *pron*: **do you want some ~?** ne vuoi ancora?, ne vuoi dell'altro; **a little ~** un altro po'

more·o·ver [mɔːˈrəʊvə(r)] *adv* inoltre

morgue [mɔːg] obitorio *m*

morn·ing [ˈmɔːnɪŋ] mattino *m*, mattina *f*; **in the ~** di mattina; *(tomorrow)* domattina; **this ~** stamattina; **tomorrow ~** domani mattina; **good ~** buongiorno

morn·ing 'sick·ness nausee *fpl* mattutine

mo·ron [ˈmɔːrɒn] F idiota *m/f*

mo·rose [məˈrəʊs] *adj* imbronciato

mor·phine [ˈmɔːfiːn] morfina *f*

mor·sel [ˈmɔːsl] pezzetto *m*

mor·tal [ˈmɔːtl] **1** *adj* mortale **2** *n* mortale *m/f*

mor·tal·i·ty [mɔːˈtælətɪ] mortalità *f inv*

mor·tar[1] [ˈmɔːtə(r)] MIL mortaio *m*

mor·tar[2] [ˈmɔːtə(r)] *cement* malta *f*

mort·gage [ˈmɔːgɪdʒ] **1** *n* mutuo *m*, ipotecario **2** *v/t* ipotecare

mor·tu·a·ry [ˈmɔːtjʊərɪ] camera *f* mortuaria

mo·sa·ic [məʊˈzeɪɪk] mosaico *m*

Mos·cow [ˈmɒskəʊ] Mosca *f*

Mos·lem [ˈmʊzlɪm] **1** *adj* islamico **2** *n* musulmano *m*, -a *f*

mosque [mɒsk] moschea *f*

mos·qui·to [mɒsˈkiːtəʊ] zanzara *f*

moss [mɒs] muschio *m*

moss·y [ˈmɒsɪ] *adj* coperto di muschio

most [məʊst] **1** *adj* la maggior parte di; **~ Saturdays** quasi tutti i sabati **2** *adv* (*very*) estremamente; **the ~ beautiful/interesting** il più bello / interessante; **that's the one I like** è quello che mi piace di più; **~ of all** soprattutto **3** *pron* la maggior parte (*of* di); **at (the) ~** al massimo; **make the ~ of** approfittare (al massimo) di

most·ly [ˈməʊstlɪ] *adv* per lo più

MOT [eməʊˈtiː] *Br* revisione *f* annuale obbligatoria dei veicoli

mo·tel [məʊˈtel] motel *m inv*

moth [mɒθ] falena *f*; (*clothes* ~) tarma *f*

'moth·ball naftalina *f*

moth·er [ˈmʌðə(r)] **1** *n* madre *f* **2** *v/t* fare da mamma a

'moth·er·board COMPUT scheda *f* madre

'moth·er·hood maternità *f inv*

Moth·er·ing 'Sun·day → *Mother's Day*

'moth·er·in·law (*pl* **mothers-in-law**) suocera *f*

moth·er·ly [ˈmʌðəlɪ] *adj* materno

moth·er·of·'pearl madreperla *f*; **'Mother's Day** Festa *f* della mamma; **'moth·er tongue** madrelingua *f*

mo·tif [məʊˈtiːf] motivo *m*

mo·tion [ˈməʊʃn] **1** *n* (*movement*) moto *m*; (*proposal*) mozione *f*; **set things in ~** metter in moto le cose **2** *v/t*: **he ~ed me forward** mi ha fatto cenno di avvicinarmi

mo·tion·less [ˈməʊʃnlɪs] *adj* immobile

mo·ti·vate [ˈməʊtɪveɪt] *v/t person* motivare

mo·ti·va·tion [məʊtɪˈveɪʃn] motivazione *f*

mo·tive [ˈməʊtɪv] motivo *m*

mo·tor [ˈməʊtə(r)] motore *m*; *Br* F car macchina *f*

'mo·tor·bike moto *f*; **'mo·tor·boat** motoscafo *m*; **mo·tor·cade** [ˈməʊtəkeɪd] corteo *m* di auto; **'mo·tor·cy·cle** motocicletta *f*; **'mo·tor·cy·clist** motociclista *m/f*; **'mo·tor home** casamobile *f*

mo·tor·ist [ˈməʊtərɪst] automobilista *m/f*

'mo·tor me·chan·ic meccanico *m*; **'mo·tor rac·ing** automobilismo *m*; **'mo·tor·scoot·er** scooter *m inv*; **'mo·tor show** salone *m* dell'automobile; **'mo·tor ve·hi·cle** autoveicolo *m*; **'mo·tor·way** *Br* autostrada *f*

mot·to [ˈmɒtəʊ] motto *m*

mould[1] [məʊld] *on food* muffa *f*

mould[2] [məʊld] **1** *n* stampo *m* **2** *v/t also fig* plasmare

M

mould·y ['məʊldɪ] *adj food* ammuffito

mound [maʊnd] (*hillock*) collinetta *f*; *in baseball* pedana *f* del lanciatore; (*pile*) mucchio *m*

mount [maʊnt] **1** *n* (*horse*) cavalcatura *f*; **Mount McKinlay** il Monte McKinlay **2** *v/t steps* salire; *horse* montare a; *bicycle* montare in; *campaign* organizzare; *jewel* montare; *photo, painting* incorniciare **3** *v/i* (*increase*) aumentare

♦ **mount up** *v/i* accumularsi

moun·tain ['maʊntɪn] montagna *f*

'**moun·tain bike** mountain bike *f inv*

moun·tain·eer [maʊntɪ'nɪə(r)] alpinista *m/f*

moun·tain·eer·ing [maʊntɪ'nɪərɪŋ] alpinismo *m*

moun·tain·ous ['maʊntɪnəs] *adj* montuoso

moun·tain 'res·cue serv·ice soccorso *m* alpino

mount·ed po'lice ['maʊntɪd] polizia *f* a cavallo

mourn [mɔːn] **1** *v/t* piangere **2** *v/i*: ~ **for** piangere la morte di

mourn·er ['mɔːnə(r)] *persona f che partecipa a un corteo funebre*

mourn·ful ['mɔːnfʊl] *adj* triste

mourn·ing ['mɔːnɪŋ] lutto *m*; **be in ~** essere in lutto; **wear ~** portare il lutto

mouse [maʊs] (*pl* **mice** [maɪs]) topo *m*; COMPUT mouse *m inv*

'**mouse mat** COMPUT tappetino *m* del mouse

mous·tache [mə'stɑːʃ] baffi *mpl*

mouth [maʊθ] *of person* bocca *f*; *of river* foce *f*

mouth·ful ['maʊθfʊl] *of food* boccone *m*; *of drink* sorsata *f*

'**mouth·or·gan** armonica *f* a bocca; '**mouth·piece** *of instrument* bocchino *m*; (*spokesperson*) portavoce *m/f*; '**mouth·wash** collutorio *m*; '**mouth·wa·ter·ing** *adj* che fa venire l'acquolina

move [muːv] **1** *n* (*step, action*) mossa *f*; *change of house* trasloco *m*; **get a ~ on!** F spicciati!; **don't make a ~!** non

ti muovere! **2** *v/t object* spostare, muovere; (*transfer*) trasferire; *emotionally* commuovere; ~ **house** traslocare **3** *v/i* muoversi, spostarsi; (*transfer*) trasferirsi

♦ **move around** *v/i in room* muoversi; *from place to place* spostarsi

♦ **move away** *v/i* allontanarsi; *move house* traslocare

♦ **move in** *v/i* trasferirsi

♦ **move on** *v/i* ripartire; *in discussion* andare avanti; **move on to sth** passare a qc

♦ **move out** *v/i of house* andare via; *of troops* ritirarsi

♦ **move up** *v/i in league* avanzare; (*make room*) spostarsi

move·ment ['muːvmənt] movimento *m*

mov·ie ['muːvɪ] film *m inv*; **go to a ~ / the ~s** andare al cinema

'**mov·ie thea·ter** *Am* cinema *m inv*

mov·ing ['muːvɪŋ] *adj which can move* mobile; *emotionally* commovente

mow [məʊ] *v/t grass* tagliare, falciare

♦ **mow down** *v/t* falciare

mow·er ['məʊə(r)] tosaerba *m inv*

MP [em'piː] *abbr* (= **Member of Parliament**) deputato *m*; (= **Military Policeman**) polizia *f* militare

mph [empiː'eɪtʃ] *abbr* (= **miles per hour**) miglia *fpl* orarie

Mr ['mɪstə(r)] signor

Mrs ['mɪsɪz] signora

Ms [mɪz] signora *appellativo m usato sia per donne sposate che nubili*

Mt *abbr* (= **Mount**) M. (= monte *m*)

much [mʌtʃ] **1** *adj* molto; **so ~ money** tanti soldi; **how ~ sugar?** quanto zucchero?; **as ~ ... as ...** tanto ... quanto ... **2** *adv* molto; **very ~** moltissimo; **too ~** troppo; **as ~ as ...** tanto quanto ...; **as ~ as a million dollars** addirittura un milione di dollari; **I thought as ~** me l'aspettavo **3** *pron* molto; **nothing ~** niente di particolare; **there's not ~ left** non ne è rimasto, -a molto, -a

muck [mʌk] (*dirt*) sporco *m*

mu·cus ['mjuːkəs] muco *m*

mud [mʌd] fango m

mud·dle ['mʌdl] **1** n disordine m; *I'm in a* ~ sono confuso **2** v/t confondere

♦ **muddle up** v/t (*mess up*) mettere in disordine; (*confuse*) confondere

mud·dy ['mʌdɪ] adj fangoso; *hands, boots* sporco di fango

mues·li ['mu:zlɪ] müsli m inv

muf·fle ['mʌfl] v/t *sound* attutire; *voice* camuffare

muf·fler ['mʌflər] Am MOT marmitta f

♦ **muffle up** v/i coprirsi bene

mug¹ [mʌg] *for tea, coffee* tazzone m; F (*face*) faccia f

mug² [mʌg] v/t (*pret & pp* **-ged**) *attack* aggredire

mug·ger ['mʌgər] aggressore m

mug·ging ['mʌgɪŋ] aggressione f

mug·gy ['mʌgɪ] adj afoso

mule [mju:l] *animal* mulo m; (*slipper*) mule f inv

♦ **mull over** [mʌl] v/t riflettere su

mul·ti·lat·er·al [mʌltɪ'lætərəl] adj POL multilaterale

mul·ti·lin·gual [mʌltɪ'lɪŋgwəl] adj multilingue inv

mul·ti·me·di·a [mʌltɪ'mi:dɪə] **1** adj multimediale **2** n multimedialità f inv

mul·ti·na·tion·al [mʌltɪ'næʃnl] **1** adj multinazionale **2** n COM multinazionale f

mul·ti·ple ['mʌltɪpl] adj multiplo

mul·ti·ple 'choice ques·tion esercizio m a scelta multipla

mul·ti·ple scle'ro·sis sclerosi f multipla

'mul·ti·plex ('cin·e·ma) cinema m inv multisale

mul·ti·pli·ca·tion [mʌltɪplɪ'keɪʃn] moltiplicazione f

mul·ti·ply ['mʌltɪplaɪ] (*pret & pp* **-ied**) **1** v/t moltiplicare **2** v/i moltiplicarsi

multi-sto·rey (car park) [mʌltɪ'stɔ:rɪ] parcheggio m a più piani

mum [mʌm] mamma f

mum·ble ['mʌmbl] **1** n borbottio m **2** v/t & v/i borbottare

mum·my ['mʌmɪ] mamma f

mumps [mʌmps] nsg orecchioni mpl

munch [mʌnʧ] v/t & v/i sgranocchiare

mu·ni·ci·pal [mju:'nɪsɪpl] adj municipale

mu·ral ['mjʊərəl] murale m

mur·der ['mɜ:də(r)] **1** n omicidio m **2** v/t *person* uccidere; *song* rovinare

mur·der·er ['mɜ:dərə(r)] omicida m/f

mur·der·ous ['mɜ:drəs] adj *rage, look* omicida

murk·y ['mɜ:kɪ] adj also fig torbido

mur·mur ['mɜ:mə(r)] **1** n mormorio m **2** v/t mormorare

mus·cle ['mʌsl] muscolo m

mus·cu·lar ['mʌskjʊlə(r)] adj *pain, strain* muscolare; *person* muscoloso

muse [mju:z] v/i riflettere

mu·se·um [mju:'zɪəm] museo m

mush·room ['mʌʃrʊm] **1** n fungo m **2** v/i crescere rapidamente

mu·sic ['mju:zɪk] musica f; *in written form* spartito m

mu·sic·al ['mju:zɪkl] **1** adj musicale; *person* portato per la musica; *voice* melodioso **2** n musical m inv

'mu·sic(·al) box carillon m inv

mu·sic·al 'in·stru·ment strumento m musicale

mu·si·cian [mju:'zɪʃn] musicista m/f

mus·sel ['mʌsl] cozza f

must [mʌst] v/aux ◊ (*necessity*): *I ~ be on time* devo arrivare in orario; *I ~* devo; *I ~n't be late* non devo far tardi ◊ (*probability*): *it ~ be about 6 o'clock* devono essere circa le sei; *they ~ have arrived by now* ormai devono essere arrivati

mus·tache Am → **moustache**

mus·tard ['mʌstəd] senape f

must·y ['mʌstɪ] adj *smell* di stantio; *room* che sa di stantio

mute [mju:t] adj muto

mut·ed ['mju:tɪd] adj tenue

mu·ti·late ['mju:tɪleɪt] v/t mutilare

mu·ti·ny ['mju:tɪnɪ] **1** n ammutinamento m **2** v/i (*pret & pp* **-ied**) ammutinarsi

M

mut·ter ['mʌtə(r)] *v/t & v/i* farfagliare

mutton ['mʌtn] montone *m*

mu·tu·al ['mjuːtʃʊəl] *adj admiration* reciproco; *friend* in comune

muz·zle ['mʌzl] **1** *n of animal* muso *m*; *for dog* museruola *f* **2** *v/t:* ~ *the press* imbavagliare la stampa

my [maɪ] *adj* il mio *m*, la mia *f*, i miei *mpl*, le mie *fpl*; ~ *bag said by man / woman* la mia valigia; ~ *sister / brother* mia sorella / mio fratello

my·op·ic [maɪ'ɒpɪk] *adj* miope

my·self [maɪ'self] *pron reflexive* mi; *emphatic* io stesso; *after prep* me

stesso; *I've hurt* ~ mi sono fatto male; ~, *I'd prefer ...* quanto a me, preferirei ...; *by* ~ da solo

mys·te·ri·ous [mɪ'stɪərɪəs] *adj* misterioso

mys·te·ri·ous·ly [mɪ'stɪərɪəslɪ] *adv* misteriosamente

mys·te·ry ['mɪstərɪ] mistero *m*

mys·tic ['mɪstɪk] *adj* mistico

mys·ti·fy ['mɪstɪfaɪ] *v/t* (*pret & pp -ied*) lasciare perplesso

myth [mɪθ] *also fig* mito *m*

myth·i·cal ['mɪθɪkl] *adj* mitico

my·thol·o·gy [mɪ'θɒlədʒɪ] mitologia *f*

N

nab [næb] *v/t* (*pret & pp -bed*) F *take for o.s.* prendere

nag [næg] (*pret & pp -ged*) **1** *v/i of person* brontolare di continuo **2** *v/t* assillare; ~ *s.o. to do sth* assillare qu perché faccia qc

nag·ging ['nægɪŋ] *adj person* brontolone; *doubt, pain* assillante

nail [neɪl] *for wood* chiodo *m*; *on finger, toe* unghia *f*

'nail clip·pers *npl* tagliaunghie *m inv*; **'nail file** limetta *f* per unghie; **'nail pol·ish** smalto *m* per unghie; **'nail pol·ish re·mov·er** solvente *m* per unghie; **'nail scis·sors** *npl* forbicine *fpl* per unghie; **'nail var·nish** smalto *m* per unghie

na·ive [naɪ'iːv] *adj* ingenuo

naked ['neɪkɪd] *adj* nudo; *to the* ~ *eye* a occhio nudo

name [neɪm] **1** *n* nome *m*; *what's your* ~? come ti chiami?; *call s.o.* ~*s* insultare qu; *make a* ~ *for o.s.* farsi un nome **2** *v/t* chiamare

♦**name after** *v/t:* *they named him after his grandfather* gli hanno messo il nome del nonno

♦**name for** *Am* → **name after**

name·ly ['neɪmlɪ] *adv* cioè

'name·sake omonimo *m*, -a *f*

'name·tag *on clothing etc* targhetta *f* col nome

nan·ny ['nænɪ] bambinaia *f*

nap [næp] *n* sonnellino *m*; **have a** ~ farsi un sonnellino

nape [neɪp]: ~ *of the neck* nuca *f*

nap·kin ['næpkɪn] (*table* ~) tovagliolo *m*; *Am* (*sanitary* ~) assorbente *m*

Na·ples ['neɪpəlz] Napoli *f*

nap·py ['næpɪ] pannolino *m*

nar·cot·ic [naː'kɒtɪk] *n* narcotico *m*

nar·rate [nə'reɪt] *v/t* raccontare, narrare

nar·ra·tion [nə'reɪʃn] narrazione *f*

nar·ra·tive ['nærətɪv] **1** *n story* racconto **2** *adj poem, style* narrativo

nar·ra·tor [nə'reɪtə(r)] narratore *m*, -trice *f*

nar·row ['nærəʊ] *adj street, bed etc* stretto; *views, mind* ristretto; *victory* di stretta misura

nar·row·ly ['nærəʊlɪ] *adv win* di stretta misura; ~ *escape sth* scampare a qc per un pelo F

nar·row-mind·ed [nærəʊ'maɪndɪd] adj di idee ristrette

na·sal ['neɪzl] adj voice nasale

nas·ty ['nɑːstɪ] adj person, thing to say, smell, weather cattivo; cut, wound, disease brutto

na·tion ['neɪʃn] nazione f

na·tion·al ['næʃənl] 1 adj nazionale 2 n cittadino m, -a f

na·tion·al 'an·them inno m nazionale

na·tion·al 'debt debito m pubblico

na·tion·al·ism ['næʃənəlɪzm] nazionalismo m

na·tion·al·i·ty [næʃə'nælətɪ] nazionalità f inv

na·tion·al·ize ['næʃənəlaɪz] v/t industry etc nazionalizzare

na·tion·al 'park parco m nazionale

na·tive ['neɪtɪv] 1 adj indigeno; ~ language madrelingua f 2 n (tribesman) indigeno m, -a f; she's a ~ of New York è originaria di New York; she speaks Chinese like a ~ parla cinese come una madrelingua

na·tive 'coun·try patria f

na·tive 'speak·er. English ~ persona f di madrelingua inglese

NATO ['neɪtəʊ] abbr (= North Atlantic Treaty Organization) NATO f

nat·u·ral ['nætʃrəl] adj naturale

nat·u·ral 'gas gas m inv naturale

nat·u·ral·ist ['nætʃrəlɪst] naturalista m/f

nat·u·ral·ize ['nætʃrəlaɪz] v/t: become ~d naturalizzarsi

nat·u·ral·ly ['nætʃərəlɪ] adv (of course) naturalmente; behave, speak con naturalezza; (by nature) per natura

nat·u·ral 'sci·ence scienze fpl naturali

nat·u·ral 'sci·en·tist studioso m, -a f di scienze naturali

na·ture ['neɪtʃə(r)] natura f

na·ture re'serve riserva f naturale

naugh·ty ['nɔːtɪ] adj cattivo; photograph, word etc spinto

nau·se·a ['nɔːzɪə] nausea f

nau·se·ate ['nɔːzɪeɪt] v/t (fig: disgust) disgustare

nau·se·at·ing ['nɔːzɪeɪtɪŋ] adj smell, taste nauseante; person disgustoso

nau·seous ['nɔːzɪəs] adj: feel ~ avere la nausea

nau·ti·cal ['nɔːtɪkl] adj nautico

'nau·ti·cal mile miglio m nautico

na·val ['neɪvl] adj navale; officer, uniform della marina

'na·val base base f navale

na·vel ['neɪvl] ombelico m

nav·i·ga·ble ['nævɪgəbl] adj river navigabile

nav·i·gate ['nævɪgeɪt] v/i in ship, in aeroplane navigare; in car fare da navigatore / -trice; COMPUT navigare

nav·i·ga·tion [nævɪ'geɪʃn] navigazione f

nav·i·ga·tor ['nævɪgeɪtə(r)] on ship, in aeroplane ufficiale m di rotta; in car navigatore m, -trice f

na·vy ['neɪvɪ] marina f militare

na·vy 'blue 1 n blu m inv scuro 2 adj blu scuro

near [nɪə(r)] 1 adv vicino 2 prep vicino a; ~ the bank vicino alla banca; do you go ~ the bank? va dalle parti della banca? 3 adj vicino; the ~est stop la fermata più vicina; in the ~ future nel prossimo futuro

near·by [nɪə'baɪ] adv live vicino

near·ly ['nɪəlɪ] adv quasi

near-sight·ed [nɪə'saɪtɪd] adj miope

neat [niːt] adj room, desk, person ordinato; whisky liscio; solution efficace; F (terrific) fantastico

ne·ces·sar·i·ly ['nesəserəlɪ] adv necessariamente

ne·ces·sa·ry ['nesəsərɪ] adj necessario; it is ~ to ... è necessario ..., bisogna ...

ne·ces·si·tate [nɪ'sesɪteɪt] v/t rendere necessario

ne·ces·si·ty [nɪ'sesɪtɪ] necessità f inv

neck [nek] collo m

neck·lace ['neklɪs] collana f

'neck·line of dress scollo m

née [neɪ] adj: Lisa Higgins ~ Smart Lisa Higgins nata Smart

need [niːd] 1 n bisogno m; if ~ be se necessario; be in ~ (be needy) essere bisognoso; **be in ~ of sth** aver bisogno di qc; **there's no ~ to be rude / upset** non c'è bisogno di essere maleducato / triste **2** v/t avere bisogno di; **you'll ~ to buy one** dovrai comprarne uno; **you don't ~ to wait** non c'è bisogno che aspetti; **I ~ to talk to you** ti devo parlare; **~ I say more?** devo aggiungere altro?

nee·dle ['niːdl] for sewing, on dial ago m; on record player puntina f

'nee·dle·work cucito m

need·y ['niːdɪ] adj bisognoso

neg·a·tive ['negətɪv] **1** adj negativo **2** n ELEC polo m negativo; PHOT negativa f; **answer in the ~** rispondere negativamente

ne·glect [nɪ'glekt] **1** n trascuratezza f **2** v/t garden, one's health trascurare; **~ to do sth** trascurare di fare qc

ne·glect·ed [nɪ'glektɪd] adj gardens, author trascurato; **feel ~** sentirsi trascurato

neg·li·gence ['neglɪdʒəns] negligenza f

neg·li·gent ['neglɪdʒənt] adj negligente

neg·li·gi·ble ['neglɪdʒəbl] adj quantity, amount trascurabile

ne·go·ti·a·ble [nɪ'gəʊʃəbl] adj salary, contract negoziabile

ne·go·ti·ate [nɪ'gəʊʃɪeɪt] **1** v/i trattare **2** v/t deal, settlement negoziare; obstacles superare; bend in road affrontare

ne·go·ti·a·tion [nɪgəʊʃɪ'eɪʃn] negoziato m, trattativa f

ne·go·ti·a·tor [nɪ'gəʊʃɪeɪtə(r)] negoziatore m, -trice f

neigh [neɪ] v/i nitrire

neigh·bor etc Am → **neighbour** etc

neigh·bour ['neɪbə(r)] vicino m, -a f

neigh·bour·hood ['neɪbəhʊd] in town quartiere m; **in the ~ of** fig intorno a

neigh·bour·ing ['neɪbərɪŋ] adj house, state confinante

neigh·bour·ly ['neɪbəlɪ] adj amichevole

nei·ther ['naɪðə(r)] **1** adj: **~ player** nessuno dei due giocatori **2** pron

nessuno m dei due, nessuna f delle due, né l'uno né l'altro, né l'una né l'altra **3** adv: **~ ... nor ...** né ... né ... **4** conj neanche; **~ do I** neanch'io

ne·on light ['niːɒn] luce f al neon

neph·ew ['nevjuː] nipote m (di zii)

nerd [nɜːd] P fesso m, -a f P; in style tamarro m P

nerve [nɜːv] nervo m; (courage) coraggio m; (impudence) faccia f tosta; **it's bad for my ~s** mi mette in agitazione; **get on s.o.'s ~s** dare sui nervi a qu

nerve-rack·ing ['nɜːrækɪŋ] adj snervante

ner·vous ['nɜːvəs] adj nervoso; **be ~ about doing sth** essere ansioso all'idea di fare qc

ner·vous 'break·down esaurimento m nervoso

ner·vous 'en·er·gy: be full of ~ essere sovraeccitato

ner·vous·ness ['nɜːvəsnɪs] nervosismo m

ner·vous 'wreck: be a ~ avere i nervi a pezzi

nest [nest] n nido m

nes·tle ['nesl] v/i rannicchiarsi

net[1] [net] for fishing retino m; for tennis rete f

net[2] [net] adj COM netto

net 'cur·tain tenda f di tulle

net 'prof·it guadagno m o utile m netto

net·tle ['netl] ortica f

'net·work of contacts, cells rete f; COMPUT network m inv

neu·rol·o·gist [njʊə'rɒlədʒɪst] neurologo m, -a f

neu·ro·sis [njʊə'rəʊsɪs] nevrosi f inv

neu·rot·ic [njʊ'rɒtɪk] adj nevrotico

neu·ter ['njuːtə(r)] v/t animal sterilizzare

neu·tral ['njuːtrl] **1** adj country neutrale; colour neutro **2** n gear folle m; **in ~** in folle

neu·tral·i·ty [njʊ'trælətɪ] neutralità f inv

neu·tral·ize ['njʊtrəlaɪz] v/t neutralizzare

nev·er ['nevə(r)] adv mai; **~! in**

disbelief ma va'!; **you're ~ going to believe this** non ci crederesti mai; **you ~ promised, did you?** non l'avrai promesso, spero!

nev·er-'end·ing *adj* senza fine

nev·er·the·less [nevəðə'les] *adv* comunque, tuttavia

new [nju:] *adj* nuovo; **this system is still ~ to me** non sono ancora abituato al sistema; **I'm ~ to the job** sono nuovo del mestiere; **that's nothing ~** non è una novità

'new·born *adj* neonato

new·com·er ['nju:kʌmə(r)] nuovo arrivato *m*, nuova arrivata *f*

new·ly ['nju:lɪ] *adv* (*recently*) recentemente

'new·ly weds [wedz] *npl* sposini *mpl*

new 'moon luna *f* nuova

news [nju:z] *nsg* notizia *f*; *on TV, radio* notiziario *m*; novità *f inv*; **any ~?** ci sono novità?; **that's ~ to me** mi giunge nuovo!

'news a·gen·cy agenzia *f* di stampa; 'news·a·gent giornalaio *m*; 'news·cast telegiornale *m*; 'news·cast·er giornalista *m/f* televisivo, -a; 'news flash notizia *f* flash; 'news·pa·per giornale *m*; 'news·read·er giornalista *m/f* radiotelevisivo, -a; 'news re·port notiziario *m*; 'news·stand edicola *f*; 'news·ven·dor edicolante *m/f*

new 'year anno *m* nuovo; **Happy New Year!** buon anno!; **New Year's 'Day** capodanno *m*; **New Year's 'Eve** San Silvestro *m*; **New Zea·land** ['zi:lənd] Nuova Zelanda *f*; **New Zea·land·er** ['zi:ləndə(r)] neozelandese *m/f*

next [nekst] **1** *adj in time* prossimo; *in space* vicino; **the ~ week / month he came back again** la settimana / il mese dopo ritornò; **who's ~?** a chi tocca? **2** *adv* dopo; **~ to** (*beside*) accanto a; (*in comparison with*) a paragone di

next 'door **1** *adj*: **~ neighbour** vicino *m*, -a *f* di casa **2** *adv live* nella casa accanto

next of 'kin parente *m/f* prossimo

nib·ble ['nɪbl] *v/t* mordicchiare

nice [naɪs] *adj person* carino, gentile; *day, weather, party* bello; *meal, food* buono; **be ~ to your sister!** sii carino con tua sorella!; **that's very ~ of you** molto gentile da parte tua!

nice·ly ['naɪslɪ] *adv written, presented* bene

nice·ties ['naɪsətɪz] *npl*: **social ~** convenevoli *mpl*

niche [ni:ʃ] *in market* nicchia *f* (di mercato); *special position* nicchia *f*

nick [nɪk] *n cut* taglietto *m*; **in the ~ of time** appena in tempo

nick·el ['nɪkl] *material* nichel *m inv*; (*Am: coin*) moneta *f* da 5 centesimi di dollaro

'nick·name *n* soprannome *m*

niece [ni:s] nipote *f* (di zii)

nig·gard·ly ['nɪgədlɪ] *adj amount* misero; *person* tirchio

night [naɪt] notte *f*; (*evening*) sera *f*; **at ~** di notte / di sera; **last ~** ieri notte / ieri sera; **travel by ~** viaggiare di notte; **during the ~** durante la notte; **stay the ~** rimanere a dormire; **a room for 2 ~s** una stanza per due notti; **work ~s** fare il turno di notte; **good ~** buona notte; **in the middle of the ~** a notte fonda

'night·cap (*drink*) bicchierino *m* bevuto prima di andare a letto; 'night·club night(-club) *m inv*; 'night·dress camicia *f* da notte; 'night·fall: **at ~** al calar della notte; 'night flight volo *m* notturno; 'night·gown camicia *f* da notte

night·ie ['naɪtɪ] F camicia *f* da notte

nigh·tin·gale ['naɪtɪŋgeɪl] usignolo *m*

'night·life vita *f* notturna

night·ly ['naɪtlɪ] *adj & adv* ogni sera; *late at night* ogni notte

'night·mare *also fig* incubo *m*; 'night por·ter portiere *m* notturno; 'night school scuola *f* serale; 'night shift turno *m* di notte; 'night·shirt camicia *f* da notte (*da uomo*); 'night·spot locale *m* notturno; 'night·time: **at ~, in the ~** di notte, la notte

nil [nɪl] SP zero *m*

nim·ble ['nɪmbl] *adj* agile

nine [naɪn] nove

nine·teen [naɪn'tiːn] diciannove

nine·teenth [naɪn'tiːnθ] *n & adj* diciannovesimo, -a

nine·ti·eth ['naɪntɪɪθ] *n & adj* novantesimo, -a

nine·ty ['naɪntɪ] novanta

ninth [naɪnθ] *n & adj* nono

nip [nɪp] (*pinch*) pizzico *m*; (*bite*) morso *m*

nip·ple ['nɪpl] capezzolo *m*

ni·tro·gen ['naɪtrədʒn] azoto *m*

no [nəʊ] **1** *adv* no **2** *adj* nessuno; **there's ~ coffee/tea left** non c'è più caffè/tè; **I have ~ family/ money** non ho famiglia/soldi; **I'm ~ linguist/expert** non sono un linguista/esperto; **~ parking** sosta vietata; **~ smoking** vietato fumare

no·bil·i·ty [nəʊ'bɪlətɪ] nobiltà *f inv*

no·ble ['nəʊbl] *adj* nobile

no·bod·y ['nəʊbədɪ] *pron* nessuno; **~ knows** nessuno lo sa; **there was ~ at home** non c'era nessuno in casa

nod [nɒd] **1** *n* cenno *m* del capo **2** *v/i* (*pret & pp* **-ded**) fare un cenno col capo; **~ in agreement** annuire

♦ **nod off** *v/i* (*fall asleep*) appisolarsi

no-hop·er [nəʊ'həʊpə(r)] F buono *m*, -a *f* a nulla

noise [nɔɪz] (*sound*) rumore *m*; *loud, unpleasant* chiasso *m*

nois·y ['nɔɪzɪ] *adj* rumoroso; *children, party* chiassoso; **don't be so ~** non fate tanto rumore

nom·i·nal ['nɒmɪnl] *adj amount* simbolico

nom·i·nate ['nɒmɪneɪt] *v/t* (*appoint*) designare; **~ s.o. for a post** proporre qu come candidato per una posizione

nom·i·na·tion [nɒmɪ'neɪʃn] (*appointing*) nomina *f*; (*proposal*) candidatura *f*; *person proposed* candidato *m*, -a *f*

nom·i·nee [nɒmɪ'niː] candidato *m*, -a *f*

non ... [nɒn] non ...

non·al·co·hol·ic *adj* analcolico

non·a·ligned *adj* non allineato

non·cha·lant ['nɒnʃələnt] *adj* noncurante

non·com·mis·sioned 'of·fi·cer sottufficiale *m*

non·com'mit·tal *adj person, response* evasivo

non·de·script ['nɒndɪskrɪpt] *adj* ordinario

none [nʌn] *pron* nessuno *m*, -a *f*; **~ of the students** nessuno degli studenti; **~ of this money is mine** neanche una lira di questi soldi è mia; **there are ~ left** non ne sono rimasti; **there is ~ left** non ne è rimasto, non è rimasto niente

non'en·ti·ty nullità *f inv*

none·the·less [nʌnðə'les] *adv* nondimeno

non·ex'ist·ent *adj* inesistente

non'fic·tion opere *fpl* non di narrativa

non·(in)'flam·ma·ble *adj* non infiammabile

non·in·ter'fer·ence, **non·in·ter'ven·tion** non intervento *m*

non-'i·ron *adj shirt* che non si stira

'no-non·sense *adj approach* pragmatico

non'pay·ment mancato pagamento *m*

non·pol'lut·ing *adj* non inquinante

non'res·i·dent *n in country* non residente *m/f*; (*in hotel*) persona *f* chi non è cliente di un albergo

non·re·turn·a·ble [nɒnrɪ'tɜːnəbl] *adj* a fondo perduto

non·sense ['nɒnsəns] sciocchezze *fpl*; **don't talk ~** non dire sciocchezze; **~, it's easy!** sciocchezze, è facile!

non'skid *adj tyres* antisdrucciolevole

non'slip *adj surface* antiscivolo *inv*

non'smok·er *person* non fumatore *m*, -trice *f*

non'stand·ard *adj* fuori standard, non di serie; *use of a word* che fa eccezione

non'stick *adj pans* antiaderente

non'stop 1 *adj flight, train* diretto; *chatter* continuo **2** *adv fly, travel* senza scalo; *chatter, argue* di continuo

non·swim·mer persona *f* chi non sa nuotare

non·u·nion *adj* non appartenente al sindacato

non·vi·o·lence non violenza *f*

non·vi·o·lent *adj* non violento

noo·dles ['nu:dlz] *npl* spaghetti *mpl* cinesi

nook [nʊk] angolino *m*

noon [nu:n] mezzogiorno *m*; **at ~** a mezzogiorno

noose [nu:s] cappio *m*

nor [nɔː(r)] *adv conj* né; **~ do I** neanch'io, neanche a me

norm [nɔːm] norma *f*

nor·mal ['nɔːml] *adj* normale

nor·mal·i·ty [nɔː'mælətɪ] normalità *f inv*

nor·mal·ize ['nɔːməlaɪz] *v/t relationships* normalizzare

nor·mal·ly ['nɔːməlɪ] *adv* (*usually*) di solito; *in a normal way* normalmente

north [nɔːθ] **1** *n* nord *m*; **to the ~ of a** nord di **2** *adj* settentrionale, nord *inv* **3** *adv travel* verso nord; **~ of a** nord di

North Am·er·i·ca America *f* del Nord; **North Am·er·i·can 1** *n* nordamericano *m*, -a *f* **2** *adj* nordamericano; **north'east** *n* nordest

nor·ther·ly ['nɔːðəlɪ] *adj wind* settentrionale; *direction* nord *inv*

nor·thern ['nɔːðən] *adj* settentrionale

nor·thern·er ['nɔːðənə(r)] settentrionale *m/f*

North Ko·re·a Corea *f* del Nord; **North Ko·re·an 1** *adj* nordcoreano **2** *n* nordcoreano *m*, -a *f*; **North 'Pole** polo *m* nord

north·wards ['nɔːðwədz] *adv travel* verso nord

north·west [nɔːð'west] *n* nordovest *m*

Nor·way ['nɔːweɪ] Norvegia *f*

Nor·we·gian [nɔː'wiːdʒn] **1** *adj* norvegese **2** *n person* norvegese *m/f*; *language* norvegese *m*

nose [nəʊz] naso *m*; **right under my**

~! proprio sotto il naso!

♦ **nose about** *v/i* F curiosare

'nose·bleed emorragia *f* nasale

nos·tal·gia [nɒ'stældʒɪə] nostalgia *f*

nos·tal·gic [nɒ'stældʒɪk] *adj* nostalgico

nos·tril ['nɒstrəl] narice *f*

nos·y ['nəʊzɪ] *adj* F curioso

not [nɒt] *adv* non; **~ this one, that one** non questo, quello; **~ a lot** non molto; **I hope ~** spero di no; **I don't know** non so; **I am ~ American** non sono americano; **he didn't help** non ha aiutato; **~ me** io no

no·ta·ble ['nəʊtəbl] *adj* notevole

no·ta·ry ['nəʊtərɪ] notaio *m*

notch [nɒtʃ] tacca *f*

note [nəʊt] *n short letter* biglietto *m*; MUS nota *f*; *memo to self* appunto *m*; *comment on text* nota *f*; **take ~s** prendere appunti; **take ~ of sth** prendere nota di qc

♦ **note down** *v/t* annotare

'note·book taccuino *m*; COMPUT notebook *m inv*

not·ed ['nəʊtɪd] *adj* noto

'note·pad bloc-notes *m inv*

'note·pa·per carta *f* da lettere

noth·ing ['nʌθɪŋ] *pron* niente; **~ but** nient'altro che; **~ much** niente di speciale; **for ~** (*for free*) gratis; (*for no reason*) per un nonnulla; **I'd like ~ better** non chiedo di meglio

no·tice ['nəʊtɪs] **1** *n on notice board, in street* avviso *m*; (*advance warning*) preavviso *m*; *in newspaper* annuncio *m*; *to leave job* preavviso *m*; *to leave house* disdetta *f*; **at short ~** con un breve preavviso; **until further ~** fino a nuovo avviso; **give s.o. his / her ~** *to quit job* dare il preavviso a qu; *to leave house* dare la disdetta a qu; **hand in one's ~** *to employer* presentare le dimissioni; **four weeks' ~** quattro settimane di preavviso; **take ~ of sth** fare caso a qc; **take no ~ of s.o. / sth** non fare caso a qu / qc **2** *v/t* notare

no·tice·a·ble ['nəʊtɪsəbl] *adj* sensibile

'notice board bacheca *f*

N

no·ti·fy ['nəʊtɪfaɪ] v/t (pret & pp -ied) informare

no·tion ['nəʊʃn] idea f

no·to·ri·ous [nəʊ'tɔːrɪəs] adj famigerato

nou·gat ['nuːgɑː] torrone m

nought [nɔːt] zero m

noun [naʊn] nome m, sostantivo m

nou·rish·ing ['nʌrɪʃɪŋ] adj nutriente

nou·rish·ment ['nʌrɪʃmənt] nutrimento m

nov·el ['nɒvl] n romanzo m

nov·el·ist ['nɒvlɪst] romanziere m, -a f

no·vel·ty ['nɒvltɪ] novità f inv

No·vem·ber [nəʊ'vembə(r)] novembre m

nov·ice ['nɒvɪs] principiante m/f

now [naʊ] adv ora, adesso; ~ and again, ~ and then ogni tanto; by ~ ormai; from ~ on d'ora in poi; right ~ subito; just ~ (proprio) adesso; ~, ~! su, su!; ~, where did I put it? dunque, dove l'ho messo?

now·a·days ['naʊədeɪz] adv oggigiorno

no·where ['nəʊweə(r)] adv da nessuna parte; there's ~ to sit non c'è posto; it's ~ near finished è ben lontano dall'essere terminato

noz·zle ['nɒzl] bocchetta f

nu·cle·ar ['njuːklɪə(r)] adj nucleare

nu·cle·ar en·er·gy energia f nucleare; **nu·cle·ar 'fis·sion** fissione f nucleare; **'nu·cle·ar-free** adj denuclearizzato; **nu·cle·ar 'phys·ics** fisica f nucleare; **nu·cle·ar 'pow·er** energia f nucleare; **nu·cle·ar 'pow·er sta·tion** centrale f nucleare; **nu·cle·ar re'ac·tor** reattore m nucleare; **nu·cle·ar 'waste** scorie fpl radioattive; **nu·cle·ar 'weap·on** arma f nucleare

nude [njuːd] 1 adj nudo 2 n painting nudo m; in the ~ nudo

nudge [nʌdʒ] v/t dare un colpetto di gomito a

nud·ist ['njuːdɪst] n nudista m/f

nui·sance ['njuːsns] seccatura f; make a ~ of o.s. dare fastidio; what a ~! che seccatura!

nuke [njuːk] v/t F distruggere con armi atomiche

null and 'void [nʌl] adj nullo

numb [nʌm] adj intirizzito; emotionally impietrito

num·ber ['nʌmbə(r)] 1 n (figure) numero m, cifra f; (quantity) quantità f inv; of hotel room, house, phone number etc numero m 2 v/t put a number on contare

'number plate MOT targa f

nu·me·ral ['njuːmərəl] numero m

nu·me·rate ['njuːmərət] adj: be ~ avere buone basi in matematica; of children saper contare

nu·me·rous ['njuːmərəs] adj numeroso

nun [nʌn] suora f

nurse [nɜːs] infermiere m, -a f

nur·se·ry ['nɜːsərɪ] school asilo m; in house stanza f dei bambini; for plants vivaio m

'nur·se·ry rhyme filastrocca f; **'nur·se·ry school** scuola f materna; **'nur·se·ry school teach·er** insegnante m/f di scuola materna

nurs·ing ['nɜːsɪŋ] professione f d'infermiere; she went into ~ è diventata infermiera

'nurs·ing home for old people casa f di riposo

nut [nʌt] noce f; for bolt dado m; ~s F (testicles) palle fpl

'nut·crack·ers npl schiaccianoci m inv

nu·tri·ent ['njuːtrɪənt] n sostanza f nutritiva

nu·tri·tion [njuː'trɪʃn] alimentazione f

nu·tri·tious [njuː'trɪʃəs] adj nutriente

nuts [nʌts] adj F (crazy) svitato; be ~ about s.o. essere pazzo di qu

'nut·shell: in a ~ in poche parole

nut·ty ['nʌtɪ] adj taste di noce; F (crazy) pazzo

ny·lon ['naɪlɒn] 1 n nylon m inv 2 adj di nylon

O

oak [əʊk] *tree* quercia *f; wood* rovere *m*

OAP [əʊeɪ'piː] *abbr* (= **old age pensioner**) pensionato *m*, -a *f*

oar [ɔː(r)] remo *m*

o·a·sis [əʊ'eɪsɪs] (*pl* **oases** [əʊ'eɪsiːz]) *also fig* oasi *f inv*

oath [əʊθ] LAW giuramento *m; (swearword)* imprecazione *f;* **on ~** sotto giuramento

'oat·meal farina *f* d'avena

oats [əʊts] *npl* avena *f*

o·be·di·ence [ə'biːdɪəns] ubbidienza *f*

o·be·di·ent [ə'biːdɪənt] *adj* ubbidiente

o·be·di·ent·ly [ə'biːdɪəntlɪ] *adv* docilmente

o·bese [əʊ'biːs] *adj* obeso

o·bes·i·ty [əʊ'biːsɪtɪ] obesità *f inv*

o·bey [ə'beɪ] *v/t parents* ubbidire a; *law* osservare

o·bit·u·a·ry [ə'bɪtjʊərɪ] *n* necrologio *m*

ob·ject¹ ['ɒbdʒɪkt] *n (thing)* oggetto *m; (aim)* scopo *m;* GRAM complemento *m*

ob·ject² [əb'dʒekt] *v/i* avere da obiettare

♦ **object to** *v/t* essere contrario a

ob·jec·tion [əb'dʒekʃn] obiezione *f*

ob·jec·tio·na·ble [əb'dʒekʃnəbl] *adj (unpleasant)* antipatico

ob·jec·tive [əb'dʒektɪv] **1** *adj* obiettivo **2** *n* obiettivo *m*

ob·jec·tive·ly [əb'dʒektɪvlɪ] *adv* obiettivamente

ob·jec·tiv·i·ty [əbdʒekt'ɪvɪtɪ] obiettività *f inv*

ob·li·ga·tion [ɒblɪ'geɪʃn] obbligo *m;* **be under an ~ to s.o.** essere in debito con qu

ob·lig·a·to·ry [ə'blɪgətrɪ] *adj* obbligatorio

o·blige [ə'blaɪdʒ] *v/t:* **much ~d!** grazie mille!

o·blig·ing [ə'blaɪdʒɪŋ] *adj* servizievole

o·blique [ə'bliːk] **1** *adj reference* indiretto **2** *n in punctuation* barra *f*

o·blit·er·ate [ə'blɪtəreɪt] *v/t city* annientare; *memory* cancellare

o·bliv·i·on [ə'blɪvɪən] oblio *m;* **fall into ~** cadere in oblio

o·bliv·i·ous [ə'blɪvɪəs] *adj:* **be ~ of sth** essere ignaro di qc

ob·long ['ɒblɒŋ] **1** *adj* rettangolare **2** *n* rettangolo *m*

ob·nox·ious [əb'nɒkʃəs] *adj* offensivo; *smell* sgradevole

ob·scene [əb'siːn] *adj* osceno; *salary, poverty* vergognoso

ob·scen·i·ty [əb'senətɪ] oscenità *f inv*

ob·scure [əb'skjʊə(r)] *adj* oscuro

ob·scu·ri·ty [əb'skjʊərətɪ] oscurità *f inv*

ob·ser·vance [əb'zɜːvns] osservanza *f*

ob·ser·vant [əb'zɜːvnt] *adj* osservante

ob·ser·va·tion [ɒbzə'veɪʃn] osservazione *f*

ob·ser·va·to·ry [əb'zɜːvətrɪ] osservatorio *m*

ob·serve [əb'zɜːv] *v/t* osservare

ob·serv·er [əb'zɜːvə(r)] osservatore *m*, -trice *f*

ob·sess [əb'ses] *v/t:* **be ~ed by / with** essere fissato con

ob·ses·sion [əb'seʃn] fissazione *f*

ob·ses·sive [əb'sesɪv] *adj person, behaviour* ossessivo

ob·so·lete ['ɒbsəliːt] *adj model* obsoleto; *word* disusato, antiquato

ob·sta·cle ['ɒbstəkl] *also fig* ostacolo

ob·ste·tri·cian [ɒbstə'trɪʃn] ostetrico *m*, -a *f*

ob·stet·rics [ɒb'stetrɪks] ostetricia f

ob·sti·na·cy ['ɒbstɪnəsɪ] ostinazione f

ob·sti·nate ['ɒbstɪnət] adj ostinato

ob·sti·nate·ly ['ɒbstɪnətlɪ] adv ostinatamente

ob·struct [əb'strʌkt] v/t road, passage ostruire; investigation, police ostacolare

ob·struc·tion [əb'strʌkʃn] on road etc ostruzione f

ob·struc·tive [əb'strʌktɪv] adj behaviour, tactics ostruzionista

ob·tru·sive [əb'truːsɪv] adj music invadente; colour stonato

ob·tain [əb'teɪn] v/t ottenere

ob·tain·a·ble [əb'teɪnəbl] adj products reperibile

ob·tuse [əb'tjuːs] adj fig ottuso

ob·vi·ous ['ɒbvɪəs] adj ovvio, evidente

ob·vi·ous·ly ['ɒbvɪəslɪ] adv ovviamente, evidentemente; ~! ovviamente!

oc·ca·sion [ə'keɪʒn] occasione f

oc·ca·sion·al [ə'keɪʒnl] adj sporadico; I like the ~ whisky bevo un whisky ogni tanto

oc·ca·sion·al·ly [ə'keɪʒnlɪ] adv ogni tanto

oc·cult [ɒ'kʌlt] 1 adj occulto 2 n: the ~ l'occulto m

oc·cu·pant ['ɒkjʊpənt] of vehicle occupante m/f; of building, flat abitante m/f

oc·cu·pa·tion [ɒkjʊ'peɪʃn] (job) professione f; of country occupazione f

oc·cu·pa·tion·al 'ther·a·pist [ɒkjʊ'peɪʃnl] ergoterapeuta m/f

oc·cu·pa·tion·al 'ther·a·py ergoterapia f

oc·cu·py ['ɒkjʊpaɪ] v/t (pret & pp -ied) occupare

oc·cur [ə'kɜː(r)] v/i (pret & pp -red) accadere; it ~red to me that ... mi è venuto in mente che ...

oc·cur·rence [ə'kʌrəns] evento m

o·cean ['əʊʃn] oceano m

o·ce·a·nog·ra·pher [əʊʃn'ɒgrəfə(r)] oceanografo m, -a f

o·ce·a·nog·ra·phy [əʊʃn'ɒgrəfɪ] oceanografia f

o'clock [ə'klɒk]: at five / six ~ alle cinque / sei; it's one ~ è l'una; it's three ~ sono le tre

Oc·to·ber [ɒk'təʊbə(r)] ottobre m

oc·to·pus ['ɒktəpəs] polpo m

OD [əʊ'diː] v/i: F ~ on drug fare un'overdose di

odd [ɒd] adj (strange) strano; (not even) dispari; the ~ one out l'eccezione f; 50 ~ 50 e rotti

'odd·ball F persona f stramba; he's an ~ è un tipo strambo

odds [ɒdz] npl: be at ~ with essere in disaccordo con; the ~ are 10 to one le probabilità sono 10 contro una; the ~ are that ... è probabile che ...; against all the ~ contro ogni aspettativa

odds and 'ends npl objects cianfrusaglie fpl; things to do cose fpl

'odds-on adj: the ~ favourite il favorito; it's ~ that ... è praticamente scontato che ...

o·di·ous ['əʊdɪəs] adj odioso

o·dor Am, **o·dour** ['əʊdə(r)] odore m

of [ɒv], [əv] prep di; the works ~ Dickens le opere di Dickens; it's made ~ steel è di acciaio; die ~ cancer morire di cancro; a friend ~ mine un mio amico; very nice ~ him molto gentile da parte sua; ~ the three this is ... dei tre questo è ...

off [ɒf] 1 prep: ~ a lane ~ the main road not far from un sentiero poco lontano dalla strada principale; leading off un sentiero che parte dalla strada principale; £20 ~ the price 20 sterline di sconto; he's ~ his food ha perso l'appetito 2 adv: be ~ of light, TV etc essere spento; of gas, tap essere chiuso; (cancelled) essere annullato; of food essere finito; she was ~ today not at work oggi non era al lavoro; you've left the lid ~ non hai messo il coperchio; we're ~ tomorrow leaving partiamo domani; I'm ~ to New York vado a New York; I must be ~ devo andare;

with his trousers / hat ~ senza pantaloni / cappello; *take a day* ~ prendere un giorno libero; *it's 3 miles* ~ dista 3 miglia; *it's a long way* ~ è molto lontano; *drive* ~ partire (in macchina); *walk* ~ allontanarsi; ~ *and on* ogni tanto **3** *adj food* andato a male; ~ *switch* interruttore *m* di spegnimento

of·fal ['ɒfl] frattaglie *fpl*

of·fence [ə'fens] LAW reato *m*; *take* ~ *at sth* offendersi per qc

of·fend [ə'fend] *v/t* (*insult*) offendere

of·fend·er [ə'fendə(r)] LAW delinquente *m/f*; *~s will be prosecuted* i trasgressori saranno perseguiti a norma di legge

of·fense *Am* → **offence**

of·fen·sive [ə'fensɪv] **1** *adj behaviour, remark*, offensivo; *smell* sgradevole **2** *n* (MIL: *attack*) offensiva *f*; *go onto the* ~ passare all'offensiva

of·fer ['ɒfə(r)] **1** *n* offerta *f* **2** *v/t* offrire; ~ *s.o. sth* offrire qc a qu

off·hand *adj attitude* disinvolto

of·fice ['ɒfɪs] ufficio *m*; (*position*) carica *f*

of·fice block complesso *m* di uffici

of·fice hours *npl* orario *m* d'ufficio

of·fi·cer ['ɒfɪsə(r)] MIL ufficiale *m*; *in police* agente *m/f*

of·fi·cial [ə'fɪʃl] **1** *adj* ufficiale **2** *n* funzionario *m*, -a *f*

of·fi·cial·ly [ə'fɪʃlɪ] *adv* ufficialmente

of·fi·ci·ate [ə'fɪʃɪeɪt] *v/i* officiare

of·fi·cious [ə'fɪʃəs] *adj* invadente

off-licence *Br* negozio *m* di alcolici

off-line *adj & adv* off-line

off-peak *adj rates* ridotto; ~ *electricity* elettricità *f* a tariffa ridotta

off-sea·son 1 *adj rates* di bassa stagione **2** *n* bassa stagione *f*

off·set *v/t* (*pret & pp* -**set**) *losses, disadvantage* compensare

off·shore *adj drilling rig, investment* off-shore *inv*

off·side 1 *adj wheel etc* destro; *on the left* sinistro **2** *adv* SP in fuorigioco

off·spring figli *mpl*; *of animal* piccoli *mpl*

off-the-'rec·ord *adj* ufficioso

'off-white *adj* bianco sporco

of·ten ['ɒfn] *adv* spesso

oil [ɔɪl] **1** *n* olio *m*; *petroleum* petrolio *m*; *for central heating* nafta *f* **2** *v/t hinges, bearings* oliare

'oil change cambio *m* dell'olio; **'oil·cloth** tela *f* cerata; **'oil com·pa·ny** compagnia *f* petrolifera; **'oil-field** giacimento *m* petrolifero; **'oil-fired** *adj central heating* a nafta; **'oil paint·ing** quadro *m* a olio; **'oil-pro·duc·ing coun·try** paese *m* produttore di petrolio; **'oil re·fin·e·ry** raffineria *f* di petrolio; **'oil rig** piattaforma *f* petrolifera; **'oil-skins** *npl* abiti *mpl* di tela cerata; **'oil slick** chiazza *f* di petrolio; **'oil tank·er** petroliera *f*; **'oil well** pozzo *m* petrolifero

oil·y ['ɔɪlɪ] *adj* unto

oint·ment ['ɔɪntmənt] pomata *f*

ok [əʊ'keɪ] *adj, adv* F: *is it* ~ *with you if …?* ti va bene se …?; *does that look* ~? ti sembra che vada bene?; *that's* ~ *by me* per me va bene; *are you* ~? well, *not hurt* stai bene?; *are you* ~ *for Friday?* ti va bene venerdì?; *he's* ~ (*is a good guy*) è in gamba

old [əʊld] *adj* vecchio; (*previous*) precedente; *how* ~ *are you / is he?* quanti anni hai / ha?; *he's getting* ~ sta invecchiando

old 'age vecchiaia *f*

old age 'pen·sion pensione *f* di anzianità

old-age 'pen·sion·er pensionato *m*, -a *f*

old 'peo·ple's home casa *f* di riposo (per anziani)

old-'fash·ioned *adj* antiquato

ol·ive ['ɒlɪv] oliva *f*

'ol·ive oil olio *m* d'oliva

O·lym·pic 'Games [ə'lɪmpɪk] *npl* Olimpiadi *fpl*, giochi *mpl* olimpici

om·e·let *Am*, **om·e·lette** ['ɒmlɪt] frittata *f*

om·i·nous ['ɒmɪnəs] *adj* sinistro

o·mis·sion [ə'mɪʃn] omissione *f*; *on purpose* esclusione *f*

o·mit [əˈmɪt] *v/t* (*pret & pp* **-ted**) omettere; *on purpose* escludere; **~ to do sth** tralasciare di fare qc

om·nip·o·tent [ɒmˈnɪpətənt] *adj* onnipotente

om·nis·ci·ent [ɒmˈnɪsɪənt] *adj* onnisciente

on [ɒn] **1** *prep* su; **~ the table/wall** sul tavolo/muro; **~ the bus/train** in autobus/treno; **get ~ the bus/ train** salire sull'autobus/sul treno; **~ TV/the radio** alla tv/radio; **~ Sunday** domenica; **~ Sundays** di domenica; **~ the 1st of June** il primo di giugno; **be ~ holiday/sale/ offer** essere in vacanza/vendita/offerta; **I'm ~ antibiotics** sto prendendo antibiotici; **this is ~ me** (*I'm paying*) offro io; **have you any money ~ you?** hai dei soldi con te?; **~ his arrival/departure** al suo arrivo/alla sua partenza; **~ hearing this** al sentire queste parole **2** *adv*: **be ~** *of light, TV etc* essere acceso; *of gas, tap* essere aperto; *of machine* essere in funzione; *of handbrake* essere inserito; **it's ~ after the news** *of programme* è dopo il notiziario; **the meeting is ~** *scheduled to happen* la riunione si fa; **put the lid ~** metti il coperchio; **with his jacket/hat ~** con la giacca/il cappello; **what's ~ tonight?** cosa c'è stasera?; **I've got something ~ tonight** *planned* stasera ho un impegno; **you're ~** (*I accept your offer etc*) d'accordo; **that's not ~** (*not allowed, not fair*) non è giusto; **~ you go** (*go ahead*) fai pure; **walk/talk ~** continuare a parlare/camminare; **and so ~** e così via; **~ and ~** *talk etc* senza sosta **3** *adj*: **the ~ switch** l'interruttore m d'accensione

once [wʌns] **1** *adv* (*one time*) una volta; (*formerly*) un tempo; **~ again, ~ more** ancora una volta; **at ~** (*immediately*) subito; **all at ~** (*suddenly*) improvvisamente; (*all*) **at ~** (*together*) contemporaneamente; **~ upon a time there was ...** c'era una volta ...; **~ in a while** ogni tanto; **~**

and for all una volta per tutte; **for ~** per una volta **2** *conj* non appena; **~ you have finished** non appena hai finito

one [wʌn] **1** *n* (*number*) uno m **2** *adj* uno, -a; **~ day** un giorno **3** *pron* uno m, -a f; **which ~?** quale?; **that ~** quello m, -a f; **this ~** questo m, -a f; **~ by ~** *enter, deal with* uno alla volta; **~ another** l'un l'altro, a vicenda; **what can ~ say/do?** cosa si può dire/fare?; **~ would have thought that ...** si sarebbe pensato che ...; **the more ~ thinks about it ...** più ci si pensa ...; **the little ~s** i piccoli; **I for ~** per quanto mi riguarda

one-'off 1 *n* fatto *f* na eccezionale; *person* persona *f* eccezionale **2** *adj* unico

one-par·ent 'fam·i·ly famiglia *f* monogenitore

one'self *pron reflexive* si; *after prep* se stesso m, -a f; **cut ~** tagliarsi; **do sth ~** fare qc da sé; **do sth by ~** fare qc da solo

one-sid·ed [wʌnˈsaɪdɪd] *adj* unilaterale

one-track 'mind *hum*: **have a ~** essere fissato col sesso

'one-way street strada *f* a senso unico

'one-way tick·et biglietto m di sola andata

on·ion [ˈʌnjən] cipolla *f*

'on-line *adj & adv* on-line *inv*

'on-line serv·ice COMPUT servizio m on-line

on·look·er [ˈɒnlʊkə(r)] astante m

on·ly [ˈəʊnlɪ] **1** *adv* solo; **not ~ X but also Y** non solo X ma anche Y; **~ just** a malapena **2** *adj* unico; **~ son** unico figlio maschio

'on·set inizio m

'on·side *adv* SP non in fuorigioco

on-the-job 'train·ing training m inv sul lavoro

on·to [ˈɒntuː] *prep*: **put sth ~ sth** mettere qc sopra qc

on·wards [ˈɒnwədz] *adv* in avanti; **from ...** ~ da ... in poi

ooze [uːz] **1** *v/i of liquid, mud* colare

2 v/t: **he ~s charm** è di una gentilezza esagerata

o·paque [əʊ'peɪk] *glass* opaco

OPEC ['əʊpek] *abbr* (= **Organization of Petroleum Exporting Countries**) OPEC *f*

o·pen ['əʊpən] **1** *adj* aperto; *flower* sbocciato; (*honest, frank*) aperto, franco; **in the ~ air** all'aria aperta **2** v/t aprire **3** v/i *of door, shop* aprirsi; *of flower* sbocciare

♦ open up v/i *of person* aprirsi

o·pen·air *adj meeting, concert* all'aperto; *pool* scoperto; **'o·pen day** giornata *f* di apertura al pubblico; **o·pen·'end·ed** *adj contract etc* aperto

o·pen·ing ['əʊpənɪŋ] *in wall etc* apertura *f*; *of film, novel etc* inizio *m*; (*job going*) posto *m* vacante

'o·pen·ing hours *npl* orario *m* d'apertura

o·pen·ly ['əʊpənlɪ] *adv* (*honestly, frankly*) apertamente

o·pen-mind·ed [əʊpən'maɪndɪd] *adj* aperto; **o·pen 'plan of·fice** open space *m inv*; **'o·pen tick·et** biglietto *m* aperto

op·e·ra ['ɒpərə] lirica *f*, opera *f*

'op·e·ra glass·es *npl* binocolo *m* da teatro; **'op·e·ra house** teatro *m* dell'opera; **'op·e·ra sing·er** cantante lirico *m*, -a *f*

op·e·rate ['ɒpəreɪt] **1** v/i *of company* operare; *of airline, bus service* essere in servizio; *of machine* funzionare; MED operare, intervenire **2** v/t *machine* far funzionare

♦ operate on v/t MED operare

'op·e·rat·ing in·struc·tions *npl* istruzioni *fpl* per l'uso

'op·e·rat·ing sys·tem COMPUT sistema *m* operativo

op·e·ra·tion [ɒpə'reɪʃn] operazione *f*; MED intervento *m* (chirurgico), operazione *f*; *of machine* funzionamento *m*; *of company* operazioni *fpl*; **have an ~** MED subire un intervento (chirurgico)

op·e·ra·tor ['ɒpəreɪtə(r)] TELEC centralinista *m/f*; *of machine* operatore

m, -trice *f*; (*tour ~*) operatore *m* turistico

o·pin·ion [ə'pɪnjən] opinione *f*, parere *m*; **in my ~** a mio parere

o'pin·ion poll sondaggio *m* d'opinione

op·po·nent [ə'pəʊnənt] avversario *m*, -a *f*

op·por·tune ['ɒpətjuːn] *adj fml* opportuno

op·por·tun·ist [ɒpə'tjuːnɪst] opportunista *m/f*

op·por·tu·ni·ty [ɒpə'tjuːnətɪ] opportunità *f inv*

op·pose [ə'pəʊz] v/t opporsi a; **be ~d to ...** essere contrario a ...; **as ~d to ...** piuttosto che ...

op·po·site ['ɒpəzɪt] **1** *adj direction* opposto; *meaning, views* contrario; *house* di fronte; **the ~ side of the road** l'altro lato della strada; **the ~ sex** l'altro sesso **2** *n* contrario *m*

op·po·site 'num·ber omologo *m*, -a *f*

op·po·si·tion [ɒpə'zɪʃn] opposizione *f*

op·press [ə'pres] v/t *the people* opprimere

op·pres·sive [ə'presɪv] *adj rule, dictator* oppressivo; *weather* opprimente

opt [ɒpt] v/t: **~ to do sth** optare per fare qc

op·ti·cal il·lu·sion ['ɒptɪkl] illusione *f* ottica

op·ti·cian [ɒp'tɪʃn] *dispensing* ottico *m*, -a *f*; *ophthalmic* optometrista *m/f*

op·ti·mism ['ɒptɪmɪzm] ottimismo *m*

op·ti·mist ['ɒptɪmɪst] ottimista *m/f*

op·ti·mis·tic [ɒptɪ'mɪstɪk] *adj attitude, view* ottimistico; *person* ottimista

op·ti·mis·tic·al·ly [ɒptɪ'mɪstɪklɪ] *adv* ottimisticamente

optimum ['ɒptɪməm] **1** *adj* ottimale **2** *n* optimum *m inv*

op·tion ['ɒpʃn] possibilità *f inv*, opzione *f*; **he had no other ~** non ha avuto scelta

op·tion·al ['ɒpʃnl] *adj* facoltativo

op·tion·al 'ex·tras *npl* optional *m inv*

or [ɔː(r)] *conj* o; *he can't hear ~ see* non può né sentire né vedere; *~ else!* o guai a te!

o·ral ['ɔːrəl] *adj* orale

or·ange ['ɒrɪndʒ] **1** *adj colour* arancione **2** *n fruit* arancia *f*; *colour* arancione *m*

or·ange·ade ['ɒrɪndʒeɪd] aranciata *f*

'**or·ange juice** succo *m* d'arancia

or·ange 'squash aranciata *f* non gasata

or·a·tor ['ɒrətə(r)] oratore *m*, -trice *f*

or·bit ['ɔːbɪt] **1** *n of earth* orbita *f*; *send sth into ~* lanciare in orbita qc **2** *v/t the earth* orbitare intorno a

or·chard ['ɔːtʃəd] frutteto *m*

or·ches·tra ['ɔːkɪstrə] orchestra *f*

or·chid ['ɔːkɪd] orchidea *f*

or·dain [ɔː'deɪn] *v/t priest* ordinare

or·deal [ɔː'diːl] esperienza *f* traumatizzante

or·der ['ɔːdə(r)] **1** *n* ordine *m*; *for goods, in restaurant* ordinazione *f*; *in ~ to do sth* così da fare qc; *he stood down in ~ that she could get the job* si è ritirato, così che lei potesse avere il lavoro; *out of ~ (not functioning)* fuori servizio; *(not in sequence)* fuori posto; *he's out of ~ (not doing the proper thing)* si sta comportando in modo scorretto **2** *v/t* ordinare; *~ s.o. to do sth* ordinare a qu di fare qc **3** *v/i* ordinare

or·der·ly ['ɔːdəlɪ] **1** *adj room, mind* ordinato; *crowd* disciplinato **2** *n in hospital* inserviente *m/f*

or·di·nal num·ber ['ɔːdɪnl] numero *m* ordinale

or·di·nar·i·ly [ɔːdɪ'neərɪlɪ] *adv (as a rule)* normalmente

or·di·nary ['ɔːdɪnərɪ] *adj* normale; *pej* ordinario; *nothing out of the ~* niente di straordinario

ore [ɔː(r)] minerale *m* grezzo

or·gan ['ɔːgən] ANAT, MUS organo *m*

or·gan·ic [ɔː'gænɪk] *adj food, fertilizer* biologico

or·gan·i·cal·ly [ɔː'gænɪklɪ] *adv grown* biologicamente

or·gan·is·m ['ɔːgənɪzm] organismo *m*

or·gan·i·za·tion [ɔːgənaɪ'zeɪʃn] organizzazione *f*

or·gan·ize ['ɔːgənaɪz] *v/t* organizzare

or·gan·ized 'crime criminalità *f inv* organizzata

or·gan·iz·er ['ɔːgənaɪzə(r)] *person* organizzatore *m*, -trice *f*

or·gas·m ['ɔːgæzm] orgasmo *m*

O·ri·ent ['ɔːrɪənt] Oriente *m*

O·ri·en·tal [ɔːrɪ'entl] **1** *adj* orientale **2** *n* orientale *m/f*

o·ri·en·tate ['ɔːrɪənteɪt] *v/t (direct)* orientare; *~ o.s. (get bearings)* orientarsi

or·i·gin ['ɒrɪdʒɪn] origine *f*; *of Chinese ~* di origine cinese

o·rig·i·nal [ə'rɪdʒənl] **1** *adj* originale **2** *n painting etc* originale *m*

o·rig·i·nal·i·ty [ərɪdʒɪn'ælətɪ] originalità *f inv*

o·rig·i·nal·ly [ə'rɪdʒənəlɪ] *adv (at first)* in origine; *~ he comes from France* è di origini francesi

o·rig·i·nate [ə'rɪdʒɪneɪt] **1** *v/t scheme, idea* dare origine a **2** *v/i of idea, belief* avere origine

o·rig·i·na·tor [ə'rɪdʒɪneɪtə(r)] *of scheme etc* ideatore *m*, -trice *f*

or·na·ment ['ɔːnəmənt] soprammobile *m*

or·na·men·tal [ɔːnə'mentl] *adj* ornamentale

or·nate [ɔː'neɪt] *adj style, architecture* ornato

or·phan ['ɔːfn] *n* orfano *m*, -a *f*

or·phan·age ['ɔːfənɪdʒ] orfanotrofio *m*

or·tho·dox ['ɔːθədɒks] *adj also fig* ortodosso

or·tho·pe·dic [ɔːθə'piːdɪk] *adj* ortopedico

os·ten·si·bly [ɒ'stensəblɪ] *adv* apparentemente

os·ten·ta·tion [ɒsten'teɪʃn] ostentazione *f*

os·ten·ta·tious [ɒsten'teɪʃəs] *adj* ostentato

os·ten·ta·tious·ly [ɒsten'teɪʃəslɪ]

adv con ostentazione

os·tra·cize ['ɒstrəsaɪz] *v/t* ostracizzare

oth·er ['ʌðə(r)] **1** *adj* altro; **the ~ day** l'altro giorno; **every ~ day** a giorni alterni; **every ~ person** una persona su due **2** *n* l'altro *m*, -a *f*; **the ~s** gli altri

oth·er·wise ['ʌðəwaɪz] *adv* altrimenti; (*differently*) diversamente

OTT [əʊtiː'tiː] *abbr* F (= **over the top**) esagerato

ot·ter ['ɒtə(r)] lontra *f*

ought [ɔːt] *v/aux*: **I/you ~ to know** dovrei/dovresti saperlo; **you ~ to have done it** avresti dovuto farlo

ounce [aʊns] oncia *f*

our ['aʊə(r)] *adj* il nostro *m*, la nostra *f*, i nostri *mpl*, le nostre *fpl*; **~ brother/sister** nostro fratello/nostra sorella

ours [aʊəz] *pron* il nostro *m*, la nostra *f*, i nostri *mpl*, le nostre *fpl*

our·selves [aʊə'selvz] *pron reflexive* ci; *emphatic* noi stessi/nois stesse; *after prep* noi; **we did it ~** l'abbiamo fatto noi (stessi/stesse); **we talked about ~** abbiamo parlato di noi; **by ~** da soli

oust [aʊst] *v/t from office* esautorare

out [aʊt]: **be ~** *of light, fire* essere spento; *of flower* essere sbocciato; *of sun* splendere; *not at home, not in building* essere fuori; *of calculations* essere sbagliato; (*be published*) essere uscito; *of secret* essere svelato; *no longer in competition* essere eliminato; *of workers* essere in sciopero; (*no longer in fashion*) essere out; **~ here in Dallas** qui a Dallas; **he's ~ in the garden** è in giardino; **(get)** ~! fuori!; **(get)** ~ **of my room!** fuori dalla mia stanza!; **that's ~!** (*out of the question*) è fuori discussione!; **he's ~ to win** *fully intends to* è deciso a vincere

out·board 'mo·tor motore *m* fuoribordo

out·break *of war, disease* scoppio *m*

out·build·ing annesso *m*

out·burst *emotional* reazione *f* vio-

lenta; **~ of anger** esplosione *f* di rabbia

'out·cast *n* emarginato *m*, -a *f*

'out·come risultato *m*

'out·cry protesta *f*

out·dat·ed *adj* sorpassato

out'do *v/t* (*pret* **-did**, *pp* **-done**) superare

out'door *adj* *toilet, activities, life* all'aperto; *swimming pool* scoperto

out'doors *adv* all'aperto

out·er ['aʊtə(r)] *adj* *wall etc* esterno

out·er 'space spazio *m* intergalattico

'out·fit (*clothes*) completo *m*; (*company, organization*) organizzazione *f*

'out·go·ing *adj* *flight, mail* in partenza; *personality* estroverso

out'grow *v/t* (*pret* **-grew**, *pp* **-grown**) *bad habits, interests* perdere

out·ing ['aʊtɪŋ] (*trip*) gita *f*

out'last *v/t* durare più di

'out·let *of pipe* scarico *m*; *for sales* punto *m* di vendita

'out·line **1** *n* *of person, building etc* profilo *m*; *of plan, novel* abbozzo *m* **2** *v/t* *plans etc* abbozzare

out'live *v/t* sopravvivere a

'out·look (*prospects*) prospettiva *f*

'out·ly·ing *adj* *areas* periferico

out'num·ber *v/t* superare numericamente

out of *prep* (*motion*) fuori; **fall ~ the window** cadere fuori dalla finestra ◊ (*position*) da **20 miles ~ Newcastle** 20 miglia da Newcastle ◊ (*cause*) per; **~ jealousy/curiosity** per gelosia/curiosità ◊ (*without*) senza; **we're ~ petrol/beer** siamo senza benzina/birra ◊ *from a group* su **5 - 10** 5 su 10

out-of-'date *adj* *passport* scaduto; *values* superato

out-of-the-way *adj* fuori mano

'out·pa·tient paziente *m/f* esterno, -a

'out·pa·tients' (clin·ic) ambulatorio *m*

out·per'form *v/t* *of machine, investment* rendere meglio di; *of company, economy* andare meglio di

'out·put **1** *n* *of factory* produzione *f*;

COMPUT output *m inv* **2** *v/t* (*pret & pp* **-ted** *or* **output**) (*produce*) produrre; COMPUT: *signal* emettere

'**out·rage 1** *n feeling* sdegno *m*; *act* atrocità *f inv* **2** *v/t* indignare

out·ra·geous [aʊt'reɪdʒəs] *adj acts* scioccante; *prices* scandaloso

'**out·right 1** *adj winner* assoluto **2** *adv win* nettamente; *kill* sul colpo

out'run *v/t* (*pret* **-ran**, *pp* **-run**) *also fig* superare; *run faster than* correre più veloce di

'out·set *n*: **at / from the ~** all' / dall'inizio

out'shine *v/t* (*pret & pp* **-shone**) eclissare

'**out·side 1** *adj surface, wall, lane* esterno **2** *adv sit, go* fuori **3** *prep* fuori di; (*apart from*) al di fuori di **4** *n of building, case etc* esterno *m*; **at the ~** al massimo

out·side 'broad·cast trasmissione *f* in esterni

out·sid·er [aʊt'saɪdə(r)] estraneo *m*, -a *f*; *in election, race* outsider *m inv*

'out·size *adj clothing* di taglia forte

'out·skirts *npl* periferia *f*

out'smart → **outwit**

out'stand·ing *adj success, writer* eccezionale; FIN: *invoice, sums* da saldare

out·stretched [aʊtstretʃt] *adj hands* teso

out'vote *v/t* mettere in minoranza

out·ward ['aʊtwəd] *adj appearance* esteriore; **~ *journey*** viaggio *m* d'andata

out·ward·ly ['aʊtwədlɪ] *adv* esteriormente

out'weigh *v/t* contare più di

out'wit *v/t* (*pret & pp* **-ted**) riuscire a gabbare

o·val ['əʊvl] *adj* ovale

o·va·ry ['əʊvərɪ] ovaia *f*

o·va·tion [əʊ'veɪʃn] ovazione *f*; **she was given a standing ~** il pubblico s'è alzato in piedi per applaudirla

ov·en ['ʌvn] *in kitchen* forno *m*; *in factory* fornace *f*

'ov·en glove, '**ov·en mitt** guanto *m* da forno; '**ov·en·proof** *adj* pirofilo; '**ov·en·read·y** *adj* pronto da mettere al forno

o·ver ['əʊvə(r)] **1** *prep* (*above*) sopra, su; (*across*) dall'altra parte; (*more than*) oltre; (*during*) nel corso di; **~ the phone** al telefono; *travel all ~ Brazil* girare tutto il Brasile; *you find them all ~ Brazil* si trovano dappertutto in Brasile; *let's talk ~ a meal* parliamone a pranzo; *we're ~ the worst* il peggio è passato; **~ and above** oltre a **2** *adv*: **be ~** (*finished*) essere finito; (*left*) essere rimasto; **~ to you** (*your turn*) tocca a te; **~ in Japan** in Giappone; **~here / there** qui / lì; *it hurts all ~* mi fa male dappertutto; *painted white all ~* tutto dipinto di bianco; *it's all ~* è finito; *I've told you ~ and ~ again* te l'ho detto mille volte; *do sth ~ again* rifare qc

o·ver·all ['əʊvərɔːl] **1** *adj length* totale **2** *adv measure* complessivamente; (*in general*) nell'insieme

o·ver·alls ['əʊvərɔːlz] *npl* tuta *f* da lavoro

o·ver·awe *v/t* intimidire; *be ~d by s.o. / sth* essere intimidito da qu / qc

o·ver·bal·ance *v/i* perdere l'equilibrio

o·ver·bear·ing *adj* autoritario

'o·ver·board *adv*: *man ~!* uomo in mare!; *go ~ for s.o. / sth* entusiasmarsi per qu / qc

'o·ver·cast *adj day, sky* nuvoloso

o·ver·charge *v/t customer* far pagare più del dovuto a

'o·ver·coat cappotto *m*

o·ver·come *v/t* (*pret* **-came**, *pp* **-come**) *difficulties, shyness* superare; *be ~ by emotion* essere sopraffatto dall'emozione

o·ver·crowd·ed *adj* sovraffollato

o·ver·do *v/t* (*pret* **-did**, *pp* **-done**) (*exaggerate*) esagerare; *in cooking* stracuocere; *you're ~ing things taking on too much* ti stai strapazzando

o·ver·done *adj meat* stracotto

'o·ver·dose *n* overdose *f inv*

'**o·ver·draft** scoperto *m* (di conto); **have an ~** avere il conto scoperto

o·ver'draw *v/t* (*pret* **-drew,** *pp* **-drawn**): **~ one's account** andare allo scoperto; **be £800 ~n** essere (allo) scoperto di 800 sterline

o·ver'dressed *adj* troppo elegante

'**o·ver·drive** MOT overdrive *m inv*

o·ver'due *adj bill, rent* arretrato; *train, baby* in ritardo

o·ver·es·ti·mate *v/t abilities, value* sovrastimare

o·ver'ex·pose *v/t photograph* sovraesporre

o·ver'flow[1] *n pipe* troppopieno *m*

o·ver'flow[2] *v/i of water* traboccare; *of river* straripare

o·ver'grown *adj garden* coperto d'erbacce; **he's an ~ baby** è un bambinone

o·ver'haul *v/t engine* revisionare; *plans* rivedere

'**o·ver·head**[1] *adj lights, cables* in alto, aereo; *railway* soprelevato

'**o·ver·head**[2] *Am nsg,* '**o·ver·heads** *npl* FIN costi *mpl* di gestione; *travel* ~ spese *fpl* di viaggio

'**o·ver·head pro·jec·tor** lavagna *f* luminosa

o·ver'hear *v/t* (*pret & pp* **-heard**) sentire per caso

o·ver'heat·ed *adj room, engine* surriscaldato

o·ver'joyed [əʊvə'dʒɔɪd] *adj* felicissimo

'**o·ver·kill**: **that's ~** è un'esagerazione

'**o·ver·land** *adj & adv* via terra

o·ver'lap *v/i* (*pret & pp* **-ped**) (*partly cover*) sovrapporsi; (*partly coincide*) coincidere

o·ver'leaf: *see* **~ a tergo**

o·ver'load *v/t* sovraccaricare

o·ver'look *v/t of tall building etc* dominare, dare su; *deliberately* chiudere un occhio su; *accidentally* non notare; **the room ~s the garden** la stanza dà sul giardino

o·ver·ly ['əʊvəlɪ] *adv* troppo; *not ~ ...* non particolarmente ...

'**o·ver·night** *adv travel* di notte; *stay* per la notte

o·ver'night 'bag piccola borsa *f* da viaggio

o·ver'paid *adj* strapagato

o·ver·pop·u·lat·ed [əʊvə'pɒpjʊleɪtɪd] *adj* sovrappopolato

o·ver'pow·er *v/t physically* sopraffare

o·ver'pow·er·ing [əʊvə'paʊrɪŋ] *adj smell* asfissiante; *sense of guilt* opprimente

o·ver'priced [əʊvə'praɪst] *adj* troppo caro

o·ver'rat·ed [əʊvə'reɪtɪd] *adj* sopravvalutato

o·ver·re'act *v/i* reagire in modo eccessivo

o·ver'ride *v/t* (*pret* **-rode,** *pp* **-ridden**) annullare; *person* annullare la decisione di; (*be more important than*) prevalere su

o·ver'rid·ing *adj concern* principale

o·ver'rule *v/t decision* annullare

o·ver'run *v/t* (*pret* **-ran,** *pp* **-run**) *country* invadere; *time* sforare; **be ~ with** essere invaso da

o·ver'seas *adv & adj* all'estero

o·ver'see *v/t* (*pret* **-saw,** *pp* **-seen**) sorvegliare

o·ver'shad·ow *v/t fig* eclissare

'**o·ver·sight** svista *f*

o·ver·sim·pli·fi·ca·tion semplificazione *f* eccessiva

o·ver'sim·pli·fy *v/t* (*pret & pp* **-ied**) semplificare troppo

o·ver'sleep *v/i* (*pret & pp* **-slept**) non svegliarsi in tempo

o·ver'state *v/t* esagerare

o·ver'state·ment esagerazione *f*

o·ver'step *v/t* (*pret & pp* **-ped**): *fig* **~ the mark** passare il segno

o·ver'take *v/t* (*pret* **-took,** *pp* **-taken**) *in work, development* superare; MOT sorpassare

o·ver'throw[1] *v/t* (*pret* **-threw,** *pp* **-thrown**) *government* rovesciare

'**o·ver·throw**[2] *n of government* rovesciamento *m*

'**o·ver·time** *Br* **1** *n* straordinario *m* **2** *adv*: **work ~** fare lo straordinario

'o·ver·ture [ˈəʊvətjʊə(r)] MUS ouverture *f inv*; **make ~s to** fare approcci a

o·ver·turn **1** *v/t vehicle, object* ribaltare; *government* rovesciare **2** *v/i of vehicle* ribaltarsi

'o·ver·view visione *f* d'insieme

o·ver·weight *adj* sovrappeso

o·ver·whelm [əʊvə'welm] *v/t with work* oberare; *with emotion* sopraffare; **be ~ed by** *by response* essere colpito da

o·ver·whelm·ing [əʊvə'welmɪŋ] *adj feeling* profondo; *majority* schiacciante

o·ver·work **1** *n* lavoro *m* eccessivo **2** *v/i* lavorare troppo **3** *v/t* far lavorare troppo

owe [əʊ] *v/t* dovere; **~ s.o. £500** dovere £500 a qu; **~ s.o. an apology** dovere delle scuse a qu; **how much**

do I ~ you? quanto le devo?

ow·ing to [ˈəʊɪŋ] *prep* a causa di

owl [aʊl] gufo *m*

own[1] [əʊn] *v/t* possedere

own[2] [əʊn] **1** *adj* proprio; **my ~ car** la mia macchina; **my very ~ mother** proprio mia madre **2** *pron:* **a car of my ~** un'auto tutta mia; **on my / his ~** da solo

♦ **own up** *v/i* confessare

own·er [ˈəʊnə(r)] proprietario *m*, -a *f*

own·er·ship [ˈəʊnəʃɪp] proprietà *f inv*

ox [ɒks] bue *m*

ox·ide [ˈɒksaɪd] ossido *m*

ox·y·gen [ˈɒksɪdʒən] ossigeno *m*

oy·ster [ˈɔɪstə(r)] ostrica *f*

oz *abbr* (= **ounce(s)**) oncia *f*

o·zone [ˈəʊzəʊn] ozono *m*

'o·zone lay·er fascia *f* o strato *m* d'ozono

P

p [piː] *abbr* (= **penny**; **pence**) penny *m inv*

PA [piːˈeɪ] *abbr* (= **personal assistant**) assistente *m/f* personale

pace [peɪs] **1** *n* (*step*) passo *m*; (*speed*) ritmo *m* **2** *v/i:* **~ up and down** camminare su e giù

'pace·mak·er MED pacemaker *m inv*; SP battistrada *m inv*

Pa·cif·ic [pəˈsɪfɪk]: **the ~ (Ocean)** il Pacifico

pac·i·fism [ˈpæsɪfɪzm] pacifismo *m*

pac·i·fist [ˈpæsɪfɪst] *n* pacifista *m/f*

pac·i·fy [ˈpæsɪfaɪ] *v/t* (*pret & pp -ied*) placare

pack [pæk] **1** *n* (*back~*) zaino *m*; *of cereal, food* confezione *f*; *of cigarettes* pacchetto *m*; *of peas etc* confezione *f*; *of cards* mazzo *m* **2** *v/t bag* fare; *item of clothing etc* mettere in valigia; *goods* imballare; *groceries* imbu-

stare **3** *v/i* fare la valigia / le valigie

pack·age [ˈpækɪdʒ] **1** *n* (*parcel*) pacco *m*; *of offers etc* pacchetto *m* **2** *v/t* confezionare

'pack·age deal *for holiday* offerta *f* tutto compreso

'pack·age tour viaggio *m* organizzato

pack·ag·ing [ˈpækɪdʒɪŋ] *also fig* confezione *f*

pack·ed [pækt] *adj* (*crowded*) affollato

pack·et [ˈpækɪt] confezione *f*; *of cigarettes, crisps* pacchetto *m*

pact [pækt] patto *m*

pad[1] [pæd] **1** *n piece of cloth etc* tampone *m*; *for writing* blocchetto *m* **2** *v/t* (*pret & pp -ded*) *with material* imbottire; *speech, report* farcire

pad[2] [pæd] *v/i* (*move quietly*) camminare a passi felpati

pad·ded ['pædɪd] *adj jacket, shoulders* imbottito

pad·ding ['pædɪŋ] *material* imbottitura *f*; *in speech etc* riempitivo *m*

pad·dle ['pædl] **1** *n for canoe* pagaia *f* **2** *v/i in canoe* pagaiare; *in water* sguazzare

pad·dling pool ['pædlɪŋpuːl] piscinetta *f* per bambini

pad·dock ['pædək] paddock *m inv*

pad·lock ['pædlɒk] **1** *n* lucchetto *m* **2** *v/t* gate chiudere col lucchetto; ~ **X to Y** fissare col lucchetto X a Y

paed·i·at·ric *etc* → **pediatric** *etc*

page[1] [peɪdʒ] *n of book etc* pagina *f*

page[2] [peɪdʒ] *v/t (call)* chiamare con l'altoparlante; *with pager* chiamare col cercapersone

pag·er ['peɪdʒə(r)] cercapersone *m inv*

paid [peɪd] *pret & pp* → **pay**

paid em·ploy·ment occupazione *f* rimunerata

pail [peɪl] secchio *m*

pain [peɪn] dolore *m*; **be in ~** soffrire; **take ~s to ...** fare il possibile per ...; **a ~ in the neck** F una rottura *f* di scatole F

pain·ful ['peɪnfʊl] *adj (distressing)* doloroso; *(laborious)* difficile; **my leg is still ~** la gamba mi fa ancora male; **it is my ~ duty to inform you ...** siamo addolorati di comunicarle ...

pain·ful·ly ['peɪnflɪ] *adv (extremely, acutely)* estremamente

pain·kill·er ['peɪnkɪlə(r)] analgesico *m*

pain·less ['peɪnlɪs] *adj* indolore

pains·tak·ing ['peɪnzteɪkɪŋ] *adj* accurato

paint [peɪnt] **1** *n for wall, car* vernice *f*; *for artist* colore *m* **2** *v/t wall etc* pitturare; *picture* dipingere **3** *v/i as art form* dipingere

paint·brush ['peɪntbrʌʃ] pennello *m*

paint·er ['peɪntə(r)] *decorator* imbianchino *m*; *artist* pittore *m*, -trice *f*

paint·ing ['peɪntɪŋ] *activity* pittura *f*, *(picture)* quadro *m*

paint·work ['peɪntwɜːk] vernice *f*

pair [peə(r)] *of objects* paio *m*; *of animals, people* coppia *f*; **a ~ of shoes** un paio di scarpe

pa·ja·mas *Am* → **pyjamas**

Pa·ki·stan [pɑːkɪ'stɑːn] Pakistan *m*

Pa·ki·sta·ni [pɑːkɪ'stɑːnɪ] **1** *n* pakistano *m*, -a *f* **2** *adj* pakistano

pal [pæl] F *(friend)* amico *m*, -a *f*

pal·ace ['pælɪs] palazzo *m* signorile

pal·ate ['pælət] palato *m*

pa·la·tial [pə'leɪʃl] *adj* sfarzoso

pale [peɪl] *adj person* pallido; ~ **pink / blue** rosa / celeste pallido

Pal·e·stine ['pæləstaɪn] Palestina *f*

Pal·e·stin·i·an [pælə'stɪnɪən] **1** *n* palestinese *m/f* **2** *adj* palestinese

pal·let ['pælɪt] pallet *m inv*

pal·lor ['pælə(r)] pallore *m*

palm[1] [pɑːm] *of hand* palma *f*

palm[2] [pɑːm] *tree* palma *f*

pal·pi·ta·tions [pælpɪ'teɪʃnz] *npl* MED palpitazioni *fpl*

pal·try ['pɔːltrɪ] *adj* irrisorio

pam·per ['pæmpə(r)] *v/t* viziare

pam·phlet ['pæmflɪt] volantino *m*

pan [pæn] **1** *n for cooking* pentola *f*; *for frying* padella *f* **2** *v/t (pret & pp -ned)* F *(criticize)* stroncare F

♦ **pan out** *v/i (develop)* svilupparse

pan·cake ['pænkeɪk] crêpe *f inv*

pan·da ['pændə] panda *m inv*

pan·de·mo·ni·um [pændɪ'məʊnɪəm] pandemonio *m*

♦ **pan·der to** ['pændə(r)] *v/t* assecondare

pane [peɪn] ~ *(of glass)* vetro *m*

pan·el ['pænl] pannello *m*; *of experts* gruppo *m*; *of judges* giuria *f*

pan·el·ling ['pænlɪŋ] rivestimento *m* a pannelli

pang [pæŋ] *of remorse* fitta *f*; ~**s of hunger** morsi *mpl* della fame

pan·ic ['pænɪk] **1** *n* panico *m* **2** *v/i (pret & pp -ked)* **don't ~** non farti prendere dal panico

'**pan·ic buy·ing** FIN *acquisto m motivato dal panico*; '**pan·ic sel·ling** FIN *vendita f motivata dal panico*; '**pan·ic-strick·en** *adj* in preda al panico

pan·o·ra·ma [pænə'rɑːmə] panorama *m*

pa·no·ra·mic [pænə'ræmɪk] adj view panoramico

pan·sy ['pænzɪ] flower viola f del pensiero

pant [pænt] v/i ansimare

pan·ties ['pæntɪz] npl mutandine fpl

pants [pænts] npl (underpants) mutande fpl; esp Am (trousers) pantaloni mpl

pan·ty·hose ['pæntɪhəʊz] Am collant mpl

pa·pal ['peɪpəl] adj pontificio

pa·per ['peɪpə(r)] 1 n material carta f; (news~) giornale m; (wall~) carta f da parati; academic relazione f; (examination ~) esame m; ~s (identity ~s, documents) documenti mpl; a piece of ~ un pezzo di carta 2 adj di carta 3 v/t room, walls tappezzare

'paperback tascabile m; paper 'bag sacchetto m di carta; 'paper boy ragazzo m che recapita i giornali a domicilio; 'paper clip graffetta f; 'paper cup bicchiere m di carta; 'paperwork disbrigo m delle pratiche

par [pɑː (r)] in golf par m inv; be on a ~ with essere allo stesso livello di; feel below ~ non sentirsi bene

par·a·chute ['pærəʃuːt] 1 n paracadute m inv 2 v/i paracadutarsi 3 v/t troops, supplies paracadutare

par·a·chut·ist ['pærəʃuːtɪst] paracadutista m/f

pa·rade [pə'reɪd] 1 n (procession) sfilata f 2 v/i sfilare 3 v/t knowledge, new car fare sfoggio di

par·a·dise ['pærədaɪs] paradiso m

par·a·dox ['pærədɒks] paradosso m

par·a·dox·i·cal [pærə'dɒksɪkl] adj paradossale

par·a·dox·i·cal·ly [pærə'dɒksɪklɪ] adv paradossalmente

par·a·graph ['pærəgrɑːf] paragrafo m

par·al·lel ['pærəlel] 1 n (in geometry) parallela f; GEOG, fig parallelo m; do two things in ~ fare due cose in parallelo 2 adj also fig parallelo 3 v/t (match) uguagliare

par·a·lyse ['pærəlaɪz] v/t also fig paralizzare

pa·ral·y·sis [pə'ræləsɪs] also fig paralisi f inv

par·a·med·ic [pærə'medɪk] n paramedico m, -a f

pa·ram·e·ter [pə'ræmɪtə(r)] parametro m

par·a·mil·i·tar·y [pærə'mɪlɪtrɪ] 1 adj paramilitare 2 n appartenente m/f ad un'organizzazione paramilitare

par·a·mount ['pærəmaʊnt] adj vitale; be ~ essere di vitale importanza

par·a·noi·a [pærə'nɔɪə] paranoia f

par·a·noid ['pærənɔɪd] adj paranoico

par·a·pher·na·li·a [pærəfə'neɪlɪə] armamentario m

par·a·phrase ['pærəfreɪz] v/t parafrasare

par·a·pleg·ic [pærə'pliːdʒɪk] n paraplegico m, -a f

par·a·site ['pærəsaɪt] also fig parassita m

par·a·sol ['pærəsɒl] parasole m

par·a·troop·er ['pærətruːpə(r)] MIL paracadutista m

par·cel ['pɑːsl] n pacco m

♦parcel up v/t impacchettare

parch [pɑːtʃ] v/t riardere; be ~ed F of person essere assetato

par·don ['pɑːdn] 1 n LAW grazia f; I beg your ~? (what did you say) prego?; I beg your ~ (I'm sorry) scusi 2 v/t scusare; LAW graziare

pare [peə(r)] v/t (peel) pelare

par·ent ['peərənt] genitore m

pa·ren·tal [pə'rentl] adj dei genitori

'par·ent company società f inv madre

par·ent-'teach·er as·so·ci·a·tion organizzazione f composta da genitori e insegnanti

par·ish ['pærɪʃ] parrocchia f

park¹ [pɑːk] n parco m

park² [pɑːk] v/t & v/i MOT parcheggiare

par·ka ['pɑːkə] parka m inv

park·ing ['pɑːkɪŋ] MOT parcheggio m; no ~ sosta f vietata

'park·ing brake Am freno m a mano;

'**par·king disc** disco *m* orario; '**parking lot** *Am* parcheggio *m*; '**parking me·ter** parchimetro *m*; '**parking place** parcheggio *m*; '**parking tick·et** multa *f* per sosta vietata

par·lia·ment ['pɑːləmənt] parlamento *m*

par·lia·men·ta·ry [pɑːljə'mentərɪ] *adj* parlamentare

pa·role [pə'rəʊl] **1** *n* libertà *f inv* vigilata; **be out on ~** essere rimesso in libertà vigilata **2** *v/t* concedere la libertà vigilata a

par·rot ['pærət] pappagallo *m*

pars·ley ['pɑːslɪ] prezzemolo *m*

part [pɑːt] **1** *n* parte *f*; *of machine* pezzo *m*; *Am: in hair* riga *f*; **take ~ in** prendere parte in **2** *adv* (*partly*) in parte **3** *v/i* separarsi **4** *v/t*: **~ one's hair** farsi la riga

♦ **part with** *v/t* separarsi da

'**part ex·change** permuta *f*; **take sth in ~ exchange** prendere qc in permuta

par·tial ['pɑːʃl] *adj* (*incomplete*) parziale; **be ~ to** avere un debole per

par·tial·ly ['pɑːʃəlɪ] *adv* parzialmente

par·ti·ci·pant [pɑː'tɪsɪpənt] partecipante *m/f*

par·ti·ci·pate [pɑː'tɪsɪpeɪt] *v/i* partecipare; **~ in sth** partecipare a qc

par·ti·ci·pa·tion [pɑːtɪsɪ'peɪʃn] partecipazione *f*

par·ti·cle ['pɑːtɪkl] PHYS particella *f*; *small amount* briciolo *m*

par·tic·u·lar [pə'tɪkjʊlə(r)] *adj* (*specific*) particolare; (*fussy*) pignolo; **in ~** in particolare

par·tic·u·lar·ly [pə'tɪkjʊləlɪ] *adv* particolarmente

part·ing ['pɑːtɪŋ] *of people* separazione *f*; *in hair* riga *f*

par·ti·tion [pɑː'tɪʃn] **1** *n* (*screen*) tramezzo *m*; (*of country*) suddivisione *f* **2** *v/t country* suddividere

♦ **partition off** *v/t* tramezzare

part·ly ['pɑːtlɪ] *adv* in parte

part·ner ['pɑːtnə(r)] COM socio *m*, -a *f*; *in relationship* partner *m/f inv*; *in*

particular activity compagno *m*, -a *f*

part·ner·ship ['pɑːtnəʃɪp] COM società *f inv*; *in particular activity* sodalizio *m*

part of 'speech GRAM parte *f* del discorso; '**part own·er** comproprietario *m*, -a *f*; '**part-time** *adj & adv* part-time; **part-'tim·er** lavoratore *m*, -trice *f* part-time

par·ty ['pɑːtɪ] **1** *n* (*celebration*) festa *f*; POL partito *m*; (*group*) gruppo *m*; **be a ~ to** essere coinvolto in **2** *v/i* (*pret & pp* **-ied**) F far baldoria

pass [pɑːs] **1** *n* for getting into a place passi *m inv*; SP passaggio *m*; *in mountains* passo *m*; **make a ~ at** fare avances a **2** *v/t* (*hand*) passare; (*go past*) passare davanti a; (*overtake*) sorpassare; (*go beyond*) superare; (*approve*) approvare; SP passare; **~ an exam** superare un esame; **~ sentence** LAW emanare la sentenza; **~ the time** passare il tempo **3** *v/i* passare; *in exam* essere promosso

♦ **pass around** *v/t* far circolare

♦ **pass away** *v/i euph* spegnersi *euph*

♦ **pass by 1** *v/t* (*go past*) passare davanti a **2** *v/i* (*go past*) passare

♦ **pass on 1** *v/t information, book, savings* passare (**to** a) **2** *v/i* (*euph: die*) mancare *euph*

♦ **pass out** *v/i* (*faint*) svenire

♦ **pass through** *v/t town* passare per

♦ **pass up** *v/t opportunity* lasciarsi sfuggire

pass·a·ble ['pɑːsəbl] *adj road* transitabile; (*acceptable*) passabile

pas·sage ['pæsɪdʒ] (*corridor*) passaggio *m*; *from poem, book* passo *m*; **the ~ of time** il passare del tempo

pas·sage·way ['pæsɪdʒweɪ] corridoio *m*

pas·sen·ger ['pæsɪndʒə(r)] passeggero *m*, -a *f*

'pas·sen·ger seat sedile *m* del passeggero

pas·ser-by [pɑːsə'baɪ] (*pl* **passers-by**) passante *m/f*

pas·sion ['pæʃn] passione *f*

pas·sion·ate ['pæ∫nət] adj appassionato

pas·sive ['pæsɪv] **1** adj passivo **2** n GRAM passivo m; **in the ~** al passivo

'pass mark EDU voto m sufficiente

Pass·o·ver ['pɑːsəʊvə(r)] REL Pasqua f ebraica

pass·port ['pɑːspɔːt] passaporto m

'pass·port control controllo m passaporti

pass·word ['pɑːswɜːd] parola f d'ordine; COMPUT password f inv

past [pɑːst] **1** adj (former) precedente; **in the ~ few days** nei giorni scorsi; **that's all ~ now** è acqua passata ormai **2** n passato m; **in the ~** nel passato **3** prep in position oltre; **it's half ~ two** sono le due e mezza; **it's ~ seven o'clock** sono le sette passate **4** adv: **run ~** passare di corsa

pas·ta ['pæstə] pasta f

paste [peɪst] **1** n (adhesive) colla f **2** v/t (stick) incollare

pas·tel ['pæstl] **1** n pastello m **2** adj pastello

pas·time ['pɑːstaɪm] passatempo m

past par·ti·ci·ple GRAM participio m passato

pas·tra·mi [pæ'strɑːmɪ] affettato m di carne di manzo speziata

pas·try ['peɪstrɪ] for pie pasta f (sfoglia); (small cake) pasticcino m

'past tense GRAM passato m

pas·ty ['peɪstɪ] adj complexion smorto

pat [pæt] **1** n colpetto m; affectionate buffetto m; **give s.o. a ~ on the back** fig dare una pacca sulla spalla a qu **2** v/t (pret & pp **-ted**) dare un colpetto a; affectionately dare un buffetto a

patch [pæt∫] **1** n on clothing pezza f; (period of time) periodo m; (area) zona f, **go through a bad ~** attraversare un brutto periodo; **~es of fog** banchi mpl di nebbia; **be not a ~ on** fig non essere niente a paragone di **2** v/t clothing rattoppare

♦ **patch up** v/t (repair temporarily) riparare alla meglio; quarrel risolvere

patch·work ['pæt∫wɜːk] **1** n patchwork m inv **2** adj quilt patchwork

patch·y ['pæt∫ɪ] adj quality irregolare; work, performance discontinuo, disuguale

pâ·té ['pæteɪ] pâté m inv

pa·tent ['peɪtnt] **1** adj palese **2** n for invention brevetto m **3** v/t invention brevettare

pa·tent·ly ['peɪtntlɪ] adv (clearly) palesemente

pa·tent 'leath·er vernice f

pa·ter·nal [pə'tɜːnl] adj paterno

pa·ter·nal·ism [pə'tɜːnlɪzm] paternalismo m

pa·ter·nal·is·tic [pətɜːnl'ɪstɪk] adj paternalistico

pa·ter·ni·ty [pə'tɜːnɪtɪ] paternità f inv

path [pɑːθ] sentiero m; fig strada f

pa·thet·ic [pə'θetɪk] adj invoking pity patetico; F (very bad) penoso

path·o·log·i·cal [pæθə'lɒdʒɪkl] adj patologico

pa·thol·o·gy [pə'θɒlədʒɪ] patologia f

pa·thol·o·gist [pə'θɒlədʒɪst] patologo m, -a f

pa·tience ['peɪ∫ns] pazienza f; Br: card game solitario m

pa·tient ['peɪ∫nt] **1** n paziente m/f **2** adj paziente; **just be ~!** abbi pazienza!

pa·tient·ly ['peɪ∫ntlɪ] adv pazientemente

pat·i·o ['pætɪəʊ] terrazza f

pat·ri·ot ['peɪtrɪət] patriota m/f

pat·ri·ot·ic [peɪtrɪ'ɒtɪk] adj patriottico

pat·ri·ot·ism ['peɪtrɪətɪzm] patriottismo m

pa·trol [pə'trəʊl] **1** n pattuglia f; **be on ~** essere di pattuglia **2** v/t (pret & pp **-led**) streets, border pattugliare

pa'trol car autopattuglia f

pa·trol·man agente m/f di pattuglia

pa·tron ['peɪtrən] of artist mecenate m, -trice f; of charity patrono m, -essa f; of shop, cinema cliente m/f

pa·tron·age ['peɪtrənɪdʒ] of artist patronato m; of charity patrocinio m

pa·tron·ize ['pætrənaɪz] v/t shop essere cliente di; *person* trattare con condiscendenza

pa·tron·iz·ing ['pætrənaɪzɪŋ] *adj* condiscendente

pa·tron 'saint patrono *m*, -a *f*

pat·ter ['pætə(r)] **1** *n* of rain etc picchiettio *m*; F of salesman imbonimento *m* **2** *v/i* picchiettare

pat·tern ['pætn] *n* on wallpaper, fabric motivo *m*, disegno *m*; for knitting, sewing (carta) modello *m*; in behaviour, events schema *m*

pat·terned ['pætənd] *adj* fantasia *inv*

paunch [pɔːntʃ] pancia *f*

pause [pɔːz] **1** *n* pausa *f* **2** *v/i* fermarsi **3** *v/t tape* fermare

pave [peɪv] *v/t* pavimentare; ~ **the way for** *fig* aprire la strada a

pave·ment ['peɪvmənt] *Br* marciapiede *m*

pav·ing stone ['peɪvɪŋ] lastra *f* di pavimentazione

paw [pɔː] **1** *n* of animal, F (hand) zampa *f* **2** *v/t* F palpare

pawn¹ [pɔːn] *n in chess* pedone *m*; *fig* pedina *f*

pawn² [pɔːn] *v/t* impegnare

'pawn·bro·ker prestatore *m*, -trice *f* su pegno

'pawn·shop monte *m* di pietà

pay [peɪ] **1** *n* paga *f*; **in the ~ of** al soldo di **2** *v/t* (*pret & pp* **paid**) pagare; ~ *s.o. a compliment* fare un complimento a qu **3** *v/i* (*pret & pp* **paid**) pagare; (*be profitable*) rendere; *it doesn't* ~ *to ...* non conviene ...; ~ *for purchase* pagare; *you'll* ~ *for this! fig* la pagherai!

♦ **pay back** *v/t person* restituire i soldi a; *loan* restituire; (*get revenge on*) farla pagare a

♦ **pay in** *v/t to bank* versare

♦ **pay off 1** *v/t debt* estinguere; *workers* liquidare; *corrupt official* comprare **2** *v/i* (*be profitable*) dare frutti

♦ **pay up** *v/i* pagare

pay·a·ble ['peɪəbl] *adj* pagabile

'pay·day giorno *m* di paga

pay·ee [peɪ'iː] beneficiario *m*, -a *f*

pay·er ['peɪə(r)] pagatore *m*, -trice *f*

pay·ment ['peɪmənt] pagamento *m*

'pay pack·et busta *f* paga; 'pay phone telefono *m* pubblico; 'pay·roll *money* stipendi *mpl*; *employees* personale *m*; *be on the* ~ essere sul libro paga; 'pay·slip busta *f* paga

PC [piː'siː] *abbr* (= *personal computer*) PC *m inv*; (= *politically correct*) politicamente corretto; (= *police constable*) agente *m* di polizia

pea [piː] pisello *m*

peace [piːs] pace *f*

peace·a·ble ['piːsəbl] *adj person* pacifico

peace·ful ['piːsfʊl] *adj* tranquillo; *demonstration* pacifico

peace·ful·ly ['piːsflɪ] *adv* tranquillamente; *demonstrate* pacificamente

peach [piːtʃ] pesca *f*; *tree* pesco *m*

pea·cock ['piːkɒk] pavone *m*

peak [piːk] **1** *n* vetta *f*; *fig* apice *m* **2** *v/i* raggiungere il livello massimo

'peak con·sump·tion periodo *m* di massimo consumo; 'peak hours *npl* ore *fpl* di punta; peak 'view·ing hours *npl* prima serata *f*

pea·nut ['piːnʌt] arachide *f*; *get paid* ~*s* F essere pagati una miseria F; *that's* ~*s to him* F sono briciole per lui

pea·nut 'but·ter burro *m* d'arachidi

pear [peə(r)] pera *f*; *tree* pero *m*

pearl [pɜːl] perla *f*

peas·ant ['peznt] contadino *m*, -a *f*

peb·ble ['pebl] ciottolo *m*

peck [pek] **1** *n* (*bite*) beccata *f*; (*kiss*) bacetto *m* **2** *v/t* (*bite*) beccare; (*kiss*) dare un bacetto a

pe·cu·li·ar [pɪ'kjuːlɪə(r)] *adj* (*strange*) strano; ~ *to* (*special*) caratteristico di

pe·cu·li·ar·i·ty [pɪkjuːlɪ'ærətɪ] (*strangeness*) stranezza *f*; (*special feature*) caratteristica *f*

ped·al ['pedl] **1** *n* of bike pedale *m* **2** *v/i turn* ~*s* pedalare; (*cycle*) andare in bicicletta

pe·dan·tic [pɪ'dæntɪk] *adj* pedante

ped·dle ['pedl] *v/t drugs* spacciare

ped·es·tal ['pedɪstl] *for statue* piedistallo *m*

P

pe·des·tri·an [pɪˈdestrɪən] n pedone m

pe·des·tri·an 'cros·sing passaggio m pedonale

pe·des·tri·an 'pre·cinct zona f pedonale

pe·di·at·ric [piːdɪˈætrɪk] adj pediatrico

pe·di·a·tri·cian [piːdɪəˈtrɪʃn] pediatra m/f

pe·di·at·rics [piːdɪˈætrɪks] pediatria f

ped·i·cure [ˈpedɪkjʊə(r)] pedicure f inv

ped·i·gree [ˈpedɪgriː] 1 n pedigree m inv 2 adj di razza pura

pee [piː] v/i F fare pipì F

peek [piːk] 1 n sbirciata f 2 v/i sbirciare F

peel [piːl] 1 n buccia f; of citrus fruit scorza f 2 v/t fruit, vegetables sbucciare 3 v/i of nose, shoulders spellarsi; of paint scrostarsi

♦ peel off 1 v/t wrapper etc togliere 2 v/i of wrapper venir via

peep [piːp] → peek

peep·hole [ˈpiːphəʊl] spioncino m

peer¹ [pɪə(r)] n (equal) pari m/f inv

peer² [pɪə(r)] v/i guardare; ~ through the mist guardare attraverso la foschia; ~ at scrutare

peeved [piːvd] adj F seccato

peg [peg] n for coat attaccapanni m inv; for tent picchetto m; off the ~ prêt-à-porter

pe·jo·ra·tive [pɪˈdʒɒrətɪv] adj peggiorativo

pel·let [ˈpelɪt] pallina f; (bullet) pallino m

pelt [pelt] 1 v/t: ~ s.o with sth tirare qc a qu 2 v/i: they ~ed along the road F sono sfrecciati per strada; it's ~ing down F piove a dirotto

pel·vis [ˈpelvɪs] pelvi f inv

pen¹ [pen] n penna f

pen² [pen] (enclosure) recinto m

pe·nal·ize [ˈpiːnəlaɪz] v/t penalizzare

pen·al·ty [ˈpenltɪ] ammenda f; in soccer rigore m; in rugby punizione f; take the ~ battere il rigore / la punizione

'pen·al·ty ar·e·a SP area f di rigore; 'pen·al·ty clause LAW penale f; 'pen·al·ty kick in soccer calcio m di rigore; in rugby calcio m di punizione; pen·al·ty 'shoot-out rigori mpl; 'pen·al·ty spot dischetto m di rigore

pence [pens] npl penny m inv

pen·cil [ˈpensɪl] matita f

pen·cil sharp·en·er temperamatite m inv

pen·dant [ˈpendənt] necklace pendaglio m

pend·ing [ˈpendɪŋ] 1 prep in attesa di 2 adj: be ~ essere in sospeso

pen·e·trate [ˈpenɪtreɪt] v/t penetrare in

pen·e·trat·ing [ˈpenɪtreɪtɪŋ] adj stare, scream penetrante; analysis perspicace

pen·e·tra·tion [penɪˈtreɪʃn] penetrazione f

'pen friend amico m, -a f di penna

pen·guin [ˈpeŋgwɪn] pinguino m

pen·i·cil·lin [penɪˈsɪlɪn] penicillina f

pe·nin·su·la [pəˈnɪnsjʊlə] penisola f

pe·nis [ˈpiːnɪs] pene m

pen·i·tence [ˈpenɪtəns] penitenza f

pen·i·tent [ˈpenɪtənt] adj pentito

pen·knife [ˈpennaɪf] temperino m

'pen name pseudonimo m

pen·nant [ˈpenənt] gagliardetto m

pen·ni·less [ˈpenɪlɪs] adj al verde

pen·ny [ˈpenɪ] penny m inv

'pen pal amico m, -a f di penna

pen·sion [ˈpenʃn] pensione f

♦ pension off v/t mandare in pensione

pen·sion·er [ˈpenʃnə(r)] pensionato m, -a f

'pen·sion fund fondo m pensioni

'pen·sion scheme schema m pensionistico

pen·sive [ˈpensɪv] adj pensieroso

Pen·ta·gon [ˈpentəgɒn]: the ~ il Pentagono

pen·tath·lon [penˈtæθlən] pentathlon m inv

Pen·te·cost [ˈpentɪkɒst] Pentecoste f

pent·house [ˈpenthaʊs] attico m

pent-up ['pentʌp] *adj* represso

pe·nul·ti·mate [pe'nʌltɪmət] *adj* penultimo

peo·ple ['piːpl] *npl* gente *f*, persone *fpl*; (*nsg: race, tribe*) popolazione *f*; **the ~** (*the citizens*) il popolo; **the American ~** gli americani; **~ say ...** si dice che ...

pep·per ['pepə(r)] *spice* pepe *m*; *vegetable* peperone *m*

pep·per·mint *sweet* mentina *f*; *flavouring* menta *f*

pep talk ['peptɔːk] *discorso m* d'incoraggiamento

per [pɜː(r)] *prep* a; **100 km ~ hour** 100 km all'ora; **£50 ~ night** 50 sterline a notte; **~ annum** all'anno

per·ceive [pə'siːv] *v/t with senses* percepire; (*view, interpret*) interpretare

per·cent [pə'sent] per cento

per·cen·tage [pə'sentɪdʒ] percentuale *f*

per·cep·ti·ble [pə'septəbl] *adj* percettibile

per·cep·ti·bly [pə'septəblɪ] *adv* percettibilmente

per·cep·tion [pə'sepʃn] *through senses* percezione *f*; (*insight*) sensibilità *f inv*

per·cep·tive [pə'septɪv] *adj person, remark* perspicace

perch [pɜːtʃ] **1** *n for bird* posatoio *m* **2** *v/i of bird* posarsi; *of person* appollaiarsi

per·co·late ['pɜːkəleɪt] *v/i of coffee* filtrare

per·co·la·tor ['pɜːkəleɪtə(r)] caffettiera *f* a filtro

per·cus·sion [pə'kʌʃn] percussioni *fpl*

per·cus·sion in·stru·ment strumento *m* a percussione

pe·ren·ni·al [pə'renɪəl] *n* BOT pianta *f* perenne

per·fect ['pɜːfɪkt] **1** *n* GRAM passato *m* prossimo **2** *adj* perfetto **3** *v/t* [pə'fekt] perfezionare

per·fec·tion [pə'fekʃn] perfezione *f*; **to ~** alla perfezione

per·fec·tion·ist [pə'fekʃnɪst] perfezionista *m/f*

per·fect·ly ['pɜːfɪktlɪ] *adv* perfettamente

per·fo·rat·ed ['pɜːfəreɪtɪd] *adj line* perforato

per·fo·ra·tions [pɜːfə'reɪʃnz] *npl* linea *fsg* perforata

per·form [pə'fɔːm] **1** *v/t* (*carry out*) eseguire; *of actors* rappresentare; *of musician* eseguire **2** *v/i of actor, musician, dancer* esibirsi; *of actor* recitare; **the car ~s well** la macchina dà ottime prestazioni

per·form·ance [pə'fɔːməns] *by actor* rappresentazione *f*; *by musician* esecuzione *f*; (*show*) spettacolo *m*; *of employee, company etc* rendimento *m*; *of machine* prestazioni *fpl*

per·form·ance car auto *f inv* di alte prestazioni

per·form·er [pə'fɔːmə(r)] artista *m/f*

per·fume ['pɜːfjuːm] profumo *m*

per·func·to·ry [pə'fʌŋktərɪ] *adj* superficiale

per·haps [pə'hæps] *adv* forse

per·il ['perəl] pericolo *m*

per·il·ous ['perələs] *adj* pericoloso

pe·rim·e·ter [pə'rɪmɪtə(r)] perimetro *m*

pe·rim·e·ter fence recinzione *f*

pe·ri·od ['pɪərɪəd] *time* periodo *m*; (*menstruation*) mestruazioni *fpl*; **I don't want to, ~!** Am non voglio, punto e basta!

pe·ri·od·ic [pɪərɪ'ɒdɪk] *adj* periodico

pe·ri·od·i·cal [pɪərɪ'ɒdɪkl] *n* periodico *m*

pe·ri·od·i·cal·ly [pɪərɪ'ɒdɪklɪ] *adv* periodicamente

pe·riph·e·ral [pə'rɪfərəl] **1** *adj not crucial* marginale **2** *n* COMPUT periferica *f*

pe·riph·e·ry [pə'rɪfərɪ] periferia *f*

per·ish ['perɪʃ] *v/i of rubber* deteriorarsi; *of person* perire

per·ish·a·ble ['perɪʃəbl] *adj food* deteriorabile

per·ish·ing ['perɪʃɪŋ] *adj* F: **it's ~** fa un freddo da cane F

per·jure ['pɜːdʒə(r)] *v/r:* **~ o.s.** spergiurare

per·ju·ry ['pɜːdʒərɪ] falso giuramento *m*

perk [pɜːk] *n of job* vantaggio *m*

♦ **perk up 1** *v/t* F tirare su di morale **2** *v/i* F animarsi

perk·y ['pɜːkɪ] *adj* F (*cheerful*) allegro

perm [pɜːm] **1** *n* permanente *f* **2** *v/t* fare la permanente a

per·ma·nent ['pɜːmənənt] *adj* permanente; *job, address* fisso

per·ma·nent·ly ['pɜːmənəntlɪ] *adv* permanentemente

per·me·a·ble ['pɜːmɪəbl] *adj* permeabile

per·me·ate ['pɜːmɪeɪt] *v/t* permeare

per·mis·si·ble [pə'mɪsəbl] *adj* permesso, ammissibile

per·mis·sion [pə'mɪʃn] permesso *m*

per·mis·sive [pə'mɪsɪv] *adj* permissivo

per·mis·sive so·ci·e·ty società *f inv* permissiva

per·mit ['pɜːmɪt] **1** *n* permesso *m* **2** *v/t* [pə'mɪt] (*pret & pp* **-ted**) permettere; ~ *s.o. to do sth* permettere a qu di fare qc

per·pen·dic·u·lar [pɜːpən'dɪkjulə(r)] *adj* perpendicolare

per·pet·u·al *adj* perenne

per·pet·u·al·ly [pə'petjuəlɪ] *adv* perennemente

per·pet·u·ate [pə'petjueɪt] *v/t* perpetuare

per·plex [pə'pleks] *v/t* lasciare perplesso

per·plexed [pə'plekst] *adj* perplesso

per·plex·i·ty [pə'pleksɪtɪ] perplessità *f inv*

per·se·cute ['pɜːsɪkjuːt] *v/t* perseguitare

per·se·cu·tion [pɜːsɪ'kjuːʃn] persecuzione *f*

per·se·cu·tor [pɜːsɪ'kjuːtə(r)] persecutore *m*, -trice *f*

per·se·ver·ance [pɜːsɪ'vɪərəns] perseveranza *f*

per·se·vere [pɜːsɪ'vɪə(r)] *v/i* perseverare

per·sist [pə'sɪst] *v/i* persistere; ~ *in* persistere in

per·sis·tence [pə'sɪstəns] (*perseverance*) perseveranza *f*; (*continuation*) persistenza *m*

per·sis·tent [pə'sɪstənt] *adj person, questions* insistente; *rain, unemployment etc* continuo

per·sis·tent·ly [pə'sɪstəntlɪ] *adv* (*continually*) continuamente

per·son ['pɜːsn] persona *f*; *in* ~ di persona

per·son·al ['pɜːsənl] *adj* personale; *don't make* ~ *remarks* non fare commenti personali

per·son·al as'sist·ant assistente *m/f* personale; **'per·son·al col·umn** annunci *mpl* personali; **per·son·al com'put·er** personal computer *m inv*; **per·son·al 'hy·giene** igiene *f* personale

per·son·al·i·ty [pɜːsə'nælətɪ] personalità *f inv*

per·son·al·ly ['pɜːsənəlɪ] *adv* personalmente; *don't take it* ~ non offenderti

per·son·al 'or·gan·iz·er agenda *f* elettronica; **per·son·al 'pro·noun** pronome *m* personale; **per·son·al 'ster·e·o** Walkman® *m inv*

per·son·i·fy [pə'sɒnɪfaɪ] *v/t* (*pret & pp* **-ied**) *of person* personificare

per·son·nel [pɜːsə'nel] *employees* personale *m*; *department* ufficio *m* del personale

per·son·nel man·a·ger direttore *m*, -trice *f* del personale

per·spec·tive [pə'spektɪv] PAINT prospettiva *f*; *get sth into* ~ vedere qc nella giusta prospettiva

per·spi·ra·tion [pɜːspɪ'reɪʃn] traspirazione *f*

per·spire [pə'spaɪə(r)] *v/i* sudare

per·suade [pə'sweɪd] *v/t* persuadere, convincere; ~ *s.o. to do sth* persuadere *o* convincere qu a fare qc

per·sua·sion [pə'sweɪʒn] persuasione *f*

per·sua·sive [pə'sweɪsɪv] *adj* persuasivo

per·ti·nent ['pɜːtɪnənt] *adj fml* pertinente

per·turb [pəˈtɜːb] v/t inquietare

per·turb·ing [pəˈtɜːbɪŋ] adj inquietante

pe·ruse [pəˈruːz] v/t fml leggere

per·va·sive [pəˈveɪsɪv] adj influence, ideas diffuso

per·verse [pəˈvɜːs] adj ostinato, irragionevole; sexually pervertito; **be ~ (awkward)** essere un bastian contrario; **take a ~ delight in doing sth** provare un piacere perverso a fare qc

per·ver·sion [pəˈvɜːʃn] sexual perversione f

per·vert [ˈpɜːvɜːt] n sexual pervertito m, -a f

pes·si·mis·m [ˈpesɪmɪzm] pessimismo m

pes·si·mist [ˈpesɪmɪst] pessimista m/f

pes·si·mist·ic [pesɪˈmɪstɪk] adj attitude, view pessimistico; person pessimista

pest [pest] animale / insetto m nocivo; F person peste f

pes·ter [ˈpestə(r)] v/t assillare; **~ s.o. to do sth** assillare qu perché faccia qc

pes·ti·cide [ˈpestɪsaɪd] pesticida m

pet [pet] **1** n animal animale m domestico; (favourite) favorito m, -a f **2** adj preferito **3** v/t (pret & pp **-ted**) animal accarezzare **4** v/i (pret & pp **-ted**) of couple pomiciare F

pet·al [ˈpetl] petalo m

♦ pe·ter out [ˈpiːtə(r)] v/i of rebellion, rain cessare; of path finire

pe·tite [pəˈtiːt] adj minuta

pe·ti·tion [pəˈtɪʃn] n petizione f

pet name nomignolo m

pet·ri·fied [ˈpetrɪfaɪd] adj terrorizzato

pet·ri·fy [ˈpetrɪfaɪ] v/t (pret & pp **-ied**) terrorizzare

pet·ro·chem·i·cal [petrəʊˈkemɪkl] adj petrolchimico

pet·rol [ˈpetrl] benzina f

pe·tro·le·um [pɪˈtrəʊlɪəm] petrolio m

pet·rol gauge spia f della benzina; '**pet·rol pump** pompa f della benzi-na; '**pet·rol sta·tion** stazione f di servizio

pet·ting [ˈpetɪŋ] petting m inv

pet·ty [ˈpetɪ] adj person, behaviour meschino; details, problem insignificante

pet·ty 'cash piccola cassa f

pet·u·lant [ˈpetjʊlənt] adj petulante

pew [pjuː] banco m (di chiesa)

pew·ter [ˈpjuːtə(r)] peltro m

phar·ma·ceu·ti·cal [fɑːməˈsjuːtɪkl] adj farmaceutico

phar·ma·ceu·ti·cals [fɑːməˈsjuːtɪklz] npl farmaceutici mpl

phar·ma·cist [ˈfɑːməsɪst] farmacista m/f

phar·ma·cy [ˈfɑːməsɪ] farmacia f

phase [feɪz] fase f

♦ phase in v/t introdurre gradualmente

♦ phase out v/t eliminare gradualmente

PhD [piːeɪtʃˈdiː] abbr (= **Doctor of Philosophy**) dottorato m di ricerca

phe·nom·e·nal [fɪˈnɒmɪnl] adj fenomenale

phe·nom·e·nal·ly [fɪˈnɒmɪnlɪ] adv straordinariamente

phe·nom·e·non [fɪˈnɒmɪnɒn] fenomeno m

phil·an·throp·ic [fɪlənˈθrɒpɪk] adj filantropico

phi·lan·thro·pist [fɪˈlænθrəpɪst] filantropo m, -a f

phi·lan·thro·py [fɪˈlænθrəpɪ] filantropia f

Phil·ip·pines [ˈfɪlɪpiːnz] npl: **the ~** le Filippine fpl

phil·is·tine [ˈfɪlɪstaɪn] n ignorante m/f

phi·los·o·pher [fɪˈlɒsəfə(r)] filosofo m, -a f

phil·o·soph·i·cal [fɪləˈsɒfɪkl] adj filosofico

phi·los·o·phy [fɪˈlɒsəfɪ] filosofia f

pho·bi·a [ˈfəʊbɪə] fobia f

phone [fəʊn] **1** n telefono m; **be on the ~** have one avere il telefono; be talking essere al telefono **2** v/t telefonare a **3** v/i telefonare

'phone book guida f telefonica,

P

elenco telefonico *m*; '**phone booth** cabina *f* telefonica; '**phone box** cabina *f* telefonica; '**phone call** telefonata *f*; '**phone card** scheda *f* telefonica; '**phone num·ber** numero *m* di telefono

pho·net·ics [fə'netɪks] fonetica *f*

pho·n(e)y ['fəʊnɪ] *adj* F falso

pho·to ['fəʊtəʊ] *n* foto *f*

'pho·to al·bum album *m* fotografico; '**pho·to·cop·i·er** fotocopiatrice *f*; '**pho·to·cop·y** 1 *n* fotocopia *f* 2 *v/t* (*pret & pp -ied*) fotocopiare

pho·to·gen·ic [fəʊtəʊ'dʒenɪk] *adj* fotogenico

pho·to·graph ['fəʊtəɡrɑːf] 1 *n* fotografia *f* 2 *v/t* fotografare

pho·tog·ra·pher [fə'tɒɡrəfə(r)] fotografo *m*, -a *f*

pho·tog·ra·phy [fə'tɒɡrəfɪ] fotografia *f*

phrase [freɪz] 1 *n* frase *f* 2 *v/t* esprimere

'phrase·book vocabolarietto *m* di frasi utili

phys·i·cal ['fɪzɪkl] 1 *adj* fisico 2 *n* MED visita *f* medica

phys·i·cal 'hand·i·cap *adj* handicap *m inv* fisico

phys·i·cal·ly ['fɪzɪklɪ] *adv* fisicamente

phys·i·cal·ly 'hand·i·cap·ped *adj*: **be ~** essere portatore *m*, -trice *f* di handicap fisico

phy·si·cian [fɪ'zɪʃn] medico *m*

phys·i·cist ['fɪzɪsɪst] fisico *m*, -a *f*

phys·ics ['fɪzɪks] fisica *f*

phys·i·o·ther·a·pist [fɪzɪəʊ'θerəpɪst] fisioterapeuta *m/f*

phys·i·o·ther·a·py [fɪzɪəʊ'θerəpɪ] fisioterapia *f*

phy·sique [fɪ'ziːk] fisico *m*

pi·a·nist ['pɪənɪst] pianista *m/f*

pi·an·o [pɪ'ænəʊ] piano *m*

pick [pɪk] 1 *n*: **take your ~** scegli quello che vuoi 2 *v/t* (*choose*) scegliere; *flowers, fruit* raccogliere; **~ one's nose** mettersi le dita nel naso 3 *v/i*: **~ and choose** fare i difficili

♦**pick at** *v/t*: **pick at one's food** mangiucchiare poco

♦**pick on** *v/t treat unfairly* prendersela con; (*select*) scegliere

♦**pick out** *v/t* (*identify*) riconoscere

♦**pick up 1** *v/t* prendere; *phone* sollevare; *baby* prendere in braccio; *from ground* raccogliere; (*collect*) andare / venire a prendere; *information* raccogliere; *in car* far salire; *man, woman* rimorchiare F; *language, skill* imparare; *habit, illness* prendere; (*buy*) trovare; *criminal* arrestare; **pick up the tab** F pagare (il conto) 2 *v/i* (*improve*) migliorare

pick·et ['pɪkɪt] 1 *n of strikers* picchetto *m* 2 *v/t* picchettare

'pick·et line cordone *m* degli scioperanti

pick·le ['pɪkl] *v/t* conservare sott'aceto

pick·les ['pɪklz] *npl* sottaceti *mpl*

'pick·pock·et borseggiatore *m*, -trice *f*

pick·y ['pɪkɪ] *adj* F difficile (da accontentare)

pic·nic ['pɪknɪk] 1 *n* picnic *m inv* 2 *v/i* (*pret & pp -ked*) fare un picnic

pic·ture ['pɪktʃə(r)] 1 *n photo* foto *f*; *painting* quadro *m*; *illustration* figura *f*; *film* film *m inv*; **put / keep s.o. in the ~** mettere / tenere al corrente qu 2 *v/t* immaginare

'pic·ture book libro *m* illustrato

pic·ture 'post·card cartolina *f* illustrata

pic·tures ['pɪktʃəz] *npl* cinema *m*

pic·tur·esque [pɪktʃə'resk] *adj* pittoresco

pie [paɪ] *sweet* torta *f*; *savoury* pasticcio *m*

piece [piːs] pezzo *m*; **a ~ of pie / bread** una fetta di torta / pane; **a ~ of advice** un consiglio; **go to ~s** crollare; **take to ~s** smontare

♦**piece together** *v/t broken plate* rimettere insieme; *facts, evidence* ricostruire

piece·meal ['piːsmiːl] *adv* poco alla volta

piece·work ['piːswɜːk] *n* lavoro *m* a cottimo

pier [pɪə(r)] *at seaside* pontile *m*

pierce [pɪəs] *v/t* (*penetrate*) trapassare; *ears* farsi i buchi in

pierc·ing ['pɪəsɪŋ] *noise* lacerante; *eyes* penetranti; *wind* pungente

pig [pɪg] *also fig* maiale *m*

pi·geon ['pɪdʒɪn] piccione *m*

'pi·geon·hole 1 *n* casella *f* **2** *v/t person* etichettare; *proposal* archiviare

pig·gy·bank ['pɪgɪbæŋk] salvadanaio *m*

pig·head·ed [pɪg'hedɪd] *adj* testardo

pig·skin pelle *f* di cinghiale; **'pig·sty** *also fig* porcile *m*; **'pig·tail** plaited treccina *f*

pile [paɪl] mucchio *m*; F **a ~ of work** un sacco di lavoro F

◆ **pile up 1** *v/i of work, bills* accumularsi **2** *v/t* ammucchiare

piles [paɪlz] *nsg* MED emorroidi *fpl*

pile-up ['paɪlʌp] MOT tamponamento *m* a catena

pil·fer·ing ['pɪlfərɪŋ] piccoli furti *mpl*

pil·grim ['pɪlgrɪm] pellegrino *m*, -a *f*

pil·grim·age ['pɪlgrɪmɪdʒ] pellegrinaggio *m*

pill [pɪl] pastiglia *f*; **the ~** la pillola; **be on the ~** prendere la pillola

pil·lar ['pɪlə(r)] colonna *f*

'pil·lar box buca *f* delle lettere (a colonnina)

pil·lion ['pɪljən] *of motor bike* sellino *m* posteriore

pil·low ['pɪləʊ] *n* guanciale *m*

'pil·low·case, 'pil·low·slip federa *f*

pi·lot ['paɪlət] **1** *n of aeroplane* pilota *m/f* **2** *v/t aeroplane* pilotare

'pi·lot plant stabilimento *m* pilota

'pi·lot scheme progetto *m* pilota

pimp [pɪmp] *n* ruffiano *m*

pim·ple ['pɪmpl] brufolo *m*

pin [pɪn] **1** *n for sewing* spillo *m*; *in bowling* birillo *m*; (*badge*) spilla *f*; ELEC spinotto *m* **2** *v/t* (*pret & pp -ned*) (*hold down*) immobilizzare; (*attach*) attaccare; *on lapel* appuntare

◆ **pin down** *v/t*: **pin s.o. down to a date** far fissare una data a qu

◆ **pin up** *v/t notice* appuntare

PIN [pɪn] *abbr* (= **personal identification number**) numero *m* di codice segreto

pin·cers ['pɪnsəz] *npl tool* tenaglie *fpl*; *of crab* chele *fpl*

pinch [pɪntʃ] **1** *n* pizzico *m*; **at a ~** al massimo **2** *v/t* pizzicare **3** *v/i of shoes* stringere

pine¹ [paɪn] *n* pino *m*; **~ furniture** mobili *mpl* di pino

pine² [paɪn] *v/i*: **~ for** soffrire per la mancanza di

pine·ap·ple ['paɪnæpl] ananas *m inv*

ping [pɪŋ] **1** *n* suono *m* metallico **2** *v/i* fare un suono metallico

ping-pong ['pɪŋpɒŋ] ping-pong *m inv*

pink [pɪŋk] *adj* rosa *inv*

pin·na·cle ['pɪnəkl] *fig* apice *m*

'pin·point *v/t* indicare con esattezza

pins and 'nee·dles *npl* formicolio *m*

'pin·stripe *adj* gessato

pint [paɪnt] pinta *f*

'pin-up (girl) pin-up *f inv*

pi·o·neer [paɪə'nɪə(r)] **1** *n fig* pioniere *m*, -a *f* **2** *v/t* essere il/la pioniere di

pi·o·neer·ing [paɪə'nɪərɪŋ] *adj work* pionieristico

pi·ous ['paɪəs] *adj* pio

pip [pɪp] *n of fruit* seme *m*

pipe [paɪp] **1** *n for smoking* pipa *f*; *for water, gas, sewage* tubo *m* **2** *v/t* trasportare con condutture

◆ **pipe down** *v/i* F far silenzio

piped mu·sic [paɪpt'mjuːzɪk] musica *f* di sottofondo

pipe·line conduttura *f*; **in the ~** *fig* in arrivo

pip·ing hot [paɪpɪŋ'hɒt] *adj* caldissimo

pi·rate ['paɪərət] *v/t software* piratare

Pis·ces ['paɪsiːz] ASTR Pesci *m/f inv*

piss [pɪs] **1** *v/i* P (*urinate*) pisciare P **2** *n* (*urine*) piscio *m* P; **take the ~out of s.o.** P prendere qu per il culo P

◆ **piss off** *v/i* P sparire; **piss off!** levati dalle palle! P

pissed [pɪst] *adj* P (*drunk*) sbronzo F; *Am* (*annoyed*) seccato

pis·tol ['pɪstl] pistola *f*

P

pis·ton ['pɪstən] pistone *m*

pit [pɪt] *n* (*hole*) buca *f*; (*coal mine*) miniera *f*

pitch¹ [pɪtʃ] *n* MUS intonazione *f*

pitch² [pɪtʃ] *v/t tent* piantare; *ball* lanciare

'pitch black *adj* buio pesto

pitch·er ['pɪtʃə(r)] *container* brocca *f*

pit·e·ous ['pɪtɪəs] *adj* pietoso

pit·fall ['pɪtfɔːl] tranello *m*

pith [pɪθ] *of citrus fruit* parte *f* bianca della scorza

pit·i·ful ['pɪtɪful] *adj sight* pietoso; *excuse, attempt* penoso

pit·i·less ['pɪtɪləs] *adj* spietato

pits [pɪts] *npl in motor racing* box *m inv*

'pit stop *in motor racing* sosta *f* ai box

pit·tance ['pɪtns] miseria *f*

pit·y ['pɪtɪ] **1** *n* pietà *f inv*; *it's a ~ that* è un peccato che; *what a ~!* che peccato!; *take ~ on* aver pietà di **2** *v/t* (*pret & pp* **-ied**) *person* avere pietà di

piv·ot ['pɪvət] *v/i* ruotare

piz·za ['piːtsə] pizza *f*

plac·ard ['plækɑːd] cartello *m*

place [pleɪs] **1** *n* posto *m*; *flat, house* casa *f*; *I've lost my ~ in book* ho perso il segno; *at my / his ~* a casa mia / sua; *in ~ of* invece di; *feel out of ~* sentirsi fuori posto; *take ~* aver luogo; *in the first ~* (*firstly*) in primo luogo **2** *v/t* (*put*) piazzare; *I can't quite ~ you* non mi ricordo dove ci siamo conosciuti; *~ an order* fare un'ordinazione

'place mat tovaglietta *f* all'americana

plac·id ['plæsɪd] *adj* placido

pla·gia·rism ['pleɪdʒərɪzm] plagio *m*

pla·gia·rize ['pleɪdʒəraɪz] *v/t* plagiare

plague [pleɪg] **1** *n* peste *f* **2** *v/t* (*bother*) tormentare

plain¹ [pleɪn] *n* pianura *f*

plain² [pleɪn] **1** *adj* (*clear, obvious*) chiaro; *not fancy* semplice; *not pretty* scialbo; *not patterned* in tinta unita; (*blunt*) franco; *~ chocolate*

cioccolato *m* fondente **2** *adv* semplicemente; *it's ~ crazy* è semplicemente matto

'plain-clothes: in ~ in borghese

plain·ly ['pleɪnlɪ] *adv* (*clearly*) chiaramente; (*bluntly*) francamente; (*simply*) semplicemente

plain-'spo·ken *adj* franco

plain·tiff ['pleɪntɪf] LAW attore *m*, -trice *f*

plain·tive ['pleɪntɪv] *adj* lamentoso

plait [plæt] **1** *n in hair* treccia *f* **2** *v/t hair* intrecciare

plan [plæn] **1** *n* (*project, intention*) piano *m*; (*drawing*) progetto *m* **2** *v/t* (*pret & pp* **-ned**) (*prepare*) organizzare; (*design*) progettare; *~ to do, ~ on doing* avere in programma di **3** *v/i* (*pret & pp* **-ned**) pianificare

plane¹ [pleɪn] *n* (*aeroplane*) aereo *m*

plane² [pleɪn] *tool* pialla *f*

plan·et ['plænɪt] pianeta *m*

plank [plæŋk] *of wood* asse *f*; *fig: of policy* punto *m*

plan·ning ['plænɪŋ] pianificazione *f*; *at the ~ stage* allo stadio di progettazione

plant¹ [plɑːnt] **1** *n* pianta *f* **2** *v/t* piantare

plant² [plɑːnt] *n* (*factory*) stabilimento *m*; (*equipment*) impianto *m*

plan·ta·tion [plæn'teɪʃn] piantagione *f*

plaque [plæk] *on wall, teeth* placca *f*

plas·ter ['plɑːstə(r)] **1** *n on wall, ceiling* intonaco *m* **2** *v/t wall, ceiling* intonacare; *be ~ed with* essere ricoperto di

plas·ter cast ingessatura *f*

plas·tic ['plæstɪk] **1** *n* plastica *f*; F (*money*) carte *fpl* di credito **2** *adj made of ~* di plastica

plas·tic 'bag sacchetto *m* di plastica;

'plas·tic mon·ey carte *fpl* di credito; **plas·tic 'sur·geon** chirurgo *m* plastico; **plas·tic 'sur·ge·ry** chirurgia *f* plastica

plate [pleɪt] *n for food* piatto *m*; *sheet of metal* lastra *f*

pla·teau ['plætəʊ] altopiano *m*

plat·form ['plætfɔːm] (*stage*) palco

m; of railway station binario *m; fig: political* piattaforma *f*

plat·i·num ['plætɪnəm] **1** *n* platino *m*
2 *adj* di platino

pla·ton·ic [pləˈtɒnɪk] *adj relationship* platonico

pla·toon [pləˈtuːn] *of soldiers* plotone *m*

plat·ter ['plætə(r)] *for meat, fish* vassoio *m*

plau·si·ble ['plɔːzəbl] *adj* plausibile

play [pleɪ] **1** *n in theatre, on TV* commedia *f; of children,* TECH, SP gioco *m*
2 *v/i of children,* SP giocare; *of musician* suonare **3** *v/t* MUS suonare; *game* giocare a; *opponent* giocare contro; (*perform: Macbeth etc*) rappresentare; *particular role* interpretare; *~ a joke on* fare uno scherzo a

♦ **play around** *v/i* F (*be unfaithful*):
his wife's been playing around sua moglie lo ha tradito; *her husband was playing around with his secretary* suo marito aveva una relazione con la segretaria

♦ **play down** *v/t* minimizzare

♦ **play up** *v/i of machine* dare noie; *of child* fare i capricci; *of tooth, bad back etc* fare male

play·act ['pleɪækt] *v/i (pretend)* fare la commedia

play·back ['pleɪbæk] playback *m inv*

play·boy ['pleɪbɔɪ] playboy *m inv*

play·er ['pleɪə(r)] SP giocatore *m*, -trice *f; musician* musicista *m/f; actor* attore *m*, -trice *f*

play·ful ['pleɪfʊl] *adj punch, mood* scherzoso; *puppy* giocherellone

play·ground ['pleɪɡraʊnd] *in school* cortile *m* per la ricreazione; *in park* parco *m* giochi

play·group asilo *m*

play·ing card ['pleɪɪŋkɑːd] carta *f* da gioco

play·ing field ['pleɪɪŋfiːld] campo *m* sportivo

play·mate ['pleɪmeɪt] compagno *m*, -a *f* di gioco

play·wright ['pleɪraɪt] commediografo *m*, -a *f*

plc [piːelˈsiː] *abbr* (= *public limited company*) società *f inv* a responsabilità limitata quotata in borsa

plea [pliː] **1** *n* appello *m*

plead [pliːd] *v/i:* ~ *for* supplicare; ~ *guilty / not guilty* dichiararsi colpevole / innocente; ~ *with* supplicare

pleas·ant ['pleznt] *adj* piacevole

please [pliːz] **1** *adv* per favore; *more tea? – yes,* ~ ancora tè? – sì, grazie; ~ *do* fai pure, prego **2** *v/t* far piacere a; ~ *yourself* fai come ti pare

pleased [pliːzd] *adj* contento; ~ *to meet you* piacere

pleas·ing ['pliːzɪŋ] *adj* piacevole

pleas·ure ['pleʒə(r)] (*happiness, satisfaction*) contentezza *f;* (*as opposed to work*) piacere *m;* (*delight*) gioia *f; it's a* ~ (*you're welcome*) è un piacere; *with* ~ con vero piacere

pleat [pliːt] *n in skirt* piega *f*

pleat·ed skirt ['pliːtɪd] gonna *f* a pieghe

pledge [pledʒ] **1** *n (promise)* promessa *f* **2** *v/t (promise)* promettere

plen·ti·ful ['plentɪfʊl] *adj* abbondante

plen·ty ['plentɪ] (*abundance*) abbondanza *f;* ~ *of* molto; *that's* ~ basta così; *there's* ~ *for everyone* ce n'è per tutti

pli·a·ble *adj* flessibile

pli·ers *npl* pinze *fpl; a pair of* ~ un paio di pinze

plight [plaɪt] situazione *f* critica

plod [plɒd] *v/i (pret & pp -ded) walk* trascinarsi

♦ **plod on** *v/i with a job* sgobbare

plod·der ['plɒdə(r)] *at work, school* sgobbone *m*, -a *f*

plot[^1] [plɒt] *n land* appezzamento *m*

plot[^2] [plɒt] **1** *n (conspiracy)* complotto *m; of novel* trama *f* **2** *v/t & v/i (pret & pp -ted)* complottare

plot·ter ['plɒtə(r)] cospiratore *m*, -trice *f;* COMPUT plotter *m inv*

plough, plow *Am* [plaʊ] **1** *n* aratro *m*
2 *v/t & v/i* arare

♦ **plough back** *v/t profits* reinvestire

pluck [plʌk] *v/t eyebrows* pinzare; *chicken* spennare

P

◆**pluck up** v/t: **pluck up courage** trovare il coraggio

plug [plʌg] **1** n for sink, bath tappo m; electrical spina f; (spark ~) candela f; for new book etc pubblicità f inv **2** v/t (pret & pp **-ged**) hole tappare; new book etc fare pubblicità a

◆**plug away** v/i F sgobbare

◆**plug in** v/t attaccare (alla presa)

plum [plʌm] **1** n susina f **2** adj: **- job** F un lavoro favoloso

plum·age ['plu:mɪdʒ] piumaggio m

plumb [plʌm] adj a piombo

◆**plumb in** v/t washing machine collegare all'impianto idraulico

plumb·er ['plʌmə(r)] idraulico m

plumb·ing ['plʌmɪŋ] pipes impianto m idraulico

plume [plu:m] n piuma f

plum·met ['plʌmɪt] v/i of aeroplane precipitare; of share prices crollare

plump [plʌmp] adj person, chicken in carne; hands, feet, face paffuto

◆**plump for** v/t scegliere

plunge [plʌndʒ] **1** n caduta f; in prices crollo m; **take the ~** fare il gran passo **2** v/i precipitare; of prices crollare **3** v/t knife conficcare; tomatoes immergere; **the city was ~d into darkness** la città fu immersa nel buio; **the news ~d him into despair** la notizia lo gettò nella disperazione

plung·ing ['plʌndʒɪŋ] adj neckline profondo

plu·per·fect ['plu:pɜ:fɪkt] n GRAM piuccheperfetto m

plu·ral ['plʊərəl] **1** n plurale m **2** adj plurale

plus [plʌs] **1** prep più **2** adj: **£500 ~** oltre 500 sterline **3** n symbol più m inv; (advantage) vantaggio m **4** conj (moreover, in addition) per di più

plush [plʌʃ] adj di lusso

'**plus sign** segno m più

ply·wood ['plaɪwʊd] compensato m

PM [pi:'em] abbr (= **Prime Minister**) primo ministro m

p.m. [pi:'em] abbr (= **post meridiem**): **at 2 ~** alle 2 del pomeriggio; **at 10.30 ~** alle 10.30 di sera

pneu·mat·ic [nju:'mætɪk] adj pneumatico

pneu·mat·ic 'drill martello m pneumatico

pneu·mo·ni·a [nju:'məʊnɪə] polmonite f

poach¹ [pəʊtʃ] v/t cook bollire; egg fare in camicia

poach² [pəʊtʃ] **1** v/i for game cacciare di frodo; for fish pescare di frodo **2** v/t cacciare / pescare di frodo

poached egg [pəʊtʃt'eg] uovo m in camicia

poach·er ['pəʊtʃə(r)] of salmon, game cacciatore / pescatore m di frodo

P.O. Box [pi:'əʊbɒks] casella f postale

pock·et ['pɒkɪt] **1** n tasca f; **line one's ~s** arricchirsi; **be out of ~** rimetterci **2** adj (miniature) in miniatura **3** v/t intascare

pock·et 'cal·cu·la·tor calcolatrice f tascabile

'**pocket book** Am (wallet) portafoglio m; (handbag) borsetta f

po·di·um ['pəʊdɪəm] podio m

po·em ['pəʊɪm] poesia f

po·et ['pəʊɪt] poeta m, -essa f

po·et·ic [pəʊ'etɪk] adj person, description poetico

po·et·ic 'jus·tice giustizia f divina

po·et·ry ['pəʊɪtrɪ] poesia f

poign·ant ['pɔɪnjənt] adj commovente

point [pɔɪnt] **1** n of pencil, knife punta f; in competition, exam punto m; (purpose) senso m; (moment) punto m; in argument, discussion punto m; in decimals virgola f; **that's beside the ~** non c'entra; **be on the ~ of** stare giusto per; **get to the ~** venire al dunque; **that's a ~** questo, in effetti, è vero; **the ~ is ...** il fatto è che ...; **you've got a ~ there** su questo, hai ragione; **I take your ~** su questo, ti do ragione; **there's no ~ in waiting / trying** non ha senso aspettare / tentare **2** v/i indicare **3** v/t gun puntare (**at** contro)

◆**point at** v/t with finger indicare col dito

♦ **point out** v/t sights, advantages indicare

♦ **point to** v/t with finger additare; (fig: indicate) far presupporre

'**point-blank 1** adj refusal, denial categorico; **at ~ range** a bruciapelo **2** adv refuse, deny categoricamente

point·ed ['pɔɪntɪd] adj remark, question significativo

point·er ['pɔɪntə(r)] for teacher bacchetta f; (hint) consiglio m; (sign, indication) indizio m

point·less ['pɔɪntləs] adj inutile; **it's ~ trying** è inutile tentare

'**point of sale** punto m vendita

'**point of view** punto m di vista

poise [pɔɪz] padronanza f di sé

poised [pɔɪzd] adj person posato

poi·son ['pɔɪzn] **1** n veleno m **2** v/t avvelenare

poi·son·ous ['pɔɪznəs] adj velenoso

poke [pəʊk] **1** n colpetto m **2** v/t (prod) dare un colpetto a; (stick) ficcare; **~ fun at** prendere in giro; **~ one's nose into** ficcare il naso in

♦ **poke around** v/i F curiosare

pok·er ['pəʊkə(r)] card game poker m inv

pok·y ['pəʊkɪ] adj F (cramped) angusto

Po·land ['pəʊlənd] Polonia f

po·lar ['pəʊlə(r)] adj polare

po·lar bear orso m polare

po·lar·ize ['pəʊləraɪz] v/t polarizzare

Pole [pəʊl] polacco m, -a f

pole¹ [pəʊl] of wood, metal paletto m

pole² [pəʊl] of earth polo m

'**pole star** stella f polare; '**pole-vault** salto m con l'asta; '**pole-vault·er** saltatore m, -trice f con l'asta

po·lice [pə'liːs] n polizia f

po·lice car auto f della polizia; **po'lice·man** poliziotto m; **po'lice state** stato m di polizia; **po'lice sta·tion** commissariato m di polizia; **po'lice·wo·man** donna f poliziotto

pol·i·cy¹ ['pɒlɪsɪ] politica f

pol·i·cy² ['pɒlɪsɪ] (insurance ~) polizza f

po·li·o ['pəʊlɪəʊ] polio f

Pol·ish ['pəʊlɪʃ] **1** adj polacco **2** n polacco m

pol·ish ['pɒlɪʃ] **1** n product lucido m; (nail ~) smalto m **2** v/t lucidare; speech rifinire

♦ **polish off** v/t food spazzolare F

♦ **polish up** v/t skill perfezionare

pol·ished ['pɒlɪʃt] adj performance impeccabile

po·lite [pə'laɪt] adj cortese

po·lite·ly [pə'laɪtlɪ] adv cortesemente

po·lite·ness [pə'laɪtnɪs] cortesia f

po·lit·i·cal [pə'lɪtɪkl] adj politico

po·lit·i·cal·ly cor·rect [pə'lɪtɪklɪ kə'rekt] adj politicamente corretto

pol·i·ti·cian [pɒlɪ'tɪʃn] uomo m politico, donna f politica

pol·i·tics ['pɒlətɪks] politica f; **what are his ~?** di che tendenze politiche è?

poll [pəʊl] **1** n (survey) sondaggio m; **the ~s** (election) le elezioni fpl; **go to the ~s** (vote) andare alle urne **2** v/t people fare un sondaggio tra; votes guadagnare

pol·len ['pɒlən] polline m

'**pol·len count** concentrazione f di polline

'**poll·ing booth** ['pəʊlɪŋ] cabina f elettorale; '**poll·ing day** giorno m delle elezioni; '**poll·ing sta·tion** seggio m elettorale

poll·ster ['pɒlstə(r)] esperto m, -a f di sondaggi

pol·lu·tant [pə'luːtənt] sostanza f inquinante

pol·lute [pə'luːt] v/t inquinare

pol·lu·tion [pə'luːʃn] inquinamento m

po·lo ['pəʊləʊ] SP polo m

'**po·lo neck** adj sweater a dolcevita

'**po·lo shirt** polo f inv

pol·y·es·ter [pɒlɪ'estə(r)] poliestere m

pol·y·sty·rene [pɒlɪ'staɪriːn] polistirolo m

pol·y·thene ['pɒlɪθiːn] polietilene m

pol·y·thene 'bag sacchetto m di plastica

P

pol·y·un·sat·u·rat·ed [pɒliʌn'sætjə- reitid] *adj* polinsaturo

pom·pous ['pɒmpəs] *adj* pomposo

pond [pɒnd] stagno *m*

pon·der ['pɒndə(r)] *v/i* riflettere

pon·tiff ['pɒntɪf] pontefice *m*

po·ny ['pəʊnɪ] pony *m inv*

'po·ny·tail coda *f* (di cavallo)

poo·dle ['puːdl] barboncino *m*

pool¹ [puːl] (*swimming ~*) piscina *f*; *of water, blood* pozza *f*

pool² [puːl] *game* biliardo *m*

pool³ [puːl] **1** *n common fund* cassa *f* comune **2** *v/t resources* mettere insieme

'pool hall sala *f* da biliardo

pools [puːlz] *npl* totocalcio *m*; *do the ~* giocare al totocalcio

'pool table tavolo *m* da biliardo

pooped [puːpt] *adj* F stanco morto

poor [pʊə(r)] **1** *adj not wealthy, unfortunate* povero; *not good* misero; *be in ~ health* essere in cattiva salute; *~ old Tony!* povero Tony! **2** *n*: *the ~* i poveri

poor·ly ['pʊəlɪ] **1** *adv* male **2** *adj* (*unwell*) indisposto

pop¹ [pɒp] **1** *n noise* schiocco *m* **2** *v/i* (*pret & pp -ped*) *of balloon etc* scoppiare **3** *v/t* (*pret & pp -ped*) *cork* stappare; *balloon* far scoppiare

pop² [pɒp] **1** *n* MUS pop *m inv* **2** *adj* pop *inv*

pop³ [pɒp] *v/t* (*pret & pp -ped*) F (*put*) ficcare F; *~ one's head around the door* sbucare con la testa dalla porta

♦ **pop in** *v/i* F (*make a brief visit*) entrare un attimo

♦ **pop out** *v/i* F (*go out for a short time*) fare un salto fuori

♦ **pop up** *v/i* F (*appear suddenly*) saltare fuori

'pop con·cert concerto *m* pop

pop·corn ['pɒpkɔːn] popcorn *m inv*

pope [pəʊp] papa *m*

'pop group gruppo *m* pop

pop·py ['pɒpɪ] papavero *m*

'pop song canzone *f* pop

pop·u·lar ['pɒpjʊlə(r)] *adj* popolare; *belief, support* diffuso

pop·u·lar·i·ty [pɒpjʊ'lærətɪ] popolarità *f inv*

pop·u·late ['pɒpjʊleɪt] *v/t* popolare

pop·u·la·tion [pɒpjʊ'leɪʃn] popolazione *f*

porce·lain ['pɔːsəlɪn] **1** *n* porcellana *f* **2** *adj* di porcellana

porch [pɔːtʃ] porticato *m*; *Am* veranda *f*

por·cu·pine ['pɔːkjʊpaɪn] porcospino *m*

pore [pɔː(r)] *of skin* poro *m*

♦ **pore over** *v/t* studiare attentamente

pork [pɔːk] maiale *m*

porn [pɔːn] *n* F porno *m* F

porn(o) [pɔːn, 'pɔːnəʊ] *adj* F porno *inv* F

por·no·graph·ic [pɔːnə'græfɪk] *adj* pornografico

porn·og·ra·phy [pɔː'nɒgrəfɪ] pornografia *f*

po·rous ['pɔːrəs] *adj* poroso

port¹ [pɔːt] *n* (*harbour, drink*) porto *m*

port² [pɔːt] *adj* (*left-hand*) babordo; *on the ~ side* a babordo

por·ta·ble ['pɔːtəbl] **1** *adj* portatile **2** *n* portatile *m*

por·ter ['pɔːtə(r)] portiere *m*

port·hole ['pɔːthəʊl] NAUT oblò *m inv*

por·tion ['pɔːʃn] *n* parte *f*; *of food* porzione *f*

por·trait ['pɔːtreɪt] **1** *n* ritratto *m* **2** *adv print* verticale

por·tray [pɔː'treɪ] *v/t of artist, photographer* ritrarre; *of actor* interpretare; *of author* descrivere

por·tray·al [pɔː'treɪəl] *by actor* rappresentazione *f*; *by author* descrizione *f*

Por·tu·gal ['pɔːtjʊgl] Portogallo *m*

Por·tu·guese [pɔːtjʊ'giːz] **1** *adj* portoghese **2** *n person* portoghese *m/f*; *language* portoghese *m*

pose [pəʊz] **1** *n* (*pretence*) posa *f* **2** *v/i for artist, photographer* posare; *~ as* farsi passare per **3** *v/t*: *~ a problem / a threat* creare un problema / una minaccia

posh [pɒʃ] *adj* F elegante; *pej* snob

po·si·tion [pə'zɪʃn] **1** *n* posizione *f*; *what would you do in my ~?* cosa faresti al mio posto? **2** *v/t* sistemare, piazzare

pos·i·tive ['pɒzətɪv] *adj* positivo; *be ~ (sure)* essere certo

pos·i·tive·ly ['pɒzətɪvlɪ] *adv* (*downright*) decisamente; (*definitely*) assolutamente; *think* in modo positivo

pos·sess [pə'zes] *v/t* possedere

pos·ses·sion [pə'zeʃn] (*ownership*) possesso *m*; *thing owned* bene *m*; *~s* averi *mpl*

pos·ses·sive [pə'zesɪv] *adj also* GRAM possessivo

pos·si·bil·i·ty [pɒsə'bɪlətɪ] possibilità *f inv*

pos·si·ble ['pɒsəbl] *adj* possibile; *the shortest / quickest ~ ...* la ... più breve / veloce possibile; *the best ~ ...* la miglior ... possibile

pos·si·bly ['pɒsəblɪ] *adv* (*perhaps*) forse; *that can't ~ be right* non è possibile che sia giusto; *could you ~ tell me ...?* potrebbe per caso dirmi ...?

post[1] [pəʊst] **1** *n of wood, metal* palo *m* **2** *v/t notice* affiggere; *profits* annunciare; *keep s.o. ~ed* tenere informato qu

post[2] [pəʊst] **1** *n* (*place of duty*) posto *m* **2** *v/t soldier, employee* assegnare; *guards* piazzare

post[3] [pəʊst] **1** *n* (*mail*) posta *f*; *by ~* per posta **2** *v/t letter* spedire (per posta); (*put in the mail*) imbucare

post·age ['pəʊstɪdʒ] affrancatura *f*

post·age stamp *fml* francobollo *m*

post·al ['pəʊstl] *adj* postale

post·al or·der vaglia *m* postale

post·box buca *f* delle lettere; **'post·card** cartolina *f*; **'post·code** codice *m* di avviamento postale; **'post·date** *v/t* postdatare

post·er ['pəʊstə(r)] manifesto *m*; *for decoration* poster *m inv*

pos·te·ri·or [pɒ'stɪərɪə(r)] *n* (*hum: buttocks*) posteriore *m*

pos·ter·i·ty [pɒ'sterətɪ] posteri *mpl*

post·grad·u·ate ['pəʊstgrædjʊɪt] **1** *n* studente *m* / studentessa *f* di un corso post-universitario **2** *adj* post-universitario

post·hu·mous ['pɒstjʊməs] *adj* postumo

post·hu·mous·ly ['pɒstjʊməslɪ] *adv* dopo la sua morte; *it was published ~* è stato pubblicato postumo

post·ing ['pəʊstɪŋ] (*assignment*) incarico *m*

post·man ['pəʊstmən] postino *m*

post·mark ['pəʊstmɑːk] timbro *m* postale

post·mor·tem [pəʊst'mɔːtəm] autopsia *f*

'post of·fice ufficio *m* postale

post·pone [pəʊst'pəʊn] *v/t* rinviare

post·pone·ment [pəʊst'pəʊnmənt] rinvio *m*

pos·ture ['pɒstʃə(r)] posizione *f*

'post·war *adj* del dopoguerra

pot[1] [pɒt] *for cooking* pentola *f*; *for coffee* caffettiera *f*; *for tea* teiera *f*; *for plant* vaso *m*

pot[2] [pɒt] F (*marijuana*) erba *f* F

po·ta·to [pə'teɪtəʊ] patata *f*

po·ta·to chips *Am*, **po·ta·to crisps** *Br npl* patatine *fpl*

'pot·bel·ly ['pɒtbelɪ] pancetta F

po·tent ['pəʊtənt] *adj* potente

po·ten·tial [pə'tenʃl] **1** *adj* potenziale **2** *n* potenziale *m*

po·ten·tial·ly [pə'tenʃəlɪ] *adv* potenzialmente

pot·hole ['pɒthəʊl] *in road* buca *f*

pot·ter ['pɒtə(r)] *n* vasaio *m*, -a *f*

pot·ter·y ['pɒtərɪ] *n activity* ceramica *f*; *items* vasellame *m*; *place* laboratorio *m* di ceramica

pot·ty ['pɒtɪ] *n for baby* vasino *m*

pouch [paʊtʃ] (*bag*) borsa *f*

poul·try ['pəʊltrɪ] *birds* volatili *mpl*; *meat* pollame *m*

pounce [paʊns] *v/i of animal* balzare; *fig* piombare

pound[1] [paʊnd] *n weight* libbra *f*; FIN sterlina *f*

pound[2] [paʊnd] *for strays* canile *m* municipale; *for cars* deposito *m* auto

pound[3] [paʊnd] *v/i of heart* battere

P

forte; **~ on** (*hammer on*) picchiare su

pound 'ster·ling sterlina *f*

pour [pɔː(r)] **1** *v/t liquid* versare **2** *v/i:* **it's ~ing (with rain)** sta diluviando

♦ **pour out** *v/t liquid* versare; *troubles* sfogarsi raccontando

pout [paʊt] *v/i* fare il broncio

pov·er·ty ['pɒvətɪ] povertà *f inv*

pov·er·ty-strick·en ['pɒvətɪstrɪkn] *adj* poverissimo

pow·der ['paʊdə(r)] **1** *n* polvere *f*, *for face* cipria *f* **2** *v/t:* **~ one's face** mettersi la cipria

'pow·der room F toilette *f inv* per signore

pow·er ['paʊə(r)] **1** *n* (*strength*) forza *f*, *of engine* potenza *f*; (*authority*) potere *m*; (*energy*) energia *f*; (*electricity*) elettricità *f inv*; **in ~** POL al potere; **fall from ~** POL perdere il potere **2** *v/t:* **~ed by atomic energy** a propulsione atomica

'pow·er-as·sis·ted steer·ing servosterzo *m*; 'pow·er cut interruzione *f* di corrente; 'pow·er fail·ure guasto *m* alla linea elettrica

pow·er·ful ['paʊəfʊl] *adj* potente

pow·er·less ['paʊəlɪs] *adj* impotente; **be ~ to ...** non poter far niente per ...

'pow·er line linea *f* elettrica; 'pow·er sta·tion centrale *f* elettrica; 'pow·er steer·ing servosterzo *m*; 'pow·er u·nit alimentatore *m*

PR [piː'ɑː(r)] *abbr* (= **public relations**) relazioni *fpl* pubbliche

prac·ti·cal ['præktɪkl] *adj* pratico

prac·ti·cal 'joke scherzo *m*

prac·ti·cal·ly ['præktɪklɪ] *adv behave, think* in modo pratico; (*almost*) praticamente

prac·tice ['præktɪs] **1** *n* pratica *f*; (*training*) esercizio *m*; (*rehearsal*) prove *fpl*; (*custom*) consuetudine *f*; **in ~** (*in reality*) in pratica; **be out of ~** essere fuori allenamento **2** *v/t & v/i Am →* **practise**

prac·tise ['præktɪs] **1** *v/t* esercitarsi in; *law, medicine* esercitare **2** *v/i* esercitarsi

prag·mat·ic [præg'mætɪk] *adj* prag matico

prag·ma·tism ['prægmətɪzm] prag matismo *m*

prai·rie ['preərɪ] prateria *f*

praise [preɪz] **1** *n* lode *f* **2** *v/t* lodare

praise·wor·thy ['preɪzwɜːðɪ] *adj* lo devole

pram [præm] carrozzina *f*

prank [præŋk] *n* birichinata *f*

prat·tle ['prætl] *v/i* cianciare

prawn [prɔːn] gamberetto *m*

pray [preɪ] *v/i* pregare

prayer [preə(r)] preghiera *f*

preach [priːtʃ] **1** *v/i* predicare **2** *v* *sermon* predicare

preach·er ['priːtʃə(r)] predicatore *m* -trice *f*

pre·am·ble [priː'æmbl] preambolo *m*

pre·car·i·ous [prɪ'keərɪəs] *adj* preca rio

pre·car·i·ous·ly [prɪ'keərɪəslɪ] *adv* precariamente

pre·cau·tion [prɪ'kɔːʃn] precauzione *f*

pre·cau·tion·a·ry [prɪ'kɔːʃnrɪ] *ad measure* di precauzione

pre·cede [prɪ'siːd] *v/t* precedere

pre·ce·dence ['presɪdəns] preceden za *f*; **take ~ over ...** avere la pre cedenza su ...

pre·ce·dent ['presɪdənt] *n* prece dente *m*

pre·ce·ding [prɪ'siːdɪŋ] *adj* prece dente

pre·cinct ['priːsɪŋkt] (*Am: district*) distretto *m*

pre·cious ['preʃəs] *adj* prezioso

pre·cip·i·tate [prɪ'sɪpɪteɪt] *v/t crisi* accelerare

pre·cip·i·ta·tion [prɪsɪpɪ'teɪʃn] *fm* precipitazione *f*

pré·cis ['preɪsiː] *n* riassunto *m*

pre·cise [prɪ'saɪs] *adj* preciso

pre·cise·ly [prɪ'saɪslɪ] *adv* precisa mente

pre·ci·sion [prɪ'sɪʒn] precisione *f*

pre·co·cious [prɪ'kəʊʃəs] *adj* chil precoce

pre·con·ceived [priːkən'siːvd] *ad*

idea preconcetto

pre·con·di·tion [priːkənˈdɪʃn] condizione *f* indispensabile

pred·a·tor [ˈpredətə(r)] *animal* predatore *m*, -trice *f*

pred·a·to·ry [ˈpredətri] *adj* rapace

pre·de·ces·sor [ˈpriːdɪsesə(r)] predecessore *m*

pre·des·ti·na·tion [priːdestiˈneɪʃn] predestinazione *f*

pre·des·tined [priːˈdestɪnd] *adj*: **be ~ to** essere predestinato a

pre·dic·a·ment [prɪˈdɪkəmənt] situazione *f* difficile

pre·dict [prɪˈdɪkt] *v/t* predire

pre·dict·a·ble [prɪˈdɪktəbl] *adj* prevedibile

pre·dic·tion [prɪˈdɪkʃn] predizione *f*

pre·dom·i·nant [prɪˈdɒmɪnənt] *adj* predominante

pre·dom·i·nant·ly [prɪˈdɒmɪnəntlɪ] *adv* prevalentemente

pre·dom·i·nate [prɪˈdɒmɪneɪt] *v/i* predominare

preen [priːn] *v/t*: **~ o.s.** *fig* farsi bello

pre·fab·ri·cat·ed [priːˈfæbrikeɪtɪd] *adj* prefabbricato

pref·ace [ˈprefɪs] *n* prefazione *f*

pre·fect [ˈpriːfekt] EDU *studente m / studentessa f dell'ultimo anno di liceo con responsabilità disciplinari*

pre·fer [prɪˈfɜː(r)] *v/t* (*pret & pp -red*) preferire; **~ X to Y** preferire X a Y; **~ to do** preferire fare

pref·er·a·ble [ˈprefərəbl] *adj* preferibile

pref·er·a·bly [ˈprefərəblɪ] *adv* preferibilmente

pref·er·ence [ˈprefərəns] preferenza *f*; **give ~ to** dare *o* accordare la preferenza a

pref·er·en·tial [prefəˈrenʃl] *adj* preferenziale

pre·fix [ˈpriːfɪks] prefisso *m*

preg·nan·cy [ˈpregnənsɪ] gravidanza *f*

preg·nant [ˈpregnənt] *adj* incinta; **get ~** restare incinta

pre·heat [ˈpriːhiːt] *v/t oven* far riscaldare

pre·his·tor·ic [priːhɪsˈtɒrɪk] *adj* preistorico

pre·judge [priːˈdʒʌdʒ] *v/t* giudicare a priori

prej·u·dice [ˈpredʒʊdɪs] **1** *n* pregiudizio *m* **2** *v/t person* influenzare; *chances* pregiudicare

prej·u·diced [ˈpredʒʊdɪst] *adj* prevenuto

prej·u·di·cial [predʒʊˈdɪʃl] *adj*: **be ~ to** essere pregiudizievole a

pre·lim·i·na·ry [prɪˈlɪmɪnərɪ] *adj* preliminare

prel·ude [ˈpreljuːd] preludio *m*

pre·mar·i·tal [priːˈmærɪtl] *adj* prematrimoniale

pre·ma·ture [ˈpremətjʊə(r)] *adj* prematuro

pre·med·i·tat·ed [priːˈmedɪteɪtɪd] *adj* premeditato

prem·i·er [ˈpremɪə(r)] *n* (*Prime Minister*) premier *m inv*

prem·i·ère [ˈpremɪeə(r)] *n* premiere *f inv*, prima *f*

prem·is·es [ˈpremɪsɪz] *npl* locali *mpl*

pre·mi·um [ˈpriːmɪəm] *n in insurance* premio *m*

pre·mo·ni·tion [preməˈnɪʃn] premonizione *f*

pre·oc·cu·pied [prɪˈɒkjʊpaɪd] *adj* preoccupato

pre·paid [ˈpriːpeɪd] *adj* prepagato

prep·a·ra·tion [prepəˈreɪʃn] preparazione *f*; **in ~ for** in vista di; **~s** preparativi *mpl*

pre·pare [prɪˈpeə(r)] **1** *v/t* preparare; **be ~d to do sth** (*willing*) essere preparato a fare qc; **be ~d for sth** (*be expecting*) essere preparato per qc **2** *v/i* prepararsi

prep·o·si·tion [prepəˈzɪʃn] preposizione *f*

pre·pos·sess·ing [priːpəˈzesɪŋ] *adj* attraente

pre·pos·ter·ous [prɪˈpɒstərəs] *adj* ridicolo

prep school [ˈprepskuːl] *scuola f privata di preparazione alla scuola superiore*

pre·req·ui·site [priːˈrekwɪzɪt] condizione *f* indispensabile

P

pre·rog·a·tive [prɪ'rɒgətɪv] prerogativa f

pre·scribe [prɪ'skraɪb] v/t of doctor prescrivere

pre·scrip·tion [prɪ'skrɪpʃn] MED ricetta f medica

pres·ence ['prezns] presenza f; **in the ~ of** in presenza di

pres·ence of 'mind presenza f di spirito

pres·ent[1] ['preznt] **1** adj (current) attuale; **be ~** essere presente **2** n: **the ~** also GRAM il presente; **at ~** al momento

pres·ent[2] ['preznt] n (gift) regalo m

pre·sent[3] [prɪ'zent] v/t award consegnare; bouquet offrire; programme presentare; **~ s.o. with sth, ~ sth to s.o.** offrire qc a qu

pre·sen·ta·tion [preznteɪʃn] presentazione f

pres·ent-day[preznt'deɪ] adj di oggi

pre·sent·er [prɪ'zentə(r)] presentatore m, -trice f

pres·ent·ly ['prezntlɪ] adv (at the moment) attualmente; (soon) tra breve

'pres·ent tense presente m

pres·er·va·tion [prezə'veɪʃn] of food conservazione f; of standards, peace etc mantenimento m

pre·ser·va·tive [prɪ'zɜ:vətɪv] n for wood; in food conservante m

pre·serve [prɪ'zɜ:v] **1** n (domain) dominio m **2** v/t standards, peace etc mantenere; wood etc proteggere; food conservare

pre·serves [prɪ'zɜ:vz] npl conserve fpl

pre·side [prɪ'zaɪd] v/i at meeting presiedere; **~ over** meeting presiedere a

pres·i·den·cy ['prezɪdənsɪ] presidenza f

pres·i·dent ['prezɪdnt] presidente m

pres·i·den·tial [prezɪ'denʃl] adj presidenziale

press [pres] **1** n: **the ~** la stampa **2** v/t button premere; (urge) far pressione su; (squeeze) stringere; clothes stirare; grapes, olives spremere **3** v/i: **~ for** fare pressioni per ottenere

'press a·gen·cy agenzia f di stampa

'press con·fer·ence conferenza f stampa

press·ing ['presɪŋ] adj urgente

press-stud ['presstʌd] (bottone m) automatico

press-up ['presʌp] flessione f sulle braccia

pres·sure ['preʃə(r)] **1** n pressione f; **be under ~** (**to do**) essere sotto pressione (per fare) **2** v/t fare delle pressioni su

'pres·sure cook·er pentola f a pressione

'pres·sur·ize ['preʃəraɪz] v/t person fare delle pressioni su

pres·tige [pre'sti:ʒ] prestigio m

pres·ti·gious [pre'stɪdʒəs] adj prestigioso

pre·sum·a·ble [prɪ'zju:məbl] adj presumibile

pre·su·ma·bly [prɪ'zju:məblɪ] adv presumibilmente

pre·sume [prɪ'zju:m] v/i presumere; **~ to do** fml permettersi di fare

pre·sump·tion [prɪ'zʌmpʃn] of innocence, guilt presunzione f

pre·sump·tu·ous [prɪ'zʌmptjʊəs] adj impertinente

pre·sup·pose [pri:sə'pəʊs] v/t presupporre

pre-tax ['pri:tæks] adj al lordo d'imposta

pre·tence [prɪ'tens] finta f

pre·tend [prɪ'tend] **1** v/t fingere **2** v/i fare finta

pre·tense Am → **pretence**

pre·ten·tious [prɪ'tenʃəs] adj pretenzioso

pre·text ['pri:tekst] pretesto m

pret·ty ['prɪtɪ] **1** adj carino **2** adv (quite) piuttosto

pre·vail [prɪ'veɪl] v/i (triumph) prevalere

pre·vail·ing [prɪ'veɪlɪŋ] adj prevalente

pre·var·i·cate [prɪ'værɪkeɪt] v/i tergiversare

pre·vent [prɪ'vent] v/t prevenire; **~ s.o. (from) doing sth** impedire a qu di fare qc

pre·ven·tion [prɪˈvenʃn] prevenzione f

pre·ven·tive [prɪˈventɪv] adj preventivo

pre·view [ˈpriːvjuː] n of film, exhibition anteprima f

pre·vi·ous [ˈpriːvɪəs] adj precedente; ~ **to** prima di

pre·vi·ous·ly [ˈpriːvɪəslɪ] adv precedentemente

pre·war [ˈpriːwɔː(r)] adj dell'anteguerra

prey [preɪ] n preda f

♦ **prey on** v/t far preda di; fig: of conman etc approfittarsi di; **prey on s.o.'s mind** preoccupare qu

price [praɪs] 1 n prezzo m 2 v/t COM fissare il prezzo di

price·less [ˈpraɪsləs] adj (valuable) di valore inestimabile

'**price tag** cartellino m del prezzo

'**price war** guerra f dei prezzi

price·y [ˈpraɪsɪ] adj F caro

prick[1] [prɪk] 1 n pain puntura f 2 v/t (jab) pungere

prick[2] [prɪk] n ∨ (penis) cazzo m ∨; person testa f di cazzo ∨

♦ **prick up** v/t: **prick up one's ears** also fig drizzare le orecchie

prick·le [ˈprɪkl] on plant spina f

prick·ly [ˈprɪklɪ] adj plant spinoso; beard ispido; (irritable) permaloso

pride [praɪd] 1 n in person, achievement orgoglio m; (self-respect) amor m proprio 2 v/t: ~ **o.s. on** vantarsi di

priest [priːst] prete m

pri·ma·ri·ly [praɪˈmeərɪlɪ] adv principalmente

pri·ma·ry [ˈpraɪmərɪ] adj principale

'**pri·ma·ry school** scuola f elementare

prime [praɪm] 1 n: **be in one's ~** essere nel fiore degli anni 2 adj example, reason principale; (very good) ottimo; **of ~ importance** della massima importanza

prime 'min·is·ter primo ministro m

'**prime time** TV TV programmi mpl tv di prima serata

prim·i·tive [ˈprɪmɪtɪv] adj also fig primitivo

prim·rose [ˈprɪmrəʊz] primula f

prince [prɪns] principe m

prin·cess [prɪnˈses] principessa f

prin·ci·pal [ˈprɪnsəpl] 1 adj principale 2 n of school preside m/f

prin·ci·pal·i·ty [prɪnsɪˈpælətɪ] principato m

prin·ci·pal·ly [ˈprɪnsəplɪ] adv principalmente

prin·ci·ple [ˈprɪnsəpl] principio m; **on ~** per principio; **in ~** in linea di principio

print [prɪnt] 1 n in book, newspaper etc caratteri mpl; photograph stampa f; mark impronta f; **out of ~** esaurito 2 v/t stampare; (use block capitals) scrivere in stampatello

♦ **print out** v/t stampare

print·ed mat·ter [ˈprɪntɪdmætə(r)] stampe fpl

print·er [ˈprɪntə(r)] person tipografo m; machine stampante f

print·ing press [ˈprɪntɪŋpres] pressa f tipografica

'**print·out** stampato m

pri·or [ˈpraɪə(r)] 1 adj precedente 2 prep: ~ **to** prima di

pri·or·i·tize [praɪˈɒrətaɪz] v/t (put in order of priority) classificare in ordine d'importanza; (give priority to) dare precedenza a

pri·or·i·ty [praɪˈɒrətɪ] priorità f inv; **have ~** avere la precedenza

pris·on [ˈprɪzn] prigione f

pris·on·er [ˈprɪznə(r)] prigioniero m, -a f; **take s.o. ~** fare prigioniero qu

pris·on·er of 'war prigioniero m di guerra

priv·a·cy [ˈprɪvəsɪ] privacy f inv

pri·vate [ˈpraɪvət] 1 adj privato 2 n MIL soldato m semplice; **in ~** in privato

pri·vate 'en·ter·prise iniziativa f privata

pri·vate·ly [ˈpraɪvətlɪ] adv (in private) in privato; (inwardly) dentro di sé; ~ **funded** finanziato da privati; ~ **owned** privato

'**pri·vate sec·tor** settore m privato

pri·va·ti·za·tion [praɪvətaɪˈzeɪʃn] privatizzazione f

P

pri·va·tize ['praɪvətaɪz] v/t privatizzare

priv·i·lege ['prɪvəlɪdʒ] special treatment privilegio m; (honour) onore m

priv·i·leged ['prɪvəlɪdʒd] adj privilegiato; (honoured) onorato

prize [praɪz] 1 n premio m 2 v/t dare molto valore a

prize-win·ner ['praɪzwɪnə(r)] vincitore m, -trice f

prize-win·ning ['praɪzwɪnɪŋ] adj vincente

pro¹ [prəʊ] n: **the ~s and cons** i pro e i contro

pro² [prəʊ] → **professional**

pro³ [prəʊ] prep: **be ~ ...** (in favour of) essere a favore di ...

prob·a·bil·i·ty [prɒbə'bɪlətɪ] probabilità f inv

prob·a·ble ['prɒbəbl] adj probabile

prob·a·bly ['prɒbəblɪ] adv probabilmente

pro·ba·tion [prə'beɪʃn] in job periodo m di prova; LAW libertà f inv vigilata; **on ~** in job in prova

pro·'ba·tion of·fi·cer funzionario m che sorveglia i vigilati

pro·'ba·tion pe·ri·od in job periodo m di prova

probe [prəʊb] 1 n (investigation) indagine f; scientific sonda f 2 v/t esplorare; (investigate) investigare

prob·lem ['prɒbləm] problema m; **no ~** non c'è problema

pro·ce·dure [prə'siːdʒə(r)] procedura f

pro·ceed [prə'siːd] 1 v/i of people proseguire; of work etc procedere 2 v/t: **to do sth** cominciare a fare qc

pro·ceed·ings [prə'siːdɪŋz] npl (events) avvenimenti mpl

pro·ceeds ['prəʊsiːdz] npl ricavato m

pro·cess ['prəʊses] 1 n processo m; **in the ~** while doing it nel far ciò 2 v/t food, raw materials trattare; data elaborare; application etc sbrigare; **~ed cheese** formaggio m fuso

pro·ces·sion [prə'seʃn] processione f

pro·claim [prə'kleɪm] v/t proclamare

proc·la·ma·tion [prɒklə'meɪʃn] proclamazione f

prod [prɒd] 1 n colpetto m 2 v/t (pret & pp **-ded**) dare un colpetto a

pro·di·gious [prə'dɪdʒəs] adj straordinario

prod·i·gy ['prɒdɪdʒɪ]: (infant) ~ bambino m, -a f prodigio

prod·uce¹ ['prɒdjuːs] n prodotti mpl

pro·duce² [prə'djuːs] v/t produrre; (bring about) dare origine a; (bring out) tirar fuori; play, play mettere in scena

pro·duc·er [prə'djuːsə(r)] produttore m, -trice f; of play regista m/f

prod·uct ['prɒdʌkt] prodotto m; (result) risultato m

pro·duc·tion [prə'dʌkʃn] produzione f; of play regia f; **a new ~ of ...** una nuova messa in scena di ...

pro·duc·tion ca·pac·i·ty capacità f inv produttiva

pro·duc·tion costs npl costi mpl di produzione

pro·duc·tive [prə'dʌktɪv] adj produttivo

pro·duc·tiv·i·ty [prɒdʌk'tɪvətɪ] produttività f inv

pro·fane [prə'feɪn] adj language sacrilego

pro·fan·i·ty [prə'fænətɪ] (swearword) imprecazione f

pro·fess [prə'fes] v/t dichiarare

pro·fes·sion [prə'feʃn] professione f

pro·fes·sion·al [prə'feʃnl] 1 adj not amateur professionale; advice, help di un esperto; piece of work da professionista; **turn ~** passare al professionismo 2 n professionista m/f

pro·fes·sion·al·ly [prə'feʃnlɪ] adv play sport a livello professionistico; (well, skilfully) in modo professionale

pro·fes·sor [prə'fesə(r)] professore m (universitario)

pro·fi·cien·cy [prə'fɪʃnsɪ] competenza f

pro·fi·cient [prə'fɪʃnt] adj competente

pro·file ['prəʊfaɪl] profilo *m*

prof·it ['profɪt] **1** *n* profitto *m* **2** *v/i*: ~ **by**, ~ **from** trarre profitto da

prof·it·a·bil·i·ty [profɪtə'bɪlətɪ] redditività *f inv*

prof·it·a·ble ['profɪtəbl] *adj* redditizio

'**prof·it cen·ter** *Am*, '**prof·it cen·tre** centro *m* di profitto

'**prof·it mar·gin** margine *m* di profitto

pro·found [prə'faʊnd] *adj* profondo

pro·found·ly [prə'faʊndlɪ] *adv* profondamente

pro·fuse [prə'fjuːs] *adj* abbondante

pro·fuse·ly [prə'fjuːslɪ] *adv* thank con grande effusione; bleed copiosamente

prog·no·sis [prog'nəʊsɪs] prognosi *f inv*

pro·gram ['prəʊgræm] **1** *n* COMPUT programma *m* **2** *v/t* (pret & pp **-med**) COMPUT programmare

pro·gram *Am*, **pro·gramme** ['prəʊgræm] **1** *n* programma *m* **2** *v/t* programmare

pro·gram·mer ['prəʊgræmə(r)] COMPUT programmatore *m*, -trice *f*

pro·gress ['prəʊgres] **1** *n* progresso *m*; **make** ~ fare progressi; **in** ~ in corso **2** *v/i* [prə'gres] (advance in time) procedere; (move on) avanzare; (make progress) fare progressi; **how is the work ~ing?** come procede il lavoro?

pro·gres·sive [prə'gresɪv] *adj* (enlightened) progressista; (which progresses) progressivo

pro·gres·sive·ly [prə'gresɪvlɪ] *adv* progressivamente

pro·hib·it [prə'hɪbɪt] *v/t* proibire

pro·hi·bi·tion [prəʊhɪ'bɪʃn] proibizione *f*; **Prohibition** il Proibizionismo

pro·hib·i·tive [prə'hɪbɪtɪv] *adj* prices proibitivo

proj·ect[1] ['prɒdʒekt] *n* (plan) piano *m*; (undertaking) progetto *m*; EDU ricerca *f*

pro·ject[2] [prə'dʒekt] **1** *v/t* figures, sales fare una proiezione di; film

proiettare **2** *v/i* (stick out) sporgere in fuori

pro·jec·tion [prə'dʒekʃn] (forecast) proiezione *f*

pro·jec·tor [prə'dʒektə(r)] for slides proiettore *m*

pro·lif·ic [prə'lɪfɪk] *adj* writer, artist prolifico

pro·log *Am*, **pro·logue** ['prəʊlɒg] prologo *m*

pro·long [prə'lɒŋ] *v/t* prolungare

prom·i·nent ['prɒmɪnənt] *adj* nose, chin sporgente; (significant) prominente

prom·is·cu·i·ty [prɒmɪ'skjuːətɪ] promiscuità *f inv*

pro·mis·cu·ous [prə'mɪskjʊəs] *adj* promiscuo

prom·ise ['prɒmɪs] **1** *n* promessa *f* **2** *v/t* promettere; ~ **to ...** promettere di ...; ~ **sth to s.o.** promettere qc a qu **3** *v/i* promettere; **I** ~ **lo** prometto

prom·is·ing ['prɒmɪsɪŋ] *adj* promettente

pro·mote [prə'məʊt] *v/t* promuovere

pro·mot·er [prə'məʊtə(r)] of sports event promoter *m/f inv*

pro·mo·tion [prə'məʊʃn] promozione *f*; **get** ~ essere promosso

prompt [prɒmpt] **1** *adj* (on time) puntuale; (speedy) tempestivo **2** *adv*: **at two o'clock** ~ alle due in punto **3** *v/t* (cause) causare; actor dare l'imbeccata a **4** *n* COMPUT prompt *m inv*

prompt·ly ['prɒmptlɪ] *adv* (on time) puntualmente; (immediately) prontamente

prone [prəʊn] *adj*: **be** ~ **to** essere soggetto a

prong [prɒŋ] dente *m*

pro·noun ['prəʊnaʊn] pronome *m*

pro·nounce [prə'naʊns] *v/t* word pronunciare; (declare) dichiarare

pro·nounced [prə'naʊnst] *adj* accent spiccato; views preciso

pron·to ['prɒntəʊ] *adv* F immediatamente

pro·nun·ci·a·tion [prənʌnsɪ'eɪʃn] pronuncia *f*

proof [pruːf] *n* prova *f*; of book bozza *f*

prop [prɒp] **1** v/t (pret & pp **-ped**) appoggiare **2** n THEA materiale m di scena

♦ **prop up** v/t also fig sostenere

prop·a·gan·da [prɒpə'gændə] propaganda f

pro·pel [prə'pel] v/t (pret & pp **-led**) spingere; of engine, fuel azionare

pro·pel·lant [prə'pelənt] in aerosol propellente m

pro·pel·ler [prə'pelə(r)] elica f

prop·er ['prɒpə(r)] adj (real) vero e proprio; (correct) giusto; (fitting) appropriato

prop·er·ly ['prɒpəli] adv (correctly) correttamente; (fittingly) in modo appropriato

'prop·er noun nome m proprio

prop·er·ty ['prɒpəti] proprietà f inv

prop·er·ty de'vel·op·er impresario m edile

proph·e·cy ['prɒfəsɪ] profezia f

proph·e·sy ['prɒfəsaɪ] v/t (pret & pp **-ied**) profetizzare

pro·por·tion [prə'pɔːʃn] proporzione f

pro·por·tion·al [prə'pɔːʃnl] adj proporzionale

pro·por·tion·al rep·re·sen·ta·tion POL rappresentanza f proporzionale

pro·pos·al [prə'pəʊzl] proposta f

pro·pose [prə'pəʊz] **1** v/t (suggest) proporre; ~ **to do sth** (plan) proporsi di fare qc **2** v/i make offer of marriage fare una proposta di matrimonio

prop·o·si·tion [prɒpə'zɪʃn] **1** n proposta f **2** v/t woman fare proposte sessuali a

pro·pri·e·tor [prə'praɪətə(r)] proprietario m, -a f

pro·pri·e·tress [prə'praɪətrɪs] proprietaria f

prose [prəʊz] prosa f

pros·e·cute ['prɒsɪkjuːt] v/t LAW intentare azione legale contro; of lawyer sostenere l'accusa contro

pros·e·cu·tion [prɒsɪ'kjuːʃn] LAW azione f giudiziaria; (lawyers) accusa f

pros·pect ['prɒspekt] **1** n (chance, likelihood) probabilità f inv; thought of something in the future prospettiva f; **~s** for company, in job prospettive fpl **2** v/i: ~ **for gold** cercare

pro·spec·tive [prə'spektɪv] adj potenziale; MP aspirante

pros·per ['prɒspə(r)] v/i prosperare

pros·per·i·ty [prɒ'sperətɪ] prosperità f inv

pros·per·ous ['prɒspərəs] adj prospero

pros·ti·tute ['prɒstɪtjuːt] n prostituta f; **male ~** prostituto m

pros·ti·tu·tion [prɒstɪ'tjuːʃn] prostituzione f

pros·trate ['prɒstreɪt] adj: **be ~ with grief** essere abbattuto dal dolore

pro·tect [prə'tekt] v/t proteggere

pro·tec·tion [prə'tekʃn] protezione f

pro'tec·tion mon·ey pizzo m F

pro·tec·tive [prə'tektɪv] adj protettivo

pro·tec·tive 'cloth·ing indumenti mpl protettivi

pro·tec·tor [prə'tektə(r)] protettore m, -trice f

pro·tein ['prəʊtiːn] proteina f

pro·test ['prəʊtest] **1** n protesta f **2** v/t [prə'test] protestare **3** v/i protestare; POL manifestare, protestare

Prot·es·tant ['prɒtɪstənt] **1** n protestante m/f **2** adj protestante

pro·test·er [prə'testə(r)] dimostrante m/f, manifestante m/f

pro·to·col ['prəʊtəkɒl] protocollo m

pro·to·type ['prəʊtətaɪp] prototipo m

pro·tract·ed [prə'træktɪd] adj prolungato

pro·trude [prə'truːd] v/i sporgere

pro·trud·ing [prə'truːdɪŋ] adj sporgente

proud [praʊd] adj orgoglioso, fiero; **be ~ of** essere fiero di

proud·ly ['praʊdlɪ] adv con orgoglio

prove [pruːv] v/t dimostrare

prov·erb ['prɒvɜːb] proverbio m

pro·vide [prə'vaɪd] v/t money, food fornire; opportunity offrire; ~ **s.o. with sth** fornire qu di qc

◆ **provide for** v/t *family* provvedere a; *of law etc* contemplare

pro·vi·ded [prə'vaɪdɪd] *conj:* ~ **(that)** *(on condition that)* a condizione che

prov·ince ['prɒvɪns] provincia f

pro·vin·cial [prə'vɪnʃl] *adj also pej* provinciale

pro·vi·sion [prə'vɪʒn] *(supply)* fornitura f; *of law,* contract disposizione f

pro·vi·sion·al [prə'vɪʒnl] *adj* provvisorio

pro·vi·so [prə'vaɪzəʊ] condizione f

prov·o·ca·tion [prɒvə'keɪʃn] provocazione f

pro·voc·a·tive [prə'vɒkətɪv] *adj* provocatorio; *sexually* provocante

pro·voke [prə'vəʊk] v/t *(cause)* causare; *(annoy)* provocare

prow [praʊ] NAUT prua f

prow·ess ['praʊɪs] abilità f inv

prowl [praʊl] v/i aggirarsi

prowl·er ['praʊlə(r)] tipo m sospetto

prox·im·i·ty [prɒk'sɪmətɪ] prossimità f inv

prox·y ['prɒksɪ] *(authority)* procura f; *person* procuratore m, -trice f, mandatario m, -a f

prude [pruːd]: **be a** ~ scandalizzarsi facilmente

pru·dence ['pruːdns] prudenza f

pru·dent ['pruːdnt] *adj* prudente

prud·ish ['pruːdɪʃ] *adj* che si scandalizza facilmente

prune¹ [pruːn] n prugna f

prune² [pruːn] v/t *plant* potare; *fig* ridurre

pry [praɪ] v/i *(pret & pp -ied)* essere indiscreto

◆ **pry into** v/t ficcare il naso in

PS ['piːes] *abbr (= postscript)* P.S. (= post scriptum m inv)

pseu·do·nym ['sjuːdənɪm] pseudonimo m

psy·chi·at·ric [saɪkɪ'ætrɪk] *adj* psichiatrico

psy·chi·a·trist [saɪ'kaɪətrɪst] psichiatra m/f

psy·chi·a·try [saɪ'kaɪətrɪ] psichiatria f

psy·chic ['saɪkɪk] *adj* psichico; **I'm not** ~! non sono un indovino!

psy·cho·an·a·lyse [saɪkəʊ'ænəlaɪz] v/t psicanalizzare

psy·cho·a·nal·y·sis [saɪkəʊən'æləsɪs] psicanalisi f

psy·cho·an·a·lyst [saɪkəʊ'ænəlɪst] psicanalista m/f

psy·cho·log·i·cal [saɪkə'lɒdʒɪkl] *adj* psicologico

psy·cho·log·i·cal·ly [saɪkə'lɒdʒɪklɪ] *adv* psicologicamente

psy·chol·o·gist [saɪ'kɒlədʒɪst] psicologo m, -a f

psy·chol·o·gy [saɪ'kɒlədʒɪ] psicologia f

psy·cho·path ['saɪkəpæθ] psicopatico m, -a f

psy·cho·so·mat·ic [saɪkəʊsə'mætɪk] *adj* psicosomatico

PT [piː'tiː] *abbr (= physical training)* educazione f fisica

PTO [piːtiː'əʊ] *abbr (= please turn over)* vedi retro

pub [pʌb] pub m inv

pu·ber·ty ['pjuːbətɪ] pubertà f inv

pu·bic hair [pjuːbɪk'heə(r)] peli mpl del pube

pub·lic ['pʌblɪk] **1** *adj* pubblico **2** *n:* **the** ~ il pubblico; **in** ~ in pubblico

pub·li·ca·tion [pʌblɪ'keɪʃn] pubblicazione f

pub·lic 'hol·i·day giorno m festivo

pub·lic·i·ty [pʌb'lɪsətɪ] pubblicità f inv

pub·li·cize ['pʌblɪsaɪz] v/t *make known* far sapere in giro; COM reclamizzare

pub·lic 'li·bra·ry biblioteca f pubblica

pub·lic lim·it·ed 'com·pa·ny società f inv a responsabilità limitata quotata in borsa

pub·lic·ly ['pʌblɪklɪ] *adv* pubblicamente

pub·lic 'pros·e·cu·tor *pubblico ministero m*; **pub·lic re'la·tions** npl relazioni fpl pubbliche; **'pub·lic school** Br scuola f privata; **'pub·lic sec·tor** settore m pubblico; **pub·lic 'trans·port** mezzi mpl pubblici

pub·lish ['pʌblɪʃ] v/t pubblicare

pub·lish·er ['pʌblɪʃə(r)] editore m

P

pub·lish·ing ['pʌblɪʃɪŋ] editoria f

'pub·lish·ing com·pa·ny casa f editrice

pud·ding ['pʊdɪŋ] *dish* budino m; *part of meal* dolce m

pud·dle ['pʌdl] n pozzanghera f

puff [pʌf] **1** n *of wind, smoke* soffio m **2** v/i (*pant*) ansimare; **~ on a cigarette** tirare boccate da una sigaretta

puff·y ['pʌfɪ] *adj eyes, face* gonfio

puke [pjuːk] v/i F vomitare

pull [pʊl] **1** n *on rope* tirata f; F (*appeal*) attrattiva f; F (*influence*) influenza f **2** v/t (*drag*) tirare; (*tug*) dare uno strappo a; *tooth* togliere **3** v/i tirare; **~ a muscle** farsi uno strappo muscolare

♦ **pull ahead** v/i *in race, competition* portarsi in testa

♦ **pull apart** v/t (*separate*) separare

♦ **pull away** v/t spostare

♦ **pull down** v/t (*lower*) tirar giù; (*demolish*) demolire

♦ **pull in** v/i *of bus, train* arrivare

♦ **pull off** v/t togliere; F *deal etc* portare a termine

♦ **pull out 1** v/t tirar fuori; *troops* (far) ritirare **2** v/i *of troops, competition*, MIL ritirarsi; *of ship* partire

♦ **pull over** v/i *of driver* accostarsi

♦ **pull through** v/i *from an illness* farcela F

♦ **pull together 1** v/i (*cooperate*) cooperare **2** v/t: **pull o.s. together** darsi una mossa F

♦ **pull up 1** v/t (*raise*) tirar su; *plant, weeds* strappare **2** v/i *of car etc* fermarsi

pul·ley ['pʊlɪ] puleggia f

pull·o·ver ['pʊləʊvə(r)] pullover m inv

pulp [pʌlp] *soft mass* poltiglia f; *of fruit* polpa f; *for paper-making* pasta f

pul·pit ['pʊlpɪt] pulpito m

pul·sate [pʌl'seɪt] v/i *of heart, blood* pulsare; *of rhythm* vibrare

pulse [pʌls] polso m

pul·ver·ize ['pʌlvəraɪz] v/t polverizzare

pump [pʌmp] **1** n pompa f **2** v/t pompare

♦ **pump up** v/t gonfiare

pump·kin ['pʌmpkɪn] zucca f

pun [pʌn] gioco m di parole

punch [pʌntʃ] **1** n *blow* pugno m; *implement* punzonatrice f **2** v/t *with fist* dare un pugno a; *hole* perforare; *ticket* forare

'punch line finale m

punc·tu·al ['pʌŋktjʊəl] *adj* puntuale

punc·tu·al·i·ty [pʌŋktjʊ'ælətɪ] puntualità f inv

punc·tu·al·ly ['pʌŋktjʊəlɪ] *adv* puntualmente

punc·tu·ate ['pʌŋktjʊeɪt] v/t mettere la punteggiatura in

punc·tu·a·tion ['pʌŋktjʊ'eɪʃn] punteggiatura f

punc·tu·a·tion mark segno m d'interpunzione

punc·ture ['pʌŋktʃə(r)] **1** n foratura f **2** v/t forare

pun·gent ['pʌndʒənt] *adj* acre; *taste* aspro

pun·ish ['pʌnɪʃ] v/t *person* punire

pun·ish·ing ['pʌnɪʃɪŋ] *adj pace, schedule* estenuante

pun·ish·ment ['pʌnɪʃmənt] punizione f

punk (rock) ['pʌŋkrɒk] MUS punk m inv

pu·ny ['pjuːnɪ] *adj person* gracile

pup [pʌp] cucciolo m

pu·pil[1] ['pjuːpl] *of eye* pupilla f

pu·pil[2] ['pjuːpl] (*student*) allievo m, -a f

pup·pet ['pʌpɪt] burattino m; *with strings* marionetta f

'pup·pet gov·ern·ment governo m fantoccio

pup·py ['pʌpɪ] cucciolo m

pur·chase[1] ['pɜːtʃəs] **1** n acquisto m **2** v/t acquistare

pur·chase[2] ['pɜːtʃəs] (*grip*) presa f

pur·chas·er ['pɜːtʃəsə(r)] acquirente m/f

pure [pjʊə(r)] *adj* puro; **~ new wool** pura lana f vergine

pure·ly ['pjʊəlɪ] *adv* puramente

ур·ga·to·ry ['pɜ:gətrɪ] purgatorio
m

urge [pɜ:dʒ] **1** *n* of political party
epurazione *f* **2** *v/t* epurare

ou·ri·fy ['pjʊərɪfaɪ] *v/t* (*pret & pp*
-ied) *water* purificare

ou·ri·tan ['pjʊərɪtən] puritano *m*, -a *f*

ou·ri·tan·i·cal [pjʊərɪ'tænɪkl] *adj* puritano

ou·ri·ty ['pjʊərɪtɪ] purezza *f*

our·ple ['pɜ:pl] *adj* viola *inv*

our·pose ['pɜ:pəs] (*aim, object*) scopo *m*; **on ~** di proposito

our·pose·ful ['pɜ:pəsfʊl] *adj* risoluto

our·pose·ly ['pɜ:pəslɪ] *adv* di proposito

ourr [pɜ:(r)] *v/i* of cat far le fusa

ourse [pɜ:s] *n for money* borsellino *m*; *Am* (*handbag*) borsetta *f*

our·sue [pə'sju:] *v/t person* inseguire; *career* intraprendere; *course of action* proseguire

our·su·er [pə'sju:ə(r)] inseguitore *m*, -trice *f*

our·suit [pə'sju:t] (*chase*) inseguimento *m*; *of happiness etc* ricerca *f*, *activity* occupazione *f*; **those in ~** gli inseguitori

ous [pʌs] pus *m inv*

oush [pʊʃ] **1** *n* (*shove*) spinta *f*; **at the ~ of a button** premendo un pulsante **2** *v/t* (*shove*) spingere; *button* premere; (*pressurize*) fare pressioni su; F *drugs* spacciare; **be ~ed for** F essere a corto di; **be ~ing 40** F essere sulla quarantina **3** *v/i* spingere

◆ push ahead *v/i* andare avanti

◆ push along *v/t cart etc* spingere

◆ push away *v/t* respingere

◆ push off **1** *v/t lid* spingere via **2** *v/i* F (*leave*) andarsene; **push off!** sparisci!

◆ push on *v/i* (*continue*) continuare

◆ push up *v/t prices* far salire

oush-but·ton ['pʊʃbʌtn] *adj* a tastiera

push-chair passeggino *m*

oush·er ['pʊʃə(r)] F *of drugs* spacciatore *m*, -trice *f*

oush-up ['pʊʃʌp] flessione *f* sulle braccia

push·y ['pʊʃɪ] *adj* F troppo intraprendente

puss, pus·sy (cat) [pʊs, 'pʊsɪ (kæt)] F micio *m*, -a *f*

◆ pussyfoot about ['pʊsɪfʊt] *v/i* F tentennare

put [pʊt] *v/t* (*pret & pp* **put**) mettere; *question* porre; **~ the cost at ...** stimare il costo intorno a ...

◆ put across *v/t ideas etc* trasmettere

◆ put aside *v/t* mettere da parte

◆ put away *v/t in cupboard etc* mettere via; *in institution* rinchiudere; (*consume*) far fuori; *money* mettere da parte

◆ put back *v/t* (*replace*) rimettere a posto

◆ put by *v/t money* mettere da parte

◆ put down *v/t* mettere giù; *deposit* versare; *rebellion* reprimere; *animal* abbattere; (*belittle*) sminuire; *in writing* scrivere; **put one's foot down** *in car* accelerare; (*be firm*) farsi valere; **put X down to Y** (*attribute*) attribuire X a Y

◆ put forward *v/t idea etc* avanzare

◆ put in *v/t* inserire; *overtime* fare; *time, effort* dedicare; *request, claim* presentare

◆ put in for *v/t* (*apply for*) fare domanda per

◆ put off *v/t light, radio, TV* spegnere; (*postpone*) rimandare; (*deter*) scoraggiare; (*repel*) disgustare; **the accident put me off driving** l'incidente mi ha fatto passare la voglia di guidare

◆ put on *v/t light, radio, TV* accendere; *tape, music* mettere su; *jacket, shoes, glasses* mettersi; *makeup* mettere; (*perform*) mettere in scena; (*assume*) affettare; **put on the brakes** frenare; **put on weight** ingrassare; **she's just putting it on** sta solo fingendo

◆ put out *v/t hand* allungare; *fire, light* spegnere

◆ put through *v/t*: **I'll put you through** (**to him**) glielo passo; **I'll put you through to sales** le passo l'ufficio vendite

P

♦ **put together** v/t (*assemble*) montare; (*organize*) organizzare

♦ **put up** v/t *hand* alzare; *person* ospitare; (*erect*) costruire; *prices* aumentare; *poster, notice* affiggere; *money* fornire; **put up for sale** mettere in vendita

♦ **put up with** v/t (*tolerate*) sopportare

putt [pʌt] v/t & v/i SP pattare

put·ty ['pʌtɪ] mastice m

puz·zle ['pʌzl] **1** n (*mystery*) mistero m; *game* rebus m inv; *jigsaw* puzzle m inv; *crossword* cruciverba m inv **2** v/t lasciar perplesso

puz·zling ['pʌzlɪŋ] adj inspiegabile

PVC [piːviːˈsiː] abbr (= **polyvinyl chloride**) PVC m inv (= polivinilcloruro m)

py·ja·mas [pəˈdʒɑːməz] npl pigiama m

py·lon ['paɪlən] pilone m

Q

quack¹ [kwæk] **1** n of duck qua qua m inv **2** v/i fare qua qua

quack² [kwæk] F (*bad doctor*) ciarlatano m, -a f; **I'm going to see the ~** vado dal dottore

quad·ran·gle ['kwɒdræŋgl] figure quadrilatero m; *courtyard* cortile m

quad·ru·ped ['kwɒdruped] quadrupede m

quad·ru·ple ['kwɒdrupl] v/i quadruplicare

quad·ru·plets ['kwɒdruplɪts] npl quattro gemelli mpl

quads [kwɒdz] npl F quattro gemelli mpl

quag·mire ['kwɒgmaɪə(r)] fig ginepraio m

quail [kweɪl] v/i perdersi d'animo

quaint [kweɪnt] adj pretty pittoresco; slightly eccentric: ideas etc curioso

quake [kweɪk] **1** n (*earthquake*) terremoto m **2** v/i also fig tremare

qual·i·fi·ca·tion [kwɒlɪfɪˈkeɪʃn] from university etc titolo m di studio; of remark etc riserva f; **have the right ~s for a job** skills avere tutti i requisiti per un lavoro

qual·i·fied ['kwɒlɪfaɪd] adj doctor, engineer etc abilitato; (*restricted*) con riserva; **I am not ~ to judge** non sono in grado di valutare

qual·i·fy ['kwɒlɪfaɪ] (*pret & pp -ied*) **1** v/t of degree, course etc abilitare; remark etc precisare **2** v/i (*get certificate etc*) ottenere la qualifica (**as** di); in competition qualificarsi; **our team has qualified for the semi-final** la nostra squadra è entrata in semifinale; **that doesn't ~ as ...** non può essere considerato ...

qual·i·ty ['kwɒlətɪ] qualità f inv

qual·i·ty con'trol controllo m (di) qualità

qualm [kwɑːm]: **have no ~s about ...** non aver scrupoli a ...

quan·da·ry ['kwɒndərɪ] n dilemma m; **be in a ~** avere un dilemma

quan·ti·fy ['kwɒntɪfaɪ] v/t (*pret & pp -ied*) quantificare

quan·ti·ty ['kwɒntɪtɪ] quantità f inv

quan·tum 'phys·ics ['kwɒntəm] teoria f fisica dei quanti

quar·an·tine ['kwɒrəntiːn] n quarantena f

quar·rel ['kwɒrəl] **1** n litigio m **2** v/i (*pret & pp -led, Am -ed*) litigare

quar·rel·some ['kwɒrəlsʌm] adj litigioso

quar·ry¹ ['kwɒrɪ] in hunt preda f

quar·ry² ['kwɒrɪ] for mining cava f

quart [kwɔːt] quarto m di gallone

quar·ter ['kwɔːtə(r)] **1** n quarto m

part of town quartiere *m*; **a ~ of an hour** un quarto d'ora; (**a**) **~ to 5** le cinque meno un quarto; (**a**) **~ past 5** le cinque e un quarto **2** *v/t* dividere in quattro parti

quar·ter·'fi·nal partita *f* dei quarti *mpl* di finale

quar·ter·'fi·nal·ist concorrente *m/f* dei quarti di finale

quar·ter·ly ['kwɔːtəlɪ] **1** *adj* trimestrale **2** *adv* trimestralmente

quar·ters ['kwɔːtəz] *npl* MIL quartieri *mpl*

quar·tet [kwɔː'tet] MUS quartetto *m*

quartz [kwɔːts] quarzo *m*

quash [kwɒʃ] *v/t* rebellion reprimere; *court decision* annullare

qua·ver ['kweɪvə(r)] **1** *n in voice* tremolio *m*; MUS croma *f* **2** *v/i of voice* tremolare

quay [kiː] banchina *f*

quay·side banchina *f*

quea·sy ['kwiːzɪ] *adj* nauseato

queen [kwiːn] regina *f*

queen 'bee ape *f* regina

queer [kwɪə(r)] *adj* (*peculiar*) strano

queer·ly ['kwɪəlɪ] *adv* stranamente

quell [kwel] *v/t* soffocare

quench [kwentʃ] *v/t also fig* spegnere

que·ry ['kwɪərɪ] **1** *n* interrogativo *m* **2** *v/t* (*pret & pp* **-ied**) *express doubt about* contestare; *check* controllare

quest [kwest] *n* ricerca *f*

ques·tion ['kwestʃn] **1** *n* domanda *f*; *matter* questione *f*; **in ~** (*being talked about*) in questione; (*in doubt*) in dubbio; **it's a ~ of money / time** è questione di soldi / tempo; **that's out of the ~** è fuori discussione **2** *v/t person* interrogare; (*doubt*) dubitare di; **that's not being ~ed** nessuno lo mette in dubbio

ques·tion·a·ble ['kwestʃnəbl] *adj* discutibile; (*dubious*) dubbio

ques·tion·er ['kwestʃnə(r)] *n* interrogatore *m*, -trice *f*

ques·tion·ing ['kwestʃnɪŋ] **1** *adj look, tone* interrogativo **2** *n* interrogatorio *m*

'ques·tion mark punto *m* interrogativo

'ques·tion mas·ter presentatore *m*, -trice *f* di quiz

ques·tion·naire [kwestʃə'neə(r)] *n* questionario *m*

queue [kjuː] **1** *n* coda *f*, fila *f* **2** *v/i* fare la fila *o* la coda

queue-jump·er ['kjuːdʒʌmpə(r)] persona *f* che non rispetta la coda

quib·ble ['kwɪbl] *v/i* cavillare

quick [kwɪk] *adj person* svelto; *reply, change* veloce; **be ~!** fai presto!, fai in fretta!; **let's have a ~ drink** beviamo qualcosina?; **can I have a ~ look?** posso dare un'occhiatina?; **that was ~!** già fatto?

quick·ie ['kwɪkɪ] F: **have a ~** *quick drink* bere qualcosina

quick·ly ['kwɪklɪ] *adv* rapidamente, in fretta

'quick·sand sabbie *fpl* mobili; **'quick·sil·ver** mercurio *m*; **quick-wit·ted** [kwɪk'wɪtɪd] *adj* sveglio

quid [kwɪd] F sterlina *f*; **50 ~** 50 sterline

qui·et ['kwaɪət] *adj voice, music* basso; *engine* silenzioso; *street, life, town* tranquillo; **keep ~ about sth** tenere segreto qc; **~!** silenzio!, stai zitto!

♦ **quieten down** ['kwaɪətn] **1** *v/t* calmare **2** *v/i* calmarsi

quiet·ly ['kwaɪətlɪ] *adv not loudly* silenziosamente, senza far rumore; (*without fuss*) semplicemente; (*peacefully*) tranquillamente

quiet·ness ['kwaɪətnɪs] *of night, street* tranquillità *f*, calma *f*; *of voice* dolcezza *f*

quilt [kwɪlt] *on bed* piumino *m*

quilt·ed ['kwɪltɪd] *adj* trapuntato

quin·ine ['kwiniːn] chinino *m*

quin·tet [kwɪn'tet] MUS quintetto *m*

quip [kwɪp] **1** *n* battuta *f* (di spirito) **2** *v/i* (*pret & pp* **-ped**) scherzare

quirk [kwɜːk] bizzarria *f*

quirk·y ['kwɜːkɪ] *adj* bizzarro

quit [kwɪt] (*pret & pp* **quit**) **1** *v/t job* mollare F; **~ doing sth** smettere di fare qc **2** *v/i* (*leave job*) licenziarsi;

COMPUT uscire; **get one's notice to ~** *from landlord* ricevere la disdetta

quite [kwaɪt] *adv* (*fairly*) abbastanza; (*completely*) completamente; **not ~ ready** non ancora pronto; **I didn't ~ understand** non ho capito bene; **is that right? – not ~** giusto? – non esattamente; **~!** esatto!; **~ a lot drink**, *change* parecchio; **~ a lot better** molto meglio; **~ a few** un bel po'; **it was ~ a surprise / change** è stata una bella sorpresa / un bel cambiamento

quits [kwɪts] *adj* **be ~ with s.o.** essere pari con qu

quit·ter ['kwɪtə(r)] F rinunciatario *m*, -a *f*

quiv·er ['kwɪvə(r)] *v/i* tremare

quiz [kwɪz] **1** *n* quiz *m inv* **2** *v/t* (*pret & pp* **-zed**) interrogare

'**quiz mas·ter** conduttore *m*, -trice *f* (di gioco a quiz)

'**quiz pro·gram** *Am*, '**quiz pro·gramme** gioco *m* a quiz

quo·ta ['kwəʊtə] quota *f*

quo·ta·tion [kwəʊ'teɪʃn] *from author* citazione *f*; *price* preventivo *m*; **give s.o. a ~ for sth** fare un preventivo a qu per qc

quo·ta·tion marks *npl* virgolette *fpl*

quote [kwəʊt] **1** *n from author* citazione *f*; *price* preventivo *m*; (*quotation mark*) virgoletta *f*; **in ~s** tra virgolette **2** *v/t text* citare; *price* stimare; **~d on the Stock Exchange** quotato in Borsa **3** *v/i*: **~ from an author** citare un autore

R

rab·bi ['ræbaɪ] rabbino *m*

rab·bit ['ræbɪt] coniglio *m*

♦ **rab·bit on** *v/i* P blaterare

rab·ble ['ræbl] marmaglia *f*

rab·ble-rous·er ['ræblraʊzə(r)] agitatore *m*, -trice *f*

ra·bies ['reɪbiːz] *nsg* rabbia *f*, idrofobia *f*

race[1] [reɪs] *n of people* razza *f*

race[2] [reɪs] **1** *n* SP gara *f*; **the ~s** (*horse races*) le corse **2** *v/i* (*run fast*) correre; **he ~d against the world champion** ha gareggiato contro il campione del mondo **3** *v/t*: **I'll ~ you** facciamo una gara

'**race·course** ippodromo *m*; '**race·horse** cavallo *m* da corsa; '**race re·la·tions** *npl* rapporti *mpl* interrazziali; '**race riot** scontri *mpl* razziali; '**race·track** pista *f*; *for horses* ippodromo *m*

ra·cial ['reɪʃl] *adj* razziale; **~ equality** parità *f inv* razziale

rac·ing ['reɪsɪŋ] corse *fpl*

'**rac·ing car** auto *f inv* da corsa

'**rac·ing driv·er** pilota *m* automobilistico

ra·cis·m ['reɪsɪzm] razzismo *m*

ra·cist ['reɪsɪst] **1** *n* razzista *m/f* **2** *adj* razzista

rack [ræk] **1** *n for parking bikes* rastrelliera *f*; *for bags on train* portabagagli *m inv*; *for CDs* porta-CD *m inv* **2** *v/t*: **~ one's brains** scervellarsi

rack·et[1] ['rækɪt] SP racchetta *f*

rack·et[2] ['rækɪt] (*noise*) baccano *m*; *criminal activity* racket *m inv*

ra·dar ['reɪdɑː(r)] radar *m inv*

'**ra·dar screen** schermo *m* radar

'**ra·dar trap** autovelox® *m*

ra·di·al 'tire *Am*, **ra·di·al 'tyre** ['reɪdɪəl] pneumatico *m* radiale

ra·di·ance ['reɪdɪəns] splendore *m*

ra·di·ant ['reɪdɪənt] *adj smile* splendente; *appearance* raggiante

ra·di·ate ['reɪdɪeɪt] *v/i of heat, light* diffondersi

ra·di·a·tion [reɪdɪ'eɪʃn] PHYS radiazione *f*

ra·di·a·tor ['reɪdɪeɪtə(r)] *in room* termosifone *m; in car* radiatore *m*

rad·i·cal ['rædɪkl] **1** *adj* radicale **2** *n* radicale *m/f*

rad·i·cal·ism ['rædɪkəlɪzm] POL radicalismo *m*

rad·i·cal·ly ['rædɪklɪ] *adv* radicalmente

ra·di·o ['reɪdɪəʊ] radio *f inv; on the ~* alla radio; *by ~* via radio

ra·di·o·ac·tive [reɪdɪəʊ'æktɪv] *adj* radioattivo; **ra·di·o·ac·tive 'waste** scorie *fpl* radioattive; **ra·di·o·ac·tiv·i·ty** [reɪdɪəʊæk'tɪvətɪ] radioattività *f inv*; **ra·di·o a'larm** radiosveglia *f*

ra·di·og·ra·pher [reɪdɪ'ɒɡrəfə(r)] radiologo *m, -a f*

ra·di·og·ra·phy [reɪdɪ'ɒɡrəfɪ] radiografia *f*

ra·di·o sta·tion stazione *f* radiofonica, radio *f inv*; **'ra·di·o tax·i** radiotaxi *m inv*; **ra·di·o'ther·a·py** radioterapia *f*

rad·ish ['rædɪʃ] ravanello *m*

ra·di·us ['reɪdɪəs] raggio *m*

raf·fle ['ræfl] *n* lotteria *f*

raft [rɑːft] zattera *f*

'raf·ter ['rɑːftə(r)] travicello *m*

rag [ræɡ] *n for cleaning etc* straccio *m*; *dressed in ~s* vestito di stracci

rage [reɪdʒ] **1** *n* rabbia *f*, collera *f*; *be in a ~* essere furioso; *be all the ~* F essere di moda **2** *v/i of person* infierire; *of storm* infuriare

'rag·ged ['ræɡɪd] *adj* stracciato

raid [reɪd] **1** *n* raid *m inv* **2** *v/t of police, robbers* fare un raid in; *fridge, orchard* fare razzia in

'raid·er ['reɪdə(r)] *on bank etc* rapinatore *m, -trice f*

rail [reɪl] *n on track* rotaia *f*; *(hand~)* corrimano *m*; *(barrier)* parapetto *m*; *curtain ~* bastone *m* per tende; *towel ~* portasciugamano *m inv*; *by ~* in treno

'rail·ings ['reɪlɪŋz] *npl around park*

etc inferriata *f*

'rail·road *etc Am* → **railway** *etc*

rail·way ['reɪlweɪ] ferrovia *f*

'rail·way line linea *f* ferroviaria

'rail·way sta·tion stazione *f* ferroviaria

rain [reɪn] **1** *n* pioggia *f*; *in the ~* sotto la pioggia **2** *v/i* piovere; *it's ~ing* sta piovendo

'rain·bow arcobaleno *m*; **'rain·coat** impermeabile *m*; **'rain·drop** goccia *f* di pioggia; **'rain·fall** piovosità *f inv*; **'rain for·est** foresta *f* pluviale; **'rain·proof** *adj fabric* impermeabile; **'rain·storm** temporale *m*

rain·y ['reɪnɪ] *adj day* di pioggia; *weather* piovoso; *it's ~* piove molto

raise [reɪz] **1** *n esp Am: in salary* aumento *m* **2** *v/t shelf, question* sollevare; *offer* aumentare; *children* allevare; *money* raccogliere

rai·sin ['reɪzn] uva *f* passa

rake [reɪk] *n for garden* rastrello *m*

♦ **rake up** *v/t leaves* rastrellare; *fig* rivangare

ral·ly ['rælɪ] *n meeting* raduno *m*; MOT rally *m inv; in tennis* scambio *m*

♦ **rally round** (*pret & pp -ied*) **1** *v/i* offrire aiuto **2** *v/t*: *rally round s.o.* aiutare qu

RAM [ræm] *abbr* COMPUT (= *random access memory*) RAM *f inv*

ram [ræm] **1** *n* montone *m* **2** *v/t* (*pret & pp -med*) *ship, car* sbattere contro

ram·ble ['ræmbl] **1** *n walk* escursione *f* **2** *v/i walk* fare passeggiate; *in speaking* divagare; *talk incoherently* vaneggiare

ram·bler ['ræmblə(r)] *walker* escursionista *m/f*

ram·bling ['ræmblɪŋ] *adj speech* sconnesso

ramp [ræmp] rampa *f*; *for raising vehicle* ponte *m* idraulico

ram·page ['ræmpeɪdʒ] **1** *v/i* scatenarsi **2** *n*: *go on the ~* scatenarsi

ram·pant ['ræmpənt] *adj inflation* dilagante

ram·part ['ræmpɑːt] bastione *m*

R

ram·shack·le ['ræmʃækl] *adj* sgangherato

ran [ræn] *pret* → **run**

ranch [rɑːntʃ] ranch *m inv*

ran·cid ['rænsɪd] *adj* rancido

ran·cour ['ræŋkə(r)] rancore *m*

R&D [ɑːrən'diː] *abbr* (= **research and development**) ricerca *f* e sviluppo *m*

ran·dom ['rændəm] **1** *adj* casuale; **~ sample** campione *m* casuale; **take a ~ sample** prendere un campione a caso **2** *n*: **at ~** a caso

ran·dy ['rændɪ] *adj* F arrapato F

rang [ræŋ] *pret* → **ring**

range [reɪndʒ] **1** *n of products* gamma *f*; *of missile, gun* gittata *f*; *of salary* scala *f*; *of voice* estensione *f*; *of mountains* catena *f*; *(shooting ~)* poligono *m* (di tiro); **at close ~** a distanza ravvicinata **2** *v/i*: **~ from X to Y** variare da X a Y

rank [ræŋk] **1** *n* MIL grado *m*; *in society* rango *m*; **the ~s** MIL la truppa **2** *v/t* classificare

♦ **rank among** *v/t* classificarsi tra

ran·kle ['ræŋkl] *v/i* bruciare

ran·sack ['rænsæk] *v/t* saccheggiare

ran·som ['rænsəm] *n* riscatto *m*; **hold s.o. to ~** tenere in ostaggio qu

'ran·som mon·ey (soldi *mpl* del) riscatto *m*

rant [rænt] *v/i*: **~ and rave** inveire

rap [ræp] **1** *n at door etc* colpo *m*; MUS rap *m inv* **2** *v/t* (*pret & pp* **-ped**) *table* etc battere

♦ **rap at** *v/t window* etc bussare a

rape[1] [reɪp] **1** *n* stupro *m* **2** *v/t* violentare

rape[2] [reɪp] *n* BOT colza *f*

'rape vic·tim vittima *f* stupro

rap·id ['ræpɪd] *adj* rapido

ra·pid·i·ty [rə'pɪdətɪ] rapidità *f inv*

rap·id·ly ['ræpɪdlɪ] *adv* rapidamente

rap·ids ['ræpɪdz] *npl* rapide *fpl*

rap·ist ['reɪpɪst] violentatore *m*

rap·port [ræ'pɔː(r)] rapporto *m*

rap·ture ['ræptʃə(r)] *n*: **go into ~s over** andare in estasi per

rap·tur·ous ['ræptʃərəs] *adj* entusiastico

rare [reə(r)] *adj* raro; *steak* al sangue

rare·ly ['reəlɪ] *adv* raramente

rar·i·ty ['reərətɪ] rarità *f inv*

ras·cal ['rɑːskl] birbante *m/f*

rash[1] [ræʃ] *n* MED orticaria *f*

rash[2] [ræʃ] *adj* action, behaviour avventato

rash·er ['ræʃə(r)] fettina *f*

rash·ly ['ræʃlɪ] *adv* avventatamente

rasp·ber·ry ['rɑːzbərɪ] lampone *m*

rat [ræt] *n* ratto *m*

rate [reɪt] **1** *n of exchange* tasso *m*; *of pay, pricing* tariffa *f*; *(speed)* ritmo *m*; **~ of interest** FIN tasso *m* d'interesse; **at this ~** (at this speed) di questo passo; **at any ~** in ogni modo **2** *v/t (consider, rank)* reputare

rather ['rɑːðə(r)] *adv* piuttosto; **I would ~ stay here** preferirei stare qui; **or would you ~ ...?** o preferiresti ...?

rat·i·fi·ca·tion [rætɪfɪ'keɪʃn] ratifica *f*

rat·i·fy ['rætɪfaɪ] *v/t* (*pret & pp* **-ied**) ratificare

rat·ings ['reɪtɪŋz] *npl* indice *m* d'ascolto

ra·ti·o ['reɪʃɪəʊ] proporzione *f*

ra·tion ['ræʃn] **1** *n* razione *f* **2** *v/t* supplies razionare

ra·tion·al ['ræʃənl] *adj* razionale

ra·tion·al·i·ty [ræʃə'nælɪtɪ] razionalità *f inv*

ra·tion·al·i·za·tion [ræʃənəlaɪ'zeɪʃn] razionalizzazione *f*

ra·tion·al·ize ['ræʃənəlaɪz] *v/t & v/i* razionalizzare

ra·tion·al·ly ['ræʃənlɪ] *adv* razionalmente

'rat race corsa *f* al successo

rat·tle ['rætl] **1** *n noise* rumore *m*; *toy* sonaglio *m* **2** *v/t* scuotere **3** *v/i* far rumore

♦ **rattle off** *v/t poem, list of names* snocciolare

♦ **rattle through** *v/t* fare di gran carriera

'rat·tle·snake serpente *m* a sonagli

rau·cous ['rɔːkəs] *adj* sguaiato

rav·age ['rævɪdʒ] **1** *n*: **the ~s of time** le ingiurie del tempo **2** *v/t*: **~d by**

war devastato dalla guerra

a·ve [reɪv] **1** v/i delirare; **~ about sth** be very enthusiastic entusiasmarsi per qc **2** n party rave m inv

'a·ven [reɪvn] corvo m

av·e·nous ['rævənəs] adj famelico

av·e·nous·ly ['rævənəslɪ] adv voracemente

ave re'view recensione f entusiastica

a·vine [rə'viːn] burrone m

av·ing ['reɪvɪŋ] adv: ~ **mad** matto da legare

a·vi·o·li ['rævɪəʊlɪ] nsg ravioli mpl

av·ish·ing ['rævɪʃɪŋ] adj incantevole

aw [rɔː] adj meat, vegetable crudo; sugar, iron grezzo

ay ma'te·ri·al materia f prima

ay [reɪ] raggio m; **a ~ of hope** un raggio di speranza

aze [reɪz] v/t: ~ **to the ground** radere al suolo

a·zor ['reɪzə(r)] rasoio m

ra·zor blade lametta f da barba

e [riː] prep COM con riferimento a

each [riːtʃ] **1** n: **within ~** vicino (**of** a); within arm's reach a portata (di mano); **out of ~** non a portata (**of** di); **keep out of ~ children** tenere lontano dalla portata dei bambini **2** v/t city etc arrivare a; decision, agreement, conclusion raggiungere; **can you ~ it?** ci arrivi?

reach out v/i allungare la mano

e·act [rɪ'ækt] v/i reagire

e·ac·tion [rɪ'ækʃn] reazione f

e·ac·tion·ar·y [rɪ'ækʃnrɪ] **1** n POL reazionario m, -a f **2** adj POL reazionario

e·ac·tor [rɪ'æktə(r)] nuclear reattore m

ead [riːd] (pret & pp read [red]) **1** v/i leggere; ~ **to s.o.** leggere a qu **2** v/t leggere; (study) studiare

read out v/t aloud leggere a voce alta

read up on v/t documentarsi su

ea·da·ble ['riːdəbl] adj handwriting leggibile; book di piacevole lettura

read·er ['riːdə(r)] person lettore m, -trice f

read·i·ly ['redɪlɪ] adv (willingly) volentieri; (easily) facilmente

read·i·ness ['redɪnɪs] for action disponibilità f inv; to agree prontezza f

read·ing ['riːdɪŋ] also from meter lettura f

'read·ing mat·ter roba f da leggere

re·ad·just [riːə'dʒʌst] **1** v/t equipment, controls regolare **2** v/i to conditions riadattarsi

read-'on·ly file COMPUT file m inv di sola lettura

read-'on·ly mem·o·ry COMPUT memoria f di sola lettura

read·y ['redɪ] adj pronto; **get (o.s.) ~** prepararsi; **get sth ~** preparare qc

read·y 'cash contanti mpl; **read·y-made** adj stew etc precotto; solution bell'e pronto; **read·y-to-wear** adj confezionato

real [riːl] adj vero

'real es·tate proprietà fpl immobiliari

re·a·lis·m ['rɪəlɪzm] realismo m

re·a·list ['rɪəlɪst] realista m/f

re·a·lis·tic [rɪə'lɪstɪk] adj realistico

re·a·lis·tic·al·ly [rɪə'lɪstɪklɪ] adv realisticamente

re·al·i·ty [rɪ'ælətɪ] realtà f inv

re·a·li·za·tion [rɪəlaɪ'zeɪʃn] realizzazione f

re·a·lize ['rɪəlaɪz] v/t rendersi conto di, realizzare; FIN realizzare; **I ~ now that ...** ora capisco che ...

real·ly ['rɪəlɪ] adv veramente; **~?** davvero?; **not ~** (not much) non proprio

real 'time n COMPUT tempo m reale

real-time adj COMPUT in tempo reale

reap [riːp] v/t mietere

re·ap·pear [riːə'pɪə(r)] v/i riapparire

reappearance [riːə'pɪərəns] ricomparsa f

rear [rɪə(r)] **1** n of building retro m; of train parte f posteriore **2** adj posteriore

rear 'end F of person posteriore m

rear-'end v/t: **be ~ed** F essere tamponato

rear 'light *of car* fanalino *m* posteriore

re·arm [ri:'ɑ:m] **1** *v/t* riarmare **2** *v/i* riarmarsi

'rear·most *adj* ultimo

re·ar·range [ri:ə'reɪnʒ] *v/t furniture* spostare; *schedule, meetings* cambiare

rear-view 'mir·ror specchietto *m* retrovisore

rea·son ['ri:zn] **1** *n faculty* ragione *f*; *(cause)* motivo *m*; **see / listen to ~** ascoltare ragione **2** *v/i*: **~ with s.o.** far ragionare con qu

rea·so·na·ble ['ri:znəbl] *adj person, price* ragionevole; *weather, health* discreto; **a ~ number of people** un discreto numero di persone

rea·so·na·bly ['ri:znəblɪ] *adv act, behave* ragionevolmente; *(quite)* abbastanza

rea·son·ing ['ri:znɪŋ] ragionamento *m*

re·as·sure [ri:ə'ʃʊə(r)] *v/t* rassicurare

re·as·sur·ing [ri:ə'ʃʊərɪŋ] *adj* rassicurante

re·bate ['ri:beɪt] *money back* rimborso *m*

reb·el ['rebl] **1** *n* ribelle *m/f*; **~ forces** forze *fpl* ribelli **2** *v/i* [rɪ'bel] *(pret & pp -led)* ribellarsi

reb·el·lion [rɪ'beljən] ribellione *f*

reb·el·lious [rɪ'beljəs] *adj* ribelle

reb·el·lious·ly [rɪ'beljəslɪ] *adv* con atteggiamento ribelle

reb·el·lious·ness [rɪ'beljəsnɪs] spirito *m* di ribellione

re·bound [rɪ'baʊnd] *v/i of ball etc* rimbalzare

re·buff [rɪ'bʌf] *n* secco rifiuto *m*

re·build ['ri:bɪld] *v/t (pret & pp -built)* ricostruire

re·buke [rɪ'bju:k] *v/t* rimproverare

re·call [rɪ'kɔ:l] *v/t* richiamare; *(remember)* ricordare

re·cap ['ri:kæp] *v/i (pret & pp -ped)* F ricapitolare

re·cap·ture [ri:'kæptʃə(r)] *v/t criminal* ricatturare; *town* riconquistare

re·cede [rɪ'si:d] *v/i of flood*

waters abbassarsi

re·ced·ing [rɪ'si:dɪŋ] *adj forehead, chin* sfuggente; **have a ~ hairline** essere stempiato

re·ceipt [rɪ'si:t] *for purchase* ricevuta *f*, scontrino *m*; **acknowledge ~ of sth** accusare ricevuta di qc; **~s** FIN introiti *mpl*

re·ceive [rɪ'si:v] *v/t* ricevere

re·ceiv·er [rɪ'si:və(r)] *of letter* destinatario *m*, -a *f*; TELEC ricevitore *m*; *for radio* apparecchio *m* ricevente

re·ceiv·er·ship [rɪ'si:vəʃɪp]: **be in ~** essere in amministrazione controllata

re·cent ['ri:snt] *adj* recente

re·cent·ly ['ri:sntlɪ] *adv* recentemente

re·cep·tion [rɪ'sepʃn] *in hotel, company* reception *f inv*; *formal party* ricevimento *m*; *(welcome)* accoglienza *f*; *on radio, mobile phone* ricezione *f*

re'cep·tion desk banco *m* della reception

re·cep·tion·ist [rɪ'sepʃnɪst] receptionist *m/f inv*

re·cep·tive [rɪ'septɪv] *adj*: **be ~ to sth** essere ricettivo verso qc

re·cess ['ri:ses] *in wall etc* rientranza *f*; *of parliament* vacanza *f*

re·ces·sion [rɪ'seʃn] *economic* recessione *f*

re·charge [ri:'tʃɑ:dʒ] *v/t battery* ricaricare

re·ci·pe ['resəpɪ] ricetta *f*

're·ci·pe book ricettario *m*

re·cip·i·ent [rɪ'sɪpɪənt] destinatario *m*, -a *f*

re·cip·ro·cal [rɪ'sɪprəkl] *adj* reciproco

re·cit·al [rɪ'saɪtl] MUS recital *m inv*

re·cite [rɪ'saɪt] *v/t poem* recitare; *details, facts* enumerare

reck·less ['reklɪs] *adj* spericolato

reck·less·ly ['reklɪslɪ] *adv behave, drive* in modo spericolato; *spend* avventatamente

reck·on ['rekən] *v/i (think, consider)* pensare

♦ **reckon on** v/t contare su

♦ **reckon with** v/t: **have s.o. / sth to reakon with** dover fare i conti con qu / qc

reck·on·ing ['rekənɪŋ] calcoli mpl

re·claim [rɪ'kleɪm] v/t land bonificare

re·cline [rɪ'klaɪn] v/i sdraiarsi

re·clin·er [rɪ'klaɪnə(r)] chair poltrona f reclinabile

re·cluse [rɪ'kluːs] eremita m/f

rec·og·ni·tion [rekəg'nɪʃn] of state, s.o.'s achievements riconoscimento m; **have changed beyond ~** essere irriconoscibile

rec·og·niz·a·ble [rekəg'naɪzəbl] adj riconoscibile

rec·og·nize ['rekəgnaɪz] v/t riconoscere; **it can be ~d by ...** si riconosce da ...

re·coil [rɪ'kɔɪl] v/i indietreggiare

ec·ol·lect [rekə'lekt] v/t rammentare

rec·ol·lec·tion [rekə'lekʃn] ricordo m

rec·om·mend [rekə'mend] v/t consigliare

rec·om·men·da·tion [rekəmen'deɪʃn] consiglio m

rec·om·pense ['rekəmpens] n fml ricompensa f; LAW risarcimento m

rec·on·cile ['rekənsaɪl] v/t people, differences riconciliare; facts conciliare; **~ o.s. to ...** rassegnarsi a ...; **they are now ~d** si sono riconciliati

ec·on·cil·i·a·tion [rekənsɪlɪ'eɪʃn] of people, differences riconciliazione f; of facts conciliazione f

e·con·di·tion [riːkən'dɪʃn] v/t ricondizionare

e·con·nais·sance [rɪ'kɒnɪsns] MIL ricognizione f

e·con·sid·er [riːkən'sɪdə(r)] **1** v/t offer, one's position riconsiderare **2** v/i ripensare

e·con·struct [riːkən'strʌkt] v/t city, crime, life ricostruire

ec·ord¹ ['rekɔːd] n MUS disco m; SP etc record m inv, primato m; written document etc nota f; in database record m inv; **~s** archivio m; **say sth off the ~** dire qc ufficiosamente;

have a criminal **~** avere precedenti penali; **he has a good ~ for punctuality / reliability** è sempre stato puntuale / affidabile

record² [rɪ'kɔːd] v/t electronically registrare; in writing annotare

'rec·ord-break·ing adj da record

re·cor·der [rɪ'kɔːdə(r)] MUS flauto m dolce

'rec·ord hold·er primatista m/f

re·cord·ing [rɪ'kɔːdɪŋ] registrazione f

re'cord·ing stu·di·o sala f di registrazione

re·cord play·er ['rekɔːd] giradischi m inv

re·count [rɪ'kaʊnt] v/t (tell) raccontare

re·count ['riːkaʊnt] **1** n of votes nuovo conteggio m **2** v/t (count again) ricontare

re·coup [rɪ'kuːp] v/t financial losses rifarsi di

re·cov·er [rɪ'kʌvə(r)] **1** v/t stolen goods recuperare **2** v/i from illness rimettersi

re·cov·er·y [rɪ'kʌvərɪ] of stolen goods recupero m; from illness guarigione f; **he has made a speedy ~** è guarito in fretta

rec·re·a·tion [rekrɪ'eɪʃn] ricreazione f

rec·re·a·tion·al [rekrɪ'eɪʃnl] adj done for pleasure ricreativo

re·cruit [rɪ'kruːt] **1** n MIL recluta f; to company neoassunto m, -a f **2** v/t new staff assumere; members arruolare

re·cruit·ment [rɪ'kruːtmənt] assunzione f; MIL, POL reclutamento m

re'cruit·ment drive campagna f di arruolamento

rec·tan·gle ['rektæŋgl] rettangolo m

rec·tan·gu·lar [rek'tæŋgjʊlə(r)] adj rettangolare

rec·ti·fy ['rektɪfaɪ] v/t (pret & pp -ied) (put right) rettificare

re·cu·pe·rate [rɪ'kjuːpəreɪt] v/i recuperare

re·cur [rɪ'kɜː(r)] (pret & pp -red) v/i

R

of error, *event* ripetersi; *of symptoms* ripresentarsi

re·cur·rent [rɪ'kʌrənt] *adj* ricorrente

re·cy·cla·ble [ri:'saɪkləbl] *adj* riciclabile

re·cy·cle [ri:'saɪkl] *v/t* riciclare

re·cy·cling [ri:'saɪklɪŋ] riciclo *m*

red [red] *adj* rosso; **in the ~** FIN in rosso

Red 'Cross Croce *f* Rossa

red·den ['redn] *v/i* (*blush*) arrossire

re·dec·o·rate [ri:'dekəreɪt] *v/t* ritinteggiare; *change wallpaper* ritappezzare

re·deem [rɪ'di:m] *v/t* *debt* estinguere; *sinners* redimere

re·deem·ing [rɪ'di:mɪŋ]: **~ feature** aspetto *m* positivo

re·demp·tion [rɪ'dempʃn] REL redenzione *f*

re·de·vel·op [ri:dɪ'veləp] *v/t* *part of town* risanare

red-hand·ed [red'hændɪd] *adj*: **catch s.o. ~** cogliere qu in flagrante; **'red·head** rosso *m*, -a *f*; **red·'hot** *adj* rovente; **red·'let·ter day** giorno *m* memorabile; **red 'light** *at traffic lights* rosso *m*; **red 'light dis·trict** quartiere *m* a luci rosse; **red 'meat** carni *fpl* rosse

re·dou·ble [ri:'dʌbl] *v/t*: **~ one's efforts** intensificare gli sforzi

red 'pep·per peperone *m* rosso

red 'tape F burocrazia *f*

re·duce [rɪ'dju:s] *v/t* ridurre

re·duc·tion [rɪ'dʌkʃn] riduzione *f*

re·dun·dan·cy [rɪ'dʌndənsɪ] *Br at work* licenziamento *m*

re'dun·dan·cy no·tice *Br* avviso *m* di licenziamento

re·'dun·dan·cy pay·ment *Br* indennità *f inv* di licenziamento

re·dun·dant [rɪ'dʌndənt] *adj* (*unnecessary*) superfluo; *Br* **be made ~ at work** essere licenziato; *Br* **make s.o. ~** licenziare qu

reed [ri:d] BOT canna *f*

reef [ri:f] *in sea* scogliera *f*

'reef knot nodo *m* piano

reek [ri:k] *v/i* puzzare; **~ of ...** puzzare di ...

reel [ri:l] *n of film* rullino *m*; *of thread* rocchetto *m*; *of tape* bobina *f*; *of fishing line* mulinello *m*

♦ **reel off** *v/t* snocciolare

re·e'lect *v/t* rieleggere

re·e'lec·tion rielezione *f*

re·'entry *of spacecraft* rientro *m*

ref [ref] F arbitro *m*

re·fer [rɪ'fɜ:(r)] **1** *v/t* (*pret & pp -red*): **~ a decision / problem to s.o.** rinviare una decisione / un problema a qu **2** *v/i*: **~ to ...** (*allude to*) riferirsi a ...; *dictionary etc* consultare ...

ref·er·ee [refə'ri:] SP arbitro *m*; *for job* referenza *f*

ref·er·ence ['refərəns] (*allusion*) allusione *f*; *for job* referenza *f*; (**~ number**) (numero *m* di) riferimento *m*; **with ~ to** con riferimento a

'ref·er·ence book opera *f* di consultazione; **'ref·er·ence li·bra·ry** biblioteca *f* di consultazione; **'ref·er·ence num·ber** numero *m* di riferimento

ref·e·ren·dum [refə'rendəm] referendum *m inv*

re·fill ['ri:fɪl] *v/t* *glass* riempire

re·fine [rɪ'faɪn] *v/t* raffinare

re·fined [rɪ'faɪnd] *adj* *manners, language* raffinato

re·fine·ment [rɪ'faɪnmənt] *to process, machine* miglioramento *m*

re·fin·e·ry [rɪ'faɪnərɪ] raffineria *f*

re·fla·tion ['ri:fleɪʃn] reflazione *f*

re·flect [rɪ'flekt] **1** *v/t light* riflettere; **be ~ed in ...** riflettersi in ... **2** *v/i* (*think*) riflettere

re·flec·tion [rɪ'flekʃn] *in water, glass etc* riflesso *m*; (*consideration*) riflessione *f*; **on ~** dopo averci riflettuto

re·flex ['ri:fleks] *in body* riflesso *m*

re·flex re'ac·tion riflesso *m*

re·form [rɪ'fɔ:m] **1** *n* riforma *f* **2** *v/t* riformare

re·form·er [rɪ'fɔ:mə(r)] riformatore *m*, -trice *f*

re·frain[1] [rɪ'freɪn] *v/i fml*: **please ~ from smoking** si prega di non fumare re·frain² [rɪ'freɪn] *n in song* ritornello *m*

re·fresh [rɪ'freʃ] *v/t person* ristorare; **feel ~ed** sentirsi ristorato

refresh·er course [rɪ'freʃə(r)] corso *m* di aggiornamento

re·fresh·ing [rɪ'freʃɪŋ] *adj drink* rinfrescante; *experience* piacevole

re·fresh·ments [rɪ'freʃmənts] *npl* rinfreschi *mpl*

re·fri·ge·rate [rɪ'frɪdʒəreɪt] *v/t*: **keep ~d** conservare in frigo

re·fri·ge·ra·tor [rɪ'frɪdʒəreɪtə(r)] frigorifero *m*

re·fu·el [riː'fjuːəl] **1** *v/t aeroplane* rifornire di carburante **2** *v/i of aeroplane, car* fare rifornimento

ref·uge ['refjuːdʒ] rifugio *m*; **take ~ from storm etc** ripararsi

ref·u·gee [refjʊ'dʒiː] rifugiato *m*, -a *f*, profugo *m*, -a *f*

refu·gee camp campo *m* profughi

re·fund ['riːfʌnd] **1** *n* rimborso *m* **2** *v/t* [rɪ'fʌnd] rimborsare

re·fus·al [rɪ'fjuːzl] rifiuto *m*

re·fuse¹ [rɪ'fjuːz] *v/t & v/i* rifiutare; **~ to do sth** rifiutare di fare qc

ref·use² ['refjuːs] (*garbage*) rifiuti *mpl*

'ref·use col·lec·tion raccolta *f* dei rifiuti

'ref·use dump discarica *f* (dei rifiuti)

re·fute [rɪ'fjuːt] *v/t* confutare

re·gain [rɪ'geɪn] *v/t control, lost territory, the lead* riconquistare

re·gal ['riːgl] *adj* regale

re·gard [rɪ'gɑːd] **1** *n*: **have great ~ for s.o.** avere molta stima di qu; **in this ~** a questo riguardo; **with ~ to** riguardo a; (*kind*) **~s** cordiali saluti; **give my ~s to Paola** saluti a Paola; **with no ~ for …** senza alcun riguardo per … **2** *v/t*: **~ s.o. / sth as sth** considerare qu / qc come qc; **as ~s …** riguardo a …

re·gard·ing [rɪ'gɑːdɪŋ] *prep* riguardo a

re·gard·less [rɪ'gɑːdlɪs] *adv* lo stesso; **~ of** senza tener conto di

re·gime [reɪ'ʒiːm] (*government*) regime *m*

re·gi·ment ['redʒɪmənt] *n* reggimento *m*

re·gion ['riːdʒən] regione *f*; **in the ~ of** intorno a

re·gion·al ['riːdʒənl] *adj* regionale

re·gis·ter ['redʒɪstə(r)] **1** *n* registro *m* **2** *v/t birth, death*: *by individual* denunciare; *by authorities* registrare; *vehicle* iscrivere; *letter* assicurare; *emotion* mostrare; **send a letter ~ed** spedire una lettera assicurata **3** *v/i at university* iscriversi; **I'm ~ed with Dr Lee** il mio medico è il dottor Lee

re·gis·tered let·ter ['redʒɪstəd] (lettera *f*) assicurata *f*

reg·is·trar [redʒɪ'strɑː(r)] *of births etc* ufficiale *m* di stato civile

re·gis·tra·tion [redʒɪ'streɪʃn] *Br* (*vehicle number*) numero *m* di targa; *at university* iscrizione *f*

re·gis·tra·tion num·ber *Br* MOT numero *m* di targa

re·gis·try of·fice ['redʒɪstrɪ] ufficio *m* di stato civile

re·gret [rɪ'gret] **1** *v/t* (*pret & pp ~ted*) rammaricarsi di; *missed opportunity* rimpiangere; **we ~ to inform you that …** siamo spiacenti di informarla che … **2** *n* rammarico *m*

re·gret·ful [rɪ'gretfəl] *adj* di rammarico

re·gret·ful·ly [rɪ'gretfəlɪ] *adv* con rammarico

re·gret·ta·ble [rɪ'gretəbl] *adj* deplorevole

re·gret·ta·bly [rɪ'gretəblɪ] *adv* purtroppo

reg·u·lar ['regjʊlə(r)] **1** *adj* regolare; (*esp Am: ordinary*) normale **2** *n at bar etc* cliente *m/f* abituale

reg·u·lar·i·ty [regjʊ'lærətɪ] regolarità *f inv*

reg·u·lar·ly ['regjʊləlɪ] *adv* regolarmente

reg·u·late ['regʊleɪt] *v/t* regolare

reg·u·la·tion [regʊ'leɪʃn] (*rule*) regolamento *m*; *control* controllo *m*

re·hab ['riːhæb] *F* riabilitazione *f*

re·ha·bil·i·tate [riːhə'bɪlɪteɪt] *v/t ex-criminal* riabilitare

re·hears·al [rɪ'hɜːsl] prova f
re·hearse [rɪ'hɜːs] v/t & v/i provare
reign [reɪn] **1** n regno m **2** v/i regnare
re·im·burse [riːɪm'bɜːs] v/t rimborsare
rein [reɪn] redine f
re·in·car·na·tion [riːɪnkɑː'neɪʃn] reincarnazione f
re·in·force [riːɪn'fɔːs] v/t rinforzare
re·in·forced con·crete [riːɪn'fɔːst] cemento m armato
re·in·force·ments [riːɪn'fɔːsmənts] npl MIL rinforzi mpl
re·in·state [riːɪn'steɪt] v/t reintegrare
re·it·e·rate [riː'ɪtəreɪt] v/t fml ripetere
re·ject [rɪ'dʒekt] v/t respingere
re·jec·tion [rɪ'dʒekʃn] rifiuto m
re·lapse ['riːlæps] n MED ricaduta f; **have a ~** avere una ricaduta
re·late [rɪ'leɪt] **1** v/t story raccontare; **~ sth to** collegare qc a qc **2** v/i: **~ to ...** be connected with riferirsi a ...; **he doesn't ~ to people** non sa stabilire un rapporto con gli altri
re·lat·ed [rɪ'leɪtɪd] adj by family imparentato; events, ideas etc collegato
re·la·tion [rɪ'leɪʃn] in family parente m/f; (connection) rapporto m; **business / diplomatic ~s** rapporti d'affari / diplomatici
re·la·tion·ship [rɪ'leɪʃnʃɪp] rapporto m
rel·a·tive ['relətɪv] **1** n parente m/f **2** adj relativo; **X is ~ to Y** X è legato a Y
rel·a·tive·ly ['relətɪvlɪ] adv relativamente
re·lax [rɪ'læks] **1** v/i rilassarsi; **~!, don't get angry** rilassati! non te la prendere **2** v/t rilassare
re·lax·a·tion [riːlæk'seɪʃn] relax m inv; of rules etc rilassamento m
re·laxed [rɪ'lækst] adj rilassato
re·lax·ing [rɪ'læksɪŋ] adj rilassante
re·lay [riː'leɪ] **1** v/t trasmettere **2** n: **~ (race)** (corsa f a) staffetta f
re·lease [rɪ'liːs] **1** n from prison rilascio m; of CD etc uscita f; of software versione f; **this film is a new ~** è un

film appena uscito **2** v/t prisoner rilasciare; handbrake togliere; film, record far uscire; information rendere noto
rel·e·gate ['relɪgeɪt] v/t relegare; **be ~d** SP essere retrocesso
rel·e·ga·tion [relɪ'geɪʃn] SP retrocessione f
re·lent [rɪ'lent] v/i cedere
re·lent·less [rɪ'lentlɪs] adj incessante, implacabile
re·lent·less·ly [rɪ'lentlɪslɪ] adv incessantemente
rel·e·vance ['reləvəns] pertinenza f
rel·e·vant ['reləvənt] adj pertinente
re·li·a·bil·i·ty [rɪlaɪə'bɪlətɪ] affidabilità f inv
re·li·a·ble [rɪ'laɪəbl] adj affidabile
re·li·a·bly [rɪ'laɪəblɪ] adv: **I am ~ informed that ...** so da fonte certa che ...
re·li·ance [rɪ'laɪəns] dipendenza f; **~ on s.o. / sth** dipendenza da qu / qc
re·li·ant [rɪ'laɪənt] adj: **be ~ on** dipendere da
rel·ic ['relɪk] reliquia f
re·lief [rɪ'liːf] sollievo m; **that's a ~** che sollievo; **in ~ in art** in rilievo
re·lieve [rɪ'liːv] v/t pressure, pain alleviare; (take over from) dare il cambio a; **be ~d** at news etc essere sollevato
re·li·gion [rɪ'lɪdʒən] religione f
re·li·gious [rɪ'lɪdʒəs] adj religioso
re·li·gious·ly [rɪ'lɪdʒəslɪ] adv (conscientiously) religiosamente
re·lin·quish [rɪ'lɪŋkwɪʃ] v/t rinunciare a
rel·ish ['relɪʃ] **1** n sauce salsa f; (enjoyment) gusto m **2** v/t idea, prospect gradire
re·live [riː'lɪv] v/t rivivere
re·lo·cate [riːlə'keɪt] v/i of business, employee trasferirsi
re·lo·ca·tion [riːlə'keɪʃn] of business, employee trasferimento m
re·luc·tance [rɪ'lʌktəns] riluttanza f
re·luc·tant [rɪ'lʌktənt] adj riluttante; **be ~ to do sth** essere restio a fare qc
re·luc·tant·ly [rɪ'lʌktəntlɪ] adv a malincuore

R

♦ **re·ly on** [rɪ'laɪ] v/t (pret & pp **-ied**) contare su; **rely on s.o. to do sth** contare su qu perché faccia qc

re·main [rɪ'meɪn] v/i rimanere

re·main·der [rɪ'meɪndə(r)] **1** n also MATH resto m **2** v/t svendere

re·main·ing [rɪ'meɪnɪŋ] adj restante

re·mains [rɪ'meɪnz] npl of body resti mpl

re·make ['riːmeɪk] n of film remake m inv

re·mand [rɪ'mɑːnd] **1** v/t: ~ **s.o. in custody** ordinare la custodia cautelare di qu **2** n: **be on** ~ essere in attesa di giudizio

re·mark [rɪ'mɑːk] **1** n commento m **2** v/t osservare

re·mar·ka·ble [rɪ'mɑːkəbl] adj notevole

♦ **re·mark·a·bly** [rɪ'mɑːkəblɪ] adv notevolmente

♦ **re·mar·ry** [riː'mærɪ] v/i (pret & pp **-ied**) risposarsi

rem·e·dy ['remədɪ] n rimedio m

♦ **re·mem·ber** [rɪ'membə(r)] **1** v/t ricordare; ~ **to lock the door** ricordati di chiudere la porta a chiave; ~ **me to her** dalle i miei saluti **2** v/i ricordare, ricordarsi

Re·mem·brance Day [rɪ'membrəns] 11 novembre, commemorazione f dei caduti in guerra

♦ **re·mind** [rɪ'maɪnd] v/t: ~ **s.o. of s.o. / sth** ricordare qu/qc a qu

re·mind·er [rɪ'maɪndə(r)] promemoria m; COM: for payment sollecito m

♦ **rem·i·nisce** [remɪ'nɪs] v/i rievocare il passato

rem·i·nis·cent [remɪ'nɪsənt] adj: **be ~ of sth** far venire in mente qc

re·miss [rɪ'mɪs] adj fml negligente

re·mis·sion [rɪ'mɪʃn] remissione f

rem·nant ['remnənt] resto m; of fabric scampolo m

re·morse [rɪ'mɔːs] rimorso m

re·morse·less [rɪ'mɔːslɪs] adj spietato

re·mote [rɪ'məʊt] adj village isolato; possibility, connection remoto; (aloof) distante; ancestor lontano

re·mote 'ac·cess COMPUT accesso m remoto

re·mote con'trol telecomando m

re·mote·ly [rɪ'məʊtlɪ] adv related, connected lontanamente; **just ~ possible** vagamente possibile

re·mote·ness [rɪ'məʊtnəs] isolamento m

re·mov·a·ble [rɪ'muːvəbl] adj staccabile

re·mov·al [rɪ'muːvl] rimozione f; from home trasloco

re'mov·al firm ditta f di traslochi

re'mov·al van furgone m dei traslochi

re·move [rɪ'muːv] v/t top, lid togliere; MED asportare; doubt, suspicion eliminare

re·mu·ner·a·tion [rɪmjuːnə'reɪʃn] rimunerazione f

re·mu·ner·a·tive [rɪ'mjuːnərətɪv] adj rimunerativo

Re·nais·sance [rɪ'neɪsəns] Rinascimento m

re·name [riː'neɪm] v/t ribattezzare; file rinominare

ren·der ['rendə(r)] v/t service rendere; ~ **s.o. helpless** rendere inermo qu

ren·der·ing ['rendərɪŋ] of piece of music interpretazione f

ren·dez·vous ['rɒndeɪvuː] (meeting) incontro m

re·new [rɪ'njuː] v/t contract, licence rinnovare; **feel ~ed** sentirsi rinato

re·new·al [rɪ'njuːəl] of contract etc rinnovo m

re·nounce [rɪ'naʊns] v/t title, rights rinunciare a

ren·o·vate ['renəveɪt] v/t ristrutturare

ren·o·va·tion [renə'veɪʃn] ristrutturazione f

re·nown [rɪ'naʊn] fama f

re·nowned [rɪ'naʊnd] adj famoso

rent [rent] **1** n affitto m; **for ~** affittasi **2** v/t flat affittare; car equipment, noleggiare; (~ out) affittare

rent·al ['rentl] for flat affitto m; for car noleggio m; for TV, phone canone m

R

'rent·al a·gree·ment contratto *m* di noleggio

rent-'free *adv* gratis

re·o·pen [ri:'əupn] *v/t & v/i* riaprire

re·or·gan·i·za·tion [ri:ɔ:gənaiz'ei·ʃn] riorganizzazione *f*

re·or·gan·ize [ri:'ɔ:gənaiz] *v/t* riorganizzare

rep [rep] COM rappresentante *m/f*

re·paint [ri:'peint] *v/t* ridipingere

re·pair [ri'peə(r)] **1** *v/t* riparare **2** *n*: **in a good / bad state of ~** in buono / cattivo stato; **~s** riparazioni *fpl*

re'pair·man tecnico *m*

re·pa·tri·ate [ri:'pætrieit] *v/t* rimpatriare

re·pa·tri·a·tion [ri:'pætri'eiʃn] rimpatrio *m*

re·pay [ri:'pei] *v/t* (*pret & pp* **-paid**) *money* restituire; *person* ripagare

re·pay·ment [ri:'peimənt] pagamento *m*

re·peal [ri'pi:l] *v/t law* abrogare

re·peat [ri'pi:t] **1** *v/t* ripetere; **am I ~ing myself?** l'ho già detto? **2** *n programme* replica *f*

re·peat 'busi·ness COM ulteriori ordini *mpl*

re·peat·ed [ri'pi:tid] *adj* ripetuto

re·peat·ed·ly [ri'pi:tidli] *adv* ripetutamente

re·peat 'or·der COM ulteriore ordine *m*

re·pel [ri'pel] *v/t* (*pret & pp* **-led**) *invaders, attack* respingere; (*disgust*) ripugnare

re·pel·lent [ri'pelənt] **1** *n* (*insect ~*) insettifugo *m* **2** *adj* ripugnante

re·pent [ri'pent] *v/i* pentirsi

re·per·cus·sions [ri:pə'kʌʃnz] *npl* ripercussioni *fpl*

rep·er·toire ['repətwɑ:(r)] repertorio *m*

rep·e·ti·tion [repi'tiʃn] ripetizione *f*

rep·e·ti·tive [ri'petitiv] *adj* ripetitivo

re·place [ri'pleis] *v/t* (*put back*) mettere a posto *v/t* (*take the place of*) sostituire

re·place·ment [ri'pleismənt] *person* sostituto *m*, -a *f*; *act* sostituzione *f*; **this is the ~ for the old model** questo è il modello che sostituisce il vecchio

re·place·ment 'part pezzo *m* di ricambio

re·play ['ri:plei] **1** *n recording* replay *m inv*; *match* spareggio *m* **2** *v/t match* rigiocare

re·plen·ish [ri'pleniʃ] *v/t container* riempire; *supplies* rifornire

rep·li·ca ['replikə] copia *f*

re·ply [ri'plai] **1** *n* risposta *f* **2** *v/t & v/i* (*pret & pp* **-ied**) rispondere

re·port [ri'pɔ:t] **1** *n* (*account*) resoconto *m*; *by journalist* servizio *m*; EDU pagella *f* **2** *v/t facts* fare un servizio su; *to authorities* denunciare; **~ one's findings to s.o.** riferire sulle proprie conclusioni a qu; **~ a person to the police** denunciare qualcuno alla polizia; **he is ~ed to be in London** si dice che sia a Londra **3** *v/i of journalist* fare un reportage; (*present o.s.*) presentarsi

♦ **report to** *v/t in business* rendere conto a

re·port·er [ri'pɔ:tə(r)] giornalista *m/f*

re·pos·sess [ri:pə'zes] *v/t* COM riprendersi

rep·re·hen·si·ble [repri'hensəbl] *adj* riprovevole

rep·re·sent [repri'zent] *v/t* rappresentare

rep·re·sen·ta·tive [repri'zentətiv] **1** *n* rappresentante *m/f* **2** *adj* (*typical*) rappresentativo

re·press [ri'pres] *v/t* reprimere

re·pres·sion [ri'preʃn] POL repressione *f*

re·pres·sive [ri'presiv] *adj* POL repressivo

re·prieve [ri'pri:v] **1** *n* LAW sospensione *f* della pena capitale; *fig* proroga *f* **2** *v/t prisoner* sospendere l'esecuzione di

rep·ri·mand ['reprimɑ:nd] *v/t* ammonire

re·print ['ri:print] **1** *n* ristampa *f* **2** *v/t* ristampare

re·pri·sal [ri'praizl] rappresaglia *f*; **take ~s** fare delle rappresaglie; **in ~**

for per rappresaglia contro

e·proach [rɪ'prəʊtʃ] **1** n rimprovero m; **be beyond ~** essere irreprensibile **2** v/t rimproverare

e·proach·ful [rɪ'prəʊtʃfʊl] adj di rimprovero

e·proach·ful·ly [rɪ'prəʊtʃfʊli] adv con aria di rimprovero

e·pro·duce [riːprə'djuːs] **1** v/t riprodurre **2** v/i riprodursi

e·pro·duc·tion [riːprə'dʌkʃn] riproduzione f

e·pro·duc·tive [riprə'dʌktɪv] adj riproduttivo

ep·tile ['reptaɪl] rettile m

e·pub·lic [rɪ'pʌblɪk] repubblica f

e·pub·li·can [rɪ'pʌblɪkn] **1** n repubblicano m, -a f **2** adj repubblicano

e·pu·di·ate [rɪ'pjuːdɪeɪt] v/t (deny) respingere

e·pul·sive [rɪ'pʌlsɪv] adj ripugnante

ep·u·ta·ble ['repjʊtəbl] adj rispettabile

ep·u·ta·tion [repjʊ'teɪʃn] reputazione f; **have a good/bad ~** avere una buona/cattiva reputazione

e·put·ed [rep'jʊtəd] adj: **be ~ to be** avere la fama di essere

e·put·ed·ly [rep'jʊtədlɪ] adv a quanto si dice

e·quest [rɪ'kwest] **1** n richiesta f; **on ~** su richiesta **2** v/t richiedere

e·qui·em ['rekwɪəm] MUS requiem m inv

e·quire [rɪ'kwaɪə(r)] v/t (need) aver bisogno di; **it ~s great care** richiede molta cura; **as ~d by law** come prescritto dalla legge; **guests are ~d to ...** i signori clienti sono pregati di ...

e·quired [rɪ'kwaɪəd] adj (necessary) necessario

e·quire·ment [rɪ'kwaɪəmənt] (need) esigenza f; (condition) requisito m

eq·ui·si·tion [rekwɪ'zɪʃn] v/t requisire

e·route [riː'ruːt] v/t aeroplane etc deviare

e·run ['riːrʌn] **1** n of programme replica f **2** v/t (pret **-ran**, pp **-run**) programme replicare

re·sched·ule [riːˈʃedjuːl] v/t stabilire di nuovo

res·cue ['reskjuː] **1** n salvataggio m; **come to s.o.'s ~** andare in aiuto a qu **2** v/t salvare

'res·cue par·ty squadra f di soccorso

re·search [rɪ'sɜːtʃ] n ricerca f
  ♦ **research into** v/t fare ricerca su

re·search and de·vel·op·ment ricerca f e sviluppo m

re·search as·sist·ant assistente ricercatore m, -trice f

re·search·er [rɪ'sɜːtʃə(r)] ricercatore m, -trice f

re·search proj·ect ricerca f

re·sem·blance [rɪ'zembləns] somiglianza f

re·sem·ble [rɪ'zembl] v/t (as)somigliare a

re·sent [rɪ'zent] v/t risentirsi per

re·sent·ful [rɪ'zentfʊl] adj pieno di risentimento

re·sent·ful·ly [rɪ'zentfʊli] adv con risentimento

re·sent·ment [rɪ'zentmənt] risentimento m

res·er·va·tion [rezə'veɪʃn] of room, table prenotazione f; mental, special area riserva f; **I have a ~** in hotel, restaurant ho prenotato

re·serve [rɪ'zɜːv] **1** n (store) riserva f; (aloofness) riserbo m; SP riserva f; **~s** FIN riserve fpl; **keep sth in ~** tenere qc di riserva **2** v/t seat, table prenotare; judgment riservarsi

re·served [rɪ'zɜːvd] adj person, manner riservato; table, seat prenotato

res·er·voir ['rezəvwɑː(r)] for water bacino m idrico

re·shuf·fle ['riːʃʌfl] **1** n POL rimpasto m **2** v/t POL rimpastare

re·side [rɪ'zaɪd] v/i fml risiedere

res·i·dence ['rezɪdəns] fml: house etc residenza f; (stay) permanenza f

'res·i·dence per·mit permesso m di residenza

'res·i·dent ['rezɪdənt] **1** n residente m/f **2** adj living in a building residente sul posto

res·i·den·tial [rezɪ'denʃl] adj district residenziale

res·i·due ['rezɪdjuː] residuo *m*

re·sign [rɪ'zaɪn] **1** *v/t position* dimettersi da; **~** *o.s.* **to** rassegnarsi a **2** *v/i from job* dimettersi

res·ig·na·tion [rezɪg'neɪʃn] *from job* dimissioni *fpl*; *mental* rassegnazione *f*

re·signed [re'zaɪnd] *adj* rassegnato; *we have become ~ to the fact that …* ci siamo rassegnati al fatto che …

re·sil·i·ent [rɪ'zɪlɪənt] *adj personality* che ha molte risorse; *material* resistente

res·in ['rezɪn] resina *f*

re·sist [rɪ'zɪst] **1** *v/t* resistere a **2** *v/i* resistere

re·sist·ance [rɪ'zɪstəns] resistenza *f*

re·sis·tant [rɪ'zɪstənt] *adj material* resistente; **~** *to heat* / *rust* resistente al calore / alla ruggine

re·sit ['riːsɪt] *v/t exam* ridare

res·o·lute ['rezəluːt] *adj* risoluto

res·o·lu·tion [rezə'luːʃn] (*decision*) risoluzione *f*; *made at New Year etc* proposito *m*; (*determination*) risolutezza *f*; *of problem* soluzione *f*; *of image* risoluzione *f*

re·solve [rɪ'zɒlv] *v/t problem, mystery* risolvere; **~** *to do sth* decidere di fare qc

re·sort [rɪ'zɔːt] *n place* località *f inv*; *holiday ~* luogo *m* di villeggiatura; *ski ~* stazione *f* sciistica; *as a last ~* come ultima risorsa

♦ resort to *v/t violence, threats* far ricorso a

♦ re·sound with [rɪ'zaʊnd] *v/t* risuonare di

re·sound·ing [rɪ'zaʊndɪŋ] *adj success, victory* clamoroso

re·source [rɪ'sɔːs] risorsa *f*; *financial ~s mpl* mezzi *mpl* economici; *leave s.o. to his own ~s* lasciare qu in balia di se stesso

re·source·ful [rɪ'sɔːsful] *adj* pieno di risorse

re·spect [rɪ'spekt] **1** *n* rispetto *m*; *show ~ to* avere rispetto per; *with ~ to* riguardo a; *in this* / *that ~* quanto a questo; *in many ~s* sotto molti aspetti; *pay one's last ~s to s.o.* rendere omaggio a qu **2** *v/t* rispettare

re·spect·a·bil·i·ty [rɪspektə'bɪlətɪ] rispettabilità *f inv*

re·spec·ta·ble [rɪ'spektəbl] *adj* rispettabile

re·spec·ta·bly [rɪ'spektəblɪ] *adv* rispettabilmente

re·spect·ful [rɪ'spektful] *adj* rispettoso

re·spect·ful·ly [rɪ'spektflɪ] *adv* con rispetto

re·spec·tive [rɪ'spektɪv] *adj* rispettivo

re·spec·tive·ly [rɪ'spektɪvlɪ] *adv* rispettivamente

res·pi·ra·tion [respɪ'reɪʃn] respirazione *f*

res·pi·ra·tor [respɪ'reɪtə(r)] MED respiratore *m*

re·spite ['respaɪt] tregua *f*; *without ~* senza tregua

re·spond [rɪ'spɒnd] *v/i* rispondere

re·sponse [rɪ'spɒns] risposta *f*

re·spon·si·bil·i·ty [rɪspɒnsɪ'bɪlətɪ] responsabilità *f inv*; *accept ~ for* assumersi la responsabilità di; *a job with more ~* un lavoro con più responsabilità

re·spon·si·ble [rɪ'spɒnsəbl] *adj* responsabile (*for* di); *job, position* di responsabilità

re·spon·sive [rɪ'spɒnsɪv] *adj audience* caloroso; *be ~ of brakes* rispondere bene

rest[1] [rest] **1** *n* riposo *m*; *set s.o.'s mind at ~* tranquillizzare qu **2** *v/i* riposare; **~** *on …* (*be based on*) basarsi su …; (*lean against*) poggiare su …; *it all ~s with him* dipende tutto da lui **3** *v/t* (*lean, balance*) appoggiare

rest[2] [rest] *n*: *the ~* il resto *m*

res·tau·rant ['restrɒnt] ristorante *m*

'res·tau·rant car RAIL vagone *m* ristorante

'rest cure cura *f* del riposo

rest·ful ['restful] *adj* riposante

'rest home casa *f* di riposo

rest·less ['restlɪs] *adj* irrequieto;

have a ~ night passare una notte agitata

rest·less·ly ['restlɪslɪ] *adv* nervosamente

res·to·ra·tion [restə'reɪʃn] restauro *m*

re·store [rɪ'stɔː(r)] *v/t building etc* restaurare; *(bring back)* restituire

re·strain [rɪ'streɪn] *v/t dog, troops* frenare; *emotions* reprimere; **~ o.s.** trattenersi

re·straint [rɪ'streɪnt] *(self-control)* autocontrollo *m*

re·strict [rɪ'strɪkt] *v/t* limitare; **I'll ~ myself to ...** mi limiterò a ...

re·strict·ed [rɪ'strɪktɪd] *adj view* limitato

re·strict·ed 'ar·e·a MIL zona *f* militare

re·stric·tion [rɪ'strɪkʃn] restrizione *f*

'rest room *Am* gabinetto *m*

re·sult [rɪ'zʌlt] *n* risultato *m*; **as a ~ of this** in conseguenza a ciò

♦ **result from** *v/i* risultare da, derivare da

♦ **result in** *v/t* dare luogo a; **this resulted in him feeling even worse** questo ha fatto sì che stesse ancora peggio

re·sume [rɪ'zjuːm] *v/t & v/i* riprendere

ré·su·mé ['rezumeɪ] *Am* curriculum vitae *m inv*

re·sump·tion [rɪ'zʌmpʃn] ripresa *f*

re·sur·face [riː'sɜːfɪs] **1** *v/t roads* asfaltare **2** *v/i (reappear)* riaffiorare

Res·ur·rec·tion [rezə'rekʃn] REL resurrezione *f*

re·sus·ci·tate [rɪ'sʌsɪteɪt] *v/t* rianimare

re·sus·ci·ta·tion [rɪsʌsɪ'teɪʃn] rianimazione *f*

re·tail ['riːteɪl] **1** *adv* al dettaglio **2** *v/i:* **~ at ...** essere in vendita a ...

re·tail·er ['riːteɪlə(r)] dettagliante *m/f*

re·tail out·let punto *m* (di) vendita

re·tail price prezzo *m* al dettaglio

re·tain [rɪ'teɪn] *v/t* conservare

re·tain·er [rɪ'teɪnə(r)] FIN onorario *m*

re·tal·i·ate [rɪ'tælɪeɪt] *v/i* vendicarsi

re·tal·i·a·tion [rɪtælɪ'eɪʃn] rappresaglia *f*; **in ~ for** per rappresaglia contro

re·tard·ed [rɪ'tɑːdɪd] *adj mentally* ritardato

rethink [riː'θɪŋk] *v/t (pret & pp -thought)* riconsiderare

re·ti·cence ['retɪsns] riservatezza *f*

re·ti·cent ['retɪsnt] *adj* riservato

re·tire [rɪ'taɪə(r)] *v/i from work* andare in pensione

re·tired [rɪ'taɪəd] *adj* in pensione

re·tire·ment [rɪ'taɪəmənt] pensione *f*; *act* pensionamento *m*

re'tire·ment age età *f inv* pensionabile

re·tir·ing [rɪ'taɪərɪŋ] *adj* riservato

re·tort [rɪ'tɔːt] **1** *n* replica *f* **2** *v/t* replicare

re·trace [rɪ'treɪs] *v/t:* **~ one's footsteps** ritornare sui propri passi

re·tract [rɪ'trækt] *v/t claws* ritrarre; *undercarriage* far rientrare; *statement* ritrattare

re·train [riː'treɪn] *v/i* riqualificarsi

re·treat [rɪ'triːt] **1** *v/i* ritirarsi **2** *n* MIL ritirata *f*; *place* rifugio *m*

re·trieve [rɪ'triːv] *v/t* recuperare

re·triev·er [rɪ'triːvə(r)] *dog* cane *m* da riporto

ret·ro·ac·tive [retrəʊ'æktɪv] *adj law etc* retroattivo

ret·ro·ac·tive·ly [retrəʊ'æktɪvlɪ] *adv* retroattivamente

ret·ro·grade ['retrəgreɪd] *adj move, decision* retrogrado

ret·ro·spect ['retrəspekt] **in ~** ripensandoci

ret·ro·spec·tive [retrə'spekt ɪv] *n* retrospettiva *f*

re·turn [rɪ'tɜːn] **1** *n* ritorno *m*; *(giving back)* restituzione *f*; COMPUT *(tasto m)* invio *m*; *in tennis* risposta *f* al servizio; **tax ~** dichiarazione *f* dei redditi; **by ~ (of post)** a stretto giro di posta; **~s (profit)** rendimento *m*; **many happy ~s (of the day)** cento di questi giorni; **in ~ for** in cambio di **2** *v/t (give back)* restituire; *(put back)* rimettere; *favour, invitation* ri-

R

cambiare **3** *v/i* (*go back, come back*) ritornare; *of symptoms, doubts etc* ricomparire

re·turn 'flight volo *m* di ritorno; **re·turn 'jour·ney** viaggio *m* di ritorno; **re'turn match** partita *f* (del girone) di ritorno; **re'turn tick·et** biglietto *m* (di) andata e ritorno

re·u·ni·fi·ca·tion [riːjuːnɪfɪ'keɪʃn] riunificazione *f*

re·u·nion [riː'juːnɪən] riunione *f*

re·u·nite [riːjuː'naɪt] *v/t* riunire

re·us·a·ble [riː'juːzəbl] *adj* riutilizzabile

re·use [riː'juːz] *v/t* riutilizzare

rev [rev] *n: ~s per minute* giri al minuto

♦ rev up *v/t* (*pret & pp -ved*) *engine* far andare su di giri

re·val·u·a·tion [riːvæljuˈeɪʃn] rivalutazione *f*

re·veal [rɪ'viːl] *v/t* (*make visible*) mostrare; (*make known*) rivelare

re·veal·ing [rɪ'viːlɪŋ] *adj remark* rivelatore; *dress* scollato

♦ revel in ['revl] *v/t* (*pret & pp -led*, *Am -ed*) godere di

rev·e·la·tion [revə'leɪʃn] rivelazione *f*

re·venge [rɪ'vendʒ] *n* vendetta *f*; **take one's ~** vendicarsi; **in - for** per vendicarsi di

rev·e·nue ['revənjuː] reddito *m*

re·ver·be·rate [rɪ'vɜːbəreɪt] *v/i of sound* rimbombare

re·vere [rɪ'vɪə(r)] *v/t* riverire

rev·e·rence ['revərəns] rispetto *m*

Rev·e·rend ['revərənd] REL reverendo *m*

rev·e·rent ['revərənt] *adj* riverente

re·verse [rɪ'vɜːs] **1** *adj sequence* opposto; **in - order** in ordine inverso **2** *n* (*opposite*) contrario *m*; (*back*) rovescio *m*; MOT retromarcia *f* **3** *v/t sequence* invertire; **~ the car** fare marcia indietro; **~ the charges** TELEC telefonare a carico del destinatario **4** *v/i* MOT fare marcia indietro

revert [rɪ'vɜːt] *v/i*: **~ to** ritornare a

re·view [rɪ'vjuː] **1** *n of book, film* recensione *f*; *of troops* rivista *f*; *of situation etc* revisione *f* **2** *v/t book, film* recensire; *troops* passare in rivista; *situation etc* riesaminare

re·view·er [rɪ'vjuːə(r)] *of book, film* critico *m*, -a *f*

re·vise [rɪ'vaɪz] **1** *v/t opinion, text* rivedere; EDU ripassare **2** *v/i* EDU ripassare

re·vi·sion [rɪ'vɪʒn] *of opinion, text* revisione *f*; *for exam* ripasso *m*

re·viv·al [rɪ'vaɪvl] *of custom, old style etc* revival *m inv*; *of patient* ripresa *f*

re·vive [rɪ'vaɪv] **1** *v/t custom, old style etc* riportare alla moda; *patient* rianimare **2** *v/i of business etc* riprendersi

re·voke [rɪ'vəʊk] *v/t licence* revocare

re·volt [rɪ'vəʊlt] **1** *n* rivolta *f* **2** *v/i* ribellarsi

re·volt·ing [rɪ'vəʊltɪŋ] *adj* (*disgusting*) schifoso

rev·o·lu·tion [revə'luːʃn] rivoluzione *f*

rev·o·lu·tion·ar·y [revə'luːʃn ərɪ] **1** *n* POL rivoluzionario *m*, -a *f* **2** *adj* rivoluzionario

rev·o·lu·tion·ize [revə'luːʃnaɪz] *v/t* rivoluzionare

re·volve [rɪ'vɒlv] *v/i* ruotare

re·volv·er [rɪ'vɒlvə(r)] revolver *m inv*

re·volv·ing 'door [rɪ'vɒlvɪŋ] porta *f* girevole

re·vue [rɪ'vjuː] THEA rivista *f*

re·vul·sion [rɪ'vʌlʃn] ribrezzo *m*

re·ward [rɪ'wɔːd] **1** *n financial* ricompensa *f*; *benefit derived* vantaggio *m* **2** *v/t financially* ricompensare

re·ward·ing [rɪ'wɔːdɪŋ] *adj experience* gratificante

re·wind [riː'waɪnd] *v/t* (*pret & pp -wound*) *film, tape* riavvolgere

re·write [riː'raɪt] *v/t* (*pret -wrote*, *pp -written*) riscrivere

rhe·to·ric ['retərɪk] retorica *f*

rhe·to·ric·al 'ques·tion [rɪ'tɒrɪkl] domanda *f* retorica

rheu·ma·tism ['ruːmətɪzm] reumatismo *m*

rhi·no·ce·ros [raɪ'nɒsərəs] rinoceronte *m*

rhu·barb ['ru:bɑ:b] rabarbaro *m*

rhyme [raɪm] **1** *n* rima *f* **2** *v/i* rimare; **~ with** fare rima con

rhythm ['rɪðm] ritmo *m*

rib [rɪb] ANAT costola *f*

rib·bon ['rɪbən] nastro *m*

rice [raɪs] riso *m*

rice 'pud·ding budino *m* di riso

rich [rɪtʃ] **1** *adj* (*wealthy*) ricco; *food* pesante **2** *n*: **the ~** i ricchi *mpl*

rich·ly ['rɪtʃlɪ] *adv deserved* pienamente

rick·et·y ['rɪkətɪ] *adj* traballante

ric·o·chet ['rɪkəʃeɪ] *v/i* rimbalzare

rid [rɪd]: **get ~ of** sbarazzarsi di

rid·dance ['rɪdns] *n* F: **good ~!** che liberazione!

rid·den ['rɪdn] *pp* → **ride**

rid·dle ['rɪdl] **1** *n* indovinello *m* **2** *v/t*: **be ~d with** essere crivellato di

ride [raɪd] **1** *n on horse* cavalcata *f*; *in vehicle* giro *m*; (*journey*) viaggio *m*; **do you want a ~ into town?** Am vuoi uno strappo in città? **2** *v/t* (*pret rode, pp ridden*): **~ a horse** andare a cavallo; **~ a bike** andare in bicicletta **3** *v/i* (*pret rode, pp ridden*) *on horse* andare a cavallo; *on bike* andare; *in vehicle* viaggiare; **he rode home** è andato a casa in bicicletta

rid·er ['raɪdə(r)] *on horse* cavallerizzo *m*, -a *f*; *on bike* ciclista *m/f*

ridge [rɪdʒ] *raised strip* sporgenza *f*; *of mountain* cresta *f*; *of roof* punta *f*

rid·i·cule ['rɪdɪkjuːl] **1** *n* ridicolo *m* **2** *v/t* ridicolizzare

ri·dic·u·lous [rɪ'dɪkjʊləs] *adj* ridicolo

ri·dic·u·lous·ly [rɪ'dɪkjʊləslɪ] *adv* incredibilmente

rid·ing ['raɪdɪŋ] *on horseback* equitazione *f*

ri·fle ['raɪfl] *n* F fucile *m*

rift [rɪft] *in earth* crepa *f*; *in party etc* spaccatura *f*

rig [rɪg] **1** *n* (*oil ~*) piattaforma *f* petrolifera **2** *v/t* (*pret & pp -ged*) *elections* manipolare

right [raɪt] **1** *adj* (*correct*) esatto; (*proper, just*) giusto; (*suitable*) adatto; *not left* destro; **be ~ of** *answer* essere esatto; *of person* avere ragione; *of clock* essere giusto; **put things ~** sistemare le cose; → **alright 2** *adv* (*directly*) proprio; (*correctly*) bene; (*completely*) completamente; *not left* a destra; **~ now** (*immediately*) subito; (*at the moment*) adesso **3** *n civil, legal etc* diritto *m*; *not left* destra *f*; **the ~** POL la destra; **on the ~** a destra; **turn to the ~, take a ~** girare a destra; **be in the ~** avere ragione; **know ~ from wrong** saper distinguere il bene dal male

right-'an·gle angolo *m* retto; **at ~s to ...** ad angolo retto con ...

right·ful ['raɪtful] *adj heir, owner etc* legittimo

'right·hand *adj* destro; **on the ~ side** a destra; **right·hand 'drive** MOT guida *f* a destra; *car* auto *f inv* con guida *f* a destra; **right·hand·ed** [raɪt'hændɪd] *adj*: **be ~** usare la (mano) destra; **right·hand 'man** braccio *m* destro; **right of 'way** *in traffic* (diritto *m* di) precedenza *f*; *across land* diritto *m* di accesso; **right 'wing** *n* POL destra *f*; SP esterno *m* destro; **right-'wing** *adj* POL di destra; **right 'wing·er** POL persona *f* di destra; **right-wing ex'trem·ism** POL estremismo *m* di destra

rig·id ['rɪdʒɪd] *adj material, principles* rigido; *attitude* inflessibile

rig·or Am → **rigour**

rig·or·ous ['rɪgərəs] *adj* rigoroso

rig·or·ous·ly ['rɪgərəslɪ] *adv check, examine* rigorosamente

rig·our ['rɪgə(r)] *of discipline* rigore *m*; **the ~s of the winter** i rigori dell'inverno

rile [raɪl] *v/t* F irritare

rim [rɪm] *of wheel* cerchione *m*; *of cup* orlo *m*; *of spectacles* montatura *f*

ring¹ [rɪŋ] (*circle*) cerchio *m*; *on finger* anello *m*; *in boxing* ring *m inv*, quadrato *m*; *at circus* pista *f*

ring² [rɪŋ] **1** *n of bell* trillo *m*; *of voice* suono *m*; **give s.o. a ~** TELEC dare un colpo di telefono a qu **2** *v/t* (*pret rang, pp rung*) *bell* suonare; TELEC

R

chimare **3** v/i (pret **rang**, pp **rung**) of bell suonare; TELEC chiamare; **please – for attention** suonare il campanello

'ring·lead·er capobanda m inv; 'ring-pull linguetta f; 'ring road circonvallazione f

rink [rɪŋk] pista f di pattinaggio su ghiaccio

rinse [rɪns] **1** n for hair colour cachet m inv **2** v/t sciacquare

ri·ot ['raɪət] **1** n sommossa f **2** v/i causare disordini

'ri·ot·er ['raɪətə(r)] dimostrante m/f

'riot police reparti mpl (di polizia) antisommossa

rip [rɪp] **1** n in cloth etc strappo m **2** v/t (pret & pp **-ped**) cloth etc strappare; **~ sth open** aprire qc strappandolo

♦ rip off v/t F customers fregare F

♦ rip up v/t letter, sheet strappare

ripe [raɪp] adj fruit maturo

rip·en ['raɪpn] v/i of fruit maturare

'ripe·ness ['raɪpnɪs] of fruit maturazione f

'rip-off n F fregatura f F

rip·ple ['rɪpl] on water increspatura f

rise [raɪz] **1** v/i (pret **rose**, pp **risen**) from chair etc alzarsi; of sun sorgere; of price, temperature aumentare; of water level salire **2** n aumento m; **~ to power** salita f al potere; **give ~ to** dare origine a

ris·en ['rɪzn] pp → rise

ris·er ['raɪzə(r)] n: **be an early / be a late ~** essere mattiniero / alzarsi sempre tardi

risk [rɪsk] **1** n rischio m; **take a ~** correre un rischio **2** v/t rischiare; **let's ~ it** proviamo

risk·y ['rɪskɪ] adj rischioso

ri·sot·to [rɪs'ɒtəʊ] risotto m

ris·qué [rɪ'skeɪ] adj osé

rit·u·al ['rɪtjʊəl] **1** n rituale m **2** adj rituale

ri·val ['raɪvl] **1** n in sport, love rivale m/f; in business concorrente m/f **2** v/t competere con; **I can't ~ that** non posso competere con quello

ri·val·ry ['raɪvlrɪ] rivalità f inv

riv·er ['rɪvə(r)] fiume m

'riv·er·bank sponda f del fiume; 'riv·er·bed letto m del fiume; 'riv·er·side **1** adj sul fiume **2** n riva f del fiume

riv·et ['rɪvɪt] **1** n ribattino m **2** v/t rivettare

riv·et·ing ['rɪvɪtɪŋ] adj avvincente

Riv·i·e·ra [rɪvɪ'eərə] n: **the Italian ~** la riviera (ligure)

road [rəʊd] strada f; **it's just down the ~** è qui vicino

'road·block posto m di blocco; 'road hog pirata m della strada; 'road hold·ing of vehicle tenuta f di strada; 'road map carta f automobilistica; road 'safe·ty sicurezza f sulle strade; 'road·side: **at the ~** sul ciglio della strada; 'road·sign cartello m stradale; 'road·way carreggiata f; 'road works npl lavori mpl stradali; 'road·wor·thy adj in buono stato di marcia

roam [rəʊm] v/i vagabondare

roar [rɔː(r)] **1** n of engine rombo m; of lion ruggito m; of traffic fragore m **2** v/i of engine rombare; of lion ruggire; of person gridare; **~ with laughter** ridere fragorosamente

roast [rəʊst] **1** n beef etc arrosto m **2** v/t chicken, potatoes arrostire; coffee beans, peanuts tostare **3** v/i of food arrostire; in hot room, climate scoppiare di caldo

roast 'beef arrosto m di manzo

'roast·ing tin [rəʊstɪŋ] teglia f per arrosti

roast 'pork arrosto m di maiale

rob [rɒb] v/t (pret & pp **-bed**) person, bank rapinare; **I've been ~bed** mi hanno rapinato

rob·ber ['rɒbə(r)] rapinatore m, -trice f

rob·ber·y ['rɒbərɪ] rapina f

robe [rəʊb] of judge toga f; of priest tonaca f; Am (dressing gown) vestaglia f

rob·in ['rɒbɪn] pettirosso m

ro·bot ['rəʊbɒt] robot m inv

ro·bust [rəʊ'bʌst] adj robusto

rock [rɒk] **1** n roccia f; MUS rock m inv; **on the ~s** drink con ghiaccio;

marriage in crisi **2** *v/t baby* cullare; *cradle* far dondolare; *(surprise)* sconvolgere **3** *v/i on chair* dondolarsi; *of boat* dondolare

rock band gruppo *m* rock; **rock 'bot·tom:** *reach ~* toccare il fondo; **'rock-bot·tom** *adj prices* bassissimo; **'rock climb·er** rocciatore *m*, -trice *f*; **rock climb·ing** roccia *f*

rock·et ['rɒkɪt] **1** *n* razzo *m* **2** *v/i of prices etc* salire alle stelle

'rock·ing chair ['rɒkɪŋ] sedia *f* a dondolo

'rock·ing horse cavallo *m* a dondolo

rock 'n' roll [rɒknˈrəʊl] rock and roll *m inv*

rock star rockstar *f inv*

rock·y ['rɒkɪ] *adj shore* roccioso; *(shaky)* instabile

rod [rɒd] sbarra *f*; *for fishing* canna *f*

rode [rəʊd] *pret* → **ride**

ro·dent ['rəʊdnt] roditore *m*

rogue [rəʊg] briccone *m*, -a *f*

role [rəʊl] ruolo *m*

role mod·el modello *m* di comportamento

roll [rəʊl] **1** *n of bread* panino *m*; *of film* rullino *m*; *of thunder* rombo *m*; *(list, register)* lista *f* **2** *v/i of ball etc* rotolare; *of boat* dondolare **3** *v/t: ~ sth into a ball* appallottolare qc; *~ sth along the ground* far rotolare qc

♦ **roll over 1** *v/i* rigirarsi **2** *v/t person, object* girare; *loan, agreement* rinnovare

♦ **roll up 1** *v/t sleeves* arrotolare **2** *v/i* F *(arrive)* arrivare

'roll call appello *m*

roll·er ['rəʊlə(r)] *for hair* bigodino *m*

'roll·er blade® *n* roller blade *m inv*;
'roll·er blind tenda *f* a rullo; **roll·er 'coast·er** ['rəʊləkəʊstə(r)] montagne *fpl* russe; **'roll·er skate** *n* pattino *m* a rotelle

'roll·ing pin ['rəʊlɪŋ] matterello *m*

ROM [rɒm] *abbr* COMPUT (= *read only memory*) ROM *f inv*

Ro·man ['rəʊmən] **1** *adj* romano **2** *n* Romano *m*, -a *f*

Ro·man 'Cath·o·lic 1 *n* REL cattoli-

co *m*, -a *f* **2** *adj* cattolico

ro·mance [rə'mæns] *(affair)* storia *f* d'amore; *novel* romanzo *m* rosa; *film* film *m inv* d'amore

ro·man·tic [rəʊ'mæntɪk] *adj* romantico

ro·man·tic·al·ly [rəʊ'mæntɪklɪ] *adv* romanticamente; *~ involved with s.o.* legato sentimentalmente a qu

Rome [rəʊm] Roma *f*

roof [ruːf] tetto *m*; *have a ~ over one's head* avere un tetto sulla testa

'roof rack MOT portabagagli *m inv*

room [ruːm] stanza *f*; *(bedroom)* camera *f* (da letto); *(space)* posto *m*; *there's no ~ for ...* non c'è posto per ...

'room mate compagno *m*, -a *f* di stanza; **'room ser·vice** servizio *m* in camera; **room 'tem·per·a·ture** temperatura *f* ambiente

room·y ['ruːmɪ] *adj house, car etc* spazioso; *clothes* ampio

root [ruːt] *n* radice *f*; *~s of person* radici *fpl*

♦ **root for** *v/t* F fare il tifo per

♦ **root out** *v/t* *(get rid of)* eradicare; *(find)* scovare

rope [rəʊp] corda *f*, fune *f*; *show s.o. the ~s* F insegnare il mestiere a qu

♦ **rope off** *v/t* transennare

ro·sa·ry ['rəʊzərɪ] REL rosario *m*

rose¹ [rəʊz] BOT rosa *f*

rose² [rəʊz] *pret* → **rise**

rose·ma·ry ['rəʊzmərɪ] rosmarino *m*

ros·trum ['rɒstrəm] podio *m*

ros·y ['rəʊzɪ] *adj* roseo

rot [rɒt] **1** *n* marciume *m* **2** *v/i (pret & pp -ted)* marcire

ro·ta ['rəʊtə] turni *mpl*; *actual document* tabella *f* dei turni; *on a ~ basis* a turno

ro·tate [rəʊ'teɪt] **1** *v/i of blades, earth* ruotare **2** *v/t* girare; *crops* avvicendare

ro·ta·tion [rəʊ'teɪʃn] *around the sun etc* rotazione *f*; *in ~* a turno

rot·ten ['rɒtn] *adj food, wood etc* marcio; F *(very bad)* schifoso F; *what ~ luck!* che scalogna!; *what a ~ thing* *to do!* che carognata!

rough [rʌf] **1** *adj* hands, skin, surface ruvido; *ground* accidentato; (*coarse*) rozzo; (*violent*) violento; *crossing* movimentato; *seas* grosso; (*approximate*) approssimativo; **~ draft** abbozzo *m* **2** *adv:* **sleep ~** dormire all'addiaccio **3** *v/t:* **~ it** F vivere senza confort **4** *n in golf* erba *f* alta
♦ **rough up** *v/t* F malmenare
rough·age ['rʌfɪdʒ] *in food* fibre *fpl*
rough·ly ['rʌflɪ] *adv* (*approximately*) circa; (*harshly*) bruscamente; **~ speaking** grosso modo
rou·lette [ruː'let] roulette *f inv*
round [raʊnd] **1** *adj* rotondo; **in figures** in cifra tonda **2** *n of postman, doctor* giro *m*; *of toast* fetta *f*; *of drinks* giro *m*; *of competition* girone *m*; *in boxing match* round *m inv* **3** *v/t the corner* girare **4** *adv & prep* → **around**
♦ **round off** *v/t edges* smussare; *meeting, night out* chiudere
♦ **round up** *v/t figure* arrotondare; *suspects, criminals* radunare
round·a·bout ['raʊndəbaʊt] **1** *adj route, way of saying sth* indiretto **2** *n on road* rotatoria *f*; **'round-the-world** *adj* intorno al mondo; **round trip 'tick·et** *Am* biglietto *m* (di) andata e ritorno; **'round-up** *of cattle* raduno *m*; *of suspects, criminals* retata *f*; *of news* riepilogo *m*
rouse [raʊz] *v/t from sleep* svegliare; *interest, emotions* risvegliare
rous·ing ['raʊzɪŋ] *adj speech, finale* entusiasmante
route [ruːt] *of car* itinerario *m*; *of plane, ship* rotta *f*; *of bus* percorso *m*
rou·tine [ruː'tiːn] **1** *adj* abituale **2** *n* routine *f*; **as a matter of ~** d'abitudine
row[1] [raʊ] *n* (*line*) fila *f*; **5 days in a ~** 5 giorni di fila
row[2] [raʊ] *v/t & v/i boat* remare
row[3] [raʊ] *n* (*quarrel*) litigio *m*; (*noise*) baccano *m*
row·dy ['raʊdɪ] *adj* turbolento
row·ing boat ['raʊɪŋ] barca *f* a remi
roy·al ['rɔɪəl] *adj* reale

roy·al·ty ['rɔɪəltɪ] (*royal persons*) reali *mpl*; *on book, recording* royalty *f inv*
rub [rʌb] *v/t* (*pret & pp -bed*) sfregare, strofinare
♦ **rub down** *v/t to clean* levigare
♦ **rub in** *v/t cream, ointment* far penetrare; **don't rub it in!** *fig* non rivoltare il coltello nella piaga!
♦ **rub off 1** *v/t dirt* levare (strofinando) **2** *v/i:* **it rubs off on you** ti si comunica
♦ **rub out** *v/t with eraser* cancellare
rub·ber ['rʌbə(r)] **1** *n* gomma *f* **2** *adj* di gomma
rub·ber 'band elastico *m*
rub·ber 'gloves *npl* guanti *mpl* di gomma
rub·bish ['rʌbɪʃ] immondizia *f*; (*poor quality*) porcheria *f*; (*nonsense*) sciocchezza *f*; **don't talk ~!** non dire sciocchezze!
'rub·bish bin pattumiera *f*
rub·ble ['rʌbl] macerie *fpl*
ru·by ['ruːbɪ] *jewel* rubino *m*
ruck·sack ['rʌksæk] zaino *m*
rud·der ['rʌdə(r)] timone *m*
rud·dy ['rʌdɪ] *adj complexion* rubicondo
rude [ruːd] *adj person, behaviour* maleducato; *language* volgare; **a ~ word** una parolaccia; **it's ~ to …** è cattiva educazione …
rude·ly ['ruːdlɪ] *adv* (*impolitely*) scortesemente
rude·ness ['ruːdnɪs] maleducazione *f*
ru·di·men·ta·ry [ruːdɪ'mentərɪ] *adj* rudimentale
ru·di·ments ['ruːdɪmənts] *npl* rudimenti *mpl*
rue·ful ['ruːfʊl] *adj* rassegnato
rue·ful·ly ['ruːfəlɪ] *adv* con aria rassegnata
ruf·fi·an ['rʌfɪən] delinquente *m/f*
ruf·fle ['rʌfl] **1** *n (on dress)* gala *f* **2** *v/t hair* scompigliare; *person* turbare; **get ~d** agitarsi
rug [rʌg] tappeto *m*; (*blanket*) coperta *f* (da viaggio)
rug·by ['rʌgbɪ] SP rugby *m inv*

rug·by 'league rugby *m inv* a tredici; **'rug·by match** partita *f* di rugby; **'rug·by play·er** giocatore *m* di rugby; **rug·by 'un·ion** rugby *m inv* a quindici

rug·ged ['rʌgɪd] *adj coastline* frastagliato; *face, features* marcato

ru·in ['ruːɪn] **1** *n* rovina *f*; **~s** rovine; **in ~s** *city, building* in rovina; *plans, career* rovinato **2** *v/t* rovinare; **be ~ed** *financially* essere rovinato

rule [ruːl] **1** *n* of club, game regola *f*; (*authority*) dominio *m*; *for measuring* metro *m* (a stecche); **as a ~** generalmente **2** *v/t country* governare; **the judge ~d that ...** il giudice ha stabilito che ... **3** *v/i of monarch* regnare

♦ **rule out** *v/t* escludere

rul·er ['ruːlə(r)] *for measuring* righello *m*; *of state* capo *m*

rul·ing ['ruːlɪŋ] **1** *n* decisione *f* **2** *adj party* di governo

rum [rʌm] *drink* rum *m inv*

rum·ble ['rʌmbl] *v/i of stomach* brontolare; *of thunder* rimbombare

♦ **rum·mage around** ['rʌmɪdʒ] *v/i* frugare

ru·mour ['ruːmə(r)] **1** *n* voce *f* **2** *v/t*: **it is ~ed that ...** corre voce che ...

rump [rʌmp] *of animal* groppa *f*

rum·ple ['rʌmpl] *v/t clothes, paper* spiegazzare

rump·'steak bistecca *f* di girello

run [rʌn] **1** *n on foot* corsa *f*; *distance* tragitto *m*; *in tights* sfilatura *f*; **go for a ~** andare a correre; **go for a ~ in the car** andare a fare un giro in macchina; **make a ~ for it** scappare; **a criminal on the ~** un evaso, un'evasa; **in the short ~ / in the long ~** sulle prime / alla lunga; **a ~ on the dollar** una forte richiesta di dollari; **it's had a three year ~** *of play* ha tenuto cartellone per tre anni **2** *v/i* (*pret* **ran**, *pp* **run**) *of person, animal* correre; *of river* scorrere; *of trains, buses* viaggiare; *of paint, makeup* sbavare; *of nose* colare; *of play* tenere il cartellone; *of software* girare; *of engine, machine*

funzionare; **don't leave the tap ~ning** non lasciare il rubinetto aperto; **~ for President** in election candidarsi alla presidenza **3** *v/t* (*pret* **ran**, *pp* **run**) correre; (*take part in: race*) partecipare a; *business, hotel, project etc* gestire; *software* lanciare; *car* usare; *risk* correre; **can I ~ you to the station?** ti porto alla stazione?; **he ran his eye down the page** diede uno sguardo alla pagina

♦ **run across** *v/t* imbattersi in

♦ **run away** *v/i* scappare

♦ **run down 1** *v/t* (*knock down*) investire; (*criticize*) parlare male di; *stocks* ridurre **2** *v/i of battery* scaricarsi

♦ **run into** *v/t* (*meet*) imbattersi in; *difficulties* trovare

♦ **run off 1** *v/i* scappare **2** *v/t* (*print off*) stampare

♦ **run out** *v/i of contract, time* scadere; *of supplies* esaurirsi

♦ **run out of** *v/t patience* perdere; *supplies* rimanere senza; **I ran out of petrol** ho finito la benzina; **we are running out of time** il tempo sta per scadere

♦ **run over 1** *v/t* (*knock down*) investire; **can we run over the details again?** possiamo rivedere i particolari? **2** *v/i of water etc* traboccare

♦ **run through** *v/t rehearse, go over* rivedere

♦ **run up** *v/t debts, large bill* accumulare; *clothes* mettere insieme

run·a·way ['rʌnəweɪ] *n* ragazzo *m*, -a *f* scappato di casa

run·'down *adj person* debilitato; *part of town, building* fatiscente

rung¹ [rʌŋ] *of ladder* piolo *m*

rung² [rʌŋ] *pp* → **ring**

run·ner ['rʌnə(r)] *athlete* velocista *m/f*

run·ner 'beans *npl* fagiolini *mpl*

run·ner-'up secondo *m*, -a *f* classificato (-a)

run·ning ['rʌnɪŋ] **1** *n* SP corsa *f*; *of business* gestione *f* **2** *adj*: **for two days ~** per due giorni di seguito

R

run·ning 'wa·ter acqua f corrente
run·ny ['rʌnɪ] adj substance liquido; nose che cola
'run-up SP rincorsa f; **in the ~ to** nel periodo che precede …
'run·way pista f
rup·ture ['rʌpʃə(r)] **1** n rottura f, MED lacerazione f; (hernia) ernia f **2** v/i of pipe etc scoppiare
ru·ral ['rʊərəl] adj rurale
ruse [ruːz] stratagemma m
rush [rʌʃ] **1** n corsa f; **do sth in a ~** fare qc di corsa; **be in a ~** andare di fretta; **what's the big ~?** che fretta c'è? **2** v/t person mettere fretta o premura in; meal mangiare in fretta; **~ s.o. to hospital / the airport** portare qu di corsa all'ospedale / aeroporto **3** v/i affrettarsi
'rush hour ora f di punta

Rus·sia ['rʌʃə] Russia f
Rus·sian ['rʌʃən] **1** adj russo **2** n russo m, -a f; language russo m
rust [rʌst] **1** n ruggine f **2** v/i arrugginirsi
rus·tle ['rʌsl] **1** n of silk, leaves fruscio m **2** v/i of silk, leaves frusciare
'rust-proof adj a prova di ruggine
rust re·mov·er ['rʌstrɪmuːvə(r)] smacchiatore m per la ruggine
rust·y ['rʌstɪ] adj also fig arrugginito; **I'm a little ~** sono un po' arrugginito
rut [rʌt] in road solco m; **be in a ~** fig essersi fossilizzato
ruth·less ['ruːθlɪs] adj spietato
ruth·less·ly adv spietatamente
ruth·less·ness ['ruːθlɪsnɪs] spietatezza f
rye [raɪ] segale f
'rye bread pane m di segale

S

sab·bat·i·cal [sə'bætɪkl] n of academic anno m sabbatico
sab·o·tage ['sæbətɑːʒ] **1** n sabotaggio m **2** v/t sabotare
sab·o·teur [sæbə'tɜː(r)] sabotatore m, -trice f
sac·cha·rin ['sækərɪn] n saccarina f
sa·chet ['sæʃeɪ] of shampoo, cream etc bustina f
sack [sæk] **1** n bag sacco m; **get the ~** F essere licenziato **2** v/t F licenziare
sa·cred ['seɪkrɪd] adj sacro
sac·ri·fice ['sækrɪfaɪs] **1** n sacrificio m; **make ~s** fig fare sacrifici **2** v/t sacrificare
sac·ri·lege ['sækrɪlɪdʒ] sacrilegio m
sad [sæd] adj triste; state of affairs deplorevole
sad·dle ['sædl] **1** n sella f **2** v/t horse sellare; **~ s.o. with sth** fig affibbiare qc a qu
sa·dis·m ['seɪdɪzm] sadismo m

sa·dist ['seɪdɪst] sadista m/f
sa·dis·tic [sə'dɪstɪk] adj sadistico
sad·ly ['sædlɪ] adv tristemente; (regrettably) purtroppo
sad·ness ['sædnɪs] tristezza f
safe [seɪf] **1** adj not dangerous sicuro; not in danger al sicuro; driver prudente; **is it ~ to walk here?** non è pericoloso camminare qui? **2** n cassaforte f
'safe·guard **1** n protezione f, salvaguardia f; **as a ~ against** per proteggersi contro **2** v/t proteggere
safe'keep·ing: **give sth to s.o. for ~** dare qc in custodia a qu
safe·ly ['seɪflɪ] adv arrive, complete first test etc senza problemi; drive prudentemente; assume tranquillamente
safe·ty ['seɪftɪ] sicurezza f
'safe·ty belt cintura f di sicurezza; 'safe·ty-con·scious adj attento ai

problemi di sicurezza; **safe·ty 'first** prudenza f; **'safe·ty pin** spilla f di sicurezza

sag [sæg] **1** n in ceiling incurvatura f **2** v/i (pret & pp **-ged**) of ceiling incurvarsi; of rope allentarsi

sa·ga ['sɑːɡə] saga f

sage [seɪdʒ] n herb salvia f

Sa·git·tar·i·us [sædʒɪ'teərɪəs] ASTR Sagittario m

said [sed] pret & pp → **say**

sail [seɪl] **1** n of boat vela f; trip veleggiata f; **go for a ~** fare un giro in barca (a vela) **2** v/t yacht pilotare **3** v/i fare vela; (depart) salpare

sail·board 1 n windsurf m inv **2** v/i fare windsurf

sail·board·ing windsurf m inv

sail·ing ['seɪlɪŋ] SP vela f

sail·ing boat barca f a vela

sail·ing ship veliero m

sail·or ['seɪlə(r)] marinaio m; **be a bad / good ~** soffrire / non soffrire il mal di mare

saint [seɪnt] santo m, -a f

sake [seɪk] n: **for my / your ~** per il mio / il tuo bene; **for the ~ of** per; **for the ~ of peace** per amor di pace

sal·ad ['sæləd] insalata f

sal·ad 'dress·ing condimento m per l'insalata

sal·a·ry ['sælərɪ] stipendio m

sal·a·ry scale scala f salariale

sale [seɪl] vendita f; **at reduced prices** svendita f, saldi mpl; **for ~ sign** in vendita; **be on ~** essere in vendita

sales [seɪlz] npl department reparto m vendite

sales as·sist·ant, **'sales clerk** Am in shop commesso m, -a f; **'sales fig·ures** npl fatturato m; **'sales·man** venditore m; **sales 'man·ag·er** direttore m, -trice f delle vendite; **'sales meet·ing** riunione f marketing e vendite; **'sales wom·an** venditrice f

sa·lient ['seɪlɪənt] adj saliente

sa·li·va [sə'laɪvə] saliva f

salm·on ['sæmən] (pl salmon) salmone m

sa·loon [sə'luːn] MOT berlina f; Am: bar bar m inv

salt [sɒlt] **1** n sale m **2** v/t food salare

'salt·cel·lar saliera f; **salt 'wa·ter** acqua f salata; **'salt-wa·ter fish** pesce m di mare

salt·y ['sɒltɪ] adj salato

sal·u·tar·y ['sæljʊtərɪ] adj experience salutare

sa·lute [sə'luːt] **1** n MIL saluto m; **take the ~** ricevere i saluti **2** v/t & v/i salutare

sal·vage ['sælvɪdʒ] v/t from wreck ricuperare

sal·va·tion [sæl'veɪʃn] salvezza f

Sal·va·tion 'Ar·my Esercito m della Salvezza

same [seɪm] **1** adj stesso **2** pron stesso; **the ~** lo stesso, la stessa; **Happy New Year – the ~ to you** Buon anno! – Grazie e altrettanto!; **he's not the ~ any more** non è più lo stesso; **all the ~** (even so) eppure; **men are all the ~** gli uomini sono tutti uguali; **it's all the ~ to me** per me è uguale **3** adv: **the ~** allo stesso modo; **I still feel the ~ about that** la penso sempre allo stesso modo

sam·ple ['sɑːmpl] **1** n campione m **2** v/t food, product provare

san·a·to·ri·um [sænə'tɔːrɪəm] casa f di cura

sanc·ti·mo·ni·ous [sæŋktɪ'məʊnɪəs] adj moraleggiante

sanc·tion ['sæŋkʃn] **1** n (approval) approvazione f; (penalty) sanzione f **2** v/t (approve) sancire

sanc·ti·ty ['sæŋktɪtɪ] santità f

sanc·tu·a·ry ['sæŋktjʊərɪ] REL santuario m; for wild animals riserva f

sand [sænd] **1** n sabbia f **2** v/t with sandpaper smerigliare

san·dal ['sændl] sandalo m

'sand·bag sacchetto m di sabbia; **'sand·blast** v/t sabbiare; **'sand dune** duna f

sand·er ['sændə(r)] tool smerigliatrice f

'sand·pa·per 1 n carta f smerigliata **2** v/t smerigliare

'sand·stone arenaria f

S

sand·wich ['sænwɪdʒ] **1** n tramezzino m **2** v/t: **be ~ed between two ...** essere incastrato tra due ...

sand·y ['sændɪ] adj beach sabbioso; full of sand pieno di sabbia; hair rossiccio

sane [seɪn] adj sano di mente

sang [sæŋ] pret → **sing**

san·i·ta·ry ['sænɪtərɪ] adj conditions igienico; installations sanitario

'san·i·ta·ry tow·el assorbente m (igienico)

san·i·ta·tion [sænɪ'teɪʃn] (sanitary installations) impianti mpl igienici; (removal of waste) fognature fpl

san·i·ty ['sænətɪ] sanità f inv mentale

sank [sæŋk] pret → **sink**

San·ta Claus ['sæntəklɔːz] Babbo m Natale

sap [sæp] **1** n in tree linfa f **2** v/t (pret & pp **-ped**) s.o.'s energy indebolire

sap·phire ['sæfaɪə(r)] n jewel zaffiro m

sar·casm ['sɑːkæzm] sarcasmo m

sar·cas·tic [sɑː'kæstɪk] adj sarcastico

sar·cas·ti·cal·ly [sɑː'kæstɪklɪ] adv sarcasticamente

sar·dine [sɑː'diːn] sardina f

Sar·din·i·a [sɑː'dɪnɪə] Sardegna f

Sar·din·i·an [sɑː'dɪnɪən] **1** adj sardo **2** n sardo m, -a f

sar·don·ic [sɑː'dɒnɪk] adj sardonico

sar·don·i·cal·ly [sɑː'dɒnɪklɪ] adv sardonicamente

sash [sæʃ] on dress fusciacca f; on uniform fascia f; on window vetro m scorrevole (di finestra a ghigliottina)

Sa·tan ['seɪtn] Satana m

satch·el ['sætʃl] for schoolchild cartella f

sat·el·lite ['sætəlaɪt] satellite m

'sat·el·lite dish antenna f parabolica

sat·el·lite TV TV f inv satellitare

sat·in ['sætɪn] adj satin m inv

sat·ire ['sætaɪə(r)] satira f

sa·tir·i·cal [sə'tɪrɪkl] adj satirico

sat·i·rist ['sætərɪst] satirista m

sat·i·rize ['sætəraɪz] v/t satireggiare

sat·is·fac·tion [sætɪs'fækʃn] soddisfazione f; is that to your ~? è di suo gradimento?

sat·is·fac·to·ry [sætɪs'fæktərɪ] adj soddisfacente; just good enough sufficiente; this is not ~ non è sufficiente

satisfy ['sætɪsfaɪ] v/t (pret & pp **-ied**) customers, needs, curiosity soddisfare; requirement rispondere a; ~ s.o.'s hunger sfamare qu; I am satisfied had enough to eat sono sazio; I am satisfied that ... (convinced) sono convinto che ...; I hope you're satisfied! sei contento?

Sat·ur·day ['sætədeɪ] sabato m

sauce [sɔːs] salsa f, sugo m

'sauce·pan pentola f

sau·cer ['sɔːsə(r)] piattino m

sauc·y ['sɔːsɪ] adj person, dress provocante

Sau·di A·ra·bi·a [saʊdɪə'reɪbɪə] Arabia f Saudita

Sau·di A·ra·bi·an [saʊdɪə'reɪbɪən] **1** adj saudita **2** n person saudita m/f

sau·na ['sɔːnə] sauna f

saun·ter ['sɔːntə(r)] v/i passeggiare; he ~ed in at 10.30 è arrivato tranquillamente alle 10.30

saus·age ['sɒsɪdʒ] salsiccia f

sav·age ['sævɪdʒ] **1** adj animal selvaggio; attack, criticism feroce **2** n selvaggio m, -a f

sav·age·ry ['sævɪdʒrɪ] ferocia f

save [seɪv] **1** v/t (rescue) salvare; money, time, effort risparmiare; (collect) raccogliere; COMPUT salvare; goal parare; you could ~ yourself a lot of effort potresti risparmiarti parecchi sforzi **2** v/i (put money aside) risparmiare; SP parare **3** n SP parata f

♦ **save up for** v/t risparmiare per

sav·er ['seɪvə(r)] person risparmiatore m, -trice f

sav·ing ['seɪvɪŋ] risparmio m

sav·ings ['seɪvɪŋz] npl risparmi mpl

'sav·ings ac·count libretto m di risparmio; **sav·ings and 'loan** Am → **building society**; **'sav·ings bank** cassa f di risparmio sa·vior *Am*, **sa·viour** ['seɪvjə(r)] REL salvatore *m*

sa·vor *etc Am* → **savour** *etc*

sa·vour ['seɪvə(r)] **1** *n* sapore *m* **2** *v/t* assaporare

sa·vour·y ['seɪvərɪ] *adj not sweet* salato (*non dolce*)

saw¹ [sɔː] **1** *n tool* sega *f* **2** *v/t* segare

saw² [sɔː] *pret* → **see**

♦ **saw off** *v/t* segare via

'saw·dust segatura *f*

sax·o·phone ['sæksəfəʊn] sassofono *m*

say [seɪ] **1** *v/t* (*pret & pp* **said**) dire; *can I ~ something?* posso dire una cosa?; *that is to ~* sarebbe a dire; *what do you ~ to that?* cosa ne dici?; *what does the note ~?* cosa dice il biglietto? **2** *n*: *have one's ~* dire la propria; *have a ~ in sth* avere voce in capitolo in qc

say·ing ['seɪɪŋ] detto *m*

scab [skæb] *on skin* crosta *f*

scaf·fold·ing ['skæfəldɪŋ] *on building* impalcature *fpl*

scald [skɔːld] *v/t* scottare; *~ o.s.* scottarsi

scale¹ [skeɪl] *on fish* scaglia *f*

scale² [skeɪl] **1** *n of map, MUS* scala *f*; *on thermometer* scala *f* graduata; *of project* portata *f*; *on a large ~* su vasta scala; *on a small ~* su scala ridotta **2** *v/t cliffs etc* scalare

♦ **scale down** *v/t* ridurre

scale 'draw·ing disegno *m* in scala

scales [skeɪlz] *npl for weighing* bilancia *fsg*

scal·lop ['skɒləp] *n* capasanta *f*

scalp [skælp] *n* cuoio *m* capelluto

scal·pel ['skælpl] bisturi *m*

scam [skæm] F truffa *f*

scam·pi ['skæmpi] gamberoni *mpl* in pastella fritti

scan [skæn] **1** *v/t* (*pret & pp* **-ned**) *horizon* scrutare; *page* scorrere; *foetus* fare l'ecografia di; *brain* fare la TAC di; COMPUT scannerizzare **2** *n* (*brain ~*) TAC *f inv*; *of foetus* ecografia *f*

♦ **scan in** *v/t* COMPUT scannerizzare

scan·dal ['skændl] scandalo *m*

scan·dal·ize ['skændəlaɪz] *v/t* scandalizzare

scan·dal·ous ['skændələs] *adj* scandaloso

Scan·di·na·vi·a [skændɪ'neɪvɪə] Scandinavia *f*

scan·ner ['skænə(r)] scanner *m inv*

scant [skænt] *adj* scarso

scant·i·ly ['skæntɪlɪ] *adv*: *~ clad* succintamente vestito

scant·y ['skæntɪ] *adj clothes* succinto

scape·goat ['skeɪpgəʊt] capro *m* espiatorio

scar [skɑː(r)] **1** *n* cicatrice *f* **2** *v/t* (*pret & pp* **-red**) *face* lasciare cicatrici su; *fig* segnare

scarce [skeəs] *adj in short supply* scarso; *make o.s. ~* squagliarsela F

scarce·ly ['skeəslɪ] *adv* appena; *there was ~ anything left* non rimaneva quasi più niente

scar·ci·ty ['skeəsɪtɪ] scarsità *f inv*

scare [skeə(r)] **1** *v/t* spaventare; *be ~d of* avere paura di **2** *n* (*panic, alarm*) panico *m*; *give s.o. a ~* mettere paura a qu

♦ **scare away** *v/t* far scappare

'scare·crow spaventapasseri *m inv*

scare·mon·ger ['skeəmʌŋgə(r)] allarmista *m/f*

scarf [skɑːf] *around neck* sciarpa *f*; *over head* foulard *m inv*

scar·let ['skɑːlət] *adj* scarlatto

scar·let 'fe·ver scarlattina *f*

scar·y ['skeərɪ] *adj* che fa paura

scath·ing ['skeɪðɪŋ] *adj* caustico

scat·ter ['skætə(r)] **1** *v/t leaflets, seeds* spargere; *crowd* disperdere **2** *v/i of people* disperdersi

scat·ter·brained ['skætəbreɪnd] *adj* sventato

scat·tered ['skætəd] *adj family, villages* sparpagliato; *~ showers* precipitazioni sparse

scat·ty ['skætɪ] *adj* sventato

scav·enge ['skævɪndʒ] *v/i* frugare tra i rifiuti

scav·eng·er ['skævɪndʒə(r)] *animal* animale *m* necrofago; (*person*) persona *f* che fruga tra i rifiuti

sce·na·ri·o [sɪ'nɑːrɪəʊ] scenario *m*

scene [si:n] scena f; (argument) scenata f; **make a ~** fare una scenata; **~s** THEA scenografia f; **jazz / rock ~** il mondo del jazz / rock; **behind the ~s** dietro le quinte

sce·ne·ry ['si:nəri] paesaggio m; THEA scenario m

scent [sent] n of roses profumo m; of animal odore m

scep·tic ['skeptik] scettico m, -a f

scep·ti·cal ['skeptikl] adj scettico

scep·ti·cal·ly ['skeptikli] adv scetticamente

scep·ti·cism ['skeptisizm] scetticismo m

sched·ule ['ʃedjuːl] 1 n of events, work programma m; for trains orario m; **be on ~** of work, of train etc essere in orario; **be behind ~** of work, of train etc essere in ritardo 2 v/t put on schedule programmare; **it's ~d for completion next month** il completamento dei lavori è previsto per il mese prossimo

sched·uled 'flight ['ʃedjuːld] volo m di linea

scheme [ski:m] 1 n (plan) piano m; (plot) complotto m 2 v/i (plot) complottare, tramare

schem·ing ['ski:mɪŋ] adj intrigante

schiz·o·phre·ni·a [skɪtsə'fri:nɪə] schizofrenia f

schiz·o·phren·ic [skɪtsə'frenɪk] 1 n schizofrenico m, -a f 2 adj schizofrenico

schol·ar ['skɒlə(r)] studioso m, -a f

schol·ar·ly ['skɒlə(r)lɪ] adj dotto

schol·ar·ship ['skɒləʃɪp] (scholarly work) erudizione f; (financial award) borsa f di studio

school [sku:l] scuola f

'school bag (satchel) cartella f; 'school·boy scolaro m; 'school·children scolari mpl; 'school days npl tempi mpl della scuola; 'school·girl scolara f; 'school·mas·ter maestro m; 'school·mate compagno m, -a f di scuola; 'school·mis·tress maestra f; 'school·teach·er insegnante m/f

sci·at·i·ca [saɪ'ætɪkə] sciatica f

sci·ence ['saɪəns] scienza f

sci·ence 'fic·tion fantascienza f

sci·en·tif·ic [saɪən'tɪfɪk] adj scientifico

sci·en·tist ['saɪəntɪst] scienziato m, -a f

scis·sors ['sɪzəz] npl forbici fpl

scoff¹ [skɒf] v/t food sbafare

scoff² [skɒf] v/i (mock) canzonare

♦ scoff at v/t deridere

scold [skəʊld] v/t sgridare

scone [skɒn] focaccina f o dolcetto m da mangiare con il tè

scoop [sku:p] 1 n for grain, flour paletta f; for ice cream cucchiaio m dosatore; of ice cream pallina f; (story) scoop m inv 2 v/t (pick up) raccogliere

♦ scoop up v/t sollevare tra le braccia

scoot·er ['sku:tə(r)] with motor scooter m inv; child's monopattino m

scope [skəʊp] portata f; (opportunity) possibilità f inv

scorch [skɔ:tʃ] v/t bruciare

scorch·ing hot ['skɔ:tʃɪŋ] adj torrido

score [skɔ:(r)] 1 n SP punteggio m; (written music) spartito m; of film etc colonna f sonora; **what's the ~?** SP a quanto sono / siamo?; **have a ~ to settle with s.o.** avere un conto in sospeso con qu; **keep (the) ~** tenere il punteggio 2 v/t goal, point segnare; (cut) incidere 3 v/i segnare; (keep the score) tenere il punteggio

'score·board segnapunti m inv

scor·er ['skɔ:rə(r)] of goal, point marcatore m, -trice f; (score-keeper) segnapunti m/f inv

scorn [skɔ:n] 1 n disprezzo m; **pour ~ on sth** deridere qc 2 v/t idea, suggestion disprezzare

scorn·ful ['skɔ:nfʊl] adj sprezzante

scorn·ful·ly ['skɔ:nfʊlɪ] adv sprezzantemente

Scor·pi·o ['skɔ:pɪəʊ] ASTR Scorpione m

Scot [skɒt] scozzese m/f

Scotch [skɒtʃ] (whisky) scotch m inv

Scotch 'tape® Am scotch® m

cot-'free *adv*: **get off** ~ farla franca

Scot-land ['skɒtlənd] Scozia *f*

Scots-man ['skɒtsmən] scozzese *m*

Scots-wom-an ['skɒtswʊmən] scozzese *f*

Scot-tish ['skɒtɪʃ] *adj* scozzese

coun-drel ['skaʊndrəl] birbante *m/f*

cour[1] ['skaʊə(r)] *v/t* (*search*) setacciare

cour[2] ['skaʊə(r)] *v/t pans* sfregare

cout [skaʊt] *n* (*boy* ~) boy-scout *m inv*

cowl [skaʊl] **1** *n* sguardo *m* torvo **2** *v/i* guardare storto

cram [skræm] *v/i* (*pret & pp* **-med**) F filare *f*

cram-ble ['skræmbl] **1** *n* (*rush*) corsa *f* **2** *v/t message* rendere indecifrabile **3** *v/i climb* inerpicarsi; **he ~d to his feet** si rialzò in fretta

cram-bled 'eggs ['skræmbld] *npl* uova *fpl* strapazzate

crap [skræp] **1** *n metal* rottame *m*; (*fight*) zuffa *f*; (*little bit*) briciolo *m* **2** *v/t* (*pret & pp* **-ped**) *plan, project* abbandonare

scrap-book album *m inv*

crape [skreɪp] **1** *n on paintwork* graffio *m* **2** *v/t paintwork, one's arm etc* graffiare; *vegetables* raschiare; ~ **a living** sbarcare il lunario

♦ **scrape through** *v/i in exam* passare per il rotto della cuffia

scrap heap cumulo *m* di rottami; **good for the** ~ da buttare via; **scrap 'met-al** rottami *mpl*; **scrap 'pa-per** carta *f* già usata

crap-py ['skræpɪ] *adj work, writing* senza capo né coda

cratch [skrætʃ] **1** *n mark* graffio *m*; **have a** ~ *to stop itching* grattarsi; **start from** ~ ricominciare da zero; **not up to** ~ non all'altezza **2** *v/t* (*mark*) graffiare; *because of itch* grattare **3** *v/i of cat, nails* graffiare

crawl [skrɔːl] **1** *n* scarabocchio *m* **2** *v/t* scarabocchiare

craw-ny ['skrɔːnɪ] *adj* scheletrico

cream [skriːm] **1** *n* urlo *m*; **~s of laughter** risate *fpl* fragorose **2** *v/i* urlare

screech [skriːtʃ] **1** *n of tyres* stridio *m*; (*scream*) strillo *m* **2** *v/i of tyres* stridere; (*scream*) strillare

screen [skriːn] **1** *n in room, hospital* paravento *m*; *of smoke* cortina *f*; *cinema, COMPUT, of television* schermo *m*; **on the** ~ *in film* sullo schermo; **on (the)** ~ COMPUT su schermo **2** *v/t* (*protect, hide*) riparare; *film* proiettare; *for security reasons* vagliare

'**screen-play** sceneggiatura *f*; '**screen sav-er** COMPUT salvaschermo *m inv*; '**screen test** *for film* provino *m*

screw [skruː] **1** *n* vite *f* (metallica); V (*sex*) scopata *f* V **2** *v/t* V scopare V; F (*cheat*) fregare F; ~ **sth to sth** avvitare qc a qc

♦ **screw up 1** *v/t eyes* strizzare; *piece of paper* appallottolare; F (*make a mess of*) mandare all'aria **2** *v/i* F (*make a bad mistake*) fare un casino F

'**screw-driv-er** cacciavite *m*

screwed 'up [skruːd'ʌp] *adj* F *psychologically* complessato

'**screw top** *on bottle* tappo *m* a vite

screw-y ['skruːɪ] *adj* F svitato

scrib-ble ['skrɪbl] **1** *n* scarabocchio *m* **2** *v/t & v/i* (*write quickly*) scarabocchiare

scrimp [skrɪmp] *v/i*: ~ **and scrape** risparmiare fino all'ultimo soldo

script [skrɪpt] *for film, play* copione *m*; (*form of writing*) scrittura *f*

scrip-ture ['skrɪptʃə(r)]: **the (Holy) Scriptures** le Sacre Scritture *fpl*

'**script-writ-er** sceneggiatore *m*, -trice *f*

scroll [skrəʊl] *n* rotolo *m* di pergamena

♦ **scroll down** *v/i* COMPUT far scorrere il testo in avanti

♦ **scroll up** *v/i* COMPUT far scorrere il testo indietro

scrounge [skraʊndʒ] *v/t* scroccare

scroung-er ['skraʊndʒə(r)] scroccone *m*, -a *f*

scrub [skrʌb] *v/t* (*pret & pp* **-bed**) *floors, hands* sfregare (con spazzola)

S

scrub·bing brush ['skrʌbɪŋ] *for floor* spazzolone *m*

scruff·y ['skrʌfɪ] *adj* trasandato

scrum [skrʌm] *in rugby* mischia *f*

♦ **scrunch up** [skrʌntʃ] *v/t plastic cup etc* accartocciare

scru·ples ['skru:plz] *npl* scrupoli *mpl*; **have no ~ about doing sth** non avere scrupoli a fare qc

scru·pu·lous ['skru:pjʊləs] *adj* scrupoloso

scru·pu·lous·ly ['skru:pjʊləslɪ] *adv (meticulously)* scrupolosamente

scru·ti·nize ['skru:tɪnaɪz] *v/t text* esaminare attentamente; *face* scrutare

scru·ti·ny ['skru:tɪnɪ] attento esame *m*; **come under ~** essere sottoposto ad attento esame

scu·ba div·ing ['sku:bə] immersione *f* subacquea

scuf·fle ['skʌfl] *n* tafferuglio *m*

sculp·tor ['skʌlptə(r)] scultore *m*, -trice *f*

sculp·ture ['skʌlptʃə(r)] scultura *f*

scum [skʌm] *on liquid* schiuma *f*; *(pej: people)* feccia *f*

sea [si:] mare *m*; **by the ~** al mare

'sea·bed fondale *m* marino; **'sea·bird** uccello *m* marino; **sea·far·ing** ['si:feərɪŋ] *adj nation* marinaro; **'sea·food** frutti *mpl* di mare; **'sea·front** lungomare *m inv*; **'sea·go·ing** *adj vessel* d'alto mare; **'sea·gull** gabbiano *m*

seal¹ [si:l] *n animal* foca *f*

seal² [si:l] *n on document* sigillo *m*; TECH chiusura *f* ermetica **2** *v/t container* chiudere ermeticamente

♦ **seal off** *v/t area* bloccare l'accesso a

'sea lev·el: **above / below ~** sopra / sotto il livello del mare

seam [si:m] *n on garment* cucitura *f*; *of ore* filone *m*

'sea·man marinaio *m*

seam·stress ['si:mstrɪs] sarta *f*

'sea·port porto *m* marittimo

'sea pow·er *nation* potenza *f* marittima

search [sɜ:tʃ] **1** *n for s.o. / sth* ricerca *f*; *of person, building* perquisizione *f*; **in ~ of** alla ricerca di **2** *v/t person,*

building, baggage perquisire; *area* perlustrare

♦ **search for** *v/t* cercare

search·ing ['sɜ:tʃɪŋ] *adj look* penetrante

'search·light riflettore *m*; **'search par·ty** squadra *f* di ricerca; **'search war·rant** mandato *m* di perquisizione

'sea·shore riva *f* (del mare)

'sea·sick *adj* con il mal di mare; **be ~** avere il mal di mare; **get ~** soffrire il mal di mare; **'sea·side** *n*: **at the ~** al mare; **go to the ~** andare al mare; **~ resort** località *f* balneare

sea·son ['si:zn] *n* stagione *f*; **in / out of ~** in / fuori stagione

sea·son·al ['si:znl] *adj* stagionale

sea·soned ['si:znd] *adj wood* stagionato; *traveller, campaigner etc* esperto

sea·son·ing ['si:znɪŋ] condimento *m*

'sea·son tick·et abbonamento *m*

seat [si:t] **1** *n* posto *m*; *of trousers* fondo *m*; POL seggio *m*; **please take a ~** si accomodi **2** *v/t (have seating for)* avere posti a sedere per; **please remain ~ed** state seduti, per favore

'seat belt cintura *f* di sicurezza

'sea ur·chin riccio *m* di mare

'sea·weed alga *f*

se·clud·ed [sɪ'klu:dɪd] *adj* appartato

se·clu·sion [sɪ'klu:ʒn] isolamento *m*

sec·ond¹ ['sekənd] **1** *n of time* secondo *m*; **just a ~** un attimo **2** *adj* secondo **3** *adv come in* secondo **4** *v/t motion* appoggiare

se·cond² [sɪ'kɒnd] *v/t*: **be ~ed to** essere assegnato a

sec·ond·a·ry ['sekəndrɪ] *adj* secondario

sec·ond·a·ry ed·u·ca·tion istruzione *f* secondaria

se·cond best *adj* secondo (dopo il migliore); **sec·ond 'big·gest** *adj* secondo in ordine di grandezza; **sec·ond 'class** *adj ticket* di seconda classe; **sec·ond 'floor** secondo piano *m*; *Am* terzo piano; **sec·ond 'gear** MOT seconda *f* (marcia); **'sec·ond hand** *n on clock* lancetta

dei secondi; '**sec·ond-hand** *adj &*
adv di seconda mano
sec·ond·ly ['sekəndlɪ] *adv* in secondo luogo
sec·ond-'rate *adj* di second'ordine
sec·ond 'thoughts: I've had ~
thoughts ci ho ripensato
se·cre·cy ['siːkrəsɪ] segretezza *f*
se·cret ['siːkrət] **1** *n* segreto *m*; *do*
sth in ~ fare qc in segreto **2** *adj* segreto
se·cret 'a·gent agente *m* segreto
sec·re·tar·i·al [sekrəˈteərɪəl] *adj*
tasks, job di segretaria
sec·re·tar·y ['sekrətərɪ] segretario
m, -a *f*; POL ministro *m*
Sec·re·tar·y of 'State *in USA* Segretario *m* di Stato
se·crete [sɪˈkriːt] *v/t (give off)* secernere; *(hide away)* nascondere
se·cre·tion [sɪˈkriːʃn] secrezione *f*
se·cre·tive ['siːkrətɪv] *adj* riservato
se·cret·ly ['siːkrətlɪ] *adv* segretamente
se·cret po'lice polizia *f* segreta
se·cret 'ser·vice servizio *m* segreto
sect [sekt] setta *f*
sec·tion ['sekʃn] sezione *f*
sec·tor ['sektə(r)] settore *m*
sec·u·lar ['sekjʊlə(r)] *adj* laico
se·cure [sɪˈkjʊə(r)] **1** *adj shelf etc* saldo *feeling* sicuro; *job* stabile **2** *v/t*
shelf etc assicurare; *s.o.'s help,*
finances assicurarsi
se·cu·ri·ty [sɪˈkjʊərətɪ] *in job* sicurezza *f*; *in relationship* stabilità *f inv;*
for investment garanzia *f*; *at airport*
etc sicurezza *f*
se'cu·ri·ties mar·ket FIN mercato *m*
dei titoli
se'cu·ri·ty a·lert stato *m* di allarme;
se'cu·ri·ty check controllo *m* di sicurezza; **se'cu·ri·ty-con·scious**
adj attento alla sicurezza; **se'cu·ri·ty forces** *npl police* forze *fpl* dell'ordine; **se'cu·ri·ty forces** *npl* forze *fpl* di sicurezza; **se'cu·ri·ty**
guard guardia *f* giurata; **se'cu·ri·ty**
risk minaccia *f* per la sicurezza
se·date [sɪˈdeɪt] *v/t* somministrare
sedativi a

se·da·tion [sɪˈdeɪʃn]: *be under ~* essere sotto l'effetto di sedativi
sed·a·tive ['sedətɪv] *n* sedativo *m*
sed·en·ta·ry ['sedntərɪ] *adj job* sedentario
sed·i·ment ['sedɪmənt] sedimento *m*
se·duce [sɪˈdjuːs] *v/t* sedurre
se·duc·tion [sɪˈdʌkʃn] seduzione *f*
se·duc·tive [sɪˈdʌktɪv] *adj smile, look*
seducente; *offer* allettante
see [siː] *v/t (pret saw, pp seen)* vedere; *(understand)* capire; *romantically*
uscire con; *I ~* capisco; *can I ~ the*
manager? vorrei vedere il direttore; *you should ~ a doctor* dovresti
andare dal medico; *~ s.o. home* accompagnare a casa qu; *I'll ~ you to*
the door t'accompagno alla porta;
~ you! F ciao! F
♦ **see about** *v/t (look into)* provvedere a; *I'll see about it* ci penso io
♦ **see off** *v/t at airport etc* salutare;
(chase away) scacciare
♦ **see out** *v/t: see s.o. out* accompagnare qu alla porta
♦ **see to** *v/t: see to sth* occuparsi di
qc; *see to it that sth gets done* assicurarsi che qc venga fatto
seed [siːd] *single seme m; collective*
semi *mpl; in tennis* testa *f* di serie; *go*
to ~ of person, district ridursi male
seed·ling ['siːdlɪŋ] semenzale *m*
seed·y ['siːdɪ] *adj bar, district* squallido
see·ing (that) ['siːɪŋ] *conj* visto che
seek [siːk] *v/t & v/i (pret & pp*
sought) cercare
seem [siːm] *v/i* sembrare; *it seems*
that ... sembra che ...
seem·ing·ly ['siːmɪŋlɪ] *adv* apparentemente
seen [siːn] *pp → see*
seep [siːp] *v/i of liquid* filtrare
♦ **seep out** *v/i of liquid* filtrare
see·saw ['siːsɔː] *n* altalena *f* (a bilico)
seethe [siːð] *v/i fig* fremere di rabbia
'**see-through** *adj dress, material* trasparente
seg·ment ['segmənt] segmento *m; of*
orange spicchio *m*

seg·ment·ed [seg'mentɪd] *adj* frazionato

seg·re·gate ['segrɪgeɪt] *v/t* separare

seg·re·ga·tion [segrɪ'geɪʃn] segregazione *f*

seis·mol·o·gy [saɪz'mɒlədʒɪ] sismologia *f*

seize [siːz] *v/t s.o., s.o.'s arm* afferrare; *power* prendere; *opportunity* cogliere; *of Customs, police etc* sequestrare

♦ **seize up** *v/i of engine* grippare

sei·zure ['siːʒə(r)] MED attacco *m*; *of drugs etc* sequestro *m*

sel·dom ['seldəm] *adv* raramente

se·lect [sɪ'lekt] **1** *v/t* selezionare **2** *adj (exclusive)* scelto

se·lec·tion [sɪ'lekʃn] scelta *f; that / those chosen* selezione *f*

se·lec·tion pro·cess procedimento *m* di selezione

se·lec·tive [sɪ'lektɪv] *adj* selettivo

self [self] (*pl* **selves** [selvz]) io *m*

self-ad·dressed 'en·ve·lope [selfə-'drest] busta *f* col proprio nome e indirizzo; **self-as'sur·ance** sicurezza *f* di sé; **self-as·sured** [selfə-'ʃʊəd] *adj* sicuro di sé; **self-cater·ing a'part·ment** appartamento *m* indipendente con cucina; **self-'cen·tered** *Am*, **self-'cen·tred** [self'sentəd] *adj* egocentrico; **self-'clean·ing** *adj even* autopulente; **self-con'fessed** [selfkən'fest] *adj* dichiarato; **self-'con·fi·dence** fiducia *f* in se stessi; **self-'con·fi·dent** *adj* sicuro di sé; **self-'con·scious** *adj* insicuro; *smile* imbarazzato; *feel ~* sentirsi a disagio; **self-'con·scious·ness** disagio *m*; **self-con·tained** [selfkən'teɪnd] *adj flat* indipendente; **self con'trol** autocontrollo *m*; **self-de'fence**, **self-de'fense** *Am personal* legittima difesa *f; of state* autodifesa *f*; **self-'dis·ci·pline** autodisciplina *f*; **self-'doubt** dubbi *mpl* personali; **self-em·ployed** [selfɪm'plɔɪd] *adj* autonomo; **self-e'steem** autostima *f*; **self-'ev·i·dent** *adj* evidente; **self-ex'pres·sion** espressione *f* di sé;

self-'gov·ern·ment autogoverno *m*; **self-'in·terest** interesse *m* personale

self·ish ['selfɪʃ] *adj* egoista

self·less ['selflɪs] *adj person* altruista; *attitude, dedication* altruistico

self-made 'man [self'meɪd] self-made man *m inv*; **self-'pit·y** autocommiserazione *f*; **self-'por·trait** autoritratto *m*; **self-pos'sessed** *adj* padrone di sé; **self-re'li·ant** *adj* indipendente; **self-re'spect** dignità *f inv*; **self-'right·eous** *adj pej* presuntuoso; **self-'sat·is·fied** *adj pej* soddisfatto di sé; **self-'ser·vice** *adj* self-service; **self-ser·vice 'res·tau·rant** self-service *m inv*; **self-taught** [self'tɔːt] *adj* autodidatta

sell [sel] (*pret & pp* **sold**) **1** *v/t* vendere; *you have to ~ yourself* devi saperti vendere **2** *v/i of products* vendere

♦ **sell out of** *v/t* esaurire; *we are sold out of candles* abbiamo esaurito le candele

♦ **sell up** *v/i* vendere

'sell-by date data *f* di scadenza; *be past its ~* essere scaduto

sell·er ['selə(r)] venditore *m*, -trice *f*

sell·ing ['selɪŋ] *n* COM vendita *f*

'sell·ing point COM punto *m* forte (che fa vendere il prodotto)

Sel·lo·tape® ['seləteɪp] scotch® *m*

se·men ['siːmən] sperma *m*

se·mes·ter [sɪ'mestər] *Am* semestre *m*

sem·i ['semɪ] *n* → **semidetached 'house**

'sem·i·cir·cle semicerchio *m*

sem·i·cir·cu·lar *adj* semicircolare

semi-'co·lon punto e virgola *m*

sem·i·con'duc·tor ELEC semiconduttore *m*

sem·i·de·tached ('house) [semɪdɪ-'tætʃt] villa *f* bifamiliare

semi'fi·nal semifinale *f*

sem·i·nar ['semɪnɑː(r)] seminario *m*

sem·i'skilled *adj* parzialmente qualificato

sen·ate ['senət] senato *m*

sen·a·tor ['senətə(r)] senatore *m*, -trice *f*

send [send] *v/t* (*pret & pp* **sent**) mandare; **~ sth to s.o.** mandare qc a qu; **~ s.o. to s.o.** mandare qu da qu; **~ her my best wishes** mandale i miei saluti

♦ **send back** *v/t* mandare indietro

♦ **send for** *v/t* doctor, help (mandare a) chiamare

♦ **send in** *v/t* troops inviare; *next interviewee* far entrare; *application form* spedire

♦ **send off** *v/t* letter, fax etc spedire; *footballer* espellere

♦ **send up** *v/t* (*mock*) prendere in giro

send·er ['sendə(r)] of letter mittente *m/f*

se·nile ['si:naıl] *adj pej* rimbambito

se·nil·i·ty [sı'nılətı] *pej* rimabambimento *m*

se·ni·or ['si:nıə(r)] *adj* (*older*) più anziano; *in rank* di grado superiore; **be ~ to s.o.** *in rank* essere di grado superiore rispetto a qu

se·ni·or 'cit·i·zen anziano *m*, -a *f*

se·ni·or·i·ty [si:nı'ɒrətı] *in job* anzianità *f inv*

sen·sa·tion [sen'seıʃn] (*feeling*) sensazione *f*; (*surprise event*) scalpore *m*; **be a ~** essere sensazionale

sen·sa·tion·al [sen'seıʃnl] *adj* sensazionale

sense [sens] **1** *n* (*meaning*) significato *m*; (*purpose, point*) senso *m*; (*common sense*) buonsenso *m*; (*sight, smell etc*) senso *m*; (*feeling*) sensazione; **in a ~** in un certo senso; **talk ~, man!** ragiona!; **come to one's ~s** tornare in sé; **it doesn't make ~** non ha senso; **there's no ~ in trying / waiting** non ha senso provare / aspettare **2** *v/t* sentire

sense·less ['senslıs] *adj* (*pointless*) assurdo

sen·si·ble ['sensəbl] *adj* person, decision assennato; *advice* sensato; *clothes, shoes* pratico

sen·si·bly ['sensəblı] *adv* assennatamente

sen·si·tive ['sensıtıv] *adj* sensibile

sen·si·tiv·i·ty [sensə'tıvıtı] sensibilità *f inv*

sen·sor ['sensə(r)] sensore *m*

sen·su·al ['sensjuəl] *adj* sensuale

sen·su·al·i·ty [sensju'ælətı] sensualità *f inv*

sen·su·ous ['sensjuəs] *adj* sensuale

sent [sent] *pret & pp →* **send**

sen·tence ['sentəns] **1** *n* GRAM frase *m*; LAW condanna *f* **2** *v/t* LAW condannare

sen·ti·ment ['sentımənt] (*sentimentality*) sentimentalismo *m*; (*opinion*) opinione *f*

sen·ti·men·tal [sentı'mentl] *adj* sentimentale

sen·ti·men·tal·i·ty [sentımen'tælətı] sentimentalismo *m*

sen·try ['sentrı] sentinella *f*

sep·a·rate ['sepərət] **1** *adj* separato **2** *v/t* ['sepəreıt] separare; **~ sth from sth** separare qc da qc **3** *v/i* of couple separarsi

sep·a·rat·ed ['sepəreıtıd] *adj* couple separato

sep·a·rate·ly ['sepərətlı] *adv* separatamente

sep·a·ra·tion [sepə'reıʃn] separazione *f*

Sep·tem·ber [sep'tembə(r)] settembre *m*

sep·tic ['septık] *adj* infetto; **go ~** of wound infettarsi

se·quel ['si:kwəl] seguito *m*

se·quence ['si:kwəns] sequenza *f*; **in ~** di seguito; **out of ~** fuori tempo; **the ~ of events** l'ordine dei fatti

se·rene [sı'ri:n] *adj* sereno

ser·geant ['sɑːdʒənt] sergente *m*

se·ri·al ['sıərıəl] *n* serial *m inv*

se·ri·al·ize ['sıərıəlaız] *v/t* novel on TV trasmettere a puntate

'se·ri·al kill·er serial killer *m/f inv*; **'se·ri·al num·ber** of product numero *m* di serie; **'se·ri·al port** COMPUT porta *f* seriale

se·ries ['sıəriːz] *nsg* serie *f inv*

se·ri·ous ['sıərıəs] *adj* illness, situation, damage grave; person, company serio; **I'm ~** dico sul serio; **listen,**

this is ~ ascolta, è una cosa seria; *we'd better take a* ~ *look at it* dovremo considerarlo seriamente

se·ri·ous·ly ['sɪərɪəslɪ] *adv injured* gravemente; *(extremely)* estremamente; ~ *though, ...* scherzi a parte, ...; ~? davvero?; *take s.o.* ~ prendere sul serio qu

se·ri·ous·ness ['sɪərɪəsnɪs] *of person* serietà *f inv*; *of situation, illness etc* gravità *f inv*

ser·mon ['sɜːmən] predica *f*

ser·vant ['sɜːvənt] domestico *m*, -a *f*

serve [sɜːv] **1** *n in tennis* servizio *m* **2** *v/t food, customer, one's country,* servire; *it* ~*s you/him right* ti/gli sta bene **3** *v/i give out food, in tennis* servire; *as politician etc* prestare servizio

♦ serve up *v/t meal* servire

serv·er ['sɜːvə(r)] COMPUT server *m inv*

ser·vice ['sɜːvɪs] **1** *n to customers, community* servizio *m*; *for vehicle, machine* manutenzione *f*; *for vehicle* revisione *f*; *in tennis* servizio *m*; *the* ~*s* MIL le forze armate **2** *v/t vehicle* revisionare; *machine* fare la manutenzione di

'ser·vice ar·e·a area *f* di servizio; 'ser·vice charge *in restaurant, club* servizio *m*; 'ser·vice in·dus·try settore *m* terziario; 'ser·vice·man MIL militare *m*; 'ser·vice pro·vid·er COMPUT fornitore *m* di servizi; 'ser·vice sec·tor settore *m* terziario; 'ser·vice sta·tion stazione *f* di servizio

ser·vi·ette [sɜːvɪ'et] tovagliolino *m*

ser·vile ['sɜːvaɪl] *adj pej* servile

serv·ing ['sɜːvɪŋ] *n of food* porzione *f*

ses·sion ['seʃn] *of parliament* sessione *f*; *with psychiatrist, consultant etc* seduta *f*

set [set] **1** *n of tools* set *m inv*; *of dishes, knives* servizio *m*; *of books* raccolta *f*; *group of people* cerchia *f*; MATH insieme *m*; *(THEA: scenery)* scenografia *f*; *where a film is made* set *m inv*; *in tennis* set *m inv*; *television* ~ televisore *m* **2** *v/t (pret* *& pp* **set)** *(place)* mettere; *film, novel etc* ambientare; *date, time, limit* fissare; *mechanism* regolare; *alarm clock* mettere; *broken limb* ingessare; *jewel* montare; *(typeset)* comporre; ~ *the table* apparecchiare (la tavola); ~ *a task for s.o.* assegnare un compito a qu **3** *v/i (pret* *& pp* **set)** *of sun* tramontare; *of glue* indurirsi **4** *adj views, ideas* rigido; *(ready)* pronto; *be dead* ~ *on (doing) sth* essere deciso a fare qc; *be very* ~ *in one's ways* essere abitudinario; ~ *book/reading in course* libro/lettura in programma; ~ *meal* menù *m inv* fisso

♦ set apart *v/t*: *set sth apart from sth* distinguere qc da qc

♦ set aside *v/t for future use* mettere da parte

♦ set back *v/t in plans etc* ritardare; *it set me back £400* F mi è costato 400 sterline

♦ set off **1** *v/i on journey* partire **2** *v/t explosion* causare; *chain reaction, alarm* far scattare

♦ set out **1** *v/i on journey* partire **2** *v/t ideas, proposal, goods* esporre; *set out to do sth (intend)* proporsi di fare qc

♦ set to *v/i start on a task* mettersi all'opera

♦ set up **1** *v/t new company* fondare; *system* mettere in opera; *equipment, machine* piazzare; F *(frame)* incastrare F **2** *v/i in business* mettersi in affari

'set·back contrattempo *m*

set·tee [se'tiː] *(couch, sofa)* divano *m*

set·ting ['setɪŋ] *n of novel etc* ambientazione *f*; *of house* posizione *f*

set·tle ['setl] **1** *v/i of bird, dust, beer* posarsi; *of building* assestarsi; *to live* stabilirsi **2** *v/t dispute* comporre; *issue, uncertainty* risolvere; *s.o.'s debts, the bill* saldare; *nerves, stomach* calmare; *that* ~*s it!* è deciso!

♦ settle down *v/i (stop being noisy)* calmarsi; *(stop wild living)* mettere la testa a posto; *in an area* stabilirsi

◆ **settle for** v/t (take, accept) accontentarsi di

◆ **settle up** v/i (pay) regolare i conti; *in hotel etc* pagare il conto

set·tled ['setld] *adj weather* stabile

set·tle·ment ['setlmənt] *of dispute* composizione f; (payment) pagamento m

set·tler ['setlə(r)] *in new country* colonizzatore m, -trice f

'**set-up** n (structure) organizzazione f; (relationship) relazione f; (frameup) montatura f

sev·en ['sevn] sette

sev·en·teen [sevn'ti:n] diciassette

sev·en·teenth [sevn'ti:nθ] diciassettesimo, -a

sev·enth ['sevnθ] *n & adj* settimo, -a

sev·en·ti·eth ['sevntiθ] *n & adj* settantesimo, -a

sev·en·ty ['sevnti] settanta

sev·er ['sevə(r)] v/t arm, cable etc recidere; *relations* troncare

sev·e·ral ['sevrl] **1** *adj* parecchi **2** *pron* parecchi m, -ie f

se·vere [sɪ'vɪə(r)] *adj illness* grave; *penalty, teacher, face* severo; *winter, weather* rigido

se·vere·ly [sɪ'vɪəlɪ] *adv punish* severamente; *speak, stare* duramente; *injured, disrupted* gravemente

se·ver·i·ty [sɪ'verətɪ] *of illness* gravità f inv; *of look etc* durezza f; *of penalty* severità f inv; *of winter* rigidità f inv

sew [səʊ] v/t & v/i (pret **-ed**, pp **sewn**) cucire

◆ **sew on** v/t button attaccare

sew·age ['su:ɪdʒ] acque fpl di scolo

'**sew·age plant** impianto m per il riciclaggio delle acque di scolo

sew·er ['su:ə(r)] fogna f

sew·ing ['səʊɪŋ] n cucito m

'**sew·ing ma·chine** macchina f da cucire

sex [seks] sesso m; **have ~ with** avere rapporti sessuali con

sex·ist ['seksɪst] **1** adj sessista **2** n sessista m/f

sex·u·al ['seksjʊəl] adj sessuale

sex·u·al as'sault violenza f sessuale;

sex·u·al ha'rass·ment molestie fpl sessuali; **sex·u·al 'in·ter·course** rapporti mpl sessuali

sex·u·al·i·ty [seksjʊ'ælətɪ] sessualità f inv

sex·u·al·ly ['seksjʊlɪ] adv sessualmente

sex·u·al·ly trans·mit·ted dis'ease [seksjʊlɪtrænz'mɪtɪd] malattia f venerea

sex·y ['seksɪ] adj sexy inv

shab·bi·ly ['ʃæbɪlɪ] adv dressed in modo trasandato; *treat* in modo meschino

shab·bi·ness ['ʃæbɪnɪs] of coat etc trasandatezza f

shab·by ['ʃæbɪ] adj coat etc trasandato; *treatment* meschino

shack [ʃæk] baracca f

shade [ʃeɪd] **1** n for lamp paralume m; of colour tonalità f inv; **in the ~** all'ombra **2** v/t from sun, light riparare

shad·ow ['ʃædəʊ] n ombra f

shad·y ['ʃeɪdɪ] adj spot all'ombra; *character, dealings* losco

shaft [ʃɑːft] of axle albero m; of mine pozzo m

shag·gy ['ʃægɪ] adj hair arruffato; *dog* dal pelo arruffato

shake [ʃeɪk] **1** n: **give sth a good ~** dare una scrollata a qc **2** v/t (pret **shook**, pp **shaken**) scuotere; *emotionally* sconvolgere; **~ hands** stringersi la mano; **~ hands with s.o.** stringere la mano a qu **3** v/i of hands, voice, building tremare

shak·en ['ʃeɪkən] **1** adj emotionally scosso **2** pp → **shake**

'**shake-up** rimpasto m

'**shak·y** ['ʃeɪkɪ] adj table etc traballante; *after illness, shock* debole; *grasp of sth, grammar etc* incerto; *voice, hand* tremante

shall [ʃæl] v/aux ◊ future: **I ~ do my best** farò del mio meglio; **I shan't see them** non li vedrò ◊ suggesting: **~ we go now?** andiamo?

shal·low ['ʃæləʊ] adj water poco profondo; *person* superficiale

sham·bles ['ʃæmblz] nsg casino m F

shame [ʃeɪm] **1** n vergogna f; **bring ~ on ...** disonorare ...; **what a ~!** che peccato!; **~ on you!** vergognati! **2** v/t: **~ s.o. into doing sth** indurre qu a fare qc per vergogna

shame·ful ['ʃeɪmfʊl] adj vergognoso

shame·ful·ly ['ʃeɪmfʊlɪ] adv vergognosamente

shame·less ['ʃeɪmlɪs] adj svergognato

sham·poo [ʃæm'puː] **1** n shampoo m inv; **a ~ and set** shampoo e messa in piega **2** v/t fare lo shampoo a

shape [ʃeɪp] **1** n forma f **2** v/t clay dar forma a; person's life, character forgiare; the future determinare

shape·less ['ʃeɪplɪs] adj dress etc informe

shape·ly ['ʃeɪplɪ] adv figure ben fatto

share [ʃeə(r)] **1** n parte f; FIN azione f; **do one's ~ of the work** fare la propria parte del lavoro **2** v/t dividere; s.o.'s feelings, opinions condividere **3** v/i dividere; **do you mind sharing with Patrick?** ti dispiace dividere con Patrick?

♦ **share out** v/t spartire

'**share·hold·er** azionista m/f

shark [ʃɑːk] fish squalo m

sharp [ʃɑːp] **1** adj knife affilato; mind, pain acuto; taste aspro **2** adv MUS in diesis; **at 3 o'clock** ~ alle 3 precise

sharp·en ['ʃɑːpn] v/t knife affilare; skills raffinare

sharp 'prac·tice pratiche fpl poco oneste

shat [ʃæt] pret & pp → **shit**

shat·ter ['ʃætə(r)] **1** v/t glass frantumare; illusions distruggere **2** v/i of glass frantumarsi

shat·tered ['ʃætəd] adj F (exhausted) esausto; (very upset) sconvolto

shat·ter·ing ['ʃætərɪŋ] adj news, experience sconvolgente; effect tremendo

shave [ʃeɪv] **1** v/t radere **2** v/i farsi la barba **3** n: **have a ~** farsi la barba; **that was a close ~** ce l'abbiamo fatta per un pelo

♦ **shave off** v/t beard tagliarsi; from piece of wood piallare

shav·en ['ʃeɪvn] adj head rasato

shav·er ['ʃeɪvə(r)] electric rasoio m

shav·ing brush ['ʃeɪvɪŋ] pennello m da barba

'**shav·ing soap** sapone m da barba

shawl [ʃɔːl] scialle m

she [ʃiː] pron lei; **~ has three children** ha tre figli; **you're funny, ~'s not** tu sei spiritoso, lei no; **there ~ is** eccola

shears [ʃɪəz] npl for gardening cesoie fpl; for sewing forbici fpl

sheath [ʃiːθ] n for knife guaina f; contraceptive preservativo m

shed[1] [ʃed] v/t (pret & pp **shed**) blood spargere; tears versare; leaves perdere; **~ light on** fig fare luce su

shed[2] [ʃed] n baracca f

sheep [ʃiːp] (pl **sheep**) pecora f

'**sheep·dog** cane m pastore

sheep·ish ['ʃiːpɪʃ] adj imbarazzato

'**sheep·skin** adj lining di montone

sheer [ʃɪə(r)] adj madness, luxury puro; drop, cliffs ripido

sheet [ʃiːt] for bed lenzuolo m; of paper foglio m; of metal, glass lastra f

shelf [ʃelf] (pl **shelves** [ʃelvz]) mensola f; **shelves** scaffale msg, ripiani mpl

shelf-life of product durata f di conservazione

shell [ʃel] **1** n of mussel etc conchiglia f; of egg guscio m; of tortoise corazza f; MIL granata f; **come out of one's ~** fig uscire dal guscio **2** v/t peas sbucciare; MIL bombardare

'**shell·fire** bombardamento m; **come under ~** essere bombardato

'**shell·fish** crostacei mpl

shel·ter ['ʃeltə(r)] **1** n (refuge) riparo m; construction rifugio m **2** v/i from rain, bombing etc ripararsi **3** v/t (protect) proteggere

shel·tered ['ʃeltəd] adj place riparato; **lead a ~ life** vivere nella bambagia

shelve [ʃelv] v/t fig accantonare

shep·herd ['ʃepəd] n pastore m

sher·ry ['ʃerɪ] sherry m inv

shield [ʃiːld] **1** n scudo m; sports trophy scudetto m; TECH schermo m di protezione f **2** v/t (*protect*) proteggere

shift [ʃɪft] **1** n (*change*) cambiamento m; *period of work* turno m **2** v/t (*move*) spostare; *stains etc* togliere **3** v/i (*move*) spostarsi; *of wind* cambiare direzione; *that's ~ing!* È un bolide!

'shift key COMPUT tasto m shift; 'shift work turni mpl; 'shift work-er turnista m/f

shift·y ['ʃɪftɪ] adj pej losco

shift-y-look·ing adj pej dall'aria losca

hilly-shally ['ʃɪlɪʃælɪ] v/i (*pret & pp -ied*) F tentennare

him·mer ['ʃɪmə(r)] v/i luccicare

shin [ʃɪn] n stinco m

shine [ʃaɪn] **1** v/i (*pret & pp shone*) *of sun, shoes, metal* splendere; *fig: of student etc* brillare **2** v/t (*pret & pp shone*) *torch etc* puntare **3** n *on shoes etc* lucentezza f

shin-gle ['ʃɪŋgl] *on beach* ciottoli mpl

shin-gles ['ʃɪŋglz] nsg MED fuoco m di Sant'Antonio

shin·y ['ʃaɪnɪ] adj *surface* lucido

ship [ʃɪp] **1** n nave f **2** v/t (*pret & pp -ped*) (*send*) spedire; (*send by sea*) spedire via mare

ship·ment ['ʃɪpmənt] (*consignment*) carico m

ship·own·er armatore m

ship·ping ['ʃɪpɪŋ] n (*sea traffic*) navigazione f; (*sending*) trasporto m (via mare)

ship·ping com·pa·ny compagnia f di navigazione

shipshape adj in perfetto ordine; 'ship·wreck **1** n naufragio m **2** v/t: *be ~ed* naufragare; 'ship·yard cantiere m navale

shirk [ʃɜːk] v/t scansare

shirk·er ['ʃɜːkə(r)] scansafatiche m/f inv

shirt [ʃɜːt] camicia f; *in his ~ sleeves* in maniche di camicia

shit [ʃɪt] **1** n P merda f P; *bad quality goods, work* stronzata f P **2** v/i (*pret & pp shat*) cagare P **3** int merda P

shit·ty ['ʃɪtɪ] adj F di merda P

shiv·er ['ʃɪvə(r)] **1** v/i rabbrividire **2** n brivido m

shock [ʃɒk] **1** n shock m inv; ELEC scossa f; *be in ~* MED essere in stato di shock **2** v/t scioccare; *be ~ed by* essere scioccato da

'shock ab·sorb·er MOT ammortizzatore m

shock·ing ['ʃɒkɪŋ] adj *behaviour, poverty* scandaloso; F *very bad* allucinante f

shock·ing·ly ['ʃɒkɪŋlɪ] adv *behave* scandalosamente; *bad, late, expensive* terribilmente

shod·dy ['ʃɒdɪ] adj *goods* scadente; *behaviour* meschino

shoe [ʃuː] scarpa f

'shoe·horn calzascarpe m inv; 'shoe·lace laccio m di scarpa; 'shoe·mak·er, 'shoe mender calzolaio m; 'shoe·shop negozio m di scarpe; 'shoe·string n: *do sth on a ~* fare qc con pochi soldi

shone [ʃɒn] pret & pp → **shine**

♦shoo away [ʃuː] v/t *children, chicken* scacciare

shook [ʃʊk] pret → **shake**

shoot [ʃuːt] **1** n BOT germoglio m **2** v/t v/t (*pret & pp shot*) sparare; *film* girare; *~ s.o. in the leg* colpire qu alla gamba; *~ s.o. for desertion* fucilare qu per diserzione

♦shoot down v/t *aeroplane* abbattere

♦shoot off v/i (*rush off*) precipitarsi

♦shoot up v/i *of prices* salire alle stelle; *of children* crescere molto; *of new suburbs, buildings etc* spuntare; F *of drug addict* farsi F

shoot·ing star ['ʃuːtɪŋ] stella f cadente

shop [ʃɒp] **1** n negozio m; *talk ~* parlare di lavoro **2** v/i (*pret & pp -ped*) fare acquisti; *go ~ping* andare a fare spese

shop as·sis·tant commesso m, -a f; 'shop·keep·er negoziante m/f; shop·lift·er ['ʃɒplɪftə(r)] taccheggiatore m, -trice f; shop·lift·ing ['ʃɒplɪftɪŋ] n taccheggio m

S

shop·per ['ʃɒpə(r)] *person* acquirente *m/f*

shop·ping ['ʃɒpɪŋ] *activity* fare spese; *items* spesa *f*; **do one's ~** fare la spesa

'**shop·ping bag** borsa *f* per la spesa; '**shop·ping cen·ter** *Am*, '**shop·ping cen·tre** centro *m* commerciale; '**shop·ping list** lista *f* della spesa; '**shop·ping mall** centro *m* commerciale

shop '**stew·ard** rappresentante *m/f* sindacale

shop '**win·dow** vetrina *f*

shore [ʃɔː(r)] riva *f*; **on ~** *not at sea* a terra

short [ʃɔːt] **1** *adj in length, distance* corto; *in height* basso; *in time* breve; **be ~ of** essere a corto di **2** *adv*: **cut a vacation / meeting ~** interrompere una vacanza / riunione; **stop a person ~** interrompere una persona; **go ~ of** fare a meno di; **in ~** in breve

short·age ['ʃɔːtɪdʒ] mancanza *f*

short '**cir·cuit** *n* corto *m* circuito; **short-com·ing** ['ʃɔːtkʌmɪŋ] difetto *m*; '**short cut** scorciatoia *f*

short·en ['ʃɔːtn] **1** *v/t* accorciare **2** *v/i* accorciarsi

'**short·fall** deficit *m inv*; *in hours etc* mancanza *f*; '**short·hand** *n* stenografia *f*; **short-'handed** *adj*: **be ~** essere a corto di personale; '**short·list** *n of candidates* rosa *f* dei candidati

short-lived ['ʃɔːtlɪvd] *adj* di breve durata

'**short·ly** ['ʃɔːtlɪ] *adv* (*soon*) tra breve; **~ before / after** poco prima / dopo

short·ness ['ʃɔːtnɪs] *of visit* brevità *f inv*; *in height* bassa statura *f*

shorts [ʃɔːts] *npl* calzoncini *mpl*

short·sight·ed [ʃɔːt'saɪtɪd] *adj also fig* miope; **short-sleeved** ['ʃɔːt-sliːvd] *adj* a maniche corte; **short-staffed** [ʃɔːt'stɑːft] *adj* a corto di personale; **short 'sto·ry** racconto *m*; **short-tem·pered** [ʃɔːt'tempəd] *adj* irascibile; '**short-term** *adj* a bre-

ve termine; '**short time** *n*: **be on ~** *of workers* lavorare a orario ridotto; '**short wave** RAD onde *fpl* corte

shot [ʃɒt] **1** *n from gun* sparo *m*; (*photograph*) foto *f*; (*injection*) puntura *f*; **be a good / poor ~** essere un buon / pessimo tiratore; **like a ~** *accept, run off* come un razzo **2** *pret & pp* → **shoot**

'**shot·gun** fucile *m* da caccia

should [ʃʊd] *v/aux*: **what ~ I do?** cosa devo fare?; **you ~n't do that** non dovresti farlo; **that ~ be long enough** dovrebbe essere lungo abbastanza; **you ~ have heard him!** avresti dovuto sentirlo!

shoul·der ['ʃəʊldə(r)] *n* ANAT spalla *f*; '**shoul·der bag** borsa *f* a tracolla; '**shoul·der blade** scapola *f*; '**shoulder strap** spallina *f*

shout [ʃaʊt] **1** *n* grido *m*, urlo *m* **2** *v/t & v/i* gridare, urlare
♦ **shout at** *v/t* urlare a

shout·ing ['ʃaʊtɪŋ] *n* urla *fpl*

shove [ʃʌv] **1** *n* spinta *f* **2** *v/t & v/i* spingere
♦ **shove in** *v/i* passare davanti; **he shoved in in front of me** mi è passato davanti
♦ **shove off** *v/i* F (*go away*) levarsi di torno

shov·el ['ʃʌvl] **1** *n* pala *f* **2** *v/t* spalare

show [ʃəʊ] **1** *n* THEA, TV spettacolo *m*; (*display*) manifestazione *f*; **on ~** *at exhibition* esposto; **it's all done for ~** *pej* è tutta una scena **2** *v/t* (*pret -ed, pp shown*) *passport, ticket* mostrare; *interest, emotion* dimostrare; *at exhibition* esporre; *film* proiettare; **~ s.o. sth, ~ sth to s.o.** mostrare qc a qu **3** *v/i* (*pret -ed, pp shown*) (*be visible*) vedersi; **does it ~?** si vede?; **what's ~ing at the cinema?** cosa danno al cinema?
♦ **show around** *v/t* far visitare
♦ **show in** *v/t* far entrare
♦ **show off 1** *v/t skills* mettere in risalto **2** *v/i pej* mettersi in mostra
♦ **show up 1** *v/t s.o.'s shortcomings etc* far risaltare; **don't show me up in public** non farmi fare brutta figura

2 v/i F (*arrive, turn up*) farsi vedere F; (*be visible*) notarsi

show busi·ness il mondo dello spettacolo

'**show·case** n vetrinetta f; *fig* vetrina f

'**show·down** regolamento m di conti

show·er ['ʃaʊə(r)] **1** n of rain acquazzone m; *to wash* doccia f; **take a ~** fare una doccia **2** v/i fare la doccia **3** v/t: **~ s.o. with praise** coprire qu di lodi

show·er cap cuffia f da doccia; '**show·er cur·tain** tenda f della doccia; '**show·er·proof** adj impermeabile

show·jump·er ['ʃəʊdʒʌmpə(r)] cavaliere m, cavallerizza f di concorso ippico

show·jump·ing concorso m ippico

'**show-off** pej esibizionista m/f

'**show·room** show-room m inv; **in ~ condition** mai usato

show·y ['ʃəʊɪ] adj appariscente

shrank [ʃræŋk] pret → **shrink**

shred [ʃred] **1** n of paper strisciolina f; of cloth brandello m; of evidence, etc briciolo m **2** v/t (pret & pp **-ded**) paper stracciare; in cooking sminuzzare

shred·der ['ʃredə(r)] for documents distruttore m di documenti

shrewd [ʃruːd] adj person, businessman scaltro; investment oculato

shrewd·ly ['ʃruːdlɪ] adv oculatamente

shrewd·ness ['ʃruːdnɪs] oculatezza f

shriek [ʃriːk] **1** n strillo m **2** v/i strillare

shrill [ʃrɪl] adj stridulo

shrimp [ʃrɪmp] gamberetto m

shrine [ʃraɪn] santuario m

shrink¹ [ʃrɪŋk] v/i (pret **shrank**, pp **shrunk**) of material restringersi; level of support etc diminuire

shrink² [ʃrɪŋk] n F (psychiatrist) strizzacervelli m/f inv

'**shrink-wrap** v/t cellofanare

'**shrink-wrap·ping** process cellofanatura f; material cellophane® m inv

shriv·el ['ʃrɪvl] v/i avvizzire

Shrove 'Tues·day [ʃrəʊv] martedì m grasso

shrub [ʃrʌb] arbusto m

shrub·be·ry ['ʃrʌbərɪ] arboreto m

shrug [ʃrʌg] **1** n alzata f di spalle **2** v/i (pret & pp **-ged**) alzare le spalle **3** v/t (pret & pp **-ged**): **~ one's shoulders** alzare le spalle

shrunk [ʃrʌŋk] pp → **shrink**

shud·der ['ʃʌdə(r)] **1** n of fear, disgust brivido m; of earth etc tremore m **2** v/i with fear, disgust rabbrividire; of earth, building tremare; **I ~ to think** non oso immaginare

shuf·fle ['ʃʌfl] **1** v/t cards mescolare **2** v/i in walking strascicare i piedi; **he ~d into the bathroom** è andato in bagno strascicando i piedi

shun [ʃʌn] v/t (pret & pp **-ned**) evitare

shut [ʃʌt] (pret & pp **shut**) **1** v/t chiudere **2** v/i of door, box chiudere; of shop, bank chiudere; **they were ~** era chiuso

♦ **shut down 1** v/t business chiudere; computer spegnere **2** v/i of business chiudere i battenti; of computer spegnersi

♦ **shut off** v/t chiudere

♦ **shut up** v/i F (be quiet) star zitto; **shut up!** zitto!

shut·ter ['ʃʌtə(r)] on window battente m; PHOT otturatore m

'**shut·ter speed** PHOT tempo m di apertura

shut·tle ['ʃʌtl] v/i fare la spola

'**shut·tle-bus** at airport bus m inv navetta; '**shut·tle·cock** SP volano m; '**shut·tle ser·vice** servizio m navetta

shy [ʃaɪ] adj timido

shy·ness ['ʃaɪnɪs] timidezza f

Si·a·mese 'twins [saɪə'miːz] npl fratelli mpl/ sorelle fpl siamesi

Si·cil·i·an [sɪ'sɪlɪən] **1** adj siciliano **2** n siciliano m, -a f

Sic·i·ly ['sɪsɪlɪ] Sicilia f

sick [sɪk] adj malato; sense of humour crudele; **I feel ~** about to vomit ho la nausea; **I'm going to be ~** vomit ho voglia di vomitare; **be ~ of** (fed up *with*) essere stufo di

sick·en ['sıkn] **1** *v/t* (*disgust*) disgustare **2** *v/i*: **be ~ing for sth** covare qc

sick·en·ing ['sıknıŋ] *adj* disgustoso

'**sick leave** *n*: **be on ~** essere in (congedo per) malattia

sick·ly ['sıklı] *adj person* delicato; *smell* stomachevole

sick·ness ['sıknıs] malattia *f*; (*vomiting*) nausea *f*

'**sick·ness ben·e·fit** *Br* indennità *f inv* di malattia

side [saɪd] *n of box, house* lato *m*; *of person, mountain* fianco *m*; *of page, record* facciata *f*; SP squadra *f*; **take ~s** (*favour one side*) prendere posizione; **take ~s with** parteggiare per; **I'm on your ~** sono dalla tua (parte); **~ by ~** fianco a fianco; **at the ~ of the road** sul ciglio della strada; **on the big** / **small ~** piuttosto grande / piccolo

♦ **side with** *v/t* prendere le parti di

'**side·board** credenza *f*; '**side·burns** *npl* basette *fpl*; '**side dish** contorno *m*; '**side ef·fect** effetto *m* collaterale; '**side·light** MOT luce *f* di posizione; '**side·line 1** *n* attività *f inv* collaterale **2** *v/t*: **feel ~d** sentirsi sminuito; '**side·step** *v/t* (*pret & pp -ped*) scansare; *fig* schivare; '**side street** via *f* laterale; '**side·track** *v/t* distrarre; **get ~ed by** essere distratto da; '**side·walk** *Am* marciapiede *m*; **side·ways** ['saɪdweɪz] *adv* di lato

siege [siːdʒ] *n* assedio *m*; **lay ~ to** assediare

sieve [sɪv] *n* setaccio *m*

sift [sɪft] *v/t* setacciare

♦ **sift through** *v/t details, data* passare al vaglio

sigh [saɪ] **1** *n* sospiro *m*; **heave a ~ of relief** tirare un respiro di sollievo **2** *v/i* sospirare

sight [saɪt] *n* vista *f*; **~s of city** luoghi *mpl* da visitare; **catch ~ of** intravedere; **know by ~** conoscere di vista; **be within ~ of** essere visibile da; **out of ~** non visibile; **out of ~ of** fuori dalla vista di; **what a ~ you are!**

come sei conciato!; **lose ~ of** *main objective etc* perdere di vista

sight·see·ing ['saɪtsiːɪŋ] *n* visita *f* turistica; **I enjoy ~** mi piace visitare i posti; **go ~** fare un giro turistico

'**sight·see·ing tour** giro *m* turistico

sight·seer ['saɪtsiːə(r)] turista *m/f*

sign [saɪn] **1** *n* (*indication*) segno *m*; (*road ~*) segnale *m*; (*outside shop*) insegna *f*; **it's a ~ of the times** è tipico dei nostri giorni **2** *v/t & v/i document* firmare

♦ **sign in** *v/i* firmare il registro (all'arrivo)

♦ **sign up** *v/i* (*join the army*) arruolarsi

sig·nal ['sıgnl] **1** *n* segnale *m*; **be sending out the right** / **wrong ~s** *fig* lanciare il messaggio giusto / sbagliato **2** *v/i of driver* segnalare

sig·na·to·ry ['sıgnətrı] *n* firmatario *m*, -a *f*

sig·na·ture ['sıgnətʃə(r)] firma *f*

sig·na·ture 'tune sigla *f* musicale

'**sig·net ring** ['sıgnıtrıŋ] anello *m* con sigillo

sig·nif·i·cance [sıg'nıfıkəns] importanza *f*; (*meaning*) significato *m*

sig·nif·i·cant [sıg'nıfıkənt] *adj event etc* significativo; (*quite large*) notevole

sig·nif·i·cant·ly [sıg'nıfıkəntlı] *adv larger, more expensive* notevolmente

sig·ni·fy ['sıgnıfaı] *v/t* (*pret & pp -ied*) significare

'**sign lan·guage** linguaggio *m* dei segni

'**sign·post** cartello *m* stradale

si·lence ['saɪləns] **1** *n* silenzio *m*; **in ~ work, march** in silenzio; **~!** silenzio! **2** *v/t* mettere a tacere

si·lenc·er ['saɪlənsə(r)] *on gun* silenziatore *m*; *on car* marmitta *f*

si·lent ['saɪlənt] *adj* silenzioso; *film* muto; **stay ~** *not comment* tacere

sil·hou·ette [sılu:'et] *n* sagoma *f*

sil·i·con ['sılıkən] silicio *m*

sil·i·con 'chip chip *m inv* al silicio

sil·i·cone ['sılıkəʊn] silicone *m*

silk [sılk] **1** *n* seta *f* **2** *adj shirt etc* di seta

silk·y ['sɪlkɪ] *adj* hair, texture setoso

sil·li·ness ['sɪlɪnɪs] stupidità *f inv*

sil·ly ['sɪlɪ] *adj* stupido

si·lo ['saɪləʊ] silo *m*

sil·ver ['sɪlvə(r)] **1** *n metal* argento *m*; ~ *objects* argenteria *f* **2** *adj ring* d'argento; *colour* argentato

sil·ver-plat·ed [sɪlvə'pleɪtɪd] *adj* placcato d'argento; **'sil·ver·ware** argenteria *f*; **sil·ver 'wed·ding** nozze *fpl* d'argento

sim·i·lar ['sɪmɪlə(r)] *adj* simile

sim·i·lar·i·ty [sɪmɪ'lærətɪ] rassomiglianza *f*

sim·i·lar·ly ['sɪmɪləlɪ] *adv* allo stesso modo

sim·mer ['sɪmə(r)] *v/i in cooking* sobbollire; *with rage* ribollire

♦ **simmer down** *v/i* calmarsi

sim·ple ['sɪmpl] *adj method, life, dress* semplice; *person* sempliciotto

sim·ple-mind·ed [sɪmpl'maɪndɪd] *adj pej* sempliciotto

sim·pli·ci·ty [sɪm'plɪsətɪ] semplicità *f inv*

sim·pli·fy ['sɪmplɪfaɪ] *v/t (pret & pp -ied)* semplificare

sim·plis·tic [sɪm'plɪstɪk] *adj* semplicistico

sim·ply ['sɪmplɪ] *adv (absolutely)* assolutamente; *in a simple way* semplicemente; *it is ~ the best* è assolutamente il migliore

sim·u·late ['sɪmjʊleɪt] *v/t* simulare

sim·ul·ta·ne·ous [sɪml'teɪnɪəs] *adj* simultaneo

sim·ul·ta·ne·ous·ly [sɪml'teɪnɪəslɪ] *adv* simultaneamente

sin [sɪn] **1** *n* peccato *m* **2** *v/i (pret & pp -ned)* peccare

since [sɪns] **1** *prep* da; ~ *last week* dalla scorsa settimana **2** *adv* da allora; *I haven't seen him* ~ non lo vedo da allora **3** *conj in expressions of time* da quando; *(seeing that)* visto che; ~ *you left* da quando sei andato via; *ever* ~ *I have known her* da quando la conosco; ~ *you don't like it* visto che non ti piace

sin·cere [sɪn'sɪə(r)] *adj* sincero

sin·cere·ly [sɪn'sɪəlɪ] *adv* con sincerità; *hope* sinceramente; *Yours* ~ Distinti saluti

sin·cer·i·ty [sɪn'serətɪ] sincerità *f inv*

sin·ful ['sɪnful] *adj* peccaminoso

sing [sɪŋ] *v/t & v/i (pret* **sang***, pp* **sung***)* cantare

singe [sɪndʒ] *v/t* bruciacchiare

sing·er ['sɪŋə(r)] cantante *m/f*

sin·gle ['sɪŋgl] **1** *adj (sole)* solo; *(not double)* singolo; *bed, sheet* a una piazza; *(not married)* single; *with reference to Europe* unico; *there wasn't a* ~ *...* non c'era nemmeno un ...; *in* ~ *file* in fila indiana **2** *n* MUS singolo *m*; *(~ room) (camera f)* singola *f*; *ticket* biglietto *m* di sola andata; *person* single *m/f inv*; **~s** *in tennis* singolo

♦ **single out** *v/t (choose)* prescegliere; *(distinguish)* distinguere

sin·gle-breast·ed [sɪŋgl'brestɪd] *adj* a un petto; **sin·gle-'hand·ed** [sɪŋgl-'hændɪd] *adj & adv* da solo; **sin·gle-mind·ed** [sɪŋgl'maɪndɪd] *adj* determinato; **Sin·gle 'Mar·ket** mercato *m* unico; **sin·gle 'moth·er** ragazza *f* madre; **sin·gle 'pa·rent** genitore *m* single; **sin·gle pa·rent 'fam·i·ly** famiglia *f* monoparentale; **sin·gle 'room** *(camera f)* singola *f*

sin·gu·lar ['sɪŋgjʊlə(r)] **1** *adj* GRAM singolare **2** *n* GRAM singolare *m*; *in the* ~ al singolare

sin·is·ter ['sɪnɪstə(r)] *adj* sinistro

sink [sɪŋk] **1** *n* lavandino *m* **2** *v/i (pret* **sank***, pp* **sunk***) of ship* affondare; *of object* andare a fondo; *of sun* calare; *of interest rates, pressure etc* scendere; *he sank onto the bed* crollò sul letto **3** *v/t (pret* **sank***, pp* **sunk***) ship (far)* affondare; *funds* investire

♦ **sink in** *v/i of liquid* penetrare; *it still hasn't really sunk in of realization* ancora non mi rendo conto

sin·ner ['sɪnə(r)] peccatore *m*, -trice *f*

si·nus ['saɪnəs] seno *m* paranasale; *my ~es are blocked* ho il naso bloccato

si·nus·i·tis [saɪnə'saɪtɪs] MED sinusite *f*

S

sip [sɪp] **1** *n* sorso *m* **2** *v/t* (*pret & pp* **-ped**) sorseggiare

sir [sɜː(r)] signore *m*; **Sir Charles** Sir Charles

si·ren ['saɪrən] sirena *f*

sir·loin ['sɜːlɔɪn] controfiletto *m*

sis·ter ['sɪstə(r)] sorella *f*; *in hospital* (infermiera *f*) caposala *f*

'sis·ter-in-law (*pl* **sisters-in-law**) cognata *f*

sit [sɪt] (*pret & pp* **sat**) **1** *v/i* sedere; (*sit down*) sedersi; *of objects* stare; *of committee, assembly etc* riunirsi **2** *v/t* *exam* dare

♦ **sit down** *v/i* sedersi

♦ **sit up** *v/i* in bed mettersi a sedere; *straighten back* star seduto bene; *wait up at night* rimanere alzato

sit·com ['sɪtkɒm] sitcom *f inv*

site [saɪt] **1** *n* luogo *m* **2** *v/t* *new offices etc* situare

sit·ting ['sɪtɪŋ] *of committee, court* sessione *f*; *for artist* seduta *f*; *for meals* turno *m*

'sit·ting room salotto *m*

sit·u·at·ed ['sɪtjʊeɪtɪd] *adj* situato; **be** ~ trovarsi

sit·u·a·tion [sɪtjʊ'eɪʃn] situazione *f*; *of building etc* posizione *f*

six [sɪks] sei

six·teen [sɪks'tiːn] sedici

six·teenth [sɪks'tiːnθ] *n & adj* sedicesimo, -a

sixth [sɪksθ] *adj* sesto

six·ti·eth ['sɪkstɪɪθ] *n & adj* sessantesimo, -a

six·ty ['sɪkstɪ] sessanta

size [saɪz] dimensioni *fpl*; *of clothes* taglia *f*, misura *f*; *of shoes* numero *m*

♦ **size up** *v/t* valutare

size·a·ble ['saɪzəbl] *adj* considerevole

siz·zle ['sɪzl] *v/i* sfrigolare

skate [skeɪt] **1** *n* pattino *m* **2** *v/i* pattinare

skate·board ['skeɪtbɔːd] *n* skateboard *m inv*

skate·board·er ['skeɪtbɔːdə(r)] skateboarder *m/f inv*

skate·board·ing ['skeɪtbɔːdɪŋ] skateboard *m inv*

skat·er ['skeɪtə(r)] pattinatore *m*, -trice *f*

skat·ing ['skeɪtɪŋ] *n* pattinaggio *m*

'skat·ing rink pista *f* di pattinaggio

skel·e·ton ['skelɪtn] scheletro *m*

'skel·e·ton key passe-partout *m inv*

'skep·tic *etc Am* → **sceptic** *etc*

sketch [sketʃ] **1** *n* abbozzo *m*; THEA sketch *m inv* **2** *v/t* abbozzare

'sketch·book album *m* da disegno

sketch·y ['sketʃɪ] *adj* *knowledge etc* lacunoso

skew·er ['skjuə(r)] *n* spiedino *m*

ski [skiː] **1** *n* sci *m inv* **2** *v/i* sciare

'ski boots *npl* scarponi *mpl* da sci

skid [skɪd] *n* sbandata *f* **2** *v/i* (*pret & pp* **-ded**) sbandare

ski·er ['skiːə(r)] sciatore *m*, -trice *f*

ski·ing ['skiːɪŋ] sci *m inv*; **go ~** andare a sciare

'ski in·struc·tor maestro *m*, -a *f* di sci

skil·ful ['skɪlfʊl] *adj* abile

skil·ful·ly ['skɪlflɪ] *adv* abilmente

'ski lift impianto *m* di risalita

skill [skɪl] (*ability*) abilità *f inv*; **what ~s do you have?** quali capacità possiede?

skilled [skɪld] *adj* abile

skilled 'work·er operaio *m*, -a *f* specializzato, -a

skill·ful *etc Am* → **skilful** *etc*

skim [skɪm] *v/t* (*pret & pp* **-med**) *surface* sfiorare; *milk* scremare

♦ **skim off** *v/t* *the best* selezionare

♦ **skim through** *v/t* *text* scorrere

skimmed 'milk [skɪmd] latte *m* scremato

skimp·y ['skɪmpɪ] *adj* *account etc* scarso; *dress* succinto

skin [skɪn] **1** *n* *of person, animal* pelle *f*; *of fruit* buccia *f* **2** *v/t* (*pret & pp* **-ned**) scoiare

'skin div·ing immersioni *fpl* subacquee

skin·flint ['skɪnflɪnt] F spilorcio *m* F

'skin graft innesto *m* epidermico

skin·ny ['skɪnɪ] *adj* magro

'skin-tight *adj* aderente

skip [skɪp] **1** *n* *little jump* salto *m* **2** *v/i* (*pret & pp* **-ped**) saltellare; *with skipping rope* saltare **3** *v/t* (*pret & pp*

'**ski pole** racchetta f da sci

skip·per ['skɪpə(r)] NAUT skipper m inv; of team capitano m

skip·ping rope ['skɪpɪŋ] corda f (per saltare)

'**ski re·sort** stazione f sciistica

skirt [skɜːt] n gonna f

'**ski run** pista f da sci

'**ski tow** sciovia f

skit·tle ['skɪtl] birillo m

skit·tles ['skɪtlz] nsg (game) birilli mpl

skive [skaɪv] v/i F fare lo scansafatiche F

skull [skʌl] cranio m

sky [skaɪ] cielo m

'**sky·light** lucernario m; '**sky·line** profilo m (contro il cielo); '**sky·scrap·er** ['skaɪskreɪpə(r)] grattacielo m

slab [slæb] of stone lastra f; of cake etc fetta f

slack [slæk] adj rope allentato; person, work negligente; period lento

slack·en ['slækn] v/t rope allentare; pace rallentare

◆ **slacken off** v/i rallentare

slacks [slæks] npl pantaloni mpl casual

◆ **slag off** [slæg] v/t P parlare male di

slain [sleɪn] pp → **slay**

slam [slæm] v/t & v/i (pret & pp **-med**) door sbattere

◆ **slam down** v/t sbattere

slan·der ['slɑːndə(r)] 1 n diffamazione f 2 v/t diffamare

slan·der·ous ['slɑːndərəs] adj diffamatorio

slang [slæŋ] slang m inv; of a specific group gergo m

slant [slɑːnt] 1 v/i pendere 2 n pendenza f; given to a story angolatura f

slant·ing ['slɑːntɪŋ] adj roof spiovente

slap [slæp] 1 n blow schiaffo m 2 v/t (pret & pp **-ped**) schiaffeggiare

'**slap·dash** adj work frettoloso; person pressapochista

slap-up 'meal F pranzo m coi fiocchi

slash [slæʃ] 1 n cut taglio m; in punctuation barra f 2 v/t skin, painting squarciare; prices, costs abbattere; ~ **one's wrists** tagliarsi le vene

slate [sleɪt] n ardesia f

slaugh·ter ['slɔːtə(r)] 1 n of animals macellazione f; of people, troops massacro m 2 v/t animals macellare; people, troops massacrare

'**slaugh·ter·house** for animals macello m

Slav [slɑːv] adj slavo

slave [sleɪv] n schiavo m, -a f

'**slave-driv·er** F negriero, -a f F

sla·ve·ry schiavitù f inv

slay [sleɪ] v/t (pret **slew**, pp **slain**) ammazzare

sleaze [sliːz] POL corruzione f

slea·zy ['sliːzɪ] adj bar, characters sordido

sled(ge) [sled, sledʒ] n slitta f

'**sledge ham·mer** mazza f

sleep [sliːp] 1 n sonno m; **go to ~** addormentarsi; **I need a good ~** ho bisogno di una bella dormita; **I couldn't get to ~** non sono riuscito a dormire 2 v/i (pret & pp **slept**) dormire

◆ **sleep in** v/i (have a long lie) dormire fino a tardi

◆ **sleep on** v/t proposal, decision dormire su; **sleep on it** dormirci su

◆ **sleep with** v/t (have sex with) andare a letto con

sleep·er ['sliːpə(r)] RAIL: on track traversina f; (sleeping car) vagone m letto; train treno m notturno; **be a light / heavy ~** avere il sonno leggero / pesante

sleep·i·ly ['sliːpɪlɪ] adv con aria assonnata

'**sleep·ing bag** ['sliːpɪŋ] sacco m a pelo; '**sleep·ing car** RAIL vagone m letto; '**sleep·ing part·ner** Br COM socio m inattivo; '**sleep·ing pill** sonnifero m

sleep·less ['sliːplɪs] adj night in bianco

'**sleep walk·er** sonnambulo m, -a f

S

'sleep walk·ing sonnambulismo *m*
sleep·y ['sli:pɪ] *adj child* assonnato;
town addormentato; **I'm ~** ho sonno
sleet [sli:t] *n* nevischio *m*
sleeve [sli:v] *of jacket etc* manica *f*
sleeve·less ['sli:vlɪs] *adj* senza maniche
sleigh [sleɪ] *n* slitta *f*
sleight of 'hand [slaɪt] gioco *m* di prestigio
slen·der ['slendə(r)] *adj figure, arms* snello; *chance, income, margin* piccolo
slept [slept] *pret & pp* → **sleep**
slew [slu:] *pret* → **slay**
slice [slaɪs] **1** *n also fig* fetta *f* **2** *v/t loaf etc* affettare
sliced 'bread [slaɪst] pane *m* a cassetta; **the greatest thing since ~** F il non plus ultra
slick [slɪk] **1** *adj performance* brillante; (*pej: cunning*) scaltro **2** *n of oil* chiazza *f* di petrolio
slid [slɪd] *pret & pp* → **slide**
slide [slaɪd] **1** *n for kids* scivolo *m*; PHOT diapositiva *f*; *in hair* fermacapelli *m inv* **2** *v/i* (*pret & pp slid*) scivolare; *of exchange rate etc* calare **3** *v/t* (*pret & pp slid*) far scivolare
slid·ing door [slaɪdɪŋ'dɔ:(r)] porta *f* scorrevole
slight [slaɪt] **1** *adj person, figure* gracile; (*small*) leggero; **no, not in the ~est** no, per nulla **2** *n* (*insult*) offesa *f*
slight·ly ['slaɪtlɪ] *adv* leggermente
slim [slɪm] **1** *adj* slanciato; *chance* scarso **2** *v/i* (*pret & pp -med*) dimagrire; **I'm ~ming** sono a dieta
slime [slaɪm] melma *f*
slim·y ['slaɪmɪ] *adj liquid* melmoso; *person* viscido
sling [slɪŋ] **1** *n for arm* fascia *f* a tracolla **2** *v/t* (*pret & pp slung*) (*throw*) lanciare
slip [slɪp] **1** *n on ice etc* scivolata *f*; (*mistake*) errore *m*; **a ~ of paper** un foglietto; **a ~ of the tongue** un lapsus; **give s.o. the ~** seminare qu **2** *v/i* (*pret & pp -ped*) *on ice etc* sci-

volare; *of quality etc* peggiorare; **he ~ped out of the room** è sgattaiolato fuori dalla stanza **3** *v/t* (*pret & pp -ped*) (*put*) far scivolare; **he ~ped it into his briefcase** l'ha fatto scivolare nella valigetta; **it ~ped my mind** mi è passato di mente
♦ slip away *v/i of time* passare; *of opportunity* andare sprecato; (*die quietly*) spirare
♦ slip off *v/t jacket etc* togliersi
♦ slip on *v/t jacket etc* infilarsi
♦ slip out *v/i* (*go out*) sgattaiolare
♦ slip up *v/i make mistake* sbagliarsi
slipped 'disc [slɪpt] ernia *f* del disco
slip·per ['slɪpə(r)] pantofola *f*
slip·per·y ['slɪpərɪ] *adj* scivoloso
'slip road rampa *f* di accesso
'slip·shod ['slɪpʃɒd] *adj* trascurato
'slip-up (*mistake*) errore *m*
slit [slɪt] **1** *n* (*tear*) strappo *m*; (*hole*) fessura *f*; *in skirt* spacco *m* **2** *v/t* (*pret & pp slit*) *envelope, packet* aprire (*tagliando*); *throat* tagliare
slith·er ['slɪðə(r)] *v/i* strisciare
sliv·er ['slɪvə(r)] scheggia *f*
slob [slɒb] *pej* sudicione *m*, -a *f*
slob·ber ['slɒbə(r)] *v/i* sbavare
slog [slɒg] *n* faticata *f*
slo·gan ['sləugən] slogan *m inv*
slop [slɒp] *v/t* (*pret & pp -ped*) rovesciare, versare
slope [sləup] **1** *n* pendenza *f*; *of mountain* pendio *m*; **built on a ~** costruito in pendio **2** *v/i* essere inclinato; **the road ~s down to the sea** la strada scende fino al mare
slop·py ['slɒpɪ] *adj work, editing* trascurato; *in dressing* sciatto; (*too sentimental*) sdolcinato
sloshed [slɒʃt] *adj* F (*drunk*) sbronzo F
slot [slɒt] **1** *n* fessura *f*; *in schedule* spazio *m*
♦ slot in (*pret & pp -ted*) **1** *v/t* infilare **2** *v/i* infilarsi
'slot ma·chine *for vending* distributore *m* automatico; *for gambling* slot-machine *f inv*
slouch [slautʃ] *v/i*: **don't ~!** su con la schiena!

slov·en·ly ['slʌvnli] *adj* sciatto
slow [sləʊ] *adj* lento; **be ~ of clock** essere indietro
♦ **slow down** *v/t & v/i* rallentare
slow·coach *Br* F lumaca *f* F
slow·down *in production* rallentamento *m*
slow·ly ['sləʊli] *adv* lentamente
slow 'mo·tion *n:* **in ~** al rallentatore
slow·ness ['sləʊnɪs] lentezza *f*
slow·poke *Am* F lumaca *f* F
slug [slʌg] *n animal* lumaca *f*
slug·gish ['slʌgɪʃ] *adj* lento
slum [slʌm] *n* slum *m inv*
slump [slʌmp] **1** *n in trade* crollo *m* **2** *v/i economically* crollare; (*collapse: of person*) accasciarsi
slung [slʌŋ] *pret & pp* → **sling**
slur [slɜː(r)] **1** *n* calunnia *f* **2** *v/t* (*pret & pp* -**red**) *words* biascicare
slurp [slɜːp] *v/t* bere rumorosamente
slurred [slɜːd] *adj speech* impappinato
slush [slʌʃ] fanghiglia *f*; (*pej: sentimental stuff*) smancerie *fpl*
slush fund fondi *mpl* neri
slush·y ['slʌʃi] *adj snow* ridotto in fanghiglia; *film, novel* sdolcinato
slut [slʌt] *pej* sgualdrina *f*
sly [slaɪ] *adj* scaltro; **on the ~** di nascosto
smack [smæk] **1** *n on the bottom* sculacciata *f*; *in the face* schiaffo *m* **2** *v/t child* picchiare; *bottom* sculacciare
small [smɔːl] **1** *adj* piccolo **2** *n:* **the ~ of the back** le reni
small 'change spiccioli *mpl*; **small hours** *npl:* **the ~** le ore *fpl* piccole; **small·pox** ['smɔːlpɒks] vaiolo *m*; **'small print** parte *f* scritta in caratteri minuti; **'small talk** conversazione *f* di circostanza
smarm·y ['smɑːmi] *adj* F untuoso
smart [smɑːt] **1** *adj* (*elegant*) elegante; (*intelligent*) intelligente; *pace* svelto; **get ~ with** fare il furbo con F **2** *v/i* (*hurt*) bruciare
smart al·ec(k) ['smɑːtælɪk] F sapientone *m* F; **'smart ass** P sapientone *m*; **'smart card** smart card *f inv*

♦ **smarten up** ['smɑːtn] *v/t* sistemare; **smarten o.s. up** mettersi in ghingheri
smart·ly ['smɑːtli] *adv dressed* elegantemente
smash [smæʃ] **1** *n noise* fracasso *m*; (*car crash*) scontro *m*; *in tennis* schiacciata *f* **2** *v/t break* spaccare; *hit hard* sbattere; **~ sth to pieces** mandare in frantumi qc **3** *v/i break* frantumarsi; **the driver ~ed into ...** l'automobilista si è schiantato contro ...
♦ **smash up** *v/t place* distruggere
smash 'hit F successone *m*
smash·ing ['smæʃɪŋ] *adj* F fantastico
smat·ter·ing ['smætərɪŋ] *of a language* infarinatura *f*
smear [smɪə(r)] **1** *n of ink etc* macchia *f*; MED striscio *m*; *on character* calunnia *f* **2** *v/t*; *character* calunniare; **~ mud over the wall** imbrattare il muro di fango
'smear cam·paign campagna *f* diffamatoria
smell [smel] **1** *n* odore *m*; **it has no ~** non ha odore; **sense of ~** olfatto *m*, odorato *m* **2** *v/t* sentire odore di; *test by smelling* sentire **3** *v/i unpleasantly* puzzare; (*sniff*) odorare; **what does it ~ of?** che odore ha?; **you ~ of beer** puzzi di birra; **it ~s good** ha un buon profumo
smell·y ['smeli] *adj* puzzolente; **it's so ~ in here** qui dentro c'è puzza
smile [smaɪl] **1** *n* sorriso *m* **2** *v/i* sorridere
♦ **smile at** *v/t* sorridere a
smirk [smɜːk] **1** *n* sorriso *m* compiaciuto **2** *v/i* sorridere con compiacimento
smog [smɒg] smog *m inv*
smoke [sməʊk] **1** *n* fumo *m*; **have a ~** fumare **2** *v/t cigarettes etc* fumare; *bacon* affumicare **3** *v/i* fumare; **I don't ~** non fumo
smok·er ['sməʊkə(r)] *person* fumatore *m*, -trice *f*
smok·ing ['sməʊkɪŋ] fumo *m*; **no ~** vietato fumare
'smok·ing com·part·ment RAIL

carrozza *m* fumatori

smok·y ['sməʊkɪ] *adj room, air* pieno di fumo

smol·der *Am* → **smoulder**

smooth [smuːð] **1** *adj surface, skin, sea liscio; sea* calmo; *transition* senza problemi; *pej: person* mellifluo **2** *v/t hair* lisciare

♦ **smooth down** *v/t with sandpaper etc* levigare

♦ **smooth out** *v/t paper, cloth* lisciare

♦ **smooth over** *v/t:* **smooth things over** appianare le cose

smooth·ly ['smuːðlɪ] *adv without any problems* senza problemi

smoth·er ['smʌðə(r)] *v/t flames, person* soffocare; *~ s.o. with kisses* coprire qu di baci

smudge [smʌdʒ] **1** *n* sbavatura *f* **2** *v/t* sbavare

smug [smʌg] *adj* compiaciuto

smug·gle ['smʌgl] *v/t* contrabbandare

smug·gler ['smʌglə(r)] contrabbandiere *m*, -a *f*

smug·gling ['smʌglɪŋ] contrabbando *m*

smug·ly ['smʌglɪ] *adv* con compiacimento

smut·ty ['smʌtɪ] *adj joke, sense of humour* sconcio

snack [snæk] *n* spuntino *m*

'**snack bar** snack bar *m inv*

snag [snæg] *n* (*problem*) problema *m*

snail [sneɪl] chiocciola *f, in cooking* lumaca *f*

snake [sneɪk] *n* serpente *m*

snap [snæp] **1** *n sound* botto *m*; PHOT foto *f* **2** *v/t* (*pret & pp* **-ped**) *break* spezzare; (*say sharply*) dire bruscamente **3** *v/i* (*pret & pp* **-ped**) *break* spezzarsi **4** *adj decision, judgement* immediato

♦ **snap up** *v/t bargains* accaparrarsi

snap·py ['snæpɪ] *adj person, mood* irritabile; F (*quick*) rapido; (*elegant*) elegante

'**snap·shot** istantanea *f*

snarl [snɑːl] **1** *n of dog* ringhio *m* **2** *v/i* ringhiare

snatch [snætʃ] **1** *v/t* afferrare; (*steal*) scippare; (*kidnap*) rapire **2** *v/i* strappare di mano

snaz·zy ['snæzɪ] *adj* F chic

sneak [sniːk] **1** *n* (*telltale*) spione *m*, -a *f* **2** *v/t* (*remove, steal*) rubare; **~ a glance at** dare una sbirciatina a **3** *v/i* (*tell tales*) fare la spia; **~ out of ...** sgattaiolare fuori da ...

sneak·ing ['sniːkɪŋ] *adj:* **have a ~ suspicion that ...** avere il vago sospetto che ...

sneak·y ['sniːkɪ] *adj* F (*crafty*) scaltro

sneer [snɪə(r)] **1** *n* sogghigno *m* **2** *v/i* sogghignare

sneeze [sniːz] **1** *n* starnuto *m* **2** *v/i* starnutire

sniff [snɪf] **1** *v/i to clear nose* tirare su col naso; *of dog* fiutare **2** *v/t smell* annusare

snig·ger ['snɪgə(r)] **1** *n* risolino *m* **2** *v/i* ridacchiare

snip [snɪp] *n* F (*bargain*) affare *m*

snip·er ['snaɪpə(r)] cecchino *m*

sniv·el ['snɪvl] *v/i pej* frignare

snob [snɒb] snob *m/f inv*

snob·ber·y ['snɒbərɪ] snobismo *m*

snob·bish ['snɒbɪʃ] *adj* snob *inv*

snook·er ['snuːkə(r)] biliardo *m*

snoop [snuːp] *n* ficcanaso *m/f inv*

♦ **snoop around** *v/i* ficcanasare

snoot·y ['snuːtɪ] *adj* snob *inv*

snooze [snuːz] **1** *n* sonnellino *m*; **have a ~** fare un sonnellino **2** *v/i* sonnecchiare

snore [snɔː(r)] *v/i* russare

snor·ing ['snɔːrɪŋ] *n* russare *m*

snor·kel ['snɔːkl] *n* boccaglio *m*

snort [snɔːt] *v/i* sbuffare

snout [snaʊt] *of pig* grugno *m; of dog* muso *m*

snow [snəʊ] **1** *n* neve *f* **2** *v/i* nevicare

♦ **snow under** *v/t:* **be snowed under with ...** essere sommerso di ...

'**snow·ball** palla *f* di neve; '**snow·bound** *adj* isolato dalla neve; '**snow chains** *npl* MOT catene *fpl* da neve; '**snow·drift** cumulo *m* di

neve; **'snow·drop** bucaneve *m inv*;
'snow·flake fiocco *m* di neve;
'snow·man pupazzo *m* di neve;
'snow·storm tormenta *f*

snow·y ['snəʊɪ] *adj weather* nevoso; *roofs, hills* innevato

snub [snʌb] **1** *n* affronto *m* **2** *v/t* (*pret & pp* **-bed**) snobbare

snub-nosed ['snʌbnəʊzd] *adj* col naso all'insù

snug [snʌg] *adj* al calduccio; (*tight-fitting*) attillato

♦ **snuggle down** ['snʌgl] *v/i* accoccolarsi

♦ **snuggle up to** *v/t* rannicchiarsi accanto a

so [səʊ] **1** *adv* così; ~ *hot/cold* così caldo/freddo; ~ *much* non così tanto; ~ *much better/easier* molto meglio/più facile; *you shouldn't eat/drink ~ much* non dovresti mangiare/bere così tanti; *I miss you* ~ mi manchi tanto; ~ *am I/do I* anch'io; ~ *is she/does she* anche lei; *and* ~ *on* e così via **2** *pron*: *I hope/think* ~ spero/penso di sì; *I don't think* ~ non credo, credo di no; *you didn't tell me – I did* – non me l'hai detto – e invece sì; *50 or* ~ circa 50 **3** *conj* (*for that reason*) così; (*in order that*) così che; *and* ~ *I missed the train* e così ho perso il treno; ~ (*that*) *I could come too* così che potessi venire anch'io; ~ *what?* E e allora?

soak [səʊk] *v/t* (*steep*) mettere a bagno; *of water, rain* inzuppare

♦ **soak up** *v/t liquid* assorbire; *soak up the sun* crogiolarsi al sole

soaked [səʊkt] *adj* fradicio; *be ~ to the skin* essere bagnato fradicio

soak·ing (*wet*) ['səʊkɪŋ] *adj* bagnato fradicio

so-and-so ['səʊənsəʊ] F *unknown person* tal dei tali *m/f inv*; (*euph: annoying person*) impiastro *m*

soap [səʊp] *n for washing* sapone *m*

'soap (**op·e·ra**) ['səʊp] soap (opera) *f inv*, telenovela *f*

soap·y ['səʊpɪ] *adj water* saponato

soar [sɔː(r)] *v/i of rocket etc* innalzar-

si; *of prices* aumentare vertiginosamente

sob [sɒb] **1** *n* singhiozzo *m* **2** *v/i* (*pret & pp* **-bed**) singhiozzare

so·ber ['səʊbə(r)] *adj* (*not drunk*) sobrio; (*serious*) serio

♦ **sober up** *v/i* smaltire la sbornia

so-'called *adj* cosiddetto

soc·cer ['sɒkə(r)] calcio *m*

'soc·cer hoo·li·gan hooligan *m/f inv*

so·cia·ble ['səʊʃəbl] *adj* socievole

so·cial ['səʊʃl] *adj* sociale

so·cial 'dem·o·crat socialdemocratico *m*, -a *f*

so·cial·is·m ['səʊʃəlizm] socialismo *m*

so·cial·ist ['səʊʃəlɪst] **1** *adj* socialista **2** *n* socialista *m/f*

so·cial·ize ['səʊʃəlaɪz] *v/i* socializzare

'soc·ial life vita *f* sociale; **so·cial 'sci·ence** scienza *f* sociale; **so·cial se'cu·ri·ty** *Br* sussidio *m* della previdenza sociale; **so·cial 'serv·i·ces** *Br npl* servizi *mpl* sociali; **'so·cial work** assistenza *f* sociale; **'so·cial work·er** assistente *m/f* sociale

so·ci·e·ty [sə'saɪətɪ] società *f inv*; (*organization*) associazione *f*

so·ci·ol·o·gist [səʊsɪ'ɒlədʒɪst] sociologo *m*, -a *f*

so·ci·ol·o·gy [səʊsɪ'ɒlədʒɪ] sociologia *f*

sock¹ [sɒk] calzino *m*

sock² [sɒk] **1** *n* F (*punch*) pugno *m* **2** *v/t* F (*punch*) dare un pugno a

sock·et ['sɒkɪt] *for light bulb* portalampada *m inv*; *in wall* presa *f* (di corrente); *of eye* orbita *f*

so·da ['səʊdə] (~ *water*) seltz *m inv*

sod·den ['sɒdn] *adj* zuppo

so·fa ['səʊfə] divano *m*

'so·fa-bed divano *m* letto

soft [sɒft] *adj pillow* soffice; *chair, skin* morbido; *light, colour* tenue; *music* soft; *voice* sommesso; (*lenient*) indulgente; *have a ~ spot for* avere un debole per

soft 'drink bibita *f* analcolica

'soft drug droga *f* leggera

soft·en ['sɒfn] **1** *v/t butter etc* ammor-

S

bidire; *position* attenuare; *impact, blow* attutire **2** *v/i of butter, ice-cream* ammorbidirsi

soft·ly ['sɒftlɪ] *adv speak* sommessamente

soft 'toy giocattolo *m* di pezza

soft·ware ['sɒftweə(r)] software *m inv*

sog·gy ['sɒgɪ] *adj* molle e pesante

soil [sɔɪl] **1** *n* (*earth*) terra *f* **2** *v/t* sporcare

so·lar 'en·er·gy ['səʊlə(r)] energia *f* solare; **'solar pan·el** pannello *m* solare; **'solar system** sistema *m* solare

sold [səʊld] *pret & pp* → **sell**

sol·dier ['səʊldʒə(r)] soldato *m*

♦ soldier on *v/i* perseverare

sole¹ [səʊl] *n of foot* pianta *f* (del piede); *of shoe* suola *f*

sole² [səʊl] *adj* unico; (*exclusive*) esclusivo

sole³ [səʊl] (*fish*) sogliola *f*

sole·ly ['səʊlɪ] *adv* solamente; **be ~ responsible** essere il solo / la sola responsabile

sol·emn ['sɒləm] *adj* solenne

so·lem·ni·ty [sə'lemnɪtɪ] solennità *f inv*

sol·emn·ly ['sɒləmlɪ] *adv* solennemente

so·li·cit [sə'lɪsɪt] *v/i of prostitute* adescare

so·lic·i·tor [sə'lɪsɪtə(r)] avvocato *m*

sol·id ['sɒlɪd] *adj* (*hard*) solido; (*without holes*) compatto; *gold, silver* massiccio; (*sturdy*) robusto; *evidence* concreto; *support* forte; **a ~ hour** un'ora intera

sol·i·dar·i·ty [sɒlɪ'dærɪtɪ] solidarietà *f inv*

so·lid·i·fy [sə'lɪdɪfaɪ] *v/i* (*pret & pp -ied*) solidificarsi

sol·id·ly ['sɒlɪdlɪ] *adv built* solidamente; *in favour of sth* all'unanimità

so·lil·o·quy [sə'lɪləkwɪ] *on stage* monologo *m*

sol·i·taire ['sɒlɪteər] *Am: card game* solitario *m*

sol·i·ta·ry ['sɒlɪtərɪ] *adj life, activity* solitario; (*single*) solo

sol·i·ta·ry con'fine·ment isolamento *m*

sol·i·tude ['sɒlɪtjuːd] solitudine *f*

so·lo ['səʊləʊ] **1** *n* MUS assolo *m* **2** *adj performance* solista; *flight* in solitario

so·lo·ist ['səʊləʊɪst] solista *m/f*

sol·u·ble ['sɒljʊbl] *adj substance* solubile; *problem* risolvibile

so·lu·tion [sə'luːʃn] soluzione *f*

solve [sɒlv] *v/t* risolvere

sol·vent ['sɒlvənt] **1** *adj financially* solvibile **2** *n* solvente *m*

som·ber *Am*, som·bre ['sɒmbə(r)] *adj* (*dark*) scuro; (*serious*) tetro

some [sʌm] **1** *adj* (*unspecified amount*) un po' di, del; (*unspecified number*) qualche, dei *m*, delle *f*; **would you like ~ water?** vuoi un po' d'acqua *o* dell'acqua?; **would you like ~ biscuits?** vuoi dei biscotti *o* qualche biscotto?; **~ people say that ...** alcuni dicono che ... **2** *pron* (*unspecified amount*) un po'; (*unspecified number*) alcuni *m*, -e *f*; **would you like ~?** ne vuoi un po'?; **give me ~** dammene un po'; **~ of the students** alcuni studenti

some·bod·y ['sʌmbədɪ] *pron* qualcuno; **'some·day** *adv* un giorno; **'some·how** *adv* (*by one means or another*) in qualche modo; (*for some unknown reason*) per qualche motivo; **'some·one** *pron* → **some·bod·y**

som·er·sault ['sʌməsɔːlt] **1** *n* capriola *f* **2** *v/i* fare una capriola

'some·thing *pron* qualcosa; **would you like ~ to drink / eat?** vuoi (qualcosa) da mangiare / bere?; **is ~ wrong?** c'è qualcosa che non va?; **'some·time** *adv* (*one of these days*) uno di questi giorni; **~ last year** l'anno scorso; **'some·times** ['sʌmtaɪmz] *adv* a volte; **'some·what** *adv* piuttosto; **'some·where 1** *adv* da qualche parte **2** *pron* un posto; **let's go ~ quiet** andiamo in un posto tranquillo

son [sʌn] figlio *m*

so·na·ta [sə'nɑːtə] MUS sonata *f*

song [sɒŋ] canzone f; of birds canto m

song-bird uccello m canoro

song-writ-er compositore m, -trice f

son-in-law (pl **sons-in-law**) genero m

son-net ['sɒnɪt] sonetto m

soon [su:n] adv presto; **as ~ as** non appena; **as ~ as possible** prima possibile; **~er or later** presto o tardi; **the ~er the better** prima è, meglio è; **how ~ can you be ready?** fra quanto sei pronto?

soot [sʊt] fuliggine f

soothe [su:ð] v/t calmare

so-phis-ti-cat-ed [sə'fɪstɪkeɪtɪd] adj sofisticato

so-phis-ti-ca-tion [sə'fɪstɪkeɪʃn] of person raffinatezza f; of machine complessità f inv

sop-py ['sɒpɪ] adj F sdolcinato

so-pra-no [sə'prɑːnəʊ] n soprano m/f

sor-did ['sɔːdɪd] adj affair, business sordido

sore [sɔː(r)] **1** adj (painful) dolorante; **is it ~?** fa male? **2** n piaga f

sore 'throat mal m di gola

sor-row ['sɒrəʊ] n dispiacere m, dolore m

sor-ry ['sɒrɪ] adj day, sight triste; (I'm) **~!** apologizing scusa!; polite form scusi!; **I'm ~** regretting mi dispiace; **I won't be ~ to leave here** non vedo l'ora di andarmene da qui; **I feel ~ for her** mi dispiace per lei

sort [sɔːt] **1** n tipo m; **~ of ...** F un po' ...; **is it finished?** – **~** F è terminato? – quasi **2** v/t separare; COMPUT ordinare

♦ **sort out** v/t papers mettere in ordine; problem risolvere; **sort things out** sistemare le cose

OS [esəʊ'es] SOS m inv

o-'so adv F così così

ought [sɔːt] pret & pp → **seek**

oul [səʊl] anima f; **the poor ~** il poverino, la poverina

ound¹ [saʊnd] **1** adj (sensible) valido; (healthy) sano; sleep profondo; structure, walls solido **2** adv: **be ~ asleep** dormire profondamente

ound² [saʊnd] **1** n suono m; (noise)

rumore m **2** v/t (pronounce) pronunciare; MED auscultare; **~ one's horn** suonare il clacson **3** v/i: **that ~s interesting** sembra interessante; **that ~s like a good idea** mi sembra un'ottima idea; **she ~ed unhappy** dalla voce sembrava infelice

♦ **sound out** v/t sondare l'opinione di

'sound bar-ri-er muro m del suono

'sound-bite slogan m inv

'sound ef-fects npl effetti mpl sonori

sound-ly ['saʊndlɪ] adv sleep profondamente; beaten battuto

'sound-proof adj insonorizzato

'sound-track colonna f sonora

soup [su:p] minestra f

'soup bowl scodella f

souped-up [su:pt'ʌp] adj F truccato F

'soup plate piatto m fondo

'soup spoon cucchiaio m da minestra

sour ['saʊə(r)] adj apple, orange aspro; milk, expression, comment acido

source [sɔːs] n fonte f; of river sorgente f

sour 'cream panna f acida

south [saʊθ] **1** adj meridionale, del sud **2** n sud m; **to the ~ of** a sud di **3** adv verso sud

South 'Af-ri-ca Repubblica f Sudafricana

South 'Af-ri-can 1 adj sudafricano **2** n sudafricano m, -a f

South A'mer-i-ca Sudamerica m

South A'mer-i-can 1 adj sudamericano **2** n sudamericano m, -a f

south-east 1 n sud-est m **2** adj sud-orientale **3** adv verso sud-est; **it's ~ of ...** è a sud-est di ...

south-'east-ern adj sud-orientale

south-er-ly ['sʌðəlɪ] adj meridionale

south-ern ['sʌðən] adj del sud

south-ern-er ['sʌðənə(r)] abitante m/f del sud

south-ern-most ['sʌðənməʊst] adj più a sud

S

South 'Pole polo *m* sud

south·wards ['saʊθwədz] *adv* verso sud

south·'west **1** *n* sud-ovest *m* **2** *adj* sud-occidentale **3** *adv* verso sud-ovest; **it's ~ of ...** è a sud-ovest di ...

south'west·ern *adj* sud-occidentale

sou·ve·nir [suːvə'nɪə(r)] souvenir *m inv*

sove·reign ['sɒvrɪn] *adj* state sovrano

sove·reign·ty ['sɒvrɪntɪ] *of state* sovranità *f inv*

So·vi·et ['səʊvɪət] *adj* sovietico

So·vi·et 'U·nion Unione *f* Sovietica

sow¹ [saʊ] *n (female pig)* scrofa *f*

sow² [səʊ] *v/t seeds* semiˉare

sown [səʊn] *pp →* **sow²**

soy·a bean ['sɔɪə] seme *m* di soia

soy(a) 'sauce salsa *f* di soia

spa [spɑː] località *f inv* termale

space [speɪs] *n* spazio *m; in car park* posto *m*

♦ space out *v/t* distanziare

'space-bar COMPUT barra *f* spaziatrice; 'space·craft veicolo *m* spaziale; 'space·ship astronave *f*; 'space shut·tle shuttle *m inv*; 'space sta·tion stazione *f* spaziale; 'space·suit tuta *f* spaziale

spa·cious ['speɪʃəs] *adj* spazioso

spade [speɪd] *for digging* vanga *f*; **~s** *in card game* picche

'spade·work *fig* preparativi *mpl*

spa·ghet·ti [spə'getɪ] *nsg* spaghetti *mpl*

Spain [speɪn] Spagna *f*

span [spæn] *v/t (pret & pp **-ned**)* coprire; *of bridge* attraversare

Span·iard ['spænjəd] spagnolo *m*, -a *f*

Span·ish ['spænɪʃ] **1** *adj* spagnolo **2** *n language* spagnolo *m*

spank [spæŋk] *v/t* sculacciare

spank·ing ['spæŋkɪŋ] sculaccione *m*

span·ner ['spænə(r)] *Br* chiave *f* inglese

spare [speə(r)] **1** *v/t (do without)* fare a meno di; **can you ~ £50?** mi puoi prestare 50 sterline?; **can you ~ the time?** hai tempo?; **have money /**

time to ~ avere soldi/tempo d'avanzo; **there were 5 to ~** *(left over, in excess)* ce n'erano 5 d'avanzo **2** *adj* in più **3** *n* ricambio *m*

spare 'part pezzo *m* di ricambio; **spare 'ribs** *npl* costine *fpl* di maiale; **spare 'room** stanza *f* degli ospiti; **spare 'time** tempo *m* libero; **spare 'tire** *Am*, **spare 'tyre** MOT ruota *f* di scorta

spar·ing ['speərɪŋ] *adj*: **be ~ with** andarci piano con F

spa·ring·ly ['speərɪŋlɪ] *adv* con moderazione

spark [spɑːk] *n* scintilla *f*

spark·ing plug ['spɑːkɪŋ] candela *f*

sparkle ['spɑːkl] *v/i* brillare

spark·ling 'wine ['spɑːklɪŋ] vino *m* frizzante

'spark plug candela *f*

spar·row ['spærəʊ] passero *m*

sparse [spɑːs] *adj vegetation* rado

sparse·ly ['spɑːslɪ] *adv*: **~ populated** scarsamente popolato

spar·tan ['spɑːtn] *adj* spartano

spas·mod·ic [spæz'mɒdɪk] *adj* irregolare

spat [spæt] *pret & pp →* **spit**

spate [speɪt] *fig* ondata *f*

spa·tial ['speɪʃl] *adj* spaziale

spat·ter ['spætə(r)] *v/t mud, paint* schizzare

speak [spiːk] *(pret* **spoke**, *pp* **spoken**) **1** *v/i* parlare; **we're not ~ing (to each other)** *(we've quarrelled)* non ci rivolgiamo la parola; **~ing** TELEC sono io **2** *v/t foreign language* parlare; *the truth* dire; **~ one's mind** dire quello che si pensa

♦ speak for *v/t* parlare a nome di

♦ speak out *v/i* prendere posizione; *say what you think* farsi sentire

♦ speak up *v/i (speak louder)* parlare ad alta voce

speak·er ['spiːkə(r)] oratore *m*, -trice *f; of sound system* cassa *f*

spear [spɪə(r)] lancia *f*

spear·mint ['spɪəmɪnt] menta *f*

spe·cial ['speʃl] *adj* speciale; *(particular)* particolare

spe·cial ef·fects *npl* effetti *mpl* speciali

spe·cial·ist ['speʃlɪst] specialista *m/f*

spe·cial·i·ty [speʃɪ'ælətɪ] specialità *f inv*

spe·cial·ize ['speʃəlaɪz] *v/i* specializzarsi; ~ **in ...** specializzarsi in; **we ~ in ...** siamo specializzati in ...

spe·cial·ly ['speʃlɪ] *adv* → **especially**

spe·cial·ty ['speʃəltɪ] *Am* specialità *f inv*

spe·cies ['spiːʃiːz] *nsg* specie *f inv*

spe·cif·ic [spə'sɪfɪk] *adj* specifico

spe·cif·i·cal·ly [spə'sɪfɪklɪ] *adv* specificamente

spec·i·fi·ca·tions [spesɪfɪ'keɪʃnz] *npl of machine etc* caratteristiche *fpl* tecniche, specifiche *fpl*

spe·ci·fy ['spesɪfaɪ] *v/t* (*pret & pp* **-ied**) specificare

spec·i·men ['spesɪmən] campione *m*

speck [spek] *of dust, soot* granello *m*

specs [speks] *npl* F (*spectacles*) occhiali *mpl*

spec·ta·cle ['spektəkl] (*impressive sight*) spettacolo *m*; (**a pair of**) **~s** (un paio di) occhiali *mpl*

spec·tac·u·lar [spek'tækjʊlə(r)] *adj* spettacolare

spec·ta·tor [spek'teɪtə(r)] spettatore *m*, -trice *f*

spec'ta·tor sport sport *m inv* spettacolo

spec·trum ['spektrəm] *fig* gamma *f*

spec·u·late ['spekjʊleɪt] *v/i* fare congetture (**on** su); FIN speculare

spec·u·la·tion [spekjʊ'leɪʃn] congetture *fpl*; FIN speculazione *f*

spec·u·la·tor ['spekjʊleɪtə(r)] FIN speculatore *m*, -trice *f*

sped [sped] *pret & pp* → **speed**

speech [spiːtʃ] (*address*) discorso *m*; *in play* monologo *m*; (*ability to speak*) parola *f*; (*way of speaking*) linguaggio *m*; **faculty / power of ~** facoltà / uso della parola; **her ~ was slurred** biascicava le parole

speech de·fect difetto *m* del linguaggio

speech·less ['spiːtʃlɪs] *adj* with shock, surprise senza parole

'speech ther·a·pist logopedista *m/f*; **speech 'ther·a·py** logopedia *f*; **'speech writ·er** ghost writer *m inv*

speed [spiːd] **1** *n* velocità *f inv*; (*quickness*) rapidità *f inv*; **at a ~ of 150 mph** a una velocità di 150 miglia orarie; **reduce your ~** rallentare **2** *v/i* (*pret & pp* **sped**) (*go quickly*) andare a tutta velocità; (*drive too quickly*) superare il limite di velocità

♦ **speed by** *v/i* sfrecciare; *of days* volare

♦ **speed up** **1** *v/i* andare più veloce **2** *v/t* accelerare

'speed·boat motoscafo *m*

'speed bump dosso *m* di rallentamento

speed·i·ly ['spiːdɪlɪ] *adv* rapidamente

speed·ing ['spiːdɪŋ] *n when driving* eccesso *m* di velocità

'speed·ing fine multa *f* per eccesso di velocità

'speed lim·it *on roads* limite *m* di velocità

speed·om·e·ter [spiː'dɒmɪtə(r)] tachimetro *m*

'speed trap *sistema m con cui la polizia individua chi supera il limite di velocità*

speed·y ['spiːdɪ] *adj* rapido

spell¹ [spel] **1** *v/t*: **how do you ~ ...?** come si scrive ...?; **could you ~ that please?** me lo può dettare lettera per lettera? **2** *v/i* sapere come si scrivono le parole

spell² [spel] *n* (*period of time*) periodo *m*; (*turn*) turno *m*

'spell·bound *adj* incantato; **'spell·check** COMPUT controllo *m* ortografico; **do a ~ on ...** fare il controllo ortografico di ...; **'spell·check·er** COMPUT correttore *m* ortografico

spell·ing ['spelɪŋ] ortografia *f*

spend [spend] *v/t* (*pret & pp* **spent**) *money* spendere; *time* passare

'spend·thrift *n pej* spendaccione *m*, -a *f*

spent [spent] *pret & pp* → **spend**

sperm [spɜ:m] spermatozoo *m*; *(semen)* sperma *m*

'**sperm bank** banca *f* dello sperma

'**sperm count** numero *m* degli spermatozoi

sphere [sfɪə(r)] *also fig* sfera *f*; **~ of influence** sfera d'influenza

spice [spaɪs] *n (seasoning)* spezia *f*

spic·y ['spaɪsɪ] *adj food* piccante

spi·der ['spaɪdə(r)] ragno *m*

'spi·der's **web** ragnatela *f*

spike [spaɪk] *n on railings* spunzone *m*; *on plant* spina *f*; *on animal* aculeo *m*; *on running shoes* chiodo *m*

spill [spɪl] **1** *v/t* versare **2** *v/i* versarsi **3** *n of oil etc* fuoriuscita *f*

spin¹ [spɪn] **1** *n* giro *m*; *on ball* effetto *m* **2** *v/t (pret & pp* **spun**) *ball* imprimere l'effetto a **3** *v/i (pret & pp* **spun**) *of wheel* girare; *my head is ~ning* mi gira la testa

spin² [spɪn] *v/t (pret & pp* **spun**) *wool, cotton* filare; *web* tessere

♦ **spin around** *v/i of person, car* girarsi

♦ **spin out** *v/t* F far durare

spin·ach ['spɪnɪdʒ] spinaci *mpl*

spin·al ['spaɪnl] *adj* spinale

spin·al 'col·umn colonna *f* vertebrale, spina *f* dorsale

spin·al 'cord midollo *m* spinale

'spin doc·tor F *persona f* incaricata di far apparire un personaggio politico nella luce migliore; '**spin-dry** *v/t* centrifugare; '**spin-dry·er** centrifuga *f*

spine [spaɪn] *of person, animal* spina *f* dorsale; *of book* dorso *m*; *on plant, hedgehog* spina *f*

spine·less ['spaɪnlɪs] *adj (cowardly)* smidollato

'spin-off applicazione *f* secondaria

spin·ster ['spɪnstə(r)] zitella *f*

spin·y ['spaɪnɪ] *adj* spinoso

spi·ral ['spaɪrəl] **1** *n* spirale *f* **2** *v/i (rise quickly)* salire vertiginosamente

spi·ral 'stair·case scala *f* a chiocciola

spire ['spaɪə(r)] spira *f*, guglia *f*

spir·it ['spɪrɪt] *n* spirito *m*; **we did it in a ~ of cooperation** abbiamo agito per spirito di collaborazione

spir·it·ed ['spɪrɪtɪd] *adj debate* animato; *defence* energico; *performance* brioso

'spir·it lev·el livella *f* a bolla d'aria

spir·its¹ ['spɪrɪts] *npl (alcohol)* superalcolici *mpl*

spir·its² ['spɪrɪts] *npl (morale)* morale *msg*; **be in good / poor ~** essere su / giù di morale

spir·i·tu·al ['spɪrɪtjʊəl] *adj* spirituale

spir·it·u·al·ism ['spɪrɪtjʊəlɪzm] spiritismo *m*

spir·it·u·al·ist ['spɪrɪtjʊəlɪst] *n* spiritista *m/f*

spit [spɪt] *v/i (pret & pp* **spat**) *of person* sputare; *it's ~ting with rain* pioviggina

♦ **spit out** *v/t food, liquid* sputare

spite [spaɪt] *n* dispetto *m*; **in ~ of** malgrado

spite·ful ['spaɪtfʊl] *adj* dispettoso

spite·ful·ly ['spaɪtfəlɪ] *adv* dispettosamente

spit·ting 'im·age ['spɪtɪŋ]: **be the ~ of s.o.** essere il ritratto sputato di qu

splash [splæʃ] **1** *n (noise)* tonfo *m*; *(small amount of liquid)* schizzo *m*; *of colour* macchia *f* **2** *v/t person* schizzare; *water, mud* spruzzare **3** *v/i* schizzare; *of waves* infrangersi

♦ **splash down** *v/i of spacecraft* ammarare

♦ **splash out** *v/i in spending* spendere un sacco di soldi (**on** per)

'splash·down ammaraggio *m*

splen·did ['splendɪd] *adj* magnifico

splen·dor *Am*, splen·dour ['splendə(r)] magnificenza *f*

splint [splɪnt] *n* MED stecca *f*

splin·ter ['splɪntə(r)] **1** *n* scheggia *f* **2** *v/i* scheggiarsi

'splin·ter group gruppo *m* scissionista

split [splɪt] **1** *n in leather* strappo *m*; *in wood* crepa *f*; *(disagreement)* spaccatura *f*; *(division, share)* divisione *f* **2** *v/t (pret & pp* **split**) *leather* strappare; *wood, logs* spaccare; *(cause disagreement in)* spaccare; *(divide)* dividere **3** v/i (pret & pp **split**) of leather strapparsi; of wood spaccarsi; (disagree) spaccarsi

♦ **split up** v/i of couple separarsi

split per·son·al·i·ty PSYCH sdoppiamento m della personalità

split·ting ['splɪtɪŋ] adj: **~ headache** feroce mal m inv di testa

splut·ter ['splʌtə(r)] v/i farfugliare

spoil [spɔɪl] v/t child viziare; surprise, party rovinare

spoil·sport F guastafeste m/f

spoilt [spɔɪlt] adj child viziato; **be ~ for choice** avere (solo) l'imbarazzo della scelta

spoke[1] [spəʊk] of wheel raggio m

spoke[2] [spəʊk] pret → **speak**

spo·ken ['spəʊkən] pp → **speak**

spokes·man ['spəʊksmən] portavoce m

spokes·per·son ['spəʊkspɜːsən] portavoce m/f

spokes·wom·an ['spəʊkswʊmən] portavoce f

sponge [spʌndʒ] n spugna f

♦ **sponge off/on** v/t F vivere alle spalle di

sponge cake pan m inv di Spagna

spong·er ['spʌndʒə(r)] F scroccone m, -a f

spon·sor ['spɒnsə(r)] **1** n for immigration garante m/f inv; for membership socio m, -a f garante; of TV programme, sports event, for fundraising sponsor m inv **2** v/t for immigration, membership garantire per; TV programme, sports event sponsorizzare

spon·sor·ship ['spɒnsəʃɪp] sponsorizzazione f

spon·ta·ne·ous [spɒn'teɪnɪəs] adj spontaneo

spon·ta·ne·ous·ly [spɒn'teɪnɪəslɪ] adv spontaneamente

spook·y ['spuːkɪ] adj F sinistro

spool [spuːl] n bobina f

spoon [spuːn] n cucchiaio m

spoon-feed v/t (pret & pp **-fed**) fig scodellare la pappa a

spoon·ful ['spuːnfʊl] cucchiaio f

spo·rad·ic [spə'rædɪk] adj sporadico

sport [spɔːt] n sport m inv

sport·ing ['spɔːtɪŋ] adj sportivo; **a ~ gesture** un gesto sportivo

'sports car [spɔːts] auto f inv sportiva; **'sports cen·ter** Am, **'sports cen·tre** indoor palazzetto m dello sport; **'sports jack·et** giacca f sportiva; **'sports·man** sportivo m; **'sports med·i·cine** medicina f dello sport; **'sports news** nsg notizie fpl sportive; **'sports page** pagina f dello sport; **'sports·wear** abbigliamento m sportivo; **'sports·wom·an** sportiva f

sport·y ['spɔːtɪ] adj sportivo

spot[1] [spɒt] n (pimple) brufolo m; caused by measles etc foruncolo m; part of pattern pois m inv; **a ~ of ...** (a little) un po' di ...

spot[2] [spɒt] n (place) posticino m; **on the ~** (in the place in question) sul posto; (immediately) immediatamente; **put s.o. on the ~** mettere in difficoltà qu

spot[3] [spɒt] v/t (pret & pp **-ted**) (notice) notare; (identify) trovare

spot 'check n controllo m casuale

spot·less ['spɒtlɪs] adj pulitissimo

'spot·light n faretto m

spot·ted ['spɒtɪd] adj fabric a pois

spot·ty ['spɒtɪ] adj with pimples brufoloso

spouse [spaʊs] fml coniuge m/f

spout [spaʊt] **1** n beccuccio m **2** v/i of liquid sgorgare **3** v/t F: **~ nonsense** ciarlare

sprain [spreɪn] **1** n slogatura f **2** v/t slogarsi

sprang [spræŋ] pret → **spring**

sprawl [sprɔːl] v/i stravaccarsi; of city estendersi; **send s.o. ~ing** of punch mandare qu a gambe all'aria

sprawl·ing ['sprɔːlɪŋ] adj city, suburbs tentacolare

spray [spreɪ] **1** n of sea water, from fountain spruzzi mpl; for hair lacca f; (container) spray m inv **2** v/t spruzzare; **~ s.o. / sth with sth** spruzzare qu / qc di qc

'spray·gun pistola f a spruzzo

spread [spred] **1** n of disease, religion

etc diffusione *f*; F *big meal* banchetto *m*; **2** *v/t* (*pret & pp* **spread**) (*lay*) stendere; *butter, jam* spalmare; *news, rumour, disease* diffondere; *arms, legs* allargare **3** *v/i* (*pret & pp* **spread**) diffondersi; *of butter* spalmarsi

'spread·sheet COMPUT spreadsheet *m inv*

spree [spri:] F: **go** (**out**) **on a ~** *having fun* andare a far baldoria; **go on a shopping ~** andare a fare spese folli

sprig [sprɪg] rametto *m*

spright·ly ['spraɪtlɪ] *adj* arzillo

spring¹ [sprɪŋ] *n season* primavera *f*

spring² [sprɪŋ] *n device* molla *f*

spring³ [sprɪŋ] **1** *n* (*jump*) balzo *m*; (*stream*) sorgente *f* **2** *v/i* (*pret* **sprang**, *pp* **sprung**) scattare; **~ from** derivare da

'spring·board trampolino *m*; **spring 'chick·en** *hum*: **she's no ~** non è più una ragazzina; **spring-'clean·ing** pulizie *fpl* di primavera; **spring 'on·ion** cipollotto *m*; '**spring·time** primavera *f*

spring·y ['sprɪŋɪ] *adj mattress, walk* molleggiato; *ground* morbido; *material* elastico

sprin·kle ['sprɪŋkl] *v/t* spruzzare; **~ sth with** cospargere qc di

sprin·kler ['sprɪŋklə(r)] *for garden* irrigatore *m*; *in ceiling* sprinkler *m inv*

sprint [sprɪnt] **1** *n*: scatto *m*; **the 100 metres ~** i cento metri piani **2** *v/i* fare uno scatto

sprint·er ['sprɪntə(r)] SP velocista *m/f*

sprout [spraʊt] **1** *v/i of seed* spuntare **2** *n* germoglio *m*; (**Brussels**) **~s** cavolini *mpl* di Bruxelles

spruce [spru:s] *adj* curato

sprung [sprʌŋ] *pp* → **spring**

spun [spʌn] *pret & pp* → **spin**

spry [spraɪ] *adj* arzillo

spud [spʌd] F patata *f*

spur [spɜ:(r)] *n* sperone *m*; *fig* sprone *m*; **on the ~ of the moment** su due piedi

♦ **spur on** *v/t* (*pret & pp* **-red**) (*encourage*) spronare

spurt [spɜ:t] **1** *n*: **put on a ~** *in race* fare uno scatto; *in work* accelerare il ritmo **2** *v/i of liquid* sprizzare

sput·ter ['spʌtə(r)] *v/i of engine* scoppiettare

spy [spaɪ] **1** *n* spia *f* **2** *v/i* (*pret & pp* **-ied**) fare la spia **3** *v/t* (*pret & pp* **-ied**) F scorgere

♦ **spy on** *v/t* spiare

squab·ble ['skwɒbl] **1** *n* bisticcio *m* **2** *v/i* bisticciare

squal·id ['skwɒlɪd] *adj* squallido

squal·or ['skwɒlə(r)] squallore *m*

squan·der ['skwɒndə(r)] *v/t money* dilapidare

square [skweə(r)] **1** *adj in shape* quadrato; **~ mile** miglio quadrato **2** *n shape* quadrato *m*; *in town* piazza *f*; *in board game* casella *f*, MATH quadrato *m*; **we're back to ~ one** siamo punto e a capo

♦ **square up** *v/i* (*settle up*) fare i conti

square 'root radice *f* quadrata

squash¹ [skwɒʃ] *n vegetable* zucca *f*

squash² [skwɒʃ] *n game* squash *m inv*

squash³ [skwɒʃ] **1** *v/t* (*crush*) schiacciare **2** *n*: *orange / lemon* ~ sciroppo *m* d'arancia / limone

squat [skwɒt] **1** *adj in shape* tozzo **2** *v/i* (*pret & pp* **-ted**) (*sit*) accovacciarsi; *illegally* occupare abusivamente

squat·ter ['skwɒtə(r)] squatter *m inv*, occupante *m/f* abusivo, -a

squeak [skwi:k] **1** *n of mouse* squittio *m*; *of hinge* cigolio *m* **2** *v/i of mouse* squittire; *of hinge* cigolare; *of shoes* scricchiolare

squeak·y ['skwi:kɪ] *adj hinge* cigolante; *shoes* scricchiolante; *voice* stridulo

squeak·y clean *adj* F pulito

squeal [skwi:l] **1** *n of pain, laughter* strillo *m*; *of brakes* stridore *m* **2** *v/i* strillare; *of brakes* stridere

squeam·ish ['skwi:mɪʃ] *adj*: **be ~** avere lo stomaco delicato

squeeze [skwi:z] **1** *n of hand,*

shoulder stretta *f*; **a ~ of lemon** una spruzzata di limone **2** *v/t hand* stringere; *orange, lemon* spremere; *sponge* strizzare

♦ **squeeze in 1** *v/i to a car etc* infilarsi **2** *v/t* infilare

♦ **squeeze up** *v/i to make space* stringersi

squid [skwɪd] calamaro *m*

squint [skwɪnt] *n* strabismo *m*

squirm [skwɜːm] *v/i* (*wriggle*) contorcersi; **~ (with embarrassment)** morire di vergogna

squir·rel ['skwɪrəl] scoiattolo *m*

squirt [skwɜːt] **1** *v/t* spruzzare **2** *n* F *pej* microbo *m* F

St *abbr* (= *saint*) S. (= santo *m*, santa *f*); (= *street*) v. (= *via f*)

stab [stæb] **1** *n* F: **have a ~ at doing sth** provare a fare qc **2** *v/t* (*pret & pp* **-bed**) *person* accoltellare

sta·bil·i·ty [stə'bɪlətɪ] stabilità *f inv*

sta·bil·ize ['steɪbɪlaɪz] **1** *v/t prices, boat* stabilizzare **2** *v/i of prices etc* stabilizzarsi

sta·ble¹ ['steɪbl] *n building* stalla *f*; *establishment* scuderia *f*

sta·ble² ['steɪbl] *adj* stabile

stack [stæk] **1** *n* (*pile*) pila *f*; (*smokestack*) ciminiera *f*; **~s of** F un sacco di F **2** *v/t* mettere in pila

sta·di·um ['steɪdɪəm] stadio *m*

staff [stɑːf] *npl* (*employees*) personale *msg*; (*teachers*) corpo *m* insegnante

staff·room *in school* sala *f* professori

stag [stæg] cervo *m*

stage¹ [steɪdʒ] *in life, project etc* fase *f*; *of journey* tappa *f*

stage² [steɪdʒ] **1** *n* THEA palcoscenico *m*; **go on the ~** *become actor* fare teatro **2** *v/t play* mettere in scena; *demonstration* organizzare

stage 'door ingresso *m* degli artisti; **'stage fright** attacco *m* di panico; **'stage hand** macchinista *m*

stag·ger ['stægə(r)] **1** *v/i* barcollare **2** *v/t* (*amaze*) sbalordire; *holidays, breaks etc* scaglionare

stag·ger·ing ['stægərɪŋ] *adj* sbalorditivo

stag·nant ['stægnənt] *adj also fig* stagnante

stag·nate [stæg'neɪt] *v/i of person, mind* vegetare

stag·na·tion [stæg'neɪʃn] ristagno *m*

'stag par·ty (festa *f* di) addio *m* al celibato

stain [steɪn] **1** *n* (*dirty mark*) macchia *f*; *for wood* mordente *m* **2** *v/t* (*dirty*) macchiare; *wood* dare il mordente a **3** *v/i of wine etc* macchiare; *of fabric* macchiarsi

stained-glass 'win·dow [steɪnd] vetrata *f* colorata

stain·less 'steel ['steɪnlɪs] **1** *n* acciaio *m* inossidabile **2** *adj* d'acciaio inossidabile

'stain re·mov·er smacchiatore *m*

stair [steə(r)] scalino *m*; **the ~s** le scale

'stair·case scala *f*

stake [steɪk] **1** *n of wood* paletto *m*; *when gambling* puntata *f*; (*investment*) partecipazione *f*; **be at ~** essere in gioco **2** *v/t tree* puntellare; *money* puntare

stale [steɪl] *adj bread* raffermo; *air* viziato; *fig: news* vecchio

'stale·mate *in chess* stallo *m*; *fig* punto *m* morto

stalk¹ [stɔːk] *n of fruit* picciolo *m*; *of plant* gambo *m*

stalk² [stɔːk] *v/t animal* seguire; *person* perseguitare (con telefonate, lettere ecc)

stalk·er ['stɔːkə(r)] persona *f* che perseguita qualcun altro con telefonate, lettere ecc

stall¹ [stɔːl] *n at market* bancarella *f*; *for cow, horse* box *m inv*

stall² [stɔːl] **1** *v/i of engine* spegnersi; *of vehicle* fermarsi; (*play for time*) temporeggiare **2** *v/t engine* far spegnere; *people* trattenere

stal·li·on ['stæljən] stallone *m*

stalls [stɔːlz] *npl* platea *f*

stal·wart ['stɔːlwət] *adj support, supporter* fedele

stam·i·na ['stæmɪnə] resistenza *f*

stam·mer ['stæmə(r)] **1** *n* balbuzie *f* **2** *v/i* balbettare

S

stamp[1] [stæmp] **1** *n for letter* franco-bollo *m*; (*date ~ etc*) timbro *m* **2** *v/t letter* affrancare; *document, passport* timbrare; **~ed addressed enve-lope** busta *f* affrancata per la risposta

stamp[2] [stæmp] *v/t*: **~ one's feet** pe-stare i piedi

'**stamp col·lec·ting** filatelia *f*; '**stamp col·lec·tion** collezione *f* di francobolli; '**stamp col·lec·tor** col-lezionista *m/f* di francobolli

♦ **stamp out** *v/t* (*eradicate*) eliminare

stam·pede [stæm'piːd] **1** *n of cattle etc* fuga *f* precipitosa; *of people* fuggi-fuggi *m inv* **2** *v/i of cattle etc* fuggire precipitosamente; *of people* precipitarsi

stance [stɑːns] (*position*) presa *f* di posizione

stand [stænd] **1** *n at exhibition* stand *m inv*; (*witness ~*) banco *m* dei testi-moni; (*support, base*) base *f*; **take the ~** LAW testimoniare **2** *v/i* (*pret & pp* **stood**) (*be situated: of person*) stare; *of object, building* trovarsi; *as opposed to sit* stare in piedi; (*rise*) alzarsi in piedi; **~ still** stare fermo; **where do you ~ on the issue?** qual è la tua posizione su questa questione? **3** *v/t* (*pret & pp* **stood**) (*tolerate*) sopportare; (*put*) mettere; **you don't ~ a chance** non hai alcuna probabilità; **~ s.o. a drink** offrire da bere a qu; **~ one's ground** non mol-lare, tenere duro

♦ **stand back** *v/i* farsi indietro

♦ **stand by 1** *v/i* (*not take action*) sta-re a guardare; (*be ready*) tenersi pronto **2** *v/t person* stare al fianco di; *decision* mantenere

♦ **stand down** *v/i* (*withdraw*) ritirarsi

♦ **stand for** *v/t* (*tolerate*) tollerare; (*mean*) significare; *freedom etc* rap-presentare

♦ **stand in for** *v/t* sostituire

♦ **stand out** *v/i* spiccare; *of person, building* distinguersi

♦ **stand up 1** *v/i* alzarsi in piedi **2** *v/t* F *on date* dare buca a F

♦ **stand up for** *v/t* difendere

♦ **stand up to** *v/t* far fronte a

stan·dard ['stændəd] **1** *adj* (*usual*) comune; *model, size* standard *inv* **2** *n* (*level*) livello *m*; (*expectation*) aspet-tativa *f*; TECH standard *m inv*; *moral* **~s** principi *mpl*; **be / not be up to ~** essere / non essere di buona qualità

stan·dard·ize ['stændədaɪz] *v/t* stan-dardizzare

'**stan·dard lamp** *Br* lampada *f* a ste-lo

stan·dard of 'li·ving tenore *m* di vita

'**stand·by 1** *n ticket* biglietto *m* stand-by; **on ~** *at airport* in lista d'at-tesa; **on ~** *of troops etc* pronto

'**stand·by pas·sen·ger** passeggero *m*, -a *f* in lista d'attesa

stand·ing ['stændɪŋ] *n in society etc* posizione *f*; (*repute*) reputazione *f*; **a musician of some ~** un musicista di una certa importanza; **a friendship of long ~** un'amicizia di lunga dura-ta

stand·ing 'or·der FIN ordine *m* per-manente

'**stand·ing room** posto *m* in piedi

stand·off·ish [stænd'ɒfɪʃ] *adj* sco-stante; '**stand·point** punto *m* di vi-sta; '**stand·still**; **be at a ~** essere fer-mo; **bring to a ~** fermare

stank [stæŋk] *pret* → **stink**

stan·za ['stænzə] *of poem* stanza *f*

sta·ple[1] ['steɪpl] *n* (*foodstuff*) ali-mento *m* base

sta·ple[2] ['steɪpl] **1** *n* (*fastener*) graffa *f* **2** *v/t* pinzare

sta·ple 'di·et alimentazione *f* base

'**sta·ple gun** pistola *f* sparachiodi

'**sta·pler** ['steɪplə(r)] pinzatrice *f*

star [stɑː(r)] **1** *n in sky* stella *f*; *fig* star *f inv* **2** *v/t* (*pret & pp* **-red**): **a film ~ring Julia Roberts** un film inter-pretato da Julia Roberts **3** *v/i* (*pret & pp* **-red**): **he ~red in Psycho** è il protagonista di Psycho

'**star·board** *adj* a tribordo

starch [stɑːtʃ] *in foodstuff* amido *m*

stare [steə(r)] **1** *n* sguardo *m* fisso **2** *v/i* fissare; **~ at** fissare

'**star·fish** stella *f* di mare

stark [stɑːk] **1** *adj landscape* desolato; *colour scheme* austero; *reminder, contrast etc* brusco **2** *adv*: ~ **naked** completamente nudo

star·ling ['stɑːlɪŋ] storno *m*

star·ry ['stɑːrɪ] *adj night* stellato

star·ry-eyed [stɑːrɪ'aɪd]] *adj person* idealista

start [stɑːt] **1** *n (beginning)* inizio *m*; **make a ~ on sth** iniziare qc; **get off to a good / bad ~** *in marriage, career* cominciare bene / male; **from the ~** dall'inizio; **well, it's a ~!** è pur sempre un inizio! **2** *v/i* iniziare, cominciare; *of engine, car* partire; **~ing from tomorrow** a partire da domani **3** *v/t* cominciare; *engine, car* mettere in moto; *business* mettere su; **~ to do sth, ~ doing sth** cominciare a fare qc

start·er ['stɑːtə(r)] *part of meal* antipasto *m*; *of car* motorino *m* d'avviamento; *in race* starter *m inv*

'starting point punto *m* di partenza

'starting sal·a·ry stipendio *m* iniziale

start·le ['stɑːtl] *v/t* far trasalire

start·ling ['stɑːtlɪŋ] *adj* sorprendente

starv·a·tion [stɑː'veɪʃn] fame *f*

starve [stɑːv] *v/i* soffrire la fame; **~ to death** morire di fame; **I'm starving** F sto morendo di fame

state[1] [steɪt] **1** *n of car, house etc* stato *m*, condizione *f*; *(country)* stato *m*; **the States** gli Stati Uniti; **be in a ~** essere agitato **2** *adj* di stato; *school* statale; *banquet etc* ufficiale

state[2] [steɪt] *v/t* dichiarare

'State De·part·ment *in USA* Ministero *m* degli Esteri

state·ment ['steɪtmənt] *to police* deposizione *f*; *(announcement)* dichiarazione *f*; *(bank ~)* estratto *m* conto

state of e·mer·gen·cy stato *m* d'emergenza

state-of-the-'art *adj* allo stato dell'arte

states·man ['steɪtsmən] statista *m*

state 'vis·it visita *f* ufficiale

stat·ic (e·lec·tric·i·ty) ['stætɪk] elettricità *f inv* statica

sta·tion ['steɪʃn] **1** *n* stazione *f* **2** *v/t guard etc* disporre; **be ~ed at** *of soldier* essere di stanza in / a

sta·tion·a·ry ['steɪʃnərɪ] *adj* fermo

sta·tion·er's ['steɪʃənərz] cartoleria *f*

sta·tion·er·y ['steɪʃənərɪ] articoli *mpl* di cancelleria

sta·tion 'man·ag·er dirigente *m* della stazione ferroviaria

'sta·tion wag·on *Am* giardiniera *f*

sta·tis·ti·cal [stə'tɪstɪkl] *adj* statistico

sta·tis·ti·cal·ly [stə'tɪstɪklɪ] *adv* statisticamente

sta·tis·ti·cian [stætɪs'tɪʃn] esperto *m*, -a *f* di statistica

sta·tis·tics [stə'tɪstɪks] *nsg science* statistica *f*; *npl figures* statistiche *fpl*

stat·ue ['stætjuː] statua *f*

sta·tus ['steɪtəs] posizione *f*

'sta·tus bar COMPUT barra *f* di stato

'sta·tus sym·bol status symbol *m inv*

stat·ute ['stætjuːt] statuto *m*

staunch [stɔːntʃ] *adj* leale

stay [steɪ] **1** *n* soggiorno *m* **2** *v/i in a place* stare; *in a condition* restare; **~ in a hotel** stare in albergo; **~ right there!** non ti muovere!; **~ put** non muoversi

♦ **stay away** *v/i* stare alla larga

♦ **stay away from** *v/t* stare alla larga da

♦ **stay behind** *v/i* rimanere

♦ **stay up** *v/i (not go to bed)* rimanere alzato

stead·i·ly ['stedɪlɪ] *adv improve etc* costantemente; *look* fisso

stead·y ['stedɪ] **1** *adj voice, hands* fermo; *job, boyfriend* fisso; *beat* regolare; *improvement, decline, progress* costante **2** *adv* **be going ~** fare coppia fissa; **~ on!** calma! **3** *v/t (pret & pp -ied) bookcase etc* rendere saldo; **~ o.s.** ritrovare l'equilibrio

steak [steɪk] bistecca *f*, carne *f* (di manzo)

steal [stiːl] *(pret* **stole**, *pp* **stolen**) **1** *v/t money etc* rubare **2** *v/i (be a thief)* rubare; **~ in / out** *(move quietly)* entrare / uscire furtivamente

S

stealth·y ['stelθɪ] *adj* furtivo

steam [stiːm] **1** *n* vapore *m* **2** *v/t food* cuocere al vapore

♦ **steam up 1** *v/i of window* appannarsi **2** *v/t:* **be steamed up** F *angry* essere furibondo

steam·er ['stiːmə(r)] *for cooking* vaporiera *f*

steam i·ron ferro *m* a vapore

steel [stiːl] **1** *n* acciaio **2** *adj* d'acciaio

steel·work·er operaio *m* di acciaieria

steel·works acciaieria *f*

steep[^1] [stiːp] *adj hill etc* ripido; F *prices* alto; **that's a bit ~ expensive** è un po' caro

steep[^2] [stiːp] *v/t (soak)* lasciare a bagno

stee·ple ['stiːpl] *n* campanile *m*

stee·ple·chase *in athletics* corsa *f* ad ostacoli

steep·ly ['stiːplɪ] *adv:* **climb ~** *of path* salire ripidamente; *of prices* salire vertiginosamente

steer[^1] [stɪə(r)] *n animal* manzo *m*

steer[^2] [stɪə(r)] *v/t car, boat* manovrare; *person* guidare; *conversation* spostare

steer·ing ['stɪərɪŋ] *of motor vehicle* sterzo *m*

steer·ing wheel volante *m*

stem[^1] [stem] *n of plant, glass* stelo *m*; *of word* radice *f*

♦ **stem from** *v/t* derivare da

stem[^2] [stem] *v/t (pret & pp -med)* *(block)* arginare

stench [stentʃ] *n* puzzo *m*

sten·cil ['stensɪl] **1** *n* stencil *m* **2** *v/t (pret & pp -led, Am -ed) pattern* disegnare con lo stencil

step [step] **1** *n (pace)* passo *m*; *(stair)* gradino *m*; *(measure)* provvedimento *m*; **~ by ~** poco a poco **2** *v/i (pret & pp -ped)* mettere il piede; **~ into / out of** salire in / scendere da

♦ **step down** *v/i from post etc* dimettersi

♦ **step forward** *v/i also fig* farsi avanti

♦ **step up** *v/t* F *(increase)* aumentare

step·broth·er fratellastro *m*; **step·daugh·ter** figliastra *f*; **step·fa·ther** patrigno *m*; **step·lad·der** scala *f* a libretto; **step·moth·er** matrigna *f*

step·ping stone ['stepɪŋ] pietra *f* di un guado; *fig* trampolino *m* di lancio

step·sis·ter sorellastra *f*

step·son figliastro *m*

ster·e·o ['sterɪəʊ] *n (sound system)* stereo *m inv*

ster·e·o·type ['sterɪəʊtaɪp] *n* stereotipo *m*

ster·ile ['steraɪl] *adj* sterile

ster·il·ize ['sterəlaɪz] *v/t* sterilizzare

ster·ling ['stɜːlɪŋ] *n* FIN sterlina *f*

stern[^1] [stɜːn] *adj* severo

stern[^2] [stɜːn] *n* NAUT poppa *f*

stern·ly ['stɜːnlɪ] *adv* severamente

ster·oids ['sterɔɪdz] *npl* anabolizzanti *mpl*

steth·o·scope ['steθəskəʊp] *n* fonendoscopio *m*

stew [stjuː] *n* spezzatino *m*

stew·ard ['stjuːəd] *n on plane, ship* steward *m inv*; *at demonstration, meeting* membro *m* del servizio d'ordine

stew·ard·ess [stjuːə'des] *on plane, ship* hostess *f inv*

stewed [stjuːd] *adj apples, plums* cotto

stick[^1] [stɪk] *n wood* rametto *m*; *(walking ~)* bastone *m*; **out in the ~s** F a casa del diavolo F

stick[^2] [stɪk] *(pret & pp stuck)* **1** *v/t with adhesive* attaccare; *needle, knife* conficcare; F *(put)* mettere **2** *v/i (jam)* bloccarsi; *(adhere)* attaccarsi

♦ **stick around** *v/i* F restare

♦ **stick by** *v/t* F: **stick by s.o.** rimanere al fianco di qu

♦ **stick out** *v/i (protrude)* sporgere; *(be noticeable)* spiccare

♦ **stick to** *v/t* F *(keep to)* attenersi a; *(follow)* seguire

♦ **stick together** *v/i* F restare uniti

♦ **stick up** *v/t poster, leaflet* affiggere

♦ **stick up for** *v/t* F difendere

stick·er ['stɪkə(r)] adesivo *m*

stick·ing plas·ter cerotto *m*

stick-in-the-mud F abitudinario m,
-a f

stick·y ['stɪkɪ] adj hands, surface appiccicoso; label adesivo

stiff [stɪf] **1** adj brush, cardboard, leather rigido; muscle, body anchilosato; mixture, paste sodo; in manner freddo; drink, competition forte; fine salato **2** adv: **be scared ~** F essere spaventato a morte F; **be bored ~** F essere annoiato a morte F

stiff·en ['stɪfn] v/i irrigidirsi

♦ **stiffen up** v/i of muscle anchilosarsi

stiff·ly ['stɪflɪ] adv rigidamente; fig freddamente

stiff·ness ['stɪfnəs] of muscles indolenzimento m; of material rigidità f; fig: of manner freddezza f

sti·fle ['staɪfl] v/t also fig soffocare

sti·fling ['staɪflɪŋ] adj soffocante

stig·ma ['stɪɡmə] vergogna f

sti·let·tos [stɪ'letəʊz] npl (shoes) scarpe fpl con tacco a spillo

still[1] [stɪl] **1** adj (motionless) immobile; without wind senza vento; drink non gas(s)ato; **it was very ~ outside** tutto era calmo fuori **2** adv: **keep / stand ~!** stai fermo!

still[2] [stɪl] adv (yet) ancora; (nevertheless) comunque; **she ~ hasn't finished** non ha ancora finito; **they are ~ my parents** sono pur sempre i miei genitori; **~ more** (even more) ancora più

still-born adj nato morto

still 'life natura f morta

stilt·ed ['stɪltɪd] adj poco naturale

stilts [stɪlts] npl trampoli mpl

stim·u·lant ['stɪmjʊlənt] stimolante m

stim·u·late ['stɪmjʊleɪt] v/t stimolare

stim·u·lat·ing ['stɪmjʊleɪtɪŋ] adj stimolante

stim·u·la·tion [stɪmjʊ'leɪʃn] stimolazione f

stim·u·lus ['stɪmjʊləs] (incentive) stimolo m

sting [stɪŋ] **1** n from bee puntura f; actual organ pungiglione m; from jellyfish pizzico m **2** v/t (pret & pp **stung**) of bee pungere; of jellyfish

pizzicare **3** v/i (pret & pp **stung**) of eyes, scratch bruciare

sting·ing ['stɪŋɪŋ] adj remark, criticism pungente

stin·gy ['stɪndʒɪ] adj F tirchio F

stink [stɪŋk] **1** n (bad smell) puzza f; F (fuss) putiferio m F; **kick up a ~** F fare un casino F **2** v/i (pret stank, pp **stunk**) (smell bad) puzzare; F (be very bad) fare schifo F

stint [stɪnt] n periodo m; **do a ~ in the army** arruolarsi nell'esercito per un periodo; **do you want to do a ~ now?** vuoi darmi il cambio?

♦ **stint on** v/t lesinare su

stip·u·late ['stɪpjʊleɪt] v/t & v/i stabilire

stip·u·la·tion [stɪpjʊ'leɪʃn] condizione f

stir [stɜ:(r)] **1** n: **give the soup a ~** mescolare la minestra; **cause a ~** fare scalpore **2** v/t (pret & pp **-red**) mescolare **3** v/i (pret & pp **-red**) of sleeping person muoversi

♦ **stir up** v/t fomentare

'stir-fry v/t (pret & pp **-ied**) saltare (in padella)

stir·ring ['stɜ:rɪŋ] adj music, speech commovente

stitch [stɪtʃ] **1** n in sewing punto m; in knitting maglia f; **~es** MED punti mpl (di sutura); **be in ~es** laughing ridere a crepapelle; **have a ~** avere una fitta al fianco **2** v/t sew cucire

♦ **stitch up** v/t wound suturare

stitch·ing ['stɪtʃɪŋ] (stitches) cucitura f

stock [stɒk] **1** n (reserves) provvista f; COM: of store stock m inv; animals bestiame m; FIN titoli mpl; for soup etc brodo m; **in ~** / **out of ~** disponibile / esaurito; **take ~** fare il punto **2** v/t COM vendere

♦ **stock up on** v/t fare provvista di

'stock·brok·er agente m/f di cambio; **'stock cube** dado m (da brodo); **'stock ex·change** borsa f valori

stock·ing ['stɒkɪŋ] calza f (da donna)

stock·ist ['stɒkɪst] rivenditore m

'stock mar·ket mercato *m* azionario; **stock·mar·ket 'crash** crollo *m* del mercato azionario; **'stock·pile 1** *n* of food, weapons scorta *f* **2** *v/t* fare scorta di; **'stock·room** magazzino *m*; **stock-'still** *adv*: **stand ~** stare immobile; **'stock·tak·ing** inventario *m*

'stock·y ['stɒkɪ] *adj* tarchiato

stodg·y ['stɒdʒɪ] *adj* food pesante

sto·i·cal ['stəʊɪkl] *adj* stoico

sto·i·cism ['stəʊɪsɪzm] stoicismo *m*

stole [stəʊl] *pret* → **steal**

stol·en ['stəʊlən] *pp* → **steal**

stom·ach ['stʌmək] **1** *n* stomaco *m*; *(abdomen)* pancia *f* **2** *v/t* *(tolerate)* sopportare

'stom·ach·ache mal *m* di stomaco

stone [stəʊn] *n* material pietra *f*; *(pebble)* sasso *m*; *(precious ~)* pietra *f* preziosa; *in fruit* nocciolo *m*

stoned [stəʊnd] *adj* F on drugs fatto F

stone-'deaf *adj* sordo (come una campana)

'stone·wall *v/i* F menare il can per l'aia

ston·y ['stəʊnɪ] *adj* ground, path sassoso

stood [stʊd] *pret* & *pp* → **stand**

stool [stuːl] *seat* sgabello *m*

stoop [stuːp] **1** *n*: **walk with a ~** camminare con la schiena curva **2** *v/i* *(bend down)* chinarsi; *(have bent back)* essere curvo

stop [stɒp] **1** *n for train, bus* fermata *f*; **come to a ~** fermarsi; **put a ~ to** mettere fine a **2** *v/t* *(pret & pp -ped)* *(put an end to)* mettere fine a; *(prevent)* fermare; *(cease)* smettere; *person, car, bus* fermare; **it has -ped raining** ha smesso di piovere; **I -ped her from leaving** le ho impedito di andar via; **~ a cheque** bloccare un assegno **3** *v/i* *(pret & pp -ped)* *(come to a halt)* fermarsi; *of rain, noise* smettere

♦ **stop by** *v/i* *(visit)* passare

♦ **stop off** *v/i* fermarsi, fare sosta; *at post office* passare a

♦ **stop over** *v/i* fare sosta

♦ **stop up** *v/t sink* intasare

'stop·gap *person* tappabuchi *m/f inv*; *thing* soluzione *f* temporanea

'stop·o·ver *n* sosta *f*; *in air travel* scalo *m* intermedio

stop·per ['stɒpə(r)] tappo *m*

'stop sign (segnale *m* di) stop *m inv*

'stop·watch cronometro *m*

stor·age ['stɔːrɪdʒ]: **put sth in ~** mettere qc in magazzino; **not much space for ~** poco spazio per riporre la roba

'stor·age ca·pac·i·ty COMPUT capacità *f* di memoria

'stor·age space spazio *m* per riporre la roba

store [stɔː(r)] **1** *n large shop* negozio *m*; *(stock)* riserva *f*; *(storehouse)* deposito *m* **2** *v/t* tenere; COMPUT memorizzare

'store·room magazzino *m*

sto·rey ['stɔːrɪ] piano *m*

stork [stɔːk] cicogna *f*

storm [stɔːm] *n* tempesta *f*

'storm warn·ing avviso *m* di tempesta

storm·y ['stɔːmɪ] *adj also fig* tempestoso

sto·ry¹ ['stɔːrɪ] *(tale)* racconto *m*; *(account)* storia *f*; *(newspaper article)* articolo *m*; F *(lie)* bugia *f*

sto·ry² ['stɔːrɪ] *Am* → **storey**

stout [staʊt] *adj person* robusto; *defender* tenace

stove [stəʊv] *for cooking* cucina *f*; *for heating* stufa *f*

stow [stəʊ] *v/t* riporre

♦ **stow away** *v/i* imbarcarsi clandestinamente

'stow·a·way *n* passeggero *m*, -a *f* clandestino, -a

strag·gler ['stræglə(r)] persona *f* che rimane indietro

straight [streɪt] **1** *adj line* retto; *hair, whisky* liscio; *back, knees* dritto; *(honest, direct)* onesto; *(tidy)* in ordine; *(conservative)* convenzionale; *(not homosexual)* etero; **keep a ~ face** non ridere **2** *adv* *(in a straight line)* dritto; *(directly, immediately)* dritto, direttamente; *(clearly: think)* con chiarezza; **stand up ~!** stai dritto!; **look s.o. ~ in the eye** guardare qu dritto negli occhi; **go ~** F *of criminal* rigare dritto; **give it to me ~** F dimmi francamente; **~ ahead** avanti dritto; **carry ~ on** proseguire dritto; **~away, ~ off** immediatamente; **~ out** *say sth* chiaro e tondo

straight·en ['streɪtn] *v/t* raddrizzare

♦ **straighten out 1** *v/t situation* sistemare; F *person* mettere in riga F **2** *v/i of road* tornare diritto

♦ **straighten up** *v/i* raddrizzarsi

straight'for·ward *adj (honest, direct)* franco; *(simple)* semplice

strain[1] [streɪn] **1** *n physical* sforzo *m; mental* tensione *f* **2** *v/t (injure)* affaticare; *fig: finances, budget* gravare su

strain[2] [streɪn] *v/t vegetables* scolare; *oil, fat etc* filtrare

strain[3] [streɪn] *n of virus* ceppo *m*

strained [streɪnd] *adj* teso

strain·er ['streɪnə(r)] *for vegetables etc* colino *m*

strait [streɪt] GEOG stretto *m*

strait·laced [streɪt'leɪst] *adj* puritano

strand[1] [strænd] *n of wool, thread* filo *m; of hair* ciocca *f*

strand[2] [strænd] *v/t* piantare in asso F; **be ~ed** essere bloccato

strange [streɪndʒ] *adj (odd, curious)* strano; *(unknown, foreign)* sconosciuto

strange·ly ['streɪndʒlɪ] *adv (oddly)* stranamente; **~ enough** strano ma vero

strang·er ['streɪndʒə(r)] *person you don't know* sconosciuto *m*, -a *f; I'm a ~ here myself* non sono di queste parti

stran·gle ['stræŋgl] *v/t person* strangolare

strap [stræp] *n of bag* tracolla *f; of bra, dress* bretellina *f*, spallina *f; of watch* cinturino *m; of shoe* listino *m*

♦ **strap in** *v/t (pret & pp -ped)* with seatbelt allacciare la cintura di sicurezza a

♦ **strap on** *v/t* allacciare

strap·less ['stræplɪs] *adj* senza spalline

stra·te·gic [strə'ti:dʒɪk] *adj* strategico

strat·e·gy ['strætədʒɪ] strategia *f*

straw[1] [strɔ:] paglia *f; that's the last ~!* questa è la goccia che fa traboccare il vaso!

straw[2] [strɔ:] *for drink* cannuccia *f*

straw·ber·ry ['strɔ:bərɪ] fragola *f*

stray [streɪ] **1** *adj animal* randagio; *bullet* vagante **2** *n dog, cat* randagio *m* **3** *v/i of animal* smarrirsi; *of child* allontanarsi; *fig: of eyes, thoughts* vagare

streak [stri:k] *of dirt, paint* stria *f; fig: of nastiness etc* vena *f* **2** *v/i move quickly* sfrecciare **3** *v/t: be ~ed with* essere striato di

streak·y ['stri:kɪ] *adj* striato

stream [stri:m] **1** *n* ruscello *m; fig: of people, complaints* fiume *m; come on ~ of plant* entrare in attività; *of oil* arrivare **2** *v/i* riversarsi

stream·er ['stri:mə(r)] stella *f* filante

'**stream·line** *v/t fig* snellire

'**stream·lined** *adj car, plane* aerodinamico; *fig: organization* snellito

street [stri:t] strada *f; in address* via *f*

'**street·car** *Am* tram *m inv;* '**street·light** lampione *m;* '**street·light·ing** illuminazione *f* stradale; '**street value** *of drugs* valore *m* di mercato; '**street·walk·er** F passeggiatrice *f;* '**street·wise** *adj* scafato F

strength [streŋθ] *of person, wind, emotion, currency* forza *f; (strong point)* punto *m* forte

strength·en ['streŋθn] **1** *v/t* rinforzare **2** *v/i* consolidarsi

stren·u·ous ['strenjʊəs] *adj* faticoso

stren·u·ous·ly ['strenjʊəslɪ] *adv deny* recisamente

stress [stres] **1** *n (emphasis)* accento *m; (tension)* stress *m inv;* **be under ~** essere sotto pressione **2** *v/t syllable* accentare; *importance etc* sottolineare

stressed 'out [strest] *adj* stressato

stress·ful ['stresfʊl] *adj* stressante

S

stretch [stretʃ] **1** *n of land, water* tratto *m*; **at a ~** (*non-stop*) di fila **2** *adj fabric* elasticizzato **3** *v/t material* tendere; *small income* far bastare; **~ the rules** F fare uno strappo (alla regola); **he ~ed out his hand** allungò la mano; **a job that ~es me** un lavoro che mi impegna **4** *v/i to relax muscles* stirarsi; *to reach sth* allungarsi; (*spread*) estendersi; *of fabric: give* cedere; *of fabric: sag* allargarsi; **~ from X to Y** (*extend*) estendersi da X a Y

stretch∙er ['stretʃə(r)] barella *f*

strict [strɪkt] *adj person* severo; *instructions, rules* tassativo

strict∙ly ['strɪktlɪ] *adv*: **be brought up ~** ricevere un'educazione rigida; **it is ~ forbidden** è severamente proibito

strictness ['strɪktnəs] severità *f inv*

strid∙den ['strɪdn] *pp* → **stride**

stride [straɪd] **1** *n* falcata *f*; **take sth in one's ~** affrontare qc senza drammi; **make great ~s** *fig* far passi da gigante **2** *v/i* (*pret* **strode**, *pp* **stridden**) procedere a grandi passi; **he strode up to me** avanzò verso di me

stri∙dent ['straɪdnt] *adj* stridulo; *fig: demands* veemente

strike [straɪk] **1** *n of workers* sciopero *m*; *of oil* scoperta *f*; **be on ~** essere in sciopero; **go on ~** entrare in sciopero **2** *v/i* (*pret & pp* **struck**) *of workers* scioperare; (*attack*) aggredire; *of disaster* colpire; *of clock* suonare **3** *v/t* (*pret & pp* **struck**) (*hit*) colpire; *match* accendere (sfregando); *of idea, thought* venire in mente a; *oil* trovare; **~ one's head against sth** battere la testa contro qc; **she struck me as being …** mi ha dato l'impressione di essere …

♦ **strike out** *v/t* depennare

'strike-break∙er crumiro *m*, -a *f*

strik∙er ['straɪkə(r)] *person on strike* scioperante *m/f*; *in football* bomber *m inv*, cannoniere *m*, punta *f*

strik∙ing ['straɪkɪŋ] *adj* (*marked*) marcato; (*eye-catching*) impressio-

nante; (*attractive*) attraente; *colour* forte

string [strɪŋ] *n* (*cord*) spago *m*; *of violin, tennis racket* corda *f*; **the ~s** MUS gli archi; **pull ~s** esercitare la propria influenza; **a ~ of** (*series*) una serie di

♦ **string along 1** *v/i* (*pret & pp* **strung**) F: **do you mind if I string along?** posso venire anch'io? **2** *v/t* (*pret & pp* **strung**) F: **string s.o. along** menare qu per il naso

♦ **string up** *v/t* F impiccare

stringed 'in∙stru∙ment [strɪŋd] strumento *m* ad arco

strin∙gent ['strɪndʒnt] *adj* rigoroso

'string play∙er suonatore *m*, -trice *f* di strumento ad arco

strip [strɪp] **1** *n* striscia *f*; (*comic ~*) fumetto *m*; *of soccer player* divisa *f* **2** *v/t* (*pret & pp* **-ped**) (*remove*) staccare; *bed* disfare; (*undress*) spogliare; **~ s.o. of sth** spogliare qu di qc **3** *v/i* (*pret & pp* **-ped**) (*undress*) spogliarsi; *of stripper* fare lo spogliarello

'strip club locale *m* di spogliarelli

stripe [straɪp] striscia *f*; *indicating rank* gallone *m*

striped [straɪpt] *adj* a strisce

'strip joint F → **strip club**

strip∙per ['strɪpə(r)] spogliarellista *f*; **male ~** spogliarellista *m*

'strip show spogliarello *m*

strip'tease spogliarello *m*

strive [straɪv] *v/i* (*pret* **strove**, *pp* **striven**): **~ to do sth** sforzarsi di fare qc; **~ for sth** lottare per (ottenere) qc

striv∙en ['strɪvn] *pp* → **strive**

strobe (**light**) [strəʊb] luce *f* stroboscopica

strode [strəʊd] *pret* → **stride**

stroke [strəʊk] **1** *n* MED ictus *m inv*; *when painting* pennellata *f*; *in swimming* bracciata *f*; *style of swimming* stile *m* di nuoto; **~ of luck** colpo di fortuna; **she never does a ~** (*of work*) non fa mai un bel niente **2** *v/t* accarezzare

stroll [strəʊl] **1** *n* passeggiata *f*; **go for**

a ~ fare una passeggiata **2** *v/i* fare due passi; **she ~ed back to the office** tornò in ufficio in tutta calma

strong [strɒŋ] *adj person, wind, drink, currency* forte; *structure* resistente; *candidate* valido; *taste, smell* intenso; *views, beliefs* fermo; *arguments* convincente; *objections* energico; ~ **support** largo consenso

'**strong·hold** *fig* roccaforte *f*

strong·ly ['strɒŋlɪ] *adv believe, object* fermamente; *built* solidamente; **feel ~ about sth** avere molto a cuore qc

strong-mind·ed [strɒŋ'maɪndɪd] *adj* risoluto; '**strong point** (punto *m*) forte *m*; '**strong·room** camera *f* blindata; **strong-'willed** [strɒŋ-'wɪld] *adj* deciso

strove [strəʊv] *pret* → **strive**

struck [strʌk] *pret & pp* → **strike**

struc·tur·al ['strʌktʃərl] *adj* strutturale

struc·ture ['strʌktʃə(r)] **1** *n something built* costruzione *f*; *of novel, society etc* struttura *f* **2** *v/t* strutturare

strug·gle ['strʌgl] **1** *n* (*fight*) collutazione *f*; *fig* lotta *f*; (*hard time*) fatica *f* **2** *v/i with a person* lottare; (*have a hard time*) faticare; ~ **to do sth** faticare a fare qc

strum [strʌm] *v/t* (*pret & pp* -**med**) strimpellare

strung [strʌŋ] *pret & pp* → **string**

strut [strʌt] *v/i* (*pret & pp* -**ted**) camminare impettito

stub [stʌb] **1** *n of cigarette* mozzicone *m*; *of cheque, ticket* matrice *f* **2** *v/t* (*pret & pp* -**bed**): ~ **one's toe** urtare il dito del piede

♦ **stub out** *v/t* spegnere

stub·ble ['stʌbl] *on man's face* barba *f* ispida

stub·born ['stʌbən] *adj person* testardo; *defence, refusal, denial* ostinato

stub·by ['stʌbɪ] *adj* tozzo

stuck [stʌk] **1** *pret & pp* → **stick 2** *adj* F: **be ~ on s.o.** essere cotto di qu F

stuck-'up *adj* F presuntuoso

stu·dent ['stjuːdnt] studente *m*, -essa *f*

stu·dent 'nurse infermiere *m*, -a *f* tirocinante

stu·dent 'teach·er insegnante *m/f* tirocinante

stu·di·o ['stjuːdɪəʊ] studio *m*; (*recording ~*) sala *f* di registrazione

stu·di·ous ['stjuːdɪəs] *adj* studioso

stud·y ['stʌdɪ] **1** *n* studio *m* **2** *v/t & v/i* (*pret & pp* -**ied**) studiare

stuff [stʌf] **1** *n* roba *f* **2** *v/t turkey* farcire; ~ **sth into sth** ficcare qc in qc

stuff·ing ['stʌfɪŋ] *for turkey* farcia *f*; *in chair, teddy bear* imbottitura *f*

stuff·y ['stʌfɪ] *adj room* mal ventilato; *person* inquadrato

stum·ble ['stʌmbl] *v/i* inciampare

♦ **stumble across** *v/t* trovare per caso

♦ **stumble over** *v/t* inciampare in; *words* incespicare in

stum·bling-block ['stʌmblɪŋ] *fig* scoglio *m*

stump [stʌmp] **1** *n of tree* ceppo *m* **2** *v/t of question, questioner* sconcertare

♦ **stump up** *v/t* F sganciare F

stun [stʌn] *v/t* (*pret & pp* -**ned**) *of blow* stordire; *of news* sbalordire

stung [stʌŋ] *pret & pp* → **sting**

stunk [stʌŋk] *pp* → **stink**

stun·ning ['stʌnɪŋ] *adj* (*amazing*) sbalorditivo; (*very beautiful*) splendido

stunt [stʌnt] *n for publicity* trovata *f* pubblicitaria; *in film* acrobazia *f*

'**stunt·man** *in film* cascatore *m*

stu·pe·fy ['stjuːpɪfaɪ] *v/t* (*pret & pp* -**ied**) sbalordire

stu·pen·dous [stjuː'pendəs] *adj* (*marvellous*) fantastico; *mistake* enorme

stu·pid ['stjuːpɪd] *adj* stupido

stu·pid·i·ty [stjuː'pɪdətɪ] stupidità *f* *inv*

stu·por ['stjuːpə(r)] stordimento *m*; **in a drunken** ~ stordito dall'alcool

stur·dy ['stɜːdɪ] *adj* robusto

stut·ter ['stʌtə(r)] *v/i* balbettare

sty [staɪ] *for pig* porcile *m*

S

style [staɪl] *n* stile *m*; (*fashion*) moda *f*; (*fashionable elegance*) classe *f*; (*hair~*) pettinatura *f*; **go out of ~** passare di moda

styl·ish ['staɪlɪʃ] *adj* elegante

styl·ist ['staɪlɪst] (*hair ~*) parrucchiere *m*, -a *f*

sub·com·mit·tee ['sʌbkəmɪtɪ] sottocommissione *f*

sub·con·scious [sʌb'kɒnʃəs] *adj* subconscio; **the ~ (mind)** il subconscio

sub·con·scious·ly [sʌb'kɒnʃəslɪ] *adv* inconsciamente

sub·con·tract [sʌbkən'trakt] *v/t* subappaltare

sub·con·trac·tor [sʌbkən'traktə(r)] subappaltatore *m*, -trice *f*

sub·di·vide [sʌbdɪ'vaɪd] *v/t* suddividere

sub·due [səb'djuː] *v/t* sottomettere

sub·dued [səb'djuːd] *adj person, voice* pacato; *light, colour* soffuso

sub·head·ing ['sʌbhedɪŋ] sottotitolo *m*

sub·hu·man [sʌb'hjuːmən] *adj* subumano

sub·ject ['sʌbdʒɪkt] **1** *n of monarch* suddito *m*, -a *f*; (*topic*) argomento *m*; EDU materia *f*; GRAM soggetto *m*; **change the ~** cambiare argomento **2** *adj:* **be ~ to** essere soggetto a; **~ to availability** nei limiti della disponibilità **3** *v/t* [səb'dʒekt] sottoporre; **be ~ed to criticism** essere criticato

sub·jec·tive [səb'dʒektɪv] *adj* soggettivo

sub·junc·tive [səb'dʒʌŋktɪv] GRAM congiuntivo *m*

sub·let ['sʌblet] *v/t* (*pret & pp* **-let**) subaffittare

sub·ma'chine gun mitra *m*

sub·ma·rine ['sʌbməriːn] sottomarino *m*, sommergibile *m*

sub·merge [səb'mɜːdʒ] **1** *v/t* sommergere **2** *v/i of submarine* immergersi

sub·mis·sion [səb'mɪʃn] (*surrender*) sottomissione *f*; *request to committee etc* richiesta *f*

sub·mis·sive [səb'mɪsɪv] *adj* sottomesso

sub·mit [səb'mɪt] (*pret & pp* **-ted**) **1** *v/t plan, proposal* presentare **2** *v/i* sottomettersi

sub·or·di·nate [sə'bɔːdɪnət] **1** *adj employee, position* subalterno **2** *n* subalterno *m*, -a *f*

sub·poe·na [sə'piːnə] **1** *n* citazione *f* **2** *v/t person* citare in giudizio

♦ **subscribe to** [səb'skraɪb] *v/t magazine etc* abbonarsi a; *theory* condividere

sub·scrib·er [səb'skraɪbə(r)] *to magazine* abbonato *m*, -a *f*

sub·scrip·tion [səb'skrɪpʃn] abbonamento *m*

sub·se·quent ['sʌbsɪkwənt] *adj* successivo

sub·se·quent·ly ['sʌbsɪkwəntlɪ] *adv* successivamente

sub·side [səb'saɪd] *v/i of waters, winds* calare; *of building* sprofondare; *of fears, panic* calmarsi

sub·sid·i·a·ry [səb'sɪdɪərɪ] *n* filiale *f*

sub·si·dize ['sʌbsɪdaɪz] *v/t* sovvenzionare

sub·si·dy ['sʌbsɪdɪ] sovvenzione *f*

♦ **subsist on** *v/t* vivere di

sub·sis·tence farm·ing [səb'sɪstəns] agricoltura *f* di sussistenza

sub·sis·tence lev·el livello *m* minimo di vita

sub·stance ['sʌbstəns] (*matter*) sostanza *f*

sub·stan·dard [sʌb'stændəd] *adj* scadente

sub·stan·tial [səb'stænʃl] *adj* considerevole; *meal* sostanzioso

sub·stan·tial·ly [səb'stænʃlɪ] *adv* (*considerably*) considerevolmente; (*in essence*) sostanzialmente

sub·stan·ti·ate [səb'stænʃɪeɪt] *v/t* comprovare

sub·stan·tive [səb'stæntɪv] *adj* sostanziale

sub·sti·tute ['sʌbstɪtjuːt] **1** *n for person* sostituto *m*, -a *f*; *for commodity* alternativa *f*; SP riserva *f* **2** *v/t:* **~ X for Y** sostituire Y con X **3** *v/i:* **~ for s.o.** sostituire qu

S

sub·sti·tu·tion [sʌbstɪˈtjuːʃn] (*act*) sostituzione *f*; **make a ~** SP fare una sostituzione

sub·ti·tle [ˈsʌbtaɪtl] *n* sottotitolo *m*

sub·tle [ˈsʌtl] *adj* hint, difference sottile; *flavour* delicato

sub·tract [səbˈtrækt] *v/t* number sottrarre

sub·urb [ˈsʌbɜːb] sobborgo *m*; **the ~s** la periferia

sub·ur·ban [səˈbɜːbən] *adj* di periferia

sub·ur·bi·a [səˈbɜːbɪə] periferia *f*

sub·ze·ro *adj*: **~ temperatures** temperature sottozero

suc·ceed [səkˈsiːd] **1** *v/i* (*be successful*) avere successo; *to throne* succedere; **~ in doing sth** riuscire a fare qc **2** *v/t* (*come after*) succedere a

suc·ceed·ing [səkˈsiːdɪŋ] *adj* successivo

suc·cess [səkˈses] successo *m*; **be a ~** avere successo

suc·cess·ful [səkˈsesfʊl] *adj* person affermato; *marriage, party* riuscito; **be ~** riuscire; **he's very ~** è arrivato

suc·cess·ful·ly [səkˈsesflɪ] *adv* con successo; **we ~ completed ...** siamo riusciti a portare a termine ...

suc·ces·sion [səkˈseʃn] (*sequence*) sfilza *f*; *to the throne* successione *f*; **in ~** di seguito

suc·ces·sive [səkˈsesɪv] *adj* successivo; **three ~ days** tre giorni di seguito

suc·ces·sor [səkˈsesə(r)] successore *m*

suc·cinct [səkˈsɪŋkt] *adj* succinto

suc·cu·lent [ˈsʌkjʊlənt] *adj* succulento

suc·cumb [səˈkʌm] *v/i* (*give in*) cedere; **~ to temptation** cedere alla tentazione

such [sʌtʃ] **1** *adj* (*of that kind*) del genere; **~ a** (*so much of a*) un/una tale; **~ as** come; **~ people** gente del ge-

nere; **he made ~ a fuss** ha fatto una tale scenata; **there is no ~ word as ...** la parola ... non esiste **2** *adv* così; **~ nice people** gente così simpatica; **as ~** (*in that capacity*) in quanto tale; **as ~** (*in itself*) di per sé

suck [sʌk] **1** *v/t* lollipop etc succhiare; **~ one's thumb** succhiarsi il dito **2** *v/i*: **it ~s** P (*is awful*) fa schifo P

♦ **suck up** *v/t* assorbire; *dust* aspirare

♦ **suck up to** *v/t* F leccare i piedi a F

suck·er [ˈsʌkə(r)] F person pollo F

suc·tion [ˈsʌkʃn] aspirazione *f*

sud·den [ˈsʌdn] *adj* improvviso; **all of a ~** all'improvviso

sud·den·ly [ˈsʌdnlɪ] *adv* improvvisamente

suds [sʌdz] *npl* (*soap ~*) schiuma *fsg*

sue [suː] **1** *v/t* fare causa a **2** *v/i* fare causa

suede [sweɪd] *n* pelle *f* scamosciata

suf·fer [ˈsʌfə(r)] **1** *v/i* (*be in great pain*) soffrire; (*deteriorate*) risentirne; **be ~ing from** avere; **~ from** soffrire di **2** *v/t* loss, setback subire

suf·fer·ing [ˈsʌfərɪŋ] *n* sofferenza *f*

suf·fi·cient [səˈfɪʃnt] *adj* sufficiente

suf·fi·cient·ly [səˈfɪʃntlɪ] *adv* abbastanza

suf·fo·cate [ˈsʌfəkeɪt] *v/t & v/i* soffocare

suf·fo·ca·tion [sʌfəˈkeɪʃn] soffocamento *m*

sug·ar [ˈʃʊɡə(r)] **1** *n* zucchero *m* **2** *v/t* zuccherare

ˈsug·ar bowl zuccheriera *f*

sug·gest [səˈdʒest] *v/t* proporre, suggerire; **I ~ that we stop now** propongo di fermarci ora

sug·ges·tion [səˈdʒestʃən] *n* proposta *f*, suggerimento *m*

su·i·cide [ˈsuːɪsaɪd] *n* suicidio *m*; **commit ~** suicidarsi

ˈsu·i·cide pact *n* patto *m* suicida

suit [suːt] **1** *n for man* vestito *m*, completo *m*; *for woman* tailleur *m* inv; *in cards* seme *m* **2** *v/t* of clothes, colour stare bene a; **~ yourself!** F fai come ti pare!; **be ~ed for sth** essere fatto per qc

sui·ta·ble [ˈsuːtəbl] *adj* adatto

sui·ta·bly ['suːtəblɪ] *adv* adeguata-mente

'**suit·case** valigia *f*

suite [swiːt] *of rooms* suite *f inv*; *of furniture* divano *m* e poltrone *fpl* coordinati; MUS suite *f inv*

sul·fur *etc Am* → **sulphur** *etc*

sulk [sʌlk] *v/i* fare il broncio

sulk·y ['sʌlkɪ] *adj* imbronciato

sul·len ['sʌlən] *adj* crucciato

sul·phur ['sʌlfə(r)] zolfo *m*

sul·phur·ic acid [sʌl'fjuːrɪk] acido *m* solforico

sul·try ['sʌltrɪ] *adj climate* afoso; *sexually* sensuale

sum [sʌm] somma *f*; *in arithmetic* addizione *f*; *a large ~ of money* una forte somma di denaro; *that's the ~ total of his efforts* quello è tutto quello che ha fatto

♦ **sum up** (*pret & pp* **-med**) **1** *v/t* (*summarize*) riassumere; (*assess*) valutare **2** *v/i* LAW riepilogare

sum·mar·ize ['sʌməraɪz] *v/t* riassumere

sum·ma·ry ['sʌmərɪ] *n* riassunto *m*

sum·mer ['sʌmə(r)] estate *f*

sum·mit ['sʌmɪt] *of mountain* vetta *f*; POL summit *m inv*

'**sum·mit meet·ing** → **summit**

sum·mon ['sʌmən] *v/t* convocare

♦ **summon up** *v/t strength* raccogliere

sum·mons ['sʌmənz] *nsg* LAW citazione *f*

sump [sʌmp] *for oil* coppa *f* dell'olio

sun [sʌn] sole *m*; *in the ~* al sole; *out of the ~* all'ombra; *he has had too much ~* ha preso troppo sole

'**sun·bathe** *v/i* prendere il sole; '**sun·bed** lettino *m* solare; '**sun·block** protezione *f* solare totale; '**sun·burn** scottatura *f*; '**sun·burnt** *adj* scottato

Sun·day ['sʌndeɪ] domenica *f*

'**sun·dial** meridiana *f*

sun·dries ['sʌndrɪz] *npl* varie *fpl*

sung [sʌŋ] *pp* → **sing**

'**sun·glass·es** *npl* occhiali *mpl* da sole

sunk [sʌŋk] *pp* → **sink**

sunk·en ['sʌŋkn] *adj cheeks* incavato

sun·ny ['sʌnɪ] *adj day* di sole; *spot* soleggiato; *disposition* allegro; *it's ~* c'è il sole

'**sun·rise** alba *f*; '**sun·set** tramonto *m*; '**sun·shade** ombrellone *m*; '**sun·shine** (luce *f* del) sole *m*; '**sun·stroke** colpo *m* di sole; '**sun·tan** abbronzatura *f*; *get a ~* abbronzarsi

su·per ['suːpə(r)] *adj* F fantastico

su·perb [suˈpɜːb] *adj* magnifico

su·per·fi·cial [suːpəˈfɪʃl] *adj* superficiale

su·per·flu·ous [suˈpɜːfluəs] *adj* superfluo

su·per·hu·man *adj efforts* sovrumano

su·per·in·tend·ent [suːpərɪnˈtendənt] *of police* commissario *m*

su·pe·ri·or [suːˈpɪərɪə(r)] **1** *adj* (*better*) superiore **2** *n in organization, society* superiore *m*

su·per·la·tive [suːˈpɜːlətɪv] **1** *adj* (*superb*) eccellente **2** *n* GRAM superlativo *m*

'**su·per·mar·ket** supermarket *m inv*, supermercato *m*

su·per·nat·u·ral 1 *adj powers* soprannaturale **2** *n*: *the ~* il soprannaturale

'**su·per·pow·er** POL superpotenza *f*

su·per·son·ic [suːpəˈsɒnɪk] *adj flight, aircraft* supersonico

su·per·sti·tion [suːpəˈstɪʃn] *n* superstizione *f*

su·per·sti·tious [suːpəˈstɪʃəs] *adj person* superstizioso

su·per·vise ['suːpəvaɪz] *v/t* supervisionare

su·per·vi·sor ['suːpəvaɪzə(r)] *at work* supervisore *m*

sup·per ['sʌpə(r)] cena *f*

sup·ple ['sʌpl] *adj person, limbs* snodato; *material* flessibile

sup·ple·ment ['sʌplɪmənt] supplemento *m*

sup·pli·er [səˈplaɪə(r)] *n* COM fornitore *m*

sup·ply [səˈplaɪ] **1** *n* fornitura *f*; *~ and demand* domanda e offerta; *supplies* rifornimenti **2** *v/t* (*pret &*

pp **-ied**) *goods* fornire; **~ s.o. with sth** fornire qc a qu; **be supplied with** *fitted with etc* essere dotato di

sup·port [sə'pɔ:t] **1** *n for structure* supporto *m*; (*backing*) sostegno *m* **2** *v/t building, structure* sostenere; *financially* mantenere; (*back*) sostenere; *football team* fare il tifo per

sup·port·er [sə'pɔ:tə(r)] sostenitore *m*, -trice *f*; *of football team etc* tifoso *m*, -a *f*

sup·port·ive [sə'pɔ:tɪv] *adj:* **be ~ towards s.o.** dare il proprio appoggio a qu

sup·pose [sə'pəuz] *v/t* (*imagine*) supporre; **I ~ so** suppongo di sì; **it is ~d to ...** (*is meant to*) dovrebbe ...; (*is said to*) dicono che ...; **you are not ~d to ...** (*not allowed to*) non dovresti ...

sup·pos·ed·ly [sə'pəuzɪdlɪ] *adv* presumibilmente

sup·pos·i·to·ry [sə'pɒzɪtrɪ] MED supposta *f*

sup·press [sə'pres] *v/t rebellion etc* reprimere

sup·pres·sion [sə'preʃn] repressione *f*

su·prem·a·cy [su:'preməsɪ] supremazia *f*

su·preme [su:'pri:m] *adj* supremo

sur·charge ['sɜːtʃɑːdʒ] *for travel* sovrapprezzo *m*; *for mail* soprattassa *f*

sure [ʃʊə(r)] **1** *adj* sicuro; **I'm ~** sono sicuro; **be ~ about sth** essere sicuro di qc; **make ~ that ...** assicurarsi che ... **2** *adv* certamente; **~ enough** infatti; **~!** F certo!

sure·ly ['ʃʊəlɪ] *adv* certamente; (*gladly*) volentieri; **~ that's not right!** non può essere!; **oh, ~ you've heard of him** non puoi non conoscerlo

sure·ty ['ʃʊərətɪ] *for loan* cauzione *f*

surf [sɜ:f] **1** *n on sea* spuma *f* **2** *v/t the Net* navigare

sur·face ['sɜ:fɪs] **1** *n of table, object, water* superficie *f*; **on the ~** *fig* superficialmente, in apparenza **2** *v/i of swimmer, submarine* risalire in su-

perficie, riemergere; (*appear*) farsi vivo

'sur·face mail posta *f* ordinaria

'surf·board tavola *f* da surf

surf·er ['sɜ:fə(r)] *on sea* surfista *m/f*

surf·ing ['sɜ:fɪŋ] surf *m inv*; **go ~** fare surf

surge [sɜ:dʒ] *n in electric current* sovratensione *f* transitoria; *in demand* impennata *f*; *of interest, financial growth etc* aumento *m*

♦ surge forward *v/i of crowd* buttarsi avanti

sur·geon ['sɜ:dʒən] chirurgo *m*

sur·ge·ry ['sɜ:dʒərɪ] intervento *m* chirurgico; *Br: place of work* ambulatorio *m*; **undergo ~** sottoporsi a un intervento chirurgico; **~ hours** orario *m* d'ambulatorio

sur·gi·cal ['sɜ:dʒɪkl] *adj* chirurgico

sur·gi·cal·ly ['sɜ:dʒɪklɪ] *adv* chirurgicamente

sur·ly ['sɜ:lɪ] *adj* scontroso

sur·mount [sə'maunt] *v/t difficulties* sormontare

sur·name ['sɜ:neɪm] cognome *m*

sur·pass [sə'pɑ:s] *v/t* superare

sur·plus ['sɜ:pləs] **1** *n* surplus *m inv* **2** *adj* eccedente

sur·prise [sə'praɪz] **1** *n* sorpresa *f*; **it'll come as no ~ to hear that ...** non ti sorprenderà sapere che ... **2** *v/t* sorprendere; **be ~d** essere sorpreso; **look ~d** avere l'aria sorpresa

sur·pris·ing [sə'praɪzɪŋ] *adj* sorprendente

sur·pris·ing·ly [sə'praɪzɪŋlɪ] *adv* sorprendentemente

sur·ren·der [sə'rendə(r)] **1** *v/i of army* arrendersi **2** *v/t weapons etc* consegnare **3** *n* resa *f*

sur·ro·gate 'moth·er ['sʌrəgət] madre *f* biologica

sur·round [sə'raund] **1** *v/t* circondare; **be ~ed by ...** essere circondato da ... **2** *n of picture etc* bordo *m*

sur·round·ing [sə'raundɪŋ] *adj* circostante

sur·round·ings [sə'raundɪŋz] *npl of village etc* dintorni *mpl*; *fig* ambiente *m*

S

sur·vey ['sɜːveɪ] **1** *n of modern literature etc* quadro *m* generale; *of building* perizia *f*; *poll* indagine *f* **2** *v/t* [sə'veɪ] (*look at*) osservare; *building* periziare

sur·vey·or [sə'veɪə(r)] perito *m*

sur·viv·al [sə'vaɪvl] sopravvivenza *f*

sur·vive [sə'vaɪv] **1** *v/i* sopravvivere; *how are you? – I'm surviving* come stai? – si tira avanti; *his two surviving daughters* le due figlie ancora in vita **2** *v/t* sopravvivere a

sur·vi·vor [sə'vaɪvə(r)] superstite *m/f*; *he's a ~ fig* se la cava sempre

sus·pect ['sʌspekt] **1** *n* indiziato *m*, -a *f* **2** *v/t* [sə'spekt] *person* sospettare; (*suppose*) supporre

sus·pect·ed [sə'spektɪd] *adj murderer* presunto; *cause, heart attack etc* sospetto

sus·pend [sə'spend] *v/t* (*hang*) sospendere; *from office, duties* sospendere

sus·pend·ers [sə'spendəz] *npl* giarrettiere *fpl*; *Am* (*braces*) bretelle *fpl*

sus·pense [sə'spens] suspense *f inv*

sus·pen·sion [sə'spenʃn] sospensione *f*

sus·pen·sion bridge ponte *m* sospeso

sus·pi·cion [sə'spɪʃn] sospetto *m*

sus·pi·cious [sə'spɪʃəs] *adj causing suspicion* sospetto; *feeling suspicion* sospettoso; *be ~ of* sospettare di

sus·tain [sə'steɪn] *v/t* sostenere

sus·tain·able [sə'steɪnəbl] *adj* sostenibile

swab [swɒb] tampone *m*

swag·ger ['swægə(r)] *n* andatura *f* spavalda

swal·low[1] ['swɒləʊ] **1** *v/t liquid, food* inghiottire **2** *v/i* inghiottire

swal·low[2] ['swɒləʊ] *n bird* rondine *f*

swam [swæm] *pret →* **swim**

swamp [swɒmp] **1** *n* palude *f* **2** *v/t: be ~ped with* essere sommerso da

swamp·y ['swɒmpɪ] *adj ground* paludoso

swan [swɒn] cigno *m*

swap [swɒp] (*pret & pp* -**ped**) **1** *v/t: ~ sth for sth* scambiare qc con qc **2** *v/i* fare scambio

swarm [swɔːm] **1** *n of bees* sciame *m* **2** *v/i: the town was ~ing with ...* la città brulicava di ...

swar·thy ['swɔːðɪ] *adj face, complexion* scuro

swat [swɒt] *v/t* (*pret & pp* -**ted**) *insect, fly* schiacciare

sway [sweɪ] **1** *n* (*influence, power*) influenza *f* **2** *v/i* barcollare

swear [sweə(r)] (*pret* **swore**, *pp* **sworn**) **1** *v/i* (*use swearword*) imprecare; *~ at s.o.* dire parolacce a qu **2** *v/t* (*promise*) giurare; *LAW, on oath* giurare

♦ **swear in** *v/t: the witness was sworn in* il testimone ha prestato giuramento

'**swear·word** parolaccia *f*

sweat [swet] **1** *n* sudore *m*; *covered in ~* tutto sudato **2** *v/i* sudare

'**sweat·band** fascia *f* asciugasudore

sweat·er ['swetə(r)] maglione *m*

'**sweat·shirt** felpa *f*

sweat·y ['swetɪ] *adj hands* sudato; *smell di* sudore

Swede [swiːd] svedese *m/f*

Swe·den ['swiːdn] Svezia *f*

Swe·dish ['swiːdɪʃ] **1** *adj* svedese **2** *n* svedese *m*

sweep [swiːp] **1** *v/t* (*pret & pp* **swept**) *floor, leaves* spazzare **2** *n* (*long curve*) curva *f*

♦ **sweep up** *v/t mess* spazzare via

sweep·ing ['swiːpɪŋ] *adj changes* radicale; *a ~ statement* una generalizzazione

sweet [swiːt] **1** *adj taste, tea* dolce; F (*kind*) gentile; F (*cute*) carino **2** *n* caramella *f*; (*dessert*) dolce *m*

sweet and 'sour *adj* agrodolce

'**sweet·corn** mais *m inv*

sweet·en ['swiːtn] *v/t drink, food* zuccherare

sweet·en·er ['swiːtnə(r)] *for drink* dolcificante *m*

'sweet·heart innamorato m, -a f

swell [swel] **1** v/i of wound, limb gonfiarsi **2** n of the sea mare m lungo

swell·ing ['sweliŋ] n MED gonfiore m

swel·ter·ing ['sweltəriŋ] adj heat, day afoso, soffocante

swept [swept] pret & pp → **sweep**

swerve [swɜːv] v/i of driver, car sterzare (bruscamente)

swift [swift] adj rapido

swim [swim] **1** v/i (pret **swam**, pp **swum**) nuotare; **go ~ming** andare a nuotare; **my head is ~ming** mi gira la testa **2** n nuotata f; **go for a ~** andare a nuotare

'swim·mer ['swimə(r)] nuotatore m, -trice f

swim·ming ['swimiŋ] nuoto m

'swim·ming baths npl piscina f pubblica; 'swim·ming cos·tume costume m da bagno; 'swim·ming pool piscina f

swin·dle ['swindl] **1** n truffa f **2** v/t truffare; **~ s.o. out of sth** estorcere qc a qu (con l'inganno)

swine [swain] F person mascalzone m

swing [swiŋ] **1** n of pendulum etc oscillazione f; for child altalena f; **a ~ to the left** una svolta verso la sinistra **2** v/t (pret & pp **swung**) far dondolare; **~ one's hips** ancheggiare **3** v/i (pret & pp **swung**) dondolare; (turn) girare; of public opinion etc indirizzarsi

'swing-'door porta f a vento

Swiss [swis] **1** adj svizzero **2** n person svizzero m, -a f; **the ~** gli svizzeri

switch [switʃ] **1** n for light interruttore m; (change) cambiamento m **2** v/t (change) cambiare **3** v/i (change) cambiare; **~ to** passare a

◆ switch off v/t spegnere

◆ switch on v/t accendere

'switch·board centralino m

'switch·o·ver to new system passaggio m

Swit·zer·land ['switsələnd] Svizzera f

swiv·el ['swivl] v/i (pret & pp **-led**,

Am **-ed**) of chair, monitor girarsi

swol·len ['swəulən] adj gonfio

swoop [swuːp] v/i of bird scendere in picchiata

◆ swoop down on v/t prey scendere in picchiata su

◆ swoop on v/t of police etc piombare su

sword [sɔːd] spada f

swore [swɔː(r)] pret → **swear**

sworn [swɔːn] pp → **swear**

swum [swʌm] pp → **swim**

swung [swʌŋ] pret & pp → **swing**

syc·a·more ['sikəmɔː] sicomoro m

syl·la·ble ['siləbl] sillaba f

syl·la·bus ['siləbəs] programma m

sym·bol ['simbəl] simbolo m

sym·bol·ic [sim'bolik] adj simbolico

sym·bol·ism ['simbəlizm] simbolismo m

sym·bol·ist ['simbəlist] simbolista m/f

sym·bol·ize ['simbəlaiz] v/t simboleggiare

sym·met·ri·c(al) [si'metrikl] adj simmetrico

sym·me·try ['simətri] simmetria f

sym·pa·thet·ic [simpə'θetik] adj (showing pity) compassionevole; (understanding) comprensivo; **be ~ towards an idea** simpatizzare per un'idea

◆ sympathize with ['simpəθaiz] v/t person, views capire

sym·pa·thiz·er ['simpəθaizə(r)] n POL simpatizzante m/f

sym·pa·thy ['simpəθi] n (pity) compassione f; (understanding) comprensione f; **don't expect any ~ from me!** non venire a lamentarti da me!

sym·pho·ny ['simfəni] sinfonia f

'sym·pho·ny or·ches·tra orchestra f sinfonica

symp·tom ['simptəm] also fig sintomo m

symp·to·mat·ic [simptə'mætik] adj: **be ~ of** fig essere sintomatico di

syn·chro·nize ['siŋkrənaiz] v/t sincronizzare

syn·o·nym ['sinənim] sinonimo m

S

sy·non·y·mous [sɪ'nɒnɪməs] *adj* sinonimo; *be ~ with fig* essere sinonimo di

syn·tax ['sɪntæks] sintassi *f inv*

syn·the·siz·er ['sɪnθəsaɪzə(r)] MUS sintetizzatore *m*

syn·thet·ic [sɪn'θetɪk] *adj* sintetico

syph·i·lis ['sɪfɪlɪs] sifilide *f*

Syr·i·a ['sɪrɪə] Siria *f*

Syr·i·an ['sɪrɪən] **1** *adj* siriano **2** *n* siriano *m*, -a *f*

sy·ringe [sɪ'rɪndʒ] *n* siringa *f*

syr·up ['sɪrəp] sciroppo *m*

sys·tem ['sɪstəm] (*method*) metodo *m*, sistema *m*; (*orderliness*) ordine *m*; (*computer*) sistema *m*; *the braking ~* il sistema di frenata; *the digestive ~* l'apparato digerente

sys·te·mat·ic [sɪstə'mætɪk] *adj* approach, person sistematico

sys·tem·at·i·cal·ly [sɪstə'mætɪklɪ] *adv* sistematicamente

sys·tems 'an·a·lyst ['sɪstəmz] COMPUT analista *m/f* di sistemi

T

tab [tæb] *n for pulling* linguetta *f*; *in text* tabulazione *f*

ta·ble ['teɪbl] *n* tavolo *m*; *of figures* tabella *f*, tavola *f*; *sit at the ~* sedersi a tavola

'ta·ble·cloth tovaglia *f*; **'ta·ble lamp** lampada *f* da tavolo; **ta·ble of 'con·tents** indice *m*; **'ta·ble·spoon** cucchiaio *m* da tavola

ta·blet ['tæblɪt] MED compressa *f*

'ta·ble ten·nis ping pong *m*

tab·loid ['tæblɔɪd] *n newspaper* quotidiano *m* formato tabloid; *pej* quotidiano *m* scandalistico

ta·boo [tə'buː] *adj* tabù *m inv*

ta·cit ['tæsɪt] *adj* tacito

ta·ci·turn ['tæsɪtɜːn] *adj* taciturno

tack [tæk] **1** *n* (*nail*) chiodino *m* **2** *v/t* (*sew*) imbastire **3** *v/i of yacht* virare di bordo

tack·le ['tækl] **1** *n* (*equipment*) attrezzatura *f*; SP: *in rugby* placcaggio *m*; *in football, hockey* contrasto *m* **2** *v/t in rugby* placcare; *in football, hockey* contrastare; *problem, intruder* affrontare

tack·y ['tækɪ] *adj paint* fresco; *glue* appiccicoso; F (*cheap, poor quality*) di cattivo gusto

tact [tækt] tatto *m*

tact·ful ['tæktfʊl] *adj* pieno di tatto

tact·ful·ly ['tæktflɪ] *adv* con grande tatto

tac·ti·cal ['tæktɪkl] *adj* tattico

tac·tics ['tæktɪks] *npl* tattica *f*

tact·less ['tæktlɪs] *adj* privo di tatto

tad·pole ['tædpəʊl] *n* girino *m*

tag [tæg] (*label*) etichetta *f*

♦ **tag along** *v/i* (*pret & pp* **-ged**) accodarsi

tail [teɪl] *n* coda *f*

'tail·back coda *f*; **'tail coat** frac *m inv*; **'tail light** luce *f* posteriore

tai·lor ['teɪlə(r)] sarto *m*, -a *f*

tai·lor-made [teɪlə'meɪd] *adj suit, solution* (fatto) su misura

'tail·wind vento *m* in coda

taint·ed ['teɪntɪd] *adj* contaminato

Tai·wan [taɪ'wɑːn] Taiwan *f*

Tai·wan·ese [taɪwə'niːz] **1** *adj* taiwanese **2** *n* taiwanese *m/f*; *dialect* taiwanese *m*

take [teɪk] *v/t* (*pret* **took**, *pp* **taken**) prendere; (*transport*) portare; (*accompany*) accompagnare; (*accept: money, gift*) accettare; *maths, French, photograph, exam, shower, stroll* fare; (*endure*) sopportare; (*require*) richiedere; *how long does it ~?*

quanto ci vuole?; **I'll ~ it when** *shopping* lo prendo

♦ **take after** *v/t* aver preso da

♦ **take apart** *v/t* (*dismantle*) smontare; F (*criticize, beat*) fare a pezzi F

♦ **take away** *v/t* *pain* far sparire; (*remove: object*) togliere; MATH sottrarre; **take sth away from s.o.** togliere qc a qu; **to take away** *food* da asporto

♦ **take back** *v/t* (*return: object*) riportare; (*receive back*) riprendere; *person* riaccompagnare; (*accept back: husband etc*) rimettersi insieme a; **I take back what I said** ritiro quello che ho detto; **that takes me back** *of music, thought etc* mi riporta al passato

♦ **take down** *v/t from shelf* tirare giù; *scaffolding* smontare; *trousers* allungare; (*write down*) annotare

♦ **take in** *v/t* (*take indoors*) portare dentro; (*give accommodation*) ospitare; (*make narrower*) stringere; (*deceive*) imbrogliare; (*include*) includere

♦ **take off 1** *v/t clothes, 10%* togliere; (*mimic*) imitare; **can you take a bit off here?** *to barber* può spuntare un po' qui?; **take a day / week off** prendere un giorno / una settimana di ferie **2** *v/i of aeroplane* decollare; (*become popular*) far presa

♦ **take on** *v/t job* intraprendere; *staff* assumere

♦ **take out** *v/t from bag, pocket* tirare fuori; *stain, appendix, tooth, word* togliere; *money from bank* prelevare; *to dinner etc* portar fuori; *insurance policy* stipulare, fare; **take it out on s.o.** prendersela con qu

♦ **take over 1** *v/t company etc* assumere il controllo di; **tourists take over the town** i turisti invadono la città **2** *v/i of new management etc* assumere il controllo; (*do sth in s.o.'s place*) dare il cambio

♦ **take to** *v/t* (*like*) prendere in simpatia; (*form habit of*) prendere l'abitudine di; **take to drink** darsi all'alcol; **he immediately took to**

the idea la nuova idea gli è piaciuta subito

♦ **take up** *v/t carpet etc* togliere; (*carry up*) portare sopra; (*shorten*) accorciare; *judo, Spanish, new job* incominciare; *offer* accettare; *space, time* occupare; **I'll take you up on your offer** accetto la tua offerta

'**take·away** *meal* piatto *m* da asporto; (*restaurant*) ristorante *m* che prepara piatti da asporto

'**take-home pay** stipendio *m* in busta

tak·en ['teɪkən] *pp → take

'**take-off** decollo *m*; (*impersonation*) imitazione *f*; '**take·o·ver** COM rilevamento *m*; '**take·o·ver bid** offerta *f* pubblica di acquisto, OPA *f*

ta·kings ['teɪkɪŋz] *npl* incassi *mpl*

tal·cum pow·der ['tælkəmpaʊdə(r)] talco *m*

tale [teɪl] storia *f*

tal·ent ['tælənt] talento *m*

tal·ent·ed ['tæləntɪd] *adj* pieno di talento; **he's not very ~** non ha molto talento

'**tal·ent scout** talent scout *m/f inv*

talk [tɔːk] **1** *v/i* parlare; **can I talk to ...?** posso parlare con ...?; **I'll ~ to him about it** gliene parlo **2** *v/t English etc* parlare; *business, politics* parlare di; **~ s.o. into doing sth** convincere qu a fare qc; **~ s.o. out of doing sth** dissuadere qu dal fare qc **3** *n* (*conversation*) conversazione *f*; (*lecture*) conferenza *f*; **~s** (*negotiations*) trattative *fpl*, negoziati *mpl*; **he's all ~** *pej* è tutto chiacchiere

♦ **talk back** *v/i* ribattere

♦ **talk down to** *v/t* trattare dall'alto in basso

♦ **talk over** *v/t* discutere di

talk·a·tive ['tɔːkətɪv] *adj* loquace

talk·ing-to ['tɔːkɪntuː] sgridata *f*

'**talk show** talk show *m inv*

tall [tɔːl] *adj* alto

tall 'or·der bella impresa *f*

tall 'sto·ry baggianata *f*

tal·ly ['tælɪ] **1** *n* conto *m* **2** *v/i* (*pret & pp -ied*) quadrare

♦ **tally with** *v/t* quadrare con

tame [teɪm] *adj animal* addomesticato; *joke etc* blando

♦ **tamper with** ['tæmpə(r)] *v/t* manomettere

tam·pon ['tæmpɒn] tampone *m*

tan [tæn] **1** *n from sun* abbronzatura *f*; *colour* marrone *m* rossiccio **2** *v/i* (*pret & pp* **-ned**) *in sun* abbronzarsi **3** *v/t* (*pret & pp* **-ned**) *leather* conciare

tan·dem ['tændəm] *bike* tandem *m inv*

tan·gent ['tændʒənt] MATH tangente *f*

tan·ge·rine [tændʒə'riːn] tangerino *m*

tan·gi·ble ['tændʒɪbl] *adj* tangibile

tan·gle ['tæŋgl] *n* nodo *m*

♦ **tangle up**: *get tangled up* *of string etc* aggrovigliarsi

tan·go ['tæŋgəʊ] *n* tango *m*

tank [tæŋk] *n* serbatoio *m*; MOT serbatoio *m*; MIL carro *m* armato; *for skin diver* bombola *f* (d'ossigeno)

tank·er ['tæŋkə(r)] *ship* nave *f* cisterna; *truck* autocisterna *f*

tanned [tænd] *adj* abbronzato

Tan·noy® ['tænɔɪ] altoparlante *m*

tan·ta·liz·ing ['tæntəlaɪzɪŋ] *adj* allettante; *smell* stuzzicante

tan·ta·mount ['tæntəmaʊnt] *adj*: *be ~ to* essere equivalente a

tan·trum ['tæntrəm] capricci *mpl*; *throw a ~* fare (i) capricci

tap [tæp] **1** *n* rubinetto *m* **2** *v/t* (*pret & pp* **-ped**) *(hit)* dare un colpetto a; *phone* mettere sotto controllo; *he was ~ping his fingers on the table* tamburellava con le dita sul tavolo

♦ **tap into** *v/t resources* attingere a

'tap dance *n* tip tap *m*

tape [teɪp] **1** *n magnetic* nastro *m* magnetico; *recorded* cassetta *f*; *(sticky)* nastro *m* adesivo; *on ~* registrato **2** *v/t conversation etc* registrare; *~ sth to sth* attaccare qc a qc col nastro adesivo

'tape deck registratore *m*; **'tape drive** COMPUT unità *f inv* di backup a nastro; **'tape meas·ure** metro *m* a nastro

tap·er ['teɪpə(r)] *v/i* assottigliarsi

♦ **taper off** *v/i of production* calare gradualmente; *of figures* decrescere

'tape re·cor·der registratore *m* a cassette

'tape re·cor·ding registrazione *f* su cassetta

ta·pes·try ['tæpɪstrɪ] arazzo *m*

tape·worm ['teɪpwɜːm] verme *m* solitario

tar [tɑː(r)] *n* catrame *m*

tar·get ['tɑːgɪt] **1** *n in shooting* bersaglio *m*; *for sales, production* obiettivo *m* **2** *v/t market* rivolgersi a

tar·get 'au·di·ence target *m inv* di pubblico; **'tar·get date** data *f* fissata; **tar·get 'fig·ure** target *m inv*; **'tar·get group** COM gruppo *m* target; **'tar·get language** lingua *f* d'arrivo; **'tar·get mar·ket** mercato *m* target

tar·iff ['tærɪf] (*price*) tariffa *f*; *(tax)* tassa *f*

tar·mac ['tɑːmæk] *at airport* pista *f*

tar·nish ['tɑːnɪʃ] *v/t metal* ossidare; *reputation* macchiare

tar·pau·lin [tɑː'pɔːlɪn] tela *f* cerata

tart[1] [tɑːt] *n* torta *f*

tart[2] [tɑːt] *n* F (*prostitute*) sgualdrina *f*, *pej: woman* stronza *f*

tar·tan ['tɑːtn] tartan *m*

task [tɑːsk] compito *m*

'task force task force *f inv*

tas·sel ['tæsl] nappa *f*

taste [teɪst] **1** *n* gusto *m*; *he has no ~* non ha nessun gusto **2** *v/t food* assaggiare; *(experience: freedom etc)* provare; *I can't ~ anything* non sento nessun sapore **3** *v/i*: *it ~s like ...* ha sapore di ...; *it ~s very nice* è molto buono

'taste buds *npl* papille *fpl* gustative

taste·ful ['teɪstfʊl] *adj* di gusto

taste·ful·ly ['teɪstfəlɪ] *adv* con gusto

taste·less ['teɪstlɪs] *adj food* insapore; *remark, person* privo di gusto

tast·ing ['teɪstɪŋ] *of wine* degustazione *f*

tast·y ['teɪstɪ] *adj* gustoso

tat·tered ['tætəd] *adj clothes, book* malridotto

tat·ters ['tætəz]: *in ~ of clothes* a brandelli; *of reputation, career* a pezzi

tat·too [tə'tu:] *n* tatuaggio *m*

tat·ty ['tætɪ] *adj* F malandato

taught [tɔːt] *pret & pp* → **teach**

taunt [tɔːnt] **1** *n* scherno *m* **2** *v/t* schernire

Taur·us ['tɔːrəs] ASTR Toro *m*

taut [tɔːt] *adj* teso

taw·dry ['tɔːdrɪ] *adj* pacchiano

tax [tæks] **1** *n* tassa; *before / after ~* al lordo / al netto di imposte **2** *v/t* tassare

tax·a·ble 'in·come reddito *m* imponibile

ta·x·a·tion [tæk'seɪʃn] tassazione *f*

'tax avoid·ance elusione *f* fiscale; **'tax brack·et** fascia *f* di reddito; **'tax code** codice *m* fiscale; **'tax-de·duct·i·ble** *adj* deducibile dalle imposte; **'tax disc** *for car* bollo *m* (di circolazione); **'tax eva·sion** evasione *f* fiscale; **'tax-free** *adj* esentasse *inv*

tax·i ['tæksɪ] taxi *m inv*

tax·i dri·ver tassista *m/f*

tax·ing ['tæksɪŋ] *adj* estenuante

tax in·spect·or ispettore *m*, -trice *f* fiscale

'tax·i rank, tax·i stand stazione *f* dei taxi

'tax·man fisco *m*; **'tax·pay·er** contribuente *m/f*; **'tax re·turn** *form* dichiarazione *f* dei redditi; **'tax year** anno *m* fiscale

TB [ti:'bi:] *abbr* (= *tuberculosis*) tbc *f* (= *tubercolosi f*)

tea [ti:] *drink* tè *m inv*; *meal* cena *f*

tea-bag ['ti:bæg] bustina *f* di tè

teach [ti:tʃ] (*pret & pp* **taught**) **1** *v/t subject* insegnare; *person* insegnare a; *~ s.o. to do sth* insegnare a qu a fare qc **2** *v/i* insegnare

ea·cher ['ti:tʃə(r)] insegnante *m/f*

ea·cher 'train·ing tirocinio *m* per insegnanti

ea·ching ['ti:tʃɪŋ] *profession* insegnamento *m*

ea·ching aid sussidio *m* didattico

tea cloth strofinaccio *m* da cucina;

'tea·cup tazza *f* da tè; **'tea drink·er** bevitore *m*, -trice *f* di tè

teak [ti:k] tek *m*

'tea leaf foglia *f* di tè

team [ti:m] *in sport* squadra *f*; *at work* équipe *f inv*

'team mate compagno *m*, -a *f* di squadra; **team 'spirit** spirito *m* d'équipe; **'team·work** lavoro *m* d'équipe

tea·pot ['ti:pɒt] teiera *f*

tear¹ [teə(r)] **1** *n in cloth etc* strappo *m* **2** *v/t* (*pret* **tore**, *pp* **torn**) *paper, cloth* strappare; *be torn between two alternatives* essere combattuto tra due alternative **3** *v/i* (*pret* **tore**, *pp* **torn**) (*run fast, drive fast*) sfrecciare

♦ **tear down** *v/t poster* strappare; *building* buttar giù

♦ **tear out** *v/t* strappare

♦ **tear up** *v/t paper* distruggere; *agreement* rompere

tear² [tɪə(r)] **1** *n in eye* lacrima *f*; *burst into ~s* scoppiare a piangere; *be in ~s* essere in lacrime

tear·drop ['tɪədrɒp] lacrima *f*

tear·ful ['tɪəful] *adj person* in lacrime; *look, voice* piangente

'tear gas gas *m inv* lacrimogeno

'tea·room sala *f* da tè

tease [ti:z] *v/t person* prendere in giro; *animal* stuzzicare

'tea serv·ice, 'tea set servizio *m* da tè; **'tea·spoon** cucchiaino *m* da caffè; **'tea strain·er** colino *m* da tè

teat [ti:t] capezzolo *m*; *made of rubber* tettarella *f*

'tea tow·el strofinaccio *m* da cucina

tech·ni·cal ['teknɪkl] *adj* tecnico

tech·ni·cal·i·ty [teknɪ'kælətɪ] (*technical nature*) tecnicismo *m*; LAW vizio *m* di procedura; *that's just a ~* è solo un dettaglio

tech·ni·cal·ly ['teknɪklɪ] *adv* tecnicamente

tech·ni·cian [tek'nɪʃn] tecnico *m*

tech·nique [tek'ni:k] tecnica *f*

tech·no·log·i·cal [teknə'lɒdʒɪkl] *adj* tecnologico

T

tech·no·lo·gy [tek'nɒlədʒɪ] tecnologia *f*

tech·no·phob·i·a [teknə'fəʊbɪə] tecnofobia *f*

ted·dy bear ['tedɪbeə(r)] orsacchiotto *m*

te·di·ous ['ti:dɪəs] *adj* noioso

tee [ti:] *n* in golf tee *m inv*

teem [ti:m] *v/i* pullulare; *be ~ing with rain* piovere a dirotto; *be ~ing with tourists / ants* pullulare di turisti / formiche

teen·age ['ti:neɪdʒ] *adj problems* degli adolescenti; *gangs* di ragazzi; *~ boy / girl* ragazzo *m* / ragazza *f* adolescente; *~ fashions* moda giovane

teen·ag·er ['ti:neɪdʒə(r)] adolescente *m/f*

teens [ti:nz] *npl* adolescenza *f*; *be in one's ~* essere adolescente; *reach one's ~* entrare nell'adolescenza

tee·ny ['ti:nɪ] *adj* F piccolissimo

teeth [ti:θ] *pl* → *tooth*

teethe [ti:ð] *v/i* mettere i denti

'**teething problems** *npl* difficoltà *fpl* iniziali

tee·to·tal [ti:'təʊtl] *adj person* astemio; *party* senza alcolici

tee·to·tal·ler [ti:'təʊtlə(r)] astemio *m*, -a *f*

tel·e·com·mu·ni·ca·tions [telɪkəmju:nɪ'keɪʃnz] telecomunicazioni *fpl*

tel·e·gram ['telɪgræm] telegramma *m*

tel·e·graph pole ['telɪgrɑ:fpəʊl] palo *m* del telegrafo

tel·e·path·ic [telɪ'pæθɪk] *adj* telepatico; *you must be ~!* devi avere poteri telepatici!

te·lep·a·thy [tɪ'lepəθɪ] telepatia *f*

tel·e·phone ['telɪfəʊn] **1** *n* telefono *m*; *be on the ~* be speaking essere al telefono; possess a phone avere il telefono **2** *v/t person* telefonare a **3** *v/i* telefonare

'**tel·e·phone bill** bolletta *f* del telefono; '**tel·e·phone book** guida *f* telefonica; '**tel·e·phone booth** cabina *f* telefonica; '**tel·e·phone box** cabina *f* telefonica; '**tel·e·phone call** telefonata *f*; '**tel·e·phone con·ver·sa·tion** conversazione *f* telefonica; '**tel·e·phone di·rec·to·ry** elenco *m* telefonico; '**tel·e·phone ex·change** centralino *m* telefonico; '**tel·e·phone mes·sage** messaggio *m* telefonico; '**tel·e·phone num·ber** numero *m* telefonico

tel·e·pho·to lens [telɪfəʊtəʊ'lenz] teleobiettivo *m*

tel·e·sales ['telɪseɪlz] vendita *f* telefonica

tel·e·scope ['telɪskəʊp] telescopio *m*

tel·e·scop·ic lens [telɪskɒpɪk'lenz] lente *f* telescopica

tel·e·thon ['telɪθɒn] telethon *m inv*

tel·e·vise ['telɪvaɪz] *v/t* trasmettere in televisione

tel·e·vi·sion ['telɪvɪʒn] televisione *f*; *set* televisione *f*, televisore *m*; *on ~* alla televisione; *watch ~* guardare la televisione

'**tel·e·vi·sion au·di·ence** pubblico *m* televisivo; '**tel·e·vi·sion li·cence** canone *m* (televisivo); '**tel·e·vision pro·gramme** programma *m* televisivo; '**tel·e·vision set** televisore *m*; '**tel·e·vision stu·di·o** studio *m* televisivo

tell [tel] (*pret & pp told*) **1** *v/t* dire; *story* raccontare; *~ s.o. sth* dire qc a qu; *don't ~ Mum* non dirlo alla mamma; *~ s.o. to do sth* dire a qu di fare qc; *I've been told that ...* mi hanno detto che ...; *it's hard to ~* è difficile a dirsi; *you never can ~* non si può mai dire; *~ X from Y* distinguere X da Y; *I can't ~ the difference between ...* non vedo nessuna differenza tra ...; *you're ~ing me!* F a chi lo dici! F **2** *v/i* (*have effect*) farsi sentire; *the heat is ~ing on him* il caldo si fa sentire su di lui; *time will ~* il tempo lo dirà

♦ **tell off** *v/t* rimproverare

tell·er ['telə(r)] in bank cassiere *m*, -a *f*

tell·ing ['telɪŋ] *adj argument* efficace; *a ~ sign* un segnale chiaro

tell·ing off rimprovero *m*; *give s.o. a ~* rimproverare qu

tell·tale ['telteɪl] **1** *adj signs* rivelatore **2** *n spione m*, spiona *f*

tel·ly ['telɪ] F tele *f*

temp [temp] **1** *n employee* impiegato *m*, -a interinale **2** *v/i* fare lavori interinali

tem·per ['tempə(r)] (*bad ~*): **have a terrible** ~ essere irascibile; **be in a** ~ essere arrabbiato; **keep one's** ~ mantenere la calma; **lose one's** ~ perdere le staffe

tem·pe·ra·ment ['temprəmənt] temperamento *m*

tem·pe·ra·men·tal [temprə'mentl] *adj* (*moody*) lunatico; *machine* imprevedibile

tem·pe·rate ['tempərət] *adj* temperato

tem·pe·ra·ture ['temprətʃə(r)] temperatura *f*; (*fever*) febbre *f*; **have a** ~ avere la febbre; **take s.o.'s** ~ prendere la temperatura a qu

tem·ple¹ ['templ] REL tempio *m*

tem·ple² ['templ] ANAT tempia *f*

tem·po ['tempəʊ] ritmo *m*; MUS tempo *m*

tem·po·rar·i·ly [tempə'reərɪlɪ] *adv* temporaneamente

tem·po·ra·ry ['tempərərɪ] *adj* temporaneo, provvisorio

tempt [tempt] *v/t* tentare

temp·ta·tion [temp'teɪʃn] tentazione *f*

tempt·ing ['temptɪŋ] *adj* allettante; *meal* appetitoso

ten [ten] dieci

te·na·cious [tɪ'neɪʃəs] *adj* tenace

te·nac·i·ty [tɪ'næsɪtɪ] tenacità *f*

ten·ant ['tenənt] inquilino *m*, -a *f*, locatario *m*, -a *f fml*; *in office* affittuario *m*, -a *f*

tend¹ [tend] *v/t* (*look after*) prendersi cura di

tend² [tend]: ~ **to do sth** tendere a fare qc, avere la tendenza a fare qc; ~ **towards sth** avere una tendenza verso qc

ten·den·cy ['tendənsɪ] tendenza *f*

ten·der¹ ['tendə(r)] *adj* (*sore*) sensibile; (*affectionate*) tenero; *steak* tenero

ten·der² ['tendə(r)] *n* COM offerta *f* ufficiale

ten·der·ness ['tendənɪs] (*soreness*) sensibilità *f*; *of kiss, steak* tenerezza *f*

ten·don ['tendən] tendine *m*

ten·nis ['tenɪs] tennis *m*

'ten·nis ball palla *f* da tennis; **'ten·nis court** campo *m* da tennis; **'ten·nis pla·yer** tennista *m/f*; **'ten·nis rack·et** racchetta *f* da tennis

ten·or ['tenə(r)] MUS tenore *m*

tense¹ [tens] *n* GRAM tempo *m*

tense² [tens] *adj voice, person* teso; *moment, atmosphere* carico di tensione

♦ **tense up** *v/i of muscles* contrarre; *of person* irrigidirsi

ten·sion ['tenʃn] tensione *f*

tent [tent] tenda *f*

ten·ta·cle ['tentəkl] tentacolo *m*

ten·ta·tive ['tentətɪv] *adj* esitante

ten·ter·hooks ['tentəhʊks]: **be on** ~ essere sulle spine

tenth [tenθ] *n & adj* decimo, -a

tep·id ['tepɪd] *adj water, reaction* tiepido

term [tɜːm] periodo *m*; *of office* durata *f* in carica; EDU: *of three months* trimestre *m*; *of two months* bimestre *m*; (*condition, word*) termine *m*; **be on good / bad ~s with s.o.** essere in buoni / cattivi rapporti con qu; **in the long / short** ~ a lungo / breve termine; **come to ~s with sth** venire a patti con qc

ter·mi·nal ['tɜːmɪnl] **1** *n at airport, for containers*, COMPUT terminale *m*; *for buses* capolinea *m inv*; ELEC morsetto *m* **2** *adj illness* in fase terminale

ter·mi·nal·ly ['tɜːmɪnəlɪ] *adv*: ~ **ill** malato (in fase) terminale

ter·mi·nate ['tɜːmɪneɪt] **1** *v/t contract, pregnancy* interrompere **2** *v/i* terminare

ter·mi·na·tion [tɜːmɪ'neɪʃn] *of contract, pregnancy* interruzione *f*

ter·mi·nol·o·gy [tɜːmɪ'nɒlədʒɪ] terminologia *f*

ter·mi·nus ['tɜːmɪnəs] *for buses* capolinea *m inv; for trains* stazione *f* di testa

ter·race ['terəs] *of houses* fila *f* di case a schiera; *on hillside, at hotel* terrazza *f*

ter·raced house [terəst'haʊs] casa *f* a schiera

ter·ra cot·ta [terə'kɒtə] *adj* di terracotta

ter·rain [tə'reɪn] terreno *m*

ter·res·tri·al [tə'restrɪəl] **1** *n* terrestre *m/f* **2** *adj television* di terra

ter·ri·ble ['terəbl] *adj* terribile

ter·ri·bly ['terəblɪ] *adv play* malissimo; *(very)* molto

ter·rif·ic [tə'rɪfɪk] *adj* eccezionale; *~!* bene!

ter·rif·i·cal·ly [tə'rɪfɪklɪ] *adv (very)* eccezionalmente

ter·ri·fy ['terɪfaɪ] *v/t (pret & pp -ied)* terrificare; *be terrified* essere terrificato

ter·ri·fy·ing ['terɪfaɪɪŋ] *adj* terrificante

ter·ri·to·ri·al [terɪ'tɔ:rɪəl] *adj* territoriale

ter·ri·to·ri·al 'wa·ters *npl* acque *fpl* territoriali

ter·ri·to·ry ['terɪtərɪ] *also fig* territorio *m*

ter·ror ['terə(r)] terrore *m*

ter·ror·is·m ['terərɪzm] terrorismo *m*

ter·ror·ist ['terərɪst] terrorista *m/f*

'ter·ror·ist at·tack attentato *m* terroristico

'ter·ror·ist or·gan·i·za·tion organizzazione *f* terroristica

ter·ror·ize ['terəraɪz] *v/t* terrorizzare

terse [tɜ:s] *adj* brusco

test [test] **1** *n* prova *f*, test *m inv; for driving, medical* esame *m; blood ~* analisi *f inv* del sangue **2** *v/t soup, bathwater* provare; *machine, theory* testare; *person, friendship* mettere alla prova; *~ the water fig* tastare il terreno

tes·ta·ment ['testəmənt] testimonianza *f (to* di); *Old / New Testament* REL Vecchio / Nuovo Testamento

'test-drive: go for a ~ fare un giro di prova

tes·ti·cle ['testɪkl] testicolo *m*

tes·ti·fy ['testɪfaɪ] *v/i (pret & pp -ied)* LAW testimoniare

tes·ti·mo·ni·al [testɪ'məʊnɪəl] referenze *fpl* scritte

tes·ti·mo·ny ['testɪmənɪ] LAW testimonianza *f*

'test tube provetta *f*

'test tube ba·by bambino *m*, -a *f* (concepito, -a) in provetta

tes·ty ['testɪ] *adj* suscettibile

te·ta·nus ['tetənəs] tetano *m*

teth·er ['teðə(r)] **1** *v/t horse* legare **2** *n: be at the end of one's ~* essere allo stremo

text [tekst] testo *m*

'text·book libro *m* di testo

tex·tile ['tekstaɪl] tessuto *m*

tex·ture ['tekstʃə(r)] consistenza *f*

Thai [taɪ] **1** *adj* tailandese **2** *n person* tailandese *m/f; language* tailandese *m*

Thai·land ['taɪlænd] Tailandia *f*

than [ðæn] *adv: older / faster ~ me* più vecchio / veloce di me; *she's more French ~ Italian* è più francese che italiana

thank [θæŋk] *v/t* ringraziare; *~ you* grazie; *no ~ you* no, grazie

thank·ful ['θæŋkfʊl] *adj* riconoscente

thank·ful·ly ['θæŋkfʊlɪ] *adv* con riconoscenza; *(luckily)* fortunatamente

thank·less ['θæŋklɪs] *adj* ingrato

thanks [θæŋks] *npl* ringraziamenti *mpl; ~!* grazie!; *~ to* grazie a

that [ðæt] **1** *adj* quel; *with masculine nouns before s+consonant, gn, ps and z* quello; *~ one* quello **2** *pron* quello *m*, -a *f; what is ~?* cos'è?; *who is ~?* chi è?; *~'s mine* è mio; *~'s tea* quello è tè; *~'s very kind* è molto gentile **3** *relative pron* che; *the person / car ~ you saw* la persona / macchina che hai visto; *the day ~ he was born* il giorno in cui è nato **4** *adv (so)* così; *~ big / expensive* così grande / caro **5** *conj* che; *I think ~ ...* credo che ...

thaw [θɔ:] *v/i of snow* sciogliersi; *of*

frozen food scongelare

he [ðə] il *m*, la *f*; i *mpl*, le *fpl*; *with masculine nouns before s+consonant, gn, ps and z* lo *m*, gli *mpl*; *before vowel* l' *m/f*, gli *mpl*; **to ~ bathroom** al bagno; **~ sooner ~ better** prima è, meglio è

he·a·ter *Am → theatre*

he·a·tre ['θɪətə(r)] teatro *m*

the·a·tre crit·ic critico *m* teatrale

he·a·tre·go·er ['θɪətəɡəʊə(r)] frequentatore *m*, -trice *f* di teatro

he·at·ri·cal [θɪ'ætrɪkl] *also fig* teatrale

heft [θeft] furto *m*

heir [ðeə(r)] *adj* il loro *m*, la loro *f*; i loro *mpl*, le loro *fpl*; *(his or her)* il suo *m*, la sua *f*, i suoi *mpl*, le sue *fpl*; **~ daughter/son** la loro figlia/il loro figlio

heirs [ðeəz] *pron* il loro *m*, la loro *f*; i loro *mpl*, le loro *fpl*; **it was an idea of ~** è stata una loro idea

hem [ðem] *pron direct object* li *m*, le *f*; *referring to things* essi *m*, esse *f*; *indirect object* loro, gli; *after preposition* loro; *referring to things* essi *m*, esse *f*; *(him or her)* lo *m*, la *f*; **I know ~** li/le conosco; **I sold it to ~** gliel'ho venduto, l'ho venduto a loro

heme [θiːm] tema *m*

theme park parco *m* a tema

theme song canzone *f* principale

hem·selves [ðem'selvz] *pron reflexive* si; *emphatic* loro stessi *mpl*, loro stesse *fpl*; *after prep* se stessi/se stesse; **they ~** loro stessi/stesse; **they enjoyed ~** si sono divertiti; **they only think about ~** pensano solo a se stessi/stesse; **by ~** *(alone)* da soli *mpl*, da sole *fpl*

hen [ðen] *adv (at that time)* allora; *(after that)* poi; *(deducing)* allora; **by ~** allora

he·o·lo·gian [θɪə'ləʊdʒɪən] teologo *m*, -a *f*

he·ol·o·gy [θɪ'ɒlədʒɪ] teologia *f*

he·o·ret·i·cal [θɪə'retɪkl] *adj* teorico *f*

he·o·ret·i·cal·ly [θɪə'retɪklɪ] *adv* teoricamente

the·o·ry ['θɪərɪ] teoria *f*; **in ~** in teoria

ther·a·peu·tic [θerə'pjuːtɪk] *adj* terapeutico

ther·a·pist ['θerəpɪst] terapista *m/f*, terapeuta *m/f*

ther·a·py ['θerəpɪ] terapia *f*

there [ðeə(r)] *adv* lì, là; *over ~* là; *down ~* laggiù; **~ is ...** c'è; **~ are ...** ci sono; **is ~ ...?** c'è ...?; **are ~ ...?** ci sono ...?; **isn't ~?** non c'è ...?; **aren't ~?** non ci sono ...?; **~ you are** giving sth ecco qui; *finding sth* ecco; *completing sth* ecco fatto; **~ and back** andata e ritorno; **~ he is!** eccolo!; **~, ~!** *comforting* su, dai!

there·a·bouts [ðeərə'baʊts] *adv* giù di lì

there·fore [ðeəfɔː(r)] *adv* quindi, pertanto

ther·mom·e·ter [θə'mɒmɪtə(r)] termometro *m*

ther·mos flask ['θɜːməsflɑːsk] termos *m inv*

ther·mo·stat ['θɜːməstæt] termostato *m*

these [ðiːz] **1** *adj* questi **2** *pron* questi *m*, -e *f*

the·sis ['θiːsɪs] (*pl* **theses** ['θiːsiːz]) tesi *f inv*

they [ðeɪ] *pron* ◊ loro; **~'re going to the theatre** vanno a teatro; **~'re going to the theatre, we're not** loro vanno a teatro, noi no; **there are** eccoli *mpl*, eccole *fpl* ◊ **if anyone looks at this, ~ will see that ...** se qualcuno lo guarda, vedrà che ...; **~ say that ...** si dice che ...; **~ are going to change the law** cambieranno la legge

thick [θɪk] *adj* spesso; *hair* folto; *fog, forest* fitto; *liquid* denso; F *(stupid)* ottuso

thick·en ['θɪkən] *v/t sauce* ispessire

thick·set ['θɪkset] *adj* tarchiato

thick·skinned ['θɪkskɪnd] *adj fig* insensibile

thief [θiːf] (*pl* **thieves** [θiːvz]) ladro *m*, -a *f*

thigh [θaɪ] coscia *f*

thim·ble ['θɪmbl] ditale *m*

thin [θɪn] *adj* sottile; *person* magro;

T

hair rado; *liquid* fluido

thing [θɪŋ] cosa *f*; **~s** (*belongings*) cose *fpl*; **how are ~s?** come vanno le cose?; **it's a good ~ you told me** è un bene che tu me l'abbia detto; **what a ~ to do / say!** che razza di cosa da fare / dire!

thing·um·a·jig ['θɪŋʌmədʒɪg] F coso *m*, cosa *f* F

think [θɪŋk] *v/i* (*pret & pp* **thought**) pensare; *I ~ so* penso *o* credo di sì; *I don't ~ so* non credo; *I ~ so too* lo penso anch'io; *what do you ~?* cosa ne pensi?; *what do you ~ of it?* cosa ne pensi?; *I can't ~ of anything more* non mi viene in mente nient'altro; *~ hard!* pensaci bene!; *I'm ~ing about emigrating* sto pensando di emigrare

♦ **think over** *v/t* riflettere su
♦ **think through** *v/t* analizzare a fondo
♦ **think up** *v/t plan* escogitare

'**think tank** comitato *m* di esperti

thin-skinned [θɪn'skɪnd] *adj fig* sensibile

third [θɜːd] *n & adj* terzo, -a

third·ly ['θɜːdlɪ] *adv* in terzo luogo

'**third-par·ty** terzi *mpl*; **third-par·ty in·sur·ance** assicurazione *f* sulla responsabilità civile; **third 'per·son** GRAM terza persona *f*; '**third-rate** *adj* scadente; **Third 'World** Terzo Mondo *m*

thirst [θɜːst] sete *f*

thirsty ['θɜːstɪ] *adj* assetato; *be ~* avere sete

thir·teen [θɜː'tiːn] tredici

thir·teenth [θɜː'tiːnθ] *n & adj* tredicesimo, -a

thir·ti·eth ['θɜːtɪɪθ] *n & adj* trentesimo, -a

thir·ty ['θɜːtɪ] trenta

this [ðɪs] **1** *adj* questo; **~ one** questo (qui) **2** *pron* questo *m*, -a *f*; **~ is easy** è facile; **~ is ...** *introducing s.o.* questo / questa è ...; TELEC sono ... **3** *adv*: **~ big / high** grande / alto così

thorn [θɔːn] spina *f*

thorn·y ['θɔːnɪ] *adj also fig* spinoso

thor·ough ['θʌrə] *adj search, know-*

ledge approfondito; *person* scrupoloso

thor·ough·bred ['θʌrəbred] *horse* purosangue *inv*

thor·ough·ly ['θʌrəlɪ] *adv clean, search for* accuratamente; *know, understand* perfettamente; *agree, spoil* completamente; **~ stupid** stupidissimo

those [ðəʊz] **1** *adj* quelli; *with masculine nouns before s+consonant, gn, ps and z* quegli **2** *pron* quelli *m*, -e *f*; *with masculine nouns before s+consonant, gn, ps and z* quegli

though [ðəʊ] **1** *conj* (*although*) benché; **~ it might fail** benché possa non riuscire; **say it as ~ you meant it** dillo come se lo sentissi davvero; **it looks as ~ ...** sembra che ... **2** *adv* però; **it's not finished ~** non è finito, però

thought [θɔːt] **1** *n* pensiero *m* **2** *pret & pp* → **think**

thought·ful ['θɔːtfʊl] *adj* pensieroso; *reply* meditato; (*considerate*) gentile

thought·ful·ly [əθɔːtflɪ] *adv* (*pensively*) con aria pensierosa; (*considerately*) gentilmente

thought·less ['θɔːtlɪs] *adj* sconsiderato

thought·less·ly ['θɔːtlɪslɪ] *adv* in modo sconsiderato

thou·sand ['θaʊznd] mille; **a ~ pounds** mille sterline; **~s of** migliaia *fpl di*

thou·sandth ['θaʊzndθ] *n & adj* millesimo, -a

thrash [θræʃ] *v/t* picchiare; SP battere
♦ **thrash about** *v/i with arms etc* sferrare colpi in aria
♦ **thrash out** *v/t solution* mettere a punto

thrash·ing ['θræʃɪŋ] botte *fpl*; SP batosta *f*

thread [θred] **1** *n* filo *m*; *of screw* filettatura *f* **2** *v/t needle* infilare il filo in; *beads* infilare

thread·bare ['θredbeə(r)] *adj* liso

threat [θret] minaccia *f*

threat·en ['θretn] *v/t* minacciare

threat·en·ing ['θretnɪŋ] *adj* minaccioso; **~ letter** lettera *f* minatoria

three [θriː] tre

three 'quart·ers tre quarti *mpl*

thresh [θreʃ] *v/t corn* trebbiare

thresh·old ['θreʃhəʊld] *of house, new era* soglia *f*; **on the ~ of** sulla soglia di

threw [θruː] *pret* → **throw**

thrift [θrɪft] parsimonia *f*

thrift·y ['θrɪftɪ] *adj* parsimonioso

thrill [θrɪl] **1** *n* emozione *f*; *physical feeling* brivido *m* **2** *v/t*: **be ~ed** essere emozionato

thrill·er ['θrɪlə(r)] giallo *m*

thrill·ing ['θrɪlɪŋ] *adj* emozionante

thrive [θraɪv] *v/i of plant* crescere rigoglioso; *of business, economy* prosperare

throat [θrəʊt] gola *f*; **have a sore ~** avere mal di gola

throat loz·enge pastiglia *f* per la gola

throb [θrɒb] *v/i* (*pret & pp* **-bed**) pulsare; *of heart* battere; *of music* rimbombare

throb·bing ['θrɒbɪŋ] pulsazione *f*; *of heart* battito *m*; *of music* rimbombo *m*

throne [θrəʊn] trono *m*

throng [θrɒŋ] *n* calca *f*

throt·tle ['θrɒtl] **1** *n on motorbike* manetta *f* di accelerazione; *on boat* leva *f* di accelerazione **2** *v/t* (*strangle*) strozzare

♦ **throttle back** *v/i* decelerare

through [θruː] **1** *prep* (*across*) attraverso; (*during*) durante; (*by means of*) tramite; **go ~ the city** attraversare la città; **~ the winter / summer** per tutto l'inverno / tutta l'estate; **arranged ~ him** organizzato tramite lui **2** *adv*: **wet ~** completamente bagnato; **watch a film ~** guardare un film fino alla fine **3** *adj*: **be ~ of couple** essersi lasciati; **have arrived**: *of news etc* essere arrivato; **you're ~** TELEC è in linea; **I'm ~ with ...** (*finished with*) ho finito con ...; **I'm ~ with him** ho chiuso con lui

through flight volo *m* diretto

through·out [θruː'aʊt] **1** *prep*: **~ the**

night per tutta la notte **2** *adv* (*in all parts*) completamente

'through train treno *m* diretto

throw [θrəʊ] **1** *v/t* (*pret* **threw**, *pp* **thrown**) lanciare; *into bin etc* gettare; *of horse* disarcionare; (*disconcert*) sconcertare; *party* dare **2** *n* lancio *m*

♦ **throw away** *v/t* buttare via, gettare

♦ **throw off** *v/t jacket etc* togliersi in fretta; *cold etc* liberarsi di

♦ **throw on** *v/t clothes* mettersi in fretta

♦ **throw out** *v/t old things* buttare via; *from bar, house etc* buttare fuori; *plan* scartare

♦ **throw up** **1** *v/t ball* lanciare; **throw up one's hands** alzare le mani al cielo **2** *v/i* (*vomit*) vomitare

'throw-a-way *adj remark* buttato lì; (*disposable*) usa e getta *inv*

'throw-in SP rimessa *f*

thrown [θrəʊn] *pp* → **throw**

thrush [θrʌʃ] *bird* tordo *m*

thrust [θrʌst] *v/t* (*pret & pp* **thrust**) (*push hard*) spingere; *knife* conficcare; **~ sth into s.o.'s hands** ficcare qc in mano a qu; **~ one's way through the crowd** farsi largo tra la folla

thud [θʌd] *n* tonfo *m*

thug [θʌg] *hooligan* teppista *m*; *tough guy* bullo *m*

thumb [θʌm] **1** *n* pollice *m* **2** *v/t*: **~ a lift** fare l'autostop

thump [θʌmp] **1** *n blow* pugno *m*; *noise* colpo *m* **2** *v/t person* dare un pugno a; **~ one's fist on the table** dare un pugno sul tavolo **3** *v/i of heart* palpitare; **~ on the door** battere alla porta

thun·der ['θʌndə(r)] *n* tuono *m*

thun·der·ous ['θʌndərəs] *adj applause* fragoroso

thun·der·storm ['θʌndəstɔːm] temporale *m*

thun·der·struck *adj* allibito

thun·der·y ['θʌndərɪ] *adj weather* temporalesco

Thurs·day ['θɜːzdeɪ] giovedì *m inv*

T

thus [ðʌs] *adv* (*in this way*) così

thwart [θwɔːt] *v/t person, plans* ostacolare

thyme [taɪm] timo *m*

thy·roid gland ['θaɪrɔɪdglænd] tiroide *f*

Ti·ber ['taɪbə(r)] Tevere *m*

tick [tɪk] **1** *n of clock* ticchettio *m; in text* segno *m* **2** *v/i of clock* ticchettare **3** *v/t with a ~* segnare

♦**tick off** *v/t* rimproverare; *item in a list* segnare

tick·et ['tɪkɪt] biglietto *m; in cloakroom* scontrino *m*

'**ti·cket col·lec·tor** bigliettaio *m*, -a *f*; '**ti·cket in·spec·tor** controllore *m*; '**ti·cket ma·chine** distributore *m* di biglietti; '**ti·cket of·fice** biglietteria *f*

tick·ing ['tɪkɪŋ] *noise* ticchettio *m*

tick·le ['tɪkl] **1** *v/t person* fare il solletico a **2** *v/i of material* dare prurito; *of person* fare il solletico

tickl·ish ['tɪklɪʃ] *adj*: **be ~** soffrire il solletico

ti·dal wave ['taɪdlweɪv] onda *f* di marea

tide [taɪd] marea *f*; **high ~** alta marea; **low ~** bassa marea; **the ~ is in / out** c'è l'alta / la bassa marea

♦**tide over** *v/t* togliere d'impiccio

ti·di·ness ['taɪdɪnɪs] ordine *m*

ti·dy ['taɪdɪ] *adj* ordinato

♦**tidy away** *v/t* (*pret & pp* **-ied**) mettere a posto

♦**tidy up 1** *v/t room, shelves* mettere in ordine; **tidy o.s. up** darsi una sistemata **2** *v/i* mettere in ordine

tie [taɪ] **1** *n* (*necktie*) cravatta *f*; (*SP: even result*) pareggio *m*; **he doesn't have any ~s** non ha legami **2** *v/t knot, hands* legare; **~ a knot** fare un nodo; **~ two ropes together** annodare due corde **3** *v/i* SP pareggiare

♦**tie down** *v/t with rope* legare; (*restrict*) vincolare

♦**tie up** *v/t person, laces, hair* legare; *boat* ormeggiare; *I'm tied up tomorrow* sono impegnato domani

tier [tɪə(r)] *of hierarchy* livello *m; in stadium* anello *m*

ti·ger ['taɪgə(r)] tigre *f*

tight [taɪt] **1** *adj clothes* stretto; *security* rigido; *rope* teso; *hard to move* bloccato; *not leaving much time* giusto; *schedule* serrato; F (*drunk*) sbronzo F **2** *adv*: **hold s.o. / sth ~** tenere qu / qc stretto; **shut sth ~** chiudere bene qc

tight·en ['taɪtn] *v/t screw* serrare; *belt* stringere; *rope* tendere; *control, security* intensificare

♦**tighten up** *v/i in discipline, security* intensificare il controllo

tight-fist·ed [taɪt'fɪstɪd] *adj* taccagno

tight·ly ['taɪtlɪ] *adv* → **tight** *adv*

tight·rope ['taɪtrəʊp] fune *f* (per funamboli)

tights [taɪts] *npl* collant *mpl*

tile [taɪl] *on floor* mattonella *f; on wall* piastrella *f; on roof* tegola *f*

till[1] [tɪl] *prep & conj* → **until**

till[2] [tɪl] *n* (*cash register*) cassa *f*

till[3] [tɪl] *v/t soil* arare

tilt [tɪlt] **1** *v/t* inclinare **2** *v/i* inclinarsi

tim·ber ['tɪmbə(r)] legname *m*

time [taɪm] tempo *m; by the clock* ora *f*; (*occasion*) volta *f; ~ is up* il tempo è scaduto; **for the ~ being** al momento; **have a good ~!** divertiti; **have a good ~!** divertiti!; **what's the ~?, what ~ is it?** che ora è?, che ore sono?; **by the ~ you finish** quando avrai finito; **the first ~** la prima volta; **four ~s** quattro volte; **~ and again** ripetutamente; **all the ~** per tutto il tempo; **I've been here for some ~** sono qui da un po'; **take your ~** fai con calma; **for a ~** per un po' (di tempo); **at any ~** in qualsiasi momento; (*and*) **about ~!** era ora!; **two / three at a ~** due / tre alla volta; **at the same ~** *speak, reply etc* contemporaneamente; (*however*) nel contempo; **in ~** in tempo; (*eventually*) col tempo; **on ~** in orario; **in no ~** in un attimo

'**time bomb** bomba *f* a orologeria; '**time clock** *in factory* bollatrice *f*;

'**time-con·sum·ing** *adj* lungo;
'**time dif·fer·ence** fuso *m* orario;
'**time-lag** scarto *m* di tempo; '**time
lim·it** limite *m* temporale
time·ly ['taɪmlɪ] *adj* tempestivo
tim·er ['taɪmə(r)] cronometro *m*; *person* cronometrista *m/f*; *on oven* timer *m inv*
'**time·sav·ing** *n* risparmio *m* di tempo; '**time·scale** *of project* cronologia *f*; '**time share** *Br* (*house, apartment*) multiproprietà *f inv*; '**time
switch** interruttore *m* a tempo;
'**time·ta·ble** orario *m*; '**time·warp**
trasposizione *f* temporale; '**time
zone** zona *f* di fuso orario
tim·id ['tɪmɪd] *adj* timido
tim·id·ly ['tɪmɪdlɪ] *adv* timidamente
tim·ing ['taɪmɪŋ] (*choosing a time*)
tempismo *m*; *that's good ~!* che
tempismo!
tin [tɪn] *metal* stagno *m*; *container* barattolo *m*
tin·foil ['tɪnfɔɪl] carta *f* stagnola
tinge [tɪndʒ] *n of colour, sadness* sfumatura *f*
tin·gle ['tɪŋgl] *v/i* pizzicare
♦ **tin·ker with** ['tɪŋkə(r)] *v/t* armeggiare con
tin·kle ['tɪŋkl] *n of bell* tintinnio *m*
tinned [tɪnd] *adj* in scatola
'**tin o·pen·er** apriscatole *m inv*
tin·sel ['tɪnsl] fili *mpl* d'argento
tint [tɪnt] **1** *n of colour* sfumatura *f*; *in
hair* riflessante *m* **2** *v/t hair* fare dei
riflessi a
tint·ed ['tɪntɪd] *glasses* fumé *inv*
ti·ny ['taɪnɪ] *adj* piccolissimo
tip¹ [tɪp] *n of stick, finger* punta *f*; *of
cigarette* filtro *m*
tip² [tɪp] **1** *n* (*piece of advice*) consiglio *m*; *money* mancia *f* **2** *v/t* (*pret
& pp* **-ped**) *waiter etc* dare la mancia
a
♦ **tip off** *v/t* fare una soffiata a
♦ **tip over** *v/t jug, liquid* rovesciare; *he
tipped water all over me* mi ha rovesciato dell'acqua addosso
'**tip-off** soffiata *f*
tipped [tɪpt] *adj cigarettes* col filtro
Tipp-Ex® *n* bianchetto *m*

tip·sy ['tɪpsɪ] *adj* alticcio
tip·toe ['tɪptəʊ]: *on* ~ sulla punta dei
piedi
tire¹ ['taɪə(r)] **1** *v/t* stancare **2** *v/i* stancarsi; *he never* ~*s of it* non se ne
stanca mai
tire² ['taɪə(r)] *Am n* → **tyre**
tired ['taɪəd] *adj* stanco; *be* ~ *of s.o.* /
sth essere stanco di qu/qc
tired·ness ['taɪədnɪs] stanchezza *f*
tire·less ['taɪəlɪs] *adj* instancabile
tire·some ['taɪəsəm] *adj* (*annoying*)
fastidioso
tir·ing ['taɪrɪŋ] *adj* stancante
Ti·rol → *Tyrol*
tis·sue ['tɪʃuː] ANAT tessuto *m*;
(*handkerchief*) fazzolettino *m* (di
carta)
'**tis·sue pa·per** carta *f* velina
tit¹ [tɪt] *bird* cincia *f*
tit² [tɪt]: ~ *for tat* pan per focaccia
tit³ [tɪt] *V* (*breast*) tetta *f* V
ti·tle ['taɪtl] titolo *m*; LAW diritto *m*
'**ti·tle-hold·er** SP detentore *m*, -trice *f*
del titolo
'**ti·tle role** *in play, film* ruolo *m* principale
tit·ter ['tɪtə(r)] *v/i* ridacchiare
to [tuː], *unstressed* [tə] **1** *prep* a; ~
Italy in Italia; ~ *Rome* a Roma; *let's
go ~ my place* andiamo a casa mia;
walk ~ the station andare a piedi
alla stazione; ~ *the north / south of
...* a nord / sud di ...; *give sth ~ s.o.*
dare qc a qu; *from Monday ~
Wednesday* da lunedì a mercoledì;
from 10 ~ 15 people tra 10 e 15 persone; *count ~ 20* contare fino a venti; *it's 5 ~ 11* sono le undici meno
cinque **2** *with verbs*: ~ *speak*, ~ *see*
parlare, vedere; *learn ~ drive* imparare a guidare; *nice ~ eat* buono da
mangiare; *too heavy ~ carry* troppo pesante da trasportare; ~ *be
honest* ... per essere franco ...; ~
learn Italian in order to per imparare l'italiano **3** *adv*: ~ *and fro* avanti
e indietro
toad [təʊd] rospo *m*
toad·stool ['təʊdstuːl] fungo *m* velenoso

toast [təʊst] **1** *n* pane *m* tostato; (*drinking*) brindisi *m inv*; **propose a ~ to s.o.** fare un brindisi in onore di qu **2** *v/t* *bread* tostare; *drinking* fare un brindisi a

to·bac·co [təˈbækəʊ] tabacco *m*

to·bac·co·nist [təˈbækənɪst] tabaccaio *m*

to·bog·gan [təˈbɒgən] *n* toboga *m inv*

to·day [təˈdeɪ] oggi

tod·dle [ˈtɒdl] *v/i* *of child* gattonare

tod·dler [ˈtɒdlə(r)] bambino *m*, -a *f* ai primi passi

to-do [təˈduː] F casino *m* F

toe [təʊ] **1** *n* dito *m* del piede; *of shoes, socks* punta *f*; **big ~** alluce *m* **2** *v/t*: **~ the line** attenersi alle direttive

toe·nail [ˈtəʊneɪl] unghia *f* del piede

tof·fee [ˈtɒfɪ] caramella *f* al mou

to·geth·er [təˈgeðə(r)] *adv* insieme

toil [tɔɪl] *n* duro lavoro *m*

toi·let [ˈtɔɪlɪt] gabinetto *m*; *place* bagno *m*, gabinetto *m*; **go to the ~** andare in bagno

'**toi·let pa·per** carta *f* igienica

toi·let·ries [ˈtɔɪlɪtrɪz] *npl* prodotti *mpl* da toilette

'**toi·let roll** rotolo *m* di carta igienica

to·ken [ˈtəʊkən] (*sign*) pegno *m*; *for gambling* gettone *m*; (*gift ~*) buono *m*

told [təʊld] *pret & pp* → **tell**

tol·e·ra·ble [ˈtɒlərəbl] *adj* *pain etc* tollerabile; (*quite good*) accettabile

tol·e·rance [ˈtɒlərəns] tolleranza *f*

tol·e·rant [ˈtɒlərənt] *adj* tollerante

tol·e·rate [ˈtɒləreɪt] *v/t* *noise, person* tollerare; **I won't ~ it!** non intendo tollerarlo!

toll[1] [təʊl] *v/i* *of bell* suonare

toll[2] [təʊl] *n* (*deaths*) bilancio *m* delle vittime

toll[3] [təʊl] *n* *for bridge, road* pedaggio *m*

'**toll booth** casello *m*

'**toll road** strada *f* a pedaggio

to·ma·to [təˈmɑːtəʊ] pomodoro *m*

to·ma·to 'ketch·up ketchup *m inv*

to·ma·to 'sauce *for pasta etc* salsa *f* o

sugo *m* di pomodoro; (*ketchup*) ketchup *m inv*

tomb [tuːm] tomba *f*

tom·boy [ˈtɒmbɔɪ] maschiaccio *m*

tomb·stone [ˈtuːmstəʊn] lapide *f*

tom·cat [ˈtɒmkæt] gatto *m* (maschio)

to·mor·row [təˈmɒrəʊ] domani; **the day after ~** dopodomani; **~ morning** domattina, domani mattina

ton [tʌn] tonnellata *f*

tone [təʊn] *of colour, musical instrument* tonalità *f inv*; *of conversation etc* tono *m*; *of neighbourhood* livello *m* sociale; **~ of voice** tono di voce

♦**tone down** *v/t* *demands, criticism* moderare il tono di

ton·er [ˈtəʊnə(r)] toner *m inv*

tongs [tɒŋz] *npl* pinze *fpl*; *for hair* ferro *m* arricciacapelli

tongue [tʌŋ] *n* lingua *f*

ton·ic [ˈtɒnɪk] MED ricostituente *m*

'**ton·ic (wa·ter)** acqua *f* tonica

to·night [təˈnaɪt] stanotte; (*this evening*) stasera

ton·sil [ˈtɒnsl] tonsilla *f*

ton·sil·li·tis [tɒnsəˈlaɪtɪs] tonsillite *f*

too [tuː] *adv* (*also*) anche; (*excessively*) troppo; **me ~** anch'io; **~ big / hot** troppo grande / caldo; **~ much rice** troppo riso; **~ many mistakes** troppi errori; **eat ~ much** mangiare troppo

took [tʊk] *pret* → **take**

tool [tuːl] attrezzo *m*; *fig* strumento *m*

toot [tuːt] *v/t* F suonare

tooth [tuːθ] (*pl* **teeth** [tiːθ]) dente *m*

'**tooth·ache** mal *m* di denti

'**tooth·brush** spazzolino *m* da denti

tooth·less [ˈtuːθlɪs] sdentato

'**tooth·paste** dentifricio *m*

'**tooth·pick** stuzzicadenti *m inv*

top [tɒp] **1** *n* *of mountain, tree* cima *f*; *of wall, screen* parte *f* alta; *of page, list, street* inizio *m*; (*lid: of bottle etc, pen*) tappo *m*; *of the class, league* testa *f*; (*clothing*) maglia *f*; (MOT: *gear*) marcia *f* più alta; **on ~ of** in cima a; **at the ~ of** *list, tree, mountain* in cima a; *league* in testa a; *page, street* all'inizio di; **get to the ~ of** *company etc* arrive in cima; **get to the ~ of mountain** arrivare alla vetta; **be over the ~** (*exaggerated*) essere esagerato **2** *adj branches* più alto; *floor* ultimo; *management* di alto livello; *official* di alto rango; *player* migliore; *speed, note* massimo **3** *v/t* (*pret & pp* **-ped**): **~ped with cream** ricoperto di crema

♦ **top up** *v/t glass* riempire; **top up the tank** fare il pieno

◆**top** '**hat** tuba *f*

top·ic ['tɒpɪk] argomento *m*

top·ic·al ['tɒpɪkl] *adj* attuale

top·less ['tɒplɪs] *adj* topless *inv*

top·most ['tɒpməʊst] *adj branches, floor* più alto

top·ping ['tɒpɪŋ] *on pizza* guarnizione *f*

top·ple ['tɒpl] **1** *v/i* crollare **2** *v/t government* far cadere

◆**top** '**se·cret** *adj* top secret *inv*

top·sy-tur·vy [tɒpsɪ'tɜːvɪ] *adj* sottosopra *inv*

torch [tɔːtʃ] *Br* pila *f*; *with flame* torcia *f*

◆**tore** [tɔː(r)] *pret* → **tear**

tor·ment ['tɔːment] **1** *n* tormento *m* **2** *v/t* [tɔː'ment] *person, animal* tormentare; **~ed by doubt** tormentato dal dubbio

torn [tɔːn] *pp* → **tear**

tor·na·do [tɔː'neɪdəʊ] tornado *m*

tor·pe·do [tɔː'piːdəʊ] **1** *n* siluro *m* **2** *v/t* silurare; *fig* far saltare

tor·rent ['tɒrənt] torrente *m*; *of lava* fiume *m*; *of abuse, words* valanga *f*

tor·ren·tial [tə'renʃl] *adj rain* torrenziale

◆**tor·toise** ['tɔːtəs] tartaruga *f*

tor·ture ['tɔːtʃə(r)] **1** *n* tortura *f* **2** *v/t* torturare

toss [tɒs] **1** *v/t ball* lanciare; *rider* disarcionare; *salad* mescolare; **~ a coin** fare testa o croce **2** *v/i*: **~ and turn** rigirarsi

◆**to·tal** ['təʊtl] **1** *n* totale *m* **2** *adj amount, disaster* totale; *stranger* perfetto

to·tal·i·tar·i·an [təʊtælɪ'teərɪən] *adj* totalitario

to·tal·ly ['təʊtəlɪ] *adv* totalmente, completamente

tot·ter ['tɒtə(r)] *v/i of person* barcollare

touch [tʌtʃ] **1** *n* tocco *m*; *sense* tatto *m*; *small detail* tocco *m*; *in rugby* touche *f*; **he felt a ~ on his shoulder** si è sentito toccare sulla spalla; **lose one's ~** perdere la mano; **kick the ball into ~** calciare la palla fuoricampo; **lose ~ with s.o.** perdere i contatti con qu; **keep in ~ with s.o.** rimanere in contatto con qu; **we kept in ~** siamo rimasti in contatto; **be out of ~** *with news* non essere al corrente; *with people* non avere contatti; **a ~ of** *little bit* un po' di ... **2** *v/t* toccare; *emotionally* commuovere **3** *v/i* toccare; *of two lines etc* toccarsi

◆**touch down** *v/i of aeroplane* atterrare; *SP* fare meta

◆**touch on** *v/t* (*mention*) accennare a

◆**touch up** *v/t photo* ritoccare; *sexually* palpeggiare

touch-and-'go: **it was ~** la situazione era critica

touch·down ['tʌtʃdaʊn] *of aeroplane* atterraggio *m*

touch·ing ['tʌtʃɪŋ] *adj* commovente

touch·line ['tʌtʃlaɪn] *SP* linea *f* laterale

'**touch screen** schermo *m* tattile

touch·y ['tʌtʃɪ] *adj person* suscettibile

tough [tʌf] *adj person* forte; *question, exam, meat, punishment* duro; *material* resistente

◆**tough·en up** ['tʌfn] *v/t person* rendere più forte

'**tough guy** F duro *m* F

tour [tʊə(r)] **1** *n* visita *f* **2** *v/t area* fare il giro di

'**tour guide** guida *f* turistica

tour·i·sm ['tʊərɪzm] turismo *m*

tour·i·st ['tʊərɪst] turista *m/f*

'**tour·ist at·trac·tion** attrazione *f* turistica; '**tour·ist in·dus·try** industria *f* del turismo; '**tour·ist (in·for·'ma·tion) of·fice** azienda *f* (autonoma) di soggiorno; '**tour·ist sea·son** stagione *f* turistica

T

tour·na·ment ['tʊənəmənt] torneo *m*

'**tour op·er·a·tor** operatore *m* turistico

tous·led ['taʊzld] *adj hair* scompigliato

tout [taʊt] *n* bagarino *m*

tow [təʊ] **1** *v/t car, boat* rimorchiare **2** *n*: *give so. a* ~ rimorchiare qu

♦ **tow away** *v/t car* portare via col carro attrezzi

to·wards [tə'wɔːdz] *prep* verso; *rude* ~ maleducato nei confronti di; *work* ~ (*achieving*) *sth* lavorare per (raggiungere) qc

tow·el ['taʊəl] asciugamano *m*

tow·er ['taʊə(r)] torre *f*

♦ **tower over** *v/t* sovrastare

'**tow·er block** condominio *m* a torre

town [taʊn] città *f inv*; *opposed to city* cittadina *f*

town 'cen·tre centro *m*; **town 'coun·cil** consiglio *m* comunale; **town 'coun·cil·lor** consigliere *m*, -a *f* comunale; **town 'hall** municipio *m*

'**tow·rope** cavo *m* da rimorchio

tox·ic ['tɒksɪk] *adj* tossico

tox·ic 'waste scorie *fpl* tossiche

tox·in ['tɒksɪn] BIO tossina *f*

toy [tɔɪ] giocattolo *m*

♦ **toy with** *v/t object* giocherellare con; *idea* accarezzare

'**toy shop** negozio *m* di giocattoli

trace [treɪs] **1** *n of substance* traccia *f* **2** *v/t* (*find*) rintracciare; (*follow: footsteps*) seguire; (*draw*) tracciare

track [træk] *n* (*path*) sentiero *m*; *on race course* pista *f*; (*race course*) circuito *m*; RAIL binario *m*; *on record, CD* brano *m*; *keep* ~ *of sth* tenersi al passo con qc; *keep record of* registrare

♦ **track down** *v/t* rintracciare

'**track·suit** tuta *f* (da ginnastica)

trac·tor ['træktə(r)] trattore *m*

trade [treɪd] **1** *n* (*commerce*) commercio *m*; (*profession, craft*) mestiere *m* **2** *v/i* (*do business*) essere in attività; ~ *in sth* commerciare in qc **3** *v/t* (*exchange*) scambiare; ~ *sth for sth* scambiare qc con qc

♦ **trade in** *v/t when buying* dare in permuta

'**trade fair** fiera *f* campionaria

'**trade·mark** marchio *m* registrato

trad·er ['treɪdə(r)] commerciante *m/f*

trade 'se·cret segreto *m* industriale

trades·man ['treɪdzmən] *plumber etc* operaio *m*; *milkman etc* fornitore *m*

trade(s) 'u·nion sindacato *m*

tra·di·tion [trə'dɪʃn] tradizione *f*

tra·di·tion·al [trə'dɪʃnl] *adj* tradizionale

tra·di·tion·al·ly [trə'dɪʃnlɪ] *adv* tradizionalmente

traf·fic ['træfɪk] *n on roads, in drugs* traffico *m*; *at airport* traffico *m* aereo

♦ **traffic in** *v/t* (*pret & pp* -**ked**) *drugs* trafficare

'**traf·fic cop** F vigile *m* (urbano); '**traf·fic is·land** isola *f* salvagente; '**traf·fic jam** ingorgo *m*; '**traf·fic lights** *npl* semaforo *m*; '**traf·fic po·lice** polizia *f* stradale; '**traf·fic sign** segnale *m* stradale; '**traf·fic war·den** ausiliario *m* (del traffico)

tra·ge·dy ['trædʒədɪ] tragedia *f*

tra·gic ['trædʒɪk] *adj* tragico

trail [treɪl] **1** *n* (*path*) sentiero *m*; *of person, animal* tracce *fpl*; *of blood* scia *f* **2** *v/t* (*follow*) seguire; (*drag*) trascinare; *caravan etc* trainare **3** *v/i* (*lag behind*) trascinarsi; *they're* ~*ing 3-1* stanno perdendo 3 a 1

trail·er ['treɪlə(r)] *pulled by vehicle* rimorchio *m*; *of film* trailer *m inv*; *Am* (*caravan*) roulotte *f inv*

train¹ [treɪn] *n* treno *m*; *go by* ~ andare in treno

train² [treɪn] **1** *v/t team, athlete* allenare; *employee* formare; *dog* addestrare **2** *v/i of team, athlete* allenarsi; *of teacher etc* fare il tirocinio

train·ee [treɪ'niː] apprendista *m/f*

train·er ['treɪnə(r)] SP allenatore *m*, -trice *f*; *of dog* addestratore *m*, -trice *f*

train·ers ['treɪnəz] *npl shoes* scarpe *fpl* da ginnastica

train·ing [treɪnɪŋ] *of new staff*

formazione *f*; SP allenamento *m*; **be in** ~ SP allenarsi; **be out of** ~ SP essere fuori allenamento

'**train·ing course** corso *m* di formazione

'**train·ing scheme** programma *m* di formazione

'**train sta·tion** stazione *f* ferroviaria

trait [treɪt] tratto *m*

trai·tor ['treɪtə(r)] traditore *m*, -trice *f*

tram [træm] tram *m inv*

tramp [træmp] **1** *n* (*vagabond*) barbone *m*, -a *f* **2** *v/i* camminare con passo pesante

tram·ple ['træmpl] *v/t*: **be ~d to death** morire travolto; **be ~d underfoot** essere calpestato

♦ **trample on** *v/t person, object* calpestare

tram·po·line ['træmpəli:n] trampolino *m*

trance [trɑːns] trance *f inv*; **go into a** ~ cadere in trance

tran·quil ['træŋkwɪl] *adj* tranquillo

tran·quil·li·ty [træŋ'kwɪlətɪ] tranquillità *f*

tran·quil·liz·er ['træŋkwɪlaɪzə(r)] tranquillante *m*

trans·act [træn'zækt] *v/t deal, business* trattare

trans·ac·tion [træn'zækʃn] transazione *f*

trans·at·lan·tic [trænzət'læntɪk] *adj* transatlantico

tran·scen·den·tal [trænsen'dentl] *adj* trascendentale

tran·script ['trænskrɪpt] trascrizione *f*

trans·fer [træns'fɜː(r)] **1** *v/t* (*pret & pp -red*) trasferire; LAW cedere **2** *v/i* (*pret & pp -red*) cambiare **3** *n* ['trænsfɜː(r)] trasferimento *m*; LAW cessione *f*; *of money* bonifico *m* bancario

trans·fer·a·ble [træns'fɜːrəbl] *adj ticket* trasferibile

'**trans·fer fee** *for football player* prezzo *m* d'acquisto

trans·form [træns'fɔːm] *v/t* trasformare

trans·for·ma·tion [trænsfə'meɪʃn] trasformazione *f*

trans·form·er [træns'fɔːmə(r)] ELEC trasformatore *m*

trans·fu·sion [træns'fjuːʒn] trasfusione *f*

tran·sis·tor [træn'zɪstə(r)] transistor *m inv*; *radio* radiolina *f*

tran·sit ['trænzɪt]: **in** ~ *of goods, passengers* in transito

tran·si·tion [træn'sɪʒn] transizione *f*

tran·si·tion·al [træn'sɪʒnl] *adj* di transizione

'**tran·sit lounge** *at airport* sala *f* passeggeri in transito

'**tran·sit pas·sen·ger** passeggero *m*, -a *f* in transito

trans·late [træns'leɪt] *v/t* tradurre

trans·la·tion [træns'leɪʃn] traduzione *f*

trans·la·tor [træns'leɪtə(r)] traduttore *m*, -trice *f*

trans·mis·sion [trænz'mɪʃn] trasmissione *f*

trans·mit [trænz'mɪt] *v/t* (*pret & pp -ted*) *news, programme, disease* trasmettere

trans·mit·ter [trænz'mɪtə(r)] *for radio, TV* trasmettitore *m*

trans·par·en·cy [træns'pærənsɪ] PHOT diapositiva *f*

trans·par·ent [træns'pærənt] *adj* trasparente

trans·plant [træns'plɑːnt] **1** *v/t* MED trapiantare **2** *n* ['trænsplɑːnt] MED trapianto *m*

trans·port [træn'spɔːt] **1** *v/t goods, people* trasportare **2** *n* ['trænspɔːt] *of goods, people* trasporto *m*; *means of transport* mezzo *m* di trasporto; **public** ~ i trasporti pubblici

trans·por·ta·tion [trænspɔː'teɪʃn] *of goods, people* trasporto *m*; **means of** ~ mezzo *m* di trasporto

trans·ves·tite [træns'vestaɪt] travestito *m*

trap [træp] **1** *n* trappola *f*; *question* tranello *m*; **set a** ~ **for s.o.** tendere una trappola a qu **2** *v/t* (*pret & pp -ped*) *animal* intrappolare; *person* incastrare; **be ~ped** *by enemy,*

T

flames, landslide etc essere intrappolato

trap·door ['træpdɔ:(r)] botola f

tra·peze [trə'piːz] trapezio m

trap·pings ['træpɪŋz] *npl of power* segni *mpl* esteriori

trash [træʃ] (*garbage*) spazzatura f; *poor product* robaccia f; *despicable person* fetente m/f

trash·y [træʃɪ] *adj goods, novel* scadente

trau·mat·ic [trɔ:'mætɪk] *adj* traumatico

trau·ma·tize ['trɔ:mətaɪz] *v/t* traumatizzare

trav·el ['trævl] **1** *n* viaggiare m; ~**s** viaggi *mpl* **2** *v/i* (*pret & pp* **-led**, *Am* **-ed**) viaggiare; *I ~ to work by train* vado a lavorare in treno **3** *v/t* (*pret & pp* **-led**, *Am* **-ed**) *miles* percorrere

'**trav·el a·gen·cy** agenzia f di viaggio; '**trav·el a·gent** agente m/f di viaggio; '**trav·el bag** borsa f da viaggio; '**trav·el ex·penses** *npl* spese *fpl* di viaggio; '**trav·el in·sur·ance** assicurazione f di viaggio

trav·el·er *Am*, **trav·el·ler** ['trævələ(r)] viaggiatore m, -trice f

'**trav·el·er's check** *Am*, '**trav·el·ler's cheque** traveller's cheque *m inv*

'**trav·el pro·gram** *Am*, '**trav·el pro·gramme** *on TV etc* programma m di viaggi

trawl·er ['trɔ:lə(r)] peschereccio m

tray [treɪ] *for food, photocopier* vassoio m; *to go in oven* teglia f

treach·er·ous ['tretʃərəs] *adj* traditore, infido

treach·er·y ['tretʃərɪ] tradimento m

tread [tred] **1** *n* passo m; *of staircase* gradino m; *of tyre* battistrada m *inv* **2** *v/i* (*pret* **trod**, *pp* **trodden**) camminare

♦ **tread on** *v/t s.o.'s foot* pestare

trea·son ['triːzn] tradimento m

trea·sure ['treʒə(r)] **1** *n also person* tesoro m **2** *v/t gift etc* custodire gelosamente

trea·sur·er ['treʒərə(r)] tesoriere m, -a f

treat [triːt] **1** *n* trattamento m speciale; *it was a real ~* è stato magnifico; *I have a ~ for you* ho una sorpresa per te; *it's my ~* (*I'm paying*) offro io **2** *v/t* trattare; *illness* curare; *~ s.o. to sth* offrire qc a qu

treat·ment ['triːtmənt] trattamento m; *of illness* cura f

treat·y ['triːtɪ] trattato m

tre·ble¹ ['trebl] *n* MUS: *boy's voice* voce f bianca; *register* alti *mpl*

tre·ble² ['trebl] **1** *adv*: ~ *the price* il triplo del prezzo **2** *v/i* triplicarsi

tree [triː] albero m

trem·ble ['trembl] *v/i* tremare

tre·men·dous [trɪ'mendəs] *adj* (*very good*) fantastico; (*enormous*) enorme

tre·men·dous·ly [trɪ'mendəslɪ] *adv* (*very*) incredibilmente; (*a lot*) moltissimo

trem·or ['tremə(r)] *of earth* scossa f

trench [trentʃ] trincea f

trend [trend] tendenza f

trend·y ['trendɪ] *adj* alla moda

tres·pass ['trespəs] *v/i* invadere una proprietà privata; *no ~ing* divieto d'accesso

♦ **trespass on** *v/t s.o.'s land, privacy* invadere; *s.o.'s rights, time* abusare di

tres·pass·er ['trespəsə(r)] intruso m, -a f

tri·al ['traɪəl] LAW processo m; *of equipment* prova f; *on ~* LAW sotto processo; *stand ~ for sth* essere processato per qc; *have sth on ~ equipment* avere qc in prova

tri·al 'pe·ri·od periodo m di prova

tri·an·gle ['traɪæŋgl] triangolo m

tri·an·gu·lar [traɪ'æŋgjʊlə(r)] *adj* triangolare

tribe [traɪb] tribù f *inv*

tri·bu·nal [traɪ'bjuːnl] tribunale m

tri·bu·ta·ry ['trɪbjʊtərɪ] *of river* affluente m

trick [trɪk] **1** *n to deceive* stratagemma m; (*knack*) trucco m; *a ~ of the light* un effetto di luce; *play a ~ on s.o.* fare uno scherzo a qu **2** *v/t* ingannare; **~ *s.o.* into doing sth** convincere qu con l'inganno a fare qc

trick·e·ry ['trɪkərɪ] truffa f

trick·le ['trɪkl] **1** n filo m; **a ~ of replies** poche risposte sporadiche **2** v/i gocciolare

trick·ster ['trɪkstə(r)] truffatore m, -trice f

trick·y ['trɪkɪ] adj (difficult) complicato

tri·cy·cle ['traɪsɪkl] triciclo m

tri·fle ['traɪfl] n (triviality) inezia f; pudding zuppa f inglese

tri·fling ['traɪflɪŋ] adj insignificante

trig·ger ['trɪgə(r)] n on gun grilletto m; on camcorder pulsante m (di accensione)

♦ trigger off v/t scatenare

trim [trɪm] **1** adj (neat) ordinato; figure snello **2** v/t (pret & pp **-med**) hair, hedge spuntare; budget, costs tagliare; (decorate: dress) ornare **3** n (light cut) spuntata f; **in good ~** in buone condizioni

trim·ming ['trɪmɪŋ] on clothes ornamento m; **with all the ~s** con tutti gli annessi e connessi

trin·ket ['trɪŋkɪt] ninnolo m

tri·o ['triːəʊ] MUS trio m

trip [trɪp] **1** n (journey) viaggio m, gita f **2** v/i (pret & pp **-ped**) (stumble) inciampare (**over** in) **3** v/t (pret & pp **-ped**) (make fall) fare inciampare

♦ trip up **1** v/t (make fall) fare inciampare; cause to make a mistake confondere **2** v/i (stumble) inciampare; (make a mistake) sbagliarsi

tripe [traɪp] trippa f

trip·le ['trɪpl] → **treble²**

trip·lets ['trɪplɪts] npl tre gemelli mpl

tri·pod ['traɪpɒd] PHOT treppiedi m inv

trite [traɪt] adj trito

tri·umph ['traɪʌmf] n trionfo m

triv·i·al ['trɪvɪəl] adj banale

triv·i·al·i·ty [trɪvɪ'ælətɪ] banalità f inv

trod [trɒd] pret → **tread**

trod·den ['trɒdn] pp → **tread**

trol·ley ['trɒlɪ] in supermarket, at

airport carrello m

trom·bone [trɒm'bəʊn] trombone m

troops [truːps] npl truppe fpl

tro·phy ['trəʊfɪ] trofeo m

trop·ic ['trɒpɪk] tropico m

trop·i·cal ['trɒpɪkl] adj tropicale

trop·ics ['trɒpɪks] npl tropici mpl

trot [trɒt] v/i (pret & pp **-ted**) trottare

trou·ble ['trʌbl] **1** n (difficulties) problemi mpl; (inconvenience) fastidio m; (disturbance) disordini mpl; **go to a lot of ~ to do sth** darsi molto da fare per fare qc; **no ~!** nessun problema!; **the ~ with you is** ... il tuo problema è ...; **get into ~** mettersi nei guai **2** v/t (worry) preoccupare; (bother, disturb) disturbare; of back, liver etc dare dei fastidi a

trou·ble-free senza problemi

trou·ble·mak·er attaccabrighe m/f

trou·ble·shoot·er (mediator) mediatore m, trice f

trou·ble·shoot·ing mediazione f; in software manual ricerca f problemi e soluzioni

trou·ble·some ['trʌbləsəm] adj fastidioso

trou·sers ['traʊzəz] npl pantaloni mpl; **a pair of ~** un paio di pantaloni

trou·ser suit tailleur m inv pantaloni

trout [traʊt] (pl trout) trota f

tru·ant ['truːənt]: **play ~** marinare la scuola

truce [truːs] tregua f

truck [trʌk] (lorry) camion m inv

trudge [trʌdʒ] **1** v/i arrancare; **~ around the shops** trascinarsi per i negozi **2** n camminata f stancante

true [truː] adj vero; **come ~ of hopes, dream** realizzarsi

tru·ly ['truːlɪ] adv davvero; **Yours ~** distinti saluti

trum·pet ['trʌmpɪt] tromba f

trum·pet·er ['trʌmpɪtə(r)] trombettiere f

trun·cheon ['trʌntʃn] manganello m

trunk [trʌŋk] of tree, body tronco m; of elephant proboscide f; (large case) baule m; Am MOT bagagliaio m inv

trunks [trʌŋks] npl for swimming calzoncini mpl da bagno

trust [trʌst] **1** n fiducia f; FIN fondo m fiduciario; COM trust m inv **2** v/t fidarsi di; **I ~ you** mi fido di te

trusted ['trʌstɪd] adj fidato

trust·ee [trʌs'tiː] amministratore m, -trice f fiduciario, -a

trust·ful, trust·ing ['trʌstful, 'trʌstɪŋ] adj fiducioso

trust·wor·thy ['trʌstwɜːðɪ] adj affidabile

truth [truːθ] verità f inv

truth·ful ['truːθful] adj account veritiero; person sincero

try [traɪ] **1** v/t (pret & pp **-ied**) provare; LAW processare; **~ to do sth** provare a fare qc, cercare di fare qc **2** v/i (pret & pp **-ied**) provare, tentare; **you must ~ harder** devi provare con più impegno **3** n tentativo m; in rugby meta f; **can I have a ~?** of food posso assaggiare?; **at doing sth** posso fare un tentativo?

♦ **try on** v/t clothes provare

♦ **try out** v/t new machine, method provare

try·ing ['traɪɪŋ] adj (annoying) difficile

T-shirt ['tiːʃɜːt] maglietta f

tub [tʌb] (bath) vasca f da bagno; of liquid tinozza f; for yoghurt, icecream barattolo m

tub·by ['tʌbɪ] adj tozzo

tube [tjuːb] (pipe) tubo m; (underground railway) metropolitana f; of toothpaste, ointment tubetto m

tube·less ['tjuːblɪs] adj tyre senza camera d'aria

tu·ber·cu·lo·sis [tjuːbɜːkjuˈləʊsɪs] tubercolosi f

tuck [tʌk] **1** n in dress pince f inv **2** v/t: **~ sth into sth** infilare qc in qc

♦ **tuck away** v/t (put away) mettere via; (eat quickly) sbafare; **be tucked away** of house, village essere nascosto

♦ **tuck in 1** v/t children rimboccare le coperte a; sheets rimboccare **2** v/i (eat) mangiare; (start eating) incominciare a mangiare

♦ **tuck up** v/t sleeves etc rimboccarsi; **tuck s.o. up in bed** rimboccare le coperte a qu

Tues·day ['tjuːzdeɪ] martedì m inv

tuft [tʌft] ciuffo m

tug [tʌg] **1** n (pull) tirata f; NAUT rimorchiatore m; **I felt a ~ at my sleeve** mi sono sentito tirare la manica **2** v/t (pret & pp **-ged**) (pull) tirare

tu·i·tion [tjuːˈɪʃn] lezioni fpl

tu·lip ['tjuːlɪp] tulipano m

tum·ble ['tʌmbl] v/i ruzzolare; of wall, prices crollare

tum·ble·down ['tʌmbldaʊn] adj in rovina, fatiscente

tum·ble-dry·er ['tʌmbldraɪə(r)] asciugatrice f

tum·bler ['tʌmblə(r)] for drinker bicchiere m (senza stelo); in circus acrobata m/f

tum·my ['tʌmɪ] F pancia f

'tum·my ache mal m di pancia

tu·mour ['tjuːmə(r)] tumore m

tu·mult ['tjuːmʌlt] tumulto m

tu·mul·tu·ous [tjuːˈmʌltjʊəs] adj tumultuoso

tu·na ['tjuːnə] tonno m; **~ salad** insalata f di tonno

tune [tjuːn] **1** n motivo m; **in ~** instrument accordato; person intonato; **out of ~** instrument scordato; person stonato **2** v/t instrument accordare; engine mettere a punto

♦ **tune in** v/i of radio, TV sintonizzarsi

♦ **tune in to** v/t radio, TV sintonizzarsi su

♦ **tune up 1** v/i of orchestra, players accordare gli strumenti **2** v/t engine mettere a punto

tune·ful ['tjuːnful] adj melodioso

tun·er ['tjuːnə(r)] (hi-fi) sintonizzatore m, tuner m inv

tune-up ['tjuːnʌp] of engine messa f a punto

tu·nic ['tjuːnɪk] tunica f; protective grembiule m; of uniform giacca f

tun·nel ['tʌnl] n galleria f, tunnel m inv

tur·bine ['tɜːbaɪn] turbina f

tur·bu·lence ['tɜːbjʊləns] *in air travel* turbolenza *f*

tur·bu·lent ['tɜːbjʊlənt] *adj* turbolento

turf [tɜːf] tappeto *m* erboso; (*piece*) zolla *f*

Tu·rin [tjʊ'rɪn] Torino *f*

Turk [tɜːk] turco *m*, -a *f*

Tur·key ['tɜːkɪ] Turchia *f*

tur·key ['tɜːkɪ] tacchino *m*

Turk·ish ['tɜːkɪʃ] **1** *adj* turco **2** *n language* turco *m*

tur·moil ['tɜːmɔɪl] agitazione *f*

turn [tɜːn] **1** *n* (*rotation*) giro *m*; *in road* curva *f*; *in variety show* numero *m*; **take ~s in doing sth** fare a turno a fare qc; **it's my ~** è il mio turno, tocca a me; **it's not your ~ yet** non è ancora il tuo turno; **take a ~ at the wheel** prendere il volante per un po'; **do s.o. a good ~** fare un favore a qu **2** *v/t wheel, corner* girare; **~ one's back on s.o.** girare le spalle a qu **3** *v/i of driver, car, wheel* girare; (*become*) diventare; **~ right/left here** gira a destra/sinistra qui; **it has ~ed sour/cold** è diventato acido/freddo; **he has ~ed 40** ha compiuto 40 anni

♦ **turn around 1** *v/t object* girare; *company* dare una svolta positiva a; (COM: *deal with*) eseguire; *order* evadere **2** *v/i of person* girarsi; *of driver* girare

♦ **turn away 1** *v/t* (*send away*) mandare via **2** *v/i* (*walk away*) andare via; (*look away*) girarsi dall'altra parte

♦ **turn back 1** *v/t edges, sheets* ripiegare **2** *v/i of walkers etc* tornare indietro; *in course of action* tirarsi indietro

♦ **turn down** *v/t offer, invitation* rifiutare; *volume, TV, heating* abbassare; *edge, collar* ripiegare

♦ **turn in 1** *v/i* (*go to bed*) andare a letto **2** *v/t to police* denunciare

♦ **turn off 1** *v/t TV, engine* spegnere; *tap* chiudere; F (*sexually*) far passare la voglia a **2** *v/i of driver* svoltare

♦ **turn on 1** *v/t TV, engine* accendere; *tap* aprire; F (*sexually*) eccitare **2** *v/i of machine* accendersi

♦ **turn out 1** *v/t lights* spegnere **2** *v/i*: **as it turned out** come è emerso; **it turned out well** è andata bene

♦ **turn over 1** *v/i in bed* girarsi; *of vehicle* capottare **2** *v/t object, page* girare; FIN fatturare

♦ **turn up 1** *v/t collar, volume, heating* alzare **2** *v/i* (*arrive*) arrivare

turn·ing ['tɜːnɪŋ] svolta *f*

'turn·ing point svolta *f* decisiva

tur·nip ['tɜːnɪp] rapa *f*

'turn·out *of people* affluenza *f*; **'turn·o·ver** FIN fatturato *m*; *of staff* ricambio *m*; **'turn·stile** cancelletto *m* girevole; **'turn·ta·ble** piatto *m*; **'turn·up** *on trousers* risvolto *m*

tur·quoise ['tɜːkwɔɪz] *adj* turchese

tur·ret ['tʌrɪt] *of castle, tank* torretta *f*

tur·tle ['tɜːtl] tartaruga *f* marina

tur·tle·neck 'sweater maglia *f* a lupetto

Tus·ca·ny ['tʌskənɪ] Toscana *f*

tusk [tʌsk] zanna *f*

tu·tor ['tjuːtə(r)] EDU *insegnante universitario che segue un piccolo gruppo di studenti*; (*private*) ~ insegnante *m/f* privato, -a

tu·to·ri·al [tjuː'tɔːrɪəl] *n at university* incontro *m* con il tutor

tu·xe·do [tʌk'siːdəʊ] *Am* smoking *m inv*

TV [tiː'viː] tv *f inv*; **on ~** alla tv

T'V din·ner piatto *m* pronto; **T'V guide** guida *f* dei programmi tv; **T'V pro·gramme** programma *m* televisivo

twang [twæŋ] **1** *n in voice* suono *m* nasale **2** *v/t guitar string* vibrare

tweez·ers ['twiːzəz] *npl* pinzette *fpl*

twelfth [twelfθ] *n & adj* dodicesimo, -a

twelve [twelv] dodici

twen·ti·eth ['twentɪɪθ] *n & adj* ventesimo, -a

twen·ty ['twentɪ] venti

twice [twaɪs] *adv* due volte; **~ as much** il doppio; **~ as fast** veloce due volte tanto

twid·dle ['twɪdl] *v/t* girare; **~ one's**

thumbs girarsi i pollici

twig [twɪg] *n* ramoscello *m*

twi·light ['twaɪlaɪt] crepuscolo *m*

twin [twɪn] gemello *m*

'twin beds *npl* due lettini *mpl*

twinge [twɪndʒ] *of pain* fitta *f*

twin·kle ['twɪŋkl] *v/i of stars, eyes* scintillare

twin 'room camera *f* a due letti

'twin town città *f inv* gemellata

twirl [twɜːl] **1** *v/t* fare roteare **2** *n of cream etc* ricciolo *m*

twist [twɪst] **1** *v/t* attorcigliare; ~ **one's ankle** prendere una storta **2** *v/i of road* snodarsi; *of river* serpeggiare **3** *n in rope* attorcigliata *f*; *in road* curva *f*; *in plot, story* svolta *f*

twist·y ['twɪstɪ] *adj road* contorto

twit [twɪt] F scemo *m*, -a *f*

twitch [twɪtʃ] **1** *n nervous* spasmo *m* **2** *v/i* (*jerk*) contrarsi

twit·ter ['twɪtə(r)] *v/i* cinguettare

two [tuː] due; *the* ~ *of them* loro due

'two-faced *adj* falso; **'two-piece** (*woman's suit*) tailleur *m inv*; **'two-stroke** *adj engine* a due tempi; **two-way 'traf·fic** traffico *m* nei

due sensi di marcia

ty·coon [taɪ'kuːn] magnate *m*

type [taɪp] **1** *n* (*sort*) tipo *m*; *what ~ of ...?* che tipo di ...? **2** *v/t & v/i* (*use a keyboard*) battere (a macchina)

type·writ·er ['taɪpraɪtə(r)] macchina *f* da scrivere

ty·phoid ['taɪfɔɪd] febbre *f* tifoide

ty·phoon [taɪ'fuːn] tifone *m*

ty·phus ['taɪfəs] tifo *m*

typ·i·cal ['tɪpɪkl] *adj* tipico; *that's ~ of you / him!* tipico!

typ·i·cal·ly ['tɪpɪklɪ] *adv*: ~ *American* tipicamente americano; *he would* ~ *arrive late* arriva sempre tardi

typ·ist ['taɪpɪst] dattilografo *m*, -a *f*

ty·ran·ni·cal [tɪ'rænɪkl] *adj* tirannico

ty·ran·nize [tɪ'rænaɪz] *v/t* tiranneggiare

ty·ran·ny ['tɪrənɪ] tirannia *f*

ty·rant ['taɪrənt] tiranno *m*, -a *f*

tyre ['taɪə(r)] gomma *f*, pneumatico *m*

Ty·rol [tɪ'rɒl] Tirolo *m*

Ty·ro·le·an [tɪrə'liːən] *adj* tirolese

Tyr·rhe·ni·an Sea [taɪ'riːnɪən] mar *m* Tirreno

U

ug·ly ['ʌglɪ] *adj* brutto

UK [juː'keɪ] *abbr* (= **United Kingdom**) Regno *m* Unito

ul·cer ['ʌlsə(r)] ulcera *f*

ul·ti·mate ['ʌltɪmət] *adj* (*best, definitive*) definitivo; (*final*) ultimo; (*basic*) fondamentale

ul·ti·mate·ly ['ʌltɪmətlɪ] *adv* (*in the end*) in definitiva

ul·ti·ma·tum [ʌltɪ'meɪtəm] ultimatum *m inv*

ul·tra·sound ['ʌltrəsaʊnd] MED ecografia *f*

ul·tra·vi·o·let [ʌltrə'vaɪələt] *adj* ultravioletto

um·bil·i·cal cord [ʌm'bɪlɪkl] cordone *m* ombelicale

um·brel·la [ʌm'brelə] ombrello *m*

um·pire ['ʌmpaɪə(r)] *n* arbitro *m*

ump·teen [ʌmp'tiːn] *adj* F ennesimo

UN [juː'en] *abbr* (= **United Nations**) ONU *f inv* (= Organizzazione *f* delle Nazioni Unite)

un·a·ble [ʌn'eɪbl] *adj*: *be ~ to do sth not know how to* non saper fare qc; *not be in a position to* non poter fare qc

un·ac·cept·a·ble [ʌnək'septəbl] *adj* inaccettabile; *it is ~ that ...* è inaccettabile che …

un·ac·count·a·ble [ʌnəˈkaʊntəbl] *adj* inspiegabile

un·ac·cus·tomed [ʌnəˈkʌstəmd] *adj:* **be ~ to sth** non essere abituato a qc

un·a·dul·ter·at·ed [ʌnəˈdʌltəreɪtɪd] *adj (fig: absolute)* puro; *activities* anti-americano

u·nan·i·mous [juːˈnænɪməs] *adj verdict* unanime; **be ~ on** essere unanimi su

u·nan·i·mous·ly [juːˈnænɪməslɪ] *adv vote, decide* all'unanimità

un·ap·proach·a·ble [ʌnəˈprəʊtʃəbl] *adj person* inavvicinabile

un·armed [ʌnˈɑːmd] *adj person* disarmato; **~ combat** combattimento senz'armi

un·as·sum·ing [ʌnəˈsjuːmɪŋ] *adj* senza pretese

un·at·tached [ʌnəˈtætʃt] *adj without a partner* libero

un·at·tend·ed [ʌnəˈtendɪd] *adj* incustodito; **leave sth ~** lasciare qc incustodito

un·au·thor·ized [ʌnˈɔːθəraɪzd] *adj* non autorizzato

un·a·void·a·ble [ʌnəˈvɔɪdəbl] *adj* inevitabile

un·a·void·a·bly [ʌnəˈvɔɪdəblɪ] *adv* inevitabilmente; **be ~ detained** essere trattenuto per cause di forza maggiore

un·a·ware [ʌnəˈweə(r)] *adj:* **be ~ of** non rendersi conto di

un·a·wares [ʌnəˈweəz] *adv:* **catch s.o. ~** prendere qu alla sprovvista

un·bal·anced [ʌnˈbælənst] *adj* non equilibrato; PSYCH squilibrato

un·bear·a·ble [ʌnˈbeərəbl] *adj* insopportabile

un·beat·a·ble [ʌnˈbiːtəbl] *adj team, quality* imbattibile

un·beat·en [ʌnˈbiːtn] *adj team* imbattuto

un·be·lie·va·ble [ʌnbɪˈliːvəbl] *adj* incredibile

un·bi·as(s)ed [ʌnˈbaɪəst] *adj* imparziale

un·block [ʌnˈblɒk] *v/t pipe* sbloccare

un·born [ʌnˈbɔːn] *adj* non ancora nato

un·break·a·ble [ʌnˈbreɪkəbl] *adj plates* infrangibile; *world record* imbattibile

un·but·ton [ʌnˈbʌtn] *v/t* sbottonare

un·called-for [ʌnˈkɔːldfɔː(r)] *adj* ingiustificato

un·can·ny [ʌnˈkænɪ] *adj resemblance, skill* sorprendente; *(worrying: feeling)* inquietante

un·ceas·ing [ʌnˈsiːsɪŋ] *adj* incessante

un·cer·tain [ʌnˈsɜːtn] *adj future, weather* incerto; *origins* dubbio; **what will happen? – it's ~** cosa succederà? – non si sa; **be ~ about sth** non essere certo su qc

un·cer·tain·ty [ʌnˈsɜːtntɪ] *of the future* incertezza *f;* **there is still ~ about …** ci sono ancora dubbi su …

un·checked [ʌnˈtʃekt] *adj:* **let sth go ~** non controllare qc

un·cle [ˈʌŋkl] zio *m*

un·com·for·ta·ble [ʌnˈkʌmftəbl] *adj* scomodo; **feel ~ about sth** sentirsi a disagio per qc; **I feel ~ with him** mi sento a disagio con lui

un·com·mon [ʌnˈkɒmən] *adj* raro; **it's not ~** non è raro

un·com·pro·mis·ing [ʌnˈkɒmprəmaɪzɪŋ] *adj* fermo; *in a negative way* intransigente

un·con·cerned [ʌnkənˈsɜːnd] *adj* indifferente; **be ~ about s.o. / sth** non darsi pensiero di qu / qc

un·con·di·tion·al [ʌnkənˈdɪʃnl] *adj* incondizionato

un·con·scious [ʌnˈkɒnʃəs] *adj* MED svenuto; PSYCH inconscio; **knock s.o. ~** stordire qu con un colpo; **be ~ of sth** *(not aware)* non rendersi conto di qc

un·con·trol·la·ble [ʌnkənˈtrəʊləbl] *adj anger, desire, children* incontrollabile

un·con·ven·tion·al [ʌnkənˈvenʃnl] *adj* poco convenzionale

un·co·op·er·a·tive [ʌnkəʊˈɒprətɪv] *adj* poco cooperativo

un·cork [ʌnˈkɔːk] *v/t bottle* stappare

U

un·cov·er [ʌnˈkʌvə(r)] v/t scoprire

un·dam·aged [ʌnˈdæmɪdʒd] adj intatto

un·daunt·ed [ʌnˈdɔːntɪd] adj: **carry on ~** continuare imperterrito

un·de·cid·ed [ʌndɪˈsaɪdɪd] adj question irrisolto; **be ~ about sth** essere indeciso su qc

un·de·ni·a·ble [ʌndɪˈnaɪəbl] adj innegabile

un·de·ni·a·bly [ʌndɪˈnaɪəblɪ] adv innegabilmente

un·der [ˈʌndə(r)] **1** prep (beneath) sotto; (less than) meno di; **it is ~ review / investigation** viene rivisto / indagato; **it is ~ construction** è in costruzione **2** adv (anaesthetized) sotto anestesia

un·der·age adj: **~ drinking** alcolismo m minorile

'un·der·arm adv throw sottinsù

'un·der·car·riage carrello m d'atterraggio

'un·der·cov·er adj agent segreto

un·der'cut v/t (pret & pp **-cut**) COM vendere a minor prezzo di

'un·der·dog: **they were the ~s** dovevano perdere

un·der'done adj meat al sangue; not cooked enough non cotto abbastanza

un·der'es·ti·mate v/t person, skills, task sottovalutare

un·der·ex'posed adj PHOT sottoesposto

un·der'fed adj malnutrito

un·der'go v/t (pret **-went**, pp **-gone**) surgery, treatment sottoporsi a; experiences vivere; **~ refurbishment** venire ristrutturato

un·der'grad·u·ate studente m, -essa f universitario, -a

'un·der·ground 1 adj passages etc sotterraneo; POL: resistance, newspaper etc clandestino **2** adv work sottoterra; **go ~** POL entrare in clandestinità **3** n RAIL metropolitana f

'un·der·growth sottobosco m

un·der'hand adj (devious) subdolo

un·der'lie v/t (pret **-lay**, pp **-lain**) (form basis of) essere alla base di

un·der'line v/t text sottolineare

un·der'ly·ing adj causes, problems di fondo

un·der'mine v/t s.o.'s position minare

un·der·neath [ʌndəˈniːθ] prep adv sotto **2** adv sotto

'un·der·pants npl mutande fpl da uomo

'un·der·pass for pedestrians sottopassaggio m

un·der·priv·i·leged [ʌndəˈprɪvɪlɪdʒd] adj svantaggiato

un·der'rate v/t sottovalutare

'un·der·shirt Am canottiera f

un·der·sized [ʌndəˈsaɪzd] adj troppo piccolo

'un·der·skirt sottogonna f

un·der·staffed [ʌndəˈstɑːft] adj a corto di personale

un·der·stand [ʌndəˈstænd] (pret & pp **-stood**) **1** v/t capire; **I ~ that you ...** mi risulta che tu ...; **they are understood to be in Canada** pare che siano in Canada **2** v/i capire

un·der·stand·able [ʌndəˈstændəbl] adj comprensibile

un·der·stand·ably [ʌndəˈstændəblɪ] adv comprensibilmente

un·der·stand·ing [ʌndəˈstændɪŋ] **1** adj person comprensivo **2** n of problem, situation comprensione f; (agreement) intesa f; **on the ~ that we agree a price** a patto che ci troviamo d'accordo sul prezzo

'un·der·state·ment understatement m inv

un·der'take v/t (pret **-took**, pp **-taken**) task intraprendere; **~ to do sth** impegnarsi a fare qc

'un·der·tak·er impresario m di pompe funebri

'un·der·tak·ing (enterprise) impresa f; (promise) promessa f

un·der'val·ue v/t sottovalutare

'un·der·wear biancheria f intima

un·der'weight adj sottopeso

'un·de·rworld criminal malavita f inv; in mythology inferi mpl

un·der'write v/t (pret **-wrote**, pp **-written**) FIN sottoscrivere

un·de·served [ˌʌndɪˈzɜːvd] adj immeritato

un·de·sir·a·ble [ˌʌndɪˈzaɪərəbl] adj features, changes indesiderato; person poco raccomandabile; ~ **ele·ment** person persona indesiderabile

un·dis·put·ed [ˌʌndɪˈspjuːtɪd] adj champion, leader indiscusso

un·do [ʌnˈduː] v/t (pret -did, pp -done) parcel, wrapping disfare; shirt sbottonare; shoes, shoelaces slacciare; s.o. else's work annullare, sciupare

un·doubt·ed·ly [ʌnˈdaʊtɪdlɪ] adv indubbiamente

un·dreamt-of [ʌnˈdremtɒv] adj riches impensato

un·dress [ʌnˈdres] 1 v/t spogliare; get ~ed spogliarsi 2 v/i spogliarsi

un·due [ʌnˈdjuː] adj (excessive) eccessivo

un·du·ly [ʌnˈdjuːlɪ] adv punished, blamed ingiustamente; (excessively) eccessivamente

un·earth [ʌnˈɜːθ] v/t ancient remains portare alla luce; (fig: find) scovare

un·earth·ly [ʌnˈɜːθlɪ] adv: at this ~ hour a quest'ora (impossibile)

un·eas·y [ʌnˈiːzɪ] adj relationship, peace precario; feel ~ about non sentirsela di

un·eat·a·ble [ʌnˈiːtəbl] adj immangiabile

un·e·co·nom·ic [ˌʌniːkəˈnɒmɪk] adj poco redditizio

un·ed·u·cat·ed [ʌnˈedjʊkeɪtɪd] adj senza istruzione

un·em·ployed [ˌʌnɪmˈplɔɪd] adj disoccupato; **the** ~ i disoccupati

un·em·ploy·ment [ˌʌnɪmˈplɔɪmənt] disoccupazione f; ~ **benefit** sussidio m di disoccupazione

un·end·ing [ʌnˈendɪŋ] adj interminabile

un·e·qual [ʌnˈiːkwəl] adj disuguale; be ~ **to the task** non essere all'altezza del compito

un·er·ring [ʌnˈerɪŋ] adj judgement, instinct infallibile

un·e·ven [ʌnˈiːvn] adj quality irregolare; ground accidentato

un·e·ven·ly [ʌnˈiːvnlɪ] adv distributed, applied in modo irregolare; ~ **matched** of two contestants mal assortiti

un·e·vent·ful [ˌʌnɪˈventfʊl] adj day, journey tranquillo

un·ex·pec·ted [ˌʌnɪkˈspektɪd] adj inatteso

un·ex·pec·ted·ly [ˌʌnɪkˈspektɪdlɪ] adv inaspettatamente

un·fair [ʌnˈfeə(r)] adj ingiusto

un·faith·ful [ʌnˈfeɪθfʊl] adj husband, wife infedele; be ~ **to s.o.** essere infedele a qu

un·fa·mil·i·ar [ˌʌnfəˈmɪljə(r)] adj sconosciuto; be ~ **with sth** non conoscere qc

un·fas·ten [ʌnˈfɑːsn] v/t belt slacciare

un·fa·vo·ra·ble Am, un·fa·vou·ra·ble [ʌnˈfeɪvərəbl] adj report, review negativo; weather conditions sfavorevole

un·feel·ing [ʌnˈfiːlɪŋ] adj person insensibile

un·fin·ished [ʌnˈfɪnɪʃt] adj job, letter, building non terminato; business in sospeso; **leave sth** ~ non terminare qc

un·fit [ʌnˈfɪt] adj physically fuori forma; be ~ **to** ... morally non essere degno di ...; ~ **to eat / drink** non commestibile / non potabile

un·flap·pa·ble [ʌnˈflæpəbl] adj F calmo, imperturbabile

un·fold [ʌnˈfəʊld] 1 v/t sheets, letter spiegare; one's arms aprire 2 v/i of story etc svolgersi; of view spiegarsi

un·fore·seen [ˌʌnfɔːˈsiːn] adj imprevisto

un·for·get·ta·ble [ˌʌnfəˈgetəbl] adj indimenticabile

un·for·giv·a·ble [ˌʌnfəˈgɪvəbl] adj imperdonabile; **that was** ~ **(of you)** è una mancanza imperdonabile

un·for·tu·nate [ʌnˈfɔːtʃənət] adj people sfortunato; event, choice of words infelice; **that's** ~ **for you** è spiacevole per lei

un·for·tu·nate·ly [ʌnˈfɔːtʃənətlɪ] adv sfortunatamente

U

un·found·ed [ʌnˈfaʊndɪd] adj infondato

un·friend·ly [ʌnˈfrendlɪ] adj poco amichevole; software di non facile uso

un·fur·nished [ʌnˈfɜːnɪʃt] adj non ammobiliato

un·god·ly [ʌnˈgɒdlɪ] adj: at this ~ hour ad un'ora impossibile

un·grate·ful [ʌnˈgreɪtfʊl] adj ingrato

un·hap·pi·ness [ʌnˈhæpɪnɪs] infelicità f inv

un·hap·py [ʌnˈhæpɪ] adj infelice; customers etc non soddisfatto; be ~ with the service / an explanation non essere soddisfatto del servizio/ della giustificazione

un·harmed [ʌnˈhɑːmd] adj illeso

un·health·y [ʌnˈhelθɪ] adj person malaticcio; conditions malsano; food, atmosphere poco sano; economy traballante; balance sheet in passivo

un·heard-of [ʌnˈhɜːdɒv] adj inaudito

un'hoped-for adj insperato

un·hurt [ʌnˈhɜːt] adj illeso

un·hy·gi·en·ic [ʌnhaɪˈdʒiːnɪk] adj non igienico

u·ni·fi·ca·tion [juːnɪfɪˈkeɪʃn] unificazione f

u·ni·form [ˈjuːnɪfɔːm] 1 n of school pupil, air hostess divisa f; of soldier divisa f, uniforme f 2 adj uniforme

u·ni·fy [ˈjuːnɪfaɪ] v/t (pret & pp -ied) unificare

u·ni·lat·e·ral [juːnɪˈlætrəl] adj unilaterale

un·i·ma·gi·na·ble [ʌnɪˈmædʒɪnəbl] adj inimmaginabile

un·i·ma·gi·na·tive [ʌnɪˈmædʒɪnətɪv] adj senza fantasia

un·im·por·tant [ʌnɪmˈpɔːtənt] adj senza importanza

un·in·hab·i·ta·ble [ʌnɪnˈhæbɪtəbl] adj inabitabile

un·in·hab·it·ed [ʌnɪnˈhæbɪtɪd] adj building disabitato; region deserto

un·in·jured [ʌnˈɪndʒəd] adj incolume

un·in·tel·li·gi·ble [ʌnɪnˈtelɪdʒəbl] adj incomprensibile

un·in·ten·tion·al [ʌnɪnˈtenʃnl] adj involontario

un·in·ten·tion·al·ly [ʌnɪnˈtenʃnlɪ] adv involontariamente

un·in·te·rest·ing [ʌnˈɪntrəstɪŋ] adj poco interessante

un·in·ter·rupt·ed [ʌnɪntəˈrʌptɪd] adj sleep, work ininterrotto

u·nion [ˈjuːnɪən] POL unione f; (trade ~) sindacato m

u·nique [juːˈniːk] adj (also very good) unico; with his own ~ humour / style con quel senso dell'umorismo / quello stile tutto suo

u·nit [ˈjuːnɪt] of measurement unità f inv; (section: of machine, structure) elemento m; (part with separate function) unità f inv; (department) reparto m; MIL unità f inv; we must work together as a ~ dobbiamo lavorare insieme come squadra

u·nit ˈcost COM costo m unitario

u·nite [juːˈnaɪt] 1 v/t unire 2 v/i unirsi

u·nit·ed [juːˈnaɪtɪd] adj unito

U·nit·ed ˈKing·dom Regno m Unito

U·nit·ed ˈNa·tions Nazioni fpl Unite

U·nit·ed ˈStates of ˈA·mer·i·ca Stati mpl Uniti (d'America)

u·ni·ty [ˈjuːnətɪ] unità f inv

u·ni·ver·sal [juːnɪˈvɜːsl] adj universale

u·ni·ver·sal·ly [juːnɪˈvɜːsəlɪ] adv universalmente

u·ni·verse [ˈjuːnɪvɜːs] universo m

u·ni·ver·si·ty [juːnɪˈvɜːsətɪ] 1 n università f inv; he is at ~ fa l'università 2 adj universitario

un·just [ʌnˈdʒʌst] adj ingiusto

un·kempt [ʌnˈkempt] adj hair scarmigliato; appearance trasandato

un·kind [ʌnˈkaɪnd] adj cattivo

un·known [ʌnˈnəʊn] 1 adj sconosciuto 2 n: a journey into the ~ un viaggio nell'ignoto

un·lead·ed [ʌnˈledɪd] adj senza piombo

un·less [ənˈles] conj a meno che; ~ he pays us tomorrow a meno che non ci paghi domani; ~ I am mistaken se non mi sbaglio

un·like [ʌn'laɪk] *prep* diverso da; *it's ~ him to drink so much* non è da lui bere così tanto; *the photograph was completely ~ her* la foto non le somigliava per niente; *~ Tom, I ...* a differenza di Tom, io ...

un·like·ly [ʌn'laɪklɪ] *adj* improbabile; *he is ~ to win* è improbabile che vinca; *it is ~ that ...* è improbabile che ...

un·lim·it·ed [ʌn'lɪmɪtɪd] *adj* illimitato

un·load [ʌn'ləʊd] *v/t lorry, goods* scaricare

un·lock [ʌn'lɒk] *v/t* aprire (con la chiave)

un·luck·i·ly [ʌn'lʌkɪlɪ] *adv* sfortunatamente

un·luck·y [ʌn'lʌkɪ] *adj day, choice, person* sfortunato; *that was so ~ for you!* che sfortuna hai avuto!

un·made-up [ʌnmeɪd'ʌp] *adj face* acqua e sapone

un·manned [ʌn'mænd] *adj spacecraft* senza equipaggio

un·mar·ried [ʌn'mærɪd] *adj* non sposato

un·mis·ta·ka·ble [ʌnmɪ'steɪkəbl] *adj* inconfondibile

un·moved [ʌn'muːvd] *adj*: *be ~ emotionally* non essere commosso

un·mu·si·cal [ʌn'mjuːzɪkl] *adj person* non portato per la musica; *sounds* disarmonico

un·nat·u·ral [ʌn'nætʃərl] *adj* non normale; *it's not ~ to be annoyed* è naturale essere seccati

un·ne·ces·sa·ry [ʌn'nesəsrɪ] *adj* non necessario; *comment, violence* gratuito

un·nerv·ing [ʌn'nɜːvɪŋ] *adj* inquietante

un·no·ticed [ʌn'nəʊtɪst] *adj* inosservato; *it went ~* passare inosservato

un·ob·tain·a·ble [ʌnəb'teɪnəbl] *adj goods* introvabile; TELEC non ottenibile

un·ob·tru·sive [ʌnəb'truːsɪv] *adj* discreto

un·oc·cu·pied [ʌn'ɒkjʊpaɪd] *adj building, house* vuoto; *post* vacante;

room libero; *he doesn't like being ~ person* non gli piace stare senza far niente

un·of·fi·cial [ʌnə'fɪʃl] *adj world record, leader* non ufficiale; *announcement* ufficioso

un·of·fi·cial·ly [ʌnə'fɪʃlɪ] *adv* non ufficialmente

un·pack [ʌn'pæk] **1** *v/t* disfare **2** *v/i* disfare le valige

un·paid [ʌn'peɪd] *adj work* non retribuito

un·pleas·ant [ʌn'pleznt] *adj person, thing to say* antipatico; *smell, taste* sgradevole; *he was very ~ to her* si è comportato malissimo con lei

un·plug [ʌn'plʌg] *v/t* (*pret & pp -ged*) *TV, computer* staccare (la spina di)

un·pop·u·lar [ʌn'pɒpjʊlə(r)] *adj person* mal visto; *decision* impopolare; *an ~ teacher with the students* un insegnante che non ha la simpatia degli studenti

un·pre·ce·den·ted [ʌn'presɪdentɪd] *adj* senza precedenti; *it was ~ for a woman to be ...* è senza precedenti che una donna sia ...

un·pre·dict·a·ble [ʌnprɪ'dɪktəbl] *adj person, weather* imprevedibile

un·pre·ten·tious [ʌnprɪ'tenʃəs] *adj person, style, hotel* senza pretese

un·prin·ci·pled [ʌn'prɪnsɪpld] *adj* senza scrupoli

un·pro·duc·tive [ʌnprə'dʌktɪv] *adj meeting, discussion* sterile; *soil* improduttivo

un·pro·fes·sion·al [ʌnprə'feʃnl] *adj person, workmanship* poco professionale; *it is ~ not to ...* è mancanza di professionalità non ...; *~ behaviour of doctor etc* scorrettezza *f* professionale

un·prof·it·a·ble [ʌn'prɒfɪtəbl] *adj* non redditizio

un·pro·nounce·a·ble [ʌnprə'naʊnsəbl] *adj* impronunciabile

un·pro·tect·ed [ʌnprə'tektɪd] *adj borders* indifeso; *machine* non riparato; *~ sex* sesso non protetto

U

un·pro·voked [ʌnprə'vəukt] *adj attack* non provocato

un·qual·i·fied [ʌn'kwɒlɪfaɪd] *adj worker, instructor* non qualificato; *doctor, teacher* non abilitato

un·ques·tio·na·bly [ʌn'kwestʃnəblɪ] *adv* (*without doubt*) indiscutibilmente

un·ques·tion·ing [ʌn'kwestʃnɪŋ] *adj attitude, loyalty* assoluto

un·rav·el [ʌn'rævl] *v/t* (*pret & pp* -led, *Am* -ed) *string* dipanare; *knitting* disfare; *mystery, complexities* risolvere

un·rea·da·ble [ʌn'riːdəbl] *adj book* illeggibile

un·re·al [ʌn'rɪəl] *adj creature* irreale; *impression* inverosimile; **this is ~!** F incredibile!

un·rea·lis·tic [ʌnrɪə'lɪstɪk] *adj person* poco realista; *expectations* poco realistico

un·rea·so·na·ble [ʌn'riːznəbl] *adj person* irragionevole; *demand, expectation* eccessivo

un·re·lat·ed [ʌnrɪ'leɪtɪd] *adj issues* senza (alcuna) attinenza; *people* non imparentato

un·re·lent·ing [ʌnrɪ'lentɪŋ] *adj* incessante

un·re·li·a·ble [ʌnrɪ'laɪəbl] *adj* poco affidabile

un·rest [ʌn'rest] agitazione *f*

un·re·strained [ʌnrɪ'streɪnd] *adj emotions* incontrollato, sfrenato

un·road·wor·thy [ʌn'rəʊdwɜːðɪ] *adj* non sicuro

un·roll [ʌn'rəʊl] *v/t carpet, scroll* srotolare

un·ru·ly [ʌn'ruːlɪ] *adj* indisciplinato

un·safe [ʌn'seɪf] *adj bridge, vehicle, wiring, district* pericoloso; **~ to drink/eat** non potabile/non commestibile; **it is ~ to ...** è rischioso ...

un·san·i·tar·y [ʌn'sænɪtrɪ] *adj conditions, drains* antigienico

un·sat·is·fac·to·ry [ʌnsætɪs'fæktrɪ] *adj* poco soddisfacente

un·sa·vou·ry [ʌn'seɪvrɪ] *adj person, reputation,* poco raccomandabile; *district* brutto

un·scathed [ʌn'skeɪðd] *adj* (*not injured*) incolume; (*not damaged*) intatto

un·screw [ʌn'skruː] *v/t* svitare

un·scru·pu·lous [ʌn'skruːpjələs] *adj* senza scrupoli

un·self·ish [ʌn'selfɪʃ] *adj person* altruista; *act, gesture, behaviour* altruistico

un·set·tled [ʌn'setld] *adj issue* irrisolto; *weather, stock market* instabile; *lifestyle* irrequieto; *bills* non pagato

un·shav·en [ʌn'ʃeɪvn] *adj* non rasato

un·sight·ly [ʌn'saɪtlɪ] *adj* brutto

un·skilled [ʌn'skɪld] *adj* non specializzato

un·so·cia·ble [ʌn'səʊʃəbl] *adj* poco socievole

un·so·phis·ti·cat·ed [ʌnsə'fɪstɪkeɪtɪd] *adj person, beliefs* semplice; *equipment* rudimentale

un·sta·ble [ʌn'steɪbl] *adj person* squilibrato; *structure, area, economy* instabile

un·stead·y [ʌn'stedɪ] *adj ladder* malsicuro; **be ~ on one's feet** non reggersi bene sulle gambe

un·stint·ing [ʌn'stɪntɪŋ] *adj support* incondizionato; *generosity* illimitato; *praise* senza riserve; **be ~ in one's efforts** prodigarsi negli sforzi

un·stuck [ʌn'stʌk] *adj:* **come ~ of** *notice etc* staccarsi; F *of plan etc* fallire

un·suc·cess·ful [ʌnsək'sesfʊl] *adj writer etc* di scarso successo; *candidate, party* sconfitto; *attempt* fallito; **he tried but was ~** ha provato ma non ha avuto fortuna

un·suc·cess·ful·ly [ʌnsək'sesflɪ] *adv try, apply* senza successo

un·suit·a·ble [ʌn'suːtəbl] *adj partner, clothing* inadatto; *thing to say, language* inappropriato; **be ~ for** non essere adatto per; **they're ~ for each other** non sono fatti l'uno per l'altra

un·sus·pect·ing [ʌnsəs'pektɪŋ] *adj* ignaro

un·swerv·ing [ʌnˈswɜːvɪŋ] *adj* loyalty, devotion incrollabile

un·think·a·ble [ʌnˈθɪŋkəbl] *adj* impensabile

un·ti·dy [ʌnˈtaɪdɪ] *adj* room, desk, hair in disordine

un·tie [ʌnˈtaɪ] *v/t* knot disfare; laces slacciare; prisoner slegare

un·til [ənˈtɪl] **1** *prep* fino a; *I can wait ~ tomorrow* posso aspettare fino a domani; *from Monday ~ Friday* da lunedì a venerdì; *not ~ Friday* non prima di venerdì; *it won't be finished ~ July* non sarà finito prima di luglio **2** *conj* finché non (non); *can you wait ~ I'm ready?* puoi aspettare che sia pronta?; *they won't do anything ~ you say so* non faranno niente finché non glielo dici tu

un·time·ly [ʌnˈtaɪmlɪ] *adj* death prematuro

un·tir·ing [ʌnˈtaɪrɪŋ] *adj* efforts instancabile

un·told [ʌnˈtəʊld] *adj* riches incalcolabile; suffering indescribile; story inedito

un·trans·lat·a·ble [ʌntrænsˈleɪtəbl] *adj* intraducibile

un·true [ʌnˈtruː] *adj* falso

un·used[1] [ʌnˈjuːzd] *adj* goods mai usato

un·used[2] [ʌnˈjuːst] *adj*: *be ~ to sth* non essere abituato a qc; *be ~ to doing sth* non essere abituato a fare qc

un·u·su·al [ʌnˈjuːʒʊəl] *adj* insolito; *it's ~ for them not to write* non è da loro non scrivere

un·u·su·al·ly [ʌnˈjuːʒʊəlɪ] *adv* insolitamente

un·veil [ʌnˈveɪl] *v/t* memorial, statue etc scoprire

un·well [ʌnˈwel] *adj*: *be / feel ~* stare / sentirsi male

un·will·ing [ʌnˈwɪlɪŋ] *adj*: *be ~ to do sth* non essere disposto a fare qc

un·will·ing·ly [ʌnˈwɪlɪŋlɪ] *adv* malvolentieri

un·wind [ʌnˈwaɪnd] (*pret & pp -wound*) **1** *v/t* tape svolgere **2** *v/i* of

tape svolgersi; of story dipanarsi; F (*relax*) rilassarsi

un·wise [ʌnˈwaɪz] *adj* avventato, imprudente

un·wrap [ʌnˈræp] *v/t* (*pret & pp -ped*) gift aprire, scartare

un·writ·ten [ʌnˈrɪtn] *adj* law, rule tacito

un·zip [ʌnˈzɪp] *v/t* (*pret & pp -ped*) dress etc aprire (la chiusura lampo di); COMPUT espandere

up [ʌp] **1** *adv*: *~ in the sky / ~ on the roof* in alto nel cielo / sul tetto; *~ here / there* quassù / lassù; *be ~* (*out of bed*) essere in piedi; of sun essere sorto; (*be built*) essere costruito; of shelves essere montato; of prices, temperature essere aumentato; (*have expired*) essere scaduto; *the road is ~* ci sono lavori in corso; *what's ~?* F che c'è?; *~ to the year 1989* fino al 1989; *he came ~ to me* mi si è avvicinato; *what are you ~ to these days?* cosa fai di bello?; *what are those kids ~ to?* cosa stanno combinando i bambini?; *be ~ to something (bad)* stare architettando qualcosa; *I don't feel ~ to it* non me la sento; *it's ~ to you* dipende da te; *it is ~ to them to solve it* their duty sta a loro risolverlo; *be ~ and about* after illness essersi ristabilito **2** *prep*: *further ~ the mountain* più in alto sulla montagna; *he climbed ~ the tree* si è arrampicato sull'albero; *they ran ~ the street* corsero per strada; *the water goes ~ this pipe* l'acqua sale su per questo tubo; *we travelled ~ to Milan* siamo arrivati fino a Milano **3** *n*: *~s and downs* alti e bassi *mpl*

'up·bring·ing educazione *f*

'up·com·ing *adj* (*forthcoming*) prossimo

up·date 1 *v/t* file, records aggiornare; *~ s.o. on sth* mettere qu al corrente di qc **2** *n* ('update) of files, records aggiornamento *m*; software version upgrade *m inv*; *can you give me an ~ on the situation?* può darmi gli ultimi aggiornamenti sulla situazione?

up'grade *v/t computers, equipment etc* aggiornare; *memory* potenziare, aumentare; *(replace with new versions)* *passenger* promuovere a una classe superiore; *product* migliorare; **I ~d the monitor** ho comprato un monitor migliore; **we could ~ you to a bigger room** possiamo offrirle una camera più grande

up·heav·al [ʌpˈhiːvl] *emotional* sconvolgimento *m*; *physical* scombussolamento *m*; *political, social* sconvolgimento *m*

up·hill [ʌpˈhɪl] **1** *adv*: **go / walk ~** salire **2** *adj* [ˈʌphɪl] *climbʰ* in salita; *struggle* arduo

up'hold *v/t (pret & pp -held) traditions, rights* sostenere; *(vindicate)* confermare

up·hol·ster·y [ʌpˈhəʊlstəri] *coverings of chairs* tappezzeria *f*; *padding of chairs* imbottitura *f*

'up·keep *of old buildings, parks etc* manutenzione *f*

'up·load *v/t* COMPUT caricare

up'mar·ket *adj restaurant, hotel* elegante; *product* di qualità

upon [əˈpɒn] *prep* → **on**

up·per [ˈʌpə(r)] *adj part of sth* superiore; *deck, rooms* di sopra; **the earth's ~ atmosphere** la parte più alta dell'atmosfera terrestre; **the ~ Thames** l'alto Tamigi

up·per 'class *adj accent* aristocratico; *family* dell'alta borghesia

up·per 'clas·ses *npl* alta borghesia *f*

'up·right 1 *adj citizen* onesto **2** *adv sit* (ben) dritto

'up·right (pi'an·o) pianoforte *m* verticale

'up·ris·ing insurrezione *f*

'up·roar *loud noise* trambusto *m*; *(protest)* protesta *f*

up'set 1 *v/t (pret & pp -set) drink, glass* rovesciare; *(make sad)* fare stare male; *(distress)* sconvolgere; *(annoy)* seccare **2** *adj (sad)* triste; *(distressed)* sconvolto; *(annoyed)* seccato; **be / get ~** prendersela

(about per); **get ~ about sth** prendersela per qc; **have an ~ stomach** avere l'intestino in disordine

up'set·ting *adj*: **it's so ~ (for me)** mi fa stare male, mi turba

'up·shot *(result, outcome)* risultato *m*

'up·side vantaggio *m*

up·side 'down *adv* capovolto; **turn sth ~** capovolgere qc

up'stairs 1 *adv* di sopra **2** *adj room* al piano di sopra

'up·start novellino *m* che si comporta in modo arrogante

up'stream *adv* a monte; **follow the river ~** risalire la corrente

'up·take: **be quick on the ~** capire le cose al volo; **be slow on the ~** essere lento nel capire

up'tight *adj* F *(nervous)* nervoso; *(inhibited)* inibito

up-to-'date *adj information* aggiornato; *fashions* più attuale

'up·turn *in economy* ripresa *f*

up·wards [ˈʌpwədz] *adv fly, move* in su; **~ of 10,000** oltre 10.000

u·ra·ni·um [jʊˈreɪniəm] uranio *m*

ur·ban [ˈɜːbən] *adj areas, population* urbano; *redevelopment* urbanistico

ur·ban·i·za·tion [ɜːbənaɪˈzeɪʃn] urbanizzazione *f*

ur·chin [ˈɜːtʃɪn] monello *m*, -a *f*

urge [ɜːdʒ] **1** *n* forte desiderio *m* **2** *v/t*: **~ s.o. to do sth** raccomandare (caldamente) a qu di fare qc

♦ **urge on** *v/t (encourage)* incitare

ur·gen·cy [ˈɜːdʒənsɪ] urgenza *f*; **the ~ of the situation** la gravità della situazione

ur·gent [ˈɜːdʒənt] *adj job, letter* urgente; **be in ~ need of sth** avere bisogno urgente di qc; **is it ~?** è urgente?

u·ri·nate [ˈjʊərɪneɪt] *v/i* orinare

u·rine [ˈjʊərɪn] urina *f*

urn [ɜːn] urna *f*

us [ʌs] *pron direct & indirect object* ci; *when two pronouns are used* ce; *after prep* noi; **they know ~** ci conoscono; **don't leave ~** non ci lasciare, non lasciarci; **she gave ~ the keys** ci ha dato le chiavi; **she gave them to ~**

ce le ha date; *that's for ~* quello è per noi; *who's that? – it's ~* chi è? – siamo noi

US [juːˈes] *abbr* (= **United States**) USA *mpl*

USA [juːesˈeɪ] *abbr* (= **United States of America**) USA *mpl*

us·a·ble [ˈjuːzəbl] *adj* utilizzabile

us·age [ˈjuːzɪdʒ] *linguistic* uso *m*

use [juːz] **1** *v/t tool, skills, knowledge* usare, utilizzare; *word, s.o.'s car* usare; *a lot of petrol* consumare; *pej: person* usare; *I could ~ a drink* F berrei volentieri qualcosa **2** *n* [juːs] uso *m*; *be of great ~ to s.o.* essere di grande aiuto a qu; *be of no ~ to s.o.* non essere d'aiuto a qu; *is that of any ~?* ti è d'aiuto?; *it's no ~* non c'è verso; *it's no ~ trying / waiting* non serve a niente provare / aspettare

♦ **use up** *v/t* finire

used¹ [juːzd] *adj car etc* usato

used² [juːst] *adj: be ~ to s.o. / sth* essere abituato a qu / qc; *get ~ to s.o. / sth* abituarsi a qu / qc; *be ~ to doing sth* essere abituato a fare qc; *get ~ to doing sth* abituarsi a fare qc

used³ [juːst]: *I ~ to know him* lo conoscevo; *I ~ to like him* un tempo mi piaceva; *I don't work there now, but I ~ to* ora non più, ma una volta lavoravo lì

use·ful [ˈjuːsfʊl] *adj information, gadget* utile; *person* di grande aiuto

use·ful·ness [ˈjuːsfʊlnɪs] utilità *f inv*

use·less [ˈjuːslɪs] *adj information, advice* inutile; F *person* incapace; *machine, computer* inservibile; *feel ~* sentirsi inutile; *it's ~ trying there isn't any point* non serve a niente provare

us·er [ˈjuːzə(r)] *of product* utente *m/f*

us·er·friend·ly *adj software, device* di facile uso

ush·er [ˈʌʃə(r)] *n* (*at wedding*) persona *f* che accompagna gli invitati ai loro posti; *in a cinema* maschera *f*

♦ **usher in** *v/t new era* inaugurare

ush·er·ette [ʌʃəˈret] maschera *f*

u·su·al [ˈjuːʒʊəl] *adj* solito; *it's not ~ for this to happen* non succede quasi mai; *as ~* come al solito; *the ~, please* il solito, per favore

u·su·al·ly [ˈjuːʒʊəlɪ] *adv* di solito

u·ten·sil [juːˈtensl] utensile *m*

u·te·rus [ˈjuːtərəs] utero *m*

u·til·i·ty [juːˈtɪlətɪ] (*usefulness*) utilità *f inv*; *public utilities* servizi pubblici

u·til·ize [ˈjuːtɪlaɪz] *v/t* utilizzare

ut·most [ˈʌtməʊst] **1** *adj* massimo **2** *n: do one's ~* fare (tutto) il possibile

ut·ter [ˈʌtə(r)] **1** *adj* totale **2** *v/t sound* emettere; *word* proferire

ut·ter·ly [ˈʌtəlɪ] *adv* totalmente

U-turn [ˈjuːtɜːn] inversione *f* a U; *fig: in policy* dietro-front *m inv*

V

va·can·cy [ˈveɪkənsɪ] *at work* posto *m* vacante; *in hotel* camera *f* libera; *~ for a driver as advert* autista cercasi; *do you have any vacancies?* avete bisogno di personale?; *"no vacancies"* "completo"

va·cant [ˈveɪkənt] *adj building* vuoto; *room* libero; *position* vacante; *look, expression* assente

va·cant·ly [ˈveɪkəntlɪ] *adv* con sguardo assente

va·cate [veɪˈkeɪt] *v/t room* lasciare libero

va·ca·tion [veɪˈkeɪʃn] *Am* vacanza *f*;

be on ~ essere in vacanza

vac·ci·nate ['væksɪneɪt] *v/t* vaccinare; ***be ~d against ...*** essere vaccinato contro ...

vac·ci·na·tion [væksɪ'neɪʃn] vaccinazione *f*

vac·cine ['væksiːn] vaccino *m*

vac·u·um ['vækjʊəm] **1** *n also fig* vuoto *m* **2** *v/t floors* passare l'aspirapolvere su

'vac·u·um clean·er aspirapolvere *m inv*; **'vac·u·um flask** termos *m inv*; **vac·u·um-'packed** *adj* sottovuoto

vag·a·bond ['vægəbɒnd] *n* vagabondo *m*, -a *f*

va·gi·na [və'dʒaɪnə] vagina *f*

va·gi·nal ['vædʒɪnl] *adj* vaginale

va·grant ['veɪɡrənt] *n* vagabondo *m*, -a *f*

vague [veɪg] *adj* vago; ***I'm still ~ about it*** non ho ancora le idee chiare al riguardo

vague·ly ['veɪglɪ] *adv* vagamente

vain [veɪn] **1** *adj person* vanitoso; *hope* vano **2** *n*: ***in ~*** invano; ***their efforts were in ~*** i loro sforzi sono stati inutili

val·en·tine ['væləntaɪn] *(card)* biglietto *m* per San Valentino; ***Valentine's Day*** San Valentino

val·et ['væleɪ] **1** *n person* cameriere *m* personale **2** *v/t* ['vælət]: ***have one's car ~ed*** far lavare la macchina dentro e fuori

'val·et ser·vice *for clothes* servizio *m* di lavanderia; *for cars* servizio *m* completo di lavaggio

val·iant ['væliənt] *adj* valoroso

val·iant·ly ['væliəntlɪ] *adv* valorosamente

val·id ['vælɪd] *adj* valido

val·i·date ['vælɪdeɪt] *v/t with official stamp* convalidare; *s.o.'s alibi* confermare

va·lid·i·ty [və'lɪdətɪ] *of reason, argument* validità *f inv*

val·ley ['vælɪ] valle *f*

val·u·a·ble ['væljʊəbl] **1** *adj* prezioso **2** *n*: ***~s*** oggetti *mpl* di valore

val·u·a·tion [vælju'eɪʃn] valutazione

f; ***at his ~*** secondo la sua valutazione

val·ue ['væljuː] **1** *n* valore *m*; ***be good ~*** essere conveniente; ***get ~ for money*** fare un affare; ***rise / fall in ~*** aumentare / perdere di valore **2** *v/t s.o.'s friendship, one's freedom* tenere a; ***I ~ your advice*** ci tengo alla tua opinione; ***have an object ~d*** far valutare un oggetto

'val·ue-ad·ded tax imposta *f* sul valore aggiunto

valve [vælv] valvola *f*

van [væn] furgone *m*

van·dal ['vændl] vandalo *m*

van·dal·is·m ['vændəlɪzm] vandalismo *m*

van·dal·ize ['vændəlaɪz] *v/t* vandalizzare

van·guard ['vænɡɑːd] *n* avanguardia *f*; ***be in the ~ of*** essere all'avanguardia di

va·nil·la [və'nɪlə] **1** *n* vaniglia *f* **2** *adj ice cream* alla vaniglia; *flavour* di vaniglia

van·ish ['vænɪʃ] *v/i* sparire

van·i·ty ['vænətɪ] *of person* vanità *f inv*

'van·i·ty case beauty-case *m inv*

van·tage point ['vɑːntɪdʒ] *on hill etc* punto *m* d'osservazione

va·por *Am* → **vapour**

va·por·ize ['veɪpəraɪz] *v/t* vaporizzare

va·pour ['veɪpə(r)] vapore *m*

'va·pour trail *of aeroplane* scia *f*

var·i·a·ble ['veərɪəbl] **1** *adj* variabile **2** *n* MATH, COMPUT variabile *f*

var·i·ant ['veərɪənt] *n* variante *f*

var·i·a·tion [veərɪ'eɪʃn] variazione *f*

var·i·cose 'vein ['værɪkəʊs] vena *f* varicosa

var·ied ['veərɪd] *adj range, diet* vario; *life* movimentato

va·ri·e·ty [və'raɪətɪ] varietà *f inv*; *(type)* tipo *m*; THEA varietà *f inv*; ***a ~ of things to do*** varie cose da fare

var·i·ous ['veərɪəs] *adj (several)* vario; *(different)* diverso

var·nish ['vɑːnɪʃ] **1** *n for wood* vernice *f*; *(nail ~)* smalto *m* **2** *v/t wood* verniciare; *nails* smaltare

var·y ['veərɪ] *v/t & v/i* (*pret & pp* **-ied**) variare **2** *v/t* variare

vase [vɑːz] vaso *m*

vas·ec·to·my [və'sektəmɪ] vasectomia *f*

vast [vɑːst] *adj desert, knowledge* vasto; *improvement* immenso

vast·ly ['vɑːstlɪ] *adv* immensamente

VAT [viːerˈtiː, væt] *abbr* (= **value added tax**) IVA *f* (=imposta *f* sul valore aggiunto)

Vat·i·can ['vætɪkən]: **the ~** il Vaticano

vau·de·ville ['vɔːdvɪl] *Am* varietà *f inv*

vault¹ [vɔːlt] *n in roof* volta *f*; *cellar* cantina *f*; **~s** *of bank* caveau *m inv*

vault² [vɔːlt] **1** *n* SP volteggio *m* **2** *v/t* saltare

VCR [viːsiːˈɑː(r)] *abbr* (= **video cassette recorder**) videoregistratore *m*

veal [viːl] (carne *f* di) vitello *m*

veer [vɪə(r)] *v/i of car* sterzare; *of wind, party* cambiare direzione

veg [vedʒ] F verdure *fpl*

ve·gan ['viːgən] **1** *n* vegaliano *m*, -a *f* **2** *adj* vegaliano

vege·ta·ble ['vedʒtəbl] verdura *f*

ve·ge·tar·i·an [vedʒɪˈteərɪən] **1** *n* vegetariano *m*, -a *f* **2** *adj* vegetariano

ve·ge·tar·i·an·ism [vedʒɪˈteərɪənɪzm] vegetarianismo *m*

veg·e·ta·tion [vedʒɪˈteɪʃn] vegetazione *f*

ve·he·mence ['viːəməns] veemenza *f*

ve·he·ment ['viːəmənt] *adj* veemente

ve·he·ment·ly ['viːəməntlɪ] *adv* veementemente

ve·hi·cle ['viːɪkl] veicolo *m*; *for information etc* mezzo *m*

veil [veɪl] **1** *n* velo *m* **2** *v/t* velare

vein [veɪn] ANAT vena *f*; **in this ~** *fig* su questo tono

Vel·cro® ['velkrəʊ] velcro *m*

ve·loc·i·ty [vɪˈlɒsətɪ] velocità *f inv*

vel·vet ['velvɪt] *n* velluto *m*

vel·vet·y ['velvɪtɪ] *adj* vellutato

ven·det·ta [ven'detə] vendetta *f*

vend·ing ma·chine ['vendɪŋ] distributore *m* automatico

vend·or ['vendə(r)] LAW venditore *m*, -trice *f*

ve·neer [vəˈnɪə(r)] *on wood* impiallacciatura *f*; *of politeness etc* parvenza *f*

ven·e·ra·ble ['venərəbl] *adj* venerabile

ven·e·rate ['venəreɪt] *v/t* venerare

ven·e·ra·tion [venəˈreɪʃn] venerazione *f*

ve·ne·re·al dis·ease [vɪˈnɪərɪəl] malattia *f* venerea

Ve·ne·tian [vəˈniːʃn] **1** *adj* veneziano **2** *n* veneziano *m*, -a *f*

ve·ne·tian 'blind veneziana *f*

ven·geance ['vendʒəns] vendetta *f*; **with a ~** a più non posso

Ven·ice ['venɪs] Venezia *f*

ven·i·son ['venɪsn] (carne *f* di) cervo *m*

ven·om ['venəm] *also fig* veleno *m*

ven·om·ous ['venəməs] *also fig* velenoso

vent [vent] *n for air* presa *f* d'aria; **give ~ to** *feelings, emotions* dare sfogo a

ven·ti·late ['ventɪleɪt] *v/t room, building* ventilare

ven·ti·la·tion [ventɪˈleɪʃn] ventilazione *f*

ven·ti·la·tion shaft condotto *m* di aerazione

ven·ti·la·tor ['ventɪleɪtə(r)] ventilatore *m*; MED respiratore *m*

ven·tril·o·quist [ven'trɪləkwɪst] ventriloquo *m*, -a *f*

ven·ture ['ventʃə(r)] **1** *n* impresa *f* **2** *v/i* avventurarsi

ven·ue ['venjuː] *for meeting, concert etc* luogo *m*

ve·ran·da [vəˈrændə] veranda *f*

verb [vɜːb] verbo *m*

verb·al ['vɜːbl] verbale

verb·al·ly ['vɜːbəlɪ] verbalmente

ver·ba·tim [vɜːˈbeɪtɪm] *adv* parola per parola

ver·dict ['vɜːdɪkt] LAW verdetto *m*; (*opinion, judgment*) giudizio *m*; **a ~**

of guilty / not guilty un verdetto di colpevolezza / non colpevolezza

verge [vɜːdʒ] *n of road* bordo *m*; *be on the ~ of ...* ruin, collapse essere sull'orlo di ...; *on the ~ of tears* sul punto di piangere

♦ **verge on** *v/t* rasentare

ver·i·fi·ca·tion [vèrɪfɪˈkeɪʃn] verifica *f*

ver·i·fy [ˈverɪfaɪ] *v/t (pret & pp -ied)* verificare

ver·mi·cel·li [vɜːmɪˈtʃelɪ] *nsg* vermicelli *mpl*

ver·min [ˈvɜːmɪn] *npl* animali *mpl* nocivi

ver·mouth [ˈvɜːməθ] vermut *m inv*

ver·nac·u·lar [vəˈnækjʊlə(r)] *n* vernacolo *m*

ver·sa·tile [ˈvɜːsətaɪl] *adj* versatile

ver·sa·til·i·ty [vɜːsəˈtɪlətɪ] versatilità *f inv*

verse [vɜːs] *poetry* poesia *f*; *part of poem, song* strofa *f*

versed [vɜːst] *adj*: *be well ~ in a subject* essere versato in una materia

ver·sion [ˈvɜːʃn] versione *f*

ver·sus [ˈvɜːsəs] *prep* SP, LAW contro

ver·te·bra [ˈvɜːtɪbrə] vertebra *f*

ver·te·brate [ˈvɜːtɪbreɪt] *n* vertebrato *m*

ver·ti·cal [ˈvɜːtɪkl] *adj* verticale

ver·ti·go [ˈvɜːtɪɡəʊ] vertigini *fpl*

ver·y [ˈverɪ] **1** *adv* molto; *was it cold? – not ~* faceva freddo? – non molto; *~ fast / easy* molto veloce / semplice, velocissimo / semplicissimo; *the ~ best* il meglio **2** *adj*: *at that ~ moment* in quel preciso momento; *that's the ~ thing I need* è proprio quello che mi serve; *the ~ thought* il solo pensiero; *right at the ~ top / bottom* proprio in cima / in fondo

ves·sel [ˈvesl] NAUT natante *m*

vest [vest] canottiera *f*; *Am (waistcoat)* gilè *m inv*

ves·tige [ˈvestɪdʒ] vestigio *m (pl* vestigia *f)*; *not a ~ of truth* neanche un'ombra di verità

vet¹ [vet] *n (veterinary surgeon)* veterinario *m*, -a *f*

vet² [vet] *v/t (pret & pp -ted)* applicants etc passare al vaglio

vet·e·ran [ˈvetərən] **1** *n* veterano *m*, -a *f*; MIL reduce *m/f* **2** *adj* veterano

vet·e·ri·na·ry 'sur·geon [ˈvetərɪnərɪ] veterinario *m*, -a *f*

ve·to [ˈviːtəʊ] **1** *n* veto *m* **2** *v/t* mettere il veto a

vex [veks] *v/t (concern, worry)* preoccupare

vexed [vekst] *adj (worried)* preoccupato; *the ~ question of ...* la questione controversa di ...

vi·a [ˈvaɪə] *prep* attraverso

vi·a·ble [ˈvaɪəbl] *adj* life form, company in grado di sopravvivere; *alternative, plan* fattibile

vi·brate [vaɪˈbreɪt] *v/i* vibrare

vi·bra·tion [vaɪˈbreɪʃn] vibrazione *f*

vic·ar [ˈvɪkə(r)] parroco *m* anglicano

vic·ar·age [ˈvɪkərɪdʒ] casa *f* del parroco

vice¹ [vaɪs] *for holding* morsa *f*

vice² [vaɪs] vizio *m*

vice 'pres·i·dent vice-presidente *m*

'vice squad buoncostume *f*

vi·ce ver·sa [vaɪsˈvɜːsə] *adv* viceversa

vi·cin·i·ty [vɪˈsɪnətɪ] *n*: *in the ~ of ...* the church etc nelle vicinanze di ...; *£500 etc* approssimativamente ...

vi·cious [ˈvɪʃəs] *adj* dog feroce attack, criticism brutale

vi·cious 'cir·cle circolo *m* vizioso

vi·cious·ly [ˈvɪʃəslɪ] *adv* brutalmente

vic·tim [ˈvɪktɪm] vittima *f*

vic·tim·ize [ˈvɪktɪmaɪz] *v/t* perseguitare

vic·tor [ˈvɪktə(r)] vincitore *m*, -trice

vic·to·ri·ous [vɪkˈtɔːrɪəs] *adj* army vittorioso; *team* vincente

vic·to·ry [ˈvɪktərɪ] vittoria *f*; *win a ~ over ...* riportare una vittoria su ...

vid·e·o [ˈvɪdɪəʊ] **1** *n* video *m inv*; *tape* videocassetta *f*; *(VCR)* videoregistratore *m* **2** *v/t* registrare

'vid·e·o cam·e·ra videocamera *f*

'vid·e·o cas·sette videocassetta *f*

'vid·e·o con·fer·ence TELEC

videoconferenza f; **'vid•e•o game** videogame m inv; **'vid•e•o•phone** videotelefono m; **'vid•e•o re•cord•er** videoregistratore m; **'vid•e•o re•cord•ing** videoregistrazione f; **'vid•e•o•tape** videocassetta f; **'vid•e•o•tape li•bra•ry** videoteca f

vie [vaɪ] v/i competere

Vi•et•nam [vɪet'næm] Vietnam m

Vi•et•nam•ese [vɪetnə'miːz] **1** adj vietnamita m/f **2** n vietnamita m/f; language vietnamita m

view [vjuː] **1** n veduta f; of situation parere m; **in ~ of** considerato; **be on ~** consideration essere esposto; **with a ~ to** con l'intenzione di **2** v/t events, situation vedere; TV programme guardare; house for sale vedere **3** v/i (watch TV) guardare la TV

view•er ['vjuːə(r)] TV telespettatore m, -trice f

'view•find•er PHOT mirino m

'view•point punto m di vista

vig•or Am → **vigour**

vig•or•ous ['vɪgərəs] adj vigoroso

vig•or•ous•ly ['vɪgərəslɪ] adv vigorosamente

vig•our ['vɪgə(r)] vigore m

vile [vaɪl] adj disgustoso

vil•la ['vɪlə] villa f

vil•lage ['vɪlɪdʒ] paese m

vil•lag•er ['vɪlɪdʒə(r)] abitante m/f (del paese)

vil•lain ['vɪlən] cattivo m, -a f; F criminal delinquente m/f

vin•di•cate ['vɪndɪkeɪt] v/t show to be correct confermare; show to be innocent scagionare; **I feel ~d by the report** il resoconto mi dà ragione

vin•dic•tive [vɪn'dɪktɪv] adj vendicativo

vin•dic•tive•ly [vɪn'dɪktɪvlɪ] adv vendicativamente

vine [vaɪn] (grape~) vite f; climber rampicante m

vin•e•gar ['vɪnɪgə(r)] aceto m

vine•yard ['vɪnjɑːd] vigneto m

vin•tage ['vɪntɪdʒ] **1** n of wine annata f **2** adj (classic) d'annata

vi•o•la [vɪ'əʊlə] MUS viola f

vi•o•late ['vaɪəleɪt] v/t violare

vi•o•la•tion [vaɪə'leɪʃn] violazione f

vi•o•lence ['vaɪələns] violenza f; **outbreaks of ~** episodi di violenza

vi•o•lent ['vaɪələnt] adj violento; **have a ~ temper** avere un carattere violento

vi•o•lent•ly ['vaɪələntlɪ] adv violentemente; **fall ~ in love** innamorarsi follemente

vi•o•let ['vaɪələt] n colour viola m; plant viola f

vi•o•lin [vaɪə'lɪn] violino m

vi•o•lin•ist [vaɪə'lɪnɪst] violinista m/f

VIP [viːaɪ'piː] abbr (= **very important person**) VIP m/f

vi•per ['vaɪpə(r)] snake vipera f

vi•ral ['vaɪrəl] adj infection virale

vir•gin ['vɜːdʒɪn] vergine m/f

vir•gin•i•ty [vɜː'dʒɪnətɪ] verginità f inv; **lose one's ~** perdere la verginità

Vir•go ['vɜːgəʊ] ASTR Vergine f

vir•ile ['vɪraɪl] adj virile

vi•ril•i•ty [vɪ'rɪlətɪ] virilità f inv

vir•tu•al ['vɜːtjʊəl] adj effettivo; COMPUT virtuale

vir•tu•al•ly ['vɜːtjʊəlɪ] adv (almost) praticamente

vir•tu•al re•al•i•ty realtà f virtuale

vir•tue ['vɜːtjuː] virtù f inv; **in ~ of** in virtù di

vir•tu•o•so [vɜːtʊ'əʊzəʊ] MUS virtuoso m, -a f

vir•tu•ous ['vɜːtjʊəs] adj virtuoso

vir•u•lent ['vɪrʊlənt] adj disease virulento; fig: attack, hatred feroce

vi•rus ['vaɪərəs] MED, COMPUT virus m inv

vi•sa ['viːzə] visto m

vise [vaɪz] Am → **vice**[1]

vis•i•bil•i•ty [vɪzə'bɪlətɪ] visibilità f inv

vis•i•ble ['vɪzəbl] adj object, difference visibile; anger evidente; **not ~ to the naked eye** invisibile ad occhio nudo

vis•i•bly ['vɪzəblɪ] adv different visibilmente; **he was ~ moved** era visibilmente emozionato

vi•sion ['vɪʒn] (eyesight) vista f; REL etc visione f

vis•it ['vɪzɪt] **1** n visita f; **pay a ~ to**

the doctor / dentist andare dal medico / dentista; *pay s.o. a ~* fare una visita a qu **2** *v/t person* andare a trovare; *place, country, city* visitare; *doctor, dentist* andare da

vis·it·ing card ['vɪzɪtɪŋ] biglietto m da visita

'vis·it·ing hours *npl at hospital* orario *m* delle visite

vis·it·or ['vɪzɪtə(r)] (*guest*) ospite *m*; *to museum etc* visitatore *m*, -trice *f*; (*tourist*) turista *m/f*

vi·sor ['vaɪzə(r)] visiera *f*

vis·u·al ['vɪzjʊəl] *adj organs, memory* visivo; *arts* figurativo

vis·u·al 'aid sussidio *m* visivo

vis·u·al dis'play u·nit videoterminale *m*

vis·u·al·ize ['vɪzjʊəlaɪz] *v/t* immaginare; (*foresee*) prevedere

vis·u·al·ly im'paired ['vɪzjʊəli] *adj* videoleso

vi·tal ['vaɪtl] *adj* (*essential*) essenziale; *it is ~ that …* è essenziale che …

vi·tal·i·ty [vaɪ'tælətɪ] *of person, city etc* vitalità *f inv*

vi·tal·ly ['vaɪtəlɪ] *adv*: *~ important* di vitale importanza

vi·tal 'or·gans *npl* organi *mpl* vitali

vi·tal sta'tis·tics *npl of woman* misure *fpl*

vit·a·min ['vɪtəmɪn] vitamina *f*

'vit·a·min pill (confetto *m* di) vitamina *f*

vit·ri·ol·ic [vɪtrɪ'ɒlɪk] *adj* caustico

vi·va·cious [vɪ'veɪʃəs] *adj* vivace

vi·vac·i·ty [vɪ'væsətɪ] vivacità *f inv*

viv·id ['vɪvɪd] *adj* vivido

viv·id·ly ['vɪvɪdlɪ] *adv* in modo vivido

V-neck ['viːnek] maglione *m* con scollo a V

vo·cab·u·la·ry [və'kæbjʊlərɪ] vocabolario *m*; *list of words* glossario *m*

vo·cal ['vəʊkl] *adj to do with the voice* vocale; *expressing opinions* eloquente; *become ~* cominciare a farsi sentire

'vo·cal cords *npl* corde *fpl* vocali

'vo·cal group MUS gruppo *m* vocale

vo·cal·ist ['vəʊkəlɪst] MUS cantante *m/f*

vo·ca·tion [və'keɪʃn] (*calling*) vocazione *f* (*for* a); (*profession*) professione *f*

vo·ca·tion·al [və'keɪʃnl] *adj guidance* professionale

vod·ka ['vɒdkə] vodka *f inv*

vogue [vəʊg] *n* moda *f*; *be in ~* essere in voga

voice [vɔɪs] **1** *n* voce *f* **2** *v/t opinions* esprimere

'voice mail segreteria *f* telefonica

void [vɔɪd] **1** *n* vuoto *m* **2** *adj*: *~ of* privo di

vol·a·tile ['vɒlətaɪl] *adj personality, moods* volubile

vol·ca·no [vɒl'keɪnəʊ] vulcano *m*

vol·ley ['vɒlɪ] *n of shots* raffica *f*; *in tennis* volée *f inv*

'vol·ley·ball pallavolo *f m*

volt [vəʊlt] volt *m inv*

volt·age ['vəʊltɪdʒ] voltaggio *m*; *high ~* alta tensione *f*

vol·ume ['vɒljuːm] volume *m*

vol·ume con'trol volume *m*

vol·un·tar·i·ly [vɒlən'teərɪlɪ] *adv* spontaneamente

vol·un·ta·ry ['vɒləntərɪ] *adj helper* volontario; *~ work* volontariato

vol·un·teer [vɒlən'tɪə(r)] **1** *n* volontario *m*, -a *f* **2** *v/i* offrirsi volontario

vo·lup·tu·ous [və'lʌptjʊəs] *adj woman, figure* giunonico

vom·it ['vɒmɪt] **1** *n* vomito *m* **2** *v/i* vomitare

♦ vomit up *v/t* vomitare

vo·ra·cious [və'reɪʃəs] *adj appetite* vorace

vo·ra·cious·ly [və'reɪʃəslɪ] *eat* voracemente; *fig: read* avidamente

vote [vəʊt] **1** *n* voto *m*; *right to vote* diritto *m* di voto **2** *v/i* POL votare; *~ for / against s.o. / sth* votare a favore di / contro qu / qc **3** *v/t*: *they ~d him President* l'hanno eletto presidente; *I ~ we stay behind* propongo di rimanere

♦ vote in *v/t new member* eleggere

♦ vote on *v/t issue* mettere ai voti

♦ vote out *v/t of office* respingere

vot·er ['vəʊtə(r)] POL elettore *m*, -trice *f*

vot·ing ['vəʊtɪŋ] POL votazione f

'**vot·ing booth** cabina f elettorale

♦ **vouch for** [vaʊtʃ] v/t truth of sth garantire; person garantire per

vouch·er ['vaʊtʃə(r)] buono m

vow [vaʊ] **1** n voto m **2** v/t: ~ **to do sth** giurare di fare qc

vow·el [vaʊl] vocale f

voy·age ['vɔɪɪdʒ] n by sea, in space viaggio m

V-sign ['viːsaɪn] for victory segno m di vittoria; **give s.o. the ~** mandare qu a quel paese

vul·gar ['vʌlgə(r)] adj person, language volgare

vul·ne·ra·ble ['vʌlnərəbl] adj vulnerabile

vul·ture ['vʌltʃə(r)] avvoltoio m

W

wad [wɒd] n of cotton wool batuffolo m; of paper fascio m; of banknotes mazzetta f

wad·dle ['wɒdl] v/i camminare ondeggiando

wade [weɪd] v/i guadare

♦ **wade through** v/t: I've still got this lot to wade through devo ancora leggermi tutto questo

wa·fer ['weɪfə(r)] biscuit cialda f; REL ostia f

'**wa·fer-thin** adj sottilissimo

waf·fle[1] ['wɒfl] n (to eat) tipo m di cialda

waf·fle[2] ['wɒfl] v/i parlare a vuoto

wag [wæg] (pret & pp -**ged**) **1** v/t finger scuotere; **the dog ~ged its tail** il cane scodinzolò **2** v/i: **the dog's tail was ~ging** il cane scodinzolava

wage[1] [weɪdʒ] v/t: ~ **war against** also fig fare la guerra a

wage[2] [weɪdʒ] n paga f; **~s** paga f

'**wage earn·er** salariato m, -a f;

'**wage freeze** blocco m dei salari;

'**wage ne·go·ti·a·tions** npl rivendicazioni fpl salariali; '**wage pack·et** fig busta f paga

wag·gle ['wægl] v/t ears, loose screw, tooth etc far muovere; ~ **one's hips** ancheggiare

wag·on Am, **wag·on** ['wægən] RAIL carro m merci; **be on the ~** F non bere alcolici

wail [weɪl] **1** n of person gemito m; of baby vagito m; of siren ululato m **2** v/i of person gemere; of baby vagire; of siren ululare

waist [weɪst] vita f

'**waist·coat** gilè m inv

'**waist·line** vita f

wait [weɪt] **1** n attesa f **2** v/i aspettare; **we'll ~ until he's ready** aspetteremo che sia pronto; **I can't ~ to …** non vedo l'ora di … **2** v/t meal ritardare

♦ **wait for** v/t aspettare; **wait for me!** aspettami!

♦ **wait on** v/t (serve) servire

♦ **wait up** v/i restare alzato ad aspettare

wait·er ['weɪtə(r)] cameriere m; ~! cameriere!

wait·ing ['weɪtɪŋ] n attesa f; **no ~ sign** divieto m di sosta

'**wait·ing list** lista f d'attesa

'**wait·ing room** sala f d'attesa

wait·ress ['weɪtrɪs] cameriera f

waive [weɪv] v/t (renoune) rinunciare a; (dispense with) fare al meno di, lasciar perdere

wake[1] [weɪk] (pret **woke**, pp **woken**) **1** v/i: ~ (**up**) svegliarsi **2** v/t svegliare

wake[2] [weɪk] n of ship scia f; **in the ~ of** fig a seguito di; **follow in the ~ of** seguire le tracce di

'**wake-up call** sveglia f (telefonica)

W

Wales [weɪlz] Galles *m*

walk [wɔːk] **1** *n* camminata *f*; *it's a long ~ to the office* è una bella camminata fino all'ufficio; *it's a short ~ to the office* l'ufficio è a due passi; *go for a ~* fare due passi **2** *v/i* camminare; *as opposed to taking the car, bus etc* andare a piedi; (*hike*) passeggiare; *learn to ~* imparare a camminare; *we ~ed for hours* abbiamo camminato per ore; *she ~ed over to the window* andò alla finestra **3** *v/t dog* portare fuori; *I'll ~ you home* ti accompagno a casa; *~ the streets* (*walk around*) girare in lungo e in largo

♦ **walk out** *v/i of husband etc, from theatre* andarsene; (*go on strike*) scendere in sciopero

♦ **walk out on** *v/t spouse, family* abbandonare

'**walk·a·bout** bagno *m* di folla; *go* ~ F *of monarch, politician* fare un bagno di folla

walk·er ['wɔːkə(r)] (*hiker*) escursionista *m/f; for baby* girello *m; for old person* deambulatore *m; be a slow / fast ~* avere il passo lento / spedito

walk·ie-'talk·ie [wɔːkɪ'tɔːkɪ] walkie-talkie *m inv*

walk·ing ['wɔːkɪŋ] *n as opposed to driving* camminare *m*; (*hiking*) escursionismo *m; it's within ~ distance* ci si arriva a piedi

'**walk·ing stick** bastone *m* da passeggio

'**walk·ing tour** escursionismo *m*

'**Walk·man**® walkman *m inv*; '**walk·out** *strike* sciopero *m* selvaggio; '**walk·over** (*easy win*) vittoria *f* facile

wall [wɔːl] *external* muro *m; internal* parete *f*; *fig: of silence etc* muro *m*; *go to the* ~ *of company* andare in rovina; *~s of a city* mura *fpl*; *drive s.o. up the* ~ F far diventare matto qu

wal·let ['wɒlɪt] portafoglio *m*

wal·lop ['wɒləp] **1** *n* F *blow* colpo *m* **2** *v/t* F colpire; *opponent* stracciare F

'**wall·pa·per 1** *n* tappezzeria *f*, carta *f* da parati **2** *v/t* tappezzare

wall-to-'wall *adj: ~ carpet* moquette *f*

wal·nut ['wɔːlnʌt] noce *f*

waltz [wɔːlts] *n* valzer *m inv*

wan [wɒn] *adj face* pallido

wan·der ['wɒndə(r)] *v/i* (*roam*) gironzolare; (*stray*) allontanarsi; *my attention began to ~* mi sono distratto

♦ **wander around** *v/i* girare

wane [weɪn] *v/i of interest, enthusiasm* calare

wan·gle ['wæŋgl] *v/t* F rimediare F

want [wɒnt] **1** *n: for ~ of* per mancanza di **2** *v/t* volere; (*need*) avere bisogno di; *~ to do sth* volere fare qc; *I ~ to stay here* voglio stare qui; *do you ~ to come too? – no, I don't ~ to* vuoi venire anche tu? – no, grazie; *you can have whatever you ~* puoi avere tutto ciò che vuoi; *it's not what I ~ed* non è quello che volevo; *she ~s you to go back* vuole che torni indietro; *he ~s a haircut* dovrebbe tagliarsi i capelli **3** *v/i: ~ for nothing* non mancare di niente

'**want ad** annuncio *m* economico

want·ed ['wɒntɪd] *adj by police* ricercato

want·ing ['wɒntɪŋ] *adj: be ~ in* mancare di

wan·ton ['wɒntən] *adj cruelty, neglect* gratuito

war [wɔː(r)] *n* guerra *f, fig* lotta *f; be at ~* essere in guerra

war·ble ['wɔːbl] *v/i of bird* gorgheggiare

ward [wɔːd] *n in hospital* corsia *f; child* minore *m* sotto tutela

♦ **ward off** *v/t blow* parare; *attacker* respingere; *cold* combattere

war·den ['wɔːdn] (*traffic ~*) vigile *m* urbano; *of hostel* direttore *m*, -trice *f; of nature reserve* guardiano *m*, -a *f; Am: of prison* agente *m/f* di custodia

ward·er ['wɔːdə(r)] agente *m/f* di custodia

'**ward·robe** *for clothes* armadio *m; clothes* guardaroba *m*

W

ware·house ['weəhaʊs] magazzino m

'**war·fare** guerra f

'**war·head** testata f

war·i·ly ['weərɪlɪ] adv con aria guardinga

warm [wɔːm] **1** adj caldo; welcome, smile caloroso; **it's ~** of weather fa caldo; **it's ~ in here** qui c'è caldo; **are you ~ enough?** ti fa freddo? **2** v/t: → **warm up**

♦ **warm up** v/t scaldare **2** v/i scaldarsi; of athlete etc fare riscaldamento

warm·heart·ed ['wɔːmhɑːtɪd] adj cordiale

warm·ly ['wɔːmlɪ] adv dressed con abiti pesanti; welcome, smile calorosamente

warmth [wɔːmθ] calore m; of welcome, smile calorosità f inv

'**warm-up** SP riscaldamento m

warn [wɔːn] v/t avvertire

warn·ing ['wɔːnɪŋ] n avvertimento m; **without ~** senza preavviso

warp [wɔːp] **1** v/t wood deformare; character segnare **2** v/i of wood deformarsi

warped [wɔːpt] adj fig contorto

'**war·plane** aereo m militare

war·rant ['wɒrənt] **1** n mandato m **2** v/t (deserve, call for) giustificare

war·ran·ty ['wɒrəntɪ] (guarantee) garanzia f; **be under ~** essere in garanzia

war·ri·or ['wɒrɪə(r)] guerriero m, -a f

'**war·ship** nave f da guerra

wart [wɔːt] verruca f

'**war·time** tempo m di guerra

war·y ['weərɪ] adj guardingo; **be ~ of** diffidare di

was [wɒz] pret → **be**

wash [wɒʃ] **1** n: **have a ~** darsi una lavata; **that skirt needs a ~** quella gonna va lavata **2** v/t lavare; **~ one's hands / hair** lavarsi le mani / i capelli **3** v/i lavarsi

♦ **wash up** v/i Br (wash the dishes) lavare i piatti

wash·a·ble ['wɒʃəbl] adj lavabile

'**wash·ba·sin**, '**wash·bowl** lavandino m

washed out [wɒʃt'aʊt] adj sfinito

wash·er ['wɒʃə(r)] for tap etc guarnizione f; → **washing machine**

wash·ing ['wɒʃɪŋ] washed clothes bucato m; clothes to be washed biancheria f da lavare; **do the ~** fare il bucato

'**wash·ing ma·chine** lavatrice f

'**wash·ing pow·der** detersivo m per bucato

wash·ing-'up: **do the ~** lavare i piatti

wash·ing-'up liq·uid detersivo m per i piatti

wasp [wɒsp] vespa f

waste [weɪst] **1** n spreco m; from industrial process rifiuti mpl; **it's a ~ of time / money** è tempo sprecato / sono soldi sprecati **2** adj material di scarto **3** v/t sprecare

♦ **waste away** v/i deperire

'**waste dis·pos·al (unit)** tritarifiuti m inv

waste·ful ['weɪstfʊl] adj person sprecone; methods, processes dispendioso

'**waste·land** distesa f desolata; **waste·'pa·per** cartaccia f; **waste-pa·per 'bas·ket** cestino m della cartaccia; '**waste prod·uct** scorie fpl industriali

watch [wɒtʃ] **1** n timepiece orologio m; MIL guardia f; **keep ~** stare all'erta **2** v/t film, TV guardare; (spy on) sorvegliare; (look after) tenere d'occhio **3** v/t guardare

♦ **watch for** v/t aspettare

♦ **watch out** v/i fare attenzione; **watch out!** attento!

♦ **watch out for** v/t fare attenzione a

'**watch·dog** fig comitato m di controllo

watch·ful ['wɒtʃfʊl] adj vigile

'**watch·mak·er** orologiaio m, -a f

wa·ter ['wɔːtə(r)] **1** n acqua f; **~s** NAUT acque (territoriali) **2** v/t plant annaffiare **3** v/i of eyes lacrimare; **my mouth is ~ing** ho l'acquolina in bocca

W

♦ **water down** v/t *drink* diluire

'**wa·ter can·non** idrante m; '**wa·ter·col·or** Am, '**wa·ter·col·our** n acquerello m; '**wa·ter·cress** crescione m

wa·tered 'down ['wɔːtəd] adj fig edulcorato

'**wa·ter·fall** cascata f

wa·ter·ing can ['wɔːtərɪŋ] annaffiatoio m

'**wa·ter·ing hole** hum bar m inv

'**wa·ter lev·el** il livello m delle acque; '**wa·ter lil·y** ninfea f; **wa·ter·logged** ['wɔːtəlɒgd] adj allagato; '**wa·ter main** conduttura f dell'acqua; '**wa·ter mark** filigrana f; '**wa·ter mel·on** anguria f, cocomero m; '**wa·ter pol·lu·tion** inquinamento m dell'acqua; '**wa·ter·proof** adj impermeabile

'**wa·ter·shed** fig svolta f; TV ora f dopo la quale sono ammessi programmi per un pubblico adulto; '**wa·ter·side** n: **at the ~** sulla riva; '**wa·ter·ski·ing** sci m inv nautico; '**wa·ter·tight** adj *compartment* stagno; fig inattaccabile; '**wa·ter·way** corso m d'acqua navigabile; '**wa·ter·wings** npl braccioli mpl; '**wa·ter·works**: **turn on the ~** F piangere

wa·ter·y ['wɔːtərɪ] adj acquoso

watt [wɒt] watt m inv

wave[1] [weɪv] n in sea onda f

wave[2] [weɪv] **1** n of hand saluto m (con la mano) **2** v/i with hand salutare (con la mano); **~ to s.o.** salutare qu (con la mano) **3** v/t *flag etc* sventolare

'**wave·length** RAD lunghezza f d'onda; **be on the same ~** fig essere sulla stessa lunghezza d'onda

wa·ver ['weɪvə(r)] v/i vacillare

wav·y ['weɪvɪ] adj *hair, line* ondulato

wax [wæks] n for floor, furniture cera f; in ear cerume m

way [weɪ] **1** n (method, manner) modo m; (manner) maniera f; (route) strada f; **this ~** (like this) così; (in this direction) da questa parte; **by the ~** (incidentally) a proposito; **by ~ of** (via) passando per; (in the form

of) come; **in a ~** (in certain respects) in un certo senso; **be under ~** essere in corso; **give ~** MOT dare la precedenza; (collapse) crollare; **X has given ~ to Y** (been replaced by) Y ha preso il posto di X; **have one's (own) ~** averla vinta; **OK, we'll do it your ~** OK, faremo come dici tu; **lead the ~** also fig fare strada; **lose one's ~** smarrirsi; **be in the ~** (be an obstruction) essere d'intralcio; **it's on the ~ to the station** è sulla strada della stazione; **I was on my ~ to the station** stavo andando alla stazione; **no ~!** neanche per sogno!; **there's no ~ he can do it** è impossibile che ce la faccia **2** adv F (much); **it's ~ too soon to decide** è veramente troppo presto per decidere; **they are ~ behind with their work** sono molto indietro con il lavoro

way 'in entrata f; **way of 'life** stile m di vita; **way 'out** n uscita f; fig: from situation via f d'uscita

we [wiː] pron noi; **~'re the best** siamo i migliori; **they're going, but ~'re not** loro vanno, noi no

weak [wiːk] adj physically, morally debole; tea, coffee leggero

weak·en ['wiːkn] **1** v/t indebolire **2** v/i indebolirsi

weak·ling ['wiːklɪŋ] morally smidollato m, -a f; physically mingherlino m, -a f

weak·ness ['wiːknɪs] debolezza f; **have a ~ for sth** (liking) avere un debole per qc

wealth [welθ] ricchezza f; **a ~ of** una grande abbondanza di

wealth·y ['welθɪ] adj ricco

weap·on ['wepən] arma f

wear [weə(r)] **1** n: **~ (and tear)** usura f; **clothes for everyday ~** vestiti per tutti i giorni; **clothes for evening ~** abiti da sera **2** v/t (pret **wore**, pp **worn**) (have on) indossare; (damage) logorare **3** v/i (pret **wore**, pp **worn**) (wear out) logorarsi; (last) durare

♦ **wear away 1** v/i consumarsi **2** v/t consumare

♦ **wear down** v/t resistance fiaccare

♦ **wear off** v/i of effect, feeling svanire

♦ **wear out 1** v/t (tire) estenuare; shoes consumare **2** v/i of shoes, carpet consumarsi

wea·ri·ly ['wɪərɪlɪ] adv stancamente

wear·ing ['weərɪŋ] adj (tiring) stancante

wear·y ['wɪərɪ] adj stanco

weath·er ['weðə(r)] **1** n tempo m; **be feeling under the ~** sentirsi poco bene **2** v/t crisis superare

'weath·er-beat·en adj segnato; **'weath·er fore·cast** previsioni fpl del tempo; **'weath·er·man** meteorologo m

weave [wiːv] **1** v/t (pret **wove**, pp **woven**) cloth tessere; basket intrecciare **2** v/i (move) zigzagare

web [web] of spider ragnatela f; **the Web** COMPUT il web m inv, la Rete f inv

webbed 'feet piedi mpl palmati

'web page pagina f web

'web site sito m web

wed·ding ['wedɪŋ] matrimonio m

'wed·ding an·ni·ver·sa·ry anniversario m di matrimonio; **'wed·ding cake** torta f nuziale; **'wed·ding day** giorno m del matrimonio; **'wed·ding dress** abito m or vestito m da sposa; **'wed·ding ring** fede f

wedge [wedʒ] **1** n to hold sth in place zeppa f; of cheese etc fetta f **2** v/t: ~ **open** tenere aperto

Wed·nes·day ['wenzdeɪ] mercoledì m inv

wee [wiː] adj F piccolo; **a ~ bit** un pochino

weed [wiːd] **1** n erbaccia f **2** v/t diserbare

♦ **weed out** v/t (remove) eliminare

'weed-kill·er diserbante m

weed·y ['wiːdɪ] adj F mingherlino

week [wiːk] settimana f; **a ~ tomorrow** una settimana a domani

'week·day giorno m feriale

week'end fine m settimana, weekend m inv; **at** or Am **on the ~** durante il fine settimana

week·ly ['wiːklɪ] **1** adj settimanale

2 n magazine settimanale m **3** adv settimanalmente

weep [wiːp] v/i (pret & pp **wept**) piangere

weep·y ['wiːpɪ] adj: **be ~** essere piagnucoloso

wee-wee 1 n F pipì f inv F; **do a ~** fare la pipì **2** v/i F fare la pipì

weigh [weɪ] v/t & v/i pesare

♦ **weigh down** v/t: **be weighed down with** with bags curvarsi sotto il peso di; with worries essere oppresso da

♦ **weigh on** v/t preoccupare

♦ **weigh up** v/t (assess) valutare

weight [weɪt] of person, object peso m; **put on / lose ~** ingrassare / dimagrire

♦ **weight down** v/t fermare con pesi

weight·less·ness ['weɪtləsnəs] assenza f di peso

'weight·lift·er pesista m/f

'weight·lift·ing sollevamento m pesi

weight·y ['weɪtɪ] adj fig: important importante

weir [wɪə(r)] chiusa f

weird [wɪəd] adj strano

weird·ly ['wɪədlɪ] adv stranamente

weird·o ['wɪədəʊ] n F pazzoide m/f

wel·come ['welkəm] **1** adj benvenuto; **make s.o. ~** accogliere bene qu; **it makes a ~ change** è un gradito cambiamento; **you're ~!** prego!; **you're ~ to try some** serviti pure **2** n also fig accoglienza f; fig: to news, proposal accoglienza f **3** v/t guests etc accogliere; fig: decision etc rallegrarsi di; **she ~s a challenge** apprezza le sfide

weld [weld] v/t saldare

weld·er ['weldə(r)] saldatore m, -trice f

wel·fare ['welfeə(r)] bene m inv

wel·fare 'state stato m sociale; **'wel·fare work** assistenza f sociale; **'wel·fare work·er** assistente m/f sociale

well[1] [wel] n for water, oil pozzo m

well[2] [wel] **1** adv bene; **~ done!** bravo!; **as ~** (too) anche; **as ~ as** in addition to oltre a; **it's just as ~ you**

W

told me hai fatto bene a dirmelo; *very* ~ *acknowledging an order* benissimo; *when you don't agree with sth but are doing it anyway* va bene; *~, ~I surprise* bene, bene!; *~ ... uncertainty, thinking* beh ... **2** *adj:* **be** ~ stare bene; *feel* ~ sentirsi bene; *get* ~ *soon!* guarisci presto!

well·'bal·anced *adj person, meal* equilibrato; *meal, diet* equilibrato; **well-be'haved** *adj* educato; **well-'be·ing** benessere *m*; **well-'built** *adj* ben fatto; *euph (fat)* robusto; **well-'done** *adj meat* ben cotto; **well-'dressed** *adj* ben vestito; **well-'earned** *adj* meritato; **well-'heeled** *adj* F danaroso

wel·lies ['weliz] *npl* F → **wellingtons**

well-in'formed *adj* ben informato

wel·ling·tons ['welɪŋtənz] *npl* stivali *mpl* di gomma

well-'known *adj* famoso; **well-'made** *adj* ben fatto; **well-'mannered** *adj* ben educato; **well-'mean·ing** *adj* spinto da buone intenzioni; **well-'off** *adj* benestante; **well-'paid** *adj* ben pagato; **well-'read** *adj* colto; **well-'timed** *adj* tempestivo; **well-to-'do** *adj* abbiente; **well-'worn** *adj* liso

Welsh [welʃ] **1** *adj* gallese **2** *n language* gallese *m*; *the* ~ i gallesi

went [went] *pret* → **go**

wept [wept] *pret & pp* → **weep**

were [wɜː(r)] *pret pl* → **be**

west [west] **1** *n* ovest *m*, occidente *m*; *the West* POL l'Occidente; *western part of a country* parte *f* occidentale del paese **2** *adj* occidentale **3** *adv* verso ovest; ~ *of* a ovest di

west·er·ly ['westəlɪ] *adj* occidentale; *in a* ~ *direction* verso ovest

west·ern ['westən] **1** *adj* occidentale; *Western* occidentale **2** *n (film)* western *m inv*

West·ern·er ['westənə(r)] occidentale *m/f*

west·ern·ized ['westənaɪzd] *adj* occidentalizzato

west·ward ['westwəd] *adv* verso ovest

wet [wet] *adj* bagnato; *(rainy)* piovoso; ~ *paint as sign* vernice fresca; *be* ~ *through* essere fradicio

wet 'blan·ket F guastafeste *m/f inv*

'wet suit *for diving* muta *f*

whack [wæk] **1** *n* F *(blow)* colpo *m*; F *(share)* parte *f* **2** *v/t* F colpire

whacked [wækt] *adj* F stanco morto

whack·ing ['wækɪŋ] *adj* F enorme

whale [weɪl] balena *f*

whal·ing ['weɪlɪŋ] caccia *f* alla balena

wharf [wɔːf] *n* banchina *f*

what [wɒt] **1** *pron* (che) cosa; ~ *is that?* (che) cos'è?; ~ *is it?* *(what do you want)* (che) cosa c'è?; ~? cosa?; *astonishment* (che) cosa?; *it's not* ~ *I meant* non è ciò che volevo dire; ~ *about some dinner?* e se mangiassimo qualcosa?; ~ *about heading home?* e se ce ne andassimo a casa?; ~ *is the date today?* quanti ne abbiamo oggi?; ~ *for? (why)* perché?; *so* ~? e allora? **2** *adj* che *inv*, quale; ~ *colour is the car?* di che colore è la macchina?; ~ *university are you at?* in quale università studi? **3** *adv:* ~ *a brilliant idea!* che bella idea!

what·ev·er [wɒt'evə(r)] **1** *pron*; *I'll do* ~ *you want* farò (tutto) quello che vuoi; ~ *I do, it'll be a probem* qualsiasi cosa faccia, ci saranno problemi; ~ *the season regardless of* in qualunque stagione; ~ *people say* qualunque cosa dica la gente; ~ *gave you that idea?* cosa mai te lo ha fatto pensare? **2** *adj* qualunque; *you have no reason* ~ *to worry* non hai nessun motivo di preoccuparti

wheat [wiːt] grano *m*, frumento *m*

whee·dle ['wiːdl] *v/t* F: ~ *sth out of s.o.* ottenere qc da qu con lusinghe

wheel [wiːl] **1** *n* ruota *f*; *(steering* ~*)* volante *m* **2** *v/t bicycle* spingere **3** *v/i of birds* roteare

♦ **wheel around** *v/i* voltarsi

'wheel·bar·row carriola *f*; **'wheel·chair** sedia *f* a rotelle; **'wheel**

clamp ceppo *m* bloccaruote

wheeze [wi:z] *v/i* ansimare

when [wen] *adv conj* quando **2** *conj* quando; **~ I was a child** quand'ero bambino

when·ev·er [wen'evə(r)] *adv (each time)* ogni volta che; *regardless of when* in qualunque momento

where [weə(r)] **1** *adv* dove **2** *conj* dove; *this is ~ I used to live* io abitavo qui

where·a·bouts [weərə'bauts] **1** *adv* dove **2** *npl*: *know s.o.'s ~* sapere dove si trova qu

where·as [weər'æz] mentre

wher·ev·er [weər'evə(r)] **1** *conj* dovunque; *~ you go* dovunque tu vada **2** *adv* dove; *~ can he be?* dove sarà mai?

whet [wet] *v/t v/t (pret & pp -ted)* *appetite* stuzzicare

wheth·er ['weðə(r)] *pron* se

which [wɪtʃ] **1** *adj* quale; *~ one is yours?* qual è il tuo? **2** *pron interrogative* quale; *relative* che; *on/in ~* su/in cui; *take one, it doesn't matter ~* prendine uno, non importa quale

which·ev·er [wɪtʃ'evə(r)] **1** *adj* qualunque **2** *pron* quello che *m*, quella che *f*; *~ of the methods* qualunque metodo

whiff [wɪf] *unpleasant* zaffata *f*; *catch a ~ of* sentire

while [waɪl] **1** *conj* mentre; *(although)* benché **2** *n*: *a long ~ ago* molto tempo fa; *wait a long ~* aspettare molto *o* lungo; *for a ~* per un po'; *in a ~* fra poco; *I'll wait a ~ longer* aspetto un altro po'

♦ **while away** *v/t* passare

whim [wɪm] capriccio *m*

whim·per ['wɪmpə(r)] **1** *n of person, baby* gemito *m*; *of animal* mugolio *m* **2** *v/i of person, baby* gemere; *of animal* mugolare

whine [waɪn] *v/i of dog* guaire; F *(complain)* piagnucolare

whip [wɪp] **1** *n* frusta *f* **2** *v/t (pret & pp -ped)* *(beat)* sbattere; *cream* montare; F *(defeat)* stracciare F

♦ **whip out** *v/t* F tirar fuori (fulmineamente)

♦ **whip up** *v/t (arouse)* sobillare; F *meal* improvvisare

whipped cream [wɪpt] panna *f* montata

whip·ping ['wɪpɪŋ] *(beating)* bastonata *f*; F *(defeat)* batosta *f*

'whip·ping cream panna *f* da montare

'whip·round F colletta *f*; *have a ~* fare una colletta

whirl [wɜ:l] **1** *n*: *my mind is in a ~* mi gira la testa **2** *v/i of blades etc* rotare; *of leaves* volteggiare; *of person* girarsi

'whirl·pool *in river* mulinello *m*; *for relaxation* vasca *f* per idromassaggio

whirr [wɜ:(r)] *v/i* ronzare

whisk [wɪsk] **1** *n* frusta *f*; *mechanical* frullino *m* **2** *v/t eggs* frullare

♦ **whisk away** *v/t* togliere in fretta

whis·kers ['wɪskəz] *npl of man* basette *fpl*; *of animal* baffi *mpl*

whis·ky whisky *m inv*

whis·per ['wɪspə(r)] **1** *n* bisbiglio *m*; *(rumour)* voce *f* **2** *v/t & v/i* bisbigliare

whis·tle ['wɪsl] **1** *n sound* fischio *m*; *device* fischietto *m* **2** *v/i* fischiare **3** *v/t* fischiettare

whis·tle-blow·er ['wɪslbləʊə(r)] F *persona f che denuncia irregolarità all'interno della propria azienda*

white [waɪt] **1** *n colour* bianco *m*; *of egg* albume *m*, bianco *m* F; *person* bianco *m*, -a *f* **2** *adj* bianco; *person* bianco; *go ~* sbiancare (in viso)

white 'Christ·mas natale *m* con la neve; **white 'cof·fee** *Br* caffè *m inv* con latte *o* panna; **white-col·lar 'work·er** impiegato *m*, -a *f*; **'White House** Casa *f* Bianca; **white 'lie** bugia *f* innocente; **white 'meat** carne *f* bianca; **'white·wash 1** *n* calce *f*; *fig* copertura *f* **2** *v/t* imbiancare (con calce); **white 'wine** vino *m* bianco

Whit·sun ['wɪtsn] Pentecoste *f*

whit·tle ['wɪtl] *v/t wood* intagliare

♦ **whittle down** *v/t* ridurre

W

whiz(z) [wɪz] *n*: *be a ~ at* F essere un genio in

♦ **whizz by**, **whizz past** *v/i of time*, *car* sfrecciare

'**whizz-kid** F mago *m*, -a *f* F

who [huː] *pron interrogative* chi; *relative* che; *the man ~ I was talking to* l'uomo con cui parlavo; *I don't know ~ to believe* non so a chi credere

who·dun(n)·it [huːˈdʌnɪt] giallo *m*

who·ev·er [huːˈevə(r)] *pron* chiunque; *(interrogative)* chi mai; *~ can that be?* chi sarà mai?

whole [həʊl] **1** *adj*: *the ~ town* tutta la città; *two ~ hours / days* ben due ore / giorni; *a ~ chicken* un pollo intero; *he drank / ate the ~ lot* ha bevuto / mangiato tutto; *it's a ~ lot easier / better* è molto più facile / meglio **2** *n* tutto *m*; *the ~ of the United States* tutti gli Stati Uniti; *on the ~* nel complesso

whole-heart·ed [həʊlˈhɑːtɪd] *adj* senza riserve; **whole-heart·ed·ly** [həʊlˈhɑːtɪdlɪ] *adv* senza riserve; **'whole·meal 'bread** pane *m* integrale; '**whole·sale 1** *adj* all'ingrosso; *fig* in massa **2** *adv* all'ingrosso; **whole·sal·er** [ˈhəʊlseɪlə(r)] grossista *m/f*; **whole·some** [ˈhəʊlsəm] *adj* sano

whol·ly [ˈhəʊlɪ] *adv* completamente

whol·ly owned 'sub·sid·i·a·ry consociata *f* interamente controllata

whom [huːm] *pron fml* chi; *to / for* a cui

whoop·ing cough [ˈhuːpɪŋ] pertosse *f*

whop·ping [ˈwɒpɪŋ] *adj* F enorme

whore [hɔː(r)] *n* puttana *f*

whose [huːz] **1** *pron interrogative* di chi; *relative* il / la cui; *~ is this?* di chi è questo?; *a man ~ wife ...* un uomo la cui moglie ...; *a country ~ economy is booming* un paese dall'economia fiorente **2** *adj* di chi; *~ bike is that?* di chi è quella bici?; *~ car are we taking?* che macchina prendiamo?

why [waɪ] *adv* perché; *that's ~* ecco perché; *~ not?* perché no?; *the reason ~ he left* il motivo per cui se ne è andato

wick·ed [ˈwɪkɪd] *adj (evil)* malvagio; *(mischievous)* malizioso

wick·er [ˈwɪkə(r)] *adj* di vimini

wick·er 'chair poltrona *f* di vimini

wick·et [ˈwɪkɪt] porta *f*

wide [waɪd] *adj* largo; *experience* vasto; *range* ampio; *be 12 metres ~* essere largo 12 metri

wide-a'wake *adj* sveglio

wide·ly [ˈwaɪdlɪ] *adv used, known* largamente; *it is ~ believed that ...* è una credenza diffusa che ...

wid·en [ˈwaɪdn] **1** *v/t* allargare **2** *v/i* allargarsi

wide-'o·pen *adj* spalancato; **wide-'rang·ing** *adj* di largo respiro; '**wide·spread** *adj* diffuso

wid·ow [ˈwɪdəʊ] *n* vedova *f*

wid·ow·er [ˈwɪdəʊə(r)] vedovo *m*

width [wɪdθ] larghezza *f*; *of fabric* altezza *f*

wield [wiːld] *v/t weapon* brandire; *power* esercitare

wife [waɪf] (*pl* **wives** [waɪvz]) moglie *f*

wig [wɪg] parrucca *f*

wig·gle [ˈwɪgl] *v/t*: *~ one's hips* ancheggiare; *loose screw etc* muovere

wild [waɪld] **1** *adj animal, flowers* selvatico; *teenager, party* scatenato; *(crazy: scheme)* folle; *applause* fragoroso; *be ~ about ...* (*keen on*) andare pazzo per ...; *go ~* impazzire; *(become angry)* andare su tutte le furie; *run ~ of children* scatenarsi; *of plants* crescere senza controllo **2** *n*: *the ~s* le zone sperdute

wil·der·ness [ˈwɪldənɪs] *empty place* deserto *m*; *fig: garden etc* giungla *f*

'**wild·fire**: *spread like ~* allargarsi a macchia d'olio; **wild'goose chase** ricerca *f* inutile; '**wild·life** fauna *f*; *~ programme* programma *m* sulla natura

wild·ly [ˈwaɪldlɪ] *adv* F terribilmente

wil·ful [ˈwɪlfʊl] *adj person* ostinato; *action* intenzionale; *action*

will¹ [wɪl] *n* LAW testamento *m*

will² [wɪl] *n* (*willpower*) volontà *f inv*

will³ [wɪl] *v/aux*: **I ~ let you know tomorrow** ti farò sapere entro domani; **~ you be there?** ci sarai?; **I won't be back** non tornerò; **you ~ call me, won't you?** mi chiamerai, vero?; **I'll pay for this – no you won't** questo lo pago io – no, lascia stare; **the car won't start** la macchina non parte; **~ you tell her that …?** dille che …; **~ you have some more tea?** vuoi dell'altro tè?; **~ you stop that!** smettila!

will·ful *Am → wilful*

will·ing ['wɪlɪŋ] *adj* disponibile; **are you ~ to pay more?** sei disposto a pagare di più?; **he was not ~ to accept** non ha voluto accettare

will·ing·ly ['wɪlɪŋlɪ] *adv* volentieri

will·ing·ness ['wɪlɪŋnɪs] disponibilità *f inv*

wil·low ['wɪləʊ] salice *m*

will·pow·er forza *f* di volontà

wil·ly-nil·ly [wɪlɪ'nɪlɪ] *adv* (*at random*) a casaccio

wilt [wɪlt] *v/i* of plant appassire

wi·ly ['waɪlɪ] *adj* astuto

wimp [wɪmp] F pappamolle *m/f*

win [wɪn] **1** *n* vittoria *f* **2** *v/t & v/i* (*pret & pp* **won**) vincere

♦ **win back** *v/t* riconquistare

wince [wɪns] *v/i* fare una smorfia

wind¹ [wɪnd] **1** *n* vento *m*; (*flatulence*) aria *f*; **get ~ of …** venire a sapere … **2** *v/t* **~ s.o.** togliere il fiato a qu

wind² [waɪnd] (*pret & pp* **wound**) **1** *v/i* of path, stream snodarsi; of plant avvolgersi **2** *v/t* avvolgere

♦ **wind down 1** *v/i*: **the party began to wind down** la gente cominciò ad andar via dalla festa **2** *v/t car window* abbassare; *business* chiudere gradualmente

♦ **wind up 1** *v/t clock* caricare; *car window* tirar su; *speech, presentation* concludere; *business, affairs, company* chiudere **2** *v/i*: **wind up in hospital** finire in ospedale

wind·bag F trombone *m*

wind·fall *fig* colpo *m* di fortuna

wind·ing ['waɪndɪŋ] *adj* tortuoso

wind in·stru·ment strumento *m* a fiato

wind·mill mulino *m*

win·dow ['wɪndəʊ] of house finestra *f*; of shop vetrina *f*; of car, train finestrino *m*; COMPUT finestra *f*; **in the ~** of shop in vetrina

win·dow box fioriera *f*; **'win·dow clean·er** lavavetri *m/f inv*; **'win·dow·pane** vetro *m* (della finestra); **'win·dow seat** on plane, train posto *m* di finestrino; **'window-shop** *v/i* (*pret & pp* -ped): **go ~ping** guardare le vetrine; **window·sill** ['wɪndəʊsɪl]

wind·screen parabrezza *m inv*; **'wind·screen wip·er** tergicristallo *m*; **'wind·shield** *Am* parabrezza *m inv* **'wind·surf·er** person windsurfista *m/f*; board windsurf *m inv*; **'wind·surf·ing** windsurf *m inv*

wind·y ['wɪndɪ] *adj* weather, day ventoso; **it's getting ~** si sta alzando il vento

wine [waɪn] vino *m*

wine bar enoteca *f*, bar *m inv*; **'wine cel·lar** cantina *f*; **'wine glass** bicchiere *m* da vino; **'wine list** lista *f* dei vini; **'wine mak·er** viticoltore *m*, -trice *f*; **'wine mer·chant** company azienda *f* vinicola; individual vinaio *m*, -a *f*

wing [wɪŋ] *n also* SP ala *f*

'wing·span apertura *f* alare

wink [wɪŋk] **1** *n* occhiolino *m*; **I didn't sleep a ~** F non ho chiuso occhio **2** *v/i* of person strizzare gli occhi; **~ at s.o.** fare l'occhiolino a qu

win·ner ['wɪnə(r)] vincitore *m*, -trice *f*

win·ning ['wɪnɪŋ] *adj* vincente

'win·ning post traguardo *m*

win·nings ['wɪnɪŋz] *npl* vincita *fsg*

win·ter ['wɪntə(r)] *n* inverno *m*

win·ter 'sports *npl* sport *m inv* invernali

win·try ['wɪntrɪ] *adj* invernale

wipe [waɪp] *v/t* (*dry*) asciugare; (*clean*) pulire; *tape* cancellare

W

♦ **wipe out** v/t (*kill*, *destroy*) distruggere; *debt* estinguere

wip·er ['waɪpə(r)] → **windscreen wiper**

wire [waɪr] **1** *adj* metallico **2** *n* fil *m* di ferro; ELEC filo *m* elettrico

wire·less ['waɪələs] radio *f inv*

wire netting rete *f* metallica

wir·ing ['waɪərɪŋ] *n* ELEC impianto *m* elettrico

wir·y ['waɪərɪ] *adj person* dal fisico asciutto

wis·dom ['wɪzdəm] saggezza *f*

'wis·dom tooth dente *m* del giudizio

wise [waɪz] *adj* saggio

'wise·crack *n* F spiritosaggine *f*

'wise guy *pej* spiritoso *m*

wise·ly ['waɪzlɪ] *adv act* saggiamente

wish [wɪʃ] **1** *n* desiderio *m*; **make a ~** esprimere un desiderio; **against his family's ~es** contro il volere della famiglia; **best ~es** for birthday *etc* tanti auguri; *as greetings* cordiali saluti **2** v/t volere; **I ~ that he'd stop** vorrei che la smettesse; **~ s.o. well** fare tanti auguri a qu; **I ~ed him good luck** gli ho augurato buona fortuna **3** v/i: **wish for** desiderare

'wish·bone forcella *f* (di pollo)

wish·ful 'think·ing ['wɪʃful] illusione *f*

wish·y-wash·y ['wɪʃwɒʃɪ] *adj person* insulso; *colour* slavato

wisp [wɪsp] *of hair* ciocca *f*; *of smoke* filo *m*

wist·ful ['wɪstful] *adj* malinconico

wist·ful·ly ['wɪstfəlɪ] *adv* malinconicamente

wit [wɪt] (*humour*) spirito *m*; *person* persona *f* di spirito; **be at one's ~s' end** non sapere più che fare; **keep one's ~s about one** non perdere la testa; **be scared out of one's ~s** essere spaventato a morte

witch [wɪtʃ] strega *f*

'witch-hunt *fig* caccia *f* alle streghe

with [wɪð] *prep* con; (*proximity*) con; (*agency*) con; (*cause*) di; (*possession*) con; **shiver ~ fear** tremare di paura; **a girl ~ blue eyes** una ragazza dagli *o* con gli occhi azzurri; **~ a**

smile / a wave con un sorriso / un gesto della mano; **are you ~ me?** (*do you understand*) mi segui?; **~ no money** senza soldi

withdraw [wɪð'drɔː] (*pret -drew*, *pp -drawn*) **1** v/t *complaint, application, troops* ritirare; *money from bank* prelevare; *troops* ritirare **2** v/i ritirarsi; ritirarsi

with·draw·al [wɪð'drɔːəl] *of complaint, application, troops* ritiro *m*; *of money* prelievo *m*; *of troops* ritiro *m*; *from drugs* crisi *f inv* di astinenza

with'draw·al symp·toms *npl* sindrome *f* da astinenza

with'drawn [wɪð'drɔːn] *adj person* chiuso

with·er ['wɪðə(r)] v/i seccare

with'hold v/t (*pret & pp -held*) *information* nascondere; *consent* rifiutare; *payment* trattenere

with'in *prep* (*inside*) dentro; *in expressions of time* nel giro di, entro; *in expressions of distance* a meno di; **is it ~ walking distance?** ci si arriva a piedi?; **we kept ~ the budget** abbiamo rispettato il budget; **it is not ~ my power** non rientra nelle mie competenze; **~ reach** a portata di mano

with'out *prep* senza; **~ you / him** senza (di) te / lui; **~ looking / asking** senza guardare / chiedere; **~ his seeing** senza che lo vedesse

with'stand v/t (*pret & pp -stood*) resistere a

wit·ness ['wɪtnɪs] **1** *n* testimone *m/f*; testimone *m/f* **2** v/t *accident, crime* essere testimone di; *signature* attestare l'autenticità di

'wit·ness box banco *m* dei testimoni

wit·ti·cis·m ['wɪtɪsɪzm] arguzia *f*

wit·ty ['wɪtɪ] *adj* arguto

wob·ble ['wɒbl] v/i *of person* vacillare; *of object* traballare

wob·bly ['wɒblɪ] *adj person* vacillante; *object* traballante; *voice, hand* tremante

wok [wɒk] wok *m inv*

woke [wəʊk] *pret* → **wake**

wok·en ['wəʊkn] *pp* → **wake**

wolf [wʊlf] **1** *n* (*pl* **wolves** [wʊlvz]) *animal* lupo *m*; (*fig: womanizer*) donnaiolo *m* **2** *v/t*: ~ (**down**) divorare

'wolf whis·tle *n* fischio *m*

'wolf-whis·tle *v/i*: ~ **at s.o.** fischiare dietro a qu

wom·an ['wʊmən] (*pl* **women** ['wɪmɪn]) donna *f*

wom·an 'doc·tor dottoressa *f*

wom·an 'driv·er autista *f*

wom·an·iz·er ['wʊmənaɪzə(r)] donnaiolo *m*

wom·an 'priest donna *f* sacerdote

womb [wuːm] utero *m*

wom·en ['wɪmɪn] *pl* → **woman**

women's lib [wɪmɪnz'lɪb] movimento *m* di liberazione della donna

women's lib·ber [wɪmɪnz'lɪbə(r)] femminista *f*

won [wʌn] *pret* & *pp* → **win**

won·der ['wʌndə(r)] **1** *n* (*amazement*) stupore *m*, meraviglia *f*; *of science etc* meraviglia *f*; *no* ~! non mi stupisce!; *it's a* ~ *that ...* è incredibile che ... **2** *v/i* pensare **3** *v/t* domandarsi; *I* ~ *if you could help* mi chiedevo se potessi aiutarmi

won·der·ful ['wʌndəfʊl] *adj* stupendo

won·der·ful·ly ['wʌndəflɪ] *adv* (*extremely*) estremamente

won't [wəʊnt] → **will not**

wood [wʊd] legno *m*; *for fire* legna *f*; (*forest*) bosco *m*

wood·ed ['wʊdɪd] *adj* boscoso

wood·en ['wʊdn] *adj* made of wood di legno

wood·peck·er ['wʊdpekə(r)] picchio *m*; 'wood·wind MUS fiati *mpl*; 'wood·work *parts made of wood* strutture *fpl* in legno; *activity* lavorazione *f* del legno

wool [wʊl] lana *f*

wool·en *Am*, wool·len ['wʊlən] **1** *adj* di lana **2** *n* indumento *m* di lana

word [wɜːd] **1** *n* parola *f*; (*news*) notizie *fpl*; (*promise*) parola *f*; *is there any* ~ *from ...?* ci sono notizie da ...?; *you have my* ~ hai la mia

parola; *have* ~s (*argue*) litigare; *have a* ~ *with s.o.* parlare con qu **2** *v/t article, letter* formulare

word·ing ['wɜːdɪŋ] formulazione *f*

word 'pro·cess·ing trattamento *m* testi

word 'pro·ces·sor *software* word processor *m inv*

wore [wɔː (r)] *pret* → **wear**

work [wɜːk] **1** *n* lavoro *m*; *out of* ~ disoccupato; *be at* ~ essere al lavoro; *I go to* ~ *by bus* vado a lavorare in autobus **2** *v/i of person* lavorare; *study* studiare; *of machine*, (*succeed*) funzionare; (*succeed*) funzionare; *I used to* ~ *with him* lavoravamo insieme; *how does it* ~? *of device* come funziona? **3** *v/t employee* far lavorare; *machine* far funzionare

◆work off *v/t bad mood, anger* sfogare; *flab* smaltire

◆work out **1** *v/t problem* capire; *solution* trovare **2** *v/i at gym* fare ginnastica; *of relationship etc* funzionare

◆work out to *v/t* (*add up to*) ammontare a

◆work up *v/t*: *work up enthusiasm* entusiasmarsi; *I worked up an appetite* mi è venuto appetito; *get worked up* (*get angry*) infuriarsi; (*get nervous*) agitarsi

work·a·ble ['wɜːkəbl] *adj solution* realizzabile

work·a·hol·ic [wɜːkə'hɒlɪk] *n* F stacanovista *m/f*

'work·day *hours of work* giornata *f* lavorativa; *not a holiday* giorno *m* feriale

work·er ['wɜːkə(r)] lavoratore *m*, -trice *f*; *she's a good* ~ lavora bene

'work·force forza *f* lavoro

work·ing ['wɜːkɪŋ] *adj day, week* lavorativo; *clothes* da lavoro; *lunch* di lavoro; *in* ~ *order* funzionante; 'work·ing class classe *f* operaia; 'work·ing-class *adj* operaio; 'work·ing con·di·tions *npl* condizioni *fpl* di lavoro; work·ing 'day → **workday**; 'work·ing hours *npl* orario *m* di lavoro; work·ing

W

'**knowledge** conoscenza *f* di base; **work·ing** '**moth·er** madre *f* che lavora

'**work·load** carico *m* di lavoro; '**work·man** operaio *m*; '**work·man·like** *adj* professionale; '**work·man·ship** fattura *f*; **work of 'art** opera *f* d'arte; '**work·out** allenamento *m*; '**work per·mit** permesso *m* di lavoro; '**work·shop** laboratorio *m*; *for mechanic* officina *f*; (*seminar*) workshop *m inv*; '**work sta·tion** work station *f inv*; '**work·top** piano *m* di lavoro; **work-to-'rule** sciopero *m* bianco

world [wɜːld] *n* mondo *m*; *the ~ of computers / the theatre* il mondo dei computer / del teatro; *out of this ~* F fantastico

World 'Cup mondiali *mpl* (di calcio)

world-'class *adj* di livello internazionale

world-'fa·mous *adj* di fama mondiale

world·ly ['wɜːldlɪ] *adj goods* materiale; *not spiritual* terreno; *power* temporale; *person* mondano

world 'pow·er potenza *f* mondiale; **world 're·cord** record *m inv* mondiale; **world 'war** guerra *f* mondiale; '**world·wide 1** *adj* mondiale **2** *adv* a livello mondiale

worm [wɜːm] *n* verme *m*

worn [wɔːn] *pp* → **wear**

worn-'out *adj shoes, carpet, part* logoro; *person* esausto, sfinito

wor·ried ['wʌrɪd] *adj* preoccupato

wor·ried·ly ['wʌrɪdlɪ] *adv* con aria preoccupata

wor·ry ['wʌrɪ] **1** *n* preoccupazione *f* **2** *v/t* (*pret & pp* -*ied*) preoccupare; (*upset*) turbare **3** *v/i* (*pret & pp* -*ied*) proccuparsi; *it will be alright, don't ~!* andrà tutto bene, non preoccuparti!

wor·ry·ing ['wʌrɪɪŋ] *adj* preoccupante

worse [wɜːs] **1** *adj* peggiore; *things will get ~* le cose peggioreranno **2** *adv* peggio

wors·en ['wɜːsn] *v/i* peggiorare

wor·ship ['wɜːʃɪp] **1** *n* culto *m* **2** *v/t* (*pret & pp* -*ped*) venerare; *fig* adorare

worst [wɜːst] **1** *adj* peggiore **2** *adv* peggio **3** *n*: *the ~* il peggio; *if the ~ comes to the ~* nel peggiore dei casi

worst-case scen·a·ri·o: *the ~* la peggiore delle ipotesi

worth [wɜːθ] **1** *adj*: *be ~* valere; *it's ~ reading / seeing* vale la pena leggerlo / vederlo; *be ~ it* valerne la pena **2** *n* valore *m*; *£20 ~ of petrol* 20 sterline di benzina

worth·less ['wɜːθlɪs] *adj object* senza valore; *person* senza valore

worth'while *adj cause* lodevole; *be ~* (*beneficial, useful*) essere utile; (*worth the effort, worth doing*) valere la pena

worth·y ['wɜːðɪ] *adj* degno; *cause* lodevole; *be ~ of* (*deserve*) meritare

would [wʊd] *v/aux*: *I ~ help if I could* ti aiuterei se potessi; *I said that I ~ go* ho detto che sarei andato; *I told him I ~ not leave unless ...* gli ho detto che non me ne sarei andato se non ...; *~ you like to go to the cinema?* vuoi andare al cinema?; *~ you mind if I smoked?* la disturba se fumo?; *~ you tell her that ...?* le dica che ...; *~ you close the door?* le dispiace chiudere la porta?; *I ~ have told you but ...* te l'avrei detto ma ...; *I ~ not have been so angry if ...* non mi sarei arrabbiato tanto se ...

wound¹ [wuːnd] **1** *n* ferita *f* **2** *v/t also with remark* ferire; *with remark* ferire

wound² [waʊnd] *pret & pp* → **wind²**

wove [wəʊv] *pret* → **weave**

wov·en ['wəʊvn] *pp* → **weave**

wow [waʊ] *int* wow

wrap [ræp] *v/t* (*pret & pp* -*ped*) *parcel, gift* incartare; (*wind, cover*) avvolgere

♦ **wrap up** *v/i against the cold* coprirsi bene

wrap·per ['ræpə(r)] incarto *m*

wrap·ping ['ræpɪŋ] involucro *m*

'**wrap·ping pa·per** carta *f* da regalo

wreath [riːθ] corona *f; for funeral co-rona f* funebre

wreck [rek] **1** *n of ship* relitto *m; of car* carcassa *f; be a nervous ~* sentirsi un rottame **2** *v/t ship* far naufragare; *car* demolire; *plans, career, marriage* distruggere

wreck·age ['rekɪdʒ] *of car, plane* rottami *mpl; of marriage, career* brandelli *mpl*

wrench [rentʃ] **1** *n tool* chiave *f* inglese; *injury* slogatura *f* **2** *v/t injure* slogarsi; (*pull*) strappare

wres·tle ['resl] *v/i* fare la lotta

♦ **wrestle with** *v/t problems* lottare con

wres·tler ['reslə(r)] lottatore *m*, -trice *f*

wrest·ling ['reslɪŋ] lotta *f* libera

wres·tling match incontro *m* di lotta libera

wrig·gle ['rɪgl] *v/i* (*squirm*) dimenarsi; *along the ground* strisciare

♦ **wriggle out of** *v/t* sottrarsi a

♦ **wring out** *v/t* (*pret & pp wrung*) *cloth* strizzare

wrin·kle ['rɪŋkl] **1** *n in skin* ruga *f; in clothes* grinza *f* **2** *v/t clothes* stropicciare **3** *v/i of clothes* stropicciarsi

wrist [rɪst] polso *m*

wrist·watch orologio *m* da polso

write [raɪt] (*pret wrote, pp written*) **1** *v/t* scrivere; *cheque* fare **2** *v/i* scrivere; *of author* scrivere; (*send a letter*) scrivere

♦ **write down** *v/t* annotare, scrivere

♦ **write off** *v/t debt* cancellare; *car* distruggere

writ·er ['raɪtə(r)] autore *m*, -trice *f; professional* scrittore *m*, -trice *f*

write-up F recensione *f*

writhe [raɪð] *v/i* contorcersi

writ·ing ['raɪtɪŋ] *as career* scrivere *m;* (*hand-writing*) scrittura *f;* (*words*) scritta *f;* (*script*) scritto *m; in ~* per iscritto

writ·ing pa·per carta *f* da lettere

writ·ten ['rɪtn] *pp* → **write**

wrong [rɒŋ] **1** *adj* sbagliato; *be ~ of person* sbagliare; *of answer* essere errato; *morally* essere ingiusto; *it's ~ to steal* non si deve rubare; *what's ~?* cosa c'è?; *there is something ~ with the car* la macchina ha qualcosa che non va **2** *adv* in modo sbagliato; *go ~ of person* sbagliare; *of marriage, plan etc* andar male **3** *n immoral action* torto *m; immorality* male *m; be in the ~* avere torto

wrong·ful ['rɒŋfʊl] *adj* illegale

wrong·ly ['rɒŋlɪ] *adv* erroneamente

wrong 'num·ber numero *m* sbagliato

wrote [rəʊt] *pret* → **write**

wrought 'i·ron [rɔːt] ferro *m* battuto

wrung [rʌŋ] *pret & pp* → **wring**

wry [raɪ] *adj* beffardo

X

xen·o·pho·bi·a [zenəʊˈfəʊbɪə] xenofobia *f*

X-ray ['eksreɪ] **1** *n* raggio *m* X; *picture* radiografia *f; have an ~* farsi fare una radiografia **2** *v/t* radiografare

xy·lo·phone [zaɪləˈfəʊn] xilofono *m*

Y

yacht [jɒt] *for pleasure* yacht *m inv*; *for racing* imbarcazione *f* da diporto

yacht·ing ['jɒtɪŋ] navigazione *f* da diporto

yachts·man ['jɒtsmən] diportista *m*

Yank [jæŋk] *n* F yankee *m inv*

yank [jæŋk] *v/t* dare uno strattone a

yap [jæp] *v/i* (*pret* & *pp* -ped) *of small dog* abbaiare; F *talk a lot* chiacchierare

yard¹ [jɑːd] *of prison, institution etc* cortile *m*; *for storage* deposito *m* all'aperto

yard² [jɑːd] *measurement* iarda *f*

'yard·stick *fig* metro *m*

yarn [jɑːn] *n* (*thread*) filato *m*; F *story* racconto *m*

yawn [jɔːn] 1 *n* sbadiglio *m* 2 *v/i* sbadigliare

year [jɪə(r)] anno *m*; *I've known here for ~s* la conosco da (tanti) anni; *it will last for ~s* durerà anni; *we were in the same ~ at school* frequentavamo lo stesso anno; *be six ~s old* avere sei anni

year·ly ['jɪəlɪ] 1 *adj* annuale 2 *adv* annualmente; *twice ~* due volte (al)l'anno

yearn [jɜːn] *v/i*: *~ to do sth* struggersi dal desiderio di fare qc

♦ yearn for *v/t* desiderare ardentemente

yearn·ing ['jɜːnɪŋ] *n* desiderio *m* struggente

yeast [jiːst] lievito *m*

yell [jel] 1 *n* urlo *m* 2 *v/t* & *v/i* urlare

yel·low ['jeləʊ] 1 *n* giallo *m* 2 *adj* giallo

yel·low 'pag·es® *npl* pagine *fpl* gialle

yelp [jelp] 1 *n* guaito *m* 2 *v/i* guaire

yen [jen] FIN yen *m inv*

yes [jes] *int* sì; *say ~* dire di sì

'yes·man *pej* yes man *m inv*

yes·ter·day ['jestədeɪ] 1 *adv* ieri; *the day before ~* l'altro ieri 2 *n* ieri *m inv*

yet [jet] 1 *adv* finora; *the fastest ~* il più veloce finora; *as ~* up to now per ora; *it is as ~ undecided* rimane ancora da decidere; *have you finished ~?* (non) hai (ancora) finito?; *he hasn't arrived ~* non è ancora arrivato; *is he here ~? – not ~* è arrivato? – non ancora; *~ bigger/ longer* ancora più grande/lungo 2 *conj* eppure; *~ I'm not sure* eppure non sono sicuro

yield [jiːld] 1 *n from fields etc* raccolto *m*; *from investment* rendita *f* 2 *v/t fruit, harvest* dare, produrre; *interest* fruttare 3 *v/i* (*give way*) cedere

yob [jɒb] P teppista *m/f*

yo·ga ['jəʊgə] yoga *m*

yog·hurt ['jɒgət] yogurt *m inv*

yolk [jəʊk] tuorlo *m*

you [juː] *pron* ◊ *subject*: *familiar singular* tu; *familiar polite plural* voi; *polite singular* lei; *do ~ know him?* lo conosci/conosce/conoscete?; *~ go, I'll stay* tu vai/lei vada/voi andate, io resto ◊ *direct object*: *familiar singular* ti; *familiar polite plural* vi; *polite singular* la; *he knows ~* ti/vi/ la conosce ◊ *indirect object*: *familiar singular* ti; *when two pronouns are used* te; *familiar polite plural* vi; *when two pronouns are used* ve; *polite singular* le; *did he talk to ~?* ti/vi/le ha parlato?; *I need to talk to ~* devo parlarti/parlarvi/parlarle; *I told ~* te/ve l'ho detto, glielo ho detto ◊ *after prep familiar singular* te; *familiar polite plural* voi; *polite singular* lei; *this is for ~* questo è per te/voi/lei ◊ *impersonal*: *~ never know* non si sa mai; *~ have to pay* si deve pagare; *fruit is good for* ~ la frutta fa bene

young [jʌŋ] *adj* giovane

young·ster ['jʌŋstə(r)] ragazzo *m*, -a *f*

your [jɔː(r)] *adj familiar singular* il tuo *m*, la tua *f*, i tuoi *mpl*, le tue *fpl*; *polite singular* il suo *m*, la sua *f*, i suoi *mpl*, le sue *fpl*; *familiar & polite plural* il vostro *m*, la vostra *f*, i vostri *mpl*, le vostre *fpl*; ~ *brother* tuo / suo / vostro fratello

yours [jɔːz] *pron familiar singular* il tuo *m*, la tua *f*, i tuoi *mpl*, le tue *fpl*; *polite singular* il suo *m*, la sua *f*, i suoi *mpl*, le sue *fpl*; *familiar & polite plural* il vostro *m*, la vostra *f*, i vostri *mpl*, le vostre *fpl*; *a friend of* ~ un tuo / suo / vostro amico; ~ *... at end of letter* saluti ...; ~ *sincerely* distinti saluti

your'self *pron reflexive* ti; *reflexive polite* si; *emphatic* tu stesso *m*, tu stessa *f*; *emphatic polite* lei stesso *m*,

lei stessa *f*; *did you hurt* ~*?* ti sei / si è fatto male?; *you said so* ~ l'hai detto tu stesso / l'ha detto lei stesso; *keep it for* ~ tienilo per te / lo tenga per sé; *by* ~ da solo

your'selves *pron reflexive* vi; *emphatic* voi stessi *mpl*, voi stesse *fpl*; *did you hurt* ~*?* vi siete fatti male?; *can you do it* ~*?* potete farlo da voi?; *by* ~ da soli *mpl*, da sole *fpl*

youth [juːθ] *n age* gioventù *f*; (*young man*) ragazzo *m*; (*young people*) giovani *mpl*

'**youth club** circolo *m* giovanile

youth·ful ['juːθful] *adj* giovanile; *ideas* giovane; *idealism* di gioventù

'**youth hos·tel** ostello *m* della gioventù

Yu·go·sla·vi·a [juːgə'slɑːvɪə] Jugoslavia *f*

Yu·go·sla·vi·an [juːgə'slɑːvɪən] **1** *adj* jugoslavo **2** *n* jugoslavo *m*, -a *f*

yup·pie ['jʌpɪ] F yuppie *m/f inv*

Z

zap [zæp] *v/t* (*pret & pp* **-ped**) F COMPUT (*delete*) cancellare; (*kill*) annientare; (*hit*) colpire; (*send*) mandare

♦ **zap along** *v/i* F *move fast* sfrecciare

zapped [zæpt] *adj* F (*exhausted*) stanchissimo

zap·per ['zæpə(r)] *for changing TV channels* telecomando *m*

zap·py ['zæpɪ] *adj* F *car, pace* veloce; (*lively, energetic*) brioso

zeal [ziːl] zelo *m*

ze·bra ['zebrə] zebra *f*

ze·bra 'cross·ing Br strisce *fpl* pedonali

ze·ro ['zɪərəʊ] zero *m*; *10 below* ~ 10 (gradi) sotto zero

♦ **zero in on** *v/t* (*identify*) identificare

ze·ro 'growth crescita *f* zero

zest [zest] (*enthusiasm*) gusto *m*; (*peel*) scorza *f*

zig-zag ['zɪgzæg] **1** *n* zigzag *m inv* **2** *v/i* (*pret & pp* **-ged**) zigzagare

zilch [zɪltʃ] F un bel niente

zinc [zɪŋk] zinco *m*

zip [zɪp] (*cerniera f*) lampo *f*

♦ **zip up** *v/t* (*pret & pp* **-ped**) *dress, jacket* allacciare; COMPUT zippare, comprimere

'**zip code** Am codice *m* di avviamento postale

zo·di·ac ['zəʊdɪæk] ASTR zodiaco *m*; *signs of the* ~ segni *mpl* zodiacali

zom·bie ['zɒmbɪ] F (*idiot*) cretino *m*, -a *f*; *feel like a* ~ *exhausted*

sentirsi uno zombie
zone [zəʊn] zona *f*
zonked [zɒŋkt] *adj* P (*exhausted*) stanco morto
zoo [zu:] zoo *m inv*
zo·o·log·i·cal [zu:ə'lɒdʒɪkl] *adj* zoo-logico

zo·ol·o·gist [zu:'ɒlədʒɪst] zoologo *m*, -a *f*
zo·ol·o·gy [zu:'ɒlədʒɪ] zoologia *f*
zoom [zu:m] *v/i* F *move fast* sfrecciare
♦ **zoom in on** *v/t* PHOT zumare su
zoom 'lens zoom *m inv*
zuc·chi·ni [zu:'ki:nɪ] *Am* zucchino *m*

Italian Verb Conjugations

You can find the conjugation pattern of an Italian verb by looking up the infinitive form in the dictionary. The numbers and letters given there after the infinitive refer to the conjugation patterns listed below.

The tables (**1a**, **2a**, **3a**, **4a**) show the full conjugations. The verb stem is given in ordinary type and the endings in *italics*. Compound tenses are given at **1a**. The three main conjugations (-are, -ere, -ire) are divided into four sets so as to illustrate the two different stress patterns of the second conjugation. Variations in form, stress pattern and vowel length are then shown for each of these four sets.

An underscore shows the stressed vowel in each conjugated form.

First Conjugation

1a mandare. The stem remains the same with regard to both spelling and pronunciation.

I. Simple Tenses

	indicativo			condizionale
pr	*imperf*	*p.r.*	*fut*	
mando	mandavo	mandai	manderò	manderei
mandi	mandavi	mandasti	manderai	manderesti
manda	mandava	mandò	manderà	manderebbe
mandiamo	mandavamo	mandammo	manderemo	manderemmo
mandate	mandavate	mandaste	manderete	mandereste
mandano	mandavano	mandarono	manderanno	manderebbero

congiuntivo		imperativo
pr	*imperf*	
mandi	mandassi	—
mandi	mandassi	manda
mandi	mandasse	mandi
mandiamo	mandassimo	mandiamo
mandiate	mandaste	mandate
mandino	mandassero	mandino

Participio presente: mandante   *Participio passato*: mandato
Gerundio presente: mandando

II. Compound Tenses

1. Active voice

(Formed by placing *avere* before the verb form *participio passato*)

Infinito
passato: aver mand*ato*

Gerundio
passato: av*e*ndo mand*ato*

Indicativo
passato pross: ho mand*ato*
trapassato prossimo: av*e*vo mand*ato*

futuro anteriore: avr*ò* mand*ato*

Condizionale
passato: avr*ei* mand*ato*

Congiuntivo
passato: *a*bbia mand*ato*
trapassato: av*e*ssi mand*ato*

2. Passive voice

(formed by placing *essere* before the verb form *participio passato*)

Infinito
presente: *e*ssere mand*ato*, -a, -i, -e
passato: *e*ssere st*a*to (st*a*ta, st*a*ti,
 st*a*te) mand*ato*, -a, -i, -e

Gerundio
presente: ess*e*ndo mand*ato*, -a, -i, -e
passato: ess*e*ndo st*a*to (st*a*ta, st*a*ti,
 st*a*te) mand*ato*, -a, -i, -e

Indicativo
presente: s*o*no mand*ato*, -a
imperf: *e*ro mand*ato*, -a
passato remoto: f*u*i mand*ato*, -a
passato prossimo: s*o*no st*a*to (st*a*ta)
 mand*ato*, -a
trap. prossimo: *e*ro st*a*to (st*a*ta)

mand*ato*, -a

fut semplice: sar*ò* mand*ato*, -a
fut anteriore: sar*ò* st*a*to (st*a*ta)
 mand*ato*, -a

Condizionale
presente: sar*ei* mand*ato*, -a
passato: sar*ei* st*a*to (st*a*ta) mand*ato*, -a

Congiuntivo
presente: s*i*a mand*ato*, -a
imperf: f*o*ssi mand*ato*, -a
passato: s*i*a st*a*to (st*a*ta) mand*ato*, -a
trapassato: f*o*ssi st*a*to (st*a*ta)
 mand*ato*, -a

Imperativo
sii mand*ato*, -a

This pattern applies to the compound tenses of all verbs

pr ind	p.r.	fut	pr congiunt	imper

1b celare. The stressed, closed *-e* in the stem becomes an open *e*.

c*e*lo	cel*ai*	celer*ò*	c*e*li	—
cel*ia*mo	cel*a*mmo	celer*e*mo	cel*ia*mo	cel*ia*mo
c*e*lano	cel*a*rono	celer*a*nno	c*e*lino	c*e*lino
		pp: cel*a*to		

1c lodare. The stressed, closed *-o* in the stem becomes an open *o*.

l*o*do	lod*ai*	loder*ò*	l*o*di	—
lod*ia*mo	lod*a*mmo	loder*e*mo	lod*ia*mo	lod*ia*mo
l*o*dano	lod*a*rono	loder*a*nno	l*o*dino	l*o*dino
		pp: lod*a*to		

1d cercare. The final consonant in the verb stem, *-c*, becomes *ch* before *i* and *e*.

c*e*rco	cerc*ai*	cercher*ò*	c*e*rchi	—
cerch*ia*mo	cerc*a*mmo	cercher*e*mo	cerch*ia*mo	cerch*ia*mo
c*e*rcano	cerc*a*rono	cercher*a*nno	c*e*rchino	c*e*rchino
		pp: cerc*a*to		

pr ind	*p.r.*	*fut*	*pr congiunt*	*imper*

1e pagare. The final consonant in the verb stem, -*g*, becomes *gh* before *i* and *e*.

pago	pagai	pagherò	paghi	—
paghiamo	pagammo	pagheremo	paghiamo	paghiamo
pagano	pagarono	pagheranno	paghino	paghino
	pp: pagato			

1f baciare. The *i* is dropped if it is followed immediately by a second *i* or an *e*.

bacio	baciai	bacerò	baci	—
baciamo	baciammo	baceremo	baciamo	baciamo
baciano	baciarono	baceranno	bacino	bacino
	pp: baciato			

1g pigliare. The *i* is dropped if it is followed immediately by a second *i*.

piglio	pigliai	piglierò	pigli	
pigliamo	piagliammo	piglieremo	pigliamo	pigliamo
pigliano	pigliarono	piglieranno	piglino	piglino
	pp: pigliato			

1h inviare. Verb forms in which the *i* is stressed retain the *i* even if it is followed by another *i*.

invio	inviai	invierò	invii	—
inviamo	inviammo	invieremo	inviamo	inviamo
inviano	inviarono	invieranno	inviino	inviino
	pp: inviato			

1i annoiare. Verbs ending in –*iare* with an unstressed *i* and a preceding vowel, drop the *i* which would be added.

annoio	annoiai	annoierò	annoi	—
annoiamo	annoiammo	annoieremo	annoiamo	annoiamo
annoiano	annoiarono	annoieranno	annoino	annoino
	pp: annoiato			

1k studiare. Verbs ending in –*iare* with an unstressed *i* and a preceding consonant, usually drop the *i* which would be added, even when the *i* in the verb stem is stressed: i.e. *tu studi*. Verbs ending in –*liare* always have -*lii*, eg *esiliare, esilii*.

studio	studiai	studierò	studi	—
studiamo	studiammo	studieremo	studiamo	studiamo
studiano	studiarono	studieranno	studino	studino
	pp: studiato			

1l abitare. In the verb forms in which the stem is stressed, the stress comes on the first syllable.

abito	abitai	abiterò	abiti	
abitiamo	abitammo	abiteremo	abitiamo	abitiamo
abitano	abitarono	abiteranno	abitino	abitino
	pp: abitato			

pr ind	p.r.	fut	pr congiunt	imper

1m collaborare. In the verb forms in which the stem is stressed, the stress comes on the second syllable.

collaboro	collaborai	collaborerò	collabori	—
collaboriamo	collaborammo	collaboreremo	collaboriamo	collaboriamo
collaborano	collaborarono	collaboreranno	collaborino	collaborino

pp: collaborato

1n aggomitolare. In the verb forms in which the stem is stressed, the stress comes on the third or fourth syllable.

aggomitolo	~mitolai	~mitolerò	~mitoli	—
~mitoliamo	~mitolammo	~mitoleremo	~mitoliamo	~mitoliamo
~mitolano	~mitolarono	~mitoleranno	~mitolino	~mitolino

pp: aggomitolato

1o giocare. The stressed –o in the stem can be extended to –uo, but this is rarer.

gi(u)oco	giocai	giocherò	gi(u)ochi	—
giochiamo	giocammo	giocheremo	giochiamo	giochiamo
gi(u)ocano	giocarono	giocheranno	gi(u)ochino	gi(u)ochino

pp: giocato

1p andare. Two stems: and- and vad-. In fut and cond the e at the start of the ending is dropped.

vado	andai	andrò	vada	—
vai	andasti	andrai	vada	va, va', vai,
va	andò	andrà	vada	vada
andiamo	andammo	andremo	andiamo	andiamo
andate	andaste	andrete	andiate	andate
vanno	andarono	andranno	vadano	vadano

pp: andato

1q stare. Verb stem sta; p.r. (stetti etc); imperf del congiunt (stessi etc) as in the 2nd Conjugation; in fut and cond e becomes a.

sto	stetti	starò	stia	—
stai	stesti	starai	stia	sta', stai
sta	stette	starà	stia	stia
stiamo	stemmo	staremo	stiamo	stiamo
state	steste	starete	stiate	state
stanno	stettero	staranno	stiano	stiano

pp: stato

1r dare. Verb stem da; imperf del congiunt dessi etc; in the p.r. alternative forms detti, dette, dettero.

do	diedi, detti	darò	dia	—
dai	desti	darai	dia	da', dai
dà	diede, dette	darà	dia	dia
diamo	demmo	daremo	diamo	diamo
date	deste	darete	diate	date
danno	diedero, dettero	daranno	diano	diano

pp: dato

Second Conjugation – First Pattern

2a temere. The stem remains the same with regard to both spelling and pronunciation.

I. Simple Tenses

	indicativo			condizionale
pr	*imperf*	*p.r.*	*fut*	
temo	temevo	temei, temetti	temerò	temerei
temo	temevo	temei, temetti	temerò	temerei
temi	temevi	temesti	temerai	temeresti
teme	temeva	temette	temerà	temerebbe
temiamo	temevamo	tememmo	temeremo	temeremmo
temete	temevate	temeste	temerete	temereste
temono	temevano	temettero, temerono	temeranno	temerebbero

	congiuntivo		imperativo
pr	*imperf*		
tema	temessi	—	
tema	temessi	temi	
tema	temesse	tema	
temiamo	temessimo	temiamo	
temiate	temeste	temete	
temano	temessero	temano	

Participio presente: temente   *Participio passato*: temuto
Gerundio presente: temendo

II. Compound Tenses

Auxiliary verb essere or avere, followed by *participio passato* (see 1a).

pr ind	*p.r.*	*fut*	*pr congiunt*	*imper*

2b avere. In *fut* and *cond* the final e in the ending is omitted.

ho	ebbi	avrò	abbia	—
hai	avesti	avrai	abbia	abbi
ha	ebbe	avrà	abbia	abbia
abbiamo	avemmo	avremo	abbiamo	abbiamo
avete	aveste	avrete	abbiate	abbiate
hanno	ebbero	avranno	abbiano	abbiano
		pp: avuto		

2c cadere. In *fut* and *cond* the final e in the ending is omitted.

cado	caddi	cadrò	cada	
cadiamo	caddemmo	cadremo	cadiamo	cadiamo
cadono	caddero	cadranno	cadano	cadano
		pp: caduto		

2d calere. Used almost exclusively in 3rd person singular; now obsolete.

cale	calse	—	caglia	—
		pp: caluto		

pr ind	p.r.	fut	pr congiunt	imper

2e dolere. In *pr, g* is added between the verb stem and the ending *o* or *a*. In *fut* and *cond l* becomes *r* and the final *e* of the ending is dropped.

dolgo	dolsi	dorrò	dolga	—
duole	dolse	dorrà	dolga	dolga
dogliamo	dolemmo	dorremo	dogliamo	dogliamo
dolgono	dolsero	dorranno	dolgano	dolgano
		pp: doluto		

2f dovere. In the forms with the emphasis on the stem vowel, *o* becomes *e*. Omission of *e* in *fut* and *cond*.

devo	dovetti	dovrò	debba, deva	—
devi	dovesti	dovrai	debba, deva	devi
deve	dovette	dovrà	debba, deva	debba, deva
dobbiamo	dovemmo	dovremo	dobbiamo	dobbiamo
dovete	doveste	dovrete	dobbiate	dovete
devono	dovettero	dovranno	debbano, devano	debbano, devano
		pp: dovuto		

2g lucere. Used only in 3rd person singular and plural of *pr dell'ind* (luce, lucono), *imperf* (luceva, lucevano), *fut* (lucerà, luceranno), *pr del congiunt* (luca, lucano), and *imperf del congiunt* (lucesse, lucessero). Also *p pr* lucente, *ger* lucendo.

2h parere. In *fut* and *cond* the final *e* in the ending is omitted.

paio	parvi	parrò	paia	—
pa(r)iamo	paremmo	parremo	pa(r)iamo	—
paiono	parvero	parranno	paiano	—
		pp: parso		

2i persuadere.

persuado	persuasi	persuaderò	persuada	—
persuadiamo	persuademmo	persuaderemo	persuadiamo	persuadiamo
persuadono	persuasero	persuaderanno	persuadano	persuadano
		pp: persuaso		

2k piacere.

piaccio	piacqui	piacerò	piaccia	—
piacciamo	piacemmo	piaceremo	piacciamo	piacciamo
piacciono	piacquero	piaceranno	piacciano	piacciano
		pp: piaciuto		

2l potere. In *fut* and *cond* the final *e* in the ending is omitted.

posso	potei	potrò	possa	—
puoi	potesti	potrai	possa	—
può	poté	potrà	possa	—
possiamo	potemmo	potremo	possiamo	—
potete	poteste	potrete	possiate	—
possono	poterono	potranno	possano	—
		pp: potuto		

pr ind	p.r.	fut	pr congiunt	imper

2m rimanere. In *pr* g is added between stem and ending *o* or *a*; *p.r.* ending in –*si* and *pp* ending in –*sto* drop the –*n* from the stem; in *fut* and *cond* n becomes *r*.

rimango	rimasi	rimarrò	rimanga	—
rimaniamo	rimanemmo	rimarremo	rimaniamo	rimaniamo
rimangono	rimasero	rimarranno	rimangano	rimangano
		pp: rimasto		

2n sapere. In *fut* and *cond* the *e* is dropped; 2nd person plural of *imperf* formed from *congiunt*.

so	seppi	saprò	sappia	—
sai	sapesti	saprai	sappia	sappi
sa	seppe	saprà	sappia	sappia
sappiamo	sapemmo	sapremo	sappiamo	sappiamo
sapete	sapeste	saprete	sappiate	sappiate
sanno	seppero	sapranno	sappiano	sappiano
		p pr: sapiente	*pp*: saputo	

2o sedere. The *e* in the stem becomes *ie* in forms with the emphasis on the stem vowel; in *pr* alternative forms with *segg*…

siedo, seggo	sedei	sederò	sieda, segga	—
sediamo	sedemmo	sederemo	sediamo	sediamo
siedono, seggono	sederono	sederanno	siedano, seggano	siedano, seggano
		pp: seduto		

2p solere. Only used in *pr*, *p.r.*, *ger* and *pp*. In *pr dell'ind* (except 2nd person singular: *suoli*) and *congiunt* it follows the pattern of *volere*.

soglio	solei	—	soglia	—
sogliamo		—	sogliamo	—
sogliono		—	sogliano	—
	ger: solendo		*pp*: solito	

2q tenere. Addition of *g* between stem and ending *o* or *a*. In *fut* and *cond* n becomes *r*.

tengo	tenni	terrò	tenga	—
tieni	tenesti	terrai	tenga	tieni
teniamo	tenemmo	terremo	teniamo	teniamo
tengono	tennero	terranno	tengano	tengano
		pp: tenuto		

2r valere. Addition of *g* between stem and ending *o* or *a*. In *fut* and *cond* n becomes *r*.

valgo	valsi	varrò	valga	—
valiamo	valemmo	varremo	valiamo	valiamo
valgono	valsero	varranno	valgano	valgano
		pp: valso		

pr ind	p.r.	fut	pr congiunt	imper

2s vedere. In *fut* and *cond* the final *e* in the ending is omitted.

vedo	vidi	vedrò	veda	—
vediamo	vedemmo	vedremo	vediamo	vediamo
vedono	videro	vedranno	vedano	vedano
		pp: visto		

2t volere. In *fut* and *cond l* becomes *r* and the final *e* of the ending is omitted; 2nd person plural of *imper* from the *congiunt*.

voglio	volli	vorrò	voglia	—
vuoi	volesti	vorrai	voglia	vogli
vuole	volle	vorrà	voglia	voglia
vogliamo	volemmo	vorremo	vogliamo	vogliamo
volete	voleste	vorrete	vogliate	vogliate
vogliono	vollero	vorranno	vogliano	vogliano
		pp: voluto		

Second Conjugation – Second Pattern

3a vendere. The stem remains the same with regard to both spelling and pronunciation.

I. Simple Tenses

| indicativo | | | | condizionale |

pr	imperf	p.r.	fut	
vendo	vendevo	vendetti, vendei	venderò	venderei
vendi	vendevi	vendesti	venderai	venderesti
vende	vendeva	vendette	venderà	venderebbe
vendiamo	vendevamo	vendemmo	venderemo	venderemmo
vendete	vendevate	vendeste	venderete	vendereste
vendono	vendevano	vendettero, venderono	venderanno	venderebbero

| congiuntivo | | imperativo |

pr	imperf	
venda	vendessi	—
venda	vendessi	vendi
venda	vendesse	venda
vendiamo	vendessimo	vendiamo
vendiate	vendeste	vendete
vendano	vendessero	vendano

Participio presente: vendente   *Participio passato*: venduto*
Gerundio presente: vendendo

---

*Participio passato of *spandere* is *spanto*.

II. Compound Tenses

Auxiliary verb *essere* or *avere*, followed by *participio passato* (see 1a).

pr ind	p.r.	fut	pr congiunt	imper

3b chiudere.

pr ind	p.r.	fut	pr congiunt	imper
chiudo	chiusi	chiuderò	chiuda	—
chiudiamo	chiudemmo	chiuderemo	chiudiamo	chiudiamo
chiudono	chiusero	chiuderanno	chiudano	chiudano
		pp: chiuso		

3c prendere.

pr ind	p.r.	fut	pr congiunt	imper
prendo	presi	prenderò	prenda	—
prendiamo	prendemmo	prenderemo	prendiamo	prendiamo
prendono	presero	prenderanno	prendano	prendano
		pp: preso		

3d fingere. The *pp* of *stringere* is *stretto*.

pr ind	p.r.	fut	pr congiunt	imper
fingo	finsi	fingerò	finga	—
fingiamo	fingemmo	fingeremo	fingiamo	fingiamo
fingono	finsero	fingeranno	fingano	fingano
		pp: finto		

3e addurre. Shorter form of *adducere*.

pr ind	p.r.	fut	pr congiunt	imper
adduco	addussi	addurrò	adduca	—
adduci	adducesti	addurrai	adduca	adduci
adduce	addusse	addurrà	adduca	adduca
adduciamo	adducemmo	addurremo	adduciamo	adduciamo
adducete	adduceste	addurrete	adduciate	adduciate
adducono	addussero	addurranno	adducano	adducano
		pp: addotto		

3f assistere. In *p.r.* alternative forms end in *–etti*.

pr ind	p.r.	fut	pr congiunt	imper
assisto	assistei	assisterò	assista	—
assistiamo	assistemmo	assisteremo	assistiamo	assistiamo
assistono	assisterono	assisteranno	assistano	assistano
		pp: assistito		

3g assolvere.

pr ind	p.r.	fut	pr congiunt	imper
assolvo	assolsi, ~vetti	assolverò	assolva	—
assolviamo	assolvemmo	assolveremo	assolviamo	assolviamo
assolvono	assolsero, assolvettero	assolveranno	assolvano	assolvano
		pp: assolto		

3h assumere.

pr ind	p.r.	fut	pr congiunt	imper
assumo	assunsi	assumerò	assuma	—
assumiamo	assumemmo	assumeremo	assumiamo	assumiamo
assumono	assunsero	assumeranno	assumano	assumano
		pp: assunto		

pr ind	p.r.	fut	pr congiunt	imper

3i bere. Conjugated according to the pattern of *bevere*. In *fut* and *cond* v becomes *r* and the *e* of the ending is dropped.

pr ind	p.r.	fut	pr congiunt	imper
bevo	bevvi, bevetti	berrò	beva	—
bevi	bevesti	berrai	beva	bevi
beve	bevve, bevette	berrà	beva	beva
beviamo	bevemmo	berremo	beviamo	beviamo
bevete	beveste	berrete	beviate	bevete
bevono	bevvero, bevettero	berranno	bevano	bevano

pp: bevuto

3k chiedere.

chiedo	chiesi	chiederò	chieda	—
chiediamo	chiedemmo	chiederemo	chiediamo	chiediamo
chiedono	chiesero	chiederanno	chiedano	chiedano

pp: chiesto

3l concedere.

concedo	concessi, concedetti	concederò	conceda	—
concediamo	concedemmo	concederemo	concediamo	concediamo
concedono	concessero, concedettero	concederanno	concedano	concedano

pp: concesso

3m connettere.

connetto	connessi, connettei	connetterò	connetta	—
connettiamo	connettemmo	connetteremo	connettiamo	connettiamo
connettono	connessero, connetterono	connetteranno	connettano	connettano

pp: connesso

3n conoscere.

conosco	conobbi	conoscerò	conosca	—
conosciamo	conoscemmo	conosceremo	conosciamo	conosciamo
conoscono	conobbero	conosceranno	conoscano	conoscano

pp: conosciuto

3o correre.

corro	corsi	correrò	corra	—
corriamo	corremmo	correremo	corriamo	corriamo
corrono	corsero	correranno	corrano	corrano

pp: corso

pr ind	p.r.	fut	pr congiunt	imper

3p cuocere. In unstressed syllables uo becomes o. Imperf cocevo or cocessi.

cuocio	cossi	cuocerò	cuocia	—
cociamo	cocemmo	cuoceremo	cociamo	cociamo
cuociono	cossero	cuoceranno	cuociano	cuociano
		pp: cotto		

3q decidere.

decido	decisi	deciderò	decida	—
decidiamo	decidemmo	decideremo	decidiamo	decidiamo
decidono	decisero	decideranno	decidano	decidano
		pp: deciso		

3r deprimere.

deprimo	depressi	deprimerò	deprima	—
deprimiamo	deprimemmo	deprimeremo	deprimiamo	deprimiamo
deprimono	depressero	deprimeranno	deprimano	deprimano
		pp: depresso		

3s devolvere.

devolvo	devolvei, devolvetti	devolverò	devolva	—
devolviamo	devolvemmo	devolveremo	devolviamo	devolviamo
devolvono	devolverono, devolvettero	devolveranno	devolvano	devolvano
		pp: devoluto, devolto		

3t dire.

dico	dissi	dirò	dica	—
dici	dicesti	dirai	dica	
dice	disse	dirà	dica	
diciamo	dicemmo	diremo	diciamo	diciamo
dite	diceste	direte	diciate	dite
dicono	dissero	diranno	dicano	dicano
		pp: detto		

3u dirigere.

dirigo	diressi	dirigerò	diriga	—
dirigiamo	dirigemmo	dirigeremo	dirigiamo	dirigiamo
dirigono	diressero	dirigeranno	dirigano	dirigano
		pp: diretto		

3v discutere.

discuto	discussi	discuterò	discuta	—
discutiamo	discutemmo	discuteremo	discutiamo	discutiamo
discutono	discussero	discuteranno	discutano	discutano
		pp: discusso		

pr ind	*p.r.*	*fut*	*pr congiunt*	*imper*

3w esigere.

esigo	esigei, esigetti	esigerò	esiga	—
esigiamo	esigemmo	esigeremo	esigiamo	esigiamo
esigono	esigerono, esigettero	esigeranno	esigano	esigano

pp: esatto

3x esimere. Has no *pp*, and the *p.r. esimei* is rarely used. Instead the corresponding forms of *esentare* are used. Otherwise regular, following the pattern of *vendere* 3a.

3y espellere.

espello	espulsi	espellerò	espella	—
espelliamo	espellemmo	espelleremo	espelliamo	espelliamo
espellono	espulsero	espelleranno	espellano	espellano

pp: espulso

3z essere. Completely irregular. *Imperf dell'ind*: ero, eri, era, eravamo, eravate, erano; *imperf del congiunt*: fossi, fossi, fosse, fossimo, foste, fossero.

sono	fui	sarò	sia	—
sei	fosti	sarai	sia	sii
è	fu	sarà	sia	sia
siamo	fummo	saremo	siamo	siamo
siete	foste	sarete	siate	siate
sono	furono	saranno	siano	siano

pp: stato

3aa fare. Shorter form of *facere*. *Imperf* regular, following the pattern of *facere*: facevo etc

faccio	feci	farò	faccia	—
fai	facesti	farai	faccia	fa', fai
fa	fece	farà	faccia	faccia
facciamo	facemmo	faremo	facciamo	facciamo
fate	faceste	farete	facciate	fate
fanno	fecero	faranno	facciano	facciano

pp: fatto

3bb fondere.

fondo	fusi	fonderò	fonda	—
fondiamo	fondemmo	fonderemo	fondiamo	fondiamo
fondono	fusero	fonderanno	fondano	fondano

pp: fuso

3cc leggere.

leggo	lessi	leggerò	legga	—
leggiamo	leggemmo	leggeremo	leggiamo	leggiamo
leggono	lessero	leggeranno	leggano	leggano

pp: letto

pr ind	p.r.	fut	pr congiunt	imper

3dd mescere.

mesco	mescei	mescerò	mesca	—
mesciamo	mescemmo	mesceremo	mesciamo	mesciamo
mescono	mescerono	mesceranno	mescano	mescano
		pp: mesciuto		

3ee mettere.

metto	misi	metterò	metta	—
mettiamo	mettemmo	metteremo	mettiamo	mettiamo
mettono	misero	metteranno	mettano	mettano
		pp: messo		

3ff muovere. In unstressed syllables *uo* becomes *o*.

muovo	mossi	muoverò	muova	—
muoviamo	movemmo	muoveremo	muoviamo	muoviamo
muovono	mossero	muoveranno	muovano	muovano
		pp: mosso		

3gg nascere.

nasco	nacqui	nascerò	nasca	—
nasciamo	nascemmo	nasceremo	nasciamo	nasciamo
nascono	nacquero	nasceranno	nascano	nascano
		pp: nato		

3hh nascondere.

nascondo	nascosi	nasconderò	nasca	—
nascondiamo	nascondemmo	nasconderemo	nascondiamo	nascondiamo
nascondono	nascosero	nasconderanno	nascondano	nascondano
		pp: nascosto		

3ii nuocere. In unstressed syllables *uo* becomes *o*.

nuoccio	nocqui	nuocerò	nuoccia	—
nociamo	nocemmo	nuoceremo	nociamo	nuociamo
nuocciono	nocquero	nuoceranno	nuocciano	nuocciano
		pp: nociuto		

3kk piovere. Used only in the 3rd person singular and plural, in the two participial forms and in the *ger*; *pr ind* piove, piovono; *p.r.* piovve, piovvero; *fut* pioverà, pioveranno; *pr congiunt* piova, piovano; *pp* piovuto.

3ll porre. When followed by an *r* in *fut* and *cond* n becomes *r*.

pongo	posi	porrò	ponga	—
poni	ponesti	porrai	ponga	poni
pone	pose	porrà	ponga	ponga
poniamo	ponemmo	porremo	poniamo	poniamo
ponete	poneste	porrete	poniate	ponete
pongono	posero	porranno	pongano	pongano
		pp: posto		

pr ind	p.r.	fut	pr congiunt	imper

3mm prefiggere.

prefiggo	prefissi	prefiggerò	prefigga	–
prefiggiamo	prefiggemmo	prefiggeremo	prefiggiamo	prefiggiamo
prefiggono	prefissero	prefiggeranno	prefiggano	prefiggano
		pp: prefisso		

3nn recere. Addition of *i* between stem and endings *o, a, u*.

recio	recetti	recerò	recia	–
reciamo	recemmo	receremo	reciamo	reciamo
reciono	recettero	receranno	reciano	reciano
		pp: reciuto		

3oo redigere.

redigo	redassi	redigerò	rediga	–
redigiamo	redigemmo	redigeremo	redigiamo	redigiamo
redigono	redassero	redigeranno	redigano	redigano
		pp: redatto		

3pp redimere.

redimo	redensi	redimerò	redima	–
redimiamo	redimemmo	redimeremo	redimiamo	redimiamo
redimono	redensero	redimeranno	redimano	redimano
		pp: redento		

3qq riflettere. In *p.r.* and in *pp* in the sense of "think about" forms usually end in *–ei* and *–uto*; in the sense of "reflect back" usually *–ssi, -sso*.

rifletto	riflettei, riflessi	rifletterò	rifletta	–
riflettiamo	riflettemmo	rifletteremo	riflettiamo	riflettiamo
riflettono	rifletterono, riflessero	rifletteranno	riflettano	riflettano
		pp: riflettuto, riflesso		

3rr rompere.

rompo	ruppi	romperò	rompa	–
rompiamo	rompemmo	romperemo	rompiamo	rompiamo
rompono	ruppero	romperanno	rompano	rompano
		pp: rotto		

3ss scegliere. The stem ending *gli* becomes *lg* before endings *o* and *a*.

scelgo	scelsi	sceglierò	scelga	–
scegli	scegliesti	sceglierai	scelga	scegli
sceglie	scelse	sceglierà	scelga	scelga
scegliamo	scegliemmo	sceglieremo	scegliamo	scegliamo
scegliete	sceglieste	sceglierete	scegliate	scegliete
scelgono	scelsero	sceglieranno	scelgano	scelgano
		pp: scelto		

pr ind	p.r.	fut	pr congiunt	imper

3tt scrivere.

scrivo	scrissi	scriverò	scriva	—
scriviamo	scrivemmo	scriveremo	scriviamo	scriviamo
scrivono	scrissero	scriveranno	scrivano	scrivano
		pp: scritto		

3uu spargere.

spargo	sparsi	spargerò	sparga	—
spargiamo	spargemmo	spargeremo	spargiamo	spargiamo
spargono	sparsero	spargeranno	spargano	spargano
		pp: sparso		

3vv spegnere. The stem sound *gn* becomes *ng* before the endings *o* and *a*.

spengo	spensi	spegnerò	spenga	—
spegni	spegnesti	spegnerai	spenga	spegni
spegne	spense	spegnerà	spenga	spenga
spegniamo	spegnemmo	spegneremo	spegniamo	spegniamo
spegnete	spegneste	spegnerete	spegniate	spegnete
spengono	spensero	spegneranno	spengano	spengano
		pp: spento		

3ww svellere.

svello	svelsi	svellerò	svella	—
svelliamo	svellemmo	svelleremo	svelliamo	svelliamo
svellono	svelsero	svelleranno	svellano	svellano
		pp: svelto		

3xx trarre.

traggo	trassi	trarrò	tragga	—
trai	traesti	trarrai	tragga	trai
trae	trasse	trarrà	tragga	tragga
traiamo	traemmo	trarremo	traiamo	traiamo
traete	traeste	trarrete	traiate	traete
traggono	trassero	trarranno	traggano	traggano
		pp: tratto		

3yy vigere. Common only in the following forms: 3rd person singular and plural of *ind pr*, *imperf* and *fut*; *cond*; *congiunt imperf* and *p pr*

Ind pr: vige, vigono; *imperf*: vigeva, vigevano; *fut*: vigerà, vigeranno. *Congiunt imperf*: vigesse, vigessero. *Cond*: vigerebbe, vigerebbero. *P pr*: vigente.

3zz vivere.

vivo	vissi	vivrò	viva	—
viviamo	vivemmo	vivremo	viviamo	viviamo
vivono	vissero	vivranno	vivano	vivano
		pp: vissuto		

Third Conjugation

4a partire. The stem remains the same with regard to both spelling and pronunciation.

I. Simple Tenses

indicativo				condizionale
pr	*imperf*	*p.r.*	*fut*	
parto*	partivo	partii	partirò	partirei
parti	partivi	partisti	partirai	partiresti
parte	partiva	partì	partirà	partirebbe
partiamo	partivamo	partimmo	partiremo	partiremmo
partite	partivate	partiste	partirete	partireste
partono*	partivano	partirono	partiranno	partirebbero

congiuntivo		imperativo
pr	*imperf*	
parta*	partissi	—
parta*	partissi	parti
parta*	partisse	parta*
partiamo	partissimo	partiamo
partiate	partiste	partite
partano*	partissero	partano*

Participio presente: partente   *Participio passato*: partito
Gerundio presente: partendo

* In *cucire* and *sdrucire* an *i* is added before *a* and *o*: *cucio*, *sdruciono* etc

II. Compound Tenses

Auxiliary verb *essere* or *avere*, followed by *participio passato* (see 1a).

pr ind	*p.r.*	*fut*	*pr congiunt*	*imper*

4b sentire. The stressed, closed −*e* of stem ending becomes an open −*e*.

sento	sentii	sentirò	senta	—
sentiamo	sentimmo	sentiremo	sentiamo	sentiamo
sentono	sentirono	sentiranno	sentano	sentano
		pp: sentito		

4c dormire. The stressed, closed −*o* of stem ending becomes an open −*o*.

dormo	dormii	dormirò	dorma	—
dormiamo	dormimmo	dormiremo	dormiamo	dormiamo
dormono	dormirono	dormiranno	dormano	dormano
		pp: dormito		

pr ind	p.r.	fut	pr congiunt	imper

4d finire. In the 1st, 2nd and 3rd person singular and 3rd person plural of *pr* (*ind* and *congiunt*) and *imper*, *isc* is added between stem and ending.

pr ind	p.r.	fut	pr congiunt	imper
finisco	finii	finirò	finisca	—
finisci	finisti	finirai	finisca	finisci
finisce	finì	finirà	finisca	finisca
finiamo	finimmo	finiremo	finiamo	finiamo
finite	finiste	finirete	finiate	finite
finiscono	finirono	finiranno	finiscano	finiscano
	pp: finito			

4e apparire.

pr ind	p.r.	fut	pr congiunt	imper
appaio, apparisco	apparvi, apparsi, apparii	apparirò	appaia, apparisca	—
appariamo	apparimmo	appariremo	appariamo	appariamo
appaiono, appariscono	apparvero, apparsero, apparirono	appariranno	appaiano, appariscano	appaiano, appariscano
	pp: apparso			

4f aprire.

pr ind	p.r.	fut	pr congiunt	imper
apro	apersi, aprii	aprirò	apra	—
apriamo	aprimmo	apriremo	apriamo	apriamo
aprono	apersero, aprirono	apriranno	aprano	aprano
	pp: aperto			

4g compire. In most forms of the *pr ind*, *pr congiunt* and *imperf*, *compire* is conjugated according to the pattern of *compiere*. An *i* is therefore added between the stem and the ending except in forms whose ending begins with an *i*.

pr ind	p.r.	fut	pr congiunt	imper
compio	compii	compirò	compia	—
compiamo	compimmo	compiremo	compiamo	compiamo
compiono	compirono	compiranno	compiano	compiano
	pp: compito, compiuto; *p pr*: compiente; *ger*: compiendo			

4h gire. Defective verb. Apart from the forms listed below, is used only in the *imperf* (*ind* and *congiunt*) and in the *cond*. This verb is now obsolete.

pr ind	p.r.	fut	pr congiunt	imper
—	—	girò	—	—
—	gisti	girai	—	—
—	gì	girà	—	—
—	gimmo	giremo	—	—
gite	giste	girete	—	gite
—	girono	giranno	—	—
	pp: gito			

pr ind	p.r.	fut	pr congiunt	imper

4i ire. Defective verb. This verb is now obsolete. It was used only in *imperf dell'ind* (*ivo* etc) and in the following forms and persons:

—	*2ⁿᵈ pers sg* isti	—	—	—
—		*1ˢᵗ pers pl* iremo	—	—
2ⁿᵈ pers pl ite	—	*2ⁿᵈ pers pl* irete	—	*2ⁿᵈ pers pl* ite
—	*3ʳᵈ pers sg* irono	*3ʳᵈ pers pl* iranno	—	—
		pp: ito		

4k morire.

muoio	morii	mor(i)rò	muoia	—
moriamo	morimmo	mor(i)remo	moriamo	moriamo
muoiono	morirono	mor(i)ranno	muoiano	muoiano
		pp: morto		

4l olire. Defective verb. Used only in *imperf dell'ind* 3ʳᵈ person singular (*oliva*) and 3ʳᵈ person plural (*olivano*) and in *p pr* (*olente*). This verb is now obsolete.

4m salire. *Pr* as 4a, adding a *g* before *o* and *a*.

salgo	salii	salirò	salga	—
saliamo	salimmo	saliremo	saliamo	saliamo
salgono	salirono	saliranno	salgano	salgano
		pp: salito		

4n udire. *Pr* as 4a, with *u* becoming *o* in the forms in which the stem is stressed.

odo	udii	ud(i)rò	oda	—
udiamo	udimmo	ud(i)remo	udiamo	udiamo
odono	udirono	ud(i)ranno	odano	odano
		pp: udito		

4o uscire.

esco	uscii	uscirò	esca	—
esci	uscisti	uscirai	esca	esci
esce	uscì	uscirà	esca	esca
usciamo	uscimmo	usciremo	usciamo	usciamo
uscite	usciste	uscirete	usciate	uscite
escono	uscirono	usciranno	escano	escano
		pp: uscito		

4p venire.

vengo	venni	verrò	venga	—
vieni	venisti	verrai	venga	vieni
viene	venne	verrà	venga	venga
veniamo	venimmo	verremo	veniamo	veniamo
venite	veniste	verrete	veniate	venite
vengono	vennero	verranno	vengano	vengano
		pp: venuto		

Note sul verbo inglese

a) Coniugazione

Modo indicativo

1. Il tempo presente mantiene la stessa forma dell'infinito in tutte le persone, ad eccezione della 3ª singolare, a cui si aggiunge una -s all'infinito; ad es. *he brings.* Se l'infinito termina con una sibilante (ch, sh, ss, zz) si aggiunge -es, ad esempio *he passes.* Questa *s* ha due diverse pronunce: dopo una consonante sorda, si pronuncia sorda, ad es. *he paints* [peɪnts]; dopo una consonante sonora, si pronuncia sonora, ad es. *he sends* [sendz]; la pronuncia di -es è sonora, inoltre, quando la *e* fa parte della desinenza oppure della lettera finale dell'infinito, ad es. *he washes* ['wɒʃɪz], *he urges* ['ɜːdʒɪz]. Nei verbi che terminano per -y, la terza persona si forma sostituendo alla *y* -ies, ad es. *he worries, he tries*; sono tuttavia regolari i verbi che all'infinito hanno una vocale davanti alla -y, ad es. *he plays.* Il verbo *to be* è irregolare in tutte le persone: *I am, you are, he is, we are, you are, they are.* Altri tre verbi fanno eccezione alla terza persona singolare: *do - he does, go - he goes, have - he has.*

   Negli altri tempi, tutte le persone restano invariate. Il **passato** ed il **participio passato** si formano aggiungendo -ed all'infinito, ad es. *I passed, passed,* oppure aggiungendo soltanto -d nei verbi che all'infinito terminano in -e, ad es. *I faced, faced.* (Sono molti i verbi irregolari; cfr. sotto). Questa desinenza -(e)d si pronuncia generalmente [t]: *passed* [pɑːst], *faced* [feɪst]; tuttavia, quando compare negli infiniti che terminano con una consonante sonora, con un suono consonantico sonoro o con una *r*, si pronuncia [d]: *warmed* [wɔːmd], *moved* [muːvd], *feared* [fɪəd]. Quando l'infinito termina con -d o -t, la desinenza -ed si pronuncia [ɪd]. Quando l'infinito termina in -y, quest'ultima si trasforma in -ie, e quindi si aggiunge la -d: *try - tried* [traɪd], *pity - pitied* ['pɪtiːd]. I **tempi passati composti** si formano con l'ausiliare *to have* ed il participio passato: **passato prossimo** *I have faced,* **trapassato prossimo** *I had faced.* Con l'ausiliare *will* (*shall*) e l'infinito si forma il **futuro,** ad es. *I shall face*; con l'ausiliare *would* (*should*) si forma il **condizionale,** ad es. *I should face.*

   Per ciascun tempo esiste inoltre la forma continuata, che si costruisce con il verbo *to be* (= essere) e il participio presente (cfr. sotto): *I am going, I was writing, I had been staying, I shall be waiting,* ecc.

2. In inglese, il **congiuntivo** non esiste quasi più, ad eccezione di alcuni casi particolari (*if I were you, so be it, it is proposed that a vote be taken,* ecc.). Al presente, mantiene la stessa forma dell'infinito per tutte le persone, *that I go, that he go,* ecc.

3. In inglese, il **participio presente** ed il **gerundio** hanno la stessa forma e si costruiscono aggiungendo all'infinito la desinenza -ing: *painting, sending.* Tuttavia: 1) nei verbi che all'infinito terminano in -e muta, la desinenza fa cadere questa vocale, ad es. *love - loving, write - writing* (fanno eccezione *dye - dyeing, singe - singeing,* che conservano la -e:); 2) il participio presente dei verbi *die, lie, vie,* ecc. si scrive *dying, lying, vying,* ecc.

4. Esiste una classe di verbi in parte irregolari, che terminano con una sola consonante preceduta da vocale semplice accentata. In questi verbi, prima di aggiungere la desinenza -ing o -ed si raddoppia la consonante:

lob	lob*bed*	lob*bing*	compel	compel*led*	compel*ling*
wed	wed*ded*	wed*ding*	control	control*led*	control*ling*
beg	beg*ged*	beg*ging*	bar	bar*red*	bar*ring*
step	step*ped*	step*ping*	stir	stir*red*	stir*ring*

I verbi che terminano per -l, quando preceduta da vocale atona, raddoppiano la consonante dei due participi nell'ortografia inglese della Gran Bretagna, ma non in quella americana:

travel travel*led, Am* traveled   travel*ling, Am* traveling

Nei verbi che terminano in -c, si sostituisce -ck alla c, prima di aggiungere le desinenze -ed e -ing:

traffic traffi*cked* traffi*cking*

5. La **forma passiva** si forma esattamente come in italiano, con il verbo *to be* ed il participio passato: *I am obliged, he was fined, they will be moved,* ecc.

b) Verbi irregolari inglesi

Si riportano le tre forme principali di ciascun verbo: infinito, passato, participio passato.

alight	alighted, alit	alighted, alit	**cling**	clung	clung
arise	arose	arisen	**come**	came	come
awake	awoke	awoken, awaked	**cost**	cost	cost
be (am, is, are)	was (were)	been	**creep**	crept	crept
bear	bore	borne	**crow**	crowed, crew	crowed
beat	beat	beaten	**cut**	cut	cut
become	became	become	**deal**	dealt	dealt
begin	began	begun	**dig**	dug	dug
behold	beheld	beheld	**do**	did	done
bend	bent	bent	**draw**	drew	drawn
beseech	besought,	besought,	**dream**	dreamt,	dreamt,
	beseeched	beseeched		dreamed	dreamed
bet	bet, betted	bet, betted	**drink**	drank	drunk
bid	bade, bid	bidden, bid	**drive**	drove	driven
bind	bound	bound	**dwell**	dwelt,	dwelt,
bite	bit	bitten		dwelled	dwelled
bleed	bled	bled	**eat**	ate	eaten
blow	blew	blown	**fall**	fell	fallen
break	broke	broken	**feed**	fed	fed
breed	bred	bred	**feel**	felt	felt
bring	brought	brought	**fight**	fought	fought
broadcast	broadcast	broadcast	**find**	found	found
build	built	built	**flee**	fled	fled
burn	burnt, burned	burnt, burned	**fling**	flung	flung
burst	burst	burst	**fly**	flew	flown
bust	bust(ed)	bust(ed)	**forbear**	forbore	forborne
buy	bought	bought	**forbid**	forbad(e)	forbidden
cast	cast	cast	**forecast**	forecast(ed)	forecast(ed)
catch	caught	caught	**forget**	forgot	forgotten
choose	chose	chosen	**forgive**	forgave	forgiven
cleave (*cut*)	clove, cleft	cloven, cleft	**forsake**	forsook	forsaken

freeze	froze	frozen
get	got	got, *Am* gotten
give	gave	given
go	went	gone
grind	ground	ground
grow	grew	grown
hang	hung, (*v/t*) hanged	hung, (*v/t*) hanged
have	had	had
hear	heard	heard
heave	heaved, NAUT hove	heaved, NAUT hove
hew	hewed	hewed, hewn
hide	hid	hidden
hit	hit	hit
hold	held	held
hurt	hurt	hurt
keep	kept	kept
kneel	knelt, kneeled	knelt, kneeled
know	knew	known
lay	laid	laid
lead	led	led
lean	leaned, leant	leaned, leant
leap	leaped, leapt	leaped, leapt
learn	learned, learnt	learned, learnt
leave	left	left
lend	lent	lent
let	let	let
lie	lay	lain
light	lighted, lit	lighted, lit
lose	lost	lost
make	made	made
mean	meant	meant
meet	met	met
mow	mowed	mowed, mown
pay	paid	paid
plead	pleaded, pled	pleaded, pled
prove	proved	proved, proven
put	put	put
quit	quit(ted)	quit(ted)
read [ri:d]	read [red]	read [red]
rend	rent	rent
rid	rid	rid
ride	rode	ridden
ring	rang	rung
rise	rose	risen
run	ran	run
saw	sawed	sawn, sawed
say	said	said
see	saw	seen
seek	sought	sought
sell	sold	sold
send	sent	sent
set	set	set
sew	sewed	sewed, sewn
shake	shook	shaken
shear	sheared	sheared, shorn
shed	shed	shed
shine	shone	shone
shit	shit(ted), shat	shit(ted), shat
shoe	shod	shod
shoot	shot	shot
show	showed	shown
shrink	shrank	shrunk
shut	shut	shut
sing	sang	sung
sink	sank	sunk
sit	sat	sat
slay	slew	slain
sleep	slept	slept
slide	slid	slid
sling	slung	slung
slink	slunk	slunk
slit	slit	slit
smell	smelt, smelled	smelt, smelled
smite	smote	smitten
sow	sowed	sown, sowed
speak	spoke	spoken
speed	sped, speeded	sped, speeded
spell	spelt, spelled	spelt, spelled
spend	spent	spent
spill	spilt, spilled	spilt, spilled
spin	spun, span	spun
spit	spat	spat
split	split	split
spoil	spoiled, spoilt	spoiled, spoilt
spread	spread	spread
spring	sprang, *Am* sprung	sprung
stand	stood	stood
stave	staved, stove	staved, stove
steal	stole	stolen
stick	stuck	stuck
sting	stung	stung
stink	stunk, stank	stunk
strew	strewed	strewed, strewn
stride	strode	stridden
strike	struck	struck
string	strung	strung
strive	strove	striven
swear	swore	sworn
sweep	swept	swept
swell	swelled	swollen
swim	swam	swum
swing	swung	swung
take	took	taken
teach	taught	taught
tear	tore	torn
tell	told	told
think	thought	thought
thrive	throve	thriven
throw	threw	thrown
thrust	thrust	thrust
tread	trod	trodden
understand	understood	understood
wake	woke, waked	woken, waked
wear	wore	worn
weave	wove	woven
wed	wed(ded)	wed(ded)
weep	wept	wept
wet	wet(ted)	wet(ted)
win	won	won
wind	wound	wound
wring	wrung	wrung
write	wrote	written

Numbers – Numerali

Cardinal numbers – I numeri cardinali

0	*zero* zero		80	*eighty* ottanta
1	*one* uno		90	*ninety* novanta
2	*two* due		100	*one/a hundred* cento
3	*three* tre		101	*one/a hundred* centouno
4	*four* quattro			*and one*
5	*five* cinque		102	*one/a hundred* centodue
6	*six* sei			*and two*
7	*seven* sette		200	*two hundred* duecento
8	*eight* otto		201	*two hundred*
9	*nine* nove			*and one* duecento uno
10	*ten* dieci		300	*three hundred* trecento
11	*eleven* undici		400	*four hundred* quattrocento
12	*twelve* dodici		500	*five hundred* cinquecento
13	*thirteen* tredici		600	*six hundred* seicento
14	*fourteen* quattordici		700	*seven hundred* settecento
15	*fifteen* quindici		800	*eight hundred* ottocento
16	*sixteen* sedici		900	*nine hundred* novecento
17	*seventeen* diciassette		1,000	*one/a thousand* mille
18	*eighteen* diciotto		1,001	*one/a thousand* milleuno/
19	*nineteen* diciannove			*and one* mille e uno
20	*twenty* venti		2,000	*two thousand* duemila
21	*twenty-one* ventuno		3,000	*three thousand* tremila
22	*twenty-two* ventidue		4,000	*four thousand* quattromila
23	*twenty-three* ventitrè		5,000	*five thousand* cinquemila
28	*twenty-eight* ventotto			
29	*twenty-nine* ventinove		10,000	*ten thousand* diecimila
30	*thirty* trenta		100,000	*one/a hundred* centomila
40	*forty* quaranta			*thousand*
50	*fifty* cinquanta		1,000,000	*one/a million* un milione
60	*sixty* sessanta		2,000,000	*two million* due milioni
70	*seventy* settanta		1,000,000,000	*one/a billion* un miliardo

Notes:

i) In Italian numbers a comma is used for decimals:

   1,25   **one point two five**   uno virgola venticinque

ii) A full stop is used where, in English, we would use a comma:

   1.000.000 = 1,000,000

Italian can also write numbers like this using a space instead of a comma:

   1 000 000 = 1,000,000

Ordinal numbers – I numeri ordinali

1st	*first*	1°	il primo, la prima
2nd	*second*	2°	secondo
3rd	*third*	3°	terzo
4th	*fourth*	4°	quarto
5th	*fifth*	5°	quinto
6th	*sixth*	6°	sesto
7th	*seventh*	7°	settimo
8th	*eighth*	8°	ottavo
9th	*ninth*	9°	nono
10th	*tenth*	10°	decimo
11th	*eleventh*	11°	undicesimo
12th	*twelfth*	12°	dodicesimo
13th	*thirteenth*	13°	tredicesimo
14th	*fourteenth*	14°	quattordicesimo
15th	*fifteenth*	15°	quindicesimo
16th	*sixteenth*	16°	sedicesimo
17th	*seventeenth*	17°	diciassettesimo
18th	*eighteenth*	18°	diciottesimo
19th	*nineteenth*	19°	diciannovesimo
20th	*twentieth*	20°	ventesimo
21st	*twenty-first*	21°	ventunesimo
22nd	*twenty-second*	22°	ventiduesimo
30th	*thirtieth*	30°	trentesimo
40th	*fortieth*	40°	quarantesimo
50th	*fiftieth*	50°	cinquantesimo
60th	*sixtieth*	60°	sessantesimo
70th	*seventieth*	70°	settantesimo
80th	*eightieth*	80°	ottantesimo
90th	*ninetieth*	90°	novantesimo
100th	*hundredth*	100°	centesimo
101st	*hundred and first*	101°	centunesimo
103rd	*hundred and third*	103°	centotreesimo
200th	*two hundredth*	200°	duecentesimo
1000th	*thousandth*	1000°	millesimo
1001st	*thousand and first*	1001°	millesimo primo
2000th	*two thousandth*	2000°	duemillesimo
1000000th	*millionth*	1000000°	milionesimo

Note:

Italian ordinal numbers are ordinary adjectives and consequently must agree:

her 13th granddaughter   la sua tredicesima nipote

Fractions – Frazioni

½	*one half, a half*	un mezzo
⅓	*one third, a third*	un terzo
⅔	*two thirds*	due terzi
¼	*one quarter, a quarter*	un quarto
¾	*three quarters*	tre quarti
⅕	*one fifth, a fifth*	un quinto
⅒	*one tenth, a tenth*	un decimo
1½	*one and a half*	uno e mezzo
2¾	*two and three quarters*	due e tre quarti
⅟₁₀₀	*one hundredth, a hundredth*	un centesimo
⅟₁₀₀₀	*one thousandth, a thousandth*	un millesimo

Approximate numbers – Valori approssimativi

a couple	un paio
about ten	una decina
about twenty	una ventina
about eighty	un'ottantina
about a hundred	un centinaio
hundreds (of people)	centinaia (di persone)
about a thousand	un migliaio
thousands	migliaia